Volume I

DOCUMENTS
of
AMERICAN HISTORY
To 1898

ninth edition

DOCUMENTS

of

AMERICAN HISTORY

two-volume edition volume I   to 1898

edited by

Henry Steele Commager

PRENTICE-HALL, INC., Englewood Cliffs, New Jersey

Library of Congress Cataloging in Publication Data

Commager, Henry Steele, ed.
  Documents of American history.

  CONTENTS: v. 1. To 1898.—v. 2. Since 1898.
  1. United States—History—Sources. I. Title.
E173.C66 1973b   973′.08
ISBN 0-13-216994-0 (v. 1)
Library of Congress Catalog Card Number: 73-11490

Printed in the United States of America

10 9 8 7 6 5 4 3

PRENTICE-HALL INTERNATIONAL, INC., *London*
PRENTICE-HALL OF AUSTRALIA, PTY. LTD., *Sydney*
PRENTICE-HALL OF CANADA, LTD., *Toronto*
PRENTICE-HALL OF INDIA PRIVATE LIMITED, *New Delhi*
PRENTICE-HALL OF JAPAN, INC., *Tokyo*

To

EVAN

WHO LIKED THEM

PREFACE

These documents are designed to illustrate the course of American history from the Age of Discovery to the present. Exigencies of space and of circumstance have required that the term document be interpreted in a very narrow sense. Properly speaking, almost everything of an original character is a document: letters, memoirs, ballads, folk-lore, poetry, fiction, newspaper reports and editorials, sermons and speeches, to say nothing of inscriptions, stamps, coins, buildings, painting and sculpture, and all the innumerable memorials which man has left in his effort to understand and organize his world. I have tried to limit my selection to documents of an official and quasi-official character, though I have been no more consistent in this than in other things. I have not included selections often, and mistakenly, referred to as "readings"; even partially to illuminate American history from letters, memoirs, travelers' descriptions, etc. would require many volumes; this material, too, should be read in its entirety rather than in excerpt, and is readily available to students.

What is presented here, then, is part of the official record, and students know that the official record is neither the whole record nor in every case the real record. I cannot say that I have been guided in my choice of material by any rigid principles of selection. The choice has been determined by the experience of the class-room, by personal interest, and by availability. I have attempted to include those documents with which students should be familiar, such as the Northwest Ordinance or *Marbury* v. *Madison;* those which are illustrative or typical, such as colonial charters or land laws; those which focussed upon themselves the attention of the country, such as the Missouri Compromise or the Lincoln-Douglas Debates; those which serve as a convenient point of departure for the study of some economic or political development, such as labor cases or party platforms; those which illuminate some phase of our social life, such as the constitution of the Brook Farm Association or the Mooney-Billings Report; those which have certain qualities of interest, eloquence or beauty, such as Lee's Farewell to his Army or Holmes' dissent in the Abrams Case.

No one can be more acutely conscious of the inadequacies of such a collection than is the editor. Students familiar with the sources of American history will find many omissions and will discover many episodes unilluminated. To most of these charges I can plead only the exigencies of space; to some I must confess personal idiosyncrasy and fallibility. Students will look in vain for Webster's Reply to Hayne or Stephen's Cornerstone speech, for Hamilton's Report on Manufactures or the Federal Reserve Act, for the diplomatic correspondence on the X.Y.Z. affair or the Trent episode. These, and scores of similar selections, were omitted because I was not able to achieve a satisfactory condensation and did not feel that they could be included *in extenso*. While I have made efforts to find documents which would illustrate phases of our social and economic history, there are fewer of these than is desirable. Such documents are hard to come by: spiritual forces do not readily translate themselves into documents. I would have liked to have included Emerson's *Divinity School Address*, Fitzhugh's *Pro Slavery Argument*, the platform of the American Economic Association; to have yielded to this temptation would have opened the flood-gates of miscellaneous source material. It cannot be pretended that presidential messages, supreme court decisions, or statutes, reveal much of the undercurrents of our social life. To discover these it would be necessary to go to church records, school reports, the minutes of fraternal orders, the records of labor organizations and agricultural societies, the records of probate courts, etc. American historians have been distressingly backward in the appreciation and publication of such material. These records therefore are not readily available, nor would a lifetime be sufficient to canvass them and take from them that which is typical.

Neither the notes nor the bibliographies which accompany these documents pretend to be extensive. In the notes I have attempted to state only what is essential for an understanding of the background of the document; the bibliographies are designed to indicate additional reading for the orientation of the document and additional bibliographical references. I have only occasionally included references to the rich deposits of material in periodicals and the publications of learned societies: for these the student will have to go to specialized bibliographical guides and to the invaluable *Writings on American History* which Miss Griffin has compiled. The documents themselves have been taken from and collated with the sources indicated. No effort has been made to standardize spelling, capitalization or punctuation, or even to correct obvious errors in the originals: to have undertaken this, even granting its propriety, would have produced confusion. I have taken very few liberties with these documents. Omissions have been indicated by the customary ellipsis sign, but I have omitted such phrases as "be it also enacted" and "done at the city of Washington, etc." without any indication. I have in most instances abbreviated Article to Art. and Section to Sec., and I have frequently substituted numbered dates for the lengthier form. I have no doubt that in the many processes of copying, collating, and printing, numerous errors have crept in; for these I beg the indulgence of the reader.

I am under obligation to many people for coöperation in the compilation of this volume. The officials of the libraries of New York University bore patiently with my demands. To my colleagues in the Department of History, Mr. Cochran, Mr. Craven, Mr. Hoffman, Mr. Musser, and Mr. Wettereau, to Mr. Stein of the Department of Economics, Mr. Thach of the Department of Government, and Dean Sommer of the Law School of New York University, I am grateful for suggestions. Without the faithful and intelligent assistance of Miss Margaret Carroll this volume could never have been prepared.

HENRY STEELE COMMAGER

PREFACE TO THE NINTH EDITION

In order to avoid an enlargement that would make *Documents of American History* unwieldy, I have had to drop some of the documents of the seventh and eighth editions. In every case these documents illustrated events which, from the perspective of 1973, seem somewhat less important than they did when originally inserted, or, as in the case of some judicial opinions, have been superseded by more recent decisions. We have included here new documents from the period since 1966—an era that has seen far-reaching developments in constitutional, political, diplomatic, and social realms. In the selection and editing of the documents I have been greatly aided by Professor Milton Cantor of the University of Massachusetts.

HENRY STEELE COMMAGER

TABLE OF CONTENTS

ix

Volume I

DOCUMENTS
of
AMERICAN HISTORY
To 1898

DOCUMENTS OF
AMERICAN HISTORY

1. PRIVILEGES AND PREROGATIVES GRANTED TO COLUMBUS
April 30, 1492

(F. N. Thorpe, ed. *Federal and State Constitutions*, Vol. I, p. 39 ff.)

For years Columbus had been presenting his scheme of sailing westward to the Indies to the sovereigns of Spain, Portugal, France and England, but without success. Finally in January 1492, the Spanish forces captured Granada and drove the Moors out of Spain, and Ferdinand and Isabella were free to consider seriously the proposals of Columbus. At first these terms were considered exorbitant and negotiations were broken off. Columbus was actually on his way to France when he was summoned back to Court, and the following terms accepted by Ferdinand and Isabella as King and Queen of Castile. The literature on Columbus is extensive. See, J. Winsor, *Christopher Columbus;* C. R. Markham, *Columbus;* H. Harrisse, *Christophe Columb,* 2 Vols.; J. B. Thacher, *Christopher Columbus,* 3 Vols. The Hakluyt Society has published the *Journal of Christopher Columbus* and two volumes of *Letters.*

FERDINAND and ELIZABETH, . . .

For as much of you, *Christopher Columbus,* are going by our command, with some of our vessels and men, to discover and subdue some Islands and Continent in the ocean, and it is hoped that by God's assistance, some of the said Islands and Continent in the ocean will be discovered and conquered by your means and conduct, therefore it is but just and reasonable, that since you expose yourself to such danger to serve us, you should be rewarded for it. And we being willing to honour and favour you for the reasons aforesaid; Our will is, That you, *Christopher Columbus,* after discovering and conquering the said Islands and Continent in the said ocean, or any of them, shall be our Admiral of the said Islands and Conti-

nent you shall so discover and conquer; and that you be our Admiral, Vice-Roy, and Governour in them, and that for the future, you may call and stile yourself, D. *Christopher Columbus,* and that your sons and successors in the said employment, may call themselves Dons, Admirals, Vice-Roys, and Governours of them; and that you may exercise the office of Admiral, with the charge of Vice-Roy and Governour of the said Islands and Continent, which you and your Lieutenants shall conquer, and freely decide all causes, civil and criminal, appertaining to the said employment of Admiral, Vice Roy, and Governour, as you shall think fit in justice, and as the Admirals of our kingdoms use to do; and that you have power to punish offenders; and you and your Lieutenants exercise the employments of Admiral, Vice-Roy, and Governour, in all things belonging to the said offices, or any of them; and that you enjoy the perquisites and salaries belonging to the said employments, and to each of them, in the same manner as the High Admiral of our kingdoms does. And by this our letter, or a copy of it signed by a *Public Notary:* We command Prince *John,* our most dearly beloved Son, the Infants, Dukes, Prelates, Marquesses, Great Masters and Military Orders, Priors, Commendaries, our Counsellors, Judges, and other Officers of Justice whatsoever, belonging to our Household, Courts, and Chancery, and Constables of Castles, Strong Houses, and others, and all Corporations, Bayliffs, Governours, Judges, Commanders, Sea Officers; and the Aldermen, Common Council, Officers, and

1

Good People of all Cities, Lands, and Places in our Kingdoms and Dominions, and in those you shall conquer and subdue, and the captains, masters, mates, and other officers and sailors, our natural subjects now being, or that shall be for the time to come, and any of them, that when you shall have discovered the said Islands and Continent in the ocean; and you, or any that shall have your commission, shall have taken the usual oath in such cases, that they for the future, look upon you as long as you live, and after you, your son and heir, and so from one heir to another forever, as our Admiral on our said Ocean, and as Vice-Roy and Governour of the said Islands and Continent, by you, *Christopher Columbus,* discovered and conquered; and that they treat you and your Lieutenants, by you appointed, for executing the employments of Admiral, Vice-Roy, and Governour, as such in all respects, and give you all the perquisites and other things belonging and appertaining to the said offices; and allow, and cause to be allowed you, all the honours, graces, concessions, prehaminences, prerogatives, immunities, and other things, or any of them which are due to you, by virtue of your commands of Admiral, Vice-Roy, and Governour, and to be observed completely, so that nothing be diminished; and that they make no objec-

tion to this, or any part of it, nor suffer it to be made; forasmuch as we from this time forward, by this our letter, bestow on you the employments of Admiral, Vice-Roy, and perpetual Governour forever; and we put you into possession of the said offices, and of every of them, and full power to use and exercise them, and to receive the perquisites and salaries belonging to them, or any of them, as was' said above. Concerning all which things, if it be requisite, and you shall desire it, We command our Chancellour, Notaries, and other Officers, to pass, seal, and deliver to you, our Letter of Privilege, in such form and legal manner, as you shall require or stand in need of. And that none of them presume to do any thing to the contrary, upon pain of our displeasure, and fortfeiture of 30 ducats for each offence. And we command him, who shall show them this our Letter, that he summon them to appear before us at our Court, where we shall then be, within fifteen days after such summons, under the said penalty. Under which same, we also command any Public Notary whatsoever, that he give to him that shows it him, a certificate under his seal, that we may know how our command is obeyed.

GIVEN at *Granada,* on the 30th of April, in the year of our Lord, 1492.—

I, THE KING, I, THE QUEEN.

2. THE PAPAL BULL *INTER CAETERA* (ALEXANDER VI)
May 4, 1493

(F. G. Davenport, ed. *European Treaties bearing on the History of the United States and its Dependencies to 1648,* p. 75 ff.)

Columbus returned from his first voyage in March, 1493, and the news of his discoveries was promptly communicated to the rulers of Spain and Portugal and to the Pope. Considerable uncertainty as to the lands discovered by Columbus existed: King John II of Portugal believed that Columbus's discoveries had really been in the region south and west of Guinea. Portuguese control over Guinea and the region to the south of Cape Bojador rested upon discoveries, papal bulls, and a treaty with Spain of 1480. King John was anxious therefore to have some decision as to the effects of Columbus's discoveries on the territorial claims of Portugal and Spain. Under these circumstances the matter was submitted to Pope Alexander VI. By the Bulls of May 3 and May 4 he drew an imaginary line of demarcation one hundred leagues west of the

Cape Verde Islands: east of this line Portugal was to have all the rights and possessions which she already held; west of this line Spain was to have the right to explore, trade, colonize, etc. The Bull of May 4 was amended by another Bull of September, 1493, specifically granting to the Spanish rulers the right to hold lands to the "eastern regions and to India". The line of demarcation of 1493 was changed the following year, Doc. No. 3. See, J. Fiske, *The Discovery of America,* Vol. II, ch. vi; E. G. Bourne, *Spain in America,* ch. iii; J. Winsor, ed. *Narrative and Critical History of America,* Vol. II; J. Winsor, *Christopher Columbus;* O. Peschel, *Die Theilung der Erde unter Papst Alexander VI und Julius II;* H. Harrisse, *Diplomatic History of America: Its First Chapter, 1452–1494.*

Alexander, bishop, servant of the servants of God, to the illustrious sovereigns, our very dear son in Christ, Ferdinand, king, and our very dear daughter in Christ, Isabella, queen of Castile. . . . We have indeed learned that you, who for a long time had intended to seek out and discover certain islands and mainlands remote and unknown and not hitherto discovered by others, to the end that you might bring to the worship of our Redeemer and the profession of the Catholic faith their residents and inhabitants, having been up to the present time greatly engaged in the siege and recovery of the kingdom itself of Granada were unable to accomplish this holy and praiseworthy purpose; but the said kingdom having at length been regained, as was pleasing to the Lord, with a wish to fulfill your desire, chose our beloved son, Christopher Columbus . . . whom you furnished with ships and men equipped for like designs, not without the greatest hardships, dangers, and expenses, to make diligent quest for these remote and unknown mainlands and islands through the sea, where hitherto no one had sailed; and they at length with divine aid and with the utmost diligence sailing in the ocean sea, discovered certain very remote islands and even mainlands that hitherto had not been discovered by others, wherein dwell very many peoples living in peace, and, as reported, going unclothed, and not eating flesh. . . . Wherefore, as becomes Catholic kings and princes . . . you have purposed . . . to bring under your sway the said mainlands and islands. . . . And in order that you may enter upon so great an undertaking with greater readiness and heartiness endowed with the benefit of our apostolic favor, we, of our own accord, not at your instance nor the request of anyone else in your regard, but out of our own sole largess and certain knowledge and out of the fullness of our apostolic power, by the authority of Almighty God conferred upon us in blessed Peter and of the vicarship of Jesus Christ, which we hold on earth, do by tenor of these presents, should any of said islands have been found by your envoys and captains, give, grant, and assign to you and your heirs and successors, kings of Castile and Leon, forever, together with all their dominions, cities, camps, places, and villages, and all rights, jurisdictions, and appurtenances, all islands and mainlands found and to be found, discovered and to be discovered towards the west and the south, by drawing and establishing a line from the Arctic pole, namely the north, to the Antarctic pole, namely the south, no matter whether the said mainlands and islands are found and to be found in the direction of India or towards any other quarter, the said line to be distant one hundred leagues towards the west and south from any of the islands commonly known as the Azores and Cape Verde. With this proviso, however, that none of the islands and mainlands, found and to be found, discovered and to be discovered, beyond that said line towards the west and south, be in the actual possession of any Christian king or prince up to the birthday of our Lord Jesus Christ just past from which the present year 1493 begins. . . . Furthermore, under penalty of excommunication *late sontentie* to be incurred *ipso facto,* should anyone thus contravene, we strictly forbid all persons of whatsoever rank, even imperial and royal, or of whatsoever estate, degree, order, or condition, to dare without your special permit or that of your aforesaid heirs and successors, to go for the purpose of trade or any other reason to the islands or mainlands . . . apostolic constitutions and ordinances and other decrees whatsoever to the contrary notwithstanding. . . . Let no one therefore, infringe, or with rash boldness contravene, this our recommendation, exhortation, requisition, gift, grant, assignment, constitution, deputation, decree, mandate, prohibition, and will. Should anyone presume to attempt this, be it known to him that he will incur the wrath of Almighty God and of the blessed apostles Peter and Paul. Given at Rome, at St. Peter's, in the year of the incarnation of our Lord 1493, the fourth of May, and the first year of our pontificate.

3. THE TREATY OF TORDESILLAS
June 7, 1494

(F. G. Davenport, ed. *European Treaties bearing on the History of the United States and its Dependencies to 1648*, p. 84 ff.)

King John of Portugal was not satisfied with the provisions of the Bull Inter Caetera, and by the Treaty of Tordesillas persuaded the Spanish crown to consent to moving the line of demarcation 370 leagues west from the Cape Verde Islands. This change gave Portugal a claim to Brazil. See, J. Fiske, *The Discovery of America,* Vol. II, ch. vi; E. G. Bourne, *Spain in America,* ch. iii; J. Winsor, ed. *Narrative and Critical History of America,* Vol. II; O. Peschel, *Die Theilung der Erde unter Papst Alexander VI und Julius II.*

. . . Whereas a certain controversy exists between the said lords, their constituents, as to what lands, of all those discovered in the ocean sea up to the present day, the date of this treaty, pertain to each one of the said parts respectively; therefore, for the sake of peace and concord, and for the preservation of the relationship and love of the said King of Portugal for the said King and Queen of Castile, Aragon, etc. it being the pleasure of their Highnesses, they . . . covenanted and agreed that a boundary or straight line be determined and drawn north and south, from pole to pole, on the said ocean sea, from the Arctic to the Antarctic pole. This boundary or line shall be drawn straight, as aforesaid, at a distant of three hundred and seventy leagues west of the Cape Verde Islands, being calculated by degrees. . . . And all lands, both islands and mainlands, found and discovered already, or to be found and discovered hereafter, by the said King of Portugal and by his vessels on this side of the said line and bound determined as above, toward the east, in either north or south latitude, on the eastern side of the said bound, provided the said bound is not crossed, shall belong to and remain in the possession of, and pertain forever to, the said King of Portugal and his successors. And all other lands, both islands and mainlands, found or to be found hereafter, . . . by the said King and Queen of Castile, Aragon, etc. and by their vessels, on the western side of the said bound, determined

as above, after having passed the said bound toward the west, in either its north or south latitude, shall belong to . . . the said King and Queen of Castile, Leon, etc. and to their successors.

Item, the said representatives promise and affirm . . . that from this date no ships shall be dispatched—namely as follows: the said King and Queen of Castile, Leon, Aragon etc. for this part of the bound . . . which pertains to the said King of Portugal . . . nor the said King of Portugal to the other side of the said bound which pertains to the said King and Queen of Castile, Aragon, etc.—for the purpose of discovering and seeking any mainlands or islands, or for the purpose of trade, barter, or conquest of any kind. But should it come to pass that the said ships of the said King and Queen of Castile . . . on sailing thus on this side of the said bound, should discover any mainlands or islands in the region pertaining, as abovesaid, to the said King of Portugal, such mainlands or islands shall belong forever to the said King of Portugal and his heirs, and their Highnesses shall order them to be surrendered to him immediately. And if the said ships of the said King of Portugal discover any islands or mainlands in the regions of the said King and Queen of Castile . . . all such lands shall belong to and remain forever in the possession of the said King and Queen of Castile . . . and their heirs, and the said King of Portugal shall cause such lands to be surrendered immediately. . . .

And by this present agreement, they . . . entreat our most Holy Father that his Holiness be pleased to confirm and approve this said agreement, according to what is set forth therein; and that he order his bulls in regard to it to be issued to the parties or to whichever of the parties may solicit them with the tenor of this agreement incorporated therein, and that he lay his censures upon those who shall violate or oppose it at any time whatsoever. . . .

4. LETTERS PATENT TO JOHN CABOT
March 5, 1496

(F. N. Thorpe, ed. *Federal and State Constitutions*, Vol. I, p. 46-7)

Giovanni Caboto was a Genoese; he came to England some time between 1484 and 1490, and settled among the merchant adventurers of Bristol. Eventually he interested Henry VII in the project of a northern route to the East, and secured a patent to find lands unknown to Christians. He set sail from Bristol May 2, 1497 and made a landfall on the Labrador coast; the expenses of the voyage were borne by the Bristol merchants. On Cabot, see C. R. Beazley, *John and Sebastian Cabot;* H. Harrisse, *John Cabot the Discoverer of North America;* C. Deane, *The Voyages of the Cabots,* in J. Winsor, *Narrative and Critical History,* Vol. III; J. A. Williamson, ed. *The Voyages of the Cabots;* J. B. Brebner, *Explorers of North America,* ch. vii.

The Letters patents of King Henry the seuenth granted vnto Iohn Cabot and his three sonnes, Lewis, Sebastian, and Sancius for the discouerie of new and vnknowen lands.

IIEnry, by the grace of God, king of Eng land and France, and lord of Ireland, to all to whom these presents shall come, Greeting.

Be it knowen that we haue giuen and granted, and by these presents do giue and grant for vs and our heires, to our welbeloued Iohn Cabot citizen of Venice, to Lewis, Sebastian, and Sancius, sonnes of the sayd Iohn, and to the heires of them, and euery of them, and their deputies, full and free authority, leaue, and power to saile to all parts, countreys, and seas of the East, of the West, and of the North, vnder our banners and ensignes, with fiue ships of what burthen or quantity soeuer they be, and as many mariners or men as they will haue with them in the sayd ships, vpon their owne proper costs and charges, to seeke out, discouer, and finde whatsoeuer isles, countreys, regions or prouinces of the heathen and infidels whatsoeuer they be, and in what part of the world soeuer they be, which before this time haue bene vnknowen to all Christians: we haue granted to them, and also to euery of them, the heires of them, and euery of them, and their deputies, and haue giuen them licence to set vp our banners and ensignes in euery village, towne, castle, isle, or maine land of them newly found. And that the aforesayd Iohn and his sonnes, or their heires and assignes may subdue, occupy and possesse all such townes, cities, castles and isles of them found, which they can subdue, occupy and possesse, as our vassals, and lieutenants, getting vnto vs the rule, title, and iurisdiction of the same villages, townes, castles, & firme land so found. Yet so that the aforesayd Iohn, and his sonnes and heires, and their deputies, be holden and bounden of all the fruits, profits, gaines, and commodities growing of such nauigation, for euery their voyage, as often as they shall arriue at our port of Bristoll (at which port they shall be bound and holden onely to arriue) all manner of necessary costs and charges by them made, being deducted, to pay vnto vs in wares or money the fift part of the capitall gaine so gotten. We giuing and granting vnto them and to their heires and deputies, that they shall be free from all paying of customes of all and singular such merchandize as they shall be free from all paying of customes of all and singular they shall bring with them from those places so newlie found.

And moreouer, we haue giuen and granted to them, their heires and deputies, that all the firme lands, isles, villages, townes, castles and places whatsoeuer they be that they shall chance to finde, may not of any other of our subjects be frequented or visited without the licence of the foresayd Iohn and his sonnes, and their deputies, vnder payne of forfeiture as well of their ships as of all and singular goods of all them that shall presume to saile to those places so found. Willing, and most straightly commanding all and singular our subjects as well on land as on sea, appointed officers, to giue good assistance to the aforesaid Iohn, and his sonnes and deputies, and that as well in arming and furnishing their ships or vessels, as in prouision of quietnesse, and in buying of victuals for their money, and all other things by them to be prouided necessary for the sayd nauigation, they do giue them all their helpe and fauour. In witnesse whereof we have caused to be made these our lettres patents. Witnesse our selfe at Westminister, the fift day of March, in the eleuenth yeere of our reigne.—

5. CHARTER TO SIR WALTER RALEGH
March 25, 1584

(F. N. Thorpe, ed. *Federal and State Constitutions*, Vol. I, p. 53 ff.)

English colonization in America may be dated from the letters patent to Sir Humphrey Gilbert of 1578. Under this grant Gilbert made two efforts to establish a colony in America; both were unsuccessful, and the second ended in the tragic death of the gallant adventurer. Sir Walter Raleigh, Gilbert's half-brother, had participated in both of Gilbert's ventures, and planned to carry on the work of colonization. Six months after Gilbert's death Raleigh received a patent couched in almost identical language as the patent of 1578. Under his charter, Raleigh sent out five expeditions to the new world, and succeeded in planting a colony on Roanoke Island, Virginia. Altogether Raleigh spent a personal fortune of some forty thousand pounds in his efforts to plant a colony in the new world, but he ended his life in the Tower of London. Raleigh, writes Professor Andrews, "was the first Englishman to demonstrate the practicability of transporting English men and women overseas to find new homes on a new soil. His colony of husbands and wives, mothers and nursing children . . . represents a new departure in English history." See, C. M. Andrews, *Our Earliest Colonial Settlements*, ch. i; L. G. Tyler, *England in America*, ch. ii; M. Waldman, *Sir Walter Raleigh;* L. Creighton, *Sir Walter Raleigh;* I. N. Tarbox, *Sir Walter Raleigh;* W. Stebbing, *Sir Walter Raleigh;* E. Edwards, *Life of Ralegh;* E. J. Payne, ed. *Voyages of the Elizabethan Seamen to America,* 1880 ed.

ELIZABETH, by the Grace of God of England, Fraunce and Ireland Queene, defender of the faith, &c. To all people to whome these presents shall come, greeting.

Knowe yee that of our especial grace, certaine science, and meere motion, . . . we give and graunt to our trustie and welbeloved servant *Walter Ralegh,* Esquire, and to his heires assignes for ever, free libertie and licence from time to time, and at all times for ever hereafter, to discover, search, finde out, and view such remote, heathen and barbarous lands, countries, and territories, not actually possessed of any Christian Prince, nor inhabited by Christian People, as to him, . . . shall seeme good, and the same to have, holde occupie and enjoy to him, . . . for ever, with all prerogatives, . . . thereto or thereabouts both by sea and land, whatsoever we by our letters patent may graunt, . . . and the said *Walter Ralegh,* his heires and assignes, . . . shall goe or travaile thither to inhabite or remaine, there to build and fortifie, at the discretion of the said *Walter Ralegh,* . . .

And we do likewise . . . give and graunt full authoritie, libertie and power to the said *Walter Ralegh,* . . . that he . . . shall . . . have, take, and leade in the saide voyage, and travaile thitherward, or to inhabit there with him, or them, and every or any of them, such and so many of our subjects as shall willingly accompanie him or them, . . .

And further that the said *Walter Ralegh,* . . . shall have . . . all the soile of all such lands, territories, and Countreis, so to bee discovered and possessed as aforesaide, and of all such Cities, castles, townes, villages, and places in the same, with the right, royalties, franchises, and jurisdictions, as well marine as other within the saide landes, or Countreis, or the seas thereunto adjoining, to be had, or used, with full power to dispose thereof, and of every part in fee-simple or otherwise, according to the order of the lawes of England, . . . : reserving always to us our heires, and successors, for all services, duties, and demaundes, the fift part of all the oare of golde and silver, that from time to time, and at all times . . . shal be there gotten and obtained: . . .

And moreover, we doe . . . give and graunt licence to the said *Walter Ralegh,* . . . that he, . . . shall and may . . . for his and their defence, encounter and expulse, repell and resist . . . all . . . as without the especiall liking and licence of the said *Walter Ralegh,* . . . shall attempt to inhabite within the said Countreis, . . . or within the space of two hundreth leagues neere to the place or places within such Countreis, . . . where the saide *Walter Ralegh,* . . . shall within sixe yeeres . . . make their dwellings. . . . And for uniting in more perfect league and amitie, of such Countreis, landes, and territories so to bee possessed and inhabited as aforesaide with our Realmes of Englande, and Ireland, and the better incouragement of men to these enterprises: we do . . . declare that all such Countreis, so hereafter to be possessed and inhabited as is aforesaide, from thencefoorth shall bee of the allegiance of us, our heires and successours. And wee doe graunt to the saide *Walter Ralegh,* . . . and to all and every of them, . . . that they . . . being either borne within our saide Realmes of Englande, . . . shall and may have all the priviledges of free Denizens, and persons native of England. . . .

And . . . we . . . do give and graunt to the said *Walter Ralegh,* . . . that hee . . . shall, within the said mentioned remote landes . . . have full and meere power and authoritie to correct, punish, pardon, governe, and rule by their and every or any of their good discretions and pollicies, as well in causes capital, or criminall, as civil, . . . all such our subjects as shall from time to time adventure themselves in the said journies or voyages, or that shall at any time hereafter inhabite any such landes, countreis, or territories as aforesaide, . . . according to such statutes, lawes and ordinances, as shall bee by him the saide *Walter Ralegh* . . . devised, or established, for the better government of the said people as aforesaid. So always as the said statutes, lawes, and ordinances may be as neere as conveniently may be, agreeable to the forme of the lawes, statutes, governement, or pollicie of England, . . .

Provided alwayes, and our will and pleasure is, and wee do hereby declare to all Christian kings, princes and states, that if the saide *Walter Ralegh,* his heires or assignes, or any of them, or any other by their licence or appointment, shall at any time or times hereafter, robbe or spoile by sea or by lande, or do any acte of unjust or unlawful hostilitie, to any of the subjects of us, our heires or successors, or to any of the subjects of any the kings, princes, rulers, governors, or estates, being then in perfect league and amitie with us, our heires and successors, and that upon such injury, or upon just complaint of any such prince, ruler, governoir, or estate, or their subjects, wee, our heires and successours, shall make open proclamation within any the portes of our Realme of England, that the saide *Walter Ralegh,* his heires and assignes, and adherents, or any to whome these our letters patents may extende, shall within the termes to be limitted, by such proclamation, make full restitution, and satisfaction of all such injuries done, so as both we and the said princes, or other so complayning, may holde us and themselves fully contented. And that if the saide *Walter Ralegh,* his heires and assignes, shall not make or cause to be made satisfaction accordingly, within such time so to be limitted, that then it shall be lawfull to us our heires and successors, to put the saide *Walter Ralegh,* his heires and assignes and adherents, and all the inhabitants of the said places to be discovered (as is aforesaide) or any of them out of our allegiance and protection, and that from and after such time of putting out of protection the said *Walter Ralegh,* his heires, assignes and adherents, and others so to be put out, and the said places within their habitation, possession and rule, shal be out of our allegeance and protection, and free for all princes and others, to pursue with hostilitie, as being not our subjects, nor by us any way to be avouched, maintained or defended, nor to be holden as any of ours, nor to our protection or dominion, or allegiance any way belonging, for that expresse mention of the cleer yeerely value of the certaintie of the premisses, or any part thereof, or of any other gift, or grant by us, or any our progenitors, or predecessors to the said *Walter Ralegh,* before this time made in these presents be not expressed, or any other grant, ordinance, provision, proclamation, or restraint to the contrarye thereof, before this time given, ordained, or provided, or any other thing, cause, or matter whatsoever, in any wise notwithstanding. In witness whereof, we have caused these our letters to be made patents. Witnesse our selves, at *Westminster,* the 25. day of March, in the sixe and twentieth yeere of our Raigne.

6. FIRST CHARTER OF VIRGINIA
April 10, 1606

(Poore, ed. *The Federal and State Constitutions*, Part II, p. 1889 ff.)

The charter to the Virginia Company granted by King James provided for the incorporation of two companies: the London Company and the Plymouth Company. It was the London Company that established the first permanent English colony in America; the expedition of one hundred and twenty settlers who left England in December, 1606, made their first landfall at Cape Henry, April 29, 1607, and planted a colony at Jamestown May 14. On the three charters of Virginia and the early history of the Colony see, W. Stith, *History of Virginia,* with numerous documents; A. Brown, *Genesis of the United States,* 2 Vols; A. Brown, *First Republic in America;* J. Fiske, *Old Virginia and her Neighbours,* Vol. I; C. M. Andrews, *The Colonial Period of American History,* Vol. I, ch. v.; L. G. Tyler, *England in America,* chs. iii–v. The records of the Virginia Company are being published by S. M. Kingsbury, ed. *Records of the Virginia Company.* On the Company see also A. Brown, *English Politics in Early Virginia History;* E. D. Neill, *History of the Virginia Company of London;* and W. F. Craven, *The Dissolution of the Virginia Company.*

I. *JAMES,* by the Grace of God, King of *England, Scotland, France,* and *Ireland,* Defender of the Faith, &c. WHEREAS our loving and well-disposed Subjects, Sir *Thomas Gates,* and Sir *George Somers,* Knights, *Richard Hackluit,* Clerk, Prebendary of *Westminster,* and *Edward-Maria Wingfield, Thomas Hanham,* and *Ralegh Gilbert,* Esqrs. *William Parker,* and *George Popham,* Gentlemen, and divers others of our loving Subjects, have been humble Suitors unto us, that We would vouchsafe unto them our Licence, to make Habitation, Plantation, and to deduce a Colony of sundry of our People into that Part of *America,* commonly called VIRGINIA, and other Parts and Territories in *America,* either appertaining unto us, or which are not now actually possessed by any *Christian* Prince or People, situate, lying, and being all along the Sea Coasts, between four and thirty Degrees of *Northerly* Latitude from the Equinoctial Line, and five and forty Degrees of the same Latitude, and in the main Land between the same four and thirty and five and forty Degrees,

and the Islands thereunto adjacent, or within one hundred Miles of the Coast thereof;

And to that End, and for the more speedy Accomplishment of their said intended Plantation and Habitation there, are desirous to divide themselves into two several Colonies and Companies; The one consisting of certain Knights, Gentlemen, Merchants, and other Adventurers, of our City of *London* and elsewhere, which are, and from time to time shall be, joined unto them, which do desire to begin their Plantation and Habitation in some fit and convenient Place, between four and thirty and one and forty Degrees of the said Latitude, alongst the Coasts of *Virginia* and Coasts of *America* aforesaid; And the other consisting of sundry Knights, Gentlemen, Merchants, and other Adventurers, of our Cities of *Bristol* and *Exeter,* and of our Town of *Plimouth,* and of other Places, which do join themselves unto that Colony, which do desire to begin their Plantation and Habitation in some fit and convenient Place, between eight and thirty Degrees and five and forty Degrees of the said Latitude, all alongst the said Coast of *Virginia* and *America,* as that Coast lyeth:

We, greatly commending, and graciously accepting of, their Desires for the Furtherance of so noble a Work, which may, by the Providence of Almighty God, hereafter tend to the Glory of his Divine Majesty, in propagating of *Christian* Religion to such People, as yet live in Darkness and miserable Ignorance of the true Knowledge and Worship of God, and may in time bring the Infidels and Savages, living in those Parts, to human Civility, and to a settled and quiet Government; Do, by these our Letters Patents, graciously accept of, and agree to, their humble and well-intended Desires;

AND do therefore, for Us, our Heirs, and Successors, GRANT and agree, that the said Sir *Thomas Gates,* Sir *George Somers, Richard Hackluit,* and *Edward-Maria Wingfield,* Adventurers of and for our City of *London,* and all such others, as are, or shall be, joined unto them of that Colony, shall be called the *first Colony;* And they shall and may begin their said first Plantation and Habitation, at any Place upon the said Coast of *Virginia* or *America,* where they shall think fit and convenient, between the said four and thirty and one and forty Degrees of the said Latitude; And that they shall have all the Lands, . . . from the said first Seat of their Plantation and Habitation by the Space of fifty Miles of *English* Statute Measure, all along the said Coast of *Virginia* and *America,* towards the *West* and *South-west,* as the Coast lyeth, . . . And also all the Lands . . . from the said Place of their first Plantation and Habitation for the space of fifty like *English* Miles, all alongst the said Coast of *Virginia* and *America,* towards the *East* and *Northeast,* or towards the *North,* as the Coast lyeth, . . . And also all the Lands . . . from the same fifty Miles every way on the Sea Coast, directly into the main Land by the Space of one hundred like *English* Miles; . . .

AND we do likewise . . . GRANT and agree, that the said *Thomas Hanham,* and *Ralegh Gilbert, William Parker,* and *George Popham,* and all others of the Town of *Plimouth* in the County of *Devon,* or elsewhere, which are, or shall be, joined unto them of that Colony, shall be called the *second Colony;* And that they shall and may begin their said Plantation and Seat of their first Abode and Habitation, at any Place upon the said Coast of *Virginia* and *America,* where they shall think fit and convenient, between eight and thirty Degrees of the said Latitude, and five and forty Degrees of the same Latitude; And that they shall have all the Lands . . . from the first Seat of their Plantation and Habitation by the Space of fifty like *English* Miles, as is aforesaid, all alongst the said Coast of *Virginia* and *America,* towards the *West* and *Southwest,* or towards the *South,* . . . And also all the Lands . . . from the said Place of their first Plantation and Habitation for the Space of fifty like Miles, all alongst the said Coast of *Virginia* and *America,* towards the *East* and *Northeast,* . . . And also all the Lands . . . from the same fifty Miles every way on the Sea Coast, directly into the main Land, by the Space of one hundred like *English* Miles. . . .

Provided always, and our Will and Pleasure herein is, that the Plantation and Habitation of such of the said Colonies, as shall last plant themselves, as aforesaid, shall not be made within one hundred like *English* Miles of the other of them, that first began to make their Plantation, as aforesaid.

AND we do also ordain . . . that each of the said Colonies shall have a Council, which shall govern and order all Matters and Causes, which shall arise, grow, or happen, to or within the same several Colonies, according to such Laws, Ordinances, and Instructions, as shall be, in that behalf, given and signed with Our Hand or Sign Manual, and pass under the Privy Seal of our Realm of *England;* Each of which Councils shall consist of thirteen Persons, to be ordained, made, and removed, from time to time, according as shall be directed and comprised in the same instructions. . . .

AND that also there shall be a Council established here in *England,* which shall, in like Manner, consist of thirteen Persons, to be, for that Purpose, appointed by Us, . . . which shall be called our *Council of Virginia;* And shall, from time to time, have the superior Managing and Direction, only of and for all Matters, that shall or may concern the Government, as well of the said several Colonies, as of and for any other Part or Place, within the aforesaid Precincts of four and thirty and five and forty Degrees, above mentioned. . . .

AND moreover, we do GRANT . . . that the said several Councils, of and for the said several Colonies, shall and lawfully may, by Virtue hereof, from time to time, without any Interruption of Us . . . , give and take Order, to dig, mine, and search for all Manner of Mines of Gold, Silver, and Copper, as well within any part of their said several Colonies, as for the said main Lands on the Backside of the same Colonies. . . . YIELDING therefore, to Us . . . the fifth Part only of all the same Gold and Silver, and the fifteenth Part of all the same Copper, so to be gotten or had. . . .

Giving and granting, by these Presents, unto the said Sir *Thomas Gates* . . . and their Associates of the said first Colony, and unto the said *Thomas Hanham* . . . and their Associates of the said second Colony . . . Power and Authority to take and surprise, by all Ways and Means whatsoever, all and every Person and Persons, with their Ships, Vessels, Goods and other Furniture, which shall be found trafficking, into any Harbour or Harbours, Creek or Creeks, or Place, within the Limits or Precincts of the said several Colonies and Plantations, not being of the same Colony, until such time, as they, being of any Realms or Dominions under our Obedience, shall pay, or agree to pay, to the Hands of the Treasurer of that Colony, within whose Limits and Precincts they shall so traffick, two and a half upon every Hundred, of any thing, so by them trafficked, bought, or sold; And being Strangers, and not Subjects under our Obeysance, until they shall pay five upon every Hundred, of such Wares and Merchandises, as they shall traffick, buy, or sell, within the Precincts of the said several Colonies, wherein they shall so traffick, buy, or sell, as aforesaid; WHICH Sums of Money, or Benefit, as aforesaid, for and during the Space of one and twenty Years, next ensuing the Date hereof, shall be wholly emploied to the Use, Benefit, and Behoof of the said several Plantations, where such Traffick shall be made; And after the said one and twenty Years ended, the same shall be taken to the Use of Us. . . .

Also we do . . . DECLARE . . . that all and every the Persons, being our Subjects, which shall dwell and inhabit within every or any of the said several Colonies and Plantations, and every of their children, which shall happen to be born within any of the Limits and Precincts of the said several Colonies and Plantations, shall HAVE and enjoy all Liberties, Franchises, and Immunities, within any of our other Dominions, to all Intents and Purposes, as if they had been abiding and born, within this our Realm of *England,* or any other of our said Dominions. . . .

And finally, we do . . . GRANT and agree, to and with the said Sir *Thomas Gates* . . . and all others of the said first Colony, that We . . . , upon Petition in that Behalf to be made, shall, . . . GIVE and GRANT unto such Persons, their Heirs, and Assigns, as the Council of that Colony, or the most Part of them, shall, for that Purpose nominate and assign, all the Lands, Tenements, and Hereditaments, which shall be within the Precincts limited for that Colony, as is aforesaid, To BE HOLDEN of Us, our Heirs, and Successors, as of our Manor at *East-Greenwich* in the County of *Kent,* in free and common Soccage only, and not in Capite: . . .

7. SECOND CHARTER OF VIRGINIA
May 23, 1609

(Poore, ed. *The Federal and State Constitutions,* Part II, p. 1893 ff.)

During the first three years of its history the affairs of the Virginia Company, both the Virginia and the Maine plantations, were badly mismanaged. The second charter made some essential changes in the first: the London and the Plymouth companies were separated; the royal council was replaced by a company council; and control of the colony was vested in the treasurer and his council. For references, see Doc. No. 6.

[After reciting the grant of 1606, the charter continues].

Now, forasmuch as divers and sundry of our loving Subjects, as well Adventurers, as Planters, of the said first Colony . . . have of late been humble Suitors unto Us, that . . . We would be pleased to grant them a further Enlargement and Explanation of the said Grant, Privileges, and Liberties, and that

such Counsellors, and other Officers, may be appointed amongst them, to manage and direct their affairs, as are willing and ready to adventure with them, as also whose Dwellings are not so far remote from the City of *London,* but that they may, at convenient Times, be ready at Hand, to give their Advice and Assistance, upon all occasions requisite.

WE . . . do . . . GIVE, GRANT, and CONfirm, to our trusty and well-beloved Subjects, [enumerates grantees] . . . , and to such, and so many, as they do, or shall hereafter, admit to be joined with them, in form hereafter in these presents expressed, whether they go in their Persons, to be Planters there in the said Plantation, or whether they go not, but adventure their monies, goods, or Chattels, that they shall be one Body or Commonalty perpetual, and shall have perpetual Succession, and one common Seal, to serve for the said Body or Commonalty, and that they, and their Successors, shall be known, called, and incorporated by the Name of, *The Treasurer and Company of Adventurers and Planters of the City of London for the first Colony in Virginia.* . . .

And we do also . . . give, grant and confirm, unto the said Treasurer and Company, and their Successors, under the Reservations, Limitations, and Declarations, hereafter expressed, all those Lands, Countries, and Territories, situate, lying, and being, in that Part of *America* called *Virginia*, from the Point of Land, called Cape or *Point Comfort,* all along the Sea Coast, to the Northward two hundred Miles, and from the said Point of *Cape Comfort,* all along the Sea Coast, to the Southward two hundred Miles, and all that Space and Circuit of Land, lying from the Sea Coast of the Precinct aforesaid, up into the Land, throughout from Sea to Sea, West, and Northwest; . . .

AND forasmuch, as the good and prosperous Success of the said Plantation cannot but chiefly depend, next under the Blessing of God, and the Support of our Royal Authority, upon the provident and good Direction of the whole Enterprize, by a careful and understanding Council, and that it is not convenient, that all the Adventurers shall be so often drawn to meet and assemble, as shall be requisite for them to have Meetings and Conference about the Affairs thereof; Therefore we DO ORDAIN, establish, and confirm, that there shall be perpetually one COUNCIL here resident, according to the Tenour of our former Letters-patents. . . .

AND further we do , . . GIVE and GRANT full Power and Authority to our said Council, here resident, . . . to nominate, make, constitute, ordain, and confirm, by such Name or Names, Stile or Stiles, as to them shall seem good, And likewise to revoke, discharge, change, and alter, as well all and singular Governors, Officers, and Ministers, which already have been made, as also which hereafter shall be by them thought fit and needful to be made or used, for the Government of the said Colony and Plantation: AND also to make, ordain, and establish all Manner of Orders, Laws, Directions, In-

structions, Forms, and Ceremonies of Government and Magistracy, fit and necessary, for and concerning the Government of the said Colony and Plantation; And the same, at all times hereafter, to abrogate, revoke, or change, . . . as they, in their good Discretion, shall think to be fittest for the Good of the Adventurers and inhabitants there. . . .

AND we do further . . . ORDAIN and establish, that the said Treasurer and Council here resident, and their Successors, or any four of them, being assembled (the Treasurer being one) shall, from time to time, have full Power and Authority, to admit and receive any other Person into their Company, Corporation, and Freedom; And further, in a General Assembly of the Adventurers, with the Consent of the greater Part, upon good Cause, to disfranchise and put out any Person or Persons, out of the said Freedom or Company. . . .

ALSO we do . . . DECLARE . . . that all and every the Persons being our Subjects, which shall go and inhabit within the said Colony and Plantation, and every their Children and Posterity; which shall happen to be born within any of the Limits thereof, shall HAVE and ENJOY all Liberties, Franchizes, and Immunities of Free Denizens and natural Subjects within any of our other Dominions to all Interests and Purposes, as if they had been abiding and born within this our realm of *England*. . . .

AND forasmuch, as it shall be necessary for all such our loving Subjects, as shall inhabit within the said Precincts of *Virginia,* aforesaid, to determine to live together, in the Fear and true Worship of Almighty God, Christian Peace, and civil Quietness, each with other, whereby every one may, with more Safety, Pleasure, and Profit, enjoy that, whereunto they shall attain with great Pain and Peril; We . . . do GIVE and GRANT unto the said Treasurer and Company, . . . and to such Governors, Officers, and Ministers, as shall be, by our said Council, constituted and appointed, . . . that they shall and may, from time to time for ever hereafter, within the said Precincts of *Virginia,* . . . have full and absolute Power and Authority, to correct, punish, pardon, govern, and rule, all such the Subjects of Us . . . as shall, from time to time, adventure themselves in any Voyage thither, or that shall, at any time hereafter, inhabit in the Precincts and Territories of the said Colony, . . .

AND further . . . in all Questions and Doubts that shall arise upon any Difficulty of Construction or Interpretation of Any thing contained either in this, or in our former Letters-patents, the same shall be . . . interpreted in most ample and beneficial manner for the said Treasurer and Company . . .

AND lastly, because the principal Effect, which we can desire or expect of this Action, is the Conversion and Reduction of the People in those Parts unto the true Worship of God and Christian Religion, in which Respect we should be loath, that any Person should be permitted to pass, that we suspected to affect the Superstitions of the Church of *Rome,* we do hereby DECLARE, that it is our Will and Pleasure, that none be permitted to pass in any Voyage, from time to time to be made into the said Country, but such, as first shall have taken the Oath of Supremacy; . . .

8. THE THIRD CHARTER OF VIRGINIA
March 12, 1612

(F. N. Thorpe, ed. *Federal and State Constitutions,* Vol. VII, p. 3803 ff.)

The third charter of Virginia added the island of Bermuda, which had been discovered by the English in 1609, to the jurisdictions of the Company, provided for more democratic government and a greater degree of independence for the Company, enlarged the powers of the Company, and instituted a lottery. The Company subsequently sold Bermuda. This charter of 1612 was annulled in 1624, when Virginia became a royal colony. See, references under Doc. 6 and W. F. Craven, *The Dissolution of the Virginia Company.*

. . . Now forasmuch as we are given to understand, that in those Seas adjoining to the said Coasts of *Virginia,* and without the Compass of those two hundred Miles by Us so granted unto the said Treasurer and Company as aforesaid, and yet not far distant from the said Colony in *Virginia,* there are or may be divers Islands lying desolate and uninhabited, some of which are already made known and discovered by the Industry, Travel, and Expences of the said Company, and others also are supposed to be and remain as yet unknown and undiscovered, all and every of which it may import the said Colony both in Safety and Policy of Trade to populate and plant; in Regard whereof, as well for the preventing of Peril, as for the better Commodity of the said Colony, they have been humble suitors unto Us, that We would be pleased to grant unto them an Enlargement of our said former Letters-patents, as well for a more ample Extent of their Limits and Territories into the Seas adjoining to and upon the Coast of *Virginia,* as also for some other Matters and Articles concerning the better government of the said Company and Colony, . . .

We therefore . . . do by these Presents give, grant, and confirm to the said Treasurer and Company of Adventurers and Planters of the city of *London* for the first Colony in *Virginia* and to their Heirs and Successors for ever, all and singular those Islands whatsoever situate and being in any Part of the Ocean Seas bordering upon the Coast of our said first Colony in *Virginia,* and being within three Hundred Leagues of any of the Parts heretofore granted to the said Treasurer and Company in our said former Letters-patents as aforesaid, and being within or between the one-and-fortieth and thirtieth Degrees of Northerly Latitude . . . Provided always, that the said Islands or any Premises herein mentioned, or by these Presents intended or meant to be granted, be not actually possessed or inhabited by any other Christian Prince or Estate, nor be within the Bounds, Limits, or Territories of the Northern Colony heretofore by Us granted to be planted by divers of our loving Subjects in the North Parts of *Virginia.* . . .

And we do hereby ordain and grant by these Presents, that the said Treasurer and Company of Adventurers and Planters aforesaid, shall and may, once every week, or oftener, at their Pleasure, hold, and keep a Court and Assembly for the better Order and Government of the said Plantation, and such Things as shall concern the same: And that any five Persons of our Council for the said first Colony in *Virginia*, for the Time being, of which Company the Treasurer, or his Deputy, to be always one, and the Number of fifteen others, at the least, of the Generality of the said Company, assembled together in such Manner, as is and hath been heretofore used and accustomed, shall be said, taken, held, and reputed to be, and shall be a *sufficient Court* of the said Company, for the handling and ordering, and dispatching of all such casual and particular Occurrences, and accidental Matters, of less Consequence and Weight, as shall from Time to Time happen, touching and concerning the said Plantation. . . .

9. ORDINANCE FOR VIRGINIA
July 24, 1621

(F. N. Thorpe, ed. *Federal and State Constitutions,* Vol. VII, p. 3810 ff.)

The first Assembly of Virginia was convened July 30, 1619 by Governor Yeardley, under the authority of the Virginia Company, and marks the beginning of representative government in America. The document authorizing the convening of this first assembly has been lost; the Ordinance of 1621 is believed to be an almost exact reproduction of the earlier one. See references to Doc. No. 6.

An ordinance and Constitution of the Treasurer, Council, and Company in England, for a Council of State and General Assembly. Dated July 24, 1621.

To all People, to whom these Presents shall come, be seen, or heard The Treasurer, Council, and Company of Adventurers and Planters for the City of *London* for the first colony of *Virginia*, send Greeting. Know ye that we, the said Treasurer, Council, and Company, taking into our careful Consideration the present State, of the said Colony of *Virginia*, and intending, by the Divine Assistance, to settle such a Form of Government there as may be to the greatest Benefit and Comfort of the People, and whereby all Injustice, Grievances, and Oppression may be prevented and kept off as much as possible from the said Colony, have thought fit to make our Entrance, by ordering and establishing such Supreme Councils, as may not only be assisting to the Governor for the time being, in the Administration of Justice, and the executing of other Duties for this office belonging, but also, by their vigilant care and Prudence, may provide, as well for a Remedy of all Inconveniences, growing from time to time, as also for advancing of Increase, Strength, Stability, and Prosperity of the said Colony:

II. We therefore, the said Treasurer, Council, and Company, by Authority directed to us from his Majesty under the Great Seal, upon mature Deliberation, do hereby order and declare, that, from henceforward, there shall be Two SUPREME COUNCILS in *Virginia*, for the better Government of the said Colony aforesaid.

III. The one of which Councils, to be called THE COUNCIL OF STATE (and whose Office shall chiefly be assisting, with their Care, Advise, and Circumspection, to the said Governor) shall be chosen, nominated, placed and displaced, from time to time, by Us, the said Treasurer, Council, and Company, and our Successors: Which Council of State shall consist, for the present, only of these Persons, as are here inserted, *viz.* Sir *Francis Wyat,* Governor of *Virginia,* Captain *Francis West,* Sir *George Yeardley,* Knight, Sir *William Neuce,* Knight Marshal of *Virginia,* Mr. *George Sandys,* Treasurer, Mr. *George Thorpe,* Deputy of the College, Captain *Thomas Neuce,* Deputy for the Company, Mr. *Pawlet,* Mr. *Leech,* Captain *Nathaniel Powel,* Mr. *Harwood,* Mr. *Samuel Macock,* Mr. *Christopher Davison,* Secretary, *Doctor Pots* Physician to the Company, Mr. *Roger Smith,* Mr. *John Berkley,* Mr. *John Rolfe,* Mr. *Ralph Hamer,* Mr. *John Pountis,* Mr. *Michael Lapworth.* Which said Counsellors and Council we earnestly pray and desire, and in his Majesty's Name strictly charge and command, that (all Factions, Partialities, and sinister Respect laid aside) they bend their Care and Endeavors to assist the said Governor; first and principally in the Advancement of the Honour and Service of God, and the Enlargement of his Kingdom amongst the Heathen People; and next, in erecting of the said Colony in due obedience to his Majesty, and all lawful Authority from his Majesty's Directions; and lastly, in maintaining the said People in Justice and *Christian* Conversation amongst themselves, and in Strength and Ability to withstand their Enemies. And this Council, to be always, or for the most Part, residing about or near the Governor.

IV. The other Council, more generally to be called by the Governor, once yearly, and no oftener, but for very extraordinary and important occasions, shall consist, for the present, of the said Council of State, and of two Burgesses out of every Town, Hundred, or other particular Plantation, to be respectively chosen by the Inhabitants; Which Council shall be called THE GENERAL ASSEMBLY, wherein (as also in the said Council of State) all Matter shall be decided, determined, and ordered, by the greater Part of the Voices then present; reserving to the Governor always a Negative Voice. And this General Assembly shall have free Power to treat, consult, and conclude, as well of all emergent Occasions concerning the Publick Weal of the said Colony and every Part thereof, as also to make, ordain, and enact such general Laws and Orders, for the Behoof of the said Colony, and the good Government thereof, as shall, from time to time, appear necessary or requisite;

V. Whereas in all other Things, we require the said General Assembly, as also the said Council of State, to imitate and follow the Policy of the Form of Government— Laws, Customs, and Manner of Trial, and other Administration of Justice, used in the Realm of *England,* as near as may be, even as ourselves, by his Majesty's Letters Patent, are required.

VI. Provided, that no Law or Ordinance, made in the said General Assembly, shall be or continue in Force or Validity, unless the same shall be solemnly ratified and confirmed, in a General Quarter Court of the said Company here in England and so ratified, be returned to them under our Seal; It being our Intent to afford the like Measure also unto the said Colony, that after the Government of the said Colony shall once have been well framed, and settled accordingly, which is to be done by Us, as by Authority derived from his Majesty, and the same shall have been so by Us declared, no Orders of Court afterwards shall bind the said Colony, unless they be ratified in like Manner in the General Assemblies. IN WITNESS whereof we have here unto set our Common Seal, the 24th of *July* 1621, and in the Year of the Reign of our Sovereign Lord, JAMES, King of *England,* &c., the —— and of Scotland the ——

10. THE LEYDEN AGREEMENT
1618

(W. Walker, *The Creeds and Platforms of Congregationalism,* p. 89–90.)

A group of London Separatists had settled in Amsterdam as early as 1593. In 1607–08 Separatists from the Scrooby Congregation joined the congregation in Amsterdam, but shortly moved to Leyden. In 1617 the Scrooby-Leyden group determined to move to America and applied to the Virginia Company for a patent to land in Virginia. To further this application, the congregation drew up these Seven Articles as assurance to the King of loyalty and orthodoxy. The King however promised only that "he would connive at them and not molest them provided they carried themselves peaceably." Eventually they secured a patent from the Virginia Company. See Doc. No. 11. On the Leyden Agreement and the Scrooby-Leyden Congregation see W. Bradford, *History of the Plymouth Plantation;* J. E. Goodwin, *The Pilgrim Republic;* L. Bacon, *The Gene-* *sis of the New England Churches;* H. M. Dexter, *Congregationalism of the Last Three Hundred Years as Seen in its Literature,* Lectures v–vii; A. E. Dunning, *Congregationalists in America,* ch. iii; G. Bancroft, in New York Hist. Soc. *Collections,* Second Ser. Vol. III; D. Plooij, *The Pilgrim Fathers from a Dutch Point of View.*

Seven Artikes which ye Church of Leyden sent to ye Counsell of England to bee considered of in respeckt of their judgements occationed about theer going to Virginia Anno 1618

1. To ye confession of fayth published in ye name of ye Church of England & to every artikell theerof wee do wth ye reformed

churches wheer wee live & also els where assent wholy.

2. As wee do acknolidg ye docktryne of fayth theer tawght so do wee ye fruites and effeckts of ye same docktryne to ye begetting of saving fayth in thousands in ye land (conformistes and reformistes as ye are called) wth whom also as wth our bretheren wee do desyer to keepe sperituall communion in peace and will pracktis in our parts all lawfull thinges.

3. The Kings Majesty wee acknoledge for Supreame Governer in his Dominion in all causes and over all parsons, and ye none maye decklyne or apeale from his authority or judgement in any cause whatsoever, byt y in all thinges obedience is dewe unto him, ether active, if ye thing commanded be not agaynst God's woord, or passive yf itt bee, except pardon can bee obtayned.

4. Wee judg itt lawfull for his Majesty to apoynt bishops; civill overseers, or officers in awthoryty onder hime, in ye severall provinces, dioses, congregatiòns or parrishes to oversee ye Churches and governe them civilly according to ye Lawes of ye Land, untto whom ye ar in all thinges to give an account & by them to bee ordered according to Godlynes.

5. The authoryty of ye present bishops in ye Land wee do acknowlidg so far forth as ye same is indeed derived from his Majesty untto them and as ye proseed in his name, whom we will also theerein honor in all things and hime in them.

6. Wee beleeve yt no sinod, classes, convocation or assembly of Ecclesiasticall officers hath any power or awthoryty att all but as ye same by ye Majestraet geven untto them.

7. And lastly, wee desyer to geve untto all Superiors dew honnor to preserve ye untiy of ye speritt wth all ye feare God, to have peace wth all men what in us lyeth & wheerin wee err to bee instructed by any.

Subscribed by
John Robinson
and
Willyam Bruster

11. THE MAYFLOWER COMPACT
November 11, 1620

(Poore, ed. *The Federal and State Constitutions*, Part I, p. 931.)

The Separatists living in Leyden, Holland, desired for various reasons to transplant their colony to America. In 1619 they secured from the Virginia Company a patent for a private plantation. The Pilgrims, reinforced by some seventy persons from London, sailed from Plymouth in September, 1620, and arrived off Cape Cod in November. Some of the London recruits were an "undesirable lot" and, Bradford tells us, boasted that they were not under the jurisdiction of the Virginia Company and "would use their owne libertie". In order to establish some form of government, therefore, the Pilgrim leaders drew up the famous Mayflower Compact. The Compact was not intended as a constitution, but was an extension of the customary church covenant to civil circumstances. Inasmuch as the Plymouth settlers were never able to secure a charter, the Mayflower compact remained the only form of constitution of the colony. See, W. Bradford, *History of the Plymouth Plantation*, various eds.; A. Young, *Chronicles of the Pilgrim Fathers, 1602-25;* E. Arber, ed. *Story of the Pilgrim Fathers, 1606-23;* J. Fiske, *Beginnings of New England;* J. G. Palfrey, *History of New England,* Vol. I; J. A. Doyle, *The English Colonies in America,* Vol. II, pt. I; E. Eggleston, *The Beginners of a Nation;* J. T. Adams, *The Founding of New England;* C. M. Andrews, *The Fathers of New England;* C. M. Andrews, *The Colonial Period of American History,* Vol. I, ch xIII; L. G. Tyler, *England in America,* ch. ix; H. L. Osgood, *American Colonies in the Seventeenth Century,* Vol. I; J. A. Goodwin, *The Pilgrim Republic;* A. Lord, "The Mayflower Compact," *Proceedings* of the Am. Antiquarian Soc., 1921; A. C. McLaughlin, *Foundations of American Constitutionalism,* ch. i; V. L. Parrington, *The Colonial Mind,* p. 16 ff.

IN The Name of God, Amen. We, whose names are underwritten, the Loyal Subjects of our dread Sovereign Lord King *James,* by the Grace of God, of *Great Britain, France,* and *Ireland,* King, *Defender of the Faith,* &c. Having undertaken for the Glory of God, and Advancement of the Christian Faith, and the Honour of our King and Country, a Voyage to plant the first colony in the northern Parts of Virginia; Do by these Presents, solemnly and mutually in the

Presence of God and one another, covenant and combine ourselves together into a civil Body Politick, for our better Ordering and Preservation, and Furtherance of the Ends aforesaid; And by Virtue hereof do enact, constitute, and frame, such just and equal Laws, Ordinances, Acts, Constitutions, and Offices, from time to time, as shall be thought most meet and convenient for the general Good of the Colony; unto which we promise all due Submission and Obedience. In WITNESS whereof we have hereunto subscribed our names at *Cape Cod* the eleventh of *November*, in the Reign of our Sovereign Lord King *James* of *England*, *France*, and *Ireland*, the eighteenth and of *Scotland*, the fifty-fourth. *Anno Domini*, 1620

Mr. John Carver
Mr. William Bradford

Mr. Stephen Hopkins
Digery Priest

Mr. Edward Winslow
Mr. William Brewster
Isaac Allerton
Miles Standish
John Alden
John Turner
Francis Eaton
James Chilton
John Craxton
John Billington
Joses Fletcher
John Goodman
Mr. Samuel Fuller
Mr. Christopher
     Martin
Mr. William Mullins
Mr. William White
Mr. Richard Warren
John Howland

Thomas Williams
Gilbert Winslow
Edmund Margesson
Peter Brown
Richard Bitteridge
George Soule
Edward Tilly
John Tilly
Francis Cooke
Thomas Rogers
Thomas Tinker
John Ridgate
Edward Fuller
Richard Clark
Richard Gardiner
Mr. John Allerton
Thomas English
Edward Doten
Edward Liester.

12. THE FIRST CHARTER OF MASSACHUSETTS
March 4, 1629

(F. N. Thorpe, ed. *Federal and State Constitutions*, Vol. III, p. 1846 ff.)

In 1620 the survivors of the Plymouth Company applied to the crown for a charter for settlement in New England, and were granted the land from the 40th to the 48th parallel, under the name of the Council for New England. It was from this body that the Pilgrims secured their patent in 1621. In 1623 the "Dorchester Adventurers" had established a fishing settlement at Cape Ann; subsequently the Adventurers, under the leadership of the Rev. John White, secured from the Council for New England a patent to this territory. This company was enlarged, and under the name of the Governor and Company of the Massachusetts Bay in New England secured the royal charter of March 4, 1629. In as much as this charter granted to the Massachusetts Bay Company territory previously granted to the Council for New England, there was some doubt about its legality. The Massachusetts Bay Company had the support of the powerful Earl of Warwick, who was titular President of the Council for New England. "Probably no one," concludes Professor C. M. Andrews, "would deny that the charter of the Massachusetts Bay Company was covertly and even 'surreptitiously' obtained". For the process by which the charter of the Company became the constitution of a colony, see Doc. No. 13. On the Charter, see, J. T. Adams, *The Founding of New England;* C. M. Andrews, *Fathers of New England;* J. Fiske, *The Beginnings of New England;* A. P. Newton, *Colonizing Activities of the English Puritans;* S. E.

Morison, *Builders of the Bay Colony;* F. Rose-Troup, *The Massachusetts Bay Company and its Predecessors;* F. Rose-Troup, *John White;* the charter and other related source material is in The Founding of Massachusetts, Mass. Hist. Society, *Proceedings,* Vol. LXII.

CHARLES, BY THE GRACE OF GOD Kinge of England . . . [there follows a recital of the patent of 1620 and the grant to Sir Henry Rosewell of 1628, which grant is by this charter confirmed, and continues:]

AND FURTHER, know yee, . . . Wee . . . doe . . . give and graunte vnto the saide Sir Henry Rosewell, Sir John Younge, Sir Richard Saltonstall, Thomas Southcott, John Humfrey, John Endecott, Symon Whetcombe, Isaak Johnson, Samuell Aldersey, John Ven, Mathewe Cradock, George Harwood, Increase Nowell, Richard Pery, Richard Bellingham, Nathaniel Wright, Samuell Vassall, Theophilus Eaton, Thomas Goffe, Thomas Adams, John Browne, Samuell Browne, Thomas Hutchins, William Vassall, William Pinchion, and George Foxcrofte, their Heires and Assignes, all that Part of Newe England in America, which lyes and extendes betweene a great River there, comonlie called Monomack River, alias Merrimack River, and a certen other River there, called Charles River, being in the Bottome of a certain Bay there, comonlie called Massachusetts, . . . ; and also all and singuler those Landes and Hereditaments whatsoever, lying within the Space of Three Englishe Myles on the South Parte of the said River, called Charles River, . . . also all and singular the Landes . . . , lying and being within the Space of Three Englishe Miles to the southward of the southermost Parte of the said Baye, called Massachusetts, ... And also all those Landes and Hereditaments whatsoever, which lye and be within the Space of Three Englishe Myles to the Northward of the saide River, called Monomack, alias Merrymack, . . . and all Landes and Hereditaments whatsoever, lyeing within the Lymitts aforesaide, North and South, in Latitude and Bredth, and in Length and Longitude, of and within all the Bredth aforesaide, throughout the mayne Landes there, from the Atlantick and Westerne Sea and Ocean on the Easte Parte, to the South Sea on the West Parte; . . . and also all Islandes in America aforesaide, in the saide Seas, . . . and all Mynes and Mynerals as well Royal mynes of Gold and Silver . . . whatsoever, in the said Landes and Premisses, . . . and free Libertie of fishing in or within any the Rivers or Waters within the Boundes and Lymytts aforesaid, and the Seas thereunto adjoining; . . .

WEE HAVE FURTHER . . . Given, graunted and confirmed, . . . vnto Sir Henry Rosewell, [etc.], and all such others as shall hereafter be admitted . . . shall . . . be, . . . one Body corporate and politique in Fact and Name, by the Name of the Governor and Company of the Massachusetts Bay in Newe-England, . . . Wee doe . . . ordeyne, . . . that by that name they shall have perpetuall Succession, and . . . shall and maie be capeable and enabled aswell to implead, and to be impleaded, and to prosecute, demaund, and aunswere, and be aunsweared vnto, in all and singuler Suites, Causes, Querrells, and Accons, of what kinde or nature soever. And also to have, take, possesse, acquire, and purchase any Landes, Tenements, or Hereditaments, or any Goodes or Chattells, . . .

AND FURTHER, . . . That . . . there shalbe one Governor, one Deputy Governor, and eighteene Assitants of the same Company,

to be from tyme to tyme constituted, elected and chosen out of the Freemen of the saide Company, . . . which said Officers shall applie themselves to take care for the best disposeing and ordering of the generall buysines and Affaires of, for, and concerning the said Landes and Premisses . . . and the Government of the People there. . . .

AND FURTHER, . . . That the Governor of the saide Company . . . shall have Authoritie from tyme to tyme . . . to give order for the assembling of the saide Company, and . . . saide Company, . . . maie once every Moneth, or oftener at their Pleasures, assemble and houlde and keepe a Courte or Assemblie of themselves, for the better ordering and directing of their Affaires, and that any seaven or more persons of the Assistants, togither with the Governor, or Deputie Governor soe assembled, . . . shalbe a full and sufficient Courte or Assemblie of the said Company, . . . and . . . WEE DOE . . . give and graunte . . . That the Governor, . . . and six of the Assistants at the least to be seaven, shall have full Power and authoritie to choose, nominate, and appointe, such and soe many others as they shall thinke fitt, . . . to be free of the said Company and Body, and them into the same to admitt; and to elect and constitute such Officers as they shall think fitt and requisite, for the ordering, mannaging, and dispatching of the Affaires of the saide Governor and Company, and their Successors; And to make Lawes and Ordinances for the Good and Welfare of the saide Company, and for the Government and ordering of the saide Landes and Plantacon, and the People inhabiting . . . the same, as to them from tyme to tyme shalbe thought meete, . . .

AND, . . . Wee doe graunte to the saide, Governor and Company, . . . That all and every the Subiects of Vs, . . . which shall . . . inhabite within the saide Landes . . . , shall have and enjoy all liberties and Immunities of free and naturall Subjects within any of the Domynions of Vs, . . . And . . . it shall and maie be lawfull, to and for the Governor . . . and such of the Assistants and Freemen of the said Company for the Tyme being as shalbe assembled in any of their generall Courts aforesaide, or in any other Courtes to be specially sumoned and assembled for that Purpose, or the greater

Parte of them . . . from tyme to tyme, to make, ordeine, and establishe all Manner of wholesome and reasonable Orders, Lawes, Statutes, and Ordinnces, Direcčons, and Instrucčons, not contrairie to the Lawes of this our Realme of England, aswell for setling of the Formes and Ceremonies of Governm^t and Magistracy, . . . and for the directing, . . . of all other Matters and Thinges, whereby our said People, . . . may be soe religiously, peaceablie, and civilly governed, as their good Life and orderlie Conversacon,

maie wynn and incite the Natives of Country, to the Knowledg and Obedience of the onlie true God and Sauior of Mankinde, and the Christian Fayth, which in our Royall Intencon, and the Adventurers free Profession, is the principall Ende of this Plantacion. . . .

Witnes ourself, at Westminster, the fourth day of March in the fourth Yeare of our Raigne.

Per Breve de Privato Sigillo,

Wolseley.

13. THE CAMBRIDGE AGREEMENT
August 26, 1629

(T. Hutchinson, *Collection of Original Papers relative to the History of the Colony of Massachusetts-Bay,* p. 25 ff.)

By this agreement some of the leading members of the Massachusetts Bay Company bound themselves to embark for America and take the charter with them. The transfer of the charter meant that a business company would be metamorphosed into a plantation. The purpose of this drastic and probably illegal action was to secure the enterprise from interference by the Government of England. For the significance of this transfer of the charter see, C. M. Andrews, *Our Earliest Colonial Settlements,* p. 67 ff.; C. M. Andrews, *The Colonial Period of American History,* Vol. I, ch. xviii.

The True Coppie of the agreement at Cambridge, August 26, 1629.

Upon due consideration of the state of the plantation now in hand for New England, wherein wee (whose names are hereunto subscribed) have engaged ourselves: and having weighed the greatnes of the worke in regard of the consequence, God's glory and the churches good: As also in regard of the difficultyes and discouragements which in all probabilityes must be forecast upon the execution of this businesse: Considering withall that this whole adventure growes upon the joint confidence we have in each others fidelity and resolution herein, so as no man of us would have adventured it without assurance of the rest: Now, for the better encouragement of ourselves and others that shall joyne with us in this action, and to the end that every man may without scruple dispose of his estate and afayres as may best fitt his preparation for this voyage, it is fully and faithfully agreed amongst us, and every of us doth hereby freely and sincerely prom-

ise and bind himselfe in the word of a christian and in the presence of God who is the searcher of all hearts, that we will so really endeavour the execution of this worke, as by God's assistance we will be ready . . . in our persons, and with such of our severall familyes as are to go with us, and such provision as we are able conveniently to furnish ourselves withall, to embarke for the said plantation by the first of March next, . . . at such port or ports of this land as shall be agreed upon by the Companie, to the end to passe the seas (under God's protection) to inhabite and continue in New England. Provided always, that before the last of September next the whole government together with the patent for the said plantation be first by an order of court legally transferred and established to remain with us and others which shall inhabite upon the said plantation . . . And we do further promise every one for himselfe, that shall fayle to be ready through his own default by the day appointed, to pay for every day's default the sum of 3£ to the vse of the rest of the Companie who shall be ready by the same day and time.

This was done by order of court the 29th of August, 1629.

Richard Saltonstall
Tho: Dudley
William Vassall
Nicko: West
Isaack Johnson
John Humfrey

Tho: Sharp
Increase Nowell
John Winthrop
Will: Pinchon
Kellam Browne
William Colbron

14. CHARTER OF FREEDOMS AND EXEMPTIONS TO PATROONS
June 7, 1629

(E. B. O'Callaghan, ed. *Documents Relative to the Colonial History of the State of New York,* Vol. II, p. 553 ff.)

This charter of privileges to the patroons established the patroon system of land tenure in New Netherland and New York. Under this charter a few patroons secured control of most of the land along the Hudson River; some of the land grants, such as those to Killian Van Rensselaer, were enormous. On the Dutch settlement of New Netherland, see E. B. O'Callaghan, *History of New Netherland,* 2 Vols.; T. A. Janvier, *Dutch Founding of New York;* A. C. Flick, ed. *History of the State of New York,* Vol. I, chs. vii–x; C. W. Rife, "Land Tenure in New Netherland"; *Essays in Colonial History presented to C. M. Andrews,* p. 41 ff.; H. L. Osgood, *American Colonies in the XVII century,* Vol. II, ch. v.

.   .   .   .   .   .

III. All such shall be acknowledged Patroons of New Netherland who shall, within the space of four years next after they have given notice to any of the Chambers of the Company here, or to the Commander or Council there, undertake to plant a Colonie there of fifty souls, upwards of fifteen years old; one-fourth part within one year, and within three years after the sending of the first, making together four years, the remainder, to the full number of fifty persons . . . ; but it is to be observed that the Company reserve the Island of the Manhattes to themselves.

IV. They shall, from the time they make known the situation of the places where they propose to settle Colonies, have the preference to all others of the absolute property of such lands as they have there chosen; but in case the situation should not afterwards please them, or they should have been mistaken as to the quality of the land, they may, after remonstrating concerning the same to the Commander and Council there, be at liberty to choose another place.

V. The Patroons, by virtue of their power, shall and may be permitted, at such places as they shall settle their Colonies, to extend their limits four leagues along the shore, that is, on one side of a navigable river, or two leagues on each side of a river, and so far into the country as the situation of the occupiers will permit; provided and conditioned that the Company keep to themselves the lands lying and remaining between the limits of Colonies, to dispose thereof, when and at such time as they shall think proper, in such manner that no person shall be allowed to come within seven or eight leagues of them without their consent, unless the situation of the land thereabout be such that the Commander and Council, for good reasons, should order otherwise. . . .

VI. They shall forever possess and enjoy all the lands lying within the aforesaid limits, together with the fruits, rights, minerals, rivers and fountains thereof; as also the chief command and lower jurisdictions, fishing, fowling and grinding, to the exclusion of all others, to be holden from the Company as a perpetual inheritance, without it ever devolving again to the Company, and in case it should devolve, to be redeemed and repossessed with twenty guilders per Colonie, to be paid to this Company, at the Chamber here or to their Commander there, within a year and six weeks after the same occurs, each at the Chamber where he originally sailed from; and further, no person or persons whatsoever shall be privileged to fish and hunt but the Patroons and such as they shall permit. And in case any one should in time prosper so much as to found one or more cities, he shall have power and authority to establish officers and magistrates there, and to make use of the title of his Colonie, acording to his pleasure and to the quality of the persons. . . .

X. The Patroons and colonists shall be privileged to send their people and effects thither, in ships belonging to the Company, provided they take the oath, and pay to the Company for bringing over the people, as mentioned in the first article. . . .

XII. Inasmuch as it is intended to people the Island of the Manhattes first, all fruits and wares that are produced on the lands situate on the North river, and lying thereabout, shall, for the present, be brought there before being sent elsewhere, . . .

XIII. All the Patroons of Colonies in New Netherland, and of Colonies on the Island of Manhattes, shall be at liberty to sail and traffic all along the coast, from Florida to Terra Neuf, provided that they do again return with all such goods as they shall get in trade to the Island of Manhattes, and pay five per cent duty to the Company, in order, if possible, that, after the necessary inventory of the goods shipped be taken, the same may be sent hither. . . .

XV. It shall be also free for the aforesaid Patroons to traffic and trade all along the coast of New Netherland and places circumjacent, with such goods as are consumed there, and receive in return for them all sorts of merchandise that may be had there, except beavers, otters, minks, and all sorts of peltry, which trade the Company reserve to themselves. But the same shall be permitted at such places where the Company have no factories, conditioned that such traders shall be obliged to bring all the peltry they can procure to the Island of Manhattes, in case it may be, at any rate, practicable, and there deliver to the Director, to be by him shipped hither with the ships and goods; or, if they should come here without going there, then to give notice thereof to the Company, that a proper account thereof may be taken, in order that they may pay to the Company one guilder for each merchantable beaver and otter skin; the property, risk and all other charges remaining on account of the Patroons or owners.

XVI. All coarse wares that the Colonists of the Patroons there shall consume, such as pitch, tar, weed-ashes, wood, grain, fish, salt, hearthstone and such like things shall be conveyed in the Company's ships, at the rate of eighteen guilders per last. . . .

XVIII. The Company promises the colonists of the Patroons that they shall be free from customs, taxes, excise, imposts or any other contributions for the space of ten years; and after the expiration of the said ten years, at the highest, such customs as the goods pay here for the present. . . .

XX. From all judgments given by the Courts of the Patroons for upwards of fifty guilders, there may be an appeal to the Company's Commander and Council in New Netherland.

XXI. In regard to such private persons as on their own account, . . . shall be inclined to go thither and settle, they shall, with the approbation of the Director and Council there, be at liberty to take up and take possession of as much land as they shall be able properly to improve, . . .

XXIII. Whosoever, whether colonists of Patroons for their Patroons, or free persons for themselves, or others for their masters, shall discover any shores, bays or other fit places for erecting fisheries, or the making of salt ponds, they may take possession thereof, and begin to work on them as their own absolute property, to the exclusion of all others. And it is consented to that the Patroons of colonists may send ships along the coast of New Netherland, on the cod fishery, . . .

XXVI. Whoever shall settle any Colonie out of the limits of the Manhattes Island, shall be obliged to satisfy the Indians for the land they shall settle upon, and they may extend or enlarge the limits of their Colonies if they settle a proportionate number of colonists thereon.

XXVII. The Patroons and colonists shall in particular, and in the speediest manner, endeavor to find out ways and means whereby they may support a Minister and Schoolmaster, that thus the service of God and zeal for religion may not grow cool and be neglected among them, and they shall, for the first, procure a Comforter of the sick there. . . .

XXIX. The Colonists shall not be permitted to make any woolen, linen or cotton cloth, nor weave any other stuffs there, on pain of being banished, and as perjurers, to be arbitrarily punished.

XXX. The Company will use their endeavors to supply the colonists with as many Blacks as they conveniently can, on the conditions hereafter to be made, in such manner, however, that they shall not be bound to do it for a longer time than they shall think proper.

XXXI. The Company promise to finish the fort on the Island of the Manhattes, and to put it in a posture of defence without delay.

15. THE CHARTER OF MARYLAND
June 20, 1632

(F. N. Thorpe, ed. *Federal and State Constitutions*, Vol. III, p. 1677 ff.)

George Calvert, first Lord Baltimore, had attempted to found a colony in Newfoundland, but discouraged by the uninviting character of his grant there persuaded Charles I to grant him a patent to land north of the Potomac. George Calvert died in April, 1632, and the charter was issued to his son, Cecil, second Lord Baltimore. The charter of Maryland was modeled after the earlier charter to the Newfoundland plantation, Avalon, which was in turn modeled after the county Palatine of Durham, a crown fief, the powers of whose lord were second only to those of the King. See, C. C. Hall, *The Lords Baltimore and the Maryland Palatinate;* M. P. Andrews, *The Founding of Maryland;* B. C. Steiner, *Beginnings of Maryland;* N. D. Mereness, *Maryland as a Proprietary Province;* W. H. Browne, *Georgius and Cecilius Calvert;* B. C. Steiner, "The First Lord Baltimore and his Colonial Projects," American Hist. Assoc. *Reports*, 1905.

. . . II. Whereas our well beloved and right trusty Subject Caecilius Calvert, Baron of Baltimore, in our Kingdom of Ireland, . . . being animated with a laudable, and pious Zeal for extending the Christian Religion, and also the Territories of our Empire, hath humbly besought Leave of Us, that he may transport, by his own Industry, and Expence, a numerous Colony of the English Nation, to a certain Region, herein after described, in a Country hitherto uncultivated, in the Parts of America, and partly occupied by Savages, having no Knowledge of the Divine Being, and that all that Region, with some certain Privileges, and Jurisdictions, appertaining unto the wholesome Government, and State of his Colony and Region aforesaid, may by our Royal Highness be given, granted, and confirmed unto him, and his Heirs.

III. Know Ye therefore, that We . . . by this our present Charter . . . do Give, Grant, and Confirm, unto the aforesaid Caecilius, now Baron of Baltimore, his Heirs, and Assigns, all that Part of the Peninsula, or Chersonese, lying in the Parts of America, between the Ocean on the East, and the Bay of Chesopeake on the West, [boundaries defined] . . .

IV. Also We do Grant . . . unto the said Baron of Baltimore . . . all Islands and Islets within the Limits aforesaid, all and singular the Islands and Islets, from the Eastern Shore of the aforesaid Region, towards the East, which have been, or shall be formed in the Sea, situate within Ten marine Leagues from the said Shore; . . . And further more the Patronages, and Advowsons of all Churches which (with the increasing Worship and Religion of Christ) within the said Region . . . , hereafter shall happen to be built, together with Licence, and Faculty of erecting and founding Churches, Chapels, and Places of Worship, in convenient and suitable Places within the Premises, and of causing the same to be dedicated and consecrated according to the Ecclesiastical Laws of our Kingdom of England, with all, and singular such, and as ample Rights, Jurisdictions, Privileges, Prerogatives, Royalties, Liberties, Immunities, and royal Rights, and Temporal Franchises whatsoever, as well by Sea as by Land, within the Region . . . aforesaid, to be had, exercised, used, and enjoyed, as any Bishop of Durham, within the Bishoprick or County Palatine of Durham, in our Kingdom of England, ever heretofore, hath had, held, used, or enjoyed or of Right could, or ought to have, hold, use, or enjoy.

V. And We do by these Presents . . . Make, Create, and Constitute Him, the now Baron of Baltimore, and his Heirs, the True and Absolute Lords and Proprietaries of the Region aforesaid, and of all other the Premises (except the before excepted) saving always the Faith and Allegiance and Sovereign Dominion due to Us . . . ; To Hold of Us as of our Castle of Windsor, in our County of Berks, in free and common Soccage, by Fealty only for all Services, and not in capite, nor by Knight's Service, Yielding therefore unto Us . . . two Indian Arrows of these Parts, to be delivered at the said Castle of Windsor, every Year, on Tuesday in Easter-Week: And also the fifth Part of all Gold and Silver Ore, which shall happen from Time to Time, to be found within the aforesaid limits.

VI. Now, That the aforesaid Region, . . . may be eminently distinguished above all other Regions of that Territory, . . . Know Ye, that . . . We do . . . Erect and Incorporate the same into a Province, and nominate the same Maryland, by which name We will that it shall from henceforth be called.

VII. And . . . We . . . do grant unto the said now Baron . . . for the good and happy Government of the said Province, free, full, and absolute Power, by the tenor of these Presents, to Ordain, Make, and Enact Laws, of what kind soever, according to their sound Discretions, whether relating to the Public State of the said Province, or the private Utility of Individuals, of and with the Advice, Assent, and Approbation of the Free-Men of the same Province, or of the greater Part of them, or of their Delegates or Deputies, whom We will shall be called together for the framing of Laws, when, and as often as Need shall require, by the aforesaid now Baron of Baltimore . . . , and in the Form which shall seem best to him . . . and duly to execute the same upon all Persons, for the Time being, within the aforesaid Province, and the Limits thereof, or under his or their Government and Power, . . . by the Imposition of Fines, Imprisonment, and other Punishment whatsoever; even if it be necessary, and the Quality of the Offence require it, by Privation of Member, or Life . . . So Nevertheless. that the Laws aforesaid be consonant to Reason and be not repugnant or contrary, but (so far as conveniently may be) agreeable to the Laws, Statutes, Customs and Rights of this Our Kingdom of England. . . .

XVII. Moreover, We will, appoint, and ordain, and by these Presents, for Us, our Heirs and Successors, do grant unto the aforesaid now Baron of Baltimore, his Heirs and Assigns, that the same Baron of Baltimore, his Heirs and Assigns, from Time to Time, forever, shall have, and enjoy the Taxes and Subsidies payable, or arising within the Ports, Harbors, and other Creeks and Places aforesaid, within the Province aforesaid, for Wares bought and sold, and Things there to be laden, or unladen, to be reasonably assessed by them, and the People there as aforesaid, on emergent Occasion; to whom We grant Power by these Presents, for Us, our Heirs and Successors, to assess and impose the said Taxes and Subsidies there, upon just Cause and in due Proportion.

XVIII. And Furthermore . . . We . . . do give . . . unto the aforesaid now Baron of Baltimore . . . full and absolute Licence, Power, and Authority . . . that he assign, alien, grant, demise, or enfeoff so many, such, and proportionate Parts and Parcels of the Premises, to any Person or Persons willing to purchase the same, as they shall think convenient, to have and to hold . . . in Fee-simple, or Fee-tail, or for Term of Life, Lives, or Years; to hold of the aforesaid now Baron of Baltimore . . . by . . . such . . . Services, Customs and Rents Of This Kind, as to the same now Baron of Baltimore . . . shall seem fit and agreeable, and not immediately of Us . . .

XIX. We also . . . do . . . grant Licence to the same Baron of Baltimore . . . to erect any Parcels of Land within the Province aforesaid, into Manors, and in every of those Manors, to have and to hold a Court-Baron, and all Things which to a Court-Baron do belong; . . .

16. FUNDAMENTAL ORDERS OF CONNECTICUT
January 14, 1639

(Poore, ed. *The Federal and State Constitutions,* Part I, p. 249 ff.)

In 1636 the Rev. Thomas Hooker led his New Town congregation into the inviting Connecticut Valley, and founded the town of Hartford. These pioneers were soon followed by others from Massachusetts Bay, and in January 1639 the freemen of the towns of Hartford, Windsor and Wethersfield assembled at Hartford and drew up the Fundamental Orders—the first written constitution that created a government. See, J. G. Palfrey, *History of New England,* Vol. I; J. Fiske, *Beginnings of New England;* B. Trumbull, *History of Connecticut,* Vol. I; J. A. Doyle, *English Colonies in America: The Puritan Colonies,* Vol. I; B. Long, *Genesis of the Constitution of the United States,* ch. iv. On Hooker, see, G. L. Walker, *Thomas Hooker;* V. L. Parrington, *The Colonial Mind,* p. 53 ff.

Forasmuch as it hath pleased the Allmighty God by the wise disposition of his divyne pruvidence so to Order and dispose of things that we the Inhabitants and Residents of Windsor, Harteford and Wethersfield are now cohabiting and dwelling in and uppon the River of Conectecotte and the Lands thereunto adioyneing; And well knowing where a people are gathered togather the word of God requires that to mayntayne the peace and union of such a people there should be an orderly and decent Government established according to God, to order and dispose of the affayres of the people at all seasons as occation shall require; doe therefore assotiate and conioyne our selves to be as one Publike State or Commonwelth; and doe, for our selves and our Successors and such as shall be adioyned to us att any tyme hereafter, enter into Combination and Confederation togather, to mayntaync and presearve the liberty and purity of the gospell of our Lord Jesus which we now professe, as also the disciplyne of the Churches, which according to the truth of the said gospell is now practised amongst us; As also in our Civell Affaires to be guided and governed according to such Lawes, Rules, Orders and decrees as shall be made, ordered & decreed, as followeth:—

1. It is Ordered . . . that there shall be yerely two generall Assemblies or Courts, the one the second thursday in Aprill, the other the second thursday in September, following; the first shall be called the Courte of Election, wherein shall be yerely Chosen . . . soe many Magestrats and other publike Officers as shall be found requisitte: Whereof one to be chosen Governour for the yeare ensueing and untill another be chosen, and noe other Magestrate to be chosen for more than one yeare; provided allwayes there be sixe chosen besids the Governour; which being chosen and sworne according to an Oath recorded for that purpose shall have power to administer iustice according to the Lawes here established, and for want thereof according to the rule of the word of God; which choise shall be made by all that are admitted freemen and

have taken the Oath of Fidellity, and doe cohabitte within this Jurisdiction, (having beene admitted Inhabitants by the major part of the Towne wherein they live,) or the major parte of such as shall be then present.

4. It is Ordered . . . that noe person be chosen Governor above once in two yeares, and that the Governor be alwayes a member of some approved congregation, and formerly of the Magestracy within this Jurisdiction; and all the Magestrats Freemen of this Commonwealth: . . .

5. It is Ordered . . . that to the aforesaid Courte of Election the severall Townes shall send their deputyes, and when the Elections are ended they may proceed in any publike searvice as at other Courts. Also the other Generall Courte in September shall be for makeing of lawes, and any other publike occation, which conserns the good of the Commonwelth.

7. It is Ordered . . . that after there are warrants given out for any of the said Generall Courts, the Constable . . . of ech Towne shall forthwith give notice dictinctly to the inhabitants of the same, . . . that at a place and tyme by him or them lymited and sett, they meet and assemble them selves togather to elect and chuse certen deputyes to be att the Generall Courte then following to agitate the afayres of the commonwelth; which said Deputyes shall be chosen by all that are admitted Inhabitants in the severall Townes and have taken the oath of fidellity; provided that non be chosen a Deputy for any Generall Courte which is not a Freeman of this Commonwelth. . . .

8. It is Ordered . . . that Wyndsor, Hartford and Wethersfield shall have power, ech Towne, to send fower of their freemen as their deputyes to every Generall Courte; and whatsoever other Townes shall be hereafter added to this Jurisdiction, they shall send so many deputyes as the Courte shall judge meete, a resonable proportion to the number of Freemen that are in the said Townes being to be attended therein; which deputyes shall have the power of the whole Towne to give their voats and alowance to all such lawes and orders as may be for the publike good, and unto which the said Townes are to be bownd.

9. It is ordered . . . that the deputyes thus chosen shall have power and liberty to appoynt a tyme and a place of meeting togather before any Generall Courte to advise and consult of all such things as may concerne the good of the publike, as also to examine their owne Elections. . . .

10. It is Ordered . . . that every Generall Courte . . . shall consist of the Governor, or some one chosen to moderate the Court, and 4 other Magestrats at lest, with the major parte of the deputyes of the severall Townes legally chosen; and in case the Freemen or major parte of them, through neglect or refusall of the Governor and major parte of the magestrats, shall call a Courte, it shall consist of the major parte of Freemen that are present or their deputyes, with a Moderator chosen by them: In which said Generall Courts shall consist the supreme power of the Commonwelth, and they only shall have power to make lawes or repeale them, to graunt levyes, to admitt of Freemen, dispose of lands undisposed of, to severall Townes or persons, and also shall have power to call ether Courte or Magestrate or any other person whatsoever into

question for any misdemeanour, and may for just causes displace or deale otherwise according to the nature of the offence; and also may deale in any other matter that concerns the good of this commonwelth, excepte election of Magestrats, which shall be done by the whole boddy of Freemen.

In which Courte the Governour or Moderator shall have power to order the Courte to give liberty of spech, and silence unceasonable and disorderly speakeings, to put all things to voate, and in case the vote be equall to have the casting voice. But non of these Courts shall be adjorned or dissolved without the consent of the major parte of the Court.

11. It is ordered . . . that when any Generall Courte uppon the occations of the Commonwelth have agreed uppon any summe or sommes of mony to be levyed uppon the severall Townes within this Jurisdiction, that a Committee be chosen to sett out and appoynt what shall be the proportion of every Towne to pay of the said levy, provided the Committees be made up of an equall number out of each Towne.

17. PLANTATION AGREEMENT AT PROVIDENCE
August 27, 1640

(F. N. Thorpe, ed. *Federal and State Constitutions,* Vol. VI, p. 3205 ff.)

In 1636 Roger Williams led a small band of settlers from Massachusetts Bay to Narragansett Bay and founded the town of Providence. In 1638 and 1639 other settlements were established, but all of these towns remained separate and independent until the charter of 1644 went into effect. In 1640 the inhabitants of Providence drew up an agreement in which, among other things, they covenanted "to hould forth liberty of conscience." On Roger Williams and the early history of Rhode Island, see O. S. Strauss, *Roger Williams;* E. Easton, *Roger Williams;* J. Ernst, *Roger Williams;* J. Ernst, *The Political Thought of Roger Williams;* V. L. Parrington, *The Colonial Mind,* p. 62 ff.; S. G. Arnold, *Rhode Island;* I. B. Richman, *Rhode Island;* E. Field, *Rhode Island,* Vol. I; J. Fiske, *Beginnings of New England;* J. T. Adams, *The Founding of New England;* J. Winsor, ed. *Narrative and Critical History,* Vol. III.

Wee, Robert Coles, Chad Browne, William Harris, and John Warner, being freely

chosen by the consent of our loving friends and neighbors the Inhabitants of this Towne of Providence, having many differences amongst us, they being freely willing and also bound themselves to stand to our Arbitration in all differences amongst us to rest contented in our determination, being so betrusted we have seriously and carefully indeavoured to weigh and consider all those differences, being desirous to bringe to unity and peace, although our abilities are farr short in the due examination of such weighty things, yet so farre as we conceive in laying all things together we have gone the fairest and equalist way to produce our peace.

II. Agreed. We have with one consent agreed that for the disposeing, of these lands that shall be disposed belonging to this towne of Providence to be in the whole Inhabitants by the choise of five men for generall disposeall of lands and also of the towne Stocke, and all Generall things and not to receive in any six dayes at townesmen, but first to give the Inhabitants notice to consider if any have just cause to shew against the receiving of him as you can apprehend, and to receive none but such as subscribe to this our determination. Also, we agree that if any of our neighbours doe apprehend himselfe wronged by these or any of these 5 disposers, that at the Generall towne meeting he may have a tryall.

Also wee agree for the towne to choose beside the other five men one or more to keepe Record of all things belonging to the towne and lying in Common.

Wee agree, as formerly hath bin the liberties of the town, so still, to hould forth liberty of Conscience.

III. Agreed, that after many Considerations and Consultations of our owne State and alsoe of States abroad in way of government, we apprehend, no way so suitable to our Condition as government by way of Arbitration. But if men agree themselves by arbitration, no State we know of disallows that, neither doe we: But if men refuse that which is but common humanity betweene man and man, then to compel such unreasonable persons to a reasonable way, we agree that the 5 disposers shall have power to compel him to choose two men himselfe, or if he refuse, for them to choose two men to arbitrate his cause, and if these foure men chosen by every partie do end the cause, then to see theire determination performed and the faultive to pay the Arbitrators for theire time spent in it: But if these foure men doe not end it, then for the 5 disposers to choose three men to put an end to it, and for the certainty thereof, wee agree the major part of the 5 disposers to choose the 3 men, and the major part of the 3 men to end the cause haveing power from the 5 disposers by a note under theire hand to performe it, and the faultive not agreeing in the first to pay the charge of the last, and for the Arbitrators to follow no imployment til the cause be ended without consent of the whole that have to doe with the cause.

Instance. In the first Arbitration the offender may offer reasonable terms of peace, and the offended may exact upon him and refuse and trouble men beyond reasonable satisfaction; so for the last arbitrators to judge where the fault was, in not agreeing in the first, to pay the charge of the last.

IV. Agreed, that if any person damnify any man, either in goods or good name, and the person offended follow not the cause upon the offendor, that if any person give notice to the 5 Disposers, they shall call the party delinquent to answer by Arbitration.

Instance. Thus, if any person abuse an other person or goods, may be for peace sake, a man will at present put it up, and it may so be resolve to revenge: therefore, for the peace of the state, the disposers are to look to it in the first place.

V. Agreed, for all the whole Inhabitants to combine ourselves to assist any man in the pursuit of any party delinquent, with all best endeavours to attack him: but if any man raise a hubbub, and there be no just cause, then for the party that raised the hubbub to satisfy men for their time lost in it.

VI. Agreed, that if any man have a difference with any of the 5 Disposers which cannot be deferred till general meeting of the towne, then he may have the Clerk call the towne together at his (discretion) for a tryall.

Instance. It may be, a man may be to depart the land, or to a farr parte of the land; or his estate may lye yppon a speedy tryall or the like case may fall out.

VII. Agreed, that the towne, by the five men shall give every man a deed of all his lands lying within the bounds of the Plantations, to hould it by for after ages.

VIII. Agreed, that the 5 disposers shall from the date hereof, meete every monthday uppon General things and at the quarterday to yeeld a new choise and give up their old Accounts.

IX. Agreed, that the Clerke shall call the 5 Disposers together at the month-day, and the generall towne together every quarter, to meete uppon general occasions from the date hereof. . . .

XI. Agreed, that all acts of disposall on both sides to stand since the difference.

XII. Agreed, that every man that hath not paid in his purchase money for his Plantation shall make up his 10s. to be 30s.

equal with the first purchasers: and for all that are received townsmen hereafter, to pay the like somme of money to the towne stocke.

These being those things wee have gener-ally concluded on, for our peace, we desireing our loving friends to receive as our absolute determination, laying ourselves downe as subjects to it.

18. THE NEW ENGLAND CONFEDERATION
May 19, 1643

(F. N. Thorpe, *Federal and State Constitutions,* Vol. I, p. 77 ff.)

The first suggestion for a union of the New England Colonies came from the magistrates and ministers of Connecticut in 1637. The proposal was renewed in 1638 and 1639; in 1640 the magistrates of Massachusetts Bay indicated acceptance of the proposal, but insisted that Rhode Island should not be admitted to the group. In 1642 the civil wars in England led to a renewal of the proposal from Massachusetts Bay, and in May 1642, delegates from Plymouth, Connecticut and New Haven met with those of the Bay colony in Boston and agreed upon the articles of Confederation. Rhode Island was consistently excluded from the Confederation. The union of the colonies of Connecticut and New Haven and the grant of a charter to Rhode Island practically put an end to the Confederation, but commissioners continued to hold meetings until 1684. See, R. Frothingham, *Rise of the Republic of the United States,* ch. ii; J. A. Doyle, *The English in America; The Puritan Colonies,* Vol. I; J. G. Palfrey, *History of New England,* Vols. I, II; L. G. Tyler, *England in America,* ch. xviii; J. Fiske, *Beginnings of New England,* ch. iv.

The Articles of Confederation between the Plantations under the Government of the Massachusetts, the Plantations under the Government of New Plymouth, the Plantations under the Government of Connecticut, and the Government of New Haven with the Plantations in Combination therewith:

Whereas we all came into these parts of America with one and the same end and aim, namely, to advance the Kingdom of our Lord Jesus Christ and to enjoy the liberties of the Gospel in purity with peace; and whereas in our settling (by a wise providence of God) we are further dispersed upon the sea coasts and rivers than was at first intended, so that we can not according to our desire with convenience communicate in one government and jurisdiction; and whereas we live encompassed with people of several nations and strange languages which hereafter may prove injurious to us or our posterity. And forasmuch as the natives have formerly committed sundry insolence and outrages upon several Plantations of the English and have of late combined themselves against us: and seeing by reason of those sad distractions in England which they have heard of, and by which they know we are hindered from that humble way of seeking advice, or reaping those comfortable fruits of protection, which at other times we might well expect. We therefore do conceive it our bounden duty, without delay to enter into a present Cosociation amongst ourselves, for mutual help and strength in all our future concernments: That, as in nation and religion, so in other respects, we be and continue one according to the tenor and true meaning of the ensuing articles; Wherefore it is fully agreed and concluded by and between the parties or Jurisdictions above named, and they jointly and severally do by these presents agree and conclude that they all be and henceforth be called by the name of the United Colonies of New England.

2. The said United Colonies for themselves and their posterities do jointly and severally hereby enter into a firm and perpetual league of friendship and amity for offence and defence, mutual advice and succor upon all just occasions both for preserving and propagating the truth and liberties of the Gospel and for their own mutual safety and welfare.

3. . . . And in reference to the Plantations which already are settled, or shall hereafter be erected, or shall settle within their limits respectively; provided no other Jurisdiction shall hereafter be taken in as a distinct head or member of this Confederation, nor shall any other Plantation or

Jurisdiction in present being, and not already in combination or under the jurisdiction of any of these Confederates, be received by any of them; nor shall any two of the Confederates join in one Jurisdiction without consent of the rest, which consent to be interpreted as is expressed in the sixth article ensuing.

4. It is by these Confederates agreed that the charge of all just wars, whether offensive or defensive, upon what part or member of this Confederation soever they fall, shall both in men, provisions, and all other disbursements be borne by all the parts of this Confederation in different proportions according to their different ability in manner following, namely, . . . that according to the different numbers which from time to time shall be found in each Jurisdiction upon a true and just account, the service of men and all charges of the war be borne by the poll: each Jurisdiction or Plantation being left to their own just course and custom of rating themselves and people according to their different estates with due respects to their qualities and exemptions amongst themselves though the Confederation take no notice of any such privilege: and that according to their different charge of each Jurisdiction and Plantation the whole advantage of the war (if it please God so to bless their endeavors) whether it be in lands, goods, or persons, shall be proportionately divided among the said Confederates.

5. It is further agreed, that if any of these Jurisdictions or any Plantation under or in combination with them, be invaded by any enemy whomsoever, upon notice and request of any three magistrates of that Jurisdiction so invaded, the rest of the Confederates without any further meeting or expostulation shall forthwith send aid to the Confederate in danger but in different proportions; namely, the Massachusetts an hundred men sufficiently armed and provided for such a service and journey, and each of the rest, forty-five so armed and provided, or any less number, if less be required according to this proportion. . . . But in any such case of sending men for present aid, whether before or after such order or alteration, it is agreed that at the meeting of the Commissioners for this Confederation,

the cause of such war or invasion be duly considered: and if it appear that the fault lay in the parties so invaded then that Jurisdiction or Plantation make just satisfaction, both to the invaders whom they have injured, and bear all the charges of the war themselves, without requiring any allowance from the rest of the Confederates towards the same. And further that if any Jurisdiction see any danger of invasion approaching, and there be time for a meeting, that in such a case three magistrates of the Jurisdiction may summon a meeting at such convenient place as themselves shall think meet, to consider and provide against the threatened danger; . . .

6. It is also agreed, that for the managing and concluding of all affairs proper, and concerning the whole Confederation two Commissioners shall be chosen by and out of each of these four Jurisdictions: namely, two for the Massachusetts, two for Plymouth, two for Connecticut, and two for New Haven, being all in Church-fellowship with us, which shall bring full power from their several General Courts respectively to hear, examine, weigh, and determine all affairs of our war, or peace, leagues, aids, charges, and numbers of men for war, division of spoils and whatsoever is gotten by conquest, receiving of more Confederates for Plantations into combination with any of the Confederates, and all things of like nature, which are the proper concomitants or consequents of such a Confederation for amity, offence, and defence: not intermeddling with the government of any of the Jurisdictions, which by the third article is preserved entirely to themselves. . . . It is further agreed that these eight Commissioners shall meet once every year besides extraordinary meetings (according to the fifth article) to consider, treat, and conclude of all affairs belonging to this Confederation, . . .

8. It is also agreed that the Commissioners for this Confederation hereafter at their meetings, whether ordinary or extraordinary, as they may have commission or opportunity, do endeavor to frame and establish agreements and orders in general cases of a civil nature, wherein all the Plantations are interested, for preserving of peace among themselves, for preventing

as much as may be all occasion of war or differences with others, as about the free and speedy passage of justice in every Jurisdiction, to all the Confederates equally as to their own, receiving those that remove from one Plantation without due certificate, how all the Jurisdictions may carry it towards the Indians, that they neither grow insolent nor be injured without due satisfaction, lest war break in upon the Confederates through such miscarriages. It is also agreed that if any servant run away from his master into any other of these confederated Jurisdictions, that in such case, upon the certificate of one magistrate in the Jurisdiction out of which the said servant fled, or upon other due proof; the said servant shall be delivered, either to his master, or any other that pursues and brings such certificate or proof. And that upon the escape of any prisoner whatsoever, or fugitive for any criminal cause, whether breaking prison, or getting from the officer, or otherwise escaping, upon the certificate of two magistrates of the Jurisdiction out of which the escape is made, that he was a prisoner, or such an offender at the time of the escape, the magistrates, or some of them of that Jurisdiction where for the present the said prisoner or fugitive abideth, shall forthwith grant such a warrant as the case will bear, for the apprehending of any such person, and the delivery of him into the hands of the officer or other person who pursues him. And if there be help required,

for the safe returning of any such offender, then it shall be granted to him that craves the same, he paying the charges thereof.

9. And for that the justest wars may be of dangerous consequence, especially to the smaller Plantations in these United Colonies, it is agreed that neither the Massachusetts, Plymouth, Connecticut, nor New Haven, nor any of the members of them, shall at any time hereafter begin, undertake, or engage themselves, or this Confederation, or any part thereof in any war whatsoever . . . without the consent and agreement of the forementioned eight Commissioners, or at least six of them, as in the sixth article is provided: and that no charge be required of any of the Confederates, in case of a defensive war, till the said Commissioners have met, and approved the justice of the war, and have agreed upon the sum of money to be levied, which sum is then to be paid by the several Confederates in proportion according to the fourth article. . . .

11. It is further agreed that if any of the Confederates shall hereafter break any of these present articles, or be any other ways injurious to any one of the other Jurisdictions; such breach of agreement or injury shall be duly considered and ordered by the Commissioners for the other Jurisdictions, that both peace and this present Confederation may be entirely preserved without violation. . . .

19. MASSACHUSETTS SCHOOL LAW OF 1642
April 14, 1642

(E. P. Cubberley, ed. *Readings in the History of Education,* p. 298–9)

This is the earliest known law on education in the American colonies. Similar laws were adopted, somewhat later, by Connecticut, New Haven, and Plymouth. See also, the law of 1647, Doc. No. 20. See bibliography in M. W. Jernegan, *The American Colonies,* p. 164.

This Coᵣt, taking into consideration the great neglect of many parents & masters in training up their children in learning & laboᵣ, & other implyments which may be proffitable to the common wealth, do hereupon order and decree, that in euery towne yᵉ chosen men appointed for managing the prudentiall affajres of the same shall hence-

forth stand charged with the care of the redresse of this evill, so as they shalbee sufficiently punished by fines for the neglect thereof, upon presentment of the grand iury, or other information or complaint in any Court within this iurisdiction; and for this end they, or the greater numbeᵣ of them, shall have power to take account from time to time of all parents and masters, and of their children, concerning their calling and implyment of their children, especially of their ability to read & understand the principles of religion & the capitall lawes of this country, and to impose fines upon such as shall refuse to render such accounts to them when they shall be required; and they shall have power, with consent of any Court or the magistrate, to put forth apprentices the children of such as they shall (find) not to be able & fitt to employ and bring them up. They shall take . . . that boyes and girles be not suffered to converse together, so as may occasion any wanton, dishonest, or immodest behavio^r; & for their better performance of this trust committed to them, they may divide the towne amongst them, appointing to every of the said townesmen a certaine number of families to have special oversight of. They are also to provide that a sufficient quantity of materialls, as hemp, flaxe, ec^{ra}, may be raised in their severall townes, & tooles & implements provided for working out the same; & for their assistance in this so needfull and beneficiall imploym^t, if they meete wth any difficulty or opposition wch they cannot well master by their own power, they may have reco^{r}se to some of the ma^{trats}, who shall take such course for their help & incuragm^t as the occasion shall require according to iustice; & the said townesmen, at the next Co^{r}t in those limits, after the end of their year, shall give a briefe account in writing of their proceedings herein, provided that they have bene so required by some Co^{r}t or magistrate a month at least before; & this order to continew for two yeares, & till the Co^{r}t shall take further order.

20. MASSACHUSETTS SCHOOL LAW OF 1647

(Records of the Governor and Company of the Massachusetts Bay in New England, Vol. II, p. 203)

This "old deluder Satan" law established the first system of public education in the American colonies. A number of towns had already established schools, and the law of 1642, Doc. No. 19, had provided for the instruction of children in reading. The purpose of the law of 1647 was that "learning might not be buried in the grave of our fathers in Church and commonwealth." Other New England States followed the example of Massachusetts within the next generation. See, G. H. Martin, *Evolution of the Massachusetts School System;* H. Suzzalo, *Rise of Local School Supervision in Massachusetts;* and articles by M. W. Jernegan in *School Review*, Vols. XXIII, XXVI–XXVIII.

It being one chiefe proiect of ye ould deluder, Satan, to keepe men from the knowledge of ye Scriptures, as in form^r times by keeping y^m in an unknowne tongue, so in these latt^r times by perswading from ye use of tongues, y^t so at least ye true sence & meaning of ye originall might be clouded by false glosses of saint seeming deceivers, y^t learning may not be buried in ye grave of o^r fath^{rs} in ye church and com-monwealth, the Lord assisting o^r endeavo^{r}s,—

It is therefore ord^{r}ed, y^t ev^{r}y towneship in this iurisdiction, aft^r ye Lord hath increased y^m number to 50 houshold^{rs}, shall then forthwth appoint one wth in their towne to teach all such children as shall resort to him to write & reade, whose wages shall be paid eith^r by ye parents or mast^{rs} of such children, or by ye inhabitants in gen^{r}all, by way of supply, as ye maior part of those y^t ord^r ye prudentials ye twone shall appoint; provided, those y^t send their children be not oppressed by paying much more y^m they can have y^m taught for in oth^r townes; & it is furth^r ordered, y^t where any towne shall increase to ye numb^r of 100 families or houshould^{rs}, they shall set up a gram-mer schoole, ye m^r thereof being able to instruct youth so farr as they shall be fitted for ye university, provided, y^t if any towne neglect ye performance hereof above one yeare, y^t every such towne shall pay 5 pounds to ye next schoole till they shall performe this order.

21. THE CAMBRIDGE PLATFORM
1648

(W. Walker, Creeds and Platforms of Congregationalism, p. 194 ff.)

The Cambridge Platform grew out of the challenge of the authority of the Congregational Church by William Vassall and others who petitioned for the removal of civil disabilities of non-members of the Church. A synod met at Cambridge, September 1, 1646, "to discuss, dispute, & cleare up . . . such questions of church government & discipline . . . as they shall thinke needfull & meete." The third session of this synod, in August 1648, adopted the Westminster Confession as its creed, and formulated the relations of church and state and the duties of the clergy in the Cambridge Platform. In 1649 this platform was laid before the Congregations and by 1651 was adopted. "This event", says Fiske, "may be regarded as completing the theocratic organization of the Puritan Commonwealth." See C. Mather, *Magnalia,* Vol. II; W. Hubbard, *General History of New England,* p. 532 ff.; J. G. Palfrey, *History of New England,* Vol. II, p. 165 ff.; H. M. Dexter, *Congregationalism,* p. 435 ff.; B. Adams, *The Emancipation of Massachusetts,* p. 79 ff.; P. Miller, *Orthodoxy in Massachusetts;* J. T. Adams, *The Founding of New England,* ch. xi.

CHAP: XVII

Of The Civil Magistrates powr in Matters Ecclesiastical

It is lawfull, profitable, & necessary for christians to gather themslves into Church estate, and therin to exercise all the ordinances of christ according unto the word, although the consent of Magistrate could not be had therunto, because the Apostles & christians in their time did frequently thus practise, when the Magistrates being all of them Jewish or pagan, & mostly persecuting enemies, would give no countenance or consent to such matters.

2. Church-government stands in no opposition to civil government of commonwelths, nor any intrencheth upon the authority of Civil Magistrates in their jurisdictions; nor any whit weakneth their hands in governing; but rather strengthneth them, & furthereth the people in yielding more hearty & conscionable obedience unto them, whatsoever some ill affected persons to the wayes of Christ have suggested to alienate the affections of Kings & Princes from the ordinances of Christ; as if the kingdome of Christ in his church could not rise & stand, without the falling and weakning of their government, which is also of Christ: whereas the contrary is most true, that they may both stand together & flourish the one being helpfull unto the other, in their distinct and due administrations.

The powr & authority of Magistrates is not for the restraining of churches, or any other good workes, but for helping in and furthering therof; & therfore the consent & countenance of Magistrates when it may be had, is not to be sleighted, or lightly esteemed; but on the contrary; it is part of that honour due to christian Magistrates to desire & crave their consent & approbation therin: which being obtayned, the churches may then proceed in their way with much more encouragement, & comfort.

4. It is not in the powr of Magistrates to compell their subjects to become church-members, & to partake at the Lords table: for the priests are reproved, that brought unworthy ones into the sanctuarie: then, as it was unlawfull for the priests, so it is unlawfull to be done by civil Magistrates. Those whom the church is to cast out if they were in, the Magistrate ought not to thrust into the church, nor to hold them therin.

5. As it is unlawfull for church-officers to meddle with the sword of the Magistrate, so it is unlawfull for the Magistrate to meddle with the work proper to church-officers. the Acts of Moses & David, who were not only Princes, but Prophets, were extraordinary; therfore not imitable. Against such usurpation the Lord witnessed, by smiting Uziah with leprosie, for presuming to offer incense.

6. It is the duty of the Magistrate, to take care of matters of religion, & to improve his civil authority for the observing of the duties commanded in the first, as well as for observing of the duties commanded in the second table. . . .

7. The object of the powr of the Magistrate, are not things meerly inward, & so not subject to his cognisance & view, as in unbeliefe hardness of heart, erronious opinions not vented; but only such things as are acted by the outward man; neither is their powr to be exercised, in commanding such acts of the outward man, & punishing the neglect therof, as are but meer inventions, & devices of men; but about such acts, as are commanded & forbidden in the word; yea such as the word doth clearly determine, though not alwayes clearly the judgment of the Magistrate or others, yet clearly in it selfe. In these he of right ought to putt

forth his authority, though oft-times actually he doth it not.

8. Idolatry, Blasphemy, Heresy, venting corrupt & pernicious opinions, that destroy the foundation, open contempt of the word preached, prophanation of the Lords day, disturbing the peaceable administration & exercise of the worship & holy things of God, & the like, are to be restrayned, & punished by civil authority.

9. If any church one or more shall grow schismaticall, rending it self from the communion of other churches, or shall walke incorrigibly or obstinately in any corrupt way of their own, contrary to the rule of the word; in such case, the Magistrate is to put forth his coercive powr, as the matter shall require. The tribes on this side Jordan intended to make warr against the other tribes, for building the altar of witness, whom they suspected to have turned away therin from following of the Lord.

Finis

22. MARYLAND TOLERATION ACT
April 21, 1649

(The Archives of Maryland, ed. by W. H. Browne, Vol. I, p. 244 ff.)

This so-called Toleration Act, passed in accordance with instructions from Lord Baltimore, was designed to secure Maryland from the charge of intolerance toward Protestantism. In 1654 the Puritans gained control of Maryland and the protection given to Catholics was withdrawn, but upon the restoration of Lord Baltimore to control, the act of 1649 was revived. The harsh provisions of the act against blasphemy were never enforced. See, G. Petrie, *Church and State in Maryland,* J. H. U. *Studies,* Vol. X; M. P. Andrews, *The Founding of Maryland,* ch. x.

Fforasmuch as in a well governed and Christian Common Wealth matters concerning Religion and the honor of God ought in the first place to bee taken, into serious consideration and endeavoured to bee settled. Be it therefore . . . enacted. . . . That whatsoever person or persons within this Province . . . shall from henceforth blaspheme God, . . . or shall deny our Saviour Jesus Christ to bee the sonne of God, or shall deny the holy Trinity the ffather sonne and holy Ghost, or the Godhead of any of the said Three persons of the Trinity or the Unity of the Godhead . . . shall be punished with death and confiscation or forfeiture of all his or her lands. . . .

. . . And whereas the inforceing of the conscience in matters of Religion hath frequently fallen out to be of dangerous Consequence in those commonwealthes where it hath been practised, And for the more quiett and peaceable governement of this Province, and the better to preserve mutuall Love and amity amongst the Inhabitants thereof. Be it

Therefore . . . enacted (except as in this present Act is before Declared and sett forth) that noe person or persons whatsoever within this Province, or the Islands, Ports, Harbors, Creekes, or havens thereunto belonging professing to believe in Jesus Christ, shall from henceforth bee any waies troubled, Molested or discountenanced for or in respect of his or her religion nor in the free exercise thereof within this Province or the Islands thereunto belonging nor any way compelled to the beleife or exercise of any other Religion against his or her consent, soe as they be not unfaithfull to the Lord Proprietary, or molest or conspire against the civill Government established or to bee established in this Province under him or his heires. And that all & every person and persons that shall presume Contrary to this Act and the true Intent and meaning thereof directly or indirectly either in person or estate willfully to wronge disturbe trouble or molest any person whatsoever within this Province professing to believe in Jesus Christ for or in respect of his or her religion or the free exercise thereof within this Province other than is provided for in this Act that such person or persons soe offending, shalbe compelled to pay trebble damages to the party soe wronged or molested, and for every such offence shall also forfeit 20^s sterling in money or the value thereof. . . , Or if the parties soe offending as aforesaid shall refuse or bee unable to recompense the party soe wronged, or to satisfy such ffyne or forfeiture, then such offender shalbe severely punished by publick whipping & imprisonment during the pleasure of the Lord proprietary, or his Leiuetenant or cheife Governor of this Province for the tyme being without baile or maineprise. . . .

23. THE NAVIGATION ACT OF 1660

(D. Pickering, *Statutes at Large,* Vol. VII, p. 452 ff.)

The Navigation laws provided the mechanism for the policy of mercantilism practiced by Great Britain as well as by the other colonizing powers of Europe. The first navigation laws were enacted in 1645; others followed in the decade of the fifties. The Act of 1660, often referred to as the First Navigation Act, systematized the laws and regulations of the preceding fifteen years. See, A. L. Beer, *Commercial Policy of England Towards the American Colonies;* A. L. Beer, *Origin of the British Colonial System,* 1578–1660; A. L. Beer, *The Old Colonial System, 1660–1754,* 2 Vols.; *Cambridge History of the British Empire,* Vol. I, ch. ix; H. E. Egerton, *Short History of British Colonial Policy;* J. T. Adams, *The Founding of New England,* ch. xii; W. J. Ashley, "The Commercial Legislation of England and the American Colonies, 1660–1760," *Quarterly Journal of Economics,* Vol. XIV; E. Channing, "The Navigation Laws," American Antiquarian Society, *Proceedings,* 1889.

An act for the encouraging and increasing of shipping and navigation

For the increase of shipping and encouragement of the navigation of this nation, wherein, under the good providence and protection of God, the wealth, safety and strength of this kingdom is so much concerned; be it enacted by the King's most excellent majesty, and by the lords and commons in this present parliament assembled, and by the authority thereof, That from and after the first day of *December* one thousand six hundred and sixty, and from thenceforward, no goods or commodities whatsoever shall be imported into or exported out of any lands, islands, plantations or territories to his Majesty belonging or in his possession, or which may hereafter belong unto or be in the possession of his Majesty, his heirs and successors, in *Asia, Africa* or *America,* in any other ship or ships, vessel or vessels whatsoever, but in such ships or vessels as do truly and without fraud belong only to the people of *England* or *Ireland,* dominion of *Wales* or town of

Berwick upon *Tweed,* or are of the built of and belonging to any the said lands, islands, plantations or territories, as the proprietors and right owners thereof, and whereof the master and three fourths of the mariners at least are *English;* under the penalty of the forfeiture and loss of all the goods and commodities which shall be imported into or exported out of any the aforesaid places in any other ship or vessel, as also of the ship or vessel. . . .

II. And be it enacted, That no alien or person not born within the allegiance of our sovereign lord the King, his heirs and successors, or naturalized, or made a free denizen, shall from and after the first day of *February,* 1661, exercise the trade or occupation of a merchant or factor in any the said places; upon pain of the forfeiture and loss of all his goods and chattels, . . . and all governors of the said lands, islands, plantations or territories, and every of them, are hereby strictly required and commanded, and all who hereafter shall be made governors of any such islands, plantations or territories, by his Majesty, his heirs or successors, shall before their entrance into their government take a solemn oath, to do their utmost, that every the aforementioned clauses, and all the matters and things therein contained, shall be punctually and *bona fide* observed according to the true intent and meaning thereof; and upon complaint and proof made before his Majesty, his heirs or successors, or such as shall be by him or them thereunto authorized and appointed, that any the said governors have been willingly and wittingly negligent in doing their duty accordingly, that the said governor so offending shall be removed from his government.

III. And it is further enacted . . . , That no goods or commodities whatsoever, of the growth, production or manufacture of *Africa, Asia* or *America,* or of any part thereof, or which are described or laid down in the usual maps or cards of those places, be imported into *England, Ireland* or *Wales,* islands of *Guernsey* and *Jersey,* or town of *Berwick* upon *Tweed,* in any other ship or ships, vessel or vessels whatsoever, but in such as do truly and without fraud belong only to the people of *England* or *Ireland,* dominion of *Wales,* or town of *Berwick* upon *Tweed* or of the lands, islands, plantations or territories in *Asia, Africa* or *America,* to his Majesty belonging, as the proprietors and right owners thereof, and whereof the master, and three fourths at least of the mariners are *English;* (2) under the penalty of the forfeiture of all such goods and commodities, and of the ship or vessel in which they were imported. . . .

IV. And it is further enacted . . . , That no goods or commodities that are of foreign growth, production or manufacture, and which are to be brought into *England, Ireland, Wales,* the islands of *Guernsey* and *Jersey,* or town of *Berwick* upon *Tweed,* in *English*-built shipping, or other shipping belonging to some of the aforesaid places, and navigated by *English* mariners, as aforesaid, shall be shipped or brought from any other place or places, country or countries, but only from those of the said growth, production or manufacture, or from those ports where the said goods and commodities can only, or are, or usually have been, first shipped for transportation, and from none other places or countries; under the penalty of the forfeiture of all such of the aforesaid goods as shall be imported from any other place or country contrary to the true intent and meaning hereof, as also of the ship in which they were imported, . . .

V. And it is further enacted . . . , That any sort of ling, stock-fish, pilchard, or any other kind of dried or salted fish, usually fished for and caught by the people of *England, Ireland, Wales,* or town of *Berwick* upon *Tweed;* or any sort of cod-fish or herring, or any oil or blubber made or that shall be made of any kind of fish whatsoever, or any whale-fins or whale-bones, which shall be imported into *England, Ireland, Wales,* or town of *Berwick* upon *Tweed,* not having been caught in vessels truly and properly belonging thereunto as proprietors and right owners thereof, and the said fish cured saved and dried, and the oil and blubber aforesaid (which shall be accounted and pay as oil) not

made by the people thereof, and shall be imported into *England, Ireland* or *Wales,* or town of *Berwick* upon *Tweed,* shall pay double aliens custom.

VI. And be it further enacted, . . . That from henceforth it shall not be lawful to any person or persons whatsoever, to load or cause to be loaden and carried in any bottom or bottoms, ship or ships, vessel or vessels whatsoever, whereof any stranger or strangers-born (unless such as shall be denizens or naturalized) be owners, part-owners or master, and whereof three fourths of the mariners at least shall not be *English,* any fish, victual, wares, goods, commodities or things, of what kind or nature soever the same shall be, from one port or creek of *England, Ireland, Wales,* islands of *Guernsey* or *Jersey,* or town of *Berwick* upon *Tweed,* to another port or creek of the same, or of any of them; under penalty for every one that shall offend contrary to the true meaning of this branch of this present act, to forfeit all such goods shall be loaden and carried in any such ship or vessel, together with the ship or vessel, . . .

VIII. And it is further enacted . . . That no goods or commodities of the growth, production or manufacture of *Muscovy,* or to any the countries, dominions or territories to the . . . emperor of *Muscovy* or *Russia* belonging, as also that no sort of masts, timber or boards, no foreign salt, pitch, tar, rosin, hemp or flax, raisins, figs, prunes, olive-oils, no sorts of corn or grain, sugar, potashes, wines, vinegar, or spirits called *aqua-vitae,* or brandy-wine, shall from after the first day of April, 1662, be imported into *England, Ireland, Wales,* or town of *Berwick* upon *Tweed,* in any ship or ships . . . but in such as do truly and without fraud belong to the people thereof, and whereof the master and three fourths of the mariners at least are *English:* and that no currans nor commodities of the growth, production or manufacture of any of the countries, islands, dominions or territories to the *Othoman* or *Turkish* empire belonging, shall from after the first day of *September,* 1661, be imported into any of the afore-mentioned places in any ship or vessel, but which is of *English*-built, and navigated. . . .

XIII. Provided also, That this act or any thing therein contained, extend not, or be meant, to restrain the importing of any *East-*

India commodities loaden in *English* built shipping, and whereof the master and three-fourths of the mariners at least are English, from the usual place or places for lading of them in any part of those seas, to the southward and eastward of *Cabo bona Esperanza,* although the said ports be not the very places of their growth. . . .

XVIII. And it is further enacted . . . That from and after the first day of *April,* 1661,

no sugars, tobacco, cotton-wool, indicoes, ginger, fustick, or other dying wood, of the growth, production or manufacture of any *English* plantations in *America, Asia* or *Africa,* shall be shipped, carried, conveyed or transported from any of the said *English* plantations to any land . . . other than to such other *English* plantations as do belong to his Majesty. . . .

24. INDEPENDENCY IN COLONIAL MASSACHUSETTS
1661, 1678

The charter of 1629 did not specifically provide that Massachusetts was bound by the laws of Parliament, and on numerous occasions leaders of the Puritan colony insisted that Massachusetts was bound only by laws passed by its legal representatives. Both John Winthrop and John Cotton apparently held this view and it is implicit in the Massachusetts Body of Liberties of 1641. The two documents below indicate the theory that "the lawes of England doe not reach America". The first, submitted to the General Court June 10, 1661, is a Declaration of Rights; the second the reply of the General Court to certain objections from the Lords of Council for Trade and Plantation to the Massachusetts laws. See, C. F. Mullett, *Fundamental Law and the American Revolution,* ch. ii; B. F. Wright, *American Interpretations of Natural Law;* A. B. Hart, ed. *Commonwealth History of Massachusetts,* Vol. I. chs. v, xvii; J. T. Adams, *Founding of New England,* ch. xii; J. Goebel, "King's Law and local custom in seventeenth century New England", *Columbia Law Rev.,* Vol. XXXI.

1. DECLARATION OF LIBERTIES. At Sessions of General Court, June 10, 1661. The Answer of the Committee unto the Matters proposed to their Consideration by the honored General Court.
(*Records of the Governor and Company of the Massachusetts Bay in New England,* Vol. IV, part 2, p. 25–6.)

Concerning our liberties

1. Wee conceive the pattent (under God) to be the first & maine foundation of our civil politye, by a Gouvernor & Company, according as is therein exprest.

2. The Gouvernor & Company are, by the pattent, a body politicke, in fact & name.

3. This body politicke is vested with power to make freemen. . . .

6. The Gouvernor, Deputy Gouvernor, Asistants, & select representatives or depu-

ties have full power and authoritie, both legislative & executive, for the gouvernment of all the people heere, whither inhabitants or straingers, both concerning eclesiasticks & in civils, without appeale, excepting lawe or lawes repugnant to the lawes of England. . . .

8. Wee conceive any imposition prejudiciall to the country contrary to any just lawe of ours, not repugnant to the lawes of England, to be an infringement of our right.

2. ANSWER TO MR. SOLICITOR'S OBJECTIONS AS TO WHAT IS DEFECTIVE IN THE LAWS OF THE COLONY. October 2, 1678.
(*Records of the Governor and Company of the Massachusetts Bay in New England,* Vol. V, p. 200–201.)

. . . To obj. 7. Your answer also therein being aprooved, the Court adds, viz, That for the acts passed in Parliament for incouraging trade and navigation, wee humbly conceive, according to the usuall sayings of the learned in the lawe, that the lawes of England are bounded within the fower seas, and doe not reach America. The subjects of his majestie here being not represented in Parliament, so wee have not looked at ourselves to be impeded in our trade by them, nor yet wee abated in our relative allegiance to his majestie. However, so soone as wee understood his majesty's pleasure, that those acts should be observed by his majesties subjects of the Massachusetts, which could not be without invading the liberties and propperties of the subject, untill the Generall Court made provission therein by a law, which they did in October, 1677, and should be strictly attended from time to time, although the same be a discouragement to trade, and a great damage to his majesties plantation, untill wee shall obteyne his majesties gracious favour for that liberty of trade, which wee are not without hopes but that his majestie will see just occasion to grant to us, for the encouraging of his good subjects in a wilderness & hard country, who, by Gods speciall blessing upon their industry, have promoted the worke of navigation, by building ships, raising seamen, and navigating them from country to country; and wee doubt not but it will appeare, upon enquiry, that this restreint upon us will be an abstraction of his majesties customes in England, and not an inlargement thereof, for that the endeavour of the merchant here is to have his bancke in England; nor doe wee beleive that ever it cann be demonstrated, that that liberty hath binn a losse to his majesties customes, especially of late yeares, for that for whatever goods from any of his majesties plantations wee pay his customes before wee have them; and having paid the duties, it seemes hard that wee may not have liberty with our fellow-subjects in England. Wee speake not thus to capitulate with his majesty, but humbly submitt the same to his royall clemency & grace. . . .

25. CONCESSIONS TO THE PROVINCE OF PENNSYLVANIA
July 11, 1681

(F. N. Thorpe, ed. *Federal and State Constitutions*, Vol. V, p. 3044 ff.)

William Penn secured a charter to Pennsylvania March 4, 1681 and immediately began to advertise his land and organize a colony. He drew up an account of the province and its advantages which was widely circulated in England and on the Continent. At the same time he began to sell shares to those who wished to join him in the enterprise and to arrange for land sales and grants. To regulate these matters he drafted a body of Conditions and Concessions, dealing chiefly with land and with Indian relations. These Concessions were not designed as a constitution or body of laws. The Frame of Government, comprising both a constitution and a series of "laws agreed upon in England" bore the dates of April 25 and May 3, 1682. The Frame of Government can be found in Thorpe, *Federal and State Constitutions*, Vol. V. The Charter, the Concessions, and numerous related documents have been conveniently collected in *Charter to William Penn and Laws of the Province of Pennsylvania*, ed. by S. George, B. M. Nead and T. McCamant. On Penn and the founding of Pennsylvania, see S. G. Fisher, *The True Willliam Penn;* B. Dobree, *William Penn;* M. R. Brailsford, *The Making of William Penn;* W. R. Shepherd, *History of Proprietary Government in Pennsylvania;* I. Sharpless, *History of Quaker Government in Pennsylvania,* 2 Vols.

Certain conditions, *or* concessions, *agreed upon by* William Penn, *Proprietary and Governor of the province of Pennsylvania, and those who are the adventurers and purchasers in the same province. . . .*

I. That so soon as it pleaseth God that the abovesaid persons arrive there, a certain quantity of land, or ground plat, shall be laid out, for a large town or city, in the most convenient place, upon the river, for health and navigation; and every purchaser and adventurer shall, by lot, have so much land therein as will answer to the proportion, which he hath bought, or taken up, upon rent: but it is to be noted, that the surveyors shall consider what roads or highways will be necessary to the cities, towns or through the lands. Great roads from city to city not to contain less than *forty* foot, in breadth, shall be first laid out and declared to be for high-ways, before the dividend of acres be laid out for the purchaser, and the like observation to be had for the streets in the towns and cities, that there may be convenient roads and streets preserved, not to be encroached upon by any planter or builder, that none may build irregularly to the damage of another. *In this, custom governs. . . .*

III. That, when the country lots are laid out, every purchaser, from *one thousand,* to *ten thousand* acres, or more, not to have above *one thousand* acres together, unless in *three* years they plant a family upon every *thousand* acres; but that all such as purchase together, lie together; and, if as many as comply with this condition, that the whole be laid out together,

VII. That, for every *fifty* acres, that shall be allotted to a servant, at the end of his service, his quit-rent shall be *two shillings* per annum, and the master, or owner of the servant, when he shall take up the other *fifty acres,* his quit-rent, shall be *four shillings* by the year, or, if the master of the servant (by reason in the indentures he is so obliged to do) allot out to the servant *fifty* acres in his own division, the said master shall have, on demand, allotted him, from the governor, the *one hundred* acres, at the chief rent of six shillings per annum.

VIII. And, for the encouragement of such as are ingenious and willing to search out gold and silver mines in this province, it is hereby agreed, that they have liberty to bore and dig in any man's property, fully paying the damages done; and in case a discovery should be made, that the discoverer have *one-fifth,* the owner of the soil (if not the discoverer) a tenth part, the Governor, *two-fifths,* and the rest to the public treasury, saving to the king the share reserved by patent.

IX. In every *hundred thousand* acres, the Governor and Proprietary, by lot, reserveth ten to himself, what shall lie but in one place.

X. That every man shall be bound to plant, or man, so much of his share of land as shall be set out and surveyed, within *three* years after it is so set out and surveyed, or else it shall be lawful for newcomers to be settled thereupon, paying to them their survey money, and they go up higher for their shares.

XI. There shall be no buying and selling, be it with an *Indian,* or one among another, of any goods to be exported, but what shall be performed in public market, when such places shall be set apart, or erected, where they shall pass the public stamp, or mark. If bad ware, and prized as good, or deceitful in proportion or weight, to forfeit the value, as if good and full weight and proportion, to the public treasury of this province, whether it be the merchandize of the *Indian,* or that of the planters.

XII. And forasmuch, as it is usual with the planters to over-reach the poor natives of the country, in trade, by goods not being good of the kind, or debased with mixtures, with which they are sensibly aggrieved, it is agreed, whatever is sold to the *Indians,* in consideration of their furs, shall be sold in the market place, and there suffer the test, whether good or bad; if good, to pass; if not good, not to be sold for good, that the natives may not be abused, nor provoked.

XIII. That no man shall, by any ways or means, in word, or deed, affront, or wrong any *Indian,* but he shall incur the same penalty of the law, as if he had committed it against his fellow planter, and if any *Indian* shall abuse, in word, or deed, any planter of this province, that he shall not be his own judge upon the *Indian,* but he shall make his complaint to the governor of the province, or his lieutenant, or deputy, or some inferior magistrate near him, who shall, to the utmost of his power, take care with the king of the said *Indian,* that all reasonable satisfaction be made to the said injured planter. . . .

XV. That the *Indians* shall have liberty to do all things relating to improvement of their ground, and providing sustenance for their families, that any of the planters shall enjoy.

XVI. That the laws, as to slanders, drunkenness, swearing, cursing, pride in apparel, trespasses, distriesses, replevins, weights, and measures, shall be the same as in *England,* till altered by law in this province. . . .

XVIII. That, in clearing the ground, care be taken to leave *one* acre of trees for every *five* acres cleared, especially to preserve oak and mulberries, for silk and shipping. . . .

WILLIAM PENN.

26. THE EARLIEST PROTEST AGAINST SLAVERY
Resolutions of Germantown Mennonites.
February 18, 1688

(P. G. Mode, ed. *Source Book and Bibliographical Guide for American Church History*, p. 552–553)

Negro slavery was first introduced to the English colonies in America in 1619; though the number of negro slaves in the seventeenth century was comparatively small, there was some protest against the institution, especially from the Quakers and Mennonites. The protest of 1688 is the earliest known protest against slavery in the American colonies. See, M. S. Locke, *Anti-Slavery in America, 1619–1808* (Radcliffe College Monographs).

This is to the monthly meeting held at Richard Worrell's:

These are the reasons why we are against the traffic of men-body, as followeth: Is there any that would be done or handled at this manner? viz., to be sold or made a slave for all the time of his life? How fearful and faint-hearted are many at sea, when they see a strange vessel, being afraid it should be a Turk, and they should be taken, and sold for slaves into Turkey. Now, what is *this* better done, than Turks do? Yea, rather it is worse for them, which say they are Christians; for we hear that the most part of such negers are brought hither against their will and consent, and that many of them are stolen. Now, though they are black, we cannot conceive there is more liberty to have them slaves, as it is to have other white ones. There is a saying, that we should do to all men like as we will be done ourselves; making no difference of what generation, descent, or colour they are. And those who steal or rob men, and those who buy or purchase them, are they not all alike? Here is liberty of conscience, which is right and reasonable; here ought to be likewise liberty of the body, except of evil-doers, which is another case. But to bring men hither, or to rob and sell them against their will, we stand against. In Europe there are many oppressed for conscience-sake; and here there are those oppressed which are of a black colour. And we who know that men must not commit adultery—some do commit adultery *in* others, separating wives from their husbands, and giving them to others: and some sell the children of these poor creatures to other men. Ah! do consider well this thing, you who do it, if you would be done at this manner—and if it is done according to Christianity! You surpass Holland and Germany in this thing. This makes an ill report in all those countries of Europe, where they hear of [it], that the Quakers do here handel men as they handel there the cattle. And for that reason some have no mind or inclination to come hither. And who shall maintain this your cause, or plead for it? Truly, we cannot do so, except you shall inform us better hereof, viz.: that Christians have liberty to practice these things. Pray, what thing in the world can be done worse towards us, than if men should rob or steal us away, and sell us for slaves to strange countries; separating husbands from their wives and children. Being now this is not done in the manner we would be done at; therefore, we contradict, and are against this traffic of men body. And we who profess that it is not lawful to steal, must, likewise, avoid to purchase such things as are stolen, but rather help to stop this robbing and stealing, if possible. And such men ought to be delivered out of the hands of the robbers, and set free as in Europe. Then is Pennsylvania to have a good report, instead, it hath now a bad one, for this sake, in other countries; Especially whereas the Europeans are desirous to know in what manner *the Quakers* do rule in *their* province; and most of them do look upon us with an envious eye. But if this is done well, what shall we say is done evil?

If once these slaves (which they say are so wicked and stubborn men,) should join themselves—fight for their freedom, and handel their masters and mistresses, as they did handel them before; will these masters and mistresses take the sword at hand and war against these poor slaves, like, as we are able to believe, some will not refuse to do? Or, have these poor negers not as much right to fight for their freedom, as you have to keep them slaves?

Now consider well this thing, if it is good or bad. And in case you find it to be good to handel these blacks in that manner, we desire and require you hereby lovingly, that you may inform us herein, which at this time never was done, viz., that Christians have such a liberty to do so. To the end we shall be satisfied on this point, and satisfy likewise our good friends and acquaintances in our native country, to whom it is a terror, or fearful thing, that men should be handelled so in Pennsylvania.

This is from our meeting at Germantown, held yᵉ 18th of the 2d month, 1688, to be delivered to the monthly meeting at Richard Worrell's.

Garret Henderich,
Derick op de Graeff,
Francis Daniel Pastorius,
Abram op de Graeff.

27. THE NAVIGATION ACT OF 1696

(D. Pickering, *Statutes at Large,* Vol. IX, p. 428 ff.)

The Navigation Act of 1696 was designed to put an end to the widespread violations and evasions of the earlier navigation acts. This act, says Professor Channing, "may be said to have added the finishing touch to the colonial system so far as shipping was concerned." For references see Doc. No. 23.

An act for preventing frauds, and regulating abuses in the plantation trade.

II. Be it enacted . . . That after the five and twentieth day of *March,* 1698, no goods or merchandizes whatsoever shall be imported into, or exported out of, any colony or plantation to his Majesty, in *Asia, Africa,* or *America,* belonging, or in his possession, . . . or shall be laden in, or carried from any one port or place in the said colonies or plantations to any other port or place in the same, the kingdom of *England,* dominion of *Wales,* or town of *Berwick* upon *Tweed,* in any ship or bottom, but what is or shall be of the built of *England,* or of the built of *Ireland,* or the said colonies or plantations, and wholly owned by the people thereof, or any of them, and navigated with the masters and three fourths of the mariners of the said places only . . . under pain of forfeiture of ship and goods. . . .

III. [Goods may be imported and exported in prize ships, the master and three fourths the mariners being English.]

VI. And for the more effectual preventing of frauds, and regulating abuses in the plantation trade in *America,* be it further enacted . . . that the officers for the collecting and managing his Majesty's revenue, and inspecting the plantation trade, in any of the said plantations, shall have the same powers and authorities, for visiting and searching of ships, and taking their entries, and for seizing and securing or bringing on shore any of the goods prohibited to be imported or exported . . . or for which any duties are payable or ought to have been paid . . . as are provided for the officers of the customs in England by the said last mentioned act made in the fourteenth year of the reign of King *Charles* the Second, and also to enter houses or warehouses, to search for and seize any such goods. . . .

IX. And it is further enacted . . . That all laws, by-laws, usages or customs, at this time, or which hereafter shall be in practice . . . in any of the said plantations, which are in any wise repugnant to the before mentioned laws, or any of them, so far as they do relate to the said plantations, or any of them, or which are any ways repugnant to this present act, or to any other law hereafter to be made in this kingdom, so far as such law shall relate to and mention the said plantations, are illegal, null and void, to all intents and purposes whatsoever. . . .

XIV. *And whereas several ships and vessels laden with tobacco, sugars, and other goods of the growth and product of his Majesty's plantations in* America, *have been discharged in several ports of the kingdoms of* Scotland *and* Ireland, *contrary to the laws and statutes now in being, under pretence that the said ships and vessels were driven thither by stress of weather, or for want of provisions, and other disabilities could not proceed on their voyage:* for remedy whereof be it enacted . . . That from and after the first day of *December,* 1696, it shall not be lawful, on any pretence whatsoever, to put on shore in the said kingdoms of *Scotland* or *Ireland,* any goods or merchandize of the growth or product of any of his Majesty's plantations aforesaid, unless the same shall have been first landed in the kingdom of *England,* dominion of *Wales,* or town of *Berwick* upon *Tweed,* and paid the rates and duties wherewith they are chargeable by law. . . .

XVI. And be it further enacted . . . That all persons and their assignees, claiming any right or propriety in any islands or tracts of land upon the continent of *America,* by charter or letters patents, shall not at any time hereafter aliene, sell or dispose of any of the said islands, tracts of lands or proprieties, other than to the natural-born subjects of *England, Ireland,* dominion of *Wales,* and town of *Berwick* upon *Tweed,* without the licence and consent of his Majesty . . . ; and all governors nominated and appointed by any such persons or proprietors, who shall be intitled to make such nomination, shall be allowed and approved of by his Majesty . . .

and shall take the oaths injoined by this or any other act to be taken by the governors or commanders in chief in other his Majesty's colonies and plantations, before their entering upon their respective governments, under the like penalty, as his Majesty's governors and commanders in chief are by the said acts liable to.

XVII. And for the more effectual prevention of frauds which may be used to elude the intention of this act, by colouring foreign ships under *English* names, be it further enacted . . . that from and after the five and twentieth day of *March,* 1698, no ship or vessel whatsoever shall be deemed or pass as a ship of the built of *England, Ireland, Wales, Berwick, Guernsey, Jersey,* or any of his Majesty's plantations in *America,* so as to be qualified to trade to, from or in any of the plantations, until the person or persons claiming property in such ship or vessel shall register the same. . . .

28. PENN'S PLAN OF UNION
1697

(E. B. O'Callaghan, ed. *Documents Relative to the Colonial History of the State of New York,* Vol. IV, p. 296–7)

This is probably the earliest of the plans of union for the English colonies in America. For Penn's plan, and other early plans such as that of Daniel Coxe, see, R. Frothingham, *Rise of the Republic of the United States,* p. 110 ff. See also, S. G. Fisher, *The True William Penn.*

A brief and plain scheme how the English colonies in the North parts of America,—viz., Boston, Connecticut, Rhode Island, New York, New Jerseys, Pennsylvania, Maryland, Virginia, and Carolina,—may be made more useful to the crown and one another's peace and safety with an universal concurrence.

1. That the several colonies before mentioned do meet once a year, and oftener if need be during the war, and at least once in two years in times of peace, by their stated and appointed deputies, to debate and resolve of such measures as are most advisable for their better understanding and the public tranquillity and safety.

2. That, in order to it, two persons, well qualified for sense, sobriety, and substance, be appointed by each province as their representatives or deputies, which in the whole make the congress to consist of twenty persons.

3. That the king's commissioner, for that purpose specially appointed, shall have the chair and preside in the said congress.

4. That they shall meet as near as conveniently may be to the most central colony for ease of the deputies.

5. Since that may in all probability be New York, both because it is near the centre of the colonies and for that it is a frontier and in the king's nomination, the governor of that colony may therefore also be the king's high commissioner during the session, after the manner of Scotland.

6. That their business shall be to hear and adjust all matters of complaint or difference between province and province. As, 1st, where persons quit their own province and go to another, that they may avoid their just debts, though they be able to pay them; 2d, where offenders fly justice, or justice cannot well be had upon such offenders in the

provinces that entertain them; 3d, to prevent or cure injuries in point of commerce; 4th, to consider the ways and means to support the union and safety of these provinces against the public enemies. In which congress the quotas of men and charges will be much easier and more equally set than it is possible for any establishment made here to do; for the provinces, knowing their own condition and one another's, can debate that matter with more freedom and satisfaction, and better adjust and balance their affairs in all respects for their common safety.

7. That, in times of war, the king's high commissioner shall be general or chief commander of the several quotas upon service against the common enemy, as he shall be advised, for the good and benefit of the whole.

29. PENNSYLVANIA CHARTER OF PRIVILEGES
October 28, 1701

(F. N. Thorpe, ed. *Federal and State Constitutions,* Vol. V, p. 3076 ff.)

The Frame of Government of 1682, proving cumbersome and unsatisfactory in detail, was replaced by the Great Charter and Frame of April 2, 1683. The following year Penn returned to England. He soon fell into disfavor with King William and in 1692 his colony was taken away from him and placed under the authority of Governor Fletcher of New York. Two years later it was restored to Penn, but Penn was not able to return to America until 1699, and meanwhile affairs became thoroughly unsatisfactory and disorganized. Under these circumstances, Penn agreed to the appointment of committees from the council and assembly to draft a new frame of government. This charter, finally agreed upon October 28, 1701, remained in force until the Revolution. For references see Doc. No. 25.

William Penn, Proprietary and Governor of the Province of *Pensilvania* and Territories thereunto belonging, To all to whom these Presents shall come, sendeth Greeting. Whereas King Charles *the Second,* by His Letters Patents, under the Great Seal of *England,* bearing Date the *Fourth* Day of *March,* in the Year *One Thousand Six Hundred and Eighty-one,* was graciously pleased to give and grant unto me, and my Heirs and Assigns for ever, this Province of *Pensilvania,* with divers great Powers and Jurisdictions for the well Government thereof. . . .

KNOW YE THEREFORE, That for the further Well-being and good Government of the said Province, and Territories and in Pursuance of the Rights and Powers beforementioned, I the said *William Penn* do declare, grant and confirm, unto all the Freemen, Planters and Adventurers, and other Inhabitants of this Province and Territories, these following Liberties, Franchises and Privileges, so far as in me lieth, to be held, enjoyed and kept, by the Freemen, Planters and Adventurers, and other Inhabitants of and in the said Province and Territories thereunto annexed, for ever.

FIRST

BECAUSE no People can be truly happy, though under the greatest Enjoyment of Civil Liberties, if abridged of the Freedom of their Consciences, as to their Religious Profession and Worship: And Almighty God being the only Lord of Conscience, Father of Lights and Spirits; and the Author as well as Object of all divine Knowledge, Faith and Worship, who only doth enlighten the Minds, and persuade and convince the Understandings of People, I do hereby grant and declare, That no Person or Persons, inhabiting in this province or Territories, who shall confess and acknowledge *One* almighty God, the Creator, Upholder and Ruler of the World; and profess him or themselves obliged to live quietly under the Civil Government, shall be in any Case molested or prejudiced, in his or their Person or Estate, because of his or their conscientious Persuasion or Practice, nor be compelled to frequent or maintain any religious Worship, Place or Ministry, contrary to his or their Mind, or to do or suffer any other Act or Thing, contrary to their religious Persuasion.

AND that all Persons who also profess to believe in *Jesus Christ,* the Saviour of the World, shall be capable (notwithstanding their other Persuasions and Practices in

Point of Conscience and Religion) to serve this Government in any Capacity, both legislatively and executively, he or they solemnly promising, when lawfully required, Allegiance to the King as Sovereign, and Fidelity to the Proprietary and Governor, and taking the Attests as now established by the Law made at *New-Castle*, in the Year *One Thousand and Seven Hundred*, entitled, *An Act directing the Attests of several Officers and Ministers*, as now amended and confirmed this present Assembly.

II For the well governing of this Province and Territories, there shall be an Assembly yearly chosen, by the Freemen thereof, to consist of *Four* Persons out of each County, of most Note for Virtue, Wisdom and Ability. . . . Which Assembly shall have Power to chuse a Speaker and other their Officers; and shall be Judges of the Qualifications and Elections of their own Members; sit upon their own Adjournments; appoint Committees; prepare Bills in order to pass into Laws; impeach Criminals, and redress Grievances; and shall have all other Powers and Privileges of an Assembly, according to the Rights of the free-born Subjects of *England*, and as is usual in any of the King's Plantations in *America*. . . .

III That the Freemen in each respective County, at the Time and Place of Meeting for Electing their Representatives to serve in Assembly, may as often as there shall be Occasion, chuse a double Number of Persons to present to the Governor for Sheriffs and Coroners to serve for *Three* Years, if so long they behave themselves well; out of which respective Elections and Presentments, the Governor shall nominate and commissionate one for each of the said Offcers, the *Third* Day after such Presentment, or else the *First* named in such Presentment, for each Office as aforesaid, shall stand and serve in that Office for the Time before respectively limited; and in Case of Death or Default, such Vacancies shall be supplied by the Governor, to serve to the End of the said Term. . . .

AND that the Justices of the respective Counties shall or may nominate and present to the Governor *Three* Persons, to serve for Clerk of the Peace for the said County, when there is a Vacancy, one of which the Governor shall commissionate within *Ten* Days after such Presentment, or else the *First*

nominated shall serve in the said Office during good Behavior.

IV THAT the Laws of this Government shall be in this Stile, viz. *By the Governor, with the Consent and Approbation of the Freemen in General Assembly met;* and shall be, after Confirmation by the Governor, forthwith recorded in the Rolls Office, and kept at *Philadelphia*, unless the Governor and Assembly shall agree to appoint another Place.

V THAT all Criminals shall have the same Privileges of Witnesses and Council as their Prosecutors.

VI THAT no Person or Persons shall or may, at any Time hereafter, be obliged to answer any Complaint, Matter or Thing whatsoever, relating to Property, before the Governor and Council, or in any other Place, but in ordinary Course of Justice, unless Appeals thereunto shall be hereafter by Law appointed.

VII THAT no Person within this Government, shall be licensed by the Governor to keep an Ordinary, Tavern or House of Publick Entertainment, but such who are first recommended to him, under the Hands of the Justices of the respective Counties, signed in open Court; which Justices are and shall be hereby impowered, to suppress and forbid any Person, keeping such Publick-House as aforesaid, upon their Misbehavior, on such Penalties as the Law doth or shall direct; and to recommend others from time to time, as they shall see Occasion. . . .

VIII BUT because the Happiness of Mankind depends so much upon the Enjoying of Liberty of their Consciences as aforesaid, I do hereby solemnly declare, promise and grant, for me, my Heirs and Assigns, That the *First* Article of this Charter relating to Liberty of Conscience, and every Part and Clause therein, according to the true Intent and Meaning thereof, shall be kept and remain, without any Alteration, inviolably for ever.

AND LASTLY, I the said *William Penn*, Proprietary and Governor of the Province of *Pensilvania*, and Territories thereunto belonging, for myself, my Heirs and Assigns, have solemnly declared, granted and confirmed, and do hereby solemnly declare, grant and confirm, That neither I, my Heirs or Assigns, shall procure or do any Thing or Things whereby the Liberties in this Charter contained and expressed, nor any Part thereof, shall be infringed or broken: And if any thing shall be procured or done, by any Person or Persons, contrary to these Presents, it shall be held of no Force or Effect. . . .

30. THE MOLASSES ACT
May 17, 1733

(D. Pickering, *Statutes at Large,* Vol. XVI, p. 374 ff.)

This Act, placing heavy duties upon the importation of rum and molasses from the French West Indies to the American colonies, was passed in response to the demand of the English merchants with interests in the British West Indies. Had it been enforced, it would have played havoc with the triangle trade of the New England merchants; fortunately for them it was not enforced. See, G. L. Beer, *Commercial Policy of England Toward the American Colonies;* E. B. Greene, *Provincial America,* ch. xvii; J. T. Adams, *Revolutionary New England,* ch. viii; W. J. Ashley, *Surveys, Historic and Economic;* C. M. Andrews, "Anglo-French Commercial Rivalry, 1700–1750", *American Hist. Rev.,* Vol. XX.

An act for the better securing and encouraging the trade of his Majesty's sugar colonies in America.

WHEREAS *the welfare and prosperity of your Majesty's sugar colonies in America are of the greatest consequence and importance to the trade, navigation and strength of this kingdom: and whereas the planters of the said sugar colonies have of late years fallen under such great discouragements, that they are unable to improve or carry on the sugar trade upon an equal footing with the foreign sugar colonies, without some advantage and relief be given to them from Great Britain:* for remedy whereof . . . be it enacted . . . , That from and after [December 25, 1733,] there shall be raised, levied, collected and paid, unto and for the use of his Majesty . . . , upon all rum or spirits of the produce or manufacture of any of the colonies or plantations in *America,* not in the possession or under the dominion of his Majesty . . . , which at any time or times within or during the continuance of this act, shall be imported or brought into any of the colonies or plantations in *America,* which now are or hereafter may be in the possession or under the dominion of his Majesty . . . , the sum of nine pence, money of *Great Britain,* . . . for every gallon thereof, and after that rate for any greater or lesser

quantity: and upon all molasses or syrups of such foreign produce or manufacture as aforesaid, which shall be imported or brought into any of the said colonies or plantations of or belonging to his Majesty, the sum of six pence of like money for every gallon thereof . . . ; and upon all sugars and paneles of such foreign growth, produce or manufacture as aforesaid, which shall be imported into any of the said colonies or plantations . . . , a duty after the rate of five shillings of like money, for every hundred weight *Avoirdupoize.* . . .

IV. And be it further enacted . . . , That from and after December 25, 1733, no sugars, paneles, syrups or molasses, of the growth, product and manufacture of any of the colonies or plantations in *America,* nor any rum or spirits of *America,* except of the growth or manufacture of his Majesty's sugar colonies there, shall be imported by any person or persons whatsoever into the kingdom of *Ireland,* but such only as shall be fairly and *bona fide* loaden and shipped in *Great Britain* in ships navigated according to the several laws now in being in that behalf, under the penalty of forfeiting all such sugar, paneles, syrups or molasses, rum or spirits, or the value thereof, together with the ship or vessel in which the same shall be imported, . . .

IX. And it is hereby further enacted . . . , That in case any sugar or paneles of the growth, produce or manufacture of any of the colonies or plantations belonging to or in the possession of his Majesty . . . , which shall have been imported into *Great Britain* after June 24, 1733, shall at any time within one year after the importation thereof, be again exported out of *Great Britain,* . . . all the residue and remainder of the subsidy or duty, by any former act or acts of parliament granted and charged on such sugar or paneles as aforesaid, shall without any delay or reward be repaid to such merchant or merchants, who do export the same, within one month after demand thereof.

X. And it is hereby further enacted . . . , That from and after June 24, 1733, for every hundred weight of sugar refined in *Great Britain* . . . , which shall be exported out of this kingdom, there shall be, by virtue of this act, repaid at the customhouse to the exporter, within one month after the demand thereof, over and above the several sums of three shillings and one shilling *per* hundred, payable by two former acts of parliament, one of them made in the ninth and tenth years of the reign of his late Majesty King *William* the Third, and the other in the second and third years of the reign of her late Majesty Queen *Anne*, the further sum of two shillings, oath or solemn affirmation as aforesaid, being first made by the refiner, that the said sugar so exported, was produced from brown and muscovado sugar, and that as he verily believes, the same was imported from some of the colonies or plantations in *America* belonging to and in the possession of the crown of *Great Britain*, and that as he verily believes the duty of the said brown and muscovado sugar was duly paid at the time of the importation thereof, and that the same was duly exported. . . .

XIII. Provided nevertheless, That nothing herein contained shall extend . . . to hinder or restrain the importation of any sugars . . . of any of the dominions belonging to the King of *Spain*, or the King of *Portugal*, from any part or place from whence such sugars might lawfully have been imported before the making of this act. . . .

31. THE ALBANY PLAN OF UNION
1754

(Works of Benjamin Franklin, ed. by J. Sparks, Vol. III, p. 36 ff.)

This plan of union, devised by Franklin, contained the germs of the solution of the problem of imperial order, ultimately solved by the Federal Constitution of the United States. An interesting discussion of the Plan is in R. Frothingham, *Rise of the Republic of the United States*, ch. iv; H. L. Osgood, *American Colonies in the Eighteenth Century*, Vol. IV, ch. xiv; A. C. McLaughlin, "The Background of American Federalism," *America and Britain*, p. 147 ff. In the document Franklin's explanatory notes are omitted.

It is proposed that humble application be made for an act of Parliament of Great Britain, by virtue of which one general government may be formed in America, including all the said colonies, within and under which government each colony may retain its present constitution, except in the particulars wherein a change may be directed by the said act, as hereafter follows.

1. That the said general government be administered by a President-General, to be appointed and supported by the crown; and a Grand Council, to be chosen by the representatives of the people of the several Colonies met in their respective assemblies.

2. That within —— months after the passing such act, the House of Representatives that happen to be sitting within that time, or that shall be especially for that purpose convened, may and shall choose members for the Grand Council, in the following proportion, that is to say,

Massachusetts Bay	7
New Hampshire	2
Connecticut	5
Rhode Island	2
New York	4
New Jersey	3
Pennsylvania	6
Maryland	4
Virginia	7
North Carolina	4
South Carolina	4
	48

3. ——who shall meet for the first time at the city of Philadelphia, being called by the President General as soon as conveniently may be after his appointment.

4. That there shall be a new election of the members of the Grand Council every three years; and, on the death or resignation of any member, his place should be supplied by a new choice at the next sitting of the Assembly of the Colony he represented.

5. That after the first three years, when the proportion of money arising out of each Colony to the general treasury can be known,

the number of members to be chosen for each Colony shall, from time to time, in all ensuing elections, be regulated by that proportion, yet so as that the number to be chosen by any one Province be not more than seven, nor less than two.

6. That the Grand Council shall meet once in every year, and oftener if occasion require, at such time and place as they shall adjourn to at the last preceding meeting, or as they shall be called to meet at by the President-General on any emergency; he having first obtained in writing the consent of seven of the members to such call, and sent duly and timely notice to the whole.

7. That the Grand Council have power to choose their speaker; and shall neither be dissolved, prorogued, nor continued sitting longer than six weeks at one time, without their own consent or the special command of the crown.

8. That the members of the Grand Council shall be allowed for their service ten shillings sterling per diem, during their session and journey to and from the place of meeting; twenty miles to be reckoned a day's journey.

9. That the assent of the President-General be requisite to all acts of the Grand Council, and that it be his office and duty to cause them to be carried into execution.

10. That the President-General, with the advice of the Grand Council, hold or direct all Indian treaties, in which the general interest of the Colonies may be concerned; and make peace or declare war with Indian nations.

11. That they make such laws as they judge necessary for regulating all Indian trade.

12. That they make all purchases from Indians, for the crown, of lands not now within the bounds of particular Colonies, or that shall not be within their bounds when some of them are reduced to more convenient dimensions.

13. That they make new settlements on such purchases, by granting lands in the King's name, reserving a quitrent to the crown for the use of the general treasury.

14. That they make laws for regulating and governing such new settlements, till the crown shall think fit to form them into particular governments.

15. That they raise and pay soldiers and build forts for the defence of any of the Colonies, and equip vessels of force to guard the coasts and protect the trade on the ocean, lakes, or great rivers; but they shall not impress men in any Colony, without the consent of the Legislature.

16. That for these purposes they have power to make laws, and lay and levy such general duties, imposts, or taxes, as to them shall appear most equal and just (considering the ability and other circumstances of the inhabitants in the several Colonies), and such as may be collected with the least inconvenience to the people; rather discouraging luxury, than loading industry with unnecessary burdens.

17. That they may appoint a General Treasurer and Particular Treasurer in each government when necessary; and, from time to time, may order the sums in the treasuries of each government into the general treasury; or draw on them for special payments, as they find most convenient.

18. Yet no money to issue but by joint orders of the President-General and Grand Council; except where sums have been appropriated to particular purposes, and the President-General is previously empowered by an act to draw such sums.

19. That the general accounts shall be yearly settled and reported to the several Assemblies.

20. That a quorum of the Grand Council, empowered to act with the President-General, do consist of twenty-five members; among whom there shall be one or more from a majority of the Colonies.

21. That the laws made by them for the purposes aforesaid shall not be repugnant, but, as near as may be, agreeable to the laws of England, and shall be transmitted to the King in Council for approbation, as soon as may be after their passing; and if not disapproved within three years after presentation, to remain in force.

22. That, in case of the death of the President-General, the Speaker of the Grand Council for the time being shall succeed, and be vested with the same powers and authorities, to continue till the King's pleasure be known.

23. That all military commission officers, whether for land or sea service, to act under this general constitution, shall be nominated

by the President-General; but the approbation of the Grand Council is to be obtained, before they receive their commissions. And all civil officers are to be nominated by the Grand Council, and to receive the President-General's approbation before they officiate.

24. But, in case of vacancy by death or removal of any officer, civil or military, under this constitution, the Governor of the Province in which such vacancy happens may appoint, till the pleasure of the President-General and Grand Council can be known.

25. That the particular military as well as civil establishments in each Colony remain in their present state, the general constitution notwithstanding; and that on sudden emergencies any Colony may defend itself, and lay the accounts of expense thence arising before the President-General and General Council, who may allow and order payment of the same, as far as they judge such accounts just and reasonable.

32. JAMES OTIS' SPEECH AGAINST THE WRITS OF ASSISTANCE
February 24, 1761

(The Works of John Adams, ed. by C. F. Adams, Vol. II, p. 521 ff.)

This famous case involved the question of the constitutionality of the writs of assistance issued from the court of exchequer in England. On the application of the surveyor-general of the port of Boston for the grant of these writs, some Boston merchants engaged Oxenbridge Thacher and James Otis to argue against their issuance. No formal record of Otis's argument exists. John Adams, however, took notes of the speech, and these are given in the first extract below. G. R. Minot in his *History of Massachusetts, 1748–1765*, Vol. II, p. 87–99, expanded these notes into a version of the argument. Adams's revision of the Minot version, is given in the second extract below. For a learned discussion of the whole question see the Appendix to J. Quincy, *Reports of Cases Argued and Adjudged in the Superior Court of Judicature of the Province of Massachusetts Bay between 1761 and 1772*, p. 479 ff., by Justice Horace Gray. Otis's argument contains one of the earliest statements of the doctrine that a law against natural law is void. For the history of this theory see, C. F. Mullett, *Fundamental Law and the American Revolution*. A copy of a writ of Assistance can be found in W. MacDonald, ed. *Select Charters, etc.*, p. 258 ff.

1. *Otis.* This writ is against the fundamental principles of law. The privilege of the House. A man who is quiet, is as secure in his house, as a prince in his castle—notwithstanding all his debts and civil processes of any kind. But—

For flagrant crimes and in cases of great public necessity, the privilege may be infringed on. For felonies an officer may break upon process and oath, that is, by a special warrant to search such a house, sworn to be suspected, and good grounds of suspicion appearing.

Make oath *coram* Lord Treasurer, or Exchequer in England, or a magistrate here, and get a special warrant for the public good, to infringe the privilege of house.

General warrant to search for felonies. Hawkins, Pleas of the Crown. Every petty officer, from the highest to the lowest; and if some of them are common, others are uncommon.

Government justices used to issue such perpetual edicts. (*Q.* With what particular reference.) But one precedent, and that in the reign of Charles II., when star chamber powers and all powers but lawful and useful powers, were pushed to extremity.

The authority of this modern practice of the Court of Exchequer. It has an Imprimatur. But what may not have? It may be owing to some ignorant Clerk of the Exchequer. But all precedents, and this among the rest, are under the control of the principles of law. Lord Talbot. Better to observe the known principles of law than any one precedent, though in the House of Lords.

As to Acts of Parliament. An act against the Constitution is void; an act against natural equity is void; and if an act of Parliament should be made, in the very words of this petition it would be void. The executive Courts must pass such acts into disuse.

8 Rep. 118 from Viner. Reason of the common law to control an act of Parliament. Iron manufacture. Noble Lord's proposal, that we should send our horses to England to be shod. If an officer will justify under a

writ, he must return it. 12. Mod. 396, perpetual writ. Statute Charles II. We have all as good right to inform as custom-house officers, and every man may have a general irreturnable commission to break houses.

By 12 of Charles, on oath before Lord Treasurer, Barons of Exchequer, or Chief Magistrate, to break, with an officer. 14 C. to issue a warrant requiring sheriffs, &c. to assist the officers to search for goods not entered or prohibited. 7 & 8. W. & M. gives officers in plantations same powers with officers in England.

Continuance of writs and processes proves no more, nor so much, as I grant a special writ of assistance on special oath for special purpose.

Pew indorsed warrant to Ware. Justice Walley searched House. Province Law. p. 114.

Bill in chancery. This Court confined their chancery power to revenue, &c.

2. . . . In the first place, may it please your Honors, I will admit that writs of one kind may be legal; that is, special writs, directed to special officers, and to search certain houses, &c. specially set forth in the writ, may be granted by the Court of Exchequer at home, upon oath made before the Lord Treasurer by the person who asks it, that he suspects such goods to be concealed in those very places he desires to search. The act of 14 Charles II, which Mr. Gridley mentions, proves this. And in this light the writ appears like a warrant from a Justice of the Peace to search for stolen goods. Your Honors will find in the old books concerning the office of a Justice of the Peace, precedents of general warrants to search suspected houses. But in more modern books you will find only special warrants to search such and such houses specially named, in which the complainant has before sworn that he suspects his goods are concealed; and you will find it adjudged that special warrants only are legal. In the same manner I rely on it, that the writ prayed for in this petition, being general, is illegal. It is a power, that places the liberty of every man in the hands of every petty officer. I say I admit that special writs of assistance, to search special places, may be granted to certain persons on oath; but I deny that the writ now prayed for

can be granted, for I beg leave to make some observations on the writ itself, before I proceed to other acts of Parliament. In the first place, the writ is universal, being directed "to all and singular Justices, Sheriffs, Constables, and other officers and subjects;" so, that, in short, it is directed to every subject in the King's dominions. Every one with this writ may be a tyrant; if this commission be legal, a tyrant in a legal manner also may control, imprison, or murder any one within the realm. In the next place, it is perpetual; there is no return. A man is accountable to no person for his doings. Every man may reign secure in his petty tyranny, and spread terror and desolation around him. In the third place, a person with this writ, in the daytime, may enter all houses, shops, &c. at will, and command all to assist him. Fourthly, by this writ not only deputies &c. but even their menial servants, are allowed to lord it over us. Now one of the most essential branches of English liberty is the freedom of one's house. A man's house is his castle; and whilst he is quiet, he is as well guarded as a prince in his castle. This writ, if it should be declared legal, would totally annihilate this privilege. Custom-house officers may enter our houses, when they please; we are commanded to permit their entry. Their menial servants may enter, may break locks, bars, and every thing in their way; and whether they break through malice or revenge, no man, no court, can inquire. Bare suspicion without oath is sufficient. This wanton exercise of his power is not a chimerical suggestion of a heated brain. I will mention some facts. Mr. Pew had one of these writs, and when Mr. Ware succeeded him, he endorsed this writ over to Mr. Ware; so that these writs are negotiable from one officer to another; and so your Honors have no opportunity of judging the persons to whom this vast power is delegated. Another instance is this: Mr. Justice Walley had called this same Mr. Ware before him, by a constable, to answer for a breach of Sabbath-day acts, or that of profane swearing. As soon as he had finished, Mr. Ware asked him if he had done. He replied, Yes/ Well then, said Mr. Ware, I will show you a little of my power. I command you to permit me to search your house for uncustomed goods. And went on to search his house from the garret to the cellar; and then served the constable in the same manner. But to show another absurdity in this writ; if it should be established, I insist upon it, every person by the 14 Charles II. has this power as well as custom-house officers. The words are, "It shall be lawful for any person or persons authorized," &c. What a scene does this open! Every man, prompted by revenge, ill humor, or wantonness, to inspect the inside of his neighbor's house, may get a writ of assistance. Others will ask it from self-defence; one arbitrary exertion will provoke another, until society be involved in tumult and in blood.

Again, these writs are not returned. Writs in their nature are temporary things. When the purposes for which they are issued are answered, they exist no more; but these live forever; no one can be called to account. Thus reason and the constitution are both against this writ. Let us see what authority there is for it. Not more than one instance can be found of it in all our law-books; and that was in the zenith of arbitrary power,

namely, in the reign of Charles II, when star-chamber powers were pushed to extremity by some ignorant clerk of the exchequer. But had this writ been in any book whatever, it would have been illegal. All precedents are under the control of the principles of law. Lord Talbot says it is better to observe these than any precedents, though in the House of Lords, the last resort of the subject. No Acts of Parliament can establish such a writ; though it should be made in the very words of the petition, it would be void. An act against the constitution is void. (vid. Viner.) But these prove no more than what I before observed, that special writs may be granted *on oath and probable suspicion*. The act of 7 & 8 William III. that the officers of the plantation shall have the same powers, &c., is confined to this sense; that an officer should show probable ground; should take his oath of it; should do this before a magistrate; and that such magistrate, if he thinks proper, should issue a special warrant to a constable to search the places. That of 6 Anne can prove no more.

33. THE PROCLAMATION OF 1763
October 7, 1763

(*Annual Register,* 1763, p. 208 ff.)

The immediate background of this famous proclamation was Pontiac's Rebellion, and its provisions were designed to be of a temporary character. The reservation of the lands west of the Appalachians appeared to deprive the Colonies of their western lands and to put an end to the widespread private speculation in these lands. See, C. W. Alvord, *The Mississippi Valley in British Politics,* 2 Vols.; C. E. Carter, *Great Britain and the Illinois Country;* V. Coffin, *Quebec and the American Revolution,* ch. v.

Whereas we have taken into our royal consideration the extensive and valuable acquisitions in America secured to our Crown by the late definitive treaty of peace concluded at Paris the 10th day of February last; and being desirous that all our loving subjects, as well of our kingdom as of our colonies in America, may avail themselves, with all convenient speed, of the great benefits and advantages which must accrue therefrom to their commerce, manufactures, and navigation; we have thought fit, with the

advice of our Privy Council, to issue this our Royal Proclamation, hereby to publish and declare to all our loving subjects that we have, with the advice of our said Privy Council, granted our letters patent under our Great Seal of Great Britain, to erect within the countries and islands ceded and confirmed to us by the said treaty, four distinct and separate governments, styled and called by the names of Quebec, East Florida, West Florida, and Grenada, and limited and bounded as follows, viz:

First, the government of Quebec, bounded on the Labrador coast by the river St. John, and from thence by a line drawn from the head of that river, through the lake St. John, to the South end of the lake Nipissim; from whence the said line, crossing the river St. Lawrence and the Lake Champlain in 45 degrees of North latitude, passes along the High Lands, which divide the rivers that empty themselves into the said river St. Lawrence, from those which fall into the sea; and also along the North coast of the Bayes des Chaleurs, and the coast of the Gulph of St. Lawrence to Cape Rosieres, and from thence crossing the mouth of the river St. Lawrence by the West end of the island of Anticosti, terminates at the aforesaid river St. John.

Secondly, The government of East Florida, bounded to the Westward by the Gulph of Mexico and the Apalachicola river; to the Northward, by a line drawn from that part of the said river where the Catahoochee and Flint rivers meet, to the source of St. Mary's river, and by the course of the said river to the Atlantic Ocean; and to the East and South by the Atlantic Ocean, and the Gulph of Florida, including all islands within six leagues of the sea coast.

Thirdly, The government of West Florida, bounded to the Southward by the Gulph of Mexico, including all islands within six leagues of the coast from the river Apalachicola to lake Pontchartrain; to the Westward by the said lake, the lake Maurepas, and the river Mississippi; to the Northward, by a line drawn due East from that part of the river Mississippi which lies in thirty-one degrees North latitude, to the river Apalachicola, or Catahoochee; and to the Eastward by the said river.

Fourthly, The government of Grenada, comprehending the island of that name, together with the Grenadines, and the islands of Dominico, St. Vincent, and Tobago.

And to the end that the open and free fishery of our subjects may be extended to, and carried on upon the coast of Labrador and the adjacent islands, we have thought fit . . . to put all that coast, from the river St. John's to Hudson's Streights, together with the islands of Anticosti and Madelane, and all other smaller islands lying upon the said coast, under the care and inspection of our governor of Newfoundland.

We have also . . . thought fit to annex the islands of St. John and Cape Breton, or Isle Royale, with the lesser islands adjacent thereto, to our government of Nova Scotia.

We have also . . . annexed to our province of Georgia, all the lands lying between the rivers Atamaha and St. Mary's.

And . . . we have . . . given express power and direction to our governors of our said colonies respectively, that so soon as the state and circumstances of the said colonies will admit thereof, they shall, with the advice and consent of the members of our council, summon and call general assemblies within the said governments respectively, in such manner and form as is used and directed in those colonies and provinces in America, which are under our immediate government; and we have also given power to the said governors, with the consent of our said councils, and the representatives of the people, so to be summoned as aforesaid, to make, constitute, and ordain laws, statutes, and ordinances for the public peace, welfare, and good government of our said colonies, and of the people and inhabitants thereof, as near as may be, agreeable to the laws of England, and under such regulations and restrictions as are used in other colonies; and in the mean time, and until such assemblies can be called as aforesaid, all persons inhabiting in, or resorting to, our said colonies, may confide in our royal protection for the enjoyment of the benefit of the laws of our realm of England: for which purpose we have given power under our great seal to the governors of our said colonies respectively, to erect and constitute, with the advice of our said councils respectively, courts of judicature and public justice within our said colonies, for the hearing and determining all causes as well criminal as civil, according to law and equity, and as near as may be, agreeable to the laws of England, with liberty to all persons who may think themselves aggrieved by the sentence of such courts, in all civil cases, to appeal, under the usual limitations and restrictions, to us, in our privy council.

And whereas it is just and reasonable, and essential to our interest and the security of our colonies, that the several nations or tribes of Indians with whom we are connected, and who live under our protection, should not be molested or disturbed in the possession of such parts of our dominions and territories as, not having been ceded to or purchased by us, are reserved to them, or any of them, as their hunting-grounds; we do therefore, with the advice of our Privy Council, declare it to be our royal will and pleasure, that no Governor or commander in chief, in any of our colonies of Quebec, East Florida, or West Florida, do presume, upon any pretence whatever, to grant warrants of survey, or pass any patents for lands beyond the bounds of their respective governments, as described in their commissions; as also that no Governor or commander in chief of our other colonies or plantations in America do presume for the present, and until our further pleasure be known, to grant warrants of survey or pass patents for any lands beyond the heads or sources of any of the rivers which fall into the Atlantic Ocean from the west or northwest; or upon any lands whatever, which, not having been ceded to or purchased by us, as aforesaid, are reserved to the said Indians, or any of them.

And we do further declare it to be our royal will and pleasure, for the present as aforesaid, to reserve under our sovereignty, protection, and dominion, for the use of the said Indians, all the land and territories not included within the limits of our said three new governments, or within the limits of the territory granted to the Hudson's Bay Company; as also all the land and territories lying to the westward of the sources of the rivers which fall into the sea from the west and northwest as aforesaid; and we do hereby strictly forbid, on pain of our displeasure, all our loving subjects from making any purchases or settlements whatever, or taking possession of any of the lands above reserved, without our special leave and license for that purpose first obtained.

And we do further strictly enjoin and require all persons whatever, who have either wilfully or inadvertently seated themselves upon any lands within the countries above described, or upon any other lands which, not having been ceded to or purchased by us, are still reserved to the said Indians as aforesaid, forthwith to remove themselves from such settlements.

And whereas great frauds and abuses have been committed in the purchasing lands of the Indians, to the great prejudice of our interests, and to the great dissatisfaction of the said Indians; in order, therefore, to prevent such irregularities for the future, and to the end that the Indians may be convinced of our justice and determined resolution to remove all reasonable cause of discontent, we do, with the advice of our Privy Council, strictly enjoin and require, that no private person do presume to make any purchase from the said Indians of any lands reserved to the said Indians within those parts of our colonies where we have thought proper to allow settlement; but that if at any time any of the said Indians should be inclined to dispose of the said lands, the same shall be purchased only for us, in our name, at some public meeting or assembly of the said Indians, to be held for that purpose by the Governor or commander in chief of our colony respectively within which they shall lie: and in case they shall lie within the limits of any proprietary government, they shall be purchased only for the use and in the name of such proprietaries, conformable to such directions and instructions as we or they shall think proper to give for that purpose. And we do, by the advice of our Privy Council, declare and enjoin, that the trade with the said Indians shall be free and open to all our subjects whatever, provided that every person who may incline to trade with the said Indians do take out a license for carrying on such trade, from the Governor or commander in chief of any of our colonies respectively where such person shall reside, and also give security to observe such regulations as we shall at any time think fit, by ourselves or commissaries to be appointed for this purpose, to direct and appoint for the benefit of the said trade. And we do hereby authorize, enjoin, and require the Governors and commanders in chief of all our colonies respectively, as well those under our immediate government as those under the government and direction of proprietaries, to grant such licenses without fee or reward, taking especial care to insert therein a condition that such license shall be void, and the security forfeited, in case the person to whom the same is granted shall refuse or neglect to observe such regulations as we shall think proper to prescribe as aforesaid.

And we do further expressly enjoin and require all officers whatever, as well military as those employed in the management and direction of Indian affairs within the territories reserved as aforesaid, for the use of the said Indians, to seize and apprehend all persons whatever who, standing charged with treasons, misprisions of treason, murders, or other felonies or misdemeanors, shall fly from justice and take refuge in the said territory, and to send them under a proper guard to the colony where the crime was committed of which they shall stand accused, in order to take their trial for the same.

Given at our Court at St. James's, the 7th day of October 1763, in the third year of our reign.

34. FRONTIER GRIEVANCES

A Remonstrance of the distressed and bleeding Frontier Inhabitants of the Province of Pennsylvania
February 13, 1764

(*Minutes of the Provincial Council of Pennsylvania,* Vol. IX, p. 138 ff.)

The various manifestations of sectionalism on the eve of the Revolution are nowhere better illustrated than in this remonstrance from the inhabitants of the frontier counties of Pennsylvania. The immediate background of the remonstrance was Pontiac's Rebellion and the raid of the so-called Paxton Boys on the civilized Conestogo Indians. See Franklin's "Narrative of the Massacres", *Works*, ed. by J. Bigelow, Vol. III, p. 260 ff. On sectionalism in Pennsylvania see W. R. Shepherd, *Proprietary Government in Pennsylvania;* C. R. Lincoln, *The Revolutionary Movement in Pennsylvania;* F. J. Turner, *The Frontier in American History,* ch. iii; G. A. Cribbs, *Frontier Policy of Pennsylvania.*

To the Honourable John Penn, Esquire, Governor of the Province of *Pennsylvania,* & of the Counties of *New Castle, Kent,* and *Sussex,* on *Delaware,* and to the Representatives of the Freemen of the said Province, in General Assembly met:

WE Matthew Smith and James Gibson, in behalf of ourselves and His Majesty's faithful and loyal Subjects, the Inhabitants of the Frontier Counties of Lancaster, York, Cumberland, Berks, and Northampton, humbly beg leave to remonstrate and to lay before you the following Grievances, which we submit to your Wisdom for Redress.

First. We apprehend that as Freemen and English Subjects, we have an indisputable Title to the same Privileges & immunities with His Majesty's other Subjects who reside in the interior Counties of Philadelphia, Chester, and Bucks, and therefore ought not to be excluded from an equal share with them in the very important Privilege of Legislation; nevertheless, contrary to the Proprietor's Charter and the acknowledged principles of common Justice & Equity, our

five counties are restrained from electing more than ten Representatives, viz: four for Lancaster, two for York, two for Cumberland, one for Berks, and one for Northampton; while the three Counties and City of Philadelphia, Chester, and Bucks, elect Twenty-Six. This we humbly conceive is oppressive, unequal, and unjust, the cause of many of our Grievances, and an infringement of our Natural privileges of Freedom & Equality; wherefore we humbly pray that we may be no longer deprived of an equal number with the three aforesaid Counties, to represent us in Assembly.

Secondly. We understand that a Bill is now before the House of Assembly, wherein it is provided that such Persons as shall be charged with killing any Indians in Lancaster County, shall not be tried in the County where the Fact was committed, but in the Counties of Philadelphia, Chester, or Bucks. This is manifestly to deprive British Subjects of their known Privileges, to cast an eternal Reproach upon whole Counties, as if they were unfit to serve their Country in the quality of Jurymen, and to contradict the well-known Laws of the British Nation in a point whereon Life, Liberty, and security essentially depend, namely, that of being tried by their equals in the neighborhood where their own, their Accusers', and the Witnesses' Character and Credit, with the Circumstances of the Fact, are best known, & instead thereof putting their Lives in the hands of Strangers who may as justly be suspected of partiallity to, as the Frontier Counties can be of prejudices against Indians; and this, too, in favour of Indians only, against His Majesty's faithful & loyal subjects. . . .

Thirdly. During the late and present

Indian War, the Frontiers of this Province have been repeatedly attacked and ravaged by Skulking parties of the Indians, who have with the most Savage Cruelty murdered Men, Women, and Children without distinction, and have reduced near a thousand Families to the most extream distress. It grieves us to the very heart to see such of our Frontier Inhabitants as have escaped Savage Fury with the loss of their parents, their Children, their Wives or Relatives, left destitute by the public, and exposed to the most cruel Poverty and Wretchedness while upwards of an Hundred and twenty of these Savages, who are with great reason suspected of being guilty of these horrid Barbarities under the Mask of Friendship, have procured themselves to be taken under the protection of the Government, with a view to elude the Fury of the brave Relatives of the murdered, and are now maintained at the public Expence. Some of these Indians now in the Barracks of Philadelphia, are confessedly a part of the Wyalusing Indians, which Tribe is now at war with us, and the others are the Moravian Indians, who, living amongst us under the Cloak of Friendship, carried on a Correspondence with our known Enemies on the Great Island. We cannot but observe with sorrow & indignation that some Persons in this Province are at pains to extenuate the barbarous Cruelties practised by these Savages on our murdered Brethren & Relatives, which are shocking to human Nature, and must pierce every Heart but that of the hardened perpetrators or their Abettors; Nor is it less distressing to hear others pleading that although the Wyalusing Tribe is at War with us, yet that part of it which is under the Protection of the Government may be friendly to the English and innocent. In what nation under the Sun was it ever the custom that when a neighboring Nation took up Arms, not an individual should be touched but only the Persons that offered Hostilities? Who ever proclaimed War with a part of a Nation, and not with the Whole? Had these Indians disapproved of the Perfidy of their Tribe, & been willing to cultivate and preserve Friendship with us, why did they not give notice of the War before it happened, as it is known to be the Result of long Deliberations, and a preconcerted Combination amongst

them? Why did they not leave their Tribe immediately, and come amongst us before there was Ground to suspect them, or War was actually waged with their Tribe? No, they stayed amongst them, were privy to their murders & Ravages, until we had destroyed their Provisions; and when they could no longer subsist at home, they come not as Deserters, but as Friends to be maintained through the Winter, that they may be able to Scalp and butcher us in the Spring.

And as to the Moravian Indians, there are strong Grounds at least to suspect their Friendship, as it is known they carried on a Correspondence with our Enemies on the Great Island. We killed three Indians going from Bethlehem to the Great Island with Blankets, Ammunition, & Provisions, which is an undeniable Proof that the Moravian Indians were in confederacy with our open Enemies; And we cannot but be filled with Indignation to hear this action of ours painted in the most odious and detestable Colours, as if we had inhumanly murdered our Guides who preserved us from perishing in the Woods, when we only killed three of our known Enemies, who attempted to shoot us when we surprized them. And besides all this, we understand that one of these very Indians is proved by the oath of Stinton's Widow, to be the very Person that murdered her Husband. How then comes it to pass that he alone, of all the Moravian Indians, should join with the enemy to murder that family? Or can it be supposed that any Enemy Indians, contrary to their known custom of making War, should penetrate into the Heart of a settled Country to burn, plunder and murder the Inhabitants, and not molest any Houses in their return, or ever be seen or heard of? Or how can we account for it, that no ravages have been committed in Northampton County, since the removal of the Moravian Indians, when the Great Cove has been struck since? These things put it beyond doubt with us that the Indians now at Philadelphia are His Majesty's Perfidious Enemies, & therefore to protect and maintain them at the Public Expence, while our suffering Brethren on the Frontiers are almost destitute of the necessaries of Life and are neglected by the Public, is sufficient to make us mad with rage, and tempt us to do what nothing but the most violent necessity can vindicate. We humbly and earnestly pray, therefore, that those Enemies of His Majesty may be removed as soon as possible out of the Province.

Fourthly. We humbly conceive that it is contrary to the maxims of good Policy, and extreamely dangerous to our Frontiers, to suffer any Indians of what tribe soever to live within the Inhabited parts of this Province while we are engaged in an Indian War, as Experience has taught us that they are all perfidious, and their claim to Freedom & Independency, puts it in their power to act as Spies, to entertain & give intelligence to our Enemies, and to furnish them with Provisions and Warlike Stores. To this fatal intercourse between our pretended Friends and open Enemies, we must ascribe the greatest of the Ravages and Murders that have been committed in the course of this and the last Indian War. We therefore pray that this grievance be taken under consideration and remedied.

Fifthly. We cannot help lamenting that no Provision has been hitherto made, that such of our Frontier Inhabitants as have been wounded in defence of the Province, their Lives and Liberties, may be taken care of and cured of their Wounds at the publick Expence. We therefore pray that this Grievance may be redressed.

Sixthly. In the late Indian war this Province, with others of His Majesty's Colonies, gave rewards for Indian Scalps, to encourage the seeking them in their own Country, as the most likely means of destroying or reducing them to reason; but no such Encouragement has been given in this War, which has damped the Spirits of many brave Men who are willing to venture their Lives in parties against the Enemy. We therefore pray that public rewards may be proposed for Indian Scalps, which may be adequate to the Dangers attending Enterprizes of this nature.

Seventhly. We daily lament that numbers of our nearest & dearest relatives are still in Captivity among the Savage Heathen, to be trained up in all their Ignorance & Barbarity, or to be tortured to death with all the contrivances of Indian Cruelty, for attempting to make their escape from Bondage; We see they pay no regard to the many solemn Promises which they have made to restore our Friends who are in Bondage amongst them. We therefore earnestly pray that no trade may hereafter be permitted to be carried on with them, until our Brethren and Relatives are brought home to us.

Eightly. We complain that a certain Society of People in this Province, in the late Indian War, & at several Treaties held by the King's representatives, openly loaded the Indians with Presents, and that J. P., a leader of the said Society, in Defiance of all Government, not only abetted our Indian Enemies, but kept up a private intelligence with them, and publickly received from them a Belt of Wampum, as if he had been our Governor or authorized by the King to treat with his Enemies. By this means the Indians have been taught to despise us as a weak and disunited people, and from this fatal Source have arose many of our Calamities under which we groan. We humbly pray therefore that this Grievance may be redressed, and that no private subject be hereafter permitted to treat with, or carry on a Correspondence with our Enemies.

Ninthly. We cannot but observe with sorrow that Fort Augusta, which has been very expensive to this Province, has afforded us but little assistance during this or the last War. The men that were stationed at that place neither helped our distressed Inhabitants to save their Crops, nor did they attack our Enemies in their Towns, or patrole on our Frontiers. We humbly request that proper measures may be taken to make that Garrison more serviceable to us in our Distress, if it can be done.

N.B. We are far from intending any Reflection against the Commanding Officer stationed at Augusta, as we presume his Conduct was always directed by those from whom he received his Orders.

SIGNED on Behalf of ourselves, and by appointment of a great number of the Frontier Inhabitants.

MATTHEW SMITH.
JAMES GIBSON.

February 13th, 1764.

35. THE STAMP ACT
March 22, 1765

(D. Pickering, *Statutes at Large,* Vol. XXVI, p. 179 ff.)

The reorganization of the Empire inaugurated in 1763 required the raising of additional revenue in the American Colonies, and as early as 1764 Grenville announced his intention of introducing a stamp tax. The colonial agents were given the opportunity to suggest alternative means of raising revenue, but though all of them protested against the stamp tax they were unable to suggest any effective alternative. The Stamp Act passed Parliament with little opposition or attention; the debate on the bill was "languid." The measure was designed to raise an additional £60,000, and the ministry optimistically hoped that it would arouse little opposition in the Colonies. For the American reaction to the Stamp Act see Docs. No. 36–39. On the Act, see R. Frothingham, *Rise of the Republic,* ch. v; G. Bancroft, *History of the United States,* author's last revision, Vol. III, chs. v–viii; C. H. Van Tyne, *Causes of the War of Independence,* ch. vi.

An act for granting and applying certain stamp duties, and other duties, in the British *colonies and plantations in* America, *towards further defraying the expences of defending, protecting, and securing the same; and for amending such parts of the several acts of parliament relating to the trade and revenues of the said colonies and plantations, as direct the manner of determining and recovering the penalties and forfeitures therein mentioned.*

WHEREAS by an act made in the last session of parliament, several duties were granted, continued, and appropriated, towards defraying the expences of defending, protecting, and securing, the British *colonies and plantations in* America: *and whereas it is just and necessary, that provision be made for raising a further revenue within your Majesty's dominions in* America, *towards defraying the said expences:* . . . be it enacted . . . , That from and after [November 1, 1765,] there shall be raised, levied, collected, and paid unto his Majesty, his heirs, and successors, throughout the colonies and plantations in *America* which now are, or hereafter may be, under the dominion of his Majesty, his heirs and successors,

For every skin or piece of vellum or parchment, or sheet or piece of paper, on which shall be ingrossed, written or printed, any declaration, plea, replication, rejoinder, demurrer, or other pleading, or any copy thereof, in any court of law within the *British* colonies and plantations in *America,* a stamp duty of three pence.

For every skin . . . on which shall be ingrossed . . . any donation, presentation, collation, or institution of or to any benefice, or any writ or instrument for the like purpose, or any register, entry, testimonial, or certificate of any degree taken in any university, academy, college, or seminary of learning . . . a stamp duty of two pounds. . . .

For every skin . . . on which shall be ingrossed . . . any note or bill of lading, which shall be signed for any kind of goods, wares, or merchandize, to be exported from, or any cocket or clearance granted within the said colonies and plantations, a stamp duty of four pence. . . .

For every skin . . . on which shall be ingrossed . . . any grant, appointment, or admission of or to any publick beneficial office or employment, for the space of one year, or any lesser time, of or above the value of twenty pounds *per annum* sterling money, in salary, fees, and perquisites . . . , (except commissions and appointments of officers of the army, navy, ordnance, or militia, of judges, and of justices of the peace) a stamp duty of ten shillings. . . .

For every skin . . . on which shall be ingrossed . . . any licence for retailing of spirituous liquors, to be granted to any person who shall take out the same . . . , a stamp duty of twenty shillings. . . .

For every skin . . . on which shall be ingrossed . . . any probate of a will, letters of administration, or of guardianship for any estate above the value of twenty pounds sterling money; within the *British* colonies and plantations upon the continent of *America,* the islands belonging thereto, and the *Bermuda* and *Bahama* islands, a stamp duty of five shillings. . . .

For every skin . . . on which shall be in-grossed . . . any bond for securing the pay-ment of any sum of money, not exceeding the sum of ten pounds sterling money, within the *British* colonies and plantations upon the continent of *America,* the islands belonging thereto, and the *Bermuda* and *Bahama* is-lands, a stamp duty of six pence. . . .

For every skin . . . on which shall be in-grossed . . . any order or warrant for sur-veying or setting out any quantity of land, not exceeding one hundred acres, issued by any governor, proprietor, or any publick of-ficer alone, or in conjunction with any other person or persons, or with any council, or any council and assembly, within the *British* colonies and plantations in *America,* a stamp duty of six pence. . . .

For every skin . . . on which shall be in-grossed . . . any such original grant . . . by which any quantity of land not exceeding one hundred acres shall be granted . . . within all other parts of the *British* dominions in *America,* a stamp duty of three shillings. [Further provision for larger grants.]

For every skin . . . on which shall be in-grossed . . . any grant, appointment, or ad-mission, of or to any publick beneficial office or employment, not herein before charged, above the value of twenty pounds *per an-num* sterling money in salary, fees, and per-quisites, or any exemplification of the same, within the *British* colonies and plantations upon the continent of *America,* the islands belonging thereto, and the *Bermuda* and *Bahama* islands (except commissions of of-ficers of the army, navy, ordnance, or militia, and of justices of the peace) a stamp duty of four pounds. . . .

For every skin . . . on which shall be in-grossed . . . any indenture, lease, convey-ance, contract, stipulation, bill of sale, char-ter party, protest, articles of apprenticeship, or covenant (except for the hire of servants not apprentices, and also except such other matters as are herein before charged) within the *British* colonies and plantations in *America,* a stamp duty of two shillings and six pence. . . .

For every skin . . . on which shall be in-grossed . . . any notarial act, bond, deed, letter of attorney, procuration, mortgage, re-lease, or other obligatory instrument, not herein before charged . . . , a stamp duty of two shillings and three pence. . . .

And for and upon every pack of playing cards, and all dice, which shall be sold or used . . . , the several stamp duties follow-ing (that is to say)

For every pack of such cards, the sum of one shilling.

And for every pair of such dice, the sum of ten shillings.

And for and upon every paper, commonly called a *pamphlet,* and upon every news paper . . . and for and upon such advertise-ments as are herein after mentioned, the respective duties following (that is to say)

For every such pamphlet and paper con-tained in half a sheet, or any lesser piece of paper . . . , a stamp duty of one half-penny, for every printed copy thereof.

For every such pamphlet and paper (being larger than half a sheet, and not exceeding one whole sheet) . . . , a stamp duty of one penny, for every printed copy thereof.

For every pamphlet and paper being larger than one whole sheet, and not exceeding six sheets in octavo, or in a lesser page, or not exceeding twelve sheets in quarto, or twenty sheets in folio . . . , a duty after the rate of one shilling for every sheet of any kind of paper which shall be contained in one printed copy thereof.

For every advertisement to be contained in any gazette, news paper, or other paper, or any pamphlet . . . , a duty of two shill-ings.

For every almanack or calendar, for any one particular year, or for any time less than a year, which shall be written or printed on one side only of any one sheet, skin, or piece of paper parchment, or vellum . . . , a stamp duty of two pence.

For every other almanack or calendar for any one particular year . . . , a stamp duty of four pence.

And for every almanack or calendar writ-ten or printed . . . , to serve for several years, duties to the same amount respectively shall be paid for every such year.

For every skin . . . on which any instru-ment, proceeding, or other matter or thing aforesaid, shall be ingrossed . . . , in any other than the *English* language, a stamp duty of double the amount of the respective duties before charged thereon. . . .

II. And also a duty of one shilling for every twenty shillings, in any sum exceeding fifty pounds, which shall be given, paid, contracted, or agreed, for, with, or in relation to any such clerk or apprentice. . . .

V. And be it further enacted . . . , That all books and pamphlets serving chiefly for the purpose of an almanack, by whatsoever name or names intituled or described, are and shall be charged with the duty imposed by this act on almanacks, but not with any of the duties charged by this act on pamphlets, or other printed papers . . .

VI. Provided always, that this act shall not extend to charge any bills of exchange, accompts, bills of parcels, bills of fees, or any bills or notes not sealed for payment of money at sight, or upon demand, or at the end of certain days of payment. . . .

XII. And be it further enacted . . . , That the said several duties shall be under the management of the commissioners, for the time being, of the duties charged on stamped vellum, parchment, and paper, in *Great Britain:* and the said commissioners are hereby impowered and required to employ such officers under them, for that purpose, as they shall think proper. . . .

XVI. And be it further enacted . . . , That no matter or thing whatsoever, by this act charged with the payment of a duty, shall be pleaded or given in evidence, or admitted in any court within the said colonies and plantations, to be good, useful, or available in law or equity, unless the same shall

be marked or stamped, in pursuance of this act, with the respective duty hereby charged thereon, or with an higher duty. . . .

LIV. And be it further enacted . . . , That all the monies which shall arise by the several rates and duties hereby granted (except the necessary charges of raising, collecting, recovering, answering, paying, and accounting for the same and the necessary charges from time to time incurred in relation to this act, and the execution thereof) shall be paid into the receipt of his Majesty's exchequer, and shall be entered separate and apart from all other monies, and shall be there reserved to be from time to time disposed of by parliament, towards further defraying the necessary expences of defending, protecting, and securing, the said colonies and plantations. . . .

LVII. . . . offences committed against any other act or acts of Parliament relating to the trade or revenues of the said colonies or plantations; shall and may be prosecuted, sued for, and recovered, in any court of record, or in any court of admiralty, in the respective colony or plantation where the offence shall be committed, or in any court of vice admiralty appointed or to be appointed, and which shall have jurisdiction within such colony, plantation, or place, (which courts of admiralty or vice admiralty are hereby respectively authorized and required to proceed, hear, and determine the same) at the election of the informer or prosecutor. . . . .

36. VIRGINIA STAMP ACT RESOLUTIONS
May 30, 1765

(Journal of the House of Burgesses of Virginia, 1761–65, p. 360)

On May 29 the Virginia House of Burgesses resolved itself into a committee of the whole to consider the Stamp Act. Patrick Henry, a new member from Louisa County, introduced seven resolutions; these were bitterly opposed by many of the tidewater leaders, but, after "torrents of sublime eloquence" from Henry, were passed. The following day, however, the House adopted the first five only, and rejected the last two. After Henry's departure, the House expunged the fifth resolution from the record. The entire series

of resolutions, however, was published in the newspapers. It is in connection with the debate on these resolutions that Henry made his "Caesar had his Brutus" speech, the actual context of which is apparently very different from that generally given. See, S. E. Morison, *Sources and Documents Illustrating the American Revolution,* p. 14 ff.; M. C. Tyler, *Patrick Henry,* p. 61 ff.; G. E. Howard, *Preliminaries of the Revolution,* ch. viii; R. Frothingham, *Rise of the Republic,* ch. v.

THE RESOLVES

Resolved, That the first adventurers and settlers of this His Majesty's Colony and Dominion of Virginia brought with them, and transmitted to their posterity, and all other His Majesty's subjects since inhabiting in this His Majesty's said Colony, all the liberties, privileges, franchises, and immunities, that have at any time been held, enjoyed, and possessed, by the people of Great Britain.

Resolved, That by two royal charters, granted by King James the First, the colonists aforesaid are declared entitled to all liberties, privileges, and immunities of denizens and natural subjects, to all intents and purposes, as if they had been abiding and born within the realm of England.

Resolved, That the taxation of the people by themselves, or by persons chosen by themselves to represent them, who can only know what taxes the people are able to bear, or the easiest method of raising them, and must themselves be affected by every tax laid on the people, is the only security against a burthensome taxation, and the distinguishing characteristick of British freedom, without which the ancient constitution cannot exist.

Resolved, That His Majesty's liege people of this his most ancient and loyal Colony have without interruption enjoyed the inestimable right of being governed by such laws, respecting their internal polity and taxation, as are derived from their own consent, with the approbation of their sovereign, or his substitute; and that the same hath never been forfeited or yielded up, but hath been constantly recognized by the kings and people of Great Britain.

Resolved therefore, That the General Assembly of this Colony have the only and sole exclusive right and power to lay taxes and impositions upon the inhabitants of this Colony, and that every attempt to vest such power in any person or persons whatsoever other than the General Assembly aforesaid has a manifest tendency to destroy British as well as American freedom.

Resolved. That His Majesty's liege people, the inhabitants of this Colony, are not bound to yield obedience to any law or ordinance whatever, designed to impose any taxation whatsoever upon them, other than the laws or ordinances of the General Assembly aforesaid.

Resolved, That any person who shall, by speaking or writing, assert or maintain that any person or persons other than the General Assembly of this Colony, have any right or power to impose or lay any taxation on the people here, shall be deemed an enemy to His Majesty's Colony.

37. INSTRUCTIONS OF THE TOWN OF BRAINTREE MASSACHUSETTS ON THE STAMP ACT
October 14, 1765

(The Works of John Adams, ed. by C. F. Adams, Vol. III, p. 465 ff.)

These instructions have a peculiar interest because they were drafted by John Adams, and announced his entrance into Massachusetts politics and into the struggle between the colonies and the mother country. The instructions were widely copied throughout Massachusetts. See, G. Chinard, *Honest John Adams,* ch. iii.

TO EBENEZER THAYER, ESQ.

SIR,— . . . We can no longer forbear complaining, that many of the measures of the late ministry, and some of the late acts of Parliament, have a tendency, in our apprehension, to divest us of our most essential rights and liberties. We shall confine ourselves, however, chiefly to the act of Parliament, commonly called the Stamp Act, by which a very burthensome, and, in our opinion, unconstitutional tax, is to be laid upon us all; and we subjected to numerous and enormous penalties, to be prosecuted, sued for, and recovered, at the option of an informer, in a court of admiralty, without a jury.

We have called this a burthensome tax, because the duties are so numerous and so high, and the embarrassments to business in this infant, sparsely-settled country so great, that it would be totally impossible for the people to subsist under it, if we had no controversy at all about the right and authority of imposing it. Considering the present scarcity of money, we have reason to think, the execution of that act for a short space of time would drain the country of its cash, strip multitudes of all their property, and reduce them to absolute beggary. And what the consequence would be to the peace of the province, from so sudden a shock and such a convulsive change in the whole course of our business and subsistence, we tremble to consider. We further apprehend this tax to be unconstitutional. We have always understood it to be a grand and fundamental principle of the constitution, that no freeman should be subject to any tax to which he has not given his own consent, in person or by proxy. And the maxims of the law, as we have constantly received them, are to the same effect, that no freeman can be separated from his property but by his own act or fault. We take it clearly, therefore, to be inconsistent with the spirit of the common law, and of the essential fundamental principles of the British constitution, that we should be subject to any tax imposed by the British Parliament; because we are not represented in that assembly in any sense, unless it be by a fiction of law, as insensible in theory as it would be injurious in practice, if such a taxation should be grounded on it.

But the most grievous innovation of all, is the alarming extension of the power of courts of admiralty. In these courts, one judge presides alone! No juries have any concern there! The law and the fact are both to be decided by the same single judge, whose commission is only during pleasure, and with whom, as we are told, the most mischievous of all customs has become established, that of taking commissions on all condemnations; so that he is under a pecuniary temptation always against the sub-

ject. . . . We have all along thought the acts of trade in this respect a grievance; but the Stamp Act has opened a vast number of sources of new crimes, which may be committed by any man, and cannot but be committed by multitudes, and prodigious penalties are annexed, and all these are to be tried by such a judge of such a court! . . . We cannot help asserting, therefore, that this part of the act will make an essential change in the constitution of juries, and it is directly repugnant to the Great Charter itself; for, by that charter, "no americament shall be assessed, but by the oath of honest and lawful men of the vicinage;" and, "no freeman shall be taken, or imprisoned, or disseized of his freehold, or liberties of free customs, nor passed upon, nor condemned, but by lawful judgment of his peers, or by the law of the land." So that this act will "make such a distinction, and create such a difference between" the subjects in Great Britain and those in America, as we could not have expected from the guardians of liberty in "both".

As these, sir, are our sentiments of this act, we, the freeholders and other inhabitants, legally assembled for this purpose, must enjoin it upon you, to comply with no measures or proposals for countenancing the same, or assisting in the execution of it, but by all lawful means, consistent with our allegiance to the King, and relation to Great Britain, to oppose the execution of it, till we can hear the success of the cries and petitions of America for relief.

We further recommend the most clear and explicit assertion and vindication of our rights and liberties to be entered on the public records, that the world may know, in the present and all future generations, that we have a clear knowledge and a just sense of them, and, with submission to Divine Providence, that we never can be slaves. . . .

38. RESOLUTIONS OF THE STAMP ACT CONGRESS
October 19, 1765

(Journal of the First Congress of the American Colonies in opposition to the Tyrannical Acts of the British Parliament, p. 27 ff.)

On the motion of James Otis, the Massachusetts House of Representatives adopted, June 8, a circular letter to the other colonies recommending a meeting of committees from the various houses of representatives in New York City in October "to consult together on the present circumstances of the colonies". The Congress met at City Hall, New York, October 7. Twenty-eight delegates from nine colonies were present: Virginia, New Hampshire, North Carolina and Georgia did not send delegates. The Congress drew up Resolutions, an address to the King, a memorial to the Lords and a petition to the House of Commons. The Resolutions were probably drafted by John Dickinson, though there is some support to the claim that they are from the pen of John Cruger of New York. For references see Doc. No. 35.

THE members of this Congress, sincerely devoted with the warmest sentiments of affection and duty to His Majesty's person and Government, inviolably attached to the present happy establishment of the Protestant succession, and with minds deeply impressed by a sense of the present and impending misfortunes of the British colonies on this continent; having considered as maturely as time will permit the circumstances of the said colonies, esteem it our indispensable duty to make the following declarations of our humble opinion respecting the most essential rights and liberties of the colonists, and of the grievances under which they labour, by reason of several late Acts of Parliament.

I. That His Majesty's subjects in these colonies owe the same allegiance to the Crown of Great Britain that is owing from his subjects born within the realm, and all due subordination to that august body the Parliament of Great Britain.

II. That His Majesty's liege subjects in these colonies are intitled to all the inherent rights and liberties of his natural born subjects within the kingdom of Great Britain.

III. That it is inseparably essential to the freedom of a people, and the undoubted right of Englishmen, that no taxes be imposed on them but with their own consent, given personally or by their representatives.

IV. That the people of these colonies are not, and from their local circumstances cannot be, represented in the House of Commons in Great Britain.

V. That the only representatives of the people of these colonies are persons chosen therein by themselves, and that no taxes ever have been, or can be constitutionally imposed on them, but by their respective legislatures.

VI. That all supplies to the Crown being free gifts of the people, it is unreasonable and inconsistent with the principles and spirit of the British Constitution, for the people of Great Britain to grant to His Majesty the property of the colonists.

VII. That trial by jury is the inherent and invaluable right of every British subject in these colonies.

VIII. That the late Act of Parliament, entitled *An Act for granting and applying certain stamp duties, and other duties, in the British colonies and plantations in America, etc.*, by imposing taxes on the inhabitants of these colonies; and the said Act, and several other Acts, by extending the jurisdiction of the courts of Admiralty beyond its ancient limits, have a manifest tendency to subvert the rights and liberties of the colonists.

IX. That the duties imposed by several late Acts of Parliament, from the peculiar circumstances of these colonies, will be extremely burthensome and grievous; and from the scarcity of specie, the payment of them absolutely impracticable.

X. That as the profits of the trade of these colonies ultimately center in Great Britain, to pay for the manufactures which they are obliged to take from thence, they eventually contribute very largely to all supplies granted there to the Crown.

XI. That the restrictions imposed by several late Acts of Parliament on the trade of these colonies will render them unable to purchase the manufactures of Great Britain.

XII. That the increase, prosperity, and happiness of these colonies depend on the full and free enjoyments of their rights and liberties, and an intercourse with Great Britain mutually affectionate and advantageous.

XIII. That it is the right of the British subjects in these colonies to petition the King or either House of Parliament.

Lastly, That it is the indispensable duty of these colonies to the best of sovereigns, to the mother country, and to themselves, to endeavour by a loyal and dutiful address to His Majesty, and humble applications to both Houses of Parliament, to procure the repeal of the Act for granting and applying certain stamp duties, of all clauses of any other Acts of Parliament, whereby the jurisdiction of the Admiralty is extended as aforesaid, and of the other late Acts for the restriction of American commerce.

39. NORTHAMPTON COUNTY RESOLUTIONS ON THE STAMP ACT
February 11, 1766

(A. C. McLaughlin, *Foundations of American Constitutionalism*, p. 126 n.)

This declaration of the county court of Northampton County, Virginia, is given as an example of the local reaction to the Stamp Act; it was one of the earliest declarations to the effect that an unconstitutional act was not binding.

Williamsburg, March 21. The following is a copy of a late order of Northampton Court, on the eastern Shore of this colony, which we are desired to insert. At a court held for Northampton county, Feb. 11, 1766.

"On the motion of the Clerk and other Officers of this Court, praying their opinion whether the act entitled 'An Act for granting and applying certain Stamp Duties, and other Duties, in America, &c,' was binding on the inhabitants of this colony, and whether they the said Officers should incur any penalties by not using stamped paper, agreeable to the directions of the said act, the Court unanimously declared it to be their opinion that the said act did not bind, affect or concern the inhabitants of this colony, in as much as they conceive the same to be unconstitutional, and that the said several officers may proceed to the execution of their respective offices without incurring any penalties by means thereof; which opinion this court doth order to be recorded. Griffin Stith, C.N.C."

Virginia Gazette, March 21, 1766.

40. PETITION OF LONDON MERCHANTS AGAINST THE STAMP ACT
January 17, 1766

(*The Parliamentary History of England*, Vol. XVI, p. 133 ff.)

The American policy of non-importation had severely injured English trade, and Parliament received numerous petitions from merchants throughout the Kingdom urging the repeal of the act. See, W. T. Laprade, "The Stamp Act in British Politics", *American Hist. Review*, Vol. XXXV, p. 735 ff.; C. H. Van Tyne, *Causes of the War of Independence*, ch. vii; D. M. Clark, *British Opinion and the American Revolution*, ch. ii.

A petition of the merchants of London, trading to North America, was presented to the House, and read; setting forth;

"That the petitioners have been long concerned in carrying on the trade between this country and the British colonies on the continent of North America; and that they have annually exported very large quantities of British manufactures, consisting of woollen goods of all kinds, cottons, linens, hardware, shoes, household furniture, and almost without exception of every other species of goods manufactured in these kingdoms, besides other articles imported from abroad, chiefly purchased with our manufactures and with the produce of our colonies; by all which, many thousand manufacturers, seamen and labourers, have been employed, to the very great and increasing benefit of this nation; and that, in return for these exports, the petitioners have received from the colonies, rice, indigo, tobacco, naval stores, oil, whale fins, furs, and lately potash, with other commodities, besides remittances by bills of exchange and bullion, obtained by the colonists in payment for articles of their produce, not required for the British market, and therefore exported to other places; and that, from the nature of this trade, consisting of British manufactures exported, and of the import of raw materials from America, many of them used in our manufactures, and all of them tending to lessen our dependence on neighbouring states, it must be deemed of the highest importance in the commercial system of this nation; and that this commerce, so beneficial to the state, and so necessary for the support of multitudes, now lies under such difficulties and discouragement, that nothing less than its utter ruin is apprehended, without the immediate interposition of parliament; and that, in consequence of the trade between the colonies and the mother country, as established and as permitted for many years, and of the experience which the petitioners have had of the readiness of the Americans to make their just remittances to the utmost of their real ability, they have been induced to make and venture such large exportations of British manufactures, as to leave the colonies indebted to the merchants of Great Britain in the sum of several millions sterling; and that at this time the colonists, when pressed for payment, appeal to past experience, in proof of their willingness; but declare it is not in their power, at present, to make good their engagements, alleging, that the taxes and restrictions laid upon them, and the extension of the jurisdiction of vice admiralty courts established by some late acts of parliament, particularly by an act passed in the fourth year of his present Majesty, for granting certain duties in the British colonies and plantations in America, and by an act passed in the fifth year of his present Majesty, for granting and applying certain stamp duties, and other duties, in the British colonies and plantations in America, with several regulations and restraints, which, if founded in acts of parliament for defined purposes, are represented to have been extended in such a manner as to disturb legal commerce and harass the fair trader, have so far interrupted the usual and former most fruitful branches of their commerce, restrained the sale of their produce, thrown the state of the several provinces into confusion, and brought on so great a number of actual bankruptcies, that the former opportunities and means of remittances and payments are utterly lost and taken from them; and that the petitioners are, by these unhappy events, reduced to the necessity of applying to the House, in order to secure themselves and their families from impending ruin; to prevent a multitude of manufacturers from becoming a burthen to the community, or else seeking their bread in other countries, to the irretrievable loss of this kingdom; and to preserve the strength of this nation entire, its commerce flourishing, the revenues increasing, our navigation, the bulwark of the kingdom, in a state of growth and extension, and the colonies, from inclination, duty, and interest, firmly attached to the mother country; and therefore praying the consideration of the premises, and entreating such relief, as to the House shall seem expedient. . . ."

41. THE DECLARATORY ACT
March 18, 1766

(D. Pickering, *Statutes at Large,* Vol. XXVII, p. 19–20.)

The obvious inability of royal officials in the colonies to enforce the Stamp Act, together with the injury to English trade resulting from the non-importation agreements, persuaded the Rockingham ministry of the expediency of a repeal of the Act. The famous examination of Franklin before the House confirmed members in their opinion that repeal was necessary. Repeal encountered firm opposition in the Lords, however, and was carried only by pressure from the King, and with the salve of the Declaratory Act. The Declaratory Act was couched in the same terms as the odious Irish Declaratory Act of 1719. For references see Docs. No. 35, 36. Franklin's examination is in his *Works,* ed. by J. Sparks, Vol. IV. For an analysis of the political theory behind the Declaratory Act see two opposing interpretations: C. H. Mc Ilwain, *The American Revolution; a Constitutional Interpretation;* R. L. Schuyler, *Parliament and the British Empire.*

An act for the better securing the dependency of his Majesty's dominions in America *upon the crown and parliament of Great Britain.*

WHEREAS *several of the houses of representatives in his Majesty's colonies and plantations in* America, *have of late, against law, claimed to themselves, or to the general assemblies of the same, the sole and exclusive right of imposing duties and taxes upon his Majesty's subjects in the said colonies and plantations; and have, in pursuance of such claim, passed certain votes, resolutions, and orders, derogatory to the legislative authority of parliament, and inconsistent with the dependency of the said colonies and plantations upon the crown of* Great Britain: . . . *be it declared . . . , That the said colonies and* plantations in *America* have been, are, and of right ought to be, subordinate unto, and dependent upon the imperial crown and parliament of *Great Britain;* and that the King's majesty, by and with the advice and consent of the lords spiritual and temporal, and commons of *Great Britain,* in parliament assembled, had, hath, and of right ought to have, full power and authority to make laws and statutes of sufficient force and validity to bind the colonies and people of *America,* subjects of the crown of *Great Britain,* in all cases whatsoever.

II. And be it further declared . . . , That all resolutions, votes, orders, and proceedings, in any of the said colonies or plantations, whereby the power and authority of the parliament of *Great Britain,* to make laws and statutes as aforesaid, is denied, or drawn into question, are, and are hereby declared to be, utterly null and void to all intents and purposes whatsoever.

42. QUARTERING ACT
March 24, 1765

(D. Pickering, *Statutes at Large,* Vol. XXVI, p. 305 ff.)

This Act, passed at the express request of General Gage, was designed to supplement the Stamp Act and the Revenue Act of 1764. The failure of New York to comply in full with the terms of the Quartering Act led to the suspension of the legislative privileges of the assembly. See E. Channing, *History of the United States,* Vol. III, p. 44 ff.; C. Becker, *Political Parties in the Province of New York.* An excellent study of the working of the Quartering Act is in S. M. Pargellis, *Lord Loudoun in North America,* ch. vii.

An act to amend and render more effectual, in his Majesty's dominions in America, *an act passed in this present session of parliament, intituled,* An act for punishing mutiny and desertion, and for the better payment of the army and their quarters. WHEREAS . . . [by the Mutiny Act of 1765] . . . *several regulations are made and enacted for the better government of the army, and their observing strict discipline, and for providing quarters for the army, and carriages on marches and other necessary occasions, and inflicting penalties on offenders against the same act, and for many other good purposes therein mentioned; but the same may not be sufficient for the forces that may be employed in his Majesty's dominions in* America: *and whereas, during the continuance of the said act, there may be occasion for marching and quartering of regiments and companies of his Majesty's forces in several parts of his Majesty's dominions in* America: *and whereas the publick houses and barracks, in his Majesty's dominions in* America, *may not be sufficient to supply quarters for such forces: and whereas it is expedient and necessary that carriages and other conveniences, upon the march of troops in his Majesty's dominions in* America, *should be supplied for that purpose:* be it enacted . . . , That for and during the continuance of this act, and no longer, it shall and may be lawful to and for the constables, tithingmen, magistrates, and other civil officers of villages, towns, townships, cities, districts, and other places, within his Majesty's dominions in *America,* and in their default or absence, for any one justice of the peace inhabiting in or near any such village, township, city, district or place, and for no others; and such constables . . . and other civil officers as aforesaid, are hereby required to billet and quarter the officers and soldiers, in his Majesty's service, in the barracks provided by the colonies; and if there shall not be sufficient room in the said barracks for the officers and soldiers, then and in such case only, to quarter and billet the residue of such officers and soldiers for whom there shall not be room in such barracks, in inns, livery stables, ale-houses, victualling-houses, and the houses of sellers of wine by retail to be drank in their own houses or places thereunto belonging, and all houses of persons selling of rum, brandy, strong water, cyder or metheglin, by retail, to be drank in houses; and in case there shall not be sufficient room for the officers and soldiers in such barracks, inns, victualling and other publick ale-houses, that in such and no other case, and upon no other account, it shall and may be lawful for the governor and council of each respective province in his Majesty's dominions in *America,* to authorize and appoint, and they are hereby directed and impowered to authorize and appoint, such proper person or persons as they shall think fit, to take, hire and make fit, and, in default of the said governor and council appointing and authorizing such person or persons, or in default of such person or persons so appointed neglecting or refusing to do their duty, in that case it shall and may be lawful for any two or more of his Majesty's justices of the peace in or near the said villages, towns, townships, cities, districts, and other places, and they are hereby required to take, hire, and make fit for the reception of his Majesty's forces, such and so many uninhabited houses, outhouses, barns, or other buildings, as shall be necessary, to quarter therein the residue of such officers and soldiers for whom there should not be room in such barracks and publick houses as aforesaid. . . .

II. And it is hereby declared and enacted, That there shall be no more billets at any time ordered, than there are effective soldiers present to be quartered therein: and in order that this service may be effectually provided for, the commander in chief in *America,* or other officer under whose orders any regiment or company shall march, shall, from time to time, give . . . as early notice as conveniently may be, in writing, signed by such commander or officer of their march, specifying their numbers and time of marching as near as may be, to the respective governors of each province through which they are to march. . . .

III. [Military officers taking upon themselves to quarter soldiers contrary to this act, or using any menace to a civil officer to deter them from their duty, to be cashiered. Persons aggrieved by being quartered on may complain to the justices, and be relieved.]

V. Provided nevertheless, and it is hereby enacted, That the officers and soldiers so quartered and billeted as aforesaid (except such as shall be quartered in the barracks, and hired uninhabited houses, or other buildings as aforesaid) shall be received and furnished with diet, and small beer, cyder, or rum mixed with water, by the owners of the inns, livery stables, alehouses, victualling-houses, and other houses in which they are allowed to be quartered and billeted by this act; paying and allowing for the same the several rates herein after mentioned to be payable, out of the subsistence-money, for diet and small beer, cyder, or rum mixed with water.

VI. Provided always, That in case any innholder, or other person, on whom any non-commission officers or private men shall be quartered by virtue of this act, . . . (except on a march, or employed in recruiting, and likewise except the recruits by them raised, for the space of seven days at most, for such non-commission officers and soldiers who are recruiting, and recruits by them raised) shall be desirous to furnish such non-commission officers or soldiers with candles, vinegar, and salt, and with small beer or cyder, not exceeding five pints, or half a pint of rum mixed with a quart of water, for each man *per diem, gratis,* and allow to such non-commission officers or soldiers the use of fire, and the necessary u[n]tensils for dressing and eating their meat, and shall give notice of such his desire to the commanding officer, and shall furnish and allow the same accordingly; then . . . the non-commission officers and soldiers so quartered shall provide their own victuals; and the officer to whom it belongs to receive, or that actually does receive, the pay and subsistence of such non-commission officers and soldiers, shall pay the several sums herein after-mentioned to be payable, out of the subsistence-money,· for diet and small beer, to the non-commission officers and soldiers aforesaid. . . .

VII. And whereas there are several barracks in several places in his Majesty's said dominions in *America,* or some of them, provided by the colonies, for the lodging and covering of soldiers in lieu of quarters, for the ease and conveniency as well of the inhabitants of and in such colonies, as of the soldiers; it is hereby further enacted, That all such officers and soldiers, so put and placed in such barracks, or in hired uninhabited houses, outhouses, barns, or other buildings, shall, from time to time, be furnished and supplied there by the persons to be authorized or appointed for that purpose by the governor and council of each respective province, or upon neglect or refusal of such governor and council in any province, then by two or more justices of the peace residing in or near·such place, with fire, candles, vinegar, and salt, bedding, utensils for dressing their victuals, and small beer or cyder, not exceeding five pints, or half a pint of rum mixed with a quart of water, to each man, without paying any thing for the same. . . .

XXX. And be it further enacted . . . That this act . . . shall continue and be in force in all his Majesty's dominions in *America* from [March 24, 1765] until [March 24, 1767].

43. THE TOWNSHEND REVENUE ACT
June 29, 1767

(D. Pickering, *Statutes at Large,* Vol. XXVII, p. 505 ff.)

On the reorganization of the Ministry in July 1766, 'Champagne Charlie' Townshend became chancellor of the exchequer; on the retirement of Chatham in October Townshend assumed the leadership in the ministry. "From this time," says Lecky, "the English government of America is little more than a series of deplorable blunders" (*History of England in the Eighteenth Century,* Vol. III, p. 379). In May 1767 Townshend brought forward three acts dealing with American affairs: a bill to suspend the New York assembly until it complied with the mutiny act; the establishment of a board of commissioners of the customs for the colonies; and a revenue act. It was expected that the revenue act would yield some £40,000, part of which was to be used for the salaries of royal governors and judges in America. Townshend died in September 1767, but the acts were enforced by his successors. On the surface the revenue acts and the reorganizations of the customs office were highly successful. Prior to 1767 the American customs had brought in some two thousand pounds annually at a cost of some nine thousand pounds; from 1768 to 1774 the American customs brought in an average of thirty thousand pounds annually, at a cost of thirteen thousand pounds. The new revenue measures excited the liveliest dissatisfaction in the American colonies. See Docs. No. 45, 46 for non-importation agreements and the Massachusetts Circular Letter. On the Townshend Acts, see, G. E. Howard, *Preliminaries of the Revolution,* ch. x; E. Channing, *History of the United States,* Vol. III, ch. IV; R. Frothingham, *Rise of the Republic,* ch. vi; C. H. Van Tyne, *Causes of the War of Independence,* ch. x; D. A. Winstanley, *Lord Chatham and the Whig Opposition.*

An act for granting certain duties in the British colonies and plantations in America; for allowing a drawback of the duties of customs upon the exportation from this kingdom, of coffee and cocoa nuts of the produce of the said colonies or plantations; for discontinuing the drawbacks payable on china earthen ware exported to America; and for

more effectually preventing the clandestine running of goods in the said colonies and plantations.

WHEREAS *it is expedient that a revenue should be raised, in your Majesty's dominions in* America, *for making a more certain and adequate provision for defraying the charge of the administration of justice, and the support of civil government, in such provinces as it shall be found necessary; and towards further defraying the expenses of defending, protecting and securing the said dominions;* . . . be it enacted. . . . That from and after the twentieth day of *November,* one thousand seven hundred and sixty seven, there shall be raised, levied, collected, and paid, unto his Majesty, his heirs, and successors, for upon and the respective Goods here in after mentioned, which shall be imported from *Great Britain* into any colony or plantation in *America* which now is or hereafter may be, under the dominion of his Majesty, his heirs, or successors, the several Rates and Duties following; that is to say,

For every hundredweight avoirdupois of crown, plate, flint, and white glass, four shillings and eight pence.

For every hundred weight avoirdupois of red lead, two shillings.

For every hundred weight avoirdupois of green glass, one shilling and two pence.

For every hundred weight avoirdupois of white lead, two shillings.

For every hundred weight avoirdupois of painters colours, two shillings.

For every pound weight avoirdupois of tea, three pence.

For every ream of paper, usually called or known by the name of *Atlas fine,* twelve shillings. . . .

IV. . . . and that all the monies that shall arise by the said duties (except the necessary charges of raising, collecting, levying, recovering, answering, paying, and accounting for the same) shall be applied, in the first place, in such manner as is herein after mentioned, in making a more certain and adequate provision for the charge of the administration of justice, and the support of civil government in such of the said colonies and plantations where it shall be found necessary; and that the residue of such duties shall be payed into the receipt of his Majesty's exchequer, and shall be entered separate and apart from all other monies paid or payable to his Majesty . . . ; and shall be there reserved, to be from time to time disposed of by parliament towards defraying the necessary expense of defending, protecting, and securing, the *British* colonies and plantations in *America.*

V. And be it further enacted . . . , That his Majesty and his successors shall be, and are hereby, impowered, from time to time, by any warrant or warrants under his or their royal sign manual or sign manuals, countersigned by the high treasurer, or any three or more of the commissioners of the treasury for the time being, to cause such monies to be applied, out of the produce of the duties granted by this act, as his Majesty, or his successors, shall think proper or necessary, for defraying the charges of the administration of justice, and the support of the civil government, within all or any of the said colonies or plantations. . . .

X. *And whereas by an act of parliament made in the fourteenth year of the reign of King Charles the Second,* intituled, An act for preventing frauds, and regulating abuses, in his Majesty's customs, *and several other acts now in force, it is lawful for any officer of his Majesty's customs, authorized by writ of assistance under the seal of his Majesty's court of exchequer, to take a constable, headborough, or other public officer inhabiting near unto the place, and in the daytime to enter and go into any house, shop cellar, warehouse, or room or other place and, in case of resistance, to break open doors, chests, trunks, and other pakage there, to seize, and from thence to bring, any kind of goods or merchandise whatsoever prohibited or uncustomed, and to put and secure the same in his Majesty's storehouse next to the place where such seizure shall be made; and whereas by an act made in the seventh and eighth years of the reign of King William the Third, intituled* An act for preventing frauds, and regulating abuses, in the plantation trade, *it is, amongst otherthings, enacted, that the officers for collecting and managing his Majesty's revenue, and inspecting the plantation trade, in America, shall have the same powers and authorities to enter houses or warehouses, to search or seize goods prohibited to be imported or exported into or out of any of the said plantations, or for which any duties are payable, or ought to have been paid; and that the like assistance shall be given to the said officers in the execution of their office, as, by the said recited act of the fourteenth year of King Charles the Second, is provided for the officers of* England: *but, no authority being expressly given by the said act, made in the seventh and eighth years of the reign of King William the Third, to any particular court to grant such writs of assistance for the officers of the customs in the said plantations, it is doubted whether such officers can legally enter houses and other places on land, to search for and seize goods, in the manner directed by the said recited acts:* To obviate which doubts for the future, and in order to carry the intention of the said recited acts into effectual execution, be it enacted . . . , That from and after the said twentieth day of *November,* one thousand seven hundred and sixty seven, such writs of assistance, to authorize and impower the officers of his Majesty's customs to enter and go into any house, warehouse, shop, cellar, or other place, in the *British* colonies or plantations in *America,* to search for and seize prohibited and uncustomed goods, in the manner directed by the said recited acts, shall and may be granted by the said superior or supreme court of justice having jurisdiction within such colony or plantation respectively. . . .

44. FUNDAMENTAL LAW AND THE BRITISH CONSTITUTION
Letters of the Massachusetts House to Ministry
January, 1768

(Bradford's *Massachusetts State Papers,* p. 137 ff.)

These addresses to the British Ministry were part of the protest of the Massachusetts General Court against the Townshend Acts of 1767. In January 1768 the Massachusetts House drew up a long letter to the Massachusetts agent, Dennis De Bredt, addresses to Shelburne, Chatham, Rockingham, Conway and Camden, the Lords of the Treasury, a petition to the King, and a circular letter to the other American colonies, Doc. No. 45. All of these documents were drafted by Samuel Adams. The extracts given below present one of the earliest formulations of the doctrine of fundamental law in the British constitution. The theory that Parliament could not pass acts contrary to fundamental law became a basic theory in American constitutional law. See also Otis's Speech on the Writs of Assistance, Doc. No. 32, the Resolutions of Virginia on the Stamp Act, Doc. No. 36, and the Massachusetts Circular Letter. The addresses of the House are given in full in Bradford's *Massachusetts State Papers,* an account of their authorship is in W. V. Wells, *Life and Public Services of Samuel Adams,* Vol. I, ch. vii. See also, C. F. Mullett, *Fundamental Law and the American Revolution;* R. G. Adams, *Political Ideas of the American Revolution;* A. C. McLaughlin, *Courts, Constitution and Parties,* ch. i.

1. Letter of the Massachusetts House to the Earl of Shelburne
January 15, 1768

There are, my Lord, fundamental rules of the constitution, which it is humbly presumed, neither the supreme legislative nor the supreme executive can alter. In all free states, the constitution is fixed; it is from thence, that the legislative derives its authority; therefore it cannot change the constitution without destroying its own foundation. If, then, the constitution of Great Britain is the common right of all British subjects, it is humbly referred to your Lordship's judgment, whether the supreme legislative of the empire may rightly leap the bounds of it, in the exercise of power over the subjects in America, any more than over those in Britain.

2. Letter of the Massachusetts House to the Marquis of Rockingham
January 22, 1768

My Lord, the superintending power of that high court over all his Majesty's subjects in the empire, and in all cases which can consist with the fundamental rules of the Constitution, was never questioned in this Province, nor, as the House concieve, in any other. But, in all free states the constitution is fixed; it is from thence that the supreme legislative as well as the supreme executive derives its authority. Neither, then, can break through the fundamental rules of the constitution without destroying their own foundation.

3. Letter of the Massachusetts House to Lord Camden
January 29, 1768

If in all free states, the constitution is fixed, and the supreme legislative power of the nation, from thence derives its authority; can that power overleap the bounds of the constitution, without subverting its own foundation? If the remotest subjects, are bound by the ties of allegiance, which this people and their forefathers have ever acknowledged; are they not by the rules of equity, intitled to all rights of that constitution, which ascertains and limits both sovereignty and allegiance? If it is an essential unalterable right in nature, ingrafted into the British constitution as a fundamental law, and ever held sacred and irrevocable by the subjects within the realm, and that what is a man's own is absolutely his own; and that no man hath a right to take it from him without his consent; may not the subjects of this province, with a decent firmness, which has always distinguished the happy subjects of Britain, plead and maintain this natural constitutional right?

45. MASSACHUSETTS CIRCULAR LETTER
February 11, 1768

(Works of Samuel Adams, ed. by H. A. Cushing, Vol. I, p. 184 ff.)

This circular letter, drawn up by Samuel Adams, informed the assemblies of the other American colonies of the measures which the Massachusetts General Court had taken with regard to the Townshend acts. On the failure of the Massachusetts House to rescind the resolution under which this letter was prepared, Governor Bernard dissolved the General Court. The Circular Letter elicited favorable responses from several of the other colonies, notably from Virginia. See, R. Frothingham, *Rise of the Republic of the United States,* ch. vi; W. V. Wells, *Life and Public Services of Samuel Adams,* Vol. I, p. 152 ff.; T. Hutchinson, *History of the Province of Massachusetts Bay,* 1749–1774.

Pro. of Massachusetts Bay, February 11, 1768.
SIR,

The House of Representatives of this Province, have taken into their serious Consideration, the great difficulties that must accrue to themselves and their Constituents, by the operation of several acts of Parliament, imposing Duties & Taxes on the American colonys. As it is a Subject in which every Colony is deeply interested, they have no reason to doubt but your Assembly is deeply impressed with its importance, & that such constitutional measures will be come into, as are proper. . . .

The House have humbly represented to the ministry, their own Sentiments that his Majesty's high Court of Parliament is the supreme legislative Power over the whole Empire; That in all free States the Constitution is fixed; & as the supreme Legislative derives its Power & Authority from the Constitution, it cannot overleap the Bounds of it, without destroying its own foundation; That the constitution ascertains & limits both Sovereignty and allegiance, &, therefore, his Majesty's American Subjects, who acknowledge themselves bound by the Ties of Allegiance, have an equitable Claim to the full enjoyment of the fundamental Rules of the British Constitution: That it is an essential, unalterable Right, in nature, ungrafted into the British Constitution, as a fundamental Law, & ever held sacred & irrevocable by the Subjects within the Realm, that what a man has honestly acquired is absolutely his own,

which he may freely give, but cannot be taken from him without his consent: That the American Subjects may, therefore, exclusive of any Consideration of Charter Rights, with a decent firmness, adapted to the Character of free men & subjects assert this natural and constitutional Right.

It is, moreover, their humble opinion, which they express with the greatest Deference to the Wisdom of the Parliament, that the Acts made there, imposing Duties on the People of this province, with the sole & express purpose of raising a Revenue, are Infringements of their natural & constitutional Rights: because, as they are not represented in the British Parliament, his Majestys Commons in Britain, by those Acts grant their Property without their consent.

This House further are of Opinion, that their Constituents, considering their local Circumstances cannot by any possibility, be represented in the Parliament, & that it will forever be impracticable, that they should be equally represented there, & consequently not at all; being separated by an Ocean of a thousand leagues: and that his Majestys Royal Predecessors, for this reason, were graciously pleased to form a subordinate legislature here, that their subjects might enjoy the unalienable Right of a Representation: Also that considering the utter impracticability of their ever being fully & equally represented in parliament, & the great Expence that must unavoidably attend even a partial representation there, this House think that a taxaticn of their Constituents, even without their Consent, grievous as it is, would be preferable to any Representation that could be admitted for them there.

Upon these principles, & also considering that were the right in Parliament ever so clear, yet, for obvious reasons, it would be beyond the rules of Equity that their Constituents should be taxed, on the manufactures of Great Britain here, in Addition to the dutys they pay for them in England, & other advantages arising to G Britain from the Acts of trade, this House have preferred a humble, dutifull, & loyal Petition, to our most gracious Sovereign, & made such Representations to his Majesty's Ministers, as they apprehended would tend to obtain redress.

They have also submitted to Consideration whether any People can be said to enjoy any degree of Freedom if the Crown in addition to its undoubted Authority of constituting a Governor, should appoint him such a Stipend as it may judge proper, without the Consent of the people & at their expence; & whether, while the Judges of the Land & other Civil officers hold not their Commissions during good Behaviour, their having salarys appointed for them by the Crown independent of the people hath not a tendency to subvert the principles of Equity & endanger the Happiness and Security of the Subject. . . .

These are the Sentiments & proceedings of this House; & as they have too much reason to believe that the enemys of the Colonies have represented them to his Majestys Ministers & the parliament as factious disloyal &

having a disposition to make themselves independent of the Mother Country, they have taken occasion, in the most humble terms, to assure his Majesty & his Ministers that with regard to the People of this province, & as they doubt not, of all the colonies the charge is unjust.

The House is fully satisfied, that your Assembly is too generous & liberal in sentiment, to believe, that this Letter proceeds from an Ambition to take the lead, or dictating to the other Assemblys: They freely submit their opinions to the Judgment of others, & shall take it kind in your house to point out to them any thing further, that may be thought necessary.

This House cannot conclude, without expressing their firm Confidence in the King our common head & Father, that the united & dutifull Supplications of his distressed American Subjects will meet with his Royal & favorable Acceptance.

46. BOSTON NON-IMPORTATION AGREEMENT
August 1, 1768
(*The Annual Register*, 1768, p. 235)

The enactment of the Townshend measures led to a renewal of the non-importation measures which had been employed at the time of the Stamp Act. As early as March 1768 merchants of Boston agreed not to import from England if merchants from New York and Philadelphia would make similar promises. The effort to establish a non-importation league, however, was unsuccessful. In August 1768 the merchants of Boston acted independently: within a few weeks similar action was taken by the merchants of other New England towns and by those of New York. Philadelphia did not fall into line until late in the following year. These and other non-importation agreements reduced importations from England by over one-half in 1768 and 1769. See, A. M. Schlesinger, *The Colonial Merchants and the American Revolution;* C. M. Andrews, *Boston Merchants and the Non-Importation Movement;* C. H. Van Tyne, *Causes of the War of Independence,* ch. x.

Agreement entered into by the Inhabitants of Boston

The merchants and traders in the town of Boston having taken into consideration the deplorable situation of the trade, and the

many difficulties it at present labours under on account of the scarcity of money, which is daily increasing for want of the other remittances to discharge our debts in Great Britain, and the large sums collected by the officers of the customs for duties on goods imported; the heavy taxes levied to discharge the debts contracted by the government in the late war; the embarrassments and restrictions laid on trade by several late acts of parliament; together with the bad success of our cod fishery, by which our principal sources of remittance are like to be greatly diminished, and we thereby rendered unable to pay the debts we owe the merchants in Great Britain, and to continue the importation of goods from thence;

We, the subscribers, in order to relieve the trade under those discouragements, to promote industry, frugality, and economy, and to discourage luxury, and every kind of extravagance, do promise and engage to and with each other as follows:

First, That we will not send for or import from Great Britain, either upon our own account, or upon commission, this fall, any other goods than what are already ordered for the fall supply.

Secondly, That we will not send for or import any kind of goods or merchandize from Great Britain, either on our own account, or on commissions, or any otherwise, from the 1st of January 1769, to the 1st of January 1770, except salt, coals, fish-hooks and lines, hemp, and duck bar lead and shot, wool-cards and card-wire.

Thirdly, That we will not purchase of any factor, or others, any kind of goods imported from Great Britain, from January 1769, to January 1770.

Fourthly, That we will not import, on our own account, or on commissions or purchase of any who shall import from any other colony in America, from January 1769, to January 1770, any tea, glass, paper, or other goods commonly imported from Great Britain.

Fifthly, That we will not, from and after the 1st of January 1769, import into this province any tea, paper, glass, or painters colours, until the act imposing duties on those articles shall be repealed.

In witness whereof, we have hereunto set our hands, this first day of August, 1768.

47. THE REGULATORS OF NORTH CAROLINA
Petition of the Inhabitants of Anson County, North Carolina
October 9, 1769

(Colonial Records of North Carolina, ed. by W. L. Saunders, Vol. VIII, p. 75 ff.)

Sectionalism, which played so important a part in colonial history, was particularly significant in the southern colonies. From Virginia to South Carolina, the backcountry of small farmers, non-slaveholding, dissenting in religion, under-represented in politics, was aligned against the tidewater. In North and South Carolina this opposition came to an open rupture. In both colonies the upcountry yeomen organized in "Regulator" bands and interfered with the courts, with the collection of rents, etc. See, J. S. Bassett, "The Regulators of North Carolina", American Hist. Assoc. *Report,* 1894; M. De L. Haywood, *Governor William Tryon;* W. A. Schaper, "Sectionalism in South Carolina," American Hist. Assoc. *Report,* 1900; F. J. Turner, *The Frontier in American History,* ch. iii.

MR. SPEAKER AND GENTLEMEN OF THE AS-
    SEMBLY:
The Petition of the Inhabitants of Anson County, being part of the Remonstrance of the Province of North Carolina,
HUMBLY SHEWETH, That the Province in general labour under general grievances, and the Western part thereof under particular ones; which we not only see but very sensibly feel, being crouch'd beneath our sufferings: and, notwithstanding our sacred priviledges, have too long yielded ourselves slaves to remorseless oppression.—Permit us to conceive it to be our inviolable right to make known our grievances, and to petition for redress; as appears in the Bill of Rights

pass'd in the reign of King Charles the first, as well as the act of Settlement of the Crown of the Revolution. We therefore beg leave to lay before you a specimen thereof; that your compassionate endeavours may tend to the relief of your injured Constituents, whose distressed condition calls aloud for aid. The alarming cries of the oppressed possibly may reach your Ears; but without your zeal how shall they ascend the throne. How relentless is the breast without sympathy, the heart that cannot bleed on a View of our calamity; to see tenderness removed, cruelty stepping in; and all our liberties and priviledges invaded and abridg'd by (as it were) domes-ticks who are conscious of their guilt and void of remorse. O how daring! how relent-less! whilst impending Judgments loudly threaten and gaze upon them, with every emblem of merited destruction.

A few of the many grievances are as follows, viz.,

1. That the poor Inhabitants in general are much oppress'd by reason of disproportionate Taxes, and those of the western Counties in particular; as they are generally in mean circumstances.

2. That no method is prescribed by Law for the payment of the Taxes of the Western counties in produce (in lieu of a Currency) as is in other Counties within this Province; to the Peoples great oppression.

3. That Lawyers, Clerks, and other pen-

tioners, in place of being obsequious Servants for the Country's use, are become a nuisance, as the business of the people is often transacted without the least degree of fairness, the intention of the law evaded, exorbitant fees extorted, and the sufferers left to mourn under their oppressions.

4. That an Attorney should have it in his power, either for the sake of ease or interest or to gratify their malevolence and spite, to commence suits to what Courts he pleases, however inconvenient it may be to the Defendant: is a very great oppression.

5. That all unlawful fees taken on Indictment, where the Defendant is acquitted by his Country (however customary it may be) is an oppression.

6. That Lawyers, Clerks, and others extorting more fees than is intended by law; is also an oppression.

7. That the violation of the King's Instructions to his delegates, their artfulness in concealing the same from him; and the great Injury the People thereby sustains: is a manifest oppression.

And for remedy whereof, we take the freedom to recommend the following mode of redress, not doubting audience and acceptance; which will not only tend to our relief, but command prayers as a duty from your humble Petitioners.

1. That at all elections each suffrage be given by Ticket & Ballot.

2. That the mode of Taxation be altered, and each person to pay in proportion to the profits arising from his Estate.

3. That no future tax be laid in Money, untill a currency is made.

4. That there may be established a Western as well as a Northern and Southern District, and a Treasurer for the same.

5. That when a currency is made it may be let out by a Loan office on Land security, and not to be call'd in by a Tax.

6. That all debts above 40s. and under £10 be tried and determined without Lawyers, by a jury of six freeholders impanneled by a Justice, and that their verdict be enter'd by the said Justice, and be a final judgment.

7. That the Chief Justice have no perquisites, but a Sallary only.

8. That Clerks be restricted in respect to fees, costs, and other things within the course of their office.

9. That Lawyers be effectually Barr'd from exacting and extorting fees.

10. That all doubts may be removed in respect to the payment of fees and costs on Indictments where the Defendant is not found guilty by the jury, and therefore acquitted.

11. That the Assembly make known by Remonstrance to the King, the conduct of the cruel and oppressive Receiver of the Quit Rents, for omitting the customary easie and effectual method of collecting by distress, and pursuing the expensive mode of commencing suits in the most distant Courts.

12. That the Assembly in like manner make known that the Governor and Council do frequently grant Lands to as many as they think proper without regard to head rights, notwithstanding the contrariety of His Majesties Instructions; by which means immense sums has been collected and numerous Patents granted, for much of the most fertile lands in this Province, that is yet uninhabited and uncultivated, environed by great numbers of poor people who are necessitated to toil in the cultivation of bad Lands whereon they hardly can subsist, who are thereby deprived of His Majesties liberality and Bounty: nor is there the least regard paid to the cultivation clause in said Patent mentioned, as many of the said Council as well as their friends and favorites enjoy large Quantities of Lands under the above-mentioned circumstances.

13. That the Assembly communicates in like manner the Violation of His Majesties Instructions respecting the Land Office by the Governor and Council, and of their own rules, customs and orders; if it be sufficiently proved that after they had granted Warrants for many Tracts of Land, and that the same was in due time survey'd and return'd, and the Patent fees timely paid into the said office; and that if a private Council was called on purpose to avoid spectators, and peremptory orders made that Patents should not be granted; and Warrants by their orders arbitrarily to have issued in the names of other Persons for the same Lands, and if when intreated by a solicitor they refus'd to render so much as a reason for their so doing, or to refund any part of the money by them extorted.

14. That some method may be pointed out

that every improvement on Lands in any of the Proprietor's part be proved when begun, by whom, and every sale made, that the eldest may have the preference of at least 300 Acres.

15. That all taxes in the following counties be paid as in other Counties in the Province, (i. e.) in the produce of the Country and that ware Houses be erected as follows, (viz.) in Anson County, at Isom Haley's ferry landing on Pe Dee river; Rowan and Orange, . . . Cumberland . . . Mecklenburg . . . and in Tryon County. . . .

16. That every denomination of People may marry according to their respective Mode, Ceremony, and custom, after due publication or Licence.

17. That Doctr Benjamin Franklin or some other known patriot be appointed Agent, to represent the unhappy state of this Province to His Majesty, and to solicit the several Boards in England:—

48. NEW YORK SONS OF LIBERTY RESOLUTIONS ON TEA
November 29, 1773

(H. Niles, *Principles and Acts of the Revolution,* 1822 ed. p. 188–9)

An act of May 1773 permitted the East India Company to export tea directly to the American Colonies free from all duties except the threepenny tax payable in America. The Company disposed of its enormous quantities of tea through its own agents, and thus had a practical monopoly on the tea business in the Colonies. It was the danger of this monopoly rather than the principle of the tea tax that aroused resentment in the Colonies. In Charleston the tea was allowed to enter but was placed in government warehouses. In Philadelphia, New York and elsewhere ships bearing tea were forced to turn back. In Boston the attempt to land tea led to the notorious Boston Tea Party of December 16, 1773. The Resolutions of the New York Sons of Liberty are given as typical of the methods employed by the Colonists. See, A. M. Schlesinger, *Colonial Merchants and the American Revolution;* C. L. Becker, *History of Political Parties in New York, 1760–1776;* H. Dawson, *The Sons of Liberty in New York;* A. C. Flick, *The American Revolution in New York;* I. Q. Leake, *Memoir of the Life and Times of General John Lamb;* M. Farrand, "The Taxation of Tea", *American Hist. Review,* Vol. III.

. . . To prevent a calamity which, of all others, is the most to be dreaded—slavery, and its terrible concomitants—we, subscribers being influenced from a regard to liberty, and disposed to use all lawful endeavors in our power, to defeat the pernicious project, and to transmit to our posterity, those blessings of freedom which our ancestors have handed down to us; and to contribute to the support of the common liberties of America, which are in danger to be subverted, *do,* for those important purposes, agree to associate together, under the name and style of the *sons of liberty of New York,* and engage our honor to, and with each other, faithfully to observe and perform the following *resolutions, viz.*

1st. *Resolved,* That whoever shall aid, or abet, or in any manner assist in the introduction of tea, from any place whatsoever, into this colony, while it is subject, by a British act to parliament, to the payment of a duty, for the purpose of raising a revenue in America, he shall be deemed an enemy to the liberties of America.

2d. *Resolved,* That whoever shall be aiding, or assisting, in the landing, or carting, or such tea, from any ship or vessel, or shall hire any house, store-house, or cellar or any place whatsoever to deposit the tea, subject to a duty as aforesaid, he shall be deemed an enemy to the liberties of America.

3d. *Resolved,* That whoever shall sell, or buy, . . . tea, or shall aid . . . in transporting such tea, . . . from this city, until the . . . revenue act shall be totally and clearly repealed, he shall be deemed an enemy to the liberties of America.

4th. *Resolved,* That whether the duties on tea, imposed by this act, be paid in Great Britain or in America, our liberties are equally affected.

5th. *Resolved,* That whoever shall transgress any of these resolutions, we will not deal with, or employ, or have any connection with him.

49. THE INTOLERABLE ACTS
1774

The Boston Tea Party of December 16, 1773 and the disturbances in Boston and Massachusetts, led Lord North to ask Parliament to vote a series of measures adequate to the emergency. March 14, the first of these notorious "intolerable acts" was laid before Parliament—the Boston Port Act. The introduction of these measures led to one of the most notable debates in Parliamentary history; see Hansard, *Parliamentary History*, Vol. XVII, *passim*. Ultimately five coercive acts received the royal signature: the Boston Port Act; the Massachusetts Government Act; the Administration of Justice Act; the Quartering Act; and the Quebec Act. The provisions of the Quartering Act, approved June 2, 1774, are essentially similar to those of the Quartering Act of 1765, Doc. No. 42. On the Intolerable Acts, see G. Bancroft, *History of the United States*, author's last revision, Vol. III, ch. xxxv, Vol. IV, chs. i, v.; E. Channing, *History*, Vol. III, ch. v.; G. E. Howard, *Preliminaries of the Revolution*, cn. xv; C. H. Van Tyne, *Causes of the War of Independence*, ch. xv; Lord Fitzmaurice, *Life of William, Earl of Shelburne*, Vol. II; F. A. Mumby, *George III and the American Revolution*: G. O. Trevelyan, *The American Revolution*, Vol. I.

1. THE BOSTON PORT ACT
March 31, 1774
(D. Pickering, *Statutes at Large*, Vol. XXX, p. 336 ff.)

The Boston Port Act, the first and most odious of the intolerable acts, was designed specifically as a punishment of Boston for the lawlessness of the Tea Party. The re-opening of the Port was made conditional upon the payment of damages for losses sustained by the East India Company. For the reaction of the colonies to the Boston Port Bill see Docs. No. 50, 51.

An act to discontinue, in such manner, and for such time as are therein mentioned, the landing and discharging, lading or shipping, of goods, wares, and merchandise, at the town, and within the harbour, of Boston, in the province of Massachuset's Bay, in North America.

WHEREAS *dangerous commotions and insurrections have been fomented and raised in the town of Boston, in the province of Massachuset's Bay, in New England, by divers ill-affected persons, to the subversion of his Majesty's government, and to the utter destruction of the publick peace, and good order of the said town; in which commotions and insurrections certain valuable cargoes of teas, being the property of the East India Company, and on board certain vessels lying within the bay or harbour of Boston, were seized and destroyed: And whereas, in the present condition of the said town and harbour, the commerce of his Majesty's subjects cannot be safely carried on there, nor the customs payable to his Majesty duly collected; and it is therefore expedient that the officers of his Majesty's customs should be forthwith removed from the said town:* . . . be it enacted . . . , That from and after June 1, 1774, it shall not be lawful for any person or persons whatsoever to lade, put, . . . off or from any quay, wharf, or other place, within the said town of *Boston*, or in or upon any part of the bay, commonly called *The Harbour of Boston*, between a certain headland or point called *Nahant Point*, . . . and a certain other headland or point called *Alderton Point*, . . . or in or upon any island, creek, landing-place, bank, or other place, within the said bay or headlands, into any ship, vessel, lighter, boat, or bottom, any goods, wares, or merchandise whatsoever, to be transported or carried into any other country, province, or place whatsoever, or into any other part of the said province of the *Massachuset's Bay*, in *New England;* or to take up, . . . within the said town, or in or upon any of the places aforesaid, out of any boat, . . . any goods, . . . to be brought from any other country, province, or place, or any other part of the said province, of the *Massachuset's Bay* in *New England*, upon pain of the forfeiture of the said goods, . . . and of the said boat, . . . and of the guns, ammunition, tackle, furniture, and stores, in or belonging to the same: And if any such goods, . . . shall, within the said town, or in any the places aforesaid, be laden or taken in from the shore into any barge, . . . to be carried on board any ship or vessel outward-bound to any other country or province, . . . or to be laden into such barge, . . . from or out of any ship or vessel coming in . . . from any other country, such barge, . . . shall be forfeited and lost. . . .

IV. Provided always, That nothing in this act contained shall extend . . . to any military or other stores of his Majesty's use, or to the ships . . . whereon the same shall be laden, which shall be commissioned by, and in the immediate pay of, his Majesty . . . ; nor to any fuel or victual brought coastwise from any part of the continent of America, for the necessary use and sustenance of the inhabitants of the town of Boston, provided the vessels wherein the same are to be carried shall be duly furnished with a cocket and let-pass, after having been duly searched by the proper officers . . . at Marblehead, in the port of Salem, . . . ; and that some officer of his Majesty's customs be also there put on board the same vessel, who is hereby authorized to go on board, and proceed with the said vessel, together with a sufficient number of persons properly armed, for his defence to the said harbour of Boston; nor in any ships . . . which may happen to be within the said harbour of Boston on or before the first day of June (1774) and may have either laden or taken on board, or be there with intent to load or take on board, or to land or discharge any goods, wares . . . provided the said ships . . . do depart . . . within fourteen days after (1 June 1774). . . .

X. Provided also, . . . That nothing herein contained . . . be construed, to enable his Majesty to appoint such port, . . . or officers, in the said town of *Boston,* or in the said bay or islands, until it shall sufficiently appear to his Majesty that full satisfaction hath been made by or on behalf of the inhabitants of the said town of *Boston* to the united company of merchants of *England* trading to the *East Indies,* for the damage sustained by the said company by the destruction of their goods sent to the said town of *Boston,* . . . and until it shall be certified to his Majesty, in council, by the governor, . . . of the said province, that reasonable satisfaction hath been made to the officers of his Majesty's revenue, and others, who suffered by the riots and insurrections above mentioned, in 1773 and 1774.

2. MASSACHUSETTS GOVERNMENT ACT
May 20, 1774
(D. Pickering, *Statutes at Large,* Vol. XXX, p. 381 ff.)

On March 28 Lord North, insisting that he wished "to take the executive power from the hands of the democratic part of the government", introduced an act for "the better regulating the government of the Province of Massachusetts Bay", which would "effectually purge the constitution of all its crudities." The Bill passed by large majorities, but eleven Lords entered a protest against it. Massachusetts largely nullified the administration of the new Act. See, G. Bancroft, *History,* author's last rev. Vol. IV, ch. iii; R. Frothingham, *Rise of the Republic,* ch. ix.

An act for the better regulating the government of the province of the Massachuset's Bay, *in* New England.

And whereas the method of electing such counsellors or assistants, . . . hath, by repeated experience, been found to be extremely ill adapted to the plan of government established in the province of the Massachusets Bay . . . , *and hath . . . for some time past, been such as had the most manifest tendency to obstruct, and, in great measure, defeat, the execution of the laws; . . . : And it hath accordingly happened, that an open resistance to the execution of the laws hath actually taken place in the town of* Boston, *and the neighbourhood thereof, . . . And whereas it is, under these circumstances, become absolutely necessary, . . . that the appointment of the said counsellors or assistants should henceforth be put upon the like footing as is established in such other of his Majesty's colonies . . . in* America, *the governors whereof are appointed by his Majesty's commission, under the great seal of* Great Britain: Be it therefore enacted . . . , that from and after August 1, 1774, so much of the charter . . . [of 1691] which relates to the time and manner of electing the assistants or counsellors for the said province, be revoked, . . . and that the offices of all counsellors and assistants, elected and appointed in pursuance thereof, shall from thenceforth cease and determine: And that, from and after the said August 1, 1774, the council, or court of assistants of the said province for the time being, shall be composed of such of the inhabitants or proprietors of lands within the same as shall be thereunto nominated and appointed by his Majesty . . . , provided, that the number of the said assistants or counsellors shall not, at any one time, exceed thirty-six, nor be less than twelve.

II. And it is hereby further enacted, That the said assistants or counsellors, so to be appointed as aforesaid, shall hold their offices respectively, for and during the pleasure of his Majesty. . . .

III. And be it further enacted . . . , That from and after July 1, 1774, it shall and may be lawful for his Majesty's governor for the time being of the said province, or, in his absence, for the lieutenant-governor, to nominate and appoint, under the seal of the province, from time to time, and also to remove, without the consent of the council, all judges of the inferior courts of common pleas, commissioners of *Oyer* and *Terminer,* the attorney general, provosts, marshals, justices of the peace, and other officers to the council or courts of justice belonging; . . .

VI. And be it further enacted . . . , That, upon every vacancy of the offices of chief justice and judges of the superior court of the said province, from and after July 1, 1774, the governor for the time being, or, in his absence, the lieutenant-governor, without the consent of the council, shall have full power and authority to nominate and appoint the persons to suceed to the said offices, who shall hold their commissions during the pleasure of his Majesty . . . ;

VII. *And whereas, by several acts of the general court, . . . the freeholders and inhabitants of the several townships, districts, and precincts, qualified, as is therein expressed, are authorized to assemble together, annually, or occasionally, upon notice given, in such manner as the said acts direct, for the choice of selectmen, constables, and other officers, and for the making and agreeing upon such necessary rules, orders, and bye-laws, for the directing, managing, and ordering, the prudential affairs of such townships, districts, and precincts, and for other purposes: and whereas a great abuse has been made of the power of calling such meetings, and the inhabitants have, contrary to the design of their institution, been misled to treat upon matters of the most general con-*

cern, and to pass many dangerous and unwarrantable resolves: for remedy whereof, be it enacted, that from and after August 1, 1774, no meeting shall be called by the select men, or at the request of any number of freeholders of any township, district, or precinct, without the leave of the governor, or, in his absence, of the lieutenant-governor, in writing, expressing the special business of the said meeting, except the annual meeting in the months of *March* or *May,* for the choice of select men, constables, and other officers, or except for the choice of persons to fill up the offices aforesaid, on the death or removal of any of the persons first elected to such offices, and also, except any meeting for the election of a representative or representatives in the general court; and that no other matter shall be treated of at such meetings. . . .

3. ADMINISTRATION OF JUSTICE ACT
May 20, 1774
(D. Pickering, *Statutes at Large,* Vol. XXX, p. 367 ff.)

This act was designed to provide for a more impartial administration of justice by transferring certain trials to another Province or to Great Britain. It was directed not only toward the maintenance of order but to the more efficient administration of the customs laws.

An act for the impartial administration of justice in the cases of persons questioned for any acts done by them in the execution of the law, or for the suppression of riots and tumults, in the province of the Massachuset's Bay, in New England.

WHEREAS *in his Majesty's province of* Massachuset's Bay, *in* New England, *an attempt hath lately been made to throw off the authority of the parliament of* Great Britain *over the said province, and an actual and avowed resistance, by open force, to the execution of certain acts of parliament, hath been suffered to take place, uncontrouled and unpunished, . . . : and whereas, in the present disordered state of the said province, it is of the utmost importance . . . to the re-establishment of lawful authority throughout the same, that neither the magistrates acting in support of the laws, nor any of his Majesty's subjects aiding and assisting them therein, or in the suppression of riots and tumults, . . . should be discouraged from the proper discharge of their duty, by an apprehension, that in case of their being questioned for any acts done therein, they may be liable to be brought to trial for the same before persons who do not acknowledge the validity of the laws, in the execution thereof, or the authority of the magistrate in support of whom, such acts had been done: in order therefore to remove every such discouragement from the minds of his Majesty's subjects, and to induce them, upon all proper occasions, to exert themselves in support of the public peace of the province, and of the authority of the King and Parliament of* Great Britain *over the same;* be it enacted . . . , That if any inquisition or indictment shall be found, or if any appeal shall be sued or preferred against any person, for murther, or other capital offence, in the province of the *Massachuset's Bay,* and it shall appear, by information given upon oath to the governor . . . of the said province, that the fact was committed by the person against whom such inquisition or indictment shall be found, or against whom such appeal shall be sued or preferred, as aforesaid, either in the execution of his duty as a magistrate, for the suppression of riots, or in the support of the laws of revenue, or in acting in his duty as an officer of revenue, or in acting under the direction and order of any magistrate, for the suppression of riots, or for the carrying into effect the laws of revenue, or in aiding and assisting in any of the cases aforesaid; and if it shall also appear, to the satisfaction of the said governor . . . that an indifferent trial cannot be had within the said province, in that case, it shall and may be lawful for the governor . . . , to direct, with the advice and consent of the council, that the inquisition, indictment, or appeal, shall be tried in some other of his Majesty's colonies, or in *Great Britain;* and for that purpose, to order the person against whom such inquisition or indictment shall be found, . . . to be sent, under sufficient custody, to the place appointed for his trial, or to admit such person to bail, taking a recognizance . . . from such person, with sufficient sureties, . . . in such sums of money as the said governor . . . shall deem reasonable, for the personal appearance of such person, if the trial shall be appointed to be had in any other colony, before the governor, . . . of such colony; and if the trial shall be appointed to be had in *Great Britain,* then before his Majesty's court of *King's Bench,* at a time to be mentioned in such recognizances; and the governor, . . . or court of *King's Bench,* where the trial is appointed to be had in *Great Britain,* upon the appearance of such person, according to such recognizance, or in custody, shall either commit such person, or admit him to bail, until such trial. . . .

II. *And, to prevent a failure of justice, from the want of evidence on the trial of any such inquisition, indictment or appeal,* be it further enacted, That the governor . . . is hereby authorised and required, to bind in recognizances to his Majesty all such witnesses as the prosecutor or person against whom such inquisition or indictment shall be found, or appeal sued or preferred, shall desire to attend the trial of the said inquisition, . . . for their personal appearance, at the time and place of such trial, to give evidence: and the said governor . . . shall thereupon appoint a reasonable sum to be allowed for the expences of every such witness . . .

VI. [Persons brought before justices etc. accused of any capital crime in the execution of their duty, to be admitted to bail.]

VIII. And be it further enacted . . . That this act . . . shall . . . be, and continue in force, for and during the term of three years.

4. THE QUEBEC ACT
June 22, 1774
(D. Pickering, *Statutes at Large,* Vol. XXX, p. 549)

The Quebec Act was not, properly speaking, one of the coercive acts. It was not designed with reference to conditions in Massachusetts or the other seaboard colonies. Nevertheless Americans regarded its provisions for religious toleration to Catholics, and for the extension of the territory of Quebec westward, as "intolerable". As a matter of fact the Quebec Act was one of the most enlightened pieces of colonial administration in the history of European colonial expansion. On the Quebec Act see V. Coffin, *The Province of Quebec and the American Revolution,* which is critical, and R. Coupland, *The Quebec Act: a Study in Statesmanship.* For the American background, see C. W. Alvord, *The Mississippi Valley in British Politics,* 2 Vols.; W. Kingsford,

History of Canada, Vol. V; A. L. Burt, *The Old Province of Quebec.*

An Act for making effectual Provision for the Government of the Province of Quebec, *in North America.*

. . . May it therefore please Your most Excellent Majesty,

That it may be enacted: [Boundaries defined, Boundaries of Proclamation of 1763 extended to include territory west to the Mississippi, north to the frontiers of the Hudson's Bay territory, and the islands in the mouth of the St. Lawrence.]

. . . And whereas the Provisions made by the said Proclamation, in respect to the Civil Government of the said Province of *Quebec,* and the Powers and Authorities given to the Governor and other Civil Officers of the said Province, by the Grants and Commissions issued in consequence thereof, have been found, upon Experience, to be inapplicable to the State and Circumstances of the said Province, the Inhabitants whereof amounted at the Conquest, to above Sixty five thousand Persons, professing the Religion of the Church of *Rome.* . . .

It is hereby declared, That His Majesty's Subjects professing the Religion of the Church of *Rome,* of, and in the said Province of *Quebec,* may have, hold, and enjoy, the free Exercise of the Religion of the Church of *Rome,* subject to the King's Supremacy, declared and established by an Act made in the First Year of the Reign of Queen Elizabeth, over all the Dominions and Countries which then did, or thereafter should, belong to the Imperial Crown of this Realm; and that the Clergy of the said Church may hold, receive, and enjoy their accustomed Dues and Rights, with respect to such Persons only as shall profess the said Religion.

Provided nevertheless, That it shall be lawful for His Majesty, His Heirs or Successors, to make such Provisions out of the rest of the said accustomed Dues and Rights, for the Encouragement of the Protestant Religion, and for the Maintenance and Support of a Protestant Clergy within the said Province, as he or they shall, from Time to Time, think necessary or expedient. . . .

And be it further enacted by the Authority aforesaid, That all His Majesty's *Canadian* Subjects within the Province of *Quebec,* the Religious Orders and Communities only excepted, may also hold and enjoy their Property and Possessions, together with all Customs and Usages, relative thereto, and all other their Civil Rights, in as large, ample and beneficial Manner, as if the said Proclamation, Commissions, Ordinances, and other Acts and Instruments, had not been made, and as may consist with their Allegiance to His Majesty, and Subjection to the Crown and Parliament of *Great Britain;* and that in all Matters of Controversy relative to Property and Civil Rights, Resort shall be had to the Laws of *Canada,* as the Rule for the Decision of the same; and all Causes that shall hereafter be instituted in any of the Courts of Justice, to be appointed within and for the said Province by His Majesty, His Heirs and Successors, shall, with respect to such Property and Rights, be determined agreeably to the said Laws and Customs of *Canada,* . . .

And whereas the Certainty and Lenity of the Criminal Law of *England,* and the Benefits and Advantages resulting from the Use of it, have been sensibly felt by the Inhabitants from an Experience of more than Nine Years, during which it has been uniformly administered; be it therefore further enacted by the Authority aforesaid, That the same shall continue to be administered, and shall be observed as Law, in the Province of *Quebec,* as well in the Description and Quality of the Offense, as in the Method of Prosecution and Trial, and the Punishment and Forfeitures thereby inflicted, to the Exclusion of every other Rule of Criminal Law, or Mode of Proceeding thereon, which did or might prevail in the said Province before the Year of our Lord One thousand seven hundred and sixtyfour; any Thing in this Act to the Contrary thereof in any Respect notwithstanding; . . .

And whereas it may be necessary to ordain many Regulations, for the future Welfare and good Government of the Province of *Quebec,* the Occasions of which cannot now be foreseen, nor without much Delay and Inconvenience be provided for, without entrusting that Authority for a certain Time, and upon proper Restrictions to Persons resident there:

And whereas it is at present inexpedient

to call an Assembly; be it therefore enacted by the Authority aforesaid, That it shall and may be lawful for His Majesty, . . . and with the Advice of the Privy Council, to constitute and appoint a Council for the Affairs of the Province of *Quebec,* to consist of such Persons resident there, not exceeding Twenty-three, nor less than Seventeen, as His Majesty, . . . shall be pleased to appoint; . . . which Council, so appointed and nominated, or the major Part thereof, shall have Power and Authority to make Ordinances for the Peace, Welfare, and good Government of the said Province with the Consent of His Majesty's Governor, or, in his Absence, of the Lieutenant Governor, or Commander in Chief for the Time being . . .

50. PENNSYLVANIA RESOLUTIONS ON THE BOSTON PORT ACT
June 20, 1774

(H. Niles, ed. *Principles and Acts of the Revolution,* 1822 ed. p. 180)

This convention, said to have been attended by over eight thousand persons, inaugurated the Revolutionary movement in Pennsylvania. The committee provided for by these resolutions instructed the regular Assembly as to the delegates and instructions for the Continental Congress. For general colonial reaction to the Boston Port Act see Docs. No. 56–57. On Pennsylvania, see C. H. Lincoln, *Revolutionary Movement in Pennsylvania;* C. J. Stillé, *Life and Times of John Dickinson,* ch. vi.

Philadelphia, June 1774

At a very large and respectable meeting of the freeholders and freemen of the city and county of Philadelphia, on June 18, 1774. Thomas Willing, John Dickinson, chairmen.
I. Resolved, That the act of parliament, for shutting up the port of Boston, is unconstitutional, oppressive to the inhabitants of that town, dangerous to the liberties of the British colonies, and that therefore, considering our brethren, at Boston, as suffering in the common cause of America.
II. That a congress of deputies from the several colonies, in North America, is the most probable and proper mode of procuring relief for our suffering brethren, obtaining redress of American grievances, securing our rights and liberties, and re-establishing peace and harmony between Great Britain and these colonies, on a constitutional foundation.
III. That a large and respectable committee be immediately appointed for the city and county of Philadelphia, to correspond with the sister colonies and with the several counties in this province, in order that all may unite in promoting and endeavoring to attain the great and valuable ends, mentioned in the foregoing resolution.
IV. That the committee nominated by this meeting shall consult together, and on mature deliberation determine, what is the most proper mode of collecting the sense of this province, and appointing deputies for the same, to attend a general congress, and having determined thereupon, shall take such measures, as by them shall be judged most expedient, for procuring this province to be represented at the said congress, in the best manner that can be devised for promoting the public welfare.
V. That the committee be instructed immediately to set on foot a subscription for the relief of such poor inhabitants of the town of Boston, as may be deprived of their means of subsistence. . . .
VI. That the committee consist of forty-three persons. . . .

51. NEW YORK CITY RESOLUTIONS ON THE BOSTON PORT ACT
July 6, 1774

(H. Niles, ed. *Principles and Acts of the Revolution,* 1822 ed. p. 174–5)

At a numerous meeting of the inhabitants of the city of New-York, convened in the fields, by a public advertisement, on Wednesday the 6th of July, 1774, Mr. Alexander M'Dougall, Chairman—

The business of the meeting being fully explained by the chairman, and the dangerous tendency of the numerous and vile arts used by the enemies of America, to divide and distract her councils, as well as the misrepresentation of the virtuous intentions of the citizens of this metropolis, in this interesting and alarming state of the liberties of America, the following resolutions were twice read, and the question being separately put on each of them, they were passed without one dissentient.

1st. Resolved, *nem. con.* That the statute commonly called the Boston port act, is oppressive to the inhabitants of that town, unconstitutional in its principles, and dangerous to the liberties of British Americans; and that, therefore, we consider our brethren at Boston, as now suffering in the common cause of these colonies.

2d. Resolved. *nem. con.* That any attack or attempt to abridge the liberties, or invade the constitution, of any of our sister colonies, is immediately an attack upon the liberties and constitution of all the British colonies.

3d. Resolved. *nem. con.* That the shutting up of any of the ports in America, with intent to exact from Americans, a submission to Parliamentary taxation, or extort a reparation of private injuries, is highly unconstitutional, and subversive of the commercial rights of the inhabitants of this continent.

4th. Resolved. *nem. con.* That it is the opinion of this meeting, that if a principal colony on this continent shall come into a joint resolution to stop all importation from, and exportation to Great Britain, till the Act of Parliament for blocking up the harbour of Boston be repealed, the same will prove the salvation of North America and her liberties, and that, on the other hand, if they continue their exports and imports, there is great reason to fear that fraud, power, and the most odious oppression, will triumph over right, justice, social happiness, and freedom:—therefore,

5th. Resolved, *nem. con.* That the deputies who shall represent this colony in the Congress of American deputies, to be held at Philadelphia, about the first of September next, are hereby instructed, empowered, and directed to engage with a majority of the principal colonies, to agree for this city, upon a non-importation from Great Britain, of all goods, wares and merchandizes until the act for blocking up the harbour of Boston be repealed, and American grievances be redressed; and also to agree to all such other measures as the Congress shall, in their wisdom, judge advansive of these great objects, and a general security of the rights and privileges of America.

6th. Resolved, *nem. con.* That this meeting will abide by, obey and observe all such resolutions, determinations and measures, which the Congress aforesaid shall come into, and direct or recommend to be done, for obtaining and securing the important ends mentioned in the foregoing resolution. And that an engagement to this effect be immediately entered into and sent to the Congress, to evince to them, our readiness and determination to co-operate with our sister colonies, for the relief of our distressed brethren of Boston as well as for the security of our common rights and privileges. . . .

8th. Resolved, *nem. con.* That a subscription should immediately be set on foot, for the relief of such poor inhabitants of Boston as are, or may be deprived of the means of subsistence, by the operation of the act of parliament for stopping up the port of Boston. . . .

9th. Resolved, *nem. con.* That the city committee of correspondence be, and they are hereby instructed to use their utmost endeavors to carry these resolutions into execution.

52. RESOLUTIONS OF FREEHOLDERS OF ALBEMARLE COUNTY
VIRGINIA
July 26, 1774

(The Writings of Thomas Jefferson, ed. by P. L. Ford, Vol. I, p. 418 ff.)

Pursuant to the instructions of the House of Burgesses of May 27, 1774—Doc. No. 53—the freeholders of Albemarle County held a meeting and subscribed to the following resolutions. The resolutions were drafted by Thomas Jefferson, and contain philosophical principles of the relations of the colonies to Parliament somewhat in advance of those generally subscribed to by the Americans. See, for an elaboration of Jefferson's position, his *Summary View of the Rights of*

British America, in *Writings,* Vol. I., and C. F. Mullett, *Fundamental Law and the American Revolution.*

At a meeting of the Freeholders of the County of Albemarle, assembled in their collective body, at the Court House of the said County, on the 26th of *July,* 1774:

Resolved, That the inhabitants of the Several States of *British America* are subject to the laws which they adopted at their first settlement, and to such others as have been since made by their respective Legislatures, duly constituted and appointed with their own consent. That no other Legislature whatever can rightly exercise authority over them; and that these privileges they hold as the common rights of mankind, confirmed by the political constitutions they have respectively assumed, and also by several charters of compact from the Crown.

Resolved, That these their natural and legal rights have in frequent instances been invaded by the Parliament of Great Britain and particularly that they were so by an act lately passed to take away the trade of the inhabitants of the town of *Boston,* in the province of *Massachusetts Bay;* that all such assumptions of unlawful power are dangerous to the right of the *British* empire in general, and should be considered as its common cause, and that we will ever be ready to join with our fellow-subjects in every part of the same, in executing all those rightful powers which God has given us, for the re-establishment and guaranteeing such their constitutional rights, when, where, and by whomsoever invaded.

It is the opinion of this meeting, that the most eligible means of effecting these purposes, will be to put an immediate stop to all imports from *Great Britain,* (cotton, osnabrigs, striped duffil, medicines, gunpowder, lead, books and printed papers, the

necessary tools and implements for the handicraft arts and manufactures excepted, for a limited term) and to all exports thereto, after the first day of *October,* which shall be in the year of our Lord, 1775; and immediately to discontinue all commercial intercourse with every part of the *British* Empire which shall not in like manner break off their commerce with *Great Britain.*

It is the opinion of this meeting, that we immediately cease to import all commodities from every part of the world, which are subjected by the *British* Parliament to the payment of duties in *America.*

It is the opinion of this meeting, that these measures should be pursued until a repeal be obtained of the Act for blocking up the harbour of *Boston;* of the Acts prohibiting or restraining internal manufactures in *America;* of the Acts imposing on any commodities duties to be paid in America; and of the Act laying restrictions on the *American* trade; and that on such repeal it will be reasonable to grant to our brethren of *Great Britain* such privileges in commerce as may amply compensate their fraternal assistance, past and future.

Resolved, However, that this meeting do submit these their opinions to the Convention of Deputies from the several counties of this Colony, and appointed to be held at *Williamsburg* on the first day of *August* next, and also to the General Congress of Deputies from the several *American* States, when and wheresoever held; and that they will concur in these or any other measures which such Convention or such Congress shall adopt as most expedient for the *American* good; and we do appoint *Thomas Jefferson* and *John Walker* our Deputies to act for this county at the said Convention, and instruct them to conform themselves to these our Resolutions and Opinions.

53. VIRGINIA INSTRUCTIONS TO THE CONTINENTAL CONGRESS
August 1, 1774

(H. Niles, ed. *Principles and Acts of the Revolution,* 1822 ed. p. 201 ff.)

On May 27, eighty-one members of the House of Burgesses of Virginia had met at the Raleigh Tavern in Williamsburg and recommended a meeting of delegates from all the colonies to a continental congress. These members requested their fellow-members of the

House of Burgesses to sound out their constituents on the question of a congress and to meet at Williamsburg August 1, 1774. At this meeting the following resolutions were drawn up and delegates chosen to the Congress. The convention further declared that it was lawful to meet the lawless acts of General Gage with force—a statement that was looked upon in England as an act of rebellion. See, R. Frothingham, *Rise of the Republic*, p. 332 ff.; C. H. Van Tyne, *Causes of the War of Independence*, p. 426 ff.; C. R. Lingley, *The Transition in Virginia;* H. J. Eckenrode, *The Revolution in Virginia;* J. M. Leake, *The Virginia Committee System and the American Revolution.*

Instructions for the deputies appointed to meet in general congress on the part of the colony of Virginia.

The unhappy disputes between Great Britain and her American colonies, . . . have compelled them to take the same into their most serious consideration; and being deprived of their usual and accustomed mode of making known their grievances, have appointed us their representatives to consider what is proper to be done in this dangerous crisis of American affairs. It being our opinion that the united wisdom of North America should be collected in a general congress of all the colonies, we have appointed the honorable Peyton Randolph, esquire, Richard Henry Lee, George Washington, Patrick Henry, Richard Bland, Benjamin Harrison, and Edmund Pendleton, esquires, deputies to represent this colony in the said congress, to be held at Philadelphia on the first Monday in September next.

And that they be the better informed of our sentiments, touching the conduct we wish them to observe on this important occasion, we desire they will express, in the first place, our faith and true allegiance to his majesty king George the third, our lawful and rightful sovereign; and that we are determined, with our lives and fortunes, to support him in the *legal* exercise of all his just rights and prerogatives; and however misrepresented, we sincerely approve of a constitutional connexion with Great Britain, and wish most ardently a return of that intercourse of affection and commercial connexion that formerly united both countries, which can only be affected by a removal of those causes of discontent which have of late unhappily divided us.

It cannot admit of a doubt but that British subjects in America, are entitled to the same rights and privileges as their fellow subjects possess in Britain; and therefore, that the power assumed by the British parliament to bind America by their statutes, in all cases whatsoever, is unconstitutional, and the source of these unhappy differences.

The end of government would be defeated by the British parliament exercising a power over the lives, the property, and the liberty of the American subjects; who are not, and from their local circumstances cannot, be there represented. Of this nature we consider the several acts of parliament for raising a revenue in America, for extending the jurisdiction of the courts of admiralty, for seizing American subjects and transporting them to Britain to be tried for crimes committed in America, and the several late oppressive acts respecting the town of Boston, and province of the Massachusetts-Bay.

The original constitution of the American colonies possessing their assemblies with the sole right of directing their internal polity, it is absolutely destructive of the end of their institution that their legislatures should be suspended, or prevented, by hasty dissolutions, from exercising their legislative powers.

Wanting the protection of Britain, we have long *acquiesced* in their acts of navigation restrictive of our commerce, which we consider as an ample recompense for such protection; but as those acts derive their efficacy from that foundation alone, we have reason to expect they will be restrained, so as to produce the reasonable purposes of Britain, without being injurious to us.

To obtain a redress of those grievances, without which the people of America can neither be safe, free, nor happy, they are willing to undergo the great inconvenience that will be derived to them from stopping all imports whatsoever from Great Britain, after the first day of November next, and also to cease exporting any commodity whatsoever, to the same place, after the 10th day of August, 1775. . . .

The proclamation issued by general Gage, in the government of the province of the Massachusetts-Bay, declaring it treason for the inhabitants of that province to assemble themselves to consider of their grievances, and form associations for their common conduct on the occasion, and requiring the civil magistrates and officers to apprehend all such persons to be tried for their supposed offences, is the most alarming process that ever appeared in a British government; . . .

That, if the said general Gage conceives he is empowered to act in this manner, as the commander in chief of his majesty's forces in America, this *odious* and *illegal* proclamation must be considered as a plain and full declaration that this *despotic viceroy* will be bound by *no law,* nor regard the constitutional rights of his majesty's subjects, whenever they interfere with the plan he has formed for oppressing the good people of the Massachusetts-Bay; and therefore, that the *executing,* or *attempting to execute* such proclamation, will justify RESISTANCE and REPRISAL.

54. VIRGINIA NON-IMPORTATION AGREEMENT
August 1, 1774

(H. Niles, ed. *Principles and Acts of the Revolution,* 1822 ed. p. 198 ff.)

The Boston Port Act aroused expressions of sympathy everywhere in the American colonies. The Boston Committee of Correspondence drew up a circular letter to the committees in other colonies recommending a suspension of trade with Great Britain; on the receipt of this letter the Virginia House of Burgesses passed a series of resolutions, drafted by Jefferson, "to oppose by all just and proper means every injury to American rights." This led to the dissolution of the House; subsequent meetings were held in the Raleigh Tavern in Williamsburg. The policy of non-intercourse was recommended by several other semi-official bodies, and was formally adopted by the Continental Congress. See Doc. No. 57; R. Frothingham, *Rise of the Republic of the United States,* ch. viii. On the relief of Boston, see Mass. Hist. Soc. *Collections,* 4th Series, Vol. IV.

At a very full meeting of the delegates from the different counties in the colony and dominion of Virginia, begun in Williamsburg, August 1st, 1774 . . .

1st. We do hereby resolve and declare that we will not either directly or indirectly, after the first day of November next, import from Great Britain, any goods, wares, or merchandize, whatever (medicines excepted) nor will we after that day import any British manufactures, either from the West Indies, or any other place. . . .

2dly. We will neither ourselves import, nor purchase any slave, or slaves, imported by any person, after the first day of November next, either from Africa, the West Indies, or any other place.

3dly. Considering the article of tea as the detestable instrument which laid the foundation of the present sufferings of our distressed friends in the town of Boston, we view it with horror, and therefore resolve that we will not, from this day, either import tea of any kind whatever, nor will we use or suffer, even such of it as is now at hand, to be used in any of our families. . . .

5thly. We do resolve, that unless American grievances be redressed before the 10th day of August, 1775, we will not, after that day, directly or indirectly, export tobacco or any other article whatever, to Great Britain, nor will we sell any such articles as we think can be exported to Great Britain with a prospect of gain. . . . And that this resolution may be the more effectually carried into execution, we do hereby recommend it to the inhabitants of this colony to refrain from the cultivation of tobacco as much as conveniently may be. . . .

8thly. In order the better to distinguish such worthy merchants and traders, who are well wishers to this colony, from those who may attempt, through motives of self-interest, to obstruct our views, we do hereby resolve that we will not, after the first day of November next, deal with any merchant or trader, who will not sign this association. . . .

9thly. Resolved. That if any person or persons shall export tobacco, or any other commodity, to Great Britain, after the 10th day of August, 1775, . . . we shall hold ourselves obliged to consider such persons . . . as inimical to the community, and as an *approver* of American *grievances;* and give it as our opinion that the public should be advertised of his conduct. . . .

55. GALLOWAY'S PLAN OF UNION
September 28, 1774

(Journals of the Continental Congress, ed. by W. C. Ford, Vol. I, p. 49 ff.)

Joseph Galloway, long a distinguished figure in Pennsylvania politics, proposed to solve the problem of colonial home rule by a plan which would give to the American colonies something approaching dominion status. This plan, at first favorably received, was ultimately defeated by a single vote, and subsequently expunged from the minutes of the Congress. John Adams observed in his Diary: "Among all the difficulties in the way of effective and united action in 1774 . . . no more alarming one happened than the plan of a proposed union between Great Britain and the Colonies presented, on the 28th of September, by Mr. Joseph Galloway." (The *Works* of John Adams, Vol. II, p. 387.) On the history of the Plan see Galloway, *Historical and Political Reflections on the Rise and Progress of the American Revolution.* See also, M. C. Tyler, *Literary History of the American Revolution,* Vol. I. p. 369 ff.; W. II. Seibert, *The Loyalists of Pennsylvania;* C. H. Lincoln, *Revolutionary Movement in Pennsylvania.*

Resolved, That this Congress will apply to His Majesty for a redress of grievances, under which his faithful subjects in America labour, and assure him that the colonies hold in abhorrence the idea of being considered independent communities on the British Government, and most ardently desire the establishment of a political union, not only among themselves, but with the mother state, upon those principles of safety and freedom which are essential in the constitution of all free governments, and particularly that of the British Legislature. And as the colonies from their local circumstances cannot be represented in the Parliament of Great Britain, they will humbly propose to His Majesty, and his two Houses of Parliament, the following plan, under which the strength of the whole Empire may be drawn together on any emergency; the interests of both countries advanced; and the rights and liberties of America secured.

A Plan of a proposed Union between Great Britain and the Colonies.

That a British and American legislature, for regulating the administration of the general affairs of America, be proposed and established in America, including all the said colonies; within and under which government, each colony shall retain its present constitution and powers of regulating and governing its own internal police in all cases whatsoever.

That the said government be administered by a President General, to be appointed by the King, and a grand council to be chosen by the Representatives of the people of the several colonies in their respective assemblies, once in every three years.

That the several assemblies shall choose members for the grand council in the following proportions, viz.: . . .

Who shall meet at the city of   for the first time, being called by the President General as soon as conveniently may be after his appointment. That there shall be a new election of members for the grand council every three years; and on the death, removal, or resignation of any member, his place shall be supplied by a new choice at the next sitting of Assembly of the colony he represented.

That the grand council shall meet once in every year if they shall think it necessary, and oftener, if occasions shall require, at such time and place as they shall adjourn to at the last preceding meeting; or as they shall be called to meet at, by the President General on any emergency.

That the grand council shall have power to choose their Speaker, and shall hold and exercise all the like rights, liberties, and privileges as are held and exercised by and in the House of Commons of Great Britain.

That the President General shall hold his office during the pleasure of the King, and his assent shall be requisite to all Acts of the grand council, and it shall be his office and duty to cause them to be carried into execution.

That the President General, by and with the advice and consent of the grand council, hold and exercise all the legislative rights, powers, and authorities, necessary for regulating and administering all the general police and affairs of the colonies, in which

Great Britain and the colonies, or any of them, the colonies in general, or more than one colony, are in any manner concerned, as well civil and criminal as commercial.

That the said President General and grand council, be an inferior and distinct branch of the British legislature, united and incorporated with it for the aforesaid general purposes; and that any of the said general regulations may originate, and be formed and digested, either in the Parliament of Great Britain, or in the said grand council; and being prepared, transmitted to the other for their approbation or dissent; and that the assent of both shall be requisite to the validity of all such general acts and statutes.

That in time of war, all bills for granting aides to the Crown, prepared by the grand council and approved by the President General, shall be valid and passed into a law, without the assent of the British Parliament.

56. DECLARATION AND RESOLVES OF THE FIRST CONTINENTAL CONGRESS
October 14, 1774

(Journals of the Continental Congress, ed. by W. C. Ford, Vol. I, p. 63 ff.)

The passage of the Intolerable Acts brought widespread demands for a congress of all the American colonies. On June 17, 1774 Samuel Adams submitted to the Massachusetts House, then assembled at Salem, a resolution that "a meeting of committees from the several colonies on this continent is highly expedient and necessary to consult upon the present state of the colonies . . . and to deliberate and determine upon wise and proper measures to be by them recommended to all the colonies for the recovery and establishment of just rights and liberties, civil and religious, and the restoration of union and harmony between Great Britain and the colonies," and that such a meeting convene in Philadelphia September 1. The resolution was adopted, and Samuel Adams, John Adams, Robert T. Paine, James Bowdoin and James Cushing were appointed delegates from Massachusetts. Most of the other colonies responded favorably to this proposal, and on September 5, delegates from all the colonies except North Carolina and Georgia assembled at Philadelphia; when the North Carolina delegation arrived, a week later, there were some fifty-five delegates in the convention. The best and liveliest account of the convention is in the Diary of John Adams, *Works,* Vol. II. See also, E. C. Burnett, ed. *Letters of Members of the Continental Congress,* Vol. I; R. Frothingham, *Rise of the Republic of the United States,* chs. viii–ix; G. E. Howard, *Preliminaries of the Revolution,* ch. xvi; C. H. Van Tyne, *Causes of the War of Independence,* chs. xvi–xvii.

Whereas, since the close of the last war, the British parliament, claiming a power of right to bind the people of America by statute in all cases whatsoever, hath, in some acts expressly imposed taxes on them, and in others, under various pretences, but in fact for the purpose of raising a revenue, hath imposed rates and duties payable in these colonies, established a board of commissioners with unconstitutional powers, and extended the jurisdiction of courts of Admiralty not only for collecting the said duties, but for the trial of causes merely arising within the body of a county.

And whereas, in consequence of other statutes, judges who before held only estates at will in their offices, have been made dependent on the Crown alone for their salaries, and standing armies kept in times of peace. And it has lately been resolved in Parliament, that by force of a statute made in the thirty-fifth year of the reign of king Henry the Eighth, colonists may be transported to England, and tried there upon accusations for treasons and misprisions, or concealments of treasons committed in the colonies; and by a late statute, such trials have been directed in cases therein mentioned.

And whereas, in the last session of Parliament, three statutes were made . . . [the Boston Port Act, the Massachusetts Government Act, the Administration of Justice Act], and another statute was then made [the Quebec Act] . . . All which statutes are impolitic, unjust, and cruel, as well as unconstitutional, and most dangerous and destructive of American rights.

And whereas, Assemblies have been frequently dissolved, contrary to the rights of the people, when they attempted to deliberate on grievances; and their dutiful, humble, loyal, & reasonable petitions to the crown for redress, have been repeatedly treated with contempt, by His Majesty's ministers of state:

The good people of the several Colonies of New-hampshire, Massachusetts-bay, Rhode-island and Providence plantations, Connecticut, New-York, New-Jersey, Pennsylvania, Newcastle Kent and Sussex on Delaware, Maryland, Virginia, North-Carolina, and South-Carolina, justly alarmed at these arbitrary proceedings of parliament and administration, have severally elected, constituted, and appointed deputies to meet, and sit in general Congress, in the city of Philadelphia, in order to obtain such establishment, as that their religion, laws, and liberties, may not be subverted:

Whereupon the deputies so appointed being now assembled, in a full and free representation of these Colonies, taking into their most serious consideration the best means of attaining the ends aforesaid, do in the first place, as Englishmen their ancestors in like cases have usually done, for asserting and vindicating their rights and liberties, declare,

That the inhabitants of the English Colonies in North America, by the immutable laws of nature, the principles of the English constitution, and the several charters or compacts, have the following Rights:

Resolved, N. C. D.

1. That they are entitled to life, liberty, and property, & they have never ceded to any sovereign power whatever, a right to dispose of either without their consent.

2. That our ancestors, who first settled these colonies, were at the time of their emigration from the mother country, entitled to all the rights, liberties, and immunities of free and natural-born subjects within the realm of England.

3. That by such emigration they by no means forfeited, surrendered, or lost any of those rights, but that they were, and their descendants now are entitled to the exercise and enjoyment of all such of them, as their local and other circumstances enable them to exercise and enjoy.

4. That the foundation of English liberty, and of all free government, is a right in the people to participate in their legislative council: and as the English colonists are not represented, and from their local and other circumstances, cannot properly be represented in the British parliament, they are entitled to a free and exclusive power of legislation in their several provincial legislatures, where their right of representation can alone be preserved, in all cases of taxation and internal polity, subject only to the negative of their sovereign, in such manner as has been heretofore used and accustomed. But, from the necessity of the case, and a regard to the mutual interest of both countries, we cheerfully consent to the operation of such acts of the British parliament, as are bona fide restrained to the regulation of our external commerce, for the purpose of securing the commercial advantages of the whole empire to the mother country, and the commercial benefits of its respective members excluding every idea of taxation, internal or external, for raising a revenue on the subjects in America without their consent.

5. That the respective colonies are entitled to the common law of England, and more especially to the great and inestimable privilege of being tried by their peers of the vicinage, according to the course of that law.

6. That they are entitled to the benefit of such of the English statutes, as existed at the time of their colonization; and which they have, by experience, respectively found to be applicable to their several local and other circumstances.

7. That these, his majesty's colonies, are likewise entitled to all the immunities and privileges granted and confirmed to them by royal charters, or secured by their several codes of provincial laws.

8. That they have a right peaceably to assemble, consider of their grievances, and petition the King; and that all prosecutions, prohibitory proclamations, and commitments for the same, are illegal.

9. That the keeping a Standing army in these colonies, in times of peace, without the consent of the legislature of that colony in which such army is kept, is against law.

10. It is indispensably necessary to good government, and rendered essential by the English constitution, that the constituent branches of the legislature be independent of each other; that, therefore, the exercise of legislative power in several colonies, by a council appointed during pleasure, by the crown, is unconstitutional, dangerous, and

destructive to the freedom of American legislation.

All and each of which the aforesaid deputies, in behalf of themselves, and their constituents, do claim, demand, and insist on, as their indubitable rights and liberties; which cannot be legally taken from them, altered or abridged by any power whatever, without their own consent, by their representatives in their several provincial legislatures.

In the course of our inquiry, we find many infringments and violations of the foregoing rights, which, from an ardent desire that harmony and mutual intercourse of affection and interest may be restored, we pass over for the present, and proceed to state such acts and measures as have been adopted since the last war, which demonstrate a system formed to enslave America.

Resolved, That the following acts of Parliament are infringements and violations of the rights of the colonists; and that the repeal of them is essentially necessary, in order to restore harmony between Great Britain and the American colonies, . . . viz.:

The several Acts of 4 Geo. 3, ch. 15 & ch. 34; 5 Geo. 3, ch. 25; 6 Geo. 3, ch. 52; 7 Geo. 3, ch. 41 & 46; 8 Geo. 3, ch. 22; which impose duties for the purpose of raising a revenue in America, extend the powers of the admiralty courts beyond their ancient limits, deprive the American subject of trial by jury, authorize the judges' certificate to indemnify the prosecutor from damages that he might otherwise be liable to, requiring oppressive security from a claimant of ships and goods seized before he shall be allowed to defend his property; and are subversive of American rights.

Also the 12 Geo. 3, ch. 24, entitled "An act for the better preserving his Majesty's dockyards, magazines, ships, ammunition, and stores," which declares a new offense in America, and deprives the American subject of a constitutional trial by jury of the vici-

nage, by authorizing the trial of any person charged with the committing any offense described in the said act, out of the realm, to be indicted and tried for the same in any shire or county within the realm.

Also the three acts passed in the last session of parliament, for stopping the port and blocking up the harbour of Boston, for altering the charter & government of the Massachusetts-bay, and that which is entitled "An Act for the better administration of Justice," &c.

Also the act passed the same session for establishing the Roman Catholick Religion in the province of Quebec, abolishing the equitable system of English laws, and erecting a tyranny there, to the great danger, from so great a dissimilarity of Religion, law, and government, of the neighbouring British colonies. . . .

Also the act passed the same session for the better providing suitable quarters for officers and soldiers in his Majesty's service in North America.

Also, that the keeping a standing army in several of these colonies, in time of peace, without the consent of the legislature of that colony in which the army is kept, is against law.

To these grievous acts and measures Americans cannot submit, but in hopes that their fellow subjects in Great-Britain will, on a revision of them, restore us to that state in which both countries found happiness and prosperity, we have for the present only resolved to pursue the following peaceable measures: 1st. To enter into a non-importation, non-consumption, and non-exportation agreement or association. 2. To prepare an address to the people of Great-Britain, and a memorial to the inhabitants of British America, & 3. To prepare a loyal address to his Majesty, agreeable to resolutions already entered into.

57. THE ASSOCIATION
October 20, 1774

(Journals of the Continental Congress, ed. by W. C. Ford, Vol. I, p. 75 ff.)

On September 27 the Continental Congress voted non-intercourse with Great Britain, and three days later a committee was appointed charged with drafting a plan to carry this resolution into effect. The committee reported October 12, and the report was adopted on the 18 and signed on the 20 October. "The signature of the Association," says Hildreth, "may be considered as the commencement of the American Union." Of particular interest are the provisions prohibiting the importation of slaves, and providing for committees of correspondence to enforce the rules of the Association. Several of the Colonies had already adopted non-importation agreements. The effect of the non-intercourse resolutions can be read in the petitions of English merchants to Parliament; see, for example, Doc. No. 58. On the Association, see R. Frothingham. *Rise of the Republic,* p. 372 ff.; A. W. Small, *The Beginnings of American Nationality;* G. E. Howard, *Preliminaries of the Revolution,* ch. xvi.

We, his majesty's most loyal subjects, the delegates of the several colonies of New-Hampshire, Massachusetts-Bay, Rhode-Island, Connecticut, New-York, New-Jersey, Pennsylvania, the three lower counties of Newcastle, Kent and Sussex on Delaware, Maryland, Virginia, North-Carolina, and South-Carolina, deputed to represent them in a continental Congress, held in the city of Philadelphia, on the 5th day of September, 1774, avowing our allegiance to his majesty, our affection and regard for our fellow-subjects in Great-Britain and elsewhere, affected with the deepest anxiety, and most alarming apprehensions, at those grievances and distresses, with which his Majesty's American subjects are oppressed; and having taken under our most serious deliberation, the state of the whole continent, find, that the present unhappy situation of our affairs is occasioned by a ruinous system of colony administration, adopted by the British ministry about the year 1763, evidently calculated for enslaving these colonies, and, with them, the British Empire. In prosecution of which system, various acts of parliament have been passed, for raising a revenue in America, for depriving the American subjects, in many instances, of the constitutional trial by jury, exposing their lives to danger, by directing a new and illegal trial beyond the seas, for crimes alleged to have been committed in America: And in prosecution of the same system, several late, cruel, and oppressive acts have been passed, respecting the town of Boston and the Massachusetts-Bay, and also an act for extending the province of Quebec, so as to border on the western frontiers of these colonies, establishing an arbitrary government therein, and discouraging the settlement of British subjects in that wide extended coun-

try; thus, by the influence of civil principles and ancient prejudices, to dispose the inhabitants to act with hostility against the free Protestant colonies, whenever a wicked ministry shall chuse so to direct them.

To obtain redress of these grievances, which threaten destruction to the lives, liberty, and property of his majesty's subjects, in North-America, we are of opinion, that a non-importation, non-consumption, and non-exportation agreement, faithfully adhered to, will prove the most speedy, effectual, and peaceable measure: And, therefore, we do, for ourselves, and the inhabitants of the several colonies, whom we represent, firmly agree and associate, under the sacred ties of virtue, honour and love of our country, as follows:

1. That from and after the first day of December next, we will not import, into British America, from Great-Britain or Ireland, any goods, wares, or merchandize whatsoever, or from any other place, any such goods, wares, or merchandise, as shall have been exported from Great-Britain or Ireland; nor will we, after that day, import any East-India tea from any part of the world; nor any molasses, syrups, paneles, coffee, or pimento, from the British plantations or from Dominica; nor wines from Madeira, or the Western Islands; nor foreign indigo.

2. We will neither import nor purchase, any slave imported after the first day of December next; after which time, we will wholly discontinue the slave trade, and will neither be concerned in it ourselves, nor will we hire our vessels, nor sell our commodities or manufactures to those who are concerned in it.

3. As a non-consumption agreement, strictly adhered to, will be an effectual security for the observation of the non-importation, we, as above, solemnly agree and associate, that from this day, we will not purchase or use any tea, imported on account of the East-India company, or any on which a duty hath been or shall be paid; and from and after the first day of March next, we will not purchase or use any East-India tea whatever; nor will we, nor shall any person for or under us, purchase or use any of those goods, wares, or merchandize, we have agreed not to import, which we shall know, or have cause to suspect, were imported after the first day of December, except such as come

under the rules and directions of the tenth article hereafter mentioned.

4. The earnest desire we have not to injure our fellow-subjects in Great-Britain, Ireland, or the West-Indies, induces us to suspend a non-exportation, until the tenth day of September, 1775; at which time, if the said acts and parts of acts of the British parliament herein after mentioned, are not repealed, we will not directly or indirectly, export any merchandize or commodity whatsoever to Great-Britain, Ireland, or the West-Indies, except rice to Europe.

5. Such as are merchants, and use the British and Irish trade, will give orders, as soon as possible, to their factors, agents and correspondents, in Great-Britain and Ireland, not to ship any goods to them, on any pretence whatsoever, as they cannot be received in America; and if any merchant, residing in Great-Britain or Ireland, shall directly or indirectly ship any goods, wares or merchandize, for America, in order to break the said non-importation agreement, or in any manner contravene the same, on such unworthy conduct being well attested, it ought to be made public; and, on the same being so done, we will not, from thenceforth, have any commercial connexion with such merchant.

6. That such as are owners of vessels will give positive orders to their captains, or masters, not to receive on board their vessels any goods prohibited by the said non-importation agreement, on pain of immediate dismission from their service.

7. We will use our utmost endeavours to improve the breed of sheep, and increase their number to the greatest extent; and to that end, we will kill them as seldom as may be, especially those of the most profitable kind; nor will we export any to the West-Indies or elsewhere; and those of us, who are or may become overstocked with, or can conveniently spare any sheep, will dispose of them to our neighbours, especially to the poorer sort, on moderate terms.

8. We will, in our several stations, encourage frugality, œconomy, and industry, and promote agriculture, arts and the manufactures of this country, especially that of wool; and will discountenance and discourage every species of extravagance and dissipation, especially all horse-racing, and all kinds of gaming, cock fighting, exhibitions of shews,

plays, and other expensive diversions and entertainments; and on the death of any relation or friend, none of us, or any of our families will go into any further mourning-dress, than a black crape or ribbon on the arm or hat, for gentlemen, and a black ribbon and necklace for ladies, and we will discontinue the giving of gloves and scarves at funerals.

9. Such as are venders of goods or merchandize will not take advantage of the scarcity of goods, that may be occasioned by this association, but will sell the same at the rates we have been respectively accustomed to do, for twelve months last past. —And if any vender of goods or merchandize shall sell such goods on higher terms, or shall, in any manner, or by any device whatsoever, violate or depart from this agreement, no person ought, nor will any of us deal with any such person, or his or her factor or agent, at any time thereafter, for any commodity whatever.

10. In case any merchant, trader, or other person, shall import any goods or merchandize, after the first day of December, and before the first day of February next, the same ought forthwith, at the election of the owner, to be either re-shipped or delivered up to the committee of the country or town, wherein they shall be imported, to be stored at the risque of the importer, until the non-importation agreement shall cease, or be sold under the direction of the committee aforesaid; and in the last-mentioned case, the owner or owners of such goods shall be reimbursed out of the sales, the first cost and charges, the profit, if any, to be applied towards relieving and employing such poor inhabitants of the town of Boston, as are immediate sufferers by the Boston port-bill; and a particular account of all goods so returned, stored, or sold, to be inserted in the public papers; and if any goods or merchandizes shall be imported after the said first day of February, the same ought forthwith to be sent back again, without breaking any of the packages thereof.

11. That a committee be chosen in every county, city, and town, by those who are qualified to vote for representatives in the legislature, whose business it shall be attentively to observe the conduct of all persons touching this association; and when it shall

be made to appear, to the satisfaction of a majority of any such committee, that any person within the limits of their appointment has violated this association, that such majority do forthwith cause the truth of the case to be published in the. gazette; to the end, that all such foes to the rights of British-America may be publicly known, and universally contemned as the enemies of American liberty; and thenceforth we respectively will break off all dealings with him or her.

12. That the committee of correspondence, in the respective colonies, do frequently inspect the entries of their customhouses, and inform each other, from time to time, of the true state thereof, and of every other material circumstance that may occur relative to this association.

13. That all manufactures of this country be sold at reasonable prices, so that no undue advantage be taken of a future scarcity of goods.

14. And we do further agree and resolve, that we will have no trade, commerce, dealings or intercourse whatsoever, with any colony or province, in North-America, which shall not accede to, or which shall hereafter violate this association, but will hold them as unworthy of the rights of freemen, and as inimical to the liberties of their country.

And we do solemnly bind ourselves and our constituents, under the ties aforesaid, to adhere to this association, until such parts of the several acts of parliament passed since the close of the last war, as impose or continue duties on tea, wine, molasses, syrups, paneles, coffee, sugar, pimento, indigo, foreign paper, glass, and painters' colours, imported into America, and extend the powers of the admiralty courts beyond their ancient limits, deprive the American subject of trial by jury, authorize the judge's certificate to indemnify the prosecutor from damages, that he might otherwise be liable to from a trial by his peers, require oppressive security from a claimant of ships or goods seized, before he shall be allowed to defend his property, are repealed.—And until that part of the act of the 12 G. 3. ch. 24, entitled "An act for the better securing his majesty's dock-yards, magazines, ships, ammunition, and stores," by which any persons charged with committing any of the offences therein described, in America, may be tried in any shire or county within the realm, is repealed—and until the four acts, passed the last session of parliament, viz. that for stopping the port and blocking up the harbour of Boston—that for altering the charter and government of the Massachusetts-Bay—and that which is entitled "An act for the better administration of justice, &c."—and that "for extending the limits of Quebec, &c." are repealed. And we recommend it to the provincial conventions, and to the committees in the respective colonies, to establish such farther regulations as they may think proper, for carrying into execution this association.

The foregoing association being determined upon by the Congress, was ordered to be subscribed by the several members thereof; and thereupon, we have hereunto set our respective names accordingly.

IN CONGRESS, PHILADELPHIA, *October 20, 1774.*

Signed, PEYTON RANDOLPH, *President.*

58. PETITION OF LONDON MERCHANTS FOR RECONCILIATION WITH AMERICA
January 23, 1775

(The Parliamentary History of England, Vol. XVIII, 1774–1777, p. 168 ff.)

Exports from England to the American colonies dropped from some two and one half million pounds in 1774 to about one-tenth that sum in 1775. Not only did the success of the Association thus threaten English merchants with ruin, but the imminent danger of hostilities with the colonies raised serious doubts as to the ability of English merchants to collect the large debts owed them by American planters. On trade, see, D. M. Clark, *British Opinion and the American Revolution,* ch. iii; on debts, see, I. Harrell, *Loyalism in Virginia.*

Mr. Alderman *Hayley* said he had a petition from the merchants of the city of London concerned in the commerce to North America, to that honourable House, and desired leave to present the same, which being given, it was brought up and read, setting forth;

"That the petitioners are all essentially interested in the trade to North America, either as exporters and importers, or as venders of British and foreign goods for exportation to that country; and that the petitioners have exported, or sold for exportation, to the British colonies in North America, very large quantities of the manufacture of Great Britain and Ireland, and in particular the staple articles of woollen, iron, and linen, also those of cotton, silk, leather, pewter, tin, copper, and brass, with almost every British manufacture; . . . and that the petitioners have likewise exported, or sold for exportation, great quantities of the various species of goods imported into this kingdom from the East-Indies, part of which receive additional manufacture in Great Britain; and that the petitioners receive returns from North America to this kingdom directly, viz. pig and bar iron, timber, staves, naval stores, tobacco, rice, indigo, deer, and other skins, beaver and furs, train oil, whalebone, bees wax, pot and pearl ashes, drugs and dyeing woods, with some bullion, and also wheat flour, Indian corn and salted provisions, when, on account of scarcity in Great Britain, those articles are permitted to be imported; . . . and that the petitioners have great reason to believe, from the best informations they can obtain, that on the balance of this extensive commerce, there is now due from the colonies in North America, to the said city only, 2,000,000 l. sterling, and upwards; and that, by the direct commerce with the colonies, and the circuitous trade thereon depending, some thousands of ships and vessels are employed, and many thousands of seamen are bred and maintained, thereby increasing the naval strength and power of Great Britain; and that, in the year 1765, there was a great stagnation of the commerce between Great Britain and her colonies, in consequence of an Act for granting and applying certain stamp duties, and other duties, in the British colonies and plantations in America, by which the merchants trading to North America, and the artificers employed in the various manufactures consumed in those countries, were subjected to many hardships; and that, in the following year, the said Act was repealed, under an ex-

press declaration of the legislature, that the continuance of the said Act would be attended with many inconveniences, and might be productive of consequences greatly detrimental to the commercial interests of these kingdoms; upon which repeal, the trade to the British colonies immediately resumed its former flourishing state; and that in the year 1767 an Act passed for granting certain duties in the British colonies and plantations in America, which imposed certain duties, to be paid in America, on tea, glass, red and white lead, painters' colours, paper, paste-board, mill-board, and scale-board, when the commerce with the colonies was again interrupted; and that in the year 1770, such parts of the said Act as imposed duties on glass, red and white lead, painters' colours, paper, paste-board, mill-board, and scale-board, were repealed, when the trade to America soon revived, except in the article of tea, on which a duty was continued, to be demanded on its importation into America, whereby that branch of our commerce was nearly lost; and that, in the year 1773, an Act passed, to allow a drawback of the duties of customs on the exportation of tea to his Majesty's colonies or plantations in America, and to empower the commissioners of the Treasury to grant licenses to the East India Company, to export tea, duty free; and by the operation of those and other laws, the minds of his Majesty's subjects in the British colonies have been greatly disquieted, a total stop is now put to the export trade with the greatest and most important part of North America, the public revenue is threatened with a large and fatal diminution, the petitioners with grievous distress, and thousands of industrious artificers and manufacturers with utter ruin; under these alarming circumstances, the petitioners receive no small comfort, from a persuasion that the representatives of the people, newly delegated to the most important of all trusts, will take the whole of these weighty matters into their most serious consideration; and therefore praying the House, that they will enter into a full and immediate examination of that system of commercial policy, which was formerly adopted, and uniformly maintained, to the happiness and advantage of both countries, and will apply such healing remedies as can alone restore and establish the commerce between Great Britain and her colonies on a permanent foundation; and that the petitioners may be heard by themselves, or agents, in support of the said petition."

59. THE BATTLE OF LEXINGTON
1775

The following two extracts present the official American and English versions of the hostilities at Lexington, April 19, 1775. It is, apparently, impossible to determine at this time who fired the first shot at Lexington, but see A. C. Mc Laughlin, et.al. eds. *Source Problems in United States History*, ch. i; A. French, *The Day of Concord and Lexington;* A. French, *General Gage's Informers,* chs. i–iii; H. Murdock, *Concord Fight.*

1. AMERICAN ACCOUNT OF THE BATTLE OF LEXINGTON: Account by the Provincial Congress at Watertown, Massachusetts
April 26, 1775
(H. Niles, ed. *Principles and Acts of the Revolution,* 1822 ed. p. 434–5.)
Watertown, April 26th, 1775.
In provincial congress of Massachusetts, to the inhabitants of Great Britain.

Friends and fellow subjects—Hostilities are at length commenced in this colony by the troops under the command of general Gage, and it being of the greatest importance, that an early, true, and authentic account of this inhuman proceeding should be known to you, the congress of this colony have transmitted the same, and from want of a session of the hon. continental congress, think it proper to address you on the alarming occasion.

By the clearest depositions relative to this transaction, it will appear that on the night preceding the nineteenth of April instant, a body of the king's troops, under the command of colonel Smith, were secretly landed at Cambridge, with an apparent design to take or destroy the military and other stores, provided for the defence of this colony, and deposited at Concord—that some inhabitants of the colony, on the night aforesaid, whilst travelling peaceably on the road, between Boston and Concord, were seized and greatly abused by armed men, who appeared to be officers of general Gage's army; that the town of Lexington, by these means, was alarmed, and a company of the inhabitants mustered on the occasion—that the regular troops on their way to Concord, marched into the said town of Lexington, and the said company, on their approach, began to disperse—that, notwithstanding this, the regulars rushed on with great violence and first began hostilities, by firing on said Lexington company, whereby they killed eight, and wounded several others—that the regulars continued their fire, until those of said company, who were neither killed nor wounded, had made their escape—that colonel Smith, with the detachment then marched to Concord, where a number of provincials were again fired on by the troops, two of them killed and several wounded, before the provincials fired on them, and provincials were again fired on by the troops, produced an engagement that lasted through the day, in which many of the provincials and more of the regular troops were killed and wounded.

To give a particular account of the ravages of the troops, as they retreated from Concord to Charlestown, would be very difficult, if not impracticable; let it suffice to say, that a great number of the houses on the road were plundered and rendered unfit for use, several were burnt, women in child-bed were driven by the soldiery naked into the streets, old men peaceably in their houses were shot dead, and such scenes exhibited as would disgrace the annals of the most uncivilised nation.

These, brethren, are marks of ministerial vengeance against this colony, for refusing, with her sister colonies, a submission to slavery; but they have not yet detached us from our loyal sovereign. We profess to be his loyal and dutiful subjects, and so hardly dealt with as we have been, are still ready, with our lives and fortunes, to defend his person, family, crown and dignity. Nevertheless, to the persecution and tyranny of his cruel ministry we will not tamely submit—appealing to Heaven for the justice of our cause, we determine to die or be free. . . .
By order,
Joseph Warren, President.

2. ENGLISH ACCOUNT OF THE BATTLE OF LEXINGTON: Report of Lieutenant-Colonel Smith to Governor Gage
April 22, 1775
(Mass. Historical Society, *Proceedings*, 1876, p. 350 ff.)

SIR,—In obedience to your Excellency's commands, I marched on the evening of the 18th inst. with the corps of grenadiers and light infantry for Concord, to execute your Excellency's orders with respect to destroying all ammunition, artillery, tents, &c, collected there, which was effected, having knocked off the trunnions of three pieces of iron ordnance, some new gun-carriages, a great number of carriage-wheels burnt, a considerable quantity of flour, some gun-powder and musquet-balls, with other small articles thrown into the river. Notwithstanding we marched with the utmost expedition and secrecy, we found the country had intelligence or strong suspicion of our coming, and fired many signal guns, and rung the alarm bells repeatedly; and were informed, when at Concord, that some cannon had been taken out of the town that day, that others, with some stores, had been carried three days before, which prevented our having an opportunity of destroying so much as might have been expected at our first setting off.

I think it proper to observe, that when I had got some miles on the march from Boston, I detached six light infantry companies to march with all expedition to seize the two bridges on different roads beyond Concord. On these companies' arrival at Lexington, I understand, from the report of Major Pitcairn, who was with them, and from many officers, that they found on a green close to the road a body of the country people drawn up in military order, with arms and accoutrements, and, as appeared after, loaded; and that they had posted some men in a dwelling and Meeting-house. Our troops advanced towards them, without any intention of injuring them, further than to inquire the reason of their being thus assembled, and, if not satisfactory, to have secured their arms; but they in confusion went off, principally to the left, only one of them fired before he went off, and three or four more jumped over a wall and fired from behind it among the soldiers; on which the troops returned it, and killed several of them. They likewise fired on the soldiers from the Meeting and dwelling-houses. . . . Rather earlier than this, on the road, a countryman from behind a wall had snapped his piece at Lieutenants Adair and Sutherland, but it flashed and did not go off. After this we saw some in the woods, but marched on to Concord without anything further happening. While at Concord we saw vast numbers assembling in many parts; at one of the bridges they marched down, with a very considerable body, on the light infantry posted there. On their coming pretty near, one of our men fired on them, which they returned; on which an action ensued, and some few were killed and wounded. In this affair, it appears that, after the bridge was quitted, they scalped and otherwise ill-treated one or two of the men who were either killed or severely wounded. . . . On our leaving Concord to return to Boston, they began to fire on us from behind the walls, ditches, trees, &c., which, as we marched, increased to a very great degree, and continued without intermission of five minutes altogether, for, I believe, upwards of eighteen miles; so that I can't think but it must have been a preconcerted scheme in them, to attack the King's troops the first favorable opportunity that offered, otherwise, I think they could not, in so short a time from our marching out, have raised such a numerous body, and for so great a space of ground. Notwithstanding the enemy's numbers, they did not make one gallant attempt during so long an action, though our men were so very much fatigued, but kept under cover.

I have the honor, &c.,

F. Smith, Lieutenant-Colonel 10th Foot.

60. ADDRESS OF THE CONTINENTAL CONGRESS TO THE INHABITANTS OF CANADA
May 29, 1775

(Journals of the Continental Congress, ed. by W. C. Ford, Vol. II, p. 68 ff.)

One of the first acts of the second Continental Congress which met May 10, 1775, was an Appeal to the inhabitants of Canada. The appeal was drafted by John Jay. Americans continued, through the early years of the war, to hug to themselves the delusion that Canadians wished to bring Canada into the American Union. In the fall of 1775 the appeal of Congress was re-enforced by a military expedition under Montgomery and Arnold which was disastrously defeated. Nothing daunted, Congress in March 1776 appointed three commissioners,—Franklin, Samuel Chase, and Charles Carroll—to proceed to Canada and persuade the Canadians to join the Americans. Even after the failure of this move, Congress provided, in the Articles of Confederation, for the admission of Canada. See J. H. Smith, *Our Struggle for the Fourteenth Colony,* Vol. I.

To the oppressed Inhabitants of Canada.
FRIENDS AND COUNTRYMEN,

Alarmed by the designs of an arbitrary Ministry, to extirpate the Rights and liberties of all America, a sense of common danger conspired with the dictates of humanity, in urging us to call your attention, by our late address, to this very important object. Since the conclusion of the late war, we have been happy in considering you as fellow-subjects, and from the commencement of the present plan for subjugating the continent, we have viewed you as fellow-sufferers with us. As we were both entitled by the bounty of an indulgent creator to freedom, and being both devoted by the cruel edicts of a despotic administration, to common ruin, we perceived the fate of the protestant and catholic colonies to be strongly linked together, and therefore invited you to join with us in re-solving to be free, and in rejecting, with disdain, the fetters of slavery, however artfully polished.

We most sincerely condole with you on the arrival of that day, in the course of which, the sun could not shine on a single freeman in all your extensive dominion. Be assured, that your unmerited degradation has engaged the most unfeigned pity of your sister colonies; and we flatter ourselves you will not, by tamely bearing the yoke, suffer that pity to be supplanted by contempt.

When hardy attempts are made to deprive men of rights, bestowed by the almighty, when avenues are cut thro' the most solemn compacts for the admission of despotism, when the plighted faith of government ceases to give security to loyal and dutiful subjects, and when the insidious stratagems and manoeuvres of peace become more terrible than the sanguinary operations of war, it is high time for them to assert those rights, and, with honest indignation, oppose the torrent of oppression rushing in upon them.

By the introduction of your present form of government, or rather present form of tyranny, you and your wives and your children are made slaves. You have nothing that you can call your own, and all the fruits of your labour and industry may be taken from you, whenever an avaritious governor and a rapacious council may incline to demand them. You are liable by their edicts to be transported into foreign countries to fight Battles in which you have no interest, and to spill your blood in conflicts from which neither honor nor emolument can be derived: Nay, the enjoyment of your very religion, in the present system, depends on a legislature in which you have no share, and over which you have no controul, and your priests are exposed to expulsion, banishment, and ruin, whenever their wealth and possessions furnish sufficient temptation. They cannot be sure that a virtuous prince will always fill the throne, and should a wicked or a careless king concur with a wicked ministry in extracting the treasure and strength of your country, it is impossible to conceive to what variety and to what extremes of wretchedness you may, under the present establishment, be reduced.

We are informed you have already been called upon to waste your lives in a contest with us. Should you, by complying in this instance, assent to your new establishment, and a war break out with France, your wealth and your sons may be sent to perish in expeditions against their islands in the West indies.

It cannot be presumed that these considerations will have no weight with you, or that you are so lost to all sense of honor. We can never believe that the present race of Canadians are so degenerated as to possess neither the spirit, the gallantry, nor the courage of their ancestors. You certainly will not permit the infamy and disgrace of such pusillanimity to rest on your own heads, and the consequences of it on your children forever.

We, for our parts, are determined to live free, or not at all; and are resolved, that posterity shall never reproach us with having brought slaves into the world.

Permit us again to repeat that we are your friends, not your enemies, and be not imposed upon by those who may endeavour to create animosities. The taking of the fort and military stores at Ticonderoga and Crown-Point, and the armed vessels on the lake, was dictated by the great law of self-preservation. They are intended to annoy us, and to cut off that friendly intercourse and communication, which has hitherto subsisted between you and us. We hope it has given you no uneasiness, and you may rely on our assurances, that these colonies will pursue no measures whatever, but such as friendship and a regard for our mutual safety and interest may suggest.

As our concern for your welfare entitles us to your friendship, we presume you will not, by doing us injury, reduce us to the disagreeable necessity of treating you as enemies.

We yet entertain hopes of your uniting with us in the defence of our common liberty, and there is yet reason to believe, that should we join in imploring the attention of our sovereign, to the unmerited and unparalleled oppressions of his American subjects, he will at length be undeceived, and forbid a licentious Ministry any longer to riot in the ruins of the rights of Mankind. . . .

61. DECLARATION OF THE CAUSES AND NECESSITY OF TAKING UP ARMS
July 6, 1775

(*Journals of the Continental Congress,* ed. by W. C. Ford, Vol. II, p. 140 ff.)

Franklin, Jay, Rutledge, Livingston, Johnson, Jefferson and Dickinson were the members of the committee appointed to draw up this declaration. The final draft is the work of Dickinson and Jefferson. On the authorship of the Declaration, see Appendix IV to C. J. Stillé, *Life and Times of John Dickinson,* Vol. I, p. 353 ff.; C. H. Van Tyne, *The War of Independence: American Phase.*

If it was possible for men, who exercise their reason to believe, that the divine Author of our existence intended a part of the human race to hold an absolute property in, and an unbounded power over others, marked out by his infinite goodness and wisdom, as the objects of a legal domination never rightfully resistible, however severe and oppressive, the inhabitants of these colonies might at least require from the parliament of Great-Britain some evidence, that this dreadful authority over them, has been granted to that body. But a reverence for our great Creator, principles of humanity, and the dictates of common sense, must convince all those who reflect upon the subject, that government was instituted to promote the welfare of mankind, and ought to be administered for the attainment of that end. The legislature of Great-Britain, however, stimulated by an inordinate passion for a power not only unjustifiable, but which they know to be peculiarly reprobated by the very constitution of that kingdom, and desperate of success in any mode of contest, where regard should be had to truth, law, or right, have at length, deserting those, attempted to effect their cruel and impolitic purpose of enslaving these colonies by violence, and have thereby rendered it necessary for us to close with their last appeal from reason to arms.—Yet, however blinded that assembly may be, by their intemperate rage for unlimited domination, so to slight justice and the opinion of mankind, we esteem ourselves bound by obligations of respect to the rest of the world, to make known the justice of our cause.

Our forefathers, inhabitants of the island of Great-Britain, left their native land, to seek on these shores a residence for civil and religious freedom. At the expense of their blood, at the hazard of their fortunes, without the least charge to the country from which they removed, by unceasing labour, and an unconquerable spirit, they effected settlements in the distant and inhospitable wilds of America, then filled with numerous and warlike nations of barbarians.—Societies or governments, vested with perfect legislatures, were formed under charters from the crown, and an harmonious intercourse was established between the colonies and the kingdom from which they derived their origin. The mutual benefits of this union became in a short time so extraordinary, as to excite astonishment. It is universally confessed, that the amazing increase of the wealth, strength, and navigation of the realm, arose from this source; and the minister, who so wisely and successfully directed the measures of Great-Britain in the late war, publicly declared, that these colonies enabled her to triumph over her enemies.—Towards the conclusion of that war, it pleased our sovereign to make a change in his counsels.—From that fatal moment, the affairs of the British empire began to fall into confusion, and gradually sliding from the summit of glorious prosperity, to which they had been advanced by the virtues and abilities of one man, are at length distracted by the convulsions, that now shake it to its deepest foundations.—The new ministry finding the brave foes of Britain, though frequently defeated, yet still contending, took up the unfortunate idea of granting them a hasty peace, and of then subduing her faithful friends.

These devoted colonies were judged to be in such a state, as to present victories without bloodshed, and all the easy emoluments of statuteable plunder.—The uninterrupted tenor of their peaceable and respectful behaviour from the beginning of colonization, their dutiful, zealous, and useful services during the war, though so recently and amply acknowledged in the most honourable manner by his majesty, by the late king, and by parliament, could not save them from the meditated innovations.—Parliament was influenced to adopt the pernicious project, and assuming a new power over them, have in the course of eleven years, given such decisive specimens of the spirit and consequences attending this power, as to leave no

doubt concerning the effects of acquiescence under it. They have undertaken to give and grant our money without our consent, though we have ever exercised an exclusive right to dispose of our own property; statutes have been passed for extending the jurisdiction of courts of admiralty, and vice-admiralty beyond their ancient limits; for depriving us of the accustomed and inestimable privilege of trial by jury, in cases affecting both life and property; for suspending the legislature of one of the colonies; for interdicting all commerce to the capital of another; and for altering fundamentally the form of government established by charter, and secured by acts of its own legislature solemnly confirmed by the crown; for exempting the "murderers" of colonists from legal trial, and in effect, from punishment; for erecting in a neighbouring province, acquired by the joint arms of Great-Britain and America, a despotism dangerous to our very existence; and for quartering soldiers upon the colonists in time of profound peace. It has also been resolved in parliament, that colonists charged with committing certain offences, shall be transported to England to be tried.

But why should we enumerate our injuries in detail? By one statute it is declared, that parliament can "of right make laws to bind us in all cases whatsoever." What is to defend us against so enormous, so unlimited a power? Not a single man of those who assume it, is chosen by us; or is subject to our controul or influence; but, on the contrary, they are all of them exempt from the operation of such laws, and an American revenue, if not diverted from the ostensible purposes for which it is raised, would actually lighten their own burdens in proportion, as they increase ours. We saw the misery to which such despotism would reduce us. We for ten years incessantly and ineffectually besieged the throne as supplicants; we reasoned, we remonstrated with parliament, in the most mild and decent language. But administration sensible that we should regard these oppressive measures as freemen ought to do, sent over fleets and armies to enforce them. The indignation of the Americans was roused, it is true; but it was the indignation of a virtuous, loyal, and affectionate people. A Congress of delegates from the United Colonies was assembled at Philadelphia, on the fifth day of last September. We resolved again to offer an humble and dutiful petition to the king, and also addressed our fellow-subjects of Great-Britain. We have pursued every temperate, every respectful measure: we have even proceeded to break off our commercial intercourse with our fellow-subjects, as the last peaceable admonition, that our attachment to no nation upon earth should supplant our attachment to liberty.— This, we flattered ourselves, was the ultimate step of the controversy: but subsequent events have shewn, how vain was this hope of finding moderation in our enemies.

Several threatening expressions against the colonies were inserted in his majesty's speech; our petition, tho' we were told it was a decent one, and that his majesty had been pleased to receive it graciously, and to promise laying it before his parliament, was huddled into both houses among a bundle of American papers, and there neglected. The lords and commons in their address, in the month of February, said, that "a rebellion at that time actually existed within the province of Massachusetts-Bay; and that those concerned in it, had been countenanced and encouraged by unlawful combinations and engagements, entered into by his majesty's subjects in several of the other colonies; and therefore they besought his majesty, that he would take the most effectual measures to inforce due obedience to the laws and authority of the supreme legislature."—Soon after, the commercial intercourse of whole colonies, with foreign countries, and with each other, was cut off by an act of parliament; by another several of them were intirely prohibited from the fisheries in the seas near their coasts, on which they always depended for their sustenance; and large reinforcements of ships and troops were immediately sent over to general Gage.

Fruitless were all the entreaties, arguments, and eloquence of an illustrious band of the most distinguished peers, and commoners, who nobly and stren[u]ously asserted the justice of our cause, to stay, or even to mitigate the heedless fury with which these accumulated and unexampled outrages were hurried on. . . .

. . . General Gage, who in the course of

the last year had taken possession of the town of Boston, in the province of Massachusetts-Bay, . . . on the 19th day of April, sent out from that place a large detachment of his army, who made an unprovoked assault on the inhabitants of the said province, at the town of Lexington, as appears by the affidavits of a great number of persons, some of whom were officers and soldiers of that detachment, murdered eight of the inhabitants, and wounded many others. From thence the troops proceeded in warlike array to the town of Concord, where they set upon another party of the inhabitants of the same province, killing several and wounding more, until compelled to retreat by the country people suddenly assembled to repel this cruel aggression. Hostilities, thus commenced by the British troops, have been since prosecuted by them without regard to faith or reputation.—The inhabitants of Boston being confined within that town by the general their governor, and having, in order to procure their dismission, entered into a treaty with him, it was stipulated that the said inhabitants having deposited their arms with their own magistrates, should have liberty to depart, taking with them their other effects. They accordingly delivered up their arms, but in open violation of honour, in defiance of the obligation of treaties, which even savage nations esteemed sacred, the governor ordered the arms deposited as aforesaid, that they might be preserved for their owners, to be seized by a body of soldiers; detained the greatest part of the inhabitants in the town, and compelled the few who were permitted to retire, to leave their most valuable effects behind. . . .

The General, further emulating his ministerial masters, by a proclamation bearing date on the 12th day of June, after venting the grossest falsehoods and calumnies against the good people of these colonies, proceeds to "declare them all, either by name or description, to be rebels and traitors, to supersede the course of the common law, and instead thereof to publish and order the use and exercise of the law martial."—His troops have butchered our countrymen, have wantonly burnt Charlestown, besides a considerable number of houses in other places; our ships and vessels are seized; the necessary supplies of provisions are intercepted, and he is exerting his utmost power to spread destruction and devastation around him.

We have received certain intelligence, that General Carleton, the Governor of Canada, is instigating the people of that province and the Indians to fall upon us; and we have but too much reason to apprehend, that schemes have been formed to excite domestic enemies against us. In brief, a part of these colonies now feel, and all of them are sure of feeling, as far as the vengeance of administration can inflict them, the complicated calamities of fire, sword, and famine. We are reduced to the alternative of chusing an unconditional submission to the tyranny of irritated ministers, or resistance by force.—The latter is our choice.—We have counted the cost of this contest, and find nothing so dreadful as voluntary slavery. —Honour, justice, and humanity, forbid us tamely to surrender that freedom which we received from our gallant ancestors, and which our innocent posterity have a right to receive from us. We cannot endure the infamy and guilt of resigning succeeding generations to that wretchedness which inevitably awaits them, if we basely entail hereditary bondage upon them.

Our cause is just. Our union is perfect. Our internal resources are great, and, if necessary, foreign assistance is undoubtedly attainable.—We gratefully acknowledge, as signal instances of the Divine favour towards us, that his Providence would not permit us to be called into this severe controversy, until we were grown up to our present strength, had been previously exercised in warlike operation, and possessed of the means of defending ourselves. With hearts fortified with these animating reflections, we most solemnly, before God and the world, declare, that, exerting the utmost energy of those powers, which our beneficent Creator hath graciously bestowed upon us, the arms we have been compelled by our enemies to assume, we will, in defiance of every hazard, with unabating firmness and perseverance, employ for the preservation of our liberties; being with one mind resolved to die freemen rather than to live slaves.

Lest this declaration should disquiet the minds of our friends and fellow-subjects in any part of the empire, we assure them that we mean not to dissolve that union which has so long and so happily subsisted between us, and which we sincerely wish to see restored.—Necessity has not yet driven us into that desperate measure, or induced us to excite any other nation to war against them.—We have not raised armies with ambitious designs of separating from Great-Britain, and establishing independent states. We fight not for glory or for conquest. We exhibit to mankind the remarkable spectacle of a people attacked by unprovoked enemies, without any imputation or even suspicion of offence. They boast of their privileges and civilization, and yet proffer no milder conditions than servitude or death.

In our own native land, in defence of the freedom that is our birth-right, and which we ever enjoyed till the late violation of it—for the protection of our property, acquired solely by the honest industry of our fore-fathers and ourselves, against violence actually offered, we have taken up arms. We shall lay them down when hostilities shall cease on the part of the aggressors, and all danger of their being renewed shall be removed, and not before.

With an humble confidence in the mercies of the supreme and impartial Judge and Ruler of the Universe, we most devoutly implore his divine goodness to protect us happily through this great conflict, to dispose our adversaries to reconciliation on reasonable terms, and thereby to relieve the empire from the calamities of civil war.

By order of Congress
JOHN HANCOCK
President.

62. PROCLAMATION OF REBELLION
August 23, 1775

(Force's *American Archives,* Fourth Series, Vol. III, p. 240)

Despite Lexington and Concord and Bunker Hill, the moderates in the Continental Congress still hoped for a reconciliation. Two days after Bunker Hill, Dickinson, the leader of the moderates, reported a draft for a final petition to the King; this was accepted by Congress July 8, 1775, and Richard Penn was authorized to present it to the King. The news of American resistance, however, determined the King to proclaim a state of rebellion. News of the Proclamation arrived in America October 31. See, R. Frothingham, *Rise of the Republic of the United States*, p. 435 ff.; C. J. Stillé, *Life and Times of John Dickinson*, Vol. I; J. Fiske, *The American Revolution*, Vol. I, ch. v.

A PROCLAMATION BY THE KING FOR SUP-
PRESSING REBELLION AND SEDITION
GEORGE R.

Whereas many of our subjects in divers parts of our Colonies and Plantations in *North America,* misled by dangerous and ill designing men, and forgetting the allegiance which they owe to the power that has protected and supported them; after various disorderly acts committed in disturbance of the publick peace, to the obstruction of lawful commerce, and to the oppression of our loyal subjects carrying on the same; have at length proceeded to open and avowed rebellion, by arraying themselves in a hostile manner, to withstand the execution of the law, and traitorously preparing, ordering and levying war against us: And whereas, there is reason to apprehend that such rebellion hath been much promoted and encouraged by the traitorous correspondence, counsels and comfort of divers wicked and desperate persons within this realm: To the end therefore, that none of our subjects may neglect or violate their duty through ignorance thereof, or through any doubt of the

protection which the law will afford to their loyalty and zeal, we have thought fit, by and with the advice of our Privy Council, to issue our Royal Proclamation, hereby declaring, that not only all our Officers, civil and military, are obliged to exert their utmost endeavours to suppress such rebellion, and to bring the traitors to justice, but that all our subjects of this Realm, and the dominions thereunto belonging, are bound by law to be aiding and assisting in the suppression of such rebellion, and to disclose and make known all traitorous conspiracies and attempts against us, our crown and dignity; and we do accordingly strictly charge and command all our Officers, as well civil as military, and all others our obedient and loyal subjects, to use their utmost endeavours to withstand and suppress such rebellion, and to disclose and make known all treasons and traitorous conspiracies which they shall know to be against us, our crown and dignity; and for that purpose, that they transmit to one of our principal Secretaries of State, or other proper officer, due and full information of all persons who shall be found carrying on correspondence with, or in any manner or degree aiding or abetting the persons now in open arms and rebellion against our Government, within any of our Colonies and Plantations in *North America,* in order to bring to condign punishment the authors, prepetrators, and abetters of such traitorous designs.

Given at our Court at *St. James's* the twenty-third day of *August,* one thousand seven hundred and seventy-five, in the fifteenth year of our reign.

GOD *save the* KING.

63. THE MOVEMENT FOR INDEPENDENCE

Instructions from the Town of Malden, Massachusetts, for a Declaration
of Independence
May 27, 1776

(H. Niles, ed. *Principles and Acts of the Revolution,* 1822 ed. p. 156–7)

On May 9 the Massachusetts House of Representatives, then sitting at Watertown, appointed a committee to bring in a resolve that the Towns of the colony instruct their representatives with respect to independence. The following day the House resolved that "The Inhabitants of each Town, in this Colony, ought in full Meeting warned for that Purpose, to advise the Person or Persons who shall be

chosen to Represent them in the next General Court, whether if the honorable Congress should, for the Safety of the said Colonies, declare them Independent of the Kingdom of Great-Britain, they the said Inhabitants will solemnly engage with their Lives and Fortunes to Support the Congress in the Measure." The instructions from Malden are typical of many voted by the towns of Massachusetts. See A. B.

Hart, ed. *Commonwealth History of Massachusetts*, Vol. III, p. 93 ff.; K. Colegrove, "New England Town Mandates", Colonial Society of Massachusetts, *Publications*, Vol. XXI, p. 411 ff.

At a legal meeting of the inhabitants of the town of Malden, (Mass.), May 27, 1776, it was voted unanimously that the following instructions be given to their representative, viz. to Mr Ezra Sargeant.

Sir—A resolution of the hon. house of representatives, calling upon the several towns in this colony to express their minds in respect to the important question of American independence, is the occasion of our now instructing you. The time was, sir, when we loved the king and the people of Great Britain with an affection truly filial; we felt ourselves interested in their glory; we shared in their joys and sorrows; we cheerfully poured the fruit of all our labours into the lap of our mother country, and without reluctance expended our blood and our treasure in their cause.

These were our sentiments toward Great Britain while she continued to act the part of a parent state; we felt ourselves happy in our connection with her, nor wished it to be dissolved; but our sentiments are altered, it is now the ardent wish of our soul that America may become a free and independent state.

A sense of unprovoked injuries will arouse the resentment of the most peaceful. Such injuries these colonies have received from Britain. Unjustifiable claims have been made by the king and his minions to tax us without our consent; these claims have been prosecuted in a manner cruel and unjust to the highest degree. The frantic policy of administration hath induced them to send fleets and armies to America; that, by depriving us of our trade, and cutting the throats of our brethren, they might awe us into submission, and erect a system of despotism in America, which should so far enlarge the influence of the crown as to enable it to rivet their shackles upon the people of Great Britain.

This plan was brought to a crisis upon the ever memorable nineteenth of April. We remember the fatal day! the expiring groans of our countrymen yet vibrate on our ears! and we now behold the flames of their peaceful dwellings ascending to Heaven! we hear their blood crying to us from the ground for vengeance! charging us, as we value the peace of their names, to have no further connection with—,who can unfeelingly hear of the slaughter of—, and composedly sleep with their blood upon his soul. The manner in which the war has been prosecuted hath confirmed us in these sentiments; piracy and murder, robbery and breach of faith, have been conspicuous in the conduct of the king's troops: defenceless towns have been attacked and destroyed: the ruins of Charlestown, which are daily in our view, daily reminds of this: the cries of the widow and the orphan demand our attention; they demand that the hand of pity should wipe the tear from their eye, and that the sword of their country should avenge their wrongs. We long entertained hope that the spirit of the British nation would once more induce them to assert their own and our rights, and bring to condign punishment the elevated villains who have trampled upon the sacred rights of men and affronted the majesty of the people. We hoped in vain; they have lost their love to freedom, they have lost their spirit of just resentment; we therefore renounce with disdain our connexion with a kingdom of slaves; we bid a final adieu to Britain.

Could an accommodation now be effected, we have reason to think that it would be fatal to the liberties of America; we should soon catch the contagion of venality and dissipation, which hath Britains to lawless domination. Were we placed in the situation we were in 1763: were the powers of appointing to offices, and commanding the militia, in the hands of governors, our arts, trade and manufactures, would be cramped; nay, more than this, the life of every man who has been active in the cause of his country would be endangered.

For these reasons, as well as many others which might be produced, we are confirmed in the opinion, that the present age would be deficient in their duty to God, their posterity and themselves, if they do not establish an American republic. This is the only form of government which we wish to see established; for we can never be willingly subject to any other King than he who, being possessed of infinite wisdom, goodness and rectitude, is alone fit to possess unlimited power.

We have freely spoken our sentiments upon this important subject, but we mean not to dictate; we have unbounded confidence in the wisdom and uprightness of the continental congress: with pleasure we recollect that this affair is under their direction; and we now instruct you, sir, to give them the strongest assurance, that, if they should declare America to be a free and independent republic, your constituents will support and defend the measure, to the last drop of their blood, and the last farthing of their treasure.

64. MECKLENBURG COUNTY RESOLUTIONS
May 20, 1775

(Documents Illustrative of the Formation of the Union of the American States, p. 6 ff.)

These resolutions, adopted in Charlotte Town, Mecklenburg County, North Carolina, were entrusted to the North Carolina delegation to the Continental Congress, but never presented. In 1819 an account of these resolutions was published, embellished with phrases taken from the Declaration of Independence; this spurious account gave rise to .the persistent myth of the Mecklenburg "Declaration of Independence." Subsequent investigation indicated that no such "declaration" had been adopted at the time, and established the real character of the resolutions. See, W. H. Hoyt, *Mecklenberg Declaration of Independence;* E. W. Sikes, *Transition of North Carolina from Colony to Commonwealth;* J. Fiske, *The American Revolution,* Vol. I, p. 150 ff.

This day the Committee met, and passed the following

RESOLVES

Whereas by an address presented to his Majesty by both Houses of Parliament in February last, the American Colonies are declared to be in a State of actual Rebellion, we conceive that all Laws and Commissions confirmed by, or derived from the Authority of the King or Parliament, are annulled and vacated, and the former civil Constitution of these Colonies for the present wholly suspended. To provide in some degree for the Exigencies of the County in the present alarming Period, we deem it proper and necessary to pass the following Resolves, *viz.*

1. That all Commissions, civil and military, heretofore granted by the Crown, to be exercised in these Colonies, are null and void, and the Constitution of each particular Colony wholly suspended.
2. That the Provincial Congress of each Province, under the Direction of the Great Continental Congress, is invested with all legislative and executive Powers within their respective Provinces; and that no other Legislative or Executive does or can exist, at this Time, in any of these Colonies.
3. As all former Laws are now suspended in this Province, and the Congress have not yet provided others, we judge it necessary, for the better Preservation of good Order, to form certain Rules and Regulations for the internal Government of this County, until Laws shall be provided for us by the Congress.
4. That the Inhabitants of this County do meet on a certain Day appointed by this Committee, and having formed themselves into nine Companies, to *wit,* eight for the County and one for the Town of *Charlotte,* do choose a Colonel and other military Officers, who shall hold and exercise their several Powers by Virtue of this Choice, and independent of *Great-Britain,* and former Constitution of this Province.
5. That for the better Preservation of the Peace and Administration of Justice, each of these Companies do choose from their own Body two discreet Freeholders, who shall be impowered each by himself, and singly, to decide and determine all Matters of Controversy arising within the said Company under the Sum of Twenty Shillings, and jointly and together all Controversies under the Sum of Forty Shillings, yet so as their Decisions may admit of Appeals to the Convention of the Select Men of the whole County; and also, that any one of these shall have Power to examine, and commit to Confinement, Persons accused of Petit Larceny.

6. That those two Select Men, thus chosen, do, jointly and together, choose from the Body of their particular Company two Persons, properly qualified to serve as Constables, who may assist them in the Execution of their Office.

7. That upon the Complaint of any Person to either of these Select Men, he do issue his Warrant, directed to the Constable, commanding him to bring the Aggressor before him or them to answer the said Complaint.

8. That these eighteen Select Men, thus appointed, to meet every third Tuesday in January, April, July, and October, at the Courthouse in *Charlotte*, to hear and determine all Matters of Controversy for Sums exceeding Forty Shillings; also Appeals: and in Cases of Felony, to commit the Person or Persons convicted thereof to close Confinement, until the Provincial Congress shall provide and establish Laws and Modes of Proceeding in all such Cases.

9. That these Eighteen Select Men, thus convened, do choose a Clerk to record the Transactions of said Convention; and that the said Clerk, upon the Application of any Persons or Persons aggrieved, do issue his Warrant to one of the Constables, to summons and warn said Offender to appear before the Convention at their next sitting, to answer the aforesaid Complaint.

10. That any Person making complaint under Oath to the Clerk, or any Member of the Convention, that he has reason to suspect that any Person or Persons indebted to him in a Sum above Forty Shillings, do intend clandestinely to withdraw from the County without paying such Debt; the Clerk, or such Member, shall issue his Warrant to the Constable, commanding him to take the said Person or Persons into safe Custody, until the next sitting of the Convention. . . .

12. That all Receivers and Collectors of Quitrents, Public and County Taxes, do pay the same into the Hands of the Chairman of this Committee, to be by them disbursed as the public Exigencies may require. And that such Receivers and Collectors proceed no farther in their Office until they be approved of by, and have given to this Committee good and sufficient Security for a faithful Return of such Monies when collected. . . .

14. That all these Officers hold their Commissions during the Pleasure of their respective Constituents.

15. That this Committee will sustain all Damages that may ever hereafter accrue to all or any of these Officers thus appointed, and thus acting, on Account of their Obedience and Conformity to these Resolves.

16. That whatever person shall hereafter receive a Commission from the Crown, or attempt to exercise any such Commission heretofore received, shall be deemed an Enemy to his Country; and upon Information being made to the Captain of the Company where he resides, the said Captain shall cause him to be apprehended, and conveyed before the two Select Men of the said Company, who upon Proof of the Fact shall commit him the said Offender, into safe Custody, until the next sitting of the Convention who shall deal with him as Prudence may direct.

17. That any Person refusing to yield Obedience to the above Resolves shall be deemed equally criminal and liable to the same Punishments as the Offenders above last mentioned.

18. That these Resolves be in full Force and Virtue, until Instructions from the General Congress of this Province, regulating the Jurisprudence of this Province, shall provide otherwise, or the legislative body of *Great-Britain* resign its unjust and arbitrary Pretentions with Respect to America.

19. That the several Militia Companies in this county do provide themselves with proper Arms and Accoutrements, and hold themselves in Readiness to execute the commands and Directions of the Provincial Congress, and of this committee.

20. That this committee do appoint Colonel Thomas Polk, and Doctor Joseph Kennedy, to purchase 300 lb. of Powder, 600 lb. of Lead, and 1000 Flints, and deposit the same in some safe place, hereafter to be appointed by the committee.

Signed by Order of the Committee.

EPH. BREVARD, Clerk of the Committee.

65. RESOLUTION FOR INDEPENDENCE
June 7, 1776

(Journals of the Continental Congress, ed. by W. C. Ford, Vol. V, p. 425)

These resolutions were introduced by Richard Henry Lee of Virginia and seconded by John Adams. The first resolution was not voted until July 2; the others were acted upon later. See, R. Frothingham, *Rise of the Republic of the United States,* p. 513 ff.

RESOLVED, That these United Colonies are, and of right ought to be, free and independent States, that they are absolved from all allegiance to the British Crown, and that all political connection between them and the State of Great Britain is, and ought to be totally dissolved.

That it is expedient forthwith to take the most effectual measures for forming foreign Alliances.

That a plan of confederation be prepared and transmitted to the respective Colonies for their consideration and approbation.

66. THE DECLARATION OF INDEPENDENCE
July 4, 1776

(F. N. Thorpe, ed. *Federal and State Constitutions,* Vol. I, p. 3 ff. The text is taken from the version in the Revised Statutes of the United States, 1878 ed., and has been collated with the facsimile of the original as printed in the original Journal of the old Congress.)

On June 7, 1776, Richard Henry Lee of Virginia introduced three resolutions one of which stated that the "colonies are, and of right ought to be, free and independent States." On the 10th a committee was appointed to prepare a declaration of independence; the committee consisted of Jefferson, John Adams, Franklin, Sherman and R. R. Livingston. This committee brought in its draft on the 28th of June, and on the 2nd of July a resolution declaring independence was adopted. July 4 the Declaration of Independence was agreed to, engrossed, signed by Hancock, and sent to the legislatures of the States. The engrossed copy of the Declaration was signed by all but one signer on August 2. On the Declaration, see C. L. Becker, *The Declaration of Independence,* esp. ch. v with its analysis of Jefferson's draft; H. Friedenwald, *The Declaration of Independence;* J. H. Hazelton, *Declaration of Independence;* J. Sanderson, *Lives of the Signers to the Declaration;* R. Frothingham, *Rise of the Republic,* ch. xi.; C. H. Van Tyne, *The War of Independence, American Phase.*

In Congress, July 4, 1776,

THE UNANIMOUS DECLARATION OF THE THIRTEEN UNITED STATES OF AMERICA,

When in the Course of human events, it becomes necessary for one people to dissolve the political bands which have connected them with another, and to assume among the Powers of the earth, the separate and equal station to which the Laws of Nature and of Nature's God entitle them, a decent respect to the opinions of mankind requires that they should declare the causes which impel them to the separation.

We hold these truths to be self-evident, that all men are created equal, that they are endowed by their Creator with certain unalienable Rights, that among these are Life, Liberty and the pursuit of Happiness. That to secure these rights, Governments are instituted among Men, deriving their just powers from the consent of the governed, That whenever any Form of Government becomes destructive of these ends, it is the Right of the People to alter or to abolish it, and to institute new Government, laying its foundation on such principles and organizing its powers in such form, as to them shall seem most likely to effect their Safety and Happiness. Prudence, indeed, will dictate that Governments long established should not be changed for light and transient causes; and accordingly all experience hath shown, that mankind are more disposed to suffer, while evils are sufferable, than to right themselves by abolishing the forms to which they are accustomed. But when a long train of abuses and usurpations, pursuing invariably the same Object evinces a design to reduce them under absolute Despotism, it is their right, it is their duty, to throw off such Government, and to provide new Guards for their future security.—Such has been the patient sufferance of these Colonies; and such is now the necessity which constrains them to alter their former Systems of Government. The history of the present King of Great Britain is a history of repeated injuries and usurpations, all having in direct object the establishment of an absolute Tyranny over these States. To prove this, let Facts be submitted to a candid world.

He has refused his Assent to Laws, the most wholesome and necessary for the public good.

He has forbidden his Governors to pass Laws of immediate and pressing importance, unless suspended in their operation till his Assent should be obtained; and when so suspended, he has utterly neglected to attend to them.

He has refused to pass other Laws for the accommodation of large districts of people, unless those people would relinquish the right of Representation in the Legislature, a right inestimable to them and formidable to tyrants only.

He has called together legislative bodies at places unusual, uncomfortable, and distant from the depository of their Public Records, for the sole purpose of fatiguing them into compliance with his measures.

He has dissolved Representative Houses repeatedly, for opposing with manly firmness his invasions on the rights of the people.

He has refused for a long time, after such dissolutions, to cause others to be elected; whereby the Legislative Powers, incapable of Annihilation, have returned to the People at large for their exercise; the State remaining in the mean time exposed to all the dangers of invasion from without, and convulsions within.

He has endeavoured to prevent the population of these States; for that purpose obstructing the Laws of Naturalization of Foreigners; refusing to pass others to encourage their migration hither, and raising the conditions of new Appropriations of Lands.

He has obstructed the Administration of Justice, by refusing his Assent to Laws for establishing Judiciary Powers.

He has made Judges dependent on his Will alone, for the tenure of their offices, and the amount and payment of their salaries.

He has erected a multitude of New Offices, and sent hither swarms of Officers to harass our People, and eat out their substance.

He has kept among us, in times of peace, Standing Armies without the Consent of our legislature.

He has affected to render the Military independent of and superior to the Civil Power.

He has combined with others to subject us to a jurisdiction foreign to our constitution, and unacknowledged by our laws; giving his Assent to their acts of pretended legislation:

For quartering large bodies of armed troops among us:

For protecting them, by a mock Trial, from Punishment for any Murders which they should commit on the Inhabitants of these States:

For cutting off our Trade with all parts of the world:

For imposing taxes on us without our Consent:

For depriving us in many cases, of the benefits of Trial by Jury:

For transporting us beyond Seas to be tried for pretended offences:

For abolishing the free System of English Laws in a neighbouring Province, establishing therein an Arbitrary government, and enlarging its Boundaries so as to render it at once an example and fit instrument for introducing the same absolute rule into these Colonies:

For taking away our Charters, abolishing our most valuable Laws, and altering fundamentally the Forms of our Governments:

For suspending our own Legislature, and declaring themselves invested with Power to legislate for us in all cases whatsoever.

He has abdicated Government here, by declaring us out of his Protection and waging War against us.

He has plundered our seas, ravaged our Coasts, burnt our towns, and destroyed the lives of our people.

He is at this time transporting large armies of foreign mercenaries to compleat the works of death, desolation and tyranny, already begun with circumstances of Cruelty & perfidy scarcely paralleled in the most barbarous ages, and totally unworthy the Head of a civilized nation.

He has constrained our fellow Citizens taken Captive on the high Seas to bear Arms against their Country, to become the executioners of their friends and Brethren, or to fall themselves by their Hands.

He has excited domestic insurrections amongst us, and has endeavoured to bring on the inhabitants of our frontiers, the merciless Indian Savages, whose known rule of warfare, is an undistinguished destruction of all ages, sexes and conditions.

In every stage of these Oppressions We have Petitioned for Redress in the most humble terms: Our repeated Petitions have been answered only by repeated injury. A Prince, whose character is thus marked by every act which may define a Tyrant, is unfit to be the ruler of a free People.

Nor have We been wanting in attention to our Brittish brethren. We have warned them from time to time of attempts by their legislature to extend an unwarrantable jurisdiction over us. We have reminded them of the circumstances of our emigration and settlement here. We have appealed to their native justice and magnanimity, and we have conjured them by the ties of our common kindred to disavow these usurpations, which, would inevitably interrupt our connections and correspondence. They too have been deaf to the voice of justice and of consanguinity. We must, therefore, acquiesce in the necessity, which denounces our Separation, and hold them, as we hold the rest of mankind, Enemies in War, in Peace Friends.

We, therefore, the Representatives of the united States of America, in General Congress, Assembled, appealing to the Supreme Judge of the world for the rectitude of our intentions, do, in the Name, and by Authority of the good People of these Colonies, solemnly publish and declare, That these United Colonies are, and of Right ought to be Free and Independent States; that they are Absolved from all Allegiance to the British Crown, and that all political connection between them and the State of Great Britain, is and ought to be totally dissolved; and that as Free and Independent States, they have full Power to levy War, conclude Peace, contract Alliances, establish Commerce, and to do all other Acts and Things which Independent States may of right do. And for the support of this Declaration, with a firm reliance on the Protection of Divine Providence, we mutually pledge to each other our Lives, our Fortunes and our sacred Honor.

JOHN HANCOCK.

New Hampshire
JOSIAH BARTLETT,
WM. WHIPPLE,
MATTHEW THORNTON.

Massachusetts-Bay
SAML. ADAMS,
JOHN ADAMS,
ROBT. TREAT PAINE,
ELBRIDGE GERRY.

Rhode Island
STEP. HOPKINS,
WILLIAM ELLERY.

Connecticut
ROGER SHERMAN,
SAM'EL HUNTINGTON,
WM. WILLIAMS,
OLIVER WOLCOTT.

New York
WM. FLOYD,
PHIL. LIVINGSTON,
FRANS. LEWIS,
LEWIS MORRIS.

Pennsylvania
ROBT. MORRIS,
BENJAMIN RUSH,
BENJA. FRANKLIN,
JOHN MORTON,
GEO. CLYMER,
JAS. SMITH,
GEO. TAYLOR,
JAMES WILSON,
GEO. ROSS.

Delaware
CAESAR RODNEY,
GEO. READ,
THO. M'KEAN.

Georgia
BUTTON GWINNETT,
LYMAN HALL,
GEO. WALTON.

Maryland
SAMUEL CHASE,
WM. PACA,
THOS. STONE,
CHARLES CARROLL of Carrollton.

Virginia
GEORGE WYTHE,
RICHARD HENRY LEE,
TH. JEFFERSON,
BENJA. HARRISON,
THS. NELSON, JR.,
FRANCIS LIGHTFOOT LEE,
CARTER BRAXTON.

North Carolina
WM. HOOPER,
JOSEPH HEWES,
JOHN PENN.

South Carolina
EDWARD RUTLEDGE,
THOS. HEYWARD, JUNR.,
THOMAS LYNCH, JUNR.,
ARTHUR MIDDLETON.

New Jersey
RICHD. STOCKTON,
JNO. WITHERSPOON,
FRAS. HOPKINSON,
JOHN HART,
ABRA. CLARK.

67. THE VIRGINIA BILL OF RIGHTS
June 12, 1776

(Poore, ed. *The Federal and State Constitutions,* Part. II, p. 1908–9)

This most famous of the Declarations of Rights of the original state constitutions was drafted by George Mason and adopted with slight changes and two additions, by the Virginia Convention of 1776. It exerted a wide influence not only in this country but in France. The article on religious freedom was drafted by Patrick Henry. See, K. Rowland, *Life of George Mason,* 3 Vols.; H. B. Grigsby, *The Virginia Convention of 1776;* G. Jellinek, *The Declaration of the Rights of Man;* B. Faÿ, *Revolutionary Spirit in France and America,* p. 263 ff.

A declaration of rights made by the representatives of the good people of Virginia, assembled in full and free convention; which rights do pertain to them and their posterity, as the basis and foundation of government.

1. That all men are by nature equally free and independent, and have certain inherent rights, of which, when they enter into a state of society, they cannot by any compact deprive or divest their posterity; namely, the enjoyment of life and liberty, with the means of acquiring and possessing property, and pursuing and obtaining happiness and safety.

2. That all power is vested in, and consequently derived from, the people; that magis-

trates are their trustees and servants, and at all times amenable to them.

3. That government is, or ought to be instituted for the common benefit, protection, and security of the people, nation, or community; of all the various modes and forms of government, that is best which is capable of producing the greatest degree of happiness and safety, and is most effectually secured against the danger of maladministration; and that when any government shall be found inadequate or contrary to these purposes, a majority of the community hath an indubitable, unalienable and indefeasible right to reform, alter or abolish it, in such manner as shall be judged most conducive to the public weal.

4. That no man, or set of men, are entitled to exclusive or separate emoluments or privileges from the community, but in consideration of publick services; which, not being descendible, neither ought the offices of magistrate, legislator or judge to be hereditary.

5. That the legislative and executive powers of the state should be separate and distinct from the judiciary; and that the members of the two first may be restrained from oppression, by feeling and participating the

burthens of the people, they should, at fixed periods, be reduced to a private station, return into that body from which they were originally taken, and the vacancies be supplied by frequent, certain, and regular elections, in which all, or any part of the former members to be again eligible or ineligible, as the laws shall direct.

6. That elections of members to serve as representatives of the people in assembly, ought to be free; and that all men having sufficient evidence of permanent common interest with, and attachment to the community, have the right of suffrage, and cannot be taxed or deprived of their property for publick uses, without their own consent, or that of their representatives so elected, nor bound by any law to which they have not, in like manner, assented for the public good.

7. That all power of suspending laws, or the execution of laws, by any authority without consent of the representatives of the people, is injurious to their rights, and ought not to be exercised.

8. That in all capital or criminal prosecutions a man hath a right to demand the cause and nature of his accusation, to be confronted with the accusers and witnesses, to call for evidence in his favour, and to a speedy trial by an impartial jury of his vicinage, without whose unanimous consent he cannot be found guilty; nor can he be compelled to give evidence against himself; that no man be deprived of his liberty, except by the law of the land or the judgment of his peers.

9. That excessive bail ought not to be required, nor excessive fines imposed, nor cruel and unusual punishments inflicted.

10. That general warrants, whereby an officer or messenger may be commanded to search suspected places without evidence of a fact committed, or to seize any person or

persons not named, or whose offence is not particularly described and supported by evidence, are grievous and oppressive, and ought not to be granted.

11. That in controversies respecting property, and in suits between man and man, the ancient trial by jury is preferable to any other, and ought to be held sacred.

12. That the freedom of the press is one of the great bulwarks of liberty, and can never be restrained but by despotick governments.

13. That a well-regulated militia, composed of the body of the people trained to arms, is the proper, natural and safe defence of a free state; that standing armies in time of peace should be avoided as dangerous to liberty; and that in all cases the military should be under strict subordination to, and governed by, the civil power.

14. That the people have a right to uniform government; and, therefore, that no government separate from, or independent of the government of Virginia, ought to be erected or established within the limits thereof.

15. That no free government, or the blessings of liberty, can be preserved to any people, but by a firm adherence to justice, moderation, temperance, frugality and virtue, and by frequent recurrence to fundamental principles.

16. That religion, or the duty which we owe to our Creator, and the manner of discharging it, can be directed only by reason and conviction, not by force or violence; and therefore all men are equally entitled to the free exercise of religion, according to the dictates of conscience; and that it is the mutual duty of all to practise Christian forbearance, love, and charity towards each other.

68. THE CONCORD TOWN MEETING DEMANDS A CONSTITUTIONAL CONVENTION

Resolutions of the Concord Town Meeting
October 21, 1776

(Facsimile in Massachusetts, *Manual of the Constitutional Convention, 1917*)

As early as May 10, 1776 Congress had passed a resolution advising the colonies to form new governments "such as shall best conduce to the happiness and safety of their constituents." The actual transformation of Colony into Commonwealth, however, was a task that challenged the talents of the wisest statesmen. How could governments be established in harmony with the principles of the Revolution; how could the theory that government originates with the people be transformed into reality? The first suggestion of the method eventually perfected by Americans—the constitutional convention—came from the town of Concord. The advice of the Concord Town Meeting, however, was not followed in the construction of the first Massachusetts constitution. Not until 1779 did Massachusetts work out a system in harmony with the Concord Resolutions. See, S. E. Morison, "History of the Constitution of Massachusetts" in *Manual of the Constitutional Convention of 1917.*

At a meeting of the Inhabitants of the Town of Concord being free & twenty one years of age and upward, met by adjournment on the twenty first Day of october 1776 to take into Consideration a Resolve of the Honourable house of Representatives of this State on the 17th of September Last the Town Resolved as followes—

Resolve 1st: That this State being at Present destitute of a Properly established form of Government, it is absolutely necessary that one should be emmediatly formed and established.

Resolved 2. That the Supreme Legislative, either in their Proper Capacity or in Joint Committee, are by no means a body proper to form & Establish a Constitution or form of Government; for Reasons following. first Because we Conceive that a Constitution in its Proper Idea intends a System of Principles Established to Secure the Subject in the Possession & enjoyment of their Rights

& Priviliges, against any Encroachments of the Governing Part. 2—Because the Same Body that forms a Constitution have of Consequence a power to alter it. 3 because a Constitution alterable by the Supreme Legislative is no Security at all to the Subject against any Encroachment of the Governing part on any, or on all of their Rights and priviliges.

Resolved 3d. That it appears to this Town highly necessary & Expedient that a Convention, or Congress be immediately Chosen, to form & establish a Constitution, by the inhabitants of the Respective Towns in this State, being free & of twenty-one years of age and upward, in Proportion as the Representatives of this State formerly were Chosen: the Convention or Congress not to Consist of a greater number than the house of assembly of this State heretofore might Consist of, Except that each Town & District shall have the Liberty to Send one Representative, or otherwise as Shall appear meet to the Inhabitants of this State in General.

Resolve 4th. that when the Convention or Congress have formed a Constitution they adjourn for a Short time and Publish their Proposed Constitution for the Inspection and Remarks of the Inhabitants of this State.

Resolved 5ly. that the honourable house of assembly of this State be Desired to Recommend it to the Inhabitants of the State to Proceed to Chuse a Convention or Congress for the Purpas abovesaid as soon as Possable.

CONCORD, October the 22d, 1776.

69. TREATY OF ALLIANCE WITH FRANCE
February 6, 1778

(Malloy, ed. *Treaties, Conventions, etc.*, Vol. I, p. 479 ff.)

This was one of two treaties concluded by the American Commissioners, Franklin, Deane, and Lee; the other was a Treaty of Amity and Commerce. The Treaty of Alliance was not warranted by the instructions from Congress, but Congress ratified it May 4, 1778. This was the first treaty of alliance ever made by the United States. The literature on the American diplomatic negotiations with France and the Treaty of Alliance is voluminous: see, F. Wharton, *Diplomatic Correspondence of the*

American Revolution, Vol. I; W. H. Trescot, *Diplomacy of the American Revolution;* E. S. Corwin, *French Policy and the American Alliance of 1778;* J. B. Perkins, *France in the American Revolution;* E. E. Hale, *Franklin in France;* and the monumental work of H. Doniol, *Historie de la Participation de la France à l'Établissement des États-Unis d'Amérique,* 5 Vols.

ART. I.—If war should break out between France and Great Britain during the continuance of the present war between the United States and England, His Majesty and the said United States shall make it a common cause and aid each other mutually with their good offices, their counsels and their forces, according to the exigence of conjunctures, as becomes good and faithful allies.

ART. II.—The essential and direct end of the present defensive alliance is to maintain effectually the liberty, sovereignty and independence absolute and unlimited, of the said United States, as well in matters of government as of commerce.

ART. III.—The two contracting parties shall each on its own part, and in the manner it may judge most proper, make all the efforts in its power against their common enemy, in order to attain the end proposed.

ART. IV.—The contracting parties agree that in case either of them should form any particular enterprise in which the concurrence of the other may be desired, the party whose concurrence is desired, shall readily, and with good faith, join to act in concert for that purpose, as far as circumstances and its own particular situation will permit; and in that case, they shall regulate, by a particular convention, the quantity and kind of succour to be furnished, and the time and manner of its being brought into action, as well as the advantages which are to be its compensation.

ART. V.—If the United States should think fit to attempt the reduction of the British power, remaining in the northern parts of America, or the islands of Bermudas, those countries or islands, in case of success, shall be confederated with or dependent upon the said United States.

ART. VI.—The Most Christian King renounces forever the possession of the islands of Bermudas, as well as of any part of the continent of North America, which before the treaty of Paris in 1763, or in virtue of that treaty, were acknowledged to belong to the Crown of Great Britain, or to the United States, heretofore called British Colonies, or which are at this time, or have lately been under the power of the King and Crown of Great Britain.

ART. VII.—If His Most Christian Majesty shall think proper to attack any of the islands situated in the Gulph of Mexico, or near that Gulph, which are at present under the power of Great Britain, all the said isles, in case of success, shall appertain to the Crown of France.

ART. VIII.—Neither of the two parties shall conclude either truce or peace with Great Britain without the formal consent of the other first obtained; and they mutually engage not to lay down their arms until the independence of the United States shall have been formally or tacitly assured by the treaty or treaties that shall terminate the war.

ART. IX.—The contracting parties declare, that being resolved to fulfil each on its own part the clauses and conditions of the present treaty of alliance, according to its own power and circumstances, there shall be no afterclaim of compensation on one side or the other, whatever may be the event of the war.

ART. X.—The Most Christian King and the United States agree to invite or admit other powers who may have received injuries from England, to make common cause with them, and to accede to the present alliance, under such conditions as shall be freely agreed to and settled between all the parties.

ART. XI.—The two parties guarantee mutually from the present time and forever against all other powers, to wit: The United States to His Most Christian Majesty, the present possessions of the Crown of France in America, as well as those which it may acquire by the future treaty of peace: And His Most Christian Majesty guarantees on his part to the United States their liberty, sovereignty and independence, absolute and unlimited, as well in matters of government as commerce, and also their possessions, and the additions or conquests that their confederation may obtain during the war, from any of the dominions now, or heretofore possessed by Great Britain in North America, conformable to the 5th and 6th articles above written, the whole as their possessions shall be fixed and assured to the said States, at the moment of the cessation of their present war with England.

ART. XII.—In order to fix more precisely the sense and application of the preceding article, the contracting parties declare, that in case of a rupture between France and England the reciprocal guarantee declared in the said article shall have its full force and effect the moment such war shall break out; and if such rupture shall not take place, the mutual obligations of the said guarantee shall not commence until the moment of the cessation of the present war between the United States and England shall have ascertained their possessions. . . .

Done at Paris, this sixth day of February, one thousand seven hundred and seventy-eight.

70. MASSACHUSETTS BILL OF RIGHTS
1780

(Poore, ed. The Federal and State Constitutions, Part. I, p. 956 ff.)

The Constitution of Massachusetts of 1778 had contained no Bill of Rights; when submitted to the vote of the freemen it was defeated by an overwhelming majority. John Adams was the chief architect of the constitution of 1780. He was responsible for the whole of the Bill of Rights with the exception of the article on Religious Freedom. See S. E. Morison in *Manual of the Constitutional Convention of 1917;* A. Nevins, *American States During and After the Revolution,* ch. v; C. F. Adams, *Life of John Adams,* ch. vi. On the Revolutionary Bills of Rights, see Doc. No. 67.

The end of the institution, maintenance, and administration of government, is to secure the existence of the body-politic, to protect it, and to furnish the individuals who compose it with the power of enjoying in safety and tranquillity their natural rights, and the blessings of life: and whenever these great objects are not obtained, the people have a right to alter the government, and to take measures necessary for their safety, prosperity, and happiness.

The body-politic is formed by a voluntary association of individuals; it is a social compact by which the whole people covenants with each citizen and each citizen with the whole people that all shall be governed by certain laws for the common good. It is the duty of the people, therefore, in framing a constitution of government, to provide for an equitable mode of making laws, as well as for an impartial interpretation and a faithful execution of them; that every man may, at all times, find his security in them.

We, therefore, the people of Massachusetts, acknowledging, with grateful hearts, the goodness of the great Legislator of the universe, in affording us, in the course of His Providence, an opportunity, deliberately and peaceably, without fraud, violence, or surprise, of entering into an original, explicit, and solemn compact with each other;

and of forming a new constitution of civil government, for ourselves and posterity; and devoutly imploring His direction in so interesting a design, do agree upon, ordain, and establish, the following Declaration of Rights, and Frame of Government, as the Constitution of the Commonwealth of Massachusetts.

PART THE FIRST

A DECLARATION OF THE RIGHTS OF THE INHABITANTS OF THE COMMONWEALTH OF MASSACHUSETTS

ARTICLE I. All men are born free and equal, and have certain natural, essential, and unalienable rights; among which may be reckoned the right of enjoying and defending their lives and liberties; that of acquiring, possessing, and protecting property; in fine, that of seeking and obtaining their safety and happiness.

II. It is the right as well as the duty of all men in society, publicly, and at stated seasons, to worship the Supreme Being, the great Creator and Preserver of the universe. And no subject shall be hurt, molested, or restrained, in his person, liberty, or estate, for worshipping God in the manner and season most agreeable to the dictates of his own conscience; or for his religious profession or sentiments; provided he doth not disturb the public peace, or obstruct others in their religious worship. . . .

As the happiness of a people and the good order and preservation of civil government essentially depend upon piety, religion, and morality, and as these cannot be generally diffused through a community but by the institution of the public worship of God and of public instructions, in piety, religion, and morality. Therefore to promote their happiness and secure the good order and preservation of their government, the people of this commonwealth have a right to invest their legislature with power to authorize and require, and the legislature shall from time to time authorize and require, the several towns . . . and other bodies—politic or religious societies, to make suitable provision, at their own expense, for the institution of the public worship of God and the support and maintenance of public Protestant teachers of piety, religion, and morality. . . .

And the people of this commonwealth . . . do invest their legislature with authority to enjoin upon all the subjects an attendance upon the instructions of the public teachers aforesaid. . . .

And every denomination of Christians, demeaning themselves peaceably and as good subjects of the commonwealth, shall be equally under the protection of the law; and no subordination of any one sect or denomination to another shall ever be established by law.

IV. The people of this commonwealth have the sole and exclusive right of governing themselves, as a free, sovereign, and independent State, and do, and forever hereafter shall, exercise and enjoy every power, jurisdiction, and right, which is not, or may not hereafter be, by them expressly delegated to the United States of America, in Congress assembled.

V. All power residing originally in the people, and being derived from them, the several magistrates and officers of government, vested with authority, whether legislative, executive, or judicial, are their substitutes and agents, and are at all times accountable to them.

VI. No man, nor corporation, or association of men, have any other title to obtain advantages, or particular and exclusive privileges, distinct from those of the community, than what arises from the consideration of services rendered to the public; and this title being in nature neither hereditary, nor transmissible to children, or descendants, or relations by blood; the idea of a man born a magistrate, lawgiver, or judge, is absurd and unnatural.

VII. Government is instituted for the common good, for the protection, safety, prosperity, and happiness of the people and not for the profit, honor or private interest of any one man, family, or class of men;

therefore the people alone have an incontestible unalienable, and indefeasible right to institute government; and to reform, alter, or totally change the same, when their protection, safety, prosperity, and happiness require it.

VIII. In order to prevent those who are vested with authority from becoming oppressors, the people have a right, at such periods and in such manner as they shall establish by their frame of government, to cause their public officers to return to private life; and to fill up vacant places by certain and regular elections and appointments.

IX. All elections ought to be free; and all the inhabitants of this commonwealth, having such qualifications as they shall establish by their frame of government, have an equal right to elect officers, and to be elected, for public employments.

X. Each individual of the society has a right to be protected by it in the enjoyment of his life, liberty, and property. . . . No part of the property of any individual can, with justice, be taken from him, or applied to public uses, without his own consent, or that of the representative body of the people. . . . And whenever the public exigencies require that the property of any individual should be appropriated to public uses, he shall receive a reasonable compensation therefor.

XI. Every subject of the commonwealth ought to find a certain remedy, by having recourse to the laws, for all injuries or wrongs which he may receive in his person, property, or character. He ought to obtain right and justice freely, and without being obliged to purchase it; completely, and without any denial; promptly, and without delay, conformably to the laws.

XII. No subject shall be held to answer for any crimes or offence, until the same is fully and plainly . . . described to him; or be compelled to accuse, or furnish evidence against himself. And every subject shall have a right to produce all proofs that may be favorable to him; to meet the witnesses against him face to face, and to be fully heard in his defence by himself, or his counsel, at his election. And no subject shall be arrested, . . . or deprived of his life, liberty, or estate, but by the judgment of his peers, or the law of the land.

And the legislature shall not make any law that shall subject any person to a capital or infamous punishment, excepting for the government of the army and navy, without trial by jury. . . .

XIV. Every subject has a right to be secure from all unreasonable searches, and seizures, of his person, his houses, his papers, and all his possessions. . . . And no warrant ought to be issued but in cases, and with the formalities prescribed by the laws.

XV. In all controversies concerning property, and in all suits between two or more persons, . . . the parties have a right to a trial by jury; and this method of procedure shall be held sacred. . . .

XVI. The liberty of the press is essential to the security of freedom in a state it ought not, therefore, to be restricted in this commonwealth.

XVII. The people have a right to keep and to bear arms for the common defence. And as, in time of peace, armies are dangerous to liberty, they ought not to be maintained without the consent of the legislature; and the military power shall always be held in an exact subordination to the civil authority, and be governed by it.

XVIII. A frequent recurrence to the fundamental principles of the constitution, and a constant adherence to those of piety, justice, moderation, temperance, industry and frugality, are absolutely necessary to preserve the advantages of liberty, and to maintain a free government. The people ought, consequently, to have a particular attention to all those principles, in the choice of their officers and representatives: and they have a right to require of their lawgivers and magistrates an exact and constant observance of them, in the formation and execution of the laws necessary for the good administration of the commonwealth.

XIX. The people have a right, in an orderly and peaceable manner to assemble to consult upon the common good; give instructions to their representatives, and to request of the legislative body, by the way of addresses, petitions, or remonstrances, redress of the wrongs done them, and of the grievances they suffer.

XX. The power of suspending the laws, or the execution of the laws, ought never to be exercised but by the legislature, or by authority derived from it, to be exercised in such particular cases only as the legislature shall expressly provide for.

XXI. The freedom of deliberation, speech, and debate, in either house of the legislature, is so essential to the rights of the people, that it cannot be the foundation of any accusation or prosecution, action or complaint, in any other court or place whatsoever.

XXII. The legislature ought frequently to assemble for the redress of grievances, for correcting, strengthening, and confirming the laws, and for making new laws, as the common good may require.

XXIII. No subsidy, charge, tax, impost, or duties ought to be established, fixed, laid, or levied, under any pretext whatsoever, without the consent of the people or their representatives in the legislature.

XXIV. Laws made to punish for actions done before the existence of such laws, and which have not been declared crimes by preceding laws, are unjust, oppressive, and inconsistent with the fundamental principles of a free government.

XXV. No subject ought, in any case, or in any time, to be declared guilty of treason or felony by the legislature.

XXVI. No magistrate or court of law shall demand excessive bail or sureties, impose excessive fines, or inflict cruel or unusual punishments.

XXVII. In time of peace, no soldier ought to be quartered in any house without the consent of the owner; and in time of war, such quarters ought not to be made but by the civil magistrate, in a manner ordained by the legislature.

XXVIII. No person can in any case be subject to law-martial, or to any penalties or pains, by virtue of that law, except those employed in the army or navy, and except the militia in actual service, but by authority of the legislature.

XXIX. It is essential to the preservation of the rights of every individual, his life, liberty, property, and character, that there be an impartial interpretation of the laws, and administration of justice. It is the right of every citizen to be tried by judges as free, impartial, and independent as the lot of humanity will admit. It is, therefore, not only the best policy, but for the security of the rights of the people, and of every citizen, that the judges of the supreme judicial court should hold their offices as long as they behave themselves well; and that they should have honorable salaries ascertained and established by standing laws.

XXX. In the government of this commonwealth, the legislative department shall never exercise the executive and judicial powers, or either of them: the executive shall never exercise the legislative and judicial powers, or either of them: the judicial shall never exercise the legislative and executive powers, or either of them: to the end it may be a government of laws and not of men.

71. THE QUOCK WALKER CASE
Massachusetts, 1783
(A. B. Hart, ed. *Commonwealth History of Massachusetts,* Vol. IV, p. 37–8)

The status of slavery in Massachusetts was, throughout the Revolutionary period, a matter of uncertainty. As early as 1770—two years before Lord Mansfield's decision in the famous Somerset case, in the case of *James* v. *Lechmere* the Superior Court of Massachusetts ruled that the plaintiff, a negro, was entitled to his freedom under the laws of the province and the terms of the royal charter. In the course of his decision in the case of *Winchendon* v. *Hatfield,* Chief Justice Parsons said, "Several negroes born in this country of imported slaves demanded their freedom of their masters by suit at law, and obtained it by a judgement of court. The defence of the master was faintly made, for such was the temper of the times, that a restless, discontented slave was worth little; and when his freedom was obtained in a course of legal proceedings, the master was not holden for his future support if he became poor. But in the first action, involving the right of the master, which came before the Supreme Judicial Court after the establishment of the Constitution, the judges declared that by virtue of the first article of the Declaration of Rights, slavery in this State was no more". This was the case of *Quock Walker* v. *Nathaniel Jennison,* 1783. Jennison, indicted for assault on Walker, justified his assault on the ground that Walker was his slave. The Court, however, speaking through Chief Justice Cushing, ruled that the first article of the Declaration of Rights had abolished slavery in Massachusetts. The case was not reported, but in 1874 Chief Justice Horace Gray read from the original notebook of Chief Justice Cushing, the following extract from his decision. See, G. H. Moore, *Notes on the History of Slavery in Massachusetts;* M. S. Locke, *Anti-Slavery in America, 1619–1808;* J. C. Hurd, *The Law of Freedom and of Bondage,* Vol. I, p. 263–4, Vol. II, p. 28–30; W. O'Brien, "Did the Jennison Case Outlaw Slavery in Massachusetts?" *William and Mary Quarterly* XVII (1960), 219.

CUSHING, C. J. As to the doctrine of slavery and the right of Christians to hold Africans in perpetual servitude, and sell and treat them as we do our horses and cattle, that (it is true) has been heretofore countenanced by the Province Laws formerly, but nowhere is it expressly enacted or established. It has been a usage—a usage which took its origin from the practice of some of the European nations, and the regulations of British government respecting the then Colonies, for the benefit of trade and wealth. But whatever sentiments have formerly prevailed in this particular or slid in upon us by the example of others, a different idea has taken place with the people of America, more favorable to the natural rights of mankind, and to that natural, innate desire of Liberty, which with Heaven (without regard to color, complexion, or shape of noses-features) has inspired all the human race. And upon this ground our Constitution of Government, by which the people of this Commonwealth have solemnly bound themselves, sets out with declaring that all men are born free and equal—and that every subject is entitled to liberty, and to have it guarded by the laws, as well as life and property—and in short is totally repugnant to the idea of being born slaves. This being the case, I think the idea of slavery is inconsistent with our own conduct and Constitution; and there can be no such thing as perpetual servitude of a rational creature, unless his liberty is forfeited by some criminal conduct or given up by personal consent or contract . . . *Verdict Guilty.*

72. THE ARTICLES OF CONFEDERATION

Agreed to by Congress November 15, 1777; ratified and in force, March 1, 1781

(Richardson, ed. *Messages and Papers,* Vol. I, p. 9 ff.)

Congress resolved June 11, 1776, that a committee should be appointed to draw up articles of confederation between the Colonies. A plan proposed by John Dickinson formed the basis of the articles as proposed to Congress and, after some debate and a few changes, adopted, November 15, 1777. Representatives of the States signed the Articles during 1778 and 1779; Maryland alone refused to ratify the Articles until Congress had arrived at some satisfactory solution of the land question. The debates on the Articles, Jefferson's Notes on the Debates, and the Official Letter of Congress accompanying the Articles, can be found in Elliot's *Debates* (1861 ed.) Vol. I, p. 69 ff. The Articles of Confederation constituted the first effort of Americans to solve the problem of imperial order, and should be studied in comparison with the Albany Plan of Union and the Constitution. On the Articles of Confederation see, R. Frothingham, *Rise of the Republic of the United States,* ch. xii; G. Bancroft, *History* Author's last rev. Vol. V, ch. xiv, A. C. McLaughlin, *Confederation and Constitution,* ch. iii; G. T. Curtis, *Constitutional History of the United States,* Vol. I.

To ALL TO WHOM these Presents shall come, we the undersigned Delegates of the States affixed to our Names send greeting. Whereas the Delegates of the United States of America in Congress assembled did on the fifteenth day of November in the Year of our Lord One Thousand Seven Hundred and Seventy seven, and in the Second Year of the Independence of America agree to certain articles of Confederation and perpetual Union between the States of Newhampshire, Massachusetts-bay, Rhodeisland and Providence Plantations, Connecticut, New York, New Jersey, Pennsylvania, Delaware, Maryland, Virginia, North-Carolina, South-Carolina and Georgia in the Words following, viz. "Articles of Confederation and perpetual Union between the states of Newhampshire, Massachusetts-bay, Rhodeisland and Providence Plantations, Connecticut, New-York, New-Jersey, Pennsylvania, Delaware, Maryland, Virginia, North-Carolina, South-Carolina and Georgia.

Art. I. The Stile of this confederacy shall be "The United States of America."

Art. II. Each state retains its sovereignty, freedom and independence, and every Power, Jurisdiction and right, which is not by this confederation expressly delegated to the United States, in Congress assembled.

Art. III. The said states hereby severally enter into a firm league of friendship with each other, for their common defence, the security of their Liberties, and their mutual and general welfare, binding themselves to assist each other, against all force offered to, or attacks made upon them, or any of them, on account of religion, sovereignty, trade, or any other pretence whatever.

Art. IV. The better to secure and perpetuate mutual friendship and intercourse among the people of the different states in this union, the free inhabitants of each of these states, paupers, vagabonds and fugitives from Justice excepted, shall be entitled to all privileges and immunities of free citizens in the several states; and the people of each state shall have free ingress and regress to and from any other state, and shall enjoy therein all the privileges of trade and commerce, subject to the same duties, impositions and restrictions as the inhabitants thereof respectively, provided that such restriction shall not extend so far as to prevent the removal of property imported into any state, to any other state of which the Owner is an inhabitant; provided also that no imposition, duties or restriction shall be laid by any state, on the property of the united states, or either of them.

If any Person guilty of, or charged with treason, felony, or other high misdemeanor in any state, shall flee from Justice, and be found in any of the united states, he shall upon demand of the Governor or executive power, of the state from which he fled, be delivered up and removed to the state having jurisdiction of his offence.

Full faith and credit shall be given in each of these states to the records, acts and judicial proceedings of the courts and magistrates of every other state.

Art. V. For the more convenient management of the general interests of the united states, delegates shall be annually appointed in such manner as the legislature of each state shall direct, to meet in Congress on the first Monday in November, in every year, with a power reserved to each state, to recal its delegates, or any of them, at any time within the year, and to send others in their stead, for the remainder of the Year.

No state shall be represented in Congress by less than two, nor by more than seven Members; and no person shall be capable of being a delegate for more than three years in any term of six years; nor shall any person, being a delegate, be capable of holding any office under the united states, for which he, or another for his benefit receives any salary, fees or emolument of any kind.

Each state shall maintain its own delegates in a meeting of the states, and while they act as members of the committee of the states.

In determining questions in the united states, in Congress assembled, each state shall have one vote.

Freedom of speech and debate in Congress shall not be impeached or questioned in any Court, or place out of Congress, and the members of congress shall be protected in their persons from arrests and imprisonments, during the time of their going to and from, and attendance on congress, except for treason, felony, or breach of the peace.

Art. VI. No state without the Consent of the united states in congress assembled, shall send any embassy to, or receive any embassy from, or enter into any conference, agreement, or alliance or treaty with any King, prince or state; nor shall any person holding any office of profit or trust under the united states, or any of them, accept of any present, emolument, office or title of any kind whatever from any king, prince or foreign state; nor shall the united states in congress assembled, or any of them, grant any title of nobility.

No two or more states shall enter into any treaty, confederation or alliance whatever between them, without the consent of the united states in congress assembled, specifying accurately the purposes for which the same is to be entered into, and how long it shall continue.

No state shall lay any imposts or duties, which may interfere with any stipulations in treaties, entered into by the united states in congress assembled, with any king, prince or state, in pursuance of any treaties already proposed by congress, to the courts of France and Spain.

No vessels of war shall be kept up in time of peace by any state, except such number only, as shall be deemed necessary by the united states in congress assembled, for the defence of such state, or its trade; nor shall any body of forces be kept up by any state, in time of peace, except such number only, as in the judgment of the united states, in congress assembled, shall be deemed requisite to garrison the forts necessary for the defence of such state; but every state shall always keep up a well regulated and disciplined militia, sufficiently armed and accoutred, and shall provide and constantly have ready for use, in public stores, a due number of field pieces and tents, and a proper quantity of arms, ammunition and camp equipage.

No state shall engage in any war without the consent of the united states in congress assembled, unless such state be actually invaded by enemies, or shall have received certain advice of a resolution being formed by some nation of Indians to invade such state, and the danger is so imminent as not to admit of a delay, till the united states in congress assembled can be consulted: nor shall any state grant commissions to any ships or vessels of war, nor letters of marque or reprisal, except it be after a declaration of war by the united states in congress assembled, and then only against the kingdom or state and the subjects thereof, against which war has been so declared, and under such regulations as shall be established by the united states in congress assembled, unless such state be infested by pirates, in which case vessels of war may be fitted out for that occasion, and kept so long as the danger shall continue, or until the united states in congress assembled shall determine otherwise.

Art. VII. When land-forces are raised by any state for the common defence, all officers of or under the rank of colonel, shall be appointed by the legislature of each state respectively by whom such forces shall be raised, or in such manner as such state shall direct, and all vacancies shall be filled up by the state which first made the appointment.

Art. VIII. All charges of war, and all other expences that shall be incurred for the common defence or general welfare, and allowed by the united states in congress assembled, shall be defrayed out of a common treasury, which shall be supplied by the several states, in proportion to the value of all land within each state, granted to or surveyed for any Person, as such land and the buildings and improvements thereon shall be estimated according to such mode as the united states in congress assembled, shall from time to time direct and appoint. The taxes for paying that proportion shall be laid and levied by the authority and direction of the legislatures of the several states within the time agreed upon by the united states in congress assembled.

Art. IX. The united states in congress assembled, shall have the sole and exclusive right and power of determining on peace and war, except in the cases mentioned in the sixth article—of sending and receiving ambassadors—entering into treaties and alliances, provided that no treaty of commerce shall be made whereby the legislative power of the respective states shall be restrained from imposing such imposts and duties on foreigners, as their own people are subjected to, or from prohibiting the exportation or importation of any species of goods or commodities whatsoever—of establishing rules for deciding in all cases, what captures on land or water shall be legal, and in what manner prizes taken by land or naval forces in the service of the united states shall be divided or appropriated.—of granting letters of marque and reprisal in times of peace—appointing courts for the trial of piracies and felonies committed on the high seas and establishing courts for receiving and determining finally appeals in all cases of captures, provided that no member of congress shall be appointed a judge of any of the said courts.

The united states in congress assembled shall also be the last resort on appeal in all disputes and differences now subsisting or that hereafter may arise between two or more states concerning boundary, jurisdiction or any other cause whatever; which authority shall always be exercised in the manner following. Whenever the legislative or executive authority or lawful agent of any state in controversy with another shall present a petition to congress. stating the matter in question and praying for a hearing, notice thereof shall be given by order of congress to the legislative or executive authority of the other state in controversy, and a day assigned for the appearance of the parties by their lawful agents, who shall then be directed to appoint by joint consent, commissioners or judges to constitute a court for hearing and determining the matter in question: but if they cannot agree, congress shall name three persons out of each of the united states, and from the list of such persons each party shall alternately strike out one, the petitioners beginning, until the number shall be reduced to thirteen; and from that number not less than seven, nor more than nine names as congress shall direct, shall in the presence of congress be drawn out by lot, and the persons whose names shall be so drawn or any five of them, shall be commissioners or judges, to hear and finally determine the controversy, so always as a major part of the judges who shall hear the cause shall agree in the determination: and if either party shall neglect to attend at the day appointed, without shewing reasons, which congress shall judge sufficient, or being present shall refuse to strike, the congress shall proceed to nominate three persons out of each state, and the secretary of congress shall strike in behalf of such party absent or refusing; and the judgment and sentence of the court to be appointed, in the manner before prescribed, shall be final and conclusive; and if any of the parties shall refuse to submit to the authority of such court, or to appear to defend their claim or cause, the court shall nevertheless proceed to pronounce sentence, or judgment, which shall in like manner be final and decisive, the judgment or sentence and other proceedings being in either case transmitted to congress, and lodged among the acts of congress for the security of the parties concerned: provided that every commissioner, before he sits in judgment, shall take an oath to be administered by one of the judges of the supreme or superior court of the state, where the cause shall be tried, "well and truly to hear and determine the matter in question, according to the best of his judgment, without favour, affection or hope of reward:" provided also that no state shall be deprived of territory for the benefit of the united states.

All controversies concerning the private right of soil claimed under different grants of two or more states, whose jurisdictions as they may respect such lands, and the states which passed such grants are adjusted, the said grants or either of them being at the same time claimed to have originated antecedent to such settlement of jurisdiction, shall on the petition of either party to the congress of the united states, be finally determined as near as may be in the same manner as is before prescribed for deciding disputes respecting territorial jurisdiction between different states.

The united states in congress assembled shall also have the sole and exclusive right and power of regulating the alloy and value of coin struck by their own authority, or by that of the respective states—fixing the standard of weights and measures throughout the united states.—regulating the trade and managing all affairs with the Indians, not members of any of the states, provided that the legislative right of any state within its own limits be not infringed or violated—establishing and regulating post-offices from one state to another, throughout all the united states, and exacting such postage on the papers passing thro' the same as may be requisite to defray the expences of the said office—appointing all officers of the land forces, in the service of the united states, excepting regimental officers.—appointing all the officers of the naval forces, and commissioning all officers whatever in the service of the united states—making rules for the government and regulation of the said land and naval forces, and directing their operations.

The united states in congress assembled shall have authority to appoint a committee, to sit in the recess of congress, to be denominated "A Committee of the States," and to consist of one delegate from each state; and to appoint such other committees and

civil officers as may be necessary for managing the general affairs of the united states under their direction—to appoint one of their number to preside, provided that no person be allowed to serve in the office of president more than one year in any term of three years; to ascertain the necessary sums of Money to be raised for the service of the united states, and to appropriate and apply the same for defraying the public expences—to borrow money, or emit bills on the credit of the united states, transmitting every half year to the respective states an account of the sums of money so borrowed or emitted,—to build and equip a navy—to agree upon the number of land forces, and to make requisitions from each state for its quota, in proportion to the number of white inhabitants in such state; which requisition shall be binding, and thereupon the legislature of each state shall appoint the regimental officers, raise the men and cloath, arm and equip them in a soldier like manner, at the expence of the united states, and the officers and men so cloathed, armed and equipped shall march to the place appointed, and within the time agreed on by the united states in congress assembled: But if the united states in congress assembled shall, on consideration of circumstances judge proper that any state should not raise men, or should raise a smaller number than its quota, and that any other state should raise a greater number of men than the quota thereof, such extra number shall be raised, officered, cloathed, armed and equipped in the same manner as the quota of such state, unless the legislature of such state shall judge that such extra number cannot be safely spared out of the same, in which case they shall raise officer, cloath, arm and equip as many of such extra number as they judge can be safely spared. And the officers and men so cloathed, armed and equipped, shall march to the place appointed, and within the time agreed on by the united states in congress assembled.

The united states in congress assembled shall never engage in a war, nor grant letters of marque and reprisal in time of peace, nor enter into any treaties or alliances, nor coin money, nor regulate the value thereof, nor ascertain the sums and expences necessary for the defence and welfare of the united states, or any of them, nor emit bills, nor borrow money on the credit of the united states, nor appropriate money, nor agree upon the number of vessels of war, to be built or purchased, or the number of land or sea forces to be raised, nor appoint a commander in chief of the army or navy, unless nine states assent to the same: nor shall a question on any other point, except for adjourning from day to day be determined, unless by the votes of a majority of the united states in congress assembled.

The congress of the united states shall have power to adjourn to any time within the year, and to any place within the united states, so that no period of adjournment be for a longer duration than the space of six Months, and shall publish the Journal of their proceedings monthly, except such parts thereof relating to treaties, alliances or military operations as in their judgment require secresy; and the yeas and nays of the delegates of each state on any question shall be entered on the Journal, when it is desired by any delegate; and the delegates of a state, or any of them, at his or their request shall be furnished with a transcript of the said Journal, except such parts as are above excepted, to lay before the legislatures of the several states.

Art X The committee of the states, or any nine of them, shall be authorised to execute, in the recess of congress, such of the powers of congress as the united states in congress assembled, by the consent of nine states, shall from time to time think expedient to vest them with; provided that no power be delegated to the said committee, for the exercise of which, by the articles of confederation, the voice of nine states in the congress of the united states assembled is requisite.

Art. XI. Canada acceding to this confederation, and joining in the measures of the united states, shall be admitted into, and entitled to all the advantages of this union: but no other colony shall be admitted into the same, unless such admission be agreed to by nine states.

Art. XII. All bills of credit emitted, monies borrowed and debts contracted by, or under the authority of congress, before the assembling of the united states, in pursuance of the present confederation, shall be deemed and considered as a charge against the united states, for payment and satisfaction whereof the said united states, and the public faith are hereby solemnly pledged.

Art. XIII. Every state shall abide by the determinations of the united states in congress assembled, on all questions which by this confederation are submitted to them. And the Articles of this confederation shall be inviolably observed by every state, and the union shall be perpetual; nor shall any alteration at any time hereafter be made in any of them; unless such alteration be agreed to in a congress of the united states, and be afterwards confirmed by the legislatures of every state.

AND WHEREAS it hath pleased the Great Governor of the World to incline the hearts of the legislatures we respectively represent in congress, to approve of, and to authorize us to ratify the said articles of confederation and perpetual union. KNOW YE that we the under-signed delegates, by virtue of the power and authority to us given for that purpose, do by these presents, in the name and in behalf of our respective constituents, fully and entirely ratify and confirm each and every of the said articles of confederation and perpetual union, and all and singular the matters and things therein contained: And we do further solemnly plight and engage the faith of our respective constituents, that they shall abide by the determinations of the united states in congress assembled, on all questions, which by the said confederation are submitted to them. And that the articles thereof shall be inviolably observed by the states we respectively represent, and that the union shall be perpetual. In Witness whereof we have hereunto set our hands in Congress. Done at Philadelphia in the state of Pennsylvania the ninth Day of July in the Year of our Lord one Thousand seven Hundred and Seventy-eight, and in the third year of the independence of America.

JOSIAH BARTLETT
JOHN WENTWORTH
Junr August 8th 1778
} On the part & behalf of the State of New Hampshire

JOHN HANCOCK
SAMUEL ADAMS
ELBRIDGE GERRY
FRANCIS DANA
JAMES LOVELL
SAMUEL HOLTEN
} On the part and behalf of The State of Massachusetts Bay

WILLIAM ELLERY
HENRY MARCHANT
JOHN COLLINS
} On the part and behalf of the State of Rhode-Island and Providence Plantations

ROGER SHERMAN
SAMUEL HUNTINGTON
OLIVER WOLCOTT
TITUS HOSMER
ANDREW ADAMS
} On the part and behalf of the State of Connecticut

JAS DUANE
FRAS LEWIS
WM DUER
GOUV MORRIS
} On the Part and Behalf of the State of New York

JNO WITHERSPOON
NATHL SCUDDER
} On the Part and in Behalf of the State of New Jersey. Novr 26, 1778.—

ROB^T MORRIS
DANIEL ROBERDEAU
JON^A BAYARD SMITH.
WILLIAM CLINGAN
JOSEPH REED 22^d
July 1778
} On the part and behalf of the State of Pennsylvania

THO M:KEAN Feby 12 1779
JOHN DICKINSON May 5th 1779
NICHOLAS VAN DYKE,
} On the part & behalf of the State of Delaware

JOHN HANSON March 1 1781
DANIEL CARROLL d^o
} On the part and behalf of the State of Maryland

RICHARD HENRY LEE
JOHN BANISTER
THOMAS ADAMS
JN^O HARVIE
FRANCIS LIGHTFOOT LEE
} On the Part and Behalf of the State of Virginia

JOHN PENN July 21st 1778
CORN^S HARNETT
JN^O WILLIAMS
} On the part and Behalf of the State of N^o Carolina

HENRY LAURENS
WILLIAM HENRY DRAYTON
JN^O MATHEWS
RICH^D HUTSON
THO^S HEYWARD Junr
} On the part & behalf of the State of South-Carolina

JN^O WALTON 24th July 1778
EDW^D TELFAIR
EDW^D LANGWORTHY
} On the part & behalf of the State of Georgia

73. COMMONWEALTH v. CATON ET. AL.
Virginia Reports, 4 Call, 5
1782

John Caton was condemned for treason by the General Court of Virginia, under the act of the assembly concerning that offence, passed in 1776, which took from the executive the power of granting pardon in such cases. The House of delegates, by resolution of June, 1782, granted him a pardon and sent it to the senate for concurrence, which was refused. Caton continued in jail under the sentence, and in October, 1782, the attorney-general moved in the general court that execution of the judgement might be awarded. The prisoner pleaded the pardon granted by the house of delegates; the attorney-general denied the validity of the pardon, as

the senate had not concurred in it, and the general court adjourned the case for novelty and difficulty, to the court of appeals. This is one of the very earliest cases in the United States where the question of the validity of an unconstitutional act was considered. It is of interest that John Marshall studied law under Judge Wythe.

WYTHE, J.: Among all the advantages which have arisen to mankind, from the study of letters, and the universal diffusion of knowledge, there is none of more importance, than the tendency they have had to produce discussions upon the respective rights of the sovereign and the subject; and upon the powers which the different branches of the government may exercise. For, by this means, tyranny has been sapped, the departments kept within their own spheres, the citizens protected, and general liberty promoted. But this beneficial result attains to higher perfection, when those who hold the purse and the sword, differing as to the powers which each may exercise, the tribunals, who hold neither, are called upon to declare the law impartially between them. For thus the pretensions of each party are fairly examined, their respective powers ascertained, and the boundaries of authority peaceably established. Under these impressions I approach the question which has been submitted to us: and although it was said the other day by one of the judges that, imitating that great and good man Lord Hale, he would sooner quit the bench than determine it, I feel no alarm; but will meet the crisis as I ought; and in the language of my oath of office, will decide it according to the best of my skill and judgement.

I have heard of an English chancellor who said, and it was nobly said, that it was his duty to protect the rights of the subject against the encroachments of the crown; and that he would do it at every hazard. But if it was his duty to protect a solitary individual against the rapacity of the sovereign, surely it is equally mine to protect one branch of the legislature and, consequently, the whole community, against the usurpations of the other: and whenever the proper occasion occurs, I shall feel the duty; and fearlessly perform it. Whenever traitors shall be fairly convicted, by the verdict of their peers, before the competent tribunal, if one branch of the legislature, without the concurrence of the other, shall attempt to rescue the offenders from the sentence of the law, I shall not hesitate, sitting in this place, to say to the general court, *Fiat justitia, ruat coelum;* and, to the usurping branch of the legislature, you attempt worse than a vain thing; for although you cannot succeed, you set an example which may convulse society to its centre. Nay more, if the whole legislature, an event to be deprecated, should attempt to overleap the bounds prescribed to them by the people, I, in administering the public justice of the country, will meet the united powers at my seat in this tribunal; and, pointing to the constitution, will say to them, here is the limit of your authority; and, hither shall you go, but no further. . . .

I am therefore of the opinion that the pardon pleaded by the prisoners, is not valid; and that it ought to be so certified to the general court.

74. TREATY OF PEACE WITH GREAT BRITAIN
September 3, 1783

(Malloy, ed. *Treaties, Conventions, etc.,* Vol. I, p. 586 ff.)

The surrender of Cornwallis at Yorktown, October 19, 1781, brought an end to the British effort to subdue the American colonies. February 27, 1782, a motion urging King George to end the war passed the House of Commons; a month later Lord North resigned, and the Rockingham Ministry entered into negotiations for a definitive peace. Congress appointed John Adams, Benjamin Franklin, John Jay, Henry Laurens, and Thomas Jefferson to conduct the negotiations, but Jefferson did not leave America, and Laurens was released from prison too late to take part in the peace conferences. The chief burden of the negotiations fell upon Franklin, and the treaty is largely a tribute to his shrewdness, persistence, and sagacity. On the Treaty, see the scholarly account by J. B. Scott, in S. F. Bemis, ed. *American Secretaries of State,* Vol. I, chs. iv–v; A. C. McLaughlin, *Confederation and Constitution,* chs. i–ii; E. G. Petty, Lord Fitzmaurice, *Life of William, Earl of Shelburne,* Vol. III.

. . . ART. I.—His Britannic Majesty acknowledges the said United States, viz. New Hampshire, Massachusetts Bay, Rhode Island, and Providence Plantations, Connecticut, New York, New Jersey, Pennsylvania, Delaware, Maryland, Virginia, North Carolina, South Carolina, and Georgia, to be free, sovereign and independent States; that he treats with them as such, and for himself, his heirs and successors, relinquishes all claims to the Government, proprietary and territorial rights of the same, and every part thereof.

ART. II.—And that all disputes which might arise in future, on the subject of the boundaries of the said United States may be prevented, it is hereby agreed and declared, that the following are, and shall be their boundaries, viz.: From the northwest angle of Nova Scotia, viz.: that angle which is formed by a line drawn due north from the source of Saint Croix River to the Highlands; along the said Highlands which divide those rivers that empty themselves into the river St. Lawrence, from those which fall into the Atlantic Ocean, to the northwesternmost head of Connecticut River; thence down along the middle of that river, to the forty-fifth degree of north latitude; from thence, by a line due west on said latitude, until it strikes the river Iroquois or Cataraquy; thence along the middle of said river into Lake Ontario, through the middle of said lake until it strikes the communication by water between that lake and Lake Erie; thence along the middle of said communication into Lake Erie, through the middle of said lake until it arrives at the water communication between that lake and Lake Huron; thence along the middle of said water communication into the Lake Huron; thence through the middle of said lake to the water communication between that lake and Lake Superior; thence through Lake Superior northward of the Isles Royal and Phelipeaux, to the Long Lake; thence through the middle of said Long Lake, and the water communication between it and the Lake of the Woods, to the said Lake of the Woods; thence through the said lake to the most northwestern point thereof, and from thence on a due west course to the river Mississippi; thence by a line to be drawn along the middle of the said river Mississippi until it shall intersect the northernmost part of the thirty-first degree of north latitude. South, by a line to be drawn due east from the determination of the line last mentioned, in the latitude of thirty-one degrees north of the Equator, to the middle of the river Appalachicola or Catahouche; thence along the middle thereof to its junction with the Flint River; thence straight to the head of St. Mary's River; and thence down along the middle of St.

Mary's River to the Atlantic Ocean. East, by a line to be drawn along the middle of the river St. Croix, from its mouth in the Bay of Fundy to its source, and from its source directly north to the aforesaid Highlands, which divide the rivers that fall into the Atlantic Ocean from those which fall into the river St. Lawrence; comprehending all islands within twenty leagues of any part of the shores of the United States, and lying between lines to be drawn due east from the points where the aforesaid boundaries between Nova Scotia on the one part, and East Florida on the other, shall respectively touch the Bay of Fundy and the Atlantic Ocean; excepting such islands as now are, or heretofore have been, within the limits of the said province of Nova Scotia.

ART. III.—It is agreed that the people of the United States shall continue to enjoy unmolested the right to take fish of every kind on the Grand Bank, and on all the other banks of Newfoundland; also in the Gulph of Saint Lawrence, and at all other places in the sea where the inhabitants of both countries used at any time heretofore to fish. And also that the inhabitants of the United States shall have liberty to take fish of every kind on such part of the coast of Newfoundland as British fishermen shall use (but not to dry or cure the same on that island) and also on the coasts, bays and creeks of all other of His Britannic Majesty's dominions in America; and that the American fishermen shall have liberty to dry and cure fish in any of the unsettled bays, harbours and creeks of Nova Scotia, Magdalen Islands, and Labrador, so long as the same shall remain unsettled; but so soon as the same or either of them shall be settled, it shall not be lawful for the said fishermen to dry or cure fish at such settlements, without a previous agreement for that purpose with the inhabitants, proprietors or possessors of the ground.

ART. IV.—It is agreed that creditors on either side shall meet with no lawful impediment to the recovery of the full value in sterling money, of all *bona fide* debts heretofore contracted.

ART. V.—It is agreed that the Congress shall earnestly recommend it to the legislatures of the respective States, to provide for the restitution of all estates, rights and properties which have been confiscated, belonging to real British subjects, and also of the estates, rights and properties of persons resident in districts in the possession of His Majesty's arms, and who have not borne arms against the said United States. And that persons of any other description shall have free liberty to go to any part or parts of any of the thirteen United States, and therein to remain twelve months, unmolested in their endeavours to obtain the restitution of such of their estates, rights and properties as may have been confiscated; and that Congress shall also earnestly recommend to the several States a reconsideration and revision of all acts or laws regarding the premises, so as to render the said laws or acts perfectly consistent, not only with justice and equity, but with that spirit of conciliation which, on the return of the blessings of .peace, should universally prevail. And that Congress shall also earnestly recommend to the several States, that the estates, rights and properties of such last mentioned persons, shall be restored to them, they refunding to any persons who may be now in possession, the *bona fide* price (where any has been given) which such persons may have paid on purchasing any of the said lands, rights or properties, since the confiscation. And it is agreed, that all persons who have any interest in confiscated lands, either by debts, marriage settlements or otherwise, shall meet with no lawful impediment in the prosecution of their just rights.

ART. VI.—That there shall be no future confiscations made, nor any prosecutions commenced against any person or persons for, or by reason of the part which he or they may have taken in the present war; and that no person shall, on that account, suffer any future loss or damage, either in his person, liberty or property; and that those who may be in confinement on such charges, at the time of the ratification of the treaty in America, shall be immediately set at liberty, and the prosecutions so commenced be discontinued.

ART. VII.—There shall be a firm and perpetual peace between His Britannic Majesty and the said States, and between the subjects of the one and the citizens of the other, wherefore all hostilities, both by sea and land, shall from henceforth cease; All prisoners on both sides shall be set at liberty, and His Britannic Majesty shall, with all convenient speed, and without causing any destruction, or carrying away any negroes or other property of the American inhabitants, withdraw all his armies, garrisons and fleets from the said United States, and from every post, place and harbour within the same; leaving in all fortifications the American artillery that may be therein; And shall also order and cause all archives, records, deeds and papers, belonging to any of the said States, or their citizens, which, in the course of the war, may have fallen into the hands of his officers, to be forthwith restored and deliver'd to the proper States and persons to whom they belong.

ART. VIII.—The navigation of the river Mississippi, from its source to the ocean, shall forever remain free and open to the subjects of Great Britain, and the citizens of the United States.

ART. IX.—In case it should so happen that any place or territory belonging to Great Britain or to the United States, should have been conquer'd by the arms of either from the other, before the arrival of the said provisional articles in America, it is agreed, that the same shall be restored without difficulty, and without requiring any compensation. . . .

75. RESOLUTION OF CONGRESS ON PUBLIC LANDS
October 10, 1780

(Journals of the Continental Congress, ed. by G. Hunt, Vol. XVIII, p. 915)

The ownership, control and administration of the western lands was one of the most acute and perplexing of the problems of the old Empire. By their charters, many of the American colonies were entitled to lands west of the Appalachians, and the Proclamation of 1763, closing these lands to settlement, aroused general resentment. With the outbreak of the Revolution, the States resumed their titles to their western lands. Many of these titles were conflicting and uncertain, and there was a widespread feeling, especially in those States that did not have title to western lands, that these lands should be surrendered to the central government. Congress, by the resolution of October 10, 1780, indicated the policy which it would follow toward any lands ceded to it by the States. See, in this connection, and for references, Docs. No. 76–79.

Resolved, that the unappropriated lands that may be ceded or relinquished to the United States, by any particular States, pursuant to the recommendation of Congress on the 6 day of September last, shall be disposed of for the common benefit of the United States, and be settled and formed into distinct republican States, which shall become members of the Federal Union, and shall have the same rights of sovereignty, freedom and independence, as the other States; that each State which shall be so

formed shall contain a suitable extent of territory, not less than one hundred nor more than one hundred and fifty miles square, or as near thereto as circumstances will admit;

That the necessary and reasonable expences which any particular State shall have incurred since the commencement of the present war, in subduing any of the British posts, or in maintaining forts or garrisons within and for the defence, or in acquiring any part of the territory that may be ceded or relinquished to the United States, shall be reimbursed;

That the said lands shall be granted and settled at such times and under such regulations as shall hereafter be agreed on by the United States in Congress assembled, or any nine or more of them.

76. VIRGINIA'S CESSION OF WESTERN LANDS TO THE UNITED STATES
December 20, 1783

(F. N. Thorpe, ed. *Federal and State Constitutions,* Vol. II, p. 955–6)

The Resolution of Congress of October 10, 1780 and the attitude of Maryland toward ratification of the Articles of Confederation gave a powerful impulse to the cession of the land claims of the States to the United States. New York and Connecticut expressed their willingness to cede their claims as early as 1781. The following year Congress accepted the New York cession. The claims of Virginia were the most extensive and the strongest of those of any State: they were based not only on charter rights but on the achievements of Clark in the Northwest. Virginia's first cession, in 1781, was coupled with conditions that were not acceptable to Congress: the cession of 1783 was promptly accepted, and the deed signed March 1, 1784. The clauses in the cession reserving military bounty lands north of the Ohio are of particular importance. See, A. C. McLaughlin, *Confederation and Constitution,* ch. vii; B. A. Hinsdale, *The Old Northwest;* F. L. Paxson, *History of the American Frontier,* chs. v–vi.

Sec. 1. Whereas the Congress of the United States did, by their act of the 6th day of September, in the year 1780, recommend to the several States in the Union, having claims to waste and unappropriated lands in the western country, a liberal cession to the United States of a portion of

their respective claims for the common benefit of the Union:

Sec. 2. And whereas this commonwealth did, on the 2d day of January, in the year 1781, yield to the Congress of the United States, for the benefit of the said States, all right, title, and claim which the said commonwealth had to the territory northwest of the river Ohio, subject to the conditions annexed to the said act of cession:

Sec. 3. And whereas the United States in Congress assembled have, by their act of the 13th of September last, stipulated the terms on which they agreed to accept the cession of this State, should the legislature approve thereof, which terms, although they do not come up to the proposition of this commonwealth, are conceived, on the whole, to approach so nearly to them as to induce this State to accept thereof, in full confidence that Congress will, in justice to this State for the liberal cession she hath made, earnestly press upon the other States claiming large tracts of waste and uncultivated territory the propriety of making cessions equally liberal for the common benefit and support of the Union:

Be it enacted by the general assembly,

That it shall and may be lawful for the delegates of this State to the Congress of the United States, . . . to . . . make over unto the United States, in Congress assembled, for the benefit of the said States, all right, title, and claim, as well of soil as jurisdiction, which this commonwealth hath to the territory or tract of country within the limits of the Virginia charter, situate, lying, and being to the northwest of the river Ohio, subject to the terms and conditions contained in the before-recited act of Congress of the 13th day of September last, that is to say: Upon condition that the territory so ceded shall be laid out and formed into States, containing a suitable extent of territory, not less than one hundred nor more than one hundred and fifty miles square, or as near thereto as circumstances will admit; and the States so formed shall be distinct republican States, and admitted members of the Federal Union, having the same rights of sovereignty, freedom, and independence as the other States; that the necessary and reasonable expences incurred by this State in subduing any British posts, or in maintaining forts or garrisons within and for the defence, or in acquiring any part of the territory so ceded or relinquished, shall be fully reimbursed by the United States; and that one commissioner shall be appointed by Congress, one by this commonwealth and another by those two commissioners, who, or a majority of them, shall be authorized and empowered to adjust and liquidate the account of the necessary and reasonable expenses incurred by the State, which they shall judge to be comprised within the intent and meaning of the act of Congress of the 10th of October, 1780, respecting such expenses. That of the French and Canadian inhabitants, and other settlers of the Kaskaskies, Saint Vincents and the neighboring villages, who have professed themselves citizens of Virginia, shall have their possessions and titles confirmed to them, and be protected in the enjoyment of their rights and liberties. That a quantity, not exceeding one hundred and fifty thousand acres,

of land, promised by this State, shall be allowed and granted to the then Colonel, now General, George Rogers Clark, and to the officers and soldiers of his regiment who marched with him when the posts of Kaskaskies and Saint Vincents were reduced, and to the officers and soldiers that have been since incorporated into the said regiment, to be laid off in one tract, the length of which not to exceed double the breadth, in such place on the northwest side of the Ohio as a majority of the officers shall choose, and to be afterwards divided among the said officers and soldiers in due proportion according to the law of Virginia. That in case the quantity of good lands on the southeast side of the Ohio, upon the waters of Cumberland River, and between Green River and Tennessee River, which have been reserved by law for the Virginia troops upon continental establishment, should, from the North Carolina line bearing in further upon the Cumberland lands than was expected, prove insufficient for their legal bounties, the deficiency should be made up to the said troops in good lands, to be laid off between the rivers Scioto and Little Miami, on the northwest side of the river Ohio, in such proportions as have been engaged to them by the laws of Virginia. That all the lands within the territory so ceded to the United States, and not reserved for or appropriated to any of the before-mentioned purposes, or disposed of in bounties to the officers and soldiers of the American Army, shall be considered as a common fund for the use and benefit of such of the United States as have become, or shall become members of the confederation or federal alliance of the said States, Virginia inclusive, according to their usual respective proportions in the general charge and expenditure, and shall be faithfully and *bona fide* disposed of for that purpose, and for no other use or purpose whatsoever: *Provided,* That the trust hereby reposed in the delegates of this State shall not be executed unless three of them, at least, are present in Congress.

77. REPORT OF GOVERNMENT FOR THE WESTERN TERRITORY
April 23, 1784

(*Journals of the Continental Congress,* ed. by J. C. Fitzpatrick, Vol. XXVI, p. 275 ff.)

Shortly after Virginia's cession of western lands had been formally completed, Jefferson introduced to Congress a plan for the organization of government in the western territory. The original plan contained two important provisions that were not finally incorporated in the Act of April 23. In the first place Jefferson proposed to create ten States out of the territory between the Ohio and the Mississippi Rivers, and provided for these potential states such names as Dolypotamia, Assenisippia and Metropotamia. In the second place Jefferson's plan contained a clause, "That after the year 1800 there shall be neither slavery nor involuntary servitude in in any of the sd. states." This clause was defeated by a vote of seven to six, even Virginia voting against its retention. Jefferson's plan can be found in various editions of his *Works,* or in Randall's *Jefferson,* Vol. I, p. 397, or in *Old South Leaflets,* Vol. VI. The Report of 1784 never went into effect. See references in Doc. No. 79.

The Committee to whom was recommitted the report of a plan for a temporary government of the western territory have agreed to the following resolutions.

Resolved, that so much of the territory ceded or to be ceded by individual states to the United States as is already purchased or shall be purchased of the Indian inhabitants & offered for sale by Congress, shall be divided into distinct states, in the following manner, as nearly as such cessions will admit; that is to say, by parallels of latitude, so that each state shall comprehend from north to south two degrees of latitude beginning to count from the completion of forty-five degrees north of the equator; and by meridians of longitude, one of which shall pass thro' the lowest point of the rapids of Ohio, and the other through the Western Cape of the mouth of the Great Kanhaway, . . .

That the settlers on any territory so purchased, and offered for sale, shall, either on their own petition, or on the order of Congress, receive authority from them with appointments of time and place for their free males of full age, within the limits of their state to meet together for the purpose of establishing a temporary government, to adopt the constitution and laws of any one of the original states, so that such laws nevertheless shall be subject to alteration by their ordinary legislature; & to erect, subject to a like alteration, counties or townships for the election of members for their legislature.

That when any such State shall have acquired twenty thousand inhabitants, on giv-ing due proof thereof to Congress, they shall receive from them authority with appointment of time and place to call a convention of representatives to establish a permanent Constitution and Government for themselves. Provided that both the temporary and permanent governments be established on these principles as their basis.

First. That they shall forever remain a part of this confederacy of the United States of America. Second. That they shall be subject to the articles of Confederation in all those cases in which the original states shall be so subject and to all the acts and ordinances of the United States in Congress assembled, conformable thereto. Third. That they shall in no case interfere with the primary disposal of the soil by the United States . . . nor with the ordinances and regulations which Congress may find necessary for securing the title to such soil to the bona fide purchasers. Fourth. That they shall be subject to pay a part of the federal debts contracted or to be contracted, to be apportioned on them by Congress, according to the same common rule & measure, by which apportionments thereof shall be made on the other states. Fifth. That no tax shall be imposed on lands, the property of the United States. Sixth. That their respective governments shall be republican. Seventh. That the lands of non-resident proprietors shall in no case, be taxed higher than those of residents . . . before the admission thereof to a vote by its delegates in Congress.

That whensoever any of the sd states shall have, of free inhabitants, as many as shall then be in any one the least numerous of the thirteen Original states, such State shall be admitted by it's delegates into the Congress of the United States on an equal footing with the said original states: provided the consent of so many states in Congress is first obtained as may at the time be competent to such admission. And in order to adopt the said Articles of Confederation to the state of Congress when it's numbers shall be thus increased, it shall be proposed to the legislatures of the states originally parties thereto, to require the assent of two thirds of the United States in Congress assembled in all those cases wherein by the said articles the assent of nine states is now required; which being agreed to by them shall be binding on the new states. Until such admission by their delegates into Congress, any of the said states after the establishment of their temporary government shall have authority to keep a sitting member in Congress, with a right of debating, but not of voting.

That measures not inconsistent with the principles of the Confedn. & necessary for the preservation of peace & good order among the settlers in any of the said new states until they shall assume a temporary Government as aforesaid, may from time to time be taken by the United States in Congress assembled.

That the preceding articles shall be formed into a charter of compact, shall be duly executed by the President of the United States in Congress assembled, under his hand & the seal of the United States, shall be promulgated and shall stand as fundamental constitutions between the thirteen original states and each of the several states now newly described, unalterable . . . but by the joint consent of the United States in Congress assembled, and of the particular state within which such alteration is proposed to be made.

78. LAND ORDINANCE OF 1785
May 20, 1785

(*Journals of the Continental Congress,* ed. by J. C. Fitzpatrick, Vol. XXVIII, p. 375 ff.)

This land ordinance laid the foundations for the public land system, followed in most essentials until 1862. Of particular importance were the provisions reserving certain lands for educational purposes. See, P. J. Treat, *The National Land System, 1785–1820,* A. C. Ford, *Colonial Precedents of our National Land System;* G. W. Knight, "History of National Land Grants for Education in the Northwest Territory," Am. Hist. Assoc. *Papers,* Vol. I.

An Ordinance for ascertaining the mode of disposing of Lands in the Western Territory.

BE it ordained by the United States in Congress assembled, that the territory ceded by individual States to the United States, which has been purchased of the Indian inhabitants, shall be disposed of in the following manner:

A surveyor from each state shall be appointed by Congress or a Committee of the States, who shall take an oath for the faithful discharge of his duty, before the Geographer of the United States. . . .

The Surveyors, as they are respectively qualified, shall proceed to divide the said territory into townships of six miles square, by lines running due north and south, and others crossing these at right angles, as near as may be, unless where the boundaries of the late Indian purchases may render the same impracticable, . . .

The first line, running due north and south as aforesaid, shall begin on the river Ohio, at a point that shall be found to be due north from the western termination of a line, which has been run as the southern boundary of the State of Pennsylvania; and the first line, running east and west, shall begin at the same point, and shall extend throughout the whole territory. Provided, that nothing herein shall be construed, as fixing the western boundary of the State of Pennsylvania. The geographer shall designate the townships, or fractional parts of townships, by numbers progressively from south to north; always beginning each range with No. 1; and the ranges shall be distinguished by their progressive numbers to the westward. The first range, extending from the Ohio to the lake Erie, being marked No. 1. The Geographer shall personally attend to the running of the first east and west line; and shall take the latitude of the extremes of the first north and south line, and of the mouths of the principal rivers.

The lines shall be measured with a chain; shall be plainly marked by chaps on the trees, and exactly described on a plat; whereon shall be noted by the surveyor, at their proper distances, all mines, salt-springs, salt-licks and mill-seats, that shall come to his knowledge, and all water-courses, mountains and other remarkable and permanent things, over and near which such lines shall pass, and also the quality of the lands.

The plats of the townships respectively,

shall be marked by subdivisions into lots of one mile square, or 640 acres, in the same direction as the external lines, and numbered from 1 to 36; always beginning the succeeding range of the lots with the number next to that with which the preceding one concluded. . . .

. . . And the geographer shall make . . . returns, from time to time, of every seven ranges as they may be surveyed. The Secretary of War shall have recourse thereto, and shall take by lot therefrom, a number of townships . . . as will be equal to one seventh part of the whole of such seven ranges, . . . for the use of the late Continental army. . . .

The board of treasury shall transmit a copy of the original plats, previously noting thereon the townships and fractional parts of townships, which shall have fallen to the several states, by the distribution aforesaid, to the commissioners of the loan-office of the several states, who, after giving notice . . . shall proceed to sell the townships or fractional parts of townships, at public vendue, in the following manner, viz.: The township or fractional part of a township No. 1, in the first range, shall be sold entire; and No. 2, in the same range, by lots; and thus in alternate order through the whole of the first range . . . provided, that none of the lands, within the said territory, be sold under the price of one dollar the acre,

to be paid in specie, or loan-office certificates, reduced to specie value, by the scale of depreciation, or certificates of liquidated debts of the United States, including interest, besides the expense of the survey and other charges thereon, which are hereby rated at thirty six dollars the township, . . . on failure of which payment, the said lands shall again be offered for sale.

There shall be reserved for the United States out of every township the four lots, being numbered 8,11,26,29, and out of every fractional part of a township, so many lots of the same numbers as shall be found thereon, for future sale. There shall be reserved the lot No. 16, of every township, for the maintenance of public schools within the said township; also one-third part of all gold, silver, lead and copper mines, to be sold, or otherwise disposed of as Congress shall hereafter direct. . . .

And Whereas Congress . . . stipulated grants of land to certain officers and soldiers of the late Continental army . . . for complying with such engagements, Be it ordained, That the secretary of war . . . determine who are the objects of the above resolutions and engagements . . . and cause the townships, or fractional parts of townships, hereinbefore reserved for the use of the late Continental army, to be drawn for in such manner as he shall deem expedient. . . .

79. RELIGIOUS LIBERTY IN VIRGINIA
Memorial of the Presbytery of Hanover
October 24, 1776

(W. H. Foote, *Sketches of Virginia, Historical and Biographical,* p. 323 ff.)

Parallel with the movement for political liberty went a demand for religious liberty. This movement was strongest in the South, where the Anglican Church had long been established by law. Ever since the days of the Great Awakening, the dissenting churches had flourished in the up-country of Virginia. The Presbyterian Church was particularly strong in the Valley, where Scotch-Irish were found in large numbers. Numerous petitions protesting against religious discrimination had been presented to the Virginia House of Burgesses in the fifties and sixties; with the coming of the Revolution these memorials became even more numerous and more emphatic. See. Doc. No. 80 and references.

To the Honorable the General Assembly of Virginia:

The Memorial of the Presbytery of Hanover humbly represents:

. . . It is well known, that in the frontier counties, which are justly supposed to contain a fifth part of the inhabitants of Virginia, the dissenters have borne the heavy burdens of purchasing glebes, building churches, and supporting the established clergy, where there are very few Episcopalians, either to assist in bearing the expense, or to reap the advantage; and that throughout the other parts of the country, there are also many thousands of zealous friends and defenders of our State, who, besides the invidious, and disadvantageous restrictions to which they have been subjected, annually pay large taxes to support an establishment, from which their consciences and principles oblige them to dissent: all which are confessedly so many violations of their natural rights; and in their consequences, a restraint upon freedom of inquiry, and private judgment.

In this enlightened age, and in a land where all, of every denomination are united in the most strenuous efforts to be free, we hope and expect that our representatives will cheerfully concur in removing every species of religious, as well as civil bondage. Certain it is, that every argument for civil liberty, gains additional strength when applied to liberty in the concerns of religion; and there is no argument in favour of establishing the Christian religion, but what may be pleaded, with equal propriety, for establishing the tenets of Mahomed by those who believe the Alcoran: or if this be not true, it is at least impossible for the magistrate to adjudge the right of preference among the various sects that profess the Christian faith, without erecting a chair of infallibility, which would lead us back to the church of Rome.

80. VIRGINIA STATUTE OF RELIGIOUS LIBERTY
January 16, 1786

(W. W. Hening, ed. *Statutes at Large of Virginia*, Vol. XII, p. 84 ff.)

The Declaration of Rights of 1776 had announced the principle of religious liberty, but the Anglican Church was still the established church. In 1777 the liberals succeeded in repealing the statutes requiring church attendance and universal support of the established church, but it was not until 1779 that the church was disestablished. Even this was not satisfactory, and Jefferson prepared a bill for absolute religious freedom and equality. This complete divorcement of church and state was bitterly opposed not only by the Episcopal but by the Presbyterian and other dissenting churches as well. The proposal to make all Christian churches state religions on equal standing and support them by taxation found favor with such men as Patrick Henry, Washington, and other conservatives. Jefferson characterized the long struggle for religious freedom as "the severest contest in which I have ever been engaged," and it was not until 1785 that his bill, sponsored in his absence by Mason, Madison, Taylor, George and W. C. Nicholas, passed the House: in January 1786 it was accepted by the Senate and became law. "Thus," wrote Madison, "in Virginia was extinguished forever the ambitious hope of making laws for the human mind", while Jefferson regarded it as one of his three memorable contributions to history. The Bill was translated into French and Italian, and aroused world-wide remark. See, H. J. Eckenrode, *Separation of Church and State in Virginia;* C. F. James, *Documentary History of the Struggle for Religious Liberty in Virginia;* R. B. Semple, *Rise and Progress of Baptists in Virginia;* F. W. Hirst, *Jefferson,* p. 130 ff.; G. Hunt, *Madison;* A. C. McLaughlin, et.al., *Source Problems in United States History,* No. iv.

An Act for establishing Religious Freedom.

I. WHEREAS Almighty God hath created the mind free; that all attempts to influence it by temporal punishments or burthens, or by civil incapacitations, tend only to beget habits of hypocrisy and meanness, and are a departure from the plan of the Holy author of our religion, who being Lord both of body and mind, yet chose not to propagate it by coercions on either, as was in his Almighty power to do; that the impious presumption of legislators and rulers, civil as well as ecclesiastical, who being themselves but fallible and uninspired men, have assumed dominion over the faith of others, setting up their own opinions and modes of thinking as the only true and infallible, and as such endeavouring to impose them on others, hath established and maintained false religions over the greatest part of the world, and through all time; that to compel a man to furnish contributions of money for the propagation of opinions which he disbelieves, is sinful and tyrannical; that even the forcing him to support this or that teacher of his own religious persuasion, is depriving him of the comfortable liberty of giving his contributions to the particular pastor whose morals he would make his pattern, and whose powers he feels most persuasive to righteousness, and is withdrawing from the ministry those temporary rewards, which proceeding from an approbation of their personal conduct, are an additional incitement to earnest and unremitting labours for the instruction of mankind; that our civil rights have no dependence on our religious opinions, any more than our opinions in physics or geometry; that therefore the proscribing any citizen as unworthy the public confidence by laying upon him an incapacity of being called to offices of trust and emolument, unless he profess or renounce this or that religious opinion, is depriving him injuriously of those privileges and advantages to which in common with his fellow-citizens he has a natural right, that it tends only to corrupt the principles of that religion it is meant to encourage, by bribing with a monopoly of worldly honours and emoluments, those who will externally profess and conform to it; that though indeed these are criminal who do not withstand such temptation, yet neither are those innocent who lay the bait in their way; that to suffer the civil magistrate to intrude his powers into the field of opinion, and to restrain the profession or propagation of principles on supposition of their ill tendency, is a dangerous fallacy, which at once destroys all religious liberty, because he being of course judge of that tendency will make his opinions the rule of judgment, and approve or condemn the sentiments of others only as they shall square with or differ from his own; that it is time enough for the rightful purposes of civil government, for its officers to interfere when principles break out into overt acts against peace and good order; and finally, that truth is great and will prevail if left to herself, that she is the proper and sufficient antagonist to error, and has nothing to fear from the conflict, unless by human interposition disarmed of her natural weapons, free argument and debate, errors ceasing to be dangerous when it is permitted freely to contradict them.

II. *Be it enacted by the General Assembly,* that no man shall be compelled to frequent or support any religious worship, place or ministry whatsoever, nor shall be enforced, restrained, molested, or burthened in his body or goods, nor shall otherwise suffer on account of his religious opinions or belief; but that all men shall be free to profess, and by argument to maintain, their opinion in matters of religion, and that the same shall in no wise diminish, enlarge or affect their civil capacities.

III. And though we well know that this assembly, elected by the people for the ordinary purposes of legislation only, have no power to restrain the acts of succeeding assemblies, constituted with powers equal to our own, and that therefore to declare this act to be irrevocable would be of no effect in law; yet as we are free to declare, and do declare, that the rights hereby asserted are of the natural rights of mankind, and that if any act shall hereafter be passed to repeal the present, or to narrow its operation, such act will be an infringement of natural right.

81. SHAYS'S REBELLION
1786

(G. R. Minot, *History of the Insurrection in Massachusetts,* p. 82 ff.)

The commercial depression of 1785–86 hit Massachusetts with particular severity. The West India trade was stopped, farm prices fell sharply, and taxation, unfairly apportioned, was intolerably heavy: the poll tax, for example, accounted for forty per cent of the entire taxes. Foreclosures on lands led to a widespread hostility against lawyers and courts, and all through the summer of 1786, town meetings demanded reforms or direct action. The legislature, however, was deaf to the appeals for reform, and in the fall of 1786 a minor rebellion broke out in central and western Massachusetts. Under the leadership of Captain Daniel Shays, infuriated mobs broke up the meetings of courts, and threatened the armory at Springfield. The outbreak excited fear and despair in the hearts of many observers, and was not without influence in persuading Americans of the desirability of a stronger central government. After the uprising had been suppressed, the legislature enacted many of the reforms advocated by the Shaysites. Minot's *History of the Insurrection* gives many of the petitions and resolutions of the town meetings. On the Rebellion see also, A. C. McLaughlin, *Confederation and Constitution*, ch. x; J. T. Adams, *New England in the Republic*, ch. vi; J. P. Warren, "The Confederation and the Shays Rebellion," *American Hist. Review*, Vol. XI; W. V. Wells, *Life and Public Services of Samuel Adams*, Vol. III, ch. lix.; A. E. Morse, *The Federalist Party in Massachusetts*, ch. iii.

1. An ADDRESS to the People of the several towns in the county of Hampshire, now at arms.

GENTLEMEN,

We have thought proper to inform you of some of the principal causes of the late risings of the people, and also of their present movement, viz.

1st. The present expensive mode of collecting debts, which by reason of the great scarcity of cash, will of necessity fill our gaols with unhappy debtors; and thereby a reputable body of people rendered incapable of being serviceable either to themselves or the community.

2d. The monies raised by impost and excise being appropriated to discharge the interest of governmental securities, and not the foreign debt, when these securities are not subject to taxation.

3d. A suspension of the writ of Habeas Corpus, by which those persons who have stepped forth to assert and maintain the rights of the people, are liable to be taken and conveyed even to the most distant part of the Commonwealth, and thereby subjected to an unjust punishment.

4th. The unlimited power granted to Justices of the Peace and Sheriffs, Deputy Sheriffs, and Constables, by the Riot Act, indemnifying them to the prosecution thereof; when perhaps, wholly actuated from a principle of revenge, hatred, and envy.

Furthermore, Be assured, that this body, now at arms, despise the idea of being instigated by British emissaries, which is so strenuously propagated by the enemies of our liberties: And also wish the most proper and speedy measures may be taken, to discharge both our foreign and domestick debt.

Per Order,

DANIEL GRAY, Chairman
of the Committee.

2. To the Printer of the Hampshire Herald.

SIR,

It has some how or other fallen to my lot to be employed in a more conspicuous manner than some others of my fellow citizens, in stepping forth on defence of the rights and privileges of the people, more especially of the county of Hampshire.

Therefore, upon the desire of the people now at arms, I take this method to publish to the world of mankind in general, particularly the people of this Commonwealth, some of the principal grievances we complain of, . . .

In the first place, I must refer you to a draught of grievances drawn up by a committee of the people, now at arms, under the signature of Daniel Gray, chairman, which is heartily approved of; some others also are here added, viz.

1st. The General Court, for certain obvious reasons, must be removed out of the town of Boston.

2d. A revision of the constitution is absolutely necessary.

3d. All kinds of governmental securities, now on interest, that have been bought of the original owners for two shillings, and the highest for six shillings and eight pence on the pound, and have received more interest than the principal cost the speculator who purchased them—that if justice was done, we verily believe, nay positively know, it would save this Commonwealth thousands of pounds.

4th. Let the lands belonging to this Commonwealth, at the eastward, be sold at the best advantage to pay the remainder of our domestick debt.

5th. Let the monies arising from impost and excise be appropriated to discharge the foreign debt.

6th. Let that act, passed by the General Court last June by a small majority of only seven, called the Supplementary Act, for twenty-five years to come, be repealed.

7th. The total abolition of the Inferiour Court of Common Pleas and General Sessions of the Peace.

8th. Deputy Sheriffs totally set aside, as a useless set of officers in the community; and Constables who are really necessary, be empowered to do the duty, by which means a large swarm of lawyers will be banished from their wonted haunts, who have been more damage to the people at large, especially the common farmers, than the savage beasts of prey.

To this I boldly sign my proper name, as a hearty wellwisher to the real rights of the people.

THOMAS GROVER

Worcester, December 7, 1786.

82. THE NORTHWEST ORDINANCE
July 13, 1787

(F. N. Thorpe, ed. *Federal and State Constitutions,* Vol. II, p. 957 ff.)

The Ordinance of April 23, 1784, Doc. No. 77, laid down the general principles of the American colonial system, but it did not provide in detail for the establishment of an administrative structure, and it was never put into effect. The immediate impulse for the Ordinance of 1787 came from a group of land speculators, members of the Ohio Company of Associates and of the Society of the Cincinnati, who wished to establish colonies in the Ohio country. The spokesmen of these groups were the Rev. Manasseh Cutler, Samuel Parsons, and General Rufus Putnam. These men succeeded in lobbying through a moribund Congress the famous Ordinance establishing a government in the Northwest territory. The authorship of the Ordinance is a matter of controversy, but it seems probable that Nathan Dane and Rufus King were the principal authors; fundamentally, of course, the Ordinance followed Jefferson's Ordinance of 1784. See B. A. Hinsdale, *The Old Northwest;* J. A. Barrett, *Evolution of the Ordinance of 1787;* W. P. and J. P. Cutler, *Life, Journals, and Correspondence of Manasseh Cutler,* 2 Vols.; R. Buell, *Memoirs of Rufus Putnam;* A. B. Hulbert, ed. *Records of the Ohio Company;* C. S. Hall, *Life and Letters of Samuel Holden Parsons;* R. King, *Ohio;* J. P. Dunn, *Indiana;* B. W. Bond, *Civilization of the Old Northwest;* J. M. Merriam, "Legislative History of the Ordinance of 1787", Am. Antiquarian Soc. *Proceedings,* N.S. Vol. V; C. R. King, *Rufus King.* Vol. I.; A. C. McLaughlin, *Confederation and Constitution,* ch. vii; F. L. Paxson, *History of the American Frontier,* chs. vii–viii; J. B. McMaster, *History of the People of the United States,* Vol. I, ch. v.

An Ordinance for the government of the Territory of the United States northwest of the River Ohio.

Be it ordained by the United States in Congress assembled, That the said territory, for the purposes of temporary government, be one district, subject, however, to be divided into two districts, as future circumstances may, in the opinion of Congress, make it expedient.

Be it ordained by the authority aforesaid, That the estates, both of resident and non-resident proprietors in the said territory, dying intestate, shall descend to, and be distributed among their children, and the descendants of a deceased child, in equal parts; the descendants of a deceased child or grandchild to take the share of their deceased parent in equal parts among them: And where there shall be no children or descendants, then in equal parts to the next of kin in equal degree; and among collaterals, the children of a deceased brother or sister of the intestate shall have, in equal parts among them, their deceased parents' share; and there shall in no case be a distinction between kindred of the whole and half-blood; saving, in all cases, to the widow of the intestate her third part of the real estate for life, and one-third part of the personal estate; and this law relative to descents and dower, shall remain in full force until altered by the legislature of the district. And until the governor and judges shall adopt laws as hereinafter mentioned, estates in the said territory may be devised or bequeathed by wills in writing, signed and sealed by him or her in whom the estate may be (being of full age), and attested by three witnesses; and real estates may be conveyed by lease and release, or bargain and sale, signed sealed and delivered by the person, being of full age, in whom the estate may be, and attested by two witnesses, provided such wills be duly proved, and such conveyances be acknowledged, or the execution thereof duly proved, and be recorded within one year after proper magistrates, courts, and registers shall be appointed for that purpose; and personal property may be transferred by delivery; saving, however to the French and Canadian inhabitants, and other settlers of the Kaskaskies, St. Vincents and the neighboring villages who have heretofore professed themselves citizens of Virginia, their laws and customs now in force among them, relative to the descent and conveyance, of property.

Be it ordained by the authority aforesaid, That there shall be appointed from time to time by Congress, a governor, whose commission shall continue in force for the term of three years, unless sooner revoked by Congress; he shall reside in the district, and have a freehold estate therein in 1,000 acres of land, while in the exercise of his office.

There shall be appointed from time to time by Congress, a secretary, whose commission shall continue in force for four years unless sooner revoked; he shall reside in the district, and have a freehold estate therein in 500 acres of land, while in the exercise of his office. It shall be his duty to keep and preserve the acts and laws passed by the legislature, and the public records of the district, and the proceedings of the governor in his executive department, and transmit authentic copies of such acts and proceedings, every six months, to the Secretary of Congress: There shall also be appointed a court to consist of three judges, any two of whom to form a court, who shall have a common law jurisdiction, and reside in the district, and have each therein a freehold estate in 500 acres of land while in the exercise of their offices; and their commissions shall continue in force during good behavior.

The governor and judges, or a majority of them, shall adopt and publish in the district such laws of the original States, criminal and civil, as may be necessary and best suited to the circumstances of the district, and report them to Congress from time to time: which laws shall be in force in the district until the organization of the General Assembly therein, unless disapproved of by Congress; but afterwards the Legislature shall have authority to alter them as they shall think fit.

The governor, for the time being, shall be commander-in-chief of the militia, appoint and commission all officers in the same below the rank of general officers; all general officers shall be appointed and commissioned by Congress.

Previous to the organization of the general assembly, the governor shall appoint such magistrates and other civil officers in each county or township, as he shall find necessary for the preservation of the peace and good order in the same: After the general assembly shall be organized, the powers and duties of the magistrates and other civil officers shall be regulated and defined by the said assembly; but all magistrates and other civil officers not herein otherwise directed, shall, during the continuance of this temporary government, be appointed by the governor.

For the prevention of crimes and injuries, the laws to be adopted or made shall have force in all parts of the district, and for the execution of process, criminal and civil, the governor shall make proper divisions thereof; and he shall proceed from time to time as circumstances may require, to lay out the parts of the district in which the Indian titles shall have been extinguished, into counties and townships, subject however to such alterations as may thereafter be made by the legislature.

So soon as there shall be five thousand free male inhabitants of full age in the district, upon giving proof thereof to the governor, they shall receive authority, with time and place, to elect representatives from their counties or townships to represent them in the general assembly: *Provided,* That, for every five hundred free male inhabitants, there shall be one representative, and so on progressively with the number of free male inhabitants shall the right of representation increase, until the number of representatives shall amount to twenty-five; after which, the number and proportion of representatives shall be regulated by the legislature: *Provided,* That no person be eligible or qualified to act as a representative unless he shall have been a citizen of one of the United States three years, and be a resident in the district, or unless he shall have resided in the district three years; and, in either case, shall likewise hold in his own right, in fee simple, two hundred acres of land within the same: *Provided, also,* That a freehold in fifty acres of land in the district, having been a citizen of one of the states, and being resident in the district, or the like freehold and two years residence in the district, shall be necessary to qualify a man as an elector of a representative.

The representatives thus elected, shall serve for the term of two years; and, in case of the death of a representative, or removal from office, the governor shall issue a writ to the county or township for which he was a member, to elect another in his stead, to serve for the residue of the term.

The general assembly or legislature shall consist of the governor, legislative council, and a house of representatives. The Legislative Council shall consist of five members, to continue in office five years, unless sooner removed by Congress; any three of whom to be a quorum: and the members of the Council shall be nominated and appointed in the following manner, to wit: As soon as representatives shall be elected, the Governor shall appoint a time and place for them to meet together; and, when met, they shall nominate ten persons, residents in the district, and each possessed of a freehold in five hundred acres of land, and return their names to Congress; five of whom Congress shall appoint and commission to serve as aforesaid; and, whenever a vacancy shall happen in the council, by death or removal from office, the house of representatives shall nominate two persons, qualified as aforesaid, for each vacancy, and return their names to Congress; one of whom Congress shall appoint and commission for the residue of the term. And every five years, four months at least before the expiration of the time of service of the members of council, the said house shall nominate ten persons, qualified as aforesaid, and return their names to Congress; five of whom Congress shall appoint and commission to serve as members of the council five years, unless sooner removed. And the governor, legislative council, and house of representatives, shall have authority to make laws in all cases, for the good government of the district, not repugnant to the principles and articles in this ordinance established and declared. And all bills, having passed by a majority in the house, and by a majority in the council, shall be referred to the governor for his assent; but no bill, or legislative act whatever, shall be of any force without his as-

sent. The governor shall have power to convene, prorogue, and dissolve the general assembly, when, in his opinion, it shall be expedient.

The governor, judges, legislative council, secretary, and such other officers as Congress shall appoint in the district, shall take an oath or affirmation of fidelity and of office; the governor before the president of congress, and all other officers before the Governor. As soon as a legislature shall be formed in the district, the council and house assembled in one room, shall have authority, by joint ballot, to elect a delegate to Congress, who shall have a seat in Congress, with a right of debating but not of voting during this temporary government.

And, for extending the fundamental principles of civil and religious liberty, which form the basis whereon these republics, their laws and constitutions are erected; to fix and establish those principles as the basis of all laws, constitutions, and governments, which forever hereafter shall be formed in the said territory: to provide also for the establishment of States, and permanent government therein, and for their admission to a share in the federal councils on an equal footing with the original States, at as early periods as may be consistent with the general interest:

It is hereby ordained and declared by the authority aforesaid, That the following articles shall be considered as articles of compact between the original States and the people and States in the said territory and forever remain unalterable, unless by common consent, to wit:

ART. 1. No person, demeaning himself in a peaceable and orderly manner, shall ever be molested on account of his mode of worship or religious sentiments, in the said territory.

ART. 2. The inhabitants of the said territory shall always be entitled to the benefits of the writ of *habeas corpus,* and of the trial by jury; of a proportionate representation of the people in the legislature; and of judicial proceedings according to the course of the common law. All persons shall be bailable, unless for capital offences, where the proof shall be evident or the presumption great. All fines shall be moderate; and no cruel or unusual punishments shall be inflicted. No man shall be deprived of his liberty or property, but by the judgment of his peers or the law of the land; and, should the public exigencies make it necessary, for the common preservation, to take any person's property, or to demand his particular services, full compensation shall be made for the same. And, in the just preservation of rights and property, it is understood and declared, that no law ought ever to be made, or have force in the said territory, that shall, in any manner whatever, interfere with or affect private contracts or engagements, *bona fide,* and without fraud, previously formed.

ART. 3. Religion, morality, and knowledge, being necessary to good government and the happiness of mankind, schools and the means of education shall forever be encouraged. The utmost good faith shall always be observed towards the Indians; their lands and property shall never be taken from them without their consent; and, in their property, rights, and liberty, they shall never be invaded or disturbed, unless in just and lawful wars authorized by Congress; but laws founded in justice and humanity, shall from time to time be made for preventing wrongs being done to them, and for preserving peace and friendship with them.

ART. 4. The said territory, and the States which may be formed therein, shall forever remain a part of this Confederacy of the United States of America, subject to the Articles of Confederation, and to such alterations therein as shall be constitutionally made; and to all the acts and ordinances of the United States in Congress assembled, conformable thereto. The inhabitants and settlers in the said territory shall be subject to pay a part of the federal debts contracted or to be contracted, and a proportional part of the expenses of government, to be apportioned on them by Congress according to the same common rule and measure by which apportionments thereof shall be made on the other States; and the taxes for paying their proportion shall be laid and levied by the authority and direction of the legislatures of the district or districts, or new States, as in the original States, within the time agreed upon by the United States in Congress assembled. The legislatures of those districts or new States, shall never interfere with the primary disposal of the soil by the United States in Congress assembled, nor with any regulations Congress may find necessary for securing the title in such soil to the *bona fide* purchasers. No tax shall be imposed on lands the property of the United States; and, in no case, shall non-resident proprietors be taxed higher than residents. The navigable waters leading into the Mississippi and St. Lawrence, and the carrying places between the same, shall be common highways and forever free, as well to the inhabitants of the said territory as to the citizens of the United States, and those of any other States that may be admitted into the confederacy, without any tax, impost, or duty therefor.

ART. 5. There shall be formed in the said territory, not less than three nor more than five States; and the boundaries of the States, as soon as Virginia shall alter her act of cession, and consent to the same, shall become fixed and established as follows, to wit: The western State in the said territory, shall be bounded by the Mississippi, the Ohio, and Wabash Rivers; a direct line drawn from the Wabash and Post Vincents, due North, to the territorial line between the United States and Canada; and, by the said territorial line, to the Lake of the Woods and Mississippi. The middle State shall be bounded by the said direct line, the Wabash from Post Vincents to the Ohio, by the Ohio, by a direct line, drawn due north from the mouth of the Great Miami, to the said territorial line, and by the said territorial line. The eastern State shall be bounded by the last mentioned direct line, the Ohio, Pennsylvania, and the said territorial line: *Provided, however,* and it is further understood and declared, that the boundaries of these three States shall be subject so far to be altered, that, if Congress shall hereafter find it expedient, they shall have authority to form one or two States in that part of the said territory which lies north of an east and west line drawn through the southerly bend or extreme of lake Michigan. And, whenever any of the said States shall have sixty thousand free inhabitants therein, such State shall be admitted, by its delegates, into the Congress of the United States, on an equal footing with the original States in all respects whatever, and shall be at liberty to form a permanent constitution and State government: *Provided,* the constitution and government so to be formed, shall be republican, and in conformity to the principles contained in these articles; and, so far as it can be consistent with the general interest of the confederacy, such admission shall be allowed at an earlier period, and when there may be a less number of free inhabitants in the State than sixty thousand.

ART. 6. There shall be neither slavery nor involuntary servitude in the said territory, otherwise than in the punishment of crimes whereof the party shall have been duly con-

victed: *Provided, always,* That any person escaping into the same, from whom labor or service is lawfully claimed in any one of the original States, such fugitive may be lawfully reclaimed and conveyed to the person claiming his or her labor or service as aforesaid.

Be it ordained by the authority aforesaid, That the resolutions of the 23rd of April 1784, relative to the subject of this ordinance, be, and the same are hereby repealed and declared null and void.

83. THE ANNAPOLIS CONVENTION

Proceedings of the Commissioners To Remedy Defects of the Federal Government, Annapolis in the State of Maryland.

Sept. 14, 1786

(Documents Illustrative of the Formation of the Union of the American States, p. 39 ff.)

Dissatisfaction with the Articles of Confederation had been growing ever since their ratification. The inability of the government of the Confederation to conclude commercial treaties with foreign nations, the mounting financial and currency difficulties, and the apparent impossibility of amending the Articles by ordinary processes, all led to a demand for a drastic revision of the Articles of Confederation. The immediate impulse for the Annapolis Convention came from a group of men who wished to open up navigation on the Potomac. In 1785 Washington invited the commissioners of Virginia and Maryland to meet at Mount Vernon and discuss the problem of communication between the East and the West. These commissioners drew up resolutions asking the co-operation of Pennsylvania in the project. Acting upon this suggestion Madison pushed through the legislature of Virginia a resolution appointing a commission to meet with other commissioners to take into consideration the state of the union. These commissioners met at Annapolis the first Monday in September 1786. See, A. C. McLaughlin, *Confederation and Constitution,* ch. xi; G. Hunt, *James Madison;* W. C. Rives, *Madison.*

To the Honorable, the Legislatures of Virginia, Delaware, Pennsylvania, New Jersey, and New York—

The Commissioners from the said States, respectively assembled at Annapolis, humbly beg leave to report.

That, pursuant to their several appointments, they met, at Annapolis in the State

of Maryland, on the eleventh day of September Instant, and having proceeded to a Communication of their Powers; they found that the States of New York, Pennsylvania, and Virginia, had, in substance, and nearly in the same terms, authorized their respective Commissioners "to meet such other Commissioners as were, or might be, appointed by the other States in the Union, at such time and place as should be agreed upon by the said Commissioners to take into consideration the trade and commerce of the United States, to consider how far an uniform system in their commercial intercourse and regulations might be necessary to their common interest and permanent harmony, and to report to the several States such an Act, relative to this great object, as when unanimously ratified by them would enable the United States in Congress assembled effectually to provide for the same." . . .

That the State of New Jersey had enlarged the object of their appointment, empowering their Commissioners, "to consider how far an uniform system in their commercial regulations and *other important matters,* might be necessary to the common interest and permanent harmony of the several States," and to report such an Act on the subject, as when ratified by them, "would enable the United States in Congress assembled, effectually to provide for the exigencies of the Union."

That appointments of Commissioners have also been made by the States of New Hampshire, Massachusetts, Rhode Island, and North Carolina, none of whom however have attended; but that no information has been received by your Commissioners, of any appointment having been made by the States of Connecticut, Maryland, South Carolina or Georgia.

That the express terms of the powers of your Commissioners supposing a deputation from all the States, and having for object the Trade and Commerce of the United States, Your Commissioners did not conceive it advisable to proceed on the business of their mission, under the Circumstance of so partial and defective a representation.

Deeply impressed however with the magnitude and importance of the object confided to them on this occasion, your Commissioners cannot forbear to indulge an expression of their earnest and unanimous wish, that speedy measures be taken, to effect a general meeting, of the States, in a future Convention, for the same, and such other purposes, as the situation of public affairs may be found to require.

If in expressing this wish, or in intimating any other sentiment, your Commissioners should seem to exceed the strict bounds of their appointment, they entertain a full confidence, that a conduct, dictated by an anxiety for the welfare of the United States, will not fail to receive an indulgent construction.

In this persuasion, your Commissioners submit an opinion, that the Idea of extending the powers of their Deputies, to other objects, than those of Commerce, which has been adopted by the State of New Jersey, was an improvement on the original plan, and will deserve to be incorporated into that of a future Convention; they are the more naturally led to this conclusion, as in the course of their reflections on the subject, they have been induced to think, that the power of regulating trade is of such comprehensive extent, and will enter so far into the general System of the foederal government, that to give it efficacy, and to obviate questions and doubts concerning its precise nature and limits, may require a correspondent adjustment of other parts of the Foederal System.

That there are important defects in the system of the Foederal Government is acknowledged by the Acts of all those States, which have concurred in the present Meeting; That the defects, upon a closer examination, may be found greater and more numerous, than even these acts imply, is at least so far probable, from the embarrassments which characterise the present State of our national affairs, foreign and domestic, as may reasonably be supposed to merit a deliberate and candid discussion, in some mode, which will unite the Sentiments and Councils of all the States. In the choice of the mode, your Commissioners are of opinion, that a Convention of Deputies from the different States, for the special and sole purpose of entering into this investigation, and digesting a plan for supplying such defects as may be discovered to exist, will be entitled to a preference from considerations, which will occur without being particularised.

Your Commissioners decline an enumeration of those national circumstances on which their opinion respecting the propriety of a future Convention, with more enlarged powers, is founded; as it would be an useless intrusion of facts and observations, most of which have been frequently the subject of public discussion, and none of which can have escaped the penetration of those to whom they would in this instance be addressed. They are however of a nature so serious, as, in the view of your Commissioners, to render the situation of the United States delicate and critical, calling for an exertion of the united virtue and wisdom of all the members of the Confederacy.

Under this impression, Your Commissioners, with the most respectful deference, beg leave to suggest their unanimous conviction that it may essentially tend to advance the interests of the union if the States, by whom they have been respectively delegated, would themselves concur, and use their endeavours to procure the concurrence of the other States, in the appointment of Commissioners, to meet at Philadelphia on the second Monday in May next, to take into consideration the situation of the United States, to devise such further provisions as shall appear to them necessary to render the constitution of the Foederal Government adequate to the exigencies of the Union; and to report such an Act for that purpose to the United States in Congress assembled, as when agreed to, by them, and afterwards confirmed by the Legislatures of every State, will effectually provide for the same.

Though your Commissioners could not with propriety address these observations and sentiments to any but the States they have the honor to represent, they have nevertheless concluded from motives of respect, to transmit copies of this Report to the United States in Congress assembled, and to the executives of the other States.

84. THE VIRGINIA OR RANDOLPH PLAN
Presented to the Federal Convention
May 29, 1787

(Hunt, G., and Scott, J. B., eds. *Debates in the Federal Convention of 1787 Reported by James Madison*, p. 23 ff. For variant texts see, *Documents Illustrative of the Formation of the Union of the American States*, p. 953 ff.)

The Randolph or Large State Plan looked to the creation of a new national government rather than a mere revision of the Articles of Confederation. Of the various plans presented to the Convention, it was not only the first, but the one which most closely approximates the finished Constitution. Note however, that the "Supreme law of the land" clause—the central clause of the Constitution—was taken not from the Randolph but from the New Jersey plan. All of the histories of the Federal Convention deal at length with the Randolph Plan. See, C. Warren, *The Making of the Constitution*, esp. p. 139 ff.; A. C. McLaughlin, *Confederation and Constitution*, ch. xii; J. B. McMaster, *History of the People of the United States*, Vol. I, p. 438 ff.

1. Resolved that the Articles of Confederation ought to be so corrected and enlarged as to accomplish the objects proposed by their institution; namely "common defence, security of liberty and general welfare."
2. Resolved therefore that the rights of suffrage in the National Legislature ought to be proportioned to the Quotas of contribution, or to the number of free inhabitants, as the one or the other rule may seem best in diffent cases.
3. Resolved that the National Legislature ought to consist of two branches.
4. Resolved that the members of the first branch of the National Legislature ought to be elected by the people of the several States every   for the terms of   ; to be of the age of   years at least, to receive liberal stipends by which they may be compensated for the devotion of their time to public service, to be ineligible to any

office established by a particular State, or under the authority of the United States, except those peculiarly belonging to the functions of the first branch, during the term of service, and for the space of   after its expiration; to be incapable of reelection for the space of   after the expiration of their term of service, and to be subject to recall.
5. Resolved that the members of the second branch of the National Legislature ought to be elected by those of the first, out of a proper number of persons nominated by the individual Legislatures, to be of the age of   years at least; to hold their offices for a term sufficient to ensure their independency; to receive liberal stipends, by which they may be compensated for the devotion of their time to public service; and to be ineligible to any office established by a particular State, or under the authority of the United States, except those peculiarly belonging to the functions of the second branch, during the term of service, and for the space of   after the expiration thereof.
6. Resolved that each branch ought to possess the right of originating Acts; that the National Legislature ought to be impowered to enjoy the Legislative Rights vested in Congress by the Confederation and moreover to legislate in all cases to which the separate States are incompetent, or in which the harmony of the United States may be interrupted by the exercise of individual Legislation; to negative all laws passed by the several States, contravening in the opin-

85. THE PATERSON OR NEW JERSEY PLAN
Presented to the Federal Convention
June 15, 1787

(Hunt, G., and Scott, J. B., eds. *Debates in the Federal Convention of 1787 Reported by James Madison,* p. 102–4. For variant texts see *Documents Illustrative of the Formation of the Union of the American States,* p. 967–8)

On the Paterson plan, see McLaughlin, *Confederation and Constitution,* p. 212 ff. Note particularly Section 6, which contains the germ of the central clause of the Constitution.

1. Resolved that the Articles of Confederation ought to be so revised, corrected, and enlarged as to render the federal Constitution adequate to the exigencies of Government, and the preservation of the Union.

2. Resolved that in addition to the powers vested in the United States in Congress, by the present existing articles of Confederation, they be authorized to pass acts for raising a revenue, by levying a duty or duties on all goods or merchandizes of foreign growth or manufacture, imported into any part of the United States, by Stamps on paper, vellum or parchment, and by a postage on all letters or packages passing through the general post-office, to be applied to such federal purposes as they shall deem proper and expedient; to make rules and regulations for the collection thereof; and the same from time to time, to alter and amend in such manner as they shall think proper: to pass Acts for the regulation of trade and commerce as well with foreign nations as with each other; provided that all punishments, fines, forfeitures and penalties to be incurred for contravening such acts rules and regulations shall be adjudged by the Common law Judiciaries of the State in which any offence contrary to the true intent and meaning of such Acts rules and regulations shall have been committed or perpetrated, with liberty of commencing in the first instance all suits and prosecutions for that purpose, in the superior common law Judiciary in such state, subject nevertheless, for the correction of errors, both in law and fact in rendering Judgement, to an appeal to the Judiciary of the United States.

3. Resolved that whenever requisitions shall be necessary, instead of the rule for making requisitions mentioned in the articles of Confederation, the United States in Congress be authorized to make such requisitions in proportion to the whole number of white and other free citizens and inhabitants of every age sex and condition including those bound to servitude for a term of years and three fifths of all other persons not comprehended in the foregoing description, except Indians not paying taxes; that if such requisitions be not complied with, in the time specified therein, to direct the collection thereof in the non-complying States and for that purpose to devise and pass acts directing and authorizing the same; provided that none of the powers hereby vested in the United States in Congress shall be exercised without the consent of at least   States, and in that proportion if the number of Confederated States should hereafter be increased or diminished.

4. Resolved that the United States in Congress be authorized to elect a federal Executive to consist of   persons, to continue in office for the term of   years, to receive punctually at stated times a fixed compensation for their services, in which no increase or diminution shall be made so as to affect the persons composing the Executive at the time of such increase or diminution, to be paid out of the federal treasury; to be incapable of holding any other office or appointment during their time of service and for   years thereafter; to be ineligible a second time, and removeable by Congress on application by a majority of the Executives of the several States; that the Executives besides their general authority to execute the federal acts ought to appoint all federal officers not otherwise provided for, and to direct all military operations; provided that none of the persons composing the federal Executive shall on any occasion take command of any troops so as personally to conduct any enterprise as General or in other capacity.

ion of the National Legislature the articles of Union; and to call forth the force of the Union against any member of the Union failing in its duty under the articles thereof.

7. Resolved that a National Executive be instituted; to be chosen by the National Legislature for the term of   years; to receive punctually, at stated times, a fixed compensation for the services rendered, in which no increase or diminution shall be made so as to affect the Magistracy, existing at the time of the increase or diminution, and to be ineligible a second time; and that besides a general authority to execute the National laws, it ought to enjoy the Executive rights vested in Congress by the Confederation.

8. Resolved that the Executive and a convenient number of the National Judiciary, ought to compose a Council or revision with authority to examine every act of the National Legislature before it shall operate, and every act of a particular Legislature before a Negative thereon shall be final; and that the dissent of the said Council shall amount to a rejection, unless the Act of the National Legislature be passed again, or that of a particular Legislature be again negatived by of the members of each branch.

9. Resolved that a National Judiciary be established to consist of one or more supreme tribunals, and of inferior tribunals to be chosen by the National Legislature, to hold their offices during good behaviour; and to receive punctually at stated times fixed compensation for their services, in which no increase or diminution shall be made so as to affect the persons actually in office at the time of such increase or diminution. That the jurisdiction of the inferior tribunals shall be to hear and determine in the first instance, and of the supreme tribunal to hear and determine in the dernier resort, all

piracies and felonies on the high seas, c
tures from an enemy; cases in which f
eigners or citizens of other States applyi
to such jurisdictions may be interested,
which respect the collection of the Nation
revenue; impeachments of any National o
ficers, and questions which may involve th
national peace and harmony.

10. Resolved that provision ought to be mad
for the admission of States lawfully arising
within the limits of the United States,
whether from a voluntary junction of Government and Territory or otherwise, with the
consent of a number of voices in the National legislature less than the whole.

11. Resolved that a Republican Government and the territory of each State, except in the instance of a voluntary junction of Government and territory, ought to be guaranteed by the United States to each State.

12. Resolved that provision ought to be made for the continuance of Congress and their authorities and privileges, until a given day after the reform of the articles of Union shall be adopted, and for the completion of all their engagements.

13. Resolved that provision ought to be made for the amendment of the Articles of Union whensoever it shall seem necessary, and that the assent of the National Legislature ought not to be required thereto.

14. Resolved that the Legislative Executive and Judiciary powers within the several States ought to be bound by oath to support the articles of Union.

15. Resolved that the amendments which shall be offered to the Confederation, by the Convention ought at a proper time, or times, after the approbation of Congress to be submitted to an assembly or assemblies of Representatives, recommended by the several Legislatures to be expressly chosen by the people, to consider and decide thereon.

5. Resolved that a federal Judiciary be established to consist of a supreme tribunal the Judges of which to be appointed by the Executive, and to hold their offices during good behaviour, to receive punctually at stated times a fixed compensation for their services in which no increase or diminution shall be made so as to affect persons actually in office at the time of such increase or diminution; that the Judiciary so established shall have authority to hear and determine in the first instance on all impeachments of federal officers, and by way of appeal in the dernier resort in all cases touching the rights of Ambassadors, in all cases of captures from an enemy, in all cases of piracies and felonies on the high Seas, in all cases in which foreigners may be interested, in the construction of any treaty or treaties, or which may arise on any of the Acts for regulation of trade, or the collection of the federal Revenue: that none of the Judiciary shall during the time they remain in office be capable of receiving or holding any other office or appointment during the time of service, or for thereafter.

6. Resolved that all Acts of the United States in Congress made by virtue and in pursuance of the powers hereby and by the articles of Confederation vested in them, and all Treaties made and ratified under the authority of the United States, shall be the supreme law of the respective States so far forth as those Acts or Treaties shall relate to the said States or their Citizens, and that the Judiciary of the several States shall be bound thereby in their decisions, any thing in the respective laws of the Individual States to the contrary notwithstanding; and that if any State, or any body of men in any State shall oppose or prevent carrying into execution such acts or treaties, the federal Executive shall be authorized to call forth the power of the Confederated States, or so much thereof as may be necessary to enforce and compel an obedience to such Acts or an observance of such Treaties.

7. Resolved that provision be made for the admission of new States into the Union.

8. Resolved the rule for naturalization ought to be the same in every State.

9. Resolved that a Citizen of one State committing an offence in another State of the Union, shall be deemed guilty of the same offence as if it had been committed by a Citizen of the State in which the offence was committed.

86. HAMILTON'S PLAN OF UNION

Presented to the Federal Convention
June 18, 1787

(*The Works of Alexander Hamilton*, ed. by H. C. Lodge, Vol. I, p. 331 ff. For variant texts, see *Documents Illustrative of the Formation of the Union of the American States*, p. 979 ff.)

Hamilton, who had long been active in the movement for strengthening the central government, and who had attended the Annapolis Convention, was a delegate to the Federal Convention from New York. He was distinctly out of sympathy with the work of the Federal Convention, as he was with the final Constitution. On June 18 he presented his own plan of Union, and explained it in an elaborate speech. The speech can be found in Madison's Notes, *Documents Illustrative, etc.*, p. 215 ff., and see note, p. 225; a somewhat different version is in the notes of Yates, *Documents Illustrative, etc.*, p. 776 ff. Hamilton's plan had no perceptible influence on the character of the Constitution.

1. The Supreme Legislative power of the United States of America to be vested in two distinct bodies of men; the one to be called the Assembly, the other the Senate who together shall form the Legislature of the United States with power to pass all laws whatsoever subject to the Negative hereafter mentioned.

2. The Assembly to consist of persons elected by the people to serve for three years.

3. The Senate to consist of persons elected to serve during good behaviour; their election to be made by electors chosen for that purpose by the people. In order to this, the States to be divided into election districts. On the death, removal or resignation of any Senator his place to be filled out of the district from which he came.

4. The supreme Executive authority of the United States to be vested in a Governor, to be elected to serve during good behaviour —His election to be made by Electors chosen by electors chosen by the people in the Election Districts aforesaid; or by electors chosen for that purpose by the respective Legislatures—provided that if an election be not made within a limited time, the President of the Senate shall be the Governor. The Governor to have a negative upon all laws about to be passed—and the execution of all laws passed—to be the Commander-in-Chief of the land and naval forces and of the militia of the United States—to have the entire direction of war when authorized or begun—to have, with the advice and approbation of the Senate, the power of making all treaties—to have the appointment of the heads or chief officers of the departments of finance, war, and foreign affairs—to have the nomination of all other officers (ambassadors to foreign nations included) subject to the approbation or rejection of the Senate—to have the power of pardoning all offences but treason, which he shall not pardon without the approbation of the Senate.

5. On the death, resignation, or removal of the Governor, his authorities to be exercised by the President of the Senate (until a successor be appointed).

6. The Senate to have the sole power of declaring war—the power of advising and approving all treaties—the power of approving or rejecting all appointments of officers except the heads or chiefs of the departments of finance, war, and foreign affairs.

7. The supreme judicial authority of the United States to be vested in twelve judges, to hold their offices during good behavior, with adequate and permanent salaries. This court to have original jurisdiction in all causes of capture, and an appellate jurisdiction (from the courts of the several States) in all causes in which the revenues of the General Government or the citizens of foreign nations are concerned.

8. The Legislature of the United States to have power to institute courts in each State for the determination of all causes of capture and of all matters relating to their revenues, or in which the citizens of foreign nations are concerned.

9. The Governor, Senators, and all officers of the United States to be liable to impeachment for mal and corrupt conduct, and upon conviction to be removed from office, and disqualified for holding any place of trust or profit. All impeachments to be tried by a court, to consist of the judges of the Supreme Court, chief or senior judge of the Superior Court of law of each State—provided that such judge hold his place during good behavior and have a permanent salary.

10. All laws of the particular States contrary to the Constitution or laws of the United States to be utterly void. And the better to prevent such laws being passed the Governor or President of each State shall be appointed by the General Government, and shall have a negative upon the laws about to be passed in the State of which he is Governor or President.

11. No State to have any forces, land or naval—and the militia of all the States to be under the sole and exclusive direction of the United States, the officers of which to be appointed and commissioned by them.

87. THE CONSTITUTION OF THE UNITED STATES

(Richardson, ed. *Messages and Papers*, Vol. I, p. 21 ff.)

Following the recommendation of the Annapolis Convention, Congress adopted, February 21, 1787, a resolution that "it is expedient that on the second Monday in May next a Convention of delegates who shall have been appointed by the several states be held at Philadelphia for the sole and express purpose of revising the Articles of Confederation." A quorum, however, did not assemble at Philadelphia until May 25, when the convention proceeded to organize. The convention continued its work throughout the summer of 1787 and on September 15 agreed to the Constitution as reported from the Committee on Style. On the 17th September the Constitution was signed, and submitted to Congress. By resolution of September 28, Congress submitted the Constitution to the States. By June 21, 1788, nine States had ratified the Constitution; Rhode Island, the last of the thirteen States to ratify, acted on May 29, 1790. Congress by resolution of September 13, 1788, fixed the date for the election of a President and the organization of the new government under the Constitution. The resolutions of Congress, the Debates and Proceedings of the Convention, the ratifications of the several States, and related material can be found in *Documents Illustrative of the Formation of the Union of the American States,* ed. by C. C. Tansill. The literature on the Constitution is voluminous. The classic analysis is the *Federalist,* written by Madison, Hamilton and Jay. Almost equally valuable is Judge Story's *Commentaries on the Constitution,* 2 vols. More recent accounts are: C. Warren, *The Making of the Constitution;* A. C. McLaughlin, *Confederation and Constitution;* M. Farrand, *Fathers of the Constitution;* M. Farrand, *Framing of the Constitution;* C. A. Beard, *Economic Interpretation of the Constitution.* The struggle over ratification can be followed in J. Elliot's *Debates in the Several State Conventions,* etc. 5 Vols.; and O. G. Libby, *Geographical Distribution of the Vote on the Federal Convention;* J. B. McMaster and F. D. Stone, *Pennsylvania and the Federal Constitution;* S. B. Harding, *Contest over Ratification in Massachusetts;* C. E. Miner, *Ratification of the Federal Constitution by the State of New York;* L. I. Trenholme, *Ratification of the Federal Constitution in North Carolina;* B. C. Steiner, *Maryland's Adoption of the Federal Constitution;* F. G. Bates, *Rhode Island and the Union;* H. G. Grigsby, *History of the Virginia Federal Convention of 1788,* 2 Vols. On the amendments, see C. Borgeaud, *Adoption and Amendment of Constitutions.*

WE THE PEOPLE of the United States, in Order to form a more perfect Union, establish Justice, insure domestic Tranquility, provide for the common defence, promote the general Welfare, and secure the Blessings of Liberty to ourselves and our Posterity, do ordain and establish this Constitution for the United States of America.

ART. I

Sec. 1. All legislative Powers herein granted shall be vested in a Congress of the United States, which shall consist of a Senate and House of Representatives.

Sec. 2. The House of Representatives shall be composed of Members chosen every second Year by the People of the several States, and the Electors in each State shall have the Qualifications requisite for Electors of the most numerous Branch of the State Legislature.

No Person shall be a Representative who shall not have attained to the Age of twenty five Years, and been seven Years a Citizen of the United States, and who shall not, when elected, be an Inhabitant of that State in which he shall be chosen.

Representatives and direct Taxes shall be apportioned among the several States which may be included within this Union, according to their respective Numbers, which shall be determined by adding to the whole Number of free Persons, including those bound to Service for a Term of Years, and excluding Indians not taxed, three fifths of all other Persons. The actual Enumeration shall be made within three Years after the first Meeting of the Congress of the United States, and within every subsequent Term of ten Years, in such Manner as they shall by Law direct. The Number of Representatives shall not exceed one for every thirty Thousand, but each State shall have at Least one Representative; and until such enumeration shall be made, the State of New Hampshire shall be entitled to chuse three, Massachusetts eight, Rhode-Island and Providence Plantations one, Connecticut five, New York six, New Jersey four, Pennsylvania eight, Delaware one, Maryland six, Virginia ten, North Carolina five, South Carolina five, and Georgia three.

When vacancies happen in the Representation from any State, the Executive Authority thereof shall issue Writs of Election to fill such Vacancies.

The House of Representatives shall chuse their Speaker and other Officers; and shall have the sole Power of Impeachment.

Sec. 3. The Senate of the United States shall be composed of two Senators from each State, chosen by the Legislature thereof, for six Years; and each Senator shall have one Vote.

Immediately after they shall be assembled in Consequence of the first Election, they shall be divided as equally as may be into three Classes. The Seats of the Senators of the first Class shall be vacated at the Expiration of the second Year, of the second Class at the Expiration of the fourth Year, and of the third Class at the Expiration of the sixth Year, so that one third may be chosen every second Year; and if Vacancies happen by Resignation, or otherwise, during the Recess of the Legislature of any State, the Executive thereof may make temporary Appointments until the next Meeting of the Legislature, which shall then fill such Vacancies.

No Person shall be a Senator who shall not have attained to the Age of thirty Years, and been nine Years a Citizens of the United States, and who shall not, when elected, be an Inhabitant of that State for which he shall be chosen.

The Vice President of the United States shall be President of the Senate, but shall have no Vote, unless they be equally divided.

The Senate shall chuse their other Officers, and also a President pro tempore, in the Absence of the Vice President, or when he shall exercise the Office of President of the United States.

The Senate shall have the sole Power to try all Impeachments. When sitting for that Purpose, they shall be on Oath or Affirmation. When the President of the United States is tried, the Chief Justice shall preside: And no Person shall be convicted without the Concurrence of two thirds of the Members present.

Judgment in Cases of Impeachment shall not extend further than to removal from Office, and disqualification to hold and enjoy any Office of honor, Trust or Profit under the United States: but the Party convicted shall nevertheless be liable and subject to Indictment, Trial, Judgment and Punishment, according to Law.

Sec. 4. The Times, Places and Manner of holding Elections for Senators and Representatives, shall be prescribed in each State by the Legislature thereof; but the Congress may at any time by Law make or alter such Regulations, except as to the Places of chusing Senators.

The Congress shall assemble at least once in every Year, and such Meeting shall be on the first Monday in December, unless they shall by Law appoint a different Day.

Sec. 5. Each House shall be the Judge of the Elections, Returns and Qualifications of its own Members, and a Majority of each shall constitute a Quorum to do Business; but a smaller Number may adjourn from day to day, and may be authorized to compel the Attendance of absent Members, in such Manner, and under such Penalties as each House may provide.

Each House may determine the Rules of its Proceedings, punish its Members for disorderly Behaviour, and, with the Concurrence of two thirds, expel a Member.

Each House shall keep a Journal of its Proceedings, and from time to time publish the same, excepting such Parts as may in their Judgment require Secrecy; and the Yeas and Nays of the Members of either House on any question shall, at the Desire of one fifth of those Present, be entered on the Journal.

Neither House, during the Session of Congress, shall, without the Consent of the other, adjourn for more than three days, nor to any other Place than that in which the two Houses shall be sitting.

Sec. 6. The Senators and Representatives shall receive a Compensation for their Services, to be ascertained by Law, and paid out of the Treasury of the United States. They shall in all Cases, except Treason, Felony and Breach of the Peace, be privileged from Arrest during their Attendance at the Session of their respective Houses, and in going to and returning from the same; and for any Speech or Debate in either House, they shall not be questioned in any other Place.

No Senator or Representative shall, during the Time for which he was elected, be appointed to any civil Office under the Authority of the United States which shall have been created, or the Emoluments whereof shall have been encreased during such time; and no Person holding any Office under the United States, shall be a Member of either House during his Continuance in Office.

Sec. 7. All Bills for raising Revenue shall originate in the House of Representatives; but the Senate may propose or concur with Amendments as on other Bills.

Every Bill which shall have passed the House of Representatives and the Senate, shall, before it become a Law, be presented to the President of the United States; If he approve he shall sign it, but if not he shall return it, with his Objections to that House in which it shall have originated, who shall enter the Objections at large on their Journal, and proceed to reconsider it. If after such Reconsideration two thirds of that House shall agree to pass the Bill, it shall be sent, together with the Objections, to the other House, by which it shall likewise be reconsidered, and if approved by two thirds of that House, it shall become a Law. But in all such Cases the Votes of both Houses shall be determined by yeas and Nays, and the Names of the Persons voting for and against the Bill shall be entered on the Journal of each House respectively. If any Bill shall not be returned by the President within ten Days (Sundays excepted) after it shall have been presented to him, the Same shall be a Law, in like Manner as if he had signed it, unless the Congress by their Adjournment prevent its Return, in which Case it shall not be a Law.

Every Order, Resolution, or Vote to which the Concurrence of the Senate and House of Representatives may be necessary (except on a question of Adjournment) shall be presented to the President of the United States; and before the Same shall take Effect, shall be approved by him, or being disapproved by him, shall be repassed by two thirds of the Senate and House of Representatives, according to the Rules and Limitations prescribed in the Case of a Bill.

Sec. 8. The Congress shall have Power To lay and collect Taxes, Duties, Imposts and Excises, to pay the Debts and provide for the common Defence and general Welfare of the United States; but all Duties, Imposts and Excises shall be uniform throughout the United States;

To borrow Money on the credit of the United States;

To regulate Commerce with foreign Nations, and among the several States, and with the Indian Tribes;

To establish an uniform Rule of Naturalization, and uniform Laws on the subject of Bankruptcies throughout the United States;

To coin Money, regulate the Value thereof, and of foreign Coin, and fix the Standard of Weights and Measures;

To provide for the Punishment of counterfeiting the Securities and current Coin of the United States;

To establish Post Offices and post Roads;

To promote the Progress of Science and useful Arts, by securing for limited Times to Authors and Inventors the exclusive Right to their respective Writings and Discoveries;

To constitute Tribunals inferior to the supreme Court;

To define and punish Piracies and Felonies committed on the high Seas, and Offences against the Law of Nations;

To declare War, grant Letters of Marque and Reprisal, and make Rules concerning Captures on Land and Water;

To raise and support Armies, but no Appropriation of Money to that Use shall be for a longer Term than two Years;

To provide and maintain a Navy;

To make Rules for the Government and Regulation of the land and naval Forces;

To provide for calling forth the Militia to execute the Laws of the Union, suppress Insurrections and repel Invasions;

To provide for organizing, arming, and disciplining, the Militia, and for governing such Part of them as may be employed in the Service of the United States, reserving to the States respectively, the Appointment of the Officers, and the Authority of training .the Militia according to the discipline prescribed by Congress;

To exercise exclusive Legislation in all Cases whatsoever, over such District (not exceeding ten Miles square) as may, by Cession of particular States, and the Acceptance of Congress, become the Seat of the Government of the United States, and to exercise like Authority over all Places purchased by the Consent of the Legislature of the State in which the Same shall be, for the Erection of Forts, Magazines, Arsenals, dock-Yards, and other needful Buildings;—And

To make all Laws which shall be necessary and proper for carrying into Execution the foregoing Powers, and all other Powers vested by this Constitution in the Government of the United States, or in any Department or Officer thereof.

Sec. 9. The Migration or Importation of such Persons as any of the States now existing shall think proper to admit, shall not be prohibited by the Congress prior to the Year one thousand eight hundred and eight, but a Tax or duty may be imposed on such Importation, not exceeding ten dollars for each Person.

The Privilege of the Writ of Habeas Corpus shall not be suspended, unless when in Cases of Rebellion or Invasion the public Safety may require it.

No Bill of Attainder or ex post facto Law shall be passed.

No Capitation, or other direct, Tax shall

be laid, unless in Proportion to the Census or Enumeration herein before directed to be taken.

No Tax or Duty shall be laid on Articles exported from any State.

No Preference shall be given by any Regulation of Commerce or Revenue to the Ports of one State over those of another: nor shall Vessels bound to, or from, one State, be obliged to enter, clear, or pay Duties in another.

No Money shall be drawn from the Treasury, but in Consequence of Appropriations made by Law; and a regular Statement and Account of the Receipts and Expenditures of all, public Money shall be published from time to time.

No Title of Nobility shall be granted by the United States: And no Person holding any Office of Profit or Trust under them, shall, without the Consent of the Congress, accept of any present, Emolument, Office, or Title, of any kind whatever, from any King, Prince or foreign State.

Sec. 10. No State shall enter into any Treaty, Alliance, or Confederation; grant Letters of Marque and Reprisal; coin Money; emit Bills of Credit; make any Thing but gold and silver Coin a Tender in Payment of Debts; pass any Bill of Attainder, ex post facto Law, or Law impairing the Obligation of Contracts, or grant any Title of Nobility.

No State shall, without the Consent of the Congress, lay any Imposts or Duties on Imports or Exports, except what may be absolutely necessary for executing it's inspection Laws: and the net Produce of all Duties and Imposts, laid by any State on Imports or Exports, shall be for the Use of the Treasury of the United States; and all such Laws shall be subject to the Revision and Controul of the Congress.

No State shall, without the Consent of Congress, lay any Duty of Tonnage, keep Troops, or Ships of War in time of Peace, enter into any Agreement or Compact with another State, or with a foreign Power, or engage in War, unless actually invaded, or in such imminent Danger as will not admit of delay.

ART. II

Sec. 1. The executive Power shall be vested in a President of the United States of America. He shall hold his Office during the Term of four Years, and, together with the Vice President, chosen for the same Term, be elected, as follows

Each State shall appoint, in such Manner as the Legislature thereof may direct, a Number of Electors, equal to the whole Number of Senators and Representatives to which the State may be entitled in the Congress: but no Senator or Representative, or Person holding an Office of Trust or Profit under the United States, shall be appointed an Elector.

The Electors shall meet in their respective States, and vote by Ballot for two Persons, of whom one at least shall not be an Inhabitant of the same State with themselves. And they shall make a List of all the Persons voted for, and of the Number of Votes for each; which List they shall sign and certify, and transmit sealed to the Seat of the Government of the United States, directed to the President of the Senate. The President of the Senate shall, in the Presence of the Senate and House of Representatives, open all the Certificates, and the Votes shall then be counted. The Person having the greatest Number of Votes shall be the President, if such Number be a Majority of the whole Number of Electors appointed; and if there be more than one who have such Majority, and have an equal Number of Votes, then the House of Representatives shall immediately chuse by Ballot one of them for President; and if no person have a Majority, then from the five highest on the List the said House shall in like Manner chuse the President. But in chusing the President, the Votes shall be taken by States, the Representation from each State having one Vote; A quorum for this Purpose shall consist of a Member or Members from two thirds of the States, and a Majority of all the States shall be necessary to a Choice. In every Case, after the Choice of the President, the Person having the greatest Number of Votes of the Electors shall be the Vice President. But if there should remain two or more who have equal Votes, the Senate shall chuse from them by Ballot the Vice President.

The Congress may determine the Time of chusing the Electors, and the Day on which they shall give their Votes; which Day shall be the same throughout the United States.

No Person except a natural born Citizen, or a Citizen of the United States, at the time of the Adoption of this Constitution, shall be eligible to the Office of President; neither shall any Person be eligible to that Office who shall not have attained to the Age of thirty five Years, and been fourteen Years a Resident within the United States.

In Case of the Removal of the President from Office, or of his Death, Resignation, or Inability to discharge the Powers and Duties of the said Office, the Same shall devolve on the Vice President, and the Congress may by Law provide for the Case of Removal, Death, Resignation or Inability, both of the President and Vice President, declaring what Officer shall then act as President, and such Officer shall act accordingly, until the Disability be removed, or a President shall be elected.

The President shall, at stated Times, receive for his Services, a Compensation, which shall neither be encreased nor diminished during the Period for which he shall have been elected, and he shall not receive within that Period any other Emolument from the United States, or any of them.

Before he enter on the Execution of his Office, he shall take the following Oath or Affirmation:—"I do solemnly swear (or affirm) that I will faithfully execute the Office of President of the United States, and will to the best of my Ability, preserve, protect and defend the Constitution of the United States."

Sec. 2. The President shall be Commander in Chief of the Army and Navy of the United States, and of the Militia of the several States, when called into the actual Service of the United States, he may require the Opinion, in writing, of the principal Officer in each of the executive Departments, upon any Subject relating to the Duties of their respective Offices, and he shall have Power to grant Reprieves and Pardons for Offences against the United States, except in Cases of Impeachment.

He shall have Power, by and with the Advice and Consent of the Senate, to make Treaties, provided two thirds of the Senators present concur; and he shall nominate, and by and with the Advice and Consent of the Senate, shall appoint Ambassadors, other

public Ministers and Consuls, Judges of the supreme Court, and all other Officers of the United States, whose Appointments are not herein otherwise provided for, and which shall be established by Law: but the Congress may by Law vest the Appointment of such inferior Officers, as they think proper, in the President alone, in the Courts of Law, or in the Heads of Departments.

The President shall have Power to fill up all Vacancies that may happen during the Recess of the Senate, by granting Commissions which shall expire at the End of their next Session.

Sec. 3. He shall from time to time give to the Congress Information of the State of the Union, and recommend to their Consideration such Measures as he shall judge necessary and expedient; he may, on extraordinary Occasions, convene both Houses, or either of them, and in Case of Disagreement between them, with Respect to the Time of Adjournment, he may adjourn them to such Time as he shall think proper; he shall receive Ambassadors and other public Ministers; he shall take Care that the Laws be faithfully executed, and shall Commission all the Officers of the United States.

Sec. 4. The President, Vice President and all civil Officers of the United States, shall be removed from Office on Impeachment for, and Conviction of, Treason, Bribery, or other high Crimes and Misdemeanors.

ART. III

Sec. 1. The judicial Power of the United States, shall be vested in one supreme Court, and in such inferior Courts as the Congress may from time to time ordain and establish. The Judges, both of the supreme and inferior Courts, shall hold their Offices during good Behaviour, and shall, at stated Times, receive for their Services, a Compensation, which shall not be diminished during their Continuance in Office.

Sec. 2. The judicial Power shall extend to all Cases, in Law and Equity, arising under this Constitution, the Laws of the United States, and Treaties made, or which shall be made, under their Authority;—to all Cases affecting Ambassadors, other public Ministers and Consuls;—to all Cases of admiralty and maritime Jurisdiction;—to Controversies to which the United States shall be a Party;—

to Controversies between two or more States; —between a State and Citizens of another State;—between Citizens of different States, —between Citizens of the same State claiming Lands under Grants of different States, and between a State, or the Citizens thereof, and foreign States, Citizens or Subjects.

In all Cases affecting Ambassadors, other public Ministers and Consuls, and those in which a State shall be Party, the supreme Court shall have original Jurisdiction. In all the other Cases before mentioned, the supreme Court shall have appellate Jurisdiction, both as to Law and Fact, with such Exceptions, and under such Regulations as the Congress shall make.

The Trial of all Crimes, except in Cases of Impeachment, shall be by Jury; and such Trial shall be held in the State where the said Crimes shall have been committed; but when not committed within any State, the Trial shall be at such Place or Places as the Congress may by Law have directed.

Sec. 3. Treason against the United States, shall consist only in levying War against them, or in adhering to their Enemies, giving them Aid and Comfort. No Person shall be convicted of Treason unless on the Testimony of two Witnesses to the same overt Act, or on Confession in open Court.

The Congress shall have Power to declare the Punishment of Treason, but no Attainder of Treason shall work Corruption of Blood, or Forfeiture except during the Life of the Person attainted.

ART. IV

Sec. 1. Full Faith and Credit shall be given in each State to the Public Acts, Records, and judicial Proceedings of every other State. And the Congress may by general Laws prescribe the Manner in which such Acts, Records and Proceedings shall be proved, and the Effect thereof.

Sec. 2. The Citizens of each State shall be entitled to all Privileges and Immunities of Citizens in the several States.

A Person charged in any State with Treason, Felony, or other Crime, who shall flee from Justice, and be found in another State, shall on Demand of the executive Authority of the State from which he fled, be delivered up, to be removed to the State having Jurisdiction of the Crime.

No Person held to Service or Labour in one State, under the Laws thereof, escaping into another, shall, in Consequence of any Law or Regulation therein, be discharged from such Service or Labour, but shall be delivered up on Claim of the Party to whom such Service or Labour may be due.

Sec. 3. New States may be admitted by the Congress into this Union; but no new States shall be formed or erected within the Jurisdiction of any other State; nor any State be formed by the Junction of two or more States, or Parts of States, without the Consent of the Legislatures of the States concerned as well as of the Congress.

The Congress shall have Power to dispose of and make all needful Rules and Regulations respecting the Territory or other Property belonging to the United States; and nothing in this Constitution shall be so construed as to Prejudice any Claims of the United States, or of any particular State.

Sec. 4. The United States shall guarantee to every State in this Union a Republican Form of Government, and shall protect each of them against Invasion; and on Application of the Legislature, or of the Executive (when the Legislature cannot be convened) against domestic Violence.

ART. V

The Congress, whenever two thirds of both Houses shall deem it necessary, shall propose Amendments to this Constitution, or, on the Application of the Legislatures of two thirds of the several States, shall call a Convention for proposing Amendments, which, in either Case, shall be valid to all Intents and Purposes, as Part of this Constitution, when ratified by the Legislatures of three fourths of the several States, or by Conventions in three fourths thereof, as the one or the other Mode of Ratification may be proposed by the Congress; Provided that no Amendment which may be made prior to the Year One thousand eight hundred and eight shall in any Manner affect the first and fourth Clauses in the Ninth Section of the first Article; and that no State, without its Consent, shall be deprived of it's equal Suffrage in the Senate.

ART. VI

All Debts contracted and Engagements

entered into, before the Adoption of this Constitution, shall be as valid against the United States under this Constitution, as under the Confederation.

This Constitution, and the Laws of the United States which shall be made in Pursuance thereof; and all Treaties made, or which shall be made, under the Authority of the United States, shall be the supreme Law of the Land; and the Judges in every State shall be bound thereby, any Thing in the Constitution or Laws of any State to the Contrary notwithstanding.

The Senators and Representatives before mentioned, and the Members of the several State Legislatures, and all executive and judicial Officers, both of the United States and of the several States, shall be bound by Oath or Affirmation, to support this Constitution; but no religious Test shall ever be required as a Qualification to any Office or public Trust under the United States.

Art. VII

The Ratification of the Conventions of nine States, shall be sufficient for the Establishment of this Constitution between the States so ratifying the Same.

Done in Convention by the Unanimous Consent of the States present the Seventeenth Day of September in the Year of our Lord one thousand seven hundred and Eighty seven and of the Independence of the United States of America the Twelfth. In witness whereof We have hereunto subscribed our Names,

Gº WASHINGTON—Presidᵗ
and deputy from Virginia

New Hampshire	{ JOHN LANGDON NICHOLAS GILMAN	Delaware	{ GEO: READ GUNNING BEDFORD jun JOHN DICKINSON RICHARD BASSETT JACO: BROOM
Massachusetts	{ NATHANIEL GORHAM RUFUS KING		
Connecticut	{ Wᴹ SAMᴸ JOHNSON ROGER SHERMAN	Maryland	{ JAMES MᶜHENRY DAN OF Sᵀ THOˢ JENIFER DANᴸ CARROLL
New York	{ ALEXANDER HAMILTON	Virginia	{ JOHN BLAIR— JAMES MADISON JR.
New Jersey	{ WIL: LIVINGSTON DAVID BREARLEY Wᴹ PATERSON JONA: DAYTON	North Carolina	{ WᴹBLOUNT RICHᴰ DOBBS SPAIGHT HU WILLIAMSON
Pensylvania	{ B FRANKLIN THOMAS MIFFLIN ROBᵀ MORRIS GEO. CLYMER THOˢ FITZSIMONS JARED INGERSOLL JAMES WILSON GOUV MORRIS	South Carolina	{ J. RUTLEDGE CHARLES COTESWORTH PINCKNEY CHARLES PINCKNEY PIERCE BUTLER
		Georgia	{ WILLIAM FEW ABR BALDWIN

Articles in addition to, and Amendment of the Constitution of the United States of America, proposed by Congress, and ratified by the Legislatures of the several States, pursuant to the fifth Article of the original Constitution.

[The first ten amendments went into effect November 3, 1791.]

Art. I

Congress shall make no law respecting an establishment of religion, or prohibiting the free exercise thereof; or abridging the freedom of speech, or of the press; or the right of the people peaceably to assemble, and to petition the government for a redress of grievances.

Art. II

A well regulated Militia, being necessary to the security of a free State, the right of the people to keep and bear Arms, shall not be infringed.

Art. III

No Soldier shall, in time of peace be quartered in any house, without the consent of the Owner, nor in time of war, but in a manner to be prescribed by law.

Art. IV

The right of the people to be secure in their persons, houses, papers, and effects, against unreasonable searches and seizures, shall not be violated, and no Warrants shall issue, but upon probable cause, supported by Oath or affirmation, and particularly describing the place to be searched, and the persons or things to be seized.

Art. V

No person shall be held to answer for a capital, or otherwise infamous crime, unless on a presentment or indictment of a Grand Jury, except in cases arising in the land or naval forces, or in the Militia, when in actual service in time of War or public danger; nor shall any person be subject for the same offence to be twice put in jeopardy of life or limb; nor shall be compelled in any criminal case to be a witness against himself, nor be deprived of life, liberty, or property, without due process of law; nor shall private property be taken for public use, without just compensation.

Art. VI

In all criminal prosecutions, the accused shall enjoy the right to a speedy and public trial, by an impartial jury of the State and district wherein the crime shall have been committed, which district shall have been previously ascertained by law, and to be informed of the nature and cause of the accusation; to be confronted with the witnesses against him; to have compulsory process for obtaining witnesses in his favor, and to have the Assistance of Counsel for his defence.

Art. VII

In Suits at common law, where the value in controversy shall exceed twenty dollars, the right of trial by jury shall be preserved, and no fact tried by a jury, shall be otherwise re-examined in any Court of the United States, than according to the rules of the common law.

Art. VIII

Excessive bail shall not be required, nor excessive fines imposed, nor cruel and unusual punishments inflicted.

Art. IX

The enumeration in the Constitution, of certain rights, shall not be construed to deny or disparage others retained by the people.

Art. X

The powers not delegated to the United States by the Constitution, nor prohibited by it to the States, are reserved to the States respectively, or to the people.

Art. XI

Jan. 8, 1798

The Judicial power of the United States shall not be construed to extend to any suit in law or equity, commenced or prosecuted against one of the United States by Citizens of another State, or by Citizens or Subjects of any Foreign State.

Art. XII

Sept. 25, 1804

The Electors shall meet in their respective states, and vote by ballot for President and Vice-President, one of whom, at least, shall not be an inhabitant of the same state with themselves; they shall name in their ballots the person voted for as President, and in distinct ballots the person voted for as

Vice-President, and they shall make distinct lists of all persons voted for as President, and of all persons voted for as Vice-President, and of the number of votes for each, which lists they shall sign and certify, and transmit sealed to the seat of the government of the United States, directed to the President of the Senate;—The President of the Senate shall, in the presence of the Senate and House of Representatives, open all the certificates and the votes shall then be counted;—The person having the greatest number of votes for President, shall be the President, if such number be a majority of the whole number of Electors appointed; and if no person have such majority, then from the persons having the highest numbers not exceeding three on the list of those voted for as President, the House of Representatives shall choose immediately, by ballot, the President. But in choosing the President, the votes shall be taken by states, the representation from each state having one vote; a quorum for this purpose shall consist of a member or members from two-thirds of the states, and a majority of all the states shall be necessary to a choice. And if the House of Representatives shall not choose a President whenever the right of choice shall devolve upon them, before the fourth day of March next following, then the Vice-President shall act as President, as in the case of the death or other constitutional disability of the President.—The person having the greatest number of votes as Vice-President, shall be the Vice-President, if such number be a majority of the whole number of Electors appointed, and if no person have a majority, then from the two highest numbers on the list, the Senate shall choose the Vice-President; a quorum for the purpose shall consist of two-thirds of the whole number of Senators, and a majority of the whole number shall be necessary to a choice. But no person constitutionally ineligible to the office of President shall be eligible to that of Vice-President of the United States.

Art. XIII

Dec. 18, 1865

Sec. 1. Neither slavery nor involuntary servitude, except as a punishment for crime whereof the party shall have been duly convicted, shall exist within the United States, or any place subject to their jurisdiction.

Sec. 2. Congress shall have power to enforce this article by appropriate legislation.

Art. XIV

July 28, 1868

Sec. 1. All persons born or naturalized in the United States, and subject to the jurisdiction thereof, are citizens of the United States and of the State wherein they reside. No State shall make or enforce any law which shall abridge the privileges or immunities of citizens of the United States; nor shall any State deprive any person of life, liberty, or property, without due process of law; nor deny to any person within its jurisdiction the equal protection of the laws.

Sec. 2. Representatives shall be apportioned among the several States according to their respective numbers, counting the whole number of persons in each State, excluding Indians not taxed. But when the right to vote at any election for the choice of electors for President and Vice President of the United States, Representatives in Congress, the Executive and Judicial officers of a State, or the members of the Legislature thereof, is denied to any of the male inhabitants of such State, being twenty-one years of age, and citizens of the United States, or in any way abridged, except for participation in rebellion, or other crime, the basis of representation therein shall be reduced in the proportion which the number of such male citizens shall bear to the whole number of male citizens twenty-one years of age in such State.

Sec. 3. No person shall be a Senator or Representative in Congress, or elector of President and Vice President, or hold any office, civil or military, under the United States, or under any State, who, having previously taken an oath, as a member of Congress, or as an officer of the United States, or as a member of any State legislature, or as an executive or judicial officer of any State, to support the Constitution of the United States, shall have engaged in insurrection or rebellion against the same, or given aid or comfort to the enemies thereof. But Congress may by a vote of two-thirds of each House, remove such disability.

Sec. 4. The validity of the public debt of the United States, authorized by law, including debts incurred for payment of pensions and bounties for services in suppressing insurrection or rebellion, shall not be questioned. But neither the United States nor any State shall assume or pay any debt or obligation incurred in aid of insurrection or rebellion against the United States, or any claim for the loss or emancipation of any slave; but all such debts, obligations and claims shall be held illegal and void.

Sec. 5. The Congress shall have power to enforce, by appropriate legislation, the provisions of this article.

ART. XV
March 30, 1870

Sec. 1. The right of citizens of the United States to vote shall not be denied or abridged by the United States or by any State on account of race, color, or previous condition of servitude—

Sec. 2. The Congress shall have power to enforce this article by appropriate legislation—

ART. XVI
February 25, 1913

The Congress shall have power to lay and collect taxes on incomes, from whatever source derived, without apportionment among the several States and without regard to any census or enumeration.

ART. XVII
May 31, 1913

The Senate of the United States shall be composed of two senators from each State, elected by the people thereof, for six years; and each Senator shall have one vote. The electors in each State shall have the qualifications requisite for electors of the most numerous branch of the State legislature.

When vacancies happen in the representation of any State in the Senate, the executive authority of such State shall issue writs of election to fill such vacancies: *Provided,* That the legislature of any State may empower the executive thereof to make temporary appointments until the people fill the vacancies by election as the legislature may direct.

This amendment shall not be so construed as to affect the election or term of any senator chosen before it becomes valid as part of the Constitution.

ART. XVIII
January 29, 1919

After one year from the ratification of this article, the manufacture, sale, or transporta-tion of intoxicating liquors within, the importation thereof into, or the exportation thereof from the United States and all territory subject to the jurisdiction thereof for beverage purposes is hereby prohibited.

The Congress and the several States shall have concurrent power to enforce this article by appropriate legislation.

This article shall be inoperative unless it shall have been ratified as an amendment to the Constitution by the legislatures of the several States, as provided in the Constitution, within seven years from the date of the submission hereof to the States by Congress.

ART. XIX
August 26, 1920

The right of citizens of the United States to vote shall not be denied or abridged by the United States or by any States on account of sex.

The Congress shall have power by appropriate legislation to enforce the provisions of this article.

ART. XX
February 6, 1933

Sec. 1. The terms of the President and Vice-President shall end at noon on the twentieth day of January, and the terms of Senators and Representatives at noon on the third day of January, of the years in which such terms would have ended if this article had not been ratified; and the terms of their successors shall then begin.

Sec. 2. The Congress shall assemble at least once in every year, and such meeting shall begin at noon on the third day of January, unless they shall by law appoint a different day.

Sec. 3. If, at the time fixed for the beginning of the term of the President, the President-elect shall have died, the Vice-President-elect shall become President. If a President shall not have been chosen before the time fixed for the beginning of his term, or if the President-elect shall have failed to qualify, then the Vice-President-elect shall act as President until a President shall have qualified; and the Congress may by law provide for the case wherein neither a President-elect nor a Vice-President-elect shall have qualified, declaring who shall then act as President, or the manner in which one who is to act shall be selected, and such person shall act accordingly until a President or Vice-President shall have qualified.

Sec. 4. The Congress may by law provide for the case of the death of any of the persons from whom the House of Representatives may choose a President whenever the right of choice shall have devolved upon them, and for the case of the death of any of the persons from whom the Senate may choose a Vice-President whenever the right of choice shall have devolved upon them.

Sec. 5. Sections 1 and 2 shall take effect on the 15th day of October following the ratification of this article.

Sec. 6. This article shall be inoperative unless it shall have been ratified as an amendment to the Constitution by the legislatures of three-fourths of the several States within seven years from the date of its submission.

ART. XXI

December 5, 1933

Sec. 1. The eighteenth article of amendment to the Constitution of the United States is hereby repealed. . . .

ART. XXII

February 26, 1951

Sec. 1. No person shall be elected to the office of the President more than twice, and no person who has held the office of President, or acted as President for more than two years of a term to which some other person was elected President shall be elected to the office of the President more than once. But this Article shall not apply to any person holding the office of President when this Article was proposed by the Congress, and shall not prevent any person who may be holding the office of President, or acting as President, during the term within which this Article becomes operative from holding the office of President or acting as President during the remainder of such term.

For articles subsequent to Article XXII see page 633.

88. OBJECTIONS TO THE FEDERAL CONSTITUTION
Letter of Robert Yates and John Lansing to the Governor of New York
1787
(J. Elliot, ed. Debates in the Several State Conventions on the Adoption of the Federal Constitution, 1861 ed., Vol. 1, p. 480 ff.)

Yates and Lansing, delegates to the Federal Convention from New York, refused to sign the Constitution; Alexander Hamilton alone signed from New York State. Opposition to the new Constitution in New York was intense, and ratification was secured only after nine other States had already ratified. See, E. W. Spaulding, *New York in the Critical Period, 1783–1789;* O. G. Libby, *Geographical Distribution of the Vote of the Thirteen States on the Federal Constitution;* C. E. Miner, *Ratification of the Federal Constitution by the State of New York.*

. . . We beg leave, briefly, to state some cogent reasons, which, among others, influenced us to decide against a consolidation of the states. These are reducible into two heads:—

1st. The limited and well-defined powers under which we acted, and which could not. on any possible construction, embrace an idea of such magnitude as to assent to a general constitution, in subversion of that of the state.

2nd. A conviction of the impracticability of establishing a general government, pervading every part of the United States, and extending essential benefits to all.

Our powers were explicit, and confined to the sole and express purpose of revising the Articles of Confederation, and reporting such alterations and provisions therein, as should render the Federal Constitution adequate to the exigencies of government, and the preservation of the Union.

From these expressions, we were led to believe that a system of consolidated government could not, in the remotest degree, have been in contemplation of the legislature of this state; for that so important a trust, as the adopting measures which tended to deprive the state government of its most essential rights of sovereignty, and to place it in a dependent situation, could not have been confided by implication; and the circumstance, that the acts of the Convention were to receive a state approbation in the last resort.

forcibly corroborated the opinion that our powers could not involve the subversion of a Constitution which, being immediately derived from the people, could only be abolished by their express consent, and not by a legislature, possessing authority vested in them for its preservation. Nor could we suppose that, if it had been the intention of the legislature to abrogate the existing confederation, they would, in such pointed terms, have directed the attention of their delegates to the revision and amendment of it, in total exclusion of every other idea.

Reasoning in this manner, we were of opinion that the leading feature of every amendment ought to be the preservation of the individual states in their uncontrolled constitutional rights, and that, in reserving these, a mode might have been devised of granting to the Confederacy, the moneys arising from a general system of revenue, the power of regulating commerce and enforcing the observance of foreign treaties, and other necessary matters of less moment.

Exclusive of our objections originating from the want of power, we entertained an opinion that a general government, however guarded by declarations of rights, or cautionary provisions, must unavoidably, in a short time, be productive of the destruction of the civil liberty of such citizens who could be effectually coerced by it, by reason of the extensive territory of the United States, the

dispersed situation of its inhabitants, and the insuperable difficulty of controlling or counteracting the views of a set of men (however unconstitutional and oppressive their acts might be) possessed of all the powers of government, and who, from their remoteness from their constituents, and necessary permanency of office, could not be supposed to be uniformly actuated by an attention to their welfare and happiness; that, however wise and energetic the principles of the general government might be, the extremities of the United States could not be kept in due submission and obedience to its laws, at the distance of many hundred miles from the seat of government; that, if the general legislature was composed of so numerous a body of men as to represent the interests of all the inhabitants of the United States, in the usual and true ideas of representation, the expense of supporting it would become intolerably burdensome; and that, if a few only were vested with a power of legislation, the interests of a great majority of the inhabitants of the United States must necessarily be unknown; or, if known, even in the first stages of the operations of the new government, unattended to.

These reasons were, in our opinion, conclusive against any system of consolidated government: to that recommended by the Convention, we suppose most of them very forcibly apply. . . .

89. BAYARD & WIFE v. SINGLETON

North Carolina Reports, 1 Martin, 42
1797

The Assembly of North Carolina, in 1785, passed a law requiring the Court to dismiss on motion any suit brought by a person whose property had been confiscated by the State during the War of Independence, against the purchasers, on affidavit of the defendants that they were purchasers from the commissioners of confiscated property. The decision of the Court is one of the earliest discussions of the right of a court to declare a legislative act void.

The Court made a few observations on our constitution and system of government. . . .

In the course of which the Judges observed that the obligation of their oaths, and the duty of their office required them in that situation, to give their opinion on that im-

portant and momentous subject; and that notwithstanding the great reluctance they might feel against involving themselves in a dispute with the Legislature of the State, yet no object of concern or respect could come in competition or authorize them to dispense with the duty they owed the public, in consequence of the trust they were invested with under the solemnity of their oaths.

That they therefore were bound to declare that they considered, that whatever disabilities the persons under whom the plaintiffs were said to derive their titles, might justly have incurred, against their maintaining or prosecuting any suits in the Courts of this State; yet that such disabilities in their nature were merely personal, and not by any means capable of being transferred to the present plaintiffs, either by descent or purchase; and that these plaintiffs being citizens of one of the United States, are citizens of this State, by the confederation of all the States; which is to be taken as a part of the law of the land, unrepealable by any act of the General Assembly.

That by the constitution every citizen had undoubtedly a right to a decision of his property by a trial by jury. For that if the Legislature could take away this right, and require him to stand condemned in his property without a trial, it might with as much authority require his life to be taken away without a trial by jury, and that he should stand condemned to die, without the formality of any trial at all: that if the members of the General Assembly could do this, they

might with equal authority, not only render themselves the Legislators of the State for life, without any further election of the people, but from thence transmit the dignity and authority of legislation down to their heirs male forever.

But that it was clear, that no act they could pass, could by any means repeal or alter the constitution, because if they could do this, they would at the same instant of time, destroy their own existence as a Legislature, and dissolve the government thereby established. Consequently the constitution (which the judicial was bound to take notice of as much as of any other law whatever) standing in full force as the fundamental law of the land, notwithstanding the act on which the present motion was groun ed, the same act must of course, in that instance, stand as abrogated and without any effect.

90. WASHINGTON'S FIRST INAUGURAL ADDRESS
April 30, 1789

(Richardson, ed. *Messages and Papers,* Vol. I, p. 51)

The first Congress was supposed to meet March 4, 1789, but not until April 2 did the House have a quorum, and the Senate did not organize until April 5. On the 6th of April the electoral votes were counted, and Washington and Adams were announced as President and Vice President. Charles Thomson was sent to notify Washington of his election, and on April 16 Washington set out from Mount Vernon for New York. For a description of the inauguration, see, *The Journal of William Maclay,* ch. i; C. Bowers, *Jefferson and Hamilton,* ch. i; R. W. Griswold, *The Republican Court;* J. B. McMaster, *With the Fathers,* p. 150 ff.

Fellow-Citizens of the Senate and of the House of Representatives:

Among the vicissitudes incident to life no event could have filled me with greater anxieties than that of which the notification was transmitted by your order, and received on the 14th day of the present month. On the one hand, I was summoned by my country, whose voice I can never hear but with veneration and love, from a retreat which I had chosen with the fondest predilection, and, in my flattering hopes, with an immutable decision, as the asylum of my declining years— a retreat which was rendered every day more necessary as well as more dear to me by the addition of habit to inclination, and of fre-

quent interruptions in my health to the gradual waste committed on it by time. On the other hand, the magnitude and difficulty of the trust to which the voice of my country called me, being sufficient to awaken in the wisest and most experienced of her citizens a distrustful scrutiny into his qualifications, could not but overwhelm with despondence one who (inheriting inferior endowments from nature and unpracticed in the duties of civil administration) ought to be peculiarly conscious of his own deficiencies. In this conflict of emotions all I dare aver is that it has been my faithful study to collect my duty from a just appreciation of every circumstance by which it might be affected. All I dare hope is that if, in executing this task, I have been too much swayed by a grateful remembrance of former instances, or by an affectionate sensibility to this transcendent proof of the confidence of my fellow-citizens, and have thence too little consulted my incapacity as well as disinclination for the weighty and untried cares before me, my error will be palliated by the motives which mislead me, and its consequences be judged by my country with some share of the partiality in which they originated.

Such being the impressions under which I

have, in obedience to the public summons, repaired to the present station, it would be peculiarly improper to omit in this first official act my fervent supplications to that Almighty Being who rules over the universe, who presides in the councils of nations, and whose providential aids can supply every human defect, that His benediction may consecrate to the liberties and happiness of the people of the United States a Government instituted by themselves for these essential purposes, and may enable every instrument employed in its administration to execute with success the functions allotted to his charge. . . . No people can be bound to acknowledge and adore the Invisible Hand which conducts the affairs of men more than those of the United States. Every step by which they have advanced to the character of an independent nation seems to have been distinguished by some token of providential agency; and in the important revolution just accomplished in the system of their united government the tranquil deliberations and voluntary consent of so many distinct communities from which the event has resulted can not be compared with the means by which most governments have been established without some return of pious gratitude, along with an humble anticipation of the future blessings which the past seem to presage. . . .

By the article establishing the executive department it is made the duty of the President "to recommend to your consideration such measures as he shall judge necessary and expedient." The circumstances under which I now meet you will acquit me from entering into that subject further than to refer to the great constitutional charter under which you are assembled, and which, in defining your powers, designates the objects to which your attention is to be given. It will be more consistent with those circumstances, and far more congenial with the feelings which actuate me, to substitute, in place of a recommendation of particular measures, the tribute that is due to the talents, the rectitude, and the patriotism which adorn the characters selected to devise and adopt them. In these honorable qualifications I behold the surest pledges that as on one side no local prejudices or attachments, no separate views nor party animosities, will misdirect the comprehensive and equal eye which ought to watch over this great assemblage of communities and interests, so, on another, that the foundation of our national policy will be laid in the pure and immutable principles of private morality, and the preëminence of free government be exemplified by all the attributes which can win the affections of its citizens and command the respect of the world. I dwell on this prospect with every satisfaction which an ardent love for my country can inspire, since there is no truth more thoroughly established than that there exists in the economy and course of nature an indissoluble union between virtue and happiness; between duty and advantage; between the genuine maxims of an honest and magnanimous policy and the solid rewards of public prosperity and felicity; since we ought to be no less persuaded that the propitious smiles of Heaven can never be expected on a nation that disregards the eternal rules of order and right which Heaven itself has ordained; and since the preservation of the sacred fire of liberty and the destiny of the republican model of government are justly considered, perhaps, as *deeply,* as *finally,* staked on the experiment intrusted to the hands of the American people.

Besides the ordinary objects submitted to your care, it will remain with your judgment to decide how far an exercise of the occasional power delegated by the fifth article of the Constitution is rendered expedient at the present juncture by the nature of objections which have been urged against the system, or by the degree of inquietude which has given birth to them. . . .

To the foregoing observations I have one to add, which will be most properly addressed to the House of Representatives. It concerns myself, and will therefore be as brief as possible. When I was first honored with a call into the service of my country, then on the eve of an arduous struggle for its liberties, the light in which I contemplated my duty required that I should renounce every pecuniary compensation. From this resolution I have in no instance departed; and being still under the impressions which produced it, I must decline as inapplicable to myself any share in the personal emoluments which may be indispensably included in a permanent provision for the executive department, and must accordingly pray that the pecuniary estimates for the station in which I am placed may during my continuance in it be limited to such actual expenditures as the public good may be thought to require.

Having thus imparted to you my sentiments as they have been awakened by the occasion which brings us together, I shall take my present leave; but not without resorting once more to the benign Parent of the Human Race in humble supplication that, since He has been pleased to favor the American people with opportunities for deliberating in perfect tranquillity, and dispositions for deciding with unparalleled unanimity on a form of government for the security of their union and the advancement of their happiness, so His divine blessing may be equally *conspicuous* in the enlarged views, the temperate consultations, and the wise measures on which the success of this Government must depend.

91. THE JUDICIARY ACT OF 1789
September 24, 1789

(*U. S. Statutes at Large,* Vol. I, p. 73 ff.)

The Constitution provided only for a Supreme Court and "such inferior Courts as the Congress may from time to time establish", thus leaving the whole question of the nature and the organization of the judiciary to the discretion of Congress. The framework of the American judicial system was created in the Act of 1789. The determination of the first Congress to create a federal judiciary was of immense importance in developing American nationalism. See, C. Warren, *Congress, The Constitution, and the Supreme Court;* S. E. Baldwin, *The American Judiciary;* C. Warren, *The Supreme Court in United States History,* 1928 ed. Vol. I, ch. i.

An Act to establish the Judicial Courts of the United States.

SEC. 1. *Be it enacted,* That the supreme court of the United States shall consist of a chief justice and five associate justices, any four of whom shall be a quorum, and shall hold annually at the seat of government two sessions, the one commencing the first Monday of February, and the other the first Monday of August. That the associate justices shall have precedence according to the date of their commissions, or when the commissions of two or more of them bear date on the same day, according to their respective ages.

SEC. 2. That the United States shall be, and they hereby are, divided into thirteen districts, to be limited and called as follows, . . .

SEC. 3. That there be a court called a District Court in each of the aforementioned districts, to consist of one judge, who shall reside in the district for which he is appointed, and shall be called a District Judge, and shall hold annually four sessions, . . .

SEC. 4. That the beforementioned districts, except those of Maine and Kentucky, shall be divided into three circuits, and be called the eastern, the middle, and the southern circuit. That the eastern circuit shall consist of the districts of New Hampshire, Massachusetts, Connecticut, and New York; that the middle circuit shall consist of the districts of New Jersey, Pennsylvania, Delaware, Maryland, and Virginia; and that the southern circuit shall consist of the districts of South Carolina and Georgia; and that there shall be held annually in each district of said circuits two courts which shall be called Circuit Courts, and shall consist of any two justices of the Supreme Court and the district judge of such districts, any two of whom shall constitute a quorum. *Provided,* That no district judge shall give a vote in any case of appeal or error from his own decision; but may assign the reasons of such his decision. . . .

SEC. 9. That the district courts shall have, exclusively of the courts of the several States, cognizance of all crimes and offences that shall be cognizable under the authority of the United States, committed within their respective districts, or upon the high seas; where no other punishment than whipping, not exceeding thirty stripes, a fine not exceeding one hundred dollars, or a term of imprisonment not exceeding six months, is to be inflicted; and shall also have exclusive original cognizance of all civil cases of admiralty and maritime jurisdiction, including all seizures under laws of impost, navigation, or trade of the United States. . . . And shall also have cognizance, concurrent with the courts of the several States, or the circuit courts, as the case may be, of all causes where an alien sues for a tort only in violation of the law of nations or a treaty of the United States. And shall also have cognizance, concurrent as last mentioned, of all suits at common law where the United States sue, and the matter in dispute amounts, exclusive of costs, to the sum or value of one hundred dollars. And shall also have jurisdiction exclusively of the courts of the several States, of all suits against consuls or vice-consuls, except for offences above the description aforesaid. And the trial of issues in fact, in the district courts, in all cases except civil causes of admiralty and maritime jurisdiction, shall be by jury. . . .

SEC. 11. That the circuit courts shall have original cognizance, concurrent with the courts of the several States, of all suits of a civil nature at common law or in equity, where the matter in dispute exceeds, exclusive of costs, the sum or value of five hundred dollars, and the United States are plaintiffs or petitioners; or an alien is a party, or the suit is between a citizen of the State where the suit is brought and a citizen of another State. And shall have exclusive cognizance of all crimes and offences cognizable under the authority of the United States, except where this act otherwise provides, or the laws of the United States shall otherwise direct, and concurrent jurisdiction with the district courts of the crimes and offences cognizable therein. . . . And the circuit courts shall also have appellate jurisdiction from the district courts under the regulations and restrictions hereinafter provided. . . .

SEC. 13. That the Supreme Court shall have exclusive jurisdiction of all controversies of a civil nature, where a state is a party, except between a state and its citizens; and except also between a state and citizens of other states, or aliens, in which latter case it shall have original but not exclusive jurisdiction. And shall have exclusively all such jurisdiction of suits or proceedings against ambassadors or other public ministers, or their domestics, or domestic servants, as a court of law can have or exercise consistently with the law of nations; and original, but not exclusive jurisdiction of all suits brought by ambassadors or other public ministers, or in which a consul or vice-consul shall be a party. And the trial of issues in fact in the Supreme Court in all actions at law against citizens of

the United States shall be by jury. The Supreme Court shall also have appellate jurisdiction from the circuit courts and courts of the several states in the cases hereinafter specially provided for; and shall have power to issue writs of prohibition to the district courts, when proceeding as courts of admiralty and maritime jurisdiction, and writs of *mandamus,* in cases warranted by the principle and usages of law, to any courts appointed, or persons holding office under the authority of the United States. . . .

SEC. 25. That a final judgment or decree in any suit, in the highest court of law or equity of a State in which a decision in the suit could be had, where is drawn in question the validity of a treaty or statute of, or an authority exercised under, the United States, and the decision is against their validity; or where is drawn in question the validity of a statute of, or an authority exercised under, any State, on the ground of their being repugnant to the constitution, treaties, or laws of the United States, and the decision is in favour of such their validity, or where is drawn in question the construction of any clause of the constitution, or of a treaty, or statute of, or commission held under, the United States, and the decision is against the title, right, privilege, or exemption, specially set up or claimed by either party, under such clause of the said Constitution, treaty, statute, or commission, may be re-examined, and reversed or affirmed in the Supreme Court of the United States upon a writ of error, the citation being signed by the chief justice, or judge or chancellor of the court rendering or passing the judgment or decree complained of, or by a justice of the Supreme Court of the United States, in the same manner and under the same regulations, and the writ shall have the same effect as if the judgment or decree complained of had been rendered or passed in a circuit court, and the proceedings upon the reversal shall also be the same, except that the Supreme Court, instead of remanding the cause for a final decision as before provided, may, at their discretion, if the cause shall have been once remanded before, proceed to a final decision of the same, and award execution. But no other error shall be assigned or regarded as a ground of reversal in any such case as aforesaid, than such as appears on the face of the record, and immediately respects the before-mentioned questions of validity or construction of the said constitution, treaties, statutes, commissions, or authorities in dispute. . . .

SEC. 35. . . . And there shall also be appointed a meet person learned in the law to act as attorney-general for the United States, who shall be sworn or affirmed to a faithful execution of his office; whose duty it shall be to prosecute and conduct all suits in the Supreme Court in which the United States shall be concerned, and to give his advice and opinion upon questions of law when required by the President of the United States, or when requested by the heads of any of the departments, touching any matters that may concern their departments, and shall receive such compensation for his services as shall by law be provided.

92. VIRGINIA RESOLUTIONS ON THE ASSUMPTION OF STATE DEBTS
December 16, 1790

(W. W. Hening, ed. *Statutes at Large of Virginia,* Vol. XIII, p. 237 ff.)

The opposition of Virginia to Hamilton's plan for the assumption of the State debts arose from the fact that Virginia had already made provision for a large part of her Revolutionary debt. The Virginia remonstrance was drafted by Patrick Henry, and caused Hamilton to remark, "This is the first symptom of a spirit which must either be killed, or will kill the Constitution of the United States."

In the House of Delegates,
Thursday, the 16th of December, 1790.

The General Assembly of the Commonwealth of Virginia to the United States in Congress assembled.

Represent,

That it is with great concern they find themselves compelled, from a sense of duty, to call the attention of Congress to an act of their last session, intitled "An act making provision for the debt of the United States," which the General Assembly conceive neither policy, justice nor the constitution warrants. Republican policy in the opinion of your memorialists could scarcely have suggested those clauses in the aforesaid act, which limit the right of the United States, in their redemption of the public debt. On the contrary they discern a striking resemblance between this system and that which was introduced into England, at the revolution; a system which has perpetuated upon that nation an enormous debt, and has moreover insinuated into the hands of the executive, an unbounded influence, which pervading every branch of the government, bears down all opposition, and daily threatens the destruction of everything that appertains to English liberty. The same causes produce the same effects! In an agricultural country like this, therefore to erect, and concentrate, and perpetuate a large monied interest, is a measure which your memorialists apprehend must in the course of human events produce one or other of two evils, the prostration of agriculture at the feet of commerce, or a change in the present form of foederal government, fatal to the existence of American liberty.

The General Assembly pass by various other parts of the said act which they apprehend will have a dangerous and impolitic tendency, and proceed to show the injustice of it as it applies to this Commonwealth. . . . Your memorialists turn away from the impolicy and injustice of the said act, and view it in another light, in which to them it appears still more odious and deformed.

During the whole discussion of the foederal constitution by the convention of Virginia, your memorialists were taught to believe "That every power not granted was retained;" under this impression and upon this positive condition, declared in the instrument of ratification, the said government was adopted by the people of this Commonwealth; but your memorialists can find no clause in the constitution authorizing Congress to assume the debts of the states! As the guardians then of the rights and interests of their constituents, as sentinels placed by them over the ministers of the foederal government, to shield it from their encroachments, or at least to sound the alarm when it is threatened with invasion, they can never reconcile it to their consciences, silently to acquiesce in a measure, which violates that hallowed maxim: a maxim on the truth and sacredness of which the foederal government depended for its adoption in this Commonwealth. But this injudicious act not only deserves the censure of the General Assembly, because it is not warranted by the constitution of the United States, but because it is repugnant to an express provision of that constitution; this provision is "That all debts contracted and engagements entered into, before the adoption of this constitution, shall be as valid against the United States under this constitution as under the confederation," which amounts to a constitutional ratification of the contracts respecting the state debts in the situation in which they existed under the confederation, and resorting to that standard there can be no doubt that in the present question the rights of states as contracting with the United States must be considered as sacred.

The General Assembly of the Commonwealth of Virginia confide so fully in the justice and wisdom of Congress upon the present occasion, as to hope that they will revise and amend the aforesaid act generally, and repeal in particular, so much of it as relates to the assumption of the state debts.

December the 23d., 1790. Agreed to by the Senate.

93. HAMILTON'S OPINION ON THE CONSTITUTIONALITY OF THE BANK
February 23, 1791

(*The Works of Alexander Hamilton*, ed. by J. C. Hamilton, Vol. IV, p. 104 ff.)

December 14, 1790, Hamilton presented to Congress his plan for the establishment of a national bank. A bill embodying most of the features of Hamilton's plan passed Congress February 8, 1791. Washington, doubtful of the constitutionality of the measure, requested Hamilton, Jefferson, and Randolph to submit written opinions on this question. For Jefferson's opinion, see Doc. No. 94. Randolph submitted two opinions, one adverse, one ambiguous. Hamilton's opinion is one of the ablest of his papers: it contained the substance of the argument subsequently adopted by Marshall in his decision in the case of *Mc Culloch* v. *Maryland*. Washington accepted Hamilton's argument, and signed the bill, February 25. On the First Bank, see, M. St. C. Clarke and D. A. Hall, *Legislative and Documentary History of the Bank of the United States*; W. G. Sumner, *History of Banking in the United States*, Vol. I.

. . . In entering upon the argument it ought to be premised that the objections of the Secretary of State and the Attorney-General are founded on a general denial of the authority of the United States to erect corporations. The latter, indeed, expressly admits, that if there be anything in the bill which is not warranted by the Constitution, it is the clause of incorporation.

Now it appears to the Secretary of the Treasury that this *general principle* is *inherent* in the very *definition* of government, and *essential* to every step of the progress to be made by that of the United States, namely:

That every power vested in a government is in its nature *sovereign*, and includes, by *force* of the *term* a right to employ all the *means* requisite and fairly applicable to the attainment of the ends of such power, and which are not precluded by restrictions and exceptions specified in the Constitution, or not immoral, or not contrary to the *essential ends* of political society. . . .

If it would be necessary to bring proof to a proposition so clear, as that which affirms that the powers of the federal government, as to *its objects*, were sovereign, there is a clause of the Constitution which would be decisive. It is that which declares that the Constitution, and the laws of the United States made in pursuance of it, . . . shall be the *supreme law of the land*. The power which can create a *supreme law of the land*, in any case, is doubtless *sovereign* as to such case.

This general and indisputable principle puts at once an end to the *abstract* question, whether the United States have power to erect a corporation; that is to say, to give a *legal* or *artificial capacity* to one or more persons, distinct from the *natural*. For it is unquestionably incident to *sovereign power* to erect corporations, and consequently to *that* of the United States, in *relation* to the *objects* intrusted to the management of the government. The difference is this: where the authority of the government is general, it can create corporations in *all cases*; where it is confined to certain branches of legislation, it can create corporations *only* in those cases. . . .

It is not denied that there are *implied* as well as *express powers,* and that the *former* are as effectually delegated as the *latter.* And for the sake of accuracy it shall be mentioned, that there is another class of powers, which may be properly denominated *resulting powers.* It will not be doubted, that if the United States should make a conquest of any of the territories of its neighbours, they would possess sovereign jurisdiction over the conquered territory. This would be rather a result, from the whole mass of the powers of the government, and from the nature of political society, than a consequence of either of the powers specially enumerated. . . .

It is conceded that *implied powers* are to be considered as delegated equally with *express ones.* Then it follows, that as a power of erecting a corporation may as well be *implied* as any other thing, it may as well be employed as an *instrument* or *mean* of carrying into execution any of the specified powers, as any other *instrument* or *mean* whatever. The only question must be, in this, as in every other case, whether the mean to be employed, or in this instance, the corporation to be erected, has a natural relation to any of the acknowledged objects or lawful ends of the government. Thus a corporation may not be erected by Congress for superintending the police of the city of Philadelphia, because they are not authorized to *regulate* the *police* of that city. But one may be erected in relation to the collection of taxes, or to the trade with foreign countries, or to the trade between the States, or with the Indian tribes; because it is the province of the federal government to *regulate* those objects and because it is incident to a general *sovereign* or *legislative* power to *regulate* a thing, to employ all the means which relate to its regulation to the best and greatest advantage. . . .

Through this mode of reasoning respecting the right of employing all the means requisite to the execution of the specified powers of the government, it is objected, that none but necessary and proper means are to be employed; and the Secretary of State maintains, that no means are to be considered as *necessary* but those without which the grant of the power would be *nugatory.* . . .

It is essential to the being of the national government, that so erroneous a conception of the meaning of the word *necessary* should be exploded.

It is certain, that neither the grammatical nor popular sense of the term requires that construction. According to both, *necessary* often means no more than *needful, requisite, incidental, useful,* or *conducive to.* . . . And it is the true one in which it is to be understood as used in the Constitution. The whole turn of the clause containing it indicates, that it was the intent of the Convention, by that clause, to give a liberal latitude to the exercise of the specified powers. The expressions have peculiar comprehensiveness. They are "to make all *laws* necessary and proper for *carrying into execution* the *foregoing powers,* and *all other powers,* vested by the Constitution in the *government* of the United States, or in any *department* or *officer* thereof.

To understand the word as the Secretary of State does, would be to depart from its obvious and popular sense, and to give it a restrictive operation, an idea never before entertained. It would be to give it the same force as if the word *absolutely* or *indispensably* had been prefixed to it. . . .

The *degree* in which a measure is necessary, can never be a *test* of the legal right to adopt it; that must be a matter of opinion, and can only be a *test* of expediency. The *relation* between the *measure* and the *end;* between the *nature* of the *mean* employed towards the execution of a power, and the object of that power, must be the criterion of constitutionality, not the more or less of *necessity* or *utility.* . . .

This restrictive interpretation of the word *necessary* is also contrary to this sound maxim of construction, namely, that the powers contained in a constitution of government, especially those which concern the general administration of the affairs of a country, its finances, trade, defence &c., ought to be construed liberally in advancement of the public good. . . . The means by which national exigencies are to be provided for, national inconveniences obviated, national prosperity promoted, are of such infinite variety, extent, and complexity, that there must of necessity be great latitude of discretion in the selection and application of those means. Hence, consequently, the necessity and propriety of exercising the authorities intrusted to a government on principles of liberal construction. . . .

But the doctrine which is contended for is not chargeable with the consequences imputed to it. It does not affirm that the national government is sovereign in all respects, but that it is sovereign to a certain extent; that is is, to the extent of the objects of its specified powers.

It leaves, therefore, a criterion of what is constitutional and of what is not so. This criterion is the *end,* to which the measure relates as a *mean.* If the *end* be clearly comprehended within any of the specified powers, and if the measure have an obvious relation to that *end,* and is not forbidden by any particular provision of the Constitution, it may safely be deemed to come within the compass of the national authority. There is also this further criterion, which may materially assist the decision; Does the proposed measure abridge a pre-existing right of any State or of any individual? If it does not, there is a strong presumption in favor of its constitutionality, and slighter relations to any declared object of the Constitution may be permitted to turn the scale. . . .

It is presumed to have been satisfactorily shown in the course of the preceding observations:

1. That the power of the government, *as to* the objects intrusted to its management, is, in its nature, sovereign.
2. That the right of erecting corporations is one inherent in, and inseparable from, the idea of sovereign power.
3. That the position, that the government of the United States can exercise no power but such as is delegated to it by its Constitution, does not militate against this principle.
4. That the word *necessary,* in the general clause, can have no *restrictive* operation derogating from the force of this principle; indeed, that the degree in which a measure is or is not *necessary,* cannot be a *test* of *constitutional right,* but of *expediency only.*
5. That the power to erect corporations is not to be considered as an *independent* or *substantive* power, but as an *incidental* and *auxiliary* one, and was therefore more properly left to implication than expressly granted.
6. That the principle in question does not extend the power of the government beyond the prescribed limits, because it only affirms a power to *incorporate* for purposes *within the sphere* of the *specified powers.*

And lastly, that the right to exercise such a power in certain cases is unequivocally granted in the most *positive* and *comprehensive* terms. . . .

A hope is entertained that it has, by this time, been made to appear, to the satisfaction of the President, that a bank has a natural relation to the power of collecting taxes—to that of regulating trade—to that of providing for the common defence—and that, as the bill under consideration contemplates the government in the light of a joint proprietor of the stock of the bank, it brings the case within the provision of the clause of the Constitution which immediately respects the property of the United States.

Under a conviction that such a relation subsists, the Secretary of the Treasury, with all deference, conceives, that it will result as a necessary consequence from the position, that all the specified powers of government are sovereign, as to the proper objects; that the incorporation of a bank is a constitutional measure; and that the objections taken to the bill, in this respect, are ill-founded. . . .

94. JEFFERSON'S OPINION ON THE CONSTITUTIONALITY OF THE BANK
February 15, 1791

(The Writings of Thomas Jefferson, ed. by H. E. Bergh, Vol. III, p. 145 ff.)

The bill for establishing a national bank, in 1791, undertakes, among other things,—
1. To form the subscribers into a corporation.
2. To enable them, in their corporate capacities, to receive grants of lands; and, so far, is against the laws of *mortmain.*
3. To make *alien* subscribers capable of holding lands; and so far is against the laws of *alienage.*

4. To transmit these lands, on the death of a proprietor, to a certain line of successors; and so far, changes the course of *descents*.

5. To put the lands out of the reach of forfeiture, or escheat; and so far, is against the laws of *forfeiture* and *escheat*.

6. To transmit personal chattels to successors, in a certain line; and so far, is against the laws of *distribution*.

7. To give them the sole and exclusive right of banking, under the national authority; and, so far, is against the laws of *monopoly*.

8. To communicate to them a power to make laws, paramount to the laws of the states; for so they must be construed, to protect the institution from the control of the state legislatures; and so probably they will be construed.

I consider the foundation of the Constitution as laid on this ground—that *all powers not delegated to the United States, by the Constitution, nor prohibited by it to the states, are reserved to the states, or to the people* (10th amend.). To take a single step beyond the boundaries thus specially drawn around the powers of Congress, is to take possession of a boundless field of power, no longer susceptible of any definition.

The incorporation of a bank, and the powers assumed by this bill, have not, in my opinion, been delegated to the United States by the Constitution.

I. *They are not among the powers specially enumerated. For these are,—*

1. A power to *lay taxes* for the purpose of paying the debts of the United States. But no debt is paid by this bill, nor any tax laid. Were it a bill to raise money, its organization in the Senate would condemn it by the Constitution.

2. To "borrow money". But this bill neither borrows money nor insures the borrowing of it. The proprietors of the bank will be just as free as any other money-holders to lend, or not to lend, their money to the public. The operation proposed in the bill, first to lend them two millions, and then borrow them back again, cannot change the nature of the latter act, which will still be a payment, and not a loan, call it by what name you please.

3. "To regulate commerce with foreign nations, and among the states, and with the Indian tribes." To erect a bank, and to regulate commerce, are very different acts. He who erects a bank creates a subject of commerce in its bills; so does he who makes a bushel of wheat, or digs a dollar out of the mines; yet neither of these persons regulates commerce thereby. To make a thing which may be bought and sold, is not to prescribe regulations for buying and selling. Besides, if this were an exercise of the power of regulating commerce, it would be void, as extending as much to the internal commerce of every state, as it is external. For the power given to Congress by the Constitution does not extend to the internal regulation of the commerce of a state . . . which remains exclusively with its own legislature; but to its external commerce only, that is to say, its commerce with another state, or with foreign nations, or with the Indian tribes. Accordingly, the bill does not propose the measure as a "regulation of trade", but as "productive of considerable advantage to trade."

Still less are these powers covered by any other of the special enumerations.

II Nor are they within either of the general phrases, which are the two following:—

1. "To lay taxes to provide for the general welfare of the United States;" that is to say, "to lay taxes *for the purpose* of providing for the general welfare;" for the laying of taxes is the *power*, and the general welfare the *purpose* for which the power is to be exercised. Congress are not to lay taxes *ad libitum, for any purpose they please;* but only to *pay the debts, or provide for the welfare, of the Union.* In like manner, they are not *to do anything they please,* to provide for the general welfare, but only to *lay taxes* for that purpose. To consider the latter phrase, not as describing the purpose of the first, but as giving a distinct and independent power to do any act they please which might be for the good of the Union, would render all the preceding and subsequent enumerations of power completely useless. It would reduce the whole instrument to a single phrase—that of instituting a Congress with power to do whatever would be for the good of the United States; and, as they would be the sole judges of the good or evil, it would be also a power to do whatever evil they pleased. It is an established rule of construction, where a phrase

will bear either of two meanings, to give it that which will allow some meaning to the other parts of the instrument, and not that which will render all the others useless. Certainly no such universal power was meant to be given them. It was intended to lace them up straitly within the enumerated powers, and those without which, as means, these powers could not be carried into effect. It is known that the very power now proposed *as a means,* was rejected *as an end by the Convention which formed the Constitution.* A proposition was made to them, to authorize Congress to open canals, and an amendatory one to empower them to incorporate. But the whole was rejected; and one of the reasons of objection urged in debate was, that they then would have a power to erect a bank, which would render great cities, where there were prejudices and jealousies on that subject, adverse to the reception of the Constitution.

2. The second general phrase is, "to make all laws *necessary* and proper for carrying into execution the enumerated powers." But they can all be carried into execution without a bank. A bank, therefore, is not *necessary,* and consequently not authorized by this phrase.

It has been much urged that a bank will give great facility or convenience in the collection of taxes. Suppose this were true; yet the Constitution allows only the means which are "necessary", not those which are merely "convenient", for effecting the enumerated powers. If such a latitude of construction be allowed to this phrase as to give any non-enumerated power, it will go to every one; for there is no one which ingenuity may not torture into a *convenience, in some way or other, to some one* of so long a list of enumerated powers. It would swallow up all the delegated powers, and reduce the whole to one phrase, as before observed. Therefore it was that the Constitution restrained them to the *necessary* means; that is to say, to those means without which

the grant of the power would be nugatory. . . .

Perhaps bank bills may be a more *convenient* vehicle than treasury orders. But a little *difference* in the degree of convenience cannot constitute the necessity which the Constitution makes the ground for assuming any non-enumerated power. . . .

Can it be thought that the Constitution intended that, for a shade or two of *convenience,* more or less, Congress should be authorized to break down the most ancient and fundamental laws of the several states such as those against mortmain, the laws of alienage, the rules of descent, the acts of distribution, the laws of escheat and forfeiture, and the laws of monopoly.

Nothing but a necessity invincible by other means, can justify such a prostration of laws, which constitute the pillars of our whole system of jurisprudence. Will Congress be too strait-laced to carry the Constitution into honest effect, unless they may pass over the foundation laws of the state governments, for the slightest convenience to theirs?

The negative of the President is the shield provided by the Constitution to protect, against the invasions of the legislature, 1. *The rights of the executive;* 2. *Of the judiciary;* 3. *Of the states and state legislatures.* The present is the case of a right remaining exclusively with the states, and is, consequently, one of those intended by the Constitution to be placed under his protection.

It must be added, however, that, unless the President's mind, on a view of everything which is urged for and against this bill, is tolerably clear that it is unauthorized by the Constitution, if the *pro* and the *con* hang so evenly as to balance his judgment, a just respect for the wisdom of the legislature would naturally decide the balance in favor of their opinion. It is chiefly for cases where they are clearly misled by error, ambition, or interest, that the Constitution has placed a check in the negative of the President.

95. CHISHOLM v. GEORGIA
2 Dallas, 419
1793

This is probably the most important of the early cases which came before the Supreme Court, and in the decision of the Court can be found a foreshadowing of the nationalism enunciated by Marshall a decade later. The case of *Chisholm* v. *Georgia* arose out of the effort of Chisholm and others, citizens of South Carolina and executors of the estate of an English creditor, to secure compensation from Georgia for property confiscated during the Revolution. The Constitution of the United States provided, Art. III. Sec. 2, that the judicial power of the United States should extend to controversies between States and between a State and the citizens of another State. Under this provision, could a citizen sue a State in the Federal Courts? That this clause authorized such suits against States was denied by Hamilton in the *Federalist,* and by Madison in the debates in the Virginia ratifying Convention. "It is not," said Madison, "in the power of individuals to call any state into court. The only operation it can have, is that, if a state should wish to bring a suit against a citizen, it must be brought before the federal court." (Elliot's *Debates,* 1861 ed. Vol. III, p. 533.) Yet in this case, the Supreme Court upheld the right of Chisholm to sue Georgia in the Supreme Court. Georgia refused to appear before the Court, denied the validity of the judgement, and threatened to punish by death any official who should attempt to execute the decree of the court. Other states also protested, and shortly after the decision an amendment was introduced which deprived the federal courts of jurisdiction in cases against one of the States by citizens of another State. This, the eleventh amendment, was ratified January 8, 1798. See C. Warren, *The Supreme Court in United States History,* 1928 ed. Vol. 1, ch. ii; L. B. Boudin, *Government by Judiciary,* Vol. I, ch. vii; H. L. Carson, *The Supreme Court;* G. J. Mc Ree, *James Iredell,* Vol. II; U. B. Phillips, "Georgia and State Rights," American Hist. Assoc. *Reports,* 1901, Vol. II.

WILSON, J. This is a case of uncommon magnitude. One of the parties to it is a State, certainly respectable, claiming to be sovereign. The question to be determined is, whether this State, so respectable and whose claim soars so high, is amenable to the jurisdiction of the Supreme Court of the United States? This question, important in itself, will depend on others, more important still; and may perhaps, be ultimately resolved into one, no less radical than this— "Do the People of the United States form a nation?". . .

To the Constitution of the United States the term sovereignty is totally unknown. There is but one place where it could have

been used with propriety. But even in that place it would not, perhaps, have comported with the delicacy of those who ordained and established that Constitution. They might have announced themselves sovereign people of the United States; but serenely conscious of the fact, they avoided the ostentatious declaration. . . .

III. I am, thirdly, and chiefly, to examine the important question now before us, by the Constitution of the United States, and the legitimate result of that valuable instrument. Under this view, the question is naturally subdivided into two others. 1. Could the Constitution of the United States vest a jurisdiction over the State of Georgia? 2. Has the Constitution vested such jurisdiction in this Court? I have already remarked, that in the practice, and even in the science of politics, there has been frequently a strong current against the natural order of things; and an inconsiderate or an interested disposition to sacrifice the end to the means. This remark deserves a more particular illustration. Even in almost every nation, which has been denominated free, the state has assumed a supercilious preëminence above the people, who have formed it: Hence the haughty notions of state independence, state sovereignty, and state supremacy. . . .

In the United States and in the several States which compose the Union, we go not so far: but still we go one step farther than we ought to go in this unnatural and inverted order of things. The states rather than the People for whose sakes the states exist, are frequently the objects which attract and arrest our principal attention. This, I believe, has produced much of the confusion and perplexity, which have appeared in several proceedings and several publications on state-politics, and on the politics, too, of the United States. Sentiments and expressions of this inaccurate kind prevail in our common, even in our convivial, language. . . . A State, I cheerfully admit, is the noblest work of Man: But, Man, himself, free and honest, is, I speak as to this world, the noblest work of God. . . .

With the strictest propriety, therefore, classical and political, our national scene opens with the most magnificent object which the nation could present: "The People of the United States" are the first personages introduced. Who were these people? They were the citizens of thirteen States, each of which had a separate constitution and government, and all of which were connected together by articles of confederation. To the purposes of public strength and felicity, that confederacy was totally inadequate. A requisition on the several States terminated its legislative authority; executive or judicial authority it had none. In order, therefore, to form a more perfect union, to establish justice, to insure domestic tranquillity, to provide for the common defense, and to secure the blessings of liberty, those people, among whom were the people of Georgia, ordained and established the present Constitution. By that Constitution legislative power is vested, executive power is vested, judicial power is vested.

The question now opens fairly to our view, could the people of those States, among whom were those of Georgia, bind those States, and Georgia among the others, by the legislative, executive, and judicial power so vested? If the principles on which I have founded myself are just and true, this question must unavoidably receive an affirmative answer. If those States were the work of those people, those people, and, that I may apply the case closely, the people of Georgia in particular, could alter, as they pleased, their former work; to any degree, they could diminish as well as enlarge it. Any or all of the former state powers they could extinguish or transfer. The inference which necessarily results is that the Constitution ordained and established by those people, and, still closely to apply the case, in particular, by the people of Georgia, could vest jurisdiction or judicial power over those States and over the State of Georgia in particular.

The next question under this head is— Has the Constitution done so? . . .

Whoever considers in a combined and comprehensive view the general texture of the Constitution will be satisfied that the people of the United States intended to form themselves into a nation for national purposes. They instituted, for such purposes, a national government, complete in all its parts, with powers legislative, executive and judiciary; and in all those powers extending over the whole nation. Is it congruous that, with regard to such purposes, any person, natural or artificial, should be permitted to claim successfully an entire exemption from the jurisdiction of the national government? Would not such claims, crowned with success, be repugnant to our very existence as a nation? When so many trains of deduction, coming from different quarters, converge and unite at last in the same point, we may safely conclude, as the legitimate result of this Constitution, that the State of Georgia is amenable to the jurisdiction of this court.

But, in my opinion, this doctrine rests not upon the legitimate result of fair and conclusive deduction from the Constitution; it is confirmed beyond all doubt by the direct and explicit declaration of the Constitution itself. "The judicial power of the United States shall extend to controversies between two States.". . . Can the most consummate degree of professional ingenuity devise a mode by which this "controversy between two States" can be brought before a court of law, and yet neither of those States be a defendant? "The judicial power of the United States shall extend to controversies between a State and citizens of another State". Could the strictest legal language . . . describe with more precise accuracy the cause now depending before the tribunal? . . .

From all, the combined inference is, that the action lies. Chief Justice Jay and Justices Blair and Cushing concurred. Justice Iredell dissented.

96. WASHINGTON'S PROCLAMATION OF NEUTRALITY
April 22, 1793

(Richardson, ed. *Messages and Papers,* Vol. I, p. 156)

The proclamation of Neutrality had the support of all the members of Washington's cabinet. Note that the word "neutrality" is nowhere used. The proclamation precipitated a pamphlet controversy between Hamilton, writing as "Pacificus" and Madison, writing as "Helvidius".

See, J. S. Bassett, *The Federalist System,* p. 86 ff.; R. Hildreth, *History of the United States,* Vol. IV, p. 411 ff.; C. M. Thomas, *American Neutrality in 1793.*

BY THE PRESIDENT OF THE UNITED STATES
OF AMERICA
A PROCLAMATION

Whereas it appears that a state of war exists between Austria, Prussia, Sardinia, Great Britain, and the United Netherlands on the one part and France on the other, and the duty and interest of the United States require that they should with sincerity and good faith adopt and pursue a conduct friendly and impartial toward the belligerent powers:

I have therefore thought fit by these presents to declare the disposition of the United States to observe the conduct aforesaid toward those powers respectively, and to exhort and warn the citizens of the United States carefully to avoid all acts and proceeding whatsoever which may in any manner tend to contravene such disposition.

And I do hereby also make known that whosoever of the citizens of the United States shall render himself liable to punishment or forfeiture under the law of nations by committing, aiding, or abetting hostilities against any of the said powers, or by carrying to any of them those articles which are deemed contraband by the modern usage of nations, will not receive the protection of the United States against such punishment or forfeiture; and further, that I have given instructions to those officers to whom it belongs to cause prosecutions to be instituted against all persons who shall, within the cognizance of the courts of the United States, violate the law of nations with respect to the powers at war, or any of them. . . .

Philadelphia, the 22d of April, 1793,

G°. WASHINGTON.

97. WASHINGTON'S PROCLAMATION ON THE WHISKEY REBELLION
August 7, 1794

(Richardson, ed. *Messages and Papers,* Vol. I, p. 158)

The excise tax of March 3, 1791 upon distilled spirits and stills was part of Hamilton's financial policy. It bore with peculiar hardship upon the inhabitants of western Pennsylvania and Virginia who were accustomed to turn their corn into whiskey because that was the only way in which it could be transported economically to the coast. The dissatisfaction of the west was so intense that it resulted in a general flouting of the law, accompanied by some violence, and Washington, on Hamilton's recommendation, ordered out the militia in order to suppress the "rebellion." See, H. H. Brackenridge, *Incidents of the Insurrection in the Western Parts of Pennsylvania;* H. Adams, *Gallatin,* p. 86 ff.; W. Findley, *History of the Insurrection in the Four Western Counties of Pennsylvania; Proceedings of the Executive of the United States Respecting the Insurgents,* 1794, with Hamilton's Report. Washington reported to Congress on his handling of the situation in his Sixth Annual Message, Richardson, ed. *Messages and Papers,* Vol. I. p. 162 ff.

BY THE PRESIDENT OF THE UNITED STATES
OF AMERICA
A PROCLAMATION

Whereas combinations to defeat the execution of the laws laying duties upon spirits distilled within the United States and upon stills have from the time of the commencement of those laws existed in some of the western parts of Pennsylvania; and

Whereas the said combinations, proceeding in a manner subversive equally of the just authority of government and of the rights of individuals, have hitherto effected their dangerous and criminal purpose by the influence of certain irregular meetings whose proceedings have tended to encourage and uphold the spirit of opposition by misrepresentations of the laws calculated to render them odious; by endeavors to deter those who might be so disposed from accepting offices under them through fear of public resentment and of injury to person and property, and to compel those who had accepted such offices by actual violence to surrender or forbear the execution of them; by circulating vindictive menaces against all those who should otherwise, directly or indirectly, aid in the execution of the said laws, or who, yielding to the dictates of conscience and to a sense of obligation, should themselves comply therewith; by actually injuring and destroying the property of persons who were understood to have so complied; by inflicting cruel and humiliating punishments upon private citizens for no other cause than that of appearing to be the friends of the laws; by intercepting the public officers on the highways, abusing, assaulting, and otherwise ill treating them; by going to their houses in the night, gaining admittance by force, taking away their papers, and committing other outrages, employing for these unwarrantable purposes the agency of armed banditti disguised in such manner as for the most part to escape discovery; and

Whereas the endeavors of the Legislature to obviate objections to the said laws by lowering the duties and by other alterations conducive to the convenience of those whom they immediately affect . . . and the endeavors of the executive officers to conciliate a compliance with the laws by explanations, by forbearance, and even by particular accommodations founded on the suggestion of local considerations, have been disappointed of their effect by the machinations of persons whose industry to excite resistance has increased with every appearance of a disposition among the people to relax in their opposition and to acquiesce in the laws, insomuch that many persons in the said western parts of Pennsylvania have at length been hardy enough to perpetrate acts which I am advised amount to treason, being overt acts of levying war against the United States, . . . avowing as the motives of these outrageous proceedings an intention to prevent by force of arms the execution of the said laws, . . . to withstand by open violence the lawful authority of the Government of the United States, and to compel thereby an alteration in the measures of the Legislature and a repeal of the laws aforesaid; and

Whereas by a law of the United States entitled "An act to provide for calling forth the militia to execute the laws of the Union, suppress insurrections, and repel invasions," it is enacted "that whenever the laws of the United States shall be opposed or the execution thereof obstructed in any State by combinations too powerful to be suppressed by the ordinary course of judicial proceedings . . . it shall be lawful for the President of the United States to call forth the militia of such State to suppress such combinations and to cause the laws to be duly executed. And if the militia of a State where such combinations may happen shall refuse or be insufficient to suppress the same, it shall be lawful for the President, if the Legislature of the United States shall not be in session, to call forth and employ such numbers of the militia of any other State or States most convenient thereto as may be necessary; . . . *Provided always,* That whenever it may be necessary in the judgment of the President to use the military force hereby directed to be called forth, the President shall forthwith, and previous thereto, by proclamation, command such insurgents to disperse and retire peaceably to their respective abodes within a limited time;" and . . .

Whereas it is in my judgment necessary under the circumstances of the case to take measures for calling forth the militia in order to suppress the combinations aforesaid, and to cause the laws to be duly executed; and I have accordingly determined so to do, feeling the deepest regret for the occasion, but withal the most solemn conviction that the essential interests of the Union demand it, that the very existence of Government and the fundamental principles of social order are materially involved in the issue, and that the patriotism and firmness of all good citizens are seriously called upon, as occasions may require, to aid in the effectual suppression of so fatal a spirit:

Wherefore, and in pursuance of the proviso above recited, I, George Washington, President of the United States, do hereby command all persons being insurgents as aforesaid, and all others whom it may concern, on or before the 1st day of September next to disperse and retire peaceably to their respective abodes. And I do moreover warn all persons whomsoever against aiding, abetting, or comforting the perpetrators of the aforesaid treasonable acts, and do require all officers and other citizens, according to their respective duties and the laws of the land, to exert their utmost endeavors to prevent and suppress such dangerous proceedings. . . .

Philadelphia, the 7th of August, 1794,

G°. WASHINGTON.

98. THE JAY TREATY
November 19, 1794

(Malloy, ed. *Treaties, Conventions, etc.*, Vol. I, p. 590 ff.)

Contrary to the provisions of the Treaty of 1783, Great Britain had retained control of the Northwest posts and had failed to make any compensation for slaves carried away during the Revolution. In addition to these grievances, of old standing, there were more recent ones arising from interference with neutral trade. War seemed imminent in 1794, when Washington nominated Chief Justice John Jay as envoy extraordinary to conclude a treaty of peace and commerce. The Jay Treaty solved some of the most important matters of dispute between the two nations, and averted war, but it contained certain features profoundly unsatisfactory to the majority of Americans. Washington hesitated some time before sending it to the Senate for ratification. After a bitter contest in the Senate, the Treaty was ratified June 24, 1795, with a reservation which suspended the obnoxious Article XII. For the debate on the Jay Treaty, see H. Adams, *Albert Gallatin;* C. Bowers, *Jefferson and Hamilton*, chs. xi–xii. A thorough history of the Treaty is S. F. Bemis, *Jay's Treaty*. The full text of the adjudications provided for by Articles 5, 6, and 7, have been edited by J. B. Moore, *International Adjudications*, Vols. I–IV. The question of appropriations for carrying out the provisions of the Treaty raised a serious constitutional problem in the House. The appropriations were finally made, but only after one of the greatest political debates in American history. For the speeches of Gallatin and Fisher Ames on appropriations for the Treaty, see A. Johnston, ed. *American Orations*, Vol. I, p. 84 ff.

ART. I. There shall be a firm, inviolable and universal peace, and a true and sincere friendship between his Britannic Majesty, his heirs and successors, and the United States of America; and between their respective countries, territories, cities, towns and people of every degree, without exception of persons or places.

ART. II. His Majesty will withdraw all his troops and garrisons from all posts and places within the boundary lines assigned by the treaty of peace to the United States. This evacuation shall take place on or before [June 1, 1796,] . . . : The United States in the mean time at their discretion, extending their settlements to any part within the said boundary line, except within the precincts or jurisdiction of any of the said posts. All settlers and traders, within the precincts or jurisdiction of the said posts, shall continue to enjoy, unmolested, all their property of every kind, and shall be protected therein. They shall be at full liberty to remain there, or to remove with all or any part of their effects; and it shall also be free to them to sell their lands, houses, or effects, or to retain the property thereof, at their discretion; such of them as shall continue to reside within the said boundary lines, shall not be compelled to become citizens of the United States, or to take any oath of allegiance to the government thereof; but they shall be at full liberty so to do if they think proper, and they shall make and declare their election within one year after the evacuation aforesaid. And all persons who shall continue there after the expiration of the said year, without having declared their intention of remaining subjects of his Britannic Majesty, shall be considered as having elected to become citizens of the United States.

ART. III. It is agreed that it shall at all times be free to his Majesty's subjects, and to the citizens of the United States, and also to the Indians dwelling on either side of the said boundary line, freely to pass and repass by land or inland navigation, into the respective territories and countries of the two parties, on the continent of America (the country within the limits of the Hudson's bay Company only excepted) and to navigate all the lakes, rivers and waters thereof, and freely to carry on trade and commerce with each other. . . . The river Mississippi shall, however, according to the treaty of peace, be entirely open to both parties; and it is further agreed, that all the ports and places on its eastern side, to whichsoever of the parties belonging, may freely be resorted to and used by both parties, in as ample a manner as any of the Atlantic ports or places of the United States, or any of the ports or places of his Majesty in Great-Britain. . . .

ART. IV. Whereas it is uncertain whether the river Mississippi extends so far to the northward, as to be intersected by a line to be drawn due west from the Lake of the Woods, in the manner mentioned in the treaty of peace . . . it is agreed, that measures shall be taken . . . for making a joint survey of the said river from one degree of latitude below the falls of St. Anthony, to the principal source or sources of the said river, and also of the parts adjacent thereto; and that if on the result of such survey, it should appear that the said river, would not be intersected by such a line as is above mentioned, the two parties will thereupon proceed by amicable negociation, to regulate the boundary line in that quarter, . . .

ART. V. Whereas doubts have arisen what river was truly intended under the name of the river St. Croix, mentioned in the said treaty of peace, and forming a part of the boundary therein described; that question shall be referred to the final decision of commissioners to be appointed. . . . The said commissioners shall, by a declaration, under their hands and seals, decide what river is the river St. Croix, intended by the treaty. . . . And both parties agree to consider such decision as final and conclusive, so as that the same shall never thereafter be called into question, or made the subject of dispute or difference between them.

ART. VI. Whereas it is alleged by divers British merchants and others his Majesty's subjects, that debts, to a considerable amount, which were bona fide contracted before the peace, still remain owing to them by citizens or inhabitants of the United States, and that by the operation of various lawful impediments since the peace, not only the full recovery of the said debts has been delayed, but also the value and security thereof have been, in several instances, impaired and lessened, so that by the ordinary course of judicial proceedings, the British creditors cannot now obtain, and actually have and receive full and adequate compensation for the losses and damages which they have thereby sustained. It is agreed, that in all such cases, where full compensation for such losses and damages cannot, for whatever reason, be actually obtained, had and received by the said creditors in the ordinary course of justice, the United States will make full and complete compensation for the same to the said creditors: But it is distinctly understood, that this provision is to extend to such losses only as have been occasioned by the lawful impediments aforesaid, . . .

ART. VII. Whereas complaints have been made by divers merchants and others, citizens of the United States, that during the course of the war in which his Majesty is now engaged, they have sustained considerable losses and damage, by reason of irregular or illegal captures or condemnations of their vessels and other property, under colour of authority or commissions from his Majesty, and that from various circumstances belonging to the said cases, adequate compensation for the losses and damages so sustained cannot now be actually obtained, had and received by the ordinary course of judicial proceedings; it is agreed, that in all such cases, where adequate compensation cannot, for whatever reason, be now actually obtained, had and received by the said merchants and others, in the ordinary course of justice, full and complete compensation for the same will be made by the British government to the said complainants. But it is distinctly understood, that this provision is not to extend to such losses or damages as have been occasioned by the manifest delay or negligence, or wilful omission of the claimant. . . .

ART. X. Neither the debts due from individuals of the one nation to individuals of the other, nor shares, nor monies which they may have in the public funds, or in the public or private banks, shall ever in any event of war or national differences be sequestered or confiscated. . . .

ART. XI. It is agreed between his Majesty and the United States of America, that there shall be a reciprocal and entirely perfect liberty of navigation and commerce between their respective people, in the manner, under the limitations and on the condtions specified in the following articles:

[Art. XII., relating to trade with the West Indies, was suspended.]

ART. XIII. His Majesty consents that the vessels belonging to the citizens of the United States of America, shall be admitted and hospitably received, in all the sea-ports and harbours of the British territories in the East-Indies. And that the citizens of the said United States, may freely carry on a trade between the said territories and the said United States, in all articles of which the importation or exportation respectively, to or from the said territories, shall not be entirely prohibited. . . . The citizens of the United States shall pay for their vessels when admitted into the said ports no other or higher tonnage-duty than shall be payable on British vessels when admitted into the ports of the United States. And they shall pay no other or higher duties or charges, on the importation or exportation of the cargoes of the said vessels, than shall be payable on the same articles when imported or exported in British vessels. But it is expressly agreed, that the vessels of the United States shall not carry any of the articles exported by them from the said British territories, to any port or place, except to some port or place in America, where the same shall be unladen, and such regulations shall be adopted by both parties, as shall from time to time be found necessary to enforce the due and faithful observance of this stipulation. It is also understood that the permission granted by this article, is not to extend to allow the vessels of the United States to carry on any part of the coasting-trade of the said British territories; but vessels going with their original cargoes, or part thereof, from one port of discharge to another, are not to be considered as carrying on the coasting-trade. Neither is this article to be construed to allow the citizens of the said states to settle or reside within the said territories, or to go into the interior parts thereof, without the permission of the British government established there. . . .

ART. XIV. There shall be between all the dominions of his Majesty in Europe and the territories of the United States, a reciprocal and perfect liberty of commerce and navigation. The people and inhabitants of the two countries respectively, shall have liberty freely and securely, and without hindrance and molestation, to come with their ships and cargoes to the lands, countries, cities, ports, places and rivers, within the dominions and territories aforesaid, to enter into the same, to resort there, and to remain and reside there, without any limitation of time.

Also to hire and possess houses and warehouses for the purposes of their commerce, and generally the merchants and traders on each side, shall enjoy the most complete protection and security for their commerce; but subject always as to what respects this article to the laws and statutes of the two countries respectively.

ART. XV. It is agreed that no other or higher duties shall be paid by the ships or merchandize of the one party in the ports of the other, than such as are paid by the like vessels or merchandize of all other nations. Nor shall any other or higher duty be imposed in one country on the importation of any articles the growth, produce or manufacture of the other, than are or shall be payable on the importation of the like articles being of the growth, produce, or manufacture of any other foreign country. Nor shall any prohibition be imposed on the exportation or importation of any articles to or from the territories of the two parties respectively, which shall not equally extend to all other nations. . . .

The two parties agree to treat for the more exact equalization of the duties on the respective navigation of their subjects and people, in such manner as may be most beneficial to the two countries. . . . In the interval it is agreed, that the United States will not impose any new or additional tonnage duties on British vessels, nor increase the now-subsisting difference between the duties payable on the importation of any articles in British or in American vessels. . . .

ART. XVII. It is agreed, that in all cases where vessels shall be captured or detained on just suspicion of having on board enemy's property, or of carrying to the enemy any of the articles which are contraband of war; the said vessel shall be brought to the nearest or most convenient port; and if any property of an enemy should be found on board such vessel, that part only which belongs to the enemy shall be made prize, and the vessel shall be at liberty to proceed with the remainder without any impediment. . . .

ART. IX. And that more abundant care may be taken for the security of the respective subjects and citizens of the contracting parties, and to prevent their suffering injuries by the men of war, or privateers of either party, all commanders of ships of war and privateers, and all others the said subjects and citizens, shall forbear doing any damage to those of the other party, or committing any outrage against them, and if they act to the contrary, they shall be punished, and shall also be bound in their persons and estates to make satisfaction and reparation for all damages, and the interest thereof, of whatever nature the said damages may be. . . .

ART. XXII. It is expressly stipulated, that neither of the said contracting parties will order or authorize any acts of reprisal against the other, on complaints of injuries or damages, until the said party shall first have presented to the other a statement thereof, verified by competent proof and evidence, and demanded justice and satisfaction, and the same shall either have been refused or unreasonably delayed.

ART. XXVI. If at any time a rupture should take place, (which God forbid) between his Majesty and the United States, the merchants and others of each of the two nations, residing in the dominions of the other, shall have the privilege of remaining and continuing their trade, so long as they behave peaceably, and commit no offence against the laws; and in case their conduct should render them suspected, and the respective governments should think proper to order them to remove, the term of twelve months from the publication of the order shall be allowed them for that purpose, to remove with their families, effects and property; but this favour shall not be extended to those who shall act contrary to the established laws; . . .

ART. XXVIII. It is agreed, that the first ten articles of this treaty shall be permanent, and that the subsequent articles, except the twelfth, shall be limited in their duration to twelve years, . . .

99. THE PINCKNEY TREATY
October 27, 1795

Treaty of Friendship, Boundaries, Commerce and Navigation Between the United States of America, and the King of Spain.

(Malloy, ed. *Treaties, Conventions, etc.* Vol. II, p. 1640 ff.)

On the conclusion of the Revolutionary War Spain, refusing to recognize the right of Great Britain to give to the United States the right to navigate the Mississippi, closed that river to Americans. Other matters of dispute between the United States and Spain concerned the boundaries of West Florida and the activities of the Spanish authorities in fomenting discontent among the Indians. Efforts of the United States to conclude a satisfactory treaty with Spain were unsuccessful in 1781 and again in 1785–6. In the early seventeen-nineties western discontent grew alarmingly and intrigues looking to separation or to an attack upon Spanish possessions attracted wide attention. The conclusion of Jay's Treaty inspired the Spanish Court with the fear that Great Britain and the United States might combine to attack Spanish possessions in the new world, and the Spanish minister, Godoy, promptly concluded with Thomas Pinckney a treaty whose provisions were highly satisfactory to Americans. The terms of the treaty, however, were not carried out for almost three years. For Pinckney's Treaty see S. F. Bemis, *Pinckney's Treaty;* A. P. Whitaker, *The Spanish-American Frontier, 1783–1795;* A. P. Whitaker, *The Mis-*

sissippi Question, 1795–1803; P. C. Phillips, *The West in the Diplomacy of the American Revolution.*

ART. I. THERE shall be a firm and inviolable peace and sincere friendship between His Catholic Majesty, his successors and subjects, and the United States, and their citizens, without exception of persons or places.

ART. II. To prevent all disputes on the subject of the boundaries which separate the territories of the two high contracting parties, it is hereby declared and agreed to as follows, to wit. The southern boundary of the United States, which divides their territory from the Spanish colonies of East and West Florida, shall be designated by a line beginning in the River Missisippi, at the northernmost part of the thirty-first degree of latitude north of the equator, which from thence shall be drawn due east to the middle of the River Apalachicola, or Catahouche, thence along the middle thereof to its junction with the Flint: thence straight to the head of St. Mary's river, and thence down the middle thereof to the Atlantic ocean. . . .

ART. IV. It is likewise agreed that the western boundary of the United States which separates them from the Spanish colony of Louissiana, is in the middle of the channel or bed of the River Missisippi, from the northern boundary of the said states to the completion of the thirty-first degree of latitude north of the equator. And His Catholic Majesty has likewise agreed that the navigation of the said river, in its whole breadth from its source to the ocean, shall be free only to his subjects and the citizens of the United States, unless he should extend this privilege to the subject of other Powers by special convention.

ART. V. The two high contracting parties shall, by all the means in their power, maintain peace and harmony among the several Indian nations who inhabit the country adjacent to the lines and rivers, which, by the preceding articles, form the boundaries of the two Floridas. . . .

And whereas several treaties of friendship exist between the two contracting parties and the said nations of Indians, it is hereby agreed that in future no treaty of alliance, or other whatever (except treaties of peace,) shall be made by either party with the Indians living within the boundary of the other, but both parties will endeavour to make the advantages of the Indian trade common and mutually beneficial to their respective subjects and citizens, observing in all things the most complete reciprocity. . . .

ART. XXII. . . . And in consequence of the stipulations contained in the IV. article, His Catholic Majesty will permit the citizens of the United States, for the space of three years from this time, to deposit their merchandizes and effects in the port of New-Orleans, and to export them from thence without paying any other duty than a fair price for the hire of the stores, and His Majesty promises either to continue this permission, if he finds during that time that it is not prejudicial to the interests of Spain, or if he should not agree to continue it there, he will assign to them, on another part of the banks of the Missisippi, an equivalent establishment. . . .

THOMAS PINCKNEY,
EL PRINCIPE DE LA PAZ,

100. WASHINGTON'S FAREWELL ADDRESS
September 17, 1796

(Richardson, ed. *Messages and Papers*, Vol. I, p. 213 ff.)

This memorable address was Washington's valedictory to the American people; its advice and injunctions have influenced American history far more than Washington himself could have anticipated. The immediate occasion for Washington's Address was the necessity of eliminating himself from the contest for the Presidency. Washington had seriously considered retiring from that office at the end of his first term, and on May 20, 1792, he had written Madison a letter containing many of the points later developed in the Farewell Address. There has been considerable controversy over the question of the authorship of the Address, and Hamilton's admirers claim that he was principally responsible for it. In July 1796 Washington sent his earlier draft of a farewell address, together with Madison's answer, to Hamilton with a request for suggestions and literary alterations. Hamilton proceeded to write an address, based almost entirely upon Washington's draft; Washington returned it to Hamilton with further suggestions, and Hamilton and John Jay polished up this draft. This second draft, however, did not please Washington as much as Hamilton's first draft, and he asked Hamilton to polish up the first draft for him. This draft was returned to Washington, who made some slight alterations and omissions, and sent it to a printer, Claypoole, who published it in the "American Daily Advertiser," September 17. Washington's, Madison's and Hamilton's drafts of the Address are given in W. C. Ford, ed. *The Writings of George Washington*, Vol. XIII. See, H. Binney, *An Inquiry into the Formation of Washington's Farewell Address;* J. C. Fitzpatrick, *George Washington Himself,* ch. lxxii.

UNITED STATES, *September 17, 1796.*
Friends and Fellow-Citizens:

The period for a new election of a citizen to administer the Executive Government of the United States being not far distant, and the time actually arrived when your thoughts must be employed in designating the person who is to be clothed with that important trust, it appears to me proper, especially as it may conduce to a more distinct expression of the public voice, that I should now apprise you of the resolution I have formed to decline being considered among the number of those out of whom a choice is to be made. . . .

The impressions with which I first undertook the arduous trust were explained on the proper occasion. In the discharge of this trust I will only say that I have, with good intentions, contributed toward the organization and administration of the Government the best exertions of which a very fallible judgment was capable. Not unconscious in the outset of the inferiority of my qualifications, experience in my own eyes, perhaps still more in the eyes of others, has strengthened the motives to diffidence of myself; and every day the increasing weight of years admonishes me more and more that the shade of retirement is as necessary to me as it will be welcome. Satisfied that if any circumstances have given peculiar value to my services they were temporary, I have the consolation to believe that, while choice and prudence invite me to quit the political scene, patriotism does not forbid it. . . .

Here, perhaps, I ought to stop. But a solicitude for your welfare which can not end with my life, and the apprehension of danger natural to that solicitude, urge me on an occasion like the present to offer to your solemn contemplation and to recommend to your frequent review some sentiments which are the result of much reflection, of no inconsiderable observation, and which appear to me all important to the permanency of your felicity as a people. . . .

Interwoven as is the love of liberty with every ligament of your hearts, no recommendation of mine is necessary to fortify or confirm the attachment.

The unity of government which constitutes you one people is also now dear to you. It is justly so, for it is a main pillar in the edifice of your real independence, the support of your tranquillity at home, your peace abroad, of your safety, of your prosperity, of that very liberty which you so highly prize. But as it is easy to foresee that from different causes and from different quarters much pains will be taken, many artifices employed, to weaken in your minds the conviction of this truth, as this is the point in your political fortress against which the batteries of internal and external enemies will be most constantly and actively (though often covertly and insidiously) directed, it is of infinite moment that you should properly estimate the immense value of your national union to your collective and individual happiness; that you should cherish a cordial, habitual, and immovable attachment to it; accustoming yourselves to think and speak of it as of the palladium of your political safety and prosperity; watching for its preservation with jealous anxiety; discountenancing whatever may suggest even a suspicion that it can in any event be abandoned, and indignantly frowning upon the first dawning of every attempt to alienate any portion of our country from the rest or to enfeeble the sacred ties which now link together the various parts.

For this you have every inducement of sympathy and interest. Citizens by birth or choice of a common country, that country has a right to concentrate your affections. The name of American, which belongs to you in your national capacity, must always exalt the just pride of patriotism more than any appellation derived from local discriminations. With slight shades of difference, you have the same religion, manners, habits, and political principles. You have in a common cause fought and triumphed together. The independence and liberty you possess are the work of joint councils and joint efforts, of common dangers, sufferings, and successes.

But these considerations, however powerfully they address themselves to your sensibility, are greatly outweighed by those which apply more immediately to your interest. Here every portion of our country finds the most commanding motives for carefully guarding and preserving the union of the whole.

The *North,* in an unrestrained intercourse with the *South,* protected by the equal laws of a common government, finds in the productions of the latter great additional resources of maritime and commercial enterprise and precious materials of manufacturing industry. The *South,* in the same intercourse, benefiting by the same agency of the *North,* sees its agriculture grow and its commerce expand. Turning partly into its own channels the seamen of the *North,* it finds its particular navigation invigorated; and while it contributes in different ways to nourish and increase the general mass of the national navigation, it looks forward to the protection of a maritime strength to which itself is unequally adapted. The *East,* in a like intercourse with the *West,* already finds, and in the progressive improvement of interior communications by land and water will more and more find, a valuable vent for the commodities which it brings from abroad or manufactures at home. The *West* derives from the *East* supplies requisite to its growth and comfort, and what is perhaps of still greater consequence, it must of necessity owe the *secure* enjoyment of indispensable *outlets* for its own productions to the weight, influence, and the future maritime strength of the Atlantic side of the Union, directed by an indissoluble community of interest as *one nation.* Any other tenure by which the *West* can hold this essential advantage, whether derived from its own separate strength or from an apostate and unnatural connection with any foreign power, must be intrinsically precarious.

While, then, every part of our country thus feels an immediate and particular interest in union, all the parts combined can not fail to find in the united mass of means and efforts greater strength, greater resource, proportionably greater security from external danger, a less frequent interruption of their peace by foreign nations, and what is of inestimable value, they must derive from union an exemption from those broils and wars between themselves which so frequently afflict neighboring countries not tied together by the same governments, which their own rivalships alone would be sufficient to produce, but which opposite foreign alliances, attachments, and intrigues would stimulate and imbitter. Hence, likewise, they will avoid the necessity of those overgrown military establishments which, under any form of government, are inauspicious to liberty, and which are to be regarded as particularly hostile to republican liberty. In this sense it is that your union ought to be considered

as a main prop of your liberty, and that the love of the one ought to endear to you the preservation of the other. . . .

Is there a doubt whether a common government can embrace so large a sphere? Let experience solve it. To listen to mere speculation in such a case were criminal. It is well worth a fair and full experiment. With such powerful and obvious motives to union affecting all parts of our country, while experience shall not have demonstrated its impracticability, there will always be reason to distrust the patriotism of those who in any quarter may endeavor to weaken its bands.

In contemplating the causes which may disturb our union it occurs as matter of serious concern that any ground should have been furnished for characterizing parties by *geographical* discriminations—*Northern* and *Southern, Atlantic* and *Western*—whence designing men may endeavor to excite a belief that there is a real difference of local interests and views. One of the expedients of party to acquire influence within particular districts is to misrepresent the opinions and aims of other districts. You can not shield yourselves too much against the jealousies and heartburnings which spring from these misrepresentations; they tend to render alien to each other those who ought to be bound together by fraternal affection. . . .

To the efficacy and permanency of your union a government for the whole is indispensable. No alliances, however strict, between the parts can be an adequate substitute. They must inevitably experience the infractions and interruptions which all alliances in all times have experienced. Sensible of this momentous truth, you have improved upon your first essay by the adoption of a Constitution of Government better calculated than your former for an intimate union and for the efficacious management of your common concerns. This Government, the offspring of our own choice, uninfluenced and unawed, adopted upon full investigation and mature deliberation, completely free in its principles, in the distribution of its powers, uniting security with energy, and containing within itself a provision for its own amendment, has a just claim to your confidence and your support. Respect for its authority, compliance with its laws, acquiescence in its measures, are duties enjoined by the fundamental maxims of true liberty. The basis of our political systems is the right of the people to make and to alter their constitutions of government. But the constitution which at any time exists till changed by an explicit and authentic act of the whole people is sacredly obligatory upon all. The very idea of the power and the right of the people to establish government presupposes the duty of every individual to obey the established government. . . .

Toward the preservation of your Government and the permanency of your present happy state, it is requisite not only that you steadily discountenance irregular oppositions to its acknowledged authority, but also that you resist with care the spirit of innovation upon its principles, however specious the pretexts. One method of assault may be to effect in the forms of the Constitution alterations which will impair the energy of the system, and thus to undermine what can not be directly overthrown. In all the changes to which you may be invited remember that time and habit are at least as necessary to fix the true character of governments as of other human institutions; that experience is the surest standard by which to test the real tendency of the existing constitution of a country; that facility in changes upon the credit of mere hypothesis and opinion exposes to perpetual change, from the endless variety of hypothesis and opinion; and remember especially that for the efficient management of your common interests in a country so extensive as ours a government of as much vigor as is consistent with the perfect security of liberty is indispensable. Liberty itself will find in such a government, with powers properly distributed and adjusted, its surest guardian. It is, indeed, little else than a name where the government is too feeble to withstand the enterprises of faction, to confine each member of the society within the limits prescribed by the laws, and to maintain all in the secure and tranquil enjoyment of the rights of person and property.

I have already intimated to you the danger of parties in the State, with particular reference to the founding of them on geographical discriminations. Let me now take a more comprehensive view, and warn you in the most solemn manner against the baneful effects of the spirit of party generally.

This spirit, unfortunately, is inseparable from our nature, having its root in the strongest passions of the human mind. It exists under different shapes in all governments, more or less stifled, controlled, or repressed; but in those of the popular form it is seen in its greatest rankness and is truly their worst enemy. . . .

It serves always to distract the public councils and enfeeble the public administration. It agitates the community with ill-founded jealousies and false alarms; kindles the animosity of one part against another; foments occasionally riot and insurrection. It opens the door to foreign influence and corruption, which find a facilitated access to the government itself through the channels of party passion. Thus the policy and the will of one country are subjected to the policy and will of another.

There is an opinion that parties in free countries are useful checks upon the administration of the government, and serve to keep alive the spirit of liberty. This within certain limits is probably true; and in governments of a monarchical cast patriotism may look with indulgence, if not with favor, upon the spirit of party. But in those of the popular character, in governments purely elective, it is a spirit not to be encouraged. From their natural tendency it is certain there will always be enough of that spirit for every salutary purpose; and there being constant danger of excess, the effort ought to be by force of public opinion to mitigate and assuage it. A fire not to be quenched, it demands a uniform vigilance to prevent its bursting into a flame, lest, instead of warming, it should consume.

It is important, likewise, that the habits of thinking in a free country should inspire caution in those intrusted with its administration to confine themselves within their respective constitutional spheres, avoiding in the exercise of the powers of one department to encroach upon another. The spirit of encroachment tends to consolidate the powers of all the departments in one, and thus to create, whatever the form of government, a real despotism. . . . If in the opinion of the people the distribution or modification of the constitutional powers be in any particular wrong, let it be corrected by an amendment in the way which the Constitution designates. But let there be no change by usurpation; for though this in one instance may be the instrument of good, it is the customary weapon by which free governments are destroyed. The precedent must always greatly overbalance in permanent evil any partial or transient benefit which the use can at any time yield.

Of all the dispositions and habits which lead to political prosperity, religion and morality are indispensable supports. In vain would that man claim the tribute of patriotism who should labor to subvert these great pillars of human happiness—these firmest props of the duties of men and citizens. The mere politician, equally with the pious man, ought to respect and to cherish them. A volume could not trace all their connections with private and public felicity. Let it simply be asked, Where is the security for property, for reputation, for life, if the sense of religious obligation *desert* the oaths which are the instruments of investigation in courts of justice? And let us with caution indulge the supposition that morality can be maintained without religion. Whatever may be conceded to the influence of refined education on minds of peculiar structure, reason and experience both forbid us to expect that national morality can prevail in exclusion of religious principle.

It is substantially true that virtue or morality is a necessary spring of popular government. The rule indeed extends with more or less force to every species of free government. Who that is a sincere friend to it can look with indifference upon attempts to shake the foundation of the fabric? Promote, then, as an object of primary importance, institutions for the general diffusion of knowledge. In proportion as the structure of a government gives force to public opinion, it is essential that public opinion should be enlightened.

As a very important source of strength and security, cherish public credit. One method of preserving it is to use it as sparingly as possible, avoiding occasions of expense by cultivating peace, but remembering also that timely disbursements to prepare for danger frequently prevent much greater disbursements to repel it; avoiding

likewise the accumulation of debt, not only by shunning occasions of expense, but by vigorous exertions in time of peace to discharge the debts which unavoidable wars have occasioned, not ungenerously throwing upon posterity the burthen which we ourselves ought to bear. . . .

Observe good faith and justice toward all nations. Cultivate peace and harmony with all. Religion and morality enjoin this conduct. And can it be that good policy does not equally enjoin it? It will be worthy of a free, enlightened, and at no distant period a great nation to give to mankind the magnanimous and too novel example of a people always guided by an exalted justice and benevolence. Who can doubt that in the course of time and things the fruits of such a plan would richly repay any temporary advantages which might be lost by a steady adherence to it? Can it be that Providence has not connected the permanent felicity of a nation with its virtue? The experiment, at least, is recommended by every sentiment which ennobles human nature. Alas! is it rendered impossible by its vices?

In the execution of such a plan nothing is more essential than that permanent, inveterate antipathies against particular nations and passionate attachments for others should be excluded, and that in place of them just and amicable feelings toward all should be cultivated. The nation which indulges toward another an habitual hatred or an habitual fondness is in some degree a slave. It is a slave to its animosity or to its affection, either of which is sufficient to lead it astray from its duty and its interest. Antipathy in one nation against another disposes each more readily to offer insult and injury, to lay hold of slight causes of umbrage, and to be haughty and intractable when accidental or trifling occasions of dispute occur

So, likewise, a passionate attachment of one nation for another produces a variety of evils. Sympathy for the favorite nation, facilitating the illusion of an imaginary common interest in cases where no real common interest exists, and infusing into one the enmities of the other, betrays the former into a participation in the quarrels and wars of the latter without adequate inducement or justification. It leads also to concessions to the favorite nation of privileges denied to others, which is apt doubly to injure the nation making the concessions by unnecessarily parting with what ought to have been retained, and by exciting jealousy, ill will, and a disposition to retaliate in the parties from whom equal privileges are withheld; and it gives to ambitious, corrupted, or deluded citizens (who devote themselves to the favorite nation) facility to betray or sacrifice the interests of their own country without odium, sometimes even with popularity, gilding with the appearances of a virtuous sense of obligation, a commendable deference for public opinion, or a laudable zeal for public good the base or foolish compliances of ambition, corruption, or infatuation. . . .

Against the insidious wiles of foreign influence (I conjure you to believe me, fellow-citizens) the jealousy of a free people ought to be *constantly* awake, since history and experience prove that foreign influence is one of the most baneful foes of republican government. But that jealousy, to be useful, must be impartial, else it becomes the instrument of the very influence to be avoided, instead of a defense against it. Excessive partiality for one foreign nation and excessive dislike of another cause those whom they actuate to see danger only on one side, and serve to veil and even second the arts of influence on the other. Real patriots who may resist the intrigues of the favorite are liable to become suspected and odious, while its tools and dupes usurp the applause and confidence of the people to surrender their interests.

The great rule of conduct for us in regard to foreign nations is, in extending our commercial relations to have with them as little *political* connection as possible. So far as we have already formed engagements let them be fulfilled with perfect good faith. Here let us stop.

Europe has a set of primary interests which to us have none or a very remote relation. Hence she must be engaged in frequent controversies, the causes of which are essentially foreign to our concerns. Hence, therefore, it must be unwise in us to implicate ourselves by artificial ties in the ordinary vicissitudes of her politics or the ordinary combinations and collisions of her friendships or enmities.

Our detached and distant situation invites and enables us to pursue a different course. If we remain one people, under an efficient government, the period is not far off when we may defy material injury from external annoyance; when we may take such an attitude as will cause the neutrality we may at any time resolve upon to be scrupulously respected; when belligerent nations, under the impossibility of making acquisitions upon us, will not lightly hazard the giving us provocation; when we may choose peace or war, as our interest, guided by justice, shall counsel.

Why forego the advantages of so peculiar a situation? Why quit our own to stand upon foreign ground? Why, by interweaving our destiny with that of any part of Europe, entangle our peace and prosperity in the toils of European ambition, rivalship, interest, humor, or caprice?

It is our true policy to steer clear of permanent alliances with any portion of the foreign world, so far, I mean, as we are now at liberty to do it; for let me not be understood as capable of patronizing infidelity to existing engagements. I hold the maxim no less applicable to public than to private affairs that honesty is always the best policy. I repeat, therefore, let those engagements be observed in their genuine sense. But in my opinion it is unnecessary and would be unwise to extend them.

Taking care always to keep ourselves by suitable establishments on a respectable defensive posture, we may safely trust to temporary alliances for extraordinary emergencies.

Harmony, liberal intercourse with all nations are recommended by policy, humanity, and interest. But even our commercial policy should hold an equal and impartial hand, neither seeking nor granting exclusive favors or preferences; consulting the natural course of things; diffusing and diversifying by gentle means the streams of commerce, but forcing nothing; establishing with powers so disposed, in order to give trade a stable course, to define the rights of our merchants, and to enable the Government to support them, conventional rules of intercourse, the best that present circumstances and mutual opinion will permit, but temporary and liable to be from time to time abandoned or varied as experience and circumstances shall dictate; constantly keeping in view that it is folly in one nation to look for disinterested favors from another; that it must pay with a portion of its independence for whatever it may accept under that character; that by such acceptance it may place itself in the condition of having given equivalents for nominal favors, and yet of being reproached with ingratitude for not giving more. There can be no greater error than to expect or calculate upon real favors from nation to nation. It is an illusion which experience must cure, which a just pride ought to discard. . . .

Though in reviewing the incidents of my Administration I am unconscious of intentional error, I am nevertheless too sensible of my defects not to think it probable that I may have committed many errors. Whatever they may be, I fervently beseech the Almighty to avert or mitigate the evils to which they may tend. I shall also carry with me the hope that my country will never cease to view them with indulgence, and that, after forty-five years of my life dedicated to its service with an upright zeal, the faults of incompetent abilities will be consigned to oblivion, as myself must soon be to the mansions of rest.

Relying on its kindness in this as in other things, and actuated by that fervent love toward it which is so natural to a man who views in it the native soil of himself and his progenitors for several generations, I anticipate with pleasing expectation that retreat in which I promise myself to realize without alloy the sweet enjoyment of partaking in the midst of my fellow-citizens the benign influence of good laws under a free government—the ever-favorite object of my heart, and the happy reward, as I trust, of our mutual cares, labors, and dangers.

G°. WASHINGTON.

101. THE ALIEN AND SEDITION ACTS
1798

The publication, in the spring of 1798, of the X Y Z correspondence raised among the Federalists a spirit of nationalism that found expression in the four acts known collectively as the Alien and Sedition Acts. The animus of these acts was directed particularly against a group of anti-Federalist editors and pamphleteers of French and English extraction, such as Thomas Cooper, Joseph Priestley, James Callender, Benjamin F. Bache, Count de Volney, V. du Pont and others. There was grave doubt as to the constitutionality of the Sedition Act, which extended the jurisdiction of the federal courts, but the question of validity never came before the courts, though in 1812 the supreme court ruled that the federal courts do not have common law jurisdiction in criminal cases. Though the Alien Acts were never enforced, a number of French refugees fled the country or went into hiding. Some twenty-five persons were arrested under the Sedition Act, and ten convicted. See, F. M. Anderson, "The Enforcement of the Alien and Sedition Laws," American Hist. Assoc. Reports, 1912; C. G. Bowers, Jefferson and Hamilton, ch. xvi–xvii; J. S. Bassett, The Federalist System, ch. xvii; J. F. Mc Laughlin, Matthew Lyon; D. Malone, Thomas Cooper; B. Faÿ, The Two Franklins.

1. THE NATURALIZATION ACT
June 18, 1798

(U. S. Statutes at Large, Vol. I, p. 566 ff.)

An Act supplementary to and to amend the act, intituled "An act to establish an uniform rule of naturalization;" and to repeal the act heretofore passed on that subject.

SECTION 1. Be it enacted . . . , That no alien shall be admitted to become a citizen of the United States, or of any state, unless . . . he shall have declared his intention to become a citizen of the United States, five years, at least, before his admission, and shall, at the time of his application to be admitted, declare and prove, to the satisfaction of the court having jurisdiction in the case, that he has resided within the United States fourteen years, at least, and within the state or territory where, or for which such court is at the time held, five years, at least, besides conforming to the other declarations, renunciations and proofs, by the said act required, any thing therein to the contrary hereof notwithstanding: *Provided,* that any alien, who was residing within the limits, and under the jurisdiction of the United States, before . . . [January 29, 1795,] . . . may, within one year after the passing of this act—and any alien who shall have made the declaration of his intention to become a citizen of the United States, in conformity to the provisions of the act [of Jan. 29, 1795], may, within four years after having made the declaration aforesaid, be admitted to become a citizen, in the manner prescribed by the said act, . . . *And provided also,* that no alien, who shall be a native, citizen, denizen or subject of any nation or state with whom the United States shall be at war, at the time of his application, shall be then admitted to become a citizen of the United States. . . .

SEC. 4. *And be it further enacted,* That all white persons, aliens, . . . who, after the passing of this act, shall continue to reside, or who shall arrive, or come to reside in any port or place within the territory of the United States, shall be reported, . . . to the clerk of the district court of the district, if living within ten miles of the port or place, in which their residence or arrival shall be, and otherwise, to the collector of such port or place, or some officer or other person there, or nearest thereto, who shall be authorized by the President of the United States, to register aliens: And report, as aforesaid, shall be made in all cases of residence, within six months from and after the passing of this act, and in all after cases, within forty-eight hours after the first arrival or coming into the territory of the United States, and shall ascertain the sex, place of birth, age, nation, place of allegiance or citizenship, condition or occupation, and place of actual or intended residence within the United States, of the alien or aliens reported, and by whom the report is made... . .

Sec. 5. *And be it further enacted,* That every alien who shall continue to reside, or who shall arrive, as aforesaid, of whom a report is required as aforesaid, who shall refuse or neglect to make such report, and to receive a certificate thereof, shall forfeit and pay the sum of two dollars; and any justice of the peace, or other civil magistrate, who has authority to require surety of the peace, shall and may, on complaint to him made thereof, cause such alien to be brought be-

fore him, there to give surety of the peace and good behaviour during his residence within the United States, or for such term as the justice or other magistrate shall deem reasonable, and until a report and registry of such alien shall be made, and a certificate thereof, received as aforesaid; and in failure of such surety, such alien shall and may be committed to the common gaol, and shall be there held, until the order which the justice or magistrate shall and may reasonably make, in the premises, shall be performed. . . .

2. THE ALIEN ACT
June 25, 1798
(U. S. Statutes at Large, Vol. I, p. 570 ff.)

An Act concerning Aliens.

SEC. 1. *Be it enacted* . . . , That it shall be lawful for the President of the United States at any time during the continuance of this act, to *order* all such *aliens* as he shall judge dangerous to the peace and safety of the United States, or shall have reasonable grounds to suspect are concerned in any treasonable or secret machinations against the government thereof, to depart out of the territory of the United States, within such time as shall be expressed in such order, which order shall be served on such alien by delivering him a copy thereof, or leaving the same at his usual abode, and returned to the office of the Secretary of State, by the marshal or other person to whom the same shall be directed. And in case any alien, so ordered to depart, shall be found at large within the United States after the time limited in such order for his departure, and not having obtained a *license* from the President to reside therein, or having obtained such *license* shall not have conformed thereto, every such alien shall, on conviction thereof, be imprisoned for a term not exceeding three years, and shall never after be admitted to become a citizen of the United States. *Provided always, and be it further enacted,* that if any alien so ordered to depart shall prove to the satisfaction of the President, by evidence to be taken before such person or persons as the President shall direct, who are for that purpose hereby authorized to administer oaths, that no injury or danger to the United States will arise from suffering such alien to reside therein, the President may grant a *license* to such alien to remain within the United States for such time as he shall judge proper, and at such place as he may designate. And the President may also require of such alien to enter into a bond to the United States, in such penal sum as he may direct, with one or more sufficient sureties to the satisfaction of the person authorized by the President to take the same, conditioned for the good behavior of such alien during his residence in the United States, and not violating his license, which license the President may revoke, whenever he shall think proper.

Sec. 2. *And be it further enacted,* That it shall be lawful for the President of the United States, whenever he may deem it necessary for the public safety, to order to be removed out of the territory thereof, any alien who may or shall be in prison in pursuance of this act; and to cause to be arrested and sent out of the United States such of those aliens as shall have been ordered to depart therefrom and shall not have obtained a license as aforesaid, in all cases where, in the opinion of the President, the public safety requires a speedy removal. And if any alien so removed or sent out of the United States by the President shall voluntarily return thereto, unless by permission of the President of the United States, such alien on conviction thereof, shall be imprisoned so long as, in the opinion of the President, the public safety may require. . . .

Sec. 6. *And be it further enacted,* That this act shall continue and be in force for and during the term of two years from the passing thereof.

3. THE ALIEN ENEMIES ACT
July 6, 1798
(U. S. Statutes at Large, Vol. I, p. 577 ff.)

An Act respecting Alien Enemies

SECTION 1. *Be it enacted . . . ,* That whenever there shall be a declared war between the United States and any foreign nation or government, or any invasion or predatory incursion shall be perpetrated, attempted, or threatened against the territory of the United States, by any foreign nation or government, . . . all natives, citizens, denizens, or subjects of the hostile nation or government, being males of the age of fourteen years and upwards, who shall be within the United States, and not actually naturalized, shall be liable to be apprehended, re-

strained, secured and removed, as alien enemies. And the President of the United States shall be, and he is hereby authorized, . . . to direct the conduct to be observed, on the part of the United States, towards the aliens who shall become liable, as aforesaid; the manner and degree of the restraint to which they shall be subject, and in what cases, and upon what security their residence shall be permitted, and to provide for the removal of those, who, not being permitted to reside within the United States, shall refuse or neglect to depart therefrom; and to establish any other regulations which shall be found necessary in the premises and for the public safety: . . .

4. THE SEDITION ACT
July 14, 1798
(U. S. Statutes at Large, Vol. I, p. 596–7)

An Act in addition to the act, entitled "An act for the punishment of certain crimes against the United States."

SEC. 1. *Be it enacted . . . ,* That if any persons shall unlawfully combine or conspire together, with intent to oppose any measure or measures of the government of the United States, which are or shall be directed by proper authority, or to impede the operation of any law of the United States, or to intimidate or prevent any person holding a place or office in or under the government of the United States, from undertaking, performing or executing his trust or duty; and if any person or persons, with intent as aforesaid, shall counsel, advise or attempt to procure any insurrection, riot, unlawful assembly, or combination, whether such conspiracy, threatening, counsel, advice, or attempt shall have the proposed effect or not, he or they shall be deemed guilty of a high misdemeanor, and on conviction, before any court of the United States having jurisdiction thereof, shall be punished by a fine not exceeding five thousand dollars, and by imprisonment during a term not less than six months nor exceeding five years; and further, at the discretion of the court may be holden to find sureties for his good behaviour in such sum, and for such time, as the said court may direct.

SEC. 2. That if any person shall write, print, utter, or publish, or shall cause or procure to be written, printed, uttered or published. or shall knowingly and willingly assist or aid in writing, printing, uttering or publishing any false, scandalous and malicious writing or writings against the government of the United States, or either house of the Congress of the United States, or the President of the United States, with intent to defame the said government, or either house of the said Congress, or the said President, or to bring them, or either of them, into contempt or disrepute; or to excite against them, or either or any of them, the hatred of the good people of the United States, or to stir up sedition within the United States, or to excite any unlawful combinations therein, for opposing or resisting any law of the United States, or any act of the President of the United States, done in pursuance of any such law, or of the powers in him vested by the constitution of the United States, or to resist, oppose, or defeat any such law or act, or to

aid, encourage or abet any hostile designs of any foreign nation against the United States, their people or government, then such person, being thereof convicted before any court of the United States having jurisdiction thereof, shall be punished by a fine not exceeding two thousand dollars, and by imprisonment not exceeding two years.

SEC. 3. That if any person shall be prosecuted under this act, for the writing or publishing any libel aforesaid, it shall be lawful for the defendant, upon the trial of the cause, to give in evidence in his defence, the truth of the matter contained in the publication charged as a libel. And the jury who shall try the cause, shall have a right to determine the law and the fact, under the direction of the court, as in other cases.

SEC. 4. That this act shall continue to be in force until March 3, 1801, and no longer. . . .

102. THE KENTUCKY AND VIRGINIA RESOLUTIONS OF 1798

The Kentucky and Virginia Resolutions of 1798 were evoked by the Alien and Sedition Acts. The Kentucky Resolutions were drafted by Jefferson, and sponsored in the Kentucky legislature by John Breckenridge. The Virginia Resolutions were drafted by Madison, and introduced by John Taylor of Caroline. These resolutions represented not so much a constitutional as a social philosophy: they were drawn up with the primary purpose not of presenting a constitutional theory but of presenting a democratic protest against what was considered a dangerous usurpation of power by the central government. The perplexing question of the proper authority to pass on problems of constitutionality had not yet been resolved in favor of the Courts, and it was not unreasonable for those who feared the centralizing tendencies of the federal government to assert that the States were the proper parties to decide this question. The resolutions of 1798 drew forth replies from several states; see Doc. No. 104. On the resolutions, see E. D. Warfield, *The Kentucky Resolutions* of 1798; N. S. Shaler, *Kentucky,* ch. x; C. W. Loring, *Nullification, Secession;* H. Von Holst, *Constitutional and Political History of the United States,* Vol. I; G. Hunt, *James Madison;* E. P. Powell, *Nullification and Secession in the United States;* A. C. McLaughlin, *Courts, Constitution and Parties,* ch. iv.

1. KENTUCKY RESOLUTIONS
November 16, 1798
(N. S. Shaler, *Kentucky,* p. 409 ff.)

I. *Resolved,* that the several States composing the United States of America, are not united on the principle of unlimited submission to their general government; but that by compact under the style and title of a Constitution for the United States and of amendments thereto, they constituted a general government for special purposes, delegated to that government certain definite powers, reserving each State to itself, the residuary mass of right to their own self-government; and that whensoever the general government assumes undelegated powers, its acts are unauthoritative, void, and of no force: That to this compact each State acceded as a State, and is an integral party, its co-States forming, as to itself, the other party: That the government created by this compact was not made the exclusive or final judge of the extent of the powers delegated to itself; since that would have made its discretion, and not the Constitution, the measure of its powers; but that as in all other cases of compact among parties having no common Judge, *each party has an equal right to judge for itself, as well of infractions as of the mode and measure of redress.*

II. *Resolved,* that the Constitution of the United States having delegated to Congress a power to punish treason, counterfeiting the securities and current coin of the United States, piracies and felonies committed on the high seas, and offenses against the laws of nations, and no other crimes whatever, and it being true as a general principle, and one of the amendments to the Constitution having also declared "that the powers not delegated to the United States by the Constitution, nor prohibited by it to the States, are reserved to the States respectively, or to the people," therefore also [the Sedition Act of July 14, 1798]; as also the act passed by them on the 27th day of June, 1798, entitled "An act to punish frauds committed on the Bank of the United States" (and all other their acts which assume to create, define, or punish crimes other than those enumerated in the Constitution), are altogether void and of no force, and that the power to create, define, and punish such other crimes is reserved, and of right appertains solely and exclusively to the respective States, each within its own Territory

III. *Resolved,* that it is true as a general principle, and is also expressly declared by one of the amendments to the Constitution that "the powers not delegated to the United States by the Constitution, nor prohibited by it to the States, are reserved to the States respectively or to the people;" and that no power over the freedom of religion, freedom of speech, or freedom of the press being delegated to the United States by the Constitution, nor prohibited by it to the States, all lawful powers respecting the same did of right remain, and were reserved to the States, or to the people: That thus was manifested their determination to retain to themselves the right of judging how far the licentiousness of speech and of the press may be abridged without lessening their useful freedom, and how far those abuses which cannot be separated from their use should be tolerated rather than the use be destroyed; and thus also they guarded against all abridgment by the United States of the freedom of religious opinions and exercises, and retained to them-

selves the right of protecting the same, as this State, by a law passed on the general demand of its citizens, had already protected them from all human restraint or interference: And that in addition to this general principle and express declaration, another and more special provision has been made by one of the amendments to the Constitution which expressly declares, that "Congress shall make no law respecting an establishment of religion, or prohibiting the free exercise thereof, or abridging the freedom of speech, or of the press," thereby guarding in the same sentence, and under the same words, the freedom of religion, of speech, and of the press, insomuch, that whatever violates either, throws down the sanctuary which covers the others, and that libels, falsehoods, defamation equally with heresy and false religion, are withheld from the cognizance of Federal tribunals. That therefore [the Sedition Act], which does abridge the freedom of the press, is not law, but is altogether void and of no effect.

IV. *Resolved,* that alien friends are under the jurisdiction and protection of the laws of the State wherein they are; that no power over them has been delegated to the United States, nor prohibited to the individual States distinct from their power over citizens; and it being true as a general principle, and one of the amendments to the Constitution having also declared that "the powers not delegated to the United States by the Constitution, nor prohibited by it to the States, are reserved to the States respectively, or to the people," the [Alien Act of June 22, 1798], which assumes power over alien friends not delegated by the Constitution, is not law, but is altogether void and of no force.

V. *Resolved,* that in addition to the general principle as well as the express declaration, that powers not delegated are reserved, another and more special provision inserted in the Constitution from abundant caution has declared, "that the migration or importation of such persons as any of the States now existing shall think proper to admit, shall not be prohibited by the Congress prior to the year 1808." That this Commonwealth does admit the migration of alien friends described as the subject of the said act concerning aliens; that a provision against prohibiting their migration is a provision against all acts equivalent thereto, or it would be nugatory;

that to remove them when migrated is equivalent to a prohibition of their migration, and is therefore contrary to the said provision of the Constitution, and void.

VI. *Resolved,* that the imprisonment of a person under the protection of the laws of this Commonwealth on his failure to obey the simple order of the President to depart out of the United States, as is undertaken by the said act entitled "An act concerning aliens," is contrary to the Constitution, one amendment to which has provided, that "no person shall be deprived of liberty without due process of law," and that another having provided "that in all criminal prosecutions, the accused shall enjoy the right to a public trial by an impartial jury, to be informed of the nature and cause of the accusation, to be confronted with the witnesses against him, to have compulsory process for obtaining witnesses in his favour, and to have the assistance of counsel for his defense," the same act undertaking to authorize the President to remove a person out of the United States who is under the protection of the law, on his own suspicion, without accusation, without jury, without public trial, without confrontation of the witnesses against him, without having witnesses in his favour, without defense, without counsel, is contrary to these provisions also of the Constitution, is therefore not law, but utterly void and of no force. That transferring the power of judging any person who is under the protection of the laws, from the courts to the President of the United States, as is undertaken by the same act concerning aliens, is against the article of the Constitution which provides, that "the judicial power of the United States shall be vested in courts, the judges of which shall hold their offices during good behavior," and that the said act is void for that reason also; and it is further to be noted, that this transfer of judiciary power is to that magistrate of the general government who already possesses all the executive, and a qualified negative in all the legislative powers.

VII. *Resolved,* that the construction applied by the general government (as is evinced by sundry of their proceedings) to those parts of the Constitution of the United States which delegate to Congress a power to lay and collect taxes, duties, imposts, and excises; to pay the debts, and provide for the common defense, and general welfare of the United States, and to make all laws which shall be necessary and proper for carrying into execution the powers vested by the Constitution in the government of the United States, or any department thereof, goes to the destruction of all the limits prescribed to their power by the Constitution: That words meant by that instrument to be subsidiary only to the execution of the limited powers ought not to be so construed as themselves to give unlimited powers, nor a part so to be taken as to destroy the whole residue of the instrument: That the proceedings of the general government under color of these articles will be a fit and necessary subject for revisal and correction at a time of greater tranquillity, while those specified in the preceding resolutions call for immediate redress.

VIII. *Resolved,* that the preceding Resolutions be transmitted to the Senators and Representatives in Congress from this Commonwealth, who are hereby enjoined to present the same to their respective Houses, and to use their best endeavors to procure, at the next session of Congress, a repeal of the aforesaid unconstitutional and obnoxious acts.

IX. *Resolved,* lastly, that the Governor of this Commonwealth be, and is hereby authorized and requested to communicate the preceding Resolutions to the Legislatures of the several States, to assure them that this Commonwealth considers Union for specified National purposes, and particularly for those specified in their late Federal Compact, to be friendly to the peace, happiness, and prosperity of all the States: that faithful to that compact according to the plain intent and meaning in which it was understood and acceded to by the several parties, it is sincerely anxious for its preservation: that it does also believe, that to take from the States all the powers of self-government, and transfer them to a general and consolidated government, without regard to the special delegations and reservations solemnly agreed to in that compact, is not for the peace, happiness, or prosperity of these States: And that, therefore, this Commonwealth is determined, as it doubts not its co-States are, tamely to submit to undelegated and consequently unlimited powers in no man or body of men on earth: that if the acts before specified should stand, these conclusions would flow from them; that the general government may place any act they think proper on the list of crimes and punish it themselves, whether enumerated or not enumerated by the Constitution as cognizable by them: that they may transfer its cognizance to the President or any other person, who may himself be the accuser, counsel, judge, and jury, whose suspicions may be the evidence, his order the sentence, his officer the executioner, and his breast the sole record of the transaction: that a very numerous and valuable description of the inhabitants of these States being by this precedent reduced as outlaws to the absolute dominion of one man, and the barrier of the Constitution thus swept away from us all, no rampart now remains against the passions and the powers of a majority of Congress, to protect from a like exportation or other more grievous punishment the minority of the same body, the legislatures, judges, governors, and counselors of the States, nor their other peaceable inhabitants who may venture to reclaim the constitutional rights and liberties of the State and people, or who for other causes, good or bad, may be obnoxious to the views or marked by the suspicions of the President, or be thought dangerous to his or their elections or other interests, public or personal: that the friendless alien has indeed been selected as the safest subject of a first experiment, but the citizen will soon follow, or rather has already followed: for, already has a sedition act marked him as its prey: that these and successive acts of the same character, unless arrested on the threshold, may tend to drive these States into revolution and blood, and will furnish new calumnies against Republican governments, and new pretexts for those who wish it to be believed, that man cannot be governed but by a rod of iron: that it would be a dangerous delusion were a confidence in the men of our choice to silence our fears for the safety of our rights: that confidence is everywhere the parent of despotism: free government is founded in jealousy and not in confidence; it is jealousy and not confidence which prescribes limited Constitutions to bind down those whom we are obliged to trust with power: that our Constitution has accordingly fixed the limits to which and no further our confidence may go; and let the honest advocate of confidence read the alien and sedition acts, and say if the Constitution has not been wise in fixing limits to the government it created, and whether we should be wise in destroying those limits; let him say what the government is if it be not a tyranny, which the men of our choice have conferred on the President, and the President of our choice has assented to and accepted over the friendly strangers, to whom the mild spirit of our country and its laws had pledged hospitality and protection: that the men of our choice have more respected the bare suspicions of the President than the solid rights of innocence, the claims of justification, the sacred force of truth, and the forms and substance of law and justice. In questions of power then let no more be heard of confidence in man, but bind him down from mischief by the claims of the Constitution. That this Commonwealth does therefore call on its co-States for an expression of their sentiments on the acts concerning aliens, and for the punishment of certain crimes herein before specified, plainly declaring whether these acts are or are not authorized by the Federal Compact. And it doubts not that their sense will be so announced as to prove their attachment unaltered to limited government, whether general or particular, and that the rights and liberties of their co-States will be exposed to no dangers by remaining embarked on a common bottom with their own: That they will concur with this Commonwealth in considering the said acts so palpably against the Constitution as to amount to an undisguised declaration, that the compact is not meant to be the measure of the powers of the general government, but that it will proceed in the exercise over these States of all powers whatsoever: That they will view this as seizing the rights of the States and consolidating them in the hands of the general government with a power assumed to bind the States (not merely in cases made Federal) but in all cases whatsoever, by laws made, not with their consent, but by others against their consent: That this would be to surrender the form of government we have chosen, and to live under one deriving its powers from its own will, and not from our authority; and that the co-States, recurring to their natural right in cases not made Federal, will concur in declaring these acts void and of no force, and will each unite with this Commonwealth in requesting their repeal at the next session of Congress.

2. VIRGINIA RESOLUTIONS
December 24, 1798
(Elliot's *Debates*, 1861 ed., Vol. IV, p. 528–529)

Resolved, That the General Assembly of Virginia doth unequivocally express a firm resolution to maintain and defend the Constitution of the United States, and the Constitution of this state, against every aggression either foreign or domestic; and that they will support the Government of the United States in all measures warranted by the former.

That this Assembly most solemnly declares a warm attachment to the union of the states, to maintain which it pledges all its powers; and that, for this end, it is their duty to watch over and oppose every infraction of those principles which constitute the only basis of that Union, because a faithful observance of them can alone secure its existence and the public happiness.

That this Assembly doth explicitly and peremptorily declare that it views the powers of the Federal Government as resulting from the compact to which the states are parties, as limited by the plain sense and intention of the instrument constituting that compact; as no further valid than they are authorized by the grants enumerated in that compact; and that, in case of a deliberate, palpable, and dangerous exercise of other powers not granted by the said compact, the states, who are parties thereto, have the right and are in duty bound to interpose for arresting the progress of the evil, and for maintaining within their respective limits the authorities, rights, and liberties appertaining to them.

That the General Assembly doth also express its deep regret, that a spirit has in sundry instances been manifested by the Federal Government to enlarge its powers by forced constructions of the constitutional charter which defines them; and that indications have appeared of a design to expound certain general phrases (which, having been copied from the very limited grant of powers in the former Articles of Confederation, were the less liable to be misconstrued) so as to destroy the meaning and effect of the particular enumeration which necessarily explains and limits the general phrases; and so as to consolidate the states, by degrees, into one sovereignty, the obvious tendency and inevitable consequence of which would be to transform the present republican system of the United States into an absolute, or, at best, a mixed monarchy.

That the General Assembly doth particularly PROTEST against the palpable and alarming infractions of the Constitution in the two late cases of the "Alien and Sedition Acts," passed at the last session of Congress; the first of which exercises a power nowhere delegated to the Federal Government, and which, by uniting legislative and judicial powers to those of [the] executive, subverts the general principles of free government, as well as the particular organization and positive provisions of the Federal Constitution: and the other of which acts exercises, in like manner, a power not delegated by the Constitution, but, on the contrary, expressly and positively forbidden by one of the amendments thereto,—a power which, more than any other, ought to produce universal alarm, because it is levelled against the right of freely examining public characters and measures, and of free communication among the people thereon, which has ever been justly deemed the only effectual guardian of every other right.

That this state having, by its Convention which ratified the Federal Constitution, expressly declared that, among other essential rights, "the liberty of conscience and of the press cannot be cancelled, abridged, restrained or modified by any authority of the United States," and from its extreme anxiety to guard these rights from every possible attack of sophistry or ambition, having, with other states, recommended an amendment for that purpose, which amendment was in due time annexed to the Constitution,—it would mark a reproachful inconsistency and criminal degeneracy, if an indifference were now shown to the palpable violation of one of the rights thus declared and secured, and to the establishment of a precedent which may be fatal to the other.

That the good people of this commonwealth, having ever felt and continuing to feel the most sincere affection for their brethren of the other states, the truest anxiety for establishing and perpetuating the union of all and the most scrupulous fidelity to that Constitution, which is the pledge of mutual friendship, and the instrument of mutual happiness, the General Assembly doth solemnly appeal to the like dispositions of the other states, in confidence that they will concur with this Commonwealth in declaring, as it does hereby declare, that the acts aforesaid are unconstitutional; and that the necessary and proper measures will be taken by each for co-operating with this state, in maintaining unimpaired the authorities, rights, and liberties reserved to the states respectively, or to the people. . . .

103. THE KENTUCKY RESOLUTIONS OF 1799
February 22, 1799

(Elliot's *Debates*, 1861 ed. Vol. IV, p. 544 ff.)

The unfavorable character of the replies of various States to the Resolutions of 1798 led to a reassertion of the principles expressed in those resolutions. The Kentucky legislature not only reaffirmed its attachment to the original resolutions, but added a resolution asserting that nullification by the States was the rightful remedy with which to meet infractions of the Constitution. In Virginia, the replies of the States were referred to a special committee of which James Madison was chairman. The report of the committee, drafted by Madison, can be found in Madison's *Writings*, ed. by G. Hunt, Vol. VI. For references, see Doc. No. 102.

The representatives of the good people of this commonwealth, in General Assembly convened, having maturely considered the answers of sundry states in the Union, to their resolutions passed the last session, respecting certain unconstitutional laws of Congress, commonly called the Alien and Sedition Laws, would be faithless, indeed, to themselves and to those they represent, were they silently to acquiesce in the principles and doctrines attempted to be maintained in all those answers, that of Virginia only excepted. To again enter the field of argument, and attempt more fully or forcibly to expose the unconstitutionality of those obnoxious laws, would, it is apprehended, be as unnecessary as unavailing. We cannot, however, but lament, that, in the discussion of those interesting subjects, by sundry of the legislatures of our sister states, unfounded suggestions, and uncandid insinuations, derogatory to the true character and principles of this commonwealth have been substituted in place of fair reasoning and sound argument. Our opinions of these alarming measures of the general government, together with our reasons for those opinions, were detailed with decency, and with temper, and submitted to the discussion and judgment of our fellow-citizens throughout the Union. Whether the like decency and temper have been observed in the answers of most of those States, who have denied or attempted to obviate the great truths contained in those resolutions, we have now only to submit to a candid world. Faithful to the true principles of the federal Union, unconscious of any designs to disturb the harmony of that Union, and anxious only to escape the fangs of despotism, the good people of this commonwealth are regardless of censure or calumniation. Lest, however, the silence of this commonwealth should be construed into an acquiescence in the doctrines and principles advanced and attempted to be maintained by the said answers, or at least those of our fellow-citizens throughout the Union who so widely differ from us on those important subjects, should be deluded by the expectation, that we shall be deterred from what we conceive our duty, or shrink from the principles contained in those resolutions—therefore,

Resolved, That this commonwealth considers the federal Union, upon the terms and for the purposes specified in the late compact, conducive to the liberty and happiness of the several states: That it does now unequivocally declare its attachment to the Union, and to that compact, agreeably to its obvious and real intention, and will be among the last to seek its dissolution: That if those who administer the general government be permitted to transgress the limits fixed by that compact, by a total disregard to the special delegations of power therein contained, an annihilation of the state governments, and the creation upon their ruins of a general consolidated government, will be the inevitable consequence: That the principle and construction contended for by sundry of the state legislatures, that the general government is the exclusive judge of the extent of the powers delegated to it, stop not short of *despotism*—since the discretion of those who administer the government, and not the *Constitution,* would be the measure of their powers: That the several states who formed that instrument being sovereign and independent, have the unquestionable right to judge of the infraction; and, *That a nullification of those sovereignties, of all unauthorized acts done under color of that instrument is the rightful remedy:* That this commonwealth does, under the most deliberate reconsideration, declare, that the said Alien and Sedition Laws are, in their opinion, palpable violations of the said Constitution; and, however cheerfully it may be disposed to surrender its opinion to a majority of its sister states, in matters of ordinary or doubtful policy, yet, in momentous regulations like the present, which so vitally wound the best rights of the citizen, it would consider a silent acquiescence as highly criminal: That although this commonwealth, as a party to the federal compact, will bow to the laws of the Union, yet, it does, at the same time declare, that it will not now, or ever hereafter, cease to oppose in a constitutional manner, every attempt at what quarter soever offered, to violate that compact. And, finally, in order that no pretext or arguments may be drawn from a supposed acquiescence, on the part of this commonwealth in the constitutionality of those laws, and be thereby used as precedents for similar future violations of the federal compact—this commonwealth does now enter against them its solemn PROTEST.

104. STATE REPLIES TO THE VIRGINIA AND KENTUCKY RESOLUTIONS
1799

(Elliot's *Debates,* 1861 ed., Vol. IV, p. 533, 539)

Every State from Maryland north replied to the Virginia and Kentucky Resolutions, disavowing, with varying degrees of indignation, the constitutional principles set forth in these Resolutions. The replies of the States are particularly interesting because of the general assertion that the judiciary rather than the legislative is the proper body to pass on the constitutionality of Congressional acts. Many of the replies are given in Elliot's *Debates,* Vol. IV, p. 532–539. See, F. M. Anderson, "Contemporary Opinion of the Virginia and Kentucky Resolutions", *American Historical Review,* Vol. V.

1. THE STATE OF RHODE ISLAND AND PROVIDENCE PLANTATIONS TO VIRGINIA
February, 1799

Certain resolutions of the Legislature of Virginia, passed on the 21st of December last, being communicated to the Assembly,—

1. *Resolved,* That, in the opinion of this legislature, the second section of the third article of the Constitution of the United States, in these words, to wit,—"The judicial power shall extend to all cases arising under the laws of the United States,"—vests in the Federal Courts, exclusively, and in the Supreme Court of the United States, ultimately, the authority of deciding on the constitutionality of any act or law of the Congress of the United States.

2. *Resolved,* That for any state legislature to assume that authority would be—

1st. Blending together legislative and judicial powers;

2d. Hazarding an interruption of the peace of the states by civil discord, in case of a diversity of opinions among the state legislatures; each state having, in that case, no resort, for vindicating its own opinions, but the strength of its own arm;

3d. Submitting most important questions of law to less competent tribunals; and,

4th. An infraction of the Constitution of the United States, expressed in plain terms.

3. *Resolved,* That, although, for the above reasons, this legislature, in their public capacity, do not feel themselves authorized to consider and decide on the constitutionality of the Sedition and Alien laws, (so called,) yet they are called upon, by the exigency of this occasion, to declare that, in their private opinions, these laws are within the powers delegated to Congress, and promotive of the welfare of the United States.

4. *Resolved,* That the governor communicate these resolutions to the supreme executive of the state of Virginia, and at the same time express to him that this legislature cannot contemplate, without extreme concern and regret, the many evil and fatal consequencies which may flow from the very unwarrantable resolutions aforesaid, of the legislature of Virginia, passed on the twenty-first day of December last.

2. NEW HAMPSHIRE RESOLUTION ON THE VIRGINIA AND KENTUCKY RESOLUTIONS
June 15, 1799

The legislature of New Hampshire, having taken into consideration certain resolutions of the General Assembly of Virginia, dated December 21, 1798; also certain resolutions of the legislature of Kentucky, of the 10th of November 1798:—

Resolved, That the legislature of New Hampshire unequivocally express a firm resolution to maintain and defend the Constitution of the United States, and the Constitution of this State, against every aggression, either foreign or domestic, and that they will support the government of the United States in all measures warranted by the former.

That the state legislatures are not the proper tribunals to determine the constitutionality of the laws of the general government; that the duty of such decision is properly and exclusively confided to the judicial department.

That, if the legislature of New Hampshire, for mere speculative purposes, were to express an opinion on the acts of the general government, commonly called "the Alien and Sedition Bills", that opinion would unreservedly be, that those acts are constitutional, and, in the present critical situation of our country, highly expedient.

That the constitutionality and expediency of the acts aforesaid have been very ably advocated and clearly demonstrated by many citizens of the United States, more especially by the minority of the General Assembly of Virginia. The legislature of New Hampshire, therefore, deem it unnecessary, by any train of arguments, to attempt further illustration of the propositions, the truth of which, it is confidently believed, at this day, is very generally seen and acknowledged.

Which report, . . . was unanimously received and adopted, one hundred and thirty-seven members being present.

105. LAND ACT OF 1800
May 10, 1800
(*U. S. Statutes at Large,* Vol. II, p. 73 ff.)

Sales under the Land Act of 1796 were disappointingly slow; in order to attract settlers and dispose of the public domain the government provided for land purchases on credit. The result was somewhat unfortunate: the credit system encouraged speculation and made collections difficult. It was discontinued by the land act of 1820, Doc. No. 122. See, P. J. Treat, *The National Land System, 1785–1820;* R. T. Hill, *The Public Domain and Democracy;* B. W. Bond, *The Civilization of the Old Northwest,* ch. x.

An Act to amend the act intituled "An act for providing for the sale of the lands of the United States, in the territory northwest of the Ohio, and above the mouth of the Kentucky River."

Sec. 1. *Be it enacted,* That for the disposal of the lands of the United States, directed to be sold by the act, intituled "An

act providing for the sale of the lands of the United States, in the territory northwest of the Ohio, and above the mouth of Kentucky river," there shall be four land offices established in the said territory: one at Cincinnati . . . one at Chilicothe . . . one at Marietta . . . and one at Steubenville. . . . Each of the said offices shall be under the direction of an officer, . . . who shall be appointed by the President of the United States, by and with the advice and consent of the Senate, . . .

Sec. 3. That the surveyor-general shall cause the townships west of the Muskingum, which by the above-mentioned act are directed to be sold in quarter townships, to be subdivided into half sections of three hundred and twenty acres each. . . .

Sec. 4. That the lands thus subdivided

. . . shall be offered for sale in sections and half sections, subdivided as before directed at the following places and times, . . . All lands, remaining unsold, at the closing of either of the public sales, may be disposed of at private sale by the registers of these respective land offices, in the manner herein after prescribed; . . .

Sec. 5. That no lands shall be sold by virtue of this act, at either public or private sale, for less than two dollars per acre, and payment may be made for the same by all purchasers, either in specie, or in evidences of the public debt of the United States, . . . and shall be made in the following manner, and under the following conditions, to wit:

1. At the time of purchase, every purchaser shall, exclusively of the fees hereafter mentioned, pay six dollars for every section, and three dollars for every half section, he may have purchased, for surveying expenses, and deposit one twentieth part of the amount of purchase money, to be forfeited, if within forty days one fourth part of the purchase money, including the said twentieth part, is not paid.

2. One fourth part of the purchase money shall be paid within forty days after the day of sale as aforesaid; another fourth part shall be paid within two years; another fourth part within three years; and another fourth part within four years after the day of sale.

3. Interest, at the rate of six per cent. a year from the day of sale shall be charged upon each of the three last payments, . . .

4. A discount at the rate of eight per cent., a year, shall be allowed on any of the three last payments, which shall be paid before the same shall become due, . . .

5. If the first payment of one fourth part of the purchase money shall not be made within forty days after the sale, the deposit, payment and fees, paid and made by the purchaser, shall be forfeited, and the lands shall . . . be disposed of at private sale, on the same terms and conditions, and in the same manner as the other lands directed by this act to be disposed of at private sale: *Provided,* that the lands which shall have been sold at public sale, and which shall, on account of such failure of payment, revert to the United States, shall not be sold at private sale, for a price less than the price that shall have been offered for the same at public sale. . . .

Sec. 16. That each person who, before the passing of this act, shall have erected . . . a grist-mill or saw-mill upon any of the lands herein directed to be sold, shall be entitled to the pre-emption of the section . . . at the rate of two dollars per acre. . . .

106. JEFFERSON'S FIRST INAUGURAL ADDRESS
March 4, 1801

(Richardson, ed. *Messages and Papers,* Vol. I, p. 322)

This address is a classic exposition of democratic philosophy, memorable alike for its confession of faith and for its literary beauty. For a brilliant but critical analysis, see H. Adams, *History of the United States During the Administration of Thomas Jefferson,* Vol. I, ch. vii. For Jefferson, see biographies by H. S. Randall, J. Parton, A. J. Nock, P. L. Ford, D. S. Muzzey, G. Chinard, F. W. Hirst, and J. T. Morse.

Friends and Fellow-Citizens:

Called upon to undertake the duties of the first executive office of our country, I avail myself of the presence of that portion of my fellow-citizens which is here assembled to express my grateful thanks for the favor with which they have been pleased to look toward me, to declare a sincere consciousness that the task is above my talents, and that I approach it with those anxious and awful presentiments which the greatness of the charge and the weakness of my powers so justly inspire. A rising nation, spread over a wide and fruitful land, traversing all the seas with the rich productions of their industry, engaged in commerce with nations who feel power and forget right, advancing rapidly to destinies beyond the reach of mortal eye—when I contemplate these transcendent objects, and see the honor, the happiness, and the hopes of this beloved country committed to the issue and the auspices of this day, I shrink from the contemplation, and humble myself before the magnitude of the undertaking. Utterly, indeed, should I despair did not the presence of many whom I here see remind me that in the other high authorities provided by our Constitution I shall find resources of wisdom, of virtue, and of zeal on which to rely under all difficulties. To you, then, gentlemen, who are charged with the sovereign functions of legislation, and to those associated with you, I look with encouragement for that guidance and support which may enable us to steer with safety the vessel in which we are all embarked amidst the conflicting elements of a troubled world.

During the contest of opinion through which we have passed the animation of discussions and of exertions has sometimes worn an aspect which might impose on strangers unused to think freely and to speak and to write what they think; but this being now decided by the voice of the nation, announced according to the rules of the Constitution, all will, of course, arrange themselves under the will of the law, and unite in common efforts for the common good. All, too, will bear in mind this sacred principle, that though the will of the majority is in all cases to prevail, that will to be rightful must be reasonable; that the minority possess their equal rights, which equal law must protect, and to violate would be oppression. Let us, then, fellow-citizens, unite with one heart and one mind. Let us restore to social intercourse that harmony and affection without which liberty and even life itself are but dreary things. And let us reflect that, having banished from our land that religious intolerance under which mankind so long bled and suffered, we have yet gained little if we countenance a political intolerance as despotic, as wicked, and capable of as bitter and bloody persecutions. During the throes and convulsions of the ancient world, during the agonizing spasms of infuriated man, seeking through blood and slaughter his long-lost liberty, it was not wonderful that the agitation of the billows should reach even this distant and peaceful shore; that this should be more felt and feared by some and less by others, and should divide opinions as to measures of safety. But every difference of opinion is not a difference of principle. We have called by different names

brethren of the same principle. We are all Republicans, we are all Federalists. If there be any among us who would wish to dissolve this Union or to change its republican form, let them stand undisturbed as monuments of the safety with which error of opinion may be tolerated where reason is left free to combat it. I know, indeed, that some honest men fear that a republican government can not be strong, that this Government is not strong enough; but would the honest patriot, in the full tide of successful experiment, abandon a government which has so far kept us free and firm on the theoretic and visionary fear that this Government, the world's best hope, may by possibility want energy to preserve itself? I trust not. I believe this, on the contrary, the strongest Government on earth. I believe it the only one where every man, at the call of the law, would fly to the standard of the law, and would meet invasions of the public order as his own personal concern. Sometimes it is said that man can not be trusted with the government of himself. Can he, then, be trusted with the government of others? Or have we found angels in the forms of kings to govern him? Let history answer this question.

Let us, then, with courage and confidence pursue our own Federal and Republican principles, our attachment to union and representative government. Kindly separated by nature and a wide ocean from the exterminating havoc of one quarter of the globe; too high-minded to endure the degradations of the others; possessing a chosen country, with room enough for our descendants to the thousandth and thousandth generation; entertaining a due sense of our equal right to the use of our own faculties, to the acquisitions of our own industry, to honor and confidence from our fellow-citizens, resulting not from birth, but from our actions and their sense of them; enlightened by a benign religion, professed, indeed, and practiced in various forms, yet all of them inculcating honesty, truth, temperance, gratitude, and the love of man; acknowledging and adoring an overruling Providence, which by all its dispensations proves that it delights in the happiness of man here and his greater happiness hereafter—with all these blessings, what more is necessary to make us a happy and a prosperous people? Still one thing more, fellow-citizens—a wise and frugal Government, which shall restrain men from injuring one another, shall leave them otherwise free to regulate their own pursuits of industry and improvement, and shall not take from the mouth of labor the bread it has earned. This is the sum of good government, and this is necessary to close the circle of our felicities.

About to enter, fellow-citizens, on the exercise of duties which comprehend everything dear and valuable to you, it is proper you should understand what I deem the essential principles of our Government, and consequently those which ought to shape its Administration. I will compress them within the narrowest compass they will bear, stating the general principle, but not all its limitations. Equal and exact justice to all men, of whatever state or persuasion, religious or political; peace, commerce, and honest friendship with all nations, entangling alliances with none; the support of the State governments in all their rights, as the most competent administrations for our domestic concerns and the surest bulwarks against antirepublican tendencies; the preservation of the General Government in its whole constitutional vigor, as the sheet anchor of our peace at home and safety abroad; a jealous care of the right of election by the people—a mild and safe corrective of abuses which are lopped by the sword of revolution where peaceable remedies are unprovided; absolute acquiescence in the decisions of the majority, the vital principle of republics, from which is no appeal but to force, the vital principle and immediate parent of despotism; a well-disciplined militia, our best reliance in peace and for the first moments of war, till regulars may relieve them; the supremacy of the civil over the military authority; economy in the public expense, that labor may be lightly burthened; the honest payment of our debts and sacred preservation of the public faith; encouragement of agriculture, and of commerce as its handmaid; the diffusion of information and arraignment of all abuses at the bar of the public reason; freedom of religion; freedom of the press, and freedom of person under the protection of the habeas corpus, and trial by juries impartially selected. These principles form the bright constellation which has gone before us and guided our steps through an age of revolution and reformation. The wisdom of our sages and blood of our heroes have been devoted to their attainment. They should be the creed of our political faith, the text of civic instruction, the touchstone by which to try the services of those we trust; and should we wander from them in moments of error or of alarm, let us hasten to retrace our steps and to regain the road which alone leads to peace, liberty, and safety.

I repair, then, fellow-citizens, to the post you have assigned me. With experience enough in subordinate offices to have seen the difficulties of this the greatest of all, I have learnt to expect that it will rarely fall to the lot of imperfect man to retire from this station with the reputation and the favor which bring him into it. Without pretensions to that high confidence you reposed in our first and greatest revolutionary character, whose preëminent services had entitled him to the first place in his country's love and destined for him the fairest page in the volume of faithful history, I ask so much confidence only as may give firmness and effect to the legal administration of your affairs. I shall often go wrong through defect of judgment. When right, I shall often be thought wrong by those whose positions will not command a view of the whole ground. I ask your indulgence for my own errors, which will never be intentional, and your support against the errors of others, who may condemn what they would not if seen in all its parts. The approbation implied by your suffrage is a great consolation to me for the past, and my future solicitude will be to retain the good opinion of those who have bestowed it in advance, to conciliate that of others by doing them all the good in my power, and to be instrumental to the happiness and freedom of all.

Relying, then, on the patronage of your good will, I advance with obedience to the work, ready to retire from it whenever you become sensible how much better choice it is in your power to make. And may that

Infinite Power which rules the destinies of the universe lead our councils to what is best, and give them a favorable issue for your peace and prosperity.

107. JEFFERSON ON THE IMPORTANCE OF NEW ORLEANS
Letter to Robert R. Livingston
April 18, 1802

(*The Writings of Thomas Jefferson*, ed. by H. E. Bergh, Vol. X, p. 311 ff.)

This famous letter to the American minister to France anticipated the formal instructions of May 1 requesting Livingston to ascertain the terms upon which France would sell New Orleans and the Floridas to the United States. At the same time Jefferson was writing to our minister in England, Rufus King, that we would "marry ourselves to the British fleet and nation" rather than see France control the Mississippi and the Gulf. For reference see Doc. No. 108.

Washington, April 18, 1802.

. . . The cession of Louisiana and the Floridas by Spain to France, works most sorely on the United States. On this subject the Secretary of State has written to you fully, yet I cannot forbear recurring to it personally, so deep is the impression it makes on my mind. It completely reverses all the political relations of the United States, and will form a new epoch in our political course. Of all nations of any consideration, France is the one which, hitherto, has offered the fewest points on which we could have any conflict of right, and the most points of a communion of interests. From these causes, we have ever looked to her as our *natural friend*, as one with which we could never have an occasion of difference. Her growth, therefore, we viewed as our own, her misfortunes ours. There is on the globe one single spot, the possessor of which is our natural and habitual enemy. It is New Orleans, through which the produce of three-eighths of our territory must pass to market, and from its fertility it will ere long yield more than half of our whole produce, and contain more than half of our inhabitants. France, placing herself in that door, assumes to us the attitude of defiance. Spain might have retained it quietly for years. Her pacific dispositions, her feeble state, would induce her to increase our facilities there, so that her possession of the place would hardly be felt by us, and it would

not, perhaps, be very long before some circumstance might arise, which might make the cession of it to us the price of something of more worth to her. Not so can it ever be in the hands of France: the impetuosity of her temper, the energy and restlessness of her character, placed in a point of eternal friction with us, and our character, which, though quiet and loving peace and the pursuit of wealth, is high-minded, despising wealth in competition with insult or injury, enterprising and energetic as any nation on earth; these circumstances render it impossible that France and the United States can continue long friends, when they meet in so irritable a position. They, as well as we, must be blind if they do not see this; and we must be very improvident if we do not begin to make arrangements on that hypothesis. The day that France takes possession of New Orleans, fixes the sentence which is to restrain her forever within her low-water mark. It seals the union of two nations, who, in conjunction, can maintain exclusive possession of the ocean. From that moment, we must marry ourselves to the British fleet and nation. We must turn all our attention to a maritime force, for which our resources place us on very high ground; and having formed and connected together a power which may render reënforcement of her settlements here impossible to France, make the first cannon which shall be fired in Europe the signal for the tearing up of any settlement she may have made, and for holding the two continents of America in sequestration for the common purposes of the United British and American nations. This is not a state of things we seek or desire. . . .

If France considers Louisiana, however, as indispensable for her views, she might perhaps be willing to look about for arrangements which might reconcile it to our interests. If anything could do this, it would be the ceding to us the island of New Orleans and the Floridas. This would certainly, in a great degree, remove the causes of jarring and irritation between us, and perhaps for such a length of time, as might produce other means of making the measure permanently conciliatory to our interests and friendships. It would, at any rate, relieve us from the necessity of taking immediate measures for countervailing such an operation by arrangements in another quarter. But still we should consider New Orleans and the Floridas as no equivalent for the risk of a quarrel with France, produced by her vicinage.

I have no doubt you have urged these considerations, on every proper occasion, with the government where you are. They are such as must have effect, if you can find means of producing thorough reflection on them by that government. . . . Every eye in the United States is now fixed on the affairs of Louisiana. Perhaps nothing since the revolutionary war, has produced more uneasy sensations through the body of the nation. Notwithstanding temporary bickerings have taken place with France, she has still a strong hold on the affections of our citizens generally. I have thought it not amiss, by way of supplement to the letters of the Secretary of State, to write you this private one, to impress you with the importance we affix to this transaction. . . .

108. THE CESSION OF LOUISIANA
April 30, 1803

(Malloy, ed. *Treaties, Conventions, etc.*, Vol. I, p. 508 ff.)

By the Treaty of Fontainebleau of 1762, France ceded Louisiana west of the Mississippi to Spain. See Shepherd, "Cession of Louisiana to Spain", *Pol. Sci. Qt.*, Vol. XIX, p. 439. By the secret Treaty of St. Ildefonso, Spain ceded this territory back to France. This substitution of a powerful for a weak neighbour along the Mississippi and at New Orleans caused consternation in the West and to Jefferson and his advisers. Congress appropriated $2,000,000 for the purchase of New Orleans, and Jefferson dispatched Monroe to co-operate with Livingston to negotiate the purchase. For reasons primarily concerned with the critical military situation on the Continent, Napoleon decided to sell to the United States the whole of Louisiana, and the cession was accordingly made. By a convention of April 30, 1803, the United States agreed to pay sixty million francs for Louisiana. The most thorough history of the negotiations is, H. Adams, *History of the United States*, Vol. I, chs. xiv–xvii, Vol. II, chs. i–vi. See also, E. W. Lyon, *Louisiana in French Diplomacy, 1759–1804;* A. P. Whitaker, *The Mississippi Question, 1795–1803;* J. K. Hosmer, *The Louisiana Purchase;* S. F. Bemis, ed. *American Secretaries of State*, Vol. III, p. 9 ff. For the Louisiana Boundary, T. M. Marshall, *History of the Western Boundary of the Louisiana Purchase*. For the constitutional questions, see *American Insurance Co.* v. *Canter*, Doc. No. 134; and E. S. Brown, *Constitutional History of the Louisiana Purchase*.

ART. I. Whereas, by the article the third of the treaty concluded at St. Idelfonso, the 1st October, 1800 between the First Consul of the French Republic and his Catholic Majesty, it was agreed as follows: "His Catholic Majesty promises and engages on his part, to cede to the French Republic, six months after the full and entire execution of the conditions and stipulations herein relative to his royal highness the duke of Parma, the colony or province of Louisiana, with the same extent that it now has in the hands of Spain, and that it had when France possessed it; and such as it should be after the treaties subsequently entered into between Spain and other states." And *whereas,* in pursuance of the Treaty, and particularly of the third article, the French Republic has an incontestible title to the domain and to the possession of the said territory:—The First Consul of the French Republic desiring to give to the United States a strong proof of his friendship, doth hereby cede to the said United States, in the name of the French Republic, forever and in full sovereignty, the said territory with all its rights and appurtenances, as fully and in the same manner as they have been acquired by the French Republic, in virtue of the above-mentioned Treaty, concluded with his Catholic Majesty.

ART. II. In the cession made by the preceding article are included the adjacent islands belonging to Louisiana, all public lots and squares, vacant lands, and all public buildings, fortifications, barracks, and other edifices which are not private property.— The Archives, papers, and documents, relative to the domain and sovereignty of Louisiana, and its dependencies, will be left in the possession of the Commissaries of the United States, and copies will be afterwards given in due form to the Magistrates and Municipal officers, of such of the said papers and documents as may be necessary to them.

ART. III. The inhabitants of the ceded territory shall be incorporated in the Union of the United States, and admitted as soon as possible, according to the principles of the Federal Constitution, to the enjoyment of all the rights, advantages and immunities of citizens of the United States; and in the mean time they shall be maintained and protected in the free enjoyment of their liberty, prop-

erty, and the Religion which they profess. . . .

ART. VII. It has been agreed between the contracting parties, that the French ships coming directly from France or any of her colonies, loaded only with the produce and manufactures of France or her said Colonies; and the ships of Spain coming directly from Spain or any of her colonies, loaded only with the produce or manufactures of Spain or her Colonies, shall be admitted during the space of twelve years in the ports of New Orleans, and in all other legal ports of entry within the ceded territory, in the same manner as the ships of the United States coming directly from France or Spain, or any of their colonies, without being subject to any other or greater duty on merchandize, or other or greater tonnage than that paid by the citizens of the United States. . . .

109. MARBURY v. MADISON
1 Cranch, 137
1803

Original proceeding for mandamus. Under the authority of the Judiciary Act of February 27, 1801, the President appointed one William Marbury justice of the peace; because of the negligence of Secretary of State Marshall the commission was not delivered, and President Jefferson instructed his Secretary of State Madison not to deliver the commission. Marbury sued for a writ of mandamus requiring Madison to deliver his commission. Marshall's opinion embraced two questions: the ethics of withholding the commission, and the right of the Supreme Court to issue a writ of mandamus. On the first question Marshall declared, in what is generally considered *obiter dicta*, that the President had no right to withhold Marbury's commission. On the second, Marshall decided that the provision of the Judiciary Act of 1789 authorizing the Supreme Court to issue a writ of mandamus, was contrary to the Constitution and therefore void. This is the first case in which the Supreme Court held a law of Congress void: not until the Dred Scott decision did the Court hold another act of Congress void. On this famous case see, A. Beveridge, *Life of John Marshall*, Vol. III, ch. iii; E. S. Corwin, *The Doctrine of Judicial Review;* A. C. McLaughlin. *The Courts, The Constitution and Parties,* ch. i; L. B. Boudin, *Government by Judiciary,* Vol. I, ch. x; C. Warren, *The Supreme Court in United States History,* (1928 ed.) Vol. I, ch. v.

MARSHALL, C. J. . . . The peculiar delicacy of this case, the novelty of some of its circumstances, and the real difficulty attending the points which occur in it, require a complete exposition of the principles on which the opinion to be given by the court is founded. . . .

In the order in which the court has viewed this subject, the following questions have been considered and decided:

1st. Has the applicant a right to the commission he demands?

2dly. If he has a right, and that right has been violated, do the laws of his country afford him a remedy?

3dly. If they do afford him a remedy, is it a *mandamus* issuing from this court? . . .

The first object of enquiry is,

Has the applicant a right to the commission he demands? . . .

It is therefore decidedly the opinion of the court, that when a commission has been signed by the President, the appointment is made; and that the commission is complete, when the seal of the United States has been affixed to it by the secretary of state. . . .

Mr. Marbury, then, since his commission was signed by the President, and sealed by the secretary of state, was appointed; and as the law creating the office, gave the officer a right to hold for five years, independent of the executive, the appointment was not revocable; but vested in the officer legal rights, which are protected by the laws of his country.

To withhold his commission, therefore, is an act deemed by the court not warranted by law, but violative of a vested legal right.

2. This brings us to the second enquiry: which is,

If he has a right, and that right has been violated, do the laws of his country afford him a remedy? . . .

The government of the United States has been emphatically termed a government of laws, and not of men. It will certainly cease to deserve this high appellation, if the laws furnish no remedy for the violation of a vested legal right.

If this obloquy is to be cast on the jurisprudence of our country, it must arise from the peculiar character of the case. . . .

By the constitution of the United States, the President is invested with certain important political powers, in the exercise of which he is to use his own discretion, and is accountable only to his country in his political character, and to his own conscience. To aid him in the performance of these duties, he is authorized to appoint certain officers, who act by his authority and in conformity with his orders.

In such cases, their acts are his acts; and whatever opinion may be entertained of the manner in which executive discretion may be used, still there exists, and can exist, no power to control that discretion. The subjects are political. . . .

The conclusion from this reasoning is, that where the heads of departments are the political or confidential agents of the executive, merely to execute the will of the President, or rather to act in cases in which the executive possesses a constitutional or legal discretion, nothing can be more perfectly clear than that their acts are only politically examinable. But where a specific duty is assigned by law, and individual rights depend upon the performance of that duty, it seems equally clear that the individual who considers himself injured, has a right to resort to the laws of his country for a remedy. . . .

It is, then, the opinion of the Court,

1st. That by signing the commission of Mr. Marbury, the president of the United States appointed him a justice of peace for the county of Washington in the district of Columbia; and that the seal of the United States, affixed thereto by the secretary of state, is conclusive testimony of the verity of the signature, and of the completion of the appointment; and that the appointment conferred on him a legal right to the office for the space of five years.

2dly. That, having this legal title to the office, he has a consequent right to the commission; a refusal to deliver which, is a plain violation of that right, for which the laws of his country afford him a remedy.

It remains to be enquired whether,

3dly. He is entitled to the remedy for which he applies. This depends on

1st. The nature of the writ applied for, and

2dly. The power of this court. . . .

This, then, is a plain case for a mandamus, either to deliver the commission, or a copy of it from the record; and it only remains to be enquired,

Whether it can issue from this court.

The act to establish the judicial courts of the United States authorizes the supreme court "to issue writs of mandamus, in cases warranted by the principles and usages of law, to any courts appointed, or persons holding office, under the authority of the United States."

The secretary of state, being a person holding an office under the authority of the United States is precisely within the letter of the description; and if this court is not authorized to issue a writ of mandamus to such an officer, it must be because the law is unconstitutional, and therefore absolutely incapable of conferring the authority and assigning the duties which its words purport to confer and assign.

The constitution vests the whole judicial power of the United States in one supreme court, and such inferior courts as congress shall, from time to time, ordain and establish. This power is expressly extended to all cases arising under the laws of the United States; and consequently, in some form, may be exercised over the present case; because the right claimed is given by a law of the United States.

In the distribution of this power it is declared, that "the supreme court shall have original jurisdiction in all cases affecting ambassadors, other public ministers and consuls, and those in which a state shall be a party. In all other cases, the supreme court shall have appellate jurisdiction." . . .

If it had been intended to leave it in the discretion of the legislature to apportion the judicial power between the supreme and inferior courts according to the will of that body, it would certainly have been useless to have proceeded further than to have defined the judicial power, and the tribunals in which it should be vested. The subsequent part of the section is mere surplusage, is entirely without meaning, if such is to be the construction. If congress remains at liberty to give this court appellate jurisdiction, where the constitution has declared their jurisdiction shall be original; and original jurisdiction where the constitution has declared it shall be appellate; the distribution of jurisdiction, made in the constitution, is form without substance.

Affirmative words are often, in their operation, negative of other objects than those affirmed; and in this case, a negative or exclusive sense must be given to them or they have no operation at all.

It cannot be presumed, that any clause in the constitution is intended to be without effect; and therefore such a construction is inadmissible, unless the words require it. . . .

The authority, therefore, given to the supreme court, by the act establishing the judicial courts of the United States, to issue writs of mandamus to public officers, appears not to be warranted by the constitution; and it becomes necessary to inquire whether a jurisdiction so conferred can be exercised.

The question whether an act repugnant to the constitution can become the law of the land, is a question deeply interesting to the United States; but, happily not of an intricacy proportioned to its interest. It seems only necessary to recognize certain principles supposed to have been long and well established, to decide it.

That the people have an original right to establish for their future government such principles as, in their opinion, shall most conduce to their own happiness, is the basis on which the whole American fabric has been erected. The exercise of this original right is a very great exertion, nor can it nor ought it to be frequently repeated. The principles therefore so established are deemed fundamental. And as the authority from which they proceed is supreme and can seldom act, they are designed to be permanent.

This original and supreme will organizes the government, and assigns to different departments their respective powers. It may either stop here or establish certain limits not to be transcended by those departments.

The government of the United States is of the latter description. The powers of the legislature are defined and limited; and that those limits may not be mistaken or forgotten, the constitution is written. To what purpose are powers limited, and to what purpose is that limitation committed to writing, if these limits may, at any time, be passed by those intended to be restrained? The distinction between a government with limited and unlimited powers is abolished if those limits do not confine the persons on whom they are imposed and if acts prohibited and acts allowed are of equal obligation. It is a proposition too plain to be contested, that the constitution controls any legislative act repugnant to it; or, that the legislature may alter the constitution by an ordinary act.

Between these alternatives there is no middle ground. The constitution is either a superior paramount law, unchangeable by ordinary means, or it is on a level with ordinary legislative acts, and, like other acts, is alterable when the legislature shall please to alter it.

If the former part of the alternative be true, then a legislative act contrary to the constitution is not law; if the latter part be true, then written constitutions are absurd attempts, on the part of the people, to limit a power in its own nature illimitable.

Certainly all those who have framed written constitutions contemplate them as forming the fundamental and paramount law of the nation, and consequently the theory of every such government must be that an act of the legislature repugnant to the Constitution is void.

This theory is essentially attached to a written constitution, and is consequently to be considered, by this court as one of the fundamental principles of our society. It is not, therefore, to be lost sight of in the further consideration of this subject.

If an act of the legislature repugnant to the constitution is void, does it, notwithstanding its invalidity, bind the courts and oblige them to give it effect? Or, in other words, though it be not law, does it constitute a rule as operative as if it was a law? This would be to overthrow in fact what was established in theory, and would seem, at first view, an absurdity too gross to be insisted on. It shall, however, receive a more attentive consideration.

It is emphatically the province and duty of the judicial department to say what the law is. Those who apply the rule to particular cases must of necessity expound and interpret that rule. If two laws conflict with each other, the courts must decide on the operation of each.

So if a law be in opposition to the constitution; if both the law and the constitution apply to a particular case, so that the court must either decide that case conformably to the law, disregarding the constitution, or conformably to the constitution, disregarding the law, the court must determine which of these conflicting rules governs the case. This is of the very essence of judicial duty.

If, then, the courts are to regard the constitution, and the constitution is superior to any ordinary act of the legislature, the constitution, and not such ordinary act, must govern the case to which they both apply.

Those, then, who controvert the principle that the constitution is to be considered in court as a paramount law, are reduced to the necessity of maintaining that courts must close their eyes on the constitution and see only the law.

This doctrine would subvert the very foundation of all written constitutions. It would declare that an act which, according to the principles and theory of our government, is entirely void, is yet, in practice, completely obligatory. It would declare that if the legislature shall do what is expressly forbidden, such act, notwithstanding the express prohibition, is in reality effectual. It would be giving to the legislature a practical and real omnipotence with the same breath which professes to restrict their powers within narrow limits. It is prescribing limits

and declaring that those limits may be passed at pleasure.

That it thus reduces to nothing what we have deemed the greatest improvement on political institutions, a written constitution, would of itself be sufficient, in America, where written constitutions have been viewed with so much reverence, for rejecting the construction. But the peculiar expressions of the constitution of the United States furnish additional arguments in favor of its rejection.

The judicial power of the United States is extended to all cases arising under the constitution.

Could it be the intention of those who gave this power to say that in using it the constitution should not be looked into? That a case arising under the constitution should be decided without examining the instrument under which it arises?

This is too extravagant to be maintained. In some cases, then, the constitution must be looked into by the judges. And if they can open it at all, what part of it are they forbidden to read or to obey?

There are many other parts of the constitution which serve to illustrate this subject.

It is declared that "no tax or duty shall be laid on articles exported from any state." Suppose a duty on the export of cotton, of tobacco, or of flour, and a suit instituted to recover it, ought judgment to be rendered in such a case? Ought the judges to close their eyes on the constitution, and only see the law?

The constitution declares "that no bill of attainder or *ex post facto* law shall be passed." If, however, such a bill should be passed, and a person should be prosecuted under it, must the court condemn to death those victims whom the constitution endeavors to preserve?

"No person," says the constitution, "shall be convicted of treason unless on the testimony of two witnesses to the same overt act, or on confession in open court."

Here the language of the constitution is addressed especially to the courts. It prescribes, directly for them, a rule of evidence not to be departed from. If the legislature should change that rule, and declare one witness, or a confession out of court, sufficient for conviction, must the constitutional principle yield to the legislative act?

From these, and many other selections which might be made, it is apparent that the framers of the constitution contemplated that instrument as a rule for the government of *courts,* as well as of the legislature. Why otherwise does it direct the judges to take an oath to support it? This oath certainly applies in an especial manner to their conduct in their official character. How immoral to impose it on them if they were to be used as the instruments, and the knowing instruments, for violating what they swear to support!

The oath of office, too, imposed by the legislature, is completely demonstrative of the legislative opinion on this subject. It is in these words: "I do solemnly swear that I will administer justice without respect to persons, and do equal right to the poor and to the rich; and that I will faithfully and impartially discharge all the duties incumbent on me as ———, according to the best of my abilities and understanding, agreeably to *the constitution* and laws of the United States." Why does a judge swear to discharge his duties agreeably to the constitution of the United States, if that constitution forms no rule for his government?—if it is closed upon him, and cannot be inspected by him?

If such be the real state of things, this is worse than solemn mockery. To prescribe, or to take this oath, becomes equally a crime.

It is also not entirely unworthy of observation, that in declaring what shall be the *supreme* law of the land, the constitution itself is first mentioned, and not the laws of the United States generally, but those only which shall be made in *pursuance* of the constitution, have that rank.

Thus, the particular phraseology of the constitution of the United States confirms and strengthens the principle, supposed to be essential to all written constitutions, that a law repugnant to the constitution is void, and that courts, as well as other departments, are bound by that instrument.

[Mandamus denied.]

110. JEFFERSON'S MESSAGE ON THE BURR CONSPIRACY
January 22, 1807

(Richardson, ed. *Messages and Papers,* Vol. I, p. 412 ff.)

On November 27, 1806, Jefferson had issued a proclamation warning citizens of the Burr conspiracy. The message below contains a more detailed account of the information upon which this proclamation was issued. Burr had surrendered to the acting Governor of Louisiana Territory January 17, 1807, but subsequently attempted to escape, only to be apprehended and sent on to Richmond for trial on the charge of treason. Two different interpretations of the Burr conspiracy are in H. Adams, *History of the United States,* Vol. III, chs. x–xiv, xix, and W. F. McCaleb, *Aaron Burr Conspiracy.* An account of the trial is in A. Beveridge, *Life of John Marshall,* Vol. III, chs. vi–ix. For Burr, see J. Parton, *Aaron Burr.*

JANUARY 22, 1807.

To the Senate and House of Representatives of the United States:

Agreeably to the request of the House of Representatives communicated in their resolution of the 16th instant, I proceed to state, under the reserve therein expressed, information received touching an illegal combination of private individuals against the peace and safety of the Union, and a military expedition planned by them against the territories of a power in amity with the United States, with the measures I have pursued for suppressing the same. . . .

Some time in the latter part of September I received intimations that designs were in agitation in the Western country unlawful and unfriendly to the peace of the Union, and that the prime mover in these was Aaron Burr, heretofore distinguished by the favor of his country. The grounds of these intimations being inconclusive, the objects uncertain, and the fidelity of that country known to be firm, the only measure taken was to urge the informants to use their best endeavors to get further insight into the designs and proceedings of the suspected persons and to communicate them to me.

It was not till the latter part of October that the objects of the conspiracy began to be perceived, but still so blended and involved in mystery that nothing distinct could be singled out for pursuit. In this state of uncertainty . . . I thought it best to send to the scene where these things were principally in transaction a person in whose integrity, understanding, and discretion entire confidence could be reposed, with instructions to investigate the plots going on, . . . and . . . to do on the spot whatever should be necessary to discover the designs of the conspirators, arrest their means, bring their persons to punishment, and to call out the force of the country to suppress any unlawful enterprise in which it should be found they were engaged. By this time it was known that many boats were under preparation, stores of provisions collecting, and an unusual number of suspicious characters in motion on the Ohio and its waters. Besides dispatching the confidential agent to that quarter, orders were at the same time sent to the governors of the Orleans and Mississippi Territories and to the commanders of the land and naval forces there to be on their guard against surprise and in constant readiness to resist any enterprise which might be attempted on the vessels, posts, or other objects under their care; and on the 8th of November instructions were forwarded to General Wilkinson to hasten an accommodation with the Spanish commandant on the Sabine, and as soon as that was effected to fall back with his principal force to the hither bank of the Mississippi for the defense of the interesting points on that river. By a letter received from that officer on the 25th of November, we learnt that a confidential agent of Aaron Burr had been deputed to him with communications, partly written in cipher and partly oral, explaining his designs, exaggerating his resources, and making such offers of emolument and command to engage him and the army in his unlawful enterprise as he had flattered himself would be successful. The General, . . . immediately dispatched a trusty officer to me with information of what had passed, . . .

The General's letter, . . . and some other information received a few days earlier, when brought together developed Burr's general designs, . . . It appeared that he contemplated two distinct objects, which might be carried on either jointly or separately, and either the one or the other first, as circumstances should direct. One of these was the severance of the Union of these States by the Alleghany Mountains; the other an attack on Mexico. A third object was provided, merely ostensible, to wit, the settlement of a pretended purchase of a tract of country on the Washita claimed by a Baron Bastrop. This was to serve as the pretext for all his preparations, an allurement for such followers as really wished to acquire settlements in that country and a cover under which to retreat in the event of a final discomfiture of both branches of his real design.

He found at once that the attachment of the Western country to the present Union was not to be shaken; that its dissolution could not be effected with the consent of its inhabitants, and that his resources were inadequate as yet to effect it by force. He took his course then at once, determined to seize on New Orleans, plunder the bank there, possess himself of the military and naval stores, and proceed on his expedition to Mexico, and to this object all his means and preparations were now directed. He collected from all the quarters where himself or his agents possessed influence all the ardent, restless, desperate, and disaffected persons who were ready for any enterprise analogous to their characters. He seduced good and well-meaning citizens, some by assurances that he possessed the confidence of the Government and was acting under its secret patronage, a pretense which procured some credit from the state of our differences with Spain, and others by offers of land in Bastrop's claim on the Washita. . . .

. . . Surmises have been hazarded that this enterprise is to receive aid from certain foreign powers; but these surmises are without proof or probability. . . .

By letters from General Wilkinson of the 14th and 18th of December, which came to hand two days after the date of the resolution of the House of Representatives— . . . I received the important affidavit a copy of which I now communicate, with extracts of so much of the letters as comes within the scope of the resolution. By these it will be seen that of three of the principal emissaries of Mr. Burr whom the General had caused to be apprehended, one had been liberated by habeas corpus, and two others, being those particularly employed in the endeavor to corrupt the general and army of the United States, have been embarked by him for ports in the Atlantic States, probably on the consideration that an impartial trial could not be expected during the present agitations of New Orleans, and that that city was not as yet a safe place for confinement. As soon as these persons shall arrive they will be delivered to the custody of the law and left to such course of trial, both as to place and process, as its functionaries may direct. The presence of the highest judicial authorities, to be assembled at this place within a few days, the means of pursuing a sounder course of proceedings here than elsewhere, and the aid of the Executive means, should the judges have occasion to use them, render it equally desirable for the criminals as for the public that, being already removed from the place where they were first apprehended, the first regular arrest should take place here, and the course of proceedings receive here its proper direction.

TH: JEFFERSON.

111. ACT TO PROHIBIT THE IMPORTATION OF SLAVES
March 2, 1807

(U. S. Statutes at Large, Vol. II, p. 426 ff.)

Article I, section 9 of the Constitution provided that "the importation of such persons as any of the States shall think proper to admit, shall not be prohibited by the Congress prior to the Year 1808. . . ." In his Sixth Annual Message, December 2, 1806 (Richardson, Vol. I, p. 405 ff.) Jefferson wrote, "I congratulate you, fellow-citizens, on the approach of the period at which you may interpose your authority constitutionally to withdraw the citizens of the United States from all further participation in those violations of human rights which have been so long continued on the unoffending inhabitants of Africa." Bills to prohibit the importation of slaves were promptly introduced into the House and the Senate. See W. E. B. Du Bois, *Suppression of the African Slave Trade;* M. S. Locke, *Anti-Slavery in America, 1619–1808;* H. Wilson, *Rise and Fall of the Slave Power in America,* Vol. I.

An Act to prohibit the importation of Slaves into any port or place within the jurisdiction of the United States, from and after the first day of January, in the year of our Lord one thousand eight hundred and eight.

Be it enacted, That from and after the first day of January, one thousand eight hundred and eight, it shall not be lawful to import or bring into the United States or the territories thereof from any foreign kingdom, place, or country, any negro, mulatto, or person of colour, as a slave, or to be held to service or labour.

Sec. 2. That no citizen of the United States, or any other person, shall, from and after the first day of January, in the year of our Lord one thousand eight hundred and eight, for himself, or themselves, or any other person whatsoever, either as master, factor, or owner, build, fit, equip, load or to otherwise prepare any ship or vessel, in any port or place within the jurisdiction of the United States, nor shall cause any ship or vessel to sail from any port or place within the same, for the purpose of procuring any negro, mulatto, or person of colour, from any foreign kingdom, place, or country, to be transported to any port or place whatsoever within the jurisdiction of the United States, to be held, sold, or disposed of as slaves, or to be held to service or labour: and if any ship or vessel shall be so fitted out for the purpose aforesaid, or shall be caused to sail so as aforesaid, every such ship or vessel, her tackle, apparel, and furniture, shall be forfeited to the United States, and shall be liable to be seized, prosecuted, and condemned in any of the circuit courts or district courts, for the district where the said ship or vessel may be found or seized. . . .

Sec. 4. If any citizen or citizens of the United States, or any person resident within the jurisdiction of the same, shall, from and after the first day of January, one thousand eight hundred and eight, take on board, receive or transport from any of the coasts or kingdoms of Africa, or from any other foreign kingdom, place, or country, any negro, mulatto, or person of colour in any ship or vessel, for the purpose of selling them in any port or place within the jurisdiction of the United States as slaves, or to be held to service or labour, or shall be in any ways aiding or abetting therein, such citizen or citizens, or person, shall severally forfeit and pay five thousand dollars, one moiety thereof to the use of any person or persons who shall sue for and prosecute the same to effect. . . .

Sec. 6. That if any person or persons whatsoever, shall, from and after the first day of January, one thousand eight hundred and eight, purchase or sell any negro, mulatto, or person, of colour, for a slave, or to be held to service or labour, who shall have been imported, or brought from any foreign kingdom, place, or country, or from the dominions of any foreign state, immediately adjoining to the United States, after the last day of December, one thousand eight hundred and seven, knowing at the time of such purchase or sale, such negro, mulatto, or person of colour, was so brought within the jurisdiction of the United States, as aforesaid, such purchaser and seller shall severally forfeit and pay for every negro, mulatto, or person of colour, so purchased or sold as aforesaid, eight hundred dollars. . . .

Sec. 7. That if any ship or vessel shall be found, from and after the first day of January, one thousand eight hundred and eight, in any river, port, bay, or harbor, or on the high seas, within the jurisdictional limits of the United States, or hovering on the coast thereof, having on board any negro, mulatto, or person of colour, for the purpose of selling them as slaves, or with intent to land the same, in any port or place within the jurisdiction of the United States, contrary to the prohibition of the act, every such ship or vessel, together with her tackle, apparel, and furniture, and the goods or effects which shall be found on board the same, shall be forfeited to the use of the United States, and may be seized, prosecuted, and condemned, in any court of the United States, having jurisdiction thereof. And it shall be lawful for the President of the United States, and he is hereby authorized, should he deem it expedient, to cause any of the armed vessels of the United States to be manned and employed to cruise on any part of the coast of the United States, or territories thereof, where he may judge attempts will be made to violate the provisions of this act, and to instruct and direct the commanders of armed vessels of the United States, to seize, take, and bring into any port of the United States all such ships or vessels, and moreover to seize, take, or bring into any port of the U. S. all ships or vessel of the U. S. wheresoever found on the high seas, contravening the provisions of this act, to be proceeded against according to law. . . .

112. COMMERCIAL WARFARE
1806–1810

The Peace of Amiens was of short duration, and in 1803 came a renewal of the European wars which soon involved the commerce of the United States. In 1805 Great Britain seized and condemned the vessel *Essex,* engaged in trade with the French West Indies: a year later Monroe reported that over 120 American vessels had been seized by the British. These depredations on neutral commerce were aggravated by the British practice of impressment. Protests proving vain, Congress on April 18, 1806, passed a non-importation act excluding many articles from importation from Great Britain. April 8, the so-called Fox's Blockade was established around the mouths of the Elbe, Weser, Trave, etc., and May 16 this blockade was extended to include all the coast from the Elbe to Brest. Napoleon retaliated with the Berlin Decree of November 21, 1806. Great Britain replied with the Order in Council of January 7, 1807 prohibiting any vessel from trading with any port of France or her Allies and the additional Order in Council of November 11 blockading all ports in Europe from which the British flag was excluded. Napoleon retaliated with the Milan Decree of December 17 declaring the British Isles in a state of blockade and that every ship searched by the British was to be regarded as enemy property. These decrees and counter-decrees not only bore severely upon American commerce, they also touched American pride and honor. The effort of William Pinkney to conclude a satisfactory treaty with Great Britain having failed, the United States established, December 22, 1807, an embargo. The Embargo Act of December 22 was supplemented by acts of January 9, 1808 and March 12, 1808. The Embargo, which Jefferson fondly believed would bring the warring Powers to terms, proved unenforceable, and it was withdrawn, March 1, 1809, in favor of another non-intercourse law. Section 11 of this act permitted the President, by proclamation, to re-open trade with Great Britain or France if either of these nations ceased to violate American rights. The British Minister Erskine having given assurances that the odious Orders in Council would be withdrawn, President Madison, by Proclamation of April 19, 1809, permitted trade with Great Britain. The action of

Erskine was disavowed by the British Government, however, and President Madison was forced, August 9, to revoke his earlier proclamation and declare the non-intercourse Act in force. This Act, however, expired in 1810, and Nathaniel Macon, Chairman of the Foreign Affairs Committee, introduced the bill known as Macon's Bill Number 2 which provided that in case either France or England should cease their violations of American commerce the non-intercourse act should be revived against the other. Meantime, by the Rambouillet Decree of March 23, 1810 Napoleon had ordered the seizure of all vessels in French ports flying the flag of the United States. Despite this chicanery, Napoleon's assurances of August 5, 1810 that in response to the proffer of the Macon Bill he would revoke all obnoxious Decrees, was accepted in good faith. By Proclamation of November 2, the President therefore withdrew restrictions on commerce with France, and on March 2, 1811 Congress passed a new non-intercourse Act directed against Great Britain. Under the circumstances English opinion demanded a revocation of the Orders in Council: at the critical moment, in May, 1812, Prime Minister Perceval was assassinated, and the revocation did not actually take place until June 23—too late to avoid war. The literature on commercial warfare of these years is extensive. Most of the documents of the controversy can be found in *American State Papers, Foreign Relations,* Vol. III; the Congressional Debates can be found in T. H. Benton, *Abridgement of the Debates of Congress, 1789–1856,* Vols. III, IV. Numerous documents are given in M. Carey, *The Olive Branch,* 10th ed. For political and diplomatic background see H. Adams, *History of the United States,* Vols. IV–VI. See also, L. Sears, *Jefferson and the Embargo;* E. Channing, *The Jeffersonian System;* chs. xvi–xx; E. Channing, *History of the United States,* Vol. IV, chs. xiv–xvi; A. T. Mahan, *Sea Power and the War of 1812;* K. C. Babcock, *Rise of American Nationality,* chs. i–iii; J. Shouler, *History of the United States,* Vol. II; H. Adams, *Albert Gallatin;* W. E. Dodd, *Nathaniel Macon;* biographies of Jefferson and Madison. On the constitutionality of the Embargo see *U. S.* v. *Brigantine William,* Hall's American Law Journal (1808) II, Federal Cases No. 16700, and C. Warren, *The Supreme Court,* (1928 ed.) Vol. II, p. 341 ff.

1. THE BERLIN DECREE
November 21, 1806

(State Papers and Publick Documents of the United States, Vol. V, p. 478)

Art. I. The British islands are declared in a state of blockade.

II. All commerce and correspondence with the British islands are prohibited. In consequence, letters or packets, addressed either to England, to an Englishman, or in the English language, shall not pass through the post-office and shall be seized.

III. Every subject of England, of whatever rank and condition soever, who shall be found in the countries occupied by our troops, or by those of our allies, shall be made a prisoner of war.

IV. All magazines, merchandise, or property whatsoever, belonging to a subject of England, shall be declared lawful prize.

V. The trade in English merchandise is forbidden; all merchandise belonging to England, or coming from its manufactories and colonies, is declared lawful prize.

VI. One half of the proceeds of the confiscation of the merchandise and property, declared good prize by the preceding articles, shall be applied to indemnify the merchants for the losses which they have suffered by the capture of merchant vessels by English cruisers.

VII. No vessel coming directly from England, or from the English colonies, or having been there since the publication of the present decree, shall be received into any port.

VIII. Every vessel contravening the above clause, by means of a false declaration, shall be seized, and the vessel and cargo confiscated, as if they were English property.

IX. Our tribunal of prizes at Paris is charged with the definitive adjudication of all the controversies, which by the French army, relative to the execution of the present decree. Our tribunal of prizes at Milan shall be charged with the definitive adjudication of the said controversies, which may arise within the extent of our kingdom of Italy.

X. The present decree shall be communicated by our minister of exterior relations, to the kings of Spain, of Naples, of Holland, and of Etruria, and to our allies, whose subjects, like ours, are the victims of the injustice and the barbarism of the English maritime laws. Our finances, our police, and our post masters general, are charged each, in what concerns him, with the execution of the present decree.

2. BRITISH ORDER IN COUNCIL
January 7, 1807
(American State Papers, Foreign Relations,
Vol. III, p. 267)

Whereas the French Government has issued certain orders, which, in violation of the usages of war, purport to prohibit the commerce of all neutral nations with His Majesty's dominions, and also to prevent such nations from trading with any other country in any articles, the growth, produce, or manufacture of His Majesty's dominions; and whereas the said Government has also taken upon itself to declare all His Majesty's dominions to be in a state of blockade, at the time when the fleets of France and her allies are themselves confined within their own ports by the superior valor and discipline of the British navy; and whereas such attempts, on the part of the enemy, would give to His Majesty an unquestionable right of retaliation, and would warrant His Majesty in enforcing the same prohibition of all commerce with France, which that power vainly hopes to effect against the commerce of His Majesty's subjects, a prohibition which the superiority of His Majesty's naval forces might enable him to support by actually investing the ports and coasts of the enemy with numerous squadrons and cruisers, so as to make the entrance or approach thereto manifestly dangerous; and whereas His Majesty, though unwilling to follow the example of his enemies by proceeding to an extremity so distressing to all nations not engaged in the war, and carrying on their accustomed trade, yet feels himself bound, by due regard to the just defense of the rights and interests of his people not to suffer such measures to be taken by the enemy, without taking some steps on his part to restrain this violence, and to retort upon them the evils of their own injustice; His Majesty is thereupon pleased, by and with the advice of his privy council, to order, and it is hereby ordered, that no vessel shall be permitted to trade from one port to another, both which ports shall belong to or be in the possession of France or her allies, or shall be so far under their control as that British vessels may not trade freely thereat; and the commanders of His Majesty's ships of war and privateers shall be, and are hereby, instructed to warn every neutral vessel coming from any such port, and destined to another such port, to discontinue her voyage, and not to proceed to any such port; and any vessel, after being so warned, or any vessel coming from any such port, after a reasonable time shall have been afforded for receiving information of this His Majesty's order, which shall be found proceeding to another such port, shall be captured and brought in, and together with her cargo shall be condemned as lawful prize; and His Majesty's principal Secretaries of State, the Lords Commissioners of the Admiralty, and the Judges of the High Court of Admiralty, and the Courts of Vice-admiralty, are to take the necessary measures herein as to them shall respectively appertain.

3. BRITISH ORDER IN COUNCIL
November 11, 1807
(Annals of the Congress of the United States,
10th Congress, 2d. session, 1808–1809, p. 1698 ff.)

Whereas certain orders, establishing an unprecedented system of warfare against this kingdom, and aimed especially at the destruction of its commerce and resources, were, sometime since, issued by the government of France, by which "the British islands were declared to be in a state of blockade," thereby subjecting to capture and condemnation all vessels, with their cargoes, which should continue to trade with his majesty's dominions:

And whereas, by the same order, "all trading in English merchandise is prohibited, and every article of merchandise belonging to England, or coming from her colonies, or of her manufacture, is declared lawful prize:"

And whereas the nations in alliance with France, and under her control, were required to give, and have given, and do give, effect to such orders:

And whereas his majesty's order of the 7th of January last has not answered the desired purpose, either of compelling the enemy to recall those orders, or of inducing neutral nations to interpose, with effect, to obtain their revocation, but, on the contrary, the same have been recently enforced with increased rigor:

And, whereas, his majesty, under these circumstances, finds himself compelled to take further measures for asserting and vindicating his just rights. . . .

His majesty is therefore pleased, by and with the advice of his privy council, to order, and it is hereby ordered, that all the ports and places of France and her allies, or of any country at war with his majesty, and all other ports or places in Europe, from which, although not at war with his majesty, the British flag is excluded, and all ports or places in the colonies belonging to his majesty's enemies, shall, from henceforth, be subject to the same restrictions in point of trade and navigation, with the exceptions hereinafter mentioned, as if the same were actually blockaded by his majesty's naval forces, in the most strict and rigorous manner: And it is hereby further ordered and declared, that all trade in articles which are of the produce or manufacture of the said countries or colonies, shall be deemed and considered to be unlawful; and that every vessel trading from or to the said countries or colonies, together with all goods and merchandise on board, and all articles of the produce or manufacture of the said countries or colonies, shall be captured and condemned as prize to the captors. . . .

And the commanders of his majesty's ships of war and privateers, and other vessels acting under his majesty's commission, shall be, and are hereby, instructed to warn every vessel which shall have commenced her voyage prior to any notice of this order, and shall be destined to any port of France, or of her allies, or of any other country at war with his majesty, or to any port or place from which the British flag, as aforesaid, is excluded, or to any colony belonging to his majesty's enemies, and which shall not have cleared out as is hereinbefore allowed, to discontinue her voyage, and to proceed to some port or place in this kingdom, or to Gibraltar or Malta; and any vessel which, after having been so warned, or after a reasonable time shall have been afforded for the arrival of information of this his majesty's order at any port or place from which she sailed, or which, after having notice of this order, shall be found in the prosecution of any voyage contrary to the restrictions contained in this order, shall be captured, and, together with her cargo, condemned as lawful prize to the captors.

And whereas countries not engaged in the war have acquiesced in these orders of France, prohibiting all trade in any articles the produce or manufacture of his majesty's dominions; and the merchants of those countries have given countenance and effect to those prohibitions by accepting from persons, styling themselves commercial agents of the enemy, resident at neutral ports, certain documents, termed "certificates of origin," being certificates obtained at the ports of shipment, declaring that the articles of the cargo are not of the produce or manufacture of his majesty's dominions, or to that effect:

And whereas this expedient has been directed by France, and submitted to by such merchants, as part of the new system of warfare directed against the trade of this kingdom, and as the most effectual instrument of accomplishing the same, and it is therefore essentially necessary to resist it:

His majesty is therefore pleased, by and with the advice of his privy council, to order, and it is hereby ordered, that if any vessel, after reasonable time shall have been afforded for receiving notice of this his majesty's order, at the port or place from which such vessel shall have cleared out, shall be found carrying any such certificate or document as aforesaid, or any document referring to or authenticating the same, such vessel shall be adjudged lawful prize to the captor, together with the goods laden therein, belonging to the person or persons by whom, or on whose behalf, any such document was put on board.

And the right honorable the lords commissioners of his majesty's treasury, his majesty's principal secretaries of state, the lords commissioners of the admiralty, and the judges of the high court of admiralty and courts of vice admiralty, are to take the necessary measures herein as to them shall respectively appertain.

W. FAWKENER.

4. THE MILAN DECREE
December 17, 1807

(State Papers and Publick Documents of the United States, Vol. VI, p. 74)

NAPOLEON, emperor of the French, king of Italy, and protector of the Rhenish confederation.

Observing the measures adopted by the British government, on the 11th November last, by which vessels belonging to neutral, friendly, or even powers the allies of England, are made liable, not only to be searched by English cruisers, but to be compulsorily detained in England, and to have a tax laid on them of so much per cent on the cargo, to be regulated by the British legislature.

Observing that by these acts the British government *denationalizes* ships of every nation in Europe, that it is not competent for any government to detract from its own independence and rights, all the sovereigns of Europe having in trust the sovereignties and independence of the flag; that if by an unpardonable weakness, and which in the eyes of posterity would be an indelible stain, if such a tyranny was allowed to be established into principles, and consecrated by useage, the English would avail themselves of it to assert it as a right, as they have availed themselves of the tolerance of government to establish the infamous principle, that the flag of a nation does not cover goods, and to have to their right of blockade an arbitrary extension, and which infringes on the sovereignty of every state; we have decreed and do decree as follows:

Art. I. Every ship, to whatever nation it may belong, that shall have submitted to be searched by an English ship, or to a voyage to England, or shall have paid any tax whatsoever to the English government, is thereby and for that alone, declared to be *denationalized,* to have forfeited the protection of its king, and to have become English property.

Art. II. Whether the ships thus *denationalized* by the arbitrary measures of the English government, enter into our ports, or those of our allies, or whether they fall into the hands of our ships of war, or of our privateers, they are declared to be good and lawful prize.

Art. III. The British islands are declared to be in a state of blockade, both by land and sea. Every ship, of whatever nation, or whatsoever the nature of its cargo may be, that sails from the ports of England, or those of the English colonies, and of the countries occupied by English troops, and proceeding to England or to the English colonies, or to countries occupied by English troops, is good and lawful prize, as contrary to the present decree, and may be captured by our ships of war, or our privateers, and adjudged to the captor.

Art. IV. These measures, which are resorted to only in just retaliation of the barbarous system adopted by England, which assimilates its legislation to that of Algiers, shall cease to have any effect with respect to all nations who shall have the firmness to compel the English government to respect their flag. They shall continue to be rigorously in force as long as that government does not return to the principle of the law of nations, which regulates the relations of civilized states in a state of war. The provisions of the present decree shall be abrogated and null, in fact, as soon as the English abide again by the principles of the law of nations, which are also the principles of justice and of honour.

All our ministers are charged with the execution of the present decree, which shall be inserted in the bulletin of the laws.

NAPOLEON.

5. THE EMBARGO ACT
December 22, 1807

(*U. S. Statutes at Large,* Vol. II, p. 451 ff.)

An Act laying an Embargo on all ships and vessels in the ports and harbors of the United States.

Be it enacted, That an embargo be, and hereby is laid on all ships and vessels in the ports and places within the limits or jurisdiction of the United States, cleared or not cleared, bound to any foreign port or place; and that no clearance be furnished to any ship or vessel bound to such foreign port or place, except vessels under the immediate direction of the President of the United States: and that the President be authorized to give such instructions to the officers of the revenue, and of the navy and revenue cutters of the United States, as shall appear best adapted for carrying the same into full effect: *Provided,* that nothing herein contained shall be construed to prevent the departure of any foreign ship or vessel, either in ballast, or with the goods, wares and merchandise on board of such foreign ship or vessel, when notified of this act.

Sec. 2. That during the continuance of this act, no registered, or sea letter vessel, having on board goods, wares and merchandise, shall be allowed to depart from one port of the United States to any other within the same, unless the master, owner, consignee or factor of such vessel shall first give bond, with one or more sureties to the collector of the district from which she is bound to depart, in a sum of double the value of the vessel and cargo, that the said goods, wares, or merchandise shall be relanded in some port of the United States, dangers of the seas excepted, which bond, and also a certificate from the collector where the same may be relanded, shall by the collector respectively be transmitted to the Secretary of the Treasury. All armed vessels possessing public commissions from any foreign power, are not to be considered as liable to the embargo laid by this act.

6. THE NON-INTERCOURSE ACT
March 1, 1809

(U. S. Statutes at Large, Vol. II, p. 528 ff.)

An Act to interdict the commercial intercourse between the United States and Great Britain and France, and their dependencies; and for other purposes.

Be it enacted, That from and after the passing of this act, the entrance of the harbors and waters of the United States and of the territories thereof, be, and the same is hereby interdicted to all public ships and vessels belonging to Great Britain or France. . . . And if any public ship or vessel as aforesaid, not being included in the exception above mentioned, shall enter any harbor or waters within the jurisdiction of the United States, or of the territories thereof, it shall be lawful for the President of the United States, or such other person as he shall have empowered for that purpose, to employ such part of the land and naval forces, or of the militia of the United States, or the territories thereof, as he shall deem necessary, to compel such ship or vessel to depart.

SEC. 2. That it shall not be lawful for any citizen or citizens of the United States or the territories thereof, nor for any person or persons residing or being in the same, to have any intercourse with, or to afford any aid or supplies to any public ship or vessel as aforesaid, which shall, contrary to the provisions of this act, have entered any harbor or waters within the jurisdiction of the United States or the territories thereof; and if any person shall, contrary to the provisions of this act, have any intercourse with such ship or vessel, or shall afford any aid to such ship or vessel,

either in repairing the said vessel or in furnishing her, her officers and crew with supplies of any kind or in any manner whatever, . . . every person so offending, shall forfeit and pay a sum not less than one hundred dollars, nor exceeding ten thousand dollars; and shall also be imprisoned for a term not less than one month, nor more than one year.

SEC. 3. That from and after the twentieth day of May next, the entrance of the harbors and waters of the United States and the territories thereof be, and the same is hereby interdicted to all ships or vessels sailing under the flag of Great Britain or France, or owned in whole or in part by any citizen or subject of either. . . . And if any ship or vessel sailing under the flag of Great Britain or France, . . . shall after the said twentieth day of May next, arrive either with or without a cargo, within the limits of the United States or of the territories thereof, such ship or vessel, together with the cargo, if any, which may be found on board, shall be forfeited, and may be seized and condemned in any court of the United States or the territories thereof, having competent jurisdiction, . . .

SEC. 4. That from and after the twentieth day of May next, it shall not be lawful to import into the United States or the territories thereof, any goods, wares or merchandise whatever, from any port or place situated in Great Britain or Ireland, or in any of the colonies or dependencies of Great Britain, nor from any port or place situated in France, or in any of her colonies or dependencies, nor from any port or place in the actual possession of either Great Britain or France. Nor shall it be lawful to import into the United States, or the territories thereof, from any foreign port or place whatever, any goods, wares or merchandise whatever, being of the growth, produce or manufacture of France, or of any of her colonies or dependencies, or being of the growth, produce or manufacture of Great Britain or Ireland, or of any of the colonies or dependencies of Great Britain, or being of the growth, produce or manufacture of any place or country in the actual possession of either France or Great Britain. . . .

SEC. 11. That the President of the United States be, and he hereby is authorized, in case either France or Great Britain shall so revoke or modify her edicts, as that they shall cease to violate the neutral commerce of the United States, to declare the same by proclamation; after which the trade of the United States, suspended by this act, and by the [Embargo Act] and the several acts supplementary thereto, may be renewed with the nation so doing. . . .

SEC. 12. That so much of the . . . [Embargo Act] and of the several acts supplementary thereto, as forbids the departure of vessels owned by citizens of the United States, and the exportation of domestic and foreign merchandise to any foreign port or place, be and the same is hereby repealed, after March 15, 1809, except so far as they relate to Great Britain or France, or their colonies or dependencies, or places in the actual possession of either. . . .

SEC. 19. That this act shall continue and be in force until the end of the next session of Congress, and no longer; and that the act laying an embargo on all ships and vessels in the ports and harbors of the United States, and the several acts supplementary thereto, shall be, and the same are hereby repealed from and after the end of the next session of Congress.

7. MACON'S BILL, No. 2
May 1, 1810

(*U. S. Statutes at Large,* Vol. II, p. 605–6)

An Act concerning the commercial intercourse between the United States and Great Britain and France and their dependencies, and for other purposes.

BE it enacted. That from and after the passage of this act, no British or French armed vessel shall be permitted to enter the harbor or waters under the jurisdiction of the United States; . . . except when they shall be forced in by distress . . . or when charged with despatches or business from their government, or coming as a public packet for the conveyance of letters; . . .

Sec. 2. That all pacific intercourse with any interdicted foreign armed vessels, the officers or crew thereof, is hereby forbidden, . . .

Sec. 4. That in case either Great Britain or France shall, before the third day of March next, so revoke or modify her edicts as that they shall cease to violate the neutral commerce of the United States, which fact

the President of the United States shall declare by proclamation, and if the other nation shall not within three months thereafter so revoke or modify her edicts in like manner, then the third, fourth, fifth, sixth, seventh, eighth, ninth, tenth, and eighteenth sections of the act, entituled "An act to interdict the commercial intercourse between the United States and Great Britain and France . . ." shall, from and after the expiration of three months from the date of the proclamation aforesaid, be revived and have full force and effect, so far as relates to the dominions, colonies, and dependencies, and to the articles the growth, produce or manufacture of the dominions, colonies and dependencies of the nation thus refusing or neglecting to revoke or modify her edicts in the manner aforesaid. And the restrictions imposed by this act shall, from the date of such proclamation, cease and be discontinued in relation to the nation revoking or modifying her decrees in the manner aforesaid.

8. THE RAMBOUILLET DECREE
March 23, 1810

(*State Papers and Publick Documents of the United States,* Vol. VII, p. 467–8)

NAPOLEON, &c.

Considering that the government of the United States, by an act dated 1st March, 1809, which forbids the entrance of the ports, harbours, and rivers of the said States, to all French vessels, orders, 1st. That after the 20th of May following, vessels under the French flag, which shall arrive in the United States, shall be seized and confiscated, as well as their cargoes; 2d. That after the same epoch, no merchandise or produce, the growth or manufacture of France or her colonies, can be imported into the said United States from any port or place whatsoever, under the penalty of seizure, confiscation, and a fine of three times the value of the merchandise; 3d. That American vessels cannot go to any port of France, of her colonies, or dependencies: We have decreed, and do decree, what follows:

ART. 1. All vessels navigating under the flag of the United States, or possessed, in whole or in part, by any citizen or subject of that power, which, counting from the 20th of May, 1809, have entered or shall enter into the ports of our empire, of our colonies, or of the countries occupied by our arms, shall be seized, and the product of the sales shall be deposited in the surplus fund (*caisse d'amortissement.*)

There shall be excepted from this regula-tion the vessels which shall be charged with despatches, or with commissions of the government of the said States, and who shall not have either cargoes or merchandise on board. . . .

NAPOLEON.

113. FLETCHER v. PECK
6 Cranch, 87
1810

Error to the U. S. circuit court of the district of Massachusetts. In 1795 the legislature of Georgia passed an act for the sale of enormous areas of her western lands. The following year a new legislature annulled the act of 1795 on the ground that it was passed fraudulently. The celebrated case of *Fletcher* v. *Peck* involved two major constitutional questions: the interpretation of the contract clause of the Federal Constitution, and the power of the court to inquire into the motives and circumstances attending the passage of a legislative act. This was the first case in which the Supreme Court held a state law void under the Constitution. See, Beveridge, *Marshall*, Vol. III ch. x; C. H. Haskins, *The Yazoo Land Companies*.

MARSHALL, C. J. . . . That the legislature of Georgia, unless restrained by its own constitution, possesses the power of disposing of the unappropriated lands within its own limits, in such manner as its own judgment shall dictate, is a proposition not to be controverted. The only question, then, presented by this demurrer, for the consideration of the court, is this, did the then constitution of the state of Georgia prohibit the legislature to dispose of the lands, which were the subject of this contract, in the manner stipulated by the contract? . . .

In the constitution of Georgia, adopted in the year 1789, the court can perceive no restriction on the legislative power, which inhibits the passage of the act of 1795. The court cannot say that, in passing that act, the legislature has transcended its powers, and violated the constitution. In overruling the demurrer, therefore, to the first plea, the circuit court committed no error. . . .

That corruption should find its way into the governments of our infant republics, and contaminate the very source of legislation, or that impure motives should contribute to the passage of a law, or the formation of a legislative contract, are circumstances most deeply to be deplored. How far a court of justice would, in any case, be competent, on proceedings instituted by the state itself, to vacate a contract thus formed, and to annul rights acquired, under that contract, by third persons having no notice of the improper means by which it was obtained, is a question which the court would approach with much circumspection. It may well be doubted, how far the validity of a law depends upon the motives of its framers, and how far the particular inducements, operating on members the supreme sovereign power of a state, to the formation of a contract by that power, are examinable in a court of justice. If the principle be conceded, that an act of the supreme sovereign power might be declared null by a court, in consequence of the means which procured it, still would there be much difficulty in saying to what extent those means must be applied to produce this effect. Must it be direct corruption? or would interest or undue influence of any kind be sufficient? Must the vitiating cause operate on a majority? or on what number of the members? Would the act be null, whatever might be the wish of the nation? or would its obligation or nullity depend upon the public sentiment? If the majority of the legislature be corrupted, it may well be doubted, whether it be within the province of the judiciary to control their conduct, and, if less than a majority act from impure motives, the principle by which judicial interference would be regulated, is not clearly discerned. Whatever difficulties this subject might present, when viewed under aspects of which it may be susceptible, this court can perceive none in the particular pleadings now under consideration. . . .

The case, as made out in the pleadings, is simply this: One individual who holds lands in the state of Georgia, under a deed covenanting that the title of Georgia was in the grantor, brings an action of covenant upon this deed and assigns as a breach that some of the members of the legislature were induced to vote in favor of the law which constituted the contract by being promised an interest in it, and that therefore the act is a mere nullity.

This solemn question cannot be brought thus collaterally and incidentally before the court. It would be indecent in the extreme, upon a private contract between two individuals, to enter into an inquiry respecting the corruption of the sovereign power of a state. If the title be plainly deduced from a legislative act which the legislature might constitutionally pass, if the act be clothed with all the requisite forms of a law, a court, sitting as a court of law, cannot sustain a suit brought by one individual against another founded on the allegation that the act is a nullity in consequence of the impure motives which influenced certain members of the legislature which passed the law. . . .

It is not intended to speak with disrespect of the legislature of Georgia, or of its acts. Far from it. The question is a general question, and is treated as one. For although such powerful objections to a legislative grant, as are alleged against this, may not again exist, yet the principle, on which alone this rescinding act is to be supported, may be applied to every case to which it shall be the will of any legislature to apply it. The principle is this: that a legislature may, by its own act, divest the vested estate of any man whatever, for reasons which shall, by itself, be deemed sufficient. . . .

In this case the legislature may have had ample proof that the original grant was obtained by practices which can never be too much reprobated, and which would have justified its abrogation so far as respected those to whom crime was imputable. But the grant, when issued, conveyed an estate in fee-simple to the grantees, clothed with all the solemnities which law can bestow. This estate was transferable; and those who purchased parts of it were not stained by that guilt which infected the original transaction. . . .

Is the power of the legislature competent to the annihilation of such title, and to a resumption of the property thus held? The principle asserted is, that one legislature is competent to repeal any act which a former legislature was competent to pass; and that one legislature cannot abridge the powers of a succeeding legislature. The correctness of this principle, so far as respects general legislation, can never be controverted. But if an act be done under a law, a succeeding legislature cannot undo it. The past cannot be recalled by the most absolute power. Conveyances have been made, those conveyances have vested legal estates, and, if those estates may be seized by the sovereign authority, still, that they originally vested is a fact, and cannot cease to be a fact. When, then, a law is in its nature a contract, when absolute rights have vested under that contract, a repeal of the law cannot divest those rights; and the act of annulling them, if legitimate, is rendered so by a power applicable to the case of every individual in the community.

It may well be doubted whether the nature of society and of the government does not prescribe some limits to the legislative power; and if any be prescribed, where are they to be found, if the property of an individual, fairly and honestly acquired, may be seized without compensation? To the legislature all legislative power is granted; but the question whether the act of transferring the property of an individual to the public be in the nature of legislative power, is well worthy of serious reflection. . . .

The validity of this rescinding act, then, might well be doubted, were Georgia a single sovereign power. But Georgia cannot be viewed as a single, unconnected, sovereign power, on whose legislature no other restrictions are imposed than may be found in its own constitution. She is a part of a large empire; she is a member of the American union; and that union has a constitution, the supremacy of which all acknowledge, and which imposes limits to the legislatures of the several states, which none claim a right to pass. The constitution of the United States declares that no state shall pass any bill of attainder, *ex post facto* law, or law impairing the obligation of contracts.

Does the case now under consideration come within this prohibitory section of the Constitution? In considering this very interesting question, we immediately ask ourselves what is a contract? Is a grant a contract? A contract is a compact between two or more parties, and is either executory or executed. An executory contract is one in which a party binds himself to do, or not to do, a particular thing; such was the law under which the conveyance was made by the governor. A contract executed is one in which the object of contract is performed; and this, says Blackstone, differs in nothing from a grant. The contract between Georgia and the purchasers was executed by the grant. A contract executed, as well as one which is executory, contains obligations binding on the parties. A grant, in its own nature, amounts to an extinguishment of the right of the grantor, and implies a contract not to reassert that right. A party is, therefore, always estopped by his own grant.

Since, then, in fact, a grant is a contract executed, the obligation of which still continues, and since the constitution uses the general term "contracts," without distinguishing between those which are executory and those which are executed, it must be construed to comprehend the latter as well as the former. A law annulling conveyances between individuals, and declaring that the grantors should stand seized of their former estates, notwithstanding those grants, would be as repugnant to the constitution as a law discharging the vendors of property from the obligation of executing their contracts by conveyances. It would be strange if a contract to convey was secured by the constitution, while an absolute conveyance remained unprotected.

If, under a fair construction of the constitution, grants are comprehended under the term "contracts," is a grant from the state excluded from the operation of the provision? Is the clause to be considered as inhibiting the State from impairing the obligation of contracts between two individuals, but as excluding from that inhibition contracts made with itself? The words themselves contain no such distinction. They are general, and are applicable to contracts of every description. If contracts made with the state are to be exempted from their operation, the exception must arise from the character of the contracting party, not from the words which are employed. . . .

It is, then, the unanimous opinion of the court, that, in this case, the estate having passed into the hands of a purchaser for a valuable consideration, without notice, the state of Georgia was restrained, either by general principles which are common to our free institutions, or by the particular provisions of the Constitution of the United States, from passing a law whereby the estate of the plaintiff in the premises so purchased could be constitutionally and legally impaired and rendered null and void. . . .

Judgment affirmed.

114. MADISON'S WAR MESSAGE
June 1, 1812

(Richardson, ed. *Messages and Papers,* Vol. I, p. 499 ff.)

Congress declared war on Great Britain June 18, 1812. On the diplomatic background of the war, see H. Adams, *History of the United States,* Vols. V VI; on the political background, J. Pratt, *Expansionists of 1812.* It was long charged that the War Hawks forced Madison to recommend a declaration of war as the price for re-election; for a careful analysis of this charge, see T. C. Smith, "War Guilt in 1812", Massachusetts Hist. Soc. *Proceedings,* Vol. LXIV, p. 319 ff.

WASHINGTON, *June 1, 1812.*
To the Senate and House of Representatives of the United States:

I communicate to Congress certain documents, being a continuation of those heretofore laid before them on the subject of our affairs with Great Britain.

Without going back beyond the renewal in 1803 of the war in which Great Britain is engaged, and omitting unrepaired wrongs of inferior magnitude, the conduct of her Government presents a series of acts hostile to the United States as an independent and neutral nation.

British cruisers have been in the continued practice of violating the American flag on the great highway of nations, and of seizing and carrying off persons sailing under it, not in the exercise of a belligerent right founded on the law of nations against an enemy, but of a municipal prerogative over British subjects. British jurisdiction is thus extended to neutral vessels in a situation where no laws can operate but the law of nations and the laws of the country to which the vessels belong, and a self-redress is assumed which, if British subjects were wrongfully detained and alone concerned, is that substitution of force for a resort to the responsible sovereign which falls within the definition of war. . . .

The practice, hence, is so far from affecting British subjects alone that, under the pretext of searching for these, thousands of American citizens, under the safeguard of public law and of their national flag, have been torn from their country and from everything dear to them; have been dragged on board ships of war of a foreign nation and exposed, under the severities of their discipline, to be exiled to the most distant and deadly climes, to risk their lives in the battles of their oppressors, and to be the melancholy instruments of taking away those of their own brethren.

Against this crying enormity, which Great Britain would be so prompt to avenge if committed against herself, the United States have in vain exhausted remonstrances and expostulations, and that no proof might be wanting of their conciliatory dispositions, and no pretext left for a continuance of the practice, the British Government was formally assured of the readiness of the United States to enter into arrangements such as could not be rejected if the recovery of British subjects were the real and the sole object. The communication passed without effect.

British cruisers have been in the practice also of violating the rights and the peace of our coasts. They hover over and harass our entering and departing commerce. To the most insulting pretensions they have added the most lawless proceedings in our very harbors, and have wantonly spilt American blood within the sanctuary of our territorial jurisdiction. . . .

Under pretended blockades, without the presence of an adequate force and sometimes without the practicability of applying one, our commerce has been plundered in every sea, the great staples of our country have been cut off from their legitimate markets, and a destructive blow aimed at our agricultural and maritime interests. In aggravation of these predatory measures they have been considered as in force from the dates of their notification, a retrospective effect being thus added, as has been done in other important cases, to the unlawfulness of the course pursued. And to render the outrage the more signal these mock blockades have been reiterated and enforced in the face of official communications from the British Government declaring as the true definition of a legal blockade "that particular ports must be actually invested and previous warning given to vessels bound to them not to enter."

Not content with these occasional expedients for laying waste our neutral trade, the cabinet of Britain resorted at length to the sweeping system of blockades, under the name of orders in council, which has been molded and managed as might best suit its political views, its commercial jealousies, or the avidity of British cruisers. . . .

Abandoning still more all respect for the neutral rights of the United States and for its own consistency, the British Government now demands as prerequisites to a repeal of its orders as they relate to the United States that a formality should be observed in the repeal of the French decrees nowise necessary to their termination nor exemplified by British usage, and that the French repeal, besides including that portion of the decrees which operates within a territorial jurisdiction, as well as that which operates on the high seas, against the commerce of the United States should not be a single and special repeal in relation to the United States, but should be extended to whatever other neutral nations unconnected with them may be affected by those decrees. . . .

It has become, indeed, sufficiently certain that the commerce of the United States is to be sacrificed, not as interfering with the belligerent rights of Great Britain; not as supplying the wants of her enemies, which she herself supplies; but as interfering with the monopoly which she covets for her own commerce and navigation. She carries on a war against the lawful commerce of a friend that she may the better carry on a commerce with an enemy—a commerce polluted by the forgeries and perjuries which are for the most part the only passports by which it can succeed. . . .

In reviewing the conduct of Great Britain toward the United States our attention is necessarily drawn to the warfare just renewed by the savages on one of our extensive frontiers—a warfare which is known to spare neither age nor sex and to be distinguished by features peculiarly shocking to humanity. It is difficult to account for the activity and combinations which have for some time been developing themselves among tribes in constant intercourse with British traders and garrisons without connecting their hostility with that influence and without recollecting the authenticated examples of such interpositions heretofore furnished by the officers and agents of that Government.

Such is the spectacle of injuries and indignities which have been heaped on our country, and such the crisis which its unexampled forbearance and conciliatory efforts have not been able to avert. . . .

Our moderation and conciliation have had no other effect than to encourage perseverance and to enlarge pretensions. We behold our seafaring citizens still the daily victims of lawless violence, committed on the great common and highway of nations, even within sight of the country which owes them protection. We behold our vessels, freighted with the products of our soil and industry, or returning with the honest proceeds of them, wrested from their lawful destinations, confiscated by prize courts no longer the organs of public law but the instruments of arbitrary edicts, and their unfortunate crews dispersed and lost, or forced or inveigled in British ports into British fleets, whilst arguments are employed in support of these aggressions which have no foundation but in a principle equally supporting a claim to regulate our external commerce in all cases whatsoever.

We behold, in fine, on the side of Great Britain a state of war against the United States, and on the side of the United States a state of peace toward Great Britain.

Whether the United States shall continue passive under these progressive usurpations and these accumulating wrongs, or, opposing force to force in defense of their national rights, shall commit a just cause into the hands of the Almighty Disposer of Events, avoiding all connections which might entangle it in the contest or views of other powers, and preserving a constant readiness to concur in an honorable reëstablishment of peace and friendship, is a solemn question which the Constitution wisely confides to the legislative department of the Government. In recommending it to their early deliberations I am happy in the assurance that the decision will be worthy the enlightened and patriotic councils of a virtuous, a free, and a powerful nation. . . .

115. REPORT AND RESOLUTIONS OF THE HARTFORD CONVENTION
January 4, 1815

(T. Dwight, *History of the Hartford Convention*, p. 368 ff.)

The dissatisfaction of New England Federalists with the Republican administration, with the accession of western territory, and with the War of 1812, culminated in the Hartford Convention of December 1814. The convention was attended by delegates from Massachusetts, Connecticut, Rhode Island, Vermont and New Hampshire. George Cabot of Massachusetts was President of the Convention; among its members were H. G. Otis, N. Dane, C. Goodrich, and Samuel Ward. Cabot exercised a moderating influence on the Convention, and the report and resolutions adopted were far from radical or treasonable. Commissioners went to Washington with the Resolutions of the Convention, but arriving just after the news of Jackson's victory at New Orleans and the Treaty of Ghent, abandoned their mission. On the Convention see Theodore Dwight, *History of the Hartford Convention;* S. E. Morison, *Harrison Gray Otis,* Vol. II, chs. xxii–xxviii; H. C. Lodge, *George Cabot;* H. Adams, *History of the United States,* Vol VIII, ch. xi.

. . . To investigate and explain the means whereby this fatal reverse has been effected, would require a voluminous discussion. Nothing more can be attempted in this report than a general allusion to the principal outlines of the policy which has produced this vicissitude. Among these may be enumerated—

First.—A deliberate and extensive system for effecting a combination among certain states, by exciting local jealousies and ambition, so as to secure to popular leaders in one section of the Union, the controul of public affairs in perpetual succession. To which primary object most other characteristics of the system may be reconciled.

Secondly.—The political intolerance displayed and avowed in excluding from office men of unexceptionable merit, for want of adherence to the executive creed.

Thirdly.—The infraction of the judiciary authority and rights, by depriving judges of their offices in violation of the constitution.

Fourthly.—The abolition of existing taxes, requisite to prepare the country for those changes to which nations are always exposed, with a view to the acquisition of popular favour.

Fifthly.—The influence of patronage in the distribution of offices, which in these states has been almost invariably made among men the least entitled to such distinction, and who have sold themselves as ready instruments for distracting public opinion, and encouraging administration to hold in contempt the wishes and remonstrances of a people thus apparently divided.

Sixthly.—The admission of new states into the Union formed at pleasure in the western region, has destroyed the balance of power which existed among the original States, and deeply affected their interest.

Seventhly.—The easy admission of naturalized foreigners, to places of trust, honour or profit, operating as an inducement to the malcontent subjects of the old world to come to these States, in quest of executive patronage, and to repay it by an abject devotion to executive measures.

Eighthly.—Hostility to Great Britain, and partiality to the late government of France, adopted as coincident with popular prejudice, and subservient to the main object, party power. Connected with these must be ranked erroneous and distorted estimates of the power and resources of those nations, of the probable results of their controversies, and of our political relations to them respectively.

Lastly and principally.—A visionary and superficial theory in regard to commerce, accompanied by a real hatred but a feigned regard to its interests, and a ruinous perseverance in efforts to render it an instrument of coercion and war.

But it is not conceivable that the obliquity of any administration could, in so short a period, have so nearly consummated the work of national ruin, unless favoured by defects in the constitution.

To enumerate all the improvements of which that instrument is susceptible, and to propose such amendments as might render it in all respects perfect, would be a task which this convention has not thought proper to assume. They have confined their attention to such as experience has demonstrated to be essential, and even among these, some are considered entitled to a more serious attention than others. They are suggested without any intentional disrespect to other states, and are meant to be such as all shall find an interest in promoting. Their object is to strengthen, and if possible to perpetuate, the union of the states, by removing the grounds of existing jealousies, and providing for a fair and equal representation, and a limitation of powers, which have been misused. . . . [There follows an analysis of the proposed amendments.]

THEREFORE RESOLVED,

That it be and hereby is recommended to the legislatures of the several states represented in this Convention, to adopt all such measures as may be necessary effectually to protect the citizens of said states from the operation and effects of all acts which have been or may be passed by the Congress of the United States, which shall contain provisions, subjecting the militia or other citizens to forcible drafts, conscriptions, or impressments, not authorised by the constitution of the United States.

Resolved, That it be and hereby is recommended to the said Legislatures, to authorize an immediate and earnest application to be made to the government of the United States, requesting their consent to some arrangement, whereby the said states may, separately or in concert, be empowered to assume upon themselves the defence of their territory against the enemy; and a reasonable portion of the taxes, collected within said States, may be paid into the respective treasuries thereof, and appropriated to the payment of the balance due said states, and to the future defence of the same. The amount so paid into the said treasuries to be credited, and the disbursements made as aforesaid to be charged to the United States.

Resolved, That it be, and hereby is, recommended to the legislatures of the aforesaid states, to pass laws (where it has not already been done) authorizing the governors or commanders-in-chief of their militia to make detachments from the same, or to form voluntary corps, as shall be most convenient and conformable to their constitutions, and to cause the same to be well armed, equipped, and disciplined, and held in readiness for service; and upon the request of the governor of either of the other states to employ the whole of such detachment or corps, as well as the regular forces of the state, or such part thereof as may be required and can be spared consistently with the safety of the state, in assisting the state, making such request to repel any invasion thereof which shall be made or attempted by the public enemy.

Resolved, That the following amendments of the constitution of the United States be recommended to the states represented as aforesaid, to be proposed by them for adoption by the state legislatures, and in such cases as may be deemed expedient by a convention chosen by the people of each state.

And it is further recommended, that the said states shall persevere in their efforts to obtain such amendments, until the same shall be effected.

First. Representatives and direct taxes shall be apportioned among the several states which may be included within this Union, according to their respective numbers of free persons, including those bound to serve for a term of years, and excluding Indians not taxed, and all other persons.

Second. No new state shall be admitted into the Union by Congress, in virtue of the power granted by the constitution, without the concurrence of two thirds of both houses.

Third. Congress shall not have power to lay any embargo on the ships or vessels of the citizens of the United States, in the ports or harbours thereof, for more than sixty days.

Fourth. Congress shall not have power, without the concurrence of two thirds of both houses, to interdict the commercial intercourse between the United States and any foreign nation, or the dependencies thereof.

Fifth. Congress shall not make or declare war, or authorize acts of hostility against any foreign nation, without the concurrence of two thirds of both houses, except such acts of hostility be in defence of the territories of the United States when actually invaded.

Sixth. No person who shall hereafter be naturalized, shall be eligible as a member of the senate or house of representatives of the United States, nor capable of holding any civil office under the authority of the United States.

Seventh. The same person shall not be elected president of the United States a second time; nor shall the president be elected from the same state two terms in succession.

Resolved, That if the application of these states to the government of the United States, recommended in a foregoing resolution, should be unsuccessful and peace should not be concluded, and the defence of these states should be neglected, as it has since the commencement of the war, it will, in the opinion of this convention, be expedient for the legislatures of the several states to appoint delegates to another convention, to meet at Boston . . . with such powers and instructions as the exigency of a crisis so momentous may require.

116. MADISON'S VETO OF BONUS BILL
March 3, 1817

(Richardson, ed. *Messages and Papers,* Vol. I, p. 584–5)

In December 1816 Calhoun introduced a bill to provide for setting aside the Bank bonus of $1,500,000 as a permanent fund for internal improvements. The bill passed Congress February, 1817; Madison's veto was his last official act. See, H. Adams, *History of the United States,* Vol. IX, p. 148 ff.; P. J. Treat, *The National Land System.*

MARCH 3, 1817.

To the House of Representatives of the United States:

Having considered the bill this day presented to me entitled "An act to set apart and pledge certain funds for internal improvements," and which sets apart and pledges funds "for constructing roads and canals, and improving the navigation of water courses, in order to facilitate, promote, and give security to internal commerce among the several States, and to render more easy and less expensive the means and provisions for the common defense," I am constrained by the insuperable difficulty I feel in reconciling the bill with the Constitution of the United States to return it with that objection to the House of Representatives, in which it originated.

The legislative powers vested in Congress are specified and enumerated in the eighth section of the first article of the Constitution, and it does not appear that the power proposed to be exercised by the bill is among the enumerated powers, or that it falls by any just interpretation within the power to make laws necessary and proper for carrying into execution those or other powers vested by the Constitution in the Government of the United States.

"The power to regulate commerce among the several States" can not include a power to construct roads and canals, and to improve the navigation of water courses in order to facilitate, promote, and secure such a commerce without a latitude of construction departing from the ordinary import of the terms strengthened by the known inconveniences which doubtless led to the grant of this remedial power to Congress.

To refer the power in question to the clause "to provide for the common defense and general welfare" would be contrary to the established and consistent rules cf interpretation, as rendering the special and careful enumeration of powers which follow the clause nugatory and improper. Such a view of the Constitution would have the effect of giving to Congress a general power of legislation instead of the defined and limited one hitherto understood to belong to them, the terms "common defense and general welfare" embracing every object and act within the purview of a legislative trust. It would have the effect of subjecting both the Constitution and laws of the several States in all cases not specifically exempted to be superseded by laws of Congress, it being expressly declared "that the Constitution of the United States and laws made in pursuance thereof shall be the supreme law of the land, and the judges of every State shall be bound thereby, anything in the constitution or laws of any State to the contrary notwithstanding." Such a view of the Constitution, finally, would have the effect of excluding the judicial authority of the United States from its participation in guarding the boundary between the legislative powers of the General and the State Governments, inasmuch as questions relating to the general welfare, being questions of policy and expediency, are unsusceptible of judicial cognizance and decision.

A restriction of the power "to provide for the common defense and general welfare" to cases which are to be provided for by the expenditure of money would still leave within the legislative power of Congress all the great and most important measures of Government, money being the ordinary and necessary means of carrying them into execution.

If a general power to construct roads and canals, and to improve the navigation of water courses, with the train of powers incident thereto, be not possessed by Congress, the assent of the States in the mode provided in the bill can not confer the power. The only cases in which the consent and cession of particular States can extend the power of Congress are those specified and provided for in the Constitution.

I am not unaware of the great importance of roads and canals and the improved navigation of water courses, and that a power in the National Legislature to provide for them might be exercised with signal advantage to the general prosperity. But seeing that such a power is not expressly given by the Constitution, and believing that it can not be deduced from any part of it without an inadmissible latitude of construction and a reliance on insufficient precedents; believing also that the permanent success of the Constitution depends on a definite partition of powers between the General and the State Governments, and that no adequate landmarks would be left by the constructive extension of the powers of Congress as proposed in the bill, I have no option but to withhold my signature from it, and to cherishing the hope that its beneficial objects may be attained by a resort for the necessary powers to the same wisdom and virtue in the nation which established the Constitution in its actual form and providently marked out in the instrument itself a safe and practicable mode of improving it as experience might suggest.

117. THE RUSH-BAGOT AGREEMENT
April 28, 1818

(Malloy, ed. *Treaties, Conventions, etc.*, Vol. I, p. 628 ff.)

This famous agreement neutralized the waters of the Great Lakes and provided for an unfortified frontier between the United States and Canada. See, J. M. Callahan, "Neutrality of the American lakes and the Anglo-American Relations" Johns Hopkins U. *Studies*, Ser. XVI.

ARRANGEMENT

BETWEEN, *the United States and Great Britain, between Richard Rush, Esq., acting as Secretary of the Department of State, and Charles Bagot, His Britannic Majesty's Envoy Extraordinary, &c.*

The naval force to be maintained upon the American lakes, by his majesty and the government of the United States, shall henceforth be confined to the following vessels on each side; that is—

On lake Ontario, to one vessel not exceeding one hundred tons burden, and armed with one eighteen pound cannon.

On the upper lakes, to two vessels, not exceeding like burden each, and armed with like force.

On the waters of lake Champlain, to one vessel not exceeding like burden, and armed with like force.

All other armed vessels on these lakes shall be forthwith dismantled, and no other vessels of war shall be there built or armed.

If either party should hereafter be desirous of annulling this stipulation, and should give notice to that effect to the other party, it shall cease to be binding after the expiration of six months from the date of such notice.

The naval force so to be limited shall be restricted to such services as will, in no respect, interfere with the proper duties of the armed vessels of the other party.

118. M'CULLOCH v. MARYLAND
4 Wheaton, 316
1819

Error to the Court of Appeals of Maryland. In 1818 Maryland passed an act imposing a tax upon the notes of all banks not chartered by the State. M'Culloch, cashier of the branch Bank of the United States at Baltimore, refused to pay the tax, and action was brought against him by the state of Maryland. Two questions were involved in this case: did Congress have the right to incorporate a bank, and was a state tax upon the bank constitutional. In his consideration of the first of these questions, Marshall relied to a large extent upon Hamilton's argument on the constitutionality of the bank, see Doc. No. 93. This was one of the most notable of Marshall's opinions, and one of the most important in construing the powers of the National Government. See, A. Beveridge, *Marshall*, Vol. IV, p. 282 ff.; C. Warren, *The Supreme Court*, (1928 ed.) Vol. I, ch. xii. This decision evoked a thorough and powerful criticism from Judge Spencer Roane of Virginia: the articles have been reprinted in the *John P. Branch Historical Papers*, 1905.

MARSHALL, C. J. . . . The first question made in this cause is, has Congress power to incorporate a bank?

It has been truly said, that this can scarcely be considered as an open question, entirely unprejudiced by the former proceedings of the nation respecting it. The principle now contested was introduced at a very early period of our history, has been recognized by many successive legislatures, and has been acted upon by the judicial department, in cases of peculiar delicacy, as a law of undoubted obligation. . . .

In discussing this question, the counsel for the State of Maryland have deemed it of some importance, in the construction of the constitution, to consider that instrument not as emanating from the people, but as the act of sovereign and independent States. The powers of the general government, it has been said, are delegated by the States, who alone are truly sovereign; and must be exercised in subordination to the States, who alone possess supreme dominion.

It would be difficult to sustain this proposition. The convention which framed the constitution was, indeed, elected by the State legislatures. But the instrument, when it came from their hands, was a mere proposal, without obligation, or pretensions to it. It was reported to the then existing Congress of the United States, with a request that it might "be submitted to a convention of Delegates, chosen in each State, by the people thereof, under the recommendation of its legislature, for their assent and ratification." This mode of proceeding was adopted; and by the Convention, by Congress, and by the State Legislatures, the instrument was submitted to the people. They acted upon it, in the only manner in which they can act safely, effectively, and wisely, on such a subject, by assembling in Convention. It is true, they assembled in their several States; and where else should they have assembled? No political dreamer was ever wild enough to think of breaking down the lines which separate the States, and of compounding the American people into one common mass. Of consequence, when they act, they act in their States. But the measures they adopt do not, on that account cease to be the measures of the people themselves, or become the measures of the state governments.

From these Conventions the constitution derives its whole authority. The government proceeds directly from the people; is "ordained and established" in the name of the people; and is declared to be ordained, "in order to form a more perfect union, establish justice, insure domestic tranquillity, and secure the blessings of liberty to themselves and to their posterity." The assent of the States, in their sovereign capacity, is implied in calling a Convention, and thus submitting that instrument to the people. But the people were at perfect liberty to accept or reject it; and their act was final. It required not the affirmance, and could not be negatived, by the State governments. The constitution, when thus adopted, was of complete obligation, and bound the State sovereignties. . . .

. . . The government of the Union, then (whatever may be the influence of this fact on the case), is emphatically and truly a government of the people. In form and in substance it emanates from them, its powers are granted by them, and are to be exercised directly on them, and for their benefit.

This government is acknowledged by all to be one of enumerated powers. The principle, that it can exercise only the powers granted to it, would seem too apparent to have required to be enforced by all those arguments which its enlightened friends, while it was depending before the people, found it necessary to urge. That principle is now universally admitted. But the question respecting the extent of the powers actually granted, is perpetually arising, and will probably continue to arise; as long as our system shall exist. In discussing these questions, the conflicting powers of the State and general governments must be brought into view, and the supremacy of their respective laws, when they are in opposition, must be settled.

If any one proposition could command the universal assent of mankind, we might expect it would be this: that the government of the Union, though limited in its powers, is supreme within its sphere of action. This would seem to result necessarily from its nature. It is the government of all; its powers are delegated by all; it represents all, and acts for all. Though any one State may be willing to control its operations, no State is willing to allow others to control them. The nation, on those subjects on which it can act, must necessarily bind its component parts. But this question is not left to mere reason: the people have, in express terms, decided it, by saying, "this constitution, and the laws of the United States, which shall be made in pursuance thereof," "shall be the supreme law of the land," and by requiring that the members of the State legislatures, and the officers of the executive and judicial departments of the States, shall take the oath of fidelity to it.

The government of the United States, then, though limited in its powers, is supreme; and its laws, when made in pursuance of the constitution, form the supreme law of the land, "anything in the constitution or laws of any State, to the contrary, notwithstanding."

Among the enumerated powers, we do not find that of establishing a bank or creating a corporation. But there is no phrase in the instrument which, like the articles of confederation, excludes incidental or implied powers; and which requires that everything granted shall be expressly and minutely described. Even the 10th amendment, which was framed for the purpose of quieting the excessive jealousies which had been excited, omits the word "expressly," and declares only that the powers "not delegated to the United States, nor prohibited to the States, are reserved to the States or to the people;" thus leaving the question, whether the particular power which may become the subject of contest, has been delegated to the one government, or prohibited to the other, to depend on a fair construction of the whole instrument. The men who drew and adopted this amendment, had experienced the embarrassments resulting from the insertion of this word in the articles of confederation, and probably omitted it to avoid those embarrassments. A constitution, to contain an accurate detail of all the subdivisions of which its great powers will admit, and of all the means by which they may be carried into execution, would partake of the prolixity of a legal code, and could scarcely be embraced by the human mind. It would probably never be understood by the public. Its nature, therefore, requires that only its great outlines should be marked, its important objects designated, and the minor ingredients which compose those objects be deduced from the nature of the objects themselves. That this idea was entertained by the framers of the American constitution, is not only to be inferred from the nature of the instrument, but from the language. Why else were some of the limitations, found in the 9th section of the first article, introduced? It is also, in some degree, warranted by their having omitted to use any restrictive term which might prevent its receiving a fair and just interpretation. In considering this question, then, we must never forget, that it is *a constitution* we are expounding.

Although, among the enumerated powers of government, we do not find the word "bank," or "incorporation," we find the great powers to lay and collect taxes; to borrow money; to regulate commerce; to declare and conduct a war; and to raise and support armies and navies. The sword and the purse, all the external relations, and no inconsiderable portion of the industry of the nation, are intrusted to its government. It can never be pretended that these vast powers draw after them others of inferior importance, merely because they are inferior. Such an idea can never be advanced. But it may, with great

reason, be contended, that a government, intrusted with such ample powers, on the due execution of which the happiness and prosperity of the nation so vitally depends, must also be intrusted with ample means for their execution. The power being given, it is the interest of the nation to facilitate its execution. It can never be their interest, and cannot be presumed to have been their intention, to clog and embarrass its execution by withholding the most appropriate means. Throughout this vast republic, from the St. Croix to the Gulph of Mexico, from the Atlantic to the Pacific, revenue is to be collected and expended, armies are to be marched and supported. The exigencies of the nation may require, that the treasure raised in the north should be transported to the south, *that* raised in the east conveyed to the west, or that this order should be reversed. Is that construction of the constitution to be preferred which would render these operations difficult, hazardous, and expensive? Can we adopt that construction (unless the words imperiously require it) which would impute to the framers of that instrument, when granting these powers for the public good, the intention of impeding their exercise by withholding a choice of means? If, indeed, such be the mandate of the constitution, we have only to obey; but that instrument does not profess to enumerate the means by which the powers it confers may be executed; nor does it prohibit the creation of a corporation, if the existence of such a being be essential to the beneficial exercise of those powers. It is, then, the subject of fair inquiry, how far such means may be employed.

It is not denied that the powers given to the government imply the ordinary means of execution. That, for example, of raising revenue and applying it to national purposes, is admitted to imply the power of conveying money from place to place, as the exigencies of the nation may require, and of employing the usual means of conveyance. But it is denied that the government has its choice of means, or that it may employ the most convenient means, if to employ them it be necessary to erect a corporation. . . .

The government which has a right to do an act, and has imposed on it the duty of performing that act, must, according to the dictates of reason, be allowed to select the means; and those who contend that it may not select any appropriate means, that one particular mode of effecting the object is excepted, take upon themselves the burden of establishing that exception.

The creation of a corporation, it is said, appertains to sovereignty. This is admitted. But to what portion of sovereignty does it appertain? Does it belong to one more than to another? In America, the powers of sovereignty are divided between the government of the Union, and those of the States. They are each sovereign, with respect to the objects committed to it, and neither sovereign with respect to the objects committed to the other. We cannot comprehend that train of reasoning which would maintain, that the extent of power granted by the people is to be ascertained, not by the nature and terms of the grant, but by its date. Some State constitutions were formed *before,* some *since* that of the United States. We cannot believe that their relation to each other is in any degree dependent upon this circumstance. Their respective powers must, we think, be precisely the same, as if they had been formed at the same time. Had they been formed at the same time, and had the people conferred on the general government the power contained in the constitution, and on the States the whole residuum of power, would it have been asserted that the government of the Union was not sovereign, with respect to those objects which were entrusted to it, in relation to which its laws were declared to be supreme? If this could not have been asserted, we cannot well comprehend the process of reasoning which maintains, that a power appertaining to sovereignty cannot be connected with that vast portion of it which is granted to the general government, so far as it is calculated to subserve the legitimate objects of that government. The power of creating a corporation, though appertaining to sovereignty, is not, like the power of making war, or levying taxes, or of regulating commerce, a great substantive and independent power, which cannot be implied as incidental to other powers, or used as a means of executing them. It is never the end for which other powers are exercised, but a means by which other objects are accomplished. No contributions are made to charity for the sake of an incorporation, but a corporation is created to administer the charity; no seminary of learning is instituted in order to be incorporated, but the corporate character is conferred to subserve the purposes of education. No city was ever built with the sole object of being incorporated, but is incorporated as affording the best means of being well governed. The power of creating a corporation is never used for its own sake, but for the purpose of effecting something else. No sufficient reason is, therefore, perceived, why it may not pass as incidental to those powers which are expressly given, if it be a direct mode of executing them.

But the constitution of the United States has not left the right of Congress to employ the necessary means, for the execution of the powers conferred on the government, to general reasoning. To its enumeration of powers is added that of making "all laws which shall be necessary and proper, for carrying into execution the foregoing powers, and all other powers vested by this constitution, in the government of the United States, or in any department thereof."

The counsel for the State of Maryland have urged various arguments, to prove that this clause, though in terms a grant of power, is not so in effect; but is really restrictive of the general right, which might otherwise be implied, of selecting means of executing the enumerated powers. . . .

But the argument on which most reliance is placed, is drawn from the peculiar language of this clause. Congress is not empowered by it to make all laws, which may have relation to the powers conferred on the government, but such only as may be *"necessary and proper"* for carrying them into execution. The word *"necessary"* is considered as controlling the whole sentence, and as limiting the right to pass laws for the execution of the granted powers, to such as are indispensable, and without which the power would be nugatory. That it excludes the choice of means, and leaves to Congress, in each case, that only which is most direct and simple.

Is it true, that this is the sense in which the word "necessary" is always used? Does it always import an absolute physical necessity, so strong, that one thing, to which another may be termed necessary cannot exist without that other? We think it does not.

If reference be had to its use, in the common affairs of the world, or in approved authors, we find that it frequently imports no more than that one thing is convenient, or useful, or essential to another. To employ the means necessary to an end, is generally understood as employing any means calculated to produce the end, and not as being confined to those single means, without which the end would be entirely unattainable. Such is the character of human language, that no word conveys to the mind, in all situations one single definite idea; and nothing is more common than to use words in a figurative sense. Almost all compositions contain words, which, taken in their rigorous sense, would convey a meaning different from that which is obviously intended. It is essential to just construction, that many words which import something excessive, should be understood in a more mitigated sense—in that sense which common usage justifies. The word "necessary" is of this description. It has not a fixed character peculiar to itself. It admits of all degrees of comparison; and is often connected with other words, which increase or diminish the impression the mind receives of the urgency it imports. A thing may be necessary, very necessary, absolutely or indispensably necessary. To no mind would the same idea be conveyed, by these several phrases. . . . This word, then, like others, is used in various senses; and, in its construction, the subject, the context, the intention of the person using them, are all to be taken into view.

Let this be done in the case under consideration. The subject is the execution of those great powers on which the welfare of a nation essentially depends. It must have been the intention of those who gave these powers, to insure, as far as human prudence could insure, their beneficial execution. This could not be done by confining the choice of means to such narrow limits as not to leave it in the power of Congress to adopt any which might be appropriate, and which were conducive to the end. This provision is made in a constitution intended to endure for ages to come, and, consequently, to be adapted to the various crises of human affairs. To have prescribed the means by which government should, in all future time, execute its powers, would have been to change, entirely, the character of the instrument, and give it

the properties of a legal code. It would have been an unwise attempt to provide, by immutable rules, for exigencies which, if foreseen at all, must have been seen dimly, and which can be best provided for as they occur. To have declared that the best means shall not be used, but those alone without which the power given would be nugatory, would have been to deprive the legislature of the capacity to avail itself of experience, to exercise its reason, and to accommodate its legislation to circumstances. . . .

This clause, as construed by the State of Maryland, would abridge and almost annihilate this useful and necessary right of the legislature to select its means. That this could not be intended is, we should think, had it not been already controverted, too apparent for controversy. . . .

The result of the most careful and attentive consideration bestowed upon this clause is, that if it does not enlarge, it cannot be construed to restrain the powers of Congress, or to impair the right of the legislature to exercise its best judgment in the selection of measures to carry into execution the constitutional powers of the government. If no other motive for its insertion can be suggested, a sufficient one is found in the desire to remove all doubts respecting the right to legislate on that vast mass of incidental powers which must be involved in the constitution, if that instrument be not a splendid bauble.

We admit, as all must admit, that the powers of the government are limited, and that its limits are not to be transcended. But we think the sound construction of the constitution must allow to the national legislature that discretion, with respect to the means by which the powers it confers are to be carried into execution, which will enable that body to perform the high duties assigned to it, in the manner most beneficial to the people. Let the end be legitimate, let it be within the scope of the constitution, and all means which are appropriate, which are plainly adapted to that end, which are not prohibited, but consist with the letter and spirit of the constitution, are constitutional. . . .

If a corporation may be employed indiscriminately with other means to carry into execution the powers of the government, no particular reason can be assigned for excluding the use of a bank, if required for its fiscal operations. To use one, must be within the discretion of Congress, if it be an appropriate mode of executing the powers of government. That it is a convenient, a useful, and essential instrument in the prosecution of its fiscal operations, is not now a subject of controversy. . . .

But were its necessity less apparent, none can deny its being an appropriate measure; and if it is, the degree of its necessity as has been very justly observed, is to be discussed in another place. Should Congress, in the execution of its powers, adopt measures which are prohibited by the constitution; or should Congress, under the pretext of executing its powers, pass laws for the accomplishment of objects not intrusted to the government, it would become the painful duty of this tribunal, should a case requiring such a decision come before it, to say that such an act was not the law of the land. But where the law is not prohibited, and is really calculated to effect any of the objects intrusted to the government, to undertake here to inquire into the degree of its necessity, would be to pass the line which circumscribes the judicial department, and to tread on legislative ground. This court disclaims all pretensions to such a power. . . .

After the most deliberate consideration, it is the unanimous and decided opinion of this court, that the act to incorporate the Bank of the United States is a law made in pursuance of the constitution, and is a part of the supreme law of the land. . . .

It being the opinion of the Court, that the act incorporating the bank is constitutional; and that the power of establishing a branch in the State of Maryland might be properly exercised by the bank itself, we proceed to inquire—

2. Whether the State of Maryland may, without violating the constitution, tax that branch?

That the power of taxation is one of vital importance; that it is retained by the States; that it is not abridged by the grant of a similar power to the government of the Union; that it is to be concurrently exercised by the two governments: are truths which have never been denied. But, such is the paramount character of the constitution,

that its capacity to withdraw any subject from the action of even this power, is admitted. The States are expressly forbidden to lay any duties on imports or exports, except what may be absolutely necessary for executing their inspection laws. If the obligation of this prohibition must be conceded—if it may restrain a state from the exercise of its taxing power on imports and exports, the same paramount character would seem to restrain, as it certainly may restrain, a state from such other exercise of this power, as is in its nature incompatible with, and repugnant to, the constitutional laws of the Union. A law, absolutely repugnant to another, as entirely repeals that other as if express terms of repeal were used.

On this ground the counsel for the bank place its claim to be exempted from the power of a State to tax its operations. There is no express provision for the case, but the claim has been sustained on a principle which so entirely pervades the constitution, is so intermixed with the materials which compose it, so interwoven with its web, so blended with its texture, as to be incapable of being separated from it, without rending it into shreds.

This great principle is, that the constitution and the laws made in pursuance thereof are supreme; that they control the constitution and laws of the respective States, and cannot be controlled by them. From this, which may be almost termed an axiom, other propositions are deduced as corollaries, on the truth or error of which, and on their application to this case, the cause has been supposed to depend. These are, 1. That a power to create implies a power to preserve. 2. That a power to destroy, if wielded by a different hand, is hostile to, and incompatible with, these powers to create and preserve. 3. That where this repugnancy exists, that authority which is supreme must control, not yield to that over which it is supreme. . . .

The power of Congress to create, and of course to continue, the bank, was the subject of the preceding part of this opinion; and is no longer to be considered as questionable.

That the power of taxing it by the States may be exercised so as to destroy it, is too obvious to be denied. But taxation is said to be an absolute power, which acknowledges no other limits than those expressly pre-scribed in the constitution, and like sovereign power of every other description, is trusted to the discretion of those who use it. . . .

The argument on the part of the State of Maryland, is, not that the states may di-rectly resist a law of Congress, but that they may exercise their acknowledged powers upon it, and that the Constitution leaves them this right in the confidence that they will not abuse it. . . .

. . . That the power to tax involves the power to destroy; that the power to destroy may defeat and render useless the power to create; that there is a plain repugnance, in conferring on one government a power to control the constitutional measures of an-other, which other, with respect to those very measures, is declared to be supreme over that which exerts the control, are propositions not to be denied. But all inconsistencies are to be reconciled by the magic of the word CONFIDENCE. Taxation, it is said, does not necessarily and unavoidably destroy. To carry it to the excess of destruction would be an abuse, to presume which, would banish that confidence which is essential to all govern-ment.

But is this a case of confidence? Would the people of any one State trust those of another with a power to control the most insignificant operations of their State govern-ment? We know they would not. Why, then, should we suppose that the people of any one State should be willing to trust those of an-other with a power to control the operations of a government to which they have con-fided their most important and most valuable interests? In the legislature of the Union alone, are all represented. The legislature of the Union alone, therefore, can be trusted by the people with the power of controlling measures which concern all, in the confidence that it will not be abused. This, then, is not a case of confidence, and we must consider it as it really is.

If we apply the principle for which the State of Maryland contends, to the constitu-tion generally, we shall find it capable of changing totally the character of that instru-ment. We shall find it capable of arresting all the measures of the government, and of prostrating it at the foot of the states. The American people have declared their consti-tution, and the laws made in pursuance thereof, to be supreme; but this principle would transfer the supremacy, in fact, to the States.

If the States may tax one instrument, em-ployed by the government in the execution of its powers, they may tax any and every other instrument. They may tax the mail; they may tax the mint; they may tax patent rights; they may tax the papers of the cus-tom-house; they may tax judicial process; they may tax all the means employed by the government, to an excess which would defeat all the ends of government. This was not in-tended by the American people. They did not design to make their government de-pendent on the States. . . .

The question is, in truth, a question of su-premacy; and if the right of the States to tax the means employed by the general gov-ernment be conceded, the declaration that the constitution, and the laws made in pur-suance thereof, shall be the supreme law of the land, is empty and unmeaning declama-tion. . . .

It has also been insisted, that, as the power of taxation in the general and State govern-ments is acknowledged to be concurrent, every argument which would sustain the right of the general government to tax banks chartered by the States, will equally sustain the right of the States to tax banks chartered by the general government.

But the two cases are not on the same reason. The people of all the States have created the general government, and have conferred upon it the general power of taxa-tion. The people of all the States, and the States themselves, are represented in Con-gress, and, by their representatives, exercise this power. When they tax the chartered in-stitutions of the States, they tax their con-stitutents; and these taxes must be uniform. But when a State taxes the operations of the government of the United States, it acts upon institutions created, not by their own con-stituents, but by people over whom they claim no control. It acts upon the measures of a government created by others as well as themselves, for the benefit of others in com-mon with themselves. The difference is that which always exists, and always must exist, between the action of the whole on a part, and the action of a part on the whole—between the laws of a government declared to be supreme, and those of a government which, when in opposition to those laws, is not supreme. . . .

The Court has bestowed on this subject its most deliberate consideration. The result is a conviction that the States have no power, by taxation or otherwise, to retard, impede, burden, or in any manner control, the operations of the constitutional laws enacted by Congress to carry into execution the powers vested in the general government. This is, we think, the unavoidable consequence of that supremacy which the constitution has declared. We are unanimously of opinion, that the law passed by the legislature of Maryland, imposing a tax on the Bank of the United States, is unconstitutional and void. . . .

Judgment Reversed.

119. TRUSTEES OF DARTMOUTH COLLEGE v. WOODWARD
4 Wheaton, 518
1819

Error to the supreme court of New Hampshire. Dartmouth College had been established in 1769 by a charter granted by King George III. In 1816 the State of New Hampshire altered this charter, and organized, under the new charter, a new board of trustees. The old board of trustees refused to accept this change, and argued that the act of New Hampshire was unconstitutional, because an impairment of contract contrary to the Federal Constitution. The opinion of the Court that a corporation charter was a contract was of considerable importance in the subsequent business history of the country. Its significance, however, was limited by the decision of the court in the *Charles River Bridge* v. *Warren Bridge* case, Doc. No. 155. There is a voluminous literature on the Dartmouth College case. See, J. M. Shirley, *Dartmouth College Causes;* A. Beveridge, *Marshall,* Vol. IV, ch. v.; E. S. Corwin, *John Marshall and the Constitution,* p. 155 ff.; C. Warren, *Supreme Court* (1928 ed.), Vol. I, p. 475 ff.; G. T. Curtis, Daniel Webster, Vol. II; C. Fuess, *Daniel Webster,* Vol. I; and the illuminating note in J. R. Long, *Cases on Constitutional Law,* p. 240.

MARSHALL, C. J.:

. . . This court can be insensible neither to the magnitude nor delicacy of this question. The validity of a legislative act is to be examined; and the opinion of the highest law tribunal of a state is to be revised: an opinion which carries with it intrinsic evidence of the diligence, of the ability, and the integrity with which it was formed. . . .

It can require no argument to prove that the circumstances of this case constitute a contract. An application is made to the crown for a charter to incorporate a religious and literary institution. In the application it is stated that large contributions have been made for the object, which will be conferred on the corporation as soon as it shall be created. The charter is granted, and on its faith the property is conveyed. Surely in this transaction every ingredient of a complete and legitimate contract is to be found. The points for consideration are, 1. Is this contract protected by the constitution of the United States? 2. Is it impaired by the acts under which the defendant holds?

1. On the first point it has been argued that the word "contract," in its broadest sense, would comprehend the political relations between the government and its citizens, would extend to offices held within a state for state purposes, and to many of those laws concerning civil institutions, which must change with circumstances, and be modified by ordinary legislation; which deeply concern the public, and which, to preserve good government, the public judgment must control. That even marriage is a contract, and its obligations are affected by the laws respecting divorces. That the clause in the constitution, if construed in its greatest latitude, would prohibit these laws. Taken in its broad, unlimited sense, the clause would be an unprofitable and vexatious interference with the internal concerns of a state, would unnecessarily and unwisely embarrass its legislation, and render immutable those civil institutions which are established for purposes of internal government, and which, to subserve those purposes, ought to vary with varying circumstances. That as the framers of the constitution could never have intended to insert in that instrument a provision so unnecessary, so mischievous, and so repugnant to its general spirit, the term "contract" must be un-

derstood in a more limited sense. That it must be understood as intended to guard against a power of at least doubtful utility, the abuse of which had been extensively felt, and to restrain the legislature in future from violating the right to property. That anterior to the formation of the constitution, a course of legislation had prevailed in many, if not in all, of the states, which weakened the confidence of man in man, and embarrassed all transactions between individuals, by dispensing with a faithful performance of engagements. To correct this mischief, by restraining the power which produced it, the state legislatures were forbidden "to pass any law impairing the obligation of contracts," that is, of contracts respecting property, under which some . . . individual could claim a right to something beneficial to himself; and that, since the clause in the constitution must in construction receive some limitation, it may be confined, and ought to be confined, to cases of this description, to cases within the mischief it was intended to remedy.

The general correctness of these observations cannot be controverted. That the framers of the constitution did not intend to restrain the states in the regulation of their civil institutions, adopted for internal government, and that the instrument they have given us is not to be so construed, may be admitted. The provision of the constitution never has been understood to embrace other contracts than those which respect property or some object of value, and confer rights which may be asserted in a court of justice. It has never been understood to restrict the general right of the legislature to legislate on the subject of divorces. . . .

The parties in this case differ less on general principles, less on the true construction of the constitution in the abstract, than on the application of those principles to this case, and on the true construction of the charter of 1769. This is the point on which the cause essentially depends. If the act of incorporation be a grant of political power, if it create a civil institution to be employed in the administration of the government, or if the funds of the college be public property, or if the state of New Hampshire, as a government, be alone interested in its transactions, the subject is one in which the legisla-

ture of the state may act according to its own judgment, unrestrained by any limitation of its power imposed by the constitution of the United States.

But if this be a *private eleemosynary institution,* endowed with a capacity to take property for objects *unconnected with government,* whose funds are bestowed by individuals on the faith of the charter; if the donors have stipulated for the future disposition and management of those funds in the manner prescribed by themselves; there may be more difficulty in the case, although neither the persons who have made these stipulations, nor those for whose benefit they were made, should be parties to the cause. Those who are no longer interested in the property may yet retain such an interest in the preservation of their own arrangements as to have a right to insist that those arrangements shall be held sacred. Or, if they have themselves disappeared, it becomes a subject of serious and anxious inquiry whether those whom they have legally empowered to represent them forever may not assert all the rights which they possessed while in being; whether, if they be without personal representatives who may feel injured by a violation of the compact, the trustees be not so completely their representatives in the eye of the law as to stand in their place, not only as respects the government of the college, but also as respects the maintenance of the college charter. It becomes then the duty of the court most seriously to examine this charter, and to ascertain its true character. . . .

Whence, then, can be derived the idea that Dartmouth College has become a public institution, and its trustees public officers. . . . Not from the source whence its funds were drawn; for its foundation is purely private and eleemosynary—not from the application of those funds, for money may be given for education and the persons receiving it do not, by being employed in the education of youth, become members of the civil government. Is it from the act of incorporation? Let this subject be considered.

A corporation is an artificial being, invisible, intangible, and existing only in contemplation of law. Being the mere creature of law, it possesses only those properties which the charter of its creation confers upon it, either expressly or as incidental to its very existence. These are such as are supposed best calculated to effect the object for which it was created. Among the most important are immortality, and, if the expression may be allowed, individuality; properties, by which a perpetual succession of many persons are considered as the same, and may act as a single individual. They enable a corporation to manage its own affairs, and to hold property without the perplexing intricacies, the hazardous and endless necessity, of perpetual conveyances for the purpose of transmitting it from hand to hand. It is chiefly for the purpose of clothing bodies of men in succession with these qualities and capacities that corporations were invented and are in use. By these means, a perpetual succession of individuals are capable of acting for the promotion of the particular object, like one immortal being. . . .

From this review of the charter, it appears that Dartmouth College is an eleemosynary institution, incorporated for the purpose of perpetuating the application of the bounty of the donors to the specified objects of that bounty; that its trustees or governors were originally named by the founder, and invested with the power of perpetuating themselves; that they are not public officers, nor is it a civil institution, participating in the administration of government; but a charity school, or a seminary of education, incorporated for the preservation of its property, and the perpetual application of that property to the objects of its creation. . . .

According to the theory of the British constitution, their Parliament is omnipotent. To annul corporate rights might give a shock to public opinion, which that government has chosen to avoid; but its power is not questioned. Had Parliament, immediately after the emanation of this charter and the execution of those conveyances which followed it, annulled the instrument, so that the living donors would have witnessed the disappointment of their hopes, the perfidy of the transaction would have been universally acknowledged. Yet then, as now, the donors would have had no interest in the property; then, as now, those who might be students would have had no rights to be violated; then, as now, it might be said that the trustees, in whom the rights of all were combined, possessed no private, individual, beneficial interest in the property confided to their protection. Yet the contract would at that time have been deemed sacred by all. What has since occurred to strip it of its inviolability? Circumstances have not changed it. In reason, in justice, and in law, it is now what it was in 1769.

This is plainly a contract to which the donors, the trustees, and the crown (to whose rights and obligations New Hampshire succeeds) were the original parties. It is a contract made on a valuable consideration. It is a contract for the security and disposition of property. It is a contract on the faith of which real and personal estate has been conveyed to the corporation. It is then a contract within the letter of the constitution, and within its spirit also, unless the fact that the property is invested by the donors in trustees for the promotion of religion and education, for the benefit of persons who are perpetually changing, though the objects remain the same, shall create a particular exception, taking this case out of the prohibition contained in the constitution.

It is more than possible that the preservation of rights of this description was not particularly in the view of the framers of the constitution when the clause under consideration was introduced into that instrument. It is probable that interferences of more frequent recurrence, to which the temptation was stronger and of which the mischief was more extensive, constituted the great motive for imposing this restriction on the state legislatures. But although a particular and a rare case may not in itself be of sufficient magnitude to induce a rule, yet it must be governed by the rule, when established, unless some plain and strong reason for excluding it can be given. It is not enough to say that this particular case was not in the mind of the convention when the article was framed, nor of the American people when it was adopted. It is necessary to go farther, and to say that, had this particular case been suggested, the language would have been so varied as to exclude it, or it would have been made a special exception. The case, being within the words of the rule, must be within its operation likewise, unless there be something in the literal construction so obviously absurd, or mischievous, or repugnant to the general spirit of the instrument as to justify those who expound the constitution in making it an exception.

On what safe and intelligible ground can this exception stand? There is no expression in the constitution, no sentiment delivered by its contemporaneous expounders, which would justify us in making it. . . .

Almost all eleemosynary corporations, those which are created for the promotion of religion, of charity, or of education, are of the same character. The law of this case is the law of all. . . .

The opinion of the court, after mature deliberation, is, that this is a contract, the obligation of which cannot be impaired without violating the constitution of the United States. This opinion appears to us to be equally supported by reason and by the former decisions of this court.

2. We next proceed to the inquiry whether its obligation has been impaired by those acts of the legislature of New Hampshire to which the special verdict refers. . . .

The obligations, then, which were created by the charter to Dartmouth College were the same in the new that they had been in the old government. The power of the government was also the same. A repeal of this charter at any time prior to the adoption of the present constitution of the United States would have been an extraordinary and unprecedented act of power, but one which could have been contested only by the restrictions upon the legislature to be found in the constitution of the state. But the constitution of the United Sates has imposed this additional limitation, that the legislature of a state shall pass no act "impairing the obligation of contracts."

It has been already stated that the act "to amend the charter and enlarge and improve the corporation of Dartmouth College" increases the number of trustees to twenty-one, gives the appointment of the additional members to the executive of the state, and creates a board of overseers, to consist of twenty-five persons, of whom twenty-one are also appointed by the executive of New Hampshire, who have power to inspect and control the most important acts of the trustees.

On the effect of this law two opinions cannot be entertained. Between acting directly and acting through the agency of trustees and overseers no essential difference is perceived. The whole power of governing the college is transformed from trustees appointed according to the will of the founder, expressed in the charter, to the executive of New Hampshire. The management and application of the funds of this eleemosynary institution, which are placed by the donors in the hands of trustees named in the charter, and empowered to perpetuate themselves, are placed by this act under the control of the government of the state. The will of the state is substituted for the will of the donors in every essential operation of the college. This is not an immaterial change. . . . This system is totally changed. The charter of 1769 exists no longer. It is reorganized; and reorganized in such a manner as to convert a literary institution, molded according to the will of its founders and placed under the control of private literary men, into a machine entirely subservient to the will of government. This may be for the advantage of this college in particular, and may be for the advantage of literature in general; but it is not according to the will of the donors, and is subversive of that contract on the faith of which their property was given. . . .

It results from this opinion, that the acts of the legislature of New Hampshire, which are stated in the special verdict found in this cause, are repugnant to the constitution of the United States; and that the judgment on this special verdict ought to have been for the plaintiffs. The judgment of the state court must, therefore, be reversed.

Mr. Justice Washington and Mr. Justice Story rendered separate concurring opinions. Mr. Justice Duvall dissented.

120. FLORIDA TREATY
February 22, 1819

(Malloy, ed. *Treaties, Conventions, etc.* Vol. II, p. 1651 ff.)

This treaty concluded long-drawn out negotiations for the cession of Florida, and marked out the western boundaries of the United States. It was later charged that Sec. J. Q. Adams had surrendered our title to Texas by this treaty. Spain held up ratification in an effort to secure from the United States a pledge not to recognize the revolting Spanish Colonies. On the Treaty, see H. B. Fuller, *Purchase of Florida;* T. M. Marshall, *Western Boundary of the Louisiana Purchase;* S. F. Bemis, ed. *American Secretaries of State,* Vol. IV, p. 7 ff.

. . . ART. II. His Catholic Majesty cedes to the United States, in full property and sovereignty, all the territories which belonged to him, situated to the eastward of the Mississippi, known by the name of East and West Florida. The adjacent islands dependent on said provinces, all public lots and squares, vacant lands, public edifices, fortifications, barracks, and other buildings, which are not private property, archives and documents, which relate directly to the property and sovereignty of said provinces, are included in this article. . . .

ART. III. The boundary line between the two countries, west of the Mississippi, shall begin on the Gulph of Mexico, at the mouth of the river Sabine, in the sea, continuing north, along the western bank of that river, to the 32d degree of latitude; thence, by a line due north, to the degree of latitude where it strikes the Rio Roxo of Natchitoches, or Red River; thence following the course of the Rio Roxo westward, to the degree of longitude 100 west from London and 23 from Washington; then, crossing the said Red River, and running thence, by a line due north, to the river Arkansas, thence, following the course of the southern bank of the Arkansas, to its source, in latitude 42 north; and thence, by that parallel of latitude, to the South Sea. The whole being as laid down in Melish's map of the United States, published at Philadelphia, improved to the first of January, 1818. But if the source of the Arkansas River shall be found to fall north or south of latitude 42, then the line shall run from the said source due north or south, as the case may be, till it meets the said parallel of latitude 42, and

thence, along the said parallel, to the South Sea: All the islands in the Sabine, and the said Red and Arkansas Rivers, throughout the course thus described, to belong to the United States; but the use of the waters, and the navigation of the Sabine to the sea, and of the said rivers Roxo and Arkansas, throughout the extent of the said boundary, on their respective banks, shall be common to the respective inhabitants of both nations. . . .

ART. V. The inhabitants of the ceded territories shall be secured in the free exercise of their religion, without any restriction. . . .

ART. VI. The inhabitants of the territories which His Catholic Majesty cedes to the United States, by this treaty, shall be incorporated in the Union of the United States, as soon as may be consistent with the principles of the Federal Constitution, and admitted to the enjoyment of all the privileges, rights, and immunities of the citizens of the United States. . . .

ART. XI. The United States, exonerating Spain from all demands in future, on account of the claims of their citizens to which the renunciations herein contained extend, and considering them entirely cancelled, undertake to make satisfaction for the same, to an amount not exceeding five millions of dollars. To ascertain the full amount and validity of those claims, a commission, to consist of three Commissioners, citizens of the United States, shall be appointed by the President, by and with the advice and consent of the Senate. . . .

ART. XV. Spanish vessels, laden only with productions of Spanish growth or manufacture, coming directly from Spain, or her colonies, "shall be admitted, for the term of twelve years, to the ports of Pensacola and St. Augustine, without paying other or higher duties on their cargoes, or of tonnage, than will be paid by the vessels of the United States. During the said term no other nation shall enjoy the same privileges within the ceded territories. . . .

121. THE MISSOURI COMPROMISE
1819–1821

The Territory of Missouri was part of the Louisiana Purchase; by the terms of this purchase the inhabitants of the Territory were

guaranteed in their liberty, property, and religion. When in 1818 Missouri petitioned for admission to the Union as a State, the question arose whether this guaranty covered property in slaves of whom there were some two or three thousand in the Territory. In the course of the discussion of the enabling act, Representative Tallmadge of New York offered an amendment excluding slavery from the State. This amendment passed the House but failed in the Senate. That summer and fall the Missouri question was the chief political issue before the country; Congress was bombarded with petitions from State legislatures and other bodies on the slavery issue. In the new Congress the positions of the House and the Senate are indicated by the passage in the House of the Taylor Amendment, in the Senate of the Thomas Amendment. The application of Maine for admission as a State offered Congress a way out of the difficulty. A conference committee reported bills to admit Maine to Statehood, and to admit Missouri with the Thomas Amendment. An act authorizing Missouri to form a state government was approved March 6, but the constitution which the Missouri Convention drew up contained a clause obnoxious to the anti-slavery element, and probably unconstitutional, and Congress refused to admit the State under this constitution. A conference committee worked out a solution to the problem which was provided in the Resolutions for the admission of Missouri of March 2. The conditions laid down were accepted by the legislature of Missouri in June, and Missouri was admitted to Statehood by proclamation of August 10. On the Missouri Compromise see F. J. Turner, *Rise of the New West*, ch. x; H. Von Holst, *Constitutional and Political History of the United States*, Vol. I, p. 324 ff.; J. B. Mc Master, *History of the People of the United States*, Vol. IV, ch. xxxix; F. C. Shoemaker, *Missouri's Struggle for Statehood, 1804–1821*; J. A. Woodburn, "Historical Significance of the Missouri Compromise," Amer. Hist. Assoc. *Report*, 1893; F. R. Hodder, "Side Lights on the Missouri Compromises" Amer. Hist. Assoc. *Report*, 1909; H. A. Trexler, *Slavery in Missouri, 1804–1865*; H. V. Ames, *State Documents on Federal Relations*, p. 193 ff.; C. R. King, *Life and Correspondence of Rufus King*, Vol. VI.

1. THE TALLMADGE AMENDMENT
February 13, 1819
(*Journal of the House of Representatives*, 15th Congress, 2nd. Sess. p. 272)

And provided also, That the further introduction of slavery or involuntary servitude be prohibited, except for the punishment of crimes, whereof the party shall be duly convicted; and that all children of slaves, born within the said state, after the admission thereof into the Union, shall be free but may be held to service until the age of twenty-five years.

2. THE TAYLOR AMENDMENT
January 26, 1820
(*Annals of the Congress of the United States*, 16th Cong. 1st. Sess. Vol. I, p. 947)

The reading of the bill proceeded as far as the fourth section; when

MR. TAYLOR, of New York, proposed to amend the bill by incorporating in that section the following provision:

Section 4, line 25, insert the following after the word "States"; "And shall ordain and establish, that there shall be neither slavery nor involuntary servitude in the said State, otherwise than in the punishment of crimes, whereof the party shall have been duly convicted: *Provided, always,* That any person escaping into the same, from whom labor or service is lawfully claimed in any other State, such fugitive may be lawfully reclaimed, and conveyed to the person claiming his or her labor or service as aforesaid: *And provided, also,* That the said provision shall not be construed to alter the condition or civil rights of any person now held to service or labor in the said Territory."

3. THE THOMAS AMENDMENT
February 17, 1820
(*Annals of the Congress of the United States*, 16th Cong. 1st Sess. Vol. I, p. 427)

And be it further enacted, That, in all that territory ceded by France to the United States, under the name of Louisiana, which lies north of thirty-six degrees and thirty minutes north latitude, excepting only such part thereof as is included within the limits of the State contemplated by this act, slavery and involuntary servitude, otherwise than in the punishment of crimes whereof the party shall have been duly convicted, shall be and is hereby forever prohibited: *Provided always,* That any person escaping into the same, from whom labor or service is lawfully claimed in any State or Territory of the United States, such fugitive may be lawfully reclaimed, and conveyed to the person claiming his or her labor or service, as aforesaid.

4. MISSOURI ENABLING ACT
March 6, 1820

(*U. S. Statutes at Large*, Vol. III, p. 545 ff.)

An Act to authorize the people of the Missouri territory to form a constitution and state government, and for the admission of such state into the Union on an equal footing with the original states, and to prohibit slavery in certain territories.

Be it enacted That the inhabitants of that portion of the Missouri territory included within the boundaries hereinafter designated, be, and they are hereby, authorized to form for themselves a constitution and state government, and to assume such name as they shall deem proper; and the said state, when formed, shall be admitted into the Union, upon an equal footing with the original states, in all respects whatsoever.

SEC. 2. That the said state shall consist of all the territory included within the following boundaries, to wit: Beginning in the middle of the Mississippi river, on the parallel of thirty-six degrees of north latitude; thence west, along that parallel of latitude, to the St. Francois river; thence up, and following the course of that river, in the middle of the main channel thereof, to the parallel of latitude of thirty-six degrees and thirty minutes; thence west, along the same, to a point where the said parallel is intersected by a meridian line passing through the middle of the mouth of the Kansas river, where the same empties into the Missouri river, thence, from the point aforesaid north, along the said meridian line, to the intersection of the parallel of latitude which passes through the rapids of the river Des Moines, making the said line to correspond with the Indian boundary line; thence east, from the point of intersection last aforesaid, along the said parallel of latitude, to the middle of the channel of the main fork of the said river Des Moines; thence down and along the middle of the main channel of the said river Des Moines, to the mouth of the same, where it empties into the Mississippi river; thence, due east, to the middle of the main channel of the Mississippi river; thence down, and following the course of the Mississippi river, in the middle of the main channel thereof, to the place of beginning: . . .

SEC. 3. That all free white male citizens of the United States, who shall have arrived at the age of twenty-one years, and have resided in said territory three months previous to the day of election, and all other persons qualified to vote for representatives to the general assembly of the said territory, shall be qualified to be elected, and they are hereby qualified and authorized to vote, and choose representatives to form a convention. . . .

SEC. 8. That in all that territory ceded by France to the United States, under the name of Louisiana, which lies north of thirty-six degrees and thirty minutes north latitude, not included within the limits of the state, contemplated by this act, slavery and involuntary servitude, otherwise than in the punishment of crimes, whereof the parties shall have been duly convicted, shall be, and is hereby, forever prohibited: *Provided always,* That any person escaping into the same, from whom labour or service is lawfully claimed, in any state or territory of the United States, such fugitive may be lawfully reclaimed and conveyed to the person claiming his or her labour or service as aforesaid.

5. THE CONSTITUTION OF MISSOURI
July 19, 1820

(Poore, ed., *Federal and State Constitutions,* Vol. II, p. 1107–8)

SEC. 26. The general assembly shall not have power to pass laws—

1. For the emancipation of slaves without the consent of their owners; or without paying them, before such emancipation, a full equivalent for such slaves so emancipated; and,

2. To prevent *bona-fide* immigrants to this State, or actual settlers therein, from bringing from any of the United States, or from any of their Territories, such persons as may there be deemed to be slaves, so long as any persons of the same description are allowed to be held as slaves by the laws of this State.

They shall have power to pass laws—

1. To prevent *bona-fide* immigrants to this State of any slaves who may have committed any high crime in any other State or Territory;

2. To prohibit the introduction of any slave for the purpose of speculation, or as an article of trade or merchandise;

3. To prohibit the introduction of any

slave, or the offspring of any slave, who here-tofore may have been, or who hereafter may be, imported from any foreign country into the United States, or any Territory thereof, in contravention of any existing statute of the United States; and,

4. To permit the owners of slaves to eman-cipate them, saving the right of creditors, where the person so emancipating will give security that the slave so emancipated shall not become a public charge.

It shall be their duty, as soon as may be, to pass such laws as may be necessary—

1. To prevent free negroes end [and] mu-lattoes from coming to and settling in this State, under any pretext whatsoever; and,

2. To oblige the owners of slaves to treat them with humanity, and to abstain from all injuries to them extending to life or limb.

6. RESOLUTION FOR THE ADMISSION OF MISSOURI
March 2, 1821

(U. S. Statutes at Large, Vol. III, p. 645)

Resolution *providing for the admission of the State of Missouri into the Union, on a certain condition.*

Resolved, That Missouri shall be admitted into this union on an equal footing with the original states, in all respects whatever, upon the fundamental condition, that the fourth clause of the twenty-sixth section of the third article of the constitution submitted on the part of said state to Congress, shall never be construed to authorize the passage of any law, and that no law shall be passed in con-formity thereto, by which any citizen, of either of the states in this Union, shall be excluded from the enjoyment of any of the privileges and immunities to which such citi-zen is entitled under the constitution of the United States: *Provided,* That the legislature of the said state, by a solemn public act, shall declare the assent of the said state to the said fundamental condition, and shall trans-mit to the President of the United States, on or before the fourth Monday in November next, an authentic copy of the said act; upon the receipt whereof, the President, by proclamation, shall announce the fact; where-upon, and without any further proceeding on the part of Congress, the admission of the said state into this Union shall be considered as complete.

122. LAND LAW OF 1820
April 24, 1820

(U. S. Statutes at Large, Vol. III, p. 566–7)

This law reduced the price of public land and put an end to the credit system established by the Act of 1800. See, P. J. Treat, *National Land System, 1785–1820;* T. Donaldson, *The Public Domain: its History with Statistics.*

An act making further provision for the sale of the public lands.

Be it enacted, That from and after the first day of July next, all the public lands of tho United States, the sale of which is, or may be authorized by law, shall, when offered at pub-lic sale, to the highest bidder, be offered in half quarter sections; and when offered at private sale, may be purchased, at the option of the purchaser, either in entire sections, half sections, quarter sections, or half quarter sections; . . .

SEC. 2. That credit shall not be allowed for the purchase money on the sale of any of the public lands which shall be sold after the first day of July next, but every purchaser of land sold at public sale thereafter, shall, on the day of purchase, make complete payment therefor; . . .

SEC. 3. That from and after the first day of July next, the price at which the public lands shall be offered for sale, shall be one dollar and twenty-five cents an acre; and at every public sale, the highest bidder, who shall make payment as aforesaid, shall be the purchaser; but no land shall be sold, either at public or private sale, for a less price than one dollar and twenty-five cents an acre; and all the public lands which shall have been offered at public sale before the first day of July next, and which shall then remain un-sold, as well as the lands that shall thereafter be offered at public sale, according to law, and remain unsold at the close of such public sales, shall be subject to be sold at private sale, by entry at the land office, at one dollar and twenty-five cents an acre, to be paid at the time of making such entry as afore-said; . . .

123. COHENS v. VIRGINIA
6 Wheaton, 264
1821

Error to the Quarterly Session Court of Norfolk, Virginia. P. J. and M. J. Cohen were prosecuted for selling lottery tickets in violation of a Virginia statute. The defendants claimed the protection of an act of Congress of 1802 establishing a lottery, but they were convicted and fined in the Virginia Court. The defendants sued out a writ of error to the Supreme Court under Sec. 25 of the Judiciary Act of 1789. This case involved the constitutionality of that Section, and the interpretation of the 11th Amendment to the Constitution. See, Beveridge, *Marshall*, Vol. IV, p. 344 ff.; Warren, *Supreme Court*, ch. xiii.

MARSHALL, C. J. . . . 1st. The first question to be considered is, whether the jurisdiction of this Court is excluded by the character of the parties, one of them being a State, and the other a citizen of that State.

The second section of the third article of the constitution defines the extent of the judicial power of the United States. Jurisdiction is given to the Courts of the Union, in two classes of cases. In the first, their jurisdiction depends on the character of the cause, whoever may be the parties. This class comprehends "all cases in law and equity arising under this constitution, the laws of the United States, and treaties made, or which shall be made, under their authority." This clause extends the jurisdiction of the Court to all the cases described, without making in its terms any exception whatever, and without any regard to the condition of the party. If there be any exception, it is to be implied against the express words of the article.

In the second class, the jurisdiction depends entirely on the character of the parties. In this are comprehended "controversies between two or more States, between a State and citizens of another State," and "between a State and foreign States, citizens or subjects." If these be the parties, it is entirely unimportant what may be the subject of controversy. Be it what it may, these parties have a constitutional right to come into the courts of the Union. . . .

A case in law or equity . . . may truly be said to arise under the constitution or a law of the United States whenever its correct solution depends on the construction of either. . . .

The jurisdiction of the Court, then, being extended by the letter of the constitution to all cases arising under it or under the laws of the United States, it follows that those who would withdraw any case of this description from that jurisdiction must sustain the exemption they claim on the spirit and true meaning of the constitution, which spirit and true meaning must be so apparent as to overrule the words which its framers have employed.

The counsel for the defendant in error have undertaken to do this; and have laid down the general proposition, that a sovereign independent State is not suable, except by its own consent.

This general proposition will not be controverted. But its consent is not requisite in each particular case. It may be given in a general law. And if a State has surrendered any portion of its sovereignty, the question, whether a liability to suit be a part of this portion, depends on the instrument by which the surrender is made. If, upon a just construction of that instrument it shall appear that the State has submitted to be sued, then it has parted with this sovereign right of judging in every case on the justice of its own pretensions, and has intrusted that power to a tribunal in whose impartiality it confides.

The American States, as well as the American people, have believed a close and firm union to be essential to their liberty and to their happiness. They have been taught by experience that this union cannot exist without a government for the whole; and they have been taught by the same experience that this government would be a mere shadow, that must disappoint all their hopes, unless invested with large portions of that sovereignty which belongs to independent States. Under the influence of this opinion, and thus instructed by experience, the American people, in the conventions of their respective States, adopted the present constitution.

If it could be doubted, whether, from its

nature, it were not supreme in all cases where it is empowered to act, that doubt would be removed by the declaration, that "this constitution, and the laws of the United States which shall be made in pursuance thereof, and all treaties made, or which shall be made, under the authority of the United States, shall be the supreme law of the land; and the judges in every State shall be bound thereby, anything in the constitution or laws of any State to the contrary notwithstanding." This is the authoritative language of the American people; and, if gentlemen please, of the American States. It marks, with lines too strong to be mistaken, the characteristic distinction between the government of the Union, and those of the States. The general government, though limited as to its objects, is supreme with respect to those objects. This principle is a part of the constitution; and if there be any who deny its necessity, none can deny its authority.

To this supreme government ample powers are confided; and if it were possible to doubt the great purposes for which they were so confided, the people of the United States have declared, that they are given "in order to form a more perfect union, establish justice, insure domestic tranquillity, provide for the common defense, promote the general welfare, and secure the blessings of liberty to themselves and their posterity." With the ample powers confided to this supreme government for these interesting purposes are connected many express and important limitations on the sovereignty of the States, which are made for the same purposes. The powers of the Union, on the great subjects of war, peace and commerce, and on many others, are in themselves limitations of the sovereignty of the States; but in addition to these, the sovereignty of the States is surrendered in many instances where the surrender can only operate to the benefit of the people, and where, perhaps, no other power is conferred on Congress than a conservative power to maintain the principles established in the constitution. The maintenance of these principles in their purity is certainly among the great duties of the government. One of the instruments by which this duty may be peaceably performed is the judicial department. It is authorized to decide all cases, of every description, arising under the constitu-

tion or laws of the United States. From this general grant of jurisdiction no exception is made of those cases in which a State may be a party. When we consider the situation of the government of the Union and of a State in relation to each other, the nature of our constitution, the subordination of the state governments to that constitution, the great purpose for which jurisdiction over all cases arising under the constitution and laws of the United States is confided to the judicial department, are we at liberty to insert in this general grant, an exception of those cases in which a State may be a party? Will the spirit of the constitution justify this attempt to control its words? We think it will not. We think a case arising under the constitution or laws of the United States is cognizable in the Courts of the Union, whoever may be the parties to that case.

Had any doubt existed with respect to the just construction of this part of the section, that doubt would have been removed by the enumeration of those cases to which the jurisdiction of the federal Courts is extended, in consequence of the character of the parties. In that enumeration, we find "controversies between two or more States, between a State and citizens of another State, and between a State and foreign States, citizens or subjects."

One of the express objects, then, for which the judicial department was established, is the decision of controversies between States, and between a State and individuals. The mere circumstance, that a State is a party, gives jurisdiction to the Court. How, then, can it be contended, that the very same instrument, in the very same section, should be so construed, as that this same circumstance should withdraw a case from the jurisdiction of the court, where the constitution or laws of the United States are supposed to have been violated? . . . The mischievous consequences of the construction contended for on the part of Virginia, are also entitled to great consideration. It would prostrate, it has been said, the government and its laws at the feet of every State in the Union. And would not this be its effect? What power of the government could be executed by its own means, in any State disposed to resist its execution by a course of legislation? The laws must be executed by individuals acting within the several States. If these individuals may be exposed to penalties, and if the Courts of the Union cannot correct the judgments by which these penalties may be enforced, the course of the government may be, at any time, arrested by the will of one of its members. Each member will possess a *veto* on the will of the whole. . . .

Different States may entertain different opinions on the true construction of the constitutional powers of Congress. . . .

But a constitution is framed for ages to come, and is designed to approach immortality as nearly as human institutions can approach it. Its course cannot always be tranquil. It is exposed to storms and tempests, and its framers must be unwise statesmen indeed, if they have not provided it, so far as its nature will permit, with the means of self-preservation from the perils it may be destined to encounter. No government ought to be so defective in its organization as not to contain within itself the means of securing the execution of its own laws against other dangers than those which occur every day. Courts of justice are the means most usually employed; and it is reasonable to expect that a government should repose on its own Courts, rather than on others. There is certainly nothing in the circumstances under which our constitution was formed, nothing in the history of the times, which would justify the opinion that the confidence reposed in the States was so implicit as to leave in them and their tribunals the power of resisting or defeating, in the form of law, the legitimate measures of the Union. . . .

It has been also urged, as an additional objection to the jurisdiction of the Court, that cases between a State and one of its own citizens, do not come within the general scope of the constitution; and were obviously never intended to be made cognizable in the federal Courts. . . .

If jurisdiction depended entirely on the character of the parties, and was not given where the parties have not an original right to come into Court, that part of the 2d section of the 3d article, which extends the judicial power to all cases arising under the constitution and laws of the United States, would be mere surplusage. It is to give jurisdiction where the character of the parties would not give it, that this very important part of the clause was inserted. It may be true, that the partiality of the State tribunals, in ordinary controversies between a State and its citizens, was not apprehended, and therefore the judicial power of the Union was not extended to such cases; but this was not the sole nor the greatest object for which this department was created. A more important, a much more interesting object, was the preservation of the constitution and laws of the United States, so far as they can be preserved by judicial authority; and therefore the jurisdiction of the Courts of the Union was expressly extended to all cases arising under that constitution and those laws. If the constitution or laws may be violated by proceedings instituted by a State against its own citizens, and if that violation may be such as essentially to affect the constitution and the laws, such as to arrest the progress of government in its constitutional course, why should these cases be excepted from that provision which expressly extends the judicial power of the Union to *all* cases arising under the constitution and laws?

After bestowing on this subject the most attentive consideration, the Court can perceive no reason founded on the character of the parties for introducing an exception which the constitution has not made; and we think that the judicial power, as originally given, extends to all cases arising under the constitution or a law of the United States, whoever may be the parties. . . .

This leads to the consideration of the 11th Amendment. . . .

It is, then, the opinion of the Court, that the defendant who removes a judgment rendered against him by a State Court into this Court, for the purpose of re-examining the question, whether that judgment be in violation of the constitution or laws of the United States, does not commence or prosecute a suit against the State, whatever may be its opinion where the effect of the writ may be to restore the party to the possession of a thing which he demands.

But should we in this be mistaken the error does not affect the case now before the Court. If this writ of error be a suit in the sense of the 11th amendment, it is not a suit commenced or prosecuted "by a citizen of another State or by a citizen or subject of any foreign State." It is not then within the amendment, but is governed by the constitution as originally framed, and we have already seen, that in its origin, the judicial power was extended to all cases arising under the constitution or laws of the United States, without respect to parties.

2d. The second objection to the jurisdiction of the Court is that its appellate power cannot be exercised, in any case, over the judgment of a State Court. This objection is sustained chiefly by arguments drawn from the supposed total separation of the judiciary of a State from that of the Union, and their entire independence of each other. The argument considers the federal judiciary as completely foreign to that of a State; and as being no more connected with it, in any respect whatever, than the Court of a foreign State. If this hypothesis be just, the argument founded on it is equally so; but if the hypothesis be not supported by the constitution, the argument fails with it.

This hypothesis is not founded on any words in the constitution which might seem to countenance it, but on the unreasonableness of giving a contrary construction to words which seem to require it, and on the incompatibility of the application of the appellate jurisdiction to the judgments of state courts with that constitutional relation which subsists between the government of the Union and the governments of those States which compose it.

Let this unreasonableness, this total incompatibility, be examined.

That the United States form, for many and for most important purposes, a single nation, has not yet been denied. In war we are one people. In making peace we are one people. In all commercial regulations we are one and the same people. In many other respects the American people are one, and the government which is alone capable of controlling and managing their interests in all these respects, is the government of the Union. It is their government, and in that character they have no other. America has chosen to be, in many respects, and to many purposes, a nation; and for all these purposes her government is complete; to all these objects it is competent. The people have declared that in the exercise of all the powers given for these objects it is supreme. It can, then, in effecting these objects, legitimately control all individuals or governments within the American territory. The constitution and laws of a State, so far as they are repugnant to the constitution and laws of the United States, are absolutely void. These States are constituent parts of the United States. They are members of one great empire—for some purposes sovereign, for some purposes subordinate.

In a government so constituted is it unreasonable that the judicial power should be competent to give efficacy to the constitutional laws of the legislature? That department can decide on the validity of the constitution or law of a State, if it be repugnant to the constitution or to a law of the United States. Is it unreasonable that it should also be empowered to decide on the judgment of a State tribunal enforcing such unconstitutional law? Is it so very unreasonable as to furnish a justification for controlling the words of the constitution? We think it is not. We think that, in a government acknowledgedly supreme with respect to objects of vital interest to the nation, there is nothing inconsistent with sound reason, nothing incompatible with the nature of government, in making all its departments supreme, so far as respects those objects, and so far as is necessary to their attainment. The exercise of the appellate power over those judgments of the state tribunals which may contravene the constitution or laws of the United States, is, we believe, essential to the attainment of those objects.

The propriety of intrusting the construction of the constitution, and laws made in pursuance thereof, to the judiciary of the Union, has not, we believe, as yet been drawn in question. It seems to be a corollary from this political axiom that the federal Courts should either possess exclusive jurisdiction in such cases, or a power to revise the judgment rendered in them by State tribunals. . . .

We are not restrained, then, by the political relations between the general and State governments from construing the words of the constitution defining the judicial power in their true sense. We are not bound to construe them more restrictively than they naturally import.

They give to the Supreme Court appellate jurisdiction in all cases arising under the constitution, laws, and treaties of the United

States. The words are broad enough to comprehend all cases of this description, in whatever court they may be decided. . . .

After having bestowed upon this question the most deliberate consideration of which we are capable, the Court is unanimously of opinion that the objections to its jurisdiction are not sustained, and that the motion ought to be overruled.

Motion denied.

After the jurisdiction of the court was thus established the case was then heard and decided on its merits. The court held that the act of Congress authorizing the lottery was confined in its operation to the city of Washington and gave the defendants no right to sell lottery tickets in Virginia, and that the Norfolk court therefore had the right to convict the defendants for violating a law of Virginia, and its judgment was therefore affirmed.

124. CHANCELLOR KENT ON UNIVERSAL SUFFRAGE

Remarks of Chancellor Kent to the New York Constitutional Convention of 1821

(*Reports of the Proceedings and Debates of the Convention of 1821,* ed. by H. N. Carter, W. L. Stone, and M. T. C. Gould, sec. 219 ff.)

The second decade of the nineteenth century witnessed a liberalizing of the constitutions of the seaboard states, resulting in part from the democratic influence of the new western states. The proposal to abolish the property qualification for suffrage in New York State aroused intense opposition from the conservatives, which was eloquently voiced by Chief Justice Ambrose Spencer and Chancellor James Kent. Despite this opposition the liberals carried the day. See, D. S. Alexander, *Political History of the State of New York,* Vol. II, ch. xxvii; J. B. Mc Master, *Acquisition of Political, Social and Industrial Rights of Man in America;* E. H. Roberts, *New York,* Vol. II; J. D. Hammond, *Political History of the State of New York,* Vol. II. On Kent, see W. J. Curtis, *James Kent;* W. Kent, *Memoirs and Letters of James Kent;* J. Horton, *James Kent.*

Chancellor Kent. . . . These are some of the fruits of our present government; and yet we seem to be dissatisfied with our present condition, and we are engaged in the bold and hazardous experiment of remodelling the constitution. Is it not fit and discreet: I speak as to wise men; is it not fit and proper that we should pause in our career, and reflect well on the immensity of the innovation in contemplation? Discontent in the midst of so much prosperity, and with such abundant means of happiness, looks like ingratitude, and as if we were disposed to arraign the goodness of Providence. Do we not expose ourselves to the danger of being deprived of the blessings we have enjoyed? . . .

The senate has hitherto been elected by the farmers of the state—by the free and independent lords of the soil, worth at least $250 in freehold estate, over and above all debts charged thereon. The governor has been chosen by the same electors, and we have hitherto elected citizens of elevated rank and character. Our assembly has been chosen by freeholders, possessing a freehold of the value of $50, or by persons renting a tenement of the yearly value of $5, and who have been rated and actually paid taxes to the state. By the report before us, we propose to annihilate, at one stroke, all those property distinctions and to bow before the idol of universal suffrage. That extreme democratic principle, when applied to the legislative and executive departments of the government, has been regarded with terror, by the wise men of every age, because in every European republic, ancient and modern, in which it has been tried, it has terminated disastrously, and been productive of corruption, injustice, violence, and tyranny. And dare we flatter ourselves that we are a peculiar people, who can run the career of history, exempted from the passions which have disturbed and corrupted the rest of mankind? If we are like other races of men, with similar follies and vices, then I greatly fear that our posterity will have reason to deplore in sackcloth and ashes, the delusion of the day. . . .

Now, sir, I wish to preserve our senate as the representative of the landed interest. I wish those who have an interest in the soil, to retain the exclusive possession of a branch in the legislature, as a strong hold in which they may find safety through all the vicissitudes which the state may be destined, in the course of Providence, to experience. I wish them to be always enabled to say that their freeholds cannot be taxed without their consent. The men of no property, together with the crowds of dependents connected with great manufacturing and commercial establishments, and the motley and undefinable population of crowded ports, may, perhaps, at some future day, under skilful management predominate in the assembly, and yet we should be perfectly safe if no laws could pass without the free consent of the owners of the soil. That security we at present enjoy; and it is that security which I wish to retain.

The apprehended danger from the experiment of universal suffrage applied to the whole legislative department, is no dream of the imagination. It is too mighty an excitement for the moral constitution of men to endure. The tendency of universal suffrage, is to jeopardize the rights of property, and the principles of liberty. There is a constant tendency in human society, and the history of every age proves it; there is a tendency in the poor to covet a share in the plunder of the rich; in the debtor to relax or avoid the obligation of contracts; in the majority to tyrannize over the minority, and trample down their rights; in the indolent and profligate, to cast the whole burthens of society upon the industrious and the virtuous; and *there is a tendency in ambitious and wicked men, to inflame these combustible materials.* It requires a vigilant government, and a firm administration of justice, to counteract that tendency. Thou shalt not covet; thou shalt not steal; are divine injunctions induced by this miserable depravity of our nature. Who can undertake to calculate with any precision, how many millions of people, this great state will contain in the course of this and the next century, and who can estimate the future extent and magnitude of our commercial ports? The disproportion between the men of property, and the men of no property, will be in every society in a ratio to its commerce, wealth, and population. We are no longer to remain plain and simple republics of farmers, like the New-England colonists, or the Dutch settlements on the Hudson. We are fast becoming a great nation, with great commerce, manufactures, population, wealth, luxuries, and with the vices and miseries that they engender. One seventh of the population of the city of Paris at this day subsists on charity, and one third of the inhabitants of that city die in the hospitals; what would become of such a city with universal suffrage? France has upwards of four, and England upwards of five millions of manufacturing and commercial labourers without property. Could these Kingdoms sustain the weight of universal suffrage? The radicals in England, with the force of that mighty engine, would at once sweep away the property, the laws, and the liberties of that island like a deluge.

The growth of the city of New-York is enough to startle and awaken those who are pursuing the *IGNIS FATUUS* of universal suffrage. . . .

125. MONROE'S VETO OF CUMBERLAND ROAD BILL
May 4, 1822

(Richardson, ed. *Messages and Papers*, Vol. II, p. 142 ff.)

A detailed and comprehensive exposition of President Monroe's constitutional objections to the Cumberland Road Bill can be found in the paper accompanying this message, Richardson, Vol. II, p. 144–183. See, J. S. Young, *Cumberland Road;* P. J. Treat, *The National Land System;* F. J. Turner, *Rise of the New West*, p. 230 ff.

WASHINGTON, *May 4, 1822.*
To the House of Representatives:
Having duly considered the bill entitled "An act for the preservation and repair of the Cumberland road," it is with deep regret, approving as I do the policy, that I am compelled to object to its passage and to return the bill to the House of Representatives, in which it originated, under a conviction that Congress do not possess the power under the Constitution to pass such a law.

A power to establish turnpikes with gates and tolls, and to enforce the collection of tolls by penalties, implies a power to adopt and execute a complete system of internal improvement. A right to impose duties to be paid by all persons passing a certain road, and on horses and carriages, as is done by this bill, involves the right to take the land from the proprietor on a valuation and to pass laws for the protection of the road from injuries, and if it exist as to one road it exists as to any other, and to as many roads as Congress may think proper to establish. A right to legislate for one of these purposes is a right to legislate for the others. It is a complete right of jurisdiction and sovereignty for all the purposes of internal improvement, and not merely the right of applying money under the power vested in Congress to make appropriations, under which power, with the consent of the States through which this road passes, the work was originally commenced, and has been so far executed. I am of opinion that Congress do not possess this power; that the States individually can not grant it, for although they may assent to the appropriation of money within their limits for such purposes, they can grant no power of jurisdiction or sovereignty by special compacts with the United States. This power can be granted only by an amendment to the Constitution and in the mode prescribed by it.

If the power exist, it must be either because it has been specifically granted to the United States or that it is incidental to some power which has been specifically granted. If we examine the specific grants of power we do not find it among them, nor is it incidental to any power which has been specifically granted.

It has never been contended that the power was specifically granted. It is claimed only as being incidental to some one or more of the powers which are specifically granted. The following are the powers from which it is said to be derived:

First, from the right to establish post-offices and post-roads; second, from the right to declare war; third, to regulate commerce; fourth, to pay the debts and provide for the common defense and general welfare; fifth, from the power to make all laws necessary and proper for carrying into execution all the powers vested by the Constitution in the Government of the United States or in any department or officer thereof; sixth and lastly, from the power to dispose of and make all needful rules and regulations respecting the territory and other property of the United States.

According to my judgment it can not be derived from either of those powers, nor from all of them united, and in consequence it does not exist. . . .

126. THE ENGLISH BACKGROUND OF THE MONROE DOCTRINE

Letter from George Canning to Richard Rush
August 20, 1823

(R. Rush, *Memoranda of a Residence at the Court of London*, p. 412)

George Canning, who was contemptuous of the Holy Alliance and its activities, became prime minister of Great Britain in September 1822. The following month the powers of Europe met at the Congress of Verona to consider the feasibility of the restoration of the Spanish monarchy in the countries of South America. Great Britain withdrew from this Congress and in March 1823 Canning instructed the English minister to Paris that England could not permit France to acquire any of the former Spanish colonies in America. August 16 Canning made informal overtures to the American minister, Rush, looking to joint action on Latin-American affairs. The letter of August 20 contains a succinct statement of Canning's position, but it did not embrace recognition of the Latin American Republics. For this reason, and because Secretary Adams felt that it would be better not "to come in as a cock-boat in the wake of the British man-of-war"

the United States did not respond to Canning's proposals. Meantime Canning had secured from Prince Polignac assurance that France would not under any circumstances act against the former Spanish colonies by force of arms. Canning was satisfied with this understanding, and did not press his original idea of a joint declaration with the United States. See references to Doc. No. 127 and H. W. V. Temperley, *The Life of Canning;* A. G. Stapleton, *Political Life of George Canning*, 3 Vols; H. W. V. Temperley, *The Foreign Policy of Canning*.

Foreign Office, Aug. 20, 1823
Private and Confidential

My dear Sir:—Before leaving Town I am desirous of bringing before you in a more distinct, but still in an unofficial and confidential shape, the question which we shortly discussed the last time that I had the pleasure of seeing you.

Is not the moment come when our Governments might understand each other as to the Spanish American Colonies? And if we can arrive at such an understanding, would it not be expedient for ourselves, and beneficial for all the world, that the principles of it should be clearly settled and plainly avowed?

For ourselves we have no disguise.

1. We conceive the recovery of the Colonies by Spain to be hopeless.

2. We conceive the question of the recognition of them, as Independent States, to be one of time and circumstances.

3. We are, however, by no means disposed to throw any impediment in the way of an arrangement between them and the mother country by amicable negotiations.

4. We aim not at the possession of any portion of them ourselves.

5. We could not see any portion of them transferred to any other Power, with indifference.

If these opinions and feelings are, as I firmly believe them to be, common to your Government with ours, why should we hesitate mutually to confide them to each other; and to declare them in the face of the world? If there be any European Power which cherishes other projects, which looks to a forcible enterprise for reducing the colonies to subjugation, on the behalf or in the name of Spain; or which meditates the acquisition of any part of them to itself, by cession or by conquest; such a declaration on the part of your government and ours would be at once the most effectual and the least offensive mode of intimating our joint misapprobation of such projects.

It would at the same time put an end to all the jealousies of Spain with respect to her remaining Colonies, and to agitation which prevails in those Colonies, an agitation which it would be but humane to allay; being determined (as we are) not to profit by encouraging it.

Do you conceive that under the power which you have recently received, you are authorized to enter into negotiation and to sign any Convention upon this subject? Do you conceive, if that be not within your competence, you could exchange with me ministerial notes upon it?

Nothing could be more gratifying to me than to join with you in such a work, and, I am persuaded, there has seldom, in the history of the world, occurred an opportunity when so small an effort of two friendly Governments might produce so unequivocal a good and prevent such extensive calamities.

I shall be absent from London but three weeks at the utmost; but never so far distant but that I can receive and reply to any communication within three or four days.

I have the honor to be

My Dear Sir, with great respect and esteem

Your obedient and faithful servant

George Canning

R. Rush, Esqr.

127. THE MONROE DOCTRINE

Extracts from President Monroe's Seventh Annual Message to Congress
December 2, 1823

(Richardson, ed. *Messages and Papers*, Vol. II, p. 207 ff.)

The literature on the Monroe Doctrine is too voluminous to detail here. See the bibliographies in F. J. Turner, *Rise of the New West*, p. 351; Channing, Hart and Turner, *Guide to the Study and Reading of American History*, Sec. 198; H. B. Meyer, *List of References on the Monroe Doctrine*. For more recent literature, see, D. Perkins, *The Monroe Doctrine, 1823–1826;* S. Bemis, ed. *American Secretaries of State and Their Diplomacy*, Vol. IV, p. 36 ff. and bibliography, p. 347 ff.; H. W. V. Temperley, *The Foreign Policy of Canning;* A. Alvarez, *The* *Monroe Doctrine*, especially the annexes. On the authorship of the Doctrine, W. C. Ford, "John Quincy Adams: His Connection with the Monroe Doctrine" in Massachusetts Hist. Soc. *Proceedings*, 2d Ser. Vol. XV, p. 373 ff. has not yet been superseded. On recognition of the Latin-American Republics, F. L. Paxson, *The Independence of the South American Republics* is still the standard treatise. The diplomatic correspondence has been collected in three volumes, W. R. Manning, ed. *Diplomatic Correspondence of the United States Concerning the Independence of the Latin Amer-*

ican Nations. A quasi-official statement of the doctrine is J. R. Clark, *Memorandum on the Monroe Doctrine*.

. . . At the proposal of the Russian Imperial Government, made through the minister of the Emperor residing here, a full power and instructions have been transmitted to the minister of the United States at St. Petersburg to arrange by amicable negotiation the respective rights and interests of the two nations on the northwest coast of this continent. A similar proposal had been made by His Imperial Majesty to the Government of Great Britain, which has likewise been acceded to. The Government of the United States has been desirous by this friendly proceeding of manifesting the great value which they have invariably attached to the friendship of the Emperor and their solicitude to cultivate the best understanding with his Government. In the discussions to which this interest has given rise and in the arrangements by which they may terminate the occasion has been judged proper for asserting, as a principle in which the rights and interests of the United States are involved, that the American continents, by the free and independent condition which they have assumed and maintain, are henceforth not to be considered as subjects for future colonization by any European powers. . . .

It was stated at the commencement of the last session that a great effort was then making in Spain and Portugal to improve the condition of the people of those countries, and that it appeared to be conducted with extraordinary moderation. It need scarcely be remarked that the result has been so far very different from what was then anticipated. Of events in that quarter of the globe, with which we have so much intercourse and from which we derive our origin, we have always been anxious and interested spectators. The citizens of the United States cherish sentiments the most friendly in favor of the liberty and happiness of their fellow-men on that side of the Atlantic. In the wars of the European powers in matters relating to themselves we have never taken any part, nor does it comport with our policy so to do. It is only when our rights are invaded or seriously menaced that we resent injuries or make preparation for our defense. With the movements in this hemisphere we are of ne-

cessity more immediately connected, and by causes which must be obvious to all enlightened and impartial observers. The political system of the allied powers is essentially different in this respect from that of America. This difference proceeds from that which exists in their respective Governments; and to the defense of our own, which has been achieved by the loss of so much blood and treasure, and matured by the wisdom of their most enlightened citizens, and under which we have enjoyed unexampled felicity, this whole nation is devoted. We owe it, therefore, to candor and to the amicable relations existing between the United States and those powers to declare that we should consider any attempt on their part to extend their system to any portion of this hemisphere as dangerous to our peace and safety. With the existing colonies or dependencies of any European power we have not interfered and shall not interfere. But with the Governments who have declared their independence and maintained it, and whose independence we have, on great consideration and on just principles, acknowledged, we could not view any interposition for the purpose of oppressing them, or controlling in any other manner their destiny, by any European power in any other light than as the manifestation of an unfriendly disposition toward the United States. In the war between those new Governments and Spain we declared our neutrality at the time of their recognition, and to this we have adhered, and shall continue to adhere, provided no change shall occur which, in the judgment of the competent authorities of this Government, shall make a corresponding change on the part of the United States indispensable to their security.

The late events in Spain and Portugal shew that Europe is still unsettled. Of this important fact no stronger proof can be adduced than that the allied powers should have thought it proper, on any principle satisfactory to themselves, to have interposed by force in the internal concerns of Spain. To what extent such interposition may be carried, on the same principle, is a question in which all independent powers whose governments differ from theirs are interested, even those most remote, and surely none more so than the United States. Our policy in regard to Europe, which was adopted at an early stage of the wars which have so long agitated that quarter of the globe, nevertheless remains the same, which is, not to interfere in the internal concerns of any of its powers; to consider the government *de facto* as the legitimate government for us; to cultivate friendly relations with it, and to preserve those relations by a frank, firm, and manly policy, meeting in all instances the just claims of every power, submitting to injuries from none. But in regard to those continents circumstances are eminently and conspicuously different. It is impossible that the allied powers should extend their political system to any portion of either continent without endangering our peace and happiness; nor can anyone believe that our southern brethren, if left to themselves, would adopt it of their own accord. It is equally impossible, therefore, that we should behold such interposition in any form with indifference. If we look to the comparative strength and resources of Spain and those new Governments, and their distance from each other, it must be obvious that she can never subdue them. It is still the true policy of the United States to leave the parties to themselves, in the hope that other powers will pursue the same course. . . .

128. PROTEST AGAINST THE CAUCUS BY THE GENERAL ASSEMBLY OF THE STATE OF TENNESSEE
1823

(Niles Register, Vol. XXV, p. 137–138)

With the breakdown of the machinery provided by the Constitution for the election of the President, there arose the practice of nominations by party caucus. The growth of the caucus system aroused widespread discontent, and the defeat of Crawford, the choice of the rump caucus of the Republican Party in 1824, marked the death of "King Caucus". The caucus system of nominations was supplanted by nominations by State legislatures and eventually by national conventions. For the origin of the caucus, see A. C. McLaughlin and A. B. Hart, *Cyclopaedia of American Government,* "caucus"; F. W. Dallinger, *Nominations for Elective Office in the United States.*

The general assembly of the State of Tennessee has taken into consideration the practice which, on former occasions, has prevailed at the City of Washington, of members of the Congress of the United States meeting in caucus, and nominating persons to be voted for as president and vice-president of the United States: and, upon the best view of the subject which this general assembly has been able to take, it is believed that the practice of congressional nominations is a violation of the spirit of the Constitution of the United States.

That instrument provides that there shall be three separate and distinct departments of the government, and great care and caution seems to have been exercised by its framers to prevent any one department from exercising the smallest degree of influence over another; and such solicitude was felt on this subject, that, in the second section of the second article, it is expressly declared, "That no *senator or representative,* or person holding an office of trust or profit under the United States, shall be appointed an elector." From this provision, it is apparent that the convention intended that the members of Congress should not be the principal and primary agents or actors in electing the president and vice-president of the United States —so far from it, they are expressly disqualified from being placed in a situation to vote for these high officers. Is there not more danger of undue influence to be apprehended, when the members of Congress meet in caucus and mutually and solemnly pledge themselves to support the individuals who may have the highest number of votes in such meeting, than there would be in permitting them to be eligible to the appointment of electors? In the latter case, a few characters, rendered ineligible by the Constitution, might succeed; but in the former, a powerful combination of influential men is formed, who may fix upon the American people their highest officers against the consent of a clear majority of the people themselves; and this may be done by the very men whom the Constitution intended to prohibit from acting on the subject. Upon an examination of the Constitution of the United States, there is but one case in which the members of Congress are permitted to act, which is in the event of a failure to make an election by the electoral college; and then the members of the House of Representatives vote by States. With what propriety the same men, who, in the year 1825, may be called on to discharge a constitutional duty, can, in the year 1824, go into a caucus and pledge themselves to support the men then nominated, cannot be discerned, especially when it might so happen that the persons thus nominated, could [not] under any circumstances, obtain a single vote from the State whose members stand pledged to support them. . . .

Upon a review of the whole question, the following reasons which admit of much amplification and enlargement, more than has been urged in the foregoing, might be con-

clusively relied on, to prove the impolicy and unconstitutionality of the Congressional nominations of candidates for the presidency and vice-presidency of the United States: 1st. A caucus nomination is against the spirit of the Constitution. 2nd. It is both inexpedient and impolitic. 3rd. Members of Congress may become the final electors, and therefore ought not to prejudge the case by pledging themselves previously to support particular candidates. 4th. It violates the equality intended to be secured by the Constitution to the weaker States. 5th. Caucus nominations may, in time (by the interference of the States), acquire the force of precedents and become authoritative, and thereby endanger the liberties of the American people.

129. GIBBONS v. OGDEN
9 Wheaton, 1
1824

Error to the New York Court for the Trial of Impeachments and Correction of Errors. The legislature of New York granted to Robert Livingston and Robert Fulton the exclusive right to navigate the waters of New York State by steamboats. This right passed to one Ogden, who sued to restrain Gibbons from operating steamboats on the Hudson River between New Jersey and New York. This is the most notable of all cases involving the interpretation of the commerce clause of the Constitution. See Beveridge, *Marshall,* Vol. IV, ch. viii; Warren, *Supreme Court,* ch. xv.

MARSHALL, C. J. The appellant contends that this decree is erroneous because the laws which purport to give the exclusive privilege it sustains are repugnant to the constitution and laws of the United States. They are said to be repugnant—1st. To that clause in the constitution which authorizes congress to regulate commerce. 2d. To that which authorizes congress to promote the progress of science and useful arts. . . .

As preliminary to the very able discussions of the constitution which we have heard from the bar,. and as having some influence on its construction, reference has been made to the political situation of these states, anterior to its formation. It has been said that they were sovereign, were completely independent, and were connected with each other only by a league. This is true. But, when these allied

sovereigns converted their league into a government, when they converted their congress of ambassadors, deputed to deliberate on their common concerns, and to recommend measures of general utility, into a legislature, empowered to enact laws on the most interesting subjects, the whole character in which the states appear underwent a change, the extent of which must be determined by a fair consideration of the instrument by which that change was effected.

This instrument contains an enumeration of powers expressly granted by the people to their government. It has been said that these powers ought to be construed strictly. But why ought they to be so construed? Is there one sentence in the constitution which gives countenance to this rule? In the last of the enumerated powers, that which grants, expressly, the means for carrying all others into execution, congress is authorized "to make all laws which shall be necessary and proper" for the purpose. But this limitation on the means which may be used, is not extended to the powers which are conferred; nor is there one sentence in the constitution, which has been pointed out by the gentlemen of the bar, or which we have been able to discern, that prescribes this rule. We do not, therefore, think ourselves justified in adopting it. What do gentlemen mean by a strict construction? If they contend only against that enlarged construction which would extend words beyond their natural and obvious import, we might question the application of the term, but should not controvert the principle. If they contend for that narrow construction which, in support of some theory not to be found in the constitution, would deny to the government those powers which the words of the grant, as usually understood, import, and which are consistent with the general views and objects of the instrument; for that narrow construction, which would cripple the government, and render it unequal to the objects for which it is declared to be instituted, and to which the powers given, as fairly understood, render it competent; then we cannot perceive the propriety of this strict contruction, nor adopt it as the rule by which the constitution is to be expounded. As men whose intentions require no concealment, generally employ the words which most directly and aptly express the ideas they intend to convey, the enlightened patriots who framed our constitution, and the people who adopted it, must be understood to have employed words in their natural sense, and to have intended what they have said.

The words are: "congress shall have power to regulate commerce with foreign nations, and among the several States, and with the Indian tribes." The subject to be regulated is commerce; and our constitution being, as was aptly said at the bar, one of enumeration, and not of definition, to ascertain the extent of the power, it becomes necessary to settle the meaning of the word. The counsel for the appellee would limit it to traffic, to buying and selling, or the interchange of commodities, and do not admit that it comprehends navigation. This would restrict a general term, applicable to many objects, to one of its significations. Commerce, undoubtedly, is traffic, but it is something more,—it is intercourse. It describes the commercial intercourse between nations, and parts of nations, in all its branches, and is regulated by prescribing rules for carrying on that intercourse. The mind can scarcely conceive a system for regulating commerce between nations which shall exclude all laws concerning navigation, which shall be silent on the admission of the vessels of the one nation into the ports of the other, and be confined to prescribing rules for the conduct of individuals, in the actual employment of buying and selling, or of barter. If commerce does not include navigation, the government of the Union has no direct power over that subject, and can make no law prescribing what shall constitute American vessels, or requiring that they shall be navigated by American seamen. Yet this power has been exercised from the commencement of the government, has been exercised with the consent of all, and has been understood by all to be a commercial regulation. All America understands, and has uniformly understood, the word "commerce" to comprehend navigation. It was so understood, and must have been so understood, when the constitution was framed. The power over commerce, including navigation, was one of the primary objects for which the people of America adopted their government, and must have been contemplated in forming it. The convention must have used the word in that sense, because all have understood it in that sense; and the attempt to restrict it comes too late.

If the opinion that "commerce," as the word is used in the constitution, comprehends navigation also, requires any additional confirmation, that additional confirmation is, we think, furnished by the words of the instrument itself. . . .

The word used in the constitution, then, comprehends, and has been always understood to comprehend, navigation within its meaning; and a power to regulate navigation is as expressly granted as if that term had been added to the word "commerce." To what commerce does this power extend? The constitution informs us, to commerce "with foreign nations, and among the several states, and with the Indian tribes." It has, we believe, been universally admitted that these words comprehend every species of commercial intercourse between the United States and foreign nations. No sort of trade can be carried on between this country and any other to which this power does not extend. It has been truly said that commerce, as the word is used in the constitution, is a unit, every part of which is indicated by the term.

If this be the admitted meaning of the word, in its application to foreign nations, it must carry the same meaning throughout the sentence, and remain a unit, unless there be some plain intelligible cause which alters it. The subject to which the power is next applied is to commerce "among the several states." The word "among" means intermingled with. A thing which is among others is intermingled with them. Commerce among the states cannot stop at the external boundary-line of each state, but may be introduced into the interior. It is not intended to say that these words comprehend that commerce which is completely internal, which is carried on between man and man in a state, or between different parts of the same state, and which does not extend to or affect other States. Such a power would be inconvenient and is certainly unnecessary. Comprehensive as the word "among" is, it may very properly be restricted to that commerce which concerns more States than one. The phrase is not one which would probably have been selected to indicate the completely interior traffic of a state, because it is not an apt phrase for that purpose; and the enumeration of the particular classes of commerce to which the power was to be extended would not have been made had the intention been to extend the power to every description. The enumeration presupposes something not enumerated; and that something, if we regard the language or the subject of the sentence, must be the exclusively internal commerce of a state. The genius and character of the whole government seem to be, that its action is to be applied to all the external concerns of the nation, and to those internal concerns which affect the states generally; but not to those which are completely within a particular state, which do not affect other states, and with which it is not necessary to interfere for the purpose of executing some of the general powers of the government. The completely internal commerce of a state then, may be considered as reserved for the state itself.

But, in regulating commerce with foreign nations, the power of congress does not stop at the jurisdictional lines of the several states. It would be a very useless power if it could not pass those lines. The commerce of the United States with foreign nations is that of the whole United States. Every district has a right to participate in it. The deep streams which penetrate our country in every direc-

tion pass through the interior of almost every state in the Union, and furnish the means of exercising this right. If congress has the power to regulate it, that power must be exercised whenever the subject exists. If it exists within the states, if a foreign voyage may commence or terminate at a port within a state, then the power of congress may be exercised within a state. . . .

The power of congress, then, whatever it may be, must be exercised within the territorial jurisdiction of the several States. The sense of the nation on this subject is unequivocally manifested by the provisions made in the laws for transporting goods by land between Baltimore and Providence, between New York and Philadelphia, and between Philadelphia and Baltimore.

We are now arrived at the inquiry, What is this power? It is the power to regulate; that is, to prescribe the rule by which commerce is to be governed. This power, like all others vested in congress, is complete in itself, may be exercised to its utmost extent, and acknowledges no limitations other than are prescribed in the constitution. These are expressed in plain terms, and do not affect the questions which arise in this case, or which have been discussed at the bar. If, as has always been understood, the sovereignty of congress, though limited to specified objects, is plenary as to those objects, the power over commerce with foreign nations, and among the several states, is vested in congress as absolutely as it would be in a single government, having in its constitution the same restrictions on the exercise of the power as are found in the constitution of the United States. . . . The power of congress, then, comprehends navigation within the limits of every state in the Union, so far as that navigation may be, in any manner, connected with "commerce with foreign nations, or among the several States, or with the Indian tribes." It may, of consequence, pass the jurisdiction line of New York, and act upon the very waters to which the prohibition now under consideration applies.

But it has been urged with great earnestness that, although the power of congress to regulate commerce with foreign nations, and among the several states, be coextensive with the subject itself, and have no other limits than are prescribed in the constitution, yet the states may severally exercise the same power within their respective jurisdictions. In support of this argument, it is said that they possessed it as an inseparable attribute of sovereignty before the formation of the constitution, and still retain it, except so far as they have surrendered it by that instrument; that this principle results from the nature of the government, and is secured by the tenth amendment; that an affirmative grant of power is not exclusive, unless in its own nature it be such that the continued exercise of it by the former possessor is inconsistent with the grant, and that this is not of that description. . . .

In discussing the question, whether this power is still in the states, in the case under consideration, we may dismiss from it the inquiry, whether it is surrendered by the mere grant to congress, or is retained until congress shall exercise the power. We may dismiss that inquiry, because it has been exercised, and the regulations which congress deemed it proper to make, are now in full operation. The sole question is, Can a State regulate commerce with foreign nations and among the States while Congress is regulating it? . . .

[Here the Chief Justice examined the acts of Congress of 1796 and 1799 directing federal officers to assist in the execution of the quarantine and health laws of a State, the act of 1803 prohibiting the importation of slaves into any State which shall itself prohibit their importation, and the act of 1789 acknowledging a concurrent power in the States to regulate the conduct of pilots.]

These acts were cited at the bar for the purpose of showing an opinion in congress, that the states possess, concurrently with the legislature of the Union, the power to regulate commerce with foreign nations and among the states. Upon reviewing them, we think, they do not establish the proposition they were intended to prove. They show the opinion that the states retain powers enabling them to pass the laws to which allusion has been made, not that those laws proceed from the particular power which has been delegated to congress.

It has been contended by the counsel for the appellant that, as the word "to regulate" implies in its nature full power over the thing to be regulated, it excludes, necessarily, the action of all others that would perform the same operation on the same thing. That regulation is designed for the entire result, applying to those parts which remain as they were, as well as to those which are altered. It produces a uniform whole, which is as much disturbed and deranged by changing what the regulating power designs to leave untouched as that on which it has operated. There is great force in this argument, and the court is not satisfied that it has been refuted.

Since, however, in exercising the power of regulating their own purely internal affairs, whether of trading or police, the states may sometimes enact laws the validity of which depends on their interfering with, and being contrary to, an act of congress passed in pursuance of the constitution, the court will enter upon the inquiry, whether the laws of New York, as expounded by the highest tribunal of that state, have, in their application to this case, come into collision with an act of congress, and deprived a citizen of a right to which that act entitles him. Should this collision exist, it will be immaterial whether those laws were passed in virtue of a concurrent power "to regulate commerce with foreign nations and among the several states," or in virtue of a power to regulate their domestic trade and police. In one case and the other the acts of New York must yield to the law of congress; and the decision sustaining the privilege they confer against a right given by a law of the Union, must be erroneous. This opinion has been frequently expressed in this court, and is founded as well on the nature of the government as on the words of the constitution. In argument, however, it has been contended that, if a law passed by a state in the exercise of its acknowledged sovereignty, comes into conflict with a law passed by congress in pursuance of the constitution, they affect the subject, and each other, like equal opposing powers. But the framers of the constitution foresaw this state of things, and provided for it by declaring the supremacy not only of itself but of the laws made in pursuance of it. The nullity of any act inconsistent with the constitution is produced by the declaration that the constitution is supreme law. . . . In every such case the act of congress, or treaty, is supreme; and the law of the state, though enacted in the exercise of powers not controverted, must yield to it. . . .

The court is aware that in stating the train of reasoning by which we have been conducted to this result, much time has been consumed in the attempt to demonstrate propositions which may have been thought axioms. . . . But it was unavoidable. . . .

Powerful and ingenious minds, taking as postulates that the powers expressly granted to the government of the Union are to be contracted, by construction, into the narrowest possible compass, and that the original powers of the states are to be retained, if any possible construction will retain them, may, by a course of well-digested, but refined and metaphysical reasoning, founded on these premises, explain away the constitution of our country and leave it a magnificent structure indeed, to look at, but totally unfit for use. They may so entangle and perplex the understanding as to obscure principles which were before thought quite plain, and induce doubts where, if the mind were to pursue its own course none would be perceived. In such a case, it is peculiarly necessary to recur to safe and fundamental principles, to sustain those principles, and, when sustained, to make them the tests of the arguments to be examined.

Decree of Court of New York reversed and annulled and bill of Aaron Ogden dismissed.

130. THE NATIONALISM OF PRESIDENT J. Q. ADAMS

Extract from First Annual Message to Congress
December 6, 1825

(Richardson, ed. *Messages and Papers,* Vol. II, p. 311 ff.)

President Adams was firmly committed to a policy of internal improvements, and the development of education and the sciences at government expense. He proposed to finance such projects by carefully conserving the public lands. Adams himself, while Secretary of State, prepared a monumental *Report on Weights and Measures,* and one of his last public acts was the dedication of an astronomical observatory. For the philosophical principles underlying this doctrine, see Brooks Adams, ed. *The Degradation of the Democratic Dogma,* introduction; B. C. Clark, *John Quincy Adams,* p. 235 ff.; F. J. Turner, *Rise of the New West,* ch. xvii; a history of internal improvement legislation is in H. G. Wheeler, *History of Congress,* Vol. II, p. 109 ff.

. . . Upon this first occasion of addressing the Legislature of the Union, with which I have been honored, in presenting to their view the execution so far as it has been effected of the measures sanctioned by them for promoting the internal improvement of our country, I can not close the communication without recommending to their calm and persevering consideration the general principle in a more enlarged extent. The great object of the institution of civil government is the improvement of the condition of those who are parties to the social compact, and no government, in whatever form constituted, can accomplish the lawful ends of its institution but in proportion as it improves the condition of those over whom it is established. Roads and canals, by multiplying and facilitating the communications and intercourse between distant regions and multitudes of men, are among the most important means of improvement. But moral, political, intellectual improvement are duties assigned by the Author of Our Existence to social no less than to individual man. For the fulfillment of those duties governments are invested with power, and to the attainment of the end—the progressive improvement of the condition of the governed—the exercise of delegated powers is a duty as sacred and indispensable as the usurpation of powers not granted is criminal and odious. Among the first, perhaps the very first, instrument for the improvement of the condition of men is knowledge, and to the acquisition of much of the knowledge adapted to the wants, the comforts, and enjoyments of human life public institutions and seminaries of learning are essential. So convinced of this was the first of my predecessors in this office, now first in the memory, as, living, he was first in the hearts, of our countrymen, that once and again in his addresses to the Congresses with whom he coöperated in the public service he earnestly recommended the establishment of seminaries of learning, to prepare for all the emergencies of peace and war—a national university and a military academy. With respect to the latter, had he lived to the present day, in turning his eyes to the institution at West Point he would have enjoyed the gratification of his most earnest wishes; but in surveying the city which has been honored with his name he would have seen the spot of earth which he had destined and bequeathed to the use and benefit of his country as the site for an university still bare and barren.

In assuming her station among the civilized nations of the earth it would seem that our country had contracted the engagement to contribute her share of mind, of labor, and of expense to the improvement of those parts of knowledge which lie beyond the reach of individual acquisition, and particularly to geographical and astronomical science. Looking back to the history only of the half century since the declaration of our independence, and observing the generous emulation with which the Governments of France, Great Britain, and Russia have devoted the genius, the intelligence, the treasures of their respective nations to the common improvement of the species in these branches of science, is it not incumbent upon us to inquire whether we are not bound by obligations of a high and honorable character to contribute our portion of energy and exertion to the common stock? The voyages of discovery prosecuted in the course of that time at the expense of those nations have not only redounded to their glory, but to the improvement of human knowledge. We have been partakers of that improvement and owe for it a sacred debt, not only of gratitude, but of equal or proportional exertion in the same common cause. Of the cost of these undertakings, if the mere expenditures of outfit, equipment, and completion of the expeditions were to be considered the only charges, it would be unworthy of a great and generous nation to take a second thought. One hundred expeditions of circumnavigation like those of Cook and La Pérouse would not burden the exchequer of the nation fitting them out so much as the ways and means of defraying a single campaign in war. But if we take into the account the lives of those benefactors of mankind of which their services in the cause of their species were the purchase, how shall the cost of those heroic

enterprises be estimated, and what compensation can be made to them or to their countries for them? Is it not by bearing them in affectionate remembrance? Is it not still more by imitating their example—by enabling countrymen of our own to pursue the same career and to hazard their lives in the same cause?

In inviting the attention of Congress to the subject of internal improvements upon a view thus enlarged it is not my design to recommend the equipment of an expedition for circumnavigating the globe for purposes of scientific research and inquiry. We have objects of useful investigation nearer home, and to which our cares may be more beneficially applied. The interior of our own territories has yet been very imperfectly explored. Our coasts along many degrees of latitude upon the shores of the Pacific Ocean, though much frequented by our spirited commercial navigators, have been barely visited by our public ships. The River of the West, first fully discovered and navigated by a countryman of our own, still bears the name of the ship in which he ascended its waters, and claims the protection of our armed national flag at its mouth. With the establishment of a military post there or at some other point of that coast, recommended by my predecessor and already matured in the deliberations of the last Congress, I would suggest the expediency of connecting the equipment of a public ship for the exploration of the whole northwest coast of this continent.

The establishment of an uniform standard of weights and measures was one of the specific objects contemplated in the formation of our Constitution, and to fix that standard was one of the powers delegated by express terms in that instrument to Congress. The Governments of Great Britain and France have scarcely ceased to be occupied with inquiries and speculations on the same subject since the existence of our Constitution, and with them it has expanded into profound, laborious, and expensive researches into the figure of the earth and the comparative length of the pendulum vibrating seconds in various latitudes from the equator to the pole. These researches have resulted in the composition and publication of several works highly interesting to the cause of science.

The experiments are yet in the process of performance. Some of them have recently been made on our own shores, within the walls of one of our own colleges, and partly by one of our own fellow-citizens. It would be honorable to our country if the sequel of the same experiments should be countenanced by the patronage of our Government, as they have hitherto been by those of France and Britain.

Connected with the establishment of an university, or separate from it, might be undertaken the erection of an astronomical observatory, with provision for the support of an astronomer, to be in constant attendance of observation upon the phenomena of the heavens, and for the periodical publication of his observations. It is with no feeling of pride as an American that the remark may be made that on the comparatively small terri-

torial surface of Europe there are existing upward of 130 of these light-houses of the skies, while throughout the whole American hemisphere there is not one. If we reflect a moment upon the discoveries which in the last four centuries have been made in the physical constitution of the universe by the means of these buildings and of observers stationed in them, shall we doubt of their usefulness to every nation? And while scarcely a year passes over our heads without bringing some new astronomical discovery to light, which we must fain receive at second hand from Europe, are we not cutting ourselves off from the means of returning light for light while we have neither observatory nor observer upon our half of the globe and the earth revolves in perpetual darkness to our unsearching eyes? . . .

131. THE PANAMA CONGRESS

Message of President Adams on the Participation of the United States in the
Panama Congress
December 26, 1825

(Richardson, ed. *Messages and Papers*, Vol. II, p. 318 ff.)

A Congress of the American nations was called by Bolívar to meet in Panama in the summer of 1826. Though Bolívar did not originally invite the United States, invitations were extended by Colombia and Mexico. President Adams adverted to the Congress in his message of December 6, 1825. The message of December 26 presents his definite acceptance of the invitation and the nominations for delegates. A subsequent message of March 15, 1826 contains a lengthy argument for American participation in the Congress. The proposal to send delegates to the Congress aroused bitter opposition in Congress, partly of a factional and partisan character, partly because it was believed that the objects of the Congress were inimical to slavery. Though the Foreign Affairs Committee of the Senate reported adversely on the mission, both Houses finally voted for participation. This action, however, came too late: Mr. Anderson died on the way to Panama, and Mr. Sergeant arrived after the Congress had adjourned. Séc. Clay's instructions to the American delegates can be found in Department of State, *Instructions*, Vol. XI; President Adams's message of March 15 in Richardson, Vol. II, p. 329 ff. Other documents are in International American Conference, Vol. IV: *The Congress of 1826 at Panama*. See also, I. B. Lockey, *Pan-Americanism: Its Beginnings;* S. F. Bemis, ed. *American*

Secretaries of State, Vol. IV, p. 137 ff.; C. Schurz, *Henry Clay,* Vol. I. On Bolivar see T. R. Ybarra, *Bolívar;* H. Augell, *Bolívar;* F. L. Petre, *Bolívar. To the Senate of the United States:*

In the message to both Houses of Congress at the commencement of the session it was mentioned that the Governments of the Republics of Colombia, of Mexico, and of Central America had severally invited the Government of the United States to be represented at the Congress of American nations to be assembled at Panama to deliberate upon objects of peculiar concernment to this hemisphere, and that this invitation had been accepted.

Although this measure was deemed to be within the constitutional competency of the Executive, I have not thought proper to take any step in it before ascertaining that my opinion of its expediency will concur with that of both branches of the Legislature, first, by the decision of the Senate upon the nominations to be laid before them, and, secondly, by the sanction of both Houses to the appropriations, without which it can not be carried into effect. . . .

It will be seen that the United States neither intend nor are expected to take part in any deliberations of a belligerent character; that the motive of their attendance is neither to contract alliances nor to engage in any undertaking or project importing hostility to any other nation.

But the Southern American nations, in the infancy of their independence, often find themselves in positions with reference to other countries with the principles applicable to which, derivable from the state of independence itself, they have not been familiarized by experience. The result of this has been that sometimes in their intercourse with the United States they have manifested dispositions to reserve a right of granting special favors and privileges to the Spanish nation as the price of their recognition. At others they have actually established duties and impositions operating unfavorably to the United States to the advantage of other European powers, and sometimes they have appeared to consider that they might interchange among themselves mutual concessions of exclusive favor, to which neither European powers nor the United States should be admitted. In most of these cases their regulations unfavorable to us have yielded to friendly expostulation and remonstrance. But it is believed to be of infinite moment that the principles of a liberal commercial inter course should be exhibited to them, and urged with disinterested and friendly persuasion upon them when all assembled for the avowed purpose of consulting together upon the establishment of such principles as may have an important bearing upon their future welfare.

The consentaneous adoption of principles of maritime neutrality, and favorable to the navigation of peace, and commerce in time of war, will also form a subject of consideration to this Congress. The doctrine that free ships make free goods and the restrictions of reason upon the extent of blockades may be established by general agreement with far more ease, and perhaps with less danger, by the general engagement to adhere to them concerted at such a meeting, than by partial treaties or conventions with each of the nations separately. An agreement between all the parties represented at the meeting that each will guard by its own means against the

establishment of any future European colony within its borders may be found advisable. This was more than two years since announced by my predecessor to the world as a principle resulting from the emancipation of both the American continents. It may be so developed to the new southern nations that they will all feel it as an essential appendage to their independence.

There is yet another subject upon which, without entering into any treaty, the moral influence of the United States may perhaps be exerted with beneficial consequences at such a meeting—the advancement of religious liberty. Some of the southern nations are even yet so far under the dominion of prejudice that they have incorporated with their political constitutions an exclusive church, without toleration of any other than the dominant sect. The abandonment of this last badge of religious bigotry and oppression may be pressed more effectually by the united exertions of those who concur in the principles of freedom of conscience upon those who are yet to be convinced of their justice and wisdom than by the solitary efforts of a minister to any one of the separate Governments. . . .

In fine, a decisive inducement with me for acceding to the measure is to show by this token of respect to the southern Republics the interest that we take in their welfare and our disposition to comply with their wishes. Having been the first to recognize their independence, and sympathized with them so far as was compatible with our neutral duties in all their struggles and sufferings to acquire it, we have laid the foundation of our future intercourse with them in the broadest principles of reciprocity and the most cordial feelings of fraternal friendship. To extend those principles to all our commercial relations with them and to hand down that friendship to future ages is congenial to the highest policy of the Union, as it will be to that of all those nations and their posterity. In the confidence that these sentiments will meet the approbation of the Senate, I nominate Richard C. Anderson, of Kentucky, and John Sergeant, of Pennsylvania, to be envoys extraordinary and ministers plenipotentiary to the assembly of American nations at Panama, and William B. Rochester, of New York, to be secretary to the mission.

132. MARTIN v. MOTT
12 Wheaton, 19
1827

The War of 1812 was violently opposed in New England and parts of New York State. In some instances this opposition took the form of denying the right of the President to call out the militia of a State. In Massachusetts, for example, the Chief Justice of the Supreme Court advised the Governor that he, and not the President, had the right to decide when the Constitutional exigency existed which required the calling of the State militia. It was this question which came before the Supreme Court in the following case. For the background of opposition to the War of 1812 see, S. E. Morison, *Life of Harrison Gray Otis,* ch. xxi; H. Adams, *History of the United States During the Administration of James Madison,* Vol. VI, ch. xvi; T. Roosevelt, *Gouverneur Morris.*

STORY, J. This is a writ of error to the judgment of the court for the trial of impeachments and the correction of errors of the State of New York, being the highest court of that state, and is brought here in virtue of the 25th section of the judiciary act of 1789, ch. 20. . . . The avowry, in substance, asserts a justification of . . . a fine and forfeiture imposed upon the original plaintiff by a court-martial, for a failure to enter the service of the United States as a militia-man, when thereto required by the President of the United States in pursuance of the act of the 28th of February, 1795. . . .

The constitution declares that Congress shall have power "to provide for calling forth the militia, to execute the laws of the Union, suppress insurrections, and repel invasions" and also "to provide for organizing, arming and disciplining the militia, and for governing such part of them as may be employed in the service of the United States". In pursuance of this authority, the act of 1795 has provided "that whenever the United States shall be invaded, or be in imminent danger of invasion from any foreign nation or Indian tribe, it shall be lawful for the President of the United States to call for such number of the militia of the state or states most convenient to the place of danger, or scene of action, as he may judge necessary to repel such invasion, and to issue his order for that purpose, to such officer or officers of the militia as he shall think proper." . . . It has

not been denied here that the act of 1795 is within the constitutional authority of Congress, or that Congress may not lawfully provide for cases of imminent danger of invasion, as well as for cases where an invasion has actually taken place. In our opinion there is no ground for a doubt on this point, even if it had been relied on, for the power to provide for repelling invasions includes the power to provide against the attempt and danger of invasion, as the necessary and proper means to effectuate the object.

. . . The power thus confided by Congress to the President is doubtless of a very high and delicate nature. A few people are naturally jealous of the exercise of military power; and the power to call the militia into actual service was certainly felt to be one of no ordinary magnitude. But it is not a power which can be executed without a correspondent responsiblity. It is, in its terms, a limited power, confined to cases of actual invasion, or of imminent danger of invasion. If it be a limited power, the question arises, by whom is the exigency to be judged of and decided? Is the President the sole and exclusive judge whether the exigency has arisen, or is it to be considered as an open question, upon which every officer to whom the orders of the President are addressed may decide for himself, and equally open to be contested by every militia-man who shall refuse to obey the orders of the President? We are all of the opinion that the authority to decide whether the exigency has arisen, belongs exclusively to the President, and that his decision is conclusive upon all other persons. We think that this construction necessarily results from the nature of the power itself, and from the manifest object contemplated by the act of Congress. . . .

If we look at the language of the act of 1795, every conclusion drawn from the nature of the power itself is strongly fortified. . . . The power itself is confined to the executive of the Union, to him who is, by the constitution, "the Commander-in-chief of the militia, when called into the actual service of the United States," whose duty it is to "take care that the laws be faithfully executed," and whose responsibility for an honest discharge of his official obligations is secured by the highest sanctions. He is necessarily constituted the judge of the existence of the exigency in the first instance, and is bound to act according to his belief of the facts. If he does so act, and decides to call forth the militia, his orders for this purpose are in strict conformity with the provisions of the law; and it would seem to follow as a necessary consequence, that every act done by a subordinate officer, in obedience to such orders, is equally justifiable. The law contemplates, under such circumstances, orders shall be given to carry the power into effect; and it cannot therefore be a correct inference that any other person has a just right to disobey them. The law does not provide for any appeal from the judgement of the President, or for any right in subordinate officers to review his decision, and in effect defeat it. Wherever a statute gives a discretionary power to any person, to be exercised by him, upon his own opinion of certain facts, it is a sound rule of construction that the statute constitutes him the sole and exclusive judge of the existence of those facts. And, in the present case, we are all of opinion that such is the true construction of the act of 1795. It is no answer that such a power may be abused, for there is no power which is not susceptible of abuse. The remedy for this, as well as for all other official misconduct, if it should occur, is to be found in the constitution itself. In a free government the danger must be remote, since in addition to the high qualities which the Executive must be presumed to possess, of public virtue and honest devotion to the public interests, the frequency of elections, and the watchfulness of the representatives of the nation, carry with them all the checks which can be useful to guard against usurpation or wanton tyranny.

Judgement reversed.

133. MASSACHUSETTS HIGH SCHOOL LAW
1827

(Laws of Massachusetts, January session, 1827, ch. cxliii)

This is the first American law providing for the establishment of high schools. Note that its provisions are mandatory rather than merely permissive. The law was not adequately enforced, however, until Horace Mann assumed control of the Massachusetts Board of Education, in 1837. Even in 1840 there were only 18 high schools in the State; by 1860 the number had increased to over one hundred. See, G. H. Martin, *Evolution of the Massachusetts Public School System*.

Be it enacted, That each town or district within this Commonwealth, containing fifty families, or householders, shall be provided with a teacher or teachers, of good morals, to instruct children in orthography, reading, writing, English grammar, geography, arithmetic, and good behavior, for such term of time as shall be equivalent to six months for one school in each year; and every town or district containing one hundred families or householders, shall be provided with such teacher or teachers, for such term of time as shall be equivalent to eighteen months, for one school in each year. In every city, town, or district, containing five hundred families, or householders shall be provided with such teacher or teachers for such term of time as shall be equivalent to twenty-four* months, shall also be provided with a master of good morals, competent to instruct, in addition to the branches of learning aforesaid, in the history of the United States, bookkeeping by single entry, geometry, surveying, algebra; and shall employ such master to instruct a school in such city, town, or district, for the benefit of all the inhabitants thereof, at least ten months in each year, exclusive of vacations, in such convenient places, or alternately at such places in such city, town, or district, as said inhabitants, at their meeting in March, or April, annually, shall determine; and in every city, or town, and district, containing four thousand inhabitants, such master shall be competent in addition to all the foregoing branches, to instruct the Latin and Greek languages, history, rhetoric, and logic.

134. AMERICAN INSURANCE COMPANY v. CANTER
1 Peters, 511
1828

Appeal from the United States circuit court for the district of South Carolina. This was a suit by the American Insurance Co. to recover a cargo of cotton which had been sold by order of the territorial legislature of Florida. The plaintiffs alleged that the territorial court which ordered the sale was not a legally constituted court because the acquisition of Florida by the United States was unconstitutional. This is the leading case on the constitutionality of the acquisition of territory. See A. Beveridge, *John Marshall,* Vol. IV, p. 142 ff.; C. Warren, *Supreme Court,* (1928 ed.) Vol. I, p. 700.

MARSHALL, C. J. The plaintiffs filed their libel in this cause in the District Court of South Carolina to obtain restitution of 356 bales of cotton . . . which had been insured by them on a voyage from New Orleans to Havre de Grace, in France. The *Point à Petre* was wrecked on the coast of Florida, the cargo saved by the inhabitants, and carried into Key West, where it was sold for the purpose of satisfying the salvors; by virtue of a decree of a court, consisting of a notary and five jurors, which was erected by an act of the territorial Legislature of Florida. The owners abandoned to the underwriters, who proceeded against the property; alleging that the sale was not made by order of a court competent to change the property. . . .

David Canter claimed the cotton as a *bona fide* purchaser, under the decree of a competent court. . . .

The district judge pronounced the decree of the Territorial Court a nullity, and awarded restitution to the libelants. . . .

The libelants and claimant both appealed. . . .

The cause depends mainly on the question whether the property in the cargo saved, was changed, by the sale at Key West. . . . Its validity has been denied, on the ground, that it was ordered by an incompetent tribunal. The tribunal was constituted by an act of the territorial legislature of Florida, passed on the 4th July, 1823, which is inserted in the record. That act purports to give the power which has been exercised; consequently, the sale is valid, if the territorial legislature was competent to enact the law.

The course which the argument has taken, will require, that, in deciding this question, the court should take into view the relation in which Florida stands to the United States.

The Constitution confers absolutely on the government of the Union the powers of making war and of making treaties; consequently, that government possesses the power of acquiring territory, either by conquest or by treaty. The usage of the world is, if a nation be not entirely subdued, to consider the holding of conquered territory as a mere military occupation, until its fate shall be determined at the treaty of peace. If it be ceded by the treaty, the acquisition is confirmed, and the ceded territory becomes a part of the nation to which it is annexed; either on the terms stipulated in the treaty of cession, or on such as its new master shall impose. On such transfer of territory, it has never been held that the relations of the inhabitants with each other undergo any change. Their relations with their former sovereign are dissolved, and new relations are created between them and the government which has acquired their territory. The same act which transfers their country transfers the allegiance of those who remain in it; and the law which may be denominated political is necessarily changed, although that which regulates the intercourse and general conduct of individuals remains in force, until altered by the newly created power of the state.

On the 2d of February, 1819, Spain ceded Florida to the United States. The 6th article of the treaty of cession contains the following provision: "The inhabitants of the territories which his Catholic Majesty cedes to the United States by this treaty shall be incorporated in the Union of the United States, as soon as may be consistent with the principles of the federal Constitution; and admitted to the enjoyment of the privileges, rights, and immunities of the citizens of the United States."

This treaty is the law of the land, and admits the inhabitants of Florida to the enjoyment of the privileges, rights and immunities of the citizens of the United States. It is unnecessary to inquire whether this is not their condition, independent of stipulation. They do not, however, participate in political power; they do not share in the government till Florida shall become a State. In the meantime Florida continues to be a territory of the United States, governed by virtue of that clause in the Constitution which empowers Congress "to make all needful rules and regulations respecting the territory or other property belonging to the United States."

Perhaps the power of governing a territory belonging to the United States which has not by becoming a State acquired the means of self-government may result necessarily from the facts that it is not within the jurisdiction of any particular State, and is within the power and jurisdiction of the United States. The right to govern may be the inevitable consequence of the right to acquire territory. Whichever may be the source whence the power is derived, the possession of it is unquestioned. In execution of it Congress, in 1822, passed "An Act for the Establishment of a Territorial Government in Florida;" and on the 3d of March, 1823, passed another act to amend the act of 1822. Under this act the territorial legislature enacted the law now under consideration. . . .

It has been contended that, by the Constitution, the judicial power of the United States extends to all cases of admiralty and maritime jurisdiction; and that the whole of this judicial power must be vested "in one supreme court, and in such inferior courts as Congress shall from time to time ordain and establish." Hence, it has been argued that Congress cannot vest admiralty jurisdiction in courts created by the territorial legislature.

We have only to pursue this subject one step further, to perceive that this provision of the Constitution does not apply to it. The next sentence declares, that "the judges both of the supreme and inferior courts, shall hold their offices during good behavior." The judges of the superior courts of Florida hold their offices for four years. These courts, then, are not constitutional courts, in which the judicial power conferred by the Constitution on the general government can be deposited. They are incapable of receiving it. They are legislative courts, created in virtue of the general right of sovereignty which exists in the government, or in virtue of that clause which enables Congress to make all needful rules and regulations, respecting the territory belonging to the United States. The jurisdiction with which they are invested, is not a part of that judicial power which is defined in the third article of the Constitution, but is conferred by Congress, in the execution of those general powers which that body possesses over the territories of the United States. Although admiralty jurisdiction can be exercised in the States, in those courts only which are established in pursuance of the third article of the Constitution; the same limitation does not extend to the territories. In legislating for them, Congress exercises the combined powers of the general, and of a state government.

We think, then, that the act of the territorial legislature erecting the court by whose decree the cargo of the *Point à Petre* was sold, is not "inconsistent with the laws and Constitution of the United States," and is valid. Consequently, the sale made in pursuance of it changed the property, and the decree of the circuit court, awarding restitution of the property to the claimant, ought to be affirmed, with costs.

Decree affirmed.

135. THE SOUTH CAROLINA PROTEST AGAINST THE TARIFF OF 1828
December 19, 1828

(Elliot's *Debates*, 1861 ed. Vol. IV, p. 580)

This protest against the "tariff of abominations" of May 20, 1828 was the concluding part of the South Carolina Exposition, drafted by Calhoun, then Vice-President of the United States. The Exposition is in Calhoun's *Works*, 1855 ed. Vol. VI. See also, references in Doc. No. 143. On Calhoun see H. Von Holst, *Calhoun;* G. Hunt, *Calhoun;* W. C. Meigs, *Calhoun,* 2 Vols. For earlier protests against the tariff and for protests from other States, see, H. V. Ames, *State Documents on Federal Relations.*

The Senate and House of Representatives of South Carolina, now met, and sitting in General Assembly, through the Hon. William Smith and the Hon. Robert Y. Hayne, their representatives in the Senate of the United States, do, in the name and on behalf of the good people of the said commonwealth, solemnly PROTEST against the system of protecting duties, lately adopted by the federal government, for the following reasons:—

1st. *Because* the good people of this commonwealth believe that the powers of Congress were delegated to it in trust for the accomplishment of certain specified objects which limit and control them, and that every exercise of them for any other purposes, is a violation of the Constitution as unwarrantable as the undisguised assumption of substantive, independent powers not granted or expressly withheld.

2d. *Because* the power to lay duties on imports is, and in its very nature can be, only a means of effecting objects specified by the Constitution; since no free government, and least of all a government of enumerated powers, can of right impose any tax, any more than a penalty, which is not at once justified by public necessity, and clearly within the scope and purview of the social compact; and since the right of confining appropriations of the public money to such legitimate and constitutional objects is as essential to the liberty of the people as their unquestionable privilege to be taxed only by their consent.

3d. *Because* they believe that the tariff law passed by Congress at its last session, and all other acts of which the principal object is the protection of manufactures, or any other branch of domestic industry, if they be considered as the exercise of a power in Congress to tax the people at its own good will and pleasure, and to apply the money raised to objects not specified in the Constitution, is a violation of these fundamental principles, a breach of a well-defined trust, and a perversion of the high powers vested in the federal government for federal purposes only.

4th. *Because* such acts, considered in the light of a regulation of commerce, are equally liable to objection; since, although the power to regulate commerce may, like all other powers, be exercised so as to protect domestic manufactures, yet it is clearly distinguishable from a power to do so *eo nomine*, both in the nature of the thing and in the common acception of the terms; and because the confounding of them would lead to the most extravagant results, since the encouragement of domestic industry implies an absolute control over all the interests, resources, and pursuits of a people, and is consistent with the idea of any other than a simple, consolidated government.

5th. *Because*, from the contemporaneous exposition of the Constitution in the numbers of the *Federalist*, (which is cited only because the Supreme Court has recognized its authority), it is clear that the power to regulate commerce was considered by the Convention as only incidentally connected with the encouragement of agriculture and manufactures; and because the power of laying imposts and duties on imports was not understood to justify in any case, a prohibition of foreign commodities, except as a means of extending commerce, by coercing foreign nations to a fair reciprocity in their intercourse with us, or for some *bona fide* commercial purpose.

6th. *Because*, whilst the power to protect manufactures is nowhere expressly granted to Congress, nor can be considered as necessary and proper to carry into effect any specified power, it seems to be expressly reserved to the states, by the 10th section of the 1st article of the Constitution.

7th. *Because* even admitting Congress to have a constitutional right to protect manufactures by the imposition of duties, or by regulations of commerce, designed principally for that purpose, yet a tariff of which the operation is grossly unequal and oppressive, is such an abuse of power as is incompatible with the principles of a free government and the great ends of civil society, justice, and equality of rights and protection.

8th. *Finally*, because South Carolina, from her climate, situation, and peculiar institutions, is, and must ever continue to be, wholly dependent upon agriculture and commerce, not only for her prosperity, but for her very existence as a state; because the valuable products of her soil—the blessings by which Divine Providence seems to have designed to compensate for the great disadvantages under which she suffers in other respects—are among the very few that can be cultivated with any profit by slave labor; and if, by the loss of her foreign commerce, these products should be confined to an inadequate market, the fate of this fertile state would be poverty and utter desolation; her citizens, in despair, would emigrate to more fortunate regions, and the whole frame and constitution of her civil policy be impaired and deranged, if not dissolved entirely.

Deeply impressed with these considerations, the representatives of the good people of this commonwealth, anxiously desiring to live in peace with their fellow-citizens, and to do all that in them lies to preserve and perpetuate the union of the states, and liberties of which it is the surest pledge, but feeling it to be their bounden duty to expose and resist all encroachments upon the true spirit of the Constitution, lest an apparant acquiescence in the system of protecting duties should be drawn into precedent—do, in the name of the commonwealth of South Carolina, claim to enter upon the Journal of the Senate their *protest* against it as unconstitutional, oppressive, and unjust.

136. THE CONSTITUTION OF A LYCEUM
1829

(Old South Leaflets No. 139)

The Lyceum movement was part of the general educational reform movement of the eighteen thirties. It was organized in 1826 by Josiah Holbrook of Massachusetts, and the various lyceums of New England were federated in 1831. In many respects similar to the Chautauqua movement of the late nineteenth and early twentieth century, the lyceums attracted to their platforms some of the most eminent intellectual leaders of the day. See, H. B. Adams, "Educational Extension in the United States," U. S. Commissioner of Education, *Report,* 1899–1900; J. S. Noffsinger, *Correspondence Schools, Lyceums, and Chautauquas.*

Constitution

Many Lyceums have adopted the following or similar articles for their Constitution:—
1. The objects of the Lyceum are the improvement of its members in useful knowledge and the advancement of Popular Education.
2. To effect these objects, they will hold meetings for reading, conversation, discussions, dissertations, illustrating the sciences, or other exercises which shall be thought expedient, and, as it is found convenient, will procure a cabinet consisting of books, apparatus for illustrating the sciences, plants, minerals, and other natural or artificial productions.
3. Any person may be Member of the Lyceum by paying into the treasury annually Two Dollars; and Twenty Dollars paid at any one time will entitle a person, his or her heirs or assigns, to one membership forever. Persons under eighteen years of age will be entitled to all the privileges of the Society, except voting, for one-half the annual sum above named. . . .

5. The delegates will meet delegates from other branches of the Lyceum in this county semi-annually, to adopt regulations for their general and mutual benefit, or to take measures to introduce uniformity and improvements into common schools, and to diffuse useful and practical knowledge generally through the community, particularly to form and aid a BOARD OF EDUCATION.
6. To raise the standard of common education, and to benefit the juvenile members of the Lyceum, a portion of the books procured shall be fitted to young minds; and teachers of schools may be permitted to use for the benefit of their pupils who are members of the Lyceum the apparatus and minerals under such restrictions as the association shall prescribe. . . .

RECOMMENDATIONS

The undersigned hereby express their opinion that popular education would be greatly advanced by measures to concentrate the views and efforts of those disposed to act in its behalf to different parts of the country.

That the formation of a Society would be the most direct and efficient measure to concentrate such views and efforts.

That the institution denominated the AMERICAN LYCEUM embraces in its plan the important objects of a National Society, for the advancement of popular education.

That it is highly desirable that an auxiliary to this Society, or a branch Lyceum, should be established in every town.

That some simple articles of apparatus are important to render Lyceums interesting, useful, and permanent, and that the articles proposed by MR. HOLBROOK are fitted to this object, and that a portion of them would be useful in district and other schools.

That a weekly meeting of teachers for us-ing apparatus, and other exercises in relation to their schools, would have a tendency to raise their qualifications and to increase the value of their services.

137. CRAIG ET. AL. V. THE STATE OF MISSOURI
4 Peters, 410
1830

Writ of error to the Supreme Court of the State of Missouri. This case concerned the constitutionality of an act of the legislature of Missouri, 27 June, 1821, to establish loan offices which were empowered to issue certificates to the amount of two hundred thousand dollars, which certificates were to be receivable at the treasury of the State of Missouri in discharge of taxes or debts due to the State and by all officers in the State in discharge of salaries and fees of office.

MARSHALL, C. J. . . . This brings us to the great question in the cause: Is the act of the Legislature of Missouri repugnant to the Constitution of the United States?

The counsel for the plaintiffs in error maintain that it is repugnant to the Constitution, because its object is the emission of bills of credit contrary to the express prohibition contained in the tenth section of the first article. . . . The clause in the Constitution which this act is supposed to violate is in these words: "No state shall emit bills of credit".

What is a bill of credit? What did the Constitution mean to forbid?

In its enlarged, and perhaps its literal sense, the term "bill of credit" may comprehend any instrument by which a State engages to pay money at a future day; thus including a certificate given for money borrowed. But the language of the Constitution itself, and the mischief to be prevented, which we know from the history of our country, equally limit the interpretation of the terms. . . . To "emit bills of credit" conveys to the mind the idea of issuing paper intended to circulate through the community for its ordinary purposes, as money, which paper is redeemable at a future day. This is the sense in which the terms have always been understood. . . .

What is the character of the certificates issued by authority of the act under consideration? What office are they to perform? Certificates signed by the auditor and treasurer of the State are to be issued by those officers to the amount of two hundred thousand dollars, of denominations not exceeding ten dollars nor less than fifty cents. The paper purports on its face to be receivable at the treasury, or at any loan-office of the State of Missouri, in discharge of taxes or debts due to the State. The law . . . also pledges the faith and funds of the State for their redemption.

It seems impossible to doubt the intention of the Legislature in passing this act, or to mistake the character of these certificates, or the office they were to perform. The denominations of the bills—from ten dollars to fifty cents—fitted them for the purpose of ordinary circulation and their reception in payment of taxes and debts to the government and to corporations, and of salaries and fees, would give them currency. They were to be put into circulation; that is, emitted by the government. . . .

But it is contended that though these certificates should be deemed bills of credit, according to the common acceptation of the term, they are not so in the sense of the Constitution because they are not made legal tender.

The Constitution itself furnishes no countenance to this distinction. The prohibition is general. It extends to all bills of credit, not to bills of a particular description. That tribunal must be bold indeed, which, without the aid of other explanatory words, could venture on this construction. It is the less admissible in this case, because the same clause of the Constitution contains a substantive prohibition to the enactment of tender laws. The Constitution, therefore, considers the emission of bills of credit and the enactment of tender laws as distinct operations, independent of each other, which may be separately performed. Both are forbidden. To sustain the one because it is not also the other; to say that bills of credit may be emitted if they be not made a tender in payment of debts, is, in effect, to expunge that distinct independent prohibition, and to read the clause as if it had been entirely omitted. We are not at liberty to do this. . . .

A majority of the court feels constrained to say that the consideration on which the note in this case was given is against the highest law of the land, and that the note itself is utterly void. In rendering judgement for the plaintiff the Court for the State of Missouri decided in favor of the validity of a law which is repugnant to the Constitution of the United States.

In the argument we have been reminded by one side of the dignity of a sovereign State; of the humiliation of her submitting herself to this tribunal; of the dangers which may result from inflicting a wound on that dignity; by the other, of the still superior dignity of the people of the United States, who

have spoken their will in terms which we cannot misunderstand.

To these admonitions we can only answer, that if the exercise of that jurisdiction which has been imposed upon us by the Constitution and laws of the United States shall be calculated to bring on those dangers which have been indicated, or if it shall be indispensable to the preservation of the Union, and consequently, of the independence and liberty of these States, these are considerations which address themselves to those departments which may with perfect propriety be influenced by them. This department can listen only to the mandates of law, and can thread only that path which is marked out by duty.

The judgement of the Supreme Court of Missouri is reversed.

138. JACKSON'S VETO OF MAYSVILLE ROAD BILL
May 27, 1830

(Richardson, ed. *Messages and Papers,* Vol. II, p. 483 ff.)

President J. Q. Adams had supported a policy of internal improvements at national expense, but Jackson, nationalistic in many respects, subscribed to doctrines of narrow construction of this question. On the veto, see, W. MacDonald, *Jacksonian Democracy,* ch. viii; E. C. Mason, *The Veto Power,* sec. 83 ff.

MAY 27, 1830.
To the House of Representatives.

Gentlemen: I have maturely considered the bill proposing to authorize "a subscription of stock in the Maysville, Washington, Paris, and Lexington Turnpike Road Company," and now return the same to the House of Representatives, in which it originated, with my objections to its passage. . . .

The constitutional power of the Federal Government to construct or promote works of internal improvement presents itself in two points of view—the first as bearing upon the sovereignty of the States within whose limits their execution is contemplated, if jurisdiction of the territory which they may occupy be claimed as necessary to their preservation and use; the second as asserting the simple right to appropriate money from the National Treasury in aid of such works when undertaken by State authority, sur-

rendering the claim of jurisdiction. In the first view the question of power is an open one, and can be decided without the embarrassments attending the other, arising from the practice of the Government. Although frequently and strenuously attempted, the power to this extent has never been exercised by the Government in a single instance. It does not, in my opinion, possess it; and no bill, therefore, which admits it can receive my official sanction.

But in the other view of the power the question is differently situated. The ground taken at an early period of the Government was "that whenever money has been raised by the general authority and is to be applied to a particular measure, a question arises whether the particular measure be within the enumerated authorities vested in Congress. If it be, the money requisite for it may be applied to it; if not, no such application can be made." The document in which this principle was first advanced is of deservedly high authority, and should be held in grateful remembrance for its immediate agency in rescuing the country from much existing abuse and for its conservative effect upon some of the most valuable principles of the Constitution. The symmetry and purity of the Government would doubtless have been better preserved if this restriction of the power of appropriation could have been maintained without weakening its ability to fulfill the general objects of its institution, an effect so likely to attend its admission, notwithstanding its apparent fitness, that every subsequent Administration of the Government, embracing a period of thirty out of the forty-two years of its existence, has adopted a more enlarged construction of the power. It is not my purpose to detain you by a minute recital of the acts which sustain this assertion, but it is proper that I should notice some of the most prominent in order that the reflections which they suggest to my mind may be better understood. . . .

The bill before me does not call for a more definite opinion upon the particular circumstances which will warrant appropriations of money by Congress to aid works of internal improvement, for although the extension of the power to apply money beyond that of carrying into effect the object for which it is appropriated has, as we have seen, been long claimed and exercised by the Federal Government, yet such grants have always been professedly under the control of the general principle that the works which might be thus aided should be "of a general, not local, national, not State," character. A disregard of this distinction would of necessity lead to the subversion of the federal system. That even this is an unsafe one, arbitrary in its nature, and liable, consequently, to great abuses, is too obvious to require the confirmation of experience. It is, however, sufficiently definite and imperative to my mind to forbid my approbation of any bill having the character of the one under consideration. I have given to its provisions all the reflection demanded by a just regard for the interests of those of our fellow-citizens who have desired its passage, and by the respect which is due to a coördinate branch of the Government, but I am not able to view it in any other light than as a measure of purely local character; or, if it can be considered national, that no further distinction between the appropriate duties of the General and State Governments need be attempted, for there can be no local interest that may not with equal propriety be denominated national. It has no connection with any established system of improvements; is exclusively within the limits of a State, starting at a point on the Ohio River and running out 60 miles to an interior town, and even as far as the State is interested conferring partial instead of general advantages.

Considering the magnitude and importance of the power, and the embarrassments to which, from the very nature of the thing, its exercise must necessarily be subjected, the real friends of internal improvement ought not to be willing to confide it to accident and chance. . . .

In the other view of the subject, and the only remaining one which it is my intention to present at this time, is involved the expediency of embarking in a system of internal improvement without a previous amendment of the Constitution explaining and defining the precise powers of the Federal Government over it. Assuming the right to appropriate money to aid in the construction of national works to be warranted by the contemporaneous and continued exposition of the Constitution, its insufficiency for the successful prosecution of them must be admitted by all candid minds. If we look to usage to define the extent of the right, that will be found so variant and embracing so much that has been overruled as to involve the whole subject in great uncertainty and to render the execution of our respective duties in relation to it replete with difficulty and embarrassment. It is in regard to such works and the acquisition of additional territory that the practice obtained its first footing. In most, if not all, other disputed questions of appropriation the construction of the Constitution may be regarded as unsettled if the right to apply money in the enumerated cases is placed on the ground of usage. . . .

If it be the wish of the people that the construction of roads and canals should be conducted by the Federal Government, it is not only highly expedient, but indispensably necessary, that a previous amendment of the Constitution, delegating the necessary power and defining and restricting its exercise with reference to the sovereignty of the States, should be made. Without it nothing extensively useful can be effected. The right to exercise as much jurisdiction as is necessary to preserve the works and to raise funds by the collection of tolls to keep them in repair can not be dispensed with. . . .

139. THE SPOILS OF VICTORY
Extract from a Speech by Mr. Marcy
1831

(*Niles' Register*, Vol. XLIII, p. 8, September 1, 1832)

In the course of the debate on Van Buren's appointment as Minister to England, Clay referred to the spoils system in New York and alleged that Van Buren had introduced this political principle into national politics. Mr. Marcy, in defending Van Buren, announced the notorious doctrine that "to the victor belong the spoils." Though the spoils system has been traced back to the Federalist machine in New York politics, this speech of Marcy's, observes Dr. Alexander, "forever . . . confirmed the belief that Van Buren was an inveterate spoilsman." For the origins of the spoils system, see H. L. McBain, *De Witt Clinton and the Origin of the Spoils System in New York*; D. R. Fox, *The Decline of Aristocracy in the Politics of New York*.

Mr. *Marcy*, one of the senators of the United States from New York, in the course of the debate on the nomination of Mr. Van Buren said—

"It may be, sir, that the politicians of New York are not so fastidious as some gentlemen are, as to disclosing the principles on which they act. They boldly *preach* what they *practice*. When they are contending for *victory*, they avow their intention of enjoying the fruits of it. If they are defeated, they expect to retire from office. If they are successful, they claim, as a matter of right, the advantages of success. They see nothing wrong in the rule that to the VICTOR belongs the spoils of the ENEMY."

140. CHEROKEE NATION v. GEORGIA
5 Peters, 1
1831

Suit for injunction to restrain the State of Georgia. In 1827 the Cherokee Indians, occupying extensive lands in northwestern Georgia, set up a government and declared themselves an independent nation. Thereupon the legislature of Georgia passed resolutions alleging ownership of all Cherokee territory and extending the laws of Georgia over the Cherokee Indians, and annulling all laws, usages and customs of the Indians. The Indians appealed to the Supreme Court for an injunction to prevent the execution of these laws. The opinion of Marshall is notable for its definition of the legal relations of the Indians with the United States government: the Indians constituted not foreign nations but domestic dependent nations in a state of pupilage. See, Beveridge, *Marshall*, Vol. IV, p. 539 ff.; A. Abel, "History of Events Resulting in Indian Consolidation West of the Mississippi River," in Am. Hist. Assoc. *Reports*, 1906, Vol. I; and references in Docs. No. 141–142.

MARSHALL, C. J. This bill is brought by the Cherokee nation, praying an injunction to restrain the state of Georgia from the execution of certain laws of that state, which, as is alleged, go directly to annihilate the Cherokee as a political society, and to seize for the use of Georgia, the lands of the nation which have been assured to them by the United States, in solemn treaties repeatedly made and still in force.

If courts were permitted to indulge their sympathies, a case better calculated to excite them can scarcely be imagined. A people, once numerous, powerful, and truly independent, found by our ancestors in the quiet and uncontrolled possession of an ample domain, gradually sinking beneath our superior policy, our arts and our arms, have yielded their lands, by successive treaties, each of which contains a solemn guarantee of the residue, until they retain no more of their formerly extensive territory than is deemed necessary to their comfortable subsistence. To preserve this remnant, the present application is made.

Before we can look into the merits of the case, a preliminary inquiry presents itself.

Has this court jurisdiction of the cause? The third article of the constitution describes the extent of the judicial power. The second section closes an enumeration of the cases to which it is extended, with "controversies between a state or citizens thereof, and foreign states, citizens or subjects." A subsequent clause of the same section gives the supreme court original jurisdiction, in all cases in which a state shall be a party. The party defendant may then unquestionably be sued in this court. May the plaintiff sue in it? Is the Cherokee nation a foreign state, in the sense in which that term is used in the constitution? The counsel for the plaintiffs have maintained the affirmative of this proposition with great earnestness and ability. So much of the argument as was intended to prove the character of the Cherokees as a state, as a distinct political society, separated from others, capable of managing its own affairs and governing itself, has in the opinion of a majority of the judges, been completely successful. They have been uniformly treated as a state, from the settlement of our country. The numerous treaties made with them by the United States, recognise them as a people capable of maintaining the relations of peace and war, of being responsible in their political character for any violation of their engagements, or for any aggression committed on the citizens of the United States, by any individual of their community. Laws have been enacted in the spirit of these treaties. The acts of our government plainly recognise the Cherokee nation as a state, and the courts are bound by those acts.

A question of much more difficulty remains. Do the Cherokees constitute a foreign state in the sense of the constitution? The counsel have shown conclusively, that they are not a state of the Union, and have insisted that, individually, they are aliens, not owing allegiance to the United States. An aggregate of aliens composing a state must, they say, be a foreign state; each individual being foreign, the whole must be foreign.

This argument is imposing, but we must examine it more closely, before we yield to it. The condition of the Indians in relation to the United States is, perhaps, unlike that of any other two people in existence. In general, nations not owing a common allegiance, are foreign to each other. The term foreign nation is, with strict propriety, applicable by either to the other. But the relation of the Indians to the United States is marked by peculiar and cardinal distinctions which exist nowhere else. The Indian territory is admitted to compose a part of the United States. In all our maps, geographical treaties, histories and laws, it is so considered. In all our intercourse with foreign nations, in our commercial regulations, in any attempt at intercourse between Indians and foreign nations, they are considered as within the jurisdictional limits of the United States, subject to many of those restraints which are imposed upon our own citizens. They acknowledge themselves, in their treaties, to be under the protection of the United States; they admit, that the United States shall have the sole and exclusive right of regulating the trade with them, and managing all their affairs as they think proper; and the Cherokees in particular were allowed by the treaty of Hopewell, which preceded the constitution, "to send a deputy of their choice, whenever they think fit, to congress." Treaties were made with some tribes, by the state of New York, under a then unsettled construction of the confederation, by which they ceded all their lands to that state, taking back a limited grant to themselves, in which they admit their dependence. Though the Indians are acknowledged to have an unquestionable, and heretofore unquestioned, right to the lands they occupy, until that right shall be extinguished by a voluntary cession to our government; yet it may well be doubted, whether those tribes which reside within the acknowledged boundaries of the United States can, with accuracy, be denominated foreign nations. They may, more correctly, perhaps, be denominated domestic dependent nations. They occupy a territory to which we assert a title independent of their will, which must take effect in point of possession, when their right of possession ceases. Meanwhile, they are in a state of pupilage; their relation to the United States resembles that of a ward to his guardian. They look to our government for protection; rely upon its kindness and its power; appeal to it for relief to their wants; and address the president as their great father. They and their country are considered by foreign nations, as well as by ourselves, as being so completely under the sovereignty and dominion of the United States, that any attempt to acquire their lands, or to form a political connection with them would be considered by all as an invasion of our territory and an act of hostility. These considerations go far to support the opinion, that the framers of our constitution had not the Indian tribes in view, when they opened the courts of the Union to controversies between a state or the citizens thereof and foreign states.

In considering this subject, the habits and usages of the Indians, in their intercourse with their white neighbors, ought not to be entirely disregarded. At the time the constitution was framed, the idea of appealing to an American court of justice for an assertion of right or a redress of wrong, had perhaps never entered the mind of an Indian or of his tribe. Their appeal was to the tomahawk, or to the government. This was well understood by the statesmen who framed the constitution of the United States, and might furnish some reason for omitting to enumerate them among the parties who might sue in the courts of the Union. Be this as it may, the peculiar relations between the United States and the Indians occupying our territory are such, that we should feel much difficulty in considering them as designated by the term foreign state, were there no other part of the constitution which might shed light on the meaning of these words. But we think that in construing them, considerable aid is furnished by that clause in the eighth section of the third article, which empowers congress to "regulate commerce with foreign nations, and among the several states, and with the Indian tribes." In this clause, they are as clearly contradistinguished, by a name appropriate to themselves, from foreign nations, as from the several states composing the Union. They are designated by a distinct appellation; and as this appellation can be applied to neither of the others, neither can the application distinguishing either of the others be, in fair construction, applied to them. The objects to which the power of regulating commerce might be directed, are divided into three distinct classes—foreign nations, the several states, and Indian tribes. When forming this article, the convention considered them as

entirely distinct. We cannot assume that the distinction was lost, in framing a subsequent article, unless there be something in its language to authorize the assumption.

The counsel for the plaintiffs contend, that the words "Indian tribes" were introduced into the article, empowering congress to regulate commerce, for the purpose of removing those doubts in which the management of Indian affairs was involved by the language of the ninth article of the confederation. Intending to give the whole of managing those affairs to the government about to be instituted, the convention conferred it explicitly; and omitted those qualifications which embarrassed the exercise of it, as granted in the confederation. This may be admitted, without weakening the construction which has been intimated. Had the Indian tribes been foreign nations, in the view of the convention, this exclusive power of regulating intercourse with them might have been, and, most probably, would have been, specifically given, in language indicating that idea, not in language contradistinguishing them from foreign nations. Congress might have been empowered "to regulate commerce with foreign nations, including the Indian tribes, and among the several states." This language would have suggested itself to statesmen who considered the Indian tribes as foreign nations, and were yet desirous of mentioning them particularly.

It has been also said, that the same words have not necessarily the same meaning attached to them, when found in different parts of the same instrument; their meaning is controlled by the context. This is undoubtedly true. In common language, the same word has various meanings, and the peculiar sense in which it is used in any sentence, is to be determined by the context. This may not be equally true with respect to proper names. "Foreign nations" is a general term, the application of which to Indian tribes, when used in the American constitution, is, at best, extremely questionable. In one article, in which a power is given to be exercised in regard to foreign nations generally, and to the Indian tribes particularly, they are mentioned as separate, in terms clearly contradistinguishing them from each other. We perceive plainly, that the constitution, in this article, does not comprehend Indian tribes in the general term "foreign nations;" not, we presume, because a tribe may not be a nation, but because it is not foreign to the United States. When, afterwards, the term "foreign state" is introduced, we cannot impute to the convention, the intention to desert its former meaning, and to comprehend Indian tribes within it, unless the context force that construction on us. We find nothing in the context, and nothing in the subject of the article, which leads to it.

The court has bestowed its best attention on this question, and, after mature deliberation, the majority is of opinion, that an Indian tribe or nation within the United States is not a foreign state, in the sense of the constitution, and cannot maintain an action in the courts of the United States.

A serious additional objection exists to the jurisdiction of the court. Is the matter of the bill the proper subject for judicial inquiry and decision? It seeks to restrain a state from the forcible exercise of legislative power over a neighboring people, asserting their independence; their right to which the state denies. On several of the matters alleged in the bill, for example, on the laws making it criminal to exercise the usual powers of self-

government in their own country, by the Cherokee nation, this court cannot interpose; at least, in the form in which those matters are presented.

That part of the bill which respects the land occupied by the Indians, and prays the aid of the court to protect their possession, may be more doubtful. The mere question of right might, perhaps, be decided by this court, in a proper case, with proper parties. But the court is asked to do more than decide on the title. The bill requires us to control the legislature of Georgia, and to restrain the exertion of its physical force. The propriety of such an interposition by the court may be well questioned; it savors too much of the exercise of political power, to be within the proper province of the judicial department. But the opinion on the point respecting parties makes it unnecessary to decide this question.

If it be true, that the Cherokee nation have rights, this is not the tribunal in which those rights are to be asserted. If it be true, that wrongs have been inflicted, and that still greater are to be apprehended, this is not the tribunal which can redress the past or prevent the future. The motion for an injunction is denied.

141. WORCESTER v. GEORGIA
6 Peters, 515
1832

Error to the Superior Court for the County of Gwinnett, Georgia. The facts are stated in the opinion below. It is of this opinion that President Jackson is reputed to have remarked: "John Marshall has made his opinion, now let him enforce it." Georgia was so incensed at judicial interference with what she considered her sovereign affairs that she refused to appear before the Court in this case, and refused likewise to obey the mandate of the Court. For the historical background of the case, see Beveridge, *Marshall*, Vol. IV, p. 547 ff.; E. M. Coulter, *Short History of Georgia*, ch. xvii; W. Lumpkin, *Removal of the Cherokee Indians from Georgia*, 2 vols.; U. B. Phillips, *Georgia and State Rights*, p. 66 ff. See also, *Cherokee Nation* v. *State of Georgia*, Doc. No. 140.

MARSHALL, C. J. This cause, in every point of view in which it can be placed, is of the deepest interest.

The defendant is a State, a member of the

Union, which has exercised the powers of government over a people who deny its jurisdiction, and are under the protection of the United States.

The plaintiff is a citizen of the State of Vermont, condemned to hard labor for four years in the penitentiary of Georgia under color of an act which he alleges to be repugnant to the Constitution, laws, and treaties of the United States.

The legislative power of a State, the controlling power of the Constitution and laws of the United States, the rights, if they have any, the political existence of a once numerous and powerful people, the personal liberty of a citizen, all are involved in the subject now to be considered. . . .

We must inquire and decide whether the act of the Legislature of Georgia under which the plaintiff in error has been prosecuted and condemned, be consistent with, or repugnant to the Constitution, laws and treaties of the United States.

It has been said at the bar that the acts of the Legislature of Georgia seize on the whole Cherokee country, parcel it out among the neighboring counties of the State, extend her code over the whole country, abolish its institutions and its laws, and annihilate its political existence.

If this be the general effect of the system, let us inquire into the effect of the particular statute and section on which the indictment is founded.

It enacts that "all white persons, residing within the limits of the Cherokee Nation on the 1st day of March next, or at any time thereafter, without a licence or permit from his excellency the governor . . . and who shall not have taken the oath hereinafter required, shall be guilty of a high misdemeanor, and upon conviction thereof, shall be punished by confinement to the penitentiary at hard labor for a term not less than four years." . . .

The extraterritorial power of every Legislature being limited in its action to its own citizens or subjects, the very passage of this act is an assertion of jurisdiction over the Cherokee Nation, and of the rights and powers consequent on jurisdiction.

The first step, then, in the inquiry which the Constitution and the laws impose on this court, is an examination of the rightfulness of this claim. . . .

From the commencement of our government Congress has passed acts to regulate trade and intercourse with the Indians; which treat them as nations, respect their rights, and manifest a firm purpose to afford that protection which treaties stipulate. All these acts, and especially that of 1802, which is still in force, manifestly consider the several Indian nations as distinct political communities, having territorial boundaries, within which their authority is exclusive, and having

a right to all the lands within those boundaries, which is not only acknowledged, but guaranteed by the United States. . . .

The Cherokee Nation, then, is a distinct community, occupying its own territory, with boundaries accurately described, in which the laws of Georgia can have no force, and which the citizens of Georgia have no right to enter but with the assent of the Cherokees themselves or in conformity with treaties and with the acts of Congress. The whole intercourse between the United States and this nation is, by our Constitution and laws, vested in the government of the United States.

The act of the State of Georgia under which the plaintiff in error was prosecuted is consequently void, and the judgement a nullity. . . . The Acts of Georgia are repugnant to the Constitution, laws, and treaties of the United States.

They interfere forcibly with the relations established between the United States and the Cherokee Nation, the regulation of which according to the settled principles of our Constitution, are committed exclusively to the government of the Union.

They are in direct hostility with treaties, repeated in a succession of years, which mark out the boundary that separates the Cherokee country from Georgia; guarantee to them all the land within their boundary; solemnly pledge the faith of the United States to restrain their citizens from trespassing on it; and recognize the pre-existing power of the nation to govern itself.

They are in equal hostility with the acts of Congress for regulating this intercourse, and giving effect to the treaties.

The forcible seizure and abduction of the plaintiff, who was residing in the nation with its permission, and by authority of the President of the United States, is also a violation of the acts which authorize the chief magistrate to exercise this authority. . . .

Judgement reversed.

142. REMOVAL OF SOUTHERN INDIANS TO INDIAN TERRITORY
Extract from Jackson's Seventh Annual Message to Congress
December 7, 1835
(Richardson, ed. *Messages and Papers*, Vol. III, p. 171 ff.)

Georgia's Indian policy, and the refusal of Jackson to sustain the Supreme Court in its in-

terpretation of the rights of the Indians, led to the plan of removing the remaining Creeks,

Cherokees, and other Indian tribes of the South to a reservation west of the Mississippi. This policy had been outlined by Jackson in his first message to Congress, and in 1830 Congress had appropriated half a million dollars for the removal of the Indians to the west. In 1834 Congress created a special Indian Territory, and by a treaty of December 29, 1835, the Indians surrendered their lands east of the Mississippi in return for five million dollars, the expenses of removal, and land. See G. Foreman, *Indian Removal;* G. Foreman, *Indians and Pioneers,* ch. xxi; W. MacDonald, *Jacksonian Democracy,* ch. x.

WASHINGTON, *December 7, 1835.*

. . . The plan of removing the aboriginal people who yet remain within the settled portions of the United States to the country west of the Mississippi River approaches its consummation. It was adopted on the most mature consideration of the condition of this race, and ought to be persisted in till the object is accomplished, and prosecuted with as much vigor as a just regard to their circumstances will permit, and as fast as their consent can be obtained. All preceding experiments for the improvement of the Indians have failed. It seems now to be an established fact that they can not live in contact with a civilized community and prosper. Ages of fruitless endeavors have at length brought us to a knowledge of this principle of intercommunication with them. The past we can not recall, but the future we can provide for. Independently of the treaty stipulations into which we have entered with the various tribes for the usufructuary rights they have ceded to us, no one can doubt the moral duty of the Government of the United States to protect and if possible to preserve and perpetuate the scattered remnants of this race which are left within our borders. In the discharge of this duty an extensive region in the West has been assigned for their permanent residence. It has been divided into districts and allotted among them. Many have already removed and others are preparing to go, and with the exception of two small bands living in Ohio and Indiana, not exceeding 1,500 persons, and of the Cherokees, all the tribes on the east side of the Mississippi, and extending from Lake Michigan to Florida, have entered into engagements which will lead to their transplantation.

The plan for their removal and reëstablishment is founded upon the knowledge we have gained of their character and habits, and has been dictated by a spirit of enlarged liberality. A territory exceeding in extent that relinquished has been granted to each tribe. Of its climate, fertility, and capacity to support an Indian population the representations are highly favorable. To these districts the Indians are removed at the expense of the United States, and with certain supplies of clothing, arms, ammunition, and other indispensable articles; they are also furnished gratuitously with provisions for the period of a year after their arrival at their new homes. In that time, from the nature of the country and of the products raised by them, they can subsist themselves by agricultural labor, if they choose to resort to that mode of life; if they do not they are upon the skirts of the great prairies, where countless herds of buffalo roam, and a short time suffices to adapt their own habits to the changes which a change of the animals destined for their food may require. Ample arrangements have also been made for the support of schools; in some instances council houses and churches are to be erected, dwellings constructed for the chiefs, and mills for common use. Funds have been set apart for the maintenance of the poor; the most necessary mechanical arts have been introduced, and blacksmiths, gunsmiths, wheelwrights, millwrights, etc., are supported among them. Steel and iron, and sometimes salt, are purchased for them, and plows and other farming utensils, domestic animals, looms, spinning wheels, cards, etc., are presented to them. And besides these beneficial arrangements, annuities are in all cases paid, amounting in some instances to more than $30 for each individual of the tribe, and in all cases sufficiently great, if justly divided and prudently expended, to enable them, in addition to their own exertions, to live comfortably. And as a stimulus for exertion, it is now provided by law that "in all cases of the appointment of interpreters or other persons employed for the benefit of the Indians a preference shall be given to persons of Indian descent, if such can be found who are properly qualified for the discharge of the duties."

Such are the arrangements for the physical comfort and for the moral improvement of the Indians. The necessary measures for their political advancement and for their separation from our citizens have not been neglected. The pledge of the United States has been given by Congress that the country destined for the residence of this people shall be forever "secured and guaranteed to them." A country west of Missouri and Arkansas has been assigned to them, into which the white settlements are not to be pushed. No political communities can be formed in that extensive region, except those which are established by the Indians themselves or by the United States for them and with their concurrence. A barrier has thus been raised for their protection against the encroachment of our citizens, and guarding the Indians as far as possible from those evils which have brought them to their present condition. Summary authority has been given by law to destroy all ardent spirits found in their country, without waiting the doubtful result and slow process of a legal seizure. I consider the absolute and unconditional interdiction of this article among these people as the first and great step in their melioration. Halfway measures will answer no purpose. These can not successfully contend against the cupidity of the seller and the overpowering appetite of the buyer. And the destructive effects of the traffic are marked in every page of the history of our Indian intercourse. . . .

143. SOUTH CAROLINA ORDINANCE OF NULLIFICATION
November 24, 1832
(*Statutes at Large of South Carolina*, Vol. I, p. 329 ff.)

The tariff of July 14, 1832 was only less unpopular than the "tariff of abominations" of 1828. The legislature of South Carolina met in special session in October, 1832 and provided for a convention to consider the tariff: the convention met in November and adopted the Ordinance of Nullification. For Jackson's Proclamation, see Doc. No. 144. See, D. F. Houston, *Critical Study of Nullification in South Carolina;* C. S. Boucher, *Nullification Movement in South Carolina;* J. G. Van Deusen, *Economic Basis of Disunion in South Carolina;* H. Von Holst, *Calhoun;* G. Hunt, *Calhoun;* J. S. Bassett, *Andrew Jackson,* Vol. II; J. Parton, *Andrew Jackson,* Vol. III; C. Bowers, *Party Battles of the Jackson Period,* ch. x.

An Ordinance to Nullify certain acts of the Congress of the United States, purporting to be laws laying duties and imposts on the importation of foreign commodities

Whereas the Congress of the United States, by various acts, purporting to be acts laying duties and imposts on foreign imports, but in reality intended for the protection of domestic manufactures, and the giving of bounties to classes and individuals engaged in particular employments, at the expense and to the injury and oppression of other classes and individuals, and by wholly exempting from taxation certain foreign commodities, such as are not produced or manufactured in the United States, to afford a pretext for imposing higher and excessive duties on articles similar to those intended to be protected, hath exceeded its just powers under the Constitution, which confers on it no authority to afford such protection, and hath violated the true meaning and intent of the Constitution, which provides for equality in imposing the burthens of taxation upon the several States and portions of the Confederacy: *And whereas* the said Congress, exceeding its just power to impose taxes and collect revenue for the purpose of effecting and accomplishing the specific objects and purposes which the Constitution of the United States authorizes it to effect and accomplish, hath raised and collected unnecessary revenue for objects unauthorized by the Constitution:—

We, therefore, the people of the State of South Carolina in Convention assembled, do declare and ordain, . . . That the several acts and parts of acts of the Congress of the United States, purporting to be laws for the imposing of duties and imposts on the importation of foreign commodities, . . . and, more especially, . . . [the tariff acts of 1828 and 1832] . . . , are unauthorized by the Constitution of the United States, and violate the true meaning and intent thereof, and are null, void, and no law, nor binding upon this State, its officers or citizens; and all promises, contracts, and obligations, made or entered into, or to be made or entered into, with purpose to secure the duties imposed by the said acts, and all judicial proceedings which shall be hereafter had in affirmance thereof, are and shall be held utterly null and void.

And it is further Ordained, That it shall not be lawful for any of the constituted authorities, whether of this State or of the United States, to enforce the payment of duties imposed by the said acts within the limits of this State; but it shall be the duty of the Legislature to adopt such measures and pass such acts as may be necessary to give full effect to this Ordinance, and to prevent the enforcement and arrest the operation of the said acts and parts of acts of the Congress of the United States within the limits of this State, from and after the 1st day of February next, . . .

And it is further Ordained, That in no case of law or equity, decided in the courts of this State, wherein shall be drawn in question the authority of this ordinance, or the validity of such act or acts of the Legislature as may be passed for the purpose of giving effect thereto, or the validity of the aforesaid acts of Congress, imposing duties, shall any appeal be taken or allowed to the Supreme Court of the United States, nor shall any copy of the record be printed or allowed for that purpose; and if any such appeal shall be attempted to be taken, the courts of this State shall proceed to execute and enforce their judgments, according to the laws and usages of the State, without reference to such attempted appeal, and the person or persons attempting to take such appeal may be dealt with as for a contempt of the court.

And it is further Ordained, That all persons now holding any office of honor, profit, or trust, civil or military, under this State, (members of the Legislature excepted), shall, within such time, and in such manner as the Legislature shall prescribe, take an oath well and truly to obey, execute, and enforce, this Ordinance, and such act or acts of the Legislature as may be passed in pursuance thereof, according to the true intent and meaning of

the same; and on the neglect or omission of any such person or persons so to do, his or their office or offices shall be forthwith vacated, . . . and no person hereafter elected to any office of honor, profit, or trust, civil or military, (members of the Legislature excepted), shall, until the Legislature shall otherwise provide and direct, enter on the execution of his office, . . . until he shall, in like manner, have taken a similar oath; and no juror shall be empannelled in any of the courts of this State, in any cause in which shall be in question this Ordinance, or any act of the Legislature passed in pursuance thereof, unless he shall first, in addition to the usual oath, have taken an oath that he will well and truly obey, execute, and enforce this Ordinance, and such act or acts of the Legislature as may be passed to carry the same into operation and effect, according to the true intent and meaning thereof.

And we, the People of South Carolina, to the end that it may be fully understood by the Government of the United States, and the people of the co-States, that we are determined to maintain this, our Ordinance and Declaration, at every hazard, *Do further Declare* that we will not submit to the application of force, on the part of the Federal Government, to reduce this State to obedience; but that we will consider the passage, by Congress, of any act . . . to coerce the State, shut up her ports, destroy or harass her commerce, or to enforce the acts hereby declared to be null and void, otherwise than through the civil tribunals of the country, as inconsistent with the longer continuance of South Carolina in the Union: and that the people of this State will thenceforth hold themselves absolved from all further obligation to maintain or preserve their political connexion with the people of the other States, and will forthwith proceed to organize a separate Government, and do all other acts and things which sovereign and independent States may of right to do.

144. JACKSON'S PROCLAMATION TO THE PEOPLE OF SOUTH CAROLINA
December 10, 1832

(Richardson, ed. *Messages and Papers,* Vol. II, p. 640 ff.)

Jackson's Proclamation was primarily concerned with the constitutional issues of nullification.

January 16, 1833 Jackson reported to Congress on nullification and presented concrete recommendations for action. See, Richardson, *Messages and Papers*, Vol. II, p. 610 ff. For references, see Doc. No. 143.

Whereas a convention assembled in the State of South Carolina have passed an ordinance by which they declare "that the several acts and parts of acts of the Congress of the United States purporting to be laws for the imposing of duties and imposts on the importation of foreign commodities, . . . are unauthorized by the Constitution of the United States, and violate the true meaning and intent thereof, and are null and void and no law," nor binding on the citizens of that State or its officers; and by the said ordinance it is further declared to be unlawful for any of the constituted authorities of the State or of the United States to enforce the payment of the duties imposed by the said acts within the same State, and that it is the duty of the legislature to pass such laws as may be necessary to give full effect to the said ordinance; and

Whereas by the said ordinance it is further ordained that in no case of law or equity decided in the courts of said State wherein shall be drawn in question the validity of the said ordinance, or of the acts of the legislature that may be passed to give it effect, or of the said laws of the United States, no appeal shall be allowed to the Supreme Court of the United States, nor shall any copy of the record be permitted or allowed for that purpose, and that any person attempting to take such appeal shall be punished as for contempt of court; and . . .

Whereas the said ordinance prescribes to the people of South Carolina a course of conduct in direct violation of their duty as citizens of the United States, contrary to the laws of their country, subversive of its Constitution, and having for its object the destruction of the Union—

To preserve this bond of our political existence from destruction, to maintain inviolate this state of national honor and prosperity, and to justify the confidence my fellow-citizens have reposed in me, I, Andrew Jackson, President of the United States, have thought proper to issue this my proclamation, stating my views of the Constitution and laws applicable to the measures adopted by the convention of South Carolina and to the reasons they have put forth to sustain them, declaring the course which duty will require me to pursue, and, appealing to the understanding and patriotism of the people, warn them of the consequences that must inevitably result from an observance of the dictates of the convention. . . .

The ordinance is founded, not on the indefeasible right of resisting acts which are plainly unconstitutional and too oppressive to be endured, but on the strange position that any one State may not only declare an act of Congress void, but prohibit its execution; that they may do this consistently with the Constitution; that the true construction of that instrument permits a State to retain its place in the Union and yet be bound by no other of its laws than those it may choose to consider as constitutional. It is true, they add, that to justify this abrogation of a law it must be palpably contrary to the Constitution; but it is evident that to give the right of resisting laws of that description, coupled with the uncontrolled right to decide what laws deserve that character, is to give the power of resisting all laws; for as by the theory there is no appeal, the reasons alleged by the State, good or bad, must prevail. If it should be said that public opinion is a sufficient check against the abuse of this power, it may be asked why it is not deemed a sufficient guard against the passage of an unconstitutional act by Congress? There is, however, a restraint in this last case which makes the assumed power of a State more indefensible, and which does not exist in the other. There are two appeals from an unconstitutional act passed by Congress—one to the judiciary, the other to the people and the States. There is no appeal from the State decision in theory, and the practical illustration shows that the courts are closed against an application to review it, both judges and jurors being sworn to decide in its favor. But reasoning on this subject is superfluous when our social compact, in express terms, declares that the laws of the United States, its Constitution, and treaties made under it are the supreme law of the land, and, for greater caution, adds "that the judges in every State shall be bound thereby, anything in the constitution or laws of any State to the contrary notwithstanding." And it may be asserted without fear of refutation that no federative government could exist without a similar provision. Look for a moment to the consequence. If South Carolina considers the revenue laws unconstitutional and has a right to prevent their execution in the port of Charleston, there would be a clear constitutional objection to their collection in every other port; and no revenue could be collected anywhere, for all imposts must be equal. It is no answer to repeat that an unconstitutional law is no law so long as the question of its legality is to be decided by the State itself, for every law operating injuriously upon any local interest will be perhaps thought, and certainly represented, as unconstitutional, and, as has been shown, there is no appeal.

If this doctrine had been established at an earlier day, the Union would have been dissolved in its infancy. The excise law in Pennsylvania, the embargo and nonintercourse law in the Eastern States, the carriage tax in Virginia, were all deemed unconstitutional, and were more unequal in their operation than any of the laws now complained of; but, fortunately, none of those States discovered that they had the right now claimed by South Carolina. The war into which we were forced to support the dignity of the nation and the rights of our citizens might have ended in defeat and disgrace, instead of victory and honor, if the States who supposed it a ruinous and unconstitutional measure had thought they possessed the right of nullifying the act by which it was declared and denying supplies for its prosecution. Hardly and unequally as those measures bore upon several members of the Union, to the legislatures of none did this efficient and peaceable remedy, as it is called, suggest itself. The discovery of this important feature in our Constitution was reserved to the present day. To the statesmen of South Carolina belongs the invention, and upon the citizens of that State will unfortunately fall the evils of reducing it to practice.

If the doctrine of a State veto upon the laws of the Union carries with it internal evidence of its impracticable absurdity, our constitutional history will also afford abundant proof that it would have been repudiated with indignation had it been proposed to form a feature in our Government.

Our present Constitution was formed . . . in vain if this fatal doctrine prevails. It was formed for important objects that are announced in the preamble, made in the name and by the authority of the people of the United States, whose delegates framed and whose conventions approved it. The most important among these objects—that which is placed first in rank, on which all the others rest—is *"to form a more perfect union."* Now, is it possible that even if there were no express provision giving supremacy to the Constitution and laws of the United States over those of the States, can it be conceived that an instrument made for the purpose of *"forming a more perfect union"* than that of the Confederation could be so constructed by the assembled wisdom of our country as to substitute for that Confederation a form of government dependent for its existence on the local interest, the party spirit, of a State, or of a prevailing faction in a State? Every man of plain, unsophisticated understanding who hears the question will give such an answer as will preserve the Union. Metaphysical subtlety, in pursuit of an impracticable theory, could alone have devised one that is calculated to destroy it.

I consider, then, the power to annul a law of the United States, assumed by one State, *incompatible with the existence of the Union, contradicted expressly by the letter of the Constitution, unauthorized by its spirit, inconsistent with every principle on which it was founded, and destructive of the great object for which it was formed.*

After this general view of the leading principle, we must examine the particular application of it which is made in the ordinance.

The preamble rests its justification on these grounds: It assumes as a fact that the obnoxious laws, although they purport to be laws for raising revenue, were in reality intended for the protection of manufactures, which purpose it asserts to be unconstitutional; that the operation of these laws is unequal; that the amount raised by them is greater than is required by the wants of the Government; and, finally, that the proceeds are to be applied to objects unauthorized by the Constitution. These are the only causes alleged to justify an open opposition to the laws of the country and a threat of seceding from the Union if any attempt should be made to enforce them. The first virtually acknowledges that the law in question was passed under a power expressly given by the Constitution to lay and collect imposts; but its constitutionality is drawn in question from the *motives* of those who passed it. However apparent this purpose may be in the present case, nothing can be more dangerous than to admit the position that an unconstitutional purpose entertained by the members who assent to a law enacted under a constitutional power shall make that law void. For how is that purpose to be ascertained? Who is to make the scrutiny? How often may bad purposes be falsely imputed, in how many cases are they concealed by false professions, in how many is no declaration of motive made? Admit this doctrine, and you give to the States an uncontrolled right to decide, and every law may be annulled under this pretext. If, therefore, the absurd and dangerous doctrine should be admitted that a State may annul an unconstitutional law, or one that it deems such, it will not apply to the present case.

The next objection is that the laws in question operate unequally. This objection may be made with truth to every law that has been or can be passed. The wisdom of man never yet contrived a system of taxation that would operate with perfect equality. If the unequal operation of a law makes it unconstitutional, and if all laws of that description may be abrogated by any State for that cause, then, indeed, is the Federal Constitution unworthy of the slightest effort for its preservation. . . . Nor did the States, when they severally ratified it, do so under the impression that a veto on the laws of the United States was reserved to them or that they could exercise it by implication. Search the debates in all their conventions, examine the speeches of the most zealous opposers of Federal authority, look at the amendments that were proposed; they are all silent—not a syllable uttered, not a vote given, not a motion made to correct the explicit supremacy given to the laws of the Union over those of the States, or to show that implication, as is now contended, could defeat it. No; we have not erred. The Constitution is still the object of our reverence, the bond of our Union, our defense in danger, the source of our prosperity in peace. It shall descend, as we have received it, uncorrupted by sophistical construction, to our posterity; and the

sacrifices of local interest, of State prejudices, of personal animosities, that were made to bring it into existence, will again be patriotically offered for its support.

The two remaining objections made by the ordinance to these laws are that the sums intended to be raised by them are greater than are required and that the proceeds will be unconstitutionally employed. . . .

The ordinance, with the same knowledge of the future that characterizes a former objection, tells you that the proceeds of the tax will be unconstitutionally applied. If this could be ascertained with certainty, the objection would with more propriety be reserved for the law so applying the proceeds, but surely can not be urged against the laws levying the duty.

These are the allegations contained in the ordinance. Examine them seriously, my fellow-citizens; judge for yourselves. I appeal to you to determine whether they are so clear, so convincing, as to leave no doubt of their correctness; and even if you should come to this conclusion, how far they justify the reckless, destructive course which you are directed to pursue. Review these objections and the conclusions drawn from them once more. What are they? Every law, then, for raising revenue, according to the South Carolina ordinance, may be rightfully annulled, unless it be so framed as no law ever will or can be framed. Congress have a right to pass laws for raising revenue and each State have a right to oppose their execution—two rights directly opposed to each other; and yet is this absurdity supposed to be contained in an instrument drawn for the express purpose of avoiding collisions between the States and the General Government by an assembly of the most enlightened statesmen and purest patriots ever embodied for a similar purpose.

In vain have these sages declared that Congress shall have power to lay and collect taxes, duties, imposts, and excises; in vain have they provided that they shall have power to pass laws which shall be necessary and proper to carry those powers into execution, that those laws and that Constitution shall be the "supreme law of the land, and that the judges in every State shall be bound thereby, anything in the constitution or laws of any State to the contrary notwithstanding;" . . . if a bare majority of the voters in any one State may, on a real or supposed knowledge of the intent with which a law has been passed, declare themselves free from its operation; . . .

The Constitution declares that the judicial powers of the United States extend to cases arising under the laws of the United States, and that such laws, the Constitution, and treaties shall be paramount to the State constitutions and laws. The judiciary act prescribes the mode by which the case may be brought before a court of the United States by appeal when a State tribunal shall decide against this provision of the Constitution. The ordinance declares there shall be no appeal—makes the State law paramount to the Constitution and laws of the United States, forces judges and jurors to swear that they will disregard their provisions, and even makes it penal in a suitor to attempt relief by appeal. It further declares that it shall not be lawful for the authorities of the United States or of that State to enforce the payment of duties imposed by the revenue laws within its limits.

Here is a law of the United States, not even pretended to be unconstitutional, repealed by the authority of a small majority of the voters of a single State. Here is a provision of the Constitution which is solemnly abrogated by the same authority.

On such expositions and reasonings the ordinance grounds not only an assertion of the right to annul the laws of which it complains, but to enforce it by a threat of seceding from the Union if any attempt is made to execute them.

This right to secede is deduced from the nature of the Constitution, which, they say, is a compact between sovereign States who have preserved their whole sovereignty and therefore are subject to no superior; that because they made the compact they can break it when in their opinion it has been departed from by the other States. Fallacious as this course of reasoning is, it enlists State pride and finds advocates in the honest prejudices of those who have not studied the nature of our Government sufficiently to see the radical error on which it rests. . . .

The Constitution of the United States, then, forms a *government,* not a league; and whether it be formed by compact between the States or in any other manner, its character is the same. It is a Government in which all the people are represented, which operates directly on the people individually, not upon the States; they retained all the power they did not grant. But each State, having expressly parted with so many powers as to constitute, jointly with the other States, a single nation, can not, from that period, possess any right to secede, because such secession does not break a league, but destroys the unity of a nation; and any injury to that unity is not only a breach which would result from the contravention of a compact, but it is an offense against the whole Union. To say that any State may at pleasure secede from the Union is to say that the United States are not a nation, because it would be a solecism to contend that any part of a nation might dissolve its connection with the other parts, to their injury or ruin, without committing any offense. Secession, like any other revolutionary act, may be morally justified by the extremity of oppression; but to call it a constitutional right is confounding the meaning of terms, and can only be done through gross error or to deceive those who are willing to assert a right, but would pause before they made a revolution or incur the penalties consequent on a failure.

Because the Union was formed by a compact, it is said the parties to that compact may, when they feel themselves aggrieved, depart from it; but it is precisely because it is a compact that they can not. A compact is an agreement or binding obligation. It may by its terms have a sanction or penalty for its breach, or it may not. If it contains no sanction, it may be broken with no other consequence than moral guilt; if it have a sanction, then the breach incurs the designated or implied penalty. A league between independent nations generally has no sanction other than a moral one; or if it should contain a penalty, as there is no common superior it can not be enforced. A government, on the contrary, always has a sanction, express or implied; and in our case it is both necessarily implied and expressly given. An attempt, by force of arms, to destroy a government is an offense, by whatever means the constitutional compact may have been formed; and such government has the right by the law of self-defense to pass acts for punishing the offender, unless that right is modified, restrained, or resumed by the constitutional act. In our system, although it is modified in the case of treason, yet authority is expressly given to pass all laws necessary to carry its powers into effect, and under this grant provision has been made for punishing acts which obstruct the due administration of the laws.

It would seem superfluous to add anything to show the nature of that union which connects us, but as erroneous opinions on this subject are the foundation of doctrines the most destructive to our peace, I must give some further development to my views on this subject. . . .

The States severally have not retained their entire sovereignty. It has been shown that in becoming parts of a nation, not members of a league, they surrendered many of their essential parts of sovereignty. The right to make treaties, declare war, levy taxes, exercise exclusive judicial and legislative powers, were all of them functions of sovereign power. The States, then, for all these important purposes were no longer sovereign. . . . How, then, with all these proofs that under all changes of our position we had, for designated purposes and with defined powers, created national governments, how is it that the most perfect of those several modes of union should now be considered as a mere league that may be dissolved at pleasure? It is from an abuse of terms. Compact is used as synonymous with league, although the true term is not employed, because it would at once show the fallacy of the reasoning. It would not do to say that our Constitution was only a league, but it is labored to prove it a compact (which in one sense it is) and then to argue that as a league is a compact every compact between nations must of course be a league, and that from such an engagement every sovereign power has a right to recede. But it has been shown that in this sense the States are not sovereign, and that even if they were, and the national Constitution had been formed by compact, there would be no right in any one State to exonerate itself from its obligations.

This, then, is the position in which we stand: A small majority of the citizens of one State in the Union have elected delegates to a State convention; that convention has ordained that all the revenue laws of the United States must be repealed, or that they are no longer a member of the Union. The governor of that State has recommended to the legislature the raising of an army to carry the secession into effect, and that he may be empowered to give clearances to vessels in the name of the State. No act of violent opposition to the laws has yet been committed, but such a state of things is hourly apprehended. And it is the intent of this instrument to *proclaim*, not only that the duty imposed on me by the Constitution "to take care that the laws be faithfully executed" shall be performed to the extent of the powers already vested in me by law, or of such others as the wisdom of Congress shall devise and intrust to me for that purpose, but to warn the citizens of South Carolina who have been deluded into an opposition to the laws of the danger they will incur by obedience to the illegal and disorganizing ordinance of the convention; to exhort those who have refused to support it to persevere in their determination to uphold the Constitution and laws of their country; and to point out to all the perilous situation into which the good people of that State have been led, and that the course they are urged to pursue is one of ruin and disgrace to the very State whose rights they affect to support. . . .

If your leaders could succeed in establishing a separation, what would be your situation? Are you united at home? Are you free from the apprehension of civil discord, with all its fearful consequences? Do our neighboring republics, every day suffering some new revolution or contending with some new insurrection, do they excite your envy? But the dictates of a high duty oblige me solemnly to announce that you can not succeed. The laws of the United States must be executed. I have no discretionary power on the subject; my duty is emphatically pronounced in the Constitution. Those who told you that you might peaceably prevent their execution deceived you; they could not have been deceived themselves. They know that a forcible opposition could alone prevent the execution of the laws, and they know that such opposition must be repelled. Their object is disunion. But be not deceived by names. Disunion by armed force is *treason.* Are you really ready to incur its guilt? If you are, on the heads of the instigators of the act be the dreadful consequences; on their heads be the dishonor, but on yours may fall the punishment. On your unhappy State will inevitably fall all the evils of the conflict you force upon the Government of your country. It can not accede to the mad project of disunion, of which you would be the first victims. Its First Magistrate can not, if he would, avoid the performance of his duty. The consequence must be fearful for you, distressing to your fellow-citizens here and to the friends of good government throughout the world. Its enemies have beheld our prosperity with a vexation they could not conceal; it was a standing refutation of their slavish doctrines, and they will point to our discord with the triumph of malignant joy. It is yet in your power to disappoint them. . . .

Fellow-citizens of the United States, the threat of unhallowed disunion, the names of those once respected by whom it is uttered, the array of military force to support it, denote the approach of a crisis in our affairs on which the continuance of our unexampled prosperity, our political existence, and perhaps that of all free governments may depend. The conjuncture demanded a free, a full, and explicit enunciation, not only of my intentions, but of my principles of action; and as the claim was asserted of a right by a State to annul the laws of the Union, and even to secede from it at pleasure, a frank exposition of my opinions in relation to the origin and form of our Government and the construction I give to the instrument by which it was created seemed to be proper.

Having the fullest confidence in the justness of the legal and constitutional opinion of my duties which has been expressed, I rely with equal confidence on your undivided support in my determination to execute the laws, to preserve the Union by all constitutional means, to arrest, if possible, by moderate and firm measures the necessity of a recourse to force; and if it be the will of Heaven that the recurrence of its primeval curse on man for the shedding of a brother's blood should fall upon our land, that it be not called down by any offensive act on the part of the United States.

Fellow-citizens, the momentous case is before you. 'On your undivided support of your Government depends the decision of the great question it involves—whether your sacred Union will be preserved and the blessing it secures to us as one people shall be perpetuated. No one can doubt that the unanimity with which that decision will be expressed will be such as to inspire new confidence in republican institutions, and that the prudence, the wisdom, and the courage which it will bring to their defense will transmit them unimpaired and invigorated to our children.

May the Great Ruler of Nations grant that the signal blessings with which He has favored ours may not, by the madness of party or personal ambition, be disregarded and lost; and may His wise providence bring those who have produced this crisis to see the folly before they feel the misery of civil strife, and inspire a returning veneration for that Union which, if we may dare to penetrate His designs, He has chosen as the only means of attaining the high destinies to which we may reasonably aspire.

ANDREW JACKSON.

145. SOUTH CAROLINA'S REPLY TO JACKSON'S PROCLAMATION
December 20, 1832
(*Statutes at Large of South Carolina* Vol. I, p. 356-7)

The Committee on federal relations, to which was referred the proclamation of the President of the United States, has had it under consideration, and recommends the adoption of the following resolutions:

Resolved, That the power vested by the Constitution and laws in the President of the United States, to issue his proclamation, does not authorize him in that mode, to interfere whenever he may think fit, in the affairs of the respective states, or that he should use it as a means of promulgating executive expositions of the Constitution, with the sanction of force thus superseding the action of other departments of the general government.

Resolved, That it is not competent to the

President of the United States, to order by proclamation the constituted authorities of a state to repeal their legislation, and that the late attempt of the President to do so is unconstitutional, and manifests a disposition to arrogate and exercise a power utterly destructive of liberty.

Resolved, That the opinions of the President, in regard to the rights of the States, are erroneous and dangerous, leading not only to the establishment of a consolidated government in the stead of our free confederacy, but to the concentration of all powers in the chief executive.

Resolved, That the proclamation of the President is the more extraordinary, that he had silently, and as it is supposed, with entire approbation, witnessed our sister state of Georgia avow, act upon, and carry into effect, even to the taking of life, principles identical with those now denounced by him in South Carolina.

Resolved, That each state of the Union has the right, whenever it may deem such a course necessary for the preservation of its liberties or vital interests, to secede peaceably from the Union, and that there is no constitutional power in the general government, much less in the executive department, of that government, to retain by force such state in the Union.

Resolved, That the primary and paramount allegiance of the citizens of this state, native or adopted, is of right due to this state.

Resolved, That the declaration of the President of the United States in his said proclamation, of his personal feelings and relations towards the State of South Carolina, is rather an appeal to the loyalty of subjects, than to the patriotism of citizens, and is a blending of official and individual character, heretofore unknown in our state papers, and revolting to our conception of political propriety.

Resolved, That the undisguised indulgence of personal hostility in the said proclamation would be unworthy of the animadversion of this legislature, but for the seldom and official form of the instrument which is made its vehicle.

Resolved, That the principles, doctrines and purposes, contained in the said proclamation are inconsistent with any just idea of a limited government, and subversive of the rights of the states and liberties of the people, and if submitted to in silence would lay a broad foundation for the establishment of monarchy.

Resolved, That while this legislature has witnessed with sorrow such a relaxation of the spirit of our institutions, that a President of the United States dare venture upon this high handed measure, it regards with indignation the menaces which are directed against it, and the concentration of a standing army on our borders—that the state will repel force by force, and relying upon the blessings of God, will maintain its liberty at all hazards.

Resolved, That copies of these resolutions be sent to our members in Congress, to be laid before that body.

146. NULLIFICATION OF THE FORCE BILL
March 18, 1833

(Statutes at Large of South Carolina, Vol. I, p. 400–401)

AN ORDINANCE
To Nullify an Act of the Congress of the United States, entitled "An Act further to provide for the Collection of Duties on Imports," commonly called the Force Bill.

We, the People of the State of South Carolina in Convention assembled, do *Declare and Ordain,* that the Act of the Congress of the United States, entitled "An Act further to provide for the collection of duties on imports," approved the second day of March, 1833, is unauthorized by the Constitution of the United States, subversive of that Constitution, and destructive of public liberty; and that the same is, and shall be deemed, null and void, within the limits of this State; and it shall be the duty of the Legislature, at such time as they may deem expedient, to adopt such measures and pass such acts as may be necessary to prevent the enforcement thereof, and to inflict proper penalties on any person who shall do any act in execution or enforcement of the same within the limits of this State.

We do further Declare and Ordain, That the allegiance of the citizens of this State, while they continue such, is due to the said State; and that obedience only, and not allegiance, is due by them to any other power or authority, to whom a control over them has been, or may be delegated by the State; and the General Assembly of the said State is hereby empowered, from time to time, when they may deem it proper, to provide for the administration to the citizens and officers of the State, or such of the said officers as they may think fit, of suitable oaths or affirmations, binding them to the observance of such allegiance; and abjuring all other allegiance; and, also, to define what shall amount to a violation of their allegiance, and to provide the proper punishment for such violation.

147. JACKSON'S VETO OF THE BANK BILL
July 10, 1832
(Richardson, ed. *Messages and Papers,* Vol. II, p. 576 ff.)

The Bill for the recharter of the Second Bank passed the Senate, June 11, and the House, July 3, 1832, with amendments in which the Senate concurred. The attempt to pass the bill over Jackson's veto failed. The veto of the recharter of the bank became the principal issue of the presidential campaign. Particularly interesting is Jackson's rejection of the finality or binding character of the opinion of the Supreme Court on a question of constitutionality. For background see, R. C. H. Catterall, *The Second Bank of the United States;* W. MacDonald, *Jacksonian Democracy,* ch. vii; W. L. Royall, *Andrew Jackson and the Bank;* J. S. Bassett, *Andrew Jackson,* Vol. II, chs. xxvii–xxviii; D. R. Dewey, *Financial History,* ch. ix.

WASHINGTON, *July 10, 1832.*
To the Senate:
The bill "to modify and continue" the act entitled "An act to incorporate the subscribers to the Bank of the United States" was presented to me on the 4th July instant. Having . . . come to the conclusion that it ought not to become a law, I herewith return it to the Senate, in which it originated, with my objections.

A bank of the United States is in many respects convenient for the Government and useful to the people. Entertaining this opinion, and deeply impressed with the belief that some of the powers and privileges possessed by the existing bank are unauthorized by the Constitution, subversive of the rights of the States, and dangerous to the liberties of the people, I felt it my duty at an early period of my Administration to call the attention of Congress to the practicability of organizing an institution combining all its advantages and obviating these objections. I sincerely regret that in the act before me I can perceive none of those modifications of the bank charter which are necessary, in my opinion, to make it compatible with justice, with sound policy, or with the Constitution of our country.

The present corporate body . . . enjoys an exclusive privilege of banking under the authority of the General Government, a monopoly of its favor and support, and, as a necessary consequence, almost a monopoly of the foreign and domestic exchange. The powers, privileges, and favors bestowed upon it in the original charter, by increasing the value of the stock far above its par value, operated as a gratuity of many millions to the stockholders. . . .

The act before me proposes another gratuity to the holders of the same stock, . . . On all hands it is conceded that its passage will increase at least 20 or 30 per cent more the market price of the stock, subject to the payment of the annuity of $200,000 per year secured by the act, thus adding in a moment one-fourth to its par value. It is not our own citizens only who are to receive the bounty of our Government. More than eight millions of the stock of this bank are held by foreigners. By this act the American Republic proposes virtually to make them a present of some millions of dollars. For these gratuities to foreigners and to some of our own opulent citizens the act secures no equivalent whatever. . . .

Every monopoly and all exclusive privileges are granted at the expense of the public, which ought to receive a fair equivalent. The many millions which this act proposes to bestow on the stockholders of the existing bank must come directly or indirectly out of the earnings of the American people. It is due to them, therefore, if their Government sell monopolies and exclusive privileges, that they should at least exact for them as much as they are worth in open market. The value of the monopoly in this case may be correctly ascertained. The twenty-eight millions of stock would probably be at an advance of 50 per cent, and command in market at least $42,000,000, subject to the payment of the present bonus. The present value of the monopoly, therefore, is $17,000,000, and this the act proposes to sell for three millions, payable in fifteen annual installments of $200,000 each.

It is not conceivable how the present stockholders can have any claim to the special favor of the Government. The present corporation has enjoyed its monopoly during the period stipulated in the original contract. If we must have such a corporation, why should not the Government sell out the whole stock and thus secure to the people the full market value of the privileges granted? Why should not Congress create and sell twenty-eight millions of stock, incorporating the purchasers with all the powers and privileges secured in this act and putting the premium upon the sales into the Treasury? . . .

The modifications of the existing charter proposed by this act are not such, in my view, as make it consistent with the rights of the States or the liberties of the people. The qualification of the right of the bank to hold real estate, the limitation of its power to establish branches, and the power reserved to Congress to forbid the circulation of small notes are restrictions comparatively of little value or importance. All the objectionable principles of the existing corporation, and most of its odious features, are retained without alleviation. . . .

Is there no danger to our liberty and independence in a bank that in its nature has so little to bind it to our country? The president of the bank has told us that most of the State banks exist by its forbearance. Should its influence become concentered, as it may under the operation of such an act as this, in the hands of a self-elected directory whose interests are identified with those of the foreign stockholders, will there not be cause to tremble for the purity of our elections in peace and for the independence of our country in war? Their power would be great whenever they might choose to exert it; but if this monopoly were regularly renewed every fifteen or twenty years on terms proposed by themselves, they might seldom in peace put forth their strength to influence elections or control the affairs of the nation. But if any private citizen or public functionary should interpose to curtail its powers or prevent a renewal of its privileges, it can not be doubted that he would be made to feel its influence. . . .

If we must have a bank with private stockholders, every consideration of sound policy and every impulse of American feeling admonishes that it should be *purely American*. Its stockholders should be composed exclusively of our own citizens, who at least ought to be friendly to our Government and willing to support it in times of difficulty and danger. . . . To a bank exclusively of American stockholders, possessing the powers and privileges granted by this act, subscriptions for $200,000,000 could be readily obtained. . . .

It is maintained by the advocates of the bank that its constitutionality in all its features ought to be considered as settled by precedent and by the decision of the Supreme Court. To this conclusion I can not assent. Mere precedent is a dangerous source of authority, and should not be regarded as deciding questions of constitutional power except where the acquiescence of the people and the States can be considered as well settled. So far from this being the case on this subject, an argument against the bank might be based on precedent. One Congress, in 1791, decided in favor of a bank; another, in 1811, decided against it. One Congress, in 1815, decided against a bank; another, in 1816, decided in its favor. Prior to the present Congress, therefore, the precedents drawn from that source were equal. If we resort to the States, the expressions of legislative, judicial, and executive opinions against the bank have been probably to those in its favor as 4 to 1. . . .

If the opinion of the Supreme Court covered the whole ground of this act, it ought not to control the coördinate authorities of this Government. The Congress, the Executive, and the Court must each for itself be guided by its own opinion of the Constitution. Each public officer who takes an oath to support the Constitution swears that he will support it as he understands it, and not as it is understood by others. It is as much the duty of the House of Representatives, of the Senate, and of the President to decide upon the constitutionality of any bill or resolution which may be presented to them for passage or approval as it is of the supreme judges when it may be brought before them for judicial decision. The opinion of the judges has no more authority over Congress than the opinion of Congress has over the judges, and on that point the President is independent of both. The authority of the Supreme Court must not, therefore, be permitted to control the Congress or the Executive when acting in their legislative capacities, but to have only such influence as the force of their reasoning may deserve.

But in the case relied upon the Supreme Court have not decided that all the features of this corporation are compatible with the Constitution. It is true that the court have said that the law incorporating the bank is a constitutional exercise of power by Congress; but taking into view the whole opinion of the court and the reasoning by which they have come to that conclusion, I understand them to have decided that inasmuch as a bank is an appropriate means for carrying into effect the enumerated powers of the General Government, therefore the law incorporating it is in accordance with that provision of the Constitution which declares that Congress shall have power "to make all laws which shall be necessary and proper for carrying those powers into execution." Having satisfied themselves that the word *"necessary"* in the Constitution means *"needful,"* *"requisite,"* *"essential,"* *"conducive to,"* and that "a bank" is a convenient, a useful, and essential instrument in the prosecution of the Government's "fiscal operations," they conclude that to "use one must be within the discretion of Congress" and that "the act to incorporate the Bank of the United States is a law made in pursuance of the Constitution;" "but," say they, *"where the law is not prohibited and is really calculated to effect any of the objects intrusted to the Govern-*

ment, to undertake here to inquire into the degree of its necessity would be to pass the line which circumscribes the judicial department and to tread on legislative ground."

The principle here affirmed is that the "degree of its necessity," involving all the details of a banking institution, is a question exclusively for legislative consideration. A bank is constitutional, but it is the province of the Legislature to determine whether this or that particular power, privilege, or exemption is "necessary and proper" to enable the bank to discharge its duties to the Government, and from their decision there is no appeal to the courts of justice. Under the decision of the Supreme Court, therefore, it is the exclusive province of Congress and the President to decide whether the particular features of this act are *necessary* and *proper* in order to enable the bank to perform conveniently and efficiently the public duties assigned to it as a fiscal agent, and therefore constitutional, or *unnecessary* and *improper,* and therefore unconstitutional.

Without commenting on the general principle affirmed by the Supreme Court, let us examine the details of this act in accordance with the rule of legislative action which they have laid down. It will be found that many of the powers and privileges conferred on it can not be supposed necessary for the purpose for which it is proposed to be created, and are not, therefore, means necessary to attain the end in view, and consequently not justified by the Constitution. . . .

The Constitution declares that "the Congress shall have power to exercise exclusive legislation in all cases whatsoever" over the District of Columbia. Its constitutional power, therefore, to establish banks in the district of Columbia and increase their capital at will is unlimited and uncontrollable by any other power than that which gave authority to the Constitution. Yet this act declares that Congress shall *not* increase the capital of existing banks, nor create other banks with capitals exceeding in the whole $6,000,000. The Constitution declares that Congress *shall* have power to exercise exclusive legislation over this District *"in all cases whatsoever,"* and this act declares they shall not. Which is the supreme law of the land? This provision can not be *"necessary"* or *"proper"* or *constitutional* unless the absurdity be admitted that whenever it be "necessary and proper" in the opinion of Congress they have a right to barter away one portion of the powers vested in them by the Constitution as a means of executing the rest. . . .

The Government is the only *"proper"* judge where its agents should reside and keep their offices, because it best knows where their presence will be *"necessary."* It can not, therefore, be *"necessary"* or *"proper"* to authorize the bank to locate branches where it pleases to perform the public service, without consulting the Government, and contrary to its will. The principle laid down by the Supreme Court concedes that Congress can not establish a bank for purposes of private speculation and gain, but only as a means of executing the delegated powers of the General Government. By the same principle a branch bank can not constitutionally be established for other than public purposes. The power which this act gives to establish two branches in any State, without the injunction or request of the Government and for other than public purposes, is not *"necessary"* to the due *execution* of the powers delegated to Congress. . . .

The principle is conceded that the States can not rightfully tax the operations of the General Government. They can not tax the money of the Government deposited in the State banks, nor the agency of those banks in remitting it; but will any man maintain that their mere selection to perform this public service for the General Government would exempt the State banks and their ordinary business from State taxation? Had the United States, instead of establishing a bank at Philadelphia, employed a private banker to keep and transmit their funds, would it have deprived Pennsylvania of the right to tax his bank and his usual banking operations? . . .

It can not be *necessary* to the character of the bank as a fiscal agent of the Government that its private business should be exempted from that taxation to which all the State banks are liable, nor can I conceive it *"proper"* that the substantive and most essential powers reserved by the States shall be thus attacked and annihilated as a means of executing the powers delegated to the General Government. It may be safely assumed that none of those sages who had an agency in forming or adopting our Constitu-

tion ever imagined that any portion of the taxing power of the States not prohibited to them nor delegated to Congress was to be swept away and annihilated as a means of executing certain powers delegated to Congress.

If our power over means is so absolute that the Supreme Court will not call in question the constitutionality of an act of Congress the subject of which "is not prohibited, and is really calculated to effect any of the objects intrusted to the Government," although, as in the case before me, it takes away powers expressly granted to Congress and rights scrupulously reserved to the States, it becomes us to proceed in our legislation with the utmost caution. Though not directly, our own powers and the rights of the States may be indirectly legislated away in the use of means to execute substantive powers. We may not enact that Congress shall not have the power of exclusive legislation over the District of Columbia, but we may pledge the faith of the United States that as a means of executing other powers it shall not be exercised for twenty years or forever. We may not pass an act prohibiting the States to tax the banking business carried on within their limits, but we may, as a means of executing our powers over other objects, place that business in the hands of our agents and then declare it exempt from State taxation in their hands. Thus may our own powers and the rights of the States, which we can not directly curtail or invade, be frittered away and extinguished in the use of means employed by us to execute other powers. That a bank of the United States, competent to all the duties which may be required by the Government, might be so organized as not to infringe on our own delegated powers or the reserved rights of the States I do not entertain a doubt. . . .

Under such circumstances the bank comes forward and asks a renewal of its charter for a term of fifteen years upon conditions which not only operate as a gratuity to the stockholders of many millions of dollars, but will sanction any abuses and legalize any encroachments. . . .

The bank is professedly established as an agent of the executive branch of the Government, and its constitutionality is maintained on that ground. Neither upon the propriety of present action nor upon the propriety of present action was the Executive consulted. It has had no opportunity to say that it neither needs nor wants an agent clothed with such powers and favored by such exemptions. There is nothing in its legitimate functions which makes it necessary or proper. Whatever interest or influence, whether public or private, has given birth to this act, it can not be found either in the wishes or necessities of the executive department, by which present action is deemed premature, and the powers conferred upon its agent not only unnecessary, but dangerous to the Government and country. . . .

There are no necessary evils in government. Its evils exist only in its abuses. If it would confine itself to equal protection, and, as Heaven does its rains, shower its favors alike on the high and the low, the rich and the poor, it would be an unqualified blessing. In the act before me there seems to be a wide and unnecessary departure from these just principles. . . .

Experience should teach us wisdom. Most of the difficulties our Government now encounters and most of the dangers which impend over our Union have sprung from an abandonment of the legitimate objects of Government by our national legislation, and the adoption of such principles as are embodied in this act. Many of our rich men have not been content with equal protection and equal benefits, but have besought us to make them richer by act of Congress. By attempting to gratify their desires we have in the results of our legislation arrayed section against section, interest against interest, and man against man, in a fearful commotion which threatens to shake the foundations of our Union. It is time to pause in our career to review our principles, and if possible revive that devoted patriotism and spirit of compromise which distinguished the sages of the Revolution and the fathers of our Union.

ANDREW JACKSON.

148. THE REMOVAL OF THE PUBLIC DEPOSITS
Jackson's Paper read to the Cabinet
September 18, 1833

(Richardson, ed. *Messages and Papers*, Vol. III, p. 5 ff.)

The veto of the bill to recharter the Bank was the principal issue of the campaign of 1832. Jackson looked upon his re-election as a public endorsement of his policy, and proceeded to the next step of his "war on the Bank" by withdrawing the public deposits from it. Secretary Duane refused to issue the order removing the deposits, and was forced to give up his office to R. B. Taney, who, on September 26, issued the order for removal and designated the Girard Bank of Philadelphia as a place of deposit. Jackson's paper read to the Cabinet and drafted by Taney, is, according to Professor MacDonald, "the most explicit statement we have of Jackson's theory regarding the status and function of a cabinet officer in our constitutional system." See, W. MacDonald, *Jacksonian Democracy*, ch. xiii; J. S. Bassett, *Andrew Jackson*. Vol. II, ch. xxix; S. Tyler, *R. B. Taney*, p. 191 ff.; D. R. Dewey, *Financial History*, p. 203 ff.

Having carefully and anxiously considered all the facts and arguments which have been submitted to him relative to a removal of the public deposits from the Bank of the United States, the President deems it his duty to communicate in this manner to his Cabinet the final conclusions of his own mind and the reasons on which they are founded, in order to put them in durable form and to prevent misconceptions. . . .

Of all the substitutes for the present bank which have been suggested, none seems to have united any considerable portion of the public in its favor. Most of them are liable to the same constitutional objections for which the present bank has been condemned, and perhaps to all there are strong objections on the score of expediency. . . .

On the whole, the President considers it as conclusively settled that the charter of the Bank of the United States will not be renewed, and he has no reasonable ground to believe that any substitute will be established. Being bound to regulate his course by the laws as they exist, and not to anticipate the interference of the legislative power for the purpose of framing new systems, it is proper for him seasonably to consider the means by which the services rendered by the Bank of the United States are to be performed after its charter shall expire.

The existing laws declare that—

The deposits of the money of the United States in places in which the said bank and branches thereof may be established shall be made in said bank or branches thereof unless the Secretary of the Treasury shall at any time otherwise order and direct, in which case the Secretary of the Treasury shall immediately lay before Congress, if in session, and, if not, immediately after the commencement of the next session, the reasons of such order or direction.

The power of the Secretary of the Treasury over the deposits is *unqualified*. The provision that he shall report his reasons to Congress is no limitation. Had it not been inserted he would have been responsible to Congress had he made a removal for any other than good reasons, and his responsibility now ceases upon the rendition of sufficient ones to Congress. The only object of the provision is to make his reasons accessible to Congress and enable that body the more readily to judge of their soundness and purity, and thereupon to make such further provision by law as the legislative power may think proper in relation to the deposit of the public money. . . .

It is a matter of surprise that a power which in the infancy of the bank was freely asserted as one of the ordinary and familiar duties of the Secretary of the Treasury should now be gravely questioned, and attempts made to excite and alarm the public mind as if some new and unheard of power was about to be usurped by the executive branch of the Government.

It is but a little more than two and a half years to the termination of the charter of the present bank. It is considered as the decision of the country that it shall then cease to exist, and no man, the President believes, has reasonable ground for expectation that any other Bank of the United States will be created by Congress.

To the Treasury Department is intrusted the safe-keeping and faithful application of the public moneys. A plan of collection different from the present must therefore be introduced and put in complete operation before the dissolution of the present bank.

When shall it be commenced? Shall no step be taken in this essential concern until the charter expires and the Treasury finds itself without an agent, its accounts in confusion, with no depository for its funds, and the whole business of the Government deranged, or shall it be delayed until six months, or a year, or two years before the expiration of the charter? It is obvious that any new system which may be substituted in the place of the Bank of the United States could not be suddenly carried into effect on the termination of its existence without serious inconvenience to the Government and the people. Its vast amount of notes are then to be redeemed and withdrawn from circulation and its immense debt collected. These operations must be gradual, otherwise much suffering and distress will be brought upon the community.

It ought to be not a work of months only, but of years, and the President thinks it can not, with due attention to the interests of the people, be longer postponed. It is safer to begin it too soon than to delay it too long. . . .

As the President presumes that the charter to the bank is to be considered as a contract on the part of the Government, it is not now in the power of Congress to disregard its stipulations; and by the terms of that contract the public money is to be deposited in the bank during the continuance of its charter unless the Secretary of the Treasury shall otherwise direct. Unless, therefore, the Secretary of the Treasury first acts, Congress have no power over the subject, for they can not add a new clause to the charter or strike one out of it without the consent of the bank, and consequently the public money must remain in that institution to the last hour of its existence unless the Secretary of the Treasury shall remove it at an earlier day. The responsibility is thus thrown upon the executive branch of the Government of deciding how long before the expiration of the charter the public interest will require the deposits to be placed elsewhere; . . . it being the duty of one of the Executive Departments to decide in the first instance, . . . whether the public deposits shall remain in the Bank of the United States until the end of its existence or be withdrawn some time before, the President has felt himself bound to examine the question carefully . . . and in his opinion the near approach of the termination of the charter and the public considerations heretofore mentioned are of themselves amply sufficient to justify the removal of the deposits, without reference to the conduct of the bank or their safety in its keeping.

But in the conduct of the bank may be found other reasons, very imperative in their character, and which require prompt action. Developments have been made from time to time of its faithlessness as a public agent, its misapplication of public funds, its interference in elections, its efforts by the machinery of committees to deprive the Government directors of a full knowledge of its concerns, and, above all, its flagrant misconduct as recently and unexpectedly disclosed in placing all the funds of the bank, including the money of the Government, at the disposition of the president of the bank as means of operating upon public opinion and procuring a new charter, without requiring him to render a voucher for their disbursement. A brief recapitulation of the facts which justify these charges, and which have come to the knowledge of the public and the President, will, he thinks, remove every reasonable doubt as to the course which it is now the duty of the President to pursue. . . .

With these facts before him in an official report from the Government directors, the President would feel that he was not only responsible for all the abuses and corruptions the bank has committed or may commit, but almost an accomplice in a conspiracy against that Government which he has sworn honestly to administer, if he did not take every step within his constitutional and legal power likely to be efficient in putting an end to these enormities. If it be possible within the scope of human affairs to find a reason for removing the Government deposits and leaving the bank to its own resource for the means of effecting its criminal designs, we have it here. Was it expected when the moneys of the United States were directed to be placed in that bank that they would be put under the control of one man empowered to spend millions without rendering a voucher or specifying the object? Can they be considered safe with the evidence before us that tens of thousands have been spent for highly improper, if not corrupt, purposes, and that the same motive may lead to the expenditure of hundreds of thousands, and even millions, more? And can we justify ourselves to the people by longer lending to it the money and power of the Government to be employed for such purposes?

It has been alleged by some as an objection to the removal of the deposits that the bank has the power, and in that event will have the disposition, to destroy the State banks employed by the Government, and bring distress upon the country. It has been the fortune of the President to encounter dangers which were represented as equally alarming, and he has seen them vanish before resolution and energy. . . . But if the President believed the bank possessed all the power which has been attributed to it, his determination would only be rendered the more inflexible. If, indeed, this corporation now holds in its hands the happiness and prosperity of the American people, it is high time to take the alarm. If the despotism be already upon us and our only safety is in the mercy of the despot, recent developments in relation to his designs and the means he employs show how necessary it is to shake it off. The struggle can never come with less distress to the people or under more favorable auspices than at the present moment.

All doubt as to the willingness of the State banks to undertake the service of the Government to the same extent and on the same terms as it is now performed by the Bank of the United States is put to rest by the report of the agent recently employed to collect information, and from that willingness their own safety in the operation may be confidently inferred. Knowing their own resources better than they can be known by others, it is not to be supposed that they would be willing to place themselves in a situation which they can not occupy without danger of annihilation or embarrassment. . . .

From all these considerations the President thinks that the State banks ought immediately to be employed in the collection and disbursement of the public revenue, and the funds now in the Bank of the United States drawn out with all convenient dispatch. . . .

As one of the most serious objections to the Bank of the United States is the power which it concentrates, care must be taken in finding other agents for the service of the Treasury not to raise up another power equally formidable. . . .

It is the desire of the President that the control of the banks and the currency shall, as far as possible, be entirely separated from the political power of the country as well as wrested from an institution which has already attempted to subject the Government to its will. In his opinion the action of the General Government on this subject ought not to extend beyond the grant in the Constitution, which only authorizes Congress "to coin money and regulate the value thereof;" all else belongs to the States and the people, and must be regulated by public opinion and the interests of trade.

In conclusion, the President must be permitted to remark that he looks upon the pending question as of higher consideration than the mere transfer of a sum of money from one bank to another. Its decision may affect the character of our Government for ages to come. Should the bank be suffered longer to use the public moneys in the accomplishment of its purposes, with the proofs of its faithlessness and corruption before our eyes, the patriotic among our citizens will despair of success in struggling against its power, and we shall be responsible for entailing it upon our country forever. Viewing it as a question of transcendent importance, both in the principles and consequences it involves, the President could not, in justice to the responsibility which he owes to the country, refrain from pressing upon the Secretary of the Treasury his view of the considera-

tions which impel to immediate action. . . .

In the remarks he has made on this all-important question he trusts the Secretary of the Treasury will see only the frank and respectful declarations of the opinions which the President has formed on a measure of great national interest deeply affecting the character and usefulness of his Administration, and not a spirit of dictation, which the President would be as careful to avoid as ready to resist. Happy will he be if the facts now disclosed produce uniformity of opinion and unity of action among the members of the Administration.

The President again repeats that he begs his Cabinet to consider the proposed measure as his own, in the support of which he shall require no one of them to make a sacrifice of opinion or principle. Its responsibility has been assumed after the most mature deliberation and reflection as necessary to preserve the morals of the people, the freedom of the press, and the purity of the elective franchise, without which all will unite in saying that the blood and treasure expended by our forefathers in the establishment of our happy system of government will have been vain and fruitless. Under these convictions he feels that a measure so important to the American people can not be commenced too soon, and he therefore names the 1st day of October next as a period proper for the change of the deposits, or sooner, provided the necessary arrangements with the State banks can be made.

ANDREW JACKSON.

149. THE LIBERATOR, Vol. I., No. 1.
January 1, 1831

(William Lloyd Garrison, 1805–1879: the Story of his Life Told by his Children, Vol. I, p. 224 ff.)

About 1828 Garrison met Benjamin Lundy, and the following year joined with him in editing the *Genius for Universal Emancipation*. Jailed for libel, he was bailed out by the philanthropist Arthur Tappan, and shortly betook himself to Boston where, with Isaac Knapp, he issued the *Liberator*. The entrance of Garrison into the anti-slavery agitation gave that movement a particularly violent and fanatical character, and he came eventually to be regarded as the leading abolitionist in the country. On Garrison see the

biography by his children, above, and L. Swift, *William Lloyd Garrison*. A severely critical estimate is in G. H. Barnes, *The Antislavery Impulse, 1830–1844*. See also bibliography in A. B. Hart, *Slavery and Abolition*.

To the Public.

In the month of August, I issued proposals for publishing *"The Liberator"* in Washington City; but the enterprise, though hailed in different sections of the country, was palsied by public indifference. Since that time, the removal of the *Genius of Universal Emancipation* to the Seat of Government has rendered less imperious the establishment of a similar periodical in that quarter.

During my recent tour for the purpose of exciting the minds of the people by a series of discourses on the subject of slavery, every place that I visited gave fresh evidence of the fact, that a greater revolution in public sentiment was to be effected in the free states —*and particularly in New England*—than at the south. I found contempt more bitter, opposition more active, detraction more relentless, prejudice more stubborn, and apathy more frozen, than among slave owners themselves. Of course, there were individual exceptions to the contrary. This state of things afflicted, but did not dishearten me. I determined, at every hazard, to lift up the standard of emancipation in the eyes of the nation, *within sight of Bunker Hill and in the birth place of liberty.* That standard is now unfurled; and long may it float, unhurt by the spoliations of time or the missiles of a desperate foe—yea, till every chain be broken, and every bondman set free! Let Southern oppressors tremble—let their secret abettors tremble—let their Northern apologists tremble—let all the enemies of the persecuted blacks tremble.

I deem the publication of my original Prospectus unnecessary, as it has obtained a wide circulation. The principles therein inculcated will be steadily pursued in this paper, excepting that I shall not array myself as the political partisan of any man. In defending the great cause of human rights, I wish to derive the assistance of all religions and of all parties.

Assenting to the "self evident truth" maintained in the American Declaration of Independence, "that all men are created equal, and endowed by their Creator with certain inalienable rights—among which are life, liberty and the pursuit of happiness," I shall strenuously contend for the immediate enfranchisement of our slave population. In Park-Street Church, on the Fourth of July, 1829, in an address on slavery, I unreflectingly assented to the popular but pernicious doctrine of *gradual* abolition. I seize this opportunity to make a full and unequivocal recantation, and thus publicly to ask pardon of my God, of my country, and of my brethren the poor slaves, for having uttered a sentiment so full of timidity, injustice and absurdity. A similar recantation, from my pen, was published in the *Genius of Universal Emancipation* at Baltimore, in September, 1829. My conscience is now satisfied.

I am aware, that many object to the severity of my language; but is there not cause for severity? I *will be* as harsh as truth, and as uncompromising as justice. On this subject, I do not wish to think, or speak, or write, with moderation. No! No! Tell a man whose house is on fire, to give a moderate alarm; tell him to moderately rescue his wife from the hands of the ravisher; tell the mother to gradually extricate her babe from the fire into which it has fallen;—but urge me not to use moderation in a cause like the present. I am in earnest —I will not equivocate—I will not excuse— I will not retreat a single inch—*AND I WILL BE HEARD.* The apathy of the people is enough to make every statue leap from its pedestal, and to hasten the resurrection of the dead.

It is pretended, that I am retarding the cause of emancipation by the coarseness of my invective, and the precipitancy of my measures. *The charge is not true.* On this question my influence,—humble as it is,—is felt at this moment to a considerable extent, and shall be felt in coming years—not perniciously, but beneficially—not as a curse, but as a blessing; and posterity will bear testimony that I was right. I desire to thank God, that he enables me to disregard "the fear of man which bringeth a snare," and to speak his truth in its simplicity and power. . . .

William Lloyd Garrison.

150. THE AMERICAN ANTI-SLAVERY SOCIETY: CONSTITUTION
December 4, 1833

The enactment of the West Indian Emancipation bill by Parliament in 1833 precipitated the organization of abolitionist sentiment in the United States in an Anti-Slavery Society. Though there was considerable opposition to such organization at the time, the insistence of Garrison carried the day, and a convention was called to meet in Philadelphia, December 4, 1833. Only a handful of delegates met, and these were dominated by Garrison, who drew up the Declaration of Sentiments. See, *William Lloyd Garrison: The Story of His Life Told by His Children,* Vol. I; A. B. Hart, *Slavery and Abolition,* ch. xii; L. Tappan, *Arthur Tappan;* S. T. Pickard, *Life and Works of J. G. Whittier;* G. H. Barnes, *The Antislavery Impulse, 1830–1844.*

1. CONSTITUTION OF THE AMERICAN ANTI-SLAVERY SOCIETY

(Platform of the American Anti-Slavery Society and its Auxiliaries, New York, 1860, p. 3–4)

Whereas the Most High God "hath made of one blood all nations of men to dwell on all the face of the earth," and hath commanded them to love their neighbors as themselves; and whereas, our National Existence is based upon this principle, as recognized in the Declaration of Independence, "that all mankind are created equal, and that they are endowed by their Creator with certain inalienable rights, among which are life, liberty, and the pursuit of happiness"; and whereas, after the lapse of nearly sixty years, since the faith and honor of the American people were pledged to this avowal, before Almighty God and the World, nearly one-sixth part of the nation are held in bondage by their fellow-citizens; and whereas, Slavery is contrary to the principles of natural justice, of our republican form of government, and of the Christian religion, and is destructive of the prosperity of the country, while it is endangering the peace, union, and liberties of the States; and whereas, we believe it the duty and interest of the masters immediately to emancipate their slaves, and that no scheme of expatriation, either voluntary or by compulsion, can remove this great and increasing evil; and whereas, we believe that it is practicable, by appeals to the consciences, hearts, and interests of the people, to awaken a public sentiment throughout the nation that will be opposed to the continuance of Slavery in any part of the Republic, and by effecting the speedy abolition of Slavery, prevent a general convulsion; and whereas, we believe we owe it to the oppressed, to our fellow-citizens who hold slaves, to our whole country, to posterity, and to God, to do all that is

lawfully in our power to bring about the extinction of Slavery, we do hereby agree, with a prayerful reliance on the Divine aid, to form ourselves into a society, to be governed by the following Constitution:—

ART. I.—This Society shall be called the AMERICAN ANTI-SLAVERY SOCIETY.

ART. II.—The object of this Society is the entire abolition of Slavery in the United States. While it admits that each State, in which Slavery exists, has, by the Constitution of the United States, the exclusive right to *legislate* in regard to its abolition in said State, it shall aim to convince all our fellow-citizens, by arguments addressed to their understandings and consciences, that Slaveholding is a heinous crime in the sight of God, and that the duty, safety, and best interests of all concerned, require its *immediate abandonment,* without expatriation. The Society will also endeavor, in a constitutional way to influence Congress to put an end to the domestic Slave trade, and to abolish Slavery in all those portions of our common country which come under its control, especially in the District of Columbia,—and likewise to prevent the extension of it to any State that may be hereafter admitted to the Union.

ART. III.—This Society shall aim to elevate the character and condition of the people of color, by encouraging their intellectual, moral and religious improvement, and by removing public prejudice, that thus they may, according to their intellectual and moral worth, share an equality with the whites, of civil and religious privileges; but this Society will never, in any way, countenance the oppressed in vindicating their rights by resorting to physical force.

ART. IV.—Any person who consents to the principles of this Constitution, who contributes to the funds of this Society, and is not a Slaveholder, may be a member of this Society, and shall be entitled to vote at the meetings. . . .

151. SOUTH CAROLINA RESOLUTIONS ON ABOLITIONIST PROPAGANDA
December 16, 1835
(Acts and Resolutions of South Carolina, 1835, p. 26 ff.)

The Southern States met abolitionist propaganda with regulatory or prohibitory legislation; most of the states south of Virginia provided severe penalties for printing or speaking anything that might incite insurrection among the slaves, or even for arguing against the institution of slavery. Several states demanded that the Federal government close the mails to abolitionist literature: the resolutions of South Carolina are given as an example of these demands. See, A. B. Hart, *Slavery and Abolition*, ch. xvi.

1. *Resolved,* That the formation of the abolition societies, and the acts and doings of certain fanatics. calling themselves abolitionists, in the non-slaveholding states of this confederacy, are in direct violation of the obligations of the compact of the union, dissocial, and incendiary in the extreme.

2. *Resolved,* That no state having a just regard for her own peace and security can acquiesce in a state of things by which such conspiracies are engendered within the limits of a friendly state, united to her by the bonds of a common league of political association, without either surrendering or compromising her most essential rights.

3. *Resolved,* That the Legislature of South Carolina, having every confidence in the justice and friendship of the non-slaveholding states, announces to her co-states her confident expectation, and she earnestly requests that the governments of these states will promptly and effectually suppress all those associations within their respective limits, purporting to be abolition societies, and that they will make it highly penal to print, publish, and distribute newspapers, pamphlets, tracts and pictorial representations calculated and having an obvious tendency to excite the slaves of the southern states to insurrection and revolt.

4. *Resolved,* That, regarding the domestic slavery of the southern states as a subject exclusively within the control of each of the said states, we shall consider every interference, by any other state of the general government, as a direct and unlawful interference, to be resisted at once, and under every possible circumstance.

5. *Resolved,* In order that a salutary negative may be put on the mischievous and unfounded assumption of some of the abolitionists—the non-slaveholding states are requested to disclaim by legislative declaration, all right, either on the part of themselves or the government of the United States, to interfere in any manner with domestic slavery, either in the states, or in the territories where it exists.

6. *Resolved,* That we should consider the abolition of slavery in the District of Columbia, as a violation of the rights of the citizens of that District, derived from the implied conditions on which that territory was ceded to the general government, and as an usurpation to be at once resisted as nothing more than the commencement of a scheme of much more extensive and flagrant injustice.

7. *Resolved,* That the legislature of South Carolina, regards with decided approbation, the measures of security adopted by the Post Office Department of the United States, in relation to the transmission of incendiary tracts. But if this highly essential and protective policy, be counteracted by congress, and the United States mail becomes a vehicle for the transmission of the mischievous documents, with which it was recently freighted we, in this contingency, expect that the Chief Magistrate of our state, will forthwith call the legislature together, that timely measures may be taken to prevent its traversing our territory. (Resolutions of transmission.)

152. TEXAS DECLARATION OF INDEPENDENCE
March 2, 1836

(Thorpe, ed., *Federal and State Constitutions*, VI, 3528)

The Texas revolution against Mexico, simmering all through the early thirties, broke out in the fall of 1835. Early in November a "consultation" at San Filipe de Austin issued a preliminary but somewhat ambiguous declaration of independence. Early in 1836, a Mexican army under Santa Anna crossed the border and the war for independence began. The first week of March witnessed the attack on the Alamo. While Travis and his 188 men were preparing to defend the Alamo, a convention met at Washington, Texas, and drew up this Declaration of Independence. On March 16, the same convention completed a constitution modeled closely upon that of the United States. On April 21, 1836, Santa Anna was defeated at San Jacinto, and Texas had won its independence. See John H. Brown, *History of Texas*, Vol. I; G. P. Garrison, *Texas;* W. C. Binkley, *The Texas Revolution;* E. C. Barker, *Life of Stephen F. Austin;* Marquis James, *The Raven: A Biography of Sam Houston;* William R. Hogan, *The Texas Republic.*

When a government has ceased to protect the lives liberty and property of its people, from whom its legitimate powers are derived, and for the advancement of whose happiness it was instituted, and so far from being a guarantee for the enjoyment of those inestimable and inalienable rights, becomes an instrument in the hands of evil rulers for their oppression: When the Federal Republican Constitution of their country, which they have sworn to support, no longer has a substantial existence, and the whole nature of their government has been forcibly changed without their consent, from a restricted federative republic, composed of sovereign states to a consolidated central military despotism in which every interest is disregarded but that of the army and the priesthood—both the eternal enemies of civil liberty, the ever-ready minions of power, and the usual instruments of tyrants:

When, long after the spirit of the constitution has departed, moderation is at length so far lost by those in power that even the semblance of freedom is removed, and the forms, themselves, of the constitution discontinued; and so far from their petitions and remonstrances being regarded, the agents who bear them are thrown into dungeons; and mercenary armies sent forth to force a new government upon them at the point of the bayonet: When, in consequence of such acts of malfeasance and abdication, on the part of the government, anarchy prevails, and Civil Society is dissolved into its original elements. In such a crisis, the first law of nature, the right of self-preservation —the inherent and unalienable right of the people to appeal to first principles and take their political affairs into their own hands in extreme cases enjoins it as a right towards themselves and a sacred obligation to their posterity to abolish such government and create another in its stead, calculated to rescue them from impending dangers, and to secure their future welfare and happiness.

Nations, as well as individuals, are amenable for their acts to the public opinion of mankind. Statement of a part of our grievance is, therefore, submitted to an impartial world, in justification of the hazardous but unavoidable step now taken of severing our political connection with the Mexican people, and assuming an independent attitude among the nations of the earth.

The Mexican government, by its colonization laws, invited and induced the Anglo-American population of Texas to colonize its wilderness under the pledged faith of a written constitution that they should continue to enjoy that constitutional liberty and republican government to which they had been habituated in the land of their birth, the United States of America. In this expectation they have been cruelly disappointed, in as much as the Mexican nation has acquiesced in the late changes made in the government by General Antonio Lopez de Santa Anna, who, having overturned the constitution of his country, now offers as the cruel alternative either to abandon our homes, acquired by so many privations, or submit to the most intolerable of all tyranny, the combined despotism of the sword and the priesthood.

It has sacrificed our welfare to the State of Coahuila, by which our interests have been continually depressed through a jealous and partial course of legislation carried on at a far distant seat of government by a hostile majority, in an unknown tongue; and this to, notwithstanding we have petitioned in the humblest terms, for the establishment of a separate state government, and have, in accordance with the provisions of the national constitution presented to the General Congress a republican constitution which was, without just cause, contemptuously rejected.

It incarcerated in a dungeon, for a long time, one of our citizens, for no other cause but a zealous endeavor to procure the acceptance of our constitution and the establishment of a state government.

It has failed and refused to secure on a firm basis, the right of trial by jury, that palladium of civil liberty, and only safe guarantee for the life, liberty, and property of the citizen.

It has failed to establish any public system of education, although possessed of almost boundless resources (the public domain) and although it is an axiom in political science, that unless a people are educated and enlightened it is idle to expect the continuance of civil liberty, or the capacity for self-government.

It has suffered the military commandants stationed among us to exercise arbitrary acts of oppression and tyranny; thus trampling upon the most sacred rights of the citizen and rendering the military superior to the civil power.

It has dissolved by force of arms, the State Congress of Coahuila and Texas, and obliged our representatives to fly for their lives from the seat of government; thus depriving us of the fundamental political right of representation.

It has demanded the surrender of a number of our citizens and ordered military detachments to seize and carry them into the interior for trial; in contempt of the civil authorities, and in defiance of the laws and the constitution.

It has made piratical attacks upon our commerce, by commissioning foreign desperadoes, and authorizing them to seize our vessels, and convey the property of our citizens to far distant ports for confiscation.

It denies us the right of worshipping the Almighty according to the dictates of our own conscience, by the support of a national religion calculated to promote the temporal interest of its human functionaries rather than the glory of the true and living God.

It has demanded us to deliver up our arms, which are essential to our defence, the rightful property of freemen, and formidable only to tyrannical governments.

It has invaded our country by sea and by land, with intent to lay waste our territory and drive us from our homes, and has now a large mercenary army advancing to carry on against us a war of extermination.

It has, through its emissaries, incited the merciless savage, with the tomahawk and scalping knife, to massacre the inhabitants of our defenceless frontiers.

It hath been, during the whole time of our connection with it, the contemptible sport and victim of successive military revolutions, and hath continually exhibited every characteristic of a weak, corrupt, and tyrannical government.

These, and other grievances, were patiently borne by the people of Texas until they reached that point at which forbearance ceases to be a virtue. We then took up arms in defence of the national constitution. We appealed to our Mexican brethren for assistance. Our appeal has been made in vain. Though months have elapsed, no sympathetic response has yet been heard from the interior. We are, therefore, forced to the melancholy conclusion that the Mexican people have acquiesced in the destruction of their liberty and the substitution therefore of a Military Government—that they are unfit to be free and incapable of self-government.

The necessity of self-preservation, therefore, now decrees our eternal political separation.

We therefore, the delegates with plenary powers, of the people of Texas, in solemn convention assembled, appealing to a candid world for the necessities of our condition, do hereby resolve and declare that our political connection with the Mexican Nation has forever ended; and that the people of Texas do now constitute a free sovereign and independent republic, and are fully invested with all the rights and attributes which properly belong to independent nations; and conscious of the rectitude of our intentions, we fearlessly and confidently commit the issue to the decision of the Supreme Arbiter of the destinies of Nations.

RICHARD ELLIS, *President*

Test:

H. S. KIMBLE, *Secretary*

153. THE SPECIE CIRCULAR
July 11, 1836
(*American State Papers, Public Lands*, Vol. VIII, p. 910)

The distribution of government funds in "pet" banks, the distribution of the surplus, and apparent prosperity led to violent speculation in public lands in the west during the second Jackson administration. Land sales rose from $2,623,-000, in 1832 to $14,757,000 in 1835, and $24,877,000 in 1836. Payment, however, was frequently in notes of local banks based on other notes of speculators. Under these circumstances Benton drafted the specie circular which was promulgated by the Secretary of the Treasury, July 11, 1836. The result of the specie circular was to check sharply the sales of public lands and to reveal the unsoundness of many of the smaller western banks. For Jackson's explanation and defence of the specie circular see Doc. No. 154. On the specie circular, see W. MacDonald, *Jacksonian Democracy*, ch. xvi; D. R. Dewey, *Financial History of the United States*, ch. x; R. G. Wellington, *Political and Sectional Influence of the Public Lands, 1828–1842*; E. G. Bourne, *History of the Surplus Revenue of 1837*.

Circular to Receivers of Public Money, and to the Deposite Banks

TREASURY DEPARTMENT, *July* 11, 1836

In consequence of complaints which have been made of frauds, speculations, and monopolies, in the purchase of the public lands, and the aid which is said to be given to effect these objects by excessive bank credits, and dangerous if not partial facilities through bank drafts and bank deposites, and the general evil influence likely to result to the public interests, and especially the safety of the great amount of money in the Treasury, and the sound condition of the currency of the country, from the further exchange of the national domain in this manner, the President of the United States has given directions, and you are hereby instructed, after the 15th day of August next, to receive in payment of the public lands nothing except what is directed by the existing laws, viz: gold and silver, and in the proper cases, Virginia land scrip; provided that till the 15th of December next, the same indulgences heretofore extended as to the kind of money received, may be continued for any quantity of land not exceeding 320 acres to each purchaser who is an actual settler or bona fide resident in the State where the sales are made.

In order to ensure the faithful execution of these instructions, all receivers are strictly prohibited from accepting for land sold, any draft, certificate, or other evidence of money, or deposite, though for specie, unless signed by the Treasurer of the United States, in conformity to the act of April 24, 1820. . . .

The principal objects of the President in adopting this measure being to repress alleged frauds, and to withhold any countenance or facilities in the power of the Government from the monopoly of the public lands in the hands of speculators and capitalists, to the injury of the actual settlers in the new States, and of emigrants in search of new homes, as well as to discourage the ruinous extension of bank issues, and bank credits, by which those results are generally supposed to be promoted, your utmost vigilance is required, and relied on, to carry this order into complete execution.

LEVI WOODBURY.

154. JACKSON'S MESSAGE ON THE SPECIE CIRCULAR

Extract from Eighth Annual Message to Congress
December 5, 1836

(Richardson, ed. *Messages and Papers*, Vol. III, p. 249)

. . . The effects of an extension of bank credits and overissues of bank paper have been strikingly illustrated in the sales of the public lands. From the returns made by the various registers and receivers in the early part of last summer it was perceived that the receipts arising from the sales of the public lands were increasing to an unprecedented amount. In effect, however, these receipts amounted to nothing more than credits in bank. The banks lent out their notes to speculators. They were paid to the receivers and immediately returned to the banks, to be lent out again and again, being mere instruments to transfer to speculators the most valuable public land and pay the Government by a credit on the books of the banks. Those credits on the books of some of the Western banks, usually called deposits, were already greatly beyond their immediate means of payment, and were rapidly increasing. Indeed, each speculation furnished means for another; for no sooner had one individual or company paid in the notes than they were immediately lent to another for a like purpose, and the banks were extending their business and their issues so largely as to alarm considerate men and render it doubtful whether these bank credits if permitted to accumulate would ultimately be of the least value to the Government. The spirit of expansion and speculation was not confined to the deposit banks, but pervaded the whole multitude of banks throughout the Union and was giving rise to new institutions to aggravate the evil.

The safety of the public funds and the interest of the people generally required that these operations should be checked; and it became the duty of every branch of the General and State Governments to adopt all legitimate and proper means to produce that salutary effect. Under this view of my duty I directed the issuing of the order which will be laid before you by the Secretary of the Treasury, requiring payment for the public lands sold to be made in specie, with an exception until the 15th of the present month

in favor of actual settlers. This measure has produced many salutary consequences. It checked the career of the Western banks and gave them additional strength in anticipation of the pressure which has since pervaded our Eastern as well as the European commercial cities. By preventing the extension of the credit system it measurably cut off the means of speculation and retarded its progress in monopolizing the most valuable of the public lands. It has tended to save the new States from a nonresident proprietorship, one of the greatest obstacles to the advancement of a new country and the prosperity of an old one. It has tended to keep open the public lands for entry by emigrants at Government prices instead of their being compelled to purchase of speculators at double or triple prices. And it is conveying into the interior large sums in silver and gold, there to enter permanently into the currency of the country and place it on a firmer foundation. It is confidently believed that the country will find in the motives which induced that order and the happy consequences which will have ensued much to commend and nothing to condemn.

It remains for Congress if they approve the policy which dictated this order to follow it up in its various bearings. Much good, in my judgment, would be produced by prohibiting sales of the public lands except to actual settlers at a reasonable reduction of price, and to limit the quantity which shall be sold to them. Although it is believed the General Government never ought to receive anything but the constitutional currency in exchange for the public lands, that point would be of less importance if the lands were sold for immediate settlement and cultivation. Indeed, there is scarcely a mischief arising out of our present land system, including the accumulating surplus of revenues, which would not be remedied at once by a restriction on land sales to actual settlers; and it promises other advantages to the country in general and to the new States in particular which can not fail to receive the most profound consideration of Congress. . . .

155. CHARLES RIVER BRIDGE v. WARREN BRIDGE
11 Peters, 420
1837

Error to the supreme court of Massachusetts. By act of 1785 the legislature of Massachusetts granted to the Charles River Bridge Company the right to build and maintain a toll bridge over the Charles River. The bridge was opened in 1786, and in 1792 the charter was extended to a period of seventy years. The charter was not, however, exclusive. In 1828 the legislature incorporated the Warren Bridge Company for the purpose of erecting a competing bridge only a few rods from the Charles River Bridge. The Warren Bridge was to be surrendered to the State as soon as the cost of construction should be recovered. The Charles River Bridge Company sued for an injunction on the ground that the construction of a competing bridge constituted an impairment of contract. The question before the court was whether the original grant should be so construed as to constitute an exclusive grant. The decision, Chief Justice Taney's first constitutional opinion, was of utmost importance in establishing the principle that legislative grants are to be construed narrowly in favor of the State, and that any ambiguity in a grant must operate against the corporation and in favor of the public. This decision modified the significance of the decision of the court in the Dartmouth College Case, and marked what some students have regarded as a retreat from the advanced position taken by the Court under Marshall. See, Warren, *Supreme Court,* (1928 ed.) Vol. II, p. 21 ff.; Boudin, *Government by Judiciary,* Vol. I, p. 385 ff.; S. Tyler, *Memoir of Roger B. Taney;* B. C. Steiner, *Life of R. B. Taney;* G. W. Biddle, "Constitutional History of the United States as Influenced by Chief-Justice Taney" in *Constitutional History of the United States as seen in the Development of American Law.*

TANEY, C. J. . . . Borrowing, as we have done, our system of jurisprudence from the English law . . . it would present a singular spectacle, if, while the courts in England are restraining, within the strictest limits, the spirit of monopoly, and exclusive privileges in nature of monopolies, and confining corporations to the privileges plainly given to them in their charter, the courts of this country should be found enlarging these privileges by implication; and construing a statute more unfavorably to the public, and to the rights of the community, than would be done in a like case in an English court of justice.

But we are not now left to determine for the first time the rules by which public grants are to be construed in this country. The subject has already been considered in this court, and the rules of construction above stated fully established. In the case of the *United States* v. *Arredondo,* 8 Pet. 738, the leading cases upon this subject are collected together by the learned judge who delivered the opinion of the court, and the principle recognized that, in grants by the public nothing passes by implication. . . .

But the case most analogous to this, and in which the question came more directly before the court, is the case of *Providence Bank* v. *Billings,* 4 Pet. 514, which was decided in 1830. In that case it appeared that the legislature of Rhode Island had chartered a bank, in the usual form of such acts of incorporation. The charter contained no stipulation on the part of the State that it would not impose a tax on the bank, nor any reservation of the right to do so. It was silent on this point. Afterwards a law was passed imposing a tax on all banks in the State, and the right to impose this tax was resisted by the Providence Bank upon the ground that if the State could impose a tax, it might tax so heavily as to render the franchise of no value, and destroy the institution, that the charter was a contract, and that a power which may in effect destroy the charter is inconsistent with it, and is impliedly renounced in granting it. But the court said that the taxing power is of vital importance and essential to the existence of government, and that the relinquishment of such a power is never to be assumed. . . . The case now before the court is, in principle, precisely the same. It is a charter from a state; the act of incorporation is silent in relation to the contested power. The argument in favor of the proprietors of the Charles River bridge, is the same, almost in words, with that used by the Providence Bank; that is, that the power claimed by the state, if it exists, may be so used as to destroy the value of the franchise they have granted to the corporation. The argument must receive the same answer; and the fact that the power has been already exercised, so as to destroy the value of the franchise, cannot in any degree affect the principle. The existence of the power does not, and cannot, depend upon the circumstance of its having been exercised or not.

It may, perhaps, be said, that in the case of the Providence Bank, this court were speaking of the taxing power; which is of vital importance to the very existence of every government. But the object and end of all government is to promote the happiness and prosperity of the community by which it is established; and it can never be assumed, that the government intended to diminish its power of accomplishing the end for which it was created. And in a country like ours, free, active and enterprising, continually advancing in numbers and wealth, new channels of communication are daily found necessary, both for travel and trade, and are essential to the comfort, convenience and prosperity of the people. A state ought never to be presumed to surrender this power, because, like the taxing power, the whole community have an interest in preserving it undiminished. And when a corporation alleges, that a state has surrendered, for seventy years, its power of improvement and public accommodation, in a great and important line of travel, along which a vast number of its citizens must daily pass, the community have a right to insist, in the language of this court, above quoted, "that its abandonment ought not to be presumed, in a case, in which the deliberate purpose of the state to abandon it does not appear." The continued existence of a government would be of no great value, if, by implications and presumptions, it was disarmed of the powers necessary to accomplish the ends of its creation, and the functions it was designed to perform, transferred to the hands of privileged corporations. The rule of construction announced by the court, was not confined to the taxing power, nor is it so limited, in the opinion delivered. On the contrary, it was distinctly placed on the ground, that the interests of the community were concerned in preserving, undiminished, the power then in question; and whenever any power of the state is said to be surrendered or diminished, whether it be the taxing power, or any other affecting the public interest, the same principle applies, and the rule of construction must be the same. No one will question, that the interests of the great body of the people of the state, would, in this instance, be affected by the surrender of this great line of travel to a single corporation, with the right to exact toll, and exclude competition, for seventy years. While the rights of private property are sacredly guarded, we must not forget, that the community also have rights, and that the happiness and well-being of every citizen depends on their faithful preservation.

Adopting the rule of construction above stated as the settled one, we proceed to apply it to the charter of 1785 to the proprietors of the Charles River bridge. This act of incorporation is in the usual form, and the privileges such as are commonly given to corporations of that kind. It confers on them the ordinary faculties of a corporation, for the purpose of building the bridge; and establishes certain rates of toll, which the company are authorized to take. This is the whole grant. There is no exclusive privilege given to them over the waters of Charles river, above or below their bridge; no right to erect another bridge themselves, nor to prevent other persons from erecting one, no engagement from the State, that another shall not be erected; and no undertaking not to sanction competition, nor to make improvements that may diminish the amount of its income. Upon all these subjects the charter is silent; and nothing is said in it about a line of travel, so much insisted on in the argument, in which they are to have exclusive privileges. No words are used from which an intention to grant any of these rights can be inferred. If the plaintiff is entitled to them, it must be implied, simply from the nature of the grant, and cannot be inferred from the words by which the grant is made. . . .

The inquiry then is, does the charter contain such a contract on the part of the State? Is there any such stipulation to be found in that instrument? It must be admitted on all hands, that there is none—no words that even relate to another bridge, or to the diminution of their tolls, or to the line of travel. If a contract on that subject can be gathered from the charter, it must be by implication, and cannot be found in the words used. Can such an agreement be implied? The rule of construction before stated is an answer to the question. In charters of this description, no rights are taken from the public, or given to the corporation, beyond those which the words of the charter, by their natural and proper construction, purport to convey. There are no words which import such a contract as the plaintiffs in error contend for, and none can be implied; and the same answer must be given to them that was given by this court to the Providence Bank. The whole community are interested in this inquiry, and they have a right to require that the power of promoting their comfort and convenience, and of advancing the public prosperity, by providing safe, convenient, and cheap ways for the transportation of produce and the purposes of travel, shall not be construed to have been surrendered or diminished by the State, unless it shall appear by plain words that it was intended to be done. . . .

Indeed, the practice and usage of almost every State in the Union old enough to have commenced the work of internal improvement, is opposed to the doctrine contended for on the part of the plaintiffs in error. Turnpike roads have been made in succession, on the same line of travel; the later ones interfering materially with the profits of the first. These corporations have, in some instances, been utterly ruined by the introduction of newer and better modes of transportation and travelling. In some cases, railroads have rendered the turnpike roads on the same line of travel so entirely useless, that the franchise of the turnpike corporation is not worth preserving. Yet in none of these cases

have the corporations supposed that their privileges were invaded, or any contract violated on the part of the State. . . .

And what would be the fruits of this doctrine of implied contracts on the part of the States, and of property in a line of travel by a corporation, if it should now be sanctioned by this court? To what results would it lead us? If it is to be found in the charter to this bridge, the same process of reasoning must discover it, in the various acts which have been passed, within the last forty years, for turnpike companies. . . . If this court should establish the principles now contended for, what is to become of the numerous railroads established on the same line of travel with turnpike companies, and which have rendered the franchises of the turnpike corporations of no value? Let it once be understood that such charters carry with them these implied contracts, and give this unknown and undefined property in a line of travelling, and you will soon find the old turnpike corporations awakening from their sleep and calling upon this court to put down the improvements which have taken their place. The millions of property which have been invested in railroads and canals upon lines of travel which had been before occupied by turnpike corporations will be put in jeopardy. We shall be thrown back to the improvements of the last century, and obliged to stand still until the claims of the old turnpike corporations shall be satisfied, and they shall consent to permit these States to avail themselves of the lights of modern science, and to partake of the benefit of those improvements which are now adding to the wealth and prosperity, and the convenience and comfort, of every other part of the civilized world. . . .

Judgment affirmed.

STORY, J., delivered a dissenting opinion in which THOMPSON, J., concurred.

156. THE *CAROLINE* AFFAIR

Message of President Van Buren
January 8, 1838

(Richardson, ed. *Messages and Papers*, Vol. III, p. 401 ff.)

Upon the failure of the Canadian Rebellion of 1837, a number of refugees seized Navy Island in the Niagara River, and from there made attacks upon the Canadian border. On December

29, Canadian militia seized the steamer, *Caroline*, then in the service of the insurgents, but on the New York shore. This invasion of American territory led to a diplomatic controversy with Great Britain that was subsequently aggravated by the arrest in New York City of a British subject, Alexander Mc Leod, on the charge of murder in connection with the attack on the *Caroline*. The documents appended to Van Buren's message give the history of the affair. See, O. E. Tiffany "Relations of the United States to the Rebellion of 1837," *Publications* of the Buffalo Historical Society, Vol. VIII; J. B. McMaster, *History of the People of the United States*, Vol. VI, p. 434 ff.; and *British and Foreign State Papers*, Vols. XXVI, XXIX, *passim*.

WASHINGTON, *January 8, 1838.*
To the Senate and House of Representatives of the United States:

In the highly excited state of feeling on the northern frontier, occasioned by the disturbances in Canada, it was to be apprehended that causes of complaint might arise on the line dividing the United States from Her Britannic Majesty's dominions. Every precaution was therefore taken on our part authorized by the existing laws, and as the troops of the Provinces were embodied on the Canadian side it was hoped that no serious violation of the rights of the United States would be permitted to occur. I regret, however, to inform you that an outrage of a most aggravated character has been committed, accompanied by a hostile though temporary invasion of our territory, producing the strongest feelings of resentment on the part of our citizens in the neighborhood and on the whole border line, and that the excitement previously existing has been alarmingly increased. To guard against the possible recurrence of any similar act I have thought it indispensable to call out a portion of the militia, to be posted on that frontier. The documents herewith presented to Congress show the character of the outrage committed, the measures taken in consequence of its occurrence, and the necessity for resorting to them. . . .

M. VAN BUREN.

STATE OF NEW YORK, *Niagara County, ss:*
Gilman Appleby, of the city of Buffalo, being sworn, says that he left the port of Buffalo on the morning of the 29th instant in the steamboat *Caroline*, owned by William Wells, of Buffalo, and bound for Schlosser, upon the east side of the Niagara River and within the United States; that this deponent commanded the said *Caroline*, and that she was cleared from Buffalo with a view to run between said Buffalo and Schlosser, carrying passengers, freight, etc.; that this deponent caused the said *Caroline* to be landed at Black Rock on her way down, and that while at Black Rock this deponent caused the American flag to be run up, and that soon after leaving Black Rock Harbor a volley of musketry was discharged at the *Caroline* from the Canada shore, but without injury; that the said *Caroline* continued her course down the Niagara River unmolested and landed outside of certain scows or boats attached to Navy Island, where a number of passengers disembarked and, as this deponent supposes, certain articles of freight were landed; . . . that at about 6 o'clock in the evening this deponent caused the said *Caroline* to be landed at Schlosser; that the crew and officers of the *Caroline* numbered ten, and that in the course of the evening twenty-three individuals, all of whom were citizens of the United States, came on board of the *Caroline* and requested this deponent and other officers of the boat to permit them to remain on board during the night, as they were unable to get lodgings at the tavern near by; these requests were acceded to, and the persons thus coming on board retired to rest, as did also the crew and officers of the *Caroline*, except such as were stationed to watch during the night; that about midnight this deponent was informed by one of the watch that several boats filled with men were making toward the *Caroline* from the river, and this deponent immediately gave the alarm, and before he was able to reach the dock the *Caroline* was boarded by some seventy or eighty men, all of whom were armed; that they immediately commenced a warfare with muskets, swords, and cutlasses upon the defenseless crew and passengers of the *Caroline* under a fierce cry of "G—d d—n them, give them no quarters; kill every man. Fire! fire!"; that the *Caroline* was abandoned without resistance, and the only effort made by either the crew or passengers seemed to be to escape slaughter; that this deponent narrowly escaped, having received several wounds, none of which, however, are of a

serious character; that immediately after the *Caroline* fell into the hands of the armed force who boarded her she was set on fire, cut loose from the dock, was towed into the current of the river, there abandoned, and soon after descended the Niagara Falls; that this deponent has made vigilant search after the individuals, thirty-three in number, who are known to have been on the *Caroline* at the time she was boarded, and twenty-one only are to be found, . . . the twelve individuals who are missing, this deponent has no doubt, were either murdered upon the steamboat or found a watery grave in the cataract of the Falls; and this deponent further says that immediately after the *Caroline* was got into the current of the stream and abandoned, as before stated, beacon lights were discovered upon the Canada shore near Chippewa, and after sufficient time had elapsed to enable the boats to reach that shore this deponent distinctly heard loud and vociferous cheering at that point; that this deponent has no doubt that the individuals who boarded the *Caroline* were a part of the British forces now stationed at Chippewa.

[Subscribed and sworn to before a commissioner, etc.]

TORONTO, UPPER CANADA, *January 8, 1838.*
His Excellency HENRY S. FOX,

Her Majesty's Minister, Washington. . . .

The governor of the State of New York complains of the cutting out and burning of the steamboat *Caroline* by order of Colonel McNab, commanding Her Majesty's forces at Chippewa, in the Province of Upper Canada, and of the destruction of the lives of some American citizens who were on board of the boat at the time she was attacked.

The act complained of was done under the following circumstances:

In Upper Canada, which contains a population of about 450,000 souls, the most perfect tranquillity prevailed up to the 4th day of December last, although in the adjoining Province of Lower Canada many of the French Canadian inhabitants had been in open rebellion against the Government for about a month preceding.

At no time since the treaty of peace with the United States in 1815 had Upper Canada been more undisturbed. The real causes of the insurrection in Lower Canada, namely, the national antipathy of the French inhabitants, did not in any degree apply in the upper Province, whose population, like the British and American inhabitants of Lower Canada, were wholly opposed to the revolt and anxious to render every service in their power in support of the Queen's authority. . . .

On the night of the 4th December the inhabitants of the city of Toronto were alarmed by the intelligence that about 500 persons armed with rifles were approaching the city; that they had murdered a gentleman of great respectability in the highway, and had made several persons prisoners. . . .

On the 7th of December an overwhelming force of militia went against them and dispersed them without losing a man, taking many prisoners, who were instantly by my order released and suffered to depart to their homes. The rest, with their leaders, fled; some have since surrendered themselves to justice; many have been taken, and some have escaped from the Province. . . .

After the dispersion of the armed insurgents near Toronto Mr. McKenzie, their leader, escaped in disguise to the Niagara River and crossed over to Buffalo. Reports had been spread there and elsewhere along the American frontier that Toronto had been burnt and that the rebels were completely successful, but the falsehood of these absurd rumors was well known before McKenzie arrived on the American side. . . .

Nevertheless, a number of American citizens in Buffalo and other towns on the frontier of the State of New York enlisted as soldiers, with the avowed object of invading Canada and establishing a provisional government. Public meetings were held to forward this design of invading a country with which the United States were at peace. Volunteers were called for, and arms, ammunition, and provisions were supplied by contributions openly made. All this was in direct and flagrant violation of the express laws of the United States, as well as of the law of nations.

The civil authority of Buffalo offered some slight shew of resistance to the movement, being urged to interpose by many of the most respectable citizens. But no real impediment was offered, and on the 13th of

December some hundreds of the citizens of the State of New York, as an armed body under the command of a Mr. Van Rensselaer, an American citizen, openly invaded and took possession of Navy Island, a part of Upper Canada, situate in the Niagara River.

Not believing that such an outrage would really be committed, no force whatever was assembled at the time to counteract this hostile movement.

In a very short time this lawless band obtained from some of the arsenals of the State of New York (clandestinely, as it is said) several pieces of artillery and other arms, which in broad daylight were openly transported to Navy Island without resistance from the American authorities. The people of Buffalo and the adjacent country continued to supply them with stores of various kinds, and additional men enlisted in their ranks.

In a few days their force was variously stated from 500 to 1,500, of whom a small proportion were rebels who had fled from Upper Canada. They began to intrench themselves, and threatened that they would in a short time make a landing on the Canadian side of the Niagara River. . . .

An official statement of the unfriendly proceedings at Buffalo was without delay (on the 13th December) made by me to his excellency the governor of the State of New York, to which no answer has been received. And after this open invasion of our territory, and when it became evident that nothing was effected at Buffalo for preventing the violation of neutrality, a special messenger was sent to your excellency at Washington to urge your interposition in the matter. . . . Soon after his departure this band of outlaws on Navy Island, . . . opened a fire from several pieces of ordnance upon the Canadian shore, which in this part is thickly settled, . . . They put several balls through a house in which a party of militiamen were quartered. . . . They killed a horse on which a man at the time was riding, but happily did no further mischief, though they fired also repeatedly with cannon and musketry upon our boats.

They continued daily to render their position more formidable, receiving constant supplies of men and warlike stores from the State of New York, . . . On the 28th De-

cember positive information was given to Colonel McNab by persons from Buffalo that a small steamboat called the *Caroline,* of about 50 tons burthen, had been hired by the pirates, who called themselves "patriots," and was to be employed in carrying down cannon and other stores and in transporting men and anything else that might be required between Fort Schlosser and Navy Island.

He resolved if she came down and engaged in this service to take or destroy her. She did come down agreeably to the information he received. She transported a piece of artillery and other stores to the island, and made repeated passages during the day between the island and the main shore.

In the night he sent a party of militia in boats, with orders to take or destroy her. They proceeded to execute the order. They found the *Caroline* moored to the wharf opposite to the inn at Fort Schlosser. In the inn there was a guard of armed men to protect her—part of the pirate force, or acting in their support. On her deck there was an armed party and a sentinel, who demanded the countersign.

Thus identified as she was with the force which in defiance of the law of nations and every principle of natural justice had invaded Upper Canada and made war upon its unoffending inhabitants, she was boarded, and after a resistance in which some desperate wounds were inflicted upon the assailants she was carried. If any peaceable citizens of the United States perished in the conflict, it was and is unknown to the captors, and it was and is equally unknown to them whether any such were there. . . .

No wanton injury was committed by the party who gallantly effected this service. They loosed the vessel from the wharf, and finding they could not tow her against the rapid current of the Niagara, they abandoned the effort to secure her, set her on fire, and let her drift down the stream.

The prisoners taken were a man who, it will be seen by the documents accompanying this dispatch, avowed himself to be a subject of Her Majesty, inhabiting Upper Canada, who had lately been traitorously in arms in that Province, and, having fled to' the United States, was then on board for the purpose of going to the camp at Navy Island; and a boy, who, being born in Lower

Canada, was probably residing in the United States, and who, being afraid to land from the boat in consequence of the firing kept up by the guard on the shore, was placed in one of the boats under Captain Drew and taken over to our side, from whence he was sent home the next day by the Falls ferry with money given him to bear his expenses. . . .

The exact position, then, of affairs on our frontier may be thus described:

An army of American citizens, joined to a very few traitors from Upper Canada, and under the command of a subject of the United States, has been raised and equipped in the State of New York against the laws of the United States and the treaties now subsisting, and are using artillery plundered from the arsenals of the State of New York in carrying on this piratical warfare against a friendly country.

The officers and Government of the United States and of the State of New York have attempted to arrest these proceedings and to control their citizens, but they have failed. Although this piratical assemblage are thus defying the civil authorities of both coun- tries, Upper Canada alone is the object of their hostilities. The Government of the United States has failed to enforce its authority by any means, civil or military, and the single question (if it be a question) is whether Upper Canada was bound to refrain from necessary acts of self-defense against a people whom their own Government either could not or would not control.

In perusing the message of His Excellency Governor Marcy to the legislature of the State of New York your excellency will probably feel some degree of surprise that after three weeks' continued hostility carried on by the citizens of New York against the people of Upper Canada his excellency seems to have considered himself not called upon to make this aggression the subject of remark for any other purpose than to complain of a solitary act of self-defense on the part of Her Majesty's Province of Upper Canada, to which such unprovoked hostilities have unavoidably led.

I have the honor to be, sir, your excellency's most obedient, humble servant,

F. B. HEAD.

157. PRE-EMPTION ACT OF 1841
September 4, 1841

(U. S. Statutes at Large, Vol. V, p. 453 ff.)

The occupation of the west, pushing ahead faster than the government land surveys, created a problem of a grave character. Individual settlers squatted on the public domain, and considered it a gross injustice when lands which they had cleared, cultivated, and improved were put up for public sale. To circumvent the government, settlers organized "Claims Associations", whose members were bound not to bid higher than a pre-arranged price. Congress, in 1841, recognized the rights of squatters and the force of public opinion by enacting a pre-emption law by which settlers were allowed to settle on a quarter section of unsurveyed public land with the right of purchase at the minimum price when such land was placed on sale. See, B. H. Hibbard, *History of Public Land Policies*, ch. ix; S. Sato, *History of the Land Question in the United States*, p. 148 ff.; R. G. Wellington, *Political and Sectional Influence of the Public Lands, 1828–1842*.

An Act to appropriate the proceeds of the *sales of public lands and to grant pre-emption rights.*

Sec. 8. That there shall be granted to each State . . . five hundred thousand acres of land for . . . internal improvements. *Provided*, that to each of the States which has already received grants for said purposes, there is hereby granted no more than a quantity of land which shall, together with the amount said State has already received . . . make five hundred thousand acres. . . .

Sec. 9. . . . That the net proceeds of the sale of said lands shall be faithfully applied to objects of internal improvement . . . namely, roads, railways, bridges, canals and improvement of water-courses, and draining of swamps. . . .

Sec. 10. That from and after the passage of this act, every . . . man, over the age of twenty-one years, and being a citizen of the United States, or having filed his declaration of intention to become a citizen . . . who since the first day of June, A. D. eighteen hundred and forty, has made . . . a settlement in person on the public lands to which the Indian title had been . . . extinguished, and which . . . shall have been surveyed prior thereto, and who shall inhabit and improve the same, and who . . . shall erect a dwelling thereon, . . . is hereby, authorized to enter with . . . the land office . . . by legal subdivisions, any number of acres not exceeding one hundred and sixty, or a quarter section of land, to include the residence of such claimant, upon paying to the United States the minimum price of such land, subject, however, to the following limitations and exceptions: No person shall be entitled to more than one pre-emptive right by virtue of this act; no person who is the proprietor of three hundred and twenty acres of land in any State or Territory of the United States, and no person who shall quit or abandon his residence on his own land to reside on the public land in the same State or Territory, shall acquire any right of preemption under this act; no lands included in any reservation . . . no lands reserved for the support of schools, nor the lands . . . to which the title has been or may be extin-

guished. by the United States at any time during the operation of this act; no sections of land reserved to the United States alternate to other sections granted to any of the States for the construction of any canal, railroad, or other . . . public improvement; no sections . . . included within the limits of any incorporated town; no portions of the public lands which have been selected as the site for a city or town; no parcel or lot of land actually settled and occupied for the purposes of trade and not agriculture; and no lands on which are situated any known salines or mines, shall be liable to entry under and by virtue of the provisions of this act. . . .

Sec. 11. That when two or more persons shall have settled on the same quarter section of land, the right of pre-emption shall be in him or her who made the first settlement, provided such persons shall conform to the other provisions of this act; and all questions as to the right of pre-emption arising between different settlers shall be settled by the register and receiver of the district within which the land is situated, subject to an appeal to and a revision by the Secretary of the Treasury of the United States. . . .

158. PRIGG v. THE COMMONWEALTH OF PENNSYLVANIA
16 Peters, 539
1842

Error to the Supreme Court of Pennsylvania. The facts of the case are stated in the opinion below. The decision of the Court, that Congress had exclusive power over the rendition of fugitive slaves, and that the states could not be obliged to enforce fugitive slave laws through state officers, led to a series of Personal Liberty Laws in northern states which largely nullified the Fugitive Slave Laws. See, for example, Doc. No. 182. See, Warren, *Supreme Court,* (1928 ed.) Vol. II, p. 83 ff.; A. B. Hart, *Slavery and Abolition,* ch. xix; M. G. Mc Dougall, *Fugitive Slaves, 1619–1865;* J. C. Hurd, *The Law of Freedom and Bondage,* Vol. II.

STORY, J. This is a writ of error to the Supreme Court of Pennsylvania, brought under the 25th section of the Judiciary Act of 1789, for the purpose of revising the judgement of that court, in a case involving the construction of the Constitution and laws of the United States.

The facts are briefly these: the plaintiff in error was indicted in the Court of Oyer and Terminer for York County for having, . . . taken and carried away from that county to the State of Maryland, a certain negro woman, named Margaret Morgan, with a design and intention of selling and disposing of, and keeping her as a slave or servant for life, contrary to a statute of Pennsylvania, passed on the 26th of March 1826. That statute in the first section, . . . provides, that if any person or persons shall from and after the passing of the act, by force and violence take and carry away . . . and shall by fraud and false pretense seduce . . . any negro or mulatto from any part of that Commonwealth, . . . shall on conviction thereof, be deemed guilty of a felony, and shall forfeit and pay a sum not less than five hundred, nor more than one thousand dollars; . . . and shall be confined and kept to hard labor, etc. . . .

The plaintiff in error pleaded not guilty to the indictment; and at the trial the jury found a special verdict, which, in substance, states, that the negro woman, Margaret Morgan was a slave for life, and held to labor and service . . . to a certain Margaret Ashmore, a citizen of Maryland; that the slave escaped and fled from Maryland into Pennsylvania in 1832; that the plaintiff in error . . . caused the said negro woman to be taken . . . as a fugitive from labor by a State constable under a warrant from a Pennsylvania magistrate; that the said negro woman was thereupon brought before the said magistrate who refused to take further cognizance of the case; and thereupon the plaintiff . . . did . . . carry away the said negro woman and her children out of Pennsylvania into Maryland. . . . The special verdict further finds, that one of the children was born in Pennsylvania, more than a year after the said negro woman had fled and escaped from Maryland. . . .

The question arising in the case as to the constitutionality of the statute of Pennsylvania, has been most elaborately argued at the bar. The counsel for the plaintiff have contended that the statute of Pennsylvania is unconstitutional, First, because Congress has the exclusive power of legislation upon the subject matter under the constitution of the United States, and under the act of the 12th of February 1793, which was passed in pursuance thereof; second, that if this power is not exclusive in Congress, still the concurrent power of the State Legislatures is suspended by the actual exercise of the power by Congress; and third, that if not suspended, still the statute of Pennsylvania, in all its provisions applicable to this case, is in direct collision with the act of Congress, and therefore is unconstitutional and void. The counsel for Pennsylvania maintain the negative of all these points.

Few questions which have ever come before this court involve more delicate and important considerations; and few upon which the public at large may be presumed to feel a more profound and pervading interest. . . .

(Upholds constitutionality of fugitive slave act of 1793.)

The remaining question is, whether the power of legislation upon this subject is exclusive in the national government, or concurrent in the States, until it is exercised by Congress. In our opinion it is exclusive; and we shall now proceed briefly to state our reasons for that opinion. . . .

In the first place it is material to state . . . that the right to seize and retake fugitive slaves and the duty to deliver them up, in whatever State of the Union they may be found, and of course the corresponding power of Congress to use the appropriate means to enforce the right and duty, derive their whole validity and obligation exclusively from the Constitution of the United States. . . . Under the Constitution it is recognized as an absolute and positive right and duty, pervading the whole Union with an equal and supreme force, uncontrolled and uncontrollable by State sovereignty or State legislation. It is therefore in a just sense a new and positive right, independent of comity, confined to no territorial limits, and bounded by no State institutions or policy. The natural inference deducible from this consideration certainly is, in the absence of any positive delegation of power to the State Legislatures, that it belongs to the legislative department of the national government, to which it owes its origin and establishment. It would be a strange anomaly, and forced construction, to suppose that the national government meant to rely for the due fulfillment of its own proper duties and the rights which it intended to secure upon State legislation, and not upon that of the Union. *A fortiori*, it would be more objectionable to suppose that a power, which was to be the same throughout the Union, should be confided to State sovereignty, which could not rightfully act beyond its own territorial limits.

In the next place, the nature of the provision and the objects to be attained by it, require that it should be controlled by one and the same will, and act uniformly by the same system of regulations throughout the Union. . . .

It is scarcely conceivable that the slaveholding States would have been satisfied with leaving to the legislation of the non-slaveholding States a power of regulation, in the absence of that of Congress, which would or might practically amount to a power to destroy the rights of the owner. . . . On the other hand, construe the right of legislation as exclusive in Congress, and every evil and every danger vanishes. The right and the duty are then co-extensive and uniform in remedy and operation throughout the whole Union. The owner has the same security, and the same remedial justice, and the same exemption from State regulation and control, through however many States he may pass with his fugitive slave in his possession. . . .

These are some of the reasons but by no means all upon which we hold the power of legislation on this subject to be exclusive in Congress. To guard, however, against any possible misconstruction of our views, it is proper to state that we are by no means to be understood, in any manner whatsoever to doubt or to interfere with the police power belonging to the States in virtue of their general sovereignty. That police power extends over all subjects within the territorial limits of the States, and has never been conceded to the United States. . . . But such regulations can never be permitted to interfere with or to obstruct the just rights of the owner to reclaim his slave, derived from the Constitution of the United States, or with the remedies prescribed by Congress to aid and enforce the same.

Upon these grounds we are of opinion that the act of Pennsylvania upon which this indictment is founded, is unconstitutional and void. . . .

Judgement reversed . . .

M'LEAN, J., dissenting. . . . The slave is found in a State where every man, black or white, is presumed to be free; and this State, to preserve the peace of its citizens, and its soil and jurisdiction from acts of violence, has prohibited the forcible abduction of persons of color. Does this law conflict with the Constitution? It clearly does not in its terms. . . .

No conflict can arise between the act of Congress and this State law. The conflict can only arise between the forcible acts of the master and the law of the State. The master exhibits no proof of right to the services of the slave, but seizes him and is about to remove him by force. I speak only of the force exerted on the slave. The law of the State presumes him to be free and prohibits his removal. Now, which shall give

way, the master or the State? The law of the State does in no case discharge, in the language of the Constitution, the slave from the service of his master.

It is a most important police regulation. And if the master violate it, is he not amenable? The offence consists in abduction of a person of color. And this is attempted to be justified upon the simple ground that the slave is property. That a slave is property must be admitted. The State law is not violated by the seizure of the slave by the master, for this is authorized by the act of Congress; but by removing him out of the State by force, and without proof of right, which the act does not authorize. Now, is not this an act which a State may prohibit? . . .

The important point is, shall the presumption of right set up by the master, unsustained by any proof, or the presumption which arises from the laws and institutions of the State, prevail. This is the true issue. The sovereignty of the State is on one side, and the asserted interest of the master on the other. That interest is protected by the paramount law, and a special, a summary, and an effectual mode of redress is given. But this mode is not pursued, and the remedy is taken into his own hands by the master.

The presumption of the State that the colored person is free may be erroneous in fact; and if so, there can be no difficulty in proving it. But may not the assertion of the master be erroneous also; and if so, how is his act of force to be remedied? The colored person is taken, and forcibly conveyed beyond the jurisdiction of the State. This force, not being authorized by the act of Congress nor by the Constitution, may be prohibited by the State. As the act covers the whole power in the Constitution, and carries out, by special enactments, its provisions, we are, in my judgement, bound by the act. We can no more, under such circumstances, administer a remedy under the Constitution in disregard of the act than we can exercise a commercial or other power in disregard of an act of Congress on the same subject.

This view respects the rights of the master and the rights of the State. It neither jeopards nor retards the reclamation of the slave. It removes all State action prejudicial to the rights of the master; and recognizes in the State a power to guard and protect its own jurisdiction, and the peace of its citizens. . . .

159. THE PEOPLE v. FISHER
N. Y. Reports, 14 Wend. 9
1835

This case illustrates the attitude of the Courts toward combinations of laborers organized for the purpose of securing higher wages, in the early decades of the nineteenth century. See Doc. No. 160.

SAVAGE, C. J. The legislature have given us their definition of conspiracies, and abrogated the common law on the subject. We must therefore see whether this case comes within the statute. The legislature have said, ". . . (6) *To commit any act injurious to the public health, to public morals, or to trade or commerce;* or for the perversion or obstruction of justice of the due administration of the laws—they shall be deemed guilty of a misdemeanor." And in section 9, it is declared that "no conspiracies, other than such as are enumerated in the last section, are punishable criminally." If the conspiracy charged in the indictment is an offence under this statute, it must be embraced under the sixth subdivision, and *is an act injurious to trade or commerce.* . . .

The question therefore is, is a conspiracy to raise the wages of journeymen shoemakers an act injurious to trade or commerce? The words *trade* and *commerce* are said by *Jacobs,* in his Law Dictionary, not to be synonymous; that commerce relates to dealings with foreign nations; trade, on the contrary, means mutual traffic among ourselves, or the buying, selling, or exchange of articles between members of the same community. That the raising of wages and a conspiracy, confederacy, or mutual agreement among journeymen for that purpose is a matter of public concern, and in which the public have a deep interest, there can be no doubt. That it was an indictable offence at common law is established by legal adjudications. . . . Such was the construction of the common law; but in *England* the subject has been thought sufficiently important to require the special attention of the legislature, and statutes were enacted in the reign of Edward 6th and George 3d, which subject workmen,

conspiring either to reduce the time of labor or to raise their wages, to the punishment of fine and imprisonment. I have found but few adjudications upon this subject; but *precedents,* in the absence of *adjudications* are some evidence of what the law is. Among these we find precedents at common law against journeymen for conspiring to raise their wages and lessen the time of labor, and to compel masters to pay for a whole day's work; against journeymen lamp-lighters, for conspiring to raise wages, and against journeymen curriers for the like offence; against salt makers, for conspiring to enhance the price of salt; . . . The immediate object in those cases, as in this, probably was to benefit the conspirators themselves; but if their individual benefit is to work a public injury, a conspiracy for such an object is against the spirit of the common law. . . .

Whatever disputes may exist among political economists upon the point, I think there can be no doubt, in a legal sense, but what the wages of labor compose a material portion of the value of manufactured articles. The products of mechanical labor compose a large proportion of the materials with which trade is carried on. By trade, I now understand traffic or mutual dealings between members of the same community, or internal trade. Coarse boots and shoes are made in many parts of our country; not for particular persons who are to wear them, but as an article of trade and commerce. Probably such is the case in Geneva, where this offence was committed. If journeymen bootmakers, by extravagant demands for wages, so enhance the price of boots made in *Geneva,* for instance, that boots made elsewhere, in *Auburn,* for example, can be sold cheaper, is not such an act injurious to trade? It is surely so to the trade of Geneva in that particular article, and that I apprehend is all that is necessary to bring the offence within the statute. It is important to the best interests of society that the price of labor be left to regulate itself, or rather be limited by the demand for it. Combinations and confederacies to *enhance* or *reduce* the prices of labor, or of any articles of trade or commerce, are injurious. They may be oppressive, by compelling the public to give more for an article of necessity or of convenience than it is worth; or on the other hand, of compelling the labor of the mechanic for less than its value. Without any officious and improper interference of the subject, the price of labor or the wages of mechanics will be regulated by the demand for the manufactured article, and the value of that which is paid for it; but the right does not exist either to enhance the price of the article, or the wages of the mechanic, by any forced and artificial means. The man who owns an article of trade or commerce is not obliged to sell it for any particular price, nor is the mechanic obliged by law to labor for any particular price. He may say that he will not make coarse boots for less than one dollar per pair, but *he has no right to say that no other mechanic shall make them for less*. The cloth merchant may say that he will not sell his goods for less than so much per yard, but has no right to say that any other merchant shall not sell for a less price. If one individual does not possess such a right over the conduct of another, no number of individuals can possess such a right. All combinations therefore

to effect such an object are injurious, not only to the individual particularly oppressed, but to the public at large. . . . It is true that no great danger is to be apprehended on account of the impracticability of . . . universal combinations. But if universally or even generally entered into, they would be prejudicial to trade and to the public; they are wrong in each particular case. Truth is, that industry requires no such means to support it. Competition is the life of trade. If the defendants cannot make coarse boots for less than one dollar per pair, let them refuse to do so; but let them not directly or indirectly undertake to say that others shall not do the work for a less price. It may be that *Pennock,* from greater industry or greater skill, made more profit by making boots at seventy-five cents per pair than the defendants at a dollar. He had a right to work for what he pleased. His employer had a right to employ him for such price as they could agree upon. The interference of the defendants was unlawful; its tendency is not only to individual oppression, but to public inconvenience and embarrassment.

I am of the opinion that the offence is indictable, and that the judgment of the general sessions of Ontario county should be reversed, and that a *venire de novo* should issue.

Judgment accordingly.

160. COMMONWEALTH v. HUNT
Mass. Reports, 4 Metcalf 45
1842

By the common law, which obtained in most American States, any combination of working men for the purpose of regulating the terms of employment or raising wages was a conspiracy. See, for example, the *Trial of James Melvin and Others for Conspiracy to Raise Wages, New York City, 1810,* American State Trials, Vol. XIII, p. 576 ff.; and *People* v. *Fisher,* Doc. No. 159. In the famous case of *Commonwealth* v. *Hunt,* Chief Justice Shaw held that a combination of working men for this purpose was not illegal.

This was an indictment against the defendants, (seven in number,) for a conspiracy. The first count alleged that the de-

fendants, together with divers other persons unknown to the grand jurors, "on the first Monday of September 1840, at Boston, being workmen and journeymen in the art and manual occupation of boot-makers, unlawfully, perniciously and deceitfully designing and intending to continue, keep up, form, and unite themselves into an unlawful club, society and combination, . . . did unlawfully assemble and meet together, and, . . . did then and there unjustly and corruptly . . . agree together, that none of them would work for any master or person whatsoever, in the said art, mystery or occupation, who should employ any workman or journeyman, or other person, in the said art, who was not a member of said club, society or combination, after notice given him to discharge such workman from the employ of such master; to the great damage and oppression, not only of their said masters employing them in said art and occupation, but also of divers other workmen and journeymen in the said art, mystery and occupation; to the evil example of all others in like case offending, and against the peace and dignity of the Commonwealth."

The second count charged that the defendants, and others unknown, at the time and place mentioned in the first count, "did unlawfully assemble, meet, conspire, confederate and agree together, not to work for any master or person who should employ any workman not being a member of a club, society or combination, called the Boston Journeymen Bootmakers' Society in Boston, in Massachusetts, or should break any of their by-laws, unless such workman should pay to said club and society such sum as should be agreed upon as a penalty for the breach of such unlawful rules, orders and by-laws; and by means of said conspiracy, they did compel one Isaac B. Wait, a master cordwainer in said Boston, to turn out of his employ one Jeremiah Horne, a journeyman bootmaker, because said Horne would not pay a sum of money to said society for an alleged penalty of some of said unjust rules, orders and by-laws.". . .

The defendants were found guilty, at the October term, 1840, of the municipal court, and thereupon several exceptions were alleged by them to the ruling of the judge at the trial. The only exception, which was considered in this court, was this: "The defendants' counsel contended that the indictment did not set forth any agreement to do a criminal act, or to do any lawful act by criminal means; and that the agreements, therein set forth, did not constitute a conspiracy indictable by any law of this Commonwealth; and they moved the court so to instruct the jury: But the judge refused so to do, and instructed the jury that the indictment against the defendants did, in his opinion, describe a confederacy among the defendants to do an unlawful act, and to effect the same by unlawful means: That the society, organized and associated for the purpose described in the indictment, was an un-

lawful conspiracy, against the laws of this Commonwealth. . . .

SHAW, C. J. . . . We have no doubt, that by the operation of the constitution of this Commonwealth, the general rules of the common law, making conspiracy an indictable offence, are in force here, and that this is included in the description of laws which had, before the adoption of the constitution, been used and approved in the Province, Colony, or State of Massachusetts Bay, and usually practised in the courts of law. . . . Still it is proper in this connexion to remark, that although the common law in regard to conspiracy in this Commonwealth is in force, yet it will not necessarily follow that every indictment at common law for this offence is a precedent for a similar indictment in this State. The general rule of the common law is, that it is a criminal and indictable offence, for two or more to confederate and combine together, by concerted means, to do that which is unlawful or criminal, to the injury of the public, or portions or classes of the community, or even to the rights of an individual. This rule of law may be equally in force as a rule of the common law, in England and in this Commonwealth; and yet it must depend upon the local laws of each country to determine, whether the purpose to be accomplished by the combination, or the concerted means of accomplishing it, be unlawful or criminal in the respective countries. All those laws of the parent country, whether rules of the common law, or early English statutes, which were made for the purpose of regulating the wages of laborers, the settlement of paupers, and making it penal for anyone to use a trade or handicraft to which he had not served a full apprenticeship—not being adapted to the circumstances of our colonial condition were not adopted, used or approved, and therefore do not come within the description of the laws adopted and confirmed by the provision of the constitution already cited. . . .

Stripped then of these introductory recitals and alleged injurious consequences, and of the qualifying epithets attached to the facts, the averment is this; that the defendants and others formed themselves into a society, and agreed not to work for any person who should employ any journeyman or other person, not a member of such society, after notice given him to discharge such workman. The manifest intent of the association is, to induce all those engaged in the same occupation to become members of it. Such a purpose is not unlawful. It would give them a power which might be exerted for useful and honorable purposes, or for dangerous and pernicious ones. If the latter were the real and actual object, and susceptible of proof, it should have been specially charged. Such an association might be used to afford each other assistance in times of poverty, sickness and distress; or to raise their intellectual, moral and social condition; or to make improvement in their art; or for other proper purposes. Or the association might be designed for purposes of oppression and injustice. . . .

Nor can we perceive that the objects of this association, whatever they may have been, were to be attained by criminal means. The means which they proposed to employ, as averred in this count, and which, as we are now to presume, were established by the proof, were, that they would not work for a person, who, after due notice, should employ a journeyman not a member of their society. Supposing the object of the association to be laudable and lawful, or at least not unlawful, are these means criminal? The case supposes that these persons are not bound by contract, but free to work for whom they please, or not to work, if they so prefer. In this state of things, we cannot perceive, that it is criminal for men to agree together to exercise their own acknowledged rights, in such a manner as best to subserve their own interests. One way to test this is, to consider the effect of such an agreement, where the object of the association is acknowledged on all hands to be a laudable one. Suppose a class of workmen, impressed with the manifold evils on intemperance, should agree with each other not to work in a shop in which ardent spirit was furnished, or not to work in a shop with any one who used it, or not to work for an employer, who should, after notice, employ a journeyman who habitually used it. The consequences might be the same. A workman, who should still persist in the use of ardent spirit, would find it more difficult to get employment; a master employing such an one might, at times, experience inconvenience in his work, in losing the services of a skilful but intemperate workman. Still it seems to us, that as the object would be lawful, and the means not unlawful, such an agreement could not be pronounced a criminal conspiracy. . . .

We think, therefore, that associations may be entered into, the object of which is to adopt measures that may have a tendency to impoverish another, that is, to diminish his gains and profits, and yet so far from being criminal or unlawful, the object may be highly meritorious and public spirited. The legality of such an association will therefore depend upon the means to be used for its accomplishment. . . .

161. THE WEBSTER-ASHBURTON TREATY
August 9, 1842

(Malloy, ed. *Treaties, Conventions, etc.* Vol. I, p. 650 ff.)

This treaty finally settled the long-standing northeastern boundary dispute between the United States and Canada. In 1827 a convention had referred the dispute to the arbitration of the King of the Netherlands, but his award had been rejected by both Great Britain and the United States. In 1838 the dispute precipitated the "Aroostook War" between the inhabitants of Maine and New Brunswick. The Webster-Ashburton Treaty embraced other outstanding disputes, particularly those which had grown out of the *Caroline* and McLeod affairs, see Doc. No. 156. The negotiations were conducted with amiability on both sides: Ashburton, the American representative of the Barings, was a personal friend of Webster's. On the northeastern boundary dispute and the Treaty, see Webster's speech, in Works, Vol. V, p. 78 ff.; J. B. Moore, *History of International Arbitrations,* Vol. I, chs. i ff.; W. F. Ganong, *The Boundaries of New Brunswick;* H. S. Burrage, *Maine in the Northeastern Boundary Controversy;* E. D. Adams, "Lord Ashburton and the Treaty of Washington," *American Hist. Rev.,* July, 1912; S. F. Bemis, ed. *American Secretaries of State,* Vol. V, p. 20 ff.

Treaty to Settle and Define Boundaries; for the Final Suppression of the African Slave-Trade; and for the Giving up of Criminals Fugitive from Justice.

ART. I. It is hereby agreed and declared that the line of boundary shall be as follows: Beginning at the monument at the source of the river St. Croix as designated and agreed to by the Commissioners under the fifth article of the treaty of 1794, between the Governments of the United States and Great Britain; thence, north, following the exploring line run and marked by the surveyors of the two Governments in the years 1817 and 1818, under the fifth article of the treaty of Ghent, to its intersection with the river St. John, and to the middle of the channel thereof; thence, up the middle of the main channel of the said river St. John, to the mouth of the river St. Francis; thence, up the middle of the channel of the said river St. Francis, and of the lakes through which it flows, to the outlet of the Lake Pohenagamook: thence, southwesterly, in a straight line, to a point on the northwest branch of the river St. John, which point shall be ten miles distant from the main branch of the St. John, in a straight line, and in the nearest direction; but if the said point shall be found to be less than seven miles from the nearest point of the summit or crest of the highlands that divide those rivers which empty themselves into the river St. Lawrence from those which fall into the river St. John, then, the said point shall be made to recede down the said northwest branch of the river St. John, to a point seven miles in a straight line from the said summit or crest; thence, in a straight line, in a course about south, eight degrees west, to the point where the parallel of latitude of 46° 25' north intersects the southwest branch of the St. John's; thence, southerly, by the said branch, to the source thereof in the highlands at the Metjarmette portage; thence, down along the said highlands which divide the waters which empty themselves into the river St. Lawrence from those which fall into the Atlantic Ocean, to the head of Hall's Stream; thence, down the middle of said stream, till the line thus run intersects the old line of boundary surveyed and marked by Valentine and Collins, previously to the year 1774, as the 45th degree of north latitude, and which has been known and understood to be the line of actual division between the States of New York and Vermont on one side, and the British province of Canada on the other; and from said point of intersection, west, along the said dividing line, as heretofore known and understood, to the Iroquois or St. Lawrence River. . . .

ART. II. It is moreover agreed, that, from the place where the joint commissioners terminated their labors under the sixth article of the treaty of Ghent, to wit: at a point in the Neebish channel, near Muddy Lake, the line shall run into and along the ship channel between St. Joseph and St. Tammany islands, to the division of the channel at or near the head of St. Joseph's island; thence, turning eastwardly and northwardly around the lower end of St. George's or Sugar island, and following the middle of the channel which divides St. George's from St. Joseph's island; thence up the east Neebish channel, nearest to St. George's island, through the middle of Lake George; thence, west of Jonas' island, into St. Mary's river, to a point in the middle of that river, about one mile above St. George's or Sugar island, so as to appropriate and assign the said island to the United States; thence, adopting the line traced on the maps by the commissioners, through the river St. Mary and Lake Superior, to a point north of Ile Royale, in said lake, one hundred yards to the north and east of Ile Chapeau, which last-mentioned island lies near the northeastern point of Ile Royale, where the line marked by the commissioners terminates; and from the last-mentioned point, southwesterly, through the middle of the sound between Ile Royale and the northwestern main land, to the mouth of Pigeon river, and up the said river, to and through the north and south Fowl Lakes, to the lakes of the height of land between Lake Superior and the Lake of the Woods; thence, along the water communication to Lake Saisaginaga, and through that lake; thence, to and through Cypress Lake, Lac du Bois Blanc, Lac la Croix, Little Vermilion Lake, and Lake Namecan, and through the several smaller lakes, straits, or streams, connecting the lakes here mentioned, to that point in Lac la Pluie, or Rainy Lake, at the Chaudière Falls, from which the commissioners traced the line to the most northwestern point of the Lake of the Woods; thence, along the said line, to the said most northwestern point, being in latitude 49° 23' 55" north, and in longitude 95° 14' 38" west from the observatory at Greenwich; thence, according to existing treaties, due south to its intersection with the 49th parallel of north latitude, and along that parallel to the Rocky mountains. It being understood that all the water communications and all the usual portages along the line from Lake Superior to the Lake of the Woods, and also Grand portage, from the shore of Lake Superior to the Pigeon river, as now actually used, shall be free and open to the use of the citizens and subjects of both countries. . . .

ART. VIII. The parties mutually stipulate that each shall prepare, equip, and maintain in service, on the coast of Africa, a sufficient and adequate squadron, or naval force of vessels, of suitable numbers and descriptions, to carry in all not less than eighty guns, to enforce, separately and respectively, the laws, rights, and obligations, of each of the two countries, for the suppression of the slave trade; the said squadrons to be independent of each other; but the two Governments stipulating, nevertheless, to give such orders to the officers commanding their respective forces as shall enable them most effectually to act in concert and co-operation, upon mutual consultation, as exigencies may arise, for the attainment of the true object of this article; copies of all such orders to be communicated by each Government to the other, respectively.

162. THE CONSTITUTION OF THE BROOK FARM ASSOCIATION
1841

(O. B. Frothingham, *Transcendentalism in New England*, p. 159 ff.)

Brook Farm, by virtue of the distinguished character of its membership and of its literary associations, is the most famous of those Utopian experiments which flourished in the generation preceding the Civil War. It was established at West Roxbury, Massachusetts, some nine miles south of Boston, and among its members were George Ripley, J. S. Dwight, Charles A. Dana, and Nathaniel Hawthorne, while almost the whole of literary Boston and Concord frequented its halls. A disastrous fire brought the experiment to an untimely end in 1846. See, L. Swift, *Brook Farm;* O. B. Frothingham, *George Ripley,* chs. iii–iv; O. B. Frothingham, *Transcendentalism in New England,* ch. vii; J. T. Codman, *Brook Farm;* J. H. Noyes, *History of American Socialisms;* M. Hillquit, *History of Socialism in the United States;* H. Semler, *Geschichte der Socialismus und Communismus in Nord America.* For other communistic experiments, see C. Nordhoff, *The Communistic Societies of the United States;* W. A. Hinds, *American Communities and Co-operative Colonies;* G. B. Lockwood, *The New Harmony Movement;* B. M. H. Shambaugh, *Amana;* A. Shaw, *Icaria;* M. A. Mikkelsen, *Bishop Hill Colony;* R. J. Hendricks, *Bethel and Aurora.* Hawthorne's *Blithedale Romance* gives a somewhat unfair picture of Brook Farm.

principles of justice and love to our social organization in accordance with the laws of Divine Providence; to substitute a system of brotherly coöperation for one of selfish competition; to secure to our children and those who may be entrusted to our care, the benefits of the highest physical, intellectual and moral education, which in the progress of knowledge the resources at our command will permit; to institute an attractive, efficient, and productive system of industry; to prevent the exercise of worldly anxiety, by the competent supply of our necessary wants; to diminish the desire of excessive accumulation, by making the acquisition of individual property subservient to upright and disinterested uses; to guarantee to each other forever the means of physical support, and of spiritual progress; and thus to impart a greater freedom, simplicity, truthfulness, refinement, and moral dignity, to our mode of life;—we the undersigned do unite in a voluntary Association, and adopt and ordain the following articles of agreement, to wit:

CONSTITUTION

In order more effectually to promote the great purposes of human culture; to establish the external relations of life on a basis of wisdom and purity; to apply the

ARTICLE I

Sec. 1. The name of this Association shall be "THE BROOK-FARM ASSOCIATION FOR INDUSTRY AND EDUCATION." All persons who shall hold one or more shares in its stock, or whose labor and skill shall be considered an equivalent for capital, may be admitted by the vote of two-thirds of the Association, as members thereof.

Sec. 2. No member of the Association shall ever be subjected to any religious test; nor shall any authority be assumed over individual freedom of opinion by the Association, nor by any one member over another; nor shall any one be held accountable to the Association, except for such overt acts, omissions of duty, as violate the principles of justice, purity, and love, on which it is founded; and in such cases the relation of any member may be suspended, or discontinued, at the pleasure of the Association.

ARTICLE II

Sec. 1. The members of this Association shall own and manage such real and personal estate in joint stock proprietorship, divided into shares of one hundred dollars, each, as may from time to time be agreed on. . . .

Sec. 4. The shareholders on their part, for themselves, their heirs and assigns, do renounce all claim on any profits accruing to the Association for the use of their capital invested in the stock of the Association, except five per cent, interest on the amount of stock held by them, payable in the manner described in the preceding section.

ARTICLE III

Sec. 1. The Association shall provide such employment for all its members as shall be adapted to their capacities, habits, and tastes; and each member shall select and perform such operations of labor, whether corporal or mental, as shall be deemed best suited to his own endowments, and the benefit of the Association.

Sec. 2. The Association guarantees to all its members, their children, and family dependents, house-rent, fuel, food, and clothing, and the other necessaries of life, without charge, not exceeding a certain fixed amount to be decided annually by the Association; no charge shall ever be made for support during inability to labor from sickness or old age, or for medical or nursing attendance, except in case of shareholders, who shall be charged therefor . . . but no charge shall be made to any members for education or the use of library and public rooms. . . .

ARTICLE V

Sec. 1. The government of the Association shall be vested in a board of Directors, divided into four departments as follows; 1st., General Direction; 2d, Direction of Education; 3d., Direction of Industry; 4th, Direction of Finance; consisting of three persons each. . . .

Sec. 5. The departments of Education and Finance shall be under the control each of its own Direction, which shall select, and in concurrence with the General Direction, shall appoint such teachers, officers, and agents, as shall be necessary to the complete and systematic organization of the department. No Directors or other officers shall be deemed to possess any rank superior to the other members of the Association, nor shall they receive any extra remuneration for their official services.

Sec. 6. The department of Industry shall be arranged in groups and series, as far as practicable, and shall consist of three primary series; to wit, Agricultural, Mechanical, and Domestic Industry. The chief of each series shall be elected every two months by the members thereof. . . .

163. DOROTHEA DIX'S MEMORIAL TO THE LEGISLATURE OF MASSACHUSETTS
January, 1843

(Old South Leaflets, No. 148)

In March 1841, Dorothea Dix, visiting a jail in East Cambridge, Massachusetts, found insane persons kept in an unheated room. The following two years she spent investigating the jails and almshouses of Massachusetts, and in January 1843 her report, dated from Dr. Channing's

house, was presented to the Legislature by some of her influential friends. The Memorial produced a profound sensation: it was referred to a committee of which Dr. Samuel G. Howe was chairman and reported with recommendations for relief. Within a short time Massachusetts made more adequate provision for her insane, and Miss Dix entered upon a larger field of philanthropic work which embraced most of the States of the American Union and several European countries. See, F. Tiffany, *Life of Dorothea Lynde Dix;* A. S. Roe, *Dorothea Dix.*

Gentlemen,—I respectfully ask to present this Memorial, believing that the cause, which actuates to and sanctions so unusual a movement, presents no equivocal claim to public consideration and sympathy. . . .

About two years since leisure afforded opportunity and duty prompted me to visit several prisons and almshouses in the vicinity of this metropolis. I found, near Boston, in the jails and asylums for the poor, a numerous class brought into unsuitable connection with criminals and the general mass of paupers. I refer to idiots and insane persons, dwelling in circumstances not only adverse to their own physical and moral improvement, but productive of extreme disadvantages to all other persons brought into association with them. I applied myself diligently to trace the causes of these evils, and sought to supply remedies. As one obstacle was surmounted, fresh difficulties appeared. Every new investigation has given depth to the conviction that it is only by decided, prompt, and vigorous legislation the evils to which I refer, and which I shall proceed more fully to illustrate, can be remedied. I shall be obliged to speak with great plainness, and to reveal many things revolting to the taste, and from which my woman's nature shrinks with peculiar sensitiveness. But truth is the highest consideration. *I tell what I have seen*—painful and shocking as the details often are—that from them you may feel more deeply the imperative obligation which lies upon you to prevent the possibility of a repetition or continuance of such outrages upon humanity. . . .

I come to present the strong claims of suffering humanity. I come to place before the Legislature of Massachusetts the condition of the miserable, the desolate, the outcast. I come as the advocate of helpless, forgotten, insane, and idiotic men and women; of beings sunk to a condition from which the most unconcerned would start with real horror; of beings wretched in our prisons, and more wretched in our almshouses. . . .

I must confine myself to few examples, but am ready to furnish other and more complete details, if required.

If my pictures are displeasing, coarse, and severe, my subjects, it must be recollected, offer no tranquil, refined, or composing features. The condition of human beings, reduced to the extremest states of degradation and misery cannot be exhibited in softened language, or adorn a polished page.

I proceed, gentlemen, briefly to call your attention to the *present* state of insane persons confined within this Commonwealth, in *cages, closets, cellars, stalls, pens! Chained, naked, beaten with rods,* and *lashed* into obedience. . . .

It is the Commonwealth, not its integral parts, that is accountable for most of the abuses which have lately and do still exist. I repeat it, it is defective legislation which perpetuates and multiplies these abuses. In illustration of my subject, I offer the following extracts from my Note-book and Journal:—

Springfield. In the jail, one lunatic woman, furiously mad, a State pauper, improperly situated, both in regard to the prisoners, the keepers, and herself. It is a case of extreme self-forgetfulness and oblivion to all the decencies of life, to describe which would be to repeat only the grossest scenes. She is much worse since leaving Worcester. In the almshouse of the same town is a woman apparently only needing judicious care, and some well-chosen employment, to make it unnecessary to confine her in solitude, in a dreary unfurnished room. Her appeals for employment and companionship are most touching, but the mistress replied "she had no time to attend to her.". . .

Lincoln. A woman in a cage. *Medford.* One idiotic subject chained, and one in a close stall for seventeen years. *Pepperell.* One often doubly chained, hand and foot; another violent; several peaceable now. *Brookfield.* One man caged, comfortable. *Granville.* One often closely confined; now losing the use of his limbs from want of exercise. *Charlemont.* One man caged. *Savoy.* One man caged. *Lenox.* Two in the jail, against whose unfit condition there the jailer protests.

Dedham. The insane disadvantageously placed in the jail. In the almshouse, two females in stalls, situated in the main building; lie in wooden bunks filled with straw; always shut up. One of these subjects is supposed curable. The overseers of the poor have declined giving her a trial at the hospital, as I was informed, on account of expense. . . .

Besides the above, I have seen many who, part of the year, are chained or caged. The use of cages all but universal. Hardly a town but can refer to some not distant period of using them; chains are less common; negligences frequent; wilful abuse less frequent than sufferings proceeding from ignorance, or want of consideration. I encountered during the last three months many poor creatures wandering reckless and unprotected through the country. . . . But I cannot particularize. In traversing the State, I have found hundreds of insane persons in every variety of circumstance and condition, many whose situation could not and need not be improved; a less number, but that very large, whose lives are the saddest pictures of human suffering and degradation.

I give a few illustrations; but description fades before reality.

Danvers. November. Visited the almshouse. A large building, much out of repair. Understand a new one is in contemplation. Here are from fifty-six to sixty inmates, one idiotic, three insane, one of the latter in close confinement at all times.

Long before reaching the house, wild shouts, snatches of rude songs, imprecations and obscene language, fell upon the ear, proceeding from the occupant of a low building, rather remote from the principal building to which my course was directed. Found the mistress, and was conducted to the place which was called "the home" of the *forlorn* maniac, a young woman, exhibiting a condition of neglect and misery blotting out the faintest idea of comfort, and outraging every sentiment of decency. She had been, I learnt, "a respectable person, industrious and worthy. Disappointments and trials shook her mind, and, finally, laid prostrate reason and self-control. She became a maniac for life. She had been at Worcester Hospital for a considerable time, and had been returned as incurable." The mistress told me she understood that, "while there, she was comfortable and decent." Alas, what a change was here exhibited! She had passed from one

degree of violence to another, in swift progress. There she stood, clinging to or beating upon the bars of her caged apartment, the contracted size of which afforded space only for increasing accumulations of filth, a *foul* spectacle. There she stood with naked arms and dishevelled hair, the unwashed frame invested with fragments of unclean garments, the air so extremely offensive, though ventilation was afforded on all sides save one, that it was not possible to remain beyond a few moments without retreating for recovery to the outward air. Irritation of body, produced by utter filth and exposure, incited her to the horrid process of tearing off her skin by inches. Her face, neck, and person were thus disfigured to hideousness. She held up a fragment just rent off. To my exclamation of horror, the mistress replied: "Oh, we can't help it. Half the skin is off sometimes. We can do nothing with her; and it makes no difference what she eats, for she consumes her own filth as readily as the food which is brought her."

Men of Massachusetts, I beg, I implore, I demand pity and protection for these of my suffering, outraged sex. Fathers, husbands, brothers, I would supplicate you for this boon; but what do I say? I dishonor you, divest you at once of Christianity and humanity, does this appeal imply distrust. If it comes burdened with a doubt of your righteousness in this legislation, then blot it out; while I declare confidence in your honor, not less than your humanity. Here you will put away the cold, calculating spirit of selfishness and self-seeking; lay off the armor of local strife and political opposition; here and now, for once, forgetful of the earthly and perishable, come up to these halls and consecrate them with one heart and one mind to works of righteousness and just judgment.

Become the benefactors of your race, the just guardians of the solemn rights you hold in trust. Raise up the fallen, succor the desolate, restore the outcast, defend the helpless, and for your eternal and great reward receive the benediction, "Well done, good and faithful servants, become rulers over many things!"

Injustice is also done to the *convicts:* it is certainly very wrong that they should be doomed day after day and night after night to listen to the ravings of madmen and madwomen. This is a kind of punishment that is not recognized by our statutes, and is what the criminal ought not to be called upon to undergo. The confinement of the criminal and of the insane in the same building is subversive of that good order and discipline which should be observed in every well-regulated prison. I do most sincerely hope that more permanent provision will be made for the pauper insane by the State, either to restore Worcester Insane Asylum to what it was originally designed to be or else make some just appropriation for the benefit of this very unfortunate class of our "fellow-beings."

Gentlemen, I commit to you this sacred cause. Your action upon this subject will affect the present and future condition of hundreds and of thousands. In this legislation, as in all things, may you exercise that "wisdom which is the breath of the power of God."

Respectfully submitted,

D. L. DIX.

164. CLAY'S RALEIGH LETTER
April 17, 1844

(*Niles' National Register,* Vol. LXVI, p. 152–3)

It was apparent, early in 1844, that Clay would be the Whig nominee for the Presidency, and it was commonly believed that Van Buren would be nominated by the Democrats. Early in 1844 Van Buren visited Clay at Ashland and came to an agreement with him to eliminate the Texas question from the campaign. Accordingly on April 17 both candidates published letters opposing immediate annexation. Van Buren's letter in all probability cost him the nomination. Clay's letter so embarrassed him in the campaign that he sought to explain it away in a series of letters known as the "Alabama letters"—but without success. Clay was defeated by Polk who was pledged to immediate annexation. The letters of Clay and Van Buren and the subsequent Alabama letters can be found in *Niles Register,* Vol. LXVI. See, C. Schurz, *Henry Clay,* Vol. II; T. C. Smith, *The Liberty and Free Soil Parties;* E. M. Shepard, *Martin Van Buren.*

TO THE EDITORS OF THE NATIONAL INTELLIGENCER

Raleigh, April 17, 1844.

Gentlemen: Subsequent to my departure from Ashland, in December last, I received various communications from popular assemblages and private individuals, requesting an expression of my opinion upon the question of the annexation of Texas to the United States. . . . The rejection of the overture of Texas, some years ago, to become annexed to the United States, had met with general acquiescence. Nothing had since occurred materially to vary the question. I had seen no evidence of a desire being entertained, on the part of any considerable portion of the American people, that Texas should become an integral part of the United States. . . . To the astonishment of the whole nation, we are now informed that a treaty of annexation has been actually concluded, and is to be submitted to the senate for its consideration. The motives for my silence, therefore, no longer remain, and I feel it to be my duty to present an exposition of my views and opinions upon the question, for what they may be worth, to the public consideration. I adopt this method as being more convenient than several replies to the respective communications which I have received.

I regret that I have not the advantage of a view of the treaty itself, so as to enable me to adapt an expression of my opinion to the actual conditions and stipulations which it contains. Not possessing that opportunity, I am constrained to treat the question according to what I presume to be the terms of the treaty. If, without the loss of national character, without the hazard of foreign war, with the general concurrence of the nation, without any danger to the integrity of the Union, and without giving an unreasonable price for Texas, the question of annexation were presented, it would appear in quite a different light from that in which, I apprehend, it is now to be regarded. . . .

Annexation and war with Mexico are identical. Now, for one, I certainly am not willing to involve this country in a foreign war for the object of acquiring Texas. I know there are those who regard such a war with indifference and as a trifling affair, on account of the weakness of Mexico, and her inability to inflict serious injury upon this country. But I do not look upon it thus lightly. I regard all wars as great calamities, to be avoided, if possible, and honorable peace as the wisest and truest policy of this country. What the United States most need are union, peace, and patience. Nor do I think that the weakness of a power should form a motive, in any case, for inducing us to engage in or to depreciate the evils of war.—Honor and good faith and justice are equally due from this country towards the weak as towards the strong. And, if an act of injustice were to be perpetrated towards any power, it would be more compatible with the dignity of the nation, and, in my judgment, less dishonorable, to inflict it upon a powerful instead of a weak foreign nation. But are we perfectly sure that we should be free from injury in a state of war with Mexico? Have we any security that countless numbers of foreign vessels, under the authority and flag of Mexico, would not prey upon our defenceless commerce in the Mexican gulf, on the Pacific ocean, and on every other sea and ocean? What commerce, on the other hand, does Mexico offer, as an indemnity for our losses, to the gallantry and enterprise of our countrymen? This view of the subject supposes that the war would be confined to the United States and Mexico as the only belligerents. But have we any certain guaranty that Mexico would obtain no allies among the great European powers? . . .

Assuming that the annexation of Texas is war with Mexico, is it competent to the treaty-making power to plunge this country into war, not only without the concurrence of, but without deigning to consult congress, to which, by the constitution, belongs exclusively the power of declaring war?

I have hitherto considered the question upon the supposition that the annexation is attempted without the assent of Mexico. If she yields her consent, that would materially affect the foreign aspect of the question, if it did not remove all foreign difficulties. On the assumption of that assent, the question would be confined to the domestic considerations which belong to it, embracing the terms and conditions upon which annexation is proposed. I do not think that Texas ought to be received into the Union, as an integral part

of it, in decided opposition to the wishes of a considerable and respectable portion of the confederacy. I think it far more wise and important to compose and harmonize the present confederacy, as it now exists, than to introduce a new element of discord and distraction into it. . . . Mr. Jefferson expressed the opinion, and others believed, that it never was in the contemplation of the framers of the constitution to add foreign territory to the confederacy, out of which new states were to be formed. The acquisitions of Louisiana and Florida may be defended upon the peculiar ground of the relation in which they stood to the states of the Union. After they were admitted, we might well pause a while, people our vast wastes, develop our resources, prepare the means of defending what we possess, and augment our strength, power, and greatness. If hereafter further territory should be wanted for an increased population, we need entertain no apprehensions but that it will be acquired by means, it is to be hoped, fair, honorable, and constitutional.

It is useless to disguise that there are those who espouse and those who oppose the annexation of Texas upon the ground of the influence which it would exert, in the balance of political power, between two great sections of the Union. I conceive that no motive for the acquisition of foreign territory would be more unfortunate, or pregnant with more fatal consequences, than that of obtaining it for the purpose of strengthening one part against another part of the common confederacy. Such a principle, put into practical operation, would menace the existence, if it did not certainly sow the seeds of a dissolution of the Union. It would be to proclaim to the world an insatiable and unquenchable thirst for foreign conquest or acquisition of territory. For if today Texas be acquired to strengthen one part of the confederacy, tomorrow Canada may be required to add strength to another. And, after that might have been obtained, still other and further acquisitions would become necessary to equalize and adjust the balance of political power. Finally, in the progress of this spirit of universal dominion, the part of the confederacy which is now weakest, would find itself still weaker from the impossibility of securing new theatres for those peculiar institutions which it is charged with being desirous to extend.

But would Texas, ultimately, really add strength to that which is now considered the weakest part of the confederacy? If my information be correct, it would not. According to that, the territory of Texas is susceptible of a division into five states of convenient size and form. Of these, two only would be adapted to those peculiar institutions to which I have referred, and the other three, lying west and north of San Antonio, being only adapted to farming and grazing purposes, from the nature of their soil, climate, and productions, would not admit of those institutions. In the end, therefore, there would be two slave and three free states probably added to the Union. If this view of the soil and geography of Texas be correct, it might serve to diminish the zeal both of those who oppose and those who are urging annexation. . . .

In the future progress of events, it is probable that there will be a voluntary or forcible separation of the British North American possessions from the parent country. I am strongly inclined to think that it will be best for the happiness of all parties that, in that event, they should be erected into a separate and independent republic. With the Canadian republic on one side, that of Texas on the other, and the United States,

the friend of both, between them, each could advance its own happiness by such constitutions, laws, and measures, as were best adapted to its peculiar condition. They would be natural allies, ready, by co-operation, to repel any European or foreign attack upon either. Each would afford a secure refuge to the persecuted and oppressed driven into exile by either of the others. They would emulate each other in improvements, in free institutions, and in the science of self-government. Whilst Texas has adopted our constitution as the model of hers, she has, in several important particulars, greatly improved upon it.

Although I have felt compelled, from the nature of the inquiries addressed to me, to extend this communication to a much greater length than I could have wished, I could not do justice to the subject, and fairly and fully expose my own opinions in a shorter space. In conclusion, they may be stated in a few words to be, that I consider the annexation of Texas, at this time, without the assent of Mexico, as a measure compromising the national character, involving us certainly in war with Mexico, probably with other foreign powers, dangerous to the integrity of the Union, inexpedient in the present financial condition of the country, and not called for by any general expression of public opinion.

I am, respectfully, your obedient servant,

HENRY CLAY.

165. THE ANNEXATION OF TEXAS

Joint Resolution of Congress annexing Texas to the United States
March 1, 1845

(U. S. Statutes at Large, Vol. V, p. 797–8)

Texas, inhabited largely by Americans, achieved independence from Mexico in 1836; independence was recognized by the United States and most of the powers of Europe, but not by Mexico. The project of annexation to the United States was continually agitated, and a treaty of annexation negotiated in 1844 which had been rejected by the Senate became the major issue of the campaign of 1844. The triumph of Polk on a platform calling for the "re-annexation" of Texas, appeared to give a mandate from the American people for annexation, and accordingly a joint resolution for annexation was pushed through Congress and approved March 1. This was the first occasion of the use of the joint resolution to achieve a desired result in foreign relations instead of a treaty, which demanded a

two-thirds vote in the Senate. Fear of English designs in Texas played a considerable rôle in hastening annexation. See, J. H. Smith, *The Annexation of Texas;* E. D. Adams, *British Interests and Activities in Texas;* S. F. Bemis, ed. *American Secretaries of State,* Vol. V, *passim;* J. S. Reeves, *American Diplomacy under Tyler and Polk.*

Resolved . . . , That Congress doth consent that the territory properly included within, and rightfully belonging to the Republic of Texas, may be erected into a new State, to be called the State of Texas, with a republican form of government, to be adopted by the people of said republic, by deputies in convention assembled, with the consent of the existing government, in order that the same may be admitted as one of the States of this Union.

2. That the foregoing consent of Congress is given upon the following conditions, and with the following guarantees, to wit: *First,* Said State to be formed, subject to the adjustment by this government of all questions of boundary that may arise with other governments; and the constitution thereof, with the proper evidence of its adoption by the people of said Republic of Texas, shall be transmitted to the President of the United States, to be laid before Congress for its final action, on or before the first day of January, one thousand eight hundred and forty-six. *Second,* Said State, when admitted into the Union, after ceding to the United States, all public edifices, fortifications, barracks, ports and harbors, navy and navy-yards, docks, magazines, arms, armaments, and all other property and means pertaining to the public defence belonging to said Republic of Texas, shall retain all the public funds, debts, taxes, and dues of every kind, which may belong to or be due and owing said republic; and shall also retain all the vacant and unappropriated lands lying within its limits, to be applied to the payment of the debts and liabilities of said Republic of Texas, and the residue of said lands, after discharging said debts and liabilities, to be disposed of as said State may direct; but in no event are said debts and liabilities to become a charge upon the Government of the United States. *Third.* New States, of convenient size, not exceeding four in number, in addition to said State of Texas, and having sufficient population, may hereafter, by the consent of said State, be formed out of the territory thereof, which shall be entitled to admission under the provisions of the federal constitution. And such States as may be formed out of that portion of said territory lying south of thirty-six degrees thirty minutes north latitude, commonly known as the Missouri compromise line, shall be admitted into the Union with or without slavery, as the people of each State asking admission may desire. And in such State or States as shall be formed out of said territory north of said Missouri compromise line, slavery, or involuntary servitude, (except for crime,) shall be prohibited.

3. That if the President of the United States shall in his judgment and discretion deem it most advisable, instead of proceeding to submit the foregoing resolution to the Republic of Texas, as an overture on the part of the United States for admission, to negotiate with that Republic; then,

Be it resolved, That a State, to be formed out of the present Republic of Texas, with suitable extent and boundaries, and with two representatives in Congress, until the next apportionment of representation, shall be admitted into the Union, by virtue of this act, on an equal footing with the existing States, as soon as the terms and conditions of such admission, and the cession of the remaining Texian territory to the United States shall be agreed upon by the Governments of Texas and the United States: And that the sum of one hundred thousand dollars be, and the same is hereby, appropriated to defray the expenses of missions and negotiations, to agree upon the terms of said admission and cession, either by treaty to be submitted to the Senate, or by articles to be submitted to the two houses of Congress, as the President may direct.

166. TEXAS AND OREGON

Extract from Polk's Inaugural Address
March 4, 1845

(Richardson, ed. *Messages and Papers,* Vol. IV, p. 379 ff.)

The Democratic campaign of 1844 had been fought on the platform of the "re-annexation of Texas and the re-occupation of Oregon". Polk, a confirmed expansionist, announced his adherence to these policies in his inaugural address. Of particular interest is Polk's statement that "our title to the country of Oregon is clear and unquestionable." See, E. I. McCormac, *James K. Polk;*

J. S. Reeves, *American Diplomacy under Tyler and Polk.*

. . . The Republic of Texas has made known her desire to come into our Union, to form a part of our Confederacy and enjoy with us the blessings of liberty secured and guaranteed by our Constitution. Texas was once a part of our country—was unwisely ceded away to a foreign power—is now independent, and possesses an undoubted right to dispose of a part or the whole of her territory and to merge her sovereignty as a separate and independent state in ours. I congratulate my country that by an act of the late Congress of the United States the assent of this Government has been given to the reunion, and it only remains for the two countries to agree upon the terms to consummate an object so important to both.

I regard the question of annexation as belonging exclusively to the United States and Texas. They are independent powers competent to contract, and foreign nations have no right to interfere with them or to take exceptions to their reunion. Foreign powers do not seem to appreciate the true character of our Government. Our Union is a confederation of independent States, whose policy is peace with each other and all the world. To enlarge its limits is to extend the dominions of peace over additional territories and increasing millions. The world has nothing to fear from military ambition in our Government. While the Chief Magistrate and the popular branch of Congress are elected for short terms by the suffrages of those millions who must in their own persons bear all the burdens and miseries of war, our Government can not be otherwise than pacific. Foreign powers should therefore look on the annexation of Texas to the United States not as the conquest of a nation seeking to extend her dominions by arms and violence, but as the peaceful acquisition of a territory once her own, by adding another member to our confederation, with the consent of that member, thereby diminishing the chances of war and opening to them new and ever-increasing markets for their products.

To Texas the reunion is important, because the strong protecting arm of our Government would be extended over her, and the vast resources of her fertile soil and genial climate would be speedily developed, while the safety of New Orleans and of our whole southwestern frontier against hostile aggression, as well as the interests of the whole Union, would be promoted by it. . . .

None can fail to see the danger to our safety and future peace if Texas remains an independent state or becomes an ally or dependency of some foreign nation more powerful than herself. Is there one among our citizens who would not prefer perpetual peace with Texas to occasional wars, which so often occur between bordering independent nations? Is there one who would not prefer free intercourse with her to high duties on all our products and manufactures which enter her ports or cross her frontiers? Is there one who would not prefer an unrestricted communication with her citizens to the frontier obstructions which must occur if she remains out of the Union? Whatever is good or evil in the local institutions of Texas will remain her own whether annexed to the United States or not. None of the present States will be responsible for them any more than they are for the local institutions of each other. They have confederated together for certain specified objects. Upon the same principle that they would refuse to form a perpetual union with Texas because of her local institutions our forefathers would have been prevented from forming our present Union. Perceiving no valid objection to the measure and many reasons for its adoption vitally affecting the peace, the safety, and the prosperity of both countries, I shall on the broad principle which formed the basis and produced the adoption of our Constitution, and not in any narrow spirit of sectional policy, endeavor by all constitutional, honorable, and appropriate means to consummate the expressed will of the people and Government of the United States by the reannexation of Texas to our Union at the earliest practicable period.

Nor will it become in a less degree my duty to assert and maintain by all constitutional means the right of the United States to that portion of our territory which lies beyond the Rocky Mountains. Our title to the country of the Oregon is "clear and unquestionable," and already are our people preparing to perfect that title by occupying it with their wives and children. But eighty years ago our population was confined on the west by the ridge of the Alleghanies. Within that period—within the lifetime, I might say, of some of my hearers—our people, increasing to many millions, have filled the eastern valley of the Mississippi, adventurously ascended the Missouri to its headsprings, and are already engaged in establishing the blessings of self-government in valleys of which the rivers flow to the Pacific. The world beholds the peaceful triumphs of the industry of our emigrants. To us belongs the duty of protecting them adequately wherever they may be upon our soil. The jurisdiction of our laws and the benefits of our republican institutions should be extended over them in the distant regions which they have selected for their homes. The increasing facilities of intercourse will easily bring the States, of which the formation in that part of our territory can not be long delayed, within the sphere of our federative Union. In the meantime every obligation imposed by treaty or conventional stipulations should be sacredly respected. . . .

167. THE REASSERTION OF THE MONROE DOCTRINE

Extract from President Polk's First Annual Message to Congress
December 2, 1845

(Richardson, ed. *Messages and Papers,* Vol. IV, p. 398 ff.)

This message of Polk's was, according to Professor Perkins, "second only in importance" to the original Monroe Doctrine. It inaugurated a new era in the history of the doctrine, and was closely connected with Polk's policy toward Oregon and Texas. Note that Polk speaks of "this continent" rather than, as in the case of Monroe, of "these continents". On the revival of the Doctrine, see, D. Perkins. *The Monroe Doctrine, 1826–1867,* ch. ii, and notes.

. . . The rapid extension of our settlements over our territories heretofore unoccupied, the addition of new States to our Confederacy, the expansion of free principles, and our rising greatness as a nation are attracting the attention of the powers of Europe, and lately the doctrine has been broached in some of them of a "balance of power" on this continent to check our advancement. The United States, sincerely desirous of preserving relations of good understanding with all nations, can not in silence permit any European interference on the North American continent, and should any such interference be attempted will be ready to resist it at any and all hazards.

It is well known to the American people and to all nations that this Government has never interfered with the relations subsisting between other governments. We have never made ourselves parties to their wars or their alliances; we have not sought their territories by conquest; we have not mingled with parties in their domestic struggles; and believing our own form of government to be the best, we have never attempted to propagate it by intrigues, by diplomacy, or by force. We may claim on this continent a like exemption from European interference. The nations of America are equally sovereign and independent with those of Europe. They possess the same rights, independent of all foreign interposition, to make war, to conclude peace, and to regulate their internal affairs. The people of the United States can not, therefore, view with indifference attempts of European powers to interfere with the independent action of the nations on this continent. The American system of government is entirely different from that of Europe. Jealousy among the different sovereigns of Europe, lest any one of them might become too powerful for the rest, has caused them anxiously to desire the establishment of what they term the "balance of power." It can not be permitted to have any application on the North American continent, and especially to the United States. We must ever maintain the principle that the people of this continent alone have the right to decide their own destiny. Should any portion of them, constituting an independent state, propose to unite themselves with our Confederacy, this will be a question for them and us to determine without any foreign interposition. We can never consent that European powers shall interfere to prevent such a union because it might disturb the "balance of power" which they may desire to maintain upon this continent. Near a quarter of a century ago the principle was distinctly announced to the world, in the annual message of one of my predecessors, that—

The American continents, by the free and independent condition which they have assumed and maintain, are henceforth not to be considered as subjects for future colonization by any European powers.

This principle will apply with greatly increased force should any European power attempt to establish any new colony in North America. In the existing circumstances of the world the present is deemed a proper occasion to reiterate and reaffirm the principle avowed by Mr. Monroe and to state my cordial concurrence in its wisdom and sound policy. The reassertion of this principle, especially in reference to North America, is at this day but the promulgation of a policy which no European power should cherish the disposition to resist. Existing rights of every European nation should be respected, but it is due alike to our safety and our interests that the efficient protection of our laws should be extended over our whole territorial limits, and that it should be distinctly announced to the world as our settled policy that no future European colony or dominion shall with our consent be planted or established on any part of the North American continent. . . .

168. POLK'S MESSAGE ON WAR WITH MEXICO
May 11, 1846

(Richardson, ed. *Messages and Papers*, Vol. IV, p. 437 ff.)

This notorious message, declaring that "Mexico . . . has shed American blood upon the American soil," led to a declaration of war, May 13. Whether the territory between the Nueces and the Rio Grande, where this act of war took place, was actually American Territory, is highly controversial. In any event Polk and his Cabinet had determined upon war as early as May 9, so that the alleged provocation for the war was not the real one. Whether Polk deserved the appellation of "the mendacious Polk" or not is a matter of opinion among historians. On the origins of the Mexican War, see, J. H. Smith, *The War with Mexico*, Vol. I; J. S. Reeves, *The Diplomacy of Tyler and Polk;* E. C. McCormac, *James K. Polk;* L. M. Sears, *John Slidell;* G. L. Rives, *The United States and Mexico*, Vol. I; N. W. Stephenson, *Texas and the Mexican War;* G. P. Garrison, *Westward Extension*, chs. xiii–xv.

To the Senate and House of Representatives:

The existing state of the relations between the United States and Mexico renders it proper that I should bring the subject to the consideration of Congress. . . .

In my message at the commencement of the present session I informed you that upon the earnest appeal both of the Congress and convention of Texas I had ordered an efficient military force to take a position "between the Nueces and the Del Norte." This had become necessary to meet a threatened invasion of Texas by the Mexican forces, for which extensive military preparations had been made. The invasion was threatened solely because Texas had determined, in accordance with a solemn resolution of the Congress of the United States, to annex herself to our Union, and under these circumstances it was plainly our duty to extend our protection over her citizens and soil.

This force was concentrated at Corpus Christi, and remained there until after I had received such information from Mexico as rendered it probable, if not certain, that the Mexican Government would refuse to receive our envoy.

Meantime Texas, by the final action of our Congress, had become an integral part of our Union. The Congress of Texas, by its act of December 19, 1836, had declared the Rio del Norte to be the boundary of that Republic. Its jurisdiction had been extended and exercised beyond the Nueces. The country between that river and the Del Norte had been represented in the Congress and in the convention of Texas, had thus taken part in the act of annexation itself, and is now included within one of our Congressional districts. Our own Congress had, moreover, with great unanimity, by the act approved December 31, 1845, recognized the country beyond the Nueces as a part of our territory by including it within our own revenue system, and a revenue officer to reside within that district has been appointed by and with the advice and consent of the Senate. It became, therefore, of urgent necessity to provide for the defense of that portion of our country. Accordingly, on the 13th of January last instructions were issued to the general in command of these troops to occupy the left bank of the Del

Norte. This river, which is the southwestern boundary of the State of Texas, is an exposed frontier.

The movement of the troops to the Del Norte was made by the commanding general under positive instructions to abstain from all aggressive acts toward Mexico or Mexican citizens and to regard the relations between that Republic and the United States as peaceful unless she should declare war or commit acts of hostility indicative of a state of war. . . .

The Mexican forces at Matamoras assumed a belligerent attitude, and on the 12th of April General Ampudia, then in command, notified General Taylor to break up his camp within twenty-four hours and to retire beyond the Nueces River, and in the event of his failure to comply with these demands announced that arms, and arms alone, must decide the question. But no open act of hostility was committed until the 24th of April. On that day General Arista, who had succeeded to the command of the Mexican forces, communicated to General Taylor that "he considered hostilities commenced and should prosecute them." A party of dragoons of 63 men and officers were on the same day dispatched from the American camp up the

Rio del Norte, on its left bank, to ascertain whether the Mexican troops had crossed or were preparing to cross the river, "became engaged with a large body of these troops, and after a short affair, in which some 16 were killed and wounded, appear to have been surrounded and compelled to surrender." . . .

The cup of forbearance had been exhausted even before the recent information from the frontier of the Del Norte. But now, after reiterated menaces, Mexico has passed the boundary of the United States, has invaded our territory and shed American blood upon the American soil. She has proclaimed that hostilities have commenced, and that the two nations are now at war.

As war exists, and, notwithstanding all our efforts to avoid it, exists by the act of Mexico herself, we are called upon by every consideration of duty and patriotism to vindicate with decision the honor, the rights, and the interests of our country. . . .

In further vindication of our rights and defense of our territory, I invoke the prompt action of Congress to recognize the existence of the war, and to place at the disposition of the Executive the means of prosecuting the war with vigor, and thus hastening the restoration of peace. . . .

169. THE OREGON TREATY
June 15, 1846

(Malloy, ed. *Treaties, Conventions, etc.*, Vol. I, p. 656)

The Oregon Treaty, establishing the boundary between the United States and British America along the 49th parallel, concluded half a century of boundary controversy in a manner highly favorable to the United States. By the convention of 1818 the United States and Great Britain had joint occupancy of the territory between the 42nd and the 54th parallels; this arrangement had been extended indefinitely in 1827, with provision for termination on one year's notice. A resolution of April 27, 1846 authorized the President to give notice of the termination of the joint occupancy agreement at his discretion. On the Oregon Treaty, see J. S. Reeves, *American Diplomacy under Tyler and Polk;* J. C. Bell, *Opening a Highway to the Pacific, 1838–1846;* F. Merk, "Oregon Pioneers and the Boundary," *American Hist. Rev.,* Vol. XXIX, p. 681 ff.; H. S. Commager, "England and the Oregon Treaty of 1846," *Oregon Historical Qt.* Vol. XXVIII.

ART. I. From the point on the forty-ninth parallel of north latitude, where the boundary laid down in existing treaties and conventions between the United States and Great Britain terminates, the line of boundary between the territories of the United States and those of her Britannic Majesty shall be continued westward along the said forty-ninth parallel of north latitude to the middle of the channel which separates the continent from Vancouver's Island, and thence southerly through the middle of the said channel, and of Fuca's Straits, to the Pacific Ocean: *Provided, however,* That the navigation of the whole of the said channel and straits, south of the forty-ninth parallel of north latitude, remain free and open to both parties.

ART. II. From the point at which the forty-ninth parallel of north latitude shall be found to intersect the great northern branch of the Columbia River, the navigation of the said branch shall be free and open to the Hudson's Bay Company, and to all British subjects trading with the same, to the point where the said branch meets the main stream of the Columbia, and thence down the said main stream to the ocean, with free access into and through the said river or rivers, it being understood that all the usual portages along the line thus described shall, in like manner, be free and open. In navigating the said river or rivers, British subjects, with their goods and produce, shall be treated on the same footing as citizens of the United States; it being, however, always understood that nothing in this article shall be construed as preventing, or intended to prevent, the government of the United States from making any regulations respecting the navigation of the said river or rivers not inconsistent with the present treaty.

ART. III. In the future appropriation of the territory south of the forty-ninth parallel of north latitude, as provided in the first article of this treaty, the possessory rights of the Hudson's Bay Company, and of all British subjects who may be already in the occupation of land or other property lawfully acquired within the said territory, shall be respected.

ART. IV. The farms, lands, and other property of every description, belonging to the Puget's Sound Agricultural Company, on the north side of the Columbia River, shall be confirmed to the said company. In case, however, the situation of those farms and lands should be considered by the United States to be of public and political importance, and the United States government should signify a desire to obtain possession of the whole, or of any part thereof, the property so required shall be transferred to the said government, at a proper valuation, to be agreed upon between the parties. . . .

170. INDEPENDENT TREASURY ACT
August 8, 1846
(*U. S. Statutes at Large,* Vol. IX, p. 69 ff.)

Van Buren, upon his accession to the Presidency, recommended the establishment of a sub-treasury system as a substitute for the National Bank. A bill incorporating this suggestion was three times defeated, but finally passed July 4, 1840, only to be repealed by the incoming Harrison administration, August 13, 1841. The victory of the Democrats in the election of 1844 insured the repassage af the act. See, D. Kinley, *The Independent Treasury System;* E. M. Shepard, *Martin Van Buren;* J. P. Phillips, *Methods of Keeping the Public Money;* A. S. Bolles, *Financial History of the United States,* Vol. II.

An Act to provide for the better Organization of the Treasury, and for the Collection, Safe-Keeping, Transfer, and Disbursement of the public Revenue.

Be it enacted . . . , That the rooms prepared and provided in the new treasury building at the seat of government for the use of the treasurer of the United States, his assistants, and clerks, and occupied by them, and also the fireproof vaults and safes erected in said rooms for the keeping of the public moneys in the possession and under the immediate control of said treasurer, and such other apartments as are provided for in this act as places of deposit of the public money, are hereby constituted and declared to be the treasury of the United States. And all moneys paid into the same shall be subject to the draft of the treasurer, drawn agreeably to appropriations made by law. . . .

SEC. 6. That the treasurer of the United States, the treasurer of the mint of the United States, the treasurers, and those acting as such, of the various branch mints, all collectors of the customs, all surveyors of the customs acting also as collectors, all assistant treasurers, all receivers of public moneys at the several land offices, all postmasters, and all public officers of whatsoever character, be, and they are hereby, required to keep safely, without loaning, using, depositing in banks, or exchanging for other funds than as allowed by this act, all the public money collected by them, or otherwise at any time placed in their possession and custody, till the same is ordered, by the proper department or officer of the government, to be transferred or paid out; and when such orders for transfer or payment are received, faithfully and promptly to make the same as directed, and to do and perform all other duties as fiscal agents of the government which may be imposed by this or any other acts of Congress, or by any regulation of the treasury department made in conformity to law; and also to do and perform all acts and duties required by law, or by direction of any of the Executive departments of the government, as agents for paying pensions, or for making any other disbursements which either of the heads of these departments may be required by law to make, and which are of a character to be made by the depositaries hereby constituted, consistently with the other official duties imposed upon them. . . .

SEC. 9. That all collectors and receivers of public money, of every character and description, within the District of Columbia, shall, as frequently as they may be directed by the Secretary of the Treasury, or the Postmaster-General so to do, pay over to the treasurer of the United States, at the treasury, all public moneys collected by them, or in their hands; . . .

SEC. 18. That on January 1, 1847, and thereafter, all duties, taxes, sales of public lands, debts, and sums of money accruing or becoming due to the United States, and also all sums due for postages or otherwise, to the general post-office department, shall be paid in gold and silver coin only, or in treasury notes issued under the authority of the United States. . . .

SEC. 19. That on April 1, 1847, and thereafter, every officer or agent engaged in making disbursements on account of the United States, or of the general post-office, shall make all payments in gold and silver coin, or in treasury notes, if the creditor agree to receive said notes in payment. . . .

171. TREATY OF GUADALUPE HIDALGO
Signed, February 2, 1848; Ratified May 30, 1848
(Malloy, ed. *Treaties, Conventions, etc.*, Vol. I, p. 1107 ff.)

This Treaty, ending the War with Mexico, was negotiated by N. P. Trist. He had been instructed to demand the cession of New Mexico and California, Lower California, and a right of way across the Isthmus of Tehuantepec. Trist's blundering, and a growing sentiment for the annexation of even more Mexican territory, led to Trist's recall; he disregarded his recall, however, and concluded the Treaty of Guadalupe Hidalgo. Polk, after some hesitation, sent the treaty to the Senate for ratification, at the same time confiding to his Diary, "if the treaty was now to be made, I should demand more territory". On the Treaty, see, J. S. Reeves, "Treaty of Guadalupe Hidalgo", *American Hist. Rev.* Vol. X, pp. 309–324; R. S. Ripley, *The War with Mexico*, Vol. II; J. H. Smith, *The War with Mexico*, Vol. II: and see, L. M. Sears, "Nicholas P. Trist, A Diplomat with Ideals," *Miss. Valley Hist. Rev.* Vol. XI, p. 85 ff.

ART. I. THERE shall be firm and universal peace between the United States of America and the Mexican Republic, and between their respective countries, territories, cities, towns, and people, without exception of place or persons. . . .

ART. V. The boundary line between the two Republics shall commence in the Gulf of Mexico, three leagues from land, opposite the mouth of the Rio Grande, otherwise called Rio Bravo del Norte, or opposite the mouth of its deepest branch, if it should have more than one branch emptying directly into the sea; from thence up the middle of that river, following the deepest channel, where it has more than one, to the point where it strikes the southern boundary of New Mexico; thence, westwardly, along the whole southern boundary of New Mexico (which runs north of the town called *Paso*) to its western termination; thence, northward, along the western line of New Mexico, until it intersects the first branch of the River Gila; (or if it should not intersect any branch of that river, then to the point on the said line nearest to such branch, and thence in a direct line to the same;) thence down the middle of the said branch and of the said river, until it empties into the Rio Colorado; thence across the Rio Colorado, following the division line between Upper and Lower California, to the Pacific Ocean. . . .

ART. VII. The River Gila, and the part of

the Rio Bravo del Norte lying below the southern boundary of New Mexico, being, agreeably to the fifth article, divided in the middle between the two republics, the navigation of the Gila and of the Bravo below said boundary shall be free and common to the vessels and citizens of both countries; and neither shall, without the consent of the other, construct any work that may impede or interrupt, in whole or in part, the exercise of this right; not even for the purpose of favoring new methods of navigation. . . .

ART. VIII. Mexicans now established in territories previously belonging to Mexico, and which remain for the future within the limits of the United States, as defined by the present treaty, shall be free to continue where they now reside, or to remove at any time to the Mexican republic, retaining the property which they possess in the said territories, or disposing thereof, and removing the proceeds wherever they please, without their being subjected, on this account, to any contribution, tax, or charge whatever. . . .

ART. XII. In consideration of the extension acquired by the boundaries of the United States, as defined in the fifth article of the present treaty, the Government of the United States engages to pay to that of the Mexican Republic the sum of fifteen millions of dollars. . . .

ART. XIII. The United States engage, moreover, to assume and pay to the claimants all the amounts now due them, and those hereafter to become due, by reason of the claims already liquidated and decided against the Mexican Republic, under the conventions between the two republics severally concluded on the eleventh day of April, eighteen hundred and thirty-nine, and on the thirtieth day of January, eighteen hundred and forty-three; so that the Mexican Republic shall be absolutely exempt, for the future, from all expense whatever on account of the said claims.

ART. XIV. The United States do furthermore discharge the Mexican Republic from all claims of citizens of the United States, not heretofore decided against the Mexican Government, which may have arisen previously to the date of the signature of this treaty; which discharge shall be final and perpetual, whether the said claims be rejected or be allowed by the board of commissioners provided for in the following article, and whatever shall be the total amount of those allowed. . . .

ART. XV. The United States, exonerating Mexico from all demands on account of the claims of their citizens mentioned in the preceding article, and considering them entirely and forever cancelled, whatever their amount may be, undertake to make satisfaction for the same, to an amount not exceeding three and one quarter millions of dollars. . . .

ART. XXI. If unhappily any disagreement should hereafter arise between the governments of the two republics, whether with respect to the interpretation of any stipulation in this treaty, or with respect to any other particular concerning the political or commercial relations of the two nations, the said governments, in the name of those nations, do promise to each other that they will endeavor, in the most sincere and earnest manner, to settle the differences so arising, and to preserve the state of peace and friendship in which the two countries are now placing themselves; using, for this end, mutual representations and pacific negotiations. And if, by these means, they should not be enabled to come to an agreement, a resort shall not, on this account, be had to reprisals, aggression, or hostility of any kind, by the one republic against the other, until the Government of that which deems itself aggrieved shall have maturely considered, in the spirit of peace and good neighborship, whether it would not be better that such difference should be settled by the arbitration of commissioners appointed on each side, or by that of a friendly nation. And should such course be proposed by either party, it shall be acceded to by the other, unless deemed by it altogether incompatible with the nature of the difference, or circumstances of the case.

172. WOMAN'S RIGHTS

The Seneca Falls Declaration of Sentiments and Resolutions
July 19, 1848

(The History of Woman Suffrage, ed. by E. C. Stanton, S. B. Anthony and M. J. Gage, Vol. I, p. 70 ff.)

Though Frances Wright, Ernestine Rose, and others had championed the cause of woman's rights early in the century, the immediate origin of the woman's rights movement of the mid-century was in the anti-slavery crusade. When at the World Anti-Slavery Convention in London, in 1840, a group of American women delegates found themselves excluded, they determined that the cause of emancipation affected them as well as slaves. The Seneca Falls Convention was the first of its kind ever held. On the early woman's rights movement, see *The History of Woman Suffrage,* Vol. I; E. A. Hecker, *Short History of Women's Rights;* B. A. Rembaugh, *The Political Status of Women in the United States;* T. Stanton and H. S. Baltch, *Elizabeth Cady Stanton;* A. D. Hallowell, *Life and Letters of James and Lucretia Mott;* K. Anthony, *Margaret Fuller.* Some interesting comments on the philosophical implications of the movement are in T. V. Smith, *The American Philosophy of Equality.*

1. DECLARATION OF SENTIMENTS

When, in the course of human events, it becomes necessary for one portion of the family of man to assume among the people of the earth a position different from that which they have hitherto occupied, but one to which the laws of nature and of nature's God entitle them, a decent respect to the opinions of mankind requires that they should declare the causes that impel them to such a course.

We hold these truths to be self-evident: that all men and women are created equal; that they are endowed by their Creator with certain inalienable rights; that among these are life, liberty, and the pursuit of happiness; that to secure these rights governments are instituted, deriving their just powers from the consent of the governed. Whenever any form of government becomes destructive of these ends, it is the right of those who suffer from it to refuse allegiance to it, and to insist upon the institution of a new government, laying its foundation on such principles, and organizing its powers in such form, as to them shall seem most likely to effect their safety and happiness. Prudence, indeed, will dictate that governments long established should not be changed for light and transient causes; and accordingly all experience hath shown that mankind are more disposed to suffer while evils are sufferable, than to right themselves by abolishing the forms to which they are accustomed. But when a long train of abuses and usurpations, pursuing invariably the same object, evinces a design to reduce them under absolute despotism, it is their duty to throw off such government, and to provide new guards for their future security. Such has been the patient sufferance of the women under this government, and such is now the necessity which constrains them to demand the equal station to which they are entitled.

The history of mankind is a history of repeated injuries and usurpations on the part of man toward woman, having in direct object the establishment of an absolute tyranny over her. To prove this, let facts be submitted to a candid world.

He has never permitted her to exercise her inalienable right to the elective franchise.

He has compelled her to submit to laws, in the formation of which she had no voice.

He has withheld from her rights which are given to the most ignorant and degraded men—both natives and foreigners.

Having deprived her of this first right of a citizen, the elective franchise, thereby leaving her without representation in the halls of legislation, he has oppressed her on all sides.

He has made her, if married, in the eye of the law, civilly dead.

He has taken from her all right in property, even to the wages she earns.

He has made her, morally, an irresponsible being, as she can commit many crimes with impunity, provided they be done in the presence of her husband. In the covenant of marriage, she is compelled to promise obedience to her husband, he becoming, to all intents and purposes, her master—the law giving him power to deprive her of her liberty, and to administer chastisement.

He has so framed the laws of divorce, as to what shall be the proper causes, and in case of separation, to whom the guardianship of the children shall be given, as to be wholly regardless of the happiness of women—the law, in all cases, going upon a false supposition of the supremacy of man, and giving all power into his hands.

After depriving her of all rights as a married woman, if single, and the owner of property, he has taxed her to support a government which recognizes her only when her property can be made profitable to it.

He has monopolized nearly all the profitable employments, and from those she is permitted to follow, she receives but a scanty remuneration. He closes against her all the avenues to wealth and distinction which he considers most honorable to himself. As a teacher of theology, medicine, or law, she is not known.

He has denied her the facilities for obtaining a thorough education, all colleges being closed against her.

He allows her in Church, as well as State, but a subordinate position, claiming Apostolic authority for her exclusion from the ministry, and, with some exceptions, from any public participation in the affairs of the Church.

He has created a false public sentiment by giving to the world a different code of morals for men and women, by which moral delinquencies which exclude women from society, are not only tolerated, but deemed of little account in man.

He has usurped the prerogative of Jehovah himself, claiming it as his right to assign for her a sphere of action, when that belongs to her conscience and to her God.

He has endeavored, in every way that he could, to destroy her confidence in her own powers, to lessen her self-respect and to make her willing to lead a dependent and abject life.

Now, in view of this entire disfranchisement of one-half the people of this country, their social and religious degradation—in view of the unjust laws above mentioned, and because women do feel themselves aggrieved, oppressed, and fraudulently deprived of their most sacred rights, we insist that they have immediate admission to all the rights and privileges which belong to them as citizens of the United States.

In entering upon the great work before us, we anticipate no small amount of misconception, misrepresentation, and ridicule; but we shall use every instrumentality within our power to effect our object. We shall employ agents, circulate tracts, petition the State and National legislatures, and endeavor to enlist the pulpit and the press in our behalf. We hope this Convention will be followed by a series of Conventions embracing every part of the country.

2. RESOLUTIONS

WHEREAS, The great precept of nature is conceded to be, that "man shall pursue his own true and substantial happiness." Blackstone in his Commentaries remarks, that this law of Nature being coeval with mankind, and dictated by God himself, is of course superior in obligation to any other. It is binding over all the globe, in all countries and at all times; no human laws are of any validity if contrary to this, and such of them as are valid, derive all their force, and all their validity, and all their authority, mediately and immediately, from this original; therefore,

Resolved, That all laws which prevent woman from occupying such a station in society as her conscience shall dictate, or which place her in a position inferior to that of man, are contrary to the great precept of nature, and therefore of no force or authority.

Resolved, That woman is man's equal— was intended to be so by the Creator, and the highest good of the race demands that she should be recognized as such.

Resolved, That the women of this country ought to be enlightened in regard to the laws under which they live, that they may no longer publish their degradation by declaring themselves satisfied with their present position, nor their ignorance, by asserting that they have all the rights they want.

Resolved, That inasmuch as man, while claiming for himself intellectual superiority, does accord to woman moral superiority, it is pre-eminently his duty to encourage her to speak and teach, as she has an opportunity, in all religious assemblies.

Resolved, That the same amount of virtue, delicacy, and refinement of behavior that is required of woman in the social state, should also be required of man, and the same transgressions should be visited with equal severity on both man and woman.

Resolved, That the objection of indelicacy and impropriety, which is so often brought against woman when she addresses a public audience, comes with a very ill-grace from those who encourage, by their attendance, her appearance on the stage, in the concert, or in feats of the circus.

Resolved, That woman has too long rested satisfied in the circumscribed limits which corrupt customs and a perverted application of the Scriptures have marked out for her, and that it is time she should move in the enlarged sphere which her great Creator has assigned her.

Resolved, That it is the duty of the women of this country to secure to themselves their sacred right to the elective franchise.

Resolved, That the equality of human rights results necessarily from the fact of the identity of the race in capabilities and responsibilities.

Resolved, That the speedy success of our cause depends upon the zealous and untiring efforts of both men and women, for the overthrow of the monopoly of the pulpit, and for the securing to women an equal participation with men in the various trades, professions, and commerce.

Resolved, therefore, That, being invested by the creator with the same capabilities, and the same consciousness of responsibility for their exercise, it is demonstrably the right and duty of woman, equally with man, to promote every righteous cause by every righteous means; and especially in regard to the great subjects of morals and religion, it is self-evidently her right to participate with her brother in teaching them, both in private and in public, by writing and by speaking, by any instrumentalities proper to be used, and in any assemblies proper to be held; and this being a self-evident truth growing out of the divinely implanted principles of human nature, any custom or authority adverse to it, whether modern or wearing the hoary sanction of antiquity, is to be regarded as a self-evident falsehood, and at war with mankind.

173. HORACE MANN ON EDUCATION AND NATIONAL WELFARE
1848

(Twelfth Annual Report of Horace Mann as Secretary of Massachusetts State Board of Education)

Horace Mann's appointment as Secretary of the newly organized Board of Education, in 1837, inaugurated a new era in the history of American education. In his annual reports Mann discussed the larger implications of education in a democracy. These reports can be found in *The Life and Work of Horace Mann,* Vols. II–V. On Mann, see biography by Mrs. Mary Mann, in Vol. I of the *Life and Work;* B. A. Hinsdale, *Horace Mann and the Common School Revival in the United States;* A. E. Winship, *Horace Mann, the Educator.*

. . . . A cardinal object which the government of Massachusetts, and all the influential men in the State, should propose to themselves, is the physical well-being of all the people,—the sufficiency, comfort, competence, of every individual in regard to food, raiment, and shelter. And these necessaries and conveniences of life should be obtained by each individual for himself, or by each family for themselves, rather than accepted from the hand of charity or extorted by poor-laws. It is not averred that this most desirable result can, in all instances, be obtained; but it is, nevertheless, the end to be aimed at. True statesmanship and true political economy, not less than true philanthropy, present this perfect theory as the goal, to be more and more closely approximated by our imperfect practice. The desire to achieve such a result cannot be regarded as an unreasonable ambition; for, though all mankind were well fed, well clothed, and well housed, they might still be half civilized.

According to the European theory, men are divided into classes,—some to toil and earn, others to seize and enjoy. According to the Massachusetts theory, all are to have an equal chance for earning, and equal security in the enjoyment of what they earn. The latter tends to equality of condition; the former, to the grossest inequalities. Tried by any Christian standard of morals, or even by any of the better sort of heathen standards, can any one hesitate, for a moment, in declaring which of the two will produce the greater amount of human welfare, and which, therefore, is the more conformable to the divine will? The European theory is blind to what constitutes the highest glory as well as the highest duty of a State. . . .

Our ambition as a State should trace itself to a different origin, and propose to itself a different object. Its flame should be lighted at the skies. Its radiance and its warmth should reach the darkest and the coldest of abodes of men. It should seek the solution of such problems as these: To what extent can competence displace pauperism? How nearly can we free ourselves from the low-minded and the vicious, not by their expatriation, but by their elevation? To what extent can the resources and powers of Nature be converted into human welfare, the peaceful arts of life be advanced, and the vast treasures of human talent and genius be developed? How much of suffering, in all its forms, can be relieved? or, what is better than relief, how much can be prevented? Cannot the classes of crimes be lessened, and the number of criminals in each class be diminished? . . .

Now two or three things will doubtless be admitted to be true, beyond all controversy, in regard to Massachusetts. By its industrial condition, and its business operations, it is exposed, far beyond any other State in the Union, to the fatal extremes of overgrown wealth and desperate poverty. Its population is far more dense than that of any other State. It is four or five times more dense than the average of all the other States taken together; and density of population has always been one of the proximate causes of social inequality. According to population and territorial extent there is far more capital in Massachusetts—capital which is movable, and instantaneously available—than in any other State in the Union; and probably both these qualifications respecting population and territory could be omitted without endangering the truth of the assertion. . . .

Now surely nothing but universal education can counterwork this tendency to the domination of capital and the servility of labor. If one class possesses all the wealth and the education, while the residue of society is ignorant and poor, it matters not by what name the relation between them may be called: the latter, in fact and in truth, will be the servile dependents and subjects of the former. But, if education be equally diffused, it will draw property after it by the strongest of all attractions; for such a thing never did happen, and never can happen, as that an intelligent and practical body of men should be permanently poor. Property and labor in different classes are essentially antagonistic; but property and labor in the same class are essentially fraternal. The people of Massachusetts have, in some degree, appreciated the truth that the unexampled prosperity of the State—its comfort, its competence, its general intelligence and virtue—is attributable to the education, more or less perfect, which all its people have received; but are they sensible of a fact equally important,— namely, that it is to this same education that two-thirds of the people are indebted for not being to-day the vassals of as severe a tyranny, in the form of capital, as the lower classes of Europe are bound to in any form of brute force?

Education then, beyond all other devices of human origin, is a great equalizer of the conditions of men,—the balance wheel of the social machinery. I do not here mean that it so elevates the moral nature as to make men disdain and abhor the oppression of their fellow men. This idea pertains to another of its attributes. But I mean that it gives each man the independence and the means by which he can resist the selfishness of other men. It does better than to disarm the poor of their hostility toward the rich: it prevents being poor. Agrarianism is the revenge of poverty against wealth. The wanton destruction of the property of others—the burning of hay-ricks, and corn-ricks, the demolition of machinery because it supersedes hand-labor, the sprinkling of vitriol on rich dresses—is only agrarianism run mad. Education prevents both the revenge and the madness. On the other hand, a fellow-feeling for one's class or caste is the common instinct of hearts not wholly sunk in selfish regard for a person or for a family. The spread of education, by enlarging the cultivated class or caste, will open a wider area over which the social feelings will expand; and, if this education should be universal and complete, it would do more than all things else to obliterate factitious distinctions in society. . . .

For the creation of wealth, then,—for the existence of a wealthy people and a wealthy nation,—intelligence is the grand condition. The number of improvers will increase as the intellectual constituency, if I may so call it, increases. In former times, and in most parts of the world even at the present day, not one man in a million has ever had such a development of mind as made it possible for him to become a contributor to art or science. . . . Let this development proceed, and contributions . . . of inestimable value, will be sure to follow. That politi-

cal economy, therefore, which busies itself about capital and labor, supply and demand, interests and rents, favorable and unfavorable balances of trade, but leaves out of account the elements of a wide-spread mental development, is naught but stupendous folly. The greatest of all the arts in political economy is to change a consumer into a producer; and the next greatest is to increase the producing power,—and this to be directly obtained by increasing his intelligence. For mere delving, an ignorant man is but little better than a swine, whom he so much resembles in his appetites, and surpasses in his power of mischief. . . .

174. THE COMPROMISE OF 1850

The new territorial accessions that resulted from the War with Mexico precipitated the slavery question into politics in an inescapable manner. As early as August, 1846, David Wilmot of Pennsylvania had introduced into the House a resolution "That as an express and fundamental condition to the acquisition of any territory from the republic of Mexico by the United States, by virtue of any treaty which may be negotiated between them . . . neither slavery nor involuntary servitude shall ever exist in any part of said territory." This resolution was never passed by Congress, but the principle it expressed was aggressively maintained by the anti-slavery element. In 1848 Oregon was organized as a Territory and the principle of the Northwest Ordinance applied, but efforts to organize California and New Mexico failed. In 1849 the people of California took matters into their own hands by adopting a constitution which prohibited slavery. With the entire country seething with excitement and threats of secession coming from everywhere in the South, the stage was set for the greatest debate in Congressional history. Clay, Webster, Calhoun, Davis, Seward, Chase and others participated in the discussion. January 29 Clay introduced his compromise resolutions. The resolutions were submitted to a committee of which Clay was chairman and reported as two bills: an Omnibus Bill covering the organization of the Territories, and a bill to prohibit the slave trade in the District of Columbia. In the course of the debates on these bills Calhoun, too feeble to speak, presented his last denunciation of Northern aggressions, Webster made his famous Seventh of March speech, and Clay his last effort to save the Union. The Omnibus Bill was finally passed in separate acts. The Bill to admit California as a State was passed and approved September 9. On the Com-

promise of 1850 see J. F. Rhodes, *History of the United States Since the Compromise of 1850,* Vol. I; H. Von Holst, *Constitutional History of the United States,* Vol. III; J. Shouler, *History of the United States,* Vol. V; E. Channing, *History of the United States,* Vol. VI, chs. iii–iv; C. Schurz, *Henry Clay,* Vol. II; C. Fuess, *Daniel Webster,* Vol. II; H. Von Holst, *Calhoun;* W. E. Dodd, *Jefferson Davis;* A. Johnson, *Stephen A. Douglas;* A. B. Hart, *Samuel P. Chase.* The important debates can be found in T. H. Benton's *Abridgement of the Debates in Congress,* Vol. XVI. The speeches of Calhoun, Webster and Clay are reprinted in A. Johnston and J. A. Woodburn, *American Orations,* Vol. II. Many interesting letters are preserved in J. S. Pike, *First Blows of the Civil War.*

1. CLAY'S RESOLUTIONS
January 29, 1850

(U. S. *Senate Journal,* 31st Congress, 1st Session, p. 118 ff.)

It being desirable, for the peace, concord, and harmony of the Union of these States, to settle and adjust amicably all existing questions of controversy between them arising out of the institution of slavery upon a fair, equitable and just basis: therefore,

1. *Resolved,* That California, with suitable boundaries, ought, upon her application to be admitted as one of the States of this Union, without the imposition by Congress of any restriction in respect to the exclusion or introduction of slavery within those boundaries.

2. *Resolved,* That as slavery does not exist by law, and is not likely to be introduced into any of the territory acquired by the United

States from the republic of Mexico, it is inexpedient for Congress to provide by law either for its introduction into, or exclusion from, any part of the said territory; and that appropriate territorial governments ought to be established by Congress in all of the said territory, not assigned as the boundaries of the proposed State of California, without the adoption of any restriction or condition on the subject of slavery.

3. *Resolved,* That the western boundary of the State of Texas ought to be fixed on the Rio del Norte, commencing one marine league from its mouth, and running up that river to the southern line of New Mexico; thence with that line eastwardly, and so continuing in the same direction to the line as established between the United States and Spain, excluding any portion of New Mexico, whether lying on the east or west of that river.

4. *Resolved,* That it be proposed to the State of Texas, that the United States will provide for the payment of all that portion of the legitimate and bona fide public debt of that State contracted prior to its annexation to the United States, and for which the duties on foreign imports were pledged by the said State to its creditors, not exceeding the sum of —— dollars, in consideration of the said duties so pledged having been no longer applicable to that object after the said annexation, but having thenceforward become payable to the United States; and upon the condition, also, that the said State of Texas shall, by some solemn and authentic act of her legislature or of a convention, relinquish to the United States any claim which it has to any part of New Mexico.

5. *Resolved,* That it is inexpedient to abolish slavery in the District of Columbia whilst that institution continues to exist in the State of Maryland, without the consent of that State, without the consent of the people of the District, and without just compensation to the owners of slaves within the District.

6. *But, resolved,* That it is expedient to prohibit, within the District, the slave trade in slaves brought into it from States or places beyond the limits of the District, either to be sold therein as merchandise, or to be transported to other markets without the District of Columbia.

7. *Resolved,* That more effectual provision ought to be made by law, according to the requirement of the constitution, for the restitution and delivery of persons bound to service or labor in any State, who may escape into any other State or Territory in the Union. And,

8. *Resolved,* That Congress has no power to promote or obstruct the trade in slaves between the slaveholding States; but that the admission or exclusion of slaves brought from one into another of them, depends exclusively upon their own particular laws.

2. THE TEXAS AND NEW MEXICO ACT
September 9, 1850
(*U. S. Statutes at Large,* Vol. IX, p. 446 ff.)

An Act proposing to the State of Texas the Establishment of her Northern and Western Boundaries, the Relinquishment by the said State of all Territory claimed by her exterior to said Boundaries, and of all her claims upon the United States, and to establish a territorial Government for New Mexico.

Be it enacted, That the following propositions shall be, and the same hereby are, offered to the State of Texas, which, when agreed to by the said State, and in an act passed by the general assembly, shall be binding and obligatory, upon the United States, and upon the said State of Texas: *Provided,* The said agreement by the said general assembly shall be given on or before the first day of December, eighteen hundred and fifty:

FIRST. The State of Texas will agree that her boundary on the north shall commence at the point at which the meridian of one hundred degrees west from Greenwich is intersected by the parallel of thirty-six degrees thirty minutes north latitude, and shall run from said point due west to the meridian of one hundred and three degrees west from Greenwich; thence her boundary shall run due south to the thirty-second degree of north latitude; thence on the said parallel of thirty-two degrees of north latitude to the Rio Bravo del Norte, and thence with the channel of said river to the Gulf of Mexico.

SECOND. The State of Texas cedes to the United States all her claim to territory exterior to the limits and boundaries which she agrees to establish by the first article of this agreement.

THIRD. The State of Texas relinquishes all claim upon the United States for liability of the debts of Texas, and for compensation or indemnity for the surrender to the United States of her ships, forts, arsenals, custom-houses, custom-house revenue, arms and munitions of war, and public buildings with their sites, which became the property of the United States at the time of the annexation.

FOURTH. The United States, in consideration of said establishment of boundaries, cession of claim to territory, and relinquishment of claims, will pay to the State of Texas the sum of ten millions of dollars in a stock bearing five per cent. interest, and redeemable at the end of fourteen years, the interest payable half-yearly at the treasury of the United States. . . .

Sec. 2. And that all that portion of the Territory of the United States bounded as follows (boundaries) . . . is hereby erected into a temporary government, by the name of the Territory of New Mexico: *Provided,* That nothing in this act contained shall be construed to inhibit the government of the United States from dividing said Territory into two or more Territories, in such manner and at such times as Congress shall deem convenient and proper, or from attaching any portion thereof to any other Territory or State: *And provided, further,* That, when admitted as a State, the said Territory, or any portion of the same, shall be received into the Union, with or without slavery, as their constitution may prescribe at the time of their admission.

3. THE UTAH ACT
(September 9, 1850)

(*U. S. Statutes at Large,* Vol. IX, p. 453 ff.)

An Act to establish a Territorial Government for Utah

Be it enacted, That all that part of the territory of the United States included within the following limits, to wit: bounded on the west by the State of California, on the north by the Territory of Oregon, and on the east by the summit of the Rocky Mountains, and on the south by the thirty-seventh parallel of north latitude, be, and the same is hereby, created into a temporary government, by the name of the Territory of Utah; and, when admitted as a State, the said Territory, or any portion of the same, shall be received into the Union, with or without slavery, as their constitution may prescribe at the time

of their admission: *Provided,* That nothing in this act contained shall be construed to inhibit the government of the United States from dividing said Territory into two or more Territories, in such manner and at such times as Congress shall deem convenient and proper, or from attaching any portion of said Territory to any other State or Territory of the United States. . . .

4. FUGITIVE SLAVE ACT
(September 18, 1850)

(*U. S. Statutes at Large,* Vol. IX, p. 462 ff.)

An Act to amend, and supplementary to, the Act entitled "An Act respecting Fugitives from Justice, and Persons escaping from the Service of their Masters," approved—[February 12, 1793].

. . . SEC. 5. That it shall be the duty of all marshals and deputy marshals to obey and execute all warrants and precepts issued under the provisions of this act, when to them directed; and should any marshal or deputy marshal refuse to receive such warrant, or other process, when tendered, or to use all proper means diligently to execute the same, he shall, on conviction thereof, be fined in the sum of one thousand dollars, to the use of such claimant, . . . and after arrest of such fugitive, by such marshal or his deputy, or whilst at any time in his custody under the provisions of this act, should such fugitive escape, whether with or without the assent of such marshal or his deputy, such marshal shall be liable, on his official bond, to be prosecuted for the benefit of such claimant, for the full value of the service or labor of said fugitive in the State, Territory, or District whence he escaped: and the better to enable the said commissioners, when thus appointed, to execute their duties faithfully and efficiently, in conformity with the requirements of the Constitution of the United States and of this act, they are hereby authorized and empowered, within their counties respectively, to appoint, . . . any one or more suitable persons, from time to time, to execute all such warrants and other process as may be issued by them in the lawful performance of their respective duties; with authority to such commissioners, or the persons to be appointed by them, to execute process as aforesaid, to summon and call to their aid the bystanders, or *posse comitatus* of the proper county, when necessary to ensure a faithful observance of the clause of the Constitution referred to, in conformity with the provisions of this act; and all good citizens are hereby commanded to aid and assist in the prompt and efficient execution of this law, whenever their services may be required, as aforesaid, for that purpose; and said warrants shall run, and be executed by said officers, any where in the State within which they are issued.

SEC. 6. That when a person held to service or labor in any State or Territory of the United States, has heretofore or shall hereafter escape into another State or Territory of the United States, the person or persons to whom such service or labor may be due, . . . may pursue and reclaim such fugitive person, either by procuring a warrant from some one of the courts, judges, or commissioners aforesaid, of the proper circuit, district, or county, for the apprehension of such fugitive from service or labor, or by seizing and arresting such fugitive, where the same can be done without process, and by taking, or causing such person to be taken, forthwith before such court, judge, or commissioner, whose duty it shall be to hear and determine the case of such claimant in a summary manner; and upon satisfactory proof being made, by deposition or affidavit, in writing, to be taken and certified by such court, judge, or commissioner, or by other satisfactory testimony, duly taken and certified by some court, . . . and with proof, also by affidavit, of the identity of the person whose service or labor is claimed to be due as aforesaid, that the person so arrested does in fact owe service or labor to the person or persons claiming him or her, in the State or Territory from which such fugitive may have escaped as aforesaid, and that said person escaped, to make out and deliver to such claimant, his or her agent or attorney, a certificate setting forth the substantial facts as to the service or labor due from such fugitive to the claimant, and of his or her escape from the State or Territory in which he or she was arrested, with authority to such claimant, . . . to use such reasonable force and restraint as may be necessary, under the circumstances of the case, to take and remove such fugitive person back to the State or Territory whence he or she may

have escaped as aforesaid. In no trial or hearing under this act shall the testimony of such alleged fugitive be admitted in evidence; and the certificates in this and the first [fourth] section mentioned, shall be conclusive of the right of the person or persons in whose favor granted, to remove such fugitive to the State or Territory from which he escaped, and shall prevent all molestation of such person or persons by any process issued by any court, judge, magistrate, or other person whomsoever.

SEC. 7. That any persons who shall knowingly and willingly obstruct, hinder, or prevent such claimant, his agent or attorney, or any person or persons lawfully assisting him, her, or them, from arresting such a fugitive from service or labor, either with or without process as aforesaid, or shall rescue, or attempt to rescue, such fugitive from service or labor, from the custody of such claimant, . . . or other person or persons lawfully assisting as aforesaid, when so arrested, . . . or shall aid, abet, or assist such person so owing service or labor as aforesaid, directly or indirectly, to escape from such claimant, . . . or shall harbor or conceal such fugitive, so as to prevent the discovery and arrest of such person, after notice or knowledge of the fact that such person was a fugitive from service or labor . . . shall, for either of said offences, be subject to a fine not exceeding one thousand dollars, and imprisonment not exceeding six months . . . ; and shall moreover forfeit and pay, by way of civil damages to the party injured by such illegal conduct, the sum of one thousand dollars, for each fugitive so lost as aforesaid. . . .

SEC. 9. That, upon affidavit made by the claimant of such fugitive, . . . that he has reason to apprehend that such fugitive will be rescued by force from his or their possession before he can be taken beyond the limits of the State in which the arrest is made, it shall be the duty of the officer making the arrest to retain such fugitive in his custody, and to remove him to the State whence he fled, and there to deliver him to said claimant, his agent, or attorney. And to this end, the officer aforesaid is hereby authorized and required to employ so many persons as he may deem necessary to overcome such force, and to retain them in his service so long as circumstances may require. . . .

SEC. 10. That when any person held to service or labor in any State or Territory, or in the District of Columbia, shall escape therefrom, the party to whom such service or labor shall be due, . . . may apply to any court of record therein, . . . and make satisfactory proof to such court, . . . of the escape aforesaid, and that the person escaping owed service or labor to such party. Whereupon the court shall cause a record to be made of the matters so proved, and also a general description of the person so escaping, with such convenient certainty as may be; and a transcript of such record, . . . being produced in any other State, Territory, or district in which the person so escaping may be found, . . . shall be held and taken to be full and conclusive evidence of the fact of escape, and that the service or labor of the person escaping is due to the party in such record mentioned. And upon the production by the said party of other and further evidence if necessary, either oral or by affidavit, in addition to what is contained in the said record of the identity of the person escaping, he or she shall be delivered up to the claimant. And the said court, commissioner, judge, or other person authorized by this act to grant certificates to claimants of fugitives, shall, upon the production of the record and other evidences aforesaid, grant to such claimant a certificate of his right to take any such person identified and proved to be owing service or labor as aforesaid, which certificate shall authorize such claimant to seize or arrest and transport such person to the State or Territory from which he escaped . . .

5. ACT ABOLISHING THE SLAVE TRADE IN THE DISTRICT OF COLUMBIA
September 20, 1850

(*U. S. Statutes at Large,* Vol. IX, p. 467 ff.)

An Act to suppress the Slave Trade in the District of Columbia.

Be it enacted . . . , That from and after January 1, 1851, it shall not be lawful to bring into the District of Columbia any slave whatever, for the purpose of being sold, or for the purpose of being placed in depot, to be subsequently transferred to any other State or place to be sold as merchandize. And if any slave shall be brought into the said District by its owner, or by the authority or consent of its owner, contrary to the provisions of this act, such slave shall thereupon become liberated and free.

Sec. 2. That it shall and may be lawful for each of the corporations of the cities of Washington and Georgetown, from time to time, and as often as may be necessary, to abate, break up, and abolish any depot or place of confinement of slaves brought into the said District as merchandize, contrary to the provisions of this act, by such appropriate means as may appear to either of the said corporations expedient and proper. And the same power is hereby vested in the Levy Court of Washington county, if any attempt shall be made, within its jurisdictional limits, to establish a depot or place of confinement for slaves brought into the said District as merchandize for sale contrary to this act.

175. THE GEORGIA PLATFORM
1850

(A. H. Stephens, *The War Between the States,* Vol. II, app. B.)

Resolutions of a Convention held at Milledgeville, Georgia, to consider the Compromise of 1850. This platform was written by Charles J. Jenkins, and represented the point of view of the Union element in Georgia. See, R. H. Shryock, *Georgia and the Union in 1850;* U. B. Phillips, "Georgia and State Rights," Am. Hist. Assoc. *Reports,* 1901, Vol. II; and references to Doc. No. 176.

To the end that the position of this State may be clearly apprehended by her Confederates of the South and of the North, and that she may be blameless of all future consequences—

Be it resolved by the people of Georgia in Convention assembled, First. That we hold the American Union secondary in importance only to the rights and principles it was designed to perpetuate. That past associations, present fruition, and future prospects, will bind us to it so long as it continues to be the safe-guard of those rights and principles.

Second. That if the thirteen original Parties to the Compact, bordering the Atlantic in a narrow belt, while their separate interests were in embryo, their peculiar tendencies scarcely developed, their revolutionary trials and triumphs still green in memory, found Union impossible without compromise, the thirty-one of this day may well yield somewhat in the conflict of opinion and policy, to preserve that Union which has extended the sway of Republican Government over a vast wilderness to another ocean, and proportionately advanced their civilization and national greatness.

Third. That in this spirit the State of Georgia has maturely considered the action of Congress, embracing a series of measures for the admission of California into the Union, the organization of Territorial Governments for Utah and New Mexico, the establishment of a boundary between the latter and the State of Texas, the suppression of the slave-trade in the District of Columbia, and the extradition of fugitive slaves, and (connected with them) the rejection of propositions to exclude slavery from the Mexican Territories, and to abolish it in the District

of Columbia; and, whilst she does not wholly approve, will abide by it as a permanent adjustment of this sectional controversy.

Fourth. That the State of Georgia, in the judgment of this Convention, will and ought to resist, even (as a last resort) to a disruption of every tie which binds her to the Union, any future Act of Congress abolishing Slavery in the District of Columbia, without the consent and petition of the slaveholders thereof, or any Act abolishing Slavery in places within the slave-holding States, purchased by the United States for the erection of forts, magazines, arsenals, dockyards, navy-yards, and other like purposes; or in any Act suppressing the slave-trade between slave-holding States; or in any refusal to admit as a State any Territory applying because of the existence of Slavery therein; or in any Act prohibiting the introduction of slaves into the Territories of Utah and New Mexico; or in any Act repealing or materially modifying the laws now in force for the recovery of fugitive slaves.

Fifth. That it is the deliberate opinion of this Convention, that upon the faithful execution of the Fugitive Slave Bill by the proper authorities, depends the preservation of our much loved Union.

176. RESOLUTIONS OF THE NASHVILLE CONVENTION
June 10, 1850

(Resolutions, Addresses, and Journal of Proceedings of the Southern Convention, p. 57 ff.)

The Nashville Convention was called by the more radical of the Southern leaders to consider what action should be taken on the Compromise of 1850. Nine slave States were represented, but the moderates were from the beginning in control of the Convention, and from the point of view of its original sponsors it was a fiasco. A second convention, attended by only a handful of delegates, met in November and drew up resolutions denouncing the Compromise and reasserting the right of secession. See, J. W. DuBose, *Life and Times of William Lowndes Yancey;* L. A. White, *Robert Barnwell Rhett;* J. Hodgson, *The Cradle of the Confederacy, or the Times of Troup, Quitman, and Yancey;* P. M. Hamer, *The Secession Movement in South Carolina, 1847–1852;* M. J. White, *Secession Movement in the United States, 1847–1852;* D. T. Herndon, "The Nashville Convention of 1850",

Alabama Hist. Soc. *Transactions,* Vol. V; A. C. Cole, "The South and the Right of Secession in the Early Fifties," *Miss. Valley Hist. Rev.,* Vol. I; R. P. Brooks, "Howell Cobb and the Crisis of 1850", *Miss. Valley Hist. Review,* Vol. IV.

1. *Resolved,* That the territories of the United States belong to the people of the several States of this Union as their common property. That the citizens of the several States have equal rights to migrate with their property to these territories, and are equally entitled to the protection of the federal government in the enjoyment of that property so long as the territories remain under the charge of that government.

2. *Resolved,* That Congress has no power to exclude from the territory of the United

States any property lawfully held in the States of the Union, and any act which may be passed by Congress to effect this result is a plain violation of the Constitution of the United States. . . .

4. *Resolved,* That to protect property existing in the several States of the Union the people of these States invested the federal government with the powers of war and negotiation and of sustaining armies and navies, and prohibited to State authorities the exercise of the same powers. They made no discrimination in the protection to be afforded or the description of the property to be defended, nor was it allowed to the federal government to determine what should be held as property. Whatever the States deal with as property the federal government is bound to recognize and defend as such. Therefore it is the sense of this Convention that all acts of the federal government which tend to denationalize property of any description recognized in the Constitution and laws of the States, or that discriminate in the degree and efficiency of the protection to be afforded to it, or which weaken or destroy the title of any citizen upon American territories, are plain and palpable violations of the fundamental law under which it exists.

5. *Resolved,* That the slaveholding States cannot and will not submit to the enactment by Congress of any law imposing onerous conditions or restraints upon the rights of masters to remove with their property into the territories of the United States, or to any law making discrimination in favor of the proprietors of other property against them. . . .

8. *Resolved,* That the performance of its duties, upon the principle we declare, would enable Congress to remove the embarrassments in which the country is now involved. The vacant territories of the United States, no longer regarded as prizes for sectional rapacity and ambition, would be gradually occupied by inhabitants drawn to them by their interests and feelings. The institutions fitted to them would be naturally applied by governments formed on American ideas, and approved by the deliberate choice of their constituents. The community would be edu-

cated and disciplined under a republican administration in habits of self government, and fitted for an association as a State, and to the enjoyment of a place in the confederacy. A community so formed and organized might well claim admission to the Union and none would dispute the validity of the claim. . . .

9. *Resolved,* That a recognition of this principle would deprive the questions between Texas and the United States of their sectional character, and would leave them for adjustment, without disturbance from sectional prejudices and passions, upon considerations of magnanimity and justice. . . .

11. *Resolved,* That in the event a dominant majority shall refuse to recognize the great constitutional rights we assert, and shall continue to deny the obligations of the Federal Government to maintain them, it is the sense of this convention that the territories should be treated as property, and divided between the sections of the Union, so that the rights of both sections be adequately secured in their respective shares. That we are aware this course is open to grave objections, but we are ready to acquiesce in the adoption of the line of 36 deg. 30 min. north latitude, extending to the Pacific ocean, as an extreme concession, upon consideration of what is due to the stability of our institution.

12. *Resolved,* That it is the opinion of this Convention that this controversy should be ended, either by a recognition of the constitutional rights of the Southern people, or by an equitable partition of the territories. That the spectacle of a confederacy of States, involved in quarrels over the fruits of a war in which the American arms were crowned with glory, is humiliating. That the incorporation of the Wilmot Proviso in the offer of settlement, a proposition which fourteen States regard as disparaging and dishonorable, is degrading to the country. A termination to this controversy by the disruption of the confederacy or by the abandonment of the territories to prevent such a result, would be a climax to the shame which attaches to the controversy which it is the paramount duty of Congress to avoid. . . .

177. CLAYTON-BULWER TREATY
April 19, 1850

(Malloy, ed. *Treaties, Conventions, etc.* Vol. I, p. 659 ff.)

The project of a canal across the Isthmus had long been agitated, and was part of Polk's foreign policy. In as much as Great Britain controlled the eastern terminus of the Nicaragua route and was expanding in Central America, the Clayton-Bulwer Treaty represented a diplomatic victory for the United States. For the abrogation of this treaty, see Doc. No. 354. On the Isthmian project see I. D. Travis, *History of the Clayton-Bulwer Treaty;* L. M. Keasby, *The Nicaragua Canal and the Monroe Doctrine;* C. H. Huberich, *The Trans-Isthmian Canal: a Study in American Diplomatic History, 1825–1904;* D. Perkins, *The Monroe Doctrine, 1826–1867,* ch. iv.

ART. I. The Governments of the United States and Great Britain hereby declare that neither the one nor the other will ever obtain or maintain for itself any exclusive control over the said ship canal; agreeing that neither will ever erect or maintain any fortifications commanding the same, or in the vicinity thereof, or occupy, or fortify, or colonize or assume, or exercise any dominion over Nicaragua, Costa Rica, the Mosquito coast, or any part of Central America; nor will either make use of any protection which either affords or may afford, or any alliance which either has or may have to or with any state or people, for the purpose of erecting or maintaining any such fortifications, or of occupying, fortifying, or colonizing Nicaragua, Costa Rica, the Mosquito coast, or any part of Central America, or of assuming or exercising dominion over the same; nor will the United States or Great Britain take advantage of any intimacy, or use any alliance, connection or influence that either may possess with any State or Government through whose territory the said canal may pass, for the purpose of acquiring or holding, directly or indirectly, for the citizens or subjects of the one, any rights or advantages in regard to commerce or navigation through the said canal which shall not be offered on the same terms to the citizens or subjects of the other.

ART. II. Vessels of the United States or Great Britain traversing the said canal shall, in case of war between the contracting parties, be exempted from blockade, detention or capture by either of the belligerents; and this provision shall extend to such a distance from the two ends of the said canal as may hereafter be found expedient to establish.

ART. III. In order to secure the construction of the said canal, the contracting parties engage that if any such canal shall be undertaken upon fair and equitable terms by any parties having the authority of the local Government or Governments through whose territory the same may pass, then the persons employed in making the said canal, and their property used, or to be used, for that object, shall be protected, from the commencement of the said canal to its completion, by the Governments of the United States and Great Britain, from unjust detention, confiscation, seizure or any violence whatsoever. . . .

ART. V. The contracting parties further engage, that when the said canal shall have been completed, they will protect it from interruption, seizure or unjust confiscation, and that they will guarantee the neutrality thereof, so that the said canal may forever be open and free, and the capital invested therein secure. Nevertheless, the Governments of the United States and Great Britain, in according their protection to the construction of the said canal, and guaranteeing its neutrality and security when completed, always understand that this protection and guarantee are granted conditionally, and may be withdrawn by both Governments, or either Government, if both Governments, or either Government, should deem that the persons or company undertaking or managing the same adopt or establish such regulations concerning the traffic thereupon as are contrary to the spirit and intention of this convention, either by making unfair discriminations in favor of the commerce of one of the contracting parties over the commerce of the other, or by imposing oppressive exactions or unreasonable tolls upon the passengers, vessels, goods, wares, merchandise or other articles. Neither party, however, shall withdraw the aforesaid protection and guarantee without first giving six months' notice to the other.

ART. VI. The contracting parties in this convention engage to invite every State with which both or either have friendly intercourse to enter into stipulations with them similar to those which they have entered into with each other, to the end that all other States may share in the honor and advantage of having contributed to a work of such general interest and importance as the canal herein contemplated. And the contracting parties likewise agree that each shall enter into treaty stipulations with such of the Central American States as they may deem advisable, for the purpose of more effectually carrying out the great design of this convention, namely, that of constructing and maintaining the said canal as a ship communication between the two oceans for the benefit of mankind, on equal terms to all, and of protecting the same; and they also agree that the good offices of either shall be employed, when requested by the other, in aiding and assisting the negotiation of such treaty stipulations; and should any differences arise as to right or property over the territory through which the said canal shall pass between the States or Governments of Central America, and such differences should in any way impede or obstruct the execution of the said canal, the Governments of the United States and Great Britain will use their good offices to settle such differences in the manner best suited to promote the interests of the said canal, and to strengthen the bonds of friendship and alliance which exist between the contracting parties.

ART. VII. It being desirable that no time should be unnecessarily lost in commencing and constructing the said canal, the Governments of the United States and Great Britain determine to give their support and encouragement to such persons or company as may first offer to commence the same, with the necessary capital, the consent of the local authorities, and on such principles as accord with the spirit and intention of this convention. . . .

ART. VIII. The Governments of the United States and Great Britain having not only desired, in entering into this convention, to accomplish a particular object, but also to establish a general principle, they hereby agree to extend their protection, by treaty stipulations, to any other practicable communications, whether by canal or railway, across the isthmus which connects North and South America, and especially to the interoceanic communications, should the same prove to be practicable, whether by canal or railway, which are now proposed to be established by the way of Tehuantepec or Panama. In granting, however, their joint protection to any such canals or railways as are by this article specified, it is always understood by the United States and Great Britain that the parties constructing or owning the same shall impose no other charges or conditions of traffic thereupon than the aforesaid Governments shall approve of as just and equitable; and that the same canals or railways, being open to the citizens and subjects of the United States and Great Britain on equal terms, shall also be open on like terms to the citizens and subjects of every other State which is willing to grant thereto such protection as the United States and Great Britain engage to afford.

178. TRIAL OF MRS. DOUGLAS FOR TEACHING COLORED CHILDREN TO READ
Norfolk, Virginia, 1853
(*American State Trials*, ed. J. D. Lawson, Vol. VII, p. 56 ff.)

The slave codes of most Southern states forbade teaching slaves to read or write; some, as those of Virginia, extended the prohibition to all negroes. Though these laws were generally disregarded, the decision of the Court below indicates that they were at times enforced. Mrs. Douglas was convicted and spent one month in jail. See U. B. Phillips, *American Negro Slavery;* C S. Sydnor, *Slavery in Mississippi.*

BAKER, J. Upon an indictment found against you for assembling with negroes to instruct them to read and write, and for associating with them in an unlawful assembly, you were found guilty, and a mere nominal fine imposed, on the last day of this court held in the month of November. . . . The Court is not called on to vindicate the policy of the law in question, for so long as it remains upon the statute book, and unrepealed, public and private justice and morality require that it should be respected and sustained. There are persons, I believe, in our community, opposed to the policy of the law in question. They profess to believe that universal intellectual culture is necessary to religious instruction and education, and that such culture is suitable to a state of slavery; and there can be no misapprehension as to your opinions on this subject, judging from the indiscreet freedom with which you spoke of your regard for the colored race in general. Such opinions in the present state of our society I regard as manifestly mischievous. It is not true that our slaves cannot be taught religious and moral duty, without being able to read the Bible and use the pen. . . .

A valuable report or document recently published in the city of New York by the Southern Aid Society sets forth many valuable and important truths upon the condition of the Southern slaves, and the utility of moral and religious instruction, apart from a knowledge of books. I recommend the careful perusal of it to all whose opinions concur with your own. It shows that a system of catechetical instruction, with a clear and simple exposition of Scripture, has been employed with gratifying success; that the slave population of the South are peculiarly susceptible of good religious influences. Their mere residence among a Christian people has wrought a great and happy change in their condition: they have been raised from the night of heathenism to the light of Christianity, and thousands of them have been brought to a saving knowledge of the Gospel.

Of the one hundred millions of the negro race, there cannot be found another so large a body as the three millions of slaves in the United States, at once so intelligent, so inclined to the Gospel, and so blessed by the elevating influence of civilization and Christianity. Occasional instances of cruelty and oppression, it is true, may sometimes occur, and probably will ever continue to take place under any system of laws; but this is not confined to wrongs committed upon the negro; wrongs are committed and cruelly practiced in a like degree by the lawless white man upon his own color; and while the negroes of our town and State are known to be surrounded by most of the substantial comforts of life, and invited both by precept and example to participate in proper, moral and religious duties, it argues, it seems to me, a sickly sensibility towards them to say their persons, and feelings, and interests are not sufficiently respected by our laws, which, in effect, tend to nullify the act of our Legislature passed for the security and protection of their masters.

. . . The first legislative provision upon this subject was introduced in the year 1831, immediately succeeding the bloody scenes of the memorable Southampton insurrection; and that law being found not sufficiently penal to check the wrongs complained of, was re-enacted with additional penalties in the year 1848, which last mentioned act, after several years' trial and experience, has been re-affirmed by adoption, and incorporated into our present code. After these several and repeated recognitions of the wisdom and propriety of the said act, it may well be said that bold and open opposition to it is a matter not to be slightly regarded, especially as we have reason to believe that every Southern slave state in our country, as a measure of self-preservation and protection, has deemed it wise and just to adopt laws with similar provisions.

There might have been no occasion for such enactments in Virginia, or elsewhere, on the subject of negro education, but as a matter of self-defense against the schemes of Northern incendiaries, and the outcry against holding our slaves in bondage. Many now living well remember how, and when, and why the anti-slavery fury began, and by what means its manifestations were made public. Our mails were clogged with abolition pamphlets and inflammatory documents, to be distributed among our Southern negroes to induce them to cut our throats. Sometimes, it may be, these libelous documents were distributed by Northern citizens professing Southern feelings, and at other times by Southern people professing Northern feelings. These, however, were not the only means resorted to by the Northern fanatics to stir up insubordination among our slaves. They scattered far and near pocket handkerchiefs, and other similar articles, with frightful engravings, and printed over with anti-slavery nonsense, with the view to work upon the feeling and ignorance of our negroes, who otherwise would have remained comfortable and happy. Under such circumstances there was but one measure of protection for the South, and that was adopted. . . . In vindication of the policy and justness of our laws, which every individual should be taught to respect, the judgment of the Court is, in addition to the proper fine and costs, that you be imprisoned for the period of one month in the jail of this city. . . .

179. APPEAL OF THE INDEPENDENT DEMOCRATS
January 19, 1854
(J. W. Schuckers, *Life and Public Services of S. P. Chase*, p. 140 ff.)

The effort of Douglas to push through the Kansas-Nebraska Bill was the immediate occasion for this "appeal", signed by six of the most prominent abolitionists in the country. More moderate Democrats like Seward refused to sign the document. The Appeal had a profound effect: it was reprinted in all of the important papers of the country, and was partly responsible for the organization of the Republican Party. For Douglas's reply to the Appeal, see *Congressional Globe*, 33 Cong. 1st Sess. XXVIII, pt. I, p. 275 ff. See A. Beveridge, *Abraham Lincoln*, Vol. II, p. 184 ff.; J. F. Rhodes, *History of the United States from the Compromise of 1850*, Vol. I, ch. v; A. Johnson, *S. A. Douglas;* A. B. Hart, *S. P. Chase*.

As Senators and Representatives in the Congress of the United States it is our duty to warn our constituents, whenever imminent danger menaces the freedom of our institutions or the permanency of the Union.

Such danger, as we firmly believe, now impends, and we earnestly solicit your prompt attention to it.

At the last session of Congress a bill for the organization of the Territory of Nebraska passed the House of Representatives by an overwhelming majority. That bill was based on the principle of excluding slavery from the new Territory. It was not taken up for consideration in the Senate and consequently failed to become a law.

At the present session a new Nebraska bill has been reported by the Senate Committee on Territories, which, should it unhappily receive the sanction of Congress, will open all the unorganized Territories of the Union to the ingress of slavery.

We arraign this bill as a gross violation of a sacred pledge; as a criminal betrayal of precious rights; as part and parcel of an atrocious plot to exclude from a vast unoccupied region immigrants from the Old World and free laborers from our own States, and convert it into a dreary region of despotism, inhabited by masters and slaves.

Take your maps, fellow citizens, we entreat you, and see what country it is which this bill gratuitously and recklessly proposes to open to slavery. . . .

This immense region, occupying the very heart of the North American Continent, and larger, by thirty-three thousand square miles, than all the existing free States—including California . . . this immense region the bill now before the Senate, without reason and without excuse, but in flagrant disregard of sound policy and sacred faith, purposes to open to slavery.

We beg your attention, fellow-citizens, to a few historical facts:

The original settled policy of the United States, clearly indicated by the Jefferson proviso of 1784 and the Ordinance of 1787, was non-extension of slavery.

In 1803 Louisiana was acquired by purchase from France. . . .

In 1818, six years later, the inhabitants of the Territory of Missouri applied to Congress for authority to form a State constitution, and for admission into the Union. There were, at that time, in the whole territory acquired from France, outside of the State of Louisiana, not three thousand slaves.

There was no apology, in the circumstances of the country, for the continuance of slavery. The original national policy was against it, and not less the plain language of the treaty under which the territory had been acquired from France.

It was proposed, therefore, to incorporate in the bill authorizing the formation of a State government, a provision requiring that the constitution of the new State should contain an article providing for the abolition of existing slavery, and prohibiting the further introduction of slaves.

This provision was vehemently and pertinaciously opposed, but finally prevailed in the House of Representatives by a decided vote. In the Senate it was rejected, and—in consequence of the disagreement between the two Houses—the bill was lost.

At the next session of Congress, the controversy was renewed with increased violence. It was terminated at length by a compromise. Missouri was allowed to come into the Union with slavery; but a section was inserted in the act authorizing her admission, excluding slavery forever from all the territory acquired from France, not included in the new State, lying north of 36° 30'. . . .

The question of the constitutionality of this prohibition was submitted by President Monroe to his cabinet. John Quincy Adams was then Secretary of State; John C. Calhoun was Secretary of War; William H. Crawford was Secretary of the Treasury; and William Wirt was Attorney-General. Each of these eminent gentlemen—three of them being from the slave states—gave a written opinion, affirming its constitutionality, and thereupon the act received the sanction of the President himself, also from a slave State.

Nothing is more certain in history than the fact that Missouri could not have been admitted as a slave State had not certain members from the free States been reconciled to the measure by the incorporation of this prohibition into the act of admission. Nothing is more certain than that this prohibition has been regarded and accepted by the whole country as a solemn compact against the extension of slavery into any part of the territory acquired from France lying north of 36° 30', and not included in the new State of Missouri. The same act— let it be ever remembered—which authorized the formation of a constitution by the State, without a clause forbidding slavery, consecrated, beyond question and beyond honest recall, the whole remainder of the Territory

to freedom and free institutions forever. For more than thirty years—during more than half our national existence under our present Constitution—this compact has been universally regarded and acted upon as inviolable American law. In conformity with it, Iowa was admitted as a free State and Minnesota has been organized as a free Territory.

It is a strange and ominous fact, well calculated to awaken the worst apprehensions and the most fearful forebodings of future calamities, that it is now deliberately proposed to repeal this prohibition, by implication or directly—the latter certainly the manlier way—and thus to subvert the compact, and allow slavery in all the yet unorganized territory.

We cannot, in this address, review the various pretenses under which it is attempted to cloak this monstrous wrong, but we must not altogether omit to notice one.

It is said that Nebraska sustains the same relations to slavery as did the territory acquired from Mexico prior to 1850, and that the pro-slavery clauses of the bill are necessary to carry into effect the compromise of that year.

No assertion could be more groundless. . . .

The statesmen whose powerful support carried the Utah and New Mexico acts never dreamed that their provisions would be ever applied to Nebraska. . . .

Here is proof beyond controversy that the principle of the Missouri act prohibiting slavery north of 36° 30', far from being abrogated by the Compromise Acts, is expressly affirmed; and that the proposed repeal of this prohibition, instead of being an affirmation of the Compromise Acts, is a repeal of a very prominent provision of the most important act of the series. It is solemnly declared in the very Compromise Acts "that nothing herein contained shall be construed to impair or qualify" the prohibition of slavery north of 36° 30'; and yet in the face of this declaration, that sacred prohibition is said to be overthrown. Can presumption further go? To all who, in any way, lean upon these compromises, we commend this exposition.

These pretenses, therefore, that the territory covered by the positive prohibition of

1820, sustains a similar relation to slavery with that acquired from Mexico, covered by no prohibition except that of disputed constitutional or Mexican law, and that the Compromises of 1850 require the incorporation of the pro-slavery clauses of the Utah and New Mexico Bill in the Nebraska act, are mere inventions, designed to cover from public reprehension meditated bad faith. Were he living now, no one would be more forward, more eloquent, or more indignant in his denunciation of that bad faith, than Henry Clay, the foremost champion of both compromises. . . .

We confess our total inability properly to delineate the character or describe the consequences of this measure. Language fails to express the sentiments of indignation and abhorrence which it inspires; and no vision less penetrating and comprehensive than that of the All-Seeing can reach its evil issues. . . .

We appeal to the people. We warn you that the dearest interests of freedom and the Union are in imminent peril. Demagogues may tell you that the Union can be maintained only by submitting to the demands of slavery. We tell you that the Union can only be maintained by the full recognition of the just claims of freedom and man. The Union was formed to establish justice and secure the blessings of liberty. When it fails to accomplish these ends it will be worthless, and when it becomes worthless it cannot long endure.

We entreat you to be mindful of that fundamental maxim of Democracy—EQUAL RIGHTS AND EXACT JUSTICE FOR ALL MEN. Do not submit to become agents in extending legalized oppression and systematized injustice over a vast territory yet exempt from these terrible evils.

We implore Christians and Christian ministers to interpose. Their divine religion requires them to behold in every man a brother, and to labor for the advancement and regeneration of the human race.

Whatever apologies may be offered for the toleration of slavery in the States, none can be offered for its extension into Territories where it does not exist, and where that extension involves the repeal of ancient law and the violation of solemn compact. Let all protest, earnestly and emphatically, by correspondence, through the press, by memorials, by resolutions of public meetings and legislative bodies, and in whatever other mode may seem expedient, against this enormous crime.

For ourselves, we shall resist it by speech and vote, and with all the abilities which God has given us. Even if overcome in the impending struggle, we shall not submit. We shall go home to our constituents, erect anew the standard of freedom, and call on the people to come to the rescue of the country from the domination of slavery. We will not despair; for the cause of human freedom is the cause of God.

> S. P. Chase
> Charles Sumner
> J. R. Giddings
> Edward Wade
> Gerritt Smith
> Alexander De Witt.

180. THE KANSAS-NEBRASKA ACT
May 30, 1854

(*U. S. Statutes at Large*, Vol. X, p. 277 ff.)

This momentous measure organized two Territories, Kansas and Nebraska, divided by the fortieth parallel; it specifically repealed the Missouri Compromise, which had come to be regarded as sacrosanct by many people in the North, and recognized the principle of "squatter sovereignty." Probably no bill ever introduced to Congress was fraught with graver consequences. Senator Douglas, who sponsored the Bill, became anathema to a large part of the North; a group of Northern Democrats, headed by Chase, issued an "Appeal of the Independent Democrats", Doc. No. 179, calling for the organization of an anti-slavery party, and in February and July of 1854 the new Republican Party came into existence. The passage of the Kansas-Nebraska Bill with its provision for "popular sovereignty" led to a struggle for the control of Kansas that soon earned for that Territory the name of "Bleeding" Kansas. Lincoln, in his debates with Douglas, attacked the theory of popular sovereignty with such skill as seriously to damage Douglas's popularity in the South and to earn for himself a national reputation. It was charged and long believed that Douglas, in his championship of this bill, was actuated solely by ambition for the Presidency. It is probable, however, that Douglas sincerely believed that the territory opened up by the Kansas-Nebraska bill would become, because of its geography and climate, free territory. He was also profoundly interested in the construction of a trans-continental railway along a Northern route, and anxious therefore to throw open the region west of Iowa to settlement. The literature on the Kansas-Nebraska Act is extensive. See, P. O. Ray, *The Repeal of the Missouri Compromise;* S. B. Dixon, *A True History of the Missouri Compromise and Its Repeal;* F. H. Hodder, "Genesis of the Kansas-Nebraska Act," Wisconsin Hist. Soc. *Proceedings,* 1912; J. F. Rhodes, *History of the United States,* Vol. I, ch. v; A. Johnson, *S. A. Douglas,* chs. viii-ix; A. J. Beveridge, *Abraham Lincoln,* Vol. II, chs. iii-iv; G. F. Milton, *The Eve of the Conflict,* ch. vii. ff.

An Act to Organize the Territories of Nebraska and Kansas.

Be it enacted . . . , That all that part of the territory of the United States included within the following limits, except such portions thereof as are hereinafter expressly exempted from the operations of this act, to wit: beginning at a point in the Missouri River where the fortieth parallel of north latitude crosses the same; thence west on said parallel to the east boundary of the Territory of Utah, on the summit of the Rocky Mountains; thence on said summit northward to the forty-ninth parallel of north latitude; thence east on said parallel to the western boundary of the territory of Minnesota; thence southward on said boundary to the Missouri River; thence down the main channel of said river to the place of beginning, be, and the same is hereby, created into a temporary government by the name of the Territory of Nebraska; and when admitted as a State or States, the said Territory, or any portion of the same, shall be received into the Union with or without slavery, as their constitution may prescribe at the time of their admission: . . .

SEC. 14. *And be it further enacted, . . .* That the Constitution, and all laws of the United States which are not locally inap-

plicable, shall have the same force and effect within the said Territory of Nebraska as elsewhere within the United States, except the eighth section of the act preparatory to the admission of Missouri into the Union, approved March 6, 1820, which, being inconsistent with the principle of non-intervention by Congress with slavery in the States and Territories, as recognized by the legislation of eighteen hundred and fifty, commonly called the Compromise Measures, is hereby declared inoperative and void; it being the true intent and meaning of this act not to legislate slavery into any Territory or State, nor to exclude it therefrom, but to leave the people thereof perfectly free to form and regulate their domestic institutions in their own way, subject only to the Constitution of the United States: *Provided,* That nothing herein contained shall be construed to revive or put in force any law or regulation which may have existed prior to the act of March 6, 1820, either protecting, establishing, prohibiting, or abolishing slavery. . . .

SEC. 19. *And be it further enacted,* That all that part of the Territory of the United States included within the following limits, except such portions thereof as are hereinafter expressly exempted from the operations of this act, to wit, beginning at a point on the western boundary of the State of Missouri, where the thirty-seventh parallel of north latitude crosses the same; thence west on said parallel to the eastern boundary of New Mexico; thence north on said boundary to latitude thirty-eight; thence following said boundary westward to the east boundary of the Territory of Utah, on the summit of the Rocky Mountains; thence northward on said summit to the fortieth parallel of latitude; thence east on said parallel to the western boundary of the State of Missouri; thence south with the western boundary of said State to the place of beginning, be, and the same is hereby, created into a temporary government by the name of the Territory of Kansas; and when admitted as a State or States, the said Territory, or any portion of the same, shall be received into the Union with or without slavery, as their constitution may prescribe at the time of their admission: . . .

181. THE OSTEND MANIFESTO
October 18, 1854

(*U. S. 33d Congress, 2d Session,* House Executive Doc. No. 93)

In August, 1854, Secretary of State Marcy instructed our minister to Spain, Pierre Soulé, to negotiate for the purchase of Cuba, and suggested a consultation with our ministers to France and England, Mr. Mason and Mr. Buchanan, for the purpose of considering European opposition to such a purchase. The three ministers accordingly met at Ostend, Belgium, and drew up the notorious Ostend Manifesto. The report was repudiated by Marcy, and Soulé resigned his mission. Buchanan's participation in the Manifesto recommended him to the Southern Democrats as a suitable candidate for the Presidency. See, S. F. Bemis, ed. *American Secretaries of State,* Vol. VI, p. 183 ff.; R. F. Nichols, *Franklin Pierce,* chs, xlvi-xlviii, and appendix; S. Webster, "Mr. Marcy, the Cuban Question and the Ostend Manifesto," *Pol. Sci. Quart.,* Vol. VIII; A. A. Ettinger, *Mission to Spain of Pierre Soulé, 1853–1855.*

Aix la Chapelle, October 18, 1854.

Sir:—The undersigned, in compliance with the wish expressed by the President in the several confidential despatches you have addressed to us, respectively, to that effect, have met in conference, first at Ostend, in Belgium, on the 9th, 10th, and 11th instant, and then at Aix la Chapelle, in Prussia, on the days next following, up to the date hereof. . . .

We have arrived at the conclusion, and are thoroughly convinced, that an immediate and earnest effort ought to be made by the government of the United States to purchase Cuba from Spain at any price for which it can be obtained, not exceeding the sum of $—.

The proposal should, in our opinion, be made in such a manner as to be presented through the necessary diplomatic forms to the Supreme Constituent Cortes about to assemble. On this momentous question, in which the people both of Spain and the United States are so deeply interested, all our proceedings ought to be open, frank, and public. They should be of such a character as to challenge the approbation of the world.

We firmly believe that, in the progress of human events, the time has arrived when the vital interests of Spain are as seriously involved in the sale, as those of the United States in the purchase, of the island and that the transaction will prove equally honorable to both nations.

Under these circumstances we cannot anticipate a failure, unless possibly through the malign influence of foreign powers who possess no right whatever to interfere in the matter.

We proceed to state some of the reasons which have brought us to this conclusion, and, for the sake of clearness, we shall specify them under two distinct heads:

1. The United States ought, if practicable, to purchase Cuba with as little delay as possible.

2. The probability is great that the government and cortes of Spain will prove willing to sell it, because this would essentially promote the highest and best interests of the Spanish people.

Then, 1. It must be clear to every reflecting mind that, from the peculiarity of its geographical position, and the considerations attendant on it, Cuba is as necessary to the North American republic as any of its present members, and that it belongs naturally to that great family of States of which the Union is the providential nursery. . . .

The natural and main outlet to the products of this entire population, the highway of their direct intercourse with the Atlantic and the Pacific States, can never be secure, but must ever be endangered whilst Cuba is a dependency of a distant power in whose possession it has proved to be a source of constant annoyance and embarrassment to their interests.

Indeed, the Union can never enjoy repose, nor possess reliable security, as long as Cuba is not embraced within its boundaries.

Its immediate acquisition by our government is of paramount importance, and we cannot doubt but that it is a consummation devoutly wished for by its inhabitants.

The intercourse which its proximity to our

coasts begets and encourages between them and the citizens of the United States, has, in the progress of time, so united their interests and blended their fortunes that they now look upon each other as if they were one people and had but one destiny.

Considerations exist which render delay in the acquisition of this island exceedingly dangerous to the United States. . . .

Cuba has thus become to us an unceasing danger, and a permanent cause of anxiety and alarm.

But we need not enlarge on these topics. It can scarcely be apprehended that foreign powers, in violation of international law, would interpose their influence with Spain to prevent our acquisition of the island. . . .

Besides, the commercial nations of the world cannot fail to perceive and appreciate the great advantages which would result to their people from a dissolution of the forced and unnatural connexion between Spain and Cuba, and the annexation of the latter to the United States. The trade of England and France with Cuba would, in that event, assume at once an important and profitable character, and rapidly extend with the increasing population and prosperity of the island.

2. But if the United States and every commercial nation would be benefited by this transfer, the interests of Spain would also be greatly and essentially promoted.

She cannot but see what such a sum of money as we are willing to pay for the island would effect in the development of her vast natural resources. . . .

Should Spain reject the present golden opportunity for developing her resources, and removing her financial embarrassments, it may never again return. . . .

Under no probable circumstances can Cuba ever yield to Spain one per cent. on the large amount which the United States are willing to pay for its acquisition. But Spain is in imminent danger of losing Cuba, without remuneration. . . .

It is not improbable, therefore, that Cuba may be wrested from Spain by a successful revolution; and in that event she will lose both the island and the price which we are now willing to pay for it—a price far beyond what was ever paid by one people to another for any province.

It may also be remarked that the settlement of this vexed question, by the cession of Cuba to the United States, would forever prevent the dangerous complications between nations to which it may otherwise give birth.

It is certain that, should the Cubans themselves organize an insurrection against the Spanish government, and should other independent nations come to the aid of Spain in the contest, no human power could, in our opinion, prevent the people and government of the United States from taking part in such a civil war in support of their neighbors and friends.

But if Spain, dead to the voice of her own interest, and actuated by stubborn pride and a false sense of honor, should refuse to sell Cuba to the United States, then the question will arise, What ought to be the course of the American government under such circumstances? Self-preservation is the first law of nature, with States as well as with individuals. All nations have, at different periods, acted upon this maxim. Although it has been made the pretext for committing flagrant injustice, as in the partition of Poland and other similar cases which history records, yet the principle itself, though often abused, has always been recognized. . . .

Our past history forbids that we should acquire the island of Cuba without the consent of Spain, unless justified by the great law of self-preservation. We must, in any event, preserve our own conscious rectitude and our own self-respect.

Whilst pursuing this course we can afford to disregard the censures of the world, to which we have been so often and so unjustly exposed.

After we shall have offered Spain a price for Cuba far beyond its present value, and this shall have been refused, it will then be time to consider the question, does Cuba, in the possession of Spain, seriously endanger our internal peace and existence of our cherished Union?

Should this question be answered in the affirmative, then, by every law, human and divine, we shall be justified in wresting it from Spain if we possess the power; and this upon the very same principle that would justify an individual in tearing down the burning house of his neighbor if there were no other means of preventing the flames from destroying his own home.

Under such circumstances we ought neither to count the cost nor regard the odds which Spain might enlist against us. We forbear to enter into the question, whether the present condition of the island would justify such a measure? We should, however, be recreant to our duty, be unworthy of our gallant forefathers, and commit base treason against our posterity, should we permit Cuba to be Africanized and become a second St. Domingo, with all its attendant horrors to the white race, and suffer the flames to extend to our own neighboring shores seriously to endanger or actually to consume the fair fabric of our Union.

We fear that the course and current of events are rapidly tending towards such a catastrophe. We, however, hope for the best, though we ought certainly to be prepared for the worst. . . .

Yours, very respectfully,
James Buchanan.
J. Y. Mason.
Pierre Soulé.
Hon. Wm. L. Marcy, Secretary of State.

182. MASSACHUSETTS PERSONAL LIBERTY ACT
May 21, 1855

(Acts and Resolves Passed by the General Court of Massachusetts in the year 1855, p. 924 ff.)

This remarkably stringent personal liberty act which practically nullified the Fugitive Slave Act of 1850, resulted from the revulsion of feeling at the time of the capture of Anthony Burns in 1854. The bill was passed over the veto of Governor Gardner. Section fourteen was directed against Judge E. G. Loring, who had returned Burns to slavery. Governor Gardner refused to remove Loring, but he was subsequently removed in 1858. See J. Parker, *Personal Liberty Laws;* J. Hurd, *The Law of Freedom and Bondage;* R. C. Hurd, *Personal Liberty and Habeas Corpus;* H. Wilson, *History of the Rise and Fall of the Slave Power,* Vol. I; C. E. Stevens, *Anthony Burns, a History;* A. B. Hart, ed. *Commonwealth History of Massachusetts,* Vol. IV, ch. xvi; C. M. Fuess, *Life of Caleb Cushing;* T. Parker, *Discourses of Slavery,* Vol. II.

An Act to protect the Rights and Liberties of the People of the Commonwealth of Massachusetts.

Sec. 1. [Act of 1842 extended.]

Sec. 2. The meaning of the one hundred and eleventh chapter of the Revised Statutes is hereby declared to be, that every person imprisoned or restrained of his liberty is entitled, as of right and of course, to the writ of *habeas corpus,* except in the cases mentioned in the second section of that chapter.

Sec. 3. The writ of *habeas corpus* may be issued by the supreme judicial court, the court of common pleas, by any justice's court or police court of any town or city, by any court of record, or by any justice of either of said courts, or by any judge of probate; and it may be issued by any justice of the peace, if no magistrate above named is known to said justice of the peace to be within five miles of the place where the party is imprisoned or restrained, and it shall be returnable before the supreme judicial court, or any one of the justices thereof, whether the court may be in session or not, and in term time or vacation. . . .

Sec. 6. If any claimant shall appear to demand the custody or possession of the person for whose benefit such writ is sued out, such claimant shall state in writing the facts on which he relies, with precision and certainty; and neither the claimant of the alleged fugitive, nor any person interested in his alleged obligation to service or labor, nor the alleged fugitive, shall be permitted to testify at the trial of the issue; and no confessions, admissions or declarations of the alleged fugitive against himself shall be given in evidence. Upon every question of fact involved in the issue, the burden of proof shall be on the claimant, and the facts alleged and necessary to be established, must be proved by the testimony of at least two credible witnesses, or other legal evidence equivalent thereto, and by the rules of evidence known and secured by the common law; and no *ex parte* deposition or affidavit shall be received in proof in behalf of the claimant, and no presumption shall arise in favor of the claimant from any proof that the alleged fugitive or any of his ancestors had actually been held as a slave, without proof that such holding was legal.

Sec. 7. If any person shall remove from the limits of this Commonwealth, or shall assist in removing therefrom, or shall come into the Commonwealth with the intention of removing or of assisting in the removing therefrom, or shall procure or assist in procuring to be so removed, any person being in the peace thereof who is not "held to service or labor" by the "party" making "claim," or who has not "escaped" from the "party" making "claim," within the meaning of those words in the constitution of the United States, on the pretence that such person is so held or has so escaped, or that his "service or labor" is so "due," or with the intent to subject him to such "service or labor," he shall be punished by a fine of not less than one thousand, nor more than five thousand dollars, and by imprisonment in the State Prison not less than one, nor more than five years. . . .

Sec. 9. No person, while holding any office of honor, trust, or emolument, under the laws of this Commonwealth, shall, in any capacity, issue any warrant or other process, or grant any certificate, under or by virtue of an act of congress [February 12, 1793] . . . or under or by virtue of an act of congress [September 18, 1853] . . . or shall in any capacity, serve any such warrant or other process.

Sec. 10. Any person who shall grant any certificate under or by virtue of the acts of congress, mentioned in the preceding section, shall be deemed to have resigned any commission from the Commonwealth which he may possess, his office shall be deemed vacant, and he shall be forever thereafter ineligible to any office of trust, honor or emolument under the laws of this Commonwealth.

Sec. 11. Any person who shall act as counsel or attorney for any claimant of any alleged fugitive from service or labor, under or by virtue of the acts of congress mentioned in the ninth section of this act, shall be deemed to have resigned any commission from the Commonwealth that he may possess, and he shall be thereafter incapacitated from appearing as counsel or attorney in the courts of this Commonwealth. . . .

Sec. 14. Any person holding any judicial office under the constitution or laws of this Commonwealth, who shall continue, for ten days after the passage of this act, to hold the office of United States commissioner, or any office . . . which qualifies him to issue any warrant or other process . . . under the [Fugitive Slave Acts] shall be deemed to have violated good behavior, to have given reason for the loss of public confidence, and furnished sufficient ground either for impeachment or for removal by address.

Sec. 15. Any sheriff, deputy sheriff, jailer, coroner, constable, or other officer of this Commonwealth, or the police of any city or town, or any district, county, city or town officer, or any officer or other member of the volunteer militia of this Commonwealth, who shall hereafter arrest . . . any person for the reason that he is claimed or adjudged to be a fugitive from service or labor, shall be punished by fine . . . and by imprisonment. . . .

Sec. 16. The volunteer militia of the Commonwealth shall not act in any manner in the seizure . . . of any person for the reason that he is claimed or adjudged to be a fugitive from service or labor. . . .

Sec. 19. No jail, prison, or other place of confinement belonging to, or used by, either the Commonwealth of Massachusetts or any county therein, shall be used for the detention or imprisonment of any person accused or convicted of any offence created by [the Federal Fugitive Slave Acts] . . . or accused or convicted of obstructing or resisting any process, warrant, or order issued under either of said acts, or of rescuing, or attempting to rescue, any person arrested or detained under any of the provisions of either of the said acts. . . .

183. AMERICAN PARTY PLATFORM
1856
(A Political Text-book for 1860, p. 23 ff.)

The American or Know-Nothing Party represented the nativist sentiment, but it attracted large numbers, North and South, who hoped that its program might distract attention from the slavery struggle and that it might effect some reconciliation between the sections. The Party nominated ex-president Millard Fillmore, and secured almost nine hundred thousand votes. It was particularly strong in Massachusetts, New York, and Maryland. On the Know-Nothings see, L. D. Scisco, *Political Nativism in New York;* L. F. Schmeckebier, *Know-Nothing Party in Maryland;* C. Stickney, *Know-Nothingism in Rhode Island;* H. J. Desmond, *The Know-Nothing Party;* T. C. Smith, *Parties and Slavery,* chs, viii, x, xii.

. . . .

2. The perpetuation of the Federal Union and Constitution, as the palladium of our civil and religious liberties, and the only sure bulwarks of American Independence.

3. *Americans must rule America;* and to this end *native*-born citizens should be selected for all State, Federal and municipal offices of government employment, in preference to all others. *Nevertheless,*

4. Persons born of American parents residing temporarily abroad, should be entitled to all the rights of native-born citizens.

5. No person should be selected for political station (whether of native or foreign birth), who recognizes any allegiance or obligation of any description to any foreign prince, potentate or power, or who refuses to recognize the Federal and State Constitutions (each within its sphere) as paramount to all other laws, as rules of political action.

6. The unqualified recognition and maintenance of the reserved rights of the several States, and the cultivation of harmony and fraternal good will between the citizens of the several States, and to this end, non-interference by Congress with questions appertaining solely to the individual States, and non-intervention by each State with the affairs of any other State.

7. The recognition of the right of native-born and naturalized citizens of the United States, permanently residing in any territory thereof, to frame their constitution and laws, and to regulate their domestic and social affairs in their own mode, subject only to the provisions of the Federal Constitution, with the privilege of admission into the Union whenever they have the requisite population for one Representative in Congress: *Provided, always,* that none but those who are citizens of the United States, under the Constitution and laws thereof, and who have a fixed residence in any such Territory, ought to participate in the formation of the Constitution, or in the enactment of laws for said Territory or State.

8. An enforcement of the principles that no State or Territory ought to admit others than citizens to the right of suffrage, or of holding political offices of the United States.

9. A change in the laws of naturalization, making a continued residence of twenty-one years, of all not heretofore provided for, an indispensable requisite for citizenship hereafter, and excluding all paupers, and persons convicted of crime, from landing upon our shores; but no interference with the vested rights of foreigners.

10. Opposition to any union between Church and State; no interference with religious faith or worship, and no test oaths for office. . . .

13. Opposition to the reckless and unwise policy of the present Administration in the general management of our national affairs, and more especially as shown in removing "Americans" (by designation) and Conservatives in principle, from office, and placing foreigners and Ultraists in their places; as shown in a truckling subserviency to the stronger, and an insolent and cowardly bravado toward the weaker powers; as shown in reopening sectional agitation, by the repeal of the Missouri Compromise; as shown in granting to unnaturalized foreigners the right of suffrage in Kansas and Nebraska; as shown in its vacillating course on the Kansas and Nebraska question; as shown in the corruptions which pervade some of the Departments of the Government; as shown in disgracing meritorious naval officers through prejudice or caprice: and as shown in the

blundering mismanagement of our foreign relations.

14. Therefore, to remedy existing evils, and prevent the disastrous consequences otherwise resulting therefrom, we would build up the "American Party" upon the principles herein before stated. . . .

184. CONSTITUTION OF THE COMMITTEE OF VIGILANTES OF SAN FRANCISCO
May 15, 1856
(*American State Trials*, ed. J. D. Lawson, Vol. XV, p. 65 ff.)

The influx of lawless elements to California at the time of the Gold Rush had led, in 1851, to the organization of Vigilance Committees who took the law into their own hands. A new outbreak of lawlessness, together with the apparent breakdown of the machinery of law-enforcement, led in 1856 to the organization of the famous San Francisco Committee of Vigilantes which H. H. Bancroft designated as "the greatest demonstration in the cause of civil righteousness, without subversion of the law or of the government that the world has ever seen." On the work of the Committee, see, H. H. Bancroft, *Popular Tribunals*, Vol. II; F. Tuthill, *History of California*. For the earlier Vigilante organization, see M. F. Williams, *History of the San Francisco Vigilance Committee of 1851,* University of California Publications in History, Vol. XII. For the workings of vigilante committees elsewhere, see N. P. Langford, *Vigilante Days and Ways;* T. J. Dimsdale, *Vigilantes of Montana*. The records of the Trial of criminals by the Vigilante Committee of 1856 can be found in *American State Trials,* Vol. XV.

Whereas, it has become apparent to the citizens of San Francisco that there is no security for life and property, either under the regulations of society, as it at present exists, or under the laws as now administered; and that by the association together of bad characters, our ballot boxes have been stolen and others substituted, or stuffed with votes that were not polled, and thereby our elections nullified, our dearest rights violated, and no other method left by which the will of the people can be manifested; therefore, the citizens whose names are hereunto attached, do unite themselves into an association for maintenance of peace and good order of society—the preservation of our lives and property, and to insure that our ballot boxes shall hereafter express the actual and unforged will of the majority of our citizens; and we do bind ourselves, each unto the other, by a solemn oath, to do and perform every just and lawful act for the maintenance of law and order, and to sustain the laws when faithfully and properly administered; but we are determined that no thief, burglar, incendiary, assassin, ballot-box stuffer, or other disturbers of the peace, shall escape punishment, either by the quibbles of the law, the insecurity of prisons, the carelessness or corruption of police, or a laxity of those who pretend to administer justice; and to secure the objects of this association, we do hereby agree:

1st. That the name and style of this association shall be the Committee of Vigilance, for the protection of the ballot-box, the lives, liberty and property of the citizens and residents of the City of San Francisco.

2d. That there shall be rooms for the deliberations of the Committee, at which there shall be some one or more members of the Committee appointed for that purpose, in constant attendance at all hours of the day and night, to receive the report of any member of the association, or of any other person or persons of any act of violence done to the person or property of any citizen of San Francisco; and if, in the judgment of the member or members of the Committee present, it be such an act as justifies or demands the interference of this Committee, either in aiding in the execution of the laws, or the prompt and summary punishment of the offender, the Committee shall be at once assembled for the purpose of taking such action as the majority of them, when assembled, shall determine upon.

3d. That it shall be the duty of any member or members of the Committee on duty at the committee rooms, whenever a general assemblage of the Committee be deemed necessary, to cause a call to be made, in such a manner as shall be found advisable.

4th. That whereas, an Executive Committee, has been chosen by the General Committee, it shall be the duty of said Executive Committee to deliberate and act upon all important questions, and decide upon the measures necessary to carry out the objects for which this association was formed.

5th. That whereas, this Committee has been organized into subdivisions, the Executive Committee shall have the power to call, when they shall so determine, upon a board of delegates, to consist of three representatives from each division, to confer with them upon matters of vital importance.

6th. That all matters of detail and government shall be embraced in a code of By-Laws.

7th. That the action of this body shall be entirely and vigorously free from all consideration of, or participation in the merits or demerits, or opinion or acts, of any and all sects, political parties, or sectional divisions in the community; and every class of orderly citizens, of whatever sect, party, or nativity, may become members of this body. No discussion of political, sectional, or sectarian subjects shall be allowed in the rooms of the association.

8th. That no persons, accused before this body, shall be punished until after fair and impartial trial and conviction.

9th. That whenever the General Committee have assembled for deliberation, the decision of the majority, upon any question that may be submitted to them by the Executive Committee, shall be binding upon the whole; provided nevertheless, that when the delegates are deliberating upon the punishment to be awarded to any criminals, no vote inflicting the death penalty shall be binding, unless passed by two-thirds of those present and entitled to vote.

10th. That all good citizens shall be eligible for admission to this body, under such regulations as may be prescribed by a committee on qualifications; and if any unworthy persons gain admission, they shall on due proof be expelled; and believing ourselves to be executors of the will of the majority of our citizens, we do pledge our sacred honor, to defend and sustain each other in carrying out the determined action of this committee, at the hazard of our lives and our fortunes.

185. DRED SCOTT v. SANDFORD
19 Howard, 393
1857

Error to the U.S. circuit court for the district of Missouri. In 1834 Dred Scott, a negro slave, was taken by his master from Missouri, a slave state, to Illinois, a free state, and hence to Wisconsin Territory where slavery was forbidden by the Missouri Compromise of 1820. Subsequently Scott was brought back to Missouri, and in 1846 he began suit to obtain his freedom, on the ground that he had become free when taken into free territory. The case was eventually brought on appeal to the Supreme Court. Three major questions were involved: whether Scott was a citizen of the State of Missouri, so as to give the Federal courts jurisdiction; whether he had been set free by his sojourn in the free state of Illinois; whether he had been set free by his sojourn in the free Territory of Wisconsin, e.g., whether the Missouri Compromise was constitutional. The Court ruled that Scott was not a citizen of the United States or of the State of Missouri and therefore not competent to sue in the Federal courts. Having thus refused jurisdiction, the court went on to pass on the other questions presented,

all of the judges giving separate opinions. Of the dissenting opinions, that by Justice Curtis dealt most elaborately with the question of citizenship.

This case, probably the most famous in the history of the Court, has been the subject of an extensive literature. See the discussion of the case and bibliographical notes in Warren, *Supreme Court,* Vol. II, ch. xxvi; C. B. Swisher, *R. B. Taney;* Hodder, "Some Phases of the Dred Scott Case," *Miss. Valley Hist. Rev.* Vol. XVI; Corwin, "Dred Scott Decision in the Light of Contemporary Legal Doctrines," A. H. R., Vol. XVII; Cattarall, "Some Antecedents of the Dred Scott Case," A. H. R., Vol. XXX; Cohn, "Dred Scott Decision in the Light of Later Events," 46 Am. Law Rev. 548.

TANEY, C. J. . . . There are two leading questions presented by the record:

1. Had the Circuit Court of the United States jurisdiction to hear and determine the case between these parties? And,

2. If it had jurisdiction, is the judgment it has given erroneous or not?

The plaintiff in error, who was also the plaintiff in the court below, was, with his wife and children, held as slaves by the defendant, in the State of Missouri, and he brought this action in the Circuit Court of the United States for that district, to assert the title of himself and his family to freedom.

The declaration is . . . that he and the defendant are citizens of different States; that is, that he is a citizen of Missouri, and the defendant a citizen of New York.

The defendant pleaded in abatement to the jurisdiction of the court, that the plaintiff was not a citizen of the State of Missouri, as alleged in his declaration, being a negro of African descent whose ancestors were of pure African blood, and who were brought into this country and sold as slaves.

To this plea the plaintiff demurred, and the defendant joined in demurrer. . . .

Before we speak of the pleas in bar, it will be proper to dispose of the questions which have arisen on the plea in abatement.

That plea denies the right of the plaintiff to sue in a court of the United States, for the reasons therein stated.

If the question raised by it is legally before us, and the court should be of opinion that the facts stated in it disqualify the plaintiff from becoming a citizen, in the sense in which that word is used in the Constitution of the United States, then the judgment of the Circuit Court is erroneous, and must be reversed. . . .

The question to be decided is, whether the facts stated in the plea are sufficient to show that the plaintiff is not entitled to sue as a citizen in a court of the United States.

This is certainly a very serious question, and one that now for the first time has been brought for decision before this court. But it is brought here by those who have a right to bring it, and it is our duty to meet it and decide it.

The question is simply this: Can a negro, whose ancestors were imported into this country, and sold as slaves, become a member of the political community formed and brought into existence by the Constitution of the United States, and as such become entitled to all the rights, and privileges, and immunities, guaranteed by that instrument to the citizen? One of which rights is the privilege of suing in a court of the United States in the cases specified in the Constitution.

It will be observed, that the plea applies to that class of persons only whose ancestors were negroes of the African race, and imported into this country, and sold and held as slaves. The only matter in issue before the court, therefore, is, whether the descendants of such slaves, when they shall be emancipated, or who are born of parents who had become free before their birth, are citizens of a State, in the sense in which the word citizen is used in the Constitution of the United States. And this being the only matter in dispute on the pleadings, the court must be understood as speaking in this opinion of that class only, that is of persons who are the descendants of Africans who were imported into this country and sold as slaves. . . .

We proceed to examine the case as presented by the pleadings.

The words "people of the United States" and "citizens" are synonymous terms, and mean the same thing. They both describe the political body who, according to our republican institutions, form the sovereignty, and who hold the power and conduct the government through their representatives. They are what we familiarly call the "sovereign people," and every citizen is one of this people, and a constituent member of this sovereignty. The question before us is, whether the class of persons described in the plea in abatement compose a portion of this people, and are constituent members of this sovereignty? We think they are not, and that they are not included, and were not intended to be included, under the word "citizens" in the Constitution, and can, therefore, claim none of the rights and privileges which that instrument provides for and secures to citizens of the United States. On the contrary, they were at that time considered as a subordinate and inferior class of beings, who had been subjugated by the dominant race, and whether emancipated or not, yet remained subject to their authority, and had no rights or privileges but such as those who held the power and the government might choose to grant them. . . .

In discussing this question, we must not confound the rights of citizenship which a state may confer within its own limits, and the rights of citizenship as a member of the Union. It does not by any means follow, because he has all the rights and privileges of a citizen of a State, that he must be a citizen of the United States. He may have all of the rights and privileges of the citizen of a State, and yet not be entitled to the rights and privileges of a citizen in any other State. For, previous to the adoption of the Constitution of the United States, every State had the undoubted right to confer on whomsoever it pleased the character of a citizen, and to endow him with all its rights. But this character, of course, was confined to the boundaries of the State, and gave him no rights or privileges in other States beyond those secured to him by the laws of nations and the comity of States. Nor have the several States surrendered the power of conferring these rights and privileges by adopting the Constitution of the United States. Each State may still confer them upon an alien, or any one it thinks proper, or upon any class or description of persons; yet he would not be a citizen in the sense in which that word is used in the Constitution of the United States, nor entitled to sue as such in one of its courts, nor to the privileges and immunities of a citizen in the other States. The rights which he would acquire would be restricted to the State which gave them. . . .

It is very clear, therefore, that no State can, by any Act or law of its own, passed since the adoption of the Constitution, introduce a new member into the political community created by the Constitution of the United States. It cannot make him a member of this community by making him a member of its own. And for the same reason it cannot introduce any person, or description of persons, who were not intended to be embraced in this new political family, which the Constitution brought into existence, but were intended to be excluded from it.

The question then arises, whether the provisions of the Constitution, in relation to the personal rights and privileges to which the citizen of a State should be entitled, embraced the negro African race, at that time in this country, or who might afterwards be imported, who had then or should afterwards be made free in any State; and to put it in the power of a single State to make him a citizen of the United States, and endue him with the

full rights of citizenship in every other State without their consent. Does the Constitution of the United States act upon him whenever he shall be made free under the laws of a State, and raised there to the rank of a citizen, and immediately clothe him with all the privileges of a citizen in every other State, and in its own courts?

The court think the affirmative of these propositions cannot be maintained. And if it cannot, the plaintiff in error could not be a citizen of the State of Missouri, within the meaning of the Constitution of the United States, and, consequently, was not entitled to sue in its courts.

It is true, every person, and every class and description of persons, who were at the time of the adoption of the Constitution recognized as citizens in the several States, became also citizens of this new political body; but none other; it was formed by them, and for them and their posterity, but for no one else. And the personal rights and privileges guarantied to citizens of this new sovereignty were intended to embrace those only who were then members of the several state communities, or who should afterwards, by birthright or otherwise, become members, according to the provisions of the Constitution and the principles on which it was founded. . . .

It becomes necessary, therefore, to determine who were citizens of the several States when the Constitution was adopted. And in order to do this, we must recur to the governments and institutions of the thirteen Colonies, when they separated from Great Britain and formed new sovereignties. . . . We must inquire who, at that time, were recognized as the people or citizens of a State. . . .

In the opinion of the court, the legislation and histories of the times, and the language used in the Declaration of Independence, show, that neither the class of persons who had been imported as slaves, nor their descendants, whether they had become free or not, were then acknowledged as a part of the people, nor intended to be included in the general words used in that memorable instrument.

It is difficult at this day to realize the state of public opinion in relation to that unfortunate race, which prevailed in the civilized and enlightened portions of the world at the time of the Declaration of Independence, and when the Constitution of the United States was framed and adopted. . . .

They had for more than a century before been regarded as beings of an inferior order; and altogether unfit to associate with the white race, either in social or political relations; and so far inferior that they had no rights which the white man was bound to respect; and that the negro might justly and lawfully be reduced to slavery for his benefit. . . . This opinion was at that time fixed and universal in the civilized portion of the white race. It was regarded as an axiom in morals as well as in politics, which no one thought of disputing, or supposed to be open to dispute; and men in every grade and position in society daily and habitually acted upon it in their private pursuits, as well as in matters of public concern, without doubting for a moment the correctness of this opinion. . . .

The legislation of the different Colonies furnishes positive and undisputable proof of this fact. . . .

The language of the Declaration of Independence is equally conclusive. . . .

This state of public opinion had undergone no change when the Constitution was adopted, as is equally evident from its provisions and language. . . .

But there are two clauses in the Constitution which point directly and specifically to the negro race as a separate class of persons, and show clearly that they were not regarded as a portion of the people or citizens of the Government then formed.

One of these clauses reserves to each of the thirteen States the right to import slaves until the year 1808, if he thinks it proper. And the importation which it thus sanctions was unquestionably of persons of the race of which we are speaking, as the traffic in slaves in the United States had always been confined to them. And by the other provision the States pledge themselves to each other to maintain the right of property of the master, by delivering up to him any slave who may have escaped from his service, and be found within their respective territories. . . . And these two provisions show, conclusively, that neither the description of persons therein referred to, nor their descendants, were embraced in any of the other provisions of the Constitution; for certainly these two clauses were not intended to confer on them or their

posterity the blessings of liberty, or any of the personal rights so carefully provided for the citizen. . . .

Indeed, when we look to the condition of this race in the several States at the time, it is impossible to believe that these rights and privileges were intended to be extended to them. . . .

The legislation of the States therefore shows, in a manner not to be mistaken, the inferior and subject condition of that race at the time the Constitution was adopted, and long afterwards, throughout the thirteen States by which that instrument was framed; and it is hardly consistent with the respect due to these States, to suppose that they regarded at that time, as fellow-citizens and members of the sovereignty, a class of beings whom they had thus stigmatized; . . . More especially, it cannot be believed that the large slave-holding States regarded them as included in the word "citizens," or would have consented to a constitution which might compel them to receive them in that character from another State. For if they were so received, and entitled to the privileges and immunities of citizens, it would exempt them from the operation of the special laws and from the police regulations which they considered to be necessary for their own safety. . . . And all of this would be done in the face of the subject race of the same color, both free and slaves, inevitably producing discontent and insubordination among them, and endangering the peace and safety of the State. . . .

But it is said that a person may be a citizen, and entitled to that character, although he does not possess all the rights which may belong to other citizens; as, for example, the right to vote, or to hold particular offices; and that yet, when he goes into another State, he is entitled to be recognized there as a citizen, although the State may measure his rights by the rights which it allows to persons of a like character or class, resident in the State, and refuse to him the full rights of citizenship.

This argument overlooks the language of the provision in the Constitution of which we are speaking.

Undoubtedly, a person may be a citizen, that is, a member of the community who form the sovereignty, although he exercises no share of the political power, and is incapacitated from holding particular offices. . . .

So, too, a person may be entitled to vote by the law of the State, who is not a citizen even of the State itself. And in some of the States of the Union foreigners not naturalized are allowed to vote. And the State may give the right to free negroes and mulattoes, but that does not make them citizens of the State, and still less of the United States. And the provision in the Constitution giving privileges and immunities in other States, does not apply to them.

Neither does it apply to a person who, being the citizen of a State, migrates to another State. For then he becomes subject to the laws of the State in which he lives, and he is no longer a citizen of the State from which he removed. And the State in which he resides may then, unquestionably, determine his *status* or condition, and place him among the class of persons who are not recognized as citizens, but belong to an inferior and subject race; and may deny him the privileges and immunities enjoyed by its citizens. . . .

. . . But if he ranks as a citizen of the State to which he belongs, within the meaning of the Constitution of the United States, then, whenever he goes into another State, the Constitution clothes him, as to the rights of person, with all the privileges and immunities which belong to citizens of the State. And if persons of the African race are citizens of a state, and of the United States, they would be entitled to all of these privileges and immunities in every State, and the State could not restrict them; for they would hold these privileges and immunities, under the paramount authority of the Federal Government, and its courts would be bound to maintain and enforce them, the Constitution and laws of the State to the contrary notwithstanding. . . .

And upon a full and careful consideration of the subject, the court is of opinion that, upon the facts stated in the plea in abatement, Dred Scott was not a citizen of Missouri within the meaning of the Constitution of the United States, and not entitled as such to sue in its courts; and, consequently, that the Circuit Court had no jurisdiction of the case, and that the judgment on the plea in abatement is erroneous. . . .

We proceed, therefore, to inquire whether the facts relied on by the plaintiff entitled him to his freedom. . . .

In considering this part of the controversy, two questions arise: 1st. Was he, together with his family, free in Missouri by reason of the stay in the territory of the United States hereinbefore mentioned? And 2d, If they were not, is Scott himself free by reason of his removal to Rock Island, in the State of Illinois, as stated in the above admissions?

We proceed to examine the first question.

The Act of Congress, upon which the plaintiff relies, declares that slavery and involuntary servitude, except as a punishment for crime, shall be forever prohibited in all that part of the territory ceded by France, under the name of Louisiana, which lies north of thirty-six degrees thirty minutes north latitude, and not included within the limits of Missouri. And the difficulty which meets us at the threshold of this part of the inquiry is, whether Congress was authorized to pass this law under any of the powers granted to it by the Constitution; for if the authority is not given by that instrument, it is the duty of this court to declare it void and inoperative, and incapable of conferring freedom upon any one who is held as a slave under the laws of any one of the States.

The counsel for the plaintiff has laid much stress upon that article in the Constitution which confers on Congress the power "to dispose of and make all needful rules and regulations respecting the territory or other property belonging to the United States;" but, in the judgment of the court, that provision has no bearing on the present controversy, and the power there given, whatever it may be, is confined, and was intended to be confined, to the territory which at that time belonged to, or was claimed by, the United States, and was within their boundaries as settled by the treaty with Great Britain, and can have no influence upon a territory afterwards acquired from a foreign Government. It was a special provision for a known and particular territory, and to meet a present emergency, and nothing more. . . .

If this clause is construed to extend to territory acquired by the present Government from a foreign nation, outside of the limits of any charter from the British Government to a colony, it would be difficult to say, why it was deemed necessary to give the Government the power to sell any vacant lands belonging to the sovereignty which might be found within it; and if this was necessary, why the grant of this power should precede the power to legislate over it and establish a Government there; and still more difficult to say, why it was deemed necessary so specially and particularly to grant the power to make needful rules and regulations in relation to any personal or movable property it might acquire there. For the words, *other property* necessarily, by every known rule of interpretation, must mean property of a different description from territory or land. And the difficulty would perhaps be insurmountable in endeavoring to account for the last member of the sentence, which provides that "nothing in this Constitution shall be so construed as to prejudice any claims of the United States or any particular State," or to say how any particular State could have claims in or to a territory ceded by a foreign Government, or to account for associating this provision with the preceding provisions of the clause, with which it would appear to have no connection. . . .

But the power of Congress over the person or property of a citizen can never be a mere discretionary power under our Constitution and form of Government. The powers of the Government and the rights and privileges of the citizen are regulated and plainly defined by the Constitution itself. And when the Territory becomes a part of the United States, the Federal Government enters into possession in the character impressed upon it by those who created it. It enters upon it with its powers over the citizen strictly defined, and limited by the Constitution, from which it derives its own existence, and by virtue of which alone it continues to exist and act as a Government and sovereignty. It has no power of any kind beyond it; and it cannot, when it enters a Territory of the United States, put off its character, and assume discretionary or despotic powers which the Constitution has denied to it. It cannot create for itself a new character separated from the citizens of the United States, and the duties it owes them under the provisions of the Constitution. The Territory being a part of the United States, the Government and the citizen both enter it under the authority of the Constitution, with their respective rights defined and marked

out; and the Federal Government can exercise no power over his person or property, beyond what that instrument confers, nor lawfully deny any right which it has reserved. . . .

The rights of private property have been guarded with equal care. Thus the rights of property are united with the rights of person, and placed on the same ground by the fifth amendment to the Constitution. . . . An Act of Congress which deprives a person of the United States of his liberty or property merely because he came himself or brought his property into a particular Territory of the United States, and who had committed no offense against the laws, could hardly be dignified with the name of due process of law. . . .

And this prohibition is not confined to the States, but the words are general, and extend to the whole territory over which the Constitution gives it power to legislate, including those portions of it remaining under territorial government, as well as that covered by States. It is a total absence of power everywhere within the dominion of the United States, and places the citizens of a territory, so far as these rights are concerned, on the same footing with citizens of the States, and guards them as firmly and plainly against any inroads which the general government might attempt, under the plea of implied or incidental powers. And if Congress itself cannot do this—if it is beyond the powers conferred on the Federal Government—it will be admitted, we presume, that it could not authorize a territorial government to exercise them. It could confer no power on any local government, established by its authority, to violate the provisions of the Constitution.

It seems, however, to be supposed, that there is a difference between property in a slave and other property, and that different rules may be applied to it in expounding the Constitution of the United States. And the laws and usages of nations, and the writings of eminent jurists upon the relation of master and slave and their mutual rights and duties, and the powers which governments may exercise over it, have been dwelt upon in the argument.

But . . . if the Constitution recognizes the right of property of the master in a slave, and makes no distinction between that description of property and other property owned by a citizen, no tribunal, acting under the authority of the United States, whether it be legislative, executive, or judicial, has a right to draw such a distinction, or deny to it the benefit of the provisions and guarantees which have been provided for the protection of private property against the encroachments of the Government.

Now . . . the right of property in a slave is distinctly and expressly affirmed in the Constitution. The right to traffic in it, like an ordinary article of merchandise and property, was guaranteed to the citizens of the United States, in every State that might desire it, for twenty years. And the Government in express terms is pledged to protect it in all future time, if the slave escapes from his owner. . . . And no word can be found in the Constitution which gives Congress a greater power over slave property, or which entitles property of that kind to less protection than property of any other description. The only power conferred is the power coupled with the duty of guarding and protecting the owner in his rights.

Upon these considerations, it is the opinion

of the court that the Act of Congress which prohibited a citizen from holding and owning property of this kind in the territory of the United States north of the line therein mentioned, is not warranted by the Constitution, and is therefore void; and that neither Dred Scott himself, nor any of his family, were made free by being carried into this territory; even if they had been carried there by the owner, with the intention of becoming a permanent resident. . . .

Upon the whole, therefore, it is the judgment of this court, that it appears by the record before us that the plaintiff in error is not a citizen of Missouri, in the sense in which that word is used in the Constitution; and that the Circuit Court of the United States, for that reason, had no jurisdiction in the case, and could give no judgment in it.

Its judgment for the defendant must, consequently, be reversed, and a mandate issued directing the suit to be dismissed for want of jurisdiction.

WAYNE, J., NELSON, J., GRIER, J., DANIEL, J., CAMPBELL, J, AND CATRON, J., filed separate concurring opinions. McLEAN, J. and CURTIS, J. dissented.

186. LINCOLN'S HOUSE DIVIDED SPEECH
Springfield, Illinois, June 17, 1858

(*Writings of Abraham Lincoln,* Constitutional ed., Vol. III, p. 1 ff.)

This speech was delivered at the close of the Republican State Convention, in the Hall of the House of Representatives. Though the "house divided" phrase had been used frequently before, it was this speech of Lincoln's that gave currency and familiarity to the phrase and the idea. For an analysis of the speech and a description of the setting, see A. Beveridge, *Abraham Lincoln,* Vol. II, p. 575 ff.

MR. PRESIDENT AND GENTLEMEN OF THE CONVENTION: If we could first know where we are, and whither we are tending, we could better judge what to do, and how to do it. We are now far into the fifth year since a policy was initiated with the avowed object and confident promise of putting an end to slavery agitation. Under the operation of that policy, that agitation has not only not ceased, but has constantly augmented. In my opinion, it will not cease until a crisis shall have been reached and passed. "A house divided against

itself cannot stand." I believe this government cannot endure permanently half slave and half free. I do not expect the Union to be dissolved; I do not expect the house to fall; but I do expect it will cease to be divided. It will become all one thing, or all the other. Either the opponents of slavery will arrest the further spread of it, and place it where the public mind shall rest in the belief that it is in the course of ultimate extinction, or its advocates will push it forward till it shall become alike lawful in all the States, old as well as new, North as well as South.

Have we no tendency to the latter condition?

Let any one who doubts, carefully contemplate that now almost complete legal combination—piece of machinery, so to speak—compounded of the Nebraska doctrine and the Dred Scott decision. Let him consider, not only what work the machinery is adapted to do, and how well adapted, but also let him study the history of its construction, and trace, if he can, or rather fail, if he can, to trace the evidences of design, and concert of action, among its chief architects, from the beginning.

The new year of 1854 found slavery excluded from more than half the States by State Constitutions, and from most of the National territory by Congressional prohibition. Four days later, commenced the struggle which ended in repealing that Congressional prohibition. This opened all the National territory to slavery, and was the first point gained. . . .

While the Nebraska Bill was passing through Congress, a *law case,* involving the question of a negro's freedom, by reason of his owner having voluntarily taken him first into a free State, and then into a territory covered by the Congressional prohibition, and held him as a slave for a long time in each, was passing through the United States Circuit Court for the District of Missouri; and both Nebraska Bill and lawsuit were brought to a decision in the same month of May, 1854. The negro's name was "Dred Scott," which name now designates the decision finally made in the case. Before the then next Presidential election, the law case came to, and was argued in, the Supreme Court of the United States; but the decision of it was deferred until after the election. Still, before the election, Senator Trumbull, on the floor of the Senate, requested the leading advocate of the Nebraska Bill to state *his opinion* whether the people of a Territory can constitutionally exclude slavery from their limits; and the latter answers: "That is a question for the Supreme Court."

The election came. Mr. Buchanan was elected, and the indorsement, such as it was, secured. That was the second point gained. . . . The Presidential inauguration came, and still no decision of the court; but the incoming President, in his inaugural address, fervently exhorted the people to abide by the forthcoming decision, whatever it might be. Then, in a few days, came the decision.

The reputed author of the Nebraska Bill finds an early occasion to make a speech at this capital indorsing the Dred Scott decision, and vehemently denouncing all opposition to it. The new President, too, seizes the early occasion of the Silliman letter to indorse and strongly construe that decision, and to express his astonishment that any different view had ever been entertained!

At length a squabble springs up between the President and the author of the Nebraska Bill, on the mere question of *fact,* whether the Lecompton Constitution was or was not in any just sense made by the people of Kansas; and in that quarrel the latter declares that all he wants is a fair vote for the people, and that he cares not whether slavery be voted *down* or voted *up.* I do not understand his declaration, that he cares not whether slavery be voted down or voted up, to be intended by him other than as an apt definition of the policy he would impress upon the public mind. . . . That principle is the only shred left of his original Nebraska doctrine. Under the Dred Scott decision "squatter sovereignty" squatted out of existence, tumbled down like temporary scaffolding; like the mould at the foundry, served through one blast, and fell back into loose sand; helped to carry an election, and then was kicked to the winds. His late joint struggle with the Republicans, against the Lecompton Constitution, involves nothing of the original Nebraska doctrine. That struggle was made on a point—the right of a people to make their own constitution—upon which he and the Republicans have never differed.

The several points of the Dred Scott decision, in connection with Senator Douglas's "care not" policy, constitute the piece of machinery, in its present state of advancement. This was the third point gained. The working points of that machinery are:

Firstly, That no negro slave, imported as such from Africa, and no descendant of such slave, can ever be a citizen of any State, in the sense of that term as used in the Constitution of the United States. This point is made in order to deprive the negro, in every possible event, of the benefit of that provision of the United States Constitution which declares that "The citizens of each State shall be entitled to all privileges and immunities of citizens in the several States."

Secondly, That, "subject to the Constitution of the United States," neither Congress nor a Territorial Legislature can exclude slavery from any United States Territory. This point is made in order that individual men may fill up the Territories with slaves, without danger of losing them as property, and thus to enhance the chances of permanency to the institution through all the future.

Thirdly, That whether the holding a negro in actual slavery in a free State makes him free, as against the holder, the United States courts will not decide, but will leave to be decided by the courts of any slave State the negro may be forced into by the master. This point is made, not to be pressed immediately; but, if acquiesced in for a while, and apparently indorsed by the people at an election, then to sustain the logical conclusion that what Dred Scott's master might lawfully do with Dred Scott, in the free State of Illinois, every other master may lawfully do with any other one, or one thousand slaves, in Illinois, or in any other free State.

Auxiliary to all this, and working hand in hand with it, the Nebraska doctrine, or what is left of it, is to educate and mould public opinion, at least Northern public opinion, not to care whether slavery is voted down or voted up. This shows exactly where we now are; and partially, also, whither we are tending. . . .

Why was the amendment, expressly declaring the right of the people, voted down? Plainly enough now,—the adoption of it would have spoiled the niche for the Dred Scott decision. Why was the court decision held up? Why even a Senator's individual opinion withheld, till after the Presidential election? Plainly enough now,—the speaking

out then would have damaged the "perfectly free" argument upon which the election was to be carried. Why the outgoing President's felicitation on the indorsement? Why the delay of a reargument? Why the incoming President's advance exhortation in favor of the decision? These things look like the cautious patting and petting of a spirited horse preparatory to mounting him, when it is dreaded that he may give the rider a fall. And why the hasty after-indorsement of the decision by the President and others?

We cannot absolutely know that all these exact adaptations are the result of preconcert. But when we see a lot of framed timbers, different portions of which we know have been gotten out at different times and places and by different workmen,—Stephen, Franklin, Roger, and James, for instance,—and when we see these timbers joined together, and see they exactly make the frame of a house or a mill, all the tenons and mortises exactly fitting, and all the lengths and proportions of the different pieces exactly adapted to their respective places, and not a piece too many or too few,—not omitting even scaffolding,—or, if a single piece be lacking, we see the place in the frame exactly fitted and prepared yet to bring such piece in,—in such a case, we find it impossible not to believe that Stephen and Franklin and Roger and James all understood one another from the beginning, and all worked upon a common plan or draft drawn up before the first blow was struck. . . .

187. THE LINCOLN–DOUGLAS DEBATES
1858

(*The Writings of Abraham Lincoln,* Constitutional ed., Vols. III–IV)

Lincoln had been a candidate for the United States Senate in 1854–55; on that memorable occasion he had thrown his vote to Lyman Trumbull and thus secured the election of Trumbull over Douglas. In June, 1858 Lincoln was chosen as the Republican candidate for the Senatorship (Doc. No. 186), and on July 24 he challenged his opponent, Douglas, to a series of joint debates. The challenge was accepted, and seven joint debates arranged for. The debates were held at Ottawa, Freeport, Jonesboro, Charleston, Galesburg, Quincy, and Alton, Illinois, from August 21 to October 15. Perhaps the most important of the debates was the second, held at

Freeport, where Lincoln forced Douglas to announce the so-called Freeport Doctrine. In the election Lincoln carried districts containing a larger population than those which Douglas carried, but Douglas received the majority of the votes of the legislature. The Debates dramatized Lincoln before the country and paved the way for his candidacy in 1860, while they distinctly embarrassed Douglas in the south. Extracts from the second, third and seventh debates are given below. The Debates have been reprinted in numerous editions. See, A. Beveridge, *Abraham Lincoln,* Vol. II, chs. ix, x; C. Sandburg, *Abraham Lincoln, The Prairie Years;* A. Johnson, *Stephen*

A. *Douglas*; G. F. Milton, *The Eve of Conflict*, ch. xx; A. C. Cole, *The Era of the Civil War*, Centennial History of Illinois, Vol. IV.

1. THE SECOND JOINT DEBATE
Freeport, August 27, 1858
LINCOLN'S OPENING SPEECH AND DOUGLAS'S REPLY

Mr. Lincoln's Speech

. . . I now proceed to propound to the Judge the interrogatories, so far as I have framed them. I will bring forward a new installment when I get them ready. I will bring them forward now only reaching to number four.

The first one is:

Question 1.—If the people of Kansas shall, by means entirely unobjectionable in all other respects, adopt a State constitution, and ask admission into the Union under it, *before* they have the requisite number of inhabitants according to the English bill,—some ninety-three thousand,—will you vote to admit them?

Q. 2. Can the people of a United States Territory, in any lawful way, against the wish of any citizen of the United States, exclude slavery from its limits prior to the formation of a State constitution?

Q. 3. If the Supreme Court of the United States shall decide that States cannot exclude slavery from their limits, are you in favor of acquiescing in, adopting, and following such decision as a rule of political action?

Q. 4. Are you in favor of acquiring additional territory, in disregard of how such acquisition may affect the nation on the slavery question? . . .

Senator Douglas's Reply

First, he desires to know if the people of Kansas shall form a constitution by means entirely proper and unobjectionable, and ask admission into the Union as a State, before they have the requisite population for a member of Congress, whether I will vote for that admission. . . . I will answer his question. In reference to Kansas, it is my opinion that as she has population enough to constitute a slave State, she has people enough for a free State. I will not make Kansas an exceptional case to the other States of the Union. I hold it to be a sound rule, of uni-

versal application, to require a Territory to contain the requisite population for a member of Congress before it is admitted as a State into the Union. I made that proposition in the Senate in 1856, and I renewed it during the last session, in a bill providing that no Territory of the United States should form a constitution and apply for admission until it had the requisite population. On another occasion I proposed that neither Kansas nor any other Territory should be admitted until it had the requisite population. Congress did not adopt any of my propositions containing this general rule, but did make an exception of Kansas. I will stand by that exception. Either Kansas must come in as a free State, with whatever population she may have, or the rule must be applied to all the other Territories alike. I therefore answer at once, that, it having been decided that Kansas has people enough for a slave State, I hold that she has enough for a free State. I hope Mr. Lincoln is satisfied with my answer; . . .

The next question propounded to me by Mr. Lincoln is, Can the people of a Territory in any lawful way, against the wishes of any citizen of the United States, exclude slavery from their limits prior to the formation of a State constitution? I answer emphatically, as Mr. Lincoln has heard me answer a hundred times from every stump in Illinois, that in my opinion the people of a Territory can, by lawful means, exclude slavery from their limits prior to the formation of a State constitution. Mr. Lincoln knew that I had answered that question over and over again. He heard me argue the Nebraska Bill on that principle all over the State in 1854, in 1855, and in 1856, and he has no excuse for pretending to be in doubt as to my position on that question. It matters not what way the Supreme Court may hereafter decide as to the abstract question whether slavery may or may not go into a Territory under the Constitution, the people have the lawful means to introduce it or exclude it as they please, for the reason that slavery cannot exist a day or an hour anywhere, unless it is supported by local police regulations. Those police regulations can only be established by the local legislature; and if the people are opposed to slavery, they will elect representatives to that body who will by unfriendly legislation effectually prevent the introduction of it into their midst. If, on the contrary, they are for it, their legislation will favor its extension. Hence, no matter what the decision of the Supreme Court may be on that abstract question, still the right of the people to make a slave Territory or a free Territory is perfect and complete under the Nebraska Bill. I hope Mr. Lincoln deems my answer satisfactory on that point. . . .

. . . The third question which Mr. Lincoln presented is, if the Supreme Court of the United States shall decide that a State of this Union cannot exclude slavery from its own limits, will I submit to it? . . . He casts an imputation upon the Supreme Court of the United States, by supposing that they would violate the Constitution of the United States. I tell him that such a thing is not possible. It would be an act of moral treason that no man on the bench could ever descend to. Mr. Lincoln himself would never in his partisan feelings so far forget what was right as to be guilty of such an act.

The fourth question of Mr. Lincoln is, Are you in favor of acquiring additional territory, in disregard as to how such acquisition may affect the Union on the slavery question? This question is very ingeniously and cunningly put.

The Black Republican creed lays it down expressly that under no circumstances shall we acquire any more territory, unless slavery is first prohibited in the country. . . . I answer that whenever it becomes necessary, in our growth and progress, to acquire more territory, that I am in favor of it, without reference to the question of slavery; and when we have acquired it, I will leave the people free to do as they please, either to make it slave or free territory, as they prefer. It is idle to tell me or you that we have territory enough. . . . I tell you, increase, and multiply, and expand, is the law of this nation's existence. You cannot limit this great Republic by mere boundary lines, saying, "Thus far shalt thou go, and no farther." Any one of you gentlemen might as well say to a son twelve years old that he is big enough, and must not grow any larger; and in order to prevent his growth, put a hoop around him to keep him to his present size. What would be the result? Either the hoop must burst and be rent asunder, or the child must die. So it would be with this great

nation. With our natural increase, growing with a rapidity unknown in any part of the globe, with the tide of emigration that is fleeing from despotism in the Old World to seek refuge in our own, there is a constant torrent pouring into this country that requires more land, more territory upon which to settle; and just as fast as our interests and our destiny require additional territory in the North, in the South, or on the islands of the ocean, I am for it; and when we acquire it, will leave the people, according to the Nebraska Bill, free to do as they please on the subject of slavery and every other question. . . .

2. THE THIRD JOINT DEBATE
Jonesboro, September 15, 1858
Lincoln's Reply to Douglas

. . . At Freeport I propounded four interrogatories to him, claiming it as a right that he should answer as many interrogatories for me as I did for him, and I would reserve myself for a future installment when I got them ready. The Judge, in answering me upon that occasion, put in what I suppose he intends as answers to all four of my interrogatories. The first one of these interrogatories I have before me, and it is in these words:

"*Question* 1. If the people of Kansas shall, by means entirely unobjectionable in all other respects, adopt a State constitution, and ask admission into the Union under it, *before* they have the requisite number of inhabitants according to the English bill,"—some ninety-three thousand,—"will you vote to admit them?"

As I read the Judge's answer in the newspaper, and as I remember it as pronounced at the time, he does not give any answer which is equivalent to yes or no,—I will or I won't. He answers at very considerable length, rather quarrelling with me for asking the question, and insisting that Judge Trumbull had done something that I ought to say something about, and finally getting out such statements as induce me to infer that he means to be understood he will, in that supposed case, vote for the admission of Kansas. I only bring this forward now for the purpose of saying that if he chooses to put a different construction upon his answer, he may do it. But if he does not, I shall from this time forward assume that he will vote for the admission of Kansas in disregard of the English bill. He has the right to remove any misunderstanding I may have. I only mention it now, that I may hereafter assume this to be the true construction of his answer, if he does not now choose to correct me.

The second interrogatory that I propounded to him was this:

"*Question* 2. Can the people of a United States Territory, in any lawful way, against the wish of any citizen of the United States, exclude slavery from its limits prior to the formation of a State Constitution?"

To this Judge Douglas answered that they can lawfully exclude slavery from the Territory prior to the formation of a constitution. He goes on to tell us how it can be done. As I understand him, he holds that it can be done by the Territorial Legislature refusing to make any enactments for the protection of slavery in the Territory, and especially by adopting unfriendly legislation to it. For the sake of clearness, I state it again: that they can exclude slavery from the Territory, 1st, by withholding what he assumes to be an indispensable assistance to it in the way of legislation; and, 2d, by unfriendly legislation. If I rightly understand him, I wish to ask your attention for a while to his position.

In the first place, the Supreme Court of the United States has decided that any Congressional prohibition of slavery in the Territories is unconstitutional; that they have reached this proposition as a conclusion from their former proposition, that the Constitution of the United States expressly recognizes property in slaves, and from that other Constitutional provision, that no person shall be deprived of property without due process of law. Hence they reach the conclusion that as the Constitution of the United States expressly recognizes property in slaves, and prohibits any person from being deprived of property without due process of law, to pass an Act of Congress by which a man who owned a slave on one side of a line would be deprived of him if he took him on the other side, is depriving him of that property without due process of law. That I understand to be the decision of the Supreme Court. I understand also that Judge Douglas adheres most firmly to that decision; and the difficulty is, how is it possible for any power to exclude slavery from the Territory, unless in violation of that decision? That is the difficulty. . . .

I hold that the proposition that slavery cannot enter a new country without police regulations is historically false. It is not true at all. I hold that the history of this country shows that the institution of slavery was originally planted upon this continent *without* these "police regulations" which the Judge now thinks necessary for the actual establishment of it. Not only so, but is there not another fact: how came this Dred Scott decision to be made? It was made upon the case of a negro being taken and actually held in slavery in Minnesota Territory, claiming his freedom because the Act of Congress prohibited his being so held there. *Will the Judge pretend that Dred Scott was not held there without police regulations?* There is at least one matter of record as to his having been held in slavery in the Territory, not only without police regulations, but in the teeth of Congressional legislation supposed to be valid at the time. This shows that there is vigor enough in slavery to plant itself in a new country even against unfriendly legislation. It takes not only law, but the *enforcement* of law to keep it out. That is the history of this country upon the subject.

I wish to ask one other question. It being understood that the Constitution of the United States guarantees property in slaves in the Territories, if there is any infringement of the right of that property, would not the United States courts, organized for the government of the Territory, apply such remedy as might be necessary in that case? It is a maxim held by the courts that there is no wrong without its remedy; and the courts have a remedy for whatever is acknowledged and treated as a wrong.

Again: I will ask you, my friends, if you were elected members of the Legislature, what would be the first thing you would have to do before entering upon your duties? *Swear to support the Constitution of the United States.* Suppose you believe, as Judge Douglas does, that the Constitution of the United States guarantees to your neighbor the right to hold slaves in that Territory; that they are his property: how can you clear your oaths unless you give him such legislation as is necessary to enable him to enjoy that property? What do you understand by supporting the Constitution of a State, or of the United States? Is it not to give such constitutional helps to the rights established by that Constitution as may be practically needed? Can you, if you swear to support the Constitution, and believe that the Constitution establishes a right, clear your oath, without giving it support? Do you support the Constitution if, knowing or believing there is a right established under it which needs specific legislation, you withhold that legislation? Do you not violate and disregard your oath? I can conceive of nothing plainer in the world. There can be nothing in the words "support the Constitution," if you may run counter to it by refusing support to any right established under the Constitution. And what I say here will hold with still more force against the Judge's doctrine of "unfriendly legislation." How could you, having sworn to support the Constitution, and believing it guaranteed the right to hold slaves in the Territories, assist in legislation *intended to defeat that right?* That would be violating your own view of the Constitution. Not only so, but if you were to do so, how long would it take the courts to hold your votes unconstitutional and void? Not a moment.

Lastly, I would ask: Is not Congress itself under obligation to give legislative support to any right that is established under the United States Constitution? I repeat the question: Is not Congress itself bound to give legislative support to any right that is established in the United States Constitution? A member of Congress swears to support the Constitution of the United States: and if he sees a right established by that Constitution which needs specific legislative protection, can he clear his oath without giving that protection? Let me ask you why many of us who are opposed to slavery upon principle give our acquiescence to a Fugitive Slave law? Why do we hold ourselves under obligations to pass such a law, and abide by it when it is passed? Because the Constitution makes provision that the owners of slaves shall have the right to reclaim them. It gives the right to reclaim slaves; and that right is, as Judge Douglas says, a barren right, unless there is legislation that will enforce it.

The mere declaration, "No person held to service or labor in one State under the laws

thereof, escaping into another, shall in consequence of any law or regulation therein be discharged from such service or labor, but shall be delivered up on claim of the party to whom such service or labor may be due," is powerless without specific legislation to enforce it. Now, on what ground would a member of Congress, who is opposed to slavery in the abstract, vote for a Fugitive law, as I would deem it my duty to do? Because there is a constitutional right which needs legislation to enforce it. And although it is distasteful to me, I have sworn to support the Constitution; and having so sworn, I cannot conceive that I do support it if I withhold from that right any necessary legislation to make it practical. And if that is true in regard to a Fugitive Slave law, is the right to have fugitive slaves reclaimed any better fixed in the Constitution than the right to hold slaves in the Territories? For this decision is a just exposition of the Constitution, as Judge Douglas thinks. Is the one right any better than the other? Is there any man who, while a member of Congress, would give support to the one any more than the other? If I wished to refuse to give legislative support to slave property in the Territories, if a member of Congress, I could not do it, holding the view that the Constitution establishes that right. If I did it at all, it would be because I deny that this decision properly construes the Constitution. But if I acknowledge, with Judge Douglas, that this decision properly construes the Constitution, I cannot conceive that I would be less than a perjured man if I should refuse in Congress to give such protection to that property as in its nature it needed.

3. THE SEVENTH JOINT DEBATE
Alton, October 15, 1858

DOUGLAS'S SPEECH, LINCOLN'S REPLY, AND
DOUGLAS'S REJOINDER

Senator Douglas's Speech

LADIES AND GENTLEMEN: It is now nearly four months since the canvass between Mr. Lincoln and myself commenced. On the 16th of June the Republican Convention assembled at Springfield and nominated Mr. Lincoln as their candidate for the United States Senate, and he, on that occasion, delivered a speech in which he laid down what he understood to be the Republican creed, and the platform on which he proposed to stand during the contest. The principal points in that speech of Mr. Lincoln's were: First, that this government could not endure permanently divided into free and slave States, as our fathers made it; that they must all become free or all become slave; all become one thing, or all become the other,—otherwise this Union could not continue to exist. I give you his opinions almost in the identical language he used. His second proposition was a crusade against the Supreme Court of the United States because of the Dred Scott decision, urging as an especial reason for his opposition to that decision that it deprived the negroes of the rights and benefits of that clause in the Constitution of the United States which guarantees to the citizens of each State all the rights, privileges, and immunities of the citizens of the several States. On the 10th of July I returned home, and delivered a speech to the people of Chicago, in which I announced it to be my purpose to appeal to the people of Illinois to sustain the course I had pursued in Congress. In that speech I joined issue with Mr. Lincoln on the points which he had presented. Thus there was an issue clear and distinct made up between us on these two propositions laid down in the speech of Mr. Lincoln at Springfield, and controverted by me in my reply to him at Chicago. On the next day, the 11th of July, Mr. Lincoln replied to me at Chicago, explaining at some length and reaffirming the positions which he had taken in his Springfield speech. In that Chicago speech he even went further than he had before, and uttered sentiments in regard to the negro being on an equality with the white man. He adopted in support of this position the argument which Lovejoy and Codding and other Abolition lecturers had made familiar in the northern and central portions of the State: to wit, that the Declaration of Independence having declared all men free and equal, by divine law, also that negro equality was an inalienable right, of which they could not be deprived. He insisted, in that speech, that the Declaration of Independence included the negro in the clause asserting that all men were created equal, and went so far as to say that if one man was allowed to take the position that it did

not include the negro, others might take the position that it did not include other men. He said that all these distinctions between this man and that man, this race and the other race, must be discarded, and we must all stand by the Declaration of Independence, declaring that all men were created equal.

The issue thus being made up between Mr. Lincoln and myself on three points, we went before the people of the State. During the following seven weeks, between the Chicago speeches and our first meeting at Ottawa, he and I addressed large assemblages of the people in many of the central counties. In my speeches I confined myself closely to those three positions which he had taken, controverting his proposition that this Union could not exist as our fathers made it, divided into free and slave States, controverting his proposition of a crusade against the Supreme Court because of the Dred Scott decision, and controverting his proposition that the Declaration of Independence included and meant the negroes as well as the white men, when it declared all men to be created equal. . . . I took up Mr. Lincoln's three propositions in my several speeches, analyzed them, and pointed out what I believed to be the radical errors contained in them. First, in regard to his doctrine that this government was in violation of the law of God, which says that a house divided against itself cannot stand, I repudiated it as a slander upon the immortal framers of our Constitution. I then said, I have often repeated, and now again assert, that in my opinion our government can endure forever, divided into free and slave States as our fathers made it,—each State having the right to prohibit, abolish, or sustain slavery, just as it pleases. This government was made upon the great basis of the sovereignty of the States, the right of each State to regulate its own domestic institutions to suit itself; and that right was conferred with the understanding and expectation that, inasmuch as each locality had separate interests, each locality must have different and distinct local and domestic institutions, corresponding to its wants and interests. Our fathers knew when they made the government that the laws and institutions which were well adapted to the Green Mountains of Vermont were unsuited to the rice plantations of South

Carolina. They knew then, as well as we know now, that the laws and institutions which would be well adapted to the beautiful prairies of Illinois would not be suited to the mining regions of California. They knew that in a republic as broad as this, having such a variety of soil, climate, and interest, there must necessarily be a corresponding variety of local laws,—the policy and institutions of each State adapted to its condition and wants. For this reason this Union was established on the right of each State to do as it pleased on the question of slavery, and every other question; and the various States were not allowed to complain of, much less interfere with, the policy of their neighbors. . . .

. . . These measures [Compromise of 1850] passed on the joint action of the two parties. They rested on the great principle that the people of each State and each Territory should be left perfectly free to form and regulate their domestic institutions to suit themselves. You Whigs and we Democrats justified them in that principle. In 1854, when it became necessary to organize the Territories of Kansas and Nebraska, I brought forward the bill on the same principle. In the Kansas-Nebraska Bill you find it declared to be the true intent and meaning of the act not to legislate slavery into any State or Territory, nor to exclude it therefrom, but to leave the people thereof perfectly free to form and regulate their domestic institutions in their own way. I stand on that same platform in 1858 that I did in 1850, 1854, and 1856. . . . It has occurred to me that in 1854 the author of the Kansas and Nebraska Bill was considered a pretty good Democrat. It has occurred to me that in 1856, when I was exerting every nerve and every energy for James Buchanan, standing on the same platform then that I do now, that I was a pretty good Democrat. They now tell me that I am not a Democrat, because I assert that the people of a Territory, as well as those of a State, have the right to decide for themselves whether slavery can or cannot exist in such Territory. . . .

I . . . further . . . say that while, under the decision of the Supreme Court, as recorded in the opinion of Chief Justice Taney, slaves are property like all other property, and can be carried into any Territory of the United States the same as any other description of property, yet when you get them there they are subject to the local law of the Territory just like all other property. You will find in a recent speech delivered by that able and eloquent statesman Hon. Jefferson Davis, at Bangor, Maine, that he took the same view of this subject that I did in my Freeport speech. He there said: "If the inhabitants of any Territory should refuse to enact such laws and police regulations as would give security to their property or to his, it would be rendered more or less valueless in proportion to the difficulties of holding it without such protection. In the case of property in the labor of man, or what is usually called slave property, the insecurity would be so great that the owner could not ordinarily retain it. Therefore, though the right would remain, the remedy being withheld, it would follow that the owner would be practically debarred, by the circumstances of the case, from taking slave property into a Territory where the sense of the inhabitants was opposed to its introduction. So much for the oft-repeated fallacy of forcing slavery upon any community."

You will also find that the distinguished Speaker of the present House of Representatives, Hon. Jas. L. Orr, construed the Kansas and Nebraska Bill in this same way in 1856, and also that great intellect of the South, Alex. H. Stephens, put the same construction upon it in Congress that I did in my Freeport speech. The whole South are rallying to the support of the doctrine that if the people of a Territory want slavery, they have a right to have it, and if they do not want it, that no power on earth can force it upon them. I hold that there is no principle on earth more sacred to all the friends of freedom than that which says that no institution, no law, no constitution, should be forced on an unwilling people contrary to their wishes; and I assert that the Kansas and Nebraska Bill contains that principle. It is the great principle contained in that bill. It is the principle on which James Buchanan was made President. Without that principle, he never would have been made President of the United States. I will never violate or abandon that doctrine, if I have to stand alone. I have resisted the blandishments and threats of power on the one side, and seduction on the other, and have stood immovably for that principle, fighting for it when assailed by Northern mobs, or threatened by Southern hostility. I have defended it against the North and the South, and I will defend it against whoever assails it, and I will follow it wherever its logical conclusions lead me. I say to you that there is but one hope, one safety for this country, and that is to stand immovably by that principle which declares the right of each State and each Territory to decide these questions for themselves. This government was founded on that principle, and must be administered in the same sense in which it was founded. . . .

Mr. Lincoln's Reply

. . . Now, irrespective of the moral aspect of this question as to whether there is a right or wrong in enslaving a negro, I am still in favor of our new Territories being in such a condition that white men may find a home,—may find some spot where they can better their condition; where they can settle upon new soil and better their condition in life. I am in favor of this, not merely (I must say it here as I have elsewhere) for our own people who are born amongst us, but as an outlet for *free white people everywhere*—the world over—in which Hans, and Baptiste, and Patrick, and all other men from all the world, may find new homes and better their conditions in life.

I have stated upon former occasions, and I may as well state again, what I understand to be the real issue in this controversy between Judge Douglas and myself. . . . The real issue in this controversy—the one pressing upon every mind—is the sentiment on the part of one class that looks upon the institution of slavery *as a wrong*, and of another class that *does not* look upon it as a wrong. The sentiment that contemplates the institution of slavery in this country as a wrong is the sentiment of the Republican party. It is the sentiment around which all their actions, all their arguments, circle, from which all their propositions radiate. They look upon it as being a moral, social, and political wrong; and while they contemplate it as such, they nevertheless have due regard for its actual existence among us, and

the difficulties of getting rid of it in any satisfactory way, and to all the constitutional obligations thrown about it. Yet, having a due regard for these, they desire a policy in regard to it that looks to its not creating any more danger. They insist that it should, as far as may be, *be treated* as a wrong; and one of the methods of treating it as a wrong is to *make provision that it shall grow no larger*. They also desire a policy that looks to a peaceful end of slavery at some time, as being wrong. These are the views they entertain in regard to it as I understand them; and all their sentiments, all their arguments and propositions, are brought within this range. I have said, and I repeat it here, that if there be a man amongst us who does not think that the institution of slavery is wrong in any one of the aspects of which I have spoken, he is misplaced, and ought not to be with us. And if there be a man amongst us who is so impatient of it as a wrong as to disregard its actual presence among us and the difficulty of getting rid of it suddenly in a satisfactory way, and to disregard the constitutional obligations thrown about it, that man is misplaced if he is on our platform. We disclaim sympathy with him in practical action. He is not placed properly with us.

On this subject of treating it as a wrong, and limiting its spread, let me say a word. Has anything ever threatened the existence of this Union save and except this very institution of slavery? What is it that we hold most dear amongst us? Our own liberty and prosperity. What has ever threatened our liberty and prosperity, save and except this institution of slavery? If this is true, how do you propose to improve the condition of things by enlarging slavery,—by spreading it out and making it bigger? You may have a wen or cancer upon your person, and not be able to cut it out, lest you bleed to death; but surely it is no way to cure it, to engraft it and spread it over your whole body. That is no proper way of treating what you regard a wrong. You see this peaceful way of dealing with it as a wrong,—restricting the spread of it, and not allowing it to go into new countries where it has not already existed. That is the peaceful way, the old-fashioned way, the way in which the fathers themselves set us the example.

On the other hand, I have said there is a sentiment which treats it as *not* being wrong. That is the Democratic sentiment of this day. . . .

. . . The Democratic policy in regard to that institution will not tolerate the merest breath, the slightest hint, of the least degree of wrong about it. Try it by some of Judge Douglas's arguments. He says he "don't care whether it is voted up or voted down" in the Territories. I do not care myself, in dealing with that expression, whether it is intended to be expressive of his individual sentiments on the subject, or only of the national policy he desires to have established. It is alike valuable for my purpose. Any man can say that who does not see anything wrong in slavery; but no man can logically say it who does see a wrong in it, because no man can logically say he don't care whether a wrong is voted up or voted down. He may say he don't care whether an indifferent thing is voted up or down, but he must logically have a choice between a right thing and a wrong thing. He contends that whatever community wants slaves has a right to have them. So they have, if it is not a wrong. But if it is a wrong, he cannot say people have a right to do wrong. He says that upon the score of equality slaves should be allowed to go in a new Territory, like other property. This is strictly logical if there is no difference between it and other property. If it and other property are equal, this argument is entirely logical. But if you insist that one is wrong and the other right, there is no use to institute a comparison between right and wrong. You may turn over everything in the Democratic policy from beginning to end, whether in the shape it takes on the statute book, in the shape it takes in the Dred Scott decision, in the shape it takes in conversation, or the shape it takes in short maxim-like arguments,—it everywhere carefully excludes the idea that there is anything wrong in it.

That is the real issue. That is the issue that will continue in this country when these poor tongues of Judge Douglas and myself shall be silent. It is the eternal struggle between these two principles—right and wrong—throughout the world. They are the two principles that have stood face to face from the beginning of time, and will ever continue to struggle. The one is the common right of humanity, and the other the divine right of kings. . . . And whenever we can get rid of the fog which obscures the real question, when we can get Judge Douglas and his friends to avow a policy looking to its perpetuation,—we can get out from among that class of men and bring them to the side of those who treat it as a wrong. Then there will soon be an end of it, and that end will be its "ultimate extinction." Whenever the issue can be distinctly made, and all extraneous matter thrown out so that men can fairly see the real difference between the parties, this controversy will soon be settled, and it will be done peaceably too. There will be no war, no violence. It will be placed again where the wisest and best men of the world placed it. . . .

I understand I have ten minutes yet. I will employ it in saying something about this argument Judge Douglas uses, while he sustains the Dred Scott decision, that the people of the Territories can still somehow exclude slavery. The first thing I ask attention to is the fact that Judge Douglas constantly said, before the decision, that whether they could or not, *was a question for the Supreme Court.* But after the court had made the decision he virtually says it is *not* a question for the Supreme Court, but for the people. And how is it he tells us they can exclude it? He says it needs "police regulations," and that admits of "unfriendly legislation." Although it is a right established by the Constitution of the United States to take a slave into a Territory of the United States and hold him as property, yet unless the Territorial Legislature will give friendly legislation, and more especially if they adopt unfriendly legislation, they can practically exclude him. Now, without meeting this proposition as a matter of fact, I pass to consider the real constitutional obligation. Let me take the gentleman who looks me in the face before me, and let us suppose that he is a member of the Territorial Legislature. The first thing he will do will be to swear that he will support the Constitution of the United States. His neighbor by his side in the Territory has slaves and needs Territorial legislation to enable him to enjoy that constitutional right. Can he withhold the legislation which his neighbor needs for the enjoyment of a right which is fixed in his favor in the Constitution of the United States which he has sworn to support? Can he withhold it without violating his oath? And, more especially, can he pass unfriendly legislation to violate his oath? Why, this is a *monstrous* sort of talk about the Constitution of the United States! *There has never been as outlandish or lawless a doctrine from the mouth of any respectable man on earth.* I do not believe it is a constitutional right to hold slaves in a Territory of the United States. I believe the decision was improperly made and I go for reversing it. Judge Douglas is furious against those who go for reversing a decision. But he is for legislating it out of all force while the law itself stands. I repeat that there has never been so monstrous a doctrine uttered from the mouth of a respectable man. . . .

I say that no man can deny his obligation to give the necessary legislation to support slavery in a Territory, who believes it is a constitutional right to have it there. No man can, who does not give the Abolitionists an argument to deny the obligation enjoined by the Constitution to enact a Fugitive State law. Try it now. It is the strongest Abolition argument ever made. I say if that Dred Scott decision is correct, then the right to hold slaves in a Territory is equally a constitutional right with the right of a slaveholder to have his runaway returned. No one can show the distinction between them. The one is express, so that we cannot deny it. The other is construed to be in the Constitution, so that he who believes the decision to be correct believes in the right. And the man who argues that by unfriendly legislation, in spite of that constitutional right, slavery may be driven from the Territories, cannot avoid furnishing an argument by which Abolitionists may deny the obligation to return fugitives, and claim the power to pass laws unfriendly to the right of the slaveholder to reclaim his fugitive. I do not know how such an argument may strike a popular assembly like this, but I defy anybody to go before a body of men whose minds are educated to estimating evidence and reasoning, and show that there is an iota of difference between the constitutional right to reclaim a fugitive and the constitutional right to hold a slave, in a

Territory, provided this Dred Scott decision is correct. I defy any man to make an argument that will justify unfriendly legislation to deprive a slaveholder of his right to hold his slave in a Territory, that will not equally, in all its length, breadth, and thickness, furnish an argument for nullifying the Fugitive Slave law. Why, there is not such an Abolitionist in the nation as Douglas, after all!

Mr. Douglas's Rejoinder

Mr. Lincoln tries to avoid the main issue by attacking the truth of my proposition that our fathers made this government divided into free and slave States, recognizing the right of each to decide all its local questions for itself. Did they not thus make it? It is true that they did not establish slavery in any of the States, or abolish it in any of them; but finding thirteen States, twelve of which were slave and one free, they agreed to form a government uniting them together as they stood, divided into free and slave States, and to guarantee forever to each State the right to do as it pleased on the slavery question. Having thus made the government, and conferred this right upon each State forever, I assert that this government can exist as they made it, divided into free and slave States, if any one State chooses to retain slavery. He says that he looks forward to a time when slavery shall be abolished everywhere. I look forward to a time when each State shall be allowed to do as it pleases. If it chooses to keep slavery forever, it is not my business, but its own; if it chooses to abolish slavery, it is its own business,—not mine. I care more for the great principle of self-government, the right of the people to rule, than I do for all the negroes in Christendom. I would not endanger the perpetuity of this Union, I would not blot out the great inalienable rights of the white man, for all the negroes that ever existed. Hence, I say, let us maintain this government on the principles that our fathers made it, recognizing the right of each State to keep slavery as long as its people determine, or to abolish it when they please. But Mr. Lincoln says that when our fathers made this government they did not look forward to the state of things now existing, and therefore he thinks the doctrine was wrong; . . .

Our fathers, I say, made this government on the principle of the right of each State to do as it pleases in its own domestic affairs, subject to the Constitution, and allowed the people of each to apply to every new change of circumstances such remedy as they may see fit to improve their condition. This right they have for all time to come.

Mr. Lincoln went on to tell you that he does not at all desire to interfere with slavery in the States where it exists, nor does his party. I expected him to say that down here. Let me ask him, then, how he expects to put slavery in the course of ultimate extinction everywhere, if he does not intend to interfere with it in the States where it exists? He says that he will prohibit it in all Territories, and the inference is, then, that unless they make free States out of them he will keep them out of the Union; for, mark you, he did not say whether or not he would vote to admit Kansas with slavery or not, as her people might apply (he forgot that, as usual, etc.): he did not say whether or not he was in favor of bringing the Territories now in existence into the Union on the principle of Clay's Compromise measures on the slavery question. I told you that he would not. His idea is that he will prohibit slavery in all the Territories and thus force them all to become free States, surrounding the slave States with a cordon of free States, and hemming them in, keeping the slaves confined to their present limits whilst they go on multiplying, until the soil on which they live will no longer feed them, and he will thus be able to put slavery in a course of ultimate extinction by starvation. He will extinguish slavery in the Southern States as the French general exterminated the Algerines when he smoked them out. He is going to extinguish slavery by surrounding the Slave States, hemming in the slaves, and starving them out of existence, as you smoke a fox out of his hole. He intends to do that in the name of humanity and Christianity, in order that we may get rid of the terrible crime and sin entailed upon our fathers of holding slaves. . . .

I ask you to look into these things, and then tell me whether the Democracy or the Abolitionists are right. I hold that the people of a Territory, like those of a State . . . have the right to decide for themselves whether slavery shall or shall not exist within their limits. The point upon which Chief Justice Taney expresses his opinion is simply this, that slaves, being property, stand on an equal footing with other property, and consequently that the owner has the same right to carry that property into a Territory that he has any other, subject to the same conditions. Suppose that one of your merchants was to take fifty or one hundred thousand dollars' worth of liquors to Kansas. He has a right to go there, under that decision; but when he gets there he finds the Maine liquor law in force, and what can he do with his property after he gets it there? He cannot sell it, he cannot use it; it is subject to the local law, and that law is against him, and the best thing he can do with it is to bring it back into Missouri or Illinois and sell it. If you take negroes to Kansas, as Colonel Jefferson Davis said in his Bangor speech, from which I have quoted to-day, you must take them there subject to the local law. If the people want the institution of slavery, they will protect and encourage it; but if they do not want it, they will withhold that protection, and the absence of local legislation protecting slavery excludes it as completely as a positive prohibition. You slaveholders of Missouri might as well understand, what you know practically, that you cannot carry slavery where the people do not want it. All you have a right to ask is that the people shall do as they please: if they want slavery, let them have it, if they do not want it, allow them to refuse to encourage it.

My friends, if, as I have said before, we will only live up to this great fundamental principle, there will be peace between the North and the South. Mr. Lincoln admits that, under the Constitution, on all domestic questions, except slavery, we ought not to interfere with the people of each State. What right have we to interfere with slavery any more than we have to interfere with any other question? He says that this slavery question is now the bone of contention. Why? Simply because agitators have combined in all the free States to make war upon it. Suppose the agitators in the States should combine in one half of the Union to make war upon the railroad system of the other half? They would thus be driven to the same sectional strife. Suppose one section makes war upon any other peculiar institution of the opposite section, and the same strife is produced. The only remedy and safety is that we shall stand by the Constitution as our fathers made it, obey the laws as they are passed, while they stand the proper test, and sustain the decisions of the Supreme Court and the constituted authorities.

188. ABLEMAN v. BOOTH
21 Howard, 506
1859

Two writs of custody to the supreme court of Wisconsin. Booth was held by Ableman, United States marshal, for violation of the fugitive slave law of September 18, 1850. The supreme court of Wisconsin discharged him from custody on a writ of *habeas corpus*. He was subsequently tried again before the United States district court, sentenced to imprisonment and fine. The supreme court of Wisconsin again ordered his release on the ground that the fugitive slave law was unconstitutional. See Warren, *Supreme Court,* (1928 ed.) Vol. II. ch. xxvii; J. Hurd, *The Law of Freedom and Bondage,* Vol. II.

TANEY, C. J. . . . It will be seen, from the foregoing statement of facts, that a judge of the supreme court of the State of Wisconsin, in the first of these cases, claimed and exercised the right to supervise and annul the proceedings of a commissioner of the United States, and to discharge a prisoner who had been committed by the commissioner for an offense against the laws of this government, and that this exercise of power by the judge was afterwards sanctioned and affirmed by the supreme court of the State.

In the second case, the state court has gone a step further, and . . . claimed and exercised this jurisdiction, but have also determined that their decision is final and conclusive upon all the courts of the United States, and ordered their clerk to disregard and refuse obedience to the writ of error issued by this court, pursuant to the act of Congress of 1789, to bring here for examination and revision the judgment of the state court.

These propositions are new in the jurisprudence of the United States, as well as of the States; and the supremacy of the state courts over the courts of the United States, in cases arising under the Constitution and laws of the United States, is now for the first time asserted and acted upon in the supreme court of a State. . . .

If the judicial power exercised in this instance has been reserved to the States, no offence against the laws of the United States can be punished by their own courts, without the permission and according to the judgement of the courts of the State in which the party happens to be imprisoned; for if the Supreme Court of Wisconsin possessed the power it has exercised in relation to offences against the act of Congress in question, it necessarily follows that they must have the same judicial authority in relation to any other law of the United States; and, consequently, their supervising and controlling power would embrace the whole criminal code of the United States, and extend to offences against our revenue laws, or any other law, intended to guard the different departments of the General Government from fraud or violence. And it would embrace all crimes, from the highest to the lowest; including felonies which are punished with death, as well as misdemeanours, which are punished by imprisonment. . . .

It would seem to be hardly necessary to do more than state the result to which these decisions of the State courts must inevitably lead. It is, of itself, a sufficient and conclusive answer; for no one will suppose that a Government which has now lasted nearly seventy years, enforcing its laws by its own tribunals, and preserving the union of the States could have lasted a single year, or fulfilled the high trusts committed to it, if offences against its laws could not have been punished without the consent of the State in which the culprit was found.

The judges of the supreme court of Wisconsin do not distinctly state from what source they suppose they have derived this judicial power. There can be no such thing as judicial authority, unless it is conferred by a government or sovereignty; and if the judges and courts of Wisconsin possess the jurisdiction they claim, they must derive it either from the United States or the State. It certainly has not been conferred on them by the United States; and it is equally clear that it was not in the power of the State to confer it, even if it had attempted to do so; for no State can authorize one of its judges or courts to exercise judicial power, by habeas corpus or otherwise, within the jurisdiction of another and independent government. And although the State of Wisconsin is sovereign within its territorial limits to a certain extent, yet that sovereignty is limited and restricted by the Constitution of the United States. . . . And the State of Wisconsin had no more power to authorize these proceedings of its judges and courts, than it would have had if the prisoner had been confined in Michigan, or in any other State of the Union, for an offense against the laws of the State in which he was imprisoned. . . .

But, as we have already said, questions of this kind must always depend upon the Constitution and laws of the United States, and not of a State. The Constitution was not formed merely to guard the States against danger from foreign nations, but mainly to secure union and harmony at home; for if this object could be attained, there would be but little danger from abroad; and to accomplish this purpose, it was felt by the statesmen who framed the Constitution, and by the people who adopted it, that it was necessary that many of the rights of sovereignty which the States then possessed should be ceded to the general government; and that, in the sphere of action assigned to it, it should be supreme, and strong enough to execute its own laws by its own tribunals, without interruption from a State or from state authorities. And it was evident that anything short of this would be inadequate to the main object for which the government was established; and that local interests, local passions or prejudices, incited and fostered by individuals for sinister purposes, would

lead to acts of aggression and injustice by one State upon the rights of another, which would ultimately terminate in violence and force, unless there was a common arbiter between them, armed with power enough to protect and guard the rights of all, by appropriate laws, to be carried into execution peaceably by its judicial tribunals.

The language of the Constitution, by which this power is granted is too plain to admit of doubt or to need comment. It declares that "this Constitution, and the laws of the United States which shall be passed in pursuance thereof, and all treaties made, or which shall be made, under the authority of the United States, shall be the supreme law of the land, and the judges in every State shall be bound thereby, anything in the constitution or laws of any State to the contrary notwithstanding."

But the supremacy thus conferred on this government could not peaceably be maintained, unless it was clothed with judicial power, equally paramount in authority to carry it into execution; for if left to the courts of justice of the several States, conflicting decisions would unavoidably take place, and the local tribunals could hardly be expected to be always free from the local influences of which we have spoken. And the Constitution and laws and treaties of the United States, and the powers granted to the federal government, would soon receive different interpretations in different States, and the government of the United States would soon become one thing in one State and another thing in another. It was essential, therefore, to its very existence as a government, that it should have the power of establishing courts of justice, altogether independent of state power, to carry into effect its own laws; and that a tribunal should be established in which all cases which might arise under the Constitution and laws and treaties of the United States, whether in a state court or in a court of the United States, should be finally and conclusively decided. Without such a tribunal, it is obvious that there would be no uniformity of judicial decision; and that the supremacy (which is but another name for independence), so carefully provided in the clause of the Constitution above referred to, could not possibly be maintained peaceably, unless it was associated with this paramount judicial authority.

Accordingly, it was conferred on the general government, in clear, precise, and comprehensive terms. . . .

The importance which the framers of the Constitution attached to such a tribunal for the purpose of preserving internal tranquillity, is strikingly manifested by the clause which gives this court jurisdiction over the sovereign States which compose this Union, when a controversy arises between them. . . . Experience has demonstrated that this power was not unwisely surrendered by the States; for in the time that has already elapsed since this government came into existence, several irritating and angry controversies have taken place between adjoining States, in relation to their respective boundaries, and which have sometimes threatened to end in force and violence, but for the power vested in this court to hear them and decide between them.

The same purposes are clearly indicated by the different language employed when conferring supremacy upon the laws of the United States, and jurisdiction upon its courts. In the first case, it provides that "this Constitution, and the laws of the United States *which shall be made in pursuance thereof,* shall be the supreme law of the land, and obligatory upon the judges in every State." The words in italics show the precision and forethought which marks every clause in the instrument. The sovereignty to be created was to be limited in its powers of legislation, and if it passed a law not authorized by its enumerated powers, it was not to be regarded as the supreme law of the land, nor were the state judges bound to carry it into execution. And as the courts of a State, and the courts of the United States, might, and indeed certainly would, often differ as to the extent of the powers conferred by the general government, it was manifested that serious controversies would arise between the authorities of the United States and of the States, which must be settled by force of arms, unless some tribunal was created to decide between them finally and without appeal.

The Constitution has accordingly provided, as far as human foresight could provide, against this danger. And in conferring judicial power upon the federal government, it declares that the jurisdiction of its courts shall extend to all cases arising under "this constitution" and the laws of the United States—leaving out the words of restriction contained in the grant of legislative power which we have above noticed. The judicial power covers every legislative act of Congress, whether it be made within the limits of its delegated powers, or be an assumption of power beyond the grants in the Constitution.

This judicial power was justly regarded as indispensable, not merely to maintain the supremacy of the laws of the United States, but also to guard the States from any encroachment upon their reserved rights by the general government. And as the Constitution is the fundamental and supreme law, if it appears that an act of Congress is not pursuant to and within the limits of the power assigned to the federal government, it is the duty of the courts of the United States to declare it unconstitutional and void. . . .

We do not question the authority of a state court, or judge, who is authorized by the laws of the State to issue the writ of habeas corpus, to issue it in any case where the party is imprisoned within its territorial limits, provided it does not appear, when the application is made, that the person imprisoned is in custody under the authority of the United States. . . . But, after the return is made, and the state judge or court judicially apprized that the party is in custody under the authority of the United States, they can proceed no further. No State judge or Court after they are judicially informed that the party is imprisoned under the authority of the United States, has any right to interfere with him, or to require him to be brought before them. And if the authority of a State, in the form of judicial process or otherwise, should attempt to control the marshal or other authorized officer or agent of the United States, in any respect, in the custody of his prisoner, it would be his duty to resist it, and to call to his aid any force that might be necessary to maintain the authority of law against illegal interference. No judicial process, whatever form it may assume, can have any lawful authority outside of the limits of the jurisdiction of the court or judge by whom it is issued; and an attempt to enforce it beyond these boundaries is nothing less than lawless violence.

And no power is more clearly conferred by the Constitution and the laws of the United States, than the power of this court to decide ultimately and finally, all cases arising under such Constitution and laws; and for that purpose to bring here for revision, by writ of error, the judgement of a state court, where such questions have arisen, and the right claimed under them is denied by the highest judicial tribunal in the State. . . .

If there was any defect of power in the commissioner, or in his mode of proceeding, it was for the tribunals of the United States to revise and correct it, and not for a state court. . . .

But although we think it unnecessary to discuss these questions, yet, as they have been decided by the state court, and are before us on the record, and we are not willing to be misunderstood, it is proper to say that, in the judgement of this court, the act of Congress commonly called the fugitive slave law is, in all of its provisions, fully authorized by the Constitution of the United States; that the commissioner had lawful authority to issue the warrant and commit the party, and that his proceedings were regular and conformable to law. . . .

Judgement of the state court reversed.

189. JOHN BROWN'S LAST SPEECH
November 2, 1859

(American State Trials, ed. by J. D. Lawson, Vol. VI, p. 800 ff.)

John Brown, most fanatical of abolitionists, planned to incite a general insurrection of slaves in Virginia and form a free state somewhere in the mountains of western Maryland and Virginia. With the aid of funds gathered in New England and New York he collected supplies and arms at a farmhouse near Harper's Ferry, Virginia, and on the night of October 16 moved on the town of Harper's Ferry and captured the government armory. United States marines under the command of Col. R. E. Lee carried the armory by assault, and captured Brown and some of his followers. He was indicted for treason and for conspiring with slaves to commit murder, convicted, and sentenced to be hanged. On Brown, see O. G. Villard, *John Brown;* F. B. Sanborn, *Life and Letters of John Brown;* R. P. Warren, *John Brown.* The trial is given in full in *American State Trials,* Vol. VI.

I have, may it please the Court, a few words to say.

In the first place, I deny everything but what I have all along admitted,—the design on my part to free the slaves. I intended certainly to have made a clean thing of that matter, as I did last winter, when I went into Missouri and there took slaves without the snapping of a gun on either side, moved them through the country, and finally left them in Canada. I designed to have done the same thing again, on a larger scale. That was all I intended. I never did intend murder, or treason, or the destruction of property, or to excite or incite slaves to rebellion, or to make insurrection.

I have another objection; and that is, it is unjust that I should suffer such a penalty. Had I interfered in the manner which I admit, and which I admit has been fairly proved (for I admire the truthfulness and candor of the greater portion of the witnesses who have testified in this case),—had I so interfered in behalf of the rich, the powerful, the intelligent, the so-called great, or in behalf of any of their friends,—either father, mother, brother, sister, wife, or children, or any of that class,—and suffered and sacrificed what I have in this interference, it would have been all right; and every man in this court would have deemed it an act worthy of reward rather than punishment.

This court acknowledges, as I suppose, the validity of the law of God. I see a book kissed here which I suppose to be the Bible, or at least the New Testament. That teaches me that all things whatsoever I would that men should do to me, I should do even so to them. It teaches me, further, to "remember them that are in bonds, as bound with them." I endeavored to act up to that instruction. I say, I am yet too young to understand that God is any respecter of persons. I believe that to have interfered as I have done—as I have always freely admitted I have done—in behalf of His despised poor, was not wrong, but right. Now, if it is deemed necessary that I should forfeit my life for the furtherance of the ends of justice, and mingle my blood further with the blood of my children and with the blood of millions in this slave country whose rights are disregarded by wicked, cruel, and unjust enactments,—I submit; so let it be done! Let me say one word further.

I feel entirely satisfied with the treatment I have received on my trial. Considering all the circumstances, it has been more generous than I expected. But I feel no consciousness of guilt. I have stated from the first what was my intention, and what was not. I never had any design against the life of any person, nor any disposition to commit trea-son, or excite slaves to rebel, or make any general insurrection. I never encouraged any man to do so, but always discouraged any idea of that kind.

Let me say, also, a word in regard to the statements made by some of those connected with me. I hear it has been stated by some of them that I have induced them to join me. But the contrary is true. I do not say this to injure them, but as regretting their weakness. There is not one of them but joined me of his own accord, and the greater part of them at their own expense. A number of them I never saw, and never had a word of conversation with, till the day they came to me; and that was for the purpose I have stated.

Now I have done.

190. RESOLUTIONS ON SECESSION FROM FLOYD COUNTY, GEORGIA
1860

(The Confederate Records of the State of Georgia, ed. by A. D. Candler, Vol. I, p. 115 ff.)

These resolutions are typical of the resolutions which were passed by many counties in Georgia on the eve of secession. The struggle between the Unionists and the dis-unionists in Georgia was more severe than elsewhere in the South with the exception of Virginia. See, I. W. Avery, *History of the State of Georgia from 1850 to 1881;* G. M. Battey, *History of Rome and Floyd County;* U. B. Phillips, *Georgia and State Rights;* H. Fielder, *Sketch of the Life and Times of Joseph E. Brown;* H. J. Pearce, *Benjamin H. Hill;* U. B. Phillips, *Life of Robert Toombs;* P. S. Flippin, *Herschel V. Johnson;* L. Pendleton, *Alexander H. Stephens.*

Whereas, the abolition sentiment of the *Northern States* first openly manifested in 1820, has for the last forty years, steadily and rapidly increased in volume, and in the intensity of hostility to the form of society, existing in the *Southern States,* and to the rights of these States as equal, independent and sovereign members of the Union; has led to long continued and ever increasing abuse and hatred of the Southern people; to ceaseless war upon their plainest Constitutional rights; to an open and shameless nullification of that provision of the constitution intended to secure the rendition of fugitive slaves, and of the laws of Congress to give it ef-fect; . . . has prompted the armed invasion of Southern soil, by stealth . . . for the diabolical purpose of inaugurating a ruthless war of the blacks against the whites throughout the Southern States; has prompted large masses of Northern people openly to sympathize with the treacherous and traitorous invaders of our country, and elevate the leader of a band of midnight assassins, and robbers . . . to the rank of a hero and a martyr . . . ; has disrupted the churches, and destroyed all national parties, and has now finally organized a party confined to a *hostile section,* and composed even there of those only who have encouraged, sympathized with, instigated, or perpetuated their long series of insults, outrages and wrongs, for the avowed purpose of making a common government, armed by us with power only for our protection, an instrument, in the hands of enemies of our destruction.

Therefore we, a portion of the people of Floyd County . . . do hereby declare:

1st. That Georgia is and of right ought to be a free, sovereign and independent State.

2d. That she came into the Union with the other States, as a sovereignty, and by virtue of that sovereignty, has the right to secede whenever, in her sovereign capacity, she shall judge such a step necessary.

3d. That in our opinion, she ought not to submit to the inauguration of Abraham Lincoln and Hannibal Hamlin, as her President and Vice-President; but should leave them to rule over those by whom alone they were elected.

4th. That we request the Legislature to announce this opinion . . . and to co-operate with the Governor in calling a Convention of the people to determine on the mode and measure of redress. . . .

6th. That we respectfully suggest to the Legislature to take immediate steps to organize and arm the forces of the State. . . .

191. CONSTITUTIONAL UNION PLATFORM
May, 1860

(K. Porter, ed. *National Party Platforms*, p. 52)

The Constitutional Union Party met at Baltimore in May, 1860, and nominated John Bell of Tennessee for President and Edward Everett of Massachusetts for the Vice-President. Bell secured the electoral votes of Tennessee, Kentucky, and Virginia, and a popular vote of some 590,000.

Whereas, Experience has demonstrated that Platforms adopted by the partisan Conventions of the country have had the effect to mislead and deceive the people, and at the same time to widen the political divisions of the country, by the creation and encouragement of geographical and sectional parties; therefore

Resolved, that it is both the part of patriotism and of duty to *recognize* no political principle other than THE CONSTITUTION OF THE COUNTRY, THE UNION OF THE STATES, AND THE ENFORCEMENT OF THE LAWS, and that, as repre-

sentatives of the Constitutional Union men of the country, in National Convention assembled, we hereby pledge ourselves to maintain, protect, and defend, separately and unitedly, these great principles of public liberty and national safety, against all enemies, at home and abroad; believing that thereby peace may once more be restored to the country; the rights of the People and of the States reëstablished, and the Government again placed in that position of justice, fraternity and equality, which, under the example and Constitution of our fathers, has solemnly bound every citizen of the United States to maintain a more perfect union, establish justice, insure domestic tranquillity, provide for the common defense, promote the general welfare, and secure the blessings of liberty to ourselves and our posterity.

192. REPUBLICAN PARTY PLATFORM
Chicago, Illinois, May 16, 1860

(*A Political Text-book for 1860,* p. 26 ff.)

The reaffirmation of the Declaration of Independence was included only after Joshua Giddings of Ohio had threatened to bolt the convention if it was omitted. This platform revealed the influence of the eastern element of the party more largely than did that of 1856. On the conventions and the election, see, E. D. Fite, *The Presidential Campaign of 1860,* ch. vi.

Resolved, That we, the delegated representatives of the Republican electors of the United States, in Convention assembled, in discharge of the duty we owe to our constituents and our country, unite in the following declarations:

1. That the history of the nation, during the last four years, has fully established the propriety and necessity of the organization and perpetuation of the Republican party, and that the causes which called it into existence are permanent in their nature, and now, more than ever before, demand its peaceful and constitutional triumph.

2. That the maintenance of the principles promulgated in the Declaration of Independence and embodied in the Federal Constitution, "That all men are created equal; that they are endowed by their Creator with certain inalienable rights; that among these

are life, liberty and the pursuit of happiness; that, to secure these rights, governments are instituted among men, deriving their just powers from the consent of the governed," is essential to the preservation of our Republican institutions; and that the Federal Constitution, the Rights of the States, and the Union of the States, must and shall be preserved.

3. That to the Union of the States this nation owes its unprecedented increase in population, its surprising development of material resources, its rapid augmentation of wealth, its happiness at home and its honor abroad; and we hold in abhorrence all schemes for Disunion, come from whatever source they may; And we congratulate the country that no Republican member of Congress has uttered or countenanced the threats of Disunion so often made by Democratic members, without rebuke and with applause from their political associates; and we denounce those threats of Disunion, in case of a popular overthrow of their ascendency, as denying the vital principles of a free government, and as an avowal of contemplated treason, which it is the imperative duty of an indignant People sternly to rebuke and forever silence.

4. That the maintenance inviolate of the rights of the States, and especially the right of each State to order and control its own domestic institutions according to its own judgment exclusively, is essential to that balance of powers on which the perfection and endurance of our political fabric depends; and we denounce the lawless invasion by armed force of the soil of any State or Territory, no matter under what pretext, as among the gravest of crimes.

5. That the present Democratic Administration has far exceeded our worst apprehensions, in its measureless subserviency to the exactions of a sectional interest, as especially evinced in its desperate exertions to force the infamous Lecompton constitution upon the protesting people of Kansas; in construing the personal relation between master and servant to involve an unqualified property in persons; in its attempted enforcement, everywhere, on land and sea, through the intervention of Congress and of the Federal Courts of the extreme pretensions of a purely local interest; and in its

general and unvarying abuse of the power intrusted to it by a confiding people. . . .

7. That the new dogma that the Constitution, of its own force, carries Slavery into any or all of the Territories of the United States, is a dangerous political heresy, at variance with the explicit provisions of that instrument itself, with contemporaneous exposition, and with legislative and judicial precedent; is revolutionary in its tendency, and subversive of the peace and harmony of the country.

8. That the normal condition of all the territory of the United States is that of freedom; That as our Republican fathers, when they had abolished slavery in all our national territory, ordained that "no person should be deprived of life, liberty, or property, without due process of law," it becomes our duty, by legislation, whenever such legislation is necessary, to maintain this provision of the Constitution against all attempts to violate it; and we deny the authority of Congress, of a territorial legislature, or of any individuals, to give legal existence to Slavery in any Territory of the United States.

9. That we brand the recent re-opening of the African slave-trade, under the cover of our national flag, aided by perversions of judicial power, as a crime against humanity and a burning shame to our country and age; and we call upon Congress to take prompt and efficient measures for the total and final suppression of that execrable traffic.

10. That in the recent vetoes, by their Federal Governors, of the acts of the Legislatures of Kansas and Nebraska, prohibiting Slavery in those Territories, we find a practical illustration of the boasted Democratic principle of Non-Intervention and Popular Sovereignty embodied in the Kansas-Nebraska bill, and a demonstration of the deception and fraud involved therein.

11. That Kansas should, of right, be immediately admitted as a State under the Constitution recently formed and adopted by her people, and accepted by the House of Representatives.

12. That, while providing revenue for the support of the General Government by duties upon imports, sound policy requires such an adjustment of these imposts as to encourage the development of the industrial interests

of the whole country; and we commend that policy of national exchanges which secures to the working men liberal wages, to agriculture remunerating prices, to mechanics and manufacturers an adequate reward for their skill, labor and enterprise, and to the nation commercial prosperity and independence.

13. That we protest against any sale or alienation to others of the Public Lands held by actual settlers, and against any view of the Homestead policy which regards the settlers as paupers or supplicants for public bounty; and we demand the passage by Congress of the complete and satisfactory Homestead measure which has already passed the house.

14. That the Republican Party is opposed to any change in our Naturalization Laws or any State legislation by which the rights of our citizenship hitherto accorded to im-migrants from foreign lands shall be abridged or impaired; and in favor of giving a full and efficient protection to the rights of all classes of citizens, whether native or naturalized, both at home and abroad.

15. That appropriations by Congress for River and Harbor improvements of a National character, required for the accommodation and security of an existing commerce, are authorized by the Constitution, and justified by the obligations of Government to protect the lives and property of its citizens.

16. That a Railroad to the Pacific Ocean is imperatively demanded by the interests of the whole country; that the Federal Government ought to render immediate and efficient aid in its construction; and that, as preliminary thereto, a daily Overland Mail should be promptly established. . . .

193. THE DEMOCRATIC PARTY PLATFORM OF 1860
June 18, 1860

(K. Porter, ed. *National Party Platforms,* p. 53)

The Democratic convention met at Charleston, S. C. in April 1860, but a victory of the Douglas forces on the floor of the convention resulted in the secession of the delegations from Alabama, Louisiana, Mississippi, Texas, Florida and a majority of those from South Carolina, Georgia and Arkansas. The remaining delegates were unable to agree upon a candidate, and the convention adjourned to Baltimore. The seceders, after a hasty meeting in Charleston, adjourned to Richmond. When the convention met in Baltimore, June 18, it was faced with contesting delegations from the Southern States, and a second secession followed. The remaining delegates nominated Douglas for the Presidency and Fitzpatrick for the Vice-Presidency. See E. D. Fite, *The Presidential Campaign of 1860,* ch. v; G. F Milton, *The Eve of Conflict,* chs. xxv xxix.

1. *Resolved,* That we, the Democracy of the Union in Convention assembled, hereby declare our affirmance of the resolutions unanimously adopted and declared as a platform of principles by the Democratic Convention at Cincinnati, in the year 1856, believing that Democratic principles are unchangeable in their nature, when applied to the same subject matters; and we recommend, as the only further resolutions, the following:

2. Inasmuch as difference of opinion exists in the Democratic party as to the nature and extent of the powers of a Territorial Legislature, and as to the powers and duties of Congress, under the Constitution of the United States, over the institution of slavery within the Territories,

Resolved, That the Democratic party will abide by the decision of the Supreme Court of the United States upon these questions of Constitutional law.

3. *Resolved,* That it is the duty of the United States to afford ample and complete protection to all its citizens, whether at home or abroad, and whether native or foreign born

4. *Resolved,* That one of the necessities of the age, in a military, commercial, and postal point of view, is speedy communication between the Atlantic and Pacific States; and the Democratic party pledge such Constitutional Government aid as will insure the construction of a Railroad to the Pacific coast, at the earliest practicable period.

5. *Resolved,* That the Democratic party are in favor of the acquisition of the Island of Cuba on such terms as shall be honorable to ourselves and just to Spain,

6. *Resolved,* That the enactments of the State Legislatures to defeat the faithful execution of the Fugitive Slave Law, are hostile in character, subversive of the Constitution, and revolutionary in their effect.

7. *Resolved,* That it is in accordance with the interpretation of the Cincinnati platform, that during the existence of the Territorial Governments the measure of restriction, whatever it may be, imposed by the Federal Constitution on the power of the Territorial Legislature over the subject of the domestic relations, as the same has been, or shall hereafter be finally determined by the Supreme Court of the United States, should be respected by all good citizens, and enforced with promptness and fidelity by every branch of the general government.

194. THE DEMOCRATIC (BRECKENRIDGE FACTION) PLATFORM
OF 1860
June, 1860
(K. Porter, ed. *National Party Platforms,* p. 54)

The seceders from the Baltimore Convention of the regular Democratic Party nominated Vice-President Breckenridge for the Presidency and Senator Lane for the Vice-Presidency. The platform and the nominations were ratified by the delegations convened at Richmond.

Resolved, That the platform adopted by the Democratic party at Cincinnati be affirmed, with the following explanatory resolutions:

1. That the Government of a Territory organized by an act of Congress is provisional and temporary, and during its existence all citizens of the United States have an equal right to settle with their property in the Territory, without their rights, either of person or property being destroyed or impaired by Congressional or Territorial legislation.

2. That it is the duty of the Federal Government, in all its departments, to protect, when necessary, the rights of persons and property in the Territories, and wherever else its constitutional authority extends.

3. That when the settlers in a Territory, having an adequate population, form a State Constitution, the right of sovereignty commences, and being consummated by admission into the Union, they stand on an equal footing with the people of other States, and the State thus organized ought to be admitted into the Federal Union, whether its Constitution prohibits or recognizes the institution of slavery.

Resolved, That the Democratic party are in favor of the acquisition of the Island of Cuba, on such terms as shall be honorable to ourselves and just to Spain, at the earliest practicable moment.

Resolved, That the enactments of State Legislatures to defeat the faithful execution of the Fugitive Slave Law are hostile in character, subversive of the Constitution, and revolutionary in their effect.

Resolved, That the Democracy of the United States recognize it as the imperative duty of this Government to protect the naturalized citizen in all his rights, whether at home or in foreign lands, to the same extent as its native-born citizens.

WHEREAS, One of the greatest necessities of the age, in a political, commercial, postal and military point of view, is a speedy communication between the Pacific and Atlantic coasts, Therefore be it

Resolved, That the National Democratic party do hereby pledge themselves to use every means in their power to secure the passage of some bills, to the extent of the constitutional authority of Congress for the construction of a Pacific Railroad from the Mississippi River to the Pacific Ocean, at the earliest practicable moment.

195. PRESIDENT BUCHANAN ON SECESSION
Extract from the Fourth Annual Message to Congress
December 3, 1860
(Richardson, ed. *Messages and Papers,* Vol. V, p. 626 ff.)

The process of secession was already under way in the South when Buchanan sent his last annual message to Congress. This message, deprecating the disruption of the Union, nevertheless announced the impotence of the Federal Government to prevent secession by force. In this opinion, Buchanan relied upon the opinion of his Attorney-general, Jeremiah S. Black, who declared that while the President should use all the force at his command to enforce the laws, he did not have the right to coerce a state. "If this view of the subject be as correct as I think it is," wrote Black, "then the Union must utterly perish at the moment when Congress shall arm one part of the people against another for any purpose beyond that of merely protecting the General Government in the exercise of its proper constitutional functions." Black's opinion is given in E. McPherson, *Political History of the Great Rebellion*, p. 51–2. On Buchanan, see G. T. Curtis, *Life of James Buchanan;* and Buchanan's own defence, *Mr. Buchanan's Administration on the Eve of the Rebellion;* P. G. Auchampaugh, *Buchanan and his Cabinet on the Eve of Secession;* and the forthcoming volume of R. F. Nichols, *The Administrative Policies of James Buchanan and his cabinet as contributing causes to the outbreak of the Civil War.*

WASHINGTON CITY, *December 3, 1860.*
Fellow-Citizens of the Senate and House of Representatives:

. . . The long-continued and intemperate interference of the Northern people with the question of slavery in the Southern States has at length produced its natural effects. The different sections of the Union are now arrayed against each other, and the time has arrived, so much dreaded by the Father of his Country, when hostile geographical parties have been formed. . . .

It can not be denied that for five and twenty years the agitation at the North against slavery has been incessant. In 1835 pictorial handbills and inflammatory appeals were circulated extensively throughout the South of a character to excite the passions of the slaves, and, in the language of General Jackson, "to stimulate them to insurrection and produce all the horrors of a servile war." This agitation has ever since been continued by the public press, by the proceedings of State and county conventions and by abolition sermons and lectures. The time of Congress has been occupied in violent speeches on this never-ending subject, and appeals, in pamphlet and other forms, indorsed by distinguished names, have been sent forth from this central point and spread broadcast over the Union.

How easy would it be for the American people to settle the slavery question forever and to restore peace and harmony to this distracted country! They, and they alone, can do it. All that is necessary to accomplish the object, and all for which the slave States have ever contended, is to be let alone and permitted to manage their domestic institutions in their own way. As sovereign States, they, and they alone, are responsible before God and the world for the slavery existing among them. For this the people of the North are not more responsible and have no more right to interfere than with similar institutions in Russia or in Brazil.

Upon their good sense and patriotic forbearance I confess I still greatly rely. Without their aid it is beyond the power of any President, no matter what may be his own political proclivities, to restore peace and harmony among the States. Wisely limited and restrained as is his power under our Constitution and laws, he alone can accomplish but little for good or for evil on such a momentous question.

And this brings me to observe that the election of any one of our fellow-citizens to the office of President does not of itself afford just cause for dissolving the Union. This is more especially true if his election has been effected by a mere plurality, and not a majority of the people, and has resulted from transient and temporary causes, which may probably never again occur. . .

After all, he is no more than the chief executive officer of the Government. His province is not to make but to execute the laws. And it is a remarkable fact in our history that, notwithstanding the repeated efforts of the antislavery party, no single act has ever passed Congress, unless we may possibly except the Missouri compromise, impairing in the slightest degree the rights of the South to their property in slaves; and it may also be observed, judging from present indications, that no probability exists of the passage of such an act by a majority of both Houses, either in the present or the next Congress. . . .

I have purposely confined my remarks to revolutionary resistance, because it has been claimed within the last few years that any State, whenever this shall be its sovereign will and pleasure, may secede from the Union in accordance with the Constitution and without any violation of the constitutional rights of the other members of the Confederacy; that as each became parties to the Union by the vote of its own people assembled in convention, so any one of them may retire from the Union in a similar manner by the vote of such a convention.

In order to justify secession as a constitutional remedy, it must be on the principle that the Federal Government is a mere voluntary association of States, to be dissolved at pleasure by any one of the contracting parties. If this be so, the Confederacy is a rope of sand, to be penetrated and dissolved by the first adverse wave of public opinion in any of the States.

Such a principle is wholly inconsistent with the history as well as the character of the Federal Constitution. . . .

It was intended to be perpetual, and not to be annulled at the pleasure of any one of the contracting parties. . . .

It may be asked, then, Are the people of the States without redress against the tyranny and oppression of the Federal Government? By no means. The right of resistance on the part of the governed against the oppression of their governments can not be denied. It exists independently of all constitutions, and has been exercised at all periods of the world's history. Under it governments have been destroyed and new ones have taken their place. It is embodied in strong and express language in our own Declaration of Independence. But the distinction must ever be observed that this is revolution against an established government, and not a voluntary secession from it by virtue of an inherent constitutional right. In short, let us look the danger fairly in the face. Secession is neither more nor less than revolution. It may or it may not be a justifiable revolution, but still it is revolution.

What, in the meantime, is the responsibility and true position of the Executive? He is bound by solemn oath, before God and the country, "to take care that the laws be faithfully executed," and from this obligation he can not be absolved by any human power. But what if the performance of this duty, in whole or in part, has been rendered impracticable by events over which he could have exercised no control? Such at the present moment is the case throughout the State of South Carolina so far as the laws of the United States to secure the administration of justice by means of the Federal judiciary are concerned. All the Federal officers within its limits through whose agency alone these laws can be carried into execution have already resigned. We no longer have a district judge, a district attorney, or a marshal in South Carolina. In fact, the whole machinery of the Federal Government necessary for the distribution of remedial justice among the people has been demolished, and it would be difficult, if not impossible, to replace it.

The only acts of Congress on the statute book bearing upon this subject are those of February 28, 1795, and March 3, 1807. These authorize the President, after he shall have ascertained that the marshal, with his *posse comitatus,* is unable to execute civil or criminal process in any particular case, to call forth the militia and employ the Army and Navy to aid him in performing this service, having first by proclamation commanded the insurgents "to disperse and retire peaceably to their respective abodes within a limited time." This duty can not by possibility be performed in a State where no judicial authority exists to issue process, and where there is no marshal to execute it, and where, even if there were such an officer, the entire population would constitute one solid combination to resist him.

The bare enumeration of these provisions proves how inadequate they are without further legislation to overcome a united opposition in a single State, not to speak of other States who may place themselves in a similar attitude. Congress alone has power to decide whether the present laws can or can not be amended so as to carry out more effectually the objects of the Constitution. . . .

Apart from the execution of the laws, so far as this may be practical, the Executive has no authority to decide what shall be the relations between the Federal Government and South Carolina. He has been invested with no such discretion. He possesses no power to change the relations heretofore existing between them, much less to acknowledge the independence of that State. This would be to invest a mere executive officer with the power of recognizing the dissolution of the confederacy among our thirty-three sovereign States.

It bears no resemblance to the recognition of a foreign *de facto* government, involving no such responsibility. Any attempt to do this would, on his part, be a naked act of usurpation. It is therefore my duty to submit to Congress the whole question in all its bearings. The course of events is so rapidly hastening forward that the emergency may soon arise when you may be called upon to decide the momentous question whether you possess the power by force of arms to compel a State to remain in the Union. I should feel myself recreant to my duty were I not to express an opinion on this important subject.

The question fairly stated is, Has the Constitution delegated to Congress the power to coerce a State into submission which is attempting to withdraw or has actually withdrawn from the Confederacy? If answered in the affirmative, it must be on the principle that the power has been conferred upon Congress to declare and to make war against a State. After much serious reflection I have arrived at the conclusion that no such power has been delegated to Congress or to any other department of the Federal Government. It is manifest upon an inspection of the Constitution that this is not among the specific and enumerated powers granted to Congress, and it is equally apparent that its exercise is not "necessary and proper for carrying into execution" any one of these powers. So far from this power having been delegated to Congress, it was expressly refused by the Convention which framed the Constitution. . . .

But if we possessed this power, would it be wise to exercise it under existing circumstances? The object would doubtless be to preserve the Union. War would not only present the most effectual means of destroying it, but would vanish all hope of its peaceable reconstruction. Besides, in the fraternal conflict a vast amount of blood and treasure would be expended, rendering future reconciliation between the States impossible. In the meantime, who can foretell what would be the sufferings and privations of the people during its existence?

The fact is that our Union rests upon public opinion, and can never be cemented by the blood of its citizens shed in civil war. If it can not live in the affections of the people, it must one day perish. Congress possesses many means of preserving it by conciliation, but the sword was not placed in their hand to preserve it by force. . . .

196. CRITTENDEN PEACE RESOLUTIONS
December 18, 1860

(E. McPherson, *Political History of the Great Rebellion*, p. 64–5)

The secession of the Southern States and the imminent danger of war led to numerous efforts to patch up some sort of a compromise. A Committee of Thirty Three, appointed to work out some compromise measures, achieved nothing. Senator Crittenden of Kentucky, bitterly opposed to secession, introduced the following resolutions to Congress, but they were rejected. While not entirely unsatisfactory to the South, they were unacceptable to Lincoln who, through Thurlow Weed, advised their rejection. Another effort to patch up peace, the Peace Conference held at the request of the legislature of Virginia, recommended a number of amendments to the Constitution, but these recommendations, too, were rejected by Congress. For various resolutions and reports, see McPherson, *Political History of the Great Rebellion*, p. 49–77. See, D. L. Dumond, *The Secession Movement, 1860–1861*, chs. viii–xii; C. Coleman, *The Life of John J. Crittenden*; M. Scrugham, *The Peaceable Americans, 1860–1861*.

Whereas, serious and alarming dissensions have arisen between the Northern and Southern States, concerning the rights and security of the rights of the slave-holding States, and especially their rights in the common territory of the United States; and whereas it is eminently desirable and proper that these dissensions which now threaten the very existence of this Union, should be permanently quieted and settled, by constitutional provision, which shall do equal justice to all sections, and thereby restore to the people that peace and good will which ought to prevail between all the citizens of the United States: Therefore,

Resolved by the Senate and House of Representatives of the United States of America in Congress Assembled, That the following articles be, and are hereby, proposed and submitted as amendments to the Constitution of the United States, . . .

Article 1. In all the territory of the United States now held, or hereafter acquired, situate North of Latitude 36° 30′, slavery or involuntary servitude, except as a punishment for crime, is prohibited while such territory shall remain under territorial government. In all the territory south of said line of latitude, slavery of the African race is hereby recognized as existing, and shall not be interfered with by Congress, but shall be protected as property by all the departments of the territorial government during its continuance. And when any Territory, north or south of said line, within such boundaries as Congress may prescribe, shall contain the population requisite for a member of Congress according to the then Federal ratio, of representation of the people of the United States, it shall, if its form of government be republican, be admitted into the Union, on an equal footing with the original States, with or without slavery, as the constitution of such new State may provide.

Art. 2. Congress shall have no power to abolish slavery in places under its exclusive jurisdiction, and situate within the limits of States that permit the holding of slaves.

Art. 3. Congress shall have no power to abolish slavery within the district of Columbia so long as it exists in the adjoining States of Virginia and Maryland, or either, not without the consent of the inhabitants, nor without just compensation first made to such owners of slaves as do not consent to such abolishment. Nor shall Congress at any time prohibit officers of the Federal Government, or members of Congress, whose duties require them to be in said District, from bringing with them their slaves, and holding them as such during the time their duties may require them to remain there, and afterwards taking them from the District.

Art. 4. Congress shall have no power to prohibit or hinder the transportation of slaves from one State to another, or to a Territory in which slaves are by law permitted to be held, whether that transportation be by land, navigable rivers, or by the sea. . . .

Art. 6. No future amendment of the Constitution shall affect the five preceding articles . . . and no amendment shall be made to the Constitution which shall authorize or give to Congress any power to abolish or interfere with slavery in any of the States by whose laws it is, or may be, allowed or permitted.

And whereas, also, besides these causes of dissension embraced in the foregoing amendments proposed to the Constitution of the United States, there are others which come within the jurisdiction of Congress, and may be remedied by its legislative power; Therefore

1. Resolved. . . . That the laws now in force for the recovery of fugitive slaves are in strict pursuance of the plain and mandatory provisions of the Constitution, and have been sanctioned as valid and constitutional by the judgment of the Supreme Court of the United States; that the slave-holding States are entitled to the faithful observance and execution of those laws, and that they ought not to be repealed, or so modified or changed as to impair their efficiency; and that laws ought to be made for the punishment of those who attempt by rescue of the slave, or other illegal means, to hinder or defeat the due execution of said laws.

2. That all State laws which conflict with the fugitive slave acts of Congress, or any other Constitutional acts of Congress, or which, in their operation, impede, hinder, or delay, the free course and due execution of any of said acts, are null and void by the present provisions of the Constitution of the United States; yet those State laws, void as they are, have given color to practices, and led to consequences which have obstructed the due administration and execution of acts of Congress, and especially the acts for the delivery of fugitive slaves, and have thereby contributed much to the discord and commotion now prevailing. Congress, therefore, in the present perilous juncture, does not deem it improper, respectfully and earnestly to recommend the repeal of those laws to the several States which have enacted them, or such legislative corrections or explanations of them as may prevent their being used or perverted to such mischievous purposes.

3. That the Act of the 18th of September, 1850, commonly called the fugitive slave law, . . . the last clause of the fifth section of said act, which authorizes a person holding a

warrant for the arrest or detention of a fugitive slave, to summon to his aid the *posse comitatus,* and which declares it to be the duty of all good citizens to assist him in its execution, ought to be so amended as to expressly limit the authority and duty to cases in which there shall be resistance or danger of resistance or rescue.

4. That the laws for the suppression of the African slave trade, and especially those prohibiting the importation of slaves in the United States, ought to be made effectual, and ought to be thoroughly executed: and all further enactments necessary to those ends ought to be promptly made.

197. MISSISSIPPI RESOLUTIONS ON SECESSION
November 30, 1860

(*Laws of Mississippi,* 1860, p. 43 ff.)

On secession in Mississippi, see D. L. Dumond, *The Secession Movement,* ch. x; J. F. H. Claiborne, *Life and Correspondence of John A. Quitman;* J. F. Garner, "The First Struggle over Secession in Mississippi," Mississippi Hist. Soc., *Publications,* Vol. IV.

Whereas, The Constitutional Union was formed by the several States in their separate sovereign capacity for the purpose of mutual advantage and protection;

That the several States are distinct sovereignties, whose supremacy is limited so far only as the same has been delegated by voluntary compact to a Federal Government, and when it fails to accomplish the ends for which it was established, the parties to the compact have the right to resume, each State for itself, such delegated powers;

That the institution of slavery existed prior to the formation of the Federal Constitution, and is recognized by its letter, and all efforts to impair its value or lessen its duration by Congress, or any of the free States, is a violation of the compact of Union and is destructive of the ends for which it was ordained, but in defiance of the principles of the Union thus established, the people of the Northern States have assumed a revolutionary position towards the Southern States;

That they have set at defiance that provision of the Constitution which was intended to secure domestic tranquillity among the States and promote their general welfare, namely: "No person held to service or labor in one State, under the laws thereof, escaping into another, shall, in consequence of any law or regulation therein, be discharged from such service or labor, but shall be delivered up on claim of the party to whom such service or labor may be due;"

That they have by voluntary associations, individual agencies and State legislation interfered with slavery as it prevails in the slaveholding States;

That they have enticed our slaves from us, and by State intervention obstructed and prevented their rendition under the fugitive slave law;

That they continue their system of agitation obviously for the purpose of encouraging other slaves to escape from service, to weaken the institution in the slave-holding States by rendering the holding of such property insecure, and as a consequence its ultimate abolition certain;

That they claim the right and demand its execution by Congress to exclude slavery from the Territories, but claim the right of protection for every species of property owned by themselves;

That they declare in every manner in which public opinion is expressed their unalterable determination to exclude from admittance into the Union any new State that tolerates slavery in its Constitution, and thereby force Congress to a condemnation of that species of property;

That they thus seek by an increase of abolition States "to acquire two-thirds of both houses" for the purpose of preparing an amendment to the Constitution of the United States, abolishing slavery in the States, and so continue the agitation that the proposed amendment shall be ratified by the Legislatures of three-fourths of the States;

That they have in violation of the comity of all civilized nations, and in violation of the comity established by the Constitution of the United States, insulted and outraged our citizens when travelling among them for pleasure, health or business, by taking their servants and liberating the same, under the forms of State laws, and subjecting their owners to degrading and ignominious punishment;

That to encourage the stealing of our property they have put at defiance that provision of the Constitution which declares that fugitives from justice (escaping) into another State, on demand of the Executive authority of that State from which he fled, shall be delivered up;

That they have sought to create domestic discord in the Southern States by incendiary publications;

That they encouraged a hostile invasion of a Southern State to excite insurrection, murder and rapine;   .

That they have deprived Southern citizens of their property and continue an unfriendly agitation of their domestic institutions, claiming for themselves perfect immunity from external interference with their domestic policy; . . .

That they have elected a majority of Electors for President and Vice-President on the ground that there exists an irreconcilable conflict between the two sections of the Confederacy in reference to their respective systems of labor and in pursuance of their hostility to us and our institutions, thus declaring to the civilized world that the powers of this Government are to be used for the dishonor and overthrow of the Southern Section of this great Confederacy. Therefore,

Be it resolved by the Legislature of the State of Mississippi, That in the opinion of those who now constitute the said Legislature, the secession of each aggrieved State is the proper remedy for these injuries.

198. SOUTH CAROLINA ORDINANCE OF SECESSION
December 20, 1860

(F. Moore, ed. *The Rebellion Record,* Vol. I, p. 2)

Immediately on the election of Lincoln to the Presidency, the legislature of South Carolina called a convention to meet December 17 to consider the question of secession. The convention, chosen by popular vote, was overwhelmingly in favor of immediate secession. It met at Charleston and on December 20 voted unanimously for secession. See, L. A. White, *Robert Barnwell Rhett,* ch. ix; J. J. Van Deusen, *Economic Basis of Disunion in South Carolina;* E. Merritt, *James Henry Hammond,* ch. vii; H. D. Capers, *Life and Times of C. G. Memminger.* See also, C. P. Denman; *The Secession Movement in Alabama;* B. B. Munford, *Virginia's Attitude Toward Slavery and Secession;* H. T. Shanks, *The Secession Movement in Virginia;* D. Dumond, *The Secession Movement, 1860–1861.*

An Ordinance to Dissolve the Union between the State of South Carolina and other

States united with her under the compact entitled the Constitution of the United States of America:

We, the people of the State of South Carolina, in Convention assembled, do declare and ordain, and it is hereby declared and ordained, that the ordinance adopted by us in Convention, on the 23d day of May, in the year of our Lord 1788, whereby the Constitution of the United States of America was ratified, and also all Acts and parts of Acts of the General Assembly of this State ratifying the amendments of the said Constitution, are hereby repealed, and that the union now subsisting between South Carolina and other States under the name of the United States of America is hereby dissolved.

199. SOUTH CAROLINA DECLARATION OF CAUSES OF SECESSION
December 24, 1860

(F. Moore, ed. *The Rebellion Record,* Vol. I, p. 3 ff.)

In justification of secession, the South Carolina Convention adopted two papers: one an Address to the People of the Slaveholding States, reported by R. B. Rhett; the other a Declaration of the Causes of Secession, reported by C. G. Memminger. An extract from the second is given below. The Address to the People can be found conveniently in E. McPherson, *Political History of the Great Rebellion,* p. 12 ff.; L. A. White, *Robert Barnwell Rhett,* p. 187 ff.; H. D. Capers, *Life and Times of C. G. Memminger.*

The people of the State of South Carolina in Convention assembled, on the 2d day of April, A. D. 1852, declared that the frequent violations of the Constitution of the United States by the Federal Government, and its encroachments upon the reserved rights of the States, fully justified this State in their withdrawal from the Federal Union; but in deference to the opinions and wishes of the other Slaveholding States, she forbore at that time to exercise this right. Since that time these encroachments have continued to increase, and further forbearance ceases to be a virtue.

And now the State of South Carolina having resumed her separate and equal place among nations, deems it due to herself, to the remaining United States of America, and to the nations of the world, that she should declare the immediate causes which have led to this act.

In 1787, Deputies were appointed by the States to revise the articles of Confederation; and on 17th September, 1787, these Deputies recommended, for the adoption of the States, the Articles of Union, known as the Constitution of the United States.

. . . Thus was established by compact between the States, a Government with defined objects and powers, limited to the express words of the grant. . . . We hold that the Government thus established is subject to the two great principles asserted in the Declaration of Independence; and we hold further, that the mode of its formation subjects it to a third fundamental principle, namely, the law of compact. We maintain that in every compact between two or more parties, the obligation is mutual; that the failure of one of the contracting parties to perform a material part of the agreement, entirely releases the obligation of the other; and that, where no arbiter is provided, each party is remitted to his own judgment to determine the fact of failure, with all its consequences.

In the present case, that fact is established with certainty. We assert that fourteen of the States have deliberately refused for years past to fulfil their constitutional obligations, and we refer to their own statutes for the proof.

The Constitution of the United States, in its fourth Article, provides as follows:

"No person held to service or labor in one State under the laws thereof, escaping into another, shall, in consequence of any law or regulation therein, be discharged from such service or labor, but shall be delivered up, on claim of the party to whom such service or labor may be due."

This stipulation was so material to the compact that without it that compact would not have been made. The greater number of the contracting parties held slaves, and they had previously evinced their estimate of the value of such a stipulation by making it a condition in the Ordinance for the government of the territory ceded by Virginia, which obligations, and the laws of the General Government, have ceased to effect the objects of the Constitution. The States of Maine, New Hampshire, Vermont, Massachusetts, Connecticut, Rhode Island, New York, Pennsylvania, Illinois, Indiana, Michigan, Wisconsin and Iowa, have enacted laws which either nullify the acts of Congress, or render useless any attempt to execute them. In many of these States the fugitive is discharged from the service of labor claimed, and in none of them has the State Government complied with the stipulation made in the Constitution. The State of New Jersey, at an early day, passed a law in conformity with her constitutional obligation; but the current of Anti-Slavery feeling has led her more recently to enact laws which render inoperative the remedies provided by her own laws and by the laws of Congress. In the State of New York even the right of transit for a slave has been denied by her tribunals; and the States of Ohio and Iowa have refused to surrender to justice fugitives charged with murder, and with inciting servile insurrection in the State of Virginia. Thus the constitutional compact has been deliberately broken and disregarded by the non-slaveholding States; and the consequence follows that South Carolina is released from her obligation. . . .

We affirm that these ends for which this Government was instituted have been defeated, and the Government itself has been destructive of them by the action of the non-slaveholding States. Those States have assumed the right of deciding upon the propriety of our domestic institutions; and have denied the rights of property established in fifteen of the States and recognized by the Constitution; they have denounced as sinful the institution of Slavery; they have permitted the open establishment among them of societies, whose avowed object is to disturb the peace of and eloin the property of the citizens of other States. They have encouraged and assisted thousands of our slaves to leave their homes; and those who remain, have been incited by emissaries, books, and pictures, to servile insurrection.

For twenty-five years this agitation has been steadily increasing, until it has now secured to its aid the power of the common Government. Observing the *forms* of the Constitution, a sectional party has found within that article establishing the Executive Department, the means of subverting the Constitution itself. A geographical line has been drawn across the Union, and all the States north of that line have united in the election of a man to the high office of President of the United States whose opinions and purposes are hostile to Slavery. He is to be intrusted with the administration of the common Government, because he has declared that "Government cannot endure permanently half slave, half free," and that the public mind must rest in the belief that Slavery is in the course of ultimate extinction.

This sectional combination for the subversion of the Constitution has been aided, in some of the States, by elevating to citizenship persons who, by the supreme law of the land, are incapable of becoming citizens; and their votes have been used to inaugurate a new policy, hostile to the South, and destructive of its peace and safety.

On the 4th of March next this party will take possession of the Government. It has announced that the South shall be excluded from the common territory, that the Judicial tribunal shall be made sectional, and that a war must be waged against Slavery until it shall cease throughout the United States.

The guarantees of the Constitution will then no longer exist; the equal rights of the States will be lost. The Slaveholding States will no longer have the power of self-government, or self-protection, and the Federal Government will have become their enemy.

Sectional interest and animosity will deepen the irritation; and all hope of remedy is rendered vain, by the fact that the public opinion at the North has invested a great political error with the sanctions of a more erroneous religious belief.

We, therefore, the people of South Carolina, by our delegates in Convention assembled, appealing to the Supreme Judge of the world for the rectitude of our intentions, have solemnly declared that the Union heretofore existing between this State and the other States of North America is dissolved, and that the State of South Carolina has resumed her position among the nations of the world, as a separate and independent state, with full power to levy war, conclude peace, contract alliances, establish commerce, and to do all other acts and things which independent States may of right do.

200. MAYOR FERNANDO WOOD'S RECOMMENDATION FOR THE SECESSION OF NEW YORK CITY
January 6, 1861

(E. McPherson, ed. *The Political History of the Great Rebellion,* p. 42 ff.)

The financial and commercial interests of New York City, with their heavy investments in the South and in the textile industries, were particularly hostile to a war policy on the part of the Federal government. Thurlow Weed made strenuous efforts to commit Lincoln to a compromise policy; Governor Morgan of New York urged moderation; and even Horace Greeley wished to let the "erring sisters go in peace." For historical background, see, D. A. Alexander, *Political History of the State of New York,* Vol. II, ch. xxvi; S. D. Brummer, *Political His-* *tory of New York State during the period of the Civil War.*

To the Honorable the Common Council:
Gentlemen: We are entering upon the public duties of the year under circumstances as unprecedented as they are gloomy and painful to contemplate. . . .

It would seem that a dissolution of the Federal Union is inevitable. . . .

If these forebodings shall be realized, and

a separation of the States shall occur, momentous considerations will be presented to the corporate authorities of this city. We must provide for the new relations which will necessarily grow out of the new condition of public affairs.

It will not only be necessary for us to settle the relations which we shall hold to other cities and States, but to establish if we can, new ones with a portion of our own State. Being the child of the Union, having drawn our sustenance from its bosom, and arisen to our present power and strength through the vigor of our mother—when deprived of her maternal advantages, we must rely upon our own resources and assume a position predicated upon the new phase which public affairs will present, and upon the inherent strength which our geographical, commercial, political, and financial preëminence imparts to us.

With our aggrieved brethren of the Slave States, we have friendly relations and a common sympathy. We have not participated in the warfare upon their constitutional rights or their domestic institutions. . . . Our ships have penetrated to every clime, and so have New York capital, energy, and enterprise found their way to every State, and, indeed, to almost every county and town of the American Union. If we have derived sustenance from the Union, so have we in return disseminated blessings for the common benefit of all. Therefore, New York has a right to expect, and should endeavor to preserve a continuance of uninterrupted intercourse with every section.

It is, however, folly to disguise the fact that, judging from the past, New York may have more cause of apprehension from the aggressive legislation of our own State than from external dangers. We have already suffered largely from this cause. For the past five years, our interests and corporate rights have been repeatedly trampled upon. Being an integral portion of the State, it has been assumed, and in effect tacitly admitted on our part by nonresistance, that all political and governmental power over us rested in the State Legislature. Even the common right of taxing ourselves for our own government, has been yielded, and we are not permitted to do so without this authority. . . .

Thus it will be seen that the political connection between the people of the city and the State has been used by the latter to our injury. The Legislature, in which the present partizan majority has the power, has become an instrument by which we are plundered to enrich their speculators, lobby agents, and Abolition politicians. . . .

How we shall rid ourselves of this odious and oppressive connection, it is not for me to determine. It is certain that a dissolution cannot be peacefully accomplished, except by the consent of the Legislature itself. Whether this can be obtained or not, is, in my judgement, doubtful. Deriving so much advantage from its power over the city, it is not probable that a partizan majority will consent to a separation—and the resort to force by violence and revolution must not be thought of for an instant. We have been distinguished as an orderly and law-abiding people. Let us do nothing to forfeit this character, or to add to the present distracted condition of public affairs.

Much, no doubt, can be said in favor of the justice and policy of a separation. . . . Why should not New York city, instead of supporting by her contributions in revenue two-thirds of the expenses of the United States, become also equally independent? As a free city, with but nominal duty on imports, her local Government could be supported without taxation upon her people. Thus we could live free from taxes, and have cheap goods nearly duty free. In this she would have the whole and united support of the Southern States, as well as all the other States to whose interests and rights under the Constitution she has always been true.

It is well for individuals or communities to look every danger squarely in the face and to meet it calmly and bravely. As dreadful as the severing of the bonds that have hitherto united the States has been in contemplation, it is now apparently a stern and inevitable fact. We have now to meet it with all the consequences, whatever they may be. If the Confederacy is broken up, the Government is dissolved, and it behooves every distinct community, as well as every individual, to take care of themselves.

When Disunion has become a fixed and certain fact, why may not New York disrupt the bands which bind her to a venal and corrupt master—to a people and a party that have plundered her revenues, attempted to ruin her commerce, taken away the power of self-government, and destroyed the Confederacy of which she was the proud Empire City? Amid the gloom which the present and prospective condition of things must cast over the country, New York, as a *Free City*, may shed the only light and hope of a future reconstruction of our once blessed Confederacy.

But I am not prepared to recommend the violence implied in these views. In stating this argument in favor of freedom "peace-

ably if we can, forcibly if we must," let me not be misunderstood. The redress can be found only in appeals to the magnanimity of the people of the whole State. The events of the past two months have no doubt effected a change in the popular sentiment of the State and National politics. This change may bring us the desired relief, and we may be able to obtain a repeal of the law to which I have referred, and a consequent restoration of our corporate rights.

FERNANDO WOOD, Mayor.

201. THE CONSTITUTION OF THE CONFEDERATE STATES OF AMERICA
March 11, 1861

(Richardson, ed. *Messages and Papers of the Confederacy,* Vol. I, p. 37 ff.)

A Provisional Constitution had been adopted February 8, 1861: it is reproduced in Jefferson Davis, *Rise and Fall of the Confederate Government,* Vol. II, appendix K. The permanent Constitution closely resembled the Constitution of the United States. Even the African slave trade was prohibited. Professor Stephenson observes that "the framers of 1861 left unstated most of their distinctive views". See, N. W. Stephenson, *The Day of the Confederacy,* ch. i.

WE, the people of the Confederate States, each State acting in its sovereign and independent character, in order to form a permanent federal government, establish justice, insure domestic tranquillity, and secure the blessings of liberty to ourselves and our posterity—invoking the favor and guidance of Almighty God—do ordain and establish this Constitution for the Confederate States of America.

ART. I

SEC. 1.—All legislative powers herein delegated shall be vested in a Congress of the Confederate States, which shall consist of a Senate and House of Representatives.

SEC. 2. (1) The House of Representatives shall be chosen every second year by the people of the several States; and the electors in each State shall be citizens of the Confederate States, and have the qualifications requisite for electors of the most numerous branch of the State Legislature; but no person of foreign birth, not a citizen of the Confederate

States, shall be allowed to vote for any officer, civil or political, State or Federal.

(2) No person shall be a Representative who shall not have attained the age of twenty-five years, and be a citizen of the Confederate States, and who shall not, when elected, be an inhabitant of that State in which he shall be chosen.

(3) Representatives and direct taxes shall be apportioned among the several States which may be included within this Confederacy, according to their respective numbers, which shall be determined by adding to the whole number of free persons, including those bound to service for a term of years, and excluding Indians not taxed, three-fifths of all slaves. The actual enumeration shall be made within three years after the first meeting of the Congress of the Confederate States, and within every subsequent term of ten years, in such manner as they shall by law direct. The number of Representatives shall not exceed one for every fifty thousand, but each State shall have at least one Representative; and until such enumeration shall be made, the State of South Carolina shall be entitled to choose six; the State of Georgia ten; the State of Alabama nine; the State of Florida two; the State of Mississippi seven; the State of Louisiana six; and the State of Texas six.

(4) When vacancies happen in the representation of any State, the Executive authority thereof shall issue writs of election to fill such vacancies.

(5) The House of Representatives shall choose their Speaker and other officers; and shall have the sole power of impeachment; except that any judicial or other federal officer resident and acting solely within the limits of any State, may be impeached by a vote of two-thirds of both branches of the Legislature thereof.

SEC. 3. (1) The Senate of the Confederate States shall be composed of two Senators from each State, chosen for six years by the Legislature thereof, at the regular session next immediately preceding the commencement of the term of service; and each Senator shall have one vote.

(2) Immediately after they shall be assembled, in consequence of the first election, they shall be divided as equally as may be into three classes. The seats of the Senators of the first class shall be vacated at the expiration of the second year; of the second class at the expiration of the fourth year; and of the third class at the expiration of the sixth year; so that one-third may be chosen every second year; and if vacancies happen by resignation or otherwise during the recess of the Legislature of any State, the Executive thereof may make temporary appointments until the next meeting of the Legislature, which shall then fill such vacancies.

(3) No person shall be a Senator, who shall not have attained the age of thirty years, and be a citizen of the Confederate States; and who shall not, when elected, be an inhabitant of the State for which he shall be chosen.

(4) The Vice-President of the Confederate States shall be President of the Senate, but shall have no vote, unless they be equally divided.

(5) The Senate shall choose their other officers, and also a President *pro tempore,* in the absence of the Vice-President, or when he shall exercise the office of President of the Confederate States.

(6) The Senate shall have sole power to try all impeachments. When sitting for that purpose they shall be on oath or affirmation. When the President of the Confederate States is tried, the Chief-Justice shall preside; and no person shall be convicted without the concurrence of two-thirds of the members present.

(7) Judgment in cases of impeachment shall not extend further than removal from office, and disqualification to hold and enjoy any office of honor, trust, or profit, under the Confederate States; but the party convicted shall, nevertheless, be liable to and subject to indictment, trial, judgment, and punishment according to law.

SEC. 4. (1) The times, places, and manner of holding elections for Senators and Representatives, shall be prescribed in each State by the Legislature thereof, subject to the provisions of this Constitution; but the Congress may, at any time, by law, make or alter such regulations, except as to the times and places of choosing Senators.

(2) The Congress shall assemble at least once in every year; and such meeting shall be on the first Monday in December, unless they shall, by law, appoint a different day.

SEC. 5. (1) Each House shall be the judge of the elections, returns, and qualifications of its own members, and a majority of each shall constitute a quorum to do business; but a smaller number may adjourn from day to day, and may be authorized to compel the attendance of absent members, in such manner and under such penalties as each House may provide.

(2) Each House may determine the rules of its proceedings, punish its members for disorderly behavior, and, with the concurrence of two-thirds of the whole number, expel a member.

(3) Each House shall keep a journal of its proceedings, and from time to time publish the same, excepting such part as may in its judgment require secrecy, and the ayes and nays of the members of either House, on any question, shall, at the desire of one-fifth of those present, be entered on the journal.

(4) Neither House, during the session of Congress, shall, without the consent of the other, adjourn for more than three days, nor to any other place than that in which the two Houses shall be sitting.

SEC. 6. (1) The Senators and Representatives shall receive a compensation for their services, to be ascertained by law, and paid out of the Treasury of the Confederate States. They shall, in all cases except treason and breach of the peace, be privileged from arrest during their attendance at the session of their respective Houses, and in going to and returning from the same; and for any speech or debate in either House, they shall not be questioned in any other place.

(2) No Senator or Representative shall, during the time for which he was elected, be appointed to any civil office under the authority of the Confederate States, which shall have been created, or the emoluments whereof shall have been increased during such time; and no person holding any office under the Confederate States shall be a member of either House during his continuance in office. But Congress may, by law, grant to the principal officer in each of the Executive Departments a seat upon the floor of either House, with the privilege of discussing any measure appertaining to his department.

SEC. 7. (1) All bills for raising revenue shall originate in the House of Representatives; but the Senate may propose or concur with amendments as on other bills.

(2) Every bill which shall have passed both Houses shall, before it becomes a law, be presented to the President of the Confederate States; if he approve he shall sign it; but if not, he shall return it with his objections to that House in which it shall have originated, who shall enter the objections at large on their journal, and proceed to reconsider it. If, after such reconsideration, two-thirds of that House shall agree to pass the bill, it shall be sent, together with the objections, to the other House, by which it shall likewise be reconsidered, and if approved by two-thirds of that House, it shall become a law. But in all such cases, the votes of both Houses shall be determined by yeas and nays, and the names of the persons voting for and against the bill shall be entered on the journal of each House respectively. If any bill shall not be returned by the President within ten days (Sundays excepted) after it shall have been presented to him, the same shall be a law, in like manner as if he had signed it, unless the Congress, by their adjournment, prevent its return; in which case it shall not be a law. The President may approve any appropriation and disapprove any other appropriation in the same bill. In such case he shall, in signing the bill, designate the appropriations disapproved; and shall return a copy of such appropriations, with his objections, to the House in which the bill shall have originated; and the same proceedings shall then be had as in case of other bills disapproved by the President.

(3) Every order, resolution, or vote, to which the concurrence of both Houses may be necessary (except on questions of adjournment) shall be presented to the President of the Confederate States; and before the same shall take effect shall be approved by him; or being disapproved by him, may be repassed by two-thirds of both Houses, according to the rules and limitations prescribed in case of a bill.

SEC. 8.—The Congress shall have power—

(1) To lay and collect taxes, duties, imposts, and excises, for revenue necessary to pay the debts, provide for the common defence, and carry on the Government of the Confederate States; but no bounties shall be granted from the treasury; nor shall any duties or taxes on importations from foreign nations be laid to promote or foster any branch of industry; and all duties, imposts, and excises shall be uniform throughout the Confederate States.

(2) To borrow money on the credit of the Confederate States.

(3) To regulate commerce with foreign nations, and among the several States, and with the Indian tribes; but neither this, nor any other clause contained in the Constitution shall be construed to delegate the power to Congress to appropriate money for any internal improvement intended to facilitate commerce; except for the purpose of furnishing lights, beacons, and buoys, and other aids to navigation upon the coasts, and the improvement of harbors, and the removing of obstructions in river navigation, in all which cases, such duties shall be laid on the navigation facilitated thereby, as may be necessary to pay the costs and expenses thereof.

(4) To establish uniform laws of naturalization, and uniform laws on the subject of bankruptcies throughout the Confederate States, but no law of Congress shall discharge any debt contracted before the passage of the same.

(5) To coin money, regulate the value thereof, and of foreign coin, and fix the standard of weights and measures.

(6) To provide for the punishment of counterfeiting the securities and current coin of the Confederate States.

(7) To establish post-offices and post-routes; but the expenses of the Post-office Department, after the first day of March, in the year of our Lord eighteen hundred and sixty-three, shall be paid out of its own revenues.

(8) To promote the progress of science and useful arts, by securing for limited times to authors and inventors the exclusive right to their respective writings and discoveries.

(9) To constitute tribunals inferior to the Supreme Court.

(10) To define and punish piracies and felonies committed on the high seas, and offences against the law of nations.

(11) To declare war, grant letters of marque and reprisal, and make rules concerning captures on land and water.

(12) To raise and support armies; but no appropriation of money to that use shall be for a longer term than two years.

(13) To provide and maintain a navy.

(14) To make rules for government and regulation of the land and naval forces.

(15) To provide for calling forth the militia to execute the laws of the Confederate States; suppress insurrections, and repel invasions.

(16) To provide for organizing, arming, and disciplining the militia, and for governing such part of them as may be employed in the service of the Confederate States; reserving to the States, respectively, the appointment of the officers, and the authority of training the militia according to the discipline prescribed by Congress.

(17) To exercise exclusive legislation, in all cases whatsoever, over such district (not exceeding ten miles square) as may, by cession of one or more States, and the acceptance of Congress, become the seat of the Government of the Confederate States; and to exercise a like authority over all places purchased by the consent of the Legislature of the State in which the same shall be, for the erection of forts, magazines, arsenals, dock-yards, and other needful buildings, and

(18) To make all laws which shall be necessary and proper for carrying into execution the foregoing powers, and all other powers vested by this Constitution in the Government of the Confederate States, or in any department or officer thereof.

SEC. 9. (1) The importation of negroes of the African race, from any foreign country, other than the slaveholding States or Territories of the United States of America, is hereby forbidden; and Congress is required to pass such laws as shall effectually prevent the same.

(2) Congress shall also have power to prohibit the introduction of slaves from any State not a member of, or Territory not belonging to, this Confederacy.

(3) The privilege of the writ of *habeas corpus* shall not be suspended, unless when in cases of rebellion or invasion the public safety may require it.

(4) No bill of attainder, or *ex post facto* law, or law denying or impairing the right of property in negro slaves shall be passed.

(5) No capitation or other direct tax shall be laid unless in proportion to the census or enumeration hereinbefore directed to be taken.

(6) No tax or duty shall be laid on articles exported from any State, except by a vote of two-thirds of both Houses.

(7) No preference shall be given by any regulation of commerce or revenue to the ports of one State over those of another.

(8) No money shall be drawn from the treasury but in consequence of appropriations made by law; and a regular statement and account of the receipts and expenditures of all public money shall be published from time to time.

(9) Congress shall appropriate no money from the treasury except by a vote of two-thirds of both Houses, taken by yeas and nays, unless it be asked and estimated for by some one of the heads of departments, and submitted to Congress by the President; or for the purpose of paying its own expenses and contingencies; or for the payment of claims against the Confederate States, the justice of which shall have been judicially declared by a tribunal for the investigation of claims against the Government, which it is hereby made the duty of Congress to establish.

(10) All bills appropriating money shall specify in federal currency the exact amount of each appropriation and the purposes for which it is made; and Congress shall grant no extra compensation to any public con-

tractor, officer, agent, or servant, after such contract shall have been made or such service rendered.

(11) No title of nobility shall be granted by the Confederate States; and no person holding any office of profit or trust under them shall, without the consent of the Congress, accept of any present, emoluments, office, or title of any kind whatever, from any king, prince, or foreign state.

(12) Congress shall make no law respecting an establishment of religion, or prohibiting the free exercise thereof; or abridging the freedom of speech or of the press; or the right of the people peaceably to assemble and petition the Government for a redress of grievances.

(13) A well-regulated militia being necessary to the security of a free State, the right of the people to keep and bear arms shall not be infringed.

(14) No soldier shall, in time of peace, be quartered in any house without the consent of the owner; nor in time of war, but in a manner prescribed by law.

(15) The right of the people to be secure in their persons, houses, papers, and against unreasonable searches and seizures, shall not be violated; and no warrant shall issue but upon probable cause, supported by oath or affirmation, and particularly describing the place to be searched, and the person or things to be seized.

(16) No person shall be held to answer for a capital or otherwise infamous crime, unless on a presentment or indictment of a grand jury, except in cases arising in the land or naval forces, or in the militia, when in actual service, in time of war, or public danger; nor shall any person be subject for the same offence to be twice put in jeopardy of life or limb; nor be compelled in any criminal case to be a witness against himself; nor be deprived of life, liberty, or property, without due process of law; nor shall any private property be taken for public use without just compensation.

(17) In all criminal prosecutions the accused shall enjoy the right to a speedy and public trial, by an impartial jury of the State and district wherein the crime shall have been committed, which district shall have been previously ascertained by law, and to be informed of the nature and cause of the accusation; to be confronted with the witnesses against him; to have compulsory process for obtaining witnesses in his favor; and to have the assistance of counsel for his defence.

(18) In suits at common law, where the value in controversy shall exceed twenty dollars, the right of trial by jury shall be preserved; and no fact so tried by a jury shall be otherwise reëxamined in any court of the Confederacy, than according to the rules of the common law.

(19) Excessive bail shall not be required, nor excessive fines imposed, nor cruel or unusual punishment inflicted.

(20) Every law, or resolution having the force of law, shall relate to but one subject, and that shall be expressed in the title.

SEC. 10. (1) No State shall enter into any treaty, alliance, or confederation; grant letters of marque and reprisals; coin money; make any thing but gold and silver coin a tender in payment of debts; pass any bill of attainder, or *ex post facto* law, or law impairing the obligation of contracts; or grant any title of nobility.

(2) No State shall, without the consent of Congress, lay any imposts or duties on imports or exports, except what may be absolutely necessary for executing its inspection laws; and the net produce of all duties and imposts, laid by any State on imports or exports, shall be for the use of the Treasury of the Confederate States; and all such laws shall be subject to the revision and control of Congress.

(3) No State shall, without the consent of Congress, lay any duty of tonnage, except on sea-going vessels, for the improvement of its rivers and harbors navigated by the said vessels; but such duties shall not conflict with any treaties of the Confederate States with foreign nations; and any surplus of revenue, thus derived, shall, after making such improvement, be paid into the common treasury; nor shall any State keep troops or ships of war in time of peace, enter into any agreement or compact with another State, or with a foreign power, or engage in war, unless actually invaded, or in such imminent danger as will not admit of delay. But when any river divides or flows through two or more

States, they may enter into compacts with each other to improve the navigation thereof.

ART. II.

SEC. 1. (1) The Executive power shall be vested in a President of the Confederate States of America. He and the Vice-President shall hold their offices for the term of six years; but the President shall not be reëligible. The President and Vice-President shall be elected as follows:

(2) Each State shall appoint, in such manner as the Legislature thereof may direct, a number of electors equal to the whole number of Senators and Representatives to which the State may be entitled in Congress; but no Senator or Representative, or person holding an office of trust or profit under the Confederate States, shall be appointed an elector.

(3) The electors shall meet in their respective States and vote by ballot for President and Vice-President, one of whom, at least, shall not be an inhabitant of the same State with themselves; they shall name in their ballots the person voted for as President, and in distinct ballots the person voted for as Vice-President, and they shall make distinct lists of all persons voted for as President, and of all persons voted for as Vice-President, and of the number of votes for each; which list they shall sign, and certify, and transmit, sealed, to the Government of the Confederate States, directed to the President of the Senate. The President of the Senate shall, in the presence of the Senate and House of Representatives, open all the certificates, and the votes shall then be counted; the person having the greatest number of votes for President shall be the President, if such number be a majority of the whole number of electors appointed; and if no person shall have such a majority, then, from the persons having the highest numbers, not exceeding three, on the list of those voted for as President, the House of Representatives shall choose immediately, by ballot, the President. But, in choosing the President, the votes shall be taken by States, the Representative from each State having one vote; a quorum for this purpose shall consist of a member or members from two-thirds of the States, and a majority of all the States shall be necessary

to a choice. And if the House of Representatives shall not choose a President, whenever the right of choice shall devolve upon them, before the fourth day of March next following, then the Vice-President shall act as President, as in case of the death, or other constitutional disability of the President.

(4) The person having the greatest number of votes as Vice-President shall be the Vice-President, if such number be a majority of the whole number of electors appointed; and if no person have a majority, then from the two highest numbers on the list, the Senate shall choose the Vice-President; a quorum for the purpose shall consist of two-thirds of the whole number of Senators, and a majority of the whole number shall be necessary for a choice.

(5) But no person constitutionally ineligible to the office of President shall be eligible to that of Vice-President of the Confederate States.

(6) The Congress may determine the time of choosing the electors, and the day on which they shall give their votes; which day shall be the same throughout the Confederate States.

(7) No person except a natural born citizen of the Confederate States, or a citizen thereof, at the time of the adoption of this Constitution, or a citizen thereof born in the United States prior to the 20th December, 1860, shall be eligible to the office of President; neither shall any person be eligible to that office who shall not have attained the age of thirty-five years, and been fourteen years a resident within the limits of the Confederate States, as they may exist at the time of his election.

(8) In case of the removal of the President from office, or of his death, resignation, or inability to discharge the powers and duties of the said office, the same shall devolve on the Vice-President; and the Congress may, by law, provide for the case of the removal, death, resignation, or inability both of the President and the Vice-President, declaring what officer shall then act as President, and such officer shall then act accordingly until the disability be removed or a President shall be elected.

(9) The President shall, at stated times, receive for his services a compensation, which

shall neither be increased nor diminished during the period for which he shall have been elected; and he shall not receive within that period any other emolument from the Confederate States, or any of them.

(10) Before he enters on the execution of the duties of his office, he shall take the following oath or affirmation:

"I do solemnly swear (or affirm) that I will faithfully execute the office of President of the Confederate States, and will, to the best of my ability, preserve, protect, and defend the Constitution thereof."

SEC. 2. (1) The President shall be commander-in-chief of the army and navy of the Confederate States, and of the militia of the several States, when called into the actual service of the Confederate States; he may require the opinion, in writing, of the principal officer in each of the Executive Departments, upon any subject relating to the duties of their respective offices; and he shall have power to grant reprieves and pardons for offences against the Confederate States, except in cases of impeachment.

(2) He shall have power, by and with the advice and consent of the Senate, to make treaties, provided two-thirds of the Senators present concur; and he shall nominate, and, by and with the advice and consent of the Senate, shall appoint ambassadors, other public ministers, and consuls, Judges of the Supreme Court, and all other officers of the Confederate States, whose appointments are not herein otherwise provided for, and which shall be established by law; but the Congress may by law vest the appointment of such inferior officers, as they think proper, in the President alone, in the courts of law, or in the heads of departments.

(3) The principal officer in each of the Executive Departments, and all persons connected with the diplomatic service, may be removed from office at the pleasure of the President. All other civil officers of the Executive Department may be removed at any time by the President, or other appointing power, when their services are unnecessary, or for dishonesty, incapacity, inefficiency, misconduct, or neglect of duty; and when so removed, the removal shall be reported to the Senate, together with the reasons therefor.

(4) The President shall have power to fill all vacancies that may happen during the recess of the Senate, by granting commissions which shall expire at the end of the next session; but no person rejected by the Senate shall be reappointed to the same office during their ensuing recess.

SEC. 3. (1) The President shall, from time to time, give to the Congress information of the state of the Confederacy, and recommend to their consideration such measures as he shall judge necessary and expedient; he may, on extraordinary occasions, convene both Houses, or either of them; and, in case of disagreement between them, with respect to the time of adjournment he may adjourn them to such time as he shall think proper; he shall receive ambassadors and other public ministers; he shall take care that the laws be faithfully executed, and shall commission all the officers of the Confederate States.

SEC. 4. (1) The President and Vice-President, and all civil officers of the Confederate States, shall be removed from office on impeachment for, or conviction of, treason, bribery, or other high crimes and misdemeanors.

ART. III.

SEC. 1. (1) The judicial power of the Confederate States shall be vested in one Superior Court, and in such inferior courts as the Congress may from time to time ordain and establish. The judges, both of the Supreme and inferior courts, shall hold their offices during good behavior, and shall, at stated times, receive for their services a compensation, which shall not be diminished during their continuance in office.

SEC. 2. (1) The judicial power shall extend to all cases arising under the Constitution, the laws of the Confederate States, or treaties made or which shall be made under their authority; to all cases affecting ambassadors, other public ministers, and consuls; to all cases of admiralty or maritime jurisdiction; to controversies to which the Confederate States shall be a party; to controversies between two or more States; between a State and citizens of another State, where the State is plaintiff; between citizens claiming lands under grants of different States, and between a State or the citizens thereof, and foreign States, citizens, or subjects; but no State shall be sued by a citizen or subject of any foreign State.

(2) In all cases affecting ambassadors, other public ministers, and consuls, and those in which a State shall be a party, the Supreme Court shall have original jurisdiction. In all the other cases before mentioned, the Supreme Court shall have appellate jurisdiction, both as to law and fact, with such exceptions, and under such regulations as the Congress shall make.

(3) The trial of all crimes, except in cases of impeachment, shall be by jury, and such trial shall be held in the State where the said crimes shall have been committed; but when not committed within any State, the trial shall be at such place or places as the Congress may by law have directed.

SEC. 3. (1) Treason against the Confederate States shall consist only in levying war against them, or in adhering to their enemies, giving them aid and comfort. No person shall be convicted of treason unless on the testimony of two witnesses to the same overt act, or on confession in open court.

(2) The Congress shall have power to declare the punishment of treason, but no attainder of treason shall work corruption of blood, or forfeiture, except during the life of the person attainted.

ART. IV.

SEC. 1. (1) Full faith and credit shall be given in each State to the public acts, records, and judicial proceedings of every other State. And the Congress may, by general laws, prescribe the manner in which such acts, records, and proceedings shall be proved, and the effect thereof.

SEC. 2. (1) The citizens of each State shall be entitled to all the privileges and immunities of citizens of the several States, and shall have the right of transit and sojourn in any State of this Confederacy, with their slaves and other property; and the right of property in said slaves shall not be thereby impaired.

(2) A person charged in any State with treason, felony, or other crime against the laws of such State, who shall flee from justice, and be found in another State, shall, on demand of the executive authority of the State from which he fled, be delivered up to be removed to the State having jurisdiction of the crime.

(3) No slave or other person held to service or labor in any State or Territory of the Confederate States, under the laws thereof, escaping or unlawfully carried into another, shall, in consequence of any law or regulation therein, be discharged from such service or labor; but shall be delivered up on claim of the party to whom such slave belongs, or to whom such service or labor may be due.

SEC. 3. (1) Other States may be admitted into this Confederacy by a vote of two-thirds of the whole House of Representatives, and two-thirds of the Senate, the Senate voting by States; but no new State shall be formed or erected within the jurisdiction of any other State; nor any State be formed by the junction of two or more States, or parts of States, without the consent of the Legislatures of the States concerned as well as of the Congress.

(2) The Congress shall have power to dispose of and make all needful rules and regulations concerning the property of the Confederate States, including the lands thereof.

(3) The Confederate States may acquire new territory; and Congress shall have power to legislate and provide governments for the inhabitants of all territory belonging to the Confederate States, lying without the limits of the several States, and may permit them, at such times, and in such manner as it may by law provide, to form States to be admitted into the Confederacy. In all such territory, the institution of negro slavery, as it now exists in the Confederate States, shall be recognized and protected by Congress and by the territorial government; and the inhabitants of the several Confederate States and Territories shall have the right to take to such territory any slaves lawfully held by them in any of the States or Territories of the Confederate States.

(4) The Confederate States shall guarantee to every State that now is or hereafter may become a member of this Confederacy, a Republican form of Government, and shall protect each of them against invasion; and on application of the Legislature, (or of the Executive when the Legislature is not in session,) against domestic violence.

ART. V.

SEC. 1. (1) Upon the demand of any three States, legally assembled in their several Conventions, the Congress shall summon a Convention of all the States, to take into consideration such amendments to the Constitution as the said States shall concur in suggesting at the time when the said demand is made; and should any of the proposed amendments to the Constitution be agreed on by the said Convention—voting by States—and the same be ratified by the Legislatures of two-thirds of the several States, or by conventions in two-thirds thereof—as the one or the other mode of ratification may be proposed by the general convention—they shall thenceforward form a part of this Constitution. But no State shall, without its consent, be deprived of its equal representation in the Senate.

ART. VI.

1.—The Government established by this Constitution is the successor of the Provisional Government of the Confederate States of America, and all the laws passed by the latter shall continue in force until the same shall be repealed or modified; and all the officers appointed by the same shall remain in office until their successors are appointed and qualified, or the offices abolished.

2. All debts contracted and engagements entered into before the adoption of this Constitution, shall be as valid against the Confederate States under this Constitution as under the Provisional Government.

3. This Constitution, and the laws of the Confederate States, made in pursuance thereof, and all treaties made, or which shall be made, under the authority of the Confederate States, shall be the supreme law of the land; and the judges in every State shall be bound thereby, any thing in the Constitution or laws of any State to the contrary notwithstanding.

4. The Senators and Representatives before mentioned, and the members of the sev-

eral State Legislatures, and all executive and judicial offices, both of the Confederate States and of the several States, shall be bound, by oath or affirmation, to support this Constitution; but no religious test shall ever be required as a qualification to any office or public trust under the Confederate States.

5. The enumeration, in the Constitution, of certain rights, shall not be construed to deny or disparage others retained by the people of the several States.

6. The powers not delegated to the Confederate States by the Constitution, nor prohibited by it to the States, are reserved to the States, respectively, or to the people thereof.

ART. VII.

1.—The ratification of the conventions of five States shall be sufficient for the establishment of this Constitution between the States so ratifying the same.

2. When five States shall have ratified this Constitution in the manner before specified, the Congress, under the provisional Constitution, shall prescribe the time for holding the election of President and Vice-President, and for the meeting of the electoral college, and for counting the votes and inaugurating the President. They shall also prescribe the time for holding the first election of members of Congress under this Constitution, and the time for assembling the same. Until the assembling of such Congress, the Congress under the provisional Constitution shall continue to exercise the legislative powers granted them; not extending beyond the time limited by the Constitution of the Provisional Government.

Adopted unanimously by the Congress of the Confederate States of South Carolina, Georgia, Florida, Alabama, Mississippi, Louisiana, and Texas, sitting in convention at the capitol, in the city of Montgomery, Ala., on the eleventh day of March, in the year eighteen hundred and sixty-one.

Howell Cobb
President of the Congress.

[Signatures]

202. LINCOLN'S FIRST INAUGURAL ADDRESS
March 4, 1861

(Richardson, ed. *Messages and Papers,* Vol. VI, p. 5 ff.)

In his first inaugural address Lincoln reiterated his constitutional doctrine that the Union was older than the States and that the contract between the States was binding and irrevocable. The last paragraph of the Inaugural was phrased by Seward. See, J. G. Nicolay and J. Hay, *Abraham Lincoln,* Vol. III; W. E. Barton, *President Lincoln,* Vol. I, ch. xiii.

FELLOW-CITIZENS OF THE UNITED STATES:
—In compliance with a custom as old as the Government itself, I appear before you to address you briefly, and to take in your presence the oath prescribed by the Constitution of the United States to be taken by the President "before he enters on the execution of his office.". . .

Apprehension seems to exist among the people of the Southern States that by the accession of a Republican administration their property and their peace and personal security are to be endangered. There has never been any reasonable cause for such apprehension. Indeed, the most ample evidence to the contrary has all the while existed and been open to their inspection. It is found in nearly all the published speeches of him who now addresses you. I do but quote from one of those speeches when I declare that "I have no purpose, directly or indirectly, to interfere with the institution of slavery in the States where it exists. I believe I have no lawful right to do so, and I have no inclination to do so." . . .

I now reiterate these sentiments; and, in doing so, I only press upon the public attention the most conclusive evidence of which the case is susceptible, that the property, peace and security of no section are to be in any wise endangered by the now incoming administration. I add, too, that all the protection which, consistently with the Constitution and the laws, can be given, will be cheerfully given to all the States when lawfully demanded, for whatever cause —as cheerfully to one section as to another. . . .

I take the official oath to-day with no mental reservations, and with no purpose to construe the Constitution or laws by any hypercritical rules. And, while I do not choose now to specify particular acts of Congress as proper to be enforced, I do suggest that it will be much safer for all, both in official and private stations, to conform to and abide by all those acts which stand unrepealed, than to violate any of them, trusting to find impunity in having them held to be unconstitutional. . . .

A disruption of the Federal Union, heretofore only menaced, is now formidably attempted.

I hold that, in contemplation of universal law and of the Constitution, the Union of these States is perpetual. Perpetuity is implied, if not expressed, in the fundamental law of all national governments. It is safe to assert that no government proper ever had a provision in its organic law for its own termination. Continue to execute all the express provisions of our national Constitution, and the Union will endure forever—it being impossible to destroy it except by some action not provided for in the instrument itself.

Again, if the United States be not a government proper, but an association of States in the nature of contract merely, can it as a contract be peaceably unmade by less than all the parties who made it? One party to a contract may violate it—break it, so to speak; but does it not require all to lawfully rescind it?

Descending from these general principles, we find the proposition that in legal contemplation the Union is perpetual confirmed by the history of the Union itself. The Union is much older than the Constitution. It was formed, in fact, by the Articles of Association in 1774. It was matured and continued by the Declaration of Independence in 1776. It was further matured, and the faith of all the then thirteen States expressly plighted and engaged that it should be perpetual, by the Articles of Confederation in 1778. And, finally, in 1787 one of the declared objects for ordaining and establishing the Constitution was "to form a more perfect Union."

But if the destruction of the Union by one or by a part only of the States be lawfully possible, the Union is less perfect than before the Constitution, having lost the vital element of perpetuity.

It follows from these views that no State upon its own mere motion can lawfully get out of the Union; that resolves and ordinances to that effect are legally void; and that acts of violence, within any State or States, against the authority of the United States, are insurrectionary or revolutionary, according to circumstances.

I therefore consider that, in view of the Constitution and the laws, the Union is unbroken; and to the extent of my ability I shall take care, as the Constitution itself expressly enjoins upon me, that the laws of the Union be faithfully executed in all the States. Doing this I deem to be only a simple duty on my part; and I shall perform it so far as practicable, unless my rightful masters, the American people, shall withhold the requisite means, or in some authoritative manner direct the contrary. I trust this will not be regarded as a menace, but only as the declared purpose of the Union that it will constitutionally defend and maintain itself.

In doing this there needs to be no bloodshed or violence; and there shall be none, unless it be forced upon the national authority. The power confided to me will be used to hold, occupy, and possess the property and places belonging to the Government, and to collect the duties and imposts; but beyond what may be necessary for these objects, there will be no invasion, no using of force against or among the people anywhere. Where hostility to the United States, in any interior locality, shall be so great and universal as to prevent competent resident citizens from holding the Federal offices, there will be no attempt to force obnoxious strangers among the people for that object. While the strict legal right may exist in the government to enforce the exercise of these offices, the attempt to do so would be so irritating, and so nearly impracticable withal, that I deem it better to forego for the time the uses of such offices.

The mails, unless repelled, will continue to be furnished in all parts of the Union. So far as possible, the people everywhere shall have that sense of perfect security which is most favorable to calm thought and reflection. The course here indicated will be followed unless current events and experience shall show a modification or change to be proper, and in every case and exigency my best discretion will be exercised according to circumstances actually existing, and with a view and a hope of a peaceful solution of the national troubles and the restoration of fraternal sympathies and affections.

That there are persons in one section or another who seek to destroy the Union at all events, and are glad of any pretext to do it, I will neither affirm nor deny; but if there be such, I need address no word to them. To those, however, who really love the Union may I not speak?

Before entering upon so grave a matter as the destruction of our national fabric, with all its benefits, its memories, and its hopes, would it not be wise to ascertain precisely why we do it? Will you hazard so desperate a step while there is any possibility that any portion of the ills you fly from have no real existence? Will you, while the certain ills you fly to are greater than all the real ones you fly from—will you risk the commission of so fearful a mistake?

All profess to be content in the Union if all constitutional rights can be maintained. Is it true, then, that any right, plainly written in the Constitution, has been denied? I think not. Happily the human mind is so constituted that no party can reach to the audacity of doing this. Think, if you can, of a single instance in which a plainly written provision of the Constitution has ever been denied. If by the mere force of numbers a majority should deprive a minority of any clearly written constitutional right, it might, in a moral point of view, justify revolution—certainly would if such a right were a vital one. But such is not our case. All the vital rights of minorities and of individuals are so plainly assured to them by affirmations and negations, guaranties and prohibitions, in the Constitution, that controversies never arise concerning them. But no organic law can ever be framed with a provision specifically applicable to every question which may occur in practical administration. No foresight can anticipate, nor any document of reasonable length contain, express provisions for all possible questions. Shall fugitives from labor be surrendered by national or by State authority? The Constitution does not expressly say. *May* Congress prohibit slavery in the Territories? The Constitution does not expressly say. *Must* Congress protect slavery in the Territories? The Constitution does not expressly say.

From questions of this class spring all our constitutional controversies, and we divide upon them into majorities and minorities. If the minority will not acquiesce, the majority must, or the Government must cease. There is no other alternative; for continuing the Government is acquiescence on one side or the other.

If a minority in such case will secede rather than acquiesce, they make a precedent which in turn will divide and ruin them; for a minority of their own will secede from them whenever a majority refuses to be controlled by such minority. For instance, why may not any portion of a new confederacy a year or two hence arbitrarily secede again, precisely as portions of the present Union now claim to secede from it? All who cherish disunion sentiments are now being educated to the exact temper of doing this.

Is there such perfect identity of interests among the States to compose a new Union as to produce harmony only, and prevent renewed secession?

Plainly, the central idea of secession is the essence of anarchy. A majority held in restraint by constitutional checks and limitations, and always changing easily with deliberate changes of popular opinions and sentiments, is the only true sovereign of a free people. Whoever rejects it does, of necessity, fly to anarchy or to despotism. Unanimity is impossible; the rule of a minority, as a permanent arrangement, is wholly inadmissible; so that, rejecting the majority principle, anarchy or despotism in some form is all that is left.

I do not forget the position assumed by some, that constitutional questions are to be decided by the Supreme Court; nor do I deny that such decisions must be binding, in any case, upon the parties to a suit, as to the object of that suit, while they are also entitled to a very high respect and consideration in all parallel cases by all other departments of the government. And, while it is obviously possible that such decision may be erroneous in any given case, still the evil effect following it, being limited to that particular case, with the chance that it may be overruled and never become a precedent for other cases, can better be borne than could the evils of a different practice. At the same time, the candid citizen must confess that if the policy of the government, upon vital questions affecting the whole people, is to be irrevocably fixed by decisions of the Supreme Court, the instant they are made, in ordinary litigation between parties in personal actions, the people will have ceased to be their own rulers, having to that extent practically resigned the government into the hands of that eminent tribunal. Nor is there in this view any assault upon the court or the judges. It is a duty from which they may not shrink to decide cases properly brought before them, and it is no fault of theirs if others seek to turn their decisions to political purposes.

One section of our country believes slavery is right, and ought to be extended, while the other believes it is wrong, and ought not to be extended. This is the only substantial dispute. The fugitive slave clause of the Constitution and the law for the suppression of the foreign slave trade are each as well enforced, perhaps, as any law can ever be in a community where the moral sense of the people imperfectly supports the law itself. The great body of the people abide by the dry legal obligation in both cases, and a few break over in each. This, I think, cannot be perfectly cured; and it would be worse in both cases after the separation of the sections than before. The foreign slave trade, now imperfectly suppressed, would be ultimately revived, without restriction, in one section, while fugitive slaves, now only partially surrendered, would not be surrendered at all by the other.

Physically speaking, we cannot separate. We cannot remove our respective sections from each other, nor build an impassable wall between them. A husband and wife may be divorced and go out of the presence and beyond the reach of each other; but the different parts of our country cannot do this. They cannot but remain face to face, and intercourse, either amicable or hostile, must continue between them. Is it possible, then, to make that intercourse more advantageous or more satisfactory after separation than before? Can aliens make treaties easier than friends can make laws? Can treaties be more faithfully enforced between aliens than laws can among friends? Suppose you go to war, you cannot fight always; and when, after much loss on both sides, and no gain on either, you cease fighting, the identical old questions as to terms of intercourse are again upon you.

This country, with its institutions, belongs to the people who inhabit it. Whenever they shall grow weary of the existing government, they can exercise their constitutional right of amending it, or their revolutionary right to dismember or overthrow it. I cannot be ignorant of the fact that many worthy and patriotic citizens are desirous of having the national Constitution amended. While I make no recommendation of amendments, I fully recognize the rightful authority of the people over the whole subject, to be exercised in either of the modes prescribed in the instrument itself, and I should, under existing circumstances, favor rather than oppose a fair opportunity being afforded the people to act upon it. I will venture to add that to me the convention mode seems preferable, in that it allows amendments to originate with the people themselves, instead of only permitting them to take or reject propositions originated by others not especially chosen for the purpose, and which might not be precisely such as they would wish to either accept or refuse. I understand a proposed amendment to the Constitution—which amendment, however, I have not seen—has passed Congress, to the effect that the Federal Government shall never interfere with the domestic institutions of the States, including that of persons held to service. To avoid misconstruction of what I have said, I depart from my purpose not to speak of particular amendments so far as to say that, holding such a provision to now be implied constitutional law, I have no objection to its being made express and irrevocable. . . .

Why should there not be a patient confidence in the ultimate justice of the people? Is there any better or equal hope in the world? In our present differences is either party without faith of being in the right? If the Almighty Ruler of nations, with his

eternal truth and justice, be on your side of the North, or on yours of the South, that truth and that justice will surely prevail by the judgment of this great tribunal of the American people.

By the frame of the government under which we live, this same people have wisely given their public servants but little power for mischief; and have, with equal wisdom, provided for the return of that little to their own hands at very short intervals. While the people retain their virtue and vigilance, no administration, by any extreme of wickedness or folly, can very seriously injure the government in the short space of four years.

My countrymen, one and all, think calmly and well upon this whole subject. Nothing valuable can be lost by taking time. If there be an object to hurry any of you in hot haste to a step which you would never take deliberately, that object will be frustrated by taking time; but no good object can be frustrated by it. Such of you as are now dissatisfied still have the old Constitution unimpaired, and, on the sensitive point, the laws of your own framing under it; while the new administration will have no immediate power, if it would, to change either. If it were admitted that you who are dissatisfied hold the right side in the dispute, there still is no single good reason for precipitate action. Intelligence, patriotism, Christianity, and a firm reliance on Him who has never yet forsaken this favored land, are still competent to adjust in the best way all our present difficulty.

In your hands, my dissatisfied fellow-countrymen, and not in mine, is the momentous issue of civil war. The government will not assail you. You can have no conflict without being yourselves the aggressors. You have no oath registered in heaven to destroy the government, while I shall have the most solemn one to "preserve, protect, and defend" it.

I am loath to close. We are not enemies, but friends. We must not be enemies. Though passion may have strained, it must not break, our bonds of affection. The mystic chords of memory, stretching from every battle-field and patriot grave to every living heart and hearthstone all over this broad land, will yet swell the chorus of the Union when again touched, as surely they will be, by the better angels of our nature.

203. DAVIS'S MESSAGE TO CONGRESS
April 29, 1861

(Richardson, ed. *Messages and Papers of the Confederacy*, Vol. I, p. 63 ff.)

Davis called the Confederate Congress together in special session April 29, 1861. In his message he analyzed again the theory of the Union and the logic of secession. In this message he also asked for authority to prosecute the war: in response to his requests Congress at this session authorized him to use all the land and naval force of the Confederacy, to issue letters of marque, raise volunteers, make loans, etc. See, J. Davis, *Rise and Fall of the Confederate Government*, Vol. I, Part IV, ch. iv.

Gentlemen of the Congress. . . .

The declaration of war made against this Confederacy by Abraham Lincoln, the President of the United States, in his proclamation issued on the 15th day of the present month, rendered it necessary, in my judgment, that you should convene at the earliest practicable moment to devise the measures necessary for the defense of the country. The occasion is indeed an extraordinary one. It justifies me in a brief review of the relations heretofore existing between us and the States which now unite in warfare against us and in a succinct statement of the events which have resulted in this warfare, to the end that mankind may pass intelligent and impartial judgment on its motives and objects. During the war waged against Great Britain by her colonies on this continent a common danger impelled them to a close alliance and to the formation of a Confederation, by the terms of which the colonies, styling themselves States, entered *"severally* into a firm league of friendship with each other for their common defense, the security of their liberties, and their mutual and general welfare, binding themselves to assist each other against all force offered to or attacks made upon them, or any of them, on account of religion, sovereignty, trade, or any other pretense whatever." In order to guard against any misconstruction of their compact, the several States made explicit declaration in a distinct article—that *"each* State *retains its* sovereignty, freedom, and independence, and every power, jurisdiction, and right which is not by this Confederation *expressly delegated* to the United States in Congress assembled."

Under this contract of alliance, the war of the Revolution was successfully waged, and resulted in the treaty of peace with Great Britain in 1783, by the terms of which the several States were *each by name* recognized to be independent. The Articles of Confederation contained a clause whereby all alterations were prohibited unless confirmed by the Legislatures of *every State* after being agreed to by the Congress; and in obedience to this provision, under the resolution of Congress of the 21st of February, 1787, the several States appointed delegates who attended a convention "for the *sole and express purpose* of revising the Articles of Confederation and reporting to Congress and the several Legislatures such alterations and provisions therein as shall, when agreed to in Congress *and confirmed by the States,* render the Federal Constitution adequate to the exigencies of Government and the preservation of the Union." It was by the delegates chosen by the *several States* under the resolution just quoted that the Constitution of the United States was framed in 1787 and submitted to the *several States* for ratification, as shown by the seventh article, which is in these words: "The ratification of the *conventions of nine States* shall be sufficient for the establishment of this Constitution *between the States* so ratifying the same." . . . The Constitution of 1787, having, however, omitted the clause already recited from the Articles of Confederation, which provided in explicit terms that each State *retained* its sovereignty and independence, some alarm was felt in the States, when invited to ratify the Constitution, lest this omission should be construed into an abandonment of their cherished principle, and they refused to be satisfied until amendments were added to the Constitution placing beyond any pretense of doubt the reservation by the States of all their sovereign rights and powers not expressly delegated to the United States by the Constitution.

Strange, indeed, must it appear to the impartial observer, but it is none the less true that all these carefully worded clauses proved unavailing to prevent the rise and growth in the Northern States of a political school which has persistently claimed that the government thus formed was not a compact *between* States, but was in effect a national government, set up *above* and *over* the States. An organization created by the States to secure the blessings of liberty and independence against *foreign* aggression, has been gradually perverted into a machine for their control in their *domestic* affairs. The *creature* has been exalted above its *creators;* the *principals* have been made subordinate to the *agent* appointed by themselves. The people of the Southern States, whose almost exclusive occupation was agriculture, early perceived a tendency in the Northern States to render the common government subservient to their own purposes by imposing burdens on commerce as a protection to their manufacturing and shipping interests. . . . By degrees, as the Northern States gained preponderance in the National Congress, self-interest taught their people to yield ready assent to any plausible advocacy of their right as a majority to govern the minority without control. They learned to listen with impatience to the suggestion of any constitutional impediment to the exercise of their will, and so utterly have the principles of the Constitution been corrupted in the Northern mind that, in the inaugural address delivered by President Lincoln in March last, he asserts as an axiom, which he plainly deems to be undeniable, that the theory of the Constitution requires that in all cases the majority shall govern; . . . This is the lamentable and fundamental error on which rests the policy that has culminated in his declaration of war against these Confederate States. In addition to the long-continued and deep-seated resentment felt by the Southern States at the persistent abuse of the powers they had delegated to the Congress, for the purpose of enriching the manufacturing and shipping classes of the North at the expense of the South, there has existed for nearly half a century another subject of discord, involving interests of such transcendent magnitude as at all times to create the apprehension in the minds of many devoted lovers of the Union that its permanence was impossible. When the several States delegated certain powers to the United States Congress, a large portion of the laboring population consisted of African slaves imported into the colonies by the mother country. In twelve out of the thirteen States negro slavery existed, and the right of property in slaves was protected by law. This property was recognized in the Constitution, and provision was made against its loss by the escape of the slave. The increase in the number of slaves by further importation from Africa was also secured by a clause forbidding Congress to prohibit the slave trade anterior to a certain date, and in no clause can there be found any delegation of power to the Congress authorizing it in any manner to legislate to the prejudice, detriment, or discouragement of the owners of that species of property, or excluding it from the protection of the Government.

The climate and soil of the Northern States soon proved unpropitious to the continuance of slave labor, whilst the converse was the case at the South. Under the unrestricted free intercourse between the two sections, the Northern States consulted their own interests by selling their slaves to the South and prohibiting slavery within their limits. The South were willing purchasers of property suitable to their wants, and paid the price of the acquisition without harboring a suspicion that their quiet possession was to be disturbed by those who were inhibited not only by want of constitutional authority, but by good faith as vendors, from disquieting a title emanating from themselves. As soon, however, as the Northern States that prohibited African slavery within their limits had reached a number sufficient to give their representation a controlling voice in the Congress, a persistent and organized system of hostile measures against the rights of the owners of slaves in the Southern States was inaugurated and gradually extended. A continuous series of measures was devised and prosecuted for the purpose of rendering insecure the tenure of property in slaves. . . . Emboldened by success, the theatre of agitation and aggression against the clearly expressed constitutional rights of the Southern States was transferred to the Congress; Senators and Representatives were sent to the common councils of the nation, whose chief title to this distinction consisted in the display of a spirit of ultra-fanaticism, and whose business was not "to promote the general welfare or insure domestic tranquillity," but to awaken the bitterest hatred against the citizens of sister States, by violent denunciation of their institutions; the transaction of public affairs was impeded by repeated efforts to usurp powers not delegated by the Constitution, for the purpose of impairing the security of property in slaves, and reducing those States which held slaves to a condition of inferiority. Finally a great party was organized for the purpose of obtaining the administration of the Government, with the avowed object of using its power for the total exclusion of the slave States from all participation in the benefits of the public domain acquired by all the States in common, whether by conquest or purchase; of surrounding them entirely by States in which slavery should be prohibited; of those rendering the property in slaves so insecure as to be comparatively worthless, and thereby annihilating in effect property worth thousands of millions of dollars. This party, thus organized, succeeded in the month of November last in the election of its candidate for the Presidency of the United States.

In the meantime, the African slaves had augmented in number from about 600,000, at the date of the adoption of the constitutional compact, to upward of 4,000,000. In moral and social condition they had been elevated from brutal savages into docile, intelligent, and civilized agricultural laborers, and supplied not only with bodily comforts but with careful religious instruction. Under the supervision of a superior race their labor had been so directed as not only to allow a gradual and marked amelioration of their own condition, but to convert hundreds of thousands of square miles of the wilderness into cultivated lands covered with a prosperous people; towns and cities had sprung into existence, and had rapidly increased in wealth and population under the social system of the South; the white population of the Southern slave-holding States had augmented from about 1,250,000 at the date of the adoption of the Constitution to more than 8,500,000, in 1860; and the productions in the South of cotton, rice, sugar, and tobacco, for the full development and continuance of which the labor of African slaves was and is indispensable, had swollen to an amount which formed nearly three-fourths of the exports of the whole United States and had become absolutely necessary to the wants of civilized man. With interests of such overwhelming magnitude imperiled, the people of the Southern States were driven by the conduct of the North to the adoption of some course of action to avert the danger with which they were openly menaced. With this view the Legislatures of the several States invited the people to select delegates to conventions to be held for the purpose of determining for themselves what measures were best adapted to meet so alarming a crisis in their history. Here it may be proper to observe that from a period as early as 1798 there had existed in *all* of the States of the Union a party almost uninterruptedly in the majority based upon the creed that each State was, in the last resort, the sole judge as well of its wrongs as of the mode and measure of redress. . . .

. . . In the exercise of a right so ancient, so well-established, and so necessary for self-preservation, the people of the Confederate States, in their conventions, determined that the wrongs which they had suffered and the evils with which they were menaced required that they should revoke the delegation of powers to the Federal Government which they had ratified in their several conventions. They consequently passed ordinances resuming all their rights as sovereign and independent States and dissolved their connection with the other States of the Union.

Having done this, they proceeded to form a new compact amongst themselves by new articles of confederation, which have been also ratified by the conventions of the several States with an approach to unanimity far exceeding that of the conventions which adopted the Constitution of 1787. They have organized their new Government in all its departments; the functions of the executive, legislative, and judicial magistrates are performed in accordance with the will of the people, as displayed not merely in a cheerful acquiescence, but in the enthusiastic support of the Government thus established by themselves; and but for the interference of the Government of the United States in this legitimate exercise of the right of a people to self-government, peace, happiness, and prosperity would now smile on our land. . . .

Jefferson Davis.

204. SEWARD'S PLAN TO AVERT CIVIL WAR
April 1, 1861

(*Writings of Abraham Lincoln,* Constitutional ed., Vol. V, p. 278 ff.)

Seward was one of the founders of the Republican Party and the most prominent of the candidates for the Republican nomination in 1860. He looked upon his appointment to the first place in the Cabinet as nothing more than his due, and entertained the idea of dominating the Presidential policy. "Seward," said Gideon Welles, "liked to be called premier". His "Thoughts for the President's Consideration" were intended to establish his dominance over the President: Lincoln's reply was a masterly rebuke, which did not alienate the Secretary of State. The best biography of Seward is F. Bancroft, *Life of William H. Seward,* 2 vols.; see especially Vol. II, chs. xxviii, xxix. See also, C. E. Macartney, *Lincoln and His Cabinet,* ch. v.; G. Bradford, *Union Portraits,* ch. vii.

Some Thoughts for the President's Consideration, April 1, 1861.

First. We are at the end of a month's administration, and yet without a policy either domestic or foreign.

Second. This, however, is not culpable, and it has even been unavoidable. The presence of the Senate, with the need to meet applications for patronage, have prevented attention to other and more grave matters.

Third. But further delay to adopt and prosecute our policies for both domestic and foreign affairs would not only bring scandal on the administration, but danger upon the country.

Fourth. To do this we must dismiss the applicants for office. But how? I suggest that we make the local appointments forthwith, leaving foreign or general ones for ulterior and occasional action.

Fifth. The policy at home. I am aware that my views are singular, and perhaps not sufficiently explained. My system is built upon this idea as a ruling one, namely, that we must CHANGE THE QUESTION BEFORE THE PUBLIC FROM ONE UPON SLAVERY, OR ABOUT SLAVERY, for a question upon UNION OR DISUNION:

In other words, from what would be regarded as a party question, to one of patriotism or union.

The occupation or evacuation of Fort Sumter, although not in fact a slavery or a party question, is so regarded. Witness the temper manifested by the Republicans in the free States, and even by the Union men in the South.

I would therefore terminate it as a safe means for changing the issue. I deem it fortunate that the last administration created the necessity.

For the rest, I would simultaneously defend and reinforce all the ports in the gulf, and have the navy recalled from foreign stations to be prepared for a blockade. Put the island of Key West under martial law.

This will raise distinctly the question of union or disunion. I would maintain every fort and possession in the South.

FOR FOREIGN NATIONS

I would demand explanations from Spain and France, categorically, at once.

I would seek explanations from Great Britain and Russia, and send agents into Canada, Mexico, and Central America to rouse a vigorous continental spirit of independence on this continent against European intervention.

And, if satisfactory explanations are not received from Spain and France,

Would convene Congress and declare war against them.

But whatever policy we adopt, there must be an energetic prosecution of it.

For this purpose it must be somebody's business to pursue and direct it incessantly.

Either the President must do it himself, and be all the while active in it, or

Devolve it on some member of his Cabinet. Once adopted, debates on it must end, and all agree and abide.

It is not in my especial province;

But I neither seek to evade nor assume responsibility.

REPLY TO SECRETARY SEWARD'S MEMORANDUM

Executive Mansion, April 1, 1861.
HON. W. H. SEWARD.

MY DEAR SIR:—Since parting with you I

have been considering your paper dated this day, and entitled "Some Thoughts for the President's Consideration." The first proposition in it is, *"First,* We are at the end of a month's administration, and yet without a policy either domestic or foreign."

At the beginning of that month, in the inaugural, I said: "The power confided to me will be used to hold, occupy, and possess the property and places belonging to the Government, and to collect the duties and imposts." This had your distinct approval at the time; and, taken in connection with the order I immediately gave General Scott, directing him to employ every means in his power to strengthen and hold the forts, comprises the exact domestic policy you now urge, with the single exception that it does not propose to abandon Fort Sumter.

Again, I do not perceive how the reinforcement of Fort Sumter would be done on a slavery or a party issue, while that of Fort Pickens would be on a more national and patriotic one.

The news received yesterday in regard to St. Domingo certainly brings a new item within the range of our foreign policy; but up to that time we have been preparing circulars and instructions to ministers and the like, all in perfect harmony, without even a suggestion that we had no foreign policy.

Upon your closing propositions—that "whatever policy we adopt, there must be an energetic prosecution of it.

"For this purpose it must be somebody's business to pursue and direct it incessantly.

"Either the President must do it himself, and be all the while active in it, or

"Devolve it on some member of his Cabinet. Once adopted, debates on it must end, and all agree and abide"—I remark that if this must be done, I must do it. When a general line of policy is adopted, I apprehend there is no danger of its being changed without good reason, or continuing to be a subject of unnecessary debate; still, upon points arising in its progress I wish, and suppose I am entitled to have, the advice of all the Cabinet.

Your obedient servant,
A. LINCOLN.

205. LINCOLN'S MESSAGE TO CONGRESS IN SPECIAL SESSION
July 4, 1861

(Richardson, ed. *Messages and Papers,* Vol. VI, p. 20 ff.)

By proclamation of April 15, 1861, Lincoln called Congress to meet in special session July 4, 1861. In the intervening period Lincoln had strained the executive authority in his effort to suppress the rebellion. The special session message informed Congress of the steps that the executive had taken and made specific recommendations for the grant of additional powers. It presented too, in a more elaborate form than the Inaugural Address, Lincoln's conception of the significance of the struggle for the preservation of the Union.

FELLOW-CITIZENS OF THE SENATE AND HOUSE OF REPRESENTATIVES:—Having been convened on an extraordinary occasion, as authorized by the Constitution, your attention is not called to any ordinary subject of legislation.

At the beginning of the present Presidential term, four months ago, the functions of the Federal Government were found to be generally suspended within the several States of South Carolina, Georgia, Alabama, Mississippi, Louisiana, and Florida, excepting only those of the Post-office Department. . . .

. . . The purpose to sever the Federal Union was openly avowed. In accordance with this purpose, an ordinance had been adopted in each of these States, declaring the States respectively to be separated from the national Union. A formula for instituting a combined government of these States had been promulgated; and this illegal organization, in the character of confederate States, was already invoking recognition, aid, and intervention from foreign powers. . . .

And this issue embraces more than the fate of these United States. It presents to the whole family of man the question whether a constitutional republic or democracy—a government of the people by the same people—can or cannot maintain its territorial integrity against its own domestic foes. It presents the question whether discontented individuals, too few in number to control administration according to organic laws in any case, can always, upon the pretenses made in this case, or on any other pretenses, or arbitrarily without any pretense, break up their government, and thus practically put an end to free government upon the earth. It forces us to ask: Is there in all republics this inherent and fatal weakness? Must a government, of necessity, be too strong for the liberties of its own people, or too weak to maintain its own existence?

So viewing the issue, no choice was left but to call out the war power of the government, and so to resist force employed for its destruction by force for its preservation. . . .

The forbearance of this government had been so extraordinary and so long continued as to lead some foreign nations to shape their action as if they supposed the early destruction of our national Union was probable. While this, on discovery, gave the executive some concern, he is now happy to say that the sovereignty and rights of the United States are now everywhere practically respected by foreign powers; and a general sympathy with the country is manifested throughout the world. . . .

It might seem, at first thought, to be of little difference whether the present movement at the South be called "secession" or "rebellion." The movers, however, well understand the difference. At the beginning they knew they could never raise their treason to any respectable magnitude by any name which implies violation of law. They knew their people possessed as much of moral sense, as much of devotion to law and order, and as much pride in and reverence for the history and government of their common country as any other civilized and patriotic people. They knew they could make no advancement directly in the teeth of these strong and noble sentiments. Accordingly, they commenced by an insidious debauching of the public mind. They invented an ingenious sophism which, if conceded, was followed by perfectly logical steps, through all the incidents, to the complete destruction of the Union. The sophism itself is that any State of the Union may consistently with the national Constitution, and therefore lawfully and peacefully, withdraw from the Union without the consent of the Union or of any other State. . . .

This sophism derives much, perhaps the whole, of its currency from the assumption that there is some omnipotent and sacred supremacy pertaining to a State—to each State of our Federal Union. Our States have neither more nor less power than that reserved to them in the Union by the Constitution—no one of them ever having been a State out of the Union. The original ones passed into the Union even before they cast off their British colonial dependence; and the new ones each came into the Union directly from a condition of dependence, excepting Texas. And even Texas in its temporary independence was never designated a State. The new ones only took the designation of States on coming into the Union, while that name was first adopted for the old ones in and by the Declaration of Independence. . . . Having never been States either in substance or in name outside of the Union, whence this magical omnipotence of "State rights," asserting a claim of power to lawfully destroy the Union itself? Much is said about the "sovereignty" of the States; but the word even is not in the national Constitution, nor, as is believed, in any of the State constitutions. What is "sovereignty" in the political sense of the term? Would it be far wrong to define it as "a political community without a political superior"? Tested by this, no one of our States except Texas ever was a sovereignty. . . . The States have their status in the Union, and they have no other legal status. If they break from this, they can only do so against law and by revolution. The Union, and not themselves separately, procured their independence and their liberty. By conquest or purchase the Union gave each of them whatever of independence or liberty it has. The Union is older than any of the States, and, in fact, it created them as States. Originally some dependent colonies made the Union, and, in turn, the Union threw off their old dependence for them, and made them States, such as they are. Not one of them ever had a State constitution independent of the Union. Of course, it is not forgotten that all the new States framed their constitutions before they entered the Union—nevertheless, dependent upon and preparatory to coming into the Union. . . .

What is now combated is the position that secession is consistent with the Constitution —is lawful and peaceful. It is not contended that there is any express law for it; and nothing should ever be implied as law which leads to unjust or absurd consequences. . . .

The seceders insist that our Constitution admits of secession. They have assumed to make a national constitution of their own, in which of necessity they have either discarded or retained the right of secession as they insist it exists in ours. If they have discarded it, they thereby admit that on principle it ought not to be in ours. If they have retained it, by their own construction of ours, they show that to be consistent they must secede from one another whenever they shall find it the easiest way of settling their debts, or effecting any other selfish or unjust object. The principle itself is one of disintegration and upon which no government can possibly endure. . . .

It may well be questioned whether there is to-day a majority of the legally qualified voters of any State except perhaps South Carolina in favor of disunion. There is much reason to believe that the Union men are the majority in many, if not in every other one, of the so-called seceded States. . . .

This is essentially a people's contest. On the side of the Union it is a struggle for maintaining in the world that form and substance of government whose leading object is to elevate the condition of men—to lift artificial weights from all shoulders; to clear the paths of laudable pursuit for all; to afford all an unfettered start, and a fair chance in the race of life. Yielding to partial and temporary departures, from necessity, this is the leading object of the government for whose existence we contend. . . .

Our popular government has often been called an experiment. Two points in it our people have already settled—the successful establishing and the successful administering of it. One still remains—its successful maintenance against a formidable internal attempt to overthrow it. It is now for them to demonstrate to the world that those who can fairly carry an election can also suppress a rebellion; that ballots are the rightful and peaceful successors of bullets; and that when ballots have fairly and constitutionally decided, there can be no successful appeal back to bullets; that there can be no successful appeal, except to ballots themselves, at succeeding elections. Such will be a great lesson of peace: teaching men that what they cannot take by an election, neither can they take it by war; teaching all the folly of being the beginners of a war. . . .

206. THE CRITTENDEN–JOHNSON RESOLUTIONS ON THE OBJECTS OF THE WAR
July, 1861

(Richardson, ed. *Messages and Addresses*, Vol. VI, p. 430)

These resolutions represented a conservative attitude toward the South and the objects of the war that shortly disappeared. The Crittenden Resolutions passed the House, July 22, 1861, with only two dissenting votes; the Johnson Resolutions passed the Senate July 25 with five dissenting votes.

THE CRITTENDEN RESOLUTIONS

Resolved by the House of Representatives of the Congress of the United States, That the present deplorable civil war has been forced upon the country by the disunionists of the Southern States now in revolt against the constitutional Government and in arms around the capital; that in this national emergency Congress, banishing all feelings of mere passion or resentment, will recollect only its duty to the whole country; that this war is not waged upon our part in any spirit of oppression, nor for any purpose of conquest or subjugation, nor purpose of overthrowing or interfering with the rights or established institutions of those States, but to defend and maintain the supremacy of the Constitution and to preserve the Union, with all the dignity, equality, and rights of the several States unimpaired; and that as soon as these objects are accomplished the war ought to cease.

THE JOHNSON RESOLUTIONS

Resolved, That the present deplorable civil war has been forced upon the country by the disunionists of the Southern States now in revolt against the constitutional Government and in arms around the capital; that in this national emergency Congress, banishing all feeling of mere passion or resentment, will recollect only its duty to the whole country; that this war is not prosecuted upon our part in any spirit of oppression, nor for any purpose of conquest or subjugation, nor purpose of overthrowing or interfering with the rights or established institutions of those States, but to defend and maintain the supremacy of the Constitution and all laws made in pursuance thereof and to preserve the Union, with all the dignity, equality, and rights of the several States unimpaired; that as soon as these objects are accomplished the war ought to cease.

207. GENERAL BUTLER'S "CONTRABANDS"

Report of General Butler to the Secretary of War July 30, 1861

(F. Moore, ed. *The Rebellion Record,* Vol. II, p. 437)

The problem of the refugee slaves was one of the most perplexing which the Government had to face. General Butler, commanding at Fortress Monroe, took matters into his own hands, and treated fugitive or captured slaves as "contraband of war". For a somewhat different solution, see Frémont's Proclamation, Doc. No. 208. The fairest discussion of Butler is in C. R. Fish's article in the *Dictionary of American Biography,* Vol. III.

Head-quarters Department of Virginia,
Fortress Monroe, July 30, 1861.
Hon. Simon Cameron, Secretary of War:—
SIR: . . . In the village of Hampton there were a large number of negroes, composed in a great measure of women and children of the men who had fled thither within my lines for protection, who had escaped from marauding parties of rebels who had been gathering up able-bodied blacks to aid them in constructing their batteries on the James and York Rivers. I have employed the men in Hampton in throwing up intrenchments, and they were working zealously and efficiently at that duty, saving our soldiers from that labor under the gleam of the mid-day sun. The women were earning substantially their own subsistence in washing, marketing, and taking care of the clothes of the soldiers, and rations were being served out to the men who worked for the support of the children. But by the evacuation of Hampton, rendered necessary by the withdrawal of troops, leaving me scarcely 5,000 men outside the Fort, including the force at Newport News, all these black people were obliged to break up their homes at Hampton, fleeing across the creek within my lines for protection and support. Indeed, it was a most distressing sight to see these poor creatures, who had trusted to the protection of the arms of the United States, and who aided the troops of the United States in their enterprise, to be thus obliged to flee from their homes, and the homes of their masters who had deserted them, and become fugitives from fear of the return of the rebel soldiery, who had threatened to shoot the men who had wrought for us, and to carry off the women who had served us, to a worse than Egyptian bondage. I have, therefore, now within the Peninsula, this side of Hampton Creek, 900 negroes, 300 of whom are able-bodied men, 30 of whom are men substantially past hard labor, 175 women, 225 children under the age of 10 years, and 170 between 10 and 18 years, and many more coming in. The questions which this state of facts presents are very embarrassing.

First, What shall be done with them? and, *Second,* What is their state and condition?

Upon these questions I desire the instructions of the Department.

The first question, however, may perhaps be answered by considering the last. Are these men, women, and children, slaves? Are they free? Is their condition that of men, women, and children, or of property, or is it a mixed relation? What their *status* was under the Constitution and laws, we all know. What has been the effect of rebellion and a state of war upon that *status?* When I adopted the theory of treating the able-bodied negro fit to work in the trenches as property liable to be used in aid of rebellion, and so contraband of war, that condition of things was in so far met, as I then and still believe, on a legal and constitutional basis. But now a new series of questions arises. Passing by women, the children, certainly, cannot be treated on that basis; if property, they must be considered the incumbrance rather than the auxiliary of an army, and, of course, in no possible legal relation could be treated as contraband. Are they property? If they were so, they have been left by their masters and owners, deserted, thrown away, abandoned, like the wrecked vessel upon the ocean. Their former possessors and owners have causelessly, traitorously, rebelliously, and, to carry out the figure, practically abandoned them to be swallowed up by the winter storm of starvation. If property, do they not become the property of the salvors? but we, their salvors, do not need and will not hold such property, and will assume no such ownership: has not, therefore, all proprietary relation ceased? Have they not become, thereupon, men, women, and children? No longer under ownership of any kind, the fearful relicts of fugitive masters, have they not by their mas-

ters' acts, and the state of war, assumed the condition, which we hold to be the normal one, of those made in God's image? Is not every constitutional, legal, and moral requirement, as well to the runaway master as their relinquished slaves, thus answered? I confess that my own mind is compelled by this reasoning to look upon them as men and women. If not free born, yet free, manumitted, sent forth from the hand that held them never to be reclaimed. . . .

In a loyal State I would put down a servile insurrection. In a state of rebellion I would confiscate that which was used to oppose my arms, and take all that property, which constituted the wealth of that State, and furnished the means by which the war is prosecuted, beside being the cause of the war; and if, in so doing, it should be objected that human beings were brought to the free enjoyment of life, liberty, and the pursuit of happiness, such objection might not require much consideration.

Pardon me for addressing the Secretary of War directly upon this question, as it involves some political considerations as well as propriety of military action. I am, sir, your obedient servant,

BENJAMIN F. BUTLER.

208. FRÉMONT'S PROCLAMATION ON SLAVES
St. Louis, August 30, 1861

(F. Moore, ed. *The Rebellion Record,* Vol. III, p. 33)

John Charles Frémont, too popular a figure to ignore, was placed in charge of the Department of the West. An ardent abolitionist, he declared martial law and issued the proclamation of August 30 confiscating the property and emancipating the slaves of rebels. While this action inspired applause from the abolitionists, it seriously embarrassed the administration, and Lincoln was forced largely to countermand it. On Frémont, see, A. Nevins, *Frémont,* ch. xxx–xxxi; C. Goodwin, *J. C. Frémont,* ch. xii.

Head-quarters Western Department.
St. Louis, Aug, 30, 1861.
CIRCUMSTANCES in my judgment are of sufficient urgency to render it necessary that the commanding General of this department should assume the administrative powers of the State. Its disorganized condition, helplessness of civil authority and the total in-

security of life, and devastation of property by bands of murderers and marauders, who infest nearly every county in the State, and avail themselves of public misfortunes, in the vicinity of a hostile force, to gratify private and neighborhood vengeance, and who find an enemy wherever they find plunder, finally demand the severest measures to repress the daily increasing crimes and outrages, which are driving off the inhabitants and ruining the State.

In this condition, the public safety and success of our arms require unity of purpose, without let or hindrance to the prompt administration of affairs. In order, therefore, to suppress disorders, maintain the public peace, and give security to the persons and property of loyal citizens, I do hereby extend and declare established martial law throughout the State of Missouri. The lines of the army occupation in this State are for the present declared to extend from Leavenworth, by way of posts of Jefferson City, Rolla, and Ironton, to Cape Girardeau on the Mississippi River. All persons who shall be taken with arms in their hands within these lines shall be tried by court-martial, and if found guilty, will be shot. Real and personal property of those who shall take up arms against the United States, or who shall be directly proven to have taken an active part with their enemies in the field, is declared confiscated to public use, and their slaves, if any they have, are hereby declared free men.

All persons who shall be proven to have destroyed, after the publication of this order, railroad tracks, bridges, or telegraph lines, shall suffer the extreme penalty of the law. All persons engaged in treasonable correspondence, in giving or procuring aid to the enemy, in fermenting turmoil, and disturbing public tranquillity, by creating or circulating false reports, or incendiary documents, are warned that they are exposing themselves.

All persons who have been led away from allegiance, are required to return to their homes forthwith. Any such absence without sufficient cause, will be held to be presumptive evidence against them. The object of this declaration is to place in the hands of military authorities power to give instantaneous effect to the existing laws, and supply such deficiencies as the conditions of the war demand; but it is not intended to suspend the ordinary tribunals of the country, where law will be administered by civil officers in the usual manner, and with their customary authority, while the same can be peaceably administered.

The commanding General will labor vigilantly for the public welfare, and, by his efforts for their safety, hopes to obtain not only acquiescence, but the active support of the people of the country.

J. C. FREMONT,
Major-General Commanding.

209. EX PARTE MERRYMAN
17 Federal Cases, 144.
1861

Circuit Court, District of Maryland. Petition for a writ of *habeas corpus.* John Merryman a citizen of Baltimore, Maryland, was arrested by order of General Keim, and imprisoned at Fort McHenry. No ground having been shown for his arrest, Chief Justice Taney authorized a writ of *habeas corpus,* commanding General Cadwalader in command of Fort McHenry to deliver up the prisoner. General Cadwalader, stating that he was acting under the authority of the President, refused to respect the writ. The Chief Justice then cited him for contempt of court, but the General refused to receive the writ of contempt. It was under these circumstances that the Chief Justice filed the following opinion. For a reply to the argument of the court, see the opinion of the Hon. Reverdy Johnson, in F. Moore, ed. *The Rebellion Record,* Vol. II, p. 185 ff. For a discussion of the case see Warren, *Supreme Court,* ch. xxviii; S. Klaus, ed. *The Milligan Case,* Introduction; J. G. Randall, *Constitutional Problems Under Lincoln;* B. C. Steiner, *Life of Roger Brooke Taney;* G. C. Sellery, *Lincoln's Suspension of Habeas Corpus,* University of Wisconsin, Bull. No. 149.

TANEY, C. J. The application in this case for a writ of *habeas corpus* is made to me under the 14th section of the Judiciary Act of 1789, which renders effectual for the citizen the constitutional privilege of the writ of *habeas corpus.* That act gives to the Courts of the United States, as well as to each justice of the Supreme Court, and to every District Judge, power to grant writs of *habeas corpus* for the purpose of an inquiry into the cause of commitment. The petition was presented to me at Washington, under the impression that I would order the prisoner to be brought before me there, but as he was confined in Fort McHenry, at the City of Baltimore, which is in my circuit, I resolved to hear it in the latter city, as obedience to the writ, under such circumstances, would not withdraw Gen. Cadwalader who had him in charge from the limits of his military command. . . .

A copy of the warrant or order, under which the prisoner was arrested, was demanded by his counsel, and refused. And it is not alleged in the return that any specific act, constituting an offence against the laws of the United States, has been charged against him upon oath; but he appears to have been arrested upon general charges of treason and rebellion, without proof, and without giving the names of the witnesses, or specifying the acts, which in the judgement of the military officer, constituted the crime. And having the prisoner thus in custody on these vague and unsupported accusations, he refuses to obey the writ of *habeas corpus,* upon the ground that he is duly authorized by the President to suspend it.

The case, then, is simply this: A military officer residing in Pennsylvania issues an order to arrest a citizen of Maryland, upon vague and indefinite charges, without any proof, so far as appears. Under this order his house is entered in the night; he is seized as a prisoner, and conveyed to Fort McHenry, and there kept in close confinement. And when a *habeas corpus* is served on the commanding officer, requiring him to produce the prisoner before a justice of the Supreme Court, in order that he may examine into the legality of the imprisonment, the answer of the officer is that he is authorized by the President to suspend the writ of *habeas corpus* at his discretion, and, in the exercise of that discretion, suspends it in this case, and on that ground refuses obedience to the writ.

As the case comes before me, therefore, I understand that the President not only claims the right to suspend the writ of *habeas corpus* himself, at his discretion, but to delegate that discretionary power to a military officer, and to leave it to him to determine whether he will or will not obey judicial process that may be served upon him.

No official notice has been given to the Courts of Justice, or to the public, by proclamation or otherwise, that the President claimed this power and had exercised it in the matter stated in the return. And I certainly listened to it with some surprise, for I had supposed it to be one of those points of constitutional law upon which there was no difference of opinion, and that it was admitted on all hands that the privilege of the writ could not be suspended except by act of Congress. . . .

The clause in the Constitution which authorizes the suspension of the privilege of the writ of *habeas corpus* is in the ninth section of the first article.

This article is devoted to the Legislative Department of the United States, and has not the slightest reference to the Executive Department. It begins by providing "that all legislative powers therein granted shall be vested in a Congress of the United States. . . ." After prescribing the manner in which these two branches of the Legislative department shall be chosen, it proceeds to enumerate specifically the legislative powers which it thereby grants and legislative powers which it expressly prohibits, and at the conclusion of this specification, a clause is inserted giving Congress "the power to make all laws which may be necessary and proper for carrying into execution the foregoing powers, and all other powers vested by this Constitution in the Government of the United States or in any department or office thereof."

The power of legislation granted by this latter clause is by its word carefully confined to the specific objects before enumerated. But as this limitation was unavoidably somewhat indefinite, it was deemed necessary to guard more effectively certain great cardinal principles essential to the liberty of the citizen and to the rights and equality of the States by denying to Congress, in express terms, any power of legislation over them. It was apprehended, it seems, that such legislation might be attempted under the pretext that it was necessary and proper to carry into execution the powers granted; and it was determined that there should be no room to doubt, where rights of such vital importance were concerned, and accordingly this clause is immediately followed by an enumeration of certain subjects to which the powers of legislation shall not extend; and the great importance which the framers of the Constitution attached to the privilege of the writ of *habeas corpus* to protect the liberty of the citizen, is proved by the fact that its suspension, except in cases of invasion and rebellion, is first in the list of prohibited power; and even in these cases the power is denied and its exercise prohibited unless the public safety shall require it. It is true that in the cases mentioned Congress is of necessity to judge whether the public safety does or does not require it; and its judgement is conclusive.

But the introduction of these words is a standing admonition to the legislative body of the danger of suspending it and of the extreme caution they should exercise before they give the Government of the United States such power over the liberty of a citizen.

It is the second Article of the Constitution that provides for the organization of the Executive Department, and enumerates the powers conferred on it, and prescribes its duties. And if the high power over the liberty of the citizens now claimed was intended to be conferred on the President, it would undoubtedly be found in plain words in this article. But there is not a word in it that can furnish the slightest ground to justify the exercise of the power. . . .

And the only power, therefore, which the President possesses, where the "life, liberty and property" of a private citizen is concerned, is the power and duties prescribed in the third section of the Second Article which requires, "that he shall take care that the laws be faithfully executed." He is not authorized to execute them himself, or through agents or officers, civil or military, appointed by himself, but he is to take care that they be faithfully carried into execution as they are expounded and adjudged by the co-ordinate branch of the government, to which that duty is assigned by the Constitution. It is thus made his duty to come in aid of the judicial authority, if it shall be resisted by force too strong to be overcome without the assistance of the Executive arm. But in exercising this power, he acts in subordination to judicial authority, assisting it to execute its process and enforce its judgements.

With such provisions in the Constitution, expressed in language too clear to be misunderstood by anyone, I can see no ground whatever for supposing that the President in any emergency or in any state of things can authorize the suspension of the privilege of the writ of *habeas corpus,* or arrest a citizen except in aid of the judicial power. He certainly does not faithfully execute the laws if he takes upon himself legislative power by suspending the writ of *habeas corpus*—and the judicial power, also, by arresting and imprisoning a person without due process of law. Nor can any argument be drawn from the

nature of sovereignty, or the necessities of government for self-defence, in times of tumult and danger. The Government of the United States is one of delegated and limited powers. It derives its existence and authority altogether from the Constitution, and neither of its branches—executive, legislative, or judicial—can exercise any of the powers of government beyond those specified and granted. . . .

To guide me to a right conclusion, I have the Commentaries on the Constitution of the United States of the late Mr. Justice Story . . . and also the clear and authoritative decision of (the Supreme) Court, given more than a half century since, and conclusively establishing the principles I have above stated. Mr. Story, speaking in his Commentaries of the *habeas corpus* clause in the Constitution, says:

"It is obvious that cases of a peculiar emergency may arise, which may justify, nay, even require, the temporary suspension of any right to the writ. . . . Hitherto no suspension of the writ has ever been authorized by Congress since the establishment of the Constitution. It would seem, as the power is given to Congress to suspend the writ of *habeas corpus* in cases of rebellion or invasion, that the right to judge whether the exigency had arisen must exclusively belong to that body". *Commentaries,* section 1,336.

And Chief Justice Marshall, in delivering the opinion of the Supreme Court in the case *ex parte* Bollman and Swartwout, uses this decisive language, in 4 Cranch, 101:

"If at any time the public safety should require the suspension of the powers vested by this act in the courts of the United States, it is for the Legislature to say so. That question depends on political considerations, on which the Legislature is to decide. Until the legislative will be expressed, this court can only see its duty, and must obey the laws."

I can add nothing to these clear and emphatic words of my great predecessor.

But the documents before me show that the military authority in this case has gone far beyond the mere suspension of the privilege of the writ of *habeas corpus*. It has, by force of arms, thrust aside the judicial authorities and officers to whom the Constitution has confided the power and duty of interpreting and administering the laws, and substituted a military government in its place, to be administered and executed by military officers. . . .

The Constitution provides, as I have before said, that "no person shall be deprived of life, liberty, or property without due process of law". It declares that "the right of the people to be secure in their persons, houses, papers, and effects against unreasonable searches and seizures shall not be violated, and no warrant shall issue but upon probable cause, supported by oath or affirmation, and particularly describing the place to be searched and the persons or things to be seized." It provides that the party accused shall be entitled to a speedy trial in a court of justice.

And these great and fundamental laws, which Congress itself could not suspend, have been disregarded and suspended, like the writ of *habeas corpus,* by a military order, supported by force of arms. Such is the case now before me; and I can only say that if the authority which the Constitution has confided to the judiciary department and judicial officers may thus upon any pretext or under any circumstances be usurped by the military power at its discretion, the people of the United States are no longer living under a Government of laws, but every citizen holds life, liberty, and property at the will and pleasure of the army officer in whose military district he may happen to be found.

In such a case my duty was too plain to be mistaken. I have exercised all the power which the Constitution and laws confer on me, but that power has been resisted by a force too strong for me to overcome. It is possible that the officer who had incurred this grave responsibility may have misunderstood his instructions, and exceeded the authority intended to be given him. I shall therefore order all the proceedings in this case, with my opinion, to be filed and recorded in the Circuit Court of the United States for the District of Maryland, and direct the clerk to transmit a copy . . . to the President of the United States. It will then remain for that high officer, in fulfillment of his constitutional obligation to "take care that the laws be faithfully executed" to determine what measure he will take to cause the civil process of the United States to be respected and enforced.

R. B. Taney

210. SECESSION OF KENTUCKY
November 20, 1861

(F. Moore, ed. *The Rebellion Record,* Vol. XII, p. 164–5)

The regularly elected legislature of Kentucky, after first attempting to maintain neutrality, eventually pledged the loyalty of the State to the Union, and provided for the expulsion of Confederate troops from the State. The Kentucky soldiers in the Confederate Army, however, called a convention to meet at Russellville, November 18, 1861. This convention drew up the following declaration of independence, and took steps to bring Kentucky into the Confederacy. See, W. C. Goodloe, *Kentucky Unionists of 1861;* E. C. Smith, *The Borderland in the Civil War,* chs. ix, xi; N. S. Shaler, *Kentucky;* T. Speed, *The Union Cause in Kentucky.*

DECLARATION OF INDEPENDENCE AND ORDINANCE OF SEPARATION

Whereas, The Federal Constitution, which created the Government of the United States, was declared by the framers thereof to be the supreme law of the land, and was intended to limit, and did expressly limit, the powers of said Government to certain general specified purposes, and did expressly reserve to the States and people all other powers whatever, and the President and Congress have treated this supreme law of the Union with contempt, and usurped to themselves the power to interfere with the rights and liberties of the States and the people, against the express provisions of the Constitution, and have thus substituted for the highest forms of rational liberty and constitutional government a central despotism, founded upon the ignorant prejudices of the masses of Northern society, and instead of giving protection, with the Constitution, to the people of fifteen States of the Union, have turned loose upon them the unrestrained and raging passions of mobs and fanatics; and because we now seek to hold our liberties, our property, our homes, and our families, under the protection of the reserved powers of the States, have blockaded our ports, invaded our soil, and waged war upon our people, for the purpose of subjugating us to their will;

And whereas, Our own honor and our duty to posterity demand that we shall not relinquish our own liberty, and shall not abandon the rights of our descendants and the world to the inestimable blessings of constitutional government, therefore,

Be it ordained, That we do hereby forever sever our connection with the Government of the United States, and in the name of the people we do hereby declare Kentucky to be a free and independent State, clothed with all the power to fix her own destiny, and to secure her own rights and liberties.

And whereas, The majority of the Legislature of Kentucky have violated their most solemn pledges made before the election, and deceived and betrayed the people; have abandoned the position of neutrality assumed by themselves and the people, and invited into the State the organized armies of Lincoln; have abdicated the Government in favor of the military despotism which they have placed around themselves, but cannot control, and have abandoned the duty of shielding the citizen with their protection; have thrown upon our people and the State the horrors and ravages of war, instead of attempting to preserve the peace; and have voted men and money for the war waged by the North for the destruction of our constitutional rights;

have violated the express words of the Constitution, by borrowing five millions of money for the support of the war, without a vote of the people; have permitted the arrest and imprisonment of our citizens, and transferred the constitutional prerogatives of the executive to a military commission of partisans; have seen the writ of *habeas corpus* suspended, without an effort for its preservation, and permitted our people to be driven in exile from their homes; have subjected our proprty to confiscation, and our persons to confinement in the penitentiary as felons, because we may choose to take part in a contest for civil liberty and constitutional government against a sectional majority, waging war against the people and institutions of thirteen States of the old Federal Union, and have done all these things deliberately, against the warnings and voice of the Governor, and the solemn remonstrances of the minority in the Senate and House of Representatives; therefore,

Be it further ordained, That the unconstitutional edicts of a factious majority of a Legislature, thus false to their pledges, their honor, and their interests, are not law, and that such a Government is unworthy of the support of a brave and free people; and we do hereby declare, that the people are absolved from all allegiance to said Government, and have the right to establish any government which to them may seem best adapted to the preservation of their rights and liberties. . . .

211. COMPENSATED EMANCIPATION

Extracts from Lincoln's Messages to Congress Recommending Compensated Emancipation
1862

(Richardson, ed. *Messages and Papers,* Vol. VI, p. 68 ff., 126 ff.)

Until the very end of the War Lincoln urged on Congress, and on the South, his plan for compensated emancipation. In his message of December 1861 he had recommended this plan to the Border States, but without effect. Shortly after the special message of March 6, Lincoln summoned members of Congress from these States, and appealed for support, but without success. On July 12, 1862, he held a conference with the senators and representatives of these States, and read to them an appeal for this policy, but again without result. The Annual

Message of December 1, 1862 contained a specific plan for compensated emancipation to which Lincoln invited the attention of Congress. See, E. C. Smith, *The Borderland in the Civil War,* p. 375 ff.; I. N. Arnold, *Lincoln and the Overthrow of Slavery.*

1. MESSAGE TO CONGRESS
March 6, 1862

FELLOW-CITIZENS OF THE SENATE AND HOUSE OF REPRESENTATIVES:—I recommend the adoption of a joint resolution by your honorable bodies which shall be substantially as follows:

"*Resolved,* That the United States ought to co-operate with any State which may adopt gradual abolishment of slavery, giving to such State pecuniary aid, to be used by such State, in its discretion, to compensate for the inconveniences, public and private, produced by such change of system."

If the proposition contained in the resolution does not meet the approval of Congress and the country, there is the end; but if it does command such approval, I deem it of importance that the States and people immediately interested should be at once distinctly notified of the fact, so that they may begin to consider whether to accept or reject it. The Federal Government would find its highest interest in such a measure, as one of the most efficient means of self-preservation. The leaders of the existing insurrection entertain the hope that this government will ultimately be forced to acknowledge the independence of some part of the disaffected region, and that all the slave States north of such part will then say, "The Union for which we have struggled being already gone, we now choose to go with the Southern section." To deprive them of this hope substantially ends the rebellion, and the initiation of emancipation completely deprives them of it as to all the States initiating it. The point is not that *all* the States tolerating slavery would very soon, if at all, initiate emancipation; but that, while the offer is equally made to all, the more northern shall by such initiation make it certain to the more southern that in no event will the former ever join the latter in their proposed confederacy. I say "initiation" because, in my judgment, gradual and not sudden emancipation is better for all. In the mere financial or pecuniary view, any member of Congress with the census tables and treasury reports before him can readily see for himself how very soon the current expenditures of this war would purchase, at fair valuation, all the slaves in any named State. Such a proposition on the part of the General Government sets up no claim of a right by Federal authority to interfere with slavery within State limits, referring, as it does, the absolute control of the subject in each case to the State and its people immediately in-

terested. It is proposed as a matter of perfectly free choice with them. . . .

The proposition now made (though an offer only), I hope it may be esteemed no offense to ask whether the pecuniary consideration tendered would not be of more value to the States and private persons concerned than are the institution and property in it in the present aspect of affairs.

While it is true that the adoption of the proposed resolution would be merely initiatory, and not within itself a practical measure, it is recommended in the hope that it would soon lead to important practical results. In full view of my great responsibility to my God and to my country, I earnestly beg the attention of Congress and the people to the subject.

Abraham Lincoln.

2. Message to Congress
December 1, 1862

. . . Our strife pertains to ourselves—to the passing generations of men—and it can without convulsion be hushed forever with the passing of one generation.

In this view I recommend the adoption of the following resolution and articles amendatory to the Constitution of the United States:

Resolved by the Senate and House of Representatives of the United States of America, in Congress assembled, (two thirds of both Houses concurring), That the following articles be proposed to the Legislatures (or conventions) of the several States as amendments to the Constitution of the United States, all or any of which articles, when ratified by three fourths of the said Legislatures (or conventions), to be valid as part or parts of the said Constitution, viz:

Art,—, Every State wherein slavery now exists which shall abolish the same therein at any time or times before the 1st day of January, A.D. 1900, shall receive compensation from the United States as follows, to wit:

The President of the United States shall deliver to every such State bonds of the United States bearing interest at the rate of —per cent. per annum to an amount equal to the aggregate sum of ———— for each slave shown to have been therein by the Eighth Census of the United States, said bonds to be delivered to such State by instalments or in one parcel at the completion of the abolishment, accordingly as the same shall have been gradual or at one time within such State; and interest shall begin to run upon any such bond only from the proper time of its delivery as aforesaid. Any State having received bonds as aforesaid and afterwards reintroducing or tolerating slavery therein shall refund to the United States the bonds so received, or the value thereof, and all interest paid thereon.

ART.—. All slaves who shall have enjoyed actual freedom by the chances of the war at any time before the end of the rebellion shall be forever free; but all owners of such who shall not have been disloyal shall be compensated for them at the same rates as is provided for States adopting abolishment of slavery, but in such way that no slave shall be twice accounted for.

ART.—. Congress may appropriate money and otherwise provide for colonizing free colored persons with their own consent at any place or places without the United States.

I beg indulgence to discuss these proposed articles at some length. Without slavery the rebellion could never have existed; without slavery it could not continue.

Among the friends of the Union there is great diversity of sentiment and of policy in regard to slavery and the African race amongst us. Some would perpetuate slavery; some would abolish it suddenly and without compensation; some would abolish it gradually and with compensation; some would remove the freed people from us, and some would retain them with us; and there are yet other minor diversities. Because of these diversities we waste much strength in struggles among ourselves. By mutual concession we should harmonize and act together. This would be compromise, but it would be compromise among the friends and not with the enemies of the Union. These articles are intended to embody a plan of such mutual concessions. If the plan shall be adopted, it is assumed that emancipation will follow, at least in several of the States.

As to the first article, the main points are, first, the emancipation; secondly, the length of time for consummating it (thirty-seven years); and, thirdly, the compensation.

The emancipation will be unsatisfactory to the advocates of perpetual slavery, but the length of time should greatly mitigate their dissatisfaction. The time spares both races from the evils of sudden derangement—in fact, from the necessity of any derangement —while most of those whose habitual course of thought will be disturbed by the measure will have passed away before its consummation. They will never see it. Another class will hail the prospect of emancipation, but will deprecate the length of time. They will feel that it gives too little to the now living slaves. But it really gives them much. It saves them from the vagrant destitution which must largely attend immediate emancipation in localities where their numbers are very great, and it gives the inspiring assurance that their posterity shall be free forever. The plan leaves to each State choosing to act under it to abolish slavery now or at the end of the century, or at any intermediate time, or by degrees extending over the whole or any part of the period, and it obliges no two States to proceed alike. It also provides for compensation, and generally the mode of making it. This, it would seem, must further mitigate the dissatisfaction of those who favor perpetual slavery, and especially of those who are to receive the compensation. Doubtless some of those who are to pay and not to receive will object. Yet the measure is both just and economical. In a certain sense the liberation of slaves is the destruction of property—property acquired by descent or by purchase, the same as any other property. It is no less true for having been often said that the people of the South are not more responsible for the original introduction of this property than are the people of the North, and when it is remembered how unhesitatingly we all use cotton and sugar and share the profits of dealing in them, it may not be quite safe to say that the South has been more responsible than the North for its continuance. If, then, for a common object this property is to be sacrificed, is it not just that it be done at a common charge?

And if with less money, or money more easily paid, we can preserve the benefits of the Union by this means than we can by the war alone, is it not also economical to do it? Let us consider it, then. Let us ascertain the sum we have expended in the war since compensated emancipation was proposed last March, and consider whether if that measure had been promptly accepted by even some of the slave States the same sum would not have done more to close the war than has been otherwise done. If so, the measure would save money, and in that view would be a prudent and economical measure. . . . The aggregate sum necessary for compensated emancipation of course would be large. But it would require no ready cash, nor the bonds even any faster than the emancipation progresses. This might not, and probably would not, close before the end of the thirty-seven years. At that time we shall probably have a hundred millions of people to share the burden, instead of thirty-one millions as now. . . .

The proposed emancipation would shorten the war, perpetuate peace, insure this increase of population, and proportionately the wealth of the country. With these we should pay all the emancipation would cost, together with our other debt, easier than we should pay our other debt without it. . . .

This fact would be no excuse for delaying payment of what is justly due, but it shows the great importance of time in this connection—the great advantage of a policy by which we shall not have to pay until we number 100,000,000 what by a different policy we would have to pay now, when we number but 31,000,000. In a word, it shows that a dollar will be much harder to pay for the war than will be a dollar for emancipation on the proposed plan. And then the latter will cost no blood, no precious life. It will be a saving of both. . . .

The third article relates to the future of the freed people. It does not oblige, but merely authorizes Congress to aid in colonizing such as may consent. This ought not to be regarded as objectionable on the one hand or on the other, insomuch as it comes to nothing unless by the mutual consent of the people to be deported and the American voters through their representatives in Congress. . . .

The plan consisting of these articles is recommended, not but that a restoration of the national authority would be accepted without its adoption.

Nor will the war nor proceedings under the proclamation of September 22, 1862, be stayed because of the *recommendation* of this plan. Its timely *adoption,* I doubt not, would bring restoration, and thereby stay both.

And notwithstanding this plan, the recommendation that Congress provide by law for compensating any State which may adopt emancipation before this plan shall have been acted upon is hereby earnestly renewed. Such would be only an advance part of the plan, and the same arguments apply to both.

This plan is recommended as a means, not in exclusion of, but additional to, all others for restoring and preserving the national authority throughout the Union. The subject is presented exclusively in its economical aspect. The plan would, I am confident, secure peace more speedily and maintain it more permanently than can be done by force alone, while all it would cost, considering amounts and manner of payment and times of payment, would be easier paid than will be the additional cost of the war if we rely solely upon force. It is much, very much, that it would cost no blood at all.

The plan is proposed as permanent constitutional law. It cannot become such without the concurrence of, first, two thirds of Congress, and afterwards three fourths of the States. The requisite three fourths of the States will necessarily include seven of the slave States. Their concurrence, if obtained, will give assurance of their severally adopting emancipation at no very distant day upon the new constitutional terms. This assurance would end the struggle now and save the Union forever. . . .

Fellow-citizens, *we* can not escape history. We of this Congress and this administration will be remembered in spite of ourselves. No personal significance or insignificance can spare one or another of us. The fiery trial through which we pass will light us down in honor or dishonor to the latest generation. We *say* we are for the Union. The world will not forget that we say this. We know how to save the Union. The world knows we do know how to save it. We, even *we here,* hold the power and bear the responsibility. In *giving* freedom to the *slave* we *assure* freedom to the *free*—honorable alike in what we give and what we preserve. We shall nobly save or meanly lose the last, best hope of earth. Other means may succeed; this could not fail. The way is plain, peaceful, generous, just—a way which if followed the world will forever applaud and God must forever bless.

ABRAHAM LINCOLN.

212. SUMNER'S RESOLUTIONS ON THE THEORY OF SECESSION
AND RECONSTRUCTION
February 11, 1862

(E. McPherson, ed. *Political History of the Great Rebellion,* p. 322)

These resolutions contain the famous state-suicide theory. See, W. A. Dunning, *Essays on the Civil War and Reconstruction,* p. 105 ff. See also, Sumner's article on "How to Treat the Rebel States", *Atlantic Monthly,* October 1863.

Resolutions declaratory of the relations between the United States and the territory once occupied by certain States, and now usurped by pretended governments, without constitutional or legal right.

Whereas certain States, rightfully belonging to the Union of the United States, have through their respective governments wickedly undertaken to abjure all those duties by which their connection with the Union was maintained; to renounce all allegiance to the Constitution; to levy war upon the national Government; and, for the consummation of this treason, have unconstitutionally and unlawfully confederated together, with the declared purpose of putting an end by force to the supremacy of the Constitution within their respective limits; and whereas this condition of insurrection, organized by pretended governments, openly exists in South Carolina, Georgia, Florida, Alabama, Mississippi, Louisiana, Texas, Arkansas, Tennessee, and Virginia, except in Eastern Tennessee and Western Virginia, and has been declared by the President of the United States, in a proclamation duly made in conformity with an act of Congress, to exist throughout this territory, with the exceptions already named; and whereas the extensive territory thus usurped by these pretended governments and organized into a hostile confederation, belongs to the United States, as an inseparable part thereof, under the sanctions of the Constitution, to be held in trust for the inhabitants in the present and future generations, and is so completely interlinked with the Union that it is forever dependent thereon; and whereas the Constitution, which is the supreme law of the land, cannot be displaced in its rightful operation within this territory, but must ever continue the supreme law thereof, notwithstanding of the doings of any pretended governments acting singly or in confederation, in order to put an end to its supremacy: Therefore—

1. *Resolved,* That any vote of secession or other act by which any State may undertake to put an end to the supremacy of the Constitution within its territory is inoperative and void against the Constitution, and when sustained by force it becomes a practical *abdication* by the State of all rights under the Constitution, while the treason which it involves still further works an instant *forfeiture* of all those functions and powers essential to the continued existence of the State as a body politic, so that from that time forward the territory falls under the exclusive jurisdiction of Congress as other territory, and the State being, according to the language of the law, *felo-de-se,* ceases to exist.

2. That any combination of men assuming to act in the place of such State, attempting to ensnare or coerce the inhabitants thereof into a confederation hostile to the Union is rebellious, treasonable, and destitute of all moral authority; and that such combination is a usurpation incapable of any constitutional existence and utterly lawless, so that every thing dependent upon it is without constitutional or legal support.

3. That the termination of a State under the Constitution necessarily causes the termination of those peculiar local institutions which, having no origin in the Constitution or in those natural rights which exist independent of the Constitution, are upheld by the sole and exclusive authority of the State.

4. That slavery, being a peculiar local institution, derived from local laws, without any origin in the Constitution or in natural rights, is upheld by the sole and exclusive authority of the State, and must therefore cease to exist legally or constitutionally when the State on which it depends no longer exists; for the incident cannot survive the principal.

5. That in the exercise of its exclusive jurisdiction over the territory once occupied by the States, it is the duty of Congress to see that the supremacy of the Constitution is

maintained in its essential principles, so that everywhere in this extensive territory slavery shall cease to exist practically, as it has already ceased to exist constitutionally or legally.

6. That any recognition of slavery in such territory, or any surrender of slaves under the pretended laws of the extinct States by any officer of the United States, civil or military, is a recognition of the pretended governments, to the exclusion of the jurisdiction of Congress under the Constitution, and is in the nature of aid and comfort to the rebellion that has been organized.

7. That any such recognition of slavery or surrender of pretended slaves, besides being a recognition of the pretended governments, giving them aid and comfort, is a denial of the rights of persons who, by the extinction of the States, have become free, so that under the Constitution, they cannot again be enslaved.

8. That allegiance from the inhabitant and protection from the Government are corresponding obligations, dependent upon each other, so that while the allegiance of every inhabitant of this territory, without distinction of color or class, is due to the United States, and cannot in any way be defeated by the action of any pretended Government, or by any pretence of property or claim to service, the corresponding obligation of protection is at the same time due by the United States to every such inhabitant, without distinction of color or class; and it follows that inhabitants held as slaves, whose paramount allegiance is due to the United States, may justly look to the national Government for protection.

9. That the duty directly cast upon Congress by the extinction of the States is reinforced by the positive prohibition of the Constitution that "no State shall enter into any confederation," or "without the consent of Congress keep troops or ships-of-war in time of peace, or enter into any agreement or compact with another State," or "grant letters of marque and reprisal," or "coin money," or "emit bills of credit," or "without the consent of Congress lay any duties on imports or exports," all of which have been done by these pretended governments, and also by the positive injunction of the Constitution, addressed to the nation, that "the United States shall guaranty to every State in this Union a republican form of government;" and that in pursuance of this duty cast upon Congress, and further enjoined by the Constitution, Congress will assume complete jurisdiction of such vacated territory where such unconstitutional and illegal things have been attempted, and will proceed to establish therein republican forms of government under the Constitution; and in the execution of this trust will provide carefully for the protection of all the inhabitants thereof, for the security of families, the organization of labor, the encouragement of industry, and the welfare of society, and will in every way discharge the duties of a just, merciful, and paternal Government.

213. INAUGURAL ADDRESS OF JEFFERSON DAVIS
February 22, 1862

(Richardson, ed. *Messages and Papers of the Confederacy,* Vol. I, p. 183 ff.)

Davis had been chosen provisional President of the Confederacy by the Montgomery Congress, and was formally inaugurated February 18. A regular election held in accordance with the Confederate Constitution, in October 1861, resulted in his election as President for a term of six years: his inaugural followed on the 22nd of February. On Davis, see his own *Rise and Fall of the Confederate Government,* 2 Vols.; W. E. Dodd, *Jefferson Davis;* A. Tate, *Jefferson Davis;* E. Cutting, *Jefferson Davis.* His writings can be found in D. Rowland, ed. *Jefferson Davis,* *Constitutionalist, His Letters, Papers and Speeches,* 10 vols.

FELLOW-CITIZENS: On this the birthday of the man most identified with the establishment of American Independence, and beneath the monument erected to commemorate his heroic virtues and those of his compatriots, we have assembled to usher into existence the permanent government of the confederate States. Through this instrumentality, under the favor of Divine Providence, we hope to perpetuate the principles of our Revolutionary fathers. The day, the memory and the purpose seem fitly associated. . . .

When a long course of class legislation, directed not to the general welfare, but to the aggrandizement of the Northern section of the Union, culminated in a warfare on the domestic institutions of the Southern States —when the dogmas of a sectional party, substituted for the provisions of the constitutional compact, threatened to destroy the sovereign rights of the States, six of those States, withdrawing from the Union, confederated together to exercise the right and perform the duty of instituting a government which would better secure the liberties for the preservation of which that Union was established.

Whatever of hope some may have entertained that a returning sense of justice would remove the danger with which our rights were threatened, and render it possible to preserve the Union of the Constitution, must have been dispelled by the malignity and barbarity of the Northern States in the prosecution of the existing war. The confidence of the most hopeful among us must have been destroyed by the disregard they have recently exhibited for all the time-honored bulwarks of civil and religious liberty. Bastiles filled with prisoners, arrested without civil process or indictment duly found; the writ of *habeas corpus* suspended by Executive mandate; a State Legislature controlled by the imprisonment of members whose avowed principles suggested to the Federal Executive that there might be another added to the list of seceded States; elections held under threats of a military power; civil officers, peaceful citizens and gentle women incarcerated for opinion's sake, proclaimed the incapacity of our late associates to administer a government as free, liberal and humane as that established for our common use.

For proof of the sincerity of our purpose to maintain our ancient institutions, we may point to the constitution of the Confederacy and the laws enacted under it, as well as to the fact that through all the necessities of an unequal struggle there has been no act on our part to impair personal liberty or the freedom of speech, of thought or of the press. The courts have been open, the judicial functions fully executed, and every right of the peaceful citizen maintained as securely as if a war of invasion had not disturbed the land.

The people of the States now confederated became convinced that the Government of the United States had fallen into the hands of a sectional majority, who would pervert that most sacred of all trusts to the destruction of the rights which it was pledged to protect. They believed that to remain longer in the Union would subject them to a continuance of a disparaging discrimination, submission to which would be inconsistent with their welfare, and intolerable to a proud people. They therefore determined to sever its bonds and establish a new confederacy for themselves.

The experiment instituted by our Revolutionary fathers, of a voluntary union of sovereign States for purposes specified in a solemn compact, had been perverted by those who, feeling power and forgetting right, were determined to respect no law but their own will. The Government had ceased to answer the ends for which it was ordained and established. To save ourselves from a revolution which, in its silent but rapid progress, was about to place us under the despotism of numbers, and to preserve in spirit, as well as in form, a system of government we believed to be peculiarly fitted to our condition, and full of promise for mankind, we determined to make a new association, composed of States homogeneous in interest, in policy and in feeling.

True to our traditions of peace and our love of justice, we sent commissioners to the United States to propose a fair and amicable settlement of all questions of public debt or property which might be in dispute. But the Government at Washington, denying our right to self-government, refused even to listen to any proposals for a peaceful separation. Nothing was then left to us but to prepare for war.

The first year in our history has been the most eventful in the annals of this continent. A new government has been established, and its machinery put in operation over an area exceeding seven hundred thousand square miles. The great principles upon which we have been willing to hazard everything that is dear to man have made conquests for us which could never have been achieved by the sword. Our Confederacy has grown from six to thirteen States; and Maryland, already united to us by hallowed memories and material interests, will, I believe, when able to speak with unstifled voice, connect her destiny with the South. . . .

The period is near at hand when our foes must sink under the immense load of debt which they have incurred, a debt which in their effort to subjugate us has already attained such fearful dimensions as will subject them to burthens which must continue to oppress them for generations to come.

We, too, have had our trials and difficulties. That we are to escape them in future is not to be hoped. It was to be expected when we entered upon this war that it would expose our people to sacrifices and cost them much, both of money and blood. But we knew the value of the object for which we struggle, and understood the nature of the war in which we were engaged. Nothing could be so bad as failure, and any sacrifice would be cheap as the price of success in such a contest. . . .

It was, perhaps, in the ordination of Providence, that we were to be taught the value of our liberties by the price which we pay for them.

The recollections of this great contest, with all its common traditions of glory, of sacrifice and of blood, will be the bond of harmony and enduring affection amongst the people; producing unity in policy, fraternity in sentiment, and joint effort in war.

Nor have the material sacrifices of the past year been made without some corresponding benefits. If the acquiescence of foreign nations in a pretended blockade has deprived us of our commerce with them, it is fast making us a self-supporting and an independent people. The blockade, if effectual and permanent, could only serve to divert our industry from the production of articles for export, and employ it in supplying commodities for domestic use.

It is a satisfaction that we have maintained the war by our unaided exertions. We have neither asked nor received assistance from any quarter. Yet the interest involved is not wholly our own. The world at large is concerned in opening our markets to its commerce. When the independence of the confederate States is recognized by the nations of the earth, and we are free to follow our interests and inclinations by cultivating foreign

trade, the Southern States will offer to manufacturing nations the most favorable markets which ever invited their commerce. Cotton, sugar, rice, tobacco, provisions, timber and naval stores, will furnish attractive exchanges. Nor would the constancy of these supplies be likely to be disturbed by war. Our confederate strength will be too great to tempt aggression; and never was there a people whose interests and principles committed them so fully to a peaceful policy as those of the confederate States. By the character of their productions they are too deeply interested in foreign commerce wantonly to disturb it. War of conquest they cannot wage, because the constitution of their confederacy admits of no coërced association. Civil war there can not be between States held together by their volition only. The rule of voluntary association, which cannot fail to be conservative, by securing just and impartial government at home, does not diminish the security of the obligations by which the confederate States may be bound to foreign nations. In proof of this it is to be remembered that, at the first moment of asserting their right of secession, these States proposed a settlement on the basis of a common liability for the obligations of the General Government.

Fellow-citizens, after the struggles of ages had consecrated the right of the Englishman to constitutional representative government, our colonial ancestors were forced to vindicate that birthright by an appeal to arms. Success crowned their efforts, and they provided for their posterity a peaceful remedy against future aggression.

The tyranny of an unbridled majority, the most odious and least responsible form of despotism, has denied us both the right and remedy. Therefore we are in arms to renew such sacrifices as our fathers made to the holy cause of constitutional liberty. At the darkest hour of our struggle the provisional gives place to the permanent government. After a series of successes and victories, which covered our arms with glory, we have recently met with serious disasters. But in the heart of a people resolved to be free, these disasters tend but to stimulate to increased resistance.

To show ourselves worthy of the inheritance bequeathed to us by the patriots of the Revolution, we must emulate that heroic devotion which made reverse to them but the crucible in which their patriotism was refined.

With confidence in the wisdom and virtue of those who will share with me the responsibility, and aid me in the conduct of public affairs; securely relying on the patriotism and courage of the people, of which the present war has furnished so many examples, I deeply feel the weight of the responsibilities I now, with unaffected diffidence, am about to assume; and, fully realizing the inequality of human power to guide and to sustain, my hope is reverently fixed on Him whose favor is ever vouchsafed to the cause which is just. With humble gratitude and adoration, acknowledging the Providence which has so visibly protected the Confederacy during its brief but eventful career, to Thee, O God! I trustingly commit myself, and prayerfully invoke thy blessing on my country and its cause.

214. HOMESTEAD ACT
May 20, 1862
(U. S. Statutes at Large, Vol. XII, p. 392 ff.)

A Homestead Act had passed both houses of Congress in 1859 only to be vetoed by President Buchanan. With the success of the Republican. party in 1860, Homestead legislation was assured. The Homestead Act brought to an end one period of American land policy and inaugurated a new policy which, with modifications, has been followed since 1862. See, B. H. Hibbard, *History of Public Land Policies*, chs. xvii-xviii; G. M. Stephenson, *A Political History of the Public Lands from 1840 to 1862*; R. T. Hill, *The Public Domain and Democracy*; J. T. DuBois and G. S. Mathews, *Galusha Grow.*

AN ACT to secure homesteads to actual settlers on the public domain.

Be it enacted, That any person who is the head of a family, or who has arrived at the age of twenty-one years, and is a citizen of the United States, or who shall have filed his declaration of intention to become such, as required by the naturalization laws of the United States, and who has never borne arms against the United States Government or given aid and comfort to its enemies, shall, from and after the first of January, eighteen hundred and sixty-three, be entitled to enter one quarter-section or a less quantity of unappropriated public lands, upon which said person may have filed a pre-emption claim, or which may, at the time the application is made, be subject to pre-emption at one dollar and twenty-five cents, or less, per acre; or eighty acres or less of such unappropriated lands, at two dollars and fifty cents per acre, to be located in a body, in conformity to the legal subdivisions of the public lands, and after the same shall have been surveyed: *Provided,* That any person owning or residing on land may, under the provisions of this act, enter other land lying contiguous to his or her said land, which shall not, with the land so already owned and occupied, exceed in the aggregate one hundred and sixty acres.

Sec. 2. That the person applying for the benefit of this act shall, upon application to the register of the land office in which he or she is about to make such entry, make affidavit before the said register or receiver that he or she is the head of a family, or is twenty-one or more years of age, or shall have performed service in the Army or Navy of the United States, and that he has never borne arms against the Government of the United States or given aid and comfort to its enemies, and that such application is made for his or her exclusive use and benefit, and that said entry is made for the purpose of actual settlement and cultivation, and not, either directly or indirectly, for the use or benefit of any other person or persons whomsoever; and upon filing the said affidavit with the register or receiver, and on payment of ten dollars, he or she shall thereupon be permitted to enter the quantity of land specified: *Provided, however,* That no certificate shall be given and patent issued therefor until the expiration of five years from the date of such entry; and if, at the expiration of such time, or at any time within two years thereafter, the person making such entry—or if he be dead, his widow; or in case of her death, his heirs or devisee; or in case of a widow making such entry, her heirs or devisee, in case of her death—shall prove by two credible witnesses that he, she, or they have resided upon or cultivated the same for the term of five years immediately succeeding the time of filing the affidavit aforesaid, and shall make affidavit that no part of said land has been alienated, and that he has borne true allegiance to the Government of the United States; then, in such case, he, she, or they, if at that time a citizen of the United States, shall be entitled to a patent, as in other cases provided for by law: *And provided, further,* That in case of the death of both father and mother, leaving an infant child or children under twenty-one years of age, the right and fee shall inure to the benefit of said infant child or children; and the executor, administrator, or guardian may, at any time within two years after the death of the surviving parent, and in accordance with the laws of the State in which such children for the time being have their domicile, sell said land for the benefit of said infants, but for no other purpose; and the purchaser shall acquire the absolute title by the purchase, and be entitled to a patent from the United States, on payment of the office fees and sum of money herein specified. . . .

215. THE PACIFIC RAILWAY ACT
July 1, 1862
(*U. S. Statutes at Large,* Vol. XII, p. 489 ff.)

The idea of a transcontinental railroad had been broached in the eighteen-forties, and the rapid growth of California after 1849 brought it sharply to the attention of the country. Throughout the fifties there was general acquiescence in the idea that the road was necessary and should be financed in part by the government, but sectional rivalries prevented any agreement on the route which the road should take. In 1853 Congress authorized a survey of various routes, and the surveys were undertaken under the direction of Secretary of War Davis, but Congress took no action on the reports of the surveys. The secession of the Southern States cleared the way for a northern route, and in 1862 the first Pacific Railway Bill, authorizing the transcontinental railroad and granting generous government aid, was passed. Two years later a second Pacific Railway Act doubled the land grants and provided that the government have a second instead of a first mortgage on the railroad property. (*Stat. at Large,* Vol. XIII, p. 356.) Altogether some 15,000,000 acres of land were granted, and some $60,000,000 lent to the Union and Central Pacific Railroads. See L. H. Haney, *A Congressional History of Railways in the United States, 1850–1887;* J. B. Sanborn, *Congressional Grants of Land in Aid of Railways;* R. E. Riegel, *The Story of the Western Railroads;* N. Trottman, *History of the Union Pacific;* K. White, *History of the Union Pacific Railway;* E. L. Sabin, *Building the Pacific Railway;* G. M. Dodge, *How We Built the Union Pacific;* J. R. Perkins, *Trails, Rails and War: The Life of General Grenville Dodge;* F. A. Cleveland and F. W. Powell, *Railroad Promotion and Capitalization.*

An Act to aid in the Construction of a Railroad and Telegraph Line from the Missouri River to the Pacific Ocean. . . .
Be it enacted, That Walter S. Burgess [names of corporators]; together with five commissioners to be appointed by the Secretary of the Interior . . . are hereby created and erected into a body corporate . . . by the name . . . of "The Union Pacific Railroad Company" . . . ; and the said corporation is hereby authorized and empowered to lay out, locate, construct, furnish, maintain and enjoy a continuous railroad and telegraph . . . from a point on the one hundredth meridian of longitude west from Greenwich, between the south margin of the valley of the Republican River and the north margin of the valley of the Platte River, to the western boundary of Nevada Territory, upon the route and terms hereinafter provided. . . .
Sec. 2. That the right of way through the public lands be . . . granted to said company for the construction of said railroad and telegraph line; and the right . . . is hereby given to said company to take from the public lands adjacent to the line of said road, earth, stone, timber, and other materials for the construction thereof; said right of way is granted to said railroad to the extent of two hundred feet in width on each side of said railroad when it may pass over the public lands, including all necessary grounds for stations, buildings, workshops, and depots,

machine shops, switches, side tracks, turn tables, and water stations. The United States shall extinguish as rapidly as may be the Indian titles to all lands falling under the operation of this act. . . .

Sec. 3. That there be . . . granted to the said company, for the purpose of aiding in the construction of said railroad and telegraph line, and to secure the safe and speedy transportation of mails, troops, munitions of war, and public stores thereon, every alternate section of public land, designated by odd numbers, to the amount of five alternate sections per mile on each side of said railroad, on the line thereof, and within the limits of ten miles on each side of said road. . . . *Provided* That all mineral lands shall be excepted from the operation of this act; but where the same shall contain timber, the timber thereon is hereby granted to said company. . . .

Sec. 5. That for the purposes herein mentioned the Secretary of the Treasury shall . . . in accordance with the provisions of this act, issue to said company bonds of the United States of one thousand dollars each, payable in thirty years after date, paying six per centum per annum interest . . . to the amount of sixteen of said bonds per mile for each section of forty miles; and to secure the repayment to the United States . . . of the amount of said bonds . . . the issue of said bonds . . . shall ipso facto constitute a first mortgage on the whole line of the railroad and telegraph. . . .

Sec. 9. That the Leavenworth, Pawnee and Western Railroad Company of Kansas are hereby authorized to construct a railroad and telegraph line . . . upon the same terms and conditions in all respects as are provided [for construction of the Union Pacific Railroad].

. . . The Central Pacific Railroad Company of California are hereby authorized to construct a railroad and telegraph line from the Pacific coast . . . to the eastern boundaries of California, upon the same terms and conditions in all respects [as are provided for the Union Pacific Railroad].

Sec. 10. . . . And the Central Pacific Rail-Road Company of California after completing its road across said State, is authorized to continue the construction of said railroad and telegraph through the Territories of the United States to the Missouri River . . . upon the terms and conditions provided in this act in relation to the Union Pacific Railroad Company, until said roads shall meet and connect. . . .

Sec. 11. That for three hundred miles of said road most mountainous and difficult of construction, to wit: one hundred and fifty miles westerly from the eastern base of the Rocky Mountains, and one hundred and fifty miles eastwardly from the western base of the Sierra Nevada mountains . . . the bonds to be issued to aid in the construction thereof shall be treble the number per mile hereinbefore provided . . . ; and between the sections last named of one hundred and fifty miles each, the bonds to be issued to aid in the construction thereof shall be double the number per mile first mentioned. . . .

216. THE MORRILL ACT
July 2, 1862
(*U. S. Statutes at Large,* Vol. XII, p. 503)

This act, granting public land for the support of industrial and agricultural education, is, with the exception of the Act of 1785, the most important piece of legislation on behalf of education ever passed. Under the terms of this act some 13,000,000 acres of the public domain have been given to the States for the establishment of mechanical and agricultural colleges: the act gave a tremendous impetus to the movement for establishing State Universities. The real "father" of the act was J. B. Turner of the University of Illinois. See, E. J. James, *Origin of the Land Grant Act of 1862;* M. T. Carriel, *Life of*

J. B. Turner; W. B. Parker, *Life and Public Services of Justin Smith Morrill;* G. W. Atherton, *Legislative Career of J. S. Morrill.* I. L. Kandel, "Federal Land Grants for Vocational Education" in Carnegie Foundation for the Advancement of Teaching, *Bulletin* No. 10, is unsympathetic to the Turner claim.

An Act donating Public Lands to the several States and Territories which may provide Colleges for the Benefit of Agriculture and the Mechanic Arts.

Be it enacted by the Senate and House of Representatives of the United States of America in Congress assembled, That there be granted to the several States, for the purposes hereinafter mentioned, an amount of public land, to be apportioned to each State a quantity equal to thirty thousand acres for each senator and representative in Congress to which the States are respectively entitled by the apportionment under the census of eighteen hundred and sixty: Provided, That no mineral lands shall be selected or purchased under the provisions of this act.

SEC. 2. And be it further enacted, That the land aforesaid, after being surveyed, shall be apportioned to the several States in sections or subdivisions of sections, not less than one quarter of a section; and whenever there are public lands in a State subject to sale at private entry at one dollar and twenty-five cents per acre, the quantity to which said State shall be entitled shall be selected from such lands within the limits of such State, and the Secretary of the Interior is hereby directed to issue to each of the States in which there is not the quantity of public lands subject to sale at private entry at one dollar and twenty-five cents per acre, to which said State may be entitled under the provisions of this act, land scrip to the amount in acres for the deficiency of its distributive share: said scrip to be sold by said States and the proceeds thereof applied to the uses and

purposes prescribed in this act, and for no other use or purpose whatsoever. . . .

SEC. 4. And be it further enacted, That all moneys derived from the sale of the lands aforesaid by the States to which the lands are apportioned, and from the sale of land scrip hereinbefore provided for, shall be invested in stocks of the United States, or of the States, or some other safe stocks, yielding not less than five per centum upon the par value of said stocks; and that the moneys so invested shall constitute a perpetual fund, the capital of which shall remain forever undiminished, (except so far as may be provided in section fifth of this act,) and the interest of which shall be inviolably appropriated, by each State which may take and claim the benefit of this act, to the endowment, support, and maintenance of at least one college where the leading object shall be, without excluding other scientific and classical studies, and including military tactics, to teach such branches of learning as are related to agriculture and mechanic arts, in such manner as the legislatures of the State may respectively prescribe, in order to promote the liberal and practical education of the industrial classes in the several pursuits and professions in life.

SEC. 5. . . .

Sixth. No State while in a condition of rebellion or insurrection against the government of the United States shall be entitled to the benefit of this Act. . . .

217. McCLELLAN OUTLINES A POLICY FOR PRESIDENT LINCOLN

Letter of General McClellan to President Lincoln
July 7, 1862

(E. McPherson, ed. *Political History of the Great Rebellion*, p. 385 ff.)

Seward was not the only prominent man who presumed to advise President Lincoln on matters of policy. McClellan's contempt for Lincoln, and his political ambitions, are well known. McClellan has revealed himself in his autobiography, *McClellan's Own Story*. The best brief interpretation is in G. Bradford, *Union Portraits*, ch. i; a severe but just analysis of his generalship is J. C. Ropes, "General McClellan" in *Critical Sketches of Some of the Federal and Confederate Commanders, Papers* of the Military Historical Society of Massachusetts, Vol. X.

General McClellan's Letter to President Lincoln.

Headquarters Army of the Potomac
July 7, 1862

Mr. President: You have been fully informed that the rebel army is in the front, with the purpose of overwhelming us by attacking our positions or reducing us by blocking our river communications. I cannot but regard our condition as critical, and I earnestly desire, in view of possible contingencies, to lay before your excellency, for your private consideration, my general views concerning the existing state of rebellion, although they do not strictly relate to the situation of this army, or strictly come within the scope of my official duties. . . .

The time has come when the government must determine upon a civil and military policy, covering the whole ground of our national trouble.

The responsibility of determining, declaring, and supporting such civil and military policy, and of directing the whole course of national affairs in regard to the rebellion, must now be assumed and exercised by you, or our cause will be lost. The Constitution gives you power, even for the present terrible exigency.

This rebellion has assumed the character of a war; as such it should be regarded, and it should be conducted upon the highest principles known to Christian civilization. It should not be a war looking to the subjugation of the people of any State, in any event. It should not be at all a war upon a population, but against armed forces and political organizations. Neither confiscation of property, political execution of persons, territorial organization of States, or forcible abolition of slavery, should be contemplated for a moment.

In prosecuting the war, all private property and unarmed persons should be strictly protected, subject only to the necessity of military operation; all private property taken for military use should be paid or receipted for; pillage and waste should be treated as high crimes; all unnecessary trespass sternly prohibited, and offensive demeanor by the military towards citizens promptly rebuked. Military arrests should not be tolerated, except in places where active hostilities exist; and oaths, not required by enactments, constitutionally made, should be neither demanded nor received.

Military government should be confined to the preservation of public order and the protection of political right. Military power should not be allowed to interfere with the relations of servitude either by supporting or impairing the authority of the master, except for repressing disorder, as in other cases. Slaves, contraband under the act of Congress, seeking military protection, should receive it. The right of the government to appropriate permanently to its own service claims to slave labor should be asserted and the right of the owner to compensation therefor should be recognized. This principle might be extended, upon grounds of military necessity and security, to all the slaves of a particular State, thus working manumission in such State; and in Missouri, perhaps in Western Virginia also, and possibly even in Maryland, the expediency of such a measure is only a question of time. A system of policy thus constitutional, and pervaded by the influences of Christianity and freedom, would receive the support of almost all truly loyal men, would deeply impress the rebel masses and all foreign nations, and it might humbly be hoped that it would commend itself to the favor of the Almighty.

Unless the principles governing the future conduct of our struggle shall be made known and approved, the effort to obtain requisite forces will be almost hopeless. A declaration of radical views, especially upon slavery, will rapidly disintegrate our present armies. . . .

In carrying out any system of policy which you may form, you will require a commander-in-chief of the army, one who possesses your confidence, understands your views, and who is competent to execute your orders, by directing the military forces of the nation to the accomplishment of the objects by you proposed. I do not seek that place for myself. I am willing to serve you in such position as you may assign to me, and I will do so as faithfully as ever subordinate served superior.

I may be on the brink of eternity; and as I hope forgiveness from my Maker, I have written this letter with sincerity towards you and from love for my country.

George B. McClellan
Major General Commanding

218. GENERAL POPE'S ADDRESS TO THE ARMY OF VIRGINIA
July 14, 1862

(F. Moore, ed. *The Rebellion Record,* Vol. V, p. 551)

In July 1862 Lincoln appointed General Halleck to the post of General-in-Chief of all the Union armies, and at the same time brought General John Pope from the west and placed him at the head of the Army of Virginia, consisting of the corps of McDowell, Banks and Frémont. Pope signallized his accession to this position by issuing the gasconade of July 14; six weeks later he suffered a disastrous defeat at the Second Battle of Bull Run. See, J. C. Ropes, *The Army Under Pope;* G. H. Gordon, *History of the campaign of the Army of Virginia under John Pope; Papers* of the Military Historical Society of Massachusetts, Vol. II: *The Virginia Campaign of General Pope.*

WASHINGTON, Monday, July 14.
To the Officers and Soldiers of the Army of Virginia:

By special assignment of the President of the United States, I have assumed command of this army. I have spent two weeks in learning your whereabouts, your condition, and your wants; in preparing you for active operations, and in placing you in positions from which you can act promptly and to the purpose.

I have come to you from the West, where we have always seen the backs of our enemies —from an army whose business it has been to seek the adversary, and to beat him when found, whose policy has been attack and not defence.

In but one instance has the enemy been able to place our Western armies in a defensive attitude. I presume that I have been called here to pursue the same system, and to lead you against the enemy. It is my purpose to do so, and that speedily.

I am sure you long for an opportunity to win the distinction you are capable of achieving—that opportunity I shall endeavor to give you.

Meantime I desire you to dismiss from your minds certain phrases which I am sorry to find much in vogue amongst you.

I hear constantly of taking strong positions and holding them—of lines of retreat, and of bases of supplies. Let us discard such ideas.

The strongest position a soldier should desire to occupy is one from which he can most easily advance against the enemy.

Let us study the probable lines of retreat of our opponents, and leave our own to take care of themselves. Let us look before us and not behind. Success and glory are in the advance. Disaster and shame lurk in the rear.

Let us act on this understanding, and it is safe to predict that your banners shall be inscribed with many a glorious deed, and that your names will be dear to your countrymen forever.

JOHN POPE,
Major-General Commanding.

219. LINCOLN AND GREELEY
August 19, 22, 1862

(F. Moore, ed. *The Rebellion Record,* Vol. XII, p. 480 ff.)

Greeley had, at the beginning of the secession movement, advocated letting the "erring sisters go in peace." Though not formally allied with the Garrison abolitionists, he had, through the columns of the *Tribune,* persistently denounced slavery. In his Prayer of Twenty Millions he demanded that Lincoln should definitely commit himself to emancipation: in this attitude Greeley spoke for a large and powerful anti-slavery element in the North, but he certainly did not speak for "twenty millions." Lincoln's reply, justifying the war as one for the preservation of the Union, is one of the most notable of his pronouncements. Greeley subsequently embarrassed the administration and himself by dallying with peace overtures from the South. See, D. Seitz, *Horace Greeley;* D. S. Alexander, *Political History of New York,* Vol. III, p. 35 ff.

1. THE PRAYER OF TWENTY MILLIONS

To Abraham Lincoln, President of the United States:

DEAR SIR: I do not intrude to tell you— for you must know already that a great proportion of those who triumphed in your election, and of all who desire the unqualified suppression of the rebellion now desolating our country, are sorely disappointed and deeply pained by the policy you seem to be pursuing with regard to the slaves of rebels. I write only to set succinctly and unmistakably before you what we require, what we think we have a right to expect, and of what we complain.

I. We require of you, as the first servant of the Republic, charged especially and pre-eminently with this duty, that you EXECUTE THE LAWS. . . .

II. We think you are strangely and disas-trously remiss in the discharge of your official and imperative duty with regard to the eman-cipating provisions of the new Confiscation Act. Those provisions were designed to fight Slavery with Liberty. They prescribe that men loyal to the Union, and willing to shed their blood in her behalf, shall no longer be held, with the nation's consent, in bondage to persistent, malignant traitors, who for twenty years have been plotting and for sixteen months have been fighting to divide and de-stroy our country. Why these traitors should be treated with tenderness by you, to the prejudice of the dearest rights of loyal men, we cannot conceive.

III. We think you are unduly influenced by the councils, the representations, the men-aces, of certain fossil politicians hailing from the Border Slave States. Knowing well that the heartily, unconditionally loyal portion of the white citizens of those States do not expect nor desire that Slavery shall be upheld to the prejudice of the Union—(for the truth of which we appeal not only to every Republican residing in those States, but to such eminent loyalists as H. Winter Davis, Parson Brown-low, the Union Central Committee of Balti-more, and to *The Nashville Union*)—we ask you to consider that Slavery is everywhere the inciting cause and sustaining base of trea-son: the most slaveholding sections of Mary-land and Delaware being this day, though un-der the Union flag, in full sympathy with the rebellion, while the free labor portions of Tennessee and of Texas, though writhing un-der the bloody heel of treason, are unconquer-ably loyal to the Union. . . . It seems to us the most obvious truth, that whatever strengthens or fortifies Slavery in the Border States strengthens also treason, and drives home the wedge intended to divide the Union. Had you, from the first, refused to recognize in those States, as here, any other than un-conditional loyalty—that which stands for the Union, whatever may become of Slavery —those States would have been, and would be, far more helpful and less troublesome to the defenders of the Union than they have been, or now are.

IV. We think timid counsels in such a crisis calculated to prove perilous, and proba-bly disastrous. It is the duty of a Govern-ment so wantonly, wickedly assailed by re-bellion as ours has been, to oppose force to force in a defiant, dauntless spirit. It can-not afford to temporize with traitors, nor with semi-traitors. It must not bribe them to be-have themselves, nor make them fair prom-ises in the hope of disarming their causeless hostility. Representing a brave and high-spirited people, it can afford to forfeit any thing else better than its own self-respect, or their admiring confidence, For our Govern-ment even to seek, after war has been made on it, to dispel the affected apprehensions of armed traitors that their cherished privi-leges may be assailed by it, is to invite insult and encourage hopes of its own downfall. The rush to arms of Ohio, Indiana, Illinois, is the true answer at once to the rebel raids of John Morgan and the traitorous sophis-tries of Beriah Magoffin.

V. We complain that the Union cause has suffered, and is now suffering immensely, from mistaken deference to rebel Slavery. Had you, sir, in your Inaugural Address, un-mistakably given notice that, in case the rebellion already commenced, were persisted in, and your efforts to preserve the Union and enforce the laws should be resisted by armed force, *you would recognize no loyal person as rightfully held in Slavery by a traitor*, we believe the rebellion would therein have received a staggering if not fatal blow. At that moment, according to the returns of the most recent elections, the Unionists were a large majority of the voters of the slave States. But they were composed in good part of the aged, the feeble, the wealthy, the timid—the young, the reckless, the aspiring, the adventurous, had already been largely lured by the gamblers and negro-traders, the politicians by trade and the conspirators by instinct, into the toils of treason. Had you then proclaimed that rebellion would strike the shackles from the slaves of every traitor, the wealthy and the cautious would have been supplied with a powerful inducement to remain loyal. . . .

VI. We complain that the Confiscation Act which you approved is habitually disre-garded by your Generals, and that no word of rebuke for them from you has yet reached the public ear. Frémont's Proclamation and Hunter's Order favoring Emancipation were promptly annulled by you; while Halleck's Number Three, forbidding fugitives from slavery to rebels to come within his lines— an order as unmilitary as inhuman, and which received the hearty approbation of every traitor in America—with scores of like tendency, have never provoked even your remonstrance. . . . And finally, we complain that you, Mr. President, elected as a Republican, knowing well what an abomination Slavery is, and how emphatically it is the core and essence of this atrocious rebellion, seem never to interfere with these atrocities, and never give a direction to your military subordinates, which does not appear to have been conceived in the interest of Slavery rather than of Freedom.

VIII. On the face of this wide earth, Mr. President, there is not one disinterested, determined, intelligent champion of the Union cause who does not feel that all attempts to put down the rebellion and at the same time uphold its inciting cause are preposterous and futile—that the rebellion, if crushed out to-morrow, would be renewed within a year if Slavery were left in full vigor—that army officers who remain to this day devoted to Slavery can at best be but half-way loyal to the Union—and that every hour of deference to Slavery is an hour of added and deepened peril to the Union. I appeal to the testimony of your ambassadors in Europe. It is freely at your service, not at mine. Ask them to tell you candidly whether the seeming subserviency of your policy to the slaveholding, slavery-upholding interest, is not the perplexity, the despair of statesmen of all parties, and be admonished by the general answer!

IX. I close as I began with the statement that what an immense majority of the loyal millions of your countrymen require of you is a frank, declared, unqualified, ungrudging execution of the laws of the land, more especially of the Confiscation Act. That act gives freedom to the slaves of rebels coming within our lines, or whom those lines may at any time inclose—we ask you to render it due obedience by publicly requiring all your subordinates to recognize and obey it. The rebels are everywhere using the late anti-negro riots in the North, as they have long used your

officers' treatment of negroes in the South, to convince the slaves that they have nothing to hope from a Union success—that we mean in that case to sell them into a bitter bondage to defray the cost of the war. Let them impress this as a truth on the great mass of their ignorant and credulous bondmen, and the Union will never be restored—never. We cannot conquer ten millions of people united in solid phalanx against us, powerfully aided by Northern sympathizers and European allies. We must have scouts, guides, spies, cooks, teamsters, diggers, and choppers from the blacks of the South, whether we allow them to fight for us or not, or we shall be baffled and repelled. As one of the millions who would gladly have avoided this struggle at any sacrifice but that of principle and honor, but who now feel that the triumph of the Union is indispensable not only to the existence of our country but to the well-being of mankind, I entreat you to render a hearty and unequivocal obedience to the law of the land.

Yours,   HORACE GREELEY.

2. PRESIDENT LINCOLN'S LETTER

Executive Mansion,
Washington, August 22, 1862.

Hon. Horace Greeley:

DEAR SIR: I have just read yours of the nineteenth, addressed to myself through the New-York *Tribune.* If there be in it any statements or assumptions of fact which I may know to be erroneous, I do not now and here controvert them. If there be in it any inferences which I may believe to be falsely drawn, I do not now and here argue against them. If there be perceptible in it an impatient and dictatorial tone, I waive it in deference to an old friend, whose heart I have always supposed to be right.

As to the policy I "seem to be pursuing," as you say, I have not meant to leave any one in doubt.

I would save the Union. I would save it the shortest way under the Constitution. The sooner the National authority can be restored, the nearer the Union will be "the Union as it was." If there be those who would not save the Union unless they could at the same time *save* Slavery, I do not agree with them. If there be those who would not save the Union unless they could at the same time *destroy*

Slavery, I do not agree with them. My paramount object in this struggle *is* to save the Union, and is *not* either to save or destroy Slavery. If I could save the Union without freeing *any* slave, I would do it; and if I could save it by freeing *all* the slaves, I would do it; and if I could do it by freeing some and leaving others alone, I would also do that. What I do about Slavery and the colored race, I do because I believe it helps to save this Union; and what I forbear, I forbear because I do *not* believe it would help to save the Union. I shall do *less* whenever I shall believe what I am doing hurts the cause, and I shall do *more* whenever I shall believe doing more will help the cause. I shall try to correct errors when shown to be errors; and I shall adopt new views so fast as they shall appear to be true views. I have here stated my purpose according to my view of *official* duty, and I intend no modification of my oft-expressed *personal* wish that all men, everywhere, could be free.   Yours,
A. LINCOLN.

220. ADDRESS TO PRESIDENT LINCOLN BY THE WORKING-MEN OF MANCHESTER, ENGLAND
December 31, 1862

(F. Moore, ed. *The Rebellion Record,* Vol. VI, p. 344)

During the Civil War the English government preserved a cautious neutrality: the opinion of the governing classes was on the whole sympathetic toward the South, that of the working-men sympathetic toward the North. Lincoln's preliminary proclamation of emancipation was a determining influence in holding England to neutrality and cementing the friendship of the liberals and the working classes. The address of the working-men of Manchester was subscribed on the eve of the formal proclamation of emancipation. For Lincoln's reply see Doc. No. 221. On the English attitude toward the War, see D. Jordan, and E. J. Pratt, *Europe and the American Civil War,* Part I; E. D. Adams, *Great Britain and the American Civil War,* 2 Vols.; H. Adams, *The Education of Henry Adams;* C. F. Adams, *Trans-Atlantic Historical Solidarity;* B. Villiers and W. H. Chesson, *Anglo-American Relations, 1861–1865;* F. L. Owsley, *King Cotton Diplomacy.*

To Abraham Lincoln, President of the United States:

As citizens of Manchester, assembled at the Free-Trade Hall, we beg to express our fraternal sentiments toward you and your country. We rejoice in your greatness as an outgrowth of England, whose blood and language you share, whose orderly and legal freedom you have applied to new circumstances, over a region immeasurably greater than our own. We honor your Free States, as a singularly happy abode for the working millions where industry is honored. One thing alone has, in the past, lessened our sympathy with your country and our confidence in it—we mean the ascendency of politicians who not merely maintained negro slavery, but desired to extend and root it more firmly. Since we have discerned, however, that the victory of the free North, in the war which has so sorely distressed us as well as afflicted you, will strike off the fetters of the slave, you have attracted our warm and earnest sympathy. We joyfully honor you, as the President, and the Congress with you, for many decisive steps toward practically exemplifying your belief in the words of your great founders: "All men are created free and equal." You have procured the liberation of the slaves in the district around Washington, and thereby made the centre of your Federation visibly free. You have enforced the laws against the slave-trade, and kept up your fleet against it, even while every ship was wanted for service in your terrible war. You have nobly decided to receive ambassadors from the negro republics of Hayti and Liberia, thus forever renouncing that unworthy prejudice which refuses the rights of humanity to men and women on account of their color. In order more effectually to stop the slave-trade, you have made with our Queen a treaty, which your Senate has ratified, for the right of mutual search. Your Congress has decreed freedom as the law forever in the vast unoccupied or half unsettled Territories which are directly subject to its legislative power. It has offered pecuniary aid to all States which will enact emancipation locally, and has forbidden your

Generals to restore fugitive slaves who seek their protection. You have entreated the slave-masters to accept these moderate offers; and after long and patient waiting, you, as Commander-in-Chief of the Army, have appointed to-morrow, the first of January, 1863, as the day of unconditional freedom for the slaves of the rebel States. Heartily do we congratulate you and your country on this humane and righteous course. We assume that you cannot now stop short of a complete uprooting of slavery. It would not become us to dictate any details, but there are broad principles of humanity which must guide you. If complete emancipation in some States be deferred, though only to a predetermined day, still in the interval, human beings should not be counted chattels. Women must have the rights of chastity and maternity, men the rights of husbands, masters the liberty of manumission. Justice demands for the black, no less than for the white, the protection of law—that his voice be heard in your courts. Nor must any such abomination be tolerated as slave-breeding States, and a slave market—if you are to earn the high reward of all your sacrifices, in the approval of the universal brotherhood and of the Divine Father. It is for your free country to decide whether any thing but immediate and total emancipation can secure the most indispensable rights of humanity against the inveterate wickedness of local laws and local executives. We implore you, for your own honor and welfare, not to faint in your providential mission. While your enthusiasm is aflame, and the tide of events runs high, let the work be finished effectually. Leave no root of bitterness to spring up and work fresh misery to your children. It is a mighty task, indeed, to reörganize the industry not only of four millions of the colored race, but of five millions of whites. Nevertheless, the vast progress you have made in the short space of twenty months fills us with hope that every stain on your freedom will shortly be removed, and that the erasure of that foul blot upon civilization and Christianity —chattel slavery—during your Presidency will cause the name of Abraham Lincoln to be honored and revered by posterity. We are certain that such a glorious consummation will cement Great Britain to the United States in close and enduring regards. Our interests, moreover, are identified with yours. We are truly one people, though locally separate. And if you have any ill-wishers here, be assured they are chiefly those who oppose liberty at home, and that they will be powerless to stir up quarrels between us, from the very day in which your country becomes, undeniably and without exception, the home of the free. Accept our high admiration of your firmness in upholding the proclamation of freedom.

221. LINCOLN'S REPLY TO THE WORKING-MEN OF MANCHESTER, ENGLAND
January 19, 1863

(*The Writings of Abraham Lincoln*, Constitutional ed., Vol. VI, p. 248)

To THE WORKING-MEN OF MANCHESTER:
  I have the honor to acknowledge the receipt of the address and resolutions which you sent me on the eve of the new year. When I came, on the 4th of March, 1861, through a free and constitutional election to preside in the Government of the United States, the country was found at the verge of civil war. Whatever might have been the cause, or whosoever the fault, one duty, paramount to all others, was before me, namely, to maintain and preserve at once the Constitution and the integrity of the Federal Republic. A conscientious purpose to perform this duty is the key to all the measures of administration which have been and to all which will hereafter be pursued. Under our frame of government and my official oath, I could not depart from this purpose if I would. It is not always in the power of governments to enlarge or restrict the scope of moral results which follow the policies that they may deem it necessary for the public safety from time to time to adopt.
  I have understood well that the duty of self-preservation rests solely with the American people; but I have at the same time

been aware that favor or disfavor of foreign nations might have a material influence in enlarging or prolonging the struggle with disloyal men in which the country is engaged. A fair examination of history has served to authorize a belief that the past actions and influences of the United States were generally regarded as having been beneficial toward mankind. I have, therefore, reckoned upon the forbearance of nations. Circumstances—to some of which you kindly allude —induce me especially to expect that if justice and good faith should be practised by the United States, they would encounter no hostile influence on the part of Great Britain. It is now a pleasant duty to acknowledge the demonstration you have given of your desire that a spirit of amity and peace toward this country may prevail in the councils of your Queen, who is respected and esteemed in your own country only more than she is by the kindred nation which has its home on this side of the Atlantic.

I know and deeply deplore the sufferings which the working-men at Manchester, and in all Europe, are called to endure in this crisis. It has been often and studiously represented that the attempt to overthrow this government, which was built upon the foundation of human rights, and to substitute for it one which should rest exclusively on the basis of human slavery, was likely to obtain the favor of Europe. Through the action of our disloyal citizens, the working-men of Europe have been subjected to severe trials, for the purpose of forcing their sanction to that attempt. Under the circumstances, I cannot but regard your decisive utterances upon the question as an instance of sublime Christian heroism which has not been surpassed in any age or in any country. It is indeed an energetic and reinspiring assurance of the inherent power of truth and of the ultimate and universal triumph of justice, humanity, and freedom. I do not doubt that the sentiments you have expressed will be sustained by your great nation; and, on the other hand, I have no hesitation in assuring you that they will excite admiration, esteem, and the most reciprocal feelings of friendship among the American people. I hail this interchange of sentiment, therefore, as an augury that whatever else may happen, whatever misfortune may befall your country or my own, the peace and friendship which now exist between the two nations will be, as it shall be my desire to make them, perpetual.

ABRAHAM LINCOLN.

222. THE EMANCIPATION PROCLAMATION
January 1, 1863
(U. S. Statutes at Large, Vol. XII, p. 1268-9)

As early as July 22, 1862, Lincoln had read to his Cabinet a preliminary draft of an emancipation proclamation. At this time Secretary Seward suggested that the proclamation should not be issued until a military victory had been won. The battle of Antietam gave Lincoln his desired opportunity; on the 22 of September he read to his Cabinet a second draft of the proclamation. After some modifications this was issued as a preliminary proclamation; the formal and definite proclamation came January 1, 1863. The *Diaries* of Welles, Chase, and Bates give interesting records of the Cabinet meetings. This proclamation was particularly important in its effect upon European, especially English, public opinion. See E. D. Adams, *Great Britain and the American Civil War*, 2 Vols.; D. Jordan and E. J. Pratt, *Europe and the American Civil War;* W. R. West, *Contemporary French Opinion on the American Civil War*. On the constitutionality of emancipation, see J. G. Randall, *Constitutional Problems Under Lincoln*, chs. xv–xvi.

BY THE PRESIDENT OF THE UNITED STATES OF AMERICA:

A Proclamation.

Whereas on the 22d day of September, A.D. 1862, a proclamation was issued by the President of the United States, containing, among other things, the following, to wit:

"That on the 1st day of January, A.D. 1863, all persons held as slaves within any State or designated part of a State the people whereof shall then be in rebellion against the United States shall be then, thenceforward, and forever free; and the executive government of the United States, including the military and naval authority thereof, will recognize and maintain the freedom of such persons and will do no act or acts to repress such persons, or any of them, in any efforts they may make for their actual freedom.

"That the executive will on the 1st day of January aforesaid, by proclamation, designate the States and parts of States, if any, in which the people thereof, respectively, shall then be in rebellion against the United States; and the fact that any State or the people thereof shall on that day be in good faith represented in the Congress of the United States by members chosen thereto at elections wherein a majority of the qualified voters of such States shall have participated shall, in the absence of strong countervailing testimony, be deemed conclusive evidence that such State and the people thereof are not then in rebellion against the United States."

Now, therefore, I, Abraham Lincoln, President of the United States, by virtue of the power in me vested as Commander-in-Chief of the Army and Navy of the United States in time of actual armed rebellion against the authority and government of the United States, and as a fit and necessary war measure for suppressing said rebellion, do, on this 1st day of January, A.D. 1863, and in accordance with my purpose so to do, publicly proclaimed for the full period of one hundred days from the first day above mentioned, order and designate as the States and parts of States wherein the people thereof, respectively, are this day in rebellion against the United States the following, to wit:

Arkansas, Texas, Louisiana (except the parishes of St. Bernard, Plaquemines, Jef-ferson, St. John, St. Charles, St. James, Ascension, Assumption, Terrebonne, Lafourche, St. Mary, St. Martin, and Orleans, including the city of New Orleans), Mississippi, Alabama, Florida, Georgia, South Carolina, North Carolina, and Virginia (except the forty-eight counties designated as West Virginia, and also the counties of Berkeley, Accomac, Northhampton, Elizabeth City, York, Princess Anne, and Norfolk, including the cities of Norfolk and Portsmouth), and which excepted parts are for the present left precisely as if this proclamation were not issued.

And by virtue of the power and for the purpose aforesaid, I do order and declare that all persons held as slaves within said designated States and parts of States are, and henceforward shall be, free; and that the Executive Government of the United States, including the military and naval authorities thereof, will recognize and maintain the freedom of said persons.

And I hereby enjoin upon the people so declared to be free to abstain from all violence, unless in necessary self-defense; and I recommend to them that, in all cases when allowed, they labor faithfully for reasonable wages.

And I further declare and make known that such persons of suitable condition will be received into the armed service of the United States to garrison forts, positions, stations, and other places, and to man vessels of all sorts in said service.

And upon this act, sincerely believed to be an act of justice, warranted by the Constitution upon military necessity, I invoke the considerate judgment of mankind and the gracious favor of Almighty God.

223. OPPOSITION TO THE EMANCIPATION PROCLAMATION

Resolutions of Illinois State Legislature
January 7, 1863

(Illinois State Register, January 7, 1863)

Lincoln's emancipation proclamation aroused widespread criticism from Northern democrats who were opposed to a war fought for the purpose of freeing the slaves. The legislature of Illinois was Democratic, and Illinois was one of the strongholds of Copperheadism and of the Knights of the Golden Circle. See, A. C. Cole, *The Era of the Civil War* (Centennial History of Illinois); E. J. Benton, *The Movement for Peace without a Victory During the Civil War.*

The constitutionality of Emancipation is discussed in J. G. Randall, *Constitutional Problems Under Lincoln,* chs. xvi–xvii.

Resolved: That the emancipation proclamation of the President of the United States is as unwarrantable in military as in civil law; a gigantic usurpation, at once converting the war, professedly commenced by the administration for the vindication of the authority of the constitution, into the crusade for the sudden, unconditional and violent liberation of 3,000,000 negro slaves; a result which would not only be a total subversion of the Federal Union but a revolution in the social organization of the Southern States, the immediate and remote, the present and far-reaching consequences of which to both races cannot be contemplated without the most dismal foreboding of horror and dismay. The proclamation invites servile insurrection as an element in this emancipation crusade—a means of warfare, the inhumanity and diabolism of which are without example in civilized warfare, and which we denounce, and which the civilized world will denounce, as an uneffaceable disgrace to the American people.

224. APPOINTMENT OF GENERAL HOOKER TO THE COMMAND OF THE ARMY OF THE POTOMAC
Letter from President Lincoln to Hooker
January 26, 1863
(The Writings of Abraham Lincoln, Constitutional ed., Vol. VI, p. 254)

After the shocking defeat of Burnside at Fredericksburg, Lincoln decided to appoint "Fighting Joe" Hooker to the command of the Army of the Potomac. At the same time the President distrusted Hooker, and many of his closest advisers felt that he was not competent to fill the position. Lincoln's letter is curious in its revelation of Lincoln's character as well as in its criticism of Hooker himself. Hooker was badly defeated at the Battle of Chancellorsville, under circumstances of an unfortunate character; just before the Battle of Gettysburg he was supplanted by General Meade. See, T. A. Dodge, *The Campaign of Chancellorsville;* J. Bigelow, *The Campaign of Chancellorsville;* A. Doubleday, *Chancellorsville and Gettysburg;* J. F. Rhodes, *History,* Vol. IV, p. 202 ff, 256 ff.

Executive Mansion, Washington, D. C.,
January 26, 1863.
MAJOR-GENERAL HOOKER.

GENERAL:—I have placed you at the head of the Army of the Potomac. Of course I have done this upon what appear to me to be sufficient reasons, and yet I think it best for you to know that there are some things in regard to which I am not quite satisfied with you. I believe you to be a brave and skilful soldier, which of course I like. I also believe you do not mix politics with your profession, in which you are right. You have confidence in yourself, which is a valuable if not an indispensable quality. You are ambitious, which within reasonable bounds does good rather than harm; but I think that during General Burnside's command of the army you have taken counsel of your ambition and thwarted him as much as you could, in which you did a great wrong to the country and to a most meritorious and honorable brother officer. I have heard, in such a way as to believe it, of your recently saying that both the army and the government needed a dictator. Of course it was not for this, but in spite of it, that I have given you the command. Only those generals who gain successes can set up dictators. What I now ask of you is military success, and I will risk the dictatorship. The government will support you to the utmost of its ability, which is neither more nor less than it has done and will do for all commanders. I much fear that the spirit that you have aided to infuse into the army, of criticising their commander and withholding confidence from him, will now turn upon you. I shall assist you as far as I can to put it down. Neither you nor Napoleon, if he were alive again, could get any good out of an army while such a spirit prevails in it. And now beware of rashness. Beware of rashness, but with energy and sleepless vigilance go forward and give us victories.

Yours very truly,
A. LINCOLN.

225. RESOLUTIONS AGAINST FOREIGN MEDIATION
March 3, 1863

(E. McPherson, *Political History of the Great Rebellion,* p. 346-7)

These resolutions were reported from the Committee on Foreign Affairs by Charles Sumner, and passed both Houses by large majorities.

WHEREAS it appears from the diplomatic correspondence submitted to Congress that a proposition, friendly in form, looking to pacification through foreign mediation, has been made to the United States by the Emperor of the French and promptly declined by the President; and whereas the idea of mediation or intervention in some shape may be regarded by foreign governments as practicable, and such governments, through this misunderstanding, may be led to proceedings tending to embarrass the friendly relations which now exist between them and the United States; and whereas, in order to remove for the future all chance of misunderstanding on this subject, and to secure for the United States the full enjoyment of that freedom from foreign interference which is one of the highest rights of independent states, it seems fit that Congress should declare its convictions thereon: Therefore

Resolved, (the House of Representatives concurring,) That while in times past the United States have sought and accepted the friendly mediation or arbitration of foreign powers for the pacific adjustment of *international* questions, where the United States were the party of the one part and some other sovereign power the party of the other part; and while they are not disposed to misconstrue the natural and humane desire of foreign powers to aid in arresting *domestic* troubles, which, widening in their influence, have afflicted other countries, especially in view of the circumstance, deeply regretted by the American people, that the blow aimed by the rebellion at the national life has fallen heavily upon the laboring population of Europe: yet, notwithstanding these things, Congress cannot hesitate to regard every proposition of foreign interference in the present contest as so far unreasonable and inadmissible that its only explanation will be found in a misunderstanding of the true state of the question, and of the real character of the war in which the republic is engaged.

2. That the United States are now grappling with an unprovoked and wicked rebellion, which is seeking the destruction of the republic that it may build a new power, whose cornerstone, according to the confession of its chief, shall be slavery; that for the suppression of this rebellion, and thus to save the republic and to prevent the establishment of such a power, the national government is now employing armies and fleets, in full faith that through these efforts all the purposes of conspirators and rebels will be crushed; that while engaged in this struggle, on which so much depends, any proposition from a foreign power, whatever form it may take, having for its object the arrest of these efforts, is, just in proportion to its influence, an encouragement to the rebellion, and to its declared pretensions, and, on this account, is calculated to prolong and embitter the conflict, to cause increased expenditure of blood and treasure, and to postpone the much-desired day of peace; that, with these convictions, and not doubting that every such proposition, although made with good intent, is injurious to the national interests, Congress will be obliged to look upon any further attempt in the same direction as an unfriendly act which it earnestly deprecates, to the end that nothing may occur abroad to strengthen the rebellion or to weaken those relations of good will with foreign powers which the United States are happy to cultivate.

3. That the rebellion from its beginning, and far back even in the conspiracy which preceded its outbreak, was encouraged by the hope of support from foreign powers; that its chiefs frequently boasted that the people of Europe were so far dependent upon regular supplies of the great southern staples that, sooner or later, their governments would be constrained to take side with the rebellion in some effective form, even to the extent of forcible intervention, if the milder form did not prevail; that the rebellion is now sustained by this hope,

which every proposition of foreign interference quickens anew, and that, without this life-giving support, it must soon yield to the just and paternal authority of the national government; that, considering these things, which are aggravated by the motive of the resistance thus encouraged, the United States regret that foreign powers have not frankly told the chiefs of the rebellion that the work in which they are engaged is hateful, and that a new government, such as they seek to found, with slavery as its acknowledged cornerstone, and with no other declared object of separate existence, is so far shocking to civilization and the moral sense of mankind that it must not expect welcome or recognition in the commonwealth of nations.

4. That the United States, confident in the justice of their cause, which is the cause, also, of good government and of human rights everywhere among men; anxious for the speedy restoration of peace, which shall secure tranquillity at home and remove all occasion of complaint abroad; and awaiting with well-assured trust the final suppression of the rebellion, through which all these things, rescued from present danger, will be secured forever, and the republic, one and indivisible, triumphant over its enemies, will continue to stand an example to mankind, *hereby announce,* as their unalterable purpose, that the war will be vigorously prosecuted, according to the humane principles of Christian states, until the rebellion shall be overcome; and they reverently invoke upon their cause the blessings of Almighty God. . . .

226. THE FRENCH IN MEXICO
1862–1866

The decision of the Mexican Congress, in July 1861 to suspend for two years all payments on foreign debts, brought to a head a situation which had long been threatening. France, Spain and Great Britain signed an agreement for joint intervention, and in 1862 took possession of Mexican custom houses. Spain and Great Britain reaching a satisfactory agreement with Mexico thereupon withdrew from the coalition, leaving France in control of the situation. A French army defeated Juarez, captured the Mexican capital, and organized a provisional government which promptly voted to establish an Empire and invited the Austrian Archduke Maximilian to the throne. Secretary Seward watched this violation of the Monroe Doctrine with profound dissatisfaction, but hesitated to antagonize Emperor Napoleon III. The despatch of March 3, 1862 sets forth the American position on intervention and assumes the honorable intentions of the signatories of the convention of 1861. The success of the Union arms by 1864 made Congress ready to assume a bolder position, but the resolution of April 4, 1864 was not passed by the Senate. After the War Seward assumed a position of inflexible hostility to the maintenance of the French regime in Mexico, and the despatch of April 16, 1866 sets forth the American attitude toward the project of Austrian military support to Emperor Maximilian. French troops were finally withdrawn from Mexico in 1867 and in June of that year the hapless Maximilian was shot. See J. B. Moore, *A Digest of International Law,* Vol. vi;

D. Perkins, *The Monroe Doctrine,* 1826–1867, ch. vii, and bibliography; E. C. Corti, *Maximilian and Charlotte of Mexico,* Vol. II; J. M. Callahan, *Evolution of Seward's Mexican Policy;* J. F. Rippy, *The United States and Mexico,* ch. xiv; C. A. Duniway, "Reasons for the Withdrawal of the French from Mexico", *American Hist. Assoc. Annual Report,* 1902, Vol. I, p. 313. On Confederate diplomacy in Mexico, see F. L. Owsley, *King Cotton Diplomacy,* ch. xvii.

1. MR. SEWARD TO MR. ADAMS
March 3, 1862

(U. S. 37th Congress, 2d Session, *House Doc.* No. 100, p. 207–8)

Department of State,
Washington, March 3, 1862.

Sir: We observe indications of a growing opinion in Europe that the demonstrations which are being made by Spanish, French, and British forces against Mexico are likely to be attended with a revolution in that country which will bring in a monarchical government there, in which the crown will be assumed by some foreign prince.

This country is deeply concerned in the peace of nations, and aims to be loyal at the same time in all its relations, as well to the allies as to Mexico. The President has therefore instructed me to submit his views on the new aspect of affairs to the parties concerned. He has relied upon the assurances given to this government by the allies that they were seeking no political objects and only a redress of grievances. He does not doubt the sincerity of the allies, and his confidence in their good faith, if it could be shaken, would be reinspired by explanations apparently made in their behalf that the governments of Spain, France, and Great Britain are not intending to intervene and will not intervene to effect a change of the constitutional form of government now existing in Mexico, or to produce any political change there in opposition to the will of the Mexican people. Indeed, he understands the allies to be unanimous in declaring that the proposed revolution in Mexico is moved only by Mexican citizens now in Europe.

The President, however, deems it his duty to express to the allies, in all candor and frankness, the opinion that no monarchical government which could be founded in Mexico, in the presence of foreign navies and armies in the waters and upon the soil of Mexico, would have any prospect of security or permanency. Secondly, that the instability of such a monarchy there would be enhanced if the throne should be assigned to any person not of Mexican nativity. That under such circumstances the new government must speedily fall unless it could draw into its support European alliances, which, relating back to the present invasion, would, in fact, make it the beginning of a permanent policy of armed European monarchical intervention injurious and practically hostile to the most general system of government on the continent of America, and this would be the beginning rather than the ending of revolution in Mexico.

These views are grounded upon some knowledge of the political sentiments and habits of society in America.

In such a case it is not to be doubted that the permanent interests and sympathies of this country would be with the other American republics. It is not intended on this occasion to predict the course of events which might happen as a consequence of the proceeding contemplated, either on this continent or in Europe. It is sufficient to say that, in the President's opinion, the emancipation of this continent from European control has been the principal fea-

ture in its history during the last century. It is not probable that a revolution in the contrary direction would be successful in an immediately succeeding century, while population in America is so rapidly increasing, resources so rapidly developing, and society so steadily forming itself upon principles of democratic American government. Nor is it necessary to suggest to the allies the improbability that European nations could steadily agree upon a policy favorable to such a counter-revolution as one conducive to their own interests, or to suggest that, however studiously the allies may act to avoid lending the aid of their land and naval forces to domestic revolutions in Mexico, the result would nevertheless be traceable to the presence of those forces there, although for a different purpose, since it may be deemed certain that but for their presence there no such revolution could probably have been attempted or even conceived.

The Senate of the United States has not, indeed, given its official sanction to the precise measures which the President has proposed for lending our aid to the existing government in Mexico, with the approval of the allies, to relieve it from its present embarrassments. This, however, is only a question of domestic administration. It would be very erroneous to regard such a disagreement as indicating any serious difference of opinion in this government or among the American people in their cordial good wishes for the safety, welfare, and stability of the republican system of government in that country.

I am, sir, your obedient servant,
William H. Seward.

2. HOUSE RESOLUTION ON FRENCH INTERVENTION IN MEXICO
April 4, 1864

(E. McPherson, *Political History of the Rebellion*, p. 349)

Resolved. That the Congress of the United States are unwilling, by silence, to leave the nations of the world under the impression that they are indifferent spectators of the deplorable events now transpiring in the Republic of Mexico; and they therefore think fit to declare that it does not accord with the policy of the United States to acknowledge a monarchical government, erected on the ruins of any republican government in America, under the auspices of any European power.

.3. MR. SEWARD TO MR. MOTLEY
April 16, 1866
(U. S. 39th Congress, 1st Session, *House Doc.* No. 93, p. 46–7)

Department of State,
Washington, April 16, 1866.

SIR: I have had the honor to receive your despatch of the 27th of March, No. 155, which brings the important announcement that a treaty, called a "military supplementary convention," was ratified on the 15th of that month between the Emperor of Austria and the Prince Maximilian, who claims to be an emperor in Mexico.

You inform me that it is expected that about one thousand volunteers will be shipped (under this treaty) from Trieste to Vera Cruz very soon, and that at least as many more will be shipped in autumn.

I have heretofore given you the President's instructions to ask for explanations, and, conditionally, to inform the government of Austria that the despatch of military expeditions by Austria under such an arrangement as the one which seems now to have been consummated would be regarded with serious concern by the United States.

The subject has now been further considered in connexion with the official information thus recently received. The time seems to have arrived when the attitude of this government in relation to Mexican affairs should be once again frankly and distinctly made known to the Emperor of Austria, and all other powers whom it may directly concern. The United States, for reasons which seem to them to be just, and to have their foundation in the laws of nations, maintain that the domestic republican government with which they are in relations of friendly communication is the only legitimate government existing in Mexico; that a war has for a period of several years been waged against that republic by the government of France; which war began with a disclaim of all political or dynastic designs that that war has subsequently taken upon

itself, and now distinctly wears the character of an European intervention to overthrow that domestic republican government, and to erect in its stead a European, imperial, military despotism by military force. The United States, in view of the character of their own political institutions, their proximity and intimate relations towards Mexico, and their just influence in the political affairs of the American continent, cannot consent to the accomplishment of that purpose by the means described. The United States have therefore addressed themselves, as they think, seasonably to the government of France, and have asked that its military forces, engaged in that objectionable political invasion, may desist from further intervention and be withdrawn from Mexico.

A copy of the last communication upon this subject, which was addressed by us to the government of France, is herewith transmitted for your special information. This paper will give you the true situation of the question. It will also enable you to satisfy the government of Vienna that the United States must be no less opposed to military intervention for political objects hereafter in Mexico by the government of Austria, than they are opposed to any further intervention of the same character in that country by France.

You will, therefore, at as early a day as may be convenient, bring the whole case, in a becoming manner, to the attention of the imperial royal government. You are authorized to state that the United States sincerely desire that Austria may find it just and expedient to come upon the same ground of non-intervention in Mexico which is maintained by the United States, and to which they have invited France.

You will communicate to us the answer of the Austrian government to this proposition.

This government could not but regard as a matter of serious concern the despatch of any troops from Austria for Mexico while the subject which you are thus directed to present to the Austrian government remains under consideration.

I am, sir, your obedient servant,
WILLIAM H. SEWARD.

227. NEW JERSEY PEACE RESOLUTIONS
March 18, 1863

(F. Moore, ed. *The Rebellion Record*, Vol. XII, p. 679 ff.)

These resolutions of the legislature of New Jersey did not meet with the approval of the New Jersey soldiers. Their protest is given in the accompanying document below. See, C. M. Knapp, *New Jersey Politics During the Civil War;* J. F. Rhodes, *History*, Vol. V, p. 317 ff.

1. NEW-JERSEY PEACE RESOLUTIONS

1. *Be it Resolved by the Senate and General Assembly of the State of New-Jersey,* That this State, in promptly answering the calls made by the President of the United States, at and since the inauguration of the war, for troops and means to assist in maintaining the power and dignity of the Federal Government, believed and confided in the professions and declarations of the President of the United States, in his inaugural address, and in the resolutions passed by Congress on the twenty-fifth day of July, 1861, in which, among other things, it was declared "that the war is not waged for conquest or subjugation, or interfering with the rights or established institutions of the States, but to maintain and defend the supremacy of the Constitution, with the rights and equality under it unimpaired, and that as soon as these objects shall be accomplished the war ought to cease;". . .

2. *And be it Resolved,* That this State having waited for the redemption of the sacred pledges of the President and Congress with a patience and forbearance only equalled in degree by the unfaltering and unswerving bravery and fidelity of her sons, conceives it to be her solemn duty, as it is her unquestioned right, to urge upon the President and Congress, in the most respectful but decided manner, the redemption of the pledges under which the troops of this State entered upon, and to this moment have continued in, the contest; . . .

3. *And be it Resolved,* That it is the deliberate sense of the people of this State that the war power within the limits of the Constitution is ample for any and all emergencies, and that all assumption of power, under whatever plea, beyond that conferred by the Constitution, is without warrant or

authority, and if permitted to continue without remonstrance, will finally encompass the destruction of the liberties of the people and the death of the Republic; and therefore, to the end that in any event the matured and deliberate sense of the people of New-Jersey may be known and declared, we, their representatives in Senate and General Assembly convened, do, in their name and in their behalf, make unto the Federal Government this our solemn

PROTEST

Against a war waged with the insurgent States for the accomplishment of unconstitutional or partisan purposes;

Against a war which has for its object the subjugation of any of the States, with a view to their reduction to territorial condition; . . .

Against the domination of the military over the civil laws in States, Territories, or districts not in a state of insurrection;

Against all arrests without warrant; against the suspension of the writ of *habeas corpus* in States and Territories sustaining the Federal Government, "where the public safety does not require it," and against the assumption of power by any person to suspend such writ, except under the express authority of Congress;

Against the creation of new States by the division of existing ones, or in any other manner not clearly authorized by the Constitution, and against the right of secession as practically admitted by the action of Congress in admitting as a new State a portion of the State of Virginia;

Against the power assumed in the proclamation of the President made January first, 1863, by which all the slaves in certain States and parts of States are for ever set free; and against the expenditures of the public moneys for the emancipation of slaves or their support at any time, under any pretence whatever;

Against any and every exercise of power upon the part of the Federal Government that is not clearly given and expressed in

428 Documents of American History

the Federal Constitution—reasserting that "the powers not delegated to the United States by the Constitution, nor prohibited by it to the States, are reserved to the States respectively, or to the people.". . .

4. *And be it Resolved,* That . . . while abating naught in her devotion to the Union of the States and the dignity and power of the Federal Government, at no time since the commencement of the present war has this State been other than willing to terminate peacefully and honorably to all a war unnecessary in its origin, fraught with horror and suffering in its prosecution, and necessarily dangerous to the liberties of all in its continuance. . . .

2. Protest of the New-Jersey Soldiers

Camp of the Eleventh New-Jersey Volunteers,
Below Falmouth, Va., March 10, 1863.

Whereas, The Legislature of our native States, . . . has sought to tarnish its high honor, and bring upon it disgrace, by the passage of resolutions tending to a dishonorable peace with armed rebels seeking to destroy our great and beneficent Government, the best ever designed for the happiness of the many; and

Whereas, We, her sons, members of the Eleventh regiment New-Jersey volunteers, citizens representing every section of the State, have left our homes to endure the fatigues, privations, and dangers incident to a soldier's life, in order to maintain our Republic in its integrity, willing to sacrifice our lives to that object; fully recognizing the impropriety of a soldier's discussion of the legislative functions of the State, yet deeming it due to ourselves, that the voice of those who offer their all in their country's

cause, be heard when weak and wicked men seek its dishonor; therefore

Resolved, That the Union of the States is the only guarantee for the preservation of our liberty and independence, and that the war for the maintenance of that Union commands *now,* as it ever has done, our best efforts and our heartfelt sympathy.

Resolved, That we consider the passage, or even the introduction of the so-called Peace Resolutions, as wicked, weak, and cowardly, tending to aid by their sympathy, the rebels seeking to destroy the Republic.

Resolved, That we regard as traitors alike the foe in arms and the secret enemies of our Government, who, at home, foment disaffection and strive to destroy confidence in our legally chosen rulers.

Resolved, That the reports spread broadcast throughout the North, by secession sympathizers, prints, and voices, that the army of which we esteem it a high honor to form a part, is demoralized and clamorous for peace on any terms, are the lying utterances of traitorous tongues, and do base injustice to our noble comrades who have never faltered in the great work, and are now not only willing but anxious to follow their gallant and chivalric leader against the strongholds of the enemy.

Resolved, That we put forth every effort, endure every fatigue, and shrink from no danger, until, under the gracious guidance of a kind Providence, every armed rebel shall be conquered, and traitors at home shall quake with fear, as the proud emblem of our national independence shall assert its power from North to South, and crush beneath its powerful folds all who dared to assail its honor, doubly hallowed by the memory of the patriot dead. . . .

228. THE GETTYSBURG ADDRESS
November 19, 1863

(*The Writings of Abraham Lincoln,* Constitutional ed., Vol. VII, p. 20)

There is considerable variation in phraseology among the various versions of this famous address. For a learned discussion of the address and comparison of facsimile manuscripts, see W. E. Barton, *Lincoln at Gettysburg.* A more popular account is C. E. Carr, *Lincoln at Gettysburg.*

Four score and seven years ago our fathers brought forth on this continent, a new nation, conceived in Liberty, and dedicated to the proposition that all men are created equal.

Now we are engaged in a great civil war,

testing whether that nation or any nation so conceived and so dedicated, can long endure. We are met on a great battle-field of that war. We have come to dedicate a portion of that field, as a final resting place for those who here gave their lives that that nation might live. It is altogether fitting and proper that we should do this.

But, in a larger sense, we can not dedicate —we can not consecrate—we can not hallow —this ground. The brave men, living and dead, who struggled here, have consecrated it, far above our poor power to add or detract. The world will little note, nor long remember what we say here, but it can never forget what they did here. It is for us the living, rather, to be dedicated here to the unfinished work which they who fought here have thus far so nobly advanced. It is rather for us to be here dedicated to the great task remaining before us—that from these honored dead we take increased devotion to that cause for which they gave the last full measure of devotion—that we here highly resolve that these dead shall not have died in vain—that this nation, under God, shall have a new birth of freedom— and that government of the people, by the people, for the people, shall not perish from the earth.

229. RECONSTRUCTION OF TENNESSEE

Lincoln's Letter to Governor Johnson
September 11, 1863

(Writings of Abraham Lincoln, Constitutional ed., Vol. VI, p. 407–8)

This letter is significant for the development of Lincoln's policy of Reconstruction. See references in Doc. No. 230 and C. R. Hall, *Andrew Johnson, Military Governor of Tennessee;* J. W. Fertig, *Secession and Reconstruction of Tennessee;* J. W. Patton, *Unionism and Reconstruction in Tennessee.*

Executive Mansion, Washington,
September 11, 1863.
HON. ANDREW JOHNSON.

MY DEAR SIR:—All Tennessee is now clear of armed insurrectionists. You need not to be reminded that it is the nick of time for reinaugurating a loyal State government. Not a moment should be lost. You and the co-operating friends there can better judge of the ways and means than can be judged by any here. I only offer a few suggestions. The reinauguration must not be such as to give control of the State and its representation in Congress to the enemies of the Union, driving its friends there into political exile. The whole struggle for Tennessee will have been profitless to both State and nation if it so ends that Governor Johnson is put down and Governor Harris put up. It must not be so. You must have it otherwise. Let the reconstruction be the work of such men only as can be trusted for the Union. Exclude all others, and trust that your government so organized will be recognized here as being the one of republican form to be guaranteed to the State, and to be protected against invasion and domestic violence. It is something on the question of time to remember that it cannot be known who is next to occupy the position I now hold, nor what he will do. I see that you have declared in favor of emancipation in Tennessee, for which may God bless you. Get emancipation into your new State government—constitution—and there will be no such word as fail for your case. The raising of colored troops, I think, will greatly help every way.

Yours very truly,
A. LINCOLN.

230. LINCOLN'S PLAN OF RECONSTRUCTION

Proclamation of Amnesty and Reconstruction
December 8, 1863

(Richardson, ed. Messages and Papers, Vol. VI, p. 213 ff.)

Lincoln had already indicated his reconstruction policy by his action during 1862 in the reconstruction of Tennessee and Louisiana. The Presidential plan, as presented in the message of

December 8, 1863, provided for the restoration of loyal governments in the seceded states when a number, equal to one tenth of the voting population of the State in 1860, should take an oath prescribed and organize a government. This Presidential plan assumed that the States were not out of the Union, and that reconstruction was a Presidential function, to be carried out through the instrumentality of the pardoning power. The opposition to this theory was announced first by the refusal of Congress to admit representatives from the reconstructed States, and, decisively, by the passage of the Wade-Davis Bill, Doc. No. 234. On Lincoln's policy, see, C. H. McCarthy, *Lincoln's Plan of Reconstruction;* C. E. Chadsey, *Reconstruction Prior to the Close of the Civil War;* J. W. Burgess, *Civil War on the Constitution,* 2 Vols.

A Proclamation

Whereas in and by the Constitution of the United States it is provided that the President "shall have power to grant reprieves and pardons for offenses against the United States, except in cases of impeachment;" and

Whereas a rebellion now exists whereby the loyal State governments of several States have for a long time been subverted, and many persons have committed and are now guilty of treason against the United States; and

Whereas, with reference to said rebellion and treason, laws have been enacted by Congress declaring forfeitures and confiscation of property and liberation of slaves, all upon terms and conditions therein stated, and also declaring that the President was thereby authorized at any time thereafter, by proclamation, to extend to persons who may have participated in the existing rebellion in any State or part thereof pardon and amnesty, with such exceptions and at such times and on such conditions as he may deem expedient for the public welfare; and

Whereas the Congressional declaration for limited and conditional pardon accords with well-established judicial exposition of the pardoning power; and

Whereas, with reference to said rebellion, the President of the United States has issued several proclamations with provisions in regard to the liberation of slaves; and

Whereas it is now desired by some persons heretofore engaged in said rebellion to resume their allegiance to the United States and to reinaugurate loyal State governments within and for their respective States:

Therefore, I, Abraham Lincoln, President of the United States, do proclaim, . . . to all persons who have, directly or by implication, participated in the existing rebellion, except as hereinafter excepted, that a full pardon is hereby granted to them and each of them, with restoration of all rights of property, except as to slaves and in property cases where rights of third parties shall have intervened, and upon the condition that every such person shall take and subscribe an oath and thenceforward keep and maintain said oath inviolate, and which oath shall be registered for permanent preservation and shall be of the tenor and effect following, to wit:

I, —— ——, do solemnly swear, in presence of Almighty God, that I will henceforth faithfully support, protect, and defend the Constitution of the United States and the Union of the States thereunder; and that I will in like manner abide by and faithfully support all acts of Congress passed during the existing rebellion with reference to slaves, so long and so far as not repealed, modified, or held void by Congress or by decision of the Supreme Court; and that I will in like manner abide by and faithfully support all proclamations of the President made during the existing rebellion having reference to slaves, so long and so far as not modified or declared void by decision of the Supreme Court. So help me God.

The persons excepted from the benefits of the foregoing provisions are all who are or shall have been civil or diplomatic officers or agents of the so-called Confederate Government; all who have left judicial stations under the United States to aid the rebellion; all who are or shall have been military or naval officers of said so-called Confederate Government above the rank of colonel in the army or of lieutenant in the navy; all who left seats in the United States Congress to aid the rebellion; all who resigned commissions in the Army or Navy of the United States and afterwards aided the rebellion; and all who have engaged in any way in treating colored persons, or white persons in charge of such, otherwise than lawfully as prisoners of war, and which persons may have been found in the United States service as soldiers, seamen, or in any other capacity.

And I do further proclaim, declare, and make known that whenever, in any of the States of Arkansas, Texas, Louisiana, Mississippi, Tennessee, Alabama, Georgia, Florida, South Carolina, and North Carolina, a number of persons, not less than one-tenth in number of the votes cast in such State at the Presidential election of the year A. D. 1860, each having taken oath aforesaid, and not having since violated it, and being a qualified voter by the election law of the State existing immediately before the so-called act of secession, and excluding all others, shall re-establish a State government which shall be republican and in nowise contravening said oath, such shall be recognized as the true government of the State, and the State shall receive thereunder the benefits of the constitutional provision which declares that "the United States shall guarantee to every State in this Union a republican form of government and shall protect each of them against invasion, and, on application of the legislature, or the executive (when the legislature can not be convened), against domestic violence."

And I do further proclaim, declare, and make known that any provision which may be adopted by such State government in relation to the freed people of such State which shall recognize and declare their permanent freedom, provide for their education, and which may yet be consistent as a temporary arrangement with their present condition as a laboring, landless, and homeless class, will not be objected to by the National Executive.

And it is suggested as not improper that in constructing a loyal State government in any State the name of the State, the boundary, the subdivisions, the constitution, and the general code of laws as before the rebellion be maintained, subject only to the modifications made necessary by the conditions hereinbefore stated, and such others, if any, not contravening said conditions and which may be deemed expedient by those framing the new State government.

To avoid misunderstanding, it may be proper to say that this proclamation, so far as it relates to State governments, has no reference to States wherein loyal State governments have all the while been maintained. And for the same reason it may be proper to further say that whether members sent to Congress from any State shall be admitted to seats constitutionally rests exclusively with the respective Houses, and not to any extent with the Executive. And, still further, that this proclamation is intended to present the people of the States wherein the national authority has been suspended and loyal State governments have been subverted a mode in and by which the national authority and loyal State governments may be re-established within said States or in any of them; and while the mode presented is the best the Executive can suggest, with his present impressions, it must not be understood that no other possible mode would be acceptable.

ABRAHAM LINCOLN.

231. THE NATIONAL BANK ACT
June 3, 1864

(U. S. Statutes at Large, Vol. XIII, p. 99 ff.)

This act amended the banking act of February 25, 1863, and created the national banking system that obtained until the passage of the Federal Reserve Act of 1913. For a history of the National Bank Act see, D. R. Dewey, *Financial History of the United States*, p. 299 ff.; J. J. Knox, *History of Banking*, p. 220 ff.; A. B. Hepburn, *History of Currency in the United States*, ch. xvii; A. M. Davis, *The Origin of the National Banking System*.

*An Act to provide a National Currency, se-*cured by a Pledge of United States Bonds, and to provide for the Circulation and Redemption thereof.

. . . Sec. 5. That associations for carrying on the business of banking may be formed by any number of persons, not less in any case than five, who shall enter into articles of association, which shall specify in general terms the object for which the association is formed, and may contain any other provisions, not inconsistent with the provisions of this act, which the association may see fit to adopt for the regulation of the business of the association and the conduct of its affairs, which said articles shall be signed by the persons uniting to form the association, and a copy of them forwarded to the comptroller of the currency, to be filed and preserved in his office. . . .

SEC. 7. That no association shall be organized under this act, with a less capital than one hundred thousand dollars, nor in a city whose population exceeds fifty thousand persons, with a less capital than two hundred thousand dollars: *Provided,* That banks with a capital of not less than fifty thousand dollars may, with the approval of the Secretary of the Treasury, be organized in any place the population of which does not exceed six thousand inhabitants.

SEC. 8. That every association formed pursuant to the provisions of this act shall . . . transact no business except such as may be incidental to its organization and necessarily preliminary, until authorized by the comptroller of the currency to commence the business of banking. Such association shall have power to adopt a corporate seal, and shall have succession by the name designated in its organization certificate, for the period of twenty years from its organization, unless sooner dissolved according to the provisions of its articles of association, or by the act of its shareholders owning two thirds of its stock, or unless the franchise shall be forfeited by a violation of this act; by such name it may make contracts . . . , and exercise under this act all such incidental powers as shall be necessary to carry on the business of banking by discounting and negotiating promissory notes, drafts, bills of exchange, and other evidences of debt; by receiving deposits; by buying and selling exchange, coin, and bullion; by loaning money on personal security; by obtaining, issuing, and circulating notes according to the provisions of this act. . . .

The shareholders of each association formed under the provisions of this act, and of each existing bank or banking association that may accept the provisions of this act, shall be held individually responsible, equally and ratably, and not one for another, for all contracts, debts, and engagements of such association to the extent of the amount of their stock therein at the par value thereof, in addition to the amount invested in such shares; except that shareholders of any banking association now existing under state laws, having not less than five millions of dollars of capital actually paid in, and a surplus of twenty per centum on hand, both to be determined by the comptroller of the currency, shall be liable only to the amount invested in their shares. . . .

SEC. 16. That every association, after having complied with the provisions of this act, preliminary to the commencement of banking business under its provisions, and before it shall be authorized to commence business, shall transfer and deliver to the treasurer of the United States any United States registered bonds bearing interest to an amount not less than thirty thousand dollars nor less than one third of the capital stock paid in, which bonds shall be deposited with the treasurer of the United States and by him safely kept in his office until the same shall be otherwise disposed of, in pursuance of the provisions of this act; and the Secretary of the Treasury is hereby authorized to receive and cancel any United States coupon bonds, and to issue in lieu thereof registered bonds of like amount, bearing a like rate of interest, and having the same time to run; and the deposit of bonds shall be, by every association, increased as its capital may be paid up or increased, so that every association shall at all times have on deposit with the treasurer registered United States bonds to the amount of at least one third of its capital stock actually paid in. . . .

SEC. 21. That upon the transfer and delivery of bonds to the treasurer, as provided in the foregoing section, the association making the same shall be entitled to receive from the comptroller of the currency circulating notes of different denominations, in blank, registered and countersigned as hereinafter provided, equal in amount to ninety per centum of the current market value of the United States bonds so transferred and delivered, but not exceeding ninety per centum of the amount of said bonds at the par value thereof, if bearing interest at a rate not less than five per centum per annum; and at no time shall the total amount of such notes, issued to any such association, exceed the amount at such time actually paid in of its capital stock.

SEC. 22. That the entire amount of notes for circulation to be issued under this act shall not exceed three hundred millions of dollars. . . .

SEC. 23. That after any such association shall have caused its promise to pay such notes on demand to be signed by the president or vice-president and cashier thereof, in such manner as to make them obligatory promissory notes, payable on demand, at its place of business, such association is hereby authorized to issue and circulate the same as money; and the same shall be received at par in all parts of the United States in payment of taxes, excises, public lands, and all other dues to the United States, except for duties on imports; and also for all salaries and other debts and demands owing by the United States to individuals, corporations, and associations within the United States, except interest on the public debt, and in redemption of the national currency. And no such association shall issue post notes or any other notes to circulate as money than such as are authorized by the foregoing provisions of this act. . . .

SEC. 26. That the bonds transferred to and deposited with the treasurer of the United States, as hereinbefore provided, by any banking association for the security of its circulating notes, shall be held exclusively for that purpose, until such notes shall be redeemed, except as provided in this act; but the comptroller of the currency shall give to any such banking association powers of attorney to receive and appropriate to its own use the interest on the bonds which it shall have so transferred to the treasurer; but such powers shall become inoperative whenever such banking association shall fail to redeem its circulating notes as aforesaid. Whenever the market or cash value of any bonds deposited with the treasurer of the United States, as aforesaid, shall be reduced below the amount of the circulation issued for the same, the comptroller of the currency is hereby authorized to demand and receive the amount of such depreciation in other United States bonds at cash value, or in money, from the association receiving said

bills, to be deposited with the treasurer of the United States as long as such depreciation continues. . . .

SEC. 30. That every association may take, receive, reserve, and charge on any loan or discount made, or upon any note, bill of exchange, or other evidences of debt, interest at the rate allowed by the laws of the state or territory where the bank is located, and no more. . . . And when no rate is fixed by the laws of the state or territory, the bank may take, receive, reserve, or charge a rate not exceeding seven per centum. . . .

SEC. 31. That every association in the cities hereinafter named shall, at all times, have on hand, in lawful money of the United States, an amount equal to at least twenty-five per centum of the aggregate amount of its notes in circulation and its deposits; and every other association shall, at all times, have on hand, in lawful money of the United States, an amount equal to at least fifteen per centum of the aggregate amount of its notes in circulation, and of its deposits. . . . *Provided*, That three fifths of said fifteen per centum may consist of balances due to an association available for the redemption of its circulating notes from associations approved by the comptroller of the currency, organized under this act, in the cities of Saint Louis, Louisville, Chicago, Detroit, Milwaukee, New Orleans, Cincinnati, Cleveland, Pittsburg, Baltimore, Philadelphia, Boston, New York, Albany, Leavenworth, San Francisco, and Washington City: *Provided, also,* That clearing-house certificates, representing specie or lawful money specially deposited for the purpose of any clearing-house association, shall be deemed to be lawful money in the possession of any association belonging to such clearing-house holding and owning such certificate, and shall be considered to be a part of the lawful money which such association is required to have under the foregoing provisions of this section: *Provided,* That the cities of Charleston and Richmond may be added to the list of cities in the national associations of which other associations may keep three fifths of their lawful money, whenever, in the opinion of the comptroller of the currency, the condition of the southern states will warrant it. And it shall be competent for the comptroller of the currency to notify any association, whose lawful money reserve as aforesaid shall be below the amount to be kept on hand as aforesaid, to make good such reserve; and if such association shall fail for thirty days thereafter so to make good its reserve of lawful money of the United States, the comptroller may, with the concurrence of the Secretary of the Treasury, appoint a receiver to wind up the business of such association, as provided in this act.

SEC. 32. That each association organized in any of the cities named in the foregoing section shall select, subject to the approval of the comptroller of the currency, an association in the city of New York, at which it will redeem its circulating notes at par. And each of such associations may keep one half of its lawful money reserve in cash deposits in the city of New York. . . .

SEC. 36. That no association shall at any time be indebted, or in any way liable, to an amount exceeding the amount of its capital stock at such time actually paid in and remaining undiminished by losses or otherwise, except on the following accounts, that is to say:—

First. On account of its notes or circulation.

Second. On account of moneys deposited with, or collected by, such association.

Third. On account of bills of exchange or drafts drawn against money actually on deposit to the credit of such association, or due thereto.

Fourth. On account of liabilities to its stockholders for dividends and reserved profits. . . .

SEC. 38. That no association, or any member thereof, shall, during the time it shall continue its banking operations, withdraw, or permit to be withdrawn, either in form of dividends or otherwise, any portion of its capital. And if losses shall at any time have been sustained by any such association equal to or exceeding its undivided profits then on hand, no dividend shall be made; and no dividend shall ever be made by any association, while it shall continue its banking operations, to an amount greater than its net profits then on hand, deducting therefrom its losses and bad debts. . . .

SEC. 41. And in lieu of all existing taxes, every association shall pay to the treasurer of the United States, in the months of January and July, a duty of one half of one per centum each half year from and after [January 1, 1864] upon the average amount of its notes in circulation, and a duty of one quarter of one per centum each ·half year upon the average amount of its deposits, and a duty of one quarter of one per centum each half year, as aforesaid, on the average amount of its capital stock beyond the amount invested in United States bonds; . . .

SEC. 44. That any bank incorporated by special law, or any banking institution organized under a general law of any state, may, by authority of this act, become a national association under its provisions, by the name prescribed in its organization certificate. . . .

SEC. 45. That all associations under this act, when designated for that purpose by the Secretary of the Treasury, shall be depositaries of public money, except receipts from customs, under such regulations as may be prescribed by the Secretary; and they may also be employed as financial agents of the government; and they shall perform all such reasonable duties, as depositaries of public moneys and financial agents of the government, as may be required of them. And the Secretary of the Treasury shall require of the association thus designated satisfactory security, by the deposit of United States bonds and otherwise, for the safe-keeping and prompt payment of the public money deposited with them, and for the faithful performance of their duties as financial agents of the government: *Provided,* That every association which shall be selected and designated as receiver or depositary of the public money shall take and receive at par all of the national currency bills, by whatever association issued, which have been paid in to the government for internal revenue, or for loans or stocks. . . .

232. PLATFORM OF NATIONAL UNION CONVENTION
Baltimore, Maryland
June 7, 1864

(The Writings of Abraham Lincoln, Constitutional ed., Vol. VII, p. 148 ff.)

The Republican Party took the name of National Union Party during the war period.

1. *Resolved,* That it is the highest duty of every American citizen to maintain against all their enemies the integrity of the Union and the paramount authority of the Constitution and laws of the United States; and that, laying aside all differences of political opinion, we pledge ourselves, as Union men, animated by a common sentiment and aiming at a common object, to do everything in our power to aid the Government in quelling by force of arms the rebellion now raging against its authority, and in bringing to the punishment due to their crimes the rebels and traitors arrayed against it.

2. *Resolved,* That we approve the determination of the Government of the United States not to compromise with rebels, or to offer them any terms of peace, except such as may be based upon an unconditional surrender of their hostility and a return to their just allegiance to the Constitution and laws of the United States, and that we call upon the Government to maintain this position, and to prosecute the war with the utmost possible vigor to the complete suppression of the rebellion, in full reliance upon the self-sacrificing patriotism, the heroic valor, and the undying devotion of the American people to their country and its free institutions.

3. *Resolved,* That as slavery was the cause, and now constitutes the strength, of this rebellion, and as it must be, always and everywhere, hostile to the principles of republican government, justice and the national safety demand its utter and complete extirpation from the soil of the republic; and that while we uphold and maintain the acts and proclamations by which the Government, in its own defense, has aimed a death-blow at this gigantic evil, we are in favor, furthermore, of such an amendment to the Constitution, to be made by the people in conformity with its provisions, as shall terminate and forever prohibit the existence of slavery within the limits or the jurisdiction of the United States.

4. *Resolved,* That the thanks of the American people are due to the soldiers and sailors of the Army and Navy, who have periled their lives in defense of their country and in vindication of the honor of its flag; that the nation owes to them some permanent recognition of their patriotism and their valor, and ample and permanent provision for those of their survivors who have received disabling and honorable wounds in the service of the country; and that the memories of those who have fallen in its defense shall be held in grateful and everlasting remembrance.

5. *Resolved,* That we approve and applaud the practical wisdom, the unselfish patriotism, and the unswerving fidelity to the Constitution and the principles of American liberty, with which Abraham Lincoln has discharged under circumstances of unparalleled difficulty the great duties and responsibilities of the Presidential office; that we approve and indorse as demanded by the emergency and essential to the preservation of the nation, and as within the provisions of the Constitution, the measures and acts which he has adopted to defend the nation against its open and secret foes; that we approve, especially, the Proclamation of Emancipation, and the employment as Union soldiers of men heretofore held in slavery; and that we have full confidence in his determination to carry these and all other constitutional measures essential to the salvation of the country into full and complete effect.

6. *Resolved,* That we deem it essential to the general welfare that harmony should prevail in the national councils, and we regard as worthy of public confidence and official trust those only who cordially indorse the principles proclaimed in these resolutions, and which should characterize the administration of the Government.

7. *Resolved,* That the Government owes to all men employed in its armies, without

regard to distinction of color, the full protection of the laws of war, and that any violation of these laws, or of the usages of civilized nations in time of war, by the rebels now in arms, should be made the subject of prompt and full redress.

8. *Resolved,* That foreign immigration, which in the past has added so much to the wealth, development of resources, and increase of power to this nation, the asylum of the oppressed of all nations, should be fostered and encouraged by a liberal and just policy.

9. *Resolved,* That we are in favor of the speedy construction of the railroad to the Pacific coast.

10. *Resolved,* That the national faith, pledged for the redemption of the public debt, must be kept inviolate, and that for this purpose we recommend economy and rigid responsibility in the public expenditures, and a vigorous and just system of taxation: and that it is the duty of every loyal State to sustain the credit and promote the use of the national currency.

11. *Resolved,* That we approve the position taken by the Government that the people of the United States can never regard with indifference the attempt of any European power to overthrow by force or to supplant by fraud the institutions of any republican government on the Western Continent, and that they will view with extreme jealousy, as menacing to the peace and independence of their own country, the efforts of any such power to obtain new footholds for monarchical governments, sustained by foreign military force, in near proximity to the United States.

233. THE CONTRACT LABOR LAW
July 4, 1864

(*U. S. Statutes at Large,* Vol. XIII, p. 386)

This law, giving validity to liens upon the wages or property of laborers imported on contract, was repealed in 1868, but the practice itself was not specifically outlawed until 1885.

Be it enacted . . .

SEC. 2. That all contracts that shall be made by emigrants to the United States in foreign countries, in conformity to regulations that may be established . . . whereby emigrants shall pledge the wages of their labor for a term not exceeding twelve months, to repay the expenses of their emigration, shall be held to be valid in law, and may be enforced in the Courts of the United States, or of the several states and territories; and such advances, if so stipulated in the contract . . . shall operate as a lien upon any land thereafter acquired by the emigrant. . . .

SEC. 5. That no person shall be qualified to fill any office under this act who shall be directly or indirectly interested in any corporation having lands for sale to immigrants, or in the carrying or transportation of immigrants . . . or who shall receive any fee or reward, or the promise thereof, for any service performed. . . .

234. THE WADE–DAVIS BILL
July 8, 1864

(Richardson, ed. *Messages and Papers,* Vol. VI, p. 223 ff.)

Congressional hostility to the Presidential plan of reconstruction, outlined in the message of December 8, 1863, grew increasingly emphatic during the following year and culminated in the passage by a close vote of the Wade-Davis bill. This bill embodied the Congressional plan of reconstruction. Lincoln did not sign the bill, and after the adjournment of Congress, issued a proclamation giving his reasons for refusing to accept the Congressional plan. See, J. G. Nicolay and J. Hay, *Abraham Lincoln,* Vol. IX, ch. v; C. H. McCarthy, *Lincoln's Plan of Reconstruction;* B. C. Steiner, *Life of Henry Winter Davis;* A. G. Riddle, *Life of Benjamin F. Wade.*

An Act to guarantee to certain States whose Governments have been usurped or over-

thrown a Republican Form of Government.

Be it enacted, That in the states declared in rebellion against the United States, the President shall, by and with the advice and consent of the Senate, appoint for each a provisional governor, . . . who shall be charged with the civil administration of such state until a state government therein shall be recognized as hereinafter provided.

SEC. 2. That so soon as the military resistance to the United States shall have been suppressed in any such state, and the people thereof shall have sufficiently returned to their obedience to the constitution and the laws of the United States, the provisional governor shall direct the marshal of the United States, as speedily as may be, to name a sufficient number of deputies, and to enroll all white male citizens of the United States, resident in the state in their respective counties, and to request each one to take the oath to support the constitution of the United States, and in his enrolment to designate those who take and those who refuse to take that oath, which rolls shall be forthwith returned to the provisional governor; and if the persons taking that oath shall amount to a majority of the persons enrolled in the state, he shall, by proclamation, invite the loyal people of the state to elect delegates to a convention charged to declare the will of the people of the state relative to the reëstablishment of a state government subject to, and in conformity with, the constitution of the United States.

SEC. 3. That the convention shall consist of as many members as both houses of the last constitutional state legislature, apportioned by the provisional governor among the counties, parishes, or districts of the state, in proportion to the white population, returned as electors, by the marshal, in compliance with the provisions of this act. The provisional governor shall, . . . provide an adequate force to keep the peace during the election.

SEC. 4. That the delegates shall be elected by the loyal white male citizens of the United States of the age of twenty-one years, and resident at the time in the county, parish, or district in which they shall offer to vote, and enrolled as aforesaid, or absent in the military service of the United States, and who shall take and subscribe the oath of allegiance to the United States in the form contained in the act of July 2, 1862; and all such citizens of the United States who are in the military service of the United States shall vote at the headquarters of their respective commands, under such regulations as may be prescribed by the provisional governor for the taking and return of their votes; but no person who has held or exercised any office, civil or military, state or confederate, under the rebel usurpation, or who has voluntarily borne arms against the United States, shall vote, or be eligible to be elected as delegate, at such election.

SEC. 5. That the said commissioners, . . . shall hold the election in conformity with this act and, . . . shall proceed in the manner used in the state prior to the rebellion. The oath of allegiance shall be taken and subscribed on the poll-book by every voter in the form above prescribed, but every person known by, or proved to, the commissioners to have held or exercised any office, civil or military, state or confederate, under the rebel usurpation, or to have voluntarily borne arms against the United States, shall be excluded, though he offer to take the oath; and in case any person who shall have borne arms against the United States shall offer to vote he shall be deemed to have borne arms voluntarily unless he shall prove the contrary by the testimony of a qualified voter. . . .

SEC. 6. That the provisional governor shall, by proclamation, convene the delegates elected as aforesaid, at the capital of the state, on a day not more than three months after the election, giving at least thirty days' notice of such day. In case the said capital shall in his judgment be unfit, he shall in his proclamation appoint another place. He shall preside over the deliberations of the convention, and administer to each delegate, before taking his seat in the convention, the oath of allegiance to the United States in the form above prescribed.

SEC. 7. That the convention shall declare, on behalf of the people of the state, their submission to the constitution and laws of the United States, and shall adopt the following provisions, hereby prescribed by the

United States in the execution of the constitutional duty to guarantee a republican form of government to every state, and incorporate them in the constitution of the state, that is to say:

First. No person who has held or exercised any office, civil or military, except offices merely ministerial, and military offices below the grade of colonel, state or confederate, under the usurping power, shall vote for or be a member of the legislature, or governor.

Second. Involuntary servitude is forever prohibited, and the freedom of all persons is guaranteed in said state.

Third. No debt, state or confederate, created by or under the sanction of the usurping power, shall be recognized or paid by the state.

SEC. 8. That when the convention shall have adopted those provisions, it shall proceed to reëstablish a republican form of government, and ordain a constitution containing those provisions, which, when adopted, the convention shall by ordinance provide for submitting to the people of the state, entitled to vote under this law, at an election to be held in the manner prescribed by the act for the election of delegates; but at a time and place named by the convention, at which election the said electors, and none others, shall vote directly for or against such constitution and form of state government, and the returns of said election shall be made to the provisional governor, who shall canvass the same in the presence of the electors, and if a majority of the votes cast shall be for the constitution and form of government, he shall certify the same, with a copy thereof, to the President of the United States, who, after obtaining the assent of congress, shall, by proclamation, recognize the government so established, and none other, as the constitutional government of the state, and from the date of such recognition, and not before, Senators and Representatives, and electors for President and Vice-President may be elected in such state, according to the laws of the state and of the United States.

SEC. 9. That if the convention shall refuse to reëstablish the state government on the conditions aforesaid, the provisional governor shall declare it dissolved; but it shall be the duty of the President, whenever he shall have reason to believe that a sufficient number of the people of the state entitled to vote under this act, in number not less than a majority of those enrolled, as aforesaid, are willing to reëstablish a state government on the conditions aforesaid, to direct the provisional governor to order another election of delegates to a convention for the purpose. . . .

SEC. 10. That, until the United States shall have recognized a republican form of state government, the provisional governor in each of said states shall see that this act, and the laws of the United States, and the laws of the state in force when the state government was overthrown by the rebellion, are faithfully executed within the state; but no law or usage whereby any person was heretofore held in involuntary servitude shall be recognized or enforced by any court or officer in such state, and the laws for the trial and punishment of white persons shall extend to all persons, and jurors shall have the qualifications of voters under this law for delegates to the convention. . . .

SEC. 11. That until the recognition of a state government as aforesaid, the provisional governor shall, under such regulations as he may prescribe, cause to be assessed, levied, and collected, for the year eighteen hundred and sixty-four, and every year thereafter, the taxes provided by the laws of such state to be levied during the fiscal year preceding the overthrow of the state government thereof, in the manner prescribed by the laws of the state, as nearly as may be; . . . The proceeds of such taxes shall be accounted for to the provisional governor, and be by him applied to the expenses of the administration of the laws in such state, subject to the direction of the President, and the surplus shall be deposited in the treasury of the United States to the credit of such state, to be paid to the state upon an appropriation therefor, to be made when a republican form of government shall be recognized therein by the United States.

SEC. 12. That all persons held to involuntary servitude or labor in the states aforesaid are hereby emancipated and discharged therefrom, and they and their posterity shall be forever free. And if any such persons or their posterity shall be restrained of liberty, under pretence of any claim to such service or labor, the courts of the United States shall, on habeas corpus, discharge them.

SEC. 13. That if any person declared free by this act, or any law of the United States, or any proclamation of the President, be restrained of liberty, with intent to be held in or reduced to involuntary servitude or labor, the person convicted before a court of competent jurisdiction of such act shall be punished by fine of not less than fifteen hundred dollars, and be imprisoned not less than five nor more than twenty years.

SEC. 14. That every person who shall hereafter hold or exercise any office, civil or military, except offices merely ministerial, and military offices below the grade of colonel, in the rebel service, state or confederate, is hereby declared not to be a citizen of the United States.

235. LINCOLN'S PROCLAMATION ON THE WADE–DAVIS BILL
July 8, 1864

(Richardson, ed. *Messages and Papers*, Vol. VI, p. 222)

BY THE PRESIDENT OF THE UNITED STATES:

A Proclamation.

Whereas at the late session Congress passed a bill "to guarantee to certain States whose governments have been usurped or overthrown a republican form of government," a copy of which is hereunto annexed; and

Whereas, the said bill was presented to the President of the United States for his approval less than one hour before the *sine die* adjournment of said session, and was not signed by him; and

Whereas the said bill contains, among other things, a plan for restoring the States in rebellion to their proper practical relation in the Union, which plan expresses the sense of Congress upon that subject, and which plan it is now thought fit to lay before the people for their consideration:

Now, therefore, I, Abraham Lincoln, President of the United States, do proclaim, declare, and make known that while I am (as I was in December last, when, by proclamation, I propounded a plan for restoration) unprepared by a formal approval of this bill to be inflexibly committed to any single plan of restoration, and while I am also unprepared to declare that the free State constitutions and governments already adopted and installed in Arkansas and Louisiana shall be set aside and held for naught, thereby repelling and discouraging the loyal citizens who have set up the same as to further effort, or to declare a constitutional competency in Congress to abolish slavery in States, but am at the same time sincerely hoping and expecting that a constitutional amendment abolishing slavery throughout the nation may be adopted, nevertheless I am fully satisfied with the system for restoration contained in the bill as one very proper plan for the loyal people of any State choosing to adopt it, and that I am and at all times shall be prepared to give the Executive aid and assistance to any such people so soon as the military resistance to the United States shall have been suppressed in any such State and the people thereof shall have sufficiently returned to their obedience to the Constitution and the laws of the United States, in which cases military governors will be appointed with directions to proceed according to the bill. . . .

ABRAHAM LINCOLN.

236. THE WADE–DAVIS MANIFESTO
August 5, 1864

(E. McPherson, ed. *Political History of the Rebellion*, p. 332 ff.)

Lincoln's pocket veto of the Wade-Davis Bill and his statement of opposition to the Congressional plan of reconstruction, provoked a vindictive attack on Lincoln and the Presidential policy by the sponsors of the bill, Benjamin Wade and Henry Winter Davis. The Manifesto was published in the New York *Tribune,* August 5, and shortly thereafter in the other leading papers of the country.

We have read without surprise, but not without indignation, the Proclamation of the President of the 8th of July. . . .

The President, by preventing this bill from becoming a law, holds the electoral votes of the rebel States at the dictation of his personal ambition.

If those votes turn the balance in his favor, is it to be supposed that his competitor, defeated by such means, will acquiesce?

If the rebel majority assert their supremacy in those States, and send votes which elect an enemy of the Government, will we not repel his claims?

And is not that civil war for the Presidency inaugurated by the votes of rebel States?

Seriously impressed with these dangers, Congress, *"the proper constituted authority,"* formally declared that there are no State governments in the rebel States, and provided for their erection at a proper time; and both the Senate and the House of Representatives rejected the Senators and Representatives chosen under the authority of what the President calls the free constitution and government of Arkansas.

The President's proclamation *"holds for naught"* this judgment, and discards the authority of the Supreme Court, and strides headlong toward the anarchy his proclamation of the 8th of December inaugurated.

If electors for President be allowed to be chosen in either of those States, a sinister light will be cast on the motives which induced the President to "hold for naught" the will of Congress rather than his government in Louisiana and Arkansas.

That judgment of Congress which the President defies was the exercise of an authority exclusively vested in Congress by the Constitution to determine what is the established government in a State, and in its own nature and by the highest judicial authority binding on all other departments of the Government. . . .

A more studied outrage on the legislative authority of the people has never been perpetrated.

Congress passed a bill; the President refused to approve it, and then by proclamation puts as much of it in force as he sees fit, and proposes to execute those parts by officers unknown to the laws of the United States and not subject to the confirmation of the Senate!

The bill directed the appointment of Provisional Governors by and with the advice and consent of the Senate.

The President, after defeating the law, proposes to appoint without law, and without the advice and consent of the Senate, *Military* Governors for the rebel States!

He has already exercised this dictatorial usurpation in Louisiana, and he defeated the bill to prevent its limitation. . . .

The President has greatly presumed on the forbearance which the supporters of his Administration have so long practiced, in view of the arduous conflict in which we are engaged, and the reckless ferocity of our political opponents.

But he must understand that our support is of a cause and not of a man; that the authority of Congress is paramount and must be respected; that the whole body of the Union men of Congress will not submit to be impeached by him of rash and unconstitutional legislation; and if he wishes our support, he must confine himself to his executive duties—to obey and execute, not make the laws—to suppress by arms armed rebellion, and leave political reorganization to Congress.

If the supporters of the Government fail to insist on this, they become responsible for the usurpations which they fail to rebuke, and are justly liable to the indignation of the people whose rights and security, committed to their keeping, they sacrifice.

Let them consider the remedy for these usurpations, and, having found it, fearlessly execute it.

237. THE HAMPTON ROADS CONFERENCE
February 3, 1865

(The Works of Abraham Lincoln, Constitutional ed., Vol. VII, p. 290, 319 ff.)

In January 1865 Francis P. Blair, Sr. was permitted to go to Richmond to discuss terms of peace with some of the leaders of the Confederacy: out of this mission came the Hampton Roads conference. Lincoln, as the instructions of January 31 indicate, first appointed Seward to conduct the unofficial negotiations with the representatives of the Confederacy; later he thought it necessary to attend the conference in person. No record was kept of this conference, but the report of Sec. Seward is apparently reliable. See also the discussion and report of the Conference in, A. H. Stephens, *War Between the States,* Vol. II, ch. xxiii, and app. R. For Blair's part in the negotiations, see W. E. Smith, *The Francis Preston Blair Family in Politics,* Vol. II, ch. xxxvii.

1. INSTRUCTIONS TO SECRETARY SEWARD

Executive Mansion,
Washington, January 31, 1865.

HON. WILLIAM H. SEWARD, Secretary of State:

You will proceed to Fortress Monroe, Virginia, there to meet and informally confer with Messrs. Stephens, Hunter, and Campbell, on the basis of my letter to F. P. Blair, Esq., of January 18, 1865, a copy of which you have. You will make known to them that three things are indispensable—to wit:

1. The restoration of the national authority throughout all the States.

2. No receding by the Executive of the United States on the slavery question from the position assumed thereon in the late annual message to Congress, and in preceding documents.

3. No cessation of hostilities short of an end of the war and the disbanding of all forces hostile to the Government.

You will inform them that all propositions of theirs, not inconsistent with the above, will be considered and passed upon in a spirit of sincere liberality. You will hear all they may choose to say and report it to me. You will not assume to definitely consummate anything.

Yours, etc.,
ABRAHAM LINCOLN.

2. MR. SEWARD TO MR. ADAMS

Department of State,
Washington, February 7, 1865.

.   .   .   .   .   .

On the morning of the 3d, the President, attended by the Secretary, received Messrs. Stephens, Hunter, and Campbell on board the United States steam transport *River Queen* in Hampton Roads. The conference was altogether informal. There was no attendance of secretaries, clerks, or other witnesses. Nothing was written or read. The conversation, although earnest and free, was calm, and courteous, and kind on both sides. The Richmond party approached the discussion rather indirectly, and at no time did they either make categorical demands, or tender formal stipulations or absolute refusals. Nevertheless, during the conference, which lasted four hours, the several points at issue between the Government and the insurgents were distinctly raised, and discussed fully, intelligently, and in an amicable spirit. What the insurgent party seemed chiefly to favor was a postponement of the question of separation, upon which the war is waged, and a mutual direction of efforts of the Government, as well as those of the insurgents, to some extrinsic policy or scheme for a season during which passions might be expected to subside, and the armies be reduced, and trade and intercourse between the people of both sections resumed. It was suggested by them that through such postponement we might now have immediate peace, with some not very certain prospect of an ultimate satisfactory adjustment of political relations between this Government and the States, section, or people now engaged in conflict with it.

This suggestion, though deliberately considered, was nevertheless regarded by the President as one of armistice or truce, and he announced that we can agree to no cessation or suspension of hostilities, except on the basis of the disbandment of the insurgent forces, and the restoration of the national authority throughout all the States in the Union. Collaterally, and in subordination to the proposition which was thus announced, the antislavery policy of the United States was reviewed in all its bearings, and the President announced that he must not be expected to depart from the positions he had heretofore assumed in his proclamation of emancipation and other documents, as these positions were reiterated in his last annual message. It was further declared by the President that the complete restoration of the national authority was an indispensable condition of any assent on our part to whatever form of peace might be proposed. The President assured the other party that, while he must adhere to these positions, he would be prepared, so far as power is lodged with the

Executive, to exercise liberality. His power, however, is limited by the Constitution; and when peace should be made, Congress must necessarily act in regard to appropriations of money and to the admission of representatives from the insurrectionary States. The Richmond party were then informed that Congress had, on the 31st ultimo, adopted by a constitutional majority a joint resolution submitting to the several States the proposition to abolish slavery throughout the Union, and that there is every reason to expect that it will be soon accepted by three fourths of the States, so as to become a part of the national organic law.

The conference came to an end by mutual acquiescence, without producing an agreement of views upon the several matters discussed, or any of them. Nevertheless, it is perhaps of some importance that we have been able to submit our opinions and views directly to prominent insurgents, and to hear them in answer in a courteous and not unfriendly manner.

I am, sir, your obedient servant,

WILLIAM H. SEWARD.

238. LINCOLN'S SECOND INAUGURAL ADDRESS
March 4, 1865

(Richardson, ed. *Messages and Papers,* Vol. VI, p. 276 ff.)

FELLOW-COUNTRYMEN:—At this second appearing to take the oath of the presidential office there is less occasion for an extended address than there was at the first. Then a statement somewhat in detail of a course to be pursued seemed fitting and proper. Now, at the expiration of four years, during which public declarations have been constantly called forth on every point and phase of the great contest which still absorbs the attention and engrosses the energies of the nation, little that is new could be presented. The progress of our arms, upon which all else chiefly depends, is as well known to the public as to myself, and it is, I trust, reasonably satisfactory and encouraging to all. With high hope for the future, no prediction in regard to it is ventured.

On the occasion corresponding to this four years ago all thoughts were anxiously directed to an impending civil war. All dreaded it, all sought to avert it. While the inaugural address was being delivered from this place, devoted altogether to *saving* the Union without war, insurgent agents were in the city seeking to *destroy* it without war—seeking to dissolve the Union and divide effects by negotiation. Both parties deprecated war, but one of them would *make* war rather than let the nation survive, and the other would *accept* war rather than let it perish, and the war came.

One eighth of the whole population was colored slaves, not distributed generally over the Union, but localized in the southern part of it. These slaves constituted a peculiar and powerful interest. All knew that this interest was somehow the cause of the war. To strengthen, perpetuate, and extend this interest was the object for which the insurgents would rend the Union even by war, while the Government claimed no right to do more than to restrict the territorial enlargement of it. Neither party expected for the war the magnitude or the duration which it has already attained. Neither anticipated that the *cause* of the conflict might cease with or even before the conflict itself should cease. Each looked for an easier triumph, and a result less fundamental and astounding. Both read the same Bible and pray to the same God, and each invokes His aid against the other. It may seem strange that any men should dare to ask a just God's assistance in wringing their bread from the sweat of other men's faces, but let us judge not, that we be not judged. The prayers of both could not be answered. That of neither has been answered fully. The Almighty has His own purposes. "Woe unto the world because of offenses; for it must needs be that offenses come, but woe to that man by whom the offense cometh." If we shall suppose that American slavery is one of those offenses which, in the providence of God, must needs come, but which, having continued through His appointed time, He now wills to remove, and that He gives to both North and South this terrible war as the woe due to those by whom the offense came, shall we discern therein any departure from those divine attributes which the believers in a living God always ascribe to Him? Fondly do we hope, fervently do we pray, that this mighty scourge of war may speedily pass away. Yet, if God wills that it continue until all the wealth piled by the bondsman's two hundred and fifty years of unrequited toil shall be sunk, and until every drop of blood drawn with the lash shall be paid by another drawn with the sword, as was said three thousand years ago, so still it must be said, "The judgments of the Lord are true and righteous altogether."

With malice toward none, with charity for all, with firmness in the right as God gives us to see the right, let us strive on to finish the work we are in, to bind up the nation's wounds, to care for him who shall have borne the battle and for his widow and his orphan, to do all which may achieve and cherish a just and lasting peace among ourselves and with all nations.

239. LINCOLN'S TERMS OF PEACE?

Admiral Porter's Report of the City Point Conference
March 27, 1865

(W. T. Sherman, *Memoirs,* Vol. II, p. 328 ff.)

On March 27th Lincoln held a conference with Grant and Sherman at City Point, Va., in which he discussed the terms for a cessation of hostilities. Serious doubts have been cast on the accuracy of Admiral Porter's recollections of this important conference.

The day of General Sherman's arrival at City Point (I think the 27th of March, 1865), I accompanied him and General Grant on board the President's flag-ship, the *Queen,* where the President received us in the upper saloon, no one but ourselves being present.

The President was in an exceedingly pleasant mood, and delighted to meet General Sherman, whom he cordially greeted.

It seems that this was the first time he had met Sherman, to remember him, since the beginning of the war, and did not remember when he had seen him before, until the general reminded him of the circumstances of their first meeting . . .

The conversation soon turned on the events of Sherman's campaign through the South, with every movement of which the President seemed familiar. . . .

The interview between the two generals and the President lasted about an hour and a half, and, as it was a remarkable one, I jotted down what I remembered of the conversation, as I have made a practice of doing during the rebellion, when any thing interesting occurred.

I don't regret having done so, as circumstances afterward occurred (Stanton's ill conduct toward Sherman) which tended to cast odium on General Sherman for allowing such liberal terms to Jos. Johnston.

Could the conversation that occurred on board the *Queen,* between the President and General Sherman, have been known, Sherman would not, and could not, have been censured. Mr. Lincoln, had he lived, would have acquitted the general of any blame, for he was only carrying out the President's wishes.

My opinion is, that Mr. Lincoln came down to City Point with the most liberal views toward the rebels. He felt confident that we would be successful, and was willing that the enemy should capitulate on the most favorable terms.

I don't know what the President would have done had he been left to himself, and had our army been unsuccessful, but he was then wrought up to a high state of excitement. He wanted peace on almost any terms, and there is no knowing what proposals he might have been willing to listen to. His heart was tenderness throughout, and, as long as the rebels laid down their arms, he did not care how it was done. I do not know how far he was influenced by General Grant, but I presume, from their long conferences, that they must have understood each other perfectly, and that the terms given to Lee after his surrender were authorized by Mr. Lincoln. I know that the latter was delighted when he heard that they had been given, and exclaimed, a dozen times, "Good!"

"All right!" "Exactly the thing!" and other similar expressions. Indeed, the President more than once told me what he supposed the terms would be: if Lee and Johnston surrendered, he considered the war ended, and that all the other rebel forces would lay down their arms at once.

· In this he proved to be right. Grant and Sherman were both of the same opinion, and so was every one else who knew any thing about the matter. . . .

After hearing General Sherman's account of his own position, and that of Johnston, at that time, the President expressed fears that the rebel general would escape south again by the railroads, and that General Sherman would have to chase him anew, over the same ground; but the general pronounced this to be impracticable. He remarked: "I have him where he cannot move without breaking up his army, which, once disbanded, can never again be got together; and I have destroyed the Southern railroads, so that they cannot be used again for a long time." General Grant remarked, "What is to prevent their laying the rails again?" "Why," said General Sherman, "my 'bummers' don't do things by halves. Every rail, after having been placed over a hot fire, has been twisted as crooked as a ram's horn, and they never can be used again."

This was the only remark made by General Grant during the interview, as he sat smoking a short distance from the President, intent, no doubt, on his own plans, which were being brought to a successful termination.

The conversation between the President and General Sherman, about the terms of surrender to be allowed Jos. Johnston, continued. Sherman energetically insisted that he could command his own terms, and that Johnston would have to yield to his demands; but the President was very decided about the matter, and insisted that the surrender of Johnston's army must be obtained on any terms.

General Grant was evidently of the same way of thinking, for, although he did not join in the conversation to any extent, yet he made no objections, and I presume had made up his mind to allow the best terms himself.

He was also anxious that Johnston should not be driven into Richmond, to reenforce the rebels there, who, from behind their strong intrenchments, would have given us incalculable trouble.

Sherman, as a subordinate officer, yielded his views to those of the President, and the terms of capitulation between himself and Johnston were exactly in accordance with Mr. Lincoln's wishes. He could not have done any thing which would have pleased the President better.

Mr. Lincoln did, in fact, arrange the (so considered) liberal terms offered General Jos. Johnston, and, whatever may have been General Sherman's private views, I feel sure that he yielded to the wishes of the President in every respect. It was Mr. Lincoln's policy that was carried out, and, had he lived long enough, he would have been but too glad to have acknowledged it. Had Mr. Lincoln lived, Secretary Stanton would have issued no false telegraphic dispatches, in the hope of killing off another general in the regular army, one who by his success had placed himself in the way of his own succession. . . .

D. D. Porter, Vice-Admiral.

(Written by the admiral in 1866, at the United States Naval Academy at Annapolis, Md., and mailed to General Sherman at St. Louis, Mo.)

240. JEFFERSON DAVIS'S LAST MESSAGE TO THE PEOPLE OF THE CONFEDERACY
April 4, 1865

(Richardson, ed. *Messages and Papers of the Confederacy*, Vol. I, p. 568 ff.)

On April 2, the Confederate Government abandoned Richmond and fled to Danville; the following day Richmond fell. President Davis's last appeal to the Confederate people reveals a stubborn determination to continue the war, but in this decision in which he was not supported by Lee, he was overruled by the course of events.

Danville, Va. April 4, 1865.

To the People of the Confederate States of America.

The General in Chief of our Army has found it necessary to make such movements of the troops as to uncover the capital and thus involve the withdrawal of the Government from the city of Richmond.

It would be unwise, even were it possible, to conceal the great moral as well as material injury to our cause that must result from the occupation of Richmond by the enemy. It is equally unwise and unworthy of us, as patriots engaged in a most sacred cause, to allow our energies to falter, our spirits to grow faint, or our efforts to become relaxed under reverses, however calamitous. While it has been to us a source of national pride that for four years of unequaled warfare we have been able, in close proximity to the center of the enemy's power, to maintain the seat of our chosen Government free from the pollution of his presence; while the memories of the heroic dead who have freely given their lives to its defense must ever remain enshrined in our hearts; while the preservation of the capital, which is usually regarded as the evidence to mankind of separate national existence, was an object very dear to us, it is also true, and should not be forgotten, that the loss which we have suffered is not without compensation. For many months the largest and finest army of the Confederacy, under the command of a leader whose presence inspires equal confidence in the troops and the people, has been greatly trammeled by the necessity of keeping constant watch over the approaches to the capital, and has thus been forced to forego more than one opportunity for promising enterprise. The hopes and confidence of the enemy have been constantly excited by the belief that their possession of Richmond would be the signal for our submission to their rule, and relieve them from the burden of war, as their failing resources admonish them it must be abandoned if not speedily brought to a successful close. It is for us, my countrymen, to show by our bearing under reverses how wretched has been the self-deception of those who have believed us less able to endure misfortune with fortitude than to encounter danger with courage. We have now entered upon a new phase of a struggle the memory of which is to endure for all ages and to shed an increasing luster upon our country.

Relieved from the necessity of guarding cities and particular points, important but not vital to our defense, with an army free to move from point to point and strike in detail the detachments and garrisons of the enemy, operating on the interior of our own country, where supplies are more accessible, and where the foe will be far removed from his own base and cut off from all succor in case of reverse, nothing is now needed to render our triumph certain but the exhibition of our own unquenchable resolve. Let us but will it, and we are free; and who, in the light of the past, dare doubt your purpose in the future?

Animated by the confidence in your spirit and fortitude, which never yet has failed me, I announce to you, fellow-countrymen, that it is my purpose to maintain your cause with my whole heart and soul; that I will never consent to abandon to the enemy one foot of the soil of any one of the States of the Confederacy. . . . If by stress of numbers we should ever be compelled to a temporary withdrawal from her limits, or those of any other border State, again and again will we return, until the baffled and exhausted enemy shall abandon in despair his endless and impossible task of making slaves of a people resolved to be free.

Let us not, then, despond, my countrymen; but, relying on the never-failing mercies and protecting care of our God, let us meet the foe with fresh defiance, with unconquered and unconquerable hearts.

Jeff'n Davis.

241. THE BURNING OF COLUMBIA, S. C.

Report of General Sherman on the Campaign of the Carolinas
April 4, 1865

(F. Moore, ed. *The Rebellion Record,* Vol. XI, p. 377)

On the night of February 17, 1865, Columbia, South Carolina, was largely destroyed by fire. It was charged at the time and is still firmly believed in some sections of the country that Sherman deliberately destroyed the city. Sherman himself placed the responsibility for the burning of the city upon Wade Hampton and the weather; subsequently he admitted that a good deal of the account given below was imaginative. General Logan in his report blames the burning upon unnamed parties who spread fire. The problem of responsibility is apparently an insoluble one, but see J. D. Hill, "The Burning of Columbia Reconsidered," *South Atlantic Quarterly,* Vol. XXV, p. 269 ff., and J. F. Rhodes, *History,* Vol. V, p. 90 ff. There is an interesting contemporary account, with some documents, in G. W. Nichols, *The Story of the Great March.*

. . . In anticipation of the occupation of the city, I had made written orders to General Howard touching the conduct of the troops. These were to destroy, absolutely, all arsenals and public property not needed for our own use, as well as all railroads, depots, and machinery useful in war to an enemy, but to spare all dwellings, colleges, schools, asylums, and harmless private property. I was the first to cross the pontoon bridge, and in company with General Howard rode into the city. The day was clear, but a perfect tempest of wind was raging. The brigade of Colonel Stone was already in the city, and was properly posted. Citizens and soldiers were on the streets, and general good order prevailed. General Wade Hampton, who commanded the Confederate rear-guard of cavalry, had, in anticipation of our capture of Columbia, ordered that all cotton, public and private, should be moved into the streets and fired, to prevent our making use of it. Bales were piled everywhere, the rope and bagging cut, and tufts of cotton were blown about in the wind, lodged in the trees and against houses, so as to resemble a snow storm. Some of these piles of cotton were burning, especially one in the very heart of the city, near the Court-house, but the fire was partially subdued by the labor of our soldiers.

During the day the Fifteenth corps passed through Columbia and out on the Camden road. The Seventeenth did not enter the town at all; and, as I have before stated, the left wing and cavalry did not come within two miles of the town.

Before one single public building had been fired by order, the smoldering fires, set by Hampton's order, were rekindled by the wind, and communicated to the buildings around. About dark they began to spread, and got beyond the control of the brigade on duty within the city. The whole of Wood's division was brought in, but it was found impossible to check the flames, which, by midnight, had become unmanageable, and raged until about four A. M., when the wind subsiding, they were got under control. I was up nearly all night, and saw Generals Howard, Logan, Woods, and others, laboring to save houses and protect families thus suddenly deprived of shelter, and of bedding and wearing apparel. I disclaim on the part of my army any agency in this fire, but on the contrary, claim that we saved what of Columbia remains unconsumed. And without hesitation, I charge General Wade Hampton with having burned his own city of Columbia, not with a malicious intent, or as the manifestations of a silly "Roman stoicism," but from folly and want of sense, in filling it with lint, cotton, and tinder. Our officers and men on duty worked well to extinguish the flames; but others not on duty, including the officers who had long been imprisoned there, rescued by us, may have assisted in spreading the fire after it had once begun, and may have indulged in unconcealed joy to see the ruin of the capital of South Carolina. During the eighteenth and nineteenth, the arsenal, railroad depots, machine shops, foundries, and other buildings were properly destroyed by detailed working parties, and the railroad track torn up and destroyed down to Kingsville and the Wateree bridge, and up in the direction of Winnsboro. . . .

242. LEE'S FAREWELL TO HIS ARMY
April 10, 1865

(Recollections and Letters of General Lee, by R. E. Lee, p. 153-4)

After the fall of Richmond, Lee pushed west towards Danville, where large supplies had been concentrated. He hoped that he might be able to effect a juncture with Johnston's army, then in North Carolina. Sheridan cut off Lee's retreat to the west, however, and on April 9 Lee surrendered his army to Grant, at Appomattox Court House. On Lee after the War, see, *Recollections and Letters of General Lee,* by his Son, R. E. Lee, p. 162 ff.; R. Winston, *Robert E. Lee;* F. L. Riley, *General Robert E. Lee After Appomattox.*

Headquarters, Army of Northern Virginia,
April 10, 1865.

After four years of arduous service, marked by unsurpassed courage and fortitude, the Army of Northern Virginia has been compelled to yield to overwhelming numbers and resources. I need not tell the survivors of so many hard-fought battles, who have remained steadfast to the last, that I have consented to this result from no distrust of them; but, feeling that valour and devotion could accomplish nothing that could compensate for the loss that would have attended the continuation of the contest, I have determined to avoid the useless sacrifice of those whose past services have endeared them to their countrymen. By the terms of the agreement, officers and men can return to their homes and remain there until exchanged. You will take with you the satisfaction that proceeds from the consciousness of duty faithfully performed; and I earnestly pray that a merciful God will extend to you His blessing and protection. With an increasing admiration of your constancy and devotion to your country, and a grateful remembrance of your kind and generous consideration of myself, I bid you an affectionate farewell.

R. E. Lee, General.

243. SURRENDER OF GENERAL JOHNSTON

Memorandum made between General Joseph E. Johnston and Major-General William T. Sherman
April 18, 1865

(Memoirs of General W. T. Sherman, Vol. II, p. 356-7)

The failure of Lee to escape from Grant and Sheridan, and the surrender of the Army of Northern Virginia, April 9, left Johnston's army the only large Confederate force still in the field. The terms of Johnston's surrender to Sherman were on the same general lines as those given by Grant to Lee and were apparently outlined by Lincoln, Doc. No. 239. These terms, however, were disapproved by Secretary Stanton, and Sherman was ordered to advance upon Johnston. Johnston agreed to new terms April 26. Stanton's disapproval of Sherman's course led to a violent altercation between the two men, in which the Secretary of War appeared in a very unhappy light. Stanton wrote of Sherman's terms, "I am distressed beyond measure at the terms. . . . They are inadmissible. There should now be literally no terms granted. We should not only brand the leading rebels with infamy, but the whole rebellion should bear the badge of the penitentiary".

(Gorham, G. C., *Life and Public Services of E. M. Stanton,* Vol. II, p. 195). Sherman's account of the incident can be found in his *Memoirs,* Vol. II, ch. xxiii. His testimony before the Committee on the War is given at length in the appendix to Nichols, *The Story of the Great March.*

Memorandum, or Basis of Agreement, made this 18th day of April, A.D. 1865, near Durham's Station, in the State of North Carolina, by and between General Joseph E. Johnston, commanding the Confederate Army, and Major-General William T. Sherman, commanding the Army of the United States in North Carolina, both present:

1. The contending armies now in the field to maintain the *status quo* until notice is

given by the commanding general of any one to its opponent, and reasonable time—say, forty-eight hours—allowed.

2. The Confederate armies now in existence to be disbanded and conducted to their several State capitals, there to deposit their arms and public property in the State Arsenal; and each officer and man to execute and file an agreement to cease from acts of war, and to abide the action of the State and Federal authority. The number of arms and munitions of war to be reported to the Chief of Ordnance at Washington City, subject to the future action of the Congress of the United States, and, in the meantime, to be used solely to maintain peace and order within the borders of the States respectively.

3. The recognition, by the Executive of the United States, of the several State governments, on their officers and Legislatures taking the oaths prescribed by the Constitution of the United States, and, where conflicting State governments have resulted from the war, the legitimacy of all shall be submitted to the Supreme Court of the United States.

4. The reestablishment of all the Federal Courts in the several States, with powers as defined by the Constitution of the United States and of the States respectively.

5. The people and inhabitants of all the States to be guaranteed, so far as the Executive can, their political rights and franchises, as well as their rights of person and property, as defined by the Constitution of the United States and of the States respectively.

6. The Executive authority of the Government of the United States not to disturb any of the people by reason of the late war, so long as they live in peace and quiet, abstain from acts of armed hostility, and obey the laws in existence at the place of their residence.

7. In general terms—the war to cease; a general amnesty, so far as the Executive of the United States can command, on condition of the disbandment of the Confederate armies, the distribution of the arms, and the resumption of peaceful pursuits by the officers and men hitherto composing said armies.

244. LINCOLN'S LAST PUBLIC ADDRESS
April 11, 1865

(*Writings of Abraham Lincoln,* Constitutional ed., Vol. VII, p. 362 ff.)

On the evening of April 11, a crowd celebrating the end of the war called at the Executive mansion. Lincoln addressed them from the balcony on the question of reconciliation and reconstruction. At the Cabinet meeting of Friday, April 14, Lincoln again spoke of the problem of reconstruction in terms similar to those of the speech of April 11. "If we were wise and discreet," he said, according to Sec. Welles, "we should re-animate the states and get their governments in successful operation, with order prevailing and the Union reëstablished, before Congress came together in December. . . . There were men in Congress who, if their motives were good were nevertheless impracticable, and who possessed feelings of hate and vindictiveness in which he did not sympathize and could not participate. He hoped there would be no persecution, no bloody work, after the war was over. None need expect he would take any part in hanging or killing those men, even the worst of them."

FELLOW-CITIZENS:—We meet this evening not in sorrow, but in gladness of heart. The evacuation of Petersburg and Richmond, and the surrender of the principal insurgent army, give hope of a righteous and speedy peace, whose joyous expression cannot be restrained. In the midst of this, however, He from whom all blessings flow must not be forgotten.

A call for a national thanksgiving is being prepared, and will be duly promulgated. . . . By these recent successes, the reinauguration of the national authority—reconstruction—which has had a large share of thought from the first, is pressed much more closely upon our attention. It is fraught with great difficulty. Unlike a case of war between independent nations, *there is no authorized organ for us to treat with*—no one man has authority to give up the rebellion for any other man. We simply must begin with and mould from disorganized and discordant elements. Nor is it a small additional embarrassment that we, the loyal people, differ among ourselves as to the mode, manner, and measure of reconstruction. As a general rule, I abstain from reading the reports of attacks upon myself, wishing not to be provoked by that to which I cannot properly offer an answer. In spite of this precaution, however, it comes to my knowledge that I am much censured for some supposed agency in setting up and seeking to sustain the new State government of Louisiana. In this I have done just so much and no more than the public knows. In the Annual Message of December, 1863, and the accompanying proclamation, I presented a plan of reconstruction, as the phrase goes, which I promised, if adopted by any State, would be acceptable to and sustained by the Executive Government of the nation. I distinctly stated that this was not the only plan which might possibly be acceptable, and I also distinctly protested that the Executive claimed no right to say when or whether members should be admitted to seats in Congress from such States. This plan was in advance submitted to the then Cabinet, and approved by every member of it. One of them suggested that I should then and in that connection apply the Emancipation Proclamation to the theretofore excepted parts of Virginia and Louisiana; that I should drop the suggestion about apprenticeship for freed people, and that I should omit the protest against my own power in regard to the admission of members of Congress. But even he approved every part and parcel of the plan which has since been employed or touched by the action of Louisiana. The new constitution of Louisiana, declaring emancipation for the whole State, practically applies the proclamation to the part previously excepted. It does not adopt apprenticeship for freed people, and is silent, as it could not well be otherwise, about the admission of members to Congress. So that, as it applied to Louisiana, every member of the Cabinet fully approved the plan. The message went to Congress, and I received many commendations of the plan, written and verbal, and not a single objection to it from any professed emancipationist came to my knowledge until after the news reached Washington that the people of Louisiana had begun to move in accordance with it. From about July, 1862, I had corresponded with different persons supposed to be interested

in seeking a reconstruction of a State government for Louisiana. When the message of 1863, with the plan before mentioned, reached New Orleans, General Banks wrote me that he was confident that the people, with his military co-operation, would reconstruct substantially on that plan. I wrote to him and some of them to try it. They tried it, and the result is known. Such has been my only agency in setting up the Louisiana government. As to sustaining it my promise is out, as before stated. But, as bad promises are better broken than kept, I shall treat this as a bad promise and break it, whenever I shall be convinced that keeping it is adverse to the public interest; but I have not yet been so convinced. I have been shown a letter on this subject, supposed to be an able one, in which the writer expresses regret that my mind has not seemed to be definitely fixed upon the question whether the seceded States, so called, are in the Union or out of it. It would perhaps add astonishment to his regret were he to learn that since I have found professed Union men endeavoring to answer that question, I have purposely forborne any public expression upon it. As appears to me, that question has not been nor yet is a practically material one, and that any discussion of it, while it thus remains practically immaterial, could have no effect other than the mischievous one of dividing our friends. As yet, whatever it may become, that question is bad as the basis of a controversy, and good for nothing at all—a merely pernicious abstraction. We all agree that the seceded States, so called, are out of their proper practical relation with the Union, and that the sole object of the Government, civil and military, in regard to those States, is to again get them into their proper practical relation. I believe that it is not only possible, but in fact easier, to do this without deciding or even considering whether those States have ever been out of the Union, than with it. Finding themselves safely at home, it would be utterly immaterial whether they had been abroad. Let us all join in doing the acts necessary to restore the proper practical relations between these States and the Union, and each forever after innocently indulge his own opinion whether, in doing the acts he brought the States from without into the Union, or only gave them proper assistance, they never having been out of it. The amount of constituency, so to speak, on which the Louisiana government rests, would be more satisfactory to all if it contained fifty thousand, or thirty thousand, or even twenty thousand, instead of twelve thousand, as it does. It is also unsatisfactory to some that the elective franchise is not given to the colored man. I would myself prefer that it were now conferred on the very intelligent, and on those who serve our cause as soldiers. Still, the question is not whether the Louisiana government, as it stands, is quite all that is desirable. The question is, Will it be wiser to take it as it is and help to improve it, or to reject and disperse? Can Louisiana be brought into proper practical relation with the Union sooner by sustaining or by discarding her new State government? Some twelve thousand voters in the heretofore Slave State of Louisiana have sworn allegiance to the Union, assumed to be the rightful political power of the State, held elections, organized a State government, adopted a Free State constitution, giving the benefit of public schools equally to black and white, and empowering the Legislature to confer the elective franchise upon the colored man. This Legislature has already voted to ratify the Constitutional Amendment recently passed by Congress, abolishing slavery throughout the nation. These twelve thousand persons are thus fully committed to the Union and to perpetuate freedom in the State—committed to the very things, and nearly all things, the nation wants—and they ask the nation's recognition and its assistance to make good this committal. Now, if we reject and spurn them, we do our utmost to disorganize and disperse them. We, in fact, say to the white man: You are worthless or worse; we will neither help you nor be helped by you. To the blacks we say: This cup of liberty which these, your old masters, held to your lips, we will dash from you, and leave you to the chances of gathering the spilled and scattered contents in some vague and undefined when, where, and how. If this course, discouraging and paralyzing both white and black, has any tendency to bring Louisiana into proper practical relations with the Union, I have so far been unable to perceive it. If, on the con-

trary, we recognize and sustain the new government of Louisiana, the converse of all this is made true. We encourage the hearts and nerve the arms of twelve thousand to adhere to their work, and argue for it, and proselyte for it, and fight for it, and feed it, and grow it, and ripen it to a complete success. The colored man, too, in seeing all united for him, is inspired with vigilance, and energy, and daring to the same end. Grant that he desires the elective franchise, will he not attain it sooner by saving the already advanced steps towards it, than by running backward over them? Concede that the new government of Louisiana is only to what it should be as the egg is to the fowl, we shall sooner have the fowl by hatching the egg than by smashing it. Again, if we reject Louisiana, we also reject one vote in favor of the proposed amendment to the National Constitution. To meet this proposition, it has been argued that no more than three fourths of those States which have not attempted secession are necessary to validly ratify the amendment. I do not commit myself against this, further than to say that such a ratification would be questionable, and sure to be persistently questioned, while a ratification by three fourths of all the States would be unquestioned and unquestionable. I repeat the question, Can Louisiana be brought into proper practical relation with the Union sooner by sustaining or by discarding her new State government? What has been said of Louisiana will apply to other States. And yet so great peculiarities pertain to each State, and such important and sudden changes occur in the same State, and withal so new and unprecedented is the whole case, that no exclusive and inflexible plan can safely be prescribed as to details and collaterals. Such exclusive and inflexible plan would surely become a new entanglement. Important principles may and must be inflexible. In the present situation as the phrase goes, it may be my duty to make some new announcement to the people of the South. I am considering, and shall not fail to act, when satisfied that action will be proper.

245. THE FREEDMEN'S BUREAU
March 3, 1865

(U. S. Statutes at Large, Vol. XIII, p. 507 ff.)

The Freedmen's Bureau was established to care for the freedmen and for the abandoned lands in the South. It was to continue for one year after the close of the war. An act of February 19, 1866, extending the life of the Freedmen's Bureau was vetoed by President Johnson. (Doc. No. 251.) July 16, 1866, a supplementary Freedmen's Bureau Act, enlarging the scope of the Bureau, was passed over the President's veto. General O. O. Howard was placed in charge of the Bureau. See, P. S. Peirce, *The Freedmen's Bureau;* L. Webster, *The Freedmen's Bureau in South Carolina;* and the documents in W. L. Fleming, *Documentary History of Reconstruction,* Vol. I.

An Act to establish a Bureau for the Relief of Freedmen and Refugees.

Be it enacted, That there is hereby established in the War Department, to continue during the present war of rebellion, and for one year thereafter, a bureau of refugees, freedmen, and abandoned lands, to which shall be committed, as hereinafter provided, the supervision and management of all abandoned lands, and the control of all subjects relating to refugees and freedmen from rebel states, or from any district of country within the territory embraced in the operations of the army, under such rules and regulations as may be prescribed by the head of the bureau and approved by the President. The said bureau shall be under the management and control of a commissioner to be appointed by the President, by and with the advice and consent of the Senate. . . .

SEC. 2. That the Secretary of War may direct such issues of provisions, clothing, and fuel, as he may deem needful for the immediate and temporary shelter and supply of destitute and suffering refugees and freedmen and their wives and children, under such rules and regulations as he may direct.

SEC. 3. That the President may, by and with the advice and consent of the Senate, appoint an assistant commissioner for each of the states declared to be in insurrection, not exceeding ten in number, who shall, under the direction of the commissioner, aid in the execution of the provisions of this act; . . . And any military officer may be detailed and assigned to duty under this act without increase of pay or allowances. . . .

SEC. 4. That the commissioner, under the direction of the President, shall have authority to set apart, for the use of loyal refugees and freedmen, such tracts of land within the insurrectionary states as shall have been abandoned, or to which the United States shall have acquired title by confiscation or sale, or otherwise, and to every male citizen, whether refugee or freedman, as aforesaid, there shall be assigned not more than forty acres of such land, and the person to whom it was so assigned shall be protected in the use and enjoyment of the land for the term of three years at an annual rent not exceeding six per centum upon the value of such land, as it was appraised by the state authorities in the year eighteen hundred and sixty, for the purpose of taxation, and in case no such appraisal can be found, then the rental shall be based upon the estimated value of the land in said year, to be ascertained in such manner as the commissioner may by regulation prescribe. At the end of said term, or at any time during said term, the occupants of any parcels so assigned may purchase the land and receive such title thereto as the United States can convey, upon paying therefor the value of the land, as ascertained and fixed for the purpose of determining the annual rent aforesaid. . . .

246. BLACK CODE OF MISSISSIPPI
1865
(Laws of Mississippi, 1865, p. 82 ff.)

The so-called Black Codes represented the Southern effort to solve the problem of the freedmen. The codes varied in harshness: those of Georgia, for example, were notably lenient; those of Louisiana and Mississippi severe. "The legislation," says Professor Fleming, "showed the combined influence of the old laws for free negroes, the vagrancy laws of the North and South for whites, the customs of slavery times, the British West Indies legislation for ex-slaves, and the regulations of the U. S. War and Treasury Departments and of the Freedmen's Bureau" *(Sequel of Appomattox,* p. 94). The laws below regulate civil rights, apprenticeship, vagrancy, and penal crimes. Most of these black laws were suspended by the military governors of the reconstructed states, and the Civil Rights Act and the Fourteenth Amendment were designed to protect the negro in his civil and legal rights. On the Black Codes, see, W. L. Fleming, *Sequel to Appomattox,* ch. iv; E. P. Oberholtzer, *History of the United States Since the Civil War,* Vol. I; and the numerous monographs on reconstruction in the States, such as those of Fleming, Garner, Reynolds, Hamilton, Ramsdell, Fertig, etc. There is a summary of the Black Codes in E. McPherson, *Political History of Reconstruction,* p. 29 ff.

1. CIVIL RIGHTS OF FREEDMEN IN MISSISSIPPI

Sec.1. *Be it enacted,* . . . That all freedmen, free negroes, and mulattoes may sue and be sued, implead and be impleaded, in all the courts of law and equity of this State, and may acquire personal property, and choses in action, by descent or purchase, and may dispose of the same in the same manner and to the same extent that white persons may: *Provided,* That the provisions of this section shall not be so construed as to allow any freedman, free negro, or mulatto to rent or lease any lands or tenements except in incorporated cities or towns, in which places the corporate authorities shall control the same. . . .

Sec. 3. . . . All freedmen, free negroes, or mulattoes who do now and have herebefore lived and cohabited together as husband and wife shall be taken and held in law as legally married, and the issue shall be taken and held as legitimate for all purposes; that it shall not be lawful for any freedman, free negro, or mulatto to intermarry with any white person; nor for any white person to intermarry with any freedman, free negro, or mulatto; and any person who shall so intermarry, shall be deemed guilty of felony, and on conviction thereof shall be confined in the State penitentiary for life; and those shall be deemed freedmen, free negroes, and mulattoes who are of pure negro blood, and those descended from a negro to the third generation, inclusive, though one ancestor in each generation may have been a white person.

Sec. 4. . . . In addition to cases in which freedmen, free negroes, and mulattoes are now by law competent witnesses, freedmen, free negroes, or mulattoes shall be competent in civil cases, when a party or parties to the suit, either plaintiff or plaintiffs, defendant or defendants, and a white person or white persons, is or are the opposing party or parties, plaintiff or plaintiffs, defendant or defendants. They shall also be competent witnesses in all criminal prosecutions where the crime charged is alleged to have been committed by a white person upon or against the person or property of a freedman, free negro, or mulatto: *Provided,* that in all cases said witnesses shall be examined in open court, on the stand; except, however, they may be examined before the grand jury, and shall in all cases be subject to the rules and tests of the common law as to competency and credibility. . . .

Sec. 6. . . . All contracts for labor made with freedmen, free negroes, and mulattoes for a longer period than one month shall be in writing, and in duplicate, attested and read to said freedman, free negro, or mulatto by a beat, city or county officer, or two disinterested white persons of the county in which the labor is to be performed, of which each party shall have one; and said contracts shall be taken and held as entire contracts, and if the laborer shall quit the service of the employer before the expiration of his term of service, without good cause, he shall forfeit his wages for that year up to the time of quitting.

Sec. 7. . . . Every civil officer shall, and every person may, arrest and carry back to his or her legal employer any freedman, free negro, or mulatto who shall have quit the service of his or her employer before the expiration of his or her term of service without good cause; and said officer and person shall be entitled to receive for arresting and carrying back every deserting employe aforesaid the sum of five dollars, and ten cents per mile from the place of arrest to the place of delivery; and the same shall be paid by the employer, and held as a set-off for so much against the wages of said deserting employe: *Provided,* that said arrested party, after being so returned, may appeal to the justice of the peace or member of the board of police of the county, who, on notice to the alleged employer, shall try summarily whether said appellant is legally employed by the alleged employer, and has good cause to quit said employer; either party shall have the right of appeal to the county court, pending which the alleged deserter shall be remanded to the alleged employer or otherwise disposed of, as shall be right and just; and the decision of the county court shall be final. . . .

Sec. 9. . . . If any person shall persuade or attempt to persuade, entice, or cause any freedman, free negro, or mulatto to desert from the legal employment of any person before the expiration of his or her term of service, or shall knowingly employ any such deserting freedman, free negro, or mulatto, or shall knowingly give or sell to any such deserting freedman, free negro, or mulatto, any food, raiment, or other thing, he or she shall be guilty of a misdemeanor, and, upon conviction, shall be fined not less than twenty-five dollars and not more than two

hundred dollars and the costs; and if said fine and costs shall not be immediately paid, the court shall sentence said convict to not exceeding two months' imprisonment in the county jail, and he or she shall moreover be liable to the party injured in damages: *Provided,* if any person shall, or shall attempt to, persuade, entice, or cause any freedman, free negro, or mulatto to desert from any legal employment of any person, with the view to employ said freedman, free negro, or mulatto without the limits of this State, such person, on conviction, shall be fined not less than fifty dollars, and not more than five hundred dollars and costs; and if said fine and costs shall not be immediately paid, the court shall sentence said convict to not exceeding six months imprisonment in the county jail. . . .

2. MISSISSIPPI APPRENTICE LAW
(*Laws of Mississippi,* 1865, p. 86)

Sec. 1. . . . It shall be the duty of all sheriffs, justices of the peace, and other civil officers of the several counties in this State, to report to the probate courts of their respective counties semi-annually, at the January and July terms of said courts, all freedmen, free negroes, and mulattoes, under the age of eighteen, in their respective counties, beats or districts, who are orphans, or whose parent or parents have not the means or who refuse to provide for and support said minors; and thereupon it shall be the duty of said probate court to order the clerk of said court to apprentice said minors to some competent and suitable person, on such terms as the court may direct, having a particular care to the interest of said minor: *Provided,* that the former owner of said minors shall have the preference when, in the opinion of the court, he or she shall be a suitable person for that purpose.

Sec. 2. . . . The said court shall be fully satisfied that the person or persons to whom said minor shall be apprenticed shall be a suitable person to have the charge and care of said minor, and fully to protect the interest of said minor. The said court shall require the said master or mistress to execute bond and security, payable to the State of Mississippi, conditioned that he or she shall furnish said minor with sufficient food and clothing; to treat said minor humanely;

furnish medical attention in case of sickness; teach, or cause to be taught, him or her to read and write, if under fifteen years old, and will conform to any law that may be hereafter passed for the regulation of the duties and relation of master and apprentice. . . .

Sec. 3. . . . In the management and control of said apprentice, said master or mistress shall have the power to inflict such moderate corporal chastisement as a father or guardian is allowed to inflict on his or her child or ward at common law: *Provided,* that in no case shall cruel or inhuman punishment be inflicted.

Sec. 4. . . . If any apprentice shall leave the employment of his or her master or mistress, without his or her consent, said master or mistress may pursue and recapture said apprentice, and bring him or her before any justice of the peace of the county, whose duty it shall be to remand said apprentice to the service of his or her master or mistress; and in the event of a refusal on the part of said apprentice so to return, then said justice shall commit said apprentice to the jail of said county, on failure to give bond, to the next term of the county court; and it shall be the duty of said court at the first term thereafter to investigate said case, and if the court shall be of opinion that said apprentice left the employment of his or her master or mistress without good cause, to order him or her to be punished, as provided for the punishment of hired freedmen, as may be from time to time provided for by law for desertion, until he or she shall agree to return to the service of his or her master or mistress: . . . if the court shall believe that said apprentice had good cause to quit his said master or mistress, the court shall discharge said apprentice from said indenture, and also enter a judgment against the master or mistress for not more than one hundred dollars, for the use and benefit of said apprentice.. . . .

3. MISSISSIPPI VAGRANT LAW
(*Laws of Mississippi,* 1865, p. 90)

Sec. 1. *Be it enacted,* etc., . . . That all rogues and vagabonds, idle and dissipated persons, beggars, jugglers, or persons practicing unlawful games or plays, runaways, common drunkards, common night-walkers, pilferers, lewd, wanton, or lascivious persons, in speech or behavior, common railers and brawlers, persons who neglect their calling or employment, misspend what they earn, or do not provide for the support of themselves or their families, or dependents, and all other idle and disorderly persons, including all who neglect all lawful business, habitually misspend their time by frequenting houses of ill-fame, gaming-houses, or tippling shops, shall be deemed and considered vagrants, under the provisions of this act, and upon conviction thereof shall be fined not exceeding one hundred dollars, with all accruing costs, and be imprisoned at the discretion of the court, not exceeding ten days.

Sec. 2. . . . All freedmen, free negroes and mulattoes in this State, over the age of eighteen years, found on the second Monday in January, 1866, or thereafter, with no lawful employment or business, or found unlawfully assembling themselves together, either in the day or night time, and all white persons so assembling themselves with freedmen, free negroes or mulattoes, or usually associating with freedmen, free negroes or mulattoes, on terms of equality, or living in adultery or fornication with a freed woman, free negro or mulatto, shall be deemed vagrants, and on conviction thereof shall be fined in a sum not exceeding, in the case of a freedman, free negro or mulatto, fifty dollars, and a white man two hundred dollars, and imprisoned at the discretion of the court, the free negro not exceeding ten days, and the white man not exceeding six months. . . .

Sec. 7. . . . If any freedman, free negro, or mulatto shall fail or refuse to pay any tax levied according to the provisions of the sixth section of this act, it shall be *prima facie* evidence of vagrancy, and it shall be the duty of the sheriff to arrest such freedman, free negro, or mulatto or such person refusing or neglecting to pay such tax, and proceed at once to hire for the shortest time such delinquent tax-payer to any one who will pay the said tax, with accruing costs, giving preference to the employer, if there be one. . . .

4. PENAL LAWS OF MISSISSIPPI
(*Laws of Mississippi, 1865,* p. 165.)

Sec.1. *Be it enacted,* . . . That no freedman, free negro or mulatto, not in the military service of the United States government, and not licensed so to do by the board of police of his or her county, shall keep or carry fire-arms of any kind, or any ammunition, dirk or bowie knife, and on conviction thereof in the county court shall be punished by fine, not exceeding ten dollars, and pay the costs of such proceedings, and all such arms or ammunition shall be forfeited to the informer; and it shall be the duty of every civil and military officer to arrest any freedman, free negro, or mulatto found with any such arms or ammunition, and cause him or her to be committed to trial in default of bail.

2. . . . Any freedman, free negro, or mulatto committing riots, routs, affrays, trespasses, malicious mischief, cruel treatment to animals, seditious speeches, insulting gestures, language, or acts, or assaults on any person, disturbance of the peace, exercising the function of a minister of the Gospel without a license from some regularly organized church, vending spirituous or intoxicating liquors, or committing any other misdemeanor, the punishment of which is not specifically provided for by law, shall, upon conviction thereof in the county court, be fined not less than ten dollars, and not more than one hundred dollars, and may be imprisoned at the discretion of the court, not exceeding thirty days.

Sec. 3. . . . If any white person shall sell, lend, or give to any freedman, free negro, or mulatto any fire-arms, dirk or bowie knife, or ammunition, or any spirituous or intoxicating liquors, such person or persons so offending, upon conviction thereof in the county court of his or her county, shall be fined not exceeding fifty dollars, and may be imprisoned, at the discretion of the court, not exceeding thirty days. . . .

Sec. 5. . . . If any freedman, free negro, or mulatto, convicted of any of the misdemeanors provided against in this act, shall fail or refuse for the space of five days, after conviction, to pay the fine and costs imposed, such person shall be hired out by the sheriff or other officer, at public outcry, to any white person who will pay said fine and all costs, and take said convict for the shortest time.

247. BLACK CODE OF LOUISIANA
1865

(Acts of the General Assembly of Louisiana Regulating Labor. Extra Session, 1865, p. 3 ff.)

On the Black Codes see Doc. No. 246 and references. See also, E. Lonn, *Reconstruction in Louisiana;* J. R. Flicken, *History of Reconstruction in Louisiana;* H. C. Warmoth, *War, Politics and Reconstruction: Stormy Days in Louisiana.*

1. AN ACT TO PROVIDE FOR AND REGULATE LABOR CONTRACTS FOR AGRICULTURAL PURSUITS.

Sec. 1. Be it enacted by the Senate and House of Representatives of the State of Louisiana in general assembly convened, That all persons employed as laborers in agricultural pursuits shall be required, during the first ten days of the month of January of each year, to make contracts for labor for the then ensuing year, or for the year next ensuing the termination of their present contracts. All contracts for labor for agricultural purposes shall be made in writing, signed by the employer, and shall be made in the presence of a Justice of the Peace and two disinterested witnesses, in whose presence the contract shall be read to the laborer, and when assented to and signed by the latter, shall be considered as binding for the time prescribed. . . .

Sec. 2. Every laborer shall have full and perfect liberty to choose his employer, but, when once chosen, he shall not be allowed to leave his place of employment until the fulfillment of his contract . . . and if they do so leave, without cause or permission, they shall forfeit all wages earned to the time of abandonment. . . .

Sec. 7. All employers failing to comply with their contracts, shall, upon conviction, be fined an amount double that due the laborer . . . to be paid to the laborer; and any inhumanity, cruelty, or neglect of duty on the part of the employer shall be summarily punished by fines . . . to be paid to the injured party. . . .

Sec. 8. Be it further enacted, &c., That in case of sickness of the laborer, wages for the time lost shall be deducted, and where the sickness is feigned for purposes of idleness, and also on refusal to work according to contract, double the amount of wages shall be deducted for the time lost; and also where rations have been furnished; and should the refusal to work continue beyond three days, the offender shall be reported to a Justice of the Peace, and shall be forced to labor on roads, levees, and other public works, without pay, until the offender consents to return to his labor.

Sec. 9. Be it further enacted, &c., That, when in health, the laborer shall work ten hours during the day in summer, and nine hours during the day in winter, unless otherwise stipulated in the labor contract; he shall obey all proper orders of his employer or his agent; take proper care of his work-mules, horses, oxen, stock; also of all agricultural implements; and employers shall have the right to make a reasonable deduction from the laborer's wages for injuries done to animals or agricultural implements committed to his care, or for bad or negligent work. Bad work shall not be allowed. Failing to obey reasonable orders, neglect of duty, and leaving home without permission will be deemed disobedience; impudence, swearing, or indecent language to or in the presence of the employer, his family, or agent, or quarreling and fighting with one another, shall be deemed disobedience. For any disobedience a fine of one dollar shall be imposed on and paid by the offender. For all lost time from work-hours, unless in case of sickness, the laborer shall be fined twenty-five cents per hour. For all absence from home without leave he will be fined at the rate of two dollars per day. Laborers will not be required to labor on the Sabbath unless by special contract. For all thefts of the laborer from the employer of agricultural products, hogs, sheep, poultry, or any other property of the employer, or willful destruction of property or injury, the laborer shall pay the employer double the amount of the value of the property stolen, destroyed, or injured, one-half to be paid to the employer and the other half to be placed in the general fund

provided for in this section. No live stock shall be allowed to laborers without the permission of the employer. Laborers shall not receive visitors during work-hours. All difficulties arising between the employers and laborers, under this section, shall be settled by the former; if not satisfactory to the laborers, an appeal may be had to the nearest Justice of the Peace and two freeholders, citizens, one of said citizens to be selected by the employer and the other by the laborer; and all fines imposed and collected under this section shall be deducted from wages due, and shall be placed in a common fund, to be divided among the other laborers on the plantation, except as provided for above. . . .

Sec. 10. Be it further enacted, &c., That for gross misconduct on the part of the laborer, such as insubordination, habitual laziness, frequent acts of violation of his contract or the laws of the State, he may be dismissed by his employer; nevertheless, the laborer shall have the right to resist his dismissal and to a redress of his wrongs by an appeal to a Justice of the Peace and two freeholders, citizens of the parish, one of the freeholders to be selected by himself and the other by his employer.

2. AN ACT RELATIVE TO APPRENTICES AND INDENTURED SERVANTS

Sec. 1. Be it enacted . . . That it shall be the duty of Sheriffs, Justices of the Peace, and other Civil officers of this State, to report . . . for each and every year, all persons under the age of eighteen years, if females, and twenty-one, if males, who are orphans, or whose parents, . . . have not the means, or who refuse to provide for and maintain said minors; and thereupon it shall be the duty of the Clerk of the District Courts . . . to examine whether the party or parties so reported from time to time, come within the purview and meaning of this Act, and, if so, to apprentice said minor or minors, in manner and form as prescribed by the Civil Code. . . .

Sec. 2. That persons, who have attained the age of majority, . . . may bind themselves to services to be performed in this State, for the term of five years, on such terms as they may stipulate, as domestic servants, and to work on farms, plantations, or in manufacturing establishments, which contracts shall be valid and binding on the parties to the same.

Sec. 3. That in all cases where the age of the minor can not be ascertained by record testimony, the Clerk of the District Courts, Mayor and President of the Police Jury, or Justices of the Peace aforesaid, shall fix the age, according to the best evidence before them. . . .

248. JOHNSON'S AMNESTY PROCLAMATION
May 29, 1865

(Richardson, ed. *Messages and Papers,* Vol. VI, p. 310 ff.)

Johnson's proclamation was similar in most respects to Lincoln's proclamation of December 8, 1863; the most important difference is to be found in section thirteen.

BY THE PRESIDENT OF THE UNITED STATES OF AMERICA.

A PROCLAMATION.

Whereas the President of the United States, on the 8th day of December, A. D. 1863, and on the 26th day of March, A. D. 1864, did, with the object to suppress the existing rebellion, to induce all persons to return to their loyalty, and to restore the authority of the United States, issue proclamations offering amnesty and pardon to certain persons who had, directly or by implication, participated in the said rebellion; and

Whereas many persons who had so engaged in said rebellion have, since the issuance of said proclamations, failed or neglected to take the benefits offered thereby; and

Whereas many persons who have been justly deprived of all claim to amnesty and pardon thereunder by reason of their participation, directly or by implication, in said rebellion and continued hostility to the Government of the United States since the date of said proclamations now desire to apply for and obtain amnesty and pardon.

To the end, therefore, that the authority of the Government of the United States may be restored and that peace, order, and freedom may be established, I, Andrew Johnson, President of the United States, do proclaim and declare that I hereby grant to all persons who have, directly or indirectly, participated in the existing rebellion, except as hereinafter excepted, amnesty and pardon, with restoration of all rights of property, except as to slaves . . . but upon the condition, nevertheless, that every such person shall take and subscribe the following oath (or affirmation) and thenceforward keep and maintain said oath inviolate, and which oath shall be registered for permanent preservation and shall be of the tenor and effect following, to wit:

I, —— ——, do solemnly swear (or affirm), in presence of Almighty God, that I will henceforth faithfully support, protect, and defend the Constitution of the United States and the Union of the States thereunder, and that I will in like manner abide by and faithfully support all laws and proclamations which have been made during the existing rebellion with reference to the emancipation of slaves. So help me God.

The following classes of persons are excepted from the benefits of this proclamation:

First. All who are or shall have been pretended civil or diplomatic officers or otherwise domestic or foreign agents of the pretended Confederate government.

Second. All who left judicial stations under the United States to aid the rebellion.

Third. All who shall have been military or naval officers of said pretended Confederate government above the rank of colonel in the army or lieutenant in the navy.

Fourth. All who left seats in the Congress of the United States to aid the rebellion.

Fifth. All who resigned or tendered resignations of their commissions in the Army or Navy of the United States to evade duty in resisting the rebellion.

Sixth. All who have engaged in any way in treating otherwise than lawfully as prisoners of war persons found in the United States service as officers, soldiers, seamen, or in other capacities.

Seventh. All persons who have been or are absentees from the United States for the purpose of aiding the rebellion.

Eighth. All military and naval officers in the rebel service who were educated by the Government in the Military Academy at West Point or the United States Naval Academy.

Ninth. All persons who held the pretended offices of governors of States in insurrection against the United States.

Tenth. All persons who left their homes within the jurisdiction and protection of the United States and passed beyond the Federal military lines into the pretended Confederate States for the purpose of aiding the rebellion.

Eleventh. All persons who have been engaged in the destruction of the commerce of the United States upon the high seas and all persons who have made raids into the United States from Canada or been engaged in destroying the commerce of the United States upon the lakes and rivers that separate the British Provinces from the United States.

Twelfth. All persons who, at the time when they seek to obtain the benefits hereof by taking the oath herein prescribed, are in military, naval, or civil confinement or custody, or under bonds of the civil, military, or naval authorities or agents of the United States as prisoners of war, or persons detained for offenses of any kind, either before or after conviction.

Thirteenth. All persons who have voluntarily participated in said rebellion and the estimated value of whose taxable property is over $20,000.

Fourteenth. All persons who have taken the oath of amnesty as prescribed in the President's proclamation of December 8, A. D. 1863, or an oath of allegiance to the Government of the United States since the date of said proclamation and who have not thenceforward kept and maintained the same inviolate.

Provided, That special application may be made to the President for pardon by any person belonging to the excepted classes, and such clemency will be liberally extended as may be consistent with the facts of the case and the peace and dignity of the United States.

The Secretary of State will establish rules and regulations for administering and recording the said amnesty oath, so as to insure its benefit to the people and guard the Government against fraud. . . .

249. PRESIDENTIAL RECONSTRUCTION

Proclamation of President Johnson for the Provisional Government of South Carolina

June 30, 1865

(Richardson, ed. *Messages and Papers,* Vol. VI, p. 326 ff.)

Johnson followed, almost *in toto* the reconstruction policy of Lincoln. Under Lincoln provisional governments had been established in four States: Louisiana, Tennessee, Arkansas and Virginia. May 29, 1865, Johnson issued his Amnesty Proclamation, and the same day a proclamation organizing a provisional government for North Carolina. Within the next two months similar proclamations for the other six states were issued. On reconstruction in South Carolina see J. P. Hollis, *Early Reconstruction Period in South Carolina;* J. S. Reynolds, *Reconstruction in South Carolina;* F. P. Simkins and R. H. Woody, *South Carolina during Reconstruction.* For special studies of reconstruction in other States see bibliography in H. K. Beale, *The Critical Year.*

BY THE PRESIDENT OF THE UNITED STATES OF AMERICA.

A PROCLAMATION.

Whereas the fourth section of the fourth article of the Constitution of the United States declares that the United States shall guarantee to every State in the Union a republican form of government and shall protect each of them against invasion and domestic violence; and

Whereas the President of the United States is by the Constitution made Commander in Chief of the Army and Navy, as well as chief civil executive officer of the

United States, and is bound by solemn oath faithfully to execute the office of President of the United States and to take care that the laws be faithfully executed; and

Whereas the rebellion which has been waged by a portion of the people of the United States against the properly constituted authorities of the Government thereof in the most violent and revolting form, but whose organized and armed forces have now been almost entirely overcome, has in its revolutionary progress deprived the people of the State of South Carolina of all civil government; and

Whereas it becomes necessary and proper to carry out and enforce the obligations of the United States to the people of South Carolina in securing them in the enjoyment of a republican form of government:

Now, therefore, in obedience to the high and solemn duties imposed upon me by the Constitution of the United States and for the purpose of enabling the loyal people of said State to organize a State government whereby justice may be established, domestic tranquillity insured, and loyal citizens protected in all their rights of life, liberty, and property, I, Andrew Johnson, President of the United States and Commander in Chief of the Army and Navy of the United States, do hereby appoint Benjamin F. Perry, of South Carolina, provisional governor of the State of South Carolina, whose duty it shall be, at the earliest practicable period, to prescribe such rules and regulations as may be necessary and proper for convening a convention composed of delegates to be chosen by that portion of the people of said State who are loyal to the United States, and no others, for the purpose of altering or amending the constitution thereof, and with authority to exercise within the limits of said State all the powers necessary and proper to enable such loyal people of the State of South Carolina to restore said State to its constitutional relations to the Federal Government and to present such a republican form of State government as will entitle the State to the guaranty of the United States therefor and its people to protection by the United States against invasion, insurrection, and domestic violence: *Provided,* That in any election that may be hereafter held for choosing delegates to any State convention

as aforesaid no person shall be qualified as an elector or shall be eligible as a member of such convention unless he shall have previously taken and subscribed the oath of amnesty as set forth in the President's proclamation of May 29, A. D. 1865, and is a voter qualified as prescribed by the constitution and laws of the State of South Carolina in force immediately before the 17th day of November, A. D. 1860, the date of the so-called ordinance of secession; and the said convention, when convened, or the legislature that may be thereafter assembled, will prescribe the qualification of electors and the eligibility of persons to hold office under the constitution and laws of the State —a power the people of the several States composing the Federal Union have rightfully exercised from the origin of the Government to the present time.

And I do hereby direct—

First. That the military commander of the department and all officers and persons in the military and naval service aid and assist the said provisional governor in carrying into effect this proclamation; and they are enjoined to abstain from in any way hindering, impeding, or discouraging the loyal people from the organization of a State government as herein authorized.

Second. That the Secretary of State proceed to put in force all laws of the United States the administration whereof belongs to the State Department applicable to the geographical limits aforesaid.

Third. That the Secretary of the Treasury proceed to nominate for appointment assessors of taxes and collectors of customs and internal revenue and such other officers of the Treasury Department as are authorized by law and put in execution the revenue laws of the United States within the geographical limits aforesaid. In making appointments the preference shall be given to qualified loyal persons residing within the districts where their respective duties are to be performed; but if suitable residents of the districts shall not be found, then persons residing in other States or districts shall be appointed.

Fourth. That the Postmaster-General proceed to establish post-offices and post routes and put into execution the postal laws of the United States within the said State, giving to loyal residents the preference of appointment; but if suitable residents are not found, then to appoint agents, etc., from other States.

Fifth. That the district judge for the judicial district in which South Carolina is included proceed to hold courts within said State in accordance with the provisions of the act of Congress. The Attorney-General will instruct the proper officers to libel and bring to judgment, confiscation, and sale property subject to confiscation and enforce the administration of justice within said

State in all matters within the cognizance and jurisdiction of the Federal courts.

Sixth. That the Secretary of the Navy take possession of all public property belonging to the Navy Department within said geographical limits and put in operation all acts of Congress in relation to naval affairs having application to the said State.

Seventh. That the Secretary of the Interior put in force the laws relating to the Interior Department applicable to the geographical limits aforesaid.

250. GENERAL GRANT'S OBSERVATIONS ON CONDITIONS IN THE SOUTH
December 18, 1865

(U. S. 39th Congress, 1st Session, *Sen. Executive Doc.* No. 2, p. 107 ff.)

In the fall of 1865 President Johnson, anxious to have reliable information on conditions in the South, sent several personal representatives through that section for purposes of observation. Among these emissaries were Carl Schurz, Harvey M. Watterson, Benjamin C. Truman, Chief Justice Chase, and General Grant. Schurz's report was a severe arraignment of the southern people and a plea for the radical policy of reconstruction: it was subsequently revealed that he was under financial obligations to the Radicals. The reports of Truman and Watterson described the South as pacified and conciliatory, and sustained the Presidential policy of reconstruction. General Grant left Washington on his trip of observation November 29, 1865, and visited Raleigh, Charleston, Savannah, Augusta, and Atlanta. His report, presented to the President December 18, was convincing testimony to the wisdom of the Presidential policy. See, L. A. Coolidge, *Life of U. S. Grant*, ch. xxiv. The Report of Schurz is bound together with Grant's; Truman's Report is in 39th Congress, 1 Sess. *Sen. Executive Doc.* No. 43. On Chase's trip, see C. G. Bowers, *The Tragic Era*, ch. iii.

. . . I am satisfied that the mass of thinking men of the south accept the present situation of affairs in good faith. The questions which have heretofore divided the sentiment of the people of the two sections —slavery and State rights, or the right of a State to secede from the Union—they regard as having been settled forever by the highest tribunal—arms—that man can resort to. I was pleased to learn from the leading men

whom I met that they not only accepted the decision arrived at as final, but, now that the smoke of battle has cleared away and time has been given for reflection, that this decision has been a fortunate one for the whole country, they receiving like benefits from it with those who opposed them in the field and in council.

Four years of war, during which law was executed only at the point of the bayonet throughout the States in rebellion, have left the people possibly in a condition not to yield that ready obedience to civil authority the American people have generally been in the habit of yielding. This would render the presence of small garrisons throughout those States necessary until such time as labor returns to its proper channel, and civil authority is fully established. I did not meet anyone, either those holding places under the government or citizens of the southern States, who think it practicable to withdraw the military from the south at present. The white and the black mutually require the protection of the general government.

There is such universal acquiescence in the authority of the general government throughout the portions of country visited by me, that the mere presence of a military force, without regard to numbers, is sufficient to maintain order. The good of the country, and economy, require that the force kept in the interior, where there are many freedmen, (elsewhere in the southern States than at forts upon the seacoast no force is necessary,) should all be white troops. The reasons for this are obvious without mentioning many of them. The presence of black troops, lately slaves, demoralizes labor, both by their advice and by furnishing in their camps a resort for the freedmen for long distances around. White troops generally excite no opposition, and therefore a small number of them can maintain order in a given district. Colored troops must be kept in bodies sufficient to defend themselves. It is not the thinking men who would use violence towards any class of troops sent among them by the general government, but the ignorant in some places might; and the late slave seems to be imbued with the idea that the property of his late master should, by right, belong to him, or at least should have no protection from the colored soldier. There is danger of collisions being brought on by such causes.

My observations lead me to the conclusion that the citizens of the southern States are anxious to return to self-government, within the Union, as soon as possible; that whilst reconstructing they want and require protection from the government; that they are in earnest in wishing to do what they think is required by the government, not humiliating to them as citizens, and that if such a course were pointed out they would pursue it in good faith. It is to be regretted that there cannot be a greater commingling, at this time, between the citizens of the two sections, and particularly of those intrusted with the law-making power.

I did not give the operations of the Freedmen's Bureau that attention I would have done if more time had been at my disposal. Conversations on the subject, however, with officers connected with the bureau, lead me to think that, in some of the States, its affairs have not been conducted with good judgment or economy, and that the belief widely spread among the freedmen of the southern States, that the lands of their former owners will, at least in part, be divided among them, has come from the agents of this bureau. This belief is seriously interfering with the willingness of the freedmen to make contracts for the coming year. In some form the Freedmen's Bureau is an absolute necessity until civil law is established and

enforced, securing to the freedmen their rights and full protection. At present, however, it is independent of the military establishment of the country, and seems to be operated by the different agents of the bureau according to their individual notions. Everywhere General Howard, the able head of the bureau, made friends by the just and fair instructions and advice he gave; but the complaint in South Carolina was that when he left, things went on as before. Many, perhaps the majority, of the agents of the Freedmen's Bureau advise the freedmen that by their own industry they must expect to live. To this end they endeavor to secure employment for them, and to see that both contracting parties comply with their engagements. In some instances, I am sorry to say, the freedman's mind does not seem to be disabused of the idea that a freedman has the right to live without care or provision for the future. The effect of the belief in division of lands is idleness and accumulation in camps, towns, and cities. In such cases I think it will be found that vice and disease will tend to the extermination or great reduction of the colored race. It cannot be expected that the opinions held by men at the south for years can be changed in a day, and therefore the freedmen require, for a few years, not only laws to protect them, but the fostering care of those who will give them good counsel, and on whom they rely.

The Freedmen's Bureau being separated from the military establishment of the country, requires all the expense of a separate organization. One does not necessarily know what the other is doing, or what orders they are acting under. It seems to me this could be corrected by regarding every officer on duty with troops in the southern States as an agent of the Freedmen's Bureau, and then have all orders from the head of the bureau sent through department commanders. This would create a responsibility that would secure uniformity of action throughout all the south; would insure the orders and instructions from the head of the bureau being carried out, and would relieve from duty and pay a large number of employes of the government.

I have the honor to be, very respectfully, your obedient servant,

U. S. Grant, Lieutenant General.

251. VETO OF FREEDMEN'S BUREAU BILL
February 19, 1866

(Richardson, ed. *Messages and Papers,* Vol. VI, p. 398 ff.)

The Freedmen's Bureau had been established by act of Congress, March 3, 1865. February 19, 1866, a new Freedmen's Bureau bill, extending the life of the bureau and enlarging its powers, was presented to President Johnson. The veto of this bill inaugurated the open warfare between the Radicals and President Johnson. July 16, a supplementary Freedmen's Bureau Act was passed over the President's veto. For the Freedmen's Bureau, see, P. S. Peirce, *The Freedmen's Bureau;* L. Webster, *The Freedmen's Bureau in South Carolina.* For the veto message, see H. Beale, *The Critical Year,* p. 80 ff.; G. F. Milton, *Age of Hate,* p. 284 ff.

WASHINGTON, *February 19, 1866.*
To the Senate of the United States:

I have examined with care the bill, which originated in the Senate and has been passed by the two Houses of Congress, to amend an act entitled "An act to establish a bureau for the relief of freedmen and refugees," and for other purposes. Having with much regret come to the conclusion that it would not be consistent with the public welfare to give my approval to the measure, I return the bill to the Senate with my objections to its becoming a law. . . .

I share with Congress the strongest desire to secure to the freedmen the full enjoyment of their freedom and property and their entire independence and equality in making contracts for their labor, but the bill before me contains provisions which in my opinion are not warranted by the Constitution and are not well suited to accomplish the end in view.

The bill proposes to establish by authority of Congress military jurisdiction over all parts of the United States containing refugees and freedmen. It would by its very nature apply with most force to those parts of the United States in which the freedmen most abound, and it expressly extends the existing temporary jurisdiction of the Freedmen's Bureau, with greatly enlarged powers, over those States "in which the ordinary course of judicial proceedings has been interrupted by the rebellion." The source from which this military jurisdiction is to emanate is none other than the President of the United States, acting through the War Department and the Commissioner of the Freedmen's Bureau. The agents to carry out this military jurisdiction are to be selected either from the Army or from civil life; the country is to be divided into districts and subdistricts, and the number of salaried agents to be employed may be equal to the number of counties or parishes in all the United States where freedmen and refugees are to be found.

The subjects over which this military jurisdiction is to extend in every part of the United States include protection to "all employees, agents, and officers of this bureau in the exercise of the duties imposed" upon them by the bill. In eleven States it is further to extend over all cases affecting freedmen and refugees discriminated against "by local law, custom, or prejudice." In those eleven States the bill subjects any white person who may be charged with depriving a freedman of "any civil rights or immunities belonging to white persons" to imprisonment or fine, or both, without, however, defining the "civil rights and immunities" which are thus to be secured to the freedmen by military law. This military jurisdiction also extends to all questions that may arise respecting contracts. The agent who is thus to exercise the office of a military judge may be a stranger, entirely ignorant of the laws of the place, and exposed to the errors of judgment to which all men are liable. The exercise of power over which there is no legal supervision by so vast a number of agents as is contemplated by the bill must, by the very nature of man, be attended by acts of caprice, injustice, and passion.

The trials having their origin under this bill are to take place without the intervention of a jury and without any fixed rules of law or evidence. The rules on which offenses are to be "heard and determined" by the numerous agents are such rules and regulations as the President, through the War Department, shall prescribe. No previous presentment is required nor any indictment charging the commission of a crime against the laws; but the trial must proceed on charges and specifications. The punishment will be, not what the law declares, but such as a court-martial may think proper; and from these arbitrary tribunals there lies no appeal, no writ of error to any of the courts in which the Constitution of the United States vests exclusively the judicial power of the country.

While the territory and the classes of actions and offenses that are made subject to this measure are so extensive, the bill itself, should it become a law, will have no limitation in point of time, but will form a part of the permanent legislation of the country. I can not reconcile a system of military jurisdiction of this kind with the words of the Constitution which declare that "no person shall be held to answer for a capital or otherwise infamous crime unless on a presentment or indictment of a grand jury, except in cases arising in the land or naval forces, or in the militia when in actual service in time of war or public danger," and that "in all criminal prosecutions the accused shall enjoy the right to a speedy and public trial by an impartial jury of the State and district wherein the crime shall have been committed." The safeguards which the experience and wisdom of ages taught our fathers to establish as securities for the protection of the innocent, the punishment of the guilty, and the equal administration of justice are to be set aside, and for the sake of a more vigorous interposition in behalf of justice we are to take the risks of the many acts of injustice that would necessarily follow from an almost countless number of agents established in every parish or county in nearly a third of the States of the Union, over whose decisions there is to be no supervision or control by the Federal courts. The power that would be thus placed in the hands of the President is such as in time of peace certainly ought never to be intrusted to any one man.

If it be asked whether the creation of such a tribunal within a State is warranted as a measure of war, the question immediately presents itself whether we are still engaged in war. Let us not unnecessarily disturb the commerce and credit and industry of the country by declaring to the American people and to the world that the United States are still in a condition of civil war. At present there is no part of our country in which the

authority of the United States is disputed. Offenses that may be committed by individuals should not work a forfeiture of the rights of whole communities. The country has returned, or is returning, to a state of peace and industry, and the rebellion is in fact at an end. The measure, therefore, seems to be as inconsistent with the actual condition of the country as it is at variance with the Constitution of the United States.

If, passing from general considerations, we examine the bill in detail, it is open to weighty objections. . . .

I can not but add another very grave objection to this bill. The Constitution imperatively declares, in connection with taxation, that each State *shall* have at least one Representative, and fixes the rule for the number to which, in future times, each State shall be entitled. It also provides that the Senate of the United States *shall* be composed of two Senators from each State, and adds with peculiar force "that no State, without its consent, shall be deprived of its equal suffrage in the Senate." The original act was necessarily passed in the absence of the States chiefly to be affected, because their people were then contumaciously engaged in the rebellion. Now the case is changed, and some, at least, of those States are attending Congress by loyal representatives, soliciting the allowance of the constitutional right for representation. At the time, however, of the consideration and the passing of this bill there was no Senator or Representative in Congress from the eleven States which are to be mainly affected by its provisions. The very fact that reports were and are made against the good disposition of the people of that portion of the country is an additional reason why they need and should have representatives of their own in Congress to explain their condition, reply to accusations, and assist by their local knowledge in the perfecting of measures immediately affecting themselves. While the liberty of deliberation would then be free and Congress would have full power to decide according to its judgment, there could be no objection urged that the States most interested had not been permitted to be heard. The principle is firmly fixed in the minds of the American people that there should be no taxation without representation. Great burdens have now to be borne by all the country, and we may best demand that they shall be borne without murmur when they are voted by a majority of the representatives of all the people. I would not interfere with the unquestionable right of Congress to judge, each House for itself, "of the elections, returns, and qualifications of its own members;" but that authority can not be construed as including the right to shut out in time of peace any State from the representation to which it is entitled by the Constitution. . . .

The bill under consideration refers to certain of the States as though they had not "been fully restored in all their constitutional relations to the United States." If they have not, let us at once act together to secure that desirable end at the earliest possible moment. It is hardly necessary for me to inform Congress that in my own judgment most of those States, so far, at least, as depends upon their own action, have already been fully restored, and are to be deemed as entitled to enjoy their constitutional rights as members of the Union. Reasoning from the Constitution itself and from the actual situation of the country, I feel not only entitled but bound to assume that with the Federal courts restored and those of the several States in the full exercise of their functions the rights and interests of all classes of people will, with the aid of the military in cases of resistance to the laws, be essentially protected against unconstitutional infringement or violation. Should this expectation unhappily fail, which I do not anticipate, then the Executive is already fully armed with the powers conferred by the act of March, 1865, establishing the Freedmen's Bureau, and hereafter, as heretofore, he can employ the land and naval forces of the country to suppress insurrection or to overcome obstructions to the laws.

In accordance with the Constitution, I return the bill to the Senate, in the earnest hope that a measure involving questions and interests so important to the country will not become a law, unless upon deliberate consideration by the people it shall receive the sanction of an enlightened public judgment.

ANDREW JOHNSON.

252. THE CIVIL RIGHTS ACT
April 9, 1866

(U. S. Statutes at Large, Vol. XIV, p. 27 ff.)

This measure, designed to protect the freedmen from such discriminating legislation as the Black codes, was first passed March 13. It was vetoed by President Johnson (Doc. No. 253), and passed over his veto April 9. The act conferred citizenship upon the negroes, legislation necessitated by the Dred Scott decision. Doubt as to the constitutionality of the measure induced Congress to enact most of its provisions into the Fourteenth Amendment. See, H. E. Flack, *Adoption of the Fourteenth Amendment;* H. White, *Life of Lyman Trumbull;* J. F. Rhodes, *History of the United States,* Vol. V, 583 ff.

An Act to protect all Persons in the United States in their Civil Rights, and furnish the Means of their Vindication.

Be it enacted, That all persons born in the United States and not subject to any foreign power, excluding Indians not taxed, are hereby declared to be citizens of the United States; and such citizens, of every race and color, without regard to any previous condition of slavery or involuntary servitude, except as a punishment for crime whereof the party shall have been duly convicted, shall have the same right, in every State and Territory in the United States, to make and enforce contracts, to sue, be parties, and give evidence, to inherit, purchase, lease, sell, hold, and convey real and personal property, and to full and equal benefit of all laws and proceedings for the security of person and property, as is enjoyed by white citizens, and shall be subject to like punishment, pains, and penalties, and to none other, any law, statute, ordinance, regulation, or custom, to the contrary notwithstanding.

SEC. 2. *And be it further enacted,* That any person who, under color of any law, statute, ordinance, regulation, or custom, shall subject, or cause to be subjected, any inhabitant of any State or Territory to the deprivation of any right secured or protected by this act, or to different punishment, pains, or penalties on account of such person having at any time been held in a condition of slavery or involuntary servitude, except as a punishment for crime whereof the party shall have been duly convicted, or by reason of his color or race, than is prescribed for the punishment of white persons, shall be deemed guilty of a misdemeanor, and, on conviction, shall be punished by fine not exceeding one thousand dollars, or imprisonment not exceeding one year, or both, in the discretion of the court.

SEC. 3. *And be it further enacted,* That the district courts of the United States, . . . shall have, exclusively of the courts of the several States, cognizance of all crimes and offences committed against the provisions of this act, and also, concurrently with the circuit courts of the United States, of all causes, civil and criminal, affecting persons who are denied or cannot enforce in the courts or judicial tribunals of the State or locality where they may be any of the rights secured to them by the first section of this act. . . .

SEC. 4. *And be it further enacted,* That the district attorneys, marshals, and deputy marshals of the United States, the commissioners appointed by the circuit and territorial courts of the United States, with powers of arresting, imprisoning, or bailing offenders against the laws of the United States, the officers and agents of the Freedmen's Bureau, and every other officer who may be specially empowered by the President of the United States, shall be, and they are hereby, specially authorized and required, at the expense of the United States, to institute proceedings against all and every person who shall violate the provisions of this act, and cause him or them to be arrested and imprisoned, or bailed, as the case may be, for trial before such court of the United States or territorial court as by this act has cognizance of the offence. . . .

SEC. 8. *And be it further enacted,* That whenever the President of the United States shall have reason to believe that offences have been or are likely to be committed against the provisions of this act within any judicial district, it shall be lawful for him, in his discretion, to direct the judge, marshal, and district attorney of such district to attend at such place within the district, and for such time as he may designate, for the purpose of the more speedy arrest and trial of persons charged with a violation of this act; and it shall be the duty of every judge or other officer, when any such requisition shall be received by him, to attend at the place and for the time therein designated.

SEC. 9. *And be it further enacted,* That it shall be lawful for the President of the United States, or such person as he may empower for that purpose, to employ such part of the land or naval forces of the United States, or of the militia, as shall be necessary to prevent the violation and enforce the due execution of this act.

SEC. 10. *And be it further enacted,* That upon all questions of law arising in any cause under the provisions of this act a final appeal may be taken to the Supreme Court of the United States.

253. VETO OF THE CIVIL RIGHTS ACT
March 27, 1866

(Richardson, ed. *Messages and Papers,* Vol. VI, p. 405 ff.)

WASHINGTON, D. C., *March 27, 1866.*
To the Senate of the United States:

I regret that the bill, which has passed both Houses of Congress, entitled "An act to protect all persons in the United States in their civil rights and furnish the means of their vindication," contains provisions which I can not approve consistently with my sense of duty to the whole people and my obligations to the Constitution of the United States. I am therefore constrained to return it to the Senate, the House in which it originated, with my objections to its becoming a law.

By the first section of the bill all persons born in the United States and not subject to any foreign power, excluding Indians not taxed, are declared to be citizens of the United States. . . . It does not purport to give these classes of persons any status as citizens of States, except that which may result from their status as citizens of the United States. The power to confer the right of State citizenship is just as exclusively with the several States as the power to confer the right of Federal citizenship is with Congress.

The right of Federal citizenship thus to be conferred on the several excepted races before mentioned is now for the first time proposed to be given by law. If, as is claimed by many, all persons who are native born already are, by virtue of the Constitution, citizens of the United States, the passage of the pending bill can not be necessary to make them such. If, on the other hand, such persons are not citizens, as may be assumed from the proposed legislation to make them such, the grave question presents itself whether, when eleven of the thirty-six States are unrepresented in Congress at the present time, it is sound policy to make our entire colored population and all other excepted classes citizens of the United States. Four millions of them have just emerged from slavery into freedom. . . . It may also be asked whether it is necessary that they should be declared citizens in order that they may be secured in the enjoyment of the civil rights proposed to be conferred by the bill. Those rights are, by Federal as well as State laws, secured to all domiciled aliens and foreigners, even before the completion of the process of naturalization; and it may safely be assumed that the same enactments are sufficient to give like protection and benefits to those for whom this bill provides special legislation. Besides, the policy of the Government from its origin to the present time seems to have been that persons who are strangers to and unfamiliar with our institutions and our laws should pass through a certain probation, at the end of which, before attaining the coveted prize, they must give evidence of their fitness to receive and to exercise the rights of citizens as contemplated by the Constitution of the United States. The bill in effect proposes a discrimination against large numbers of intelligent, worthy, and patriotic foreigners, and in favor of the negro, to whom, after long years of bondage, the avenues to freedom and intelligence have just now been suddenly opened. . . .

The first section of the bill also contains an enumeration of the rights to be enjoyed by these classes so made citizens "in every State and Territory in the United States." These rights are "to make and enforce contracts; to sue, be parties, and give evidence; to inherit, purchase, lease, sell, hold, and convey real and personal property," and to have "full and equal benefit of all laws and proceedings for the security of person and property as is enjoyed by white citizens." So, too, they are made subject to the same punishment, pains, and penalties in common with white citizens, and to none other. Thus a perfect equality of the white and colored races is attempted to be fixed by Federal law in every State of the Union over the vast field of State jurisdiction covered by these enumerated rights. In no one of these can any State ever exercise any power of discrimination between the different races. . . .

Hitherto every subject embraced in the enumeration of rights contained in this bill has been considered as exclusively belonging to the States. They all relate to the internal police and economy of the respective States. They are matters which in each State concern the domestic condition of its people, varying in each according to its own peculiar circumstances and the safety and well-being of its own citizens. I do not mean to say that upon all these subjects there are not Federal restraints—as, for instance, in the State power of legislation over contracts there is a Federal limitation that no State shall pass a law impairing the obligations of contracts; and, as to crimes, that no State shall pass an *ex post facto* law; and, as to money, that no State shall make anything but gold and silver a legal tender; but where can we find a Federal prohibition against the power of any State to discriminate, as do most of them, between aliens and citizens, between artificial persons, called corporations, and natural persons, in the right to hold real estate? If it be granted that Congress can repeal all State laws discriminating between whites and blacks in the subjects covered by this bill, why, it may be asked, may not Congress repeal in the same way all State laws discriminating between the two races on the subjects of suffrage and office? If Congress can declare by law who shall hold lands, who shall testify, who shall have capacity to make a contract in a State, then Congress can by law also declare who, without regard to color or race, shall have the right to sit as a juror or as a judge, to hold any office, and, finally, to vote "in every State and Territory of the United States." As respects the Territories, they come within the power of Congress, for as to them the lawmaking power is the Federal power; but as to the States no similar provision exists vesting in Congress the power "to make rules and regulations" for them.

The object of the second section of the bill is to afford discriminating protection to colored persons in the full enjoyment of all the rights secured to them by the preceding section. . . .

This provision of the bill seems to be unnecessary, as adequate judicial remedies could be adopted to secure the desired end without invading the immunities of legislators, always important to be preserved in the interest of public liberty; without assailing the independence of the judiciary, always essential to the preservation of individual rights; and without impairing the efficiency of ministerial officers, always necessary for the maintenance of public peace and order. The remedy proposed by this section seems to be in this respect not only anomalous, but unconstitutional; for the Constitution guarantees nothing with certainty if it does not insure to the several States the right of making and executing laws in regard to all matters arising within their jurisdiction, subject only to the restriction that in cases of conflict with the Constitution and constitutional laws of the United States the latter should be held to be the supreme law of the land. . . .

It is clear that in States which deny to persons whose rights are secured by the first section of the bill any one of those rights all criminal and civil cases affecting them will, by the provisions of the third section, come under the exclusive cognizance of the Federal tribunals. It follows that if, in any State which denies to a colored person any one of all those rights, that person should commit a crime against the laws of a State—murder, arson, rape, or any other crime—all protection and punishment through the courts of the State are taken away, and he can only be tried and punished in the Federal courts. How is the criminal to be tried? If the offense is provided for and punished by Federal law, that law, and not the State law, is to govern. It is only when the offense does not happen to be within the purview of Federal law that the Federal courts are to try

and punish him under any other law. Then resort is to be had to "the common law, as modified and changed" by State legislation, "so far as the same is not inconsistent with the Constitution and laws of the United States." So that over this vast domain of criminal jurisprudence provided by each State for the protection of its own citizens and for the punishment of all persons who violate its criminal laws, Federal law, whenever it can be made to apply, displaces State law. The question here naturally arises, from what source Congress derives the power to transfer to Federal tribunals certain classes of cases embraced in this section. . . . This section of the bill undoubtedly comprehends cases and authorizes the exercise of powers that are not, by the Constitution, within the jurisdiction of the courts of the United States. To transfer them to those courts would be an exercise of authority well calculated to excite distrust and alarm on the part of all the States, for the bill applies alike to all of them—as well to those that have as to those that have not been engaged in rebellion. . . .

The fourth section of the bill provides that officers and agents of the Freedmen's Bureau shall be empowered to make arrests, and also that other officers may be specially commissioned for that purpose by the President of the United States. It also authorizes circuit courts of the United States and the superior courts of the Territories to appoint, without limitation, commissioners, who are to be charged with the performance of *quasi* judicial duties. The fifth section empowers the commissioners so to be selected by the courts to appoint in writing, under their hands, one or more suitable persons from time to time to execute warrants and other processes described by the bill. These numerous official agents are made to constitute a sort of police, in addition to the military, and are authorized to summon a *posse comitatus*, and even to call to their aid such portion of the land and naval forces of the United States, or of the militia, "as may be necessary to the performance of the duty with which they are charged." This extraordinary power is to be conferred upon agents irresponsible to the Government and to the people, to whose number the discretion of the commissioners is the only limit, and in whose hands such authority might be made a terrible engine of wrong, oppression, and fraud. . . .

The ninth section authorizes the President, or such person as he may empower for that purpose, "to employ such part of the land or naval forces of the United States, or of the militia, as shall be necessary to prevent the violation and enforce the due execution of this act." This language seems to imply a permanent military force, that is to be always at hand, and whose only business is to be the enforcement of this measure over the vast region where it is intended to operate. . . .

In all our history, in all our experience as a people living under Federal and State law, no such system as that contemplated by the details of this bill has ever before been proposed or adopted. They establish for the security of the colored race safeguards which go infinitely beyond any that the General Government has ever provided for the white race. In fact, the distinction of race and color is by the bill made to operate in favor of the colored and against the white race. They interfere with the municipal legislation of the States, with the relations existing exclusively between a State and its citizens, or between inhabitants of the same State—an absorption and assumption of power by the General Government which, if acquiesced in, must sap and destroy our federative system of limited powers and break down the barriers which preserve the rights of the States. It is another step, or rather stride, toward centralization and the concentration of all legislative powers in the National Government. The tendency of the bill must be to resuscitate the spirit of rebellion and to arrest the progress of those influences which are more closely drawing around the States the bonds of union and peace. . . .

ANDREW JOHNSON.

254. REPORT OF THE JOINT COMMITTEE ON RECONSTRUCTION
June 20, 1866
(*Report of the Joint Committee on Reconstruction*, p. 4 ff.)

A Committee of six Senators and nine Representatives, of which Senator Fessenden was chairman, was appointed in December 1865 "to inquire into the condition of the states which formed the so-called Confederate States of America, and report whether they, or any of them, are entitled to be represented in either house of Congress." The *Report* recommended that the Confederate states were not entitled to representation; it also maintained the authority of Congress, rather than of the Executive, over the process of reconstruction. The *Report* was published separately, and also with a voluminous body of testimony collected by various sub-committees. Of great importance is B. B. Kendrick, *Journal of the Joint Committee of Fifteen on Reconstruction*.

A claim for the immediate admission of senators and representatives from the so-called Confederate States has been urged, which seems to your committee not to be founded either in reason or in law, and which cannot be passed without comment. Stated in a few words, it amounts to this: That inasmuch as the lately insurgent States had no legal right to separate themselves from the Union, they still retain their position as States, and consequently the people thereof have a right to immediate representation in Congress without the interposition of any conditions whatever. . . . It has even been contended that until such admission all legislation affecting their interests is, if not unconstitutional, at least unjustifiable and oppressive.

It is believed by your Committee that these propositions are not only wholly untenable, but, if admitted, would tend to the destruction of the government. . . . It cannot, we think, be denied that the war thus waged was a civil war of the greatest magnitude. The people waging it were necessarily subject to all the rules which, by the law of nations, control a contest of that character, and to all the legitimate consequences following it. One of these consequences was that, within the limits prescribed by humanity, the conquered rebels were at the mercy of the conquerors. . . .

It is moreover contended . . . that from the peculiar nature and character of our government . . . from the moment rebellion lays down its arms and actual hostilities cease all political rights of rebellious communities are at once restored; that because the people of a state of the Union were once an organized community within the Union, they necessarily so remain, and their right to be represented in Congress at any and all times, and to participate in the government of the country under all circumstances, admits of neither question nor dispute. If this is indeed true, then is the government of the United States powerless for its own protection, and flagrant rebellion, carried to the extreme of civil war, is a pastime which any state may play at, not only certain that it can lose nothing in any event, but may even be the gainer by defeat. If rebellion succeeds it accomplishes its purpose and destroys the government. If it fails, the war has been barren of results, and the battle may still be fought out in the legislative halls of the country. Treason, defeated in the field, has only to take possession of Congress, and the cabinet.

Your committee do not deem it either necessary or proper to discuss the question whether the late Confederate States are still States of this Union, or can ever be otherwise. Granting this profitless abstraction about which so many words have been wasted, it by no means follows that the people of those States may not place themselves in a position to abrogate the powers and privileges incident to a State of the Union, and deprive themselves of all pretence of right to exercise those powers and enjoy those privileges. . . .

Equally absurd is the pretence that the legislative authority of the nation must be inoperative so far as they are concerned, while they, by their own act, have lost the right to take part in it. Such a proposition carries its own refutation on its face. . . .

It is the opinion of your committee—

I. That the States lately in rebellion were, at the close of the war, disorganized communities, without civil government, and without constitutions or other forms, by virtue of which political relation could legally exist between them and the federal government.

II. That Congress cannot be expected to recognize as valid the election of representatives from disorganized communities, which, from the very nature of the case, were unable to present their claim to representation under those established and recognized rules,

the observance of which has been hitherto required.

III. That Congress would not be justified in admitting such communities to a participation in the government of the country without first providing such constitutional or other guarantees as will tend to secure the civil rights of all citizens of the republic; a just equality of representation; protection against claims founded in rebellion and crime; a temporary restoration of the right of suffrage to those who have not actively participated in the efforts to destroy the Union and overthrow the government, and the exclusion from position of public trust of, at least, a portion of those whose crimes have proved them to be enemies of the Union, and unworthy of public confidence. . . .

We now propose to re-state, as briefly as possible, the general facts and principles applicable to all the States recently in rebellion:

. . . Third. Having voluntarily deprived themselves of representation in Congress for the criminal purpose of destroying the Union, and having reduced themselves, by the act of levying war, to the condition of public enemies, they have no right to complain of temporary exclusion from Congress; but on the contrary . . . the burden now rests upon them, before claiming to be reinstated in their former condition, to show that they are qualified to resume federal relations. . . .

Fourth. Having . . . forfeited all civil and political rights and privileges under the federal Constitution, they can only be restored thereto by the permission and authority of that constitutional power against which they rebelled and by which they were subdued.

Fifth. These rebellious enemies were conquered by the people of the United States acting through all the co-ordinate branches of the government, and not by the executive department alone. The powers of conqueror are not so vested in the President that he can fix and regulate the terms of settlement and confer congressional representation on conquered rebels and traitors. . . . The authority to restore rebels to political power in the federal Government can be exercised only with the concurrence of all the departments in which political power is vested. . . .

. . . Eighth. . . . No proof has been afforded to Congress of a constituency in any one of the so-called Confederate States, unless we except the State of Tennessee, qualified to elect senators and representatives in Congress. No State Constitution, or amendment to a State Constitution, has had the sanction of the people. All the so-called legislation of State conventions and legislatures has been had under military dictation. If the President may, at his will and under his own authority, whether as military commander or chief executive, qualify persons to appoint senators and elect representatives, and empower others to appoint and elect them, he thereby practically controls the organization of the legislative department. The constitu-

tional form of government is thereby practically destroyed, and its power absorbed in the Executive. . . .

Ninth. The necessity of providing adequate safeguards for the future, before restoring the insurrectionary States to a participation in the direction of public affairs, is apparent from the bitter hostility to the government and people of the United States yet existing throughout the conquered territory. . . .

Tenth. The conclusion of your committee therefore is, that the so-called Confederate States are not, at present, entitled to representation in the Congress of the United States. . . .

255. PRESIDENT JOHNSON ON THE RESTORATION OF THE SOUTHERN STATES TO THE UNION

Second Annual Message to Congress
December 3, 1866

(Richardson, ed. *Messages and Papers,* Vol. VI, p. 445 ff.)

WASHINGTON, *December 3, 1866.*
Fellow-Citizens of the Senate and House of Representatives:

. . . In my message of the 4th of December, 1865, Congress was informed of the measures which had been instituted by the Executive with a view to the gradual restoration of the States in which the insurrection occurred to their relations with the General Government. Provisional governors had been appointed, conventions called, governors elected, legislatures assembled, and Senators and Representatives chosen to the Congress of the United States. Courts had been opened for the enforcement of laws long in abeyance. The blockade had been removed, custom-houses reestablished, and the internal-revenue laws put in force, in order that the people might contribute to the national income. Postal operations had been renewed, and efforts were being made to restore them to their former condition of efficiency. The States themselves had been asked to take part in the high function of amending the Constitution, and of thus sanctioning the extinction of African slavery as one of the legitimate results of our internecine struggle.

Having progressed thus far, the executive department found that it had accomplished nearly all that was within the scope of its constitutional authority. One thing, however,

yet remained to be done before the work of restoration could be completed, and that was the admission to Congress of loyal Senators and Representatives from the States whose people had rebelled against the lawful authority of the General Government. This question devolved upon the respective Houses, which by the Constitution are made the judges of the elections, returns, and qualifications of their own members, and its consideration at once engaged the attention of Congress. . . .

All of the States in which the insurrection had existed promptly amended their constitutions so as to make them conform to the great change thus effected in the organic law of the land; declared null and void all ordinances and laws of secession; repudiated all pretended debts and obligations created for the revolutionary purposes of the insurrection, and proceeded in good faith to the enactment of measures for the protection and amelioration of the condition of the colored race. Congress, however, yet hesitated to admit any of these States to representation, and it was not until toward the close of the eighth month of the session that an exception was made in favor of Tennessee by the admission of her Senators and Representatives.

I deem it a subject of profound regret that

Congress has thus far failed to admit to seats loyal Senators and Representatives from the other States whose inhabitants, with those of Tennessee, had engaged in the rebellion. Ten States—more than one-fourth of the whole number—remain without representation; the seats of fifty members in the House of Representatives and of twenty members in the Senate are yet vacant, not by their own consent, not by a failure of election, but by the refusal of Congress to accept their credentials. Their admission, it is believed, would have accomplished much toward the renewal and strengthening of our relations as one people and removed serious cause for discontent on the part of the inhabitants of those States. It would have accorded with the great principle enunciated in the Declaration of American Independence that no people ought to bear the burden of taxation and yet be denied the right of representation. It would have been in consonance with the express provisions of the Constitution that "each State shall have at least one Representative" and "that no State, without its consent, shall be deprived of its equal suffrage in the Senate." These provisions were intended to secure to every State and to the people of every State the right of representation in each House of Congress; and so important was it deemed by the framers of the Constitution that the equality of the States in the Senate should be preserved that not even by an amendment of the Constitution can any State, without its consent, be denied a voice in that branch of the National Legislature.

It is true it has been assumed that the existence of the States was terminated by the rebellious acts of their inhabitants, and that, the insurrection having been suppressed, they were thenceforward to be considered merely as conquered territories. The legislative, executive, and judicial departments of the Government have, however, with great distinctness and uniform consistency, refused to sanction an assumption so incompatible with the nature of our republican system and with the professed objects of the war. Throughout the recent legislation of Congress the undeniable fact makes itself apparent that these ten political communities are nothing less than States of this Union. At the very commencement of the rebellion each House declared, with a unanimity as remarkable as it

was significant, that the war was not "waged upon our part in any spirit of oppression, nor for any purpose of conquest or subjugation, nor purpose of overthrowing or interfering with the rights or established institutions of those States, but to defend and maintain the supremacy of the Constitution and all laws made in pursuance thereof, and to preserve the Union, with all the dignity, equality, and rights of the several States unimpaired; and that as soon as these objects" were "accomplished the war ought to cease." . . .

The action of the executive department of the Government upon this subject has been equally definite and uniform, and the purpose of the war was specifically stated in the proclamation issued by my predecessor on the 2nd day of September, 1862. It was then solemnly proclaimed and declared "that hereafter, as heretofore, the war will be prosecuted for the object of practically restoring the constitutional relation between the United States and each of the States and the people thereof in which States that relation is or may be suspended or disturbed."

The recognition of the States by the judicial department of the Government has also been clear and conclusive in all proceedings affecting them as States had in the Supreme, circuit, and district courts.

In the admission of Senators and Representatives from any and all of the States there can be no just ground of apprehension that persons who are disloyal will be clothed with the powers of legislation, for this could not happen when the Constitution and the laws are enforced by a vigilant and faithful Congress. Each House is made the "judge of the elections, returns, and qualifications of its own members," and may, "with the concurrence of two-thirds, expel a member." . . .

The Constitution of the United States makes it the duty of the President to recommend to the consideration of Congress "such measures as he shall judge necessary and expedient." I know of no measure more imperatively demanded by every consideration of national interest, sound policy, and equal justice than the admission of loyal members from the now unrepresented States. This would consummate the work of restoration and exert a most salutary influence in the reestablishment of peace, harmony, and fraternal feeling. It would tend greatly to renew the confidence of the American people in the vigor and stability of their institutions. It would bind us more closely together as a nation and enable us to show to the world the inherent and recuperative power of a government founded upon the will of the people and established upon the principles of liberty, justice, and intelligence. . . .

In our efforts to preserve "the unity of government which constitutes us one people" by restoring the States to the condition which they held prior to the rebellion, we should be cautious, lest, having rescued our nation from perils of threatened disintegration, we resort to consolidation, and in the end absolute despotism, as a remedy for the recurrence of similar troubles. The war having terminated, and with it all occasion for the exercise of powers of doubtful constitutionality, we should hasten to bring legislation within the boundaries prescribed by the Constitution and to return to the ancient landmarks established by our fathers for the guidance of succeeding generations. . . .

256. EX PARTE MILLIGAN
4 Wallace, 2
1866

Certificate from the United States circuit court for the District of Indiana. By an act of March 3, 1863, Congress authorized the President to suspend the writ of *habeas corpus,* and under this authority President Lincoln, September 15, 1863, suspended the writ in cases where officers held persons for offenses against the military or naval service. Milligan, a civilian, was arrested, tried by a military commission, found guilty of fomenting insurrection, and sentenced to be hanged. He petitioned the United States circuit court for a writ of *habeas corpus.*

The decision of the Court in this case, one of the most notable in our history, condemned military tribunals in sections where the civil courts were open, and, by implication, raised serious doubts as to the legality of Congressional reconstruction. A thorough discussion of the case can be found in *The Milligan Case,* ed. by S. Klaus. See also in this connection the opinion of Taney in *ex parte Merryman,* Doc. No. 209. A standard work on the constitutional problems of the war is W. Whiting, *War Powers under the Constitution of the United States.* An excellent briefer discussion can be found in W. A. Dunning, *Essays on the Civil War and Reconstruction,* chs. i, ii. On Copperhead activities see I. W. Ayer, *The Great Northwest Conspiracy;* F. A. Stiger, *History of the Order of Sons of Liberty;* J. L. Vallandigham, *Life of Clement L. Vallandigham.*

DAVIS, J. . . . The importance of the main question presented by this record cannot be overstated; for it involves the very framework of the government and the fundamental principles of American liberty.

During the late wicked rebellion, the temper of the times did not allow that calmness in deliberation and discussion so necessary to a correct conclusion of a purely judicial question. *Then,* considerations of safety were mingled with the exercise of power; and feelings and interests prevailed which are happily terminated. *Now,* that the public safety is assured, this question, as well as all others, can be discussed and decided without passion or the admixture of any element not required to form a legal judgment. We approach the investigation of this case, fully sensible of the magnitude of the inquiry and the necessity of full and cautious deliberation. . . .

The controlling question in the case is this: Upon the *facts* stated in Milligan's petition, and the exhibits filed, had the military commission mentioned in it *jurisdiction,* legally, to try and sentence him? Milligan, not a resident of one of the rebellious states, or a prisoner of war, but a citizen of Indiana for twenty years past, and never in the military or naval service, is, while at his home, arrested by the military power of the United States, imprisoned, and, on certain criminal charges preferred against him, tried, convicted, and sentenced to be hanged by a military commission, organized under the direction of the military commander of the military district of Indiana. Had this tribunal the legal power and authority to try and punish this man?

No graver question was ever considered by this court, nor one which more nearly concerns the rights of the whole people; for it is the birthright of every American citizen when charged with crime, to be tried and punished according to law. The power of punishment is alone through the means which the laws have provided for that purpose, and if they are ineffectual, there is an immunity from punishment no matter how great an offender the individual may be, or how much his crimes may have shocked the sense of justice of the country, or endangered its safety. By the protection of the law human rights are secured; withdraw that protection, and they are at the mercy of wicked rulers, or the clamor of an excited people. If there was law to justify this military trial, it is not our province to interfere; if there was not, it is our duty to declare the nullity of the whole proceedings. The decision of this question does not depend on argument or judicial precedents, numerous and highly illustrative as they are. These precedents inform us of the extent of the struggle to preserve liberty, and to relieve those in civil life from military trials. The founders of our government were familiar with the history of that struggle, and secured in a written Constitution every right which the people had wrested from power during a contest of ages. By that Constitution and the laws authorized by it this question must be determined. The provisions of that instrument on the administration of criminal justice are too plain and direct to leave room for misconstruction or doubt of their true meaning. Those applicable to this case are found in that clause of the original Constitution which says, "That the trial of all crimes, except in case of impeachment, shall be by jury"; and in the fourth, fifth, and sixth articles of the amendments. . . .

Time has proven the discernment of our ancestors; for even these provisions, expressed in such plain English words, that it would seem the ingenuity of man could not evade them, are *now,* after the lapse of more than seventy years, sought to be avoided. . . . The Constitution of the United States is a law for rulers and people, equally in war and in peace, and covers with the shield of its protection all classes of men, at all times, and under all circumstances. No doctrine involving more pernicious consequences was ever invented by the wit of man than that any of its provisions can be suspended during any of the great exigencies of government. Such a doctrine leads directly to anarchy or despotism, but the theory of necessity on which it is based is false; for the government, within the Constitution, has all the powers granted to it which are necessary to preserve its existence; as has been happily proved by the result of the great effort to throw off its just authority.

Have any of the rights guaranteed by the Constitution been violated in the case of Milligan? and if so, what are they?

Every trial involves the exercise of judicial power; and from what source did the military commission that tried him derive their authority? Certainly no part of the judicial power of the country was conferred on them; because the Constitution expressly vests it "in one Supreme Court and such inferior courts as the Congress may from time to time ordain and establish," and it is not pretended that the commission was a court ordained and established by Congress. They cannot justify on the mandate of the President, because he is controlled by law, and has his appropriate sphere of duty, which is to execute, not to make, the laws; and there is "no unwritten criminal code to which resort can be had as a source of jurisdiction."

But it is said that the jurisdiction is complete under the "laws and usages of war."

It can serve no useful purpose to inquire what those laws and usages are, whence they originated, where found, and on whom they operate; they can never be applied to citizens in states which have upheld the authority of the government, and where the courts are open and their process unobstructed. This court has judicial knowledge that in Indiana the federal authority was always unopposed, and its courts always open to hear criminal accusations and redress grievances; and no usage of war could sanction a military trial there for any offense whatever of a citizen in civil life, in nowise connected with the military service. Congress could grant no such power; and to the honor of our national legislature be it said, it has never been provoked by the state of the country even to attempt its exercise. One of the plainest constitutional provisions was, therefore, infringed when Milligan was tried by a court not ordained and established by Congress, and not composed of judges appointed during good behavior.

Why was he not delivered to the circuit court of Indiana to be proceeded against according to law? No reason of necessity could be urged against it; because Congress had declared penalties against the offenses charged, provided for their punishment, and directed that court to hear and determine them. And soon after this military tribunal was ended, the circuit court met, peacefully transacted its business, and adjourned. It needed no bayonets to protect it, and required no military aid to execute its judgments. It was held in a state, eminently distinguished for patriotism, by judges commissioned during the rebellion who were provided with juries, upright, intelligent, and selected by a marshal appointed by the President. The government had no right to conclude that Milligan, if guilty, would not receive in that court merited punishment; for its records disclose that it was constantly engaged in the trial of similar offenses, and was never interrupted in its administration of criminal justice. If it was dangerous, in the distracted condition of affairs, to leave Milligan unrestrained of his liberty, because he "conspired against the government, afforded aid and comfort to rebels, and incited the people to insurrection," the *law* said, arrest him, confine him closely, render him powerless to do further mischief; and then present his case to the grand jury of the district, with proofs of his guilt, and, if indicted, try him according to the course of the common law. If this had been done, the Constitution would have been vindicated, the law of 1863 enforced, and the securities for personal liberty preserved and defended.

Another guarantee of freedom was broken when Milligan was denied a trial by jury. The great minds of the country have differed on the correct interpretation to be given to the various provisions of the federal Constitution; and judicial decision has been often invoked to settle their true meaning; but until recently no one ever doubted that the right of trial by jury was forfeited in the organic law against the power of attack. It is *now* assailed; but if ideas can be expressed in words, and language has any meaning, *this right*—one of the most valuable in a free country—is preserved to every one accused of crime who is not attached to the army, or navy, or militia in actual service. . . .

It is claimed that martial law covers with its broad mantle the proceedings of this military commission. The proposition is this: that in a time of war the commander of an armed force (if, in his opinion, the exigencies of the country demand it, and of which he is to judge) has the power, within the lines of his military district, to suspend all civil rights and their remedies, and subject citizens as well as soldiers to the rule of *his will;* and in the exercise of his lawful authority cannot be restrained, except by his superior officer or the President of the United States.

If this position is sound to the extent claimed, then when war exists, foreign or domestic, and the country is subdivided into military departments for mere convenience, the commander of one of them can, if he chooses, within his limits, on the plea of necessity, with the approval of the Executive, substitute military force for, and to the exclusion of, the laws, and punish all persons, as he thinks right and proper, without fixed or certain rules.

The statement of this proposition shows its importance; for, if true, republican government is a failure, and there is an end of liberty regulated by law. Martial law, established on such a basis, destroys every guarantee of the Constitution, and effectually renders the "military independent of, and superior to, the civil power,"—the attempt to do which by the king of Great Britain was deemed by our fathers such an offense, that they assigned it to the world as one of the causes which impelled them to declare their independence. Civil liberty and this kind of martial law cannot endure together; the antagonism is irreconcilable; and, in the conflict, one or the other must perish.

This nation, as experience has proved, cannot always remain at peace, and has no right to expect that it will always have wise and humane rulers, sincerely attached to the principles of the Constitution. Wicked men, ambitious of power, with hatred of liberty and contempt of law, may fill the place once occupied by Washington and Lincoln; and if this right is conceded, and the calamities of war again befall us, the dangers to human liberty are frightful to contemplate. If our fathers had failed to provide for just such a contingency, they would have been false to the trust reposed in them. They knew—the history of the world told them—the nation they were founding, be its existence short' or long, would be involved in war; how often or how long continued, human foresight could not tell; and that unlimited power, wherever lodged at such a time, was especially hazardous to freemen. For this, and other equally weighty reasons, they secured the inheritance they had fought to maintain, by incorporating in a written Constitution the safeguards which time had proved were essential to its preservation. Not one of these safeguards can the President, or Congress, or the judiciary disturb, except the one concerning the writ of habeas corpus.

It is essential to the safety of every government that, in a great crisis like the one we have just passed through, there should be a power somewhere of suspending the writ of habeas corpus. In every war, there are men of previously good character, wicked enough to counsel their fellow-citizens to resist the measures deemed necessary by a good government to sustain its just authority and overthrow its enemies; and their influence may lead to dangerous combinations. In the emergency of the times, an immediate public investigation according to law may not be possible; and yet the peril to the country may be too imminent to suffer such persons to go at large. Unquestionably, there is then an exigency which demands that the government, if it should see fit, in the exercise of a proper discretion, to make arrests, should not be required to produce the persons arrested in answer to a writ of habeas corpus. The Constitution goes no further. It does not say after a writ of habeas corpus is denied a citizen, that he shall be tried otherwise than by the course of the common law; if it had intended this result, it was easy by the use of direct words to have accomplished it. The illustrious men who framed that instrument were guarding the foundations of civil liberty against the abuses of unlimited power; they were full of wisdom, and the lessons of history informed them that a trial by an established court, assisted by an impartial jury, was the only sure way of protecting the citizen against oppression and wrong. Knowing this, they limited the suspension to one great right, and left the rest to remain forever inviolable. But, it is insisted that the safety of the country in time of war demands that this broad claim for martial law shall be sustained. If this were true, it could be well said

that a country, preserved at the sacrifice of all the cardinal principles of liberty, is not worth the cost of preservation. Happily, it is not so.

It will be borne in mind that this is not a question of the power to proclaim martial law, when war exists in a community and the courts and civil authorities are overthrown. Nor is it a question what rule a military commander, at the head of his army, can impose on states in rebellion to cripple their resources and quell the insurrection. The jurisdiction claimed is much more extensive. The necessities of the service, during the late rebellion, required that the loyal states should be placed within the limits of certain military districts and commanders appointed in them; and, it is urged, that this, in a military sense, constituted them the theatre of military operations; and, as in this case, Indiana had been and was again threatened with invasion by the enemy, the occasion was furnished to establish martial law. The conclusion does not follow from the premises. If armies were collected in Indiana, they were to be employed in another locality, where the laws were obstructed and the national authority disputed. On *her* soil there was no hostile foot; if once invaded, that invasion was at an end, and with it all pretext for martial law. Martial law cannot arise from a *threatened* invasion. The necessity must be actual and present; the invasion real, such as effectually closes the courts and deposes the civil administration.

It is difficult to see how the *safety* of the country required martial law in Indiana. If any of her citizens were plotting treason, the power of arrest could secure them, until the government was prepared for their trial, when the courts were open and ready to try them. It was as easy to protect witnesses before a civil as a military tribunal; and as there could be no wish to convict, except on sufficient legal evidence, surely an ordained and established court was better able to judge of this than a military tribunal composed of gentlemen not trained to the profession of the law.

It follows, from what has been said on this subject, that there are occasions when martial rule can be properly applied. If, in foreign invasion or civil war, the courts are actually closed, and it is impossible to administer criminal justice according to law, *then,* on the theatre of active military operations, where war really prevails, there is a necessity to furnish a substitute for the civil authority, thus overthrown, to preserve the safety of the army and society; and as no power is left but the military, it is allowed to govern by martial rule until the laws can have their free course. As necessity creates the rule, so it limits its duration; for, if this government is continued *after* the courts are reinstated, it is a gross usurpation of power. Martial rule can never exist where the courts are open, and in the proper and unobstructed ex-ercise of their jurisdiction. It is also confined to the locality of actual war. Because, during the late rebellion it could have been enforced in Virginia, where the national authority was overturned and the courts driven out, it does not follow that it should obtain in Indiana, where that authority was never disputed, and justice was always administered. . . .

Mr. Chief Justice Chase, for himself and Mr. Justice Wayne, Mr. Justice Swayne, and Mr. Justice Miller, delivered an opinion in which he differed from the court in several important points, but concurred in the judgement in the case.

257. EFFORTS TO ENCOURAGE IMMIGRATION
South Carolina Immigration Bill
1866
(*South Carolina Statutes at Large,* Vol. XIII, p. 380)

The demand for industrial labor, the opening up of the west, and the disorganization of the labor system of the South, all led to official as well as unofficial efforts to encourage immigration. Most Southern States attempted to attract immigrants to take the place of the negro worker, but uniformly without success. In South Carolina a state commissioner of agriculture was created and a pamphlet advertising the attractions of the state published in several languages and distributed widely throughout northern Europe. See, F. B. Simkins and R. H. Woody, *South Carolina During Reconstruction,* p. 243 ff.

To Encourage Immigration to South Carolina

1. *Be it enacted* by the Senate and House of Representatives, now met and sitting in General Assembly, and by the authority of the same, That for the purpose of encouraging, promoting and protecting European immigration to and in this State, the sum of ten thousand dollars be appropriated from the contingent fund, to be expended under the direction of the Government, for the purposes and in the manner hereinafter provided.

2. That the Governor, by and with the advice and consent of the Senate, shall appoint a Commissioner of Immigration, who shall open an office in the fire-proof building in Charleston, to perform such duties as may appertain to his office, and shall be paid for his services the salary of fifteen hundred dollars per annum out of the fund aforesaid, in quarterly payments.

3. That it shall be the duty of said Commissioner of Immigration to advertise in all the gazettes of the State for lands for sale; to cause such lands, after having been duly laid off, platted and described, at the expense of the owner or owners of said lands, to be appraised by three disinterested persons, and their titles to be examined by the Attorney General or Solicitors of the State, and endorsed by them, as the case may be; to open a book or books for the registry of the same, together with the price demanded and the conditions of payment. And in case such lands be selected by any immigrant, to superintend the transfer of title and other necessary instruments and proceedings of conveyance.

4. That the said Commissioner shall periodically publish, advertise and cause to be distributed in the Northern and European ports and states, descriptive lists of such lands as have been registered and offered for sale, together with this Act, and a statement of such advantages as this State offers in soil, climate, productions, social improvements, etc., to the industrious, orderly and frugal European immigrant.

258. EX PARTE GARLAND
4 Wallace, 333
1867

Petition to the Supreme Court. Garland, a citizen of Arkansas, had been admitted to practice before the Supreme Court in 1860. He subsequently served in the Confederate Army, but received from the President a full pardon for all offences. An Act of Congress of January 24, 1865, excluded from practice before the Supreme Court any one who could not take an oath that he had never fought against the United States. Garland challenged the constitutionality of this law. This is the first case in which an act of Congress was held unconstitutional by a vote of five to four.

FIELD, J. . . . The petitioner . . . now produces his pardon, and asks permission to continue to practise as an attorney and counsellor of the court without taking the oath required by the act of January 24, 1865, and the rule of the court, which he is unable to take, by reason of the offices he held under the Confederate government. He rests his application principally upon two grounds:

1st. That the act of January 24, 1865, so far as it affects his status in the court, is unconstitutional and void; and,

2. That, if the act be constitutional, he is released from compliance with its provisions by the pardon of the President. . . .

The statute is directed against parties who have offended in any of the particulars embraced by these clauses. And its object is to exclude them from the profession of the law, or at least from its practice in the courts of the United States. As the oath prescribed cannot be taken by these parties, the act, as against them, operates as a legislative decree of perpetual exclusion. And exclusion from any of the professions or any of the ordinary avocations of life for past conduct can be regarded in no other light than as punishment for such conduct. The exaction of the oath is the mode provided for ascertaining the parties upon whom the act is intended to operate, and instead of lessening, increases its objectionable character. All enactments of this kind partake of the nature of bills of pains and penalties, and are subject to the constitutional inhibition against the passage of bills of attainder, under which general designation they are included.

In the exclusion which the statute adjudges it imposes a punishment for some of the acts specified which were not punishable at the time they were committed; and for other of the acts it adds a new punishment to that before prescribed, and it is thus brought within the further inhibition of the Constitution against the passage of an ex post facto law. . . .

The profession of an attorney and counsellor is not like an office created by an act of Congress, which depends for its continuance, its powers, and its emoluments upon the will of its creator, and the possession of which may be burdened with any conditions not prohibited by the Constitution. Attorneys and counsellors are not officers of the United States; they are not elected or appointed in the manner prescribed by the Constitution for the election and appointment of such officers. They are officers of the court, admitted as such by its order, upon evidence of their possessing sufficient legal learning and fair private character. . . . They hold their office during good behavior, and can only be deprived of it for misconduct ascertained and declared by the judgment of the court after opportunity to be heard has been afforded. Their admission or their exclusion is not the exercise of a mere ministerial power. It is the exercise of judicial power, and has been so held in numerous cases. . . .

The legislature may undoubtedly prescribe qualifications for the office, to which he must conform, as it may where it has exclusive jurisdiction, prescribe qualifications for the pursuit of any of the ordinary avocations of life. The question, in this case, is not as to the power of Congress to prescribe qualifications, but whether that power has been exercised as a means for the infliction of punishment, against the prohibition of the Constitution. . . .

This view is strengthened by a consideration of the effect of the pardon produced by the petitioner, and the nature of the pardoning power of the President.

The Constitution provides that the President "shall have power to grant reprieves and pardons for offenses against the United

States, except in cases of impeachment."

The power thus conferred is unlimited, with the exception stated. It extends to every offense known to the law, and may be exercised at any time after its commission, either before legal proceedings are taken, or during their pendency, or after conviction and judgment. This power of the President is not subject to legislative control. Congress can neither limit the effect of his pardon, nor exclude from its exercise any class of offenders. The benign prerogative of mercy reposed in him cannot be fettered by any legislative restrictions.

Such being the case, the inquiry arises as to the effect and operation of a pardon, and on this point all the authorities concur. A pardon reaches both the punishment prescribed for the offense and the guilt of the offender; and when the pardon is full, it releases the punishment and blots out of existence the guilt, so that in the eye of the law the offender is as innocent as if he had never committed the offense. If granted before conviction, it prevents any of the penalties and disabilities consequent upon conviction from attaching; if granted after conviction, it removes the penalties and disabilities, and restores him to all his civil rights; it makes him, as it were, a new man, and gives him a new credit and capacity. . . . The pardon produced by the petitioner is a full pardon

"for all offenses by him committed, arising from participation, direct or implied, in the Rebellion," and is subject to certain conditions which have been complied with. The effect of this pardon is to relieve the petitioner from all penalties and disabilities attached to the offense of treason, committed by his participation in the Rebellion. So far as that offense is concerned, he is thus placed beyond the reach of punishment of any kind. But to exclude him, by reason of that offense, from continuing in the enjoyment of a previously acquired right, is to enforce a punishment for that offense notwithstanding the pardon. If such exclusion can be effected by the exaction of an expurgatory oath covering the offense, the pardon may be avoided, and that accomplished indirectly which cannot be reached by direct legislation. It is not within the constitutional power of Congress to inflict punishment beyond the reach of executive clemency. From the petitioner, therefore, the oath required by the act of January 24th, 1865, could not be exacted, even if that act were not subject to any other objection than the one thus stated.

It follows, from the views expressed, that the prayer of the petitioner must be granted. . . . And it is so ordered.

MILLER, J., with whom concurred WAITE, C. J., and Justices SWAYNE and DAVIS, delivered a dissenting opinion.

259. MISSISSIPPI v. JOHNSON
4 Wallace, 475
1867

Suit in the Supreme Court by the State of Mississippi to enjoin President Johnson from enforcing the Reconstruction Acts of 1867 on the ground that they were unconstitutional. With the failure of Mississippi to secure a decision from the Court on this question, Georgia filed a suit to restrain Secretary Stanton from enforcing the acts. *Georgia* v. *Stanton*, 6 Wallace, 50. See, W. A. Dunning, *Reconstruction, Political and Economic,* ch. xvi; J. W. Burgess, *Reconstruction and the Constitution,* p. 144 ff.; Warren, *The Supreme Court,* Vol. II, ch. xxx.

CHASE, C. J. A motion was made, some days since, in behalf of the State of Mississippi, for leave to file a bill in the name of the State, praying this court perpetually to enjoin and restrain Andrew Johnson, President of the

United States, and E. O. C. Ord, general commanding in the District of Mississippi and Arkansas, from executing, or in any manner carrying out, certain acts of Congress therein named.

The acts referred to are those of March 2d and March 23d, 1867, commonly known as the Reconstruction Acts. . . . The single point which requires consideration is this: Can the President be restrained by injunction from carrying into effect an act of Congress alleged to be unconstitutional?

It is assumed by the counsel for the State of Mississippi, that the President, in the execution of the Reconstruction Acts, is required to perform a mere ministerial duty. In this assumption there is, we think, a confounding of the terms ministerial and executive, which are by no means equivalent in import.

A ministerial duty, the performance of which may, in proper cases, be required of the head of a department, by judicial process, is one in respect to which nothing is left to discretion. It is a simple, definite duty, arising under conditions admitted or proved to exist, and imposed by law. . . .

Very different is the duty of the President in the exercise of the power to see that the laws are faithfully executed, and among these laws the acts named in the bill. By the first of these acts he is required to assign generals to command in the several military districts, and to detail sufficient military force to enable such officers to discharge their duties under the law. By the supplementary act, other duties are imposed on the several commanding generals, and these duties must necessarily be performed under the supervision of the President as commander in chief. The duty thus imposed on the President is in no just sense ministerial. It is purely executive and political.

An attempt on the part of the judicial department of the government to enforce the performance of such duties by the President might be justly characterized, in the language of Chief Justice Marshall, as "an absurd and excessive extravagance."

It is true that in the instance before us the interposition of the court is not sought to en force action by the executive under constitutional legislation, but to restrain such action under legislation alleged to be unconstitutional. But we are unable to perceive that this circumstance takes the case out of the general principles which forbid judicial interference with the exercise of executive discretion.

It was admitted in the argument that the application now made to us is without a precedent; and this is of much weight against it. . . .

The fact that no such application was ever before made in any case indicates the general judgment of the profession that no such application should be entertained.

It will hardly be contended that Congress [the court?] can interpose, in any case, to restrain the enactment of an unconstitutional law; and yet how can the right to judicial interposition to prevent such an enactment, when the purpose is evident and the execution of that purpose certain, be distinguished, in principle, from the right to such interposition against the execution of such a law by the President?

The Congress is the legislative department of the government; the President is the executive department. Neither can be restrained in its action by the judicial department; though the acts of both, when performed, are, in proper cases, subject to its cognizance.

The impropriety of such interference will be clearly seen upon consideration of its possible consequences.

Suppose the bill filed and the injunction prayed for allowed. If the President refuse obedience, it is needless to observe that the court is without power to enforce its process. If, on the other hand, the President complies with the order of the court and refuses to execute the acts of Congress, is it not clear that a collision may occur between the executive and legislative departments of the government? May not the House of Representatives impeach the President for such refusal? And in that case could this court interfere, in behalf of the President, thus endangered by compliance with its mandate, and restrain by injunction the Senate of the United States from sitting as a court of impeachment? Would the strange spectacle be offered to the public world of an attempt by this court to arrest proceedings in that court?

These questions answer themselves. . . .

It has been suggested that the bill contains a prayer that, if the relief sought cannot be had against Andrew Johnson, as President, it may be granted against Andrew Johnson as a citizen of Tennessee. But it is plain that relief as against the execution of an act of Congress by Andrew Johnson, is relief against its execution by the President. A bill praying an injunction against the execution of an act of Congress by the incumbent of the presidential office cannot be received, whether it describes him as President or as a citizen of a State.

The motion for leave to file the bill is therefore denied.

260. THE FIRST RECONSTRUCTION ACT
March 2, 1867

(*U. S. Statutes at Large,* Vol. XIV, p. 428 ff.)

The triumph of the Radicals in the elections of 1866 gave them a free hand in the development of a reconstruction policy. The famous Act of March 2, 1867, contained the general principles of congressional reconstruction. There was grave doubt about the constitutionality of some of the provisions of this act, but the efforts of Southern States to bring the question before the Supreme Court were unavailing. For the argument against the constitutionality of the measure, see Johnson's veto message, Document No. 261. On the history of the Act, see J. F. Rhodes, *History of the United States,* Vol. VI; J. W. Burgess, *Reconstruction and the Constitution;* W. L. Fleming, *The Sequel of Appomattox,* chs. v–vi; C. E. Chadsey, *The Struggle Between President Johnson and Congress over Reconstruction;* J. A. Woodburn, *Thaddeus Stevens,* chs. xiii–xviii; G. F. Milton, *The Age of Hate,* ch. xvii; B. B. Kendrick, *The Journal of the Joint Committee of Fifteen.* For the political background, H. K. Beale, *The Critical Year,* is invaluable. For military government, see W. A. Dunning, *Essays on the Civil War and Reconstruction,* chs. iii–iv; and the numerous monographs on reconstruction in the States; see bibliographies in W. A. Dunning, *Reconstruction,* and in H. K. Beale, *Critical Year.*

An Act to provide for the more efficient Government of the Rebel States

WHEREAS no legal State governments or adequate protection for life or property now exists in the rebel States of Virginia, North Carolina, South Carolina, Georgia, Mississippi, Alabama, Louisiana, Florida, Texas, and Arkansas; and whereas it is necessary that peace and good order should be enforced in said States until loyal and republican State governments can be legally established: Therefore,

Be it enacted, That said rebel States shall be divided into military districts and made subject to the military authority of the United States as hereinafter prescribed, and for that purpose Virginia shall constitute the first district; North Carolina and South Carolina the second district; Georgia, Alabama, and Florida the third district; Mississippi and Arkansas the fourth district; and Louisiana and Texas the fifth district.

SEC. 2. That it shall be the duty of the President to assign to the command of each of said districts an officer of the army, not below the rank of brigadier-general, and to detail a sufficient military force to enable such officer to perform his duties and enforce his authority within the district to which he is assigned.

SEC. 3. That it shall be the duty of each officer assigned as aforesaid, to protect all persons in their rights of persons and property, to suppress insurrection, disorder, and violence, and to punish, or cause to be punished, all disturbers of the public peace and criminals; and to this end he may allow local civil tribunals to take jurisdiction of and to try offenders, or, when in his judgment it may be necessary for the trial of offenders, he shall have power to organize military commissions or tribunals for that purpose, and all interference under color of State authority with the exercise of military authority under this act, shall be null and void.

SEC. 4. That all persons put under military arrest by virtue of this act shall be tried without unnecessary delay, and no cruel or unusual punishment shall be inflicted, and no sentence of any military commission or tribunal hereby authorized, affecting the life or liberty of any person, shall be executed until it is approved by the officer in command of the district, and the laws and regulations for the government of the army shall not be affected by this act, except in so far as they conflict with its provisions: *Provided,* That no sentence of death under the provisions of this act shall be carried into effect without the approval of the President.

SEC. 5. That when the people of any one of said rebel States shall have formed a constitution of government in conformity with the Constitution of the United States in all respects, framed by a convention of delegates elected by the male citizens of said State, twenty-one years old and upward, of whatever race, color, or previous condition, who have been resident in said State for one year previous to the day of such election, except such as may be disfranchised for participation in the rebellion or for felony at common law, and when such constitution shall provide that the elective franchise shall be enjoyed by all such persons as have the qualifications herein stated for electors of delegates, and when such constitution shall be ratified by a majority of the persons voting on the question of ratification who are qualified as electors for delegates, and when such constitution shall have been submitted to Congress for examination and approval, and Congress shall have approved the same, and when said State, by a vote of its legislature elected under said constitution, shall have adopted the amendment to the Constitution of the United States, proposed by the Thirty-ninth Congress, and known as article fourteen, and when said article shall have become a part of the Constitution of the United States said State shall be declared entitled to representation in Congress, and senators and representatives shall be admitted therefrom on their taking the oath prescribed by law, and then and thereafter the preceding sections of this act shall be inoperative in said State: *Provided,* That no person excluded from the privilege of holding office by said proposed amendment to the Constitution of the United States, shall be eligible to election as a member of the convention to frame a constitution for any of said rebel States, nor shall any such person vote for members of such convention.

SEC. 6. That, until the people of said rebel States shall be by law admitted to representation in the Congress of the United States, any civil governments which may exist therein shall be deemed provisional only, and in all respects subject to the paramount authority of the United States at any time to abolish, modify, control, or supersede the same; and in all elections to any office under such provisional governments all persons shall be entitled to vote, and none others, who are entitled to vote, under the provisions of the fifth section of this act; and no persons shall be eligible to any office under any such provisional governments who would be disqualified from holding office under the provisions of the third *article* of said constitutional amendment.

261. VETO OF THE FIRST RECONSTRUCTION ACT
March 2, 1867

(Richardson, ed. *Messages and Papers,* Vol. VI, p. 498 ff.)

Dunning states that this veto message was drafted by J. S. Black.

WASHINGTON, *March 2, 1867*
To the House of Representatives:

I have examined the bill "to provide for the more efficient government of the rebel States" with the care and anxiety which its transcendent importance is calculated to awaken. I am unable to give it my assent, for reasons so grave that I hope a statement of them may have some influence on the minds of the patriotic and enlightened men with whom the decision must ultimately rest.

The bill places all the people of the ten States therein named under the absolute domination of military rulers; and the preamble undertakes to give the reason upon which the measure is based and the ground upon which it is justified. It declares that there exists in those States no legal governments and no adequate protection for life or property, and asserts the necessity of enforcing peace and good order within their limits. Is this true as matter of fact?

It is not denied that the States in question have each of them an actual government, with all the powers—executive, judicial, and legislative—which properly belong to a free state. They are organized like the other States of the Union, and, like them, they make, administer, and execute the laws which concern their domestic affairs. An existing *de facto* government, exercising such functions as these, is itself the law of the state upon all matters within its jurisdiction. To pronounce the supreme law-making power of an established state illegal is to say that law itself is unlawful.

The provisions which these governments have made for the preservation of order, the suppression of crime, and the redress of private injuries are in substance and principle the same as those which prevail in the Northern States and in other civilized countries. . . .

The bill, however, would seem to show upon its face that the establishment of peace and good order is not its real object. The fifth section declares that the preceding sections shall cease to operate in any State where certain events shall have happened. . . .

All these conditions must be fulfilled before the people of any of these States can be relieved from the bondage of military domination; but when they are fulfilled, then immediately the pains and penalties of the bill are to cease, no matter whether there be peace and order or not, and without any reference to the security of life or property. The excuse given for the bill in the preamble is admitted by the bill itself not to be real. The military rule which it establishes is plainly to be used, not for any purpose of order or for the prevention of crime, but solely as a means of coercing the people into the adoption of principles and measures to which it is known that they are opposed, and upon which they have an undeniable right to exercise their own judgment.

I submit to Congress whether this measure is not in its whole character, scope, and object without precedent and without authority, in palpable conflict with the plainest provisions of the Constitution, and utterly destructive to those great principles of liberty and humanity for which our ancestors on both sides of the Atlantic have shed so much blood and expended so much treasure.

The ten States named in the bill are divided into five districts. For each district an officer of the Army, not below the rank of a brigadier-general, is to be appointed to rule over the people; and he is to be supported with an efficient military force to enable him to perform his duties and enforce his authority. Those duties and that authority, as defined by the third section of the bill, are "to protect all persons in their rights of person and property, to suppress insurrection, disorder, and violence, and to punish or cause to be punished all disturbers of the public peace or criminals." The power thus given to the commanding officer over all the people of each district is that of an absolute monarch. His mere will is to take the place of all law. The law of the States is now the only rule applicable to the subjects placed under his con-

trol, and that is completely displaced by the clause which declares all interference of State authority to be null and void. He alone is permitted to determine what are rights of person or property, and he may protect them in such way as in his discretion may seem proper. It places at his free disposal all the lands and goods in his district, and he may distribute them without let or hindrance to whom he pleases. Being bound by no State law, and there being no other law to regulate the subject, he may make a criminal code of his own; and he can make it as bloody as any recorded in history, or he can reserve the privilege of acting upon the impulse of his private passions in each case that arises. He is bound by no rules of evidence; there is, indeed, no provision by which he is authorized or required to take any evidence at all. Everything is a crime which he chooses to call so, and all persons are condemned whom he pronounces to be guilty. He is not bound to keep and record or make any report of his proceedings. He may arrest his victims wherever he finds them, without warrant, accusation, or proof of probable cause. If he gives them a trial before he inflicts the punishment, he gives it of his grace and mercy, not because he is commanded so to do. . . .

It is also provided that "he shall have power to organize military commissions or tribunals;" but this power he is not commanded to exercise. . . . Instead of mitigating the harshness of his single rule, such a tribunal would be used much more probably to divide the responsibility of making it more cruel and unjust.

Several provisions dictated by the humanity of Congress have been inserted in the bill, apparently to restrain the power of the commanding officer; but it seems to me that they are of no avail for that purpose. . . .

It is plain that the authority here given to the military officer amounts to absolute despotism. But to make it still more unendurable, the bill provides that it may be delegated to as many subordinates as he chooses to appoint, for it declares that he shall "punish or cause to be punished." Such a power has not been wielded by any monarch in England for more than five hundred years. In all that time no people who speak the English language have borne such servitude. It reduces the whole population of the ten States—all persons, of every color, sex, and condition, and every stranger within their limits—to the most abject and degrading slavery. No master ever had a control so absolute over the slaves as this bill gives to the military officers over both white and colored persons. . . .

I come now to a question which is, if possible, still more important. Have we the power to establish and carry into execution a measure like this? I answer, Certainly not, if we derive our authority from the Constitution and if we are bound by the limitations which it imposes.

This proposition is perfectly clear, that no branch of the Federal Government—executive, legislative, or judicial—can have any just powers except those which it derives through and exercises under the organic law of the Union. Outside of the Constitution we have no legal authority more than private citizens, and within it we have only so much as that instrument gives us. This broad principle limits all our functions and applies to all subjects. It protects not only the citizens of States which are within the Union, but it shields every human being who comes or is brought under our jurisdiction. We have no right to do in one place more than in another that which the Constitution says we shall not do at all. If, therefore, the Southern States were in truth out of the Union, we could not treat their people in a way which the fundamental law forbids.

Some persons assume that the success of our arms in crushing the opposition which was made in some of the States to the execution of the Federal laws reduced those States and all their people—the innocent as well as the guilty—to the condition of vassalage and gave us a power over them which the Constitution does not bestow or define or limit. No fallacy can be more transparent than this. Our victories subjected the insurgents to legal obedience, not to the yoke of an arbitrary despotism. . . .

Invasion, insurrection, rebellion, and domestic violence were anticipated when the Government was framed, and the means of repelling and suppressing them were wisely provided for in the Constitution; but it was not thought necessary to declare that the States in which they might occur should be expelled from the Union. Rebellions, which were invariably suppressed, occurred prior to

that out of which these questions grow; but the States continued to exist and the Union remained unbroken. In Massachusetts, in Pennsylvania, in Rhode Island, and in New York, at different periods in our history, violent and armed opposition to the United States was carried on; but the relations of those States with the Federal Government were not supposed to be interrupted or changed thereby after the rebellious portions of their population were defeated and put down. It is true that in these earlier cases there was no formal expression of a determination to withdraw from the Union, but it is also true that in the Southern States the ordinances of secession were treated by all the friends of the Union as mere nullities and are now acknowledged to be so by the States themselves. If we admit that they had any force or validity or that they did in fact take the States in which they were passed out of the Union, we sweep from under our feet all the grounds upon which we stand in justifying the use of Federal force to maintain the integrity of the Government.

This is a bill passed by Congress in time of peace. There is not in any one of the States brought under its operation either war or insurrection. The laws of the States and of the Federal Government are all in undisturbed and harmonious operation. The courts, State and Federal, are open and in the full exercise of their proper authority. Over every State comprised in these five military districts, life, liberty, and property are secured by State laws and Federal laws, and the National Constitution is everywhere in force and everywhere obeyed. What, then, is the ground on which this bill proceeds? The title of the bill announces that it is intended "for the more efficient government" of these ten States. It is recited by way of preamble that no legal State governments "nor adequate protection for life or property" exist in those States, and that peace and good order should be thus enforced. The first thing which arrests attention upon these recitals, which prepare the way for martial law, is this, that the only foundation upon which martial law can exist under our form of government is not stated or so much as pretended. Actual war, foreign invasion, domestic insurrection—none of these appear; and none of these, in fact, exist. It is not even recited that any sort of war or insurrection is threatened. Let us pause here to consider, upon this question of constitutional law and the power of Congress, a recent decision of the Supreme Court of the United States in *ex parte* Milligan. . . .

I need not say to the representatives of the American people that their Constitution forbids the exercise of judicial power in any way but one—that is, by the ordained and established courts. It is equally well known that in all criminal cases a trial by jury is made indispensable by the express words of that instrument. I will not enlarge on the inestimable value of the right thus secured to every freeman or speak of the danger to public liberty in all parts of the country which must ensue from a denial of it anywhere or upon any pretense. A very recent decision of the Supreme Court has traced the history, vindicated the dignity, and made known the value of this great privilege so clearly that nothing more is needed. To what extent a violation of it might be excused in time of war or public danger may admit of discussion, but we are providing now for a time of profound peace, when there is not an armed soldier within our borders except those who are in the service of the Government. It is in such a condition of things that an act of Congress is proposed which, if carried out, would deny a trial by the lawful courts and juries to 9,000,000 American citizens and to their posterity for an indefinite period. It seems to be scarcely possible that anyone should seriously believe this consistent with a Constitution which declares in simple, plain, and unambiguous language that all persons shall have that right and that no person shall ever in any case be deprived of it. The Constitution also forbids the arrest of the citizen without judicial warrant, founded on probable cause. This bill authorizes an arrest without warrant, at the pleasure of a military commander. The Constitution declares that "no person shall be held to answer for a capital or otherwise infamous crime unless on presentment by a grand jury." This bill holds every person not a soldier answerable for all crimes and all charges without any presentment. The Constitution declares that "no person shall be deprived of life, liberty, or property without due process of law." This bill sets aside all process of law, and makes the citizen answerable in his person and property to the will of one man, and as to his life to the

will of two. Finally, the Constitution declares that "the privilege of the writ of *habeas corpus* shall not be suspended unless when, in case of rebellion or invasion, the public safety may require it;" whereas this bill declares martial law (which of itself suspends this great writ) in time of peace, and authorizes the military to make the arrest, and gives to the prisoner only one privilege, and that is a trial "without unnecessary delay." He has no hope of release from custody, except the hope, such as it is, of release by acquittal before a military commission.

The United States are bound to guarantee to each State a republican form of government. Can it be pretended that this obligation is not probably broken if we carry out a measure like this, which wipes away every vestige of republican government in ten States and puts the life, property, liberty, and honor of all the people in each of them under the domination of a single person clothed with unlimited authority?

The purpose and object of the bill—the general intent which pervades it from beginning to end—is to change the entire structure and character of the State governments and to compel them by force to the adoption of organic laws and regulations which they are unwilling to accept if left to themselves. The negroes have not asked for the privilege of voting; the vast majority of them have no idea what it means. This bill not only thrusts it into their hands, but compels them, as well as the whites, to use it in a particular way. If they do not form a constitution with prescribed articles in it and afterwards elect a legislature which will act upon certain measures in a prescribed way, neither blacks nor whites can be relieved from the slavery which the bill imposes upon them. Without pausing here to consider the policy or impolicy of Africanizing the southern part of our territory, I would simply ask the attention of Congress to that manifest, well-known, and universally acknowledged rule of constitutional law which declares that the Federal Government has no jurisdiction, authority, or power to regulate such subjects for any State. To force the right of suffrage out of the hands of the white people and into the hands of the negroes is an arbitrary violation of this principle. . . .

The bill also denies the legality of the gov-

ernments of ten of the States which participated in the ratification of the amendment to
the Federal Constitution abolishing slavery
forever within the jurisdiction of the United
States and practically excludes them from the
Union. If this assumption of the bill be correct, their concurrence can not be considered
as having been legally given, and the important fact is made to appear that the consent
of three-fourths of the States—the requisite
number—has not been constitutionally obtained to the ratification of that amendment,
thus leaving the question of slavery where it
stood before the amendment was officially declared to have become a part of the Constitution.

That the measure proposed by this bill does
violate the Constitution in the particulars
mentioned and in many other ways which I
forbear to enumerate is too clear to admit of
the least doubt. . . .

It is a part of our public history which can
never be forgotten that both Houses of Congress, in July, 1861, declared in the form of a
solemn resolution that the war was and should
be carried on for no purpose of subjugation,
but solely to enforce the Constitution and
laws, and that when this was yielded by the
parties in rebellion the contest should cease,
with the constitutional rights of the States
and of individuals unimpaired. This resolution was adopted and sent forth to the world
unanimously by the Senate and with only two
dissenting voices in the House. It was accepted by the friends of the Union in the
South as well as in the North as expressing
honestly and truly the object of the war. On
the faith of it many thousands of persons in
both sections gave their lives and their fortunes to the cause. To repudiate it now by
refusing to the States and to the individuals
within them the rights which the Constitution and laws of the Union would secure
to them is a breach of our plighted honor for
which I can imagine no excuse and to which
I can not voluntarily become a party. . . .

ANDREW JOHNSON.

262. THE TENURE OF OFFICE ACT
March 2, 1867

(U. S. Statutes at Large, Vol. XIV, p. 430 ff.)

The struggle between Johnson and the Radicals
over Reconstruction had been referred to the
voters, and the elections of the fall of 1866 were
overwhelmingly favorable to the Radicals. The
thirty-ninth Congress which met in December
1866 was dominated by such Radical leaders as
Stevens, Sumner, Wilson, Boutwell, Wade,
Chandler, and others. The Tenure of Office Act
was one of three momentous bills passed March
2, 1867. The question of the power of the
President to remove officials appointed by and
with the advice of the Senate had long been
a controversial one; it was not, indeed, settled
until 1926 (see Doc. No. 459). It was highly uncertain whether the Act was originally designed
to afford permanence of tenure to the members
of Johnson's cabinet who had been appointed by
President Lincoln. See Johnson's veto message,
Doc. No. 263. Johnson's removal of Secretary
Stanton, in alleged violation of the Tenure of
Office Act, was the principal charge in the
impeachment proceedings. See, C. E. Chadsey,
*The Struggle Between President Johnson and
Congress over Reconstruction;* W. A. Dunning,
Reconstruction, ch. vi; J. F. Rhodes, *History of
the United States,* Vol. VI; J. W. Burgess, *Re-
construction and the Constitution;* biographies
of Johnson by Milton, Stryker, Winston.

*An Act regulating the Tenure of certain Civil
Offices.*

Be it enacted, That every person holding
any civil office to which he has been appointed
by and with the advice and consent of the
Senate, and every person who shall hereafter
be appointed to any such office, and shall become duly qualified to act therein, is, and
shall be entitled to hold such office until a successor shall have been in like manner appointed and duly qualified, except as herein
otherwise provided: *Provided,* That the Secretaries of State, of the Treasury, of War, of
the Navy, and of the Interior, the Postmaster-General, and the Attorney-General, shall
hold their offices respectively for and during
the term of the President by whom they may
have been appointed and for one month thereafter, subject to removal by and with the advice and consent of the Senate.

SEC. 2. That when any officer appointed as aforesaid, excepting judges of the United States courts, shall, during a recess of the Senate, be shown, by evidence satisfactory to the President, to be guilty of misconduct in office, or crime, or for any reason shall become incapable or legally disqualified to perform its duties, in such case, and in no other, the President may suspend such officer and designate some suitable person to perform temporarily the duties of such office until the next meeting of the Senate, and until the case shall be acted upon by the Senate . . . ; and in such case it shall be the duty of the President, within twenty days after the first day of such next meeting of the Senate, to report to the Senate such suspension, with the evidence and reasons for his action in the case, and the name of the person so designated to perform the duties of such office. And if the Senate shall concur in such suspension and advise and consent to the removal of such officer, they shall so certify to the President, who may thereupon remove such officer, and, by and with the advice and consent of the Senate, appoint another person to such office. But if the Senate shall refuse to concur in such suspension, such officer so suspended shall forthwith resume the functions of his office, and the powers of the person so· performing its duties in his stead shall cease, and the official salary and emoluments of such officer shall, during such suspension, belong to the person so performing the duties thereof, and not to the officer so suspended. . . .

SEC. 3. That the President shall have power to fill all vacancies which may happen during the recess of the Senate, by reason of death or resignation, by granting commissions which shall expire at the end of their next session thereafter. . . .

SEC. 4. That nothing in this act contained shall be construed to extend the term of any office the duration of which is limited by law.

SEC. 5. That if any person shall, contrary to the provisions of this act, accept any appointment to or employment in any office, or shall hold or exercise or attempt to hold or exercise, any such office or employment, he shall be deemed, and is hereby declared to be, guilty of a high misdemeanor, and, upon trial and conviction thereof, he shall be punished therefor by a fine not exceeding ten thousand dollars, or by imprisonment not exceeding five years, or both said punishments, in the discretion of the court.

SEC. 6. That every removal, appointment, or employment, made, had, or exercised, contrary to the provisions of this act, . . . shall be deemed, and are hereby declared to be, high misdemeanors, and, upon trial and conviction thereof, every person guilty thereof shall be punished by a fine not exceeding ten thousand dollars, or by imprisonment not exceeding five years, or both said punishments, in the discretion of the court. . . .

263. VETO OF TENURE OF OFFICE ACT
March 2, 1867

(Richardson, ed. *Messages and Papers,* Vol. VI, p. 492 ff.)

According to Welles, the veto message was drafted by Secretaries Seward and Stanton.

WASHINGTON, *March 2, 1867.*
To the Senate of the United States:

I have carefully examined the bill "to regulate the tenure of certain civil offices." . . . In effect the bill provides that the President shall not remove from their places any of the civil officers whose terms of service are not limited by law without the advice and consent of the Senate of the United States. The bill in this respect conflicts, in my judgment, with the Constitution of the United States. The question, as Congress is well aware, is by no means a new one. That the power of removal is constitutionally vested in the President of the United States is a principle which has been not more distinctly declared by judicial authority and judicial commentators than it has been uniformly practiced upon by the legislative and executive departments of the Government. . . .

The question has often been raised in subsequent times of high excitement, and the practice of the Government has, nevertheless, conformed in all cases to the decision thus early made.

The question was revived during the Administration of President Jackson, who made, as is well recollected, a very large number of removals, which were made an occasion of close and rigorous scrutiny and remonstrance. The subject was long and earnestly debated in the Senate, and the early construction of the Constitution was, nevertheless, freely accepted as binding and conclusive upon Congress.

The question came before the Supreme Court of the United States in January, 1839, *ex parte* Hennen. It was declared by the court on that occasion that the power of removal from office was a subject much disputed, and upon which a great diversity of opinion was entertained in the early history of the Government. This related, however, to the power of the President to remove officers appointed with the concurrence of the Senate, and the great question was whether the removal was to be by the President alone or with the concurrence of the Senate, both constituting the appointing power. No one denied the power of the President and Senate jointly to remove where the tenure of the office was not fixed by the Constitution, which was a full recognition of the principle that the power of removal was incident to the power of appointment; but it was very early adopted as a practical construction of the Constitution that this power was vested in the President alone, . . .

Thus has the important question presented by this bill been settled, in the language of the late Daniel Webster . . . by construction, settled by precedent, settled by the practice of the Government, and settled by statute. The events of the last war furnished a prac-

tical confirmation of the wisdom of the Constitution as it has hitherto been maintained in many of its parts, including that which is now the subject of consideration. When the war broke out, rebel enemies, traitors, abettors, and sympathizers were found in every Department of the Government, as well in the civil service as in the land and naval military service. They were found in Congress and among the keepers of the Capitol; in foreign missions; in each and all the Executive Departments; in the judicial service; in the post-office, and among the agents for conducting Indian affairs. Upon probable suspicion they were promptly displaced by my predecessor, so far as they held their offices under executive authority, and their duties were confided to new and loyal successors. No complaints against that power or doubts of its wisdom were entertained in any quarter. I sincerely trust and believe that no such civil war is likely to occur again. I can not doubt, however, that in whatever form and on whatever occasion sedition can raise an effort to hinder or embarrass or defeat the legitimate action of this Government, whether by preventing the collection of revenue, or disturbing the public peace, or separating the States, or betraying the country to a foreign enemy, the power of removal from office by the Executive, as it has heretofore existed and been practiced, will be found indispensable.

Under these circumstances, as a depositary of the executive authority of the nation, I do not feel at liberty to unite with Congress in reversing it by giving my approval to the bill. . . .

264. COMMAND OF THE ARMY ACT
March 2, 1867

(U. S. Statutes at Large, Vol. XIV, p. 485 ff.)

Congress inserted in the Army Appropriation act of March 2, 1867, provisions which virtually deprived the President of the command of the army by requiring that he issue all military orders through the General of the army. Johnson approved of the bill, in order not to defeat the appropriations, but he entered a protest against those sections depriving him of command of the army. See, Richardson, Vol. VI, p. 472. For references, see Doc. No. 262.

An Act making appropriations for the sup-

port of the army for the year ending June, 30, 1868 *and for other purposes.*

SEC. 2. *And be it further enacted,* That the headquarters of the General of the army of the United States shall be at the city of Washington, and all orders and instructions relating to military operations issued by the President or Secretary of War shall be issued through the General of the army, and, in case of his inability, through the next in rank. The General of the army shall not be removed, suspended, or relieved from command, or assigned to duty elsewhere than at said headquarters, except at his own request, without the previous approval of the Senate; and any orders or instructions relating to military operations issued contrary to the requirements of this section shall be null and void; and any officer who shall issue orders or instructions contrary to the provisions of this section shall be deemed guilty of a misdemeanor in office; and any officer of the army who shall transmit, convey, or obey any orders or instructions so issued contrary to the provisions of this section, knowing that such orders were so issued, shall be liable to imprisonment for not less than two nor more than twenty years, upon conviction thereof in any court of competent jurisdiction. . . .

265. THE SECOND RECONSTRUCTION ACT
March 23, 1867

(*U. S. Statutes at Large*, Vol. XV, p. 2 ff.)

This act provided in detail for the processes by which the military commanders were to reconstruct the Southern States. For references see Doc. No. 260.

An Act supplementary to an Act entitled "An Act to provide for the more efficient Government of the Rebel States," passed March 2, 1867, and to facilitate Restoration.

Be it enacted . . . , That before . . . September 1, 1867 . . . , the commanding general in each district defined by . . . [the act of March 2, 1867] . . . , shall cause a registration to be made of the male citizens of the United States, twenty-one years of age and upwards, resident in each county or parish in the State or States included in his district, which registration shall include only those persons who are qualified to vote for delegates by the act aforesaid, and who shall have taken and subscribed the following oath or affirmation: "I, —— ——, do solemnly swear (or affirm), in the presence of Almighty God, that I am a citizen of the State of ——; that I have resided in said State for —— months next preceding this day, and now reside in the county of ——, or the parish of ——, in said State (as the case may be); that I am twenty-one years old; that I have not been disfranchised for participation in any rebellion or civil war against the United States, or for felony committed against the laws of any State or of the United States; that I have never been a member of any State legislature, nor held any executive or judicial office in any State, and afterwards engaged in insurrection or rebellion against the United States, or given aid or comfort to the enemies thereof; that I have never taken an oath as a member of Congress of the United States, or as an officer of the United States, or as a member of any State legislature, or as an executive or judicial officer of any State, to support the Constitution of the United States, and afterwards engaged in insurrection or rebellion against the United States, or given aid or comfort to the enemies thereof; that I will faithfully support the Constitution and obey the laws of the United States, and will, to the best of my ability, encourage others so to do, so help me God." . . .

SEC. 2. That after the completion of the registration hereby provided for in any State, at such time and places therein as the commanding general shall appoint and direct, of which at least thirty days' public notice shall be given, an election shall be held of delegates to a convention for the purpose of establishing a constitution and civil government for such State loyal to the Union, said convention in each State, except Virginia, to consist of the same number of members as the most numerous branch of the State legislature of such State . . . [in 1860] . . . , to be apportioned among the several districts, counties, or parishes of such State by the commanding general, giving to each representation in the ration of voters registered as aforesaid as nearly as may be. The convention in Virginia shall consist of the same number of members as represented the territory now constituting Virginia in the most numerous branch of the legislature of said State . . . [in 1860] . . . , to be apportioned as aforesaid.

SEC. 3. That at said election the registered voters of each State shall vote for or against a convention to form a constitution therefor under this act. And the commanding general . . . shall ascertain and declare the total vote in each State . . . If a majority of the votes given on that question shall be for a convention, then such convention shall be held as hereinafter provided; but if a majority of said votes shall be against a convention, then no such convention shall be held under this act: *Provided,* That such convention shall not be held unless a majority of all such registered voters shall have voted on the question of holding such convention.

SEC. 4. That the commanding general of each district shall appoint as many boards of registration as may be necessary, consisting of three loyal officers or persons, to make and complete the registration, superintend the election, and make return to him of the votes, lists of voters, and of the persons elected as delegates by a plurality of the votes cast at said election; and upon receiving said returns he shall open the same, ascertain the persons elected as delegates, according to the returns of the officers who conducted said election, and make proclamation thereof; and if a majority of the votes given on that question shall be for a convention, the commanding general, within sixty days from the date of election, shall notify the delegates to assemble in convention, at a time and place to be mentioned in the notification, and said convention, when organized, shall proceed to frame a constitution and civil government according to the provisions of this act, and the act to which it is supplementary; and when the same shall have been so framed, said constitution shall be submitted by the convention for ratifica-tion to the persons registered under the provisions of this act at an election to be conducted by the officers or persons appointed or to be appointed by the commanding general, as hereinbefore provided, and to be held after the expiration of thirty days from the date of notice thereof, to be given by said convention; and the returns thereof shall be made to the commanding general of the district.

SEC. 5. That if, according to said returns, the constitution shall be ratified by a majority of the votes of the registered electors . . . at least one half of all the registered voters voting upon the question of such ratification, the president of the convention shall transmit a copy of the same, duly certified, to the President of the United States, who shall forthwith transmit the same to Congress . . . ; and if it shall moreover appear to Congress that the election was one at which all the registered and qualified electors in the State had an opportunity to vote freely and without restraint, fear, or the influence of fraud, and if the Congress shall be satisfied that such constitution meets the approval of a majority of all the qualified electors in the State, and if the said constitution shall be declared by Congress to be in conformity with the provisions of the act to which this is supplementary, and the other provisions of said act shall have been complied with, and the said constitution shall be approved by Congress, the State shall be declared entitled to representation, and senators and representatives shall be admitted therefrom as therein provided.

266. VETO OF THE SECOND RECONSTRUCTION ACT
March 23, 1867

(Richardson, ed. *Messages and Papers,* Vol. VI, p. 531 ff.)

WASHINGTON, *March 23, 1867.*

To the House of Representatives:

I have considered the bill entitled "An act supplementary to an act entitled 'An act to provide for the more efficient government of the rebel States,' passed March 2, 1867, and to facilitate restoration," and now return it to the House of Representatives with my objections.

This bill provides for elections in the ten States brought under the operation of the original act to which it is supplementary. Its details are principally directed to the elections for the formation of the State constitutions, but by the sixth section of the bill "all elections" in these States occurring while the original act remains in force are brought within its purview. Referring to these details, it will be found that, first of all, there is to be a registration of the voters. No one whose name has not been admitted on the list is to be allowed to vote at any of these elections. To ascertain who is entitled to registration, reference is made necessary, by the express language of the supplement, to the original act and to the pending bill. The fifth section of the original act provides, as to voters, that they shall be "male citizens of the State, 21 years old and upward, of whatever race, color, or previous condition, who have been residents of said State for one year." This is the general qualification, followed, however, by many exceptions. No one can be registered, according to the original act, "who may be disfranchised for participation in the rebellion"—a provision which left undetermined the question as to what amounted to disfranchisement, and whether without a judicial sentence the act itself produced that effect. This supplemental bill superadds an oath, to be taken by every person before his name can be admitted upon the registration, that he has "not been disfranchised for participation in any rebellion or civil war against the United States." It thus imposes upon every person the necessity and responsibility of deciding for himself, under the peril of punishment by a military commission if he makes a mistake, what works disfranchisement by participation in rebellion and what amounts to such participation. . . .

The fourth section of the bill provides "that the commanding general of each district shall appoint as many boards of registration as may be necessary, consisting of three loyal officers or persons." The only qualification stated for these officers is that they must be "loyal." They may be persons in the military service or civilians, residents of the State or strangers. Yet these persons are to exercise most important duties and are vested with unlimited discretion. They are to decide what names shall be placed upon the register and from their decision there is to be no appeal. They are to superintend the elections and to decide all questions which may arise. They are to have the custody of the ballots and to make return of the persons elected. Whatever frauds or errors they may commit must pass without redress. All that is left for the commanding general is to receive the returns of the elections, open the same, and ascertain who are chosen "according to the returns of the officers who conducted said elections." By such means and with this sort of agency are the conventions of delegates to be constituted.

As the delegates are to speak for the people, common justice would seem to require

that they should have authority from the people themselves. No convention so constituted will in any sense represent the wishes of the inhabitants of these States, for under the all-embracing exceptions of these laws, by a construction which the uncertainty of the clause as to disfranchisement leaves open to the board of officers, the great body of the people may be excluded from the polls and from all opportunity of expressing their own wishes or voting for delegates who will faithfully reflect their sentiments.

I do not deem it necessary further to investigate the details of this bill. No consideration could induce me to give my approval to such an election law for any purpose, and especially for the great purpose of framing the constitution of a State. If ever the American citizen should be left to the free exercise of his own judgment it is when he is engaged in the work of forming the fundamental law under which he is to live. That work is his work, and it can not properly be taken out of his hands. All this legislation proceeds upon the contrary assumption that the people of each of these States shall have no constitution except such as may be arbitrarily dictated by Congress and formed under the restraint of military rule. A plain statement of facts makes this evident.

In all these States there are existing constitutions, framed in the accustomed way by the people. Congress, however, declares that these constitutions are not "loyal and republican," and requires the people to form them anew. What, then, in the opinion of Congress, is necessary to make the constitution of a State "loyal and republican"? The original act answers the question: It is universal negro suffrage—a question which the Federal Constitution leaves exclusively to the States themselves. All this legislative machinery of martial law, military coercion, and political disfranchisement is avowedly for that purpose and none other. The existing constitutions of the ten States conform to the acknowledged standards of loyalty and republicanism. Indeed, if there are degrees in republican forms of government, their constitutions are more republican now than when these States, four of which were members of the original thirteen, first became members of the Union.

Congress does not now demand that a single provision of their constitutions be changed except such as confine suffrage to the white population. It is apparent, therefore, that these provisions do not conform to the standard of republicanism which Congress seeks to establish. That there may be no mistake, it is only necessary that reference should be made to the original act, which declares "such constitution shall provide that the elective franchise shall be enjoyed by all such persons as have the qualifications herein stated for electors of delegates." What class of persons is here meant clearly appears in the same section; that is to say, "the male citizens of said State 21 years old and upward, of whatever race, color, or previous condition, who have been resident in said State for one year previous to the day of such election."

Without these provisions no constitution which can be framed in any one of the ten States will be of any avail with Congress. This, then, is the test of what the constitution of a State of this Union must contain to make it republican. Measured by such a standard, how few of the States now composing the Union have republican constitutions! If in the exercise of the constitutional guaranty that Congress shall secure to every State a republican form of government universal suffrage for blacks as well as whites is a *sine qua non,* the work of reconstruction may as well begin in Ohio as in Virginia, in Pennsylvania as in North Carolina. . . .

ANDREW JOHNSON

267. THE THIRD RECONSTRUCTION ACT
July 19, 1867

(*U. S. Statutes at Large,* Vol. XV, p. 14 ff.)

This act was designed to clear up the ambiguities of the Acts of March 2 and March 23, 1867, particularly with reference to the oath required by the second of those acts. This act was drafted by Sec. Stanton. See, G. C. Gorham, *Life and Public Services of Stanton,* Vol. II, and references to Doc. No. 260.

An Act supplementary to an Act entitled "An Act to provide for the more efficient Government of the Rebel States," passed [March 2, 1867], *and the Act supplementary thereto, passed* [March 23, 1867].

Be it enacted, That it is hereby declared to have been the true intent and meaning . . . [of the acts of March 2 and March 23, 1867] . . . , that the governments then existing in the rebel States of Virginia, North Carolina, South Carolina, Georgia, Mississippi, Alabama, Louisiana, Florida, Texas, and Arkansas were not legal State governments; and that thereafter said governments, if continued, were to be continued subject in all respects to the military commanders of the respective districts, and to the paramount authority of Congress.

SEC. 2. That the commander of any district named in said act shall have power, subject to the disapproval of the General of the army of the United States, and to have effect till disapproved, whenever in the opinion of such commander the proper administration of said act shall require it, to suspend or remove from office, or from the performance of official duties and the exercise of official powers, any officer or person holding or exercising, or professing to hold or exercise, any civil or military office or duty in such district under any power, election, appointment or authority derived from, or granted by, or claimed under, any so-called State or the government thereof, or any municipal or other division thereof, and upon such suspension or removal such commander, subject to the disapproval of the General as aforesaid, shall have power to provide from time to time for the performance of the said duties of such officer or person so suspended or removed, by the detail of some competent officer or soldier of the army, or by the appointment of some other person, to perform the same, and to fill vacancies occasioned by death, resignation, or otherwise.

SEC. 3. That the General of the army of the United States shall be invested with all the powers of suspension, removal, appointment, and detail granted in the preceding section to district commanders.

SEC. 4. That the acts of the officers of the army already done in removing in said districts persons exercising the functions of civil officers, and appointing others in their stead, are hereby confirmed: *Provided,* That any person heretofore or hereafter appointed by any district commander to exercise the functions of any civil office, may be removed either by the military officer in command of the district, or by the General of the army. And it shall be the duty of such commander to remove from office as aforesaid all persons who are disloyal to the government of the United States, or who use their official influence in any manner to hinder, delay, prevent, or obstruct the due and proper administration of this act and the acts to which it is supplementary.

SEC. 5. That the boards of registration provided for in the act [of March 23, 1867] shall have power, and it shall be their duty before allowing the registration of any person, to ascertain, upon such facts or information as they can obtain, whether such person is entitled to be registered under said act, and the oath required by said act shall not be conclusive on such question, and no person shall be registered unless such board shall decide that he is entitled thereto; and such board shall also have power to examine, under oath, . . . any one touching the qualification of any person claiming registration; . . . *Provided,* That no person shall be disqualified as member of any board of registration by reason of race or color.

SEC. 6. That the true intent and meaning of the oath prescribed in said supplementary act is, (among other things,) that no person who has been a member of the legislature of any State, or who has held any executive or judicial office in any State, whether he has taken an oath to support the Constitution of the United States or not, and whether he was holding such office at the commencement of the rebellion, or had held it before, and who has afterwards engaged in insurrection or rebellion against the United States, or given aid or comfort to the enemies thereof, is entitled to be registered or to vote; and the words "executive or judicial office in any State" in said oath mentioned shall be construed to include all civil offices created by law for the administration of any general law of a State, or for the administration of justice. . . .

SEC. 10. That no district commander or member of the board of registration, or any of the officers or appointees acting under them, shall be bound in his action by any opinion of any civil officer of the United States.

SEC. 11. That all provisions of this act and of the acts to which this is supplementary shall be construed liberally, to the end that all the intents thereof may be fully and perfectly carried out.

268. THE PURCHASE OF ALASKA
March 30, 1867

(Malloy, ed. *Treaties, Conventions, etc.* Vol. II, p. 1521 ff.)

The purchase of Alaska was regarded, at the time, as "Seward's folly"; it was lobbied through Congress by Robert Walker of Mississippi, to the accompaniment of rumors of bribery. See, F. Bancroft, *Seward,* Vol. II, ch. xlii; J. M. Callahan, *The Alaska Purchase and Americo-Canadian Relations,* W. Va. Studies in History, Series I. On Walker, see W. E. Dodd, *Robert J. Walker, Imperialist.*

CONVENTION FOR THE CESSION OF THE
RUSSIAN POSSESSIONS IN NORTH
AMERICA TO THE UNITED STATES
Concluded March 30, 1867. Ratifications exchanged at Washington, June 20, 1867.
Proclaimed June 20, 1867.
. . . ART. I. . . . His Majesty the Emperor of all the Russias agrees to cede to the United States, by this Convention, immediately upon the exchange of the ratifications

thereof, all the territory and dominion now possessed by his said Majesty on the continent of America and in the adjacent islands, the same being contained within the geographical limits herein set forth, to wit: The eastern limit is the line of demarcation between the Russian and the British possessions in North America, as established by the convention between Russia and Great Britain, of February 28—16, 1825, and described in Articles III. and IV. of said convention, in the following terms: . . .

" 'IV. With reference to the line of demarcation laid down in the preceding article, it is understood—

" '1st. That the island called Prince of Wales Island shall belong wholly to Russia,' . . .

" '2d. That whenever the summit of the

mountains which extend in a direction parallel to the coast from the 56th degree of north latitude to the point of intersection of the 141st degree of west longitude shall prove to be at the distance of more than ten marine leagues from the ocean, the limit between the British possessions and the line of coast which is to belong to Russia as above mentioned, (that is to say, the limit to the possessions ceded by this convention,) shall be formed by a line parallel to the winding of the coast, and which shall never exceed the distance of ten marine leagues therefrom.' " . . .

ART. II. . . . In the cession of territory and dominion made by the preceding article are included the right of property in all public lots and squares, vacant lands, and all public buildings, fortifications, barracks, and other edifices which are not private individual property. It is, however, understood and agreed, that the churches which have been built in the ceded territory by the Russian Government, shall remain the property of such members of the Greek Oriental Church resident in the territory as may choose to worship therein. . . .

ART. III. . . . The inhabitants of the ceded territory, according to their choice, reserving their natural allegiance, may return to Russia within three years; but, if they should prefer to remain in the ceded territory, they, with the exception of uncivilized native tribes, shall be admitted to the enjoyment of all the rights, advantages, and immunities of citizens of the United States, and shall be maintained and protected in the free enjoyment of their liberty, property, and religion. The uncivilized tribes will be subject to such laws and regulations as the United States may from time to time adopt in regard to aboriginal tribes of that country. . . .

ART. VI. In consideration of the cession aforesaid, the United States agree to pay at the Treasury in Washington . . . seven million two hundred thousand dollars in gold. . . .

269. THE IMPEACHMENT OF PRESIDENT JOHNSON
1868

(Richardson, ed. *Messages and Papers*, Vol. VI, p. 709 ff., 755 ff.)

The House of Representatives resolved, February 24, 1868, to impeach President Johnson. On March 2 and 3 articles of impeachment were agreed upon by the House and on March 4 presented to the Senate. J. A. Bingham, G. S. Boutwell, J. F. Wilson, B. F. Butler, T. Williams, J. A. Logan, and T. Stevens were the House managers of the impeachment. The Senate voted on the articles, May 16 and 26, 1868. See, D. M. De Witt, *Impeachment and Trial of Andrew Johnson;* W. A. Dunning, *Essays on Civil War and Reconstruction,* p. 253 ff.; G. F. Milton, *The Age of Hate,* chs. xxi-xxvi; L. P. Stryker, *Andrew Johnson,* chs. lxiii lxxx; C. G. Bowers, *The Tragic Era,* ch. ix.

IN THE HOUSE OF REPRESENTATIVES,
UNITED STATES,
March 2, 1868.

ARTICLES EXHIBITED BY THE HOUSE OF REPRESENTATIVES OF THE UNITED STATES, IN THE NAME OF THEMSELVES AND ALL THE PEOPLE OF THE UNITED STATES, AGAINST ANDREW JOHNSON, PRESIDENT OF THE UNITED STATES, IN MAINTENANCE AND SUPPORT OF THEIR IMPEACHMENT AGAINST HIM FOR HIGH CRIMES AND MISDEMEANORS IN OFFICE.

ARTICLE I. That said Andrew Johnson, President of the United States, on the 21st day of February, A. D. 1868, at Washington, in the district of Columbia, unmindful of the high duties of his office, of his oath of office, and of the requirement of the Constitution that he should take care that the laws be faithfully executed, did unlawfully and in violation of the Constitution and laws of the United States issue an order in writing for the removal of Edwin M. Stanton from the office of Secretary for the Department of War, said Edwin M. Stanton having been theretofore duly appointed and commissioned, by and with the advice and consent of the Senate of the United States, as such Secretary; and said Andrew Johnson, President of the United States, on the 12th day of August, A. D. 1867, and during the recess of said Senate, having suspended by his order Edwin M. Stanton from said office, and within twenty days after the first day of the next meeting of said Senate—that is to say, on the 12th day of December, in the year last aforesaid—having reported to said Senate such suspension, with the evidence and reasons for his action in the case and the name of the person designated to perform the duties of such office temporarily until the next meeting of the Senate; and said Senate thereafterwards, on the 13th day of January, A. D. 1868, having duly considered the evidence and reasons reported by said Andrew Johnson for said suspension, and having refused to concur in said suspension, whereby and by force of the provisions of an act entitled "An act regulating the tenure of certain civil offices," passed March 2, 1867, said Edwin M. Stanton did forthwith resume the functions of his office, whereof the said Andrew Johnson had then and there due notice; and said Edwin M. Stanton, by reason of the premises, on said 21st day of February, being lawfully entitled to hold said office of Secretary for the Department of War; which said order for the removal of said Edwin M. Stanton is in substance as follows; that is to say:

EXECUTIVE MANSION,
Washington, D. C., February 21, 1868.
HON. EDWIN M. STANTON,
Washington, D. C.

SIR: By virtue of the power and authority vested in me as President by the Constitution and laws of the United States, you are hereby removed from office as Secretary for the Department of War, and your functions as such will terminate upon the receipt of this communication.

You will transfer to Brevet Major-General Lorenzo Thomas, Adjutant-General of the Army, who has this day been authorized and empowered to act as Secretary of War *ad interim,* all records, books, papers, and other public property now in your custody and charge.

Respectfully, yours,
ANDREW JOHNSON.

which order was unlawfully issued with intent then and there to violate the act entitled "An act regulating the tenure of certain civil offices," passed March 2, 1867 . . . whereby said Andrew Johnson, President of the United States, did then and there commit and was guilty of a high misdemeanor in office.

ART. II. That on said 21st day of February, A. D. 1868, at Washington, in the District

of Columbia, said Andrew Johnson, President of the United States, . . . did, with intent to violate the Constitution of the United States and the act aforesaid, issue and deliver to one Lorenzo Thomas a letter of authority in substance as follows; that is to say:

EXECUTIVE MANSION,
Washington, D. C., February 21, 1868.
Brevet Major-General LORENZO THOMAS,
Adjutant-General United States Army, Washington, D. C.

SIR: The Hon. Edwin M. Stanton having been this day removed from office as Secretary for the Department of War, you are hereby authorized and empowered to act as Secretary of War *ad interim,* and will immediately enter upon the discharge of the duties pertaining to that office.

Mr. Stanton has been instructed to transfer to you all the records, books, papers, and other public property now in his custody and charge.

Respectfully, yours,
ANDREW JOHNSON.

then and there being no vacancy in said office of Secretary for the Department of War; whereby said Andrew Johnson, President of the United States, did then and there commit and was guilty of a high misdemeanor in office.

ART. III. That said Andrew Johnson, President of the United States, on the 21st day of February, A. D. 1868, at Washington, in the District of Columbia, did commit and was guilty of a high misdemeanor in office in this, that without authority of law, while the Senate of the United States was then and there in session, he did appoint one Lorenzo Thomas to be Secretary for the Department of War *ad interim,* without the advice and consent of the Senate, and with intent to violate the Constitution of the United States, . . .

ART. IV. That said Andrew Johnson, President of the United States, . . . did unlawfully conspire with one Lorenzo Thomas, and with other persons to the House of Representatives unknown, with intent, by intimidation and threats, unlawfully to hinder and prevent Edwin M. Stanton, then and there the Secretary for the Department of War, . . . from holding said office of Secretary for the Department of War, contrary to and in violation of the Constitution of the United States and of the provisions of an act entitled "An act to define and punish certain conspiracies," approved July 31, 1861; . . .

ART. V. That said Andrew Johnson, President of the United States, . . . did unlawfully conspire with one Lorenzo Thomas, and with other persons to the House of Representatives unknown, to prevent and hinder the execution of an act entitled "An act regulating the tenure of certain civil offices," passed March 2, 1867. . . .

ART. VI. That said Andrew Johnson, President of the United States, . . . did unlawfully conspire with one Lorenzo Thomas by force to seize, take, and possess the property of the United States in the Department of War, and then and there in the custody and charge of Edwin M. Stanton, Secretary for said Department, contrary to the provisions of an act entitled "An act to define and punish certain conspiracies," approved July 31, 1861, and with intent to violate and disregard an act entitled "An act regulating the tenure of certain civil offices," passed March 2, 1867; . . .

ART. VII. That said Andrew Johnson, President of the United States, . . . did unlawfully conspire with one Lorenzo Thomas with intent unlawfully to seize, take, and possess the property of the United States in the Department of War, in the custody and charge of Edwin M. Stanton, Secretary for said Department, with intent to violate and disregard the act entitled "An act regulating the tenure of certain civil offices, passed March 2, 1867; . . .

ART. VIII. That said Andrew Johnson, President of the United States, . . . with intent unlawfully to control the disbursement of the moneys appropriated for the military service and for the Department of War, . . . did unlawfully, and in violation of the Constitution of the United States, and without the advice and consent of the Senate of the United States, . . . there being no vacancy in the office of Secretary for the Department of War, and with intent to violate and disregard the act aforesaid, then and there issue and deliver to one Lorenzo Thomas a letter of authority, . . .

ART. IX. That said Andrew Johnson, President of the United States, on the 22d day of February, A. D. 1868, . . . in disregard of

the Constitution and the laws of the United States duly enacted, as Commander in Chief of the Army of the United States, did bring before himself then and there William H. Emory, a major-general by brevet in the Army of the United States, actually in command of the Department of Washington and the military forces thereof, and did then and there, as such Commander in Chief, declare to and instruct said Emory that part of a law of the United States, passed March 2, 1867, entitled "An Act making appropriations for the support of the Army for the year ending June 30, 1868, and for other purposes," especially the second section thereof, which provides, among other things, that "all orders and instructions relating to military operations issued by the President or Secretary of War shall be issued through the General of the Army, and in case of his inability through the next in rank," was unconstitutional . . . with intent thereby to induce said Emory, in his official capacity as commander of the Department of Washington, to violate the provisions of said act and to take and receive, act upon, and obey such orders as he, the said Andrew Johnson, might make and give, and which should not be issued through the General of the Army of the United States, according to the provisions of said act, . . .

March 3, 1868.

The following additional articles of impeachment were agreed to, viz:

ART. X. That said Andrew Johnson, President of the United States, unmindful of the high duties of his office and the dignity and proprieties thereof, and of the harmony and courtesies which ought to exist and be maintained between the executive and legislative branches of the Government of the United States, . . . did attempt to bring into disgrace, ridicule, hatred, contempt, and reproach the Congress of the United States and the several branches thereof, to impair and destroy the regard and respect of all the good people of the United States for the Congress and legislative power thereof (which all officers of the Government ought inviolably to preserve and maintain), and to excite the odium and resentment of all the good people of the United States against Congress and the laws by it duly and constitutionally enacted; and, in pursuance of his said design and intent,

openly and publicly, and before divers assemblages of the citizens of the United States,
. . . did, on the 18th day of August, A. D.
1866, and on divers other days and times, . . .
make and deliver with a loud voice certain intemperate, inflammatory, and scandalous harangues, and did therein utter loud threats
and bitter menaces, as well against Congress
as the laws of the United States, duly enacted
thereby, amid the cries, jeers, and laughter of
the multitudes then assembled and in hearing,
which are set forth in the several specifications hereinafter written in substance and effect; that is to say:

Specification first.—In this, that at Washington, . . . in the Executive Mansion, to a
committee of citizens who called upon the
President of the United States, speaking of
and concerning the Congress of the United
States, said Andrew Johnson, President of the
United States, . . . on the 18th day of
August, A. D. 1866, did in a loud voice declare in substance and effect, among other
things; that is to say: . . .

We have witnessed in one department of the
Government every endeavor to prevent the restoration of peace, harmony, and union. We have
seen hanging upon the verge of the Government,
as it were, a body called, or which assumes to be,
the Congress of the United States, while in fact
it is a Congress of only a part of the States. We
have seen this Congress pretend to be for the
Union, when its every step and act tended to
perpetuate disunion and make a disruption of the
States inevitable. . . . We have seen Congress
gradually encroach, step by step, upon constitutional rights, and violate, day after day and
month after month, fundamental principles of
the Government. We have seen a Congress that
seemed to forget that there was a limit to the
sphere and scope of legislation. We have seen a
Congress in a minority assume to exercise power
which, allowed to be consummated, would result in despotism or monarchy itself.

Specification second.—In this, that at
Cleveland, in the State of Ohio, . . . on the
3d day of September, A. D. 1866, before a
public assemblage of citizens and others, said
Andrew Johnson, President of the United
States, speaking of and concerning the Congress of the United States, did in a loud voice
declare in substance and effect, among other
things; that is to say:

I will tell you what I did do. I called upon
your Congress that is trying to break up the
Government. . . .

In conclusion, besides that, Congress had taken
much pains to poison their constituents against
him. But what had Congress done? Have they
done anything to restore the Union of these
States? No. On the contrary, they have done
everything to prevent it. And because he stood
now where he did when the rebellion commenced,
he had been denounced as a traitor. Who had
run greater risks or made greater sacrifices than
himself? But Congress, factious and domineer-
ing, had undertaken to poison the minds of the
American people.

Specification third.—In this, that at St.
Louis, in the State of Missouri, . . . on the
8th day of September, A. D. 1866, . . . said
Andrew Johnson, President of the United
States, speaking of and concerning the Congress of the United States, did in a loud voice
declare in substance and effect, among other
things; that is to say:

Go on . . . if you will go back and ascertain the
cause of the riot at New Orleans, perhaps you
will not be so prompt in calling out "New Orleans." If you will take up the riot at New Orleans
and trace it back to its source or its immediate
cause, you will find out who was responsible for
the blood that was shed there. If you will take up
the riot at New Orleans and trace it back to the
Radical Congress, you will find that the riot at
New Orleans was substantially planned. . . .
You will also find that that convention did assemble, in violation of law, and the intention of
that convention was to supersede the reorganized
authorities in the State government of Louisiana,
which had been recognized by the Government
of the United States; and every man engaged in
that rebellion in that convention, with the intention of superseding and upturning the civil
government which had been recognized by the
Government of the United States, I say that he
was a traitor to the Constitution of the United
States; and hence you find that another rebellion
was commenced, *having its origin in the Radical
Congress.* . . .

And I have been traduced, I have been slan-
dered, I have been maligned, I have been called
Judas Iscariot and all that. Now, my countrymen, here to-night, it is very easy to indulge in
epithets; it is easy to call a man a Judas and cry
out "traitor;" but when he is called upon to give
arguments and facts he is very often found wanting. Judas Iscariot—Judas. There was a Judas,
and he was one of the twelve apostles. Oh, yes;
the twelve apostles had a Christ. The twelve

apostles had a Christ, and he never could have had a Judas unless he had had twelve apostles. If I have played the Judas, who has been my Christ that I have played the Judas with? Was it Thad. Stevens? Was it Wendell Phillips? Was it Charles Sumner? These are the men that stop and compare themselves with the Savior, and everybody that differs with them in opinion, and to try to stay and arrest their diabolical and nefarious policy, is to be denounced as a Judas. . . .

which said utterances, declarations, threats, and harangues, highly censurable in any, are peculiarly indecent and unbecoming in the Chief Magistrate of the United States, by means whereof said Andrew Johnson has brought the high office of the President of the United States into contempt, ridicule, and disgrace, to the great scandal of all good citizens; whereby said Andrew Johnson, President of the United States, did commit and was then and there guilty of a high misdemeanor in office.

ART. XI. That said Andrew Johnson, President of the United States, . . . did on the 18th day of August, A. D. 1866, at the city of Washington, in the District of Columbia, by public speech, declare and affirm in substance that the Thirty-ninth Congress of the United States was not a Congress of the United States authorized by the Constitution to exercise legislative power under the same, but, on the contrary, was a Congress of only part of the States; thereby denying and intending to deny that the legislation of said Congress was valid or obligatory upon him, the said Andrew Johnson, except in so far as he saw fit to approve the same, . . . in pursuance of said declaration the said Andrew Johnson, President of the United States, . . . on the 21st day of February, A. D. 1868, at the city of Washington, in the District of Columbia, did unlawfully, and in disregard of the requirement of the Constitution that he should take care that the laws be faithfully executed, attempt to prevent the execution of an act entitled "An act regulating the tenure of certain civil offices," passed March 2, 1867, by unlawfully devising and contriving, and attempting to devise and contrive, means by which he should prevent Edwin M. Stanton from forthwith resuming the functions of the office of Secretary for the Department of War, notwithstanding the refusal of the Senate to concur in the suspension theretofore by said Andrew Johnson of said Edwin M. Stanton from said office of Secretary for the Department of War, and also by further unlawfully devising and contriving, and attempting to devise and contrive, means then and there to prevent the execution of an act entitled "An act making appropriations for the support of the Army for the fiscal year ending June 30, 1868, and for other purposes," approved March 2, 1867, and also to prevent the execution of an act entitled "An act to provide for the more efficient government of the rebel States," passed March 2, 1867, whereby the said Andrew Johnson, President of the United States, did then, to wit, on the 21st day of February, A. D. 1868, at the city of Washington, commit and was guilty of a high misdemeanor in office.

SATURDAY, MAY 16, 1868.
THE UNITED STATES vs. ANDREW JOHNSON, PRESIDENT.

The Chief Justice stated that, in pursuance of the order of the Senate, he would first proceed to take the judgment of the Senate on the eleventh article. The roll of the Senate was called, with the following result:

The Senators who voted "guilty" are Messrs. Anthony, Cameron, Cattell, Chandler, Cole, Conkling, Conness, Corbett, Cragin, Drake, Edmunds, Ferry, Frelinghuysen, Harlan, Howard, Howe, Morgan, Morrill of Maine, Morrill of Vermont, Morton, Nye, Patterson of New Hampshire, Pomeroy, Ramsey, Sherman, Sprague, Stewart, Sumner, Thayer, Tipton, Wade, Williams, Willey, Wilson, and Yates—35.

The Senators who voted "not guilty" are Messrs. Bayard, Buckalew, Davis, Dixon, Doolittle, Fessenden, Fowler, Grimes, Henderson, Hendricks, Johnson, McCreery, Norton, Patterson of Tennessee, Ross, Saulsbury, Trumbull, Van Winkle, and Vickers—19.

The Chief Justice announced that upon this article thirty-five Senators had voted "guilty" and nineteen Senators "not guilty," and declared that two-thirds of the Senators present not having pronounced him guilty, Andrew Johnson, President of the United States, stood acquitted of the charges contained in the eleventh article of impeachment.

TUESDAY, MAY 26, 1868.
THE UNITED STATES *vs.* ANDREW
JOHNSON, PRESIDENT.

The Senate ordered that the vote be taken upon the second article of impeachment. The roll of the Senate was called, with the following result:

The Senators who voted "guilty" are Messrs. Anthony, Cameron, Cattell, Chandler, Cole, Conkling, Conness, Corbett, Cragin, Drake, Edmunds, Ferry, Frelinghuysen, Harlan, Howard, Howe, Morgan, Morrill of Maine, Morrill of Vermont, Morton, Nye, Patterson of New Hampshire, Pomeroy, Ramsey, Sherman, Sprague, Stewart, Sumner, Thayer, Tipton, Wade, Willey, Williams, Wilson, and Yates—35.

The Senators who voted "not guilty" are Messrs. Bayard, Buckalew, Davis, Dixon, Doolittle, Fessenden, Fowler, Grimes, Henderson, Hendricks, Johnson, McCreery, Norton, Patterson of Tennessee, Ross, Saulsbury, Trumbull, Van Winkle, and Vickers—19.

The Chief Justice announced that upon this article thirty-five Senators had voted "guilty" and nineteen Senators had voted "not guilty," and declared that two-thirds of the Senators present not having pronounced him guilty, Andrew Johnson, President of the United States, stood acquitted of the charges contained in the second article of impeachment.

The Senate ordered that the vote be taken upon the third article of impeachment. The roll of the Senate was called, with the following result:

The Senators who voted "guilty" are Messrs. Anthony, Cameron, Cattell, Chandler, Cole, Conkling, Conness, Corbett, Cragin, Drake, Edmunds, Ferry, Frelinghuysen, Harlan, Howard, Howe, Morgan, Morrill of Maine, Morrill of Vermont, Morton, Nye, Patterson of New Hampshire, Pomeroy, Ramsey, Sherman, Sprague, Stewart, Sumner, Thayer, Tipton, Wade, Willey, Williams, Wilson, and Yates—35.

The Senators who voted "not guilty" are Messrs. Bayard, Buckalew, Davis, Dixon, Doolittle, Fessenden, Fowler, Grimes, Henderson, Hendricks, Johnson, McCreery, Norton, Patterson of Tennessee, Ross, Saulsbury,

Trumbull, Van Winkle, and Vickers—19.

The Chief Justice announced that upon this article thirty-five Senators had voted "guilty" and nineteen Senators had voted "not guilty," and declared that two-thirds of the Senators present not having pronounced him guilty, Andrew Johnson, President of the United States, stood acquitted of the charges contained in the third article.

No objection being made, the secretary, by direction of the Chief Justice, entered the judgment of the Senate upon the second, third, and eleventh articles, as follows:

The Senate having tried Andrew Johnson, President of the United States, upon articles of impeachment exhibited against him by the House of Representatives, and two-thirds of the Senators present not having found him guilty of the charges contained in the second, third, and eleventh articles of impeachment, it is therefore

Ordered and adjudged, That the said Andrew Johnson, President of the United States, be, and he is, acquitted of the charges in said articles made and set forth.

A motion "that the Senate sitting for the trial of the President upon articles of impeachment do now adjourn without day" was adopted by a vote of 34 yeas to 16 nays.

Those who voted in the affirmative are Messrs. Anthony, Cameron, Cattell, Chandler, Cole, Conkling, Corbett, Cragin, Drake, Edmunds, Ferry, Frelinghuysen, Harlan, Howard, Morgan, Morrill of Maine, Morrill of Vermont, Morton, Nye, Patterson of New Hampshire, Pomeroy, Ramsey, Sherman, Sprague, Stewart, Sumner, Thayer, Tipton, Van Winkle, Wade, Willey, Williams, Wilson, and Yates.

Those who voted in the negative are Messrs. Bayard, Buckalew, Davis, Dixon, Doolittle, Fowler, Henderson, Hendricks, Johnson, McCreery, Norton, Patterson of Tennessee, Ross, Saulsbury, Trumbull, and Vickers.

The Chief Justice declared the Senate sitting as a court of impeachment for the trial of Andrew Johnson, President of the United States, upon articles of impeachment exhibited against him by the House of Representatives, adjourned without day.

270. FOURTH RECONSTRUCTION ACT
March 11, 1868

(*U. S. Statutes at Large,* Vol. XV, p. 41)

The Second Reconstruction Act, Doc. No. 265, provided for the ratification of the new state constitutions only where they were accepted by a majority of the registered voters. The defeat of the Alabama Constitution in February 1868 by the absence from the polls of a majority of the registered voters led Congress to pass the Act of March 11, 1868. Under the provisions of this Act a number of constitutions were ratified and in the summer of 1868 Congress admitted seven of the southern States to the Union. For references, see Doc. No. 260.

An Act to amend the Act [of March 23, 1867]

Be it enacted, That hereafter any election authorized by the act [of March 23, 1867], shall be decided by a majority of the votes actually cast; and at the election in which the question of the adoption or rejection of any constitution is submitted, any person duly registered in the State may vote in the election district where he offers to vote when he has resided therein for ten days next preceding such election, upon presentation of his certificate of registration, his affidavit, or other satisfactory evidence, under such regulations as the district commanders may prescribe.

SEC. 2. *And be it further enacted,* That the constitutional convention of any of the States mentioned in the acts to which this is amendatory may provide that at the time of voting upon the ratification of the constitution the registered voters may vote also for members of the House of Representatives of the United States, and for all elective officers provided for by the said constitution; and the same election officers who shall make the return of the votes cast on the ratification or rejection of the constitution, shall enumerate and certify the votes cast for members of Congress.

271. THE KU KLUX KLAN
Organization and Principles
1868

(J. C. Lester and D. L. Wilson, *The Ku Klux Klan* . . . ed. by W. L. Fleming, p. 154 ff.)

The Ku Klux Klan, one of the two largest of the secret organizations that flourished in the South during Reconstruction, was founded in 1865 at Pulaski, Tennessee. The order grew rapidly in 1867 and 1868; a general organization was perfected in May 1867 at which a constitution was adopted. General Bedford Forrest was the first Grand Wizard of the Order. The Order was effective in frightening the negro out of his unnatural alliance with the Union Leagues, but it was used as a cloak for lawlessness and violence and formally disbanded in 1869. Its activities continued, however, for some time after this date. Congress took cognizance of the Order and similar secret societies such as the Knights of the White Camelia, by passing the Ku Klux Klan Acts of May 31, 1870 and April 20, 1871, Doc. No. 273. A Congressional Ku Klux Klan Committee sat during the summer of 1871 and took thirteen volumes of testimony on conditions in the South. See, *Report of the Joint Select Committee* . . . U.S. 42d Cong. 2d Sess. Sen. Report, No. 41. On the Ku Klux Klan see also, W. L. Fleming, *Sequel to Appomattox,* ch. xi; W. G. Brown, *The Lower South in American History,* ch. iv; W. A. Sinclair, *The Aftermath of Slavery.*

Organization and Principles of the Ku Klux Klan

Appellation

This Organization shall be styled and denominated, the Order of the * * *

Creed

We, the Order of the * * * , reverentially acknowledge the majesty and supremacy of the Divine Being, and recognize the goodness and providence of the same. And we recognize our relation to the United States Government, the supremacy of the Constitution, the Constitutional Laws thereof, and the Union of States thereunder.

Character and objects of the Order

This is an institution of Chivalry, Humanity, Mercy, and Patriotism; embodying in its genius and its principles all that is chivalric in conduct, noble in sentiment, generous in manhood, and patriotic in purpose; its peculiar objects being

First: To protect the weak, the innocent, and the defenseless, from the indignities, wrongs, and outrages of the lawless, the violent, and the brutal; to relieve the injured and oppressed; to succor the suffering and unfortunate, and especially the widows and orphans of Confederate soldiers.

Second: To protect and defend the Constitution of the United States, and all laws passed in conformity thereto, and to protect the States and the people thereof from all invasion from any source whatever.

Third: To aid and assist in the execution of all constitutional laws, and to protect the people from unlawful seizure, and from trial except by their peers in conformity to the laws of the land.

Titles

Sec. 1. The officers of this Order shall consist of a Grand Wizard of the Empire, and his ten Genii; a Grand Dragon of the Realm, and his eight Hydras; a Grand Titan of the Dominion, and his six Furies; a Grand Giant of the Province, and his four Goblins; a Grand Cyclops of the Den, and his two Night Hawks; a Grand Magi, a Grand Monk, a Grand Scribe, a Grand Exchequer, a Grand Turk, and a Grand Sentinel.

Sec. 2. The body politic of this Order shall be known and designated as "Ghouls."

Territory and its Divisions

Sec. 1. The territory embraced within the jurisdiction of this Order shall be coterminous with the States of Maryland, Virginia, North Carolina, South Carolina, Georgia, Florida, Alabama, Mississippi, Louisiana, Texas, Arkansas, Missouri, Kentucky, and Tennessee; all combined constituting the Empire.

Sec. 2. The Empire shall be divided into four departments, the first to be styled the Realm, and coterminous with the boundaries of the several States; the second to be styled the Dominion and to be coterminous with such counties as the Grand Dragons of the several Realms may assign to the charge of the Grand Titan. The third to be styled the Province, and to be coterminous with the several counties; *provided* the Grand Titan may, when he deems it necessary, assign two Grand Giants to one Province, prescribing, at the same time, the jurisdiction of each. The fourth department to be styled the Den, and shall embrace such part of a Province as the Grand Giant shall assign to the charge of a Grand Cyclops. . . .

Interrogations to be asked

1st. Have you ever been rejected, upon application for membership in the * * * , or have you ever been expelled from the same?

2d. Are you now, or have you ever been, a member of the Radical Republican party, or either of the organizations known as the "Loyal League" and the "Grand Army of the Republic?"

3d. Are you opposed to the principles and policy of the Radical party, and to the Loyal League, and the Grand Army of the Republic, so far as you are informed of the character and purposes of those organizations?

4th. Did you belong to the Federal army during the late war, and fight against the South during the existence of the same?

5th. Are you opposed to negro equality, both social and political?

6th. Are you in favor of a white man's government in this country?

7th. Are you in favor of Constitutional liberty, and a Government of equitable laws instead of a Government of violence and oppression?

8th. Are you in favor of maintaining the Constitutional rights of the South?

9th. Are you in favor of the re-enfranchisement and emancipation of the white men of the South, and the restitution of the Southern people to all their rights, alike proprietary, civil, and political?

10th. Do you believe in the inalienable right of self-preservation of the people against the exercise of arbitrary and unlicensed power? . . .

. . . 9. The most profound and rigid secrecy concerning any and everything that relates to the Order, shall at all times be maintained.

10. Any member who shall reveal or betray the secrets of this Order, shall suffer the extreme penalty of the law.

272. THE FOURTEENTH AMENDMENT
July 28, 1868

(F. N. Thorpe, ed. *Federal and State Constitutions*, Vol. I, p. 31)

Widespread doubt as to the constitutionality of the Civil Rights Act, Doc. No. 252, led to the formulation, by the Joint Committee of Fifteen, of this amendment to the Constitution. It was first submitted to the legislatures of the States in June, 1866. Rejected by most of the southern States, its ratification was made a condition of restoration to the Union. Ratification, thus being obtained, was announced July 28, 1868. New Jersey, Ohio, and Oregon subsequently rescinded their ratification. The revolutionary character of the Fourteenth Amendment justifies its insertion at this point. The Amendment for the first time defined citizenship, and for the first time threw the protection of the Federal Government around rights that might be invaded by the State governments—thus reversing the traditional relationship. The first section of the Amendment has given rise to more adjudication than any other part of the Constitution. There appears to be little support to the so-called conspiracy theory that the framers of the amendment deliberately phrased the amendment so that it would protect the property and rights of corporations against State legislation. See, B. B. Kendrick, *The Journal of the Joint Committee of Fifteen on Reconstruction;* H. E. Flack, *The Adoption of the Fourteenth Amendment;* C. Warren, *Supreme Court,* Vol. II, chs. xxx–xxxii; L. Boudin, *Government by Judiciary,* Vol. II, chs. xxiii, xxxvi; Graham, "The Conspiracy Theory of the Fourteenth Amendment," 47 Yale L. J. 371; Boudin, "Truth and Fiction about the Fourteenth Amendment," 16 N. Y. U. L. Qt. Rev. 19. F. J. Swayze, "Judicial Construction of the Fourteenth Amendment," 26 Harv. Law R. 1.

ART. XIV.

SEC. 1. All persons born or naturalized in the United States, and subject to the jurisdiction thereof, are citizens of the United States and of the State wherein they reside. No State shall make or enforce any law which shall abridge the privileges or immunities of citizens of the United States; nor shall any State deprive any person of life, liberty, or property, without due process of law; nor deny to any person within its jurisdiction the equal protection of the laws.

SEC. 2. Representatives shall be apportioned among the several States according to their respective numbers, counting the whole number of persons in each State, excluding Indians not taxed. But when the right to vote at any election for the choice of electors for President and Vice-President of the United States, Representatives in Congress, the Executive and Judicial officers of a State, or the members of the Legislature thereof, is denied to any of the male inhabitants of such State, being twenty-one years of age, and citizens of the United States, or in any way abridged, except for participation in rebellion, or other crime, the basis of representation therein shall be reduced in the proportion which the number of such male citizens shall bear to the whole number of male citizens twenty-one years of age in such State.

SEC. 3. No person shall be a Senator or Representative in Congress, or elector of President and Vice-President, or hold any office, civil or military, under the United States, or under any State, who, having previously taken an oath, as a member of Congress, or as an officer of the United States, or as a member of any State legislature, or as an executive or judicial officer of any State, to support the Constitution of the United States, shall have engaged in insurrection or rebellion against the same, or given aid or comfort to the enemies thereof. But Congress may by a vote of two-thirds of each House, remove such disability.

SEC. 4. The validity of the public debt of the United States, authorized by law, including debts incurred for payment of pensions and bounties for services in suppressing insurrection or rebellion, shall not be questioned. But neither the United States nor any State shall assume or pay any debt or obligation incurred in aid of insurrection or rebellion against the United States, or any claim for the loss or emancipation of any slave; but all such debts, obligations and claims shall be held illegal and void.

SEC. 5. The Congress shall have power to enforce, by appropriate legislation, the provisions of this article.

273. ACT TO ENFORCE THE FOURTEENTH AMENDMENT
April 20, 1871

(*U. S. Statutes at Large*, Vol. XVII, p. 13 ff.)

This so-called Ku Klux Act was the most important of several Civil Rights Acts designed to insure for the negro the full benefits of the thirteenth, fourteenth and fifteenth amendments. Similar acts had been passed May 31, 1870 and February 28, 1871. An act designed to secure social equality for the negro was passed March 1, 1875 (see Doc. No. 291). In 1876 the Supreme Court, in *U. S.* v. *Reese,* 92 U. S. 214 and *U. S.* v. *Cruikshank,* 92 U. S. 542, declared certain sections of the Civil Rights Act of May 31, 1870 unconstitutional, and thus anticipated its attitude toward the Ku Klux and Civil Rights Acts. In 1883, in *U. S.* v. *Harris,* 106 U. S. 629, the Court held parts of the Act of April 20, 1871 unconstitutional; in *The Civil Rights Cases,* 109 U. S. 3, it held the Civil Rights Act unconstitutional. Efforts to repeal these force acts were not successful until the second Cleveland administration. See, W. W. Davis, "The Federal Enforcement Acts," in *Studies in Southern History and Politics;* W. A. Dunning, *Essays on the Civil War and Reconstruction,* p. 353 ff.; C. Warren, *The Supreme Court* (1928 ed.), Vol. II, ch. xxxiv,

An Act to enforce the Provisions of the Fourteenth Amendment to the Constitution of the United States, and for other Purposes.

*Be it enacted . . . ,*That any person who, under color of any law, statute, ordinance, regulation, custom, or usage of any State, shall subject, or cause to be subjected, any person within the jurisdiction of the United States to the deprivation of any rights, privileges, or immunities secured by the Constitution of the United States, shall, any such law, statute, ordinance, regulation, custom, or usage of the State to the contrary notwithstanding, be liable to the party injured in any action at law, suit in equity, or other proper proceeding for redress; such proceeding to be prosecuted in the several district or circuit courts of the United States, with and subject to the same rights of appeal, review upon error, and other remedies provided in like cases in such courts, under the provisions of the [Civil Rights Act of 1866], and the other remedial laws of the United States which are in their nature applicable in such cases.

SEC. 2. That if two or more persons within any State or Territory of the United States shall conspire together to overthrow, or to put down, or to destroy by force the government of the United States, or to levy war against the United States, or to oppose by force the authority of the government of the United States, or by force, intimidation, or threat to prevent, hinder, or delay the execution of any law of the United States, or by force to seize, take, or possess any property of the United States contrary to the authority thereof, or by force, intimidation, or threat to prevent any person from accepting or holding any office or trust or place of confidence under the United States, or from discharging the duties thereof, or by force, intimidation, or threat to induce any officer of the United States to leave any State, district, or place where his duties as such officer might lawfully be performed, or to injure him in his person or property on account of his lawful discharge of the duties of his office, or to injure his person while engaged in the lawful discharge of the duties of his office, or to injure his property so as to molest, interrupt, hinder, or impede him in the discharge of his official duty, or by force, intimidation, or threat to deter any party or witness in any court of the United States from attending such court, or from testifying in any matter pending in such court fully, freely, and truthfully, or to injure any such party or witness in his person or property on account of his having so attended or testified, or by force, intimidation, or threat to influence the verdict, presentment, or indictment, of any juror or grand juror in any court of the United States, or to injure such juror in his person or property on account of any verdict, presentment, or indictment lawfully assented to by him, or on account of his being or having been such juror, or shall conspire together, or go in disguise upon the public highway or upon the premises of another for the purpose, either directly or indirectly, of depriving any person or any class of persons of the equal protection of the laws, or of equal privileges or immunities under the laws, or for the purpose of preventing or hindering the constituted authorities of any State from giving or securing to all persons within such

State the equal protection of the laws, or shall conspire together for the purpose of in any manner impeding, hindering, obstructing, or defeating the due course of justice in any State or Territory, with intent to deny to any citizen of the United States the due and equal protection of the laws, or to injure any person in his person or his property for lawfully enforcing the right of any person or class of persons to the equal protection of the laws, or by force, intimidation, or threat to prevent any citizen of the United States lawfully entitled to vote from giving his support or advocacy in a lawful manner towards or in favor of the election of any lawfully qualified person as an elector of President or Vice-President of the United States, or as a member of the Congress of the United States, or to injure any such citizen in his person or property on account of such support or advocacy, each and every person so offending shall be deemed guilty of a high crime, and, upon conviction thereof in any district or circuit court of the United States or district or supreme court of any Territory of the United States having jurisdiction of similar offences, shall be punished by a fine not less than five hundred nor more than five thousand dollars, or by imprisonment, with or without hard labor, as the court may determine, for a period of not less than six months nor more than six years, as the court may determine, or by both such fine and imprisonment as the court shall determine. . . .

Sec. 3. That in all cases where insurrection, domestic violence, unlawful combinations, or conspiracies in any State shall so obstruct or hinder the execution of the laws thereof, and of the United States, as to deprive any portion or class of the people of such State of any of the rights, privileges, or immunities, or protection, named in the Constitution and secured by this act, and the constituted authorities of such State shall either be unable to protect, or shall, from any cause, fail in or refuse protection of the people in such rights, such facts shall be deemed a denial by such State of the equal protection of the laws to which they are entitled under the Constitution of the United States; and in all such cases . . . it shall be lawful for the President, and it shall be his duty to take such measures, by the employment of the militia or the land and naval forces of the United States, or of either, or by other means, as he may deem necessary for the suppression of such insurrection, domestic violence, or combinations. . . .

Sec. 4. That whenever in any State or part of a State the unlawful combinations named in the preceding section of this act shall be organized and armed, and so numerous and powerful as to be able, by violence, to either overthrow or set at defiance the constituted authorities of such State, and of the United States within such State, or when the constituted authorities are in complicity with, or shall connive at the unlawful purposes of, such powerful and armed combinations; and whenever, by reason of either or all of the causes aforesaid, the conviction of such offenders and the preservation of the public safety shall become in such district impracticable, in every such case such combinations shall be deemed a rebellion against the government of the United States, and during the continuance of such rebellion, and within the limits of the district which shall be so under the sway thereof, such limits to be prescribed by proclamation, it shall be lawful for the President of the United States, when in his judgment the public safety shall require it, to suspend the privileges of the writ of habeas corpus, to the end that such rebellion may be overthrown: Provided, That all the provisions of the second section of [the Habeas Corpus Act of March 3, 1863], which relate to the discharge of prisoners other than prisoners of war, and to the penalty for refusing to obey the order of the court, shall be in full force so far as the same are applicable to the provisions of this section: Provided further, That the President shall first have made proclamation, as now provided by law, commanding such insurgents to disperse: And provided also, That the provisions of this section shall not be in force after the end of the next regular session of Congress.

Sec. 5. That no person shall be a grand or petit juror in any court of the United States upon any inquiry, hearing, or trial of any suit, proceeding, or prosecution based upon or arising under the provisions of this act who shall, in the judgment of the court, be in complicity with any such combination or conspiracy; and every such juror shall, before entering upon any such inquiry, hearing, or trial, take and subscribe an oath in open court that he has never, directly or indirectly, counselled, advised, or voluntarily aided any such combination or conspiracy. . . .

SEC. 6. That any person or persons, having knowledge that any of the wrongs conspired to be done and mentioned in the second section of this act are about to be committed, and having power to prevent or aid in preventing the same, shall neglect or refuse to do so, and such wrongful act shall be committed, such person or persons shall be liable to the person injured . . . for all damages caused by any such wrongful act which such first-named person or persons by reasonable diligence could have prevented. . . .

274. THE DEMOCRATIC PLATFORM OF 1868
July 4, 1868

(K. Porter, ed. *National Party Platforms*, p. 64 ff.)

Reconstruction and the money question were the principal issues of the campaign of 1868. The Democratic Convention met in New York City in July 1868 and adopted a platform incorporating Pendleton's "Ohio idea" on money, but nominated for the Presidency Horatio Seymour of New York, a hard money man. The second place on the ticket went to Frank Blair of Missouri. Seymour polled 2,709,000 votes, but secured only 80 votes in the electoral college. Only the money and reconstruction planks of the platform are given. See, C. H. Coleman, *The Election of 1868;* W. H. Smith, *The Francis Preston Blair Family in Politics,* Vol. II, ch. xlii.

. . . 3. Payment of the public debt of the United States as rapidly as practicable. All moneys drawn from the people by taxation, except so much as is requisite for the necessities of the government, economically administered, being honestly applied to such payment, and where the obligations of the government do not expressly state upon their face, or the law under which they were issued does not provide, that they shall be paid in coin, they ought, in right and in justice, to be paid in the lawful money of the United States. . . .

5. One currency for the government and the people, the laborer and the office-holder, the pensioner and the soldier, the producer and the bond-holder. . . .

8. . . . In demanding these measures and reforms we arraign the Radical party for its disregard of right, and the unparalleled oppression and tyranny which have marked its career.

After the most solemn and unanimous pledge of both Houses of Congress to prosecute the war exclusively for the maintenance of the government and the preservation of the Union under the Constitution, it has repeatedly violated that most sacred pledge, under which alone was rallied that noble volunteer army which carried our flag to victory.

Instead of restoring the Union, it has, so far as in its power, dissolved it, and subjected ten States, in time of profound peace, to military despotism and negro supremacy.

It has nullified there the right of trial by jury; it has abolished the *habeas corpus,* that most sacred writ of liberty; it has overthrown the freedom of speech and of the press; it has substituted arbitrary seizures and arrests, and military trials and secret star-chamber inquisitions, for the constitutional tribunals; it has disregarded in time of peace the right of the people to be free from searches and seizures; it has entered the post and telegraph offices, and even the private rooms of individuals, and seized their private papers and letters without any specific charge or notice of affidavit, as required by the organic law; it has converted the American capitol into a Bastile; it has established a system of spies and official espionage to which no constitutional monarchy of Europe would now dare to resort; it has abolished the right of appeal, on important constitutional questions, to the Supreme Judicial tribunal, and threatens to curtail, or destroy, its original jurisdiction, which is irrevocably vested by the Constitution; while the learned Chief Justice has been subjected to the most atrocious calumnies, merely because he would not prostitute his high office to the support of the false and partisan charges preferred against the President. Its corruption and extravagance have exceeded anything known in history, and by its frauds and monopolies it has nearly doubled the burden of the debt created by the war; it has stripped the President of his constitutional power of appointment, even of his own Cabinet. Under its repeated assaults the pillars of the government are rocking on their base, and should it succeed in November next and inaugurate its President, we will meet, as a subjected and conquered people, amid the ruins of liberty and the scattered fragments of the Constitution.

And we do declare and resolve, That ever since the people of the United States threw off all subjection to the British crown, the privilege and trust of suffrage have belonged to the several States, and have been granted, regulated, and controlled exclusively by the political power of each State respectively, and that any attempt by congress, on any pretext whatever, to deprive any State of this right, or interfere with its exercise, is a flagrant usurpation of power, which can find no warrant in the Constitution; and if sanctioned by the people will subvert our form of government, and can only end in a single centralized and consolidated government, in which the separate existence of the States will be entirely absorbed, and an unqualified despotism be established in place of a federal union of co-equal States; and that we regard the reconstruction acts so-called, of Congress, as such an usurpation, and unconstitutional, revolutionary, and void. . . .

275. PRESIDENT JOHNSON'S RECOMMENDATION FOR THE REVALUATION OF THE PUBLIC DEBT

Extract from Fourth Annual Message to Congress
December 9, 1868

(Richardson, ed. *Messages and Papers,* Vol. VI, p. 677)

President Johnson's biographers have largely ignored his financial ideas and policies. There is a brief discussion in H. Beale, *The Critical Year,* ch. x.

. . . In my message to Congress December 4, 1865, it was suggested that a policy should be devised which, without being oppressive to the people, would at once begin to effect a reduction of the debt, and, if persisted in, discharge it fully within a definite number of years. The Secretary of the Treasury forcibly recommends legislation of this character, and justly urges that the longer it is deferred the more difficult must become its accomplishment. We should follow the wise precedents established in 1789 and 1816, and without further delay make provision for the payment of our obligations at as early a period as may be practicable. The fruits of their labors should be enjoyed by our citizens rather than used to build up and sustain moneyed monopolies in our own and other lands. Our foreign debt is already computed by the Secretary of the Treasury at $850,-000,000; citizens of foreign countries receive interest upon a large portion of our securities, and American taxpayers are made to contribute large sums for their support. The idea that such a debt is to become permanent should be at all times discarded as involving taxation too heavy to be borne, and payment once in every sixteen years, at the present rate of interest, of an amount equal to the original sum. This vast debt, if permitted to become permanent and increasing, must eventually be gathered into the hands of a few, and enable them to exert a dangerous and controlling power in the affairs of the Government. The borrowers would become servants to the lenders, the lenders the masters of the people. We now pride ourselves upon having given freedom to 1,000,000 of the colored race; it will then be our shame that 40,000,000 of people, by their own toleration of usurpation and profligacy, have suffered themselves to become enslaved, and merely exchanged slave owners for new taskmasters in the shape of bondholders and taxgatherers. Besides, permanent debts pertain to monarchical governments, and, tending to monopolies, perpetuities, and class legislation, are totally irreconcilable with free institutions. Introduced into our republican system, they would gradually but surely sap its foundations, eventually subvert our governmental fabric, and erect upon its ruins a moneyed aristocracy. It is our sacred duty to transmit unimpaired to our posterity the blessings of liberty which were bequeathed to us by the founders of the Republic, and by our example teach those who are to follow us carefully to avoid the dangers which threaten a free and independent people.

Various plans have been proposed for the payment of the public debt. However they may have varied as to the time and mode in which it should be redeemed, there seems to be a general concurrence as to the propriety and justness of a reduction in the present rate of interest. The Secretary of the Treasury in his report recommends 5 per cent; Congress, in a bill passed prior to adjournment on the 27th of July last, agreed upon 4 and 4½ per cent; while by many 3 per cent has been held to be an amply sufficient return for the investment. The general impression as to the exorbitancy of the existing rate of interest has led to an inquiry in the public mind respecting the consideration which the Government has actually received for its bonds, and the conclusion is becoming prevalent that the amount which it obtained was in real money three or four hundred per cent less than the obligations which it issued in return. It can not be denied that we are paying an extravagant percentage for the use of the money borrowed, which was paper currency, greatly depreciated below the value of coin. This fact is made apparent when we consider that bondholders receive from the Treasury upon each dollar they own in Government securities 6 per cent in gold, which is nearly or quite equal to 9 per cent in currency; that the bonds are then converted into capital for the national banks, upon which those institutions issue their circulation, bearing 6 per cent interest; and that

they are exempt from taxation by the Government and the States, and thereby enhanced 2 per cent in the hands of the holders. We thus have an aggregate of 17 per cent which may be received upon each dollar by the owners of Government securities. A system that produces such results is justly regarded as favoring a few at the expense of the many, and has led to the further inquiry whether our bondholders, in view of the large profits which they have enjoyed, would themselves be averse to a settlement of our indebtedness upon a plan which would yield them a fair remuneration and at the same time be just to the taxpayers of the nation. Our national credit should be sacredly observed, but in making provision for our creditors we should not forget what is due to the masses of the people. It may be assumed that the holders of our securities have already received upon their bonds a larger amount than their original investment, measured by a gold standard. Upon this statement of facts it would seem but just and equitable that the 6 per cent interest now paid by the Government should be applied to the reduction of the principal in semi-annual installments, which in sixteen years and eight months would liquidate the entire national debt. Six per cent in gold would at present rates be equal to 9 per cent in currency, and equivalent to the payment of the debt one and a half times in a fraction less than seventeen years. This, in connection with all the other advantages derived from their investment, would afford to the public creditors a fair and liberal compensation for the use of their capital, and with this they should be satisfied. The lessons of the past admonish the lender that it is not well to be over-anxious in exacting from the borrower rigid compliance with the letter of the bond. . . .

276. GRANT'S FIRST INAUGURAL ADDRESS
March 4, 1869

(Richardson, ed. *Messages and Addresses*, Vol. VII, p. 6 ff.)

On the election of 1868, see C. H. Coleman, *The Election of 1868;* for the Grant administration see J. F. Rhodes, *History*, Vol. VII and forthcoming studies by W. B. Hesseltine and by A. Nevins; on Grant after Appomattox, see A.

Badeau, *Grant in Peace;* L. A. Coolidge, *U. S. Grant*, ch. xxx ff.

Citizens of the United States:
   Your suffrages having elected me to the

office of President of the United States, I have, in conformity to the Constitution of our country, taken the oath of office prescribed therein. I have taken this oath without mental reservation and with the determination to do to the best of my ability all that is required of me. The responsibilities of the position I feel, but accept them without fear. The office has come to me unsought; I commence its duties untrammeled. I bring to it a conscious desire and determination to fill it to the best of my ability to the satisfaction of the people.

On all leading questions agitating the public mind I will always express my views to Congress and urge them according to my judgment, and when I think it advisable will exercise the constitutional privilege of interposing a veto to defeat measures which I oppose; but all laws will be faithfully executed, whether they meet my approval or not.

I shall on all subjects have a policy to recommend, but none to enforce against the will of the people. Laws are to govern all alike—those opposed as well as those who favor them. I know no method to secure the repeal of bad or obnoxious laws so effective as their stringent execution.

The country having just emerged from a great rebellion, many questions will come before it for settlement in the next four years which preceding Administrations have never had to deal with. In meeting these it is desirable that they should be approached calmly, without prejudice, hate, or sectional pride, remembering that the greatest good to the greatest number is the object to be attained.

This requires security of person, property, and free religious and political opinion in every part of our common country, without regard to local prejudice. All laws to secure these ends will receive my best efforts for their enforcement.

A great debt has been contracted in securing to us and our posterity the Union. The payment of this, principal and interest, as well as the return to a specie basis as soon as it can be accomplished without material detriment to the debtor class or to the country at large, must be provided for. To protect the national honor, every dollar of Government indebtedness should be paid in gold, unless otherwise expressly stipulated in the contract. Let it be understood that no repudiator of one farthing of our public debt will be trusted in public place, and it will go far toward strengthening a credit which ought to be the best in the world, and will ultimately enable us to replace the debt with bonds bearing less interest than we now pay. To this should be added a faithful collection of the revenue, a strict accountability to the Treasury for every dollar collected, and the greatest practicable retrenchment in expenditure in every department of Government.

When we compare the paying capacity of the country now, with the ten States in poverty from the effects of war, but soon to emerge, I trust, into greater prosperity than ever before, with its paying capacity twenty-five years ago, and calculate what it probably will be twenty-five years hence, who can doubt the feasibility of paying every dollar then with more ease than we now pay for useless luxuries? Why, it looks as though Providence had bestowed upon us a strong box in the precious metals locked up in the sterile mountains of the far West, and which we are now forging the key to unlock, to meet the very contingency that is now upon us.

Ultimately it may be necessary to insure the facilities to reach these riches, and it may be necessary also that the General Government should give its aid to secure this access; but that should only be when a dollar of obligation to pay secures precisely the same sort of dollar to use now, and not before. Whilst the question of specie payments is in abeyance the prudent business man is careful about contracting debts payable in the distant future. The nation should follow the same rule. A prostrate commerce is to be rebuilt and all industries encouraged.

The young men of the country—those who from their age must be its rulers twenty-five years hence—have a peculiar interest in maintaining the national honor. A moment's reflection as to what will be our commanding influence among the nations of the earth in their day, if they are only true to themselves, should inspire them with national pride. All divisions—geographical, political, and religious—can join in this common sentiment. How the public debt is to be paid or specie payments resumed is not so important as that a plan should be adopted and acquiesced in. A united determination to do is worth more than divided counsels upon the method of doing. Legislation upon this subject may not be necessary now, nor even advisable, but it will be when the civil law is more fully restored in all parts of the country and trade resumes its wonted channels. . . .

The question of suffrage is one which is likely to agitate the public so long as a portion of the citizens of the nation are excluded from its privileges in any State. It seems to me very desirable that this question should be settled now, and I entertain the hope and express the desire that it may be by the ratification of the fifteenth article of amendment to the Constitution.

In conclusion I ask patient forbearance one toward another throughout the land, and a determined effort on the part of every citizen to do his share toward cementing a happy union; and I ask the prayers of the nation to Almighty God in behalf of this consummation.

277. VEAZIE BANK v. FENNO
8 Wallace, 533
1869

Certificate from the U.S. circuit court for the district of Maine. This case involved the constitutionality of the act of Congress of July 13, 1866 imposing a tax of ten per cent on state bank notes.

CHASE, C. J. . . . It will be seen that when the policy of taxing bank circulation was first adopted in 1863, Congress was inclined to discriminate for, rather than against, the circulation of the State banks; but that when the country had been sufficiently furnished with a national currency by the issues of United States notes and of National bank notes, the discrimination was turned, and very decidedly turned, in the opposite direction.

The general question now before us is, whether or not the tax of ten per cent., imposed on State banks . . . is repugnant to the Constitution of the United States.

In support of the position that the act of Congress, so far as it provides for the levy and collection of this tax, is repugnant to the Constitution, two propositions have been argued with much force and earnestness.

The first is that the tax in question is a direct tax, and has not been apportioned among the States agreeably to the Constitution.

The second is that the act imposing the tax impairs a franchise granted by the State, and that Congress has no power to pass any law with that intent or effect. . . .

The difficulty of defining with accuracy the terms used in the clause of the Constitution which confers the powers of taxation upon Congress, was felt in the Convention which framed that instrument, and has always been experienced by courts when called upon to determine their meaning. . . .

Much diversity of opinion has always prevailed upon the question, what are direct taxes? Attempts to answer it by reference to the definitions of political economists have been frequently made, but without satisfactory results. The enumeration of the different kinds of taxes which Congress was authorized to impose was probably made with very little reference to this question. The great work of Adam Smith, the first comprehensive treatise on political economy in the English language, had then been recently published; but in this work, though there are passages which refer to the characteristic difference between direct and indirect taxation, there is nothing which affords any valuable light on the use of the words "direct taxes" in the Constitution.

We are obliged, therefore, to resort to historical evidence, and to seek the meaning of words in the use and in the opinion of those whose relations to the government, and means of knowledge, warranted them in speaking with authority.

And, considered in this light, the meaning and application of the rule, as to direct taxes, appears to us quite clear.

It is, as we think, distinctly shown in every act of Congress on the subject. . . .

This review shows that personal property, contracts, occupations, and the like, have never been regarded by Congress as proper subjects of direct tax. . . .

It may rightly be affirmed, therefore, that in the practical construction of the Constitution by Congress, direct taxes have been limited to taxes on land and appurtenances, and taxes on polls or capitation taxes.

And this construction is entitled to great consideration especially in the absence of anything adverse to it in the discussions of the Convention which framed, and of the conventions which ratified, the Constitution. . . .

It follows necessarily that the power to tax without apportionment extends to all other objects. Taxes on other objects are included under the heads of taxes not direct, duties, imposts, and excises, and must be laid and collected by the rule of uniformity. The tax under consideration is a tax on bank circulation, and may very well be classed under the head of duties. Certainly it is not, in the sense of the Constitution, a direct tax. It may be said to come within the same category of taxation as the tax on incomes of insurance companies, . . .

It is insisted, however, that the tax in the case before us is excessive, and so excessive as to indicate a purpose on the part of Congress to destroy the franchise of the bank, and is, therefore, beyond the constitutional power of Congress.

The first answer to this is that the judicial cannot prescribe to the legislative departments of the government limitations upon the exercise of its acknowledged powers. The power to tax may be exercised oppressively upon persons, but the responsibility of the legislature is not to the courts, but to the people by whom its members are elected. So if a particular tax bears heavily upon a corporation, or a class of corporations, it cannot, for that reason only, be pronounced contrary to the Constitution.

But there is another answer which vindicates equally the wisdom and power of Congress.

It cannot be doubted that under the Con-

stitution the power to provide a circulation of coin is given to Congress. And it is settled by the uniform practice of the government and by repeated decisions, that Congress may constitutionally authorize the emission of bills of credit. It is not important here, to decide whether the quality of legal tender, in payment of debts, can be constitutionally imparted to these bills; it is enough to say, that there can be no question of the power of the government to emit them; to make them receivable in payment of debts to itself; to fit them for use by those who see fit to use them in all the transactions of commerce; to provide for their redemption; to make them a currency, uniform in value and description, and convenient and useful for circulation. These powers, until recently, were only partially and occasionally exercised. Lately, however, Congress has undertaken to supply a currency for the entire country. . . .

Having thus, in the exercise of undisputed constitutional powers, undertaken to provide a currency for the whole country, it cannot be questioned that Congress may, constitutionally, secure the benefit of it to the people by appropriate legislation. To this end, Congress has denied the quality of legal tender to foreign coins, and has provided by law against the imposition of counterfeit and base coin on the community. To the same end, Congress may restrain, by suitable enactments, the circulation as money of any notes not issued under its own authority. Without this power, indeed, its attempts to secure a sound and uniform currency for the country must be futile.

Viewed in this light, as well as in the other light of a duty on contracts or property, we cannot doubt the constitutionality of the tax under consideration. . . .

NELSON, J., delivered a dissenting opinion in which DAVIS, J., concurred.

278. TEXAS v. WHITE
7 Wallace, 700
1869

Suit by Texas in the Supreme Court of the United States. During the Civil War the government of Texas disposed of some United States bonds, in payment of supplies for the Confederate government. The Reconstruction gov-

ernment of Texas brought suit to enjoin the defendants from receiving payment on these bonds, on the ground that the State government of the Confederacy was not a legal government and therefore the disposition of the bonds was illegal. This celebrated case is the leading case on the question of the theory of secession and of reconstruction. See, Warren, *The Supreme Court* (1928 ed.), Vol. II, p. 488 ff.; Dunning, *Essays on the Civil War and Reconstruction*, ch. ii.

CHASE, C. J. . . . The first inquiries to which our attention was directed by counsel arose upon the allegations . . . that the State, having severed her relations with a majority of the States of the Union, and having by her ordinance of secession attempted to throw off her allegiance to the Constitution, and the government of the United States, has so far changed her status as to be disabled from prosecuting suits in the National courts. . . .

. . . It is not to be questioned that this court has original jurisdiction of suits by States against citizens of other States, or that the States entitled to invoke this jurisdiction must be States of the Union. But it is equally clear that no such jurisdiction has been conferred upon this court of suits by any other political communities than such States.

If, therefore, it is true that the State of Texas was not at the time of filing this bill, or is not now, one of the United States, we have no jurisdiction of this suit, and it is our duty to dismiss it. . . .

In the Constitution the term "State" most frequently expresses the combined idea just noticed, of people, territory, and government. A State, in the ordinary sense of the Constitution, is a political community of free citizens, occupying a territory of defined boundaries and organized under a government sanctioned and limited by a written constitution, and established by the consent of the governed. It is the union of such States, under a common constitution, which forms the distinct and greater political unit, which the Constitution designates as the United States, and makes of the people and States which compose it one people and one country. . . .

The Republic of Texas was admitted into the Union, as a State, on the 27th of December, 1845. By this act the new State, and the people of the new State, were invested with all the rights, and became subject to all the responsibilities and duties of the original States under the Constitution.

From the date of admission until 1861 the State was represented in the Congress of the United States by her senators and representatives, and her relations as a member of the Union remained unimpaired. In that year, acting upon the theory that the rights of a State under the Constitution might be renounced, and her obligations thrown off at pleasure, Texas undertook to sever the bond thus formed, and to break up her constitutional relations with the United States. . . .

The position thus assumed could only be maintained by arms, and Texas accordingly took part, with the other Confederate States, in the war of rebellion, which these events made inevitable. During the whole of that war there was no governor, or judge, or any other state officer in Texas, who recognized the National authority. Nor was any officer of the United States permitted to exercise any authority whatever under the National government within the limits of the State, except under the immediate protection of the National military forces.

Did Texas, in consequence of these acts, cease to be a State? Or, if not, did the State cease to be a member of the Union?

It is needless to discuss at length the question whether the right of a State to withdraw from the Union for any cause, regarded by itself as sufficient, is consistent with the Constitution of the United States.

The Union of the States was never a purely artificial and arbitrary relation. It began among the Colonies, and grew out of common origin, mutual sympathies, kindred principles, similar interests, and geographical relations. It was confirmed and strengthened by the necessities of war, and received definite form, and character, and sanction from the Articles of Confederation. By these the Union was solemnly declared to be "perpetual." And when these Articles were found to be inadequate to the exigencies of the country, the Constitution was ordained "to form a more perfect Union." It is difficult to convey the idea of indissoluble unity more clearly than by these words. What can be indissoluble if a perpetual Union made more perfect, is not?

But the perpetuity and indissolubility of the Union by no means implies the loss of distinct and individual existence, or of the right of self-government by the States. Under the Articles of Confederation each State retained its sovereignty, freedom, and independence, and every power, jurisdiction, and right not expressly delegated to the United States. Under the Constitution, though the powers of the States were much restricted, still, all powers not delegated to the United States, nor prohibited to the States, are reserved to the States, respectively, or to the people. And we have already had occasion to remark at this term, that "the people of each State compose a State, having, its own government, and endowed with all the functions essential to separate and independent existence," and that "without the States in union, there could be no such political body as the United States." Not only, therefore, can there be no loss of separate and independent autonomy to the States, through their union under the Constitution, but it may be not unreasonably said that the preservation of the States, and the maintenance of their governments, are as much within the design and care of the Constitution as the preservation of the Union and the maintenance of the National government. The Constitution, in all its provisions, looks to an indestructible Union, composed of indestructible States.

When, therefore, Texas became one of the United States, she entered into an indissoluble relation. All the obligations of perpetual union, and all the guaranties of republican government in the Union, attached at once to the State. The act which consummated her admission into the Union was something more than a compact; it was the incorporation of a new member into the political body. And it was final. The union between Texas and the other States was as complete, as perpetual, and as indissoluble as the union between the original States. There was no place for reconsideration or revocation except through revolution, or through consent of the States.

Considered therefore as transactions under the Constitution, the ordinance of secession, adopted by the convention and ratified by a majority of the citizens of Texas, and all the acts of her legislature intended to give effect to that ordinance, were absolutely void. They were utterly without operation in law. The obligations of the State, as a member of the Union, and of every citizen of the State,

remained perfect and unimpaired. It certainly follows that the State did not cease to be a State, nor her citizens to be citizens of the Union. If this were otherwise, the State must have become foreign, and her citizens foreigners. The war must have become a war for conquest and subjugation.

Our conclusion therefore is, that Texas continued to be a State, and a State of the Union, notwithstanding the transactions to which we have referred.

But in order to the exercise by a State, of the right to sue in this court, there needs to be a state government, competent to represent the State in its relations with the National government, so far at least as the institution and prosecution of a suit is concerned.

And it is by no means a logical conclusion, from the premises which we have endeavored to establish, that the governmental relations of Texas to the Union remained unaltered. . . . No one has been bold enough to contend that, while Texas was controlled by a government hostile to the United States, and in affiliation with a hostile confederation, waging war upon the United States, senators chosen by her legislature, or representatives elected by her citizens, were entitled to seats in Congress, or that any suit, instituted in her name, could be entertained in this court. All admit that, during this condition of civil war, the rights of the State as a member, and of her people as citizens of the Union, were suspended. The government and the citizens of the State, refusing to recognize their constitutional obligations, assumed the character of enemies, and incurred the consequences of rebellion.

These new relations imposed new duties upon the United States. The first was that of suppressing the rebellion. The next was that of re-establishing the broken relations of the State with the Union. The first of these duties having been performed, the next necessarily engaged the attention of the National government.

The authority for the performance of the first had been found in the power to suppress insurrection and carry on war; for the performance of the second, authority was derived from the obligation of the United States to guarantee to every State in the Union a republican form of government. The latter, indeed, in the case of a rebellion which involves the government of a State, and for the time excludes the National authority from its limits, seems to be a necessary complement to the former.

Of this the case of Texas furnishes a striking illustration. When the war closed there was no government in the State except that which had been organized for the purpose of waging war against the United States. That government immediately disappeared. . . .

There being no government in Texas in constitutional relations with the Union, it became the duty of the United States to provide for the restoration of such a government. . . .

It is not important to review, at length, the measures which have been taken under this power, by the executive and legislative departments of the National government. It is proper, however, to observe the almost immediately after the cessation of organized hostilities, and while the war yet smouldered in Texas, the President of the United States issued his proclamation appointing a provisional governor for the State, and providing for the assembling of a convention, with a view to the re-establishment of a republican government, under an amended constitution, and to the restoration of the State to her proper constitutional relations. A convention was accordingly assembled, the constitution amended, elections held, and a state government, acknowledging its obligations to the Union, established.

Whether the action thus taken was, in all respects, warranted by the Constitution, it is not now necessary to determine. The power exercised by the President was supposed, doubtless, to be derived from his constitutional functions as commander-in-chief; and, so long as the war continued, it cannot be denied that he might institute temporary government within insurgent districts, occupied by the National forces, or take measures, in any State, for the restoration of state government faithful to the Union, employing, however, in such efforts, only such means and agents as were authorized by constitutional laws.

But the power to carry into effect the clause of the guaranty is primarily a legislative power, and resides in Congress. . . .

The action of the President must, therefore, be considered as provisional, and in that light it seems to have been regarded by Congress. It was taken after the term of the 38th Congress had expired. The 39th Congress, which assembled in December, 1865, followed by the 40th Congress, which met in March, 1867, proceeded, after long deliberation, to adopt various measures for reorganization and restoration. These measures were embodied in proposed amendments to the Constitution, and in the acts known as the Reconstruction Acts, which have been so far carried into effect, that a majority of the States which were engaged in the rebellion have been restored to their constitutional relations, under forms of government, adjudged to be republican by Congress, through the admission of their "Senators and Representatives into the councils of the Union."

Nothing in the case before us requires the court to pronounce judgment upon the constitutionality of any particular provision of these acts. . . .

What has thus been said generally describes, with sufficient accuracy, the situation of Texas. A provisional governor of the State was appointed by the President in 1865; in 1866 a governor was elected by the people under the constitution of that year; at a subsequent date a governor was appointed by the commander of the district. Each of the three exercised executive functions and actually represented the State in the executive department.

In the case before us each has given his sanction to the prosecution of the suit, and we find no difficulty, without investigating the legal title of either to the executive office, in holding that the sanction thus given sufficiently warranted the action of the solicitor and counsel in behalf of the State. The necessary conclusion is that the suit was instituted and is prosecuted by competent authority. . . .

[The court then considered the validity of the acts of the state government during the period of secession and held the transfer of the bonds by that government void.]

It follows that the title of the State was not divested by the act of the insurgent government in entering into this contract. . . .

On the whole case, therefore, our conclusion is that the State of Texas is entitled to the relief sought by her bill, and a decree must be made accordingly.

GRIER, J., delivered a dissenting opinion in which Justices SWAYNE and MILLER concurred.

279. GRANT'S APPEAL FOR THE ANNEXATION OF SANTO DOMINGO
May 31, 1870

(Richardson, ed. *Messages and Papers,* Vol. VII, p. 61 ff.)

Grant, who was anxious to secure the annexation of the Dominican Republic, sent his secretary Babcock to Santo Domingo to survey the situation; Babcock returned with a treaty of annexation. Grant submitted this irregular document to his Cabinet only to meet unanimous opposition. A more formal treaty was then drawn up and submitted to the Senate January 10, 1870; on the 15th of March the Committee on Foreign Relations reported adversely on ratification and Sumner delivered his famous "Naboth's Vineyard" speech, which cost him the Chairmanship of the Foreign Relations Committee. For his opposition to the Treaty, Attorney General E. R. Hoar was forced to resign. See, S. F. Bemis, ed. *American Secretaries of State,* Vol. VII, p. 147 ff.; E. L. Pierce, *Memoir and Letters of Charles Sumner,* Vol. IV, 425 ff.; A. Nevins, *Hamilton Fish and the Grant Administration.*

EXECUTIVE MANSION, *May 31, 1870.*
To the Senate of the United States:

I transmit to the Senate, for consideration with a view to its ratification, an additional article to the treaty of the 29th of November last, for the annexation of the Dominican Republic to the United States, stipulating for an extension of the time for exchanging the ratifications thereof, signed in this city on the 14th instant by the plenipotentiaries of the parties.

It was my intention to have also negotiated with the plenipotentiary of San Domingo amendments to the treaty of annexation to obviate objections which may be urged against the treaty as it is now worded; but on reflection I deem it better to submit to the Senate the propriety of their amending the treaty as follows: First, to specify that the obligations of this Government shall not exceed the $1,500,000 stipulated in the treaty; secondly, to determine the manner of appointing the agents to receive and disburse the same; thirdly, to determine the class of creditors who shall take precedence in the settlement of their claims; and, finally, to insert such amendments as may suggest themselves to the minds of Senators to carry out in good faith the conditions of the treaty submitted to the Senate of the United States in January last, according to the spirit and intent of that treaty. From the most reliable information I can obtain, the sum specified in the treaty will pay every just claim against the Republic of San Domingo and leave a balance sufficient to carry on a Territorial government until such time as new laws for providing a Territorial revenue can be enacted and put in force.

I feel an unusual anxiety for the ratification of this treaty, because I believe it will redound greatly to the glory of the two countries interested, to civilization, and to the extirpation of the institution of slavery.

The doctrine promulgated by President Monroe has been adhered to by all political parties, and I now deem it proper to assert the equally important principle that hereafter no territory on this continent shall be regarded as subject of transfer to a European power.

The Government of San Domingo has voluntarily sought this annexation. It is a weak power, numbering probably less than 120,000 souls, and yet possessing one of the richest territories under the sun, capable of supporting a population of 10,000,000 people in luxury. The people of San Domingo are not capable of maintaining themselves in their present condition, and must look for outside support.

They yearn for the protection of our free institutions and laws, our progress and civilization. Shall we refuse them?

I have information which I believe reliable that a European power stands ready now to offer $2,000,000 for the possession of Samana Bay alone. If refused by us, with what grace can we prevent a foreign power from attempting to secure the prize?

The acquisition of San Domingo is desirable because of its geographical position. It commands the entrance to the Caribbean Sea and the Isthmus transit of commerce. It possesses the richest soil, best and most capacious harbors, most salubrious climate, and the most valuable products of the forest, mine, and soil of any of the West India Islands. Its possession by us will in a few years build up a coastwise commerce of immense magnitude, which will go far toward restoring to us our lost merchant marine. It will give to us those articles which we consume so largely and do not produce, thus equalizing our exports and imports.

In case of foreign war it will give us command of all the islands referred to, and thus prevent an enemy from ever again possessing himself of rendezvous upon our very coast.

At present our coast trade between the States bordering on the Atlantic and those bordering on the Gulf of Mexico is cut into by the Bahamas and the Antilles. Twice we must, as it were, pass through foreign countries to get by sea from Georgia to the west coast of Florida.

San Domingo, with a stable government, under which her immense resources can be developed, will give remunerative wages to tens of thousands of laborers not now on the island.

This labor will take advantage of every available means of transportation to abandon the adjacent islands and seek the blessings of freedom and its sequence—each inhabitant receiving the reward of his own labor. Porto Rico and Cuba will have to abolish slavery, as a measure of self-preservation to retain their laborers.

San Domingo will become a large consumer of the products of Northern farms and manufactories. The cheap rate at which her citizens can be furnished with food, tools, and machinery will make it necessary that the contiguous islands should have the same advantages in order to compete in the production of sugar, coffee, tobacco, tropical fruits, etc. This will open to us a still wider market for our products.

The production of our own supply of these articles will cut off more than one hundred millions of our annual imports, besides largely increasing our exports. With such a picture it is easy to see how our large debt abroad is ultimately to be extinguished. With a balance of trade against us (including interest on bonds held by foreigners and money spent by our citizens traveling in foreign lands) equal to the entire yield of the precious metals in this country, it is not so easy to see how this result is to be otherwise accomplished.

The acquisition of San Domingo is an adherence to the "Monroe doctrine;" it is a measure of national protection; it is asserting our just claim to a controlling influence over the great commercial traffic soon to flow from east to west by the way of the Isthmus of Darien; it is to build up our merchant marine; it is to furnish new markets for the products of our farms, shops, and manufactories; it is to make slavery insupportable in Cuba and Porto Rico at once and ultimately so in Brazil; it is to settle the unhappy condition of Cuba, and end an exterminating conflict; it is to provide honest means of paying our honest debts, without overtaxing the people; it is to furnish our citizens with the necessaries of everyday life at cheaper rates than ever before; and it is, in fine, a rapid stride toward that greatness which the intelligence, industry, and enterprise of the citizens of the United States entitle this country to assume among nations.

U. S. GRANT.

280. THE LEGAL TENDER CASES
12 Wallace, 457
1871

These were two cases involving the constitutionality of the legal tender acts of 1862 and 1863. The first case, *Knox* v. *Lee,* came on a writ of error from the Western District of Texas; the second, *Parker* v. *Davis,* came on a writ of error to the Supreme Judicial Court of Massachusetts. In the case of *Hepburn* v. *Griswold,* 8 Wallace 603, the Court, which then consisted of only eight judges, held the legal tender acts of 1862 and 1863 unconstitutional by a vote of five to three. Shortly before this decision was announced Justice Grier resigned.

There were therefore two vacancies on the Court, and President Grant promptly filled them by the appointment of J. P. Bradley and W. Strong. Both of these justices maintained the constitutionality of the legal tender acts, Justice Strong delivering the opinion of the Court in the Legal Tender Cases. It was at the time freely charged that President Grant had packed the Court. On the Legal Tender Cases see C. Warren, *Supreme Court*, 1928 ed., Vol. II, ch. xxxi; H. L. Carson, *The Supreme Court*, p. 442 ff.; L. Boudin, *Government by Judiciary*, Vol. II, ch. xxv; G. Bancroft, *A Plea for the Constitution of the United States Wounded in the House of its Guardians;* G. F. Hoar, *The Charge of Packing the Court Against President Grant and Attorney-General Hoar;* E. J. James, *The Legal Tender Decisions.*

STRONG, J., The controlling questions in these cases are the following: Are the acts of Congress, known as the legal tender acts, constitutional when applied to contracts made before their passage; and, secondly, Are they valid as applicable to debts contracted since their enactment? . . . It would be difficult to overestimate the consequences which must follow our decision. They will affect the entire business of the country, and take hold of the possible continued existence of the government. If it be held by this court that Congress has no constitutional power, under any circumstances, or in any emergency, to make treasury notes a legal tender for the payment of all debts (a power confessedly possessed by every independent sovereignty other than the United States), the government is without those means of self-preservation which, all must admit, may, in certain contingencies, become indispensable, even if they were not when the acts of Congress now called in question were enacted.

The consequences of which we have spoken, serious as they are, must be accepted, if there is a clear incompatibility between the Constitution and the legal tender acts. But we are unwilling to precipitate them upon the country unless such incompatibility plainly appears. A decent respect for a co-ordinate branch of the government demands that the judiciary should presume, until the contrary is clearly shown, that there has been no transgression of power by Congress—all the members of which act under the obligation of an oath of fidelity to the Constitution. . . .

Nor can it be questioned that, when investigating the nature and extent of the powers conferred by the Constitution upon Congress, it is indispensable to keep in view the objects for which those powers were granted. This is the universal rule of construction applied alike to statutes, wills, contracts, and constitutions. If the general purpose of the instrument is ascertained, the language of its provisions must be construed with reference to that purpose and so as to subserve it. In no other way can the intent of the framers of the instrument be discovered. And there are more urgent reasons for looking to the ultimate purpose in examining the powers conferred by a constitution than there are in construing a statute, a will, or a contract. We do not expect to find in a constitution minute details. It is necessarily brief and comprehensive. It prescribes outlines, leaving the filling up to be deduced from the outlines. . . .

If these are correct principles, if they are proper views of the manner in which the Constitution is to be understood, the powers conferred upon Congress must be regarded as related to each other, and all means for a common end. Each is but part of a system, a constituent of one whole. No single power is the ultimate end for which the Constitution was adopted. It may, in a very proper sense, be treated as a means for the accomplishment of a subordinate object, but that object is itself a means designed for an ulterior purpose. Thus the power to levy and collect taxes, to coin money and regulate its value, to raise and support armies, or to provide for and maintain a navy, are instruments for the paramount object, which was to establish a government, sovereign within its sphere, with capability of self preservation, thereby forming a union more perfect than that which existed under the old Confederacy.

The same may be asserted also of all the non-enumerated powers included in the authority expressly given "to make all laws which shall be necessary and proper for carrying into execution the specified powers vested in Congress, and all other powers vested by the Constitution in the government of the United States, or in any department or officer thereof." It is impossible to know what those non-enumerated powers are, and what is their nature and extent, without considering the purposes they were intended to subserve. Those purposes, it must be noted, reach beyond the mere execution of all powers definitely intrusted to Congress and mentioned in detail. They embrace the execution of all other powers vested by the Constitution in the government of the United States, or in any department or officer thereof. It certainly was intended to confer upon the government the power of self-preservation. . . .

That would appear, then, to be a most unreasonable construction of the Constitution which denies to the government created by it, the right to employ freely every means, not prohibited, necessary for its preservation, and for the fulfillment of its acknowledged duties. Such a right, we hold, was given by the last clause of the eighth section of its first article. The means or instrumentalities referred to in that clause, and authorized, are not enumerated or defined. In the nature of things enumeration and specification were impossible. But they were left to the discretion of Congress, subject only to the restrictions that they be not prohibited, and be necessary and proper for carrying into execution the enumerated powers given to Congress, and all other powers vested in the government of the United States, or in any department or officer thereof.

And here it is to be observed it is not indispensable to the existence, of any power claimed for the federal government that it can be found specified in the words of the Constitution, or clearly and directly traceable to some one of the specified powers. Its existence may be deduced fairly from more than one of the substantive powers expressly defined, or from them all combined. It is allowable to group together any number of them and infer from them all that the power claimed has been conferred. . . . And it is of importance to observe that Congress has often exercised, without question, powers that are not expressly given nor ancillary to any single enumerated power. Powers thus exercised are what are called by Judge Story, in his Commentaries on the Constitution, resulting powers, arising from the aggregate powers of the government. He instances the right to sue and make contracts. Many others might be given. The oath required by law from officers of the government is one. So is

building a capitol or a presidential mansion, and so also is the penal code. . . .

Indeed, the whole history of the government and of congressional legislation has exhibited the use of a very wide discretion, even in times of peace and in the absence of any trying emergency, in the selection of the necessary and proper means to carry into effect the great objects for which the government was framed, and this discretion has generally been unquestioned, or, if questioned, sanctioned by this court. . . .

Before we can hold the Legal Tender Acts unconstitutional, we must be convinced they were not appropriate means, or means conducive to the execution of any or all of the powers of Congress, or of the government, not appropriate in any plain degree (for we are not judges of the degree of appropriateness), or we must hold that they were prohibited. This brings us to the inquiry whether they were, when enacted, appropriate instrumentalities for carrying into effect, or executing any of the known powers of Congress, or of any department of the government. Plainly, to this inquiry, a consideration of the time when they were enacted, and of the circumstances in which the government then stood, is important. It is not to be denied that acts may be adapted to the exercise of lawful power, and appropriate to it, in seasons of exigency, which would be inappropriate at other times.

We do not propose to dilate at length upon the circumstances in which the country was placed, when Congress attempted to make treasury notes a legal tender. They are of too recent occurrence to justify enlarged description. Suffice it to say that a civil war was then raging which seriously threatened the overthrow of the government and the destruction of the Constitution itself. It demanded the equipment and support of large armies and navies, and the employment of money to an extent beyond the capacity of all ordinary sources of supply. Meanwhile the public treasury was nearly empty, and the credit of the government, if not stretched to its utmost tension, had become nearly exhausted. . . .

It was at such a time and in such circumstances that Congress was called upon to devise means for maintaining the army and navy, for securing the large supplies of money needed, and, indeed, for the preservation of the government created by the Constitution. It was at such a time and in such an emergency that the Legal Tender Acts were passed. Now, if it were certain that nothing else would have supplied the absolute necessities of the treasury, that nothing else would have enabled the government to maintain its armies and navy, that nothing else would have saved the government and the Constitution from destruction, while the Legal Tender Acts would, could any one be bold enough to assert that Congress transgressed its powers? . . .

But if it be conceded that some other means might have been chosen for the accomplishment of these legitimate and necessary ends, the concession does not weaken the argument. . . . At best this is mere conjecture. But admitting it to be true, what does it prove? Nothing more than that Congress had the choice of means for a legitimate end, each appropriate and adapted to that end, though, perhaps, in different degrees. What then? Can this court say that it ought to have adopted one rather than the other? . . .

We hold the acts of Congress constitutional as applied to contracts made either before or after their passage. In so holding we overrule so much of what was decided in *Hepburn* v. *Griswold*, 8 Wallace, 603, as ruled the acts unwarranted by the Constitution so far as applied to contracts made before their enactment. . . .

Judgment in each case affirmed.

CHASE, C. J. and CLIFFORD, J., NELSON, J. and FIELD, J. dissenting.

281. THE TREATY OF WASHINGTON
May 8, 1871

(Malloy, ed. *Treaties, Conventions, etc.* Vol. I, p. 700 ff.)

The failure of the Johnson-Clarendon Convention of 1869 left Anglo-American relations in an unsatisfactory state. The Treaty of Washington provided for the arbitration of the most pressing problem of our relations with Great Britain —the Alabama Claims. The Treaty represented a triumph of the ideas of Secretary of State Fish over those of Charles Sumner. On the Treaty of Washington, see C. Cushing, *The Treaty of Washington;* J. C. Bancroft Davis, *Mr. Fish and the Treaty of Washington;* D. H. Chamberlain, *Charles Sumner and the Treaty of Washington;* S. F. Bemis, ed. *American Secretaries of State,* Vol. VII, p. 165 ff.; *Papers Relating to the Treaty of Washington,* in *Foreign Relations of the United States,* 1872, Part II.

TREATY RELATIVE TO CLAIMS, FISHERIES, NAVIGATION OF THE ST. LAWRENCE, ETC., AMERICAN LUMBER ON THE RIVER St. JOHN; BOUNDARY.

ART. I. Whereas differences have arisen between the Government of the United States and the Government of Her Britannic Majesty, and still exist, growing out of the acts committed by the several vessels which have given rise to the claims generically known as the "Alabama Claims:"

And whereas Her Britannic Majesty has authorized her High Commissioners and Plenipotentiaries to express, in a friendly spirit, the regret felt by Her Majesty's Government for the escape, under whatever circumstances, of the Alabama and other vessels from British ports, and for the depredations committed by those vessels:

Now, in order to remove and adjust all complaints and claims on the part of the United States, and to provide for the speedy settlement of such claims which are not admitted by Her Britannic Majesty's Government, the high contracting parties agree that all the said claims, growing out of acts committed by the aforesaid vessels and generically known as the "Alabama Claims," shall be referred to a tribunal of arbitration to be composed of five Arbitrators, to be appointed in the following manner, that is to say: One shall be named by the President of the United States; one shall be named by Her Britannic Majesty; His Majesty the King of Italy shall be requested to name one; the President of the Swiss Confederation shall be requested to name one; and His Majesty the Emperor of Brazil shall be requested to name one. . . .

ART. II. The Arbitrators shall meet at Geneva, in Switzerland, at the earliest convenient day . . . and shall proceed impartially and carefully to examine and decide all questions that shall be laid before them on the part of the Governments of the United States and Her Britannic Majesty respectively. All questions considered by the tribunal, including the final award, shall be decided by a majority of all the Arbitrators. . . .

ART. VI. In deciding the matters submitted to the Arbitrators, they shall be governed by the following three rules, . . . and by such principles of international law not inconsistent therewith as the Arbitrators shall determine to have been applicable to the case.

RULES.

A neutral Government is bound—

First, to use due diligence to prevent the fitting out, arming, or equipping, within its jurisdiction, of any vessel which it has reasonable ground to believe is intended to cruise or to carry on war against any Power with which it is at peace; and also to use like diligence to prevent the departure from its jurisdiction of any vessel intended to cruise or carry on war as above, such vessel having been specially adapted, in whole or in part, within such jurisdiction, to warlike use.

Secondly, not to permit or suffer either belligerent to make use of its ports or waters as the base of naval operations against the other, or for the purpose of renewal or augmentation of military supplies or arms, or the recruitment of men.

Thirdly, to exercise due diligence in its own ports and waters, and, as to all persons within its jurisdiction, to prevent any violation of the foregoing obligations and duties.

Her Britannic Majesty has commanded her High Commissioners and Plenipotentiaries to declare that Her Majesty's Government cannot assent to the foregoing rules as a statement of principles of international law which were in force at the time when the claims mentioned in Article I. arose, but that Her Majesty's Government, in order to evince its desire of strengthening the friendly relations between the two countries, and of making satisfactory provision for the future, agrees that in deciding the questions between the two countries arising out of those claims, the Arbitrators should assume that Her Majesty's Government had undertaken to act upon the principles set forth in these rules.

And the high contracting parties agree to observe these rules as between themselves in future, and to bring them to the knowledge of other maritime Powers, and to invite them to accede to them.

ART. VII. . . . The said tribunal shall first determine as to each vessel separately whether Great Britain has, by any act or omission, failed to fulfil any of the duties set forth in the foregoing three rules, or recognized by the principles of international law not inconsistent with such rules. . . . In case the tribunal find that Great Britain has failed to fulfil any duty or duties as aforesaid, it may, if it think proper, proceed to award a sum in gross to be paid by Great Britain to the United States for all the claims referred to it. . . .

282. THE COLLECTOR v. DAY
11 Wallace, 113
1871

Error to the U.S. circuit court for the district of Massachusetts. This case involved the constitutionality of a federal income tax on the salary of a State official. The dissenting opinion expresses a view more widely held today than at the time of its announcement.

NELSON, J. The case presents the question whether or not it is competent for Congress, under the Constitution of the United States, to impose a tax upon a salary of a judicial officer of a State?

In *Dobbins* v. *The Commissioners of Erie County,* 16 Peters, 435, it was decided that it was not competent for the legislature of a

State to levy a tax upon the salary or emoluments of an officer of the United States. The decision was placed mainly upon the ground that the officer was a means or instrumentality employed for carrying into effect some of the legitimate powers of the government, which could not be interfered with by taxation or otherwise by the States, and that the salary or compensation for the service of the officer was inseparably connected with the office; that if the officer, as such, was exempt, the salary assigned for his support or maintenance while holding the office was also, for like reasons, equally exempt. . . .

We shall now proceed to show that, upon the same construction of that instrument, and for like reasons, that government is prohibited from taxing the salary of the judicial officer of a State. . . .

The general government, and the States, although both exist within the same territorial limits, are separate and distinct sovereignties, acting separately and independently of each other, within their respective spheres. The former in its appropriate sphere is supreme but the States within the limits of their powers not granted, or, in the language of the Tenth Amendment, "reserved," are as independent of the general government as that government within its sphere is independent of the States.

The relations existing between the two governments are well stated by the present Chief Justice [CHASE] in the case of *Lane County* v. *Oregon,* 7 Wallace, 76. "Both the States and the United States," he observed, "existed before the Constitution. The people, through that instrument, established a more perfect union, by substituting a National government, acting with ample powers directly upon the citizens, instead of the Confederate government, which acted with powers greatly restricted, only upon the States. But, in many of the articles of the Constitution, the necessary existence of the States, and within their proper spheres, the independent authority of the States, are distinctly recognized. To them nearly the whole charge of interior regulation is committed or left; to them, and to the people, all powers, not expressly delegated to the National government, are reserved." Upon looking into the Constitution, it will be found that but few of the articles in that instrument could be carried into practical effect without the existence of the States.

Two of the great departments of the government, the executive and legislative, depend upon the exercise of the powers, or upon the people of the States. The Constitution guarantees to the States a republican form of government, and protects each against invasion or domestic violence. Such being the separate and independent condition of the States in our complex system, as recognized by the Constitution, and the existence of which is so indispensable, that, without them, the general government itself would disappear from the family of nations, it would seem to follow, as a reasonable, if not a necessary consequence, that the means and instrumentalities employed for carrying on the operations of their governments, for preserving their existence, and fulfilling the high and responsible duties assigned to them in the Constitution, should be left free and unimpaired, should not be liable to be crippled, much less defeated, by the taxing power of another government, which power acknowledges no limits but the will of the legislative body imposing the tax. And, more especially, those means and instrumentalities which are the creation of their sovereign and reserved rights, one of which is the establishment of the judicial department, and the appointment of officers to administer their laws. Without this power, and the exercise of it, we risk nothing in saying that no one of the States under the form of government guaranteed by the Constitution could long preserve its existence. . . .

The supremacy of the general government, therefore, so much relied on in the argument of the counsel for the plaintiff in error, in respect to the question before us, cannot be maintained. The two governments are upon an equality, and the question is whether the power "to lay and collect taxes" enables the general government to tax the salary of a judicial officer of the State, which officer is a means or instrumentality employed to carry into execution one of its most important functions, the administration of the laws, and which concerns the exercise of a right reserved to the States?

. . . In respect to the reserved powers, the State is as sovereign and independent as the general government. And if the means and instrumentalities employed by that government to carry into operation the powers granted to it are, necessarily, and, for the sake of self-preservation, exempt from taxation by the States, why are not those of the States depending upon their reserved powers, for like reasons, equally exempt from federal taxation? Their unimpaired existence in the one case is as essential as in the other. It is admitted that there is no express provision in the Constitution that prohibits the general government from taxing the means and instrumentalities of the States, nor is there any prohibiting the States from taxing the means and instrumentalities of that government. In both cases the exemption rests upon necessary implication, and is upheld by the great law of self-preservation; as any government, whose means employed in conducting its operations, if subject to the control of another and distinct government, can exist only at the mercy of that government. Of what avail are these means if another power may tax them at discretion? . . .

Judgment affirmed.

Mr. Justice BRADLEY dissenting,

I dissent from the opinion of the court in this case, because it seems to me that the general government has the same power of taxing the income of officers of the state governments as it has of taxing that of its own officers. It is the common government of all alike; and every citizen is presumed to trust his own government in the matter of taxation. No man ceases to be a citizen of the United States by being an officer under the state government. I cannot accede to the doctrine that the general government is to be regarded as in any sense foreign or antagonistic to the state governments, their officers, or people; nor can I agree that a presumption can be admitted that the general government will act in a manner hostile to the existence or functions of the state governments, which are constituent parts of the system or body politic forming the basis on which the general government is founded. The taxation by the state governments of the instruments em-

ployed by the general government in the exercise of its powers, is a very different thing. Such taxation involves an interference with the powers of a government in which other states and their citizens are equally interested with the state which imposes the taxation. In my judgment, the limitation of the power of taxation in the general government, which the present decision establishes, will be found very difficult of control. Where are we to stop in enumerating the functions of the state governments which will be interfered with by federal taxation? If a state incorporates a railroad to carry out its purposes of internal improvement, or a bank to aid its financial arrangements, reserving, perhaps, a percentage on the stock or profits, for the supply of its own treasury, will the bonds or stock of such an institution be free from federal taxation? How can we now tell what the effect of this decision will be? I cannot but regard it as founded on a fallacy, and that it will lead to mischievous consequences. I am as much opposed as any one can be to any interference by the general government with the just powers of the state governments. But no concession of any of the just powers of the general government can easily be recalled. I, therefore, consider it my duty to at least record my dissent when such concession appears to be made. An extended discussion of the subject would answer no useful purpose.

283. LIBERAL REPUBLICAN PARTY PLATFORM
Cincinnati, Ohio
May 1; 1872

(K. Porter, ed. *National Party Platforms*, p. 77 ff.)

The Liberal Republican movement represented a reaction from the Radical Republican policy toward the South and from the corruption of the Grant administration. The movement had its genesis in Sumner's break with Grant over the Santo Domingo affair and in a party division in Missouri. The Cincinnati convention nominated Horace Greeley for the Presidency, and the Democrats in their Baltimore Convention accepted this candidate. See, E. D. Ross, *The Liberal Republican Movement;* T. S. Barclay, *The Liberal Republican Movement in Missouri;* E. P. Oberholtzer, *History of the United States Since the Civil War,* Vol. III, ch. i.

Cincinnati, Ohio, May 1, 1872

We, the Liberal Republicans of the United States, in National Convention assembled at Cincinnati, proclaim the following principles as essential to just government:

1. We recognize the equality of all men before the law, and hold that it is the duty of Government, in its dealings with the people to mete out equal and exact justice to all, of whatever nativity, race, color, or persuasion, religious or political.

2. We pledge ourselves to maintain the

union of these States, emancipation and en-franchisement, and to oppose any reopening of the questions settled by the Thirteenth, Fourteenth, and Fifteenth Amendments to the Constitution.

3. We demand the immediate and absolute removal of all disabilities imposed on account of the Rebellion, which was finally subdued seven years ago, believing that universal am-nesty will result in complete pacification in all sections of the country.

4. Local self-government, with impartial suffrage, will guard the rights of all citizens more securely than any centralized power. The public welfare requires the supremacy of the civil over the military authority, and freedom of person under the protection of the *habeas corpus*. We demand for the individual the largest liberty consistent with public or-der; for the State self-government, and for the nation a return to the methods of peace and the constitutional limitations of power.

5. The Civil Service of the Government has become a mere instrument of partisan tyranny and personal ambition, and an ob-ject of selfish greed. It is a scandal and re-proach upon free institutions, and breeds a demoralization dangerous to the perpetuity of republican government. We therefore re-gard such thorough reforms of the Civil Serv-ice as one of the most pressing necessities of the hour; that honesty, capacity, and fidelity, constitute the only valid claims to public em-ployment; that the offices of the Government cease to be a matter of arbitrary favoritism and patronage, and that public station be-come again a post of honor. To this end it is imperatively required that no President shall be a candidate for re-election.

6. We demand a system of Federal taxa-tion which shall not unnecessarily interfere with the industry of the people, and which

shall provide the means necessary to pay the expenses of the Government economically ad-ministered, the pensions, the interest on the public debt, and a moderate reduction an-nually of the principal thereof; and, recog-nizing that there are in our midst honest but irreconcilable differences of opinion with re-gard to the respective systems of Protection and Free Trade, we remit the discussion of the subject to the people in their Congres-sional Districts, and to the decision of Con-gress thereon, wholly free of Executive inter-ference or dictation.

7. The public credit must be sacredly maintained, and we denounce repudiation in every form and guise.

8. A speedy return to specie payment is demanded alike by the highest considerations of commercial morality and honest govern-ment.

9. We remember with gratitude the hero-ism and sacrifices of the soldiers and sailors of the republic, and no act of ours shall ever detract from their justly-earned fame, or the full reward of their patriotism.

10. We are opposed to all further grants of land to railroads or other corporations. The public domain should be held sacred to actual settlers.

11. We hold that it is the duty of the Government, in its intercourse with foreign nations, to cultivate the friendship of peace, by treating with all on fair and equal terms, regarding it alike dishonorable either to de-mand what is not right, or to submit to what is wrong.

12. For the promotion and success of these vital principles, and the support of the can-didates nominated by this convention we in-vite and cordially welcome the cooperation of all patriotic citizens, without regard to previous affiliations.

284. THE SLAUGHTER-HOUSE CASES
16 Wallace, 36
1873

Error to the supreme court of Louisiana. In 1869 the legislature of Louisiana, in order to protect the health of the people of New Orleans, granted to a slaughter-house company for twenty-five years the exclusive privilege of con-ducting a slaughter-house within the city limits

of New Orleans. The validity of the act was challenged on the ground that it violated the Fourteenth Amendment. The opinion of the court is memorable as one of the earliest in-terpretations of the Fourteenth Amendment. Note especially the scant consideration given by the Court to the due process clause of the Amendment. See Warren, *Supreme Court,* Vol. II, ch. xxxii.

MILLER, J. . . . The plaintiffs in error . . . allege that the statute is a violation of the Constitution of the United States in these several particulars:

That it creates an involuntary servitude forbidden by the Thirteenth Article of Amendment;

That it abridges the privileges and immunities of citizens of the United States;

That it denies to the plaintiffs the equal protection of the laws; and,

That it deprives them of their property without due process of law; contrary to the provisions of the first section of the Fourteenth Article of Amendment.

This court is thus called upon for the first time to give construction of these articles. . . .

Twelve articles of amendment were added to the federal Constitution soon after the original organization of the government under it in 1789. . . . Within the last eight years three other articles of amendment of vast importance have been added by the voice of the people to that now venerable instrument.

The most cursory glance at these articles discloses a unity of purpose, when taken in connection with the history of the times, which cannot fail to have an important bearing on any question of doubt concerning their true meaning. Nor can such doubts, when any reasonably exist, be safely and rationally solved without a reference to that history; for in it is found the occasion and the necessity for recurring again to the great source of power in this country, the people of the States, for additional guarantees of human rights; additional powers to the federal government; additional restraints upon those of the States. . . .

We repeat, then, in the light of this recapitulation of events, almost too recent to be called history, but which are familiar to us all; and on the most casual examination of the language of these amendments, no one can fail to be impressed with the one pervading purpose found in them all, lying at the foundation of each, and without which none of them would have been even suggested; we mean the freedom of the slave race, the security and firm establishment of that freedom, and the protection of the newly-made freeman and citizen from the oppressions of those who had formerly exercised unlimited dominion over him. It is true that only the Fifteenth Amendment, in terms, mentions the negro by speaking of his color and his slavery. But it is just as true that each of the other articles was addressed to the grievances of that race, and designed to remedy them as the Fifteenth.

We do not say that no one else but the negro can share in this protection. Both the language and spirit of these articles are to have their fair and just weight in any question of construction. Undoubtedly while negro slavery alone was in the mind of the Congress which proposed the thirteenth article, it forbids any other kind of slavery, now or hereafter. If Mexican peonage or the Chinese coolie labor system shall develop slavery of the Mexican or Chinese race within our territory, this amendment may safely be trusted to make it void. And so if other rights are assailed by the States which properly and necessarily fall within the protection of these articles, that protection will apply, though the party interested may not be of African descent. But what we do say, and what we wish to be understood is, that in any fair and just construction of any section or phrase of these amendments, it is necessary to look to the purpose which we have said was the pervading spirit of them all, the evil which they were designed to remedy, and the process of continued addition to the Constitution, until that purpose was supposed to be accomplished, as far as constitutional law can accomplish it.

The first section of the fourteenth article, to which our attention is more specially invited, opens with a definition of citizenship—not only citizenship of the United States, but citizenship of the States. No such definition was previously found in the Constitution, nor had any attempt been made to define it by act of Congress. . . . It had been said by eminent judges that no man was a citizen of the United States, except as he was a citizen of one of the States composing the Union. Those, therefore, who had been born and resided always in the District of Columbia or in the Territories, though within the United States, were not citizens. Whether this proposition was sound or not had never been judicially decided. But it had been held by this court, in the celebrated Dred Scott Case, only a few years before the outbreak of the civil war, that a man of African descent, whether a slave or not, could not be a citizen of a State or of the United States. This decision, while it met the condemnation of some of the ablest statesmen and constitutional lawyers of the country, had never been overruled; and if it was to be accepted as a constitutional limitation of the right of citizenship, then all the negro race who had recently been made freemen, were still, not only not citizens, but were incapable of becoming so by anything short of an amendment to the Constitution.

To remove this difficulty primarily, and to establish a clear and comprehensive definition of citizenship which should declare what should constitute citizenship of the United States, and also citizenship of a State, the first clause of the first section was framed.

"All persons born or naturalized in the United States, and subject to the jurisdiction thereof, are citizens of the United States and of the State wherein they reside." . . .

It is quite clear, then, that there is a citizenship of the United States, and a citizenship of a State, which are distinct from each other, and which depend upon different characteristics or circumstances in the individual.

We think this distinction and its explicit recognition in this amendment of great weight in this argument, because the next paragraph of this same section, which is the one mainly relied on by the plaintiffs in error, speaks only of privileges and immunities of citizens of the United States, and does not speak of those of citizens of the several States. The argument, however, in favor of the plaintiffs rests wholly on the assumption that the citizenship is the same, and the privileges and immunities guaranteed by the clause are the same.

The language is, "No State shall make or enforce any law which shall abridge the privileges or immunities of citizens of *the United States*." It is a little remarkable, if this clause was intended as a protection to the citizen of a State against the legislative power of his own State, that the word citizen of the State should be left out when it is so carefully used, and used in contradistinction to citizens of the

United States, in the very sentence which precedes it. It is too clear for argument that the change in phraseology was adopted understandingly and with a purpose.

Of the privileges and immunities of the citizen of the United States, and of the privileges and immunities of the citizen of the State, and what they respectively are, we will presently consider; but we wish to state here that it is only the former which are placed by this clause under the protection of the federal Constitution, and that the latter, whatever they may be, are not intended to have any additional protection by this paragraph of the amendment.

If, then, there is a difference between the privileges and immunities belonging to a citizen of the United States as such, and those belonging to the citizen of the State as such, the latter must rest for their security and protection where they have heretofore rested; for they are not embraced by this paragraph of the amendment.

The first occurrence of the words "privileges and immunities" in our constitutional history, is to be found in the fourth of the Articles of the old Confederation. . . .

In the Constitution of the United States, which superseded the Articles of Confederation, the corresponding provision is found in section two of the fourth article, in the following words: "The citizens of each State shall be entitled to all the privileges and immunities of citizens of the several States."

There can be but little question that the purpose of both these provisions is the same, and that the privileges and immunities intended are the same in each. In the Articles of the Confederation we have some of these specifically mentioned, and enough perhaps to give some general idea of the class of civil rights meant by the phrase.

Fortunately we are not without judicial construction of this clause of the Constitution. . . .

The constitutional provision there alluded to did not create those rights, which it called privileges and immunities of citizens of the States. It threw around them in that clause no security for the citizens of the State in which they were claimed or exercised. Nor did it profess to control the power of the state governments over the rights of its own citizens.

Its sole purpose was to declare to the several States, that whatever those rights, as you grant or establish them to your own citizens, or as you limit or qualify, or impose restrictions on their exercise, the same, neither more nor less, shall be the measure of the rights of citizens of other States within your jurisdiction. . . . But with the exception of . . . a few . . . restrictions, the entire domain of the privileges and immunities of citizens of the States, as above defined, lay within the constitutional and legislative power of the States, and without that of the federal government. Was it the purpose of the Fourteenth Amendment, by the simple declaration that no State should make or enforce any law which shall abridge the privileges and immunities of citizens of the United States, to transfer the security and protection of all the civil rights which we have mentioned, from the States to the federal government? And where it is declared that Congress shall have the power to enforce that article, was it intended to bring within the power of Congress the entire domain of civil rights heretofore belonging exclusively to the States?

All this and more must follow, if the proposition of the plaintiffs in error be sound. For not only are these rights subject to the control of Congress whenever in its discretion any of them are supposed to be abridged by state legislation, but that body may also pass laws in advance, limiting and restricting the exercise of legislative power by the States, in their most ordinary and usual functions, as in its judgment it may think proper on all such subjects. And still further, such a construction followed by the reversal of the judgments of the Supreme Court of Louisiana in these cases, would constitute this court a perpetual censor upon all legislation of the States, on the civil rights of their own citizens, with authority to nullify such as it did not approve as consistent with those rights, as they existed at the time of the adoption of this amendment. The argument, we admit, is not always the most conclusive which is drawn from the consequences urged against the adoption of a particular construction of an instrument. But when, as in the case before us, these consequences are so serious, so far-reaching and pervading, so great a departure from the structure and spirit of

our institutions; when the effect is to fetter and degrade the state governments by subjecting them to the control of Congress, in the exercise of powers heretofore universally conceded to them of the most ordinary and fundamental character; when in fact it radically changes the whole theory of the relations of the state and federal governments to each other and of both these governments to the people; the argument has a force that is irresistible, in the absence of language which expresses such a purpose too clearly to admit of doubt.

We are convinced that no such results were intended by the Congress which proposed these amendments, nor by the legislatures of the States which ratified them.

Having shown that the privileges and immunities relied on in the argument are those which belong to citizens of the States as such, and that they are left to the state governments for security and protection, and not by this article placed under the special care of the federal government, we may hold ourselves excused from defining the privileges and immunities of citizens of the United States which no State can abridge, until some case involving those privileges may make it necessary to do so. . . .

But it is useless to pursue this branch of the inquiry, since we are of opinion that the rights claimed by these plaintiffs in error, if they have any existence, are not privileges and immunities of citizens of the United States within the meaning of the clause of the Fourteenth Amendment under consideration. . . .

The argument has not been much pressed in these cases that the defendant's charter deprives the plaintiffs of their property without due process of law, or that it denies to them the equal protection of the law. The first of these paragraphs has been in the Constitution since the adoption of the Fifth Amendment, as a restraint upon the federal power. It is also to be found in some form of expression in the constitutions of nearly all the States, as a restraint upon the power of the States. This law, then, has practically been the same as it now is during the existence of the government, except so far as the present amendment may place the restraining power over the States in this matter in the hands of the federal government.

We are not without judicial interpretation, therefore, both state and national, of the meaning of this clause. And it is sufficient to say that under no construction of that provision that we have ever seen, or any that we deem admissible, can the restraint imposed by the State of Louisiana upon the exercise of their trade by the butchers of New Orleans be held to be a deprivation of property within the meaning of that provision.

"Nor shall any State deny to any person within its jurisdiction the equal protection of the laws."

In the light of the history of these amendments, and the pervading purpose of them, which we have already discussed, it is not difficult to give a meaning to this clause. The existence of laws in the States where the newly emancipated negroes resided, which discriminated with gross injustice and hardship against them as a class, was the evil to be remedied by this clause, and by it such laws are forbidden.

If, however, the States did not conform their laws to its requirements, then by the fifth section of the article of amendment Congress was authorized to enforce it by suitable legislation. We doubt very much whether any action of a State not directed by way of discrimination against the negroes as a class, or on account of their race, will ever be held to come within the purview of this provision. It is so clearly a provision for that race and that emergency, that a strong case would be necessary for its application to any other. But as it is a State that is to be dealt with, and not alone the validity of its laws, we may safely leave that matter until Congress shall have exercised its power, or some case of state oppression, by denial of equal justice in its courts, shall have claimed a decision at our hands. We find no such case in the one before us, and do not deem it necessary to go over the argument again, as it may have relation to this particular clause of the amendment. . . .

Judgment affirmed.

Justice FIELD delivered a dissenting opinion in which Chief Justice CHASE and Justices BRADLEY and SWAYNE concurred.

285. "THE CRIME OF '73"
Coinage Act of February 12, 1873
(U. S. Statutes at Large, Vol. XVII, p. 424 ff.)

This act revising the coinage system of the country omitted from the coinage the standard silver dollar of 412½ grains. This demonetization of silver came later to be known as the "crime of '73". What gave significance to the demonetization of silver was the enormous increase in the American production of silver due to new discoveries of silver ore in the west. The charge that the omission of silver dollars from the coinage was part of a gold conspiracy is rejected by most students of our financial history, but it was an article of faith with a large part of the American people for twenty years. See, J. L. Laughlin, *History of Bimetallism;* A. D. Noyes, *Forty Years of American Finance; Report of the Monetary Commission of 1876;* A. B. Hepburn, *History of Currency in the United States,* ch. xv; W. H. Harvey, *Coin's Financial School.*

An Act revising and amending the Laws relative to the Mints, Assay-offices, and Coinage of the United States.

SEC. 14. That the gold coins of the United States shall be a one-dollar piece, which, at the standard weight of twenty-five and eight tenths grains, shall be the unit of value; a quarter-eagle, or two-and-a-half dollar piece; a three-dollar piece; a half-eagle, or five-dollar piece; an eagle, or ten-dollar piece; and a double eagle, or twenty-dollar piece . . . ; which coins shall be a legal tender in all payments at their nominal value when not below the standard weight and limit of tolerance provided in this act for the single piece, and, when reduced in weight, below said standard and tolerance, shall be a legal tender at valuation in proportion to their actual weight. . . .

SEC. 15. That the silver coins of the United States shall be a trade-dollar, a half-dollar, or fifty-cent piece, a quarter-dollar, or twenty-five-cent piece, a dime, or ten-cent piece; . . . and said coins shall be a legal tender at their nominal value for any amount not exceeding five dollars in any one payment.

SEC. 16. That the minor coins of the

United States shall be a five-cent piece, a three-cent piece, and a one-cent piece . . . ; which coins shall be a legal tender, at their nominal value, for any amount not exceeding twenty-five cents in any one payment.

SEC. 17. That no coins, either of gold, silver, or minor coinage, shall hereafter be issued from the mint other than those of the denominations, standards, and weights herein set forth.

286. CITIZENS' SAVINGS & LOAN ASSOCIATION v. TOPEKA
20 Wallace, 655
1874

Error to the United States circuit court for the district of Kansas. This case involved the validity of an act of the legislature of Kansas authorizing the sale of bonds for the benefit of a bridge manufacturing company. The city of Topeka, which had issued the bonds in the first instance, claimed that the law was void and the issue unconstitutional. This is the leading case for the doctrine that taxes may not be imposed for other than public purposes. For a discussion of the question of what constitutes public purposes, see Green v. Frazier, Doc. No. 441.

MILLER, J. . . . We find ample reason to sustain the demurrer on the second ground on which it is argued by counsel and sustained by the circuit court.

That proposition is that the act authorizes the towns and other municipalities to which it applies, by issuing bonds or loaning their credit, to take the property of the citizen under the guise of taxation to pay these bonds, and use it in aid of the enterprises of others which are not of a public character, thus perverting the right of taxation, which can only be exercised for a public use, to the aid of individual interests and personal purposes of profit and gain.

The proposition as thus broadly stated is not new, nor is the question which it raises difficult of solution.

If these municipal corporations, which are in fact subdivisions of the State, and which for many reasons are vested with quasi legislative powers, have a fund or other property out of which they can pay the debts which they contract, without resort to taxation, it may be within the power of the legislature of the State to authorize them to use it in aid of projects strictly private or personal, but which would in a secondary manner contribute to the public good; or where there is property or money vested in a corporation of the kind for a particular use, as public worship or charity, the legislature may pass laws

authorizing them to make contracts in reference to this property, and incur debts payable from that source.

But such instances are few and exceptional, and the proposition is a very broad one, that debts contracted by municipal corporations must be paid, if paid at all, out of taxes which they may lawfully levy, and that all contracts creating debts to be paid in future, not limited to payment from some other source, imply an obligation to pay by taxation.

It follows that in this class of cases the right to contract must be limited by the right to tax, and if in the given case no tax can lawfully be levied to pay the debt, the contract itself is void for want of authority to make it. . . . The validity of a contract which can only be fulfilled by a resort to taxation depends on the power to lay the tax for that purpose. . . .

. . . We assume that unless the legislature of Kansas had the right to authorize the counties and towns in that State to lay taxes to be used as an aid of manufacturing enterprises, conducted by individuals, or private corporations, for purposes of gain, the law is void, and the bonds issued under it are also void.

We proceed to the inquiry whether such a power exists in the legislature of the State of Kansas.

We have already said the question is not new. The subject of the aid voted to the railways by counties and towns has been brought to the attention of the courts of almost every State in the Union. It has been thoroughly discussed and is still the subject of discussion in those courts. It is quite true that a decided preponderance of authority is to be found in favor of the proposition that the legislatures of the States, unless restricted by some special provisions of their constitutions, may confer upon those municipal bodies the right to take stock in corporations created to build railroads, and to lend their credit to such corporations. Also to levy the necessary taxes on the inhabitants, and on property within their limits to general taxation, to enable them to pay the debts thus incurred. . . .

In all these cases, however, the decision has turned upon the question whether the taxation by which this aid was afforded to the building of railroads was for a public purpose. Those who came to the conclusion that it was, held the laws for that purpose valid. Those who could not reach that conclusion held them void. In all the controversy this has been the turning point of the judgements of the courts. And it is safe to say that no court has held debts created in aid of railroad companies by counties or towns, valid on any other ground than that the purpose for which the taxes were levied was a public use. . . .

We have referred to this history of the contest over aid to railroads by taxation, to show that the strongest advocates for the validity of these laws never placed it on the ground of the unlimited power in the state legislature to tax the people, but conceded that where the purpose for which the tax was to be issued, could no longer be justly claimed to have this public character, but was purely in aid of private or personal objects, the law authorizing it was beyond the legislative power, and was an unauthorized invasion of private right. . . .

Of all the powers conferred upon government that of taxation is most liable to abuse. Given a purpose or object for which taxation may be lawfully used, and the extent of its exercise is in its very nature unlimited. It is true that express limitation on the amount of tax to be levied or the things to be taxed may be imposed by constitution or statute, but in most instances for which taxes are levied, as the support of government, the prosecution of war, the national defence, any limitation is unsafe. The entire resources of the people should in some instances be at the disposal of the government.

The power to tax is, therefore, the strongest, the most pervading of all the powers of government, reaching directly or indirectly to all classes of the people. It was said by Chief Justice Marshall, in the case of Mc-

Culloch v. *State of Maryland,* that the power to tax is the power to destroy. A striking instance of the truth of the proposition is seen in the fact that the existing tax of ten per cent, imposed by the United States on the circulation of all other banks than the national banks, drove out of existence every state bank of circulation within a year or two after its passage. This power can as readily be employed against one class of individuals and in favor of another, so as to ruin the one class and give unlimited wealth and prosperity to the other, if there is no implied limitation of the uses for which the power may be exercised.

To lay with one hand the power of the government on the property of the citizen, and with the other to bestow it upon favored individuals to aid private enterprises and build up private fortunes, is none the less a robbery because it is done under the forms of law and is called taxation. This is not legislation. It is a decree under legislative forms.

Nor is it taxation. A "tax," says Webster's Dictionary, "is a rate or sum of money assessed on the person or property of a citizen by government for the use of the nation or state." "Taxes are burdens or charges imposed by the legislature upon persons or property to raise money for public purposes." Cooley on Constitutional Limitations, 479. . . .

We have established, we think, beyond cavil that there can be no lawful tax which is not laid for a public purpose. It may not be easy to draw the line in all cases so as to decide what is a public purpose in this sense and what is not.

It is undoubtedly the duty of the legislature which imposes or authorizes municipalities to impose a tax to see that it is not to be used for purposes of private interest instead of a public use, and the courts can only be justified in interposing when a violation of this principle is clear and the reason for interference cogent. And in deciding whether, in the given case, the object for which the taxes are assessed falls upon the one side or the other of this line, they must be governed mainly by the course and usage of the government, the objects for which taxes have been customarily and by long course of legislation levied, what objects or purposes have been considered necessary to the support and for the proper use of the government, whether state or municipal. Whatever lawfully pertains to this and is sanctioned by time and the acquiescence of the people may well be held to belong to the public use, and proper for the maintenance of good government, though this may not be the only criterion of rightful taxation.

But in the case before us, in which the towns are authorized to contribute aid by way of taxation to any class of manufacturers, there is no difficulty in holding that this is not such a public purpose as we have been considering. If it be said that a benefit results to the local public of a town by es-

tablishing manufactures, the same may be said of any other business or pursuit which employs capital or labor. The merchant, the mechanic, the inn-keeper, the banker, the builder, the steamboat owner are equally promoters of the public good, and equally deserving the aid of the citizens by forced contributions. No line can be drawn in favor of the manufacturer which would not open the coffers of the public treasury to the importunities of two-thirds of the business men of the city or town. . . .

Judgment affirmed.

CLIFFORD, J. dissenting.

287. THE GRANGER MOVEMENT

The two documents below illustrate the local and the general character of the Granger movement. The first indicates the anti-railroad character of the movement in the middle western States; the second emphasizes the social rather than the economic character of the movement. The first is taken from J. Periam, *The Groundswell*, p. 286 ff.; the second from *Proceedings of the Seventh Session of the National Grange of the Patrons of Husbandry*, Feb. 4, 1874. Both are reprinted in J. R. Commons, ed. *Documentary History of American Industrial Society*, Vol. X. For background, see S. J. Buck, *The Granger Movement; The Agrarian Crusade; A. E. Paine, Granger Movement in Illinois.*

1. RESOLUTIONS OF SPRINGFIELD, ILLINOIS, FARMERS' CONVENTION
April 2, 1873

1. Resolved, by the farmers of Illinois, in mass meeting assembled, that all chartered monopolies, not regulated and controlled by law, have proved detrimental to the public prosperity, corrupting in their management, and dangerous to republican institutions.

2. Resolved, that the railways of the world, except in those countries where they have been held under the strict regulation and supervision of the government, have proved themselves arbitrary, extortionate and as opposed to free institutions and free commerce between states as were the feudal barons of the middle ages.

3. Resolved, that we hold, declare and resolve, that this despotism, which defies our laws, plunders our shippers, impoverishes our people, and corrupts our government, shall

be subdued and made to subserve the public interest at whatever cost. . . .

5. Resolved, that in view of the present extortions, we look with alarm upon the future of an interest which can combine in the hands of a few men a capital of nearly $250,000,000, and we believe it essential to the prosperity of all classes that this contest continue until these corporations acknowledge the supremacy of law.

6. Resolved, that we regard it as the undoubted power, and the imperative duty of the legislature, to pass laws fixing reasonable maximum rates for freight and passengers, without classification of roads, and that we urge upon our General Assembly the passage of such laws. . . .

9. Resolved, that we urge the passage of a bill enforcing the principle that railroads are public highways, and requiring railroads to make connections with all roads whose tracks meet or cross their own, and to receive and transmit cars and trains offered over their roads at reasonable maximum rates, whether offered at such crossings, or at stations along their roads, and empowering the making of connections by municipal corporations for that purpose, and for public use. . . .

12. Resolved, that we indorse most fully the action of those who tender legal rates of fare upon the railroads, and refuse to pay more; and that it is the duty of the legislature to provide by law for the defense by the State of Illinois of suits commenced, or that hereafter may be commenced by rail-

road companies against individuals who have in good faith insisted, or hereafter may insist, upon the right to ride in railroads at legal rates.

13. Resolved, that the presentation of railroad passes to our legislators, whatever may be the spirit and intent with which they are accepted, are demoralizing in their influence; and we look to our legislature, now in session, to rise above personal considerations of pecuniary interest or convenience, and to pass a law making it a misdemeanor for any Senator, or other state or county officers, to accept any railroad pass. . . .

14. Whereas, the constitution of 1848, Article X, prohibits the legislature from granting special railroad charters . . . therefore, Resolved, that it is extremely doubtful whether any railroad charter granted since April 1, 1848, by the legislature of Illinois, is of any validity, and that the vested rights of railroad monopolies in this state exist only by assumption of the monopolies and the sufferance of the people. . . .

15. Whereas, the constitution of 1870, Article XI, Section 13, prohibits any railroad company from issuing watered stock . . . and whereas, this article of the constitution has probably been violated by nearly all the railroad companies in the state; therefore, Resolved, that it is the duty of the railroad commissioners to look carefully into this matter, and to commence proceedings in all clear cases by *quo warranto,* or otherwise, against all railroad companies which have disregarded this important provision of the organic law of the state. . . .

18. Resolved, that we are in favor of the immediate repeal of the protective duties on iron, steel, lumber, and all materials which enter into the construction of railroad cars, steamships, sailing vessels, agricultural implements, etc. and that we urge upon Congress immediate action for this purpose, that cheap railroads and cheap ships are necessary to cheap freights, and that we invite the railroad companies to co-operate with us to that end. . . .

2. DECLARATION OF PURPOSE OF NATIONAL GRANGE
1874

1. PREAMBLE. Profoundly impressed with the truth that the National Grange of the United States should definitely proclaim to the world its general objects, we hereby unanimously make this Declaration of Purposes of the Patrons of Husbandry:

GENERAL OBJECTS. 1. United by the strong and faithful tie of agriculture, we mutually resolve to labor for the good of our Order, our country, and mankind.

2. We heartily indorse the motto: "In essentials, unity; in non-essentials, liberty; in all things, charity."

SPECIFIC OBJECTS. 3. We shall endeavor to advance our cause by laboring to accomplish the following objects:

To develop a better and higher manhood and womanhood among ourselves. To enhance the comforts and attractions of our homes, and strengthen our attachments to our pursuits. To foster mutual understanding and coöperation. To maintain inviolate our laws, and to emulate each other in labor to hasten the good time coming. To reduce our expenses, both individual and corporate. To buy less and produce more, in order to make our farms self-sustaining. To diversify our crops, and crop no more than we can cultivate. To condense the weight of our exports, selling less in the bushel and more on hoof and in fleece; less in lint, and more in warp and woof. To systematize our work, and calculate intelligently on probabilities. To discountenance the credit system, the mortgage system, the fashion system, and every other system tending to prodigality and bankruptcy.

We propose meeting together, talking together, working together, buying together, selling together, and in general acting together for our mutual protection and advancement, as occasion may require. We shall avoid litigation as much as possible by arbitration in the Grange. We shall constantly strive to secure entire harmony, goodwill, vital brotherhood among ourselves, and to make our order perpetual. We shall earnestly endeavor to suppress personal, local, sectional, and national prejudices, all unhealthy rivalry, all selfish ambition. Faithful adherence to these principles will insure our mental, moral, social, and material advancement.

BUSINESS RELATIONS. 4. For our business interests, we desire to bring producers and consumers, farmers and manufacturers into the most direct and friendly relations possible. Hence we must dispense with a surplus of middlemen, not that we are unfriendly to them, but we do not need them. Their surplus and their exactions diminish our profits.

We wage no aggressive warfare against any other interest whatever. On the contrary, all our acts and all our efforts, so far as business is concerned, are not only for the benefit of the producer and consumer, but also for all other interests that tend to bring these two parties into speedy and economical contact. Hence we hold that transportation companies of every kind are necessary to our success, that their interests are intimately connected with our interests, and harmonious action is mutually advantageous, keeping in view the first sentence in our declaration of principles of action that "Individual happiness depends upon general prosperity."

We shall, therefore, advocate for every state the increase in every practicable way, of all facilities for transporting cheaply to the seaboard, or between home producers and consumers, all the productions of our country. We adopt it as our fixed purpose to "open out the channels in nature's great arteries that the life-blood of commerce may flow freely."

We are not enemies of railroads, navigable and irrigating canals, nor of any corporation that will advance our industrial interests, nor of any laboring classes.

In our noble Order there is no communism, no agrarianism.

We are opposed to such spirit and management of any corporation or enterprise as tends to oppress the people and rob them of their just profits. We are not enemies to capital, but we oppose the tyranny of monopolies. We long to see the antagonism between capital and labor removed by common consent, and by an enlightened statesmanship worthy of the nineteenth century. We are opposed to excessive salaries, high rates of interest, and exorbitant per cent profits in trade. They greatly increase our burdens, and do not bear a proper proportion to the profits of producers. We desire only self-protection and the protection of every true interest of our land by legitimate transactions, legitimate trade, and legitimate profits.

EDUCATION. We shall advance the cause of education among ourselves and for our children, by all just means within our power. We especially advocate for our agricultural and industrial colleges that practical agriculture, domestic science, and all the arts which adorn the home, be taught in their courses of study.

THE GRANGE NOT PARTISAN. 5. We emphatically and sincerely assert the oft-repeated truth taught in our organic law, that the Grange, National, State, or Subordinate, is not a political or party organization. No Grange, if true to its obligations, can discuss political or religious questions, nor call political conventions, nor nominate candidates, nor even discuss their merits in its meetings.

Yet the principles we teach underlie all true politics, all true statesmanship, and, if properly carried out, will tend to purify the whole political atmosphere of our country. For we seek the greatest good to the greatest number.

We must always bear in mind that no one, by becoming a Patron of Husbandry, gives up that inalienable right and duty which belongs to every American citizen, to take a proper interest in the politics of his country.

On the contrary, it is right for every member to do all in his power legitimately to influence for good the action of any political party to which he belongs. It is his duty to do all he can in his own party to put down bribery, corruption, and trickery; to see that none but competent, faithful, and honest men, who will unflinchingly stand by our industrial interests, are nominated for all positions of trust; and to have carried out the principle which should always characterize every Patron, that the office should seek the man, and not the man the office.

We acknowledge the broad principle that difference of opinion is no crime, and hold that "progress toward truth is made by differences of opinion," while "the fault lies in bitterness of controversy."

We desire a proper equality, equity, and fairness; protection for the weak, restraint upon the strong; in short, justly distributed burdens and justly distributed power. These are American ideas, the very essence of American independence, and to advocate the contrary is unworthy of the sons and daughters of an American republic.

We cherish the belief that sectionalism is, and of right should be, dead and buried with the past. Our work is for the present and the future. In our agricultural brotherhood and its purposes we shall recognize no north, no south, no east, no west.

It is reserved by every Patron, as the right of a freeman, to affiliate with any party that will best carry out his principles.

OUTSIDE COÖPERATION. 6. Ours being peculiarly a farmers' institution, we cannot admit all to our ranks. Many are excluded by the nature of our organization, not because they are professional men, or artisans, or laborers, but because they have not a sufficient direct interest in tilling the soil, or may have some interest in conflict with our purposes. But we appeal to all good citizens for their cordial coöperation to assist in our efforts toward reform, that we may eventually remove from our midst the last vestige of tyranny and corruption. We hail the general desire for fraternal harmony, equitable compromises, and earnest coöperation, as an omen of our future success.

7. It shall be an abiding principle with us to relieve any of our oppressed and suffering brotherhood by any means at our command.

Last, but not least, we proclaim it among our purposes to inculcate a proper appreciation of the abilities and sphere of woman, as is indicated by admitting her to membership and position in our order.

Imploring the continued assistance of our Divine Master to guide us in our work, we here pledge ourselves to faithful and harmonious labor for all future time, to return by our united efforts to the wisdom, justice, fraternity, and political purity of our forefathers.

288. GRANT'S RECOMMENDATION OF RESUMPTION OF SPECIE PAYMENTS

Extracts from President Grant's First Annual Message and Sixth Annual Message to Congress
December 6, 1869 and December 7, 1874

(Richardson, ed. *Messages and Papers*, Vol. VII, p. 29–30, p. 285 ff.)

For references see Doc. No. 289.

1. . . . . Among the evils growing out of the rebellion, and not yet referred to, is that of an irredeemable currency. It is an evil which I hope will receive your most earnest attention. It is a duty, and one of the highest duties, of Government to secure to the citizen a medium of exchange of fixed, unvarying value. This implies a return to a specie basis, and no substitute for it can be devised. It should be commenced now and reached at the earliest practicable moment consistent with a fair regard to the interests of the debtor class. Immediate resumption, if practicable, would not be desirable. It would compel the debtor class to pay, beyond their contracts, the premium on gold at the date of their purchase, and would bring bankruptcy and ruin to thousands. Fluctuation, however, in the paper value of the measure of all values (gold) is detrimental to the interests of trade. It makes the man of business an involuntary gambler, for in all sales where future payment is to be made both parties speculate as to what will be the value of the currency to be paid and received. I earnestly recommend to you, then, such legislation as will insure a gradual return to specie payments and put an immediate stop to fluctuations in the value of currency.

The methods to secure the former of these results are as numerous as are the speculators on political economy. To secure the latter I see but one way, and that is to authorize the Treasury to redeem its own paper, at a fixed price, whenever presented, and to withhold from circulation all currency so redeemed until sold again for gold.

The vast resources of the nation, both developed and undeveloped, ought to make our credit the best on earth. With a less burden of taxation than the citizen has endured for six years past, the entire public debt could be paid in ten years. But it is not desirable that the people should be taxed to pay it in that time. Year by year the ability to pay increases in a rapid ratio. But the burden of interest ought to be reduced as rapidly as can be done without the violation of contract. The public debt is represented in great part by bonds having from five to twenty and from ten to forty years to run, bearing interest at the rate of 6 per cent and 5 per cent, respectively. It is optional with the Government to pay these bonds at any period after the expiration of the least time mentioned upon their face. The time has already expired when a great part of them may be taken up, and is rapidly approaching when all may be. It is believed that all which are now due may be replaced by bonds bearing a rate of interest not exceeding 4½ per cent, and as rapidly as the remainder become due that they may be replaced in the same way. To accomplish this it may be necessary to authorize the interest to be paid at either of three or four of the money centers of Europe, or by any assistant treasurer of the United States, at the option of the holder of the bond. I suggest this subject for the consideration of Congress, and also, simultaneously with this, the propriety of redeeming our currency, as before suggested, at its market value at the time the law goes into effect, increasing the rate at which currency shall be bought and sold from day to day or week to week, at the same rate of interest as Government pays upon its bonds. . . .

2. . . . In view of the pledges of the American Congress when our present legal-tender system was adopted, and debt contracted, there should be no delay—certainly no unnecessary delay—in fixing by legislation a method by which we will return to specie. To the accomplishment of this end I invite your special attention. I believe firmly that there can be no prosperous and permanent revival of business and industries until a policy is adopted—with legislation to carry it out—looking to a return to a specie basis. It is easy to conceive that the debtor and speculative classes may think it of value to them to make so-called money abundant until they can throw a portion of their burdens upon others. But even these, I believe, would be disappointed in the result if a course should be pursued which will keep in doubt the value of the legal-tender medium of exchange. A revival of productive industry is needed by all classes; by none more than the holders of property, of whatever sort, with debts to liquidate from realization upon its

sale. But admitting that these two classes of citizens are to be benefited by expansion, would it be honest to give it? Would not the general loss be too great to justify such relief? Would it not be just as honest and prudent to authorize each debtor to issue his own legal-tenders to the extent of his liabilities? Than to do this, would it not be safer, for fear of overissues by unscrupulous creditors, to say that all debt obligations are obliterated in the United States, and now we commence anew, each possessing all he has at the time free from incumbrance? These propositions are too absurd to be entertained for a moment by thinking or honest people. Yet every delay in preparation for final resumption partakes of this dishonesty, and is only less in degree as the hope is held out that a convenient season will at last arrive for the good work of redeeming our pledges to commerce. It will never come, in my opinion, except by positive action by Congress, or by national disasters which will destroy, for a time at least, the credit of the individual and the State at large. A sound currency might be reached by total bankruptcy and discredit of the integrity of the nation and of individuals. I believe it is in the power of Congress at this session to devise such legislation as will renew confidence, revive all the industries, start us on a career of prosperity to last for many years and to save the credit of the nation and of the people. Steps toward the return to a specie basis are the great requisites to this devoutly to be sought for end. There are others which I may touch upon hereafter.

A nation dealing in a currency below that of specie in value labors under two great disadvantages: First, having no use for the world's acknowledged medium of exchange, gold and silver, these are driven out of the country because there is no need for their use; second, the medium of exchange in use being of a fluctuating value—for, after all, it is only worth just what it will purchase of gold and silver, metals having an intrinsic value just in proportion to the honest labor it takes to produce them—a larger margin must be allowed for profit by the manufacturer and producer. It is months from the date of production to the date of realization. Interest upon capital must be charged, and risk of fluctuation in the value of that which is to be received in payment added. Hence high prices, acting as a protection to the foreign producer, who receives nothing in exchange for the products of his skill and labor except a currency good, at a stable value, the world over. It seems to me that nothing is clearer than that the greater part of the burden of existing prostration, for the want of a sound financial system, falls upon the working man, who must after all produce the wealth, and the salaried man, who superintends and conducts business. The burden falls upon them in two ways—by the deprivation of employment and by the decreased purchasing power of their salaries. It is the duty of Congress to devise the method of correcting the evils which are acknowledged to exist, and not mine. But I will venture to suggest two or three things which seem to me as absolutely necessary to a return to specie payments, the first great requisite in a return to prosperity. The legal-tender clause to the law authorizing the issue of currency

by the National Government should be repealed, to take effect as to all contracts entered into after a day fixed in the repealing act—not to apply, however, to payments of salaries by Government, or for other expenditures now provided by law to be paid in currency, in the interval pending between repeal and final resumption. Provision should be made by which the Secretary of the Treasury can obtain gold as it may become necessary from time to time from the date when specie redemption commences. To this might and should be added a revenue sufficiently in excess of expenses to insure an accumulation of gold in the Treasury to sustain permanent redemption.

I commend this subject to your careful consideration, believing that a favorable solution is attainable, and if reached by this Congress that the present and future generations will ever gratefully remember it as their deliverer from a thraldom of evil and disgrace. . . .

289. THE RESUMPTION OF SPECIE PAYMENTS
January 14, 1875

(*U. S. Statutes at Large,* Vol. XVIII, p. 296)

The financial stringency brought about by the panic of 1873 resulted in an effort to increase the issuance of legal tender notes to $400,000,000 which was defeated only by Grant's veto. This veto was the turning point in the greenback agitation; early in 1875 Congress provided for the resumption of specie payments, and the reduction of greenback circulation to $300,000,000. Hayes, elected in 1876, appointed John Sherman Secretary of the Treasury, and Sherman accumulated a gold reserve sufficient to insure successful resumption January 1, 1879. The result was that greenbacks reached par shortly before resumption. The reduction in the circulation of greenbacks provided for by the act of 1875 was stopped when $346,681,000 was outstanding. See, D. R. Dewey, *Financial History,* ch. xv; J. Sherman, *Recollections,* Vol. I, p. 507 ff., Vol. II, p. 636 ff.; A. D. Noyes, *Forty Years of American Finance;* A. S. Bolles, *Financial History of the United States,* Vol. III; *Specie Resumption and the Refunding of the National Debt,* Executive Doc. XVII, 46th Congress, 2nd Session; D. C. Barrett, *Greenbacks and the Resumption of Specie Payments, 1862–1879;* A. B. Hepburn, *A History of Currency in the United States,* chs. xii, xiii.

An act to provide for the resumption of specie payments.

*Be it enacted . . . ,*That the Secretary of the Treasury is hereby authorized and required, as rapidly as practicable, to cause to be coined at the mints of the United States, silver coins of the denominations of ten, twenty-five, and fifty cents, of standard value, and to issue them in redemption of an equal number and amount of fractional currency of similar denominations, or, at his discretion, he may issue such silver coins through the mints, the subtreasuries, public depositaries, and post-offices of the United States; and, upon such issue, he is hereby authorized and required to redeem an equal amount of such fractional currency, until the whole amount of such fractional currency outstanding shall be redeemed.

SEC. 2. That so much of section 3524 of the Revised Statutes of the United States as provides for a charge of one-fifth of one per centum for converting standard gold bullion into coin is hereby repealed, and hereafter no charge shall be made for that service.

SEC. 3. That section 5177 of the Revised Statutes of the United States, limiting the aggregate amount of circulating-notes of national banking-associations, be, and is hereby, repealed; and each existing banking-association may increase its circulating-notes in accordance with existing law without respect to said aggregate limit; and new banking-associations may be organized in accordance with existing law without respect to said aggregate limit; and the provisions of law for the withdrawal and redistribution of national-bank currency among the several States and Territories are hereby repealed. And whenever, and so often, as circulating-notes shall be issued to any such banking-association, so increasing its capital or circulating-notes, or so newly organized as aforesaid, it shall be the duty of the Secretary of the Treasury to redeem the legal-tender United States notes in excess only of three hundred million of dollars, to the amount of eighty per centum of the sum of national-bank notes so issued to any such banking-association as aforesaid,

and to continue such redemption as such circulating-notes are issued until there shall be outstanding the sum of three hundred million dollars of such legal-tender United States notes, and no more. And on and after January 1, 1879, the Secretary of the Treasury shall redeem, in coin, the United States legal-tender notes then outstanding on their presentation for redemption, at the office of the assistant treasurer of the United States in the city of New York, in sums of not less than fifty dollars. And to enable the Secretary of the Treasury to prepare and provide for the redemption in this act authorized or required, he is authorized to use any surplus revenues, from time to time, in the Treasury not otherwise appropriated, and to issue, sell, and dispose of, at not less than par, in coin, either of the descriptions of bonds of the United States described in the . . . Act of July 14, 1870 . . . , with like qualities, privileges, and exemptions, to the extent necessary to carry this act into full effect, and to use the proceeds thereof for the purposes aforesaid. . . .

290. MINOR v. HAPPERSETT
21 Wallace, 162
1875

Error to the supreme court of Missouri. This case involved the interpretation of the relation of the Fourteenth Amendment to the right to vote, with particular reference to the privileges and immunities clause of that Amendment.

WAITE, C. J. The question is presented in this case, whether, since the adoption of the Fourteenth Amendment, a woman, who is a citizen of the United States and of the State of Missouri, is a voter in that State, notwithstanding the provision of the constitution and laws of the State, which confine the right of suffrage to men alone. . . .

It is contended that the provisions of the Constitution and laws of the State of Missouri, which confine the right of suffrage and registration therefor to men, are in violation of the Constitution of the United States, and therefore void. The argument is, that as a woman, born or naturalized in the United States and subject to the jurisdiction thereof, is a citizen of the United States and of the State in which she resides, she has the right

of suffrage as one of the privileges and immunities of her citizenship, which the State cannot by its laws or constitution abridge.

There is no doubt that women may be citizens. They are persons, and by the Fourteenth Amendment "all persons born or naturalized in the United States and subject to the jurisdiction thereof" are expressly declared to be "citizens of the United States and of the State wherein they reside." But, in our opinion, it did not need this amendment to give them that position. Before its adoption the Constitution of the United States did not in terms prescribe who should be citizens of the United States or of the several States, yet there were necessarily such citizens without such provision. . . .

For convenience it has been found necessary to give a name to this membership. The object is to designate by a title the person and the relation he bears to the nation. For this purpose the words "subject," "inhabitant," and "citizen" have been used, and the choice between them is sometimes made to depend upon the form of the government. Citizen is now more commonly employed, however, and as it has been considered better suited to the description of one living under a republican government, it was adopted by nearly all of the States upon their separation from Great Britain, and was afterwards adopted in the Articles of Confederation and in the Constitution of the United States. When used in this sense it is understood as conveying the idea of membership of a nation, and nothing more. . . .

. . . Sex has never been made one of the elements of citizenship in the United States. In this respect men have never had an advantage over women. The same laws precisely apply to both. The Fourteenth Amendment did not affect the citizenship of women any more than it did of men. In this particular, therefore, the rights of Mrs. Minor do not depend upon the amendment. She has always been a citizen from her birth, and entitled to all the privileges and immunities of citizenship. . . .

If the right of suffrage is one of the necessary privileges of a citizen of the United States, then the constitution and laws of Missouri confining it to men are in violation of the Constitution of the United States, as amended, and consequently void. The direct question is, therefore, presented whether all citizens are necessarily voters.

The Constitution does not define the privileges and immunities of citizens. For that definition we must look elsewhere. In this case we need not determine what they are, but only whether suffrage is necessarily one of them.

It certainly is nowhere made so in express terms. The United States has no voters in the States of its own creation. The elective officers of the United States are all elected directly or indirectly by state voters. . . .

The Amendment did not add to the privileges and immunities of a citizen. It simply furnished an additional guaranty for the protection of such as he already had. No new voters were necessarily made by it. Indirectly it may have had that effect, because it may have increased the number of citizens entitled to suffrage under the constitution and laws of the States, but it operates for this purpose, if at all, through the States and the state laws, and not directly upon the citizen.

It is clear therefore, we think, that the Constitution has not added the right of suffrage to the privileges and immunities of citizenship as they existed at the time it was adopted. This makes it proper to inquire whether suffrage was co-extensive with the citizenship of the States at the time of its adoption. If it was, then it may with force be argued that suffrage was one of the rights which belonged to citizenship, and in the enjoyment of which every citizen must be protected. But if it was not, the contrary may with propriety be assumed.

When the Federal Constitution was adopted, all the States, with the exception of Rhode Island and Connecticut, had constitutions of their own. . . . Upon an examination of these constitutions we find that in no State were all citizens permitted to vote. . . .

In this condition of the law in respect to suffrage in the several States it cannot for a moment be doubted that if it had been intended to make all citizens of the United States voters, the framers of the Constitution would not have left it to implication. . . .

It is true that the United States guarantees to every State a republican form of government. . . . The guaranty is of a republican form of government. No particular government is designated as republican, neither is the exact form to be guaranteed, in any manner especially designated. Here, as in other parts of the instrument, we are compelled to resort elsewhere to ascertain what was intended.

The guaranty necessarily implies a duty on the part of the States themselves to provide such a government. All the States had governments when the Constitution was adopted. In all the people participated to some extent, through their representatives elected in the manner specially provided. These governments the Constitution did not change. They were accepted precisely as they were, and it is, therefore, to be presumed that they were such as it was the duty of the States to provide. Thus we have unmistakable evidence of what was republican in form, within the meaning of that term as employed in the Constitution.

As we have seen, all the citizens of the States were not invested with the right of suffrage. In all, save perhaps New Jersey, this right was only bestowed upon men and not upon all of them. Under these circumstances it is certainly now too late to contend that a government is not republican, within the meaning of this guaranty in the Constitution, because women are not made voters. . . .

Certainly if the courts can consider any question settled, this is one. For nearly ninety years the people have acted upon the idea that the Constitution, when it conferred citizenship, did not necessarily confer the right of suffrage. . . .

Being unanimously of the opinion that the Constitution of the United States does not confer the right of suffrage upon any one, and that the constitutions and laws of the several States which commit that important trust to men alone are not necessarily void, we affirm the judgement.

291. THE CIVIL RIGHTS ACT
March 1, 1875

(U. S. Statutes at Large, Vol. XVIII, p. 335 ff.)

For history and references, see Doc. No. 273.

An act to protect all citizens in their civil and legal rights

Whereas it is essential to just government we recognize the equality of all men before the law, and hold that it is the duty of government in its dealings with the people to mete out equal and exact justice to all, of whatever nativity, race, color, or persuasion, religious or political; and it being the appropriate object of legislation to enact great fundamental principles into law: Therefore,

Be it enacted, That all persons within the jurisdiction of the United States shall be entitled to the full and equal enjoyment of the accommodations, advantages, facilities, and privileges of inns, public conveyances on land or water, theaters, and other places of public amusement; subject only to the conditions and limitations established by law, and applicable alike to citizens of every race and color, regardless of any previous condition of servitude.

SEC. 2. That any person who shall violate the foregoing section by denying to any citizen, except for reasons by law applicable to citizens of every race and color, and regardless of any previous condition of servitude, the full enjoyment of any of the accommodations, advantages, facilities, or privileges in said section enumerated, or by aiding or inciting such denial, shall, for every such offense, forfeit and pay the sum of five hundred dollars to the person aggrieved thereby, . . . and shall also, for every such offense, be deemed guilty of a misdemeanor, and, upon conviction thereof, shall be fined not less than five hundred nor more than one thousand dollars, or shall be imprisoned not less than thirty days nor more than one year . . .

SEC. 3. That the district and circuit courts of the United States shall have, exclusively of the courts of the several States, cognizance of all crimes and offenses against, and violations of, the provisions of this act . . .

SEC. 4. That no citizen possessing all other qualifications which are or may be prescribed by law shall be disqualified for service as grand or petit juror in any court of the United States, or of any State, on account of race, color, or previous condition of servitude; and any officer or other person charged with any duty in the selection or summoning of jurors who shall exclude or fail to summon any citizen for the cause aforesaid shall, on conviction thereof, be deemed guilty of a misdemeanor, and be fined not more than five thousand dollars.

SEC. 5. That all cases arising under the provisions of this act . . . shall be renewable by the Supreme Court of the United States, without regard to the sum in controversy. . . .

292. CIVIL RIGHTS CASES
109 U. S. 3
1883

These were five cases, appealed from different circuit courts, involving the validity and interpretation of the Civil Rights Act of March 1, 1875. (Doc. No. 291.) In each case a colored person had been denied some accommodation or privilege on account of color. The opinion of the Court that the rights which this law attempted to protect were social rather than civil rights, and that the Federal Government had no jurisdiction over these matters, practically put an end to the effort of the Federal Government to enforce the guaranties of the Fourteenth Amendment. See, Warren, *Supreme Court* (1928 ed.), Vol. II, ch. xxxiv; W. A. Dunning, *Essays on Civil War and Reconstruction,* p. 363 ff.; W. W. Davis, "The Federal Enforcement Acts," *Studies in Southern History and Politics.*

BRADLEY, J. [After holding that the statute derived no support from the Fourteenth Amendment].

. . . But the power of Congress to adopt direct and primary, as distinguished from corrective legislation, on the subject in hand, is sought in the second place, from the Thirteenth Amendment, which abolishes slavery. . . .

It is true that slavery cannot exist without law any more than property in lands and goods can exist without law, and therefore the Thirteenth Amendment may be regarded as nullifying all state laws which establish or uphold slavery. But it has a reflex character also, establishing and decreeing universal civil and political freedom throughout the United States; and it is assumed that the power in Congress to enforce the articles by appropriate legislation, clothes Congress with power to pass all laws necessary and proper for abolishing all badges and incidents of slavery in the United States; and upon this assumption it is claimed that this is sufficient authority for declaring by law that all persons shall have equal accommodations and privileges in all inns, public conveyances, and places of public amusement; the argument being that the denial of such equal accommodations and privileges is in itself a subjection to a species of servitude within the meaning of the amendment. Conceding the major proposition to be true, that Congress has a right to enact all necessary and proper laws for the obliteration and prevention of slavery with all its badges and incidents, is the minor proposition also true, that the denial to any person of admission to the accommodations and privileges of an inn, a public conveyance, or a theatre, does subject that person to any form of servitude, or tend to fasten upon him any badge of slavery? If it does not, then

power to pass the law is not found in the Thirteenth Amendment. . . .

But is there any similarity between such servitudes and a denial by the owner of an inn, a public conveyance, or a theatre, of its accommodations and privileges to an individual, even though the denial be founded on the race or color of that individual? Where does any slavery or servitude, or badge of either, arise from such an act of denial? Whether it might not be a denial of a right which, if sanctioned by the state law, would be obnoxious to the prohibitions of the Fourteenth Amendment, is another question. But what has it to do with the question of slavery? . . .

The long existence of African slavery in this country gave us very distinct notions of what it was, and what were its necessary incidents. Compulsory service of the slave for the benefit of the master, restraint of his movements except by the master's will, disability to hold property, to make contracts, to have a standing in court, to be a witness against a white person, and such like burdens and incapacities were the inseparable incidents of the institution. . . . Can the act of a mere individual, the owner of the inn, the public conveyance, or place of amusement, refusing the accommodation, be justly regarded as imposing any badge of slavery or servitude upon the applicant, or only as inflicting an ordinary civil injury, properly cognizable by the laws of the State, and presumably subject to redress by those laws until the contrary appears?

After giving to these questions all the consideration which their importance demands, we are forced to the conclusion that such an act of refusal has nothing to do with slavery or involuntary servitude, and that if it is violative of any right of the party, his redress is to be sought under the laws of the State; or, if those laws are adverse to his rights and do not protect him, his remedy will be found in the corrective legislation which Congress has adopted, or may adopt, for counteracting the effect of state laws, or state action, prohibited by the Fourteenth Amendment. It would be running the slavery argument into the ground to make it apply to every act of discrimination which a person may see fit to make as to the guests he will entertain, or as to the people he will take into his coach or cab or car, or admit to his concert or theatre, or deal with in other matters of intercourse or business. . . .

When a man has emerged from slavery, and by the aid of beneficent legislation has shaken off the inseparable concomitants of that state, there must be some stage in the progress of his elevation when he takes the rank of a mere citizen, and ceases to be the special favorite of the laws, and when his rights as a citizen, or a man, are to be protected in the ordinary modes by which other men's rights are protected. There were thousands of free colored people in this country before the abolition of slavery, enjoying all the essential rights of life, liberty and property the same as white citizens; yet no one, at that time, thought that it was any invasion of his personal status as a freeman because he was not admitted to all the privileges enjoyed by white citizens, or because he was subjected to discriminations in the enjoyment of accommodations in inns, public conveyances and places of amusement. Mere discriminations on account of race or color were not regarded as badges of slavery. If, since that time, the enjoyment of equal rights in all these respects has become established by constitutional enactment, it is not by force of the Thirteenth Amendment (which merely abolishes slavery), but by force of the Fourteenth and Fifteenth Amendments.

On the whole we are of the opinion that no countenance of authority for the passage of the law in question can be found in either the Thirteenth or Fourteenth Amendment of the Constitution; and no other ground of authority for its passage being suggested, it must necessarily be declared void, at least so far as its operation in the several States is concerned. . . .

HARLAN, J., delivered a dissenting opinion.

293. EX PARTE YARBROUGH
110 U. S. 651
1884

Petition for a writ of *habeas corpus* for release of persons convicted and imprisoned for conspiracy to prevent a negro from voting at an election for a member of Congress, contrary to Federal laws safeguarding the right to vote at Congressional elections. It was alleged by Yarbrough that these laws were unconstitutional.

MILLER, J. . . . Stripped of its technical verbiage, the offence charged in this indictment is that the defendants conspired to intimidate Berry Saunders, a citizen of African descent, in the exercise of his right to vote for a member of the Congress of the United States, and in the execution of that conspiracy they beat, bruised, wounded and otherwise maltreated him; and in the second count, that they did this on account of his race, color, and previous condition of servitude, by going in disguise and assaulting him on the public highway and on his own premises. . . .

. . . That a government whose essential character is republican, whose executive head and legislative body are both elective, whose most numerous and powerful branch of the legislature is elected by the people directly, has no power by appropriate laws to secure this election from the influence of violence, of corruption, and of fraud, is a proposition so startling as to arrest attention and demand the gravest consideration.

If this government is anything more than a mere aggregation of delegated agents of other states and governments, each of which is superior to the general government, it must have the power to protect the elections on which its existence depends from violence and corruption.

If it has not this power, it is left helpless before the two great natural and historical enemies of all republics, open violence and insidious corruption.

The proposition that it has no such power is supported by the old argument often heard, often repeated, and in this court never assented to, that when a question of the power of Congress arises the advocate of the power must be able to place his finger on words which expressly grant it. . . . Because there is no *express* power to provide for preventing violence exercised on the voter as a means of controlling his vote, no such law can be enacted. It destroys at one blow, in construing the Constitution of the United States, the doctrine universally applied to all instruments of writing, that what is implied is as much a part of the instrument as what is expressed. This principle, in its application to the Constitution of the United States, more than to almost any other writing, is a necessity, by reason of the inherent inability to put into words all derivative powers,—a difficulty which the instrument itself recognizes by conferring on Congress the authority to pass all laws necessary and proper to carry into execution the powers expressly granted, and all other powers vested in the government or any branch of it by the Constitution. Article 1, section 8, clause 18.

We know of no express authority to pass laws to punish theft or burglary of the treasury of the United States. Is there therefore no power in the Congress to protect the treasury by punishing such theft and burglary?

Are the mails of the United States, and the money carried in them, to be left at the mercy of robbers and of thieves who may handle the mail, because the Constitution contains no express words of power in Congress to enact laws for the punishment of those offences? The principle, if sound, would abolish the entire criminal jurisdiction of the courts of the United States, and the laws which confer that jurisdiction.

It is said that the states can pass the necessary law on this subject, and no necessity exists for such action by Congress. But the existence of state laws punishing the counterfeiting of the coin of the United States has never been held to supersede the acts of Congress passed for that purpose, or to justify the United States in failing to enforce its own laws to protect the circulation of the coin which it issues. . . .

So, also, has the Congress been slow to exercise the powers expressly conferred upon it in relation to elections by the fourth section of the first article of the Constitution. This section declares that: "The times, places, and manner of holding elections for Senators and Representatives shall be prescribed in each State by the legislature thereof; but the Congress may at any time make or alter such regulations, except as to the place of choosing Senators." . . .

Will it be denied that it is in the power of that body to provide laws for the proper conduct of those elections? To provide, if necessary, the officers who shall conduct them and make return of the result? And especially to provide, in an election held under its own authority, for security of life and limb to the voter while in the exercise of this function? Can it be doubted that Congress can, by law, protect the act of voting, the place where it is done, and the man who votes from personal violence or intimidation, and the election itself from corruption or fraud?

If this be so, and it is not doubted, are such powers annulled because an election for state officers is held at the same time and place? Is it any less important that the election of members of Congress should be the free choice of all the electors, because state officers are to be elected at the same time?

These questions answer themselves; and it is only because the Congress of the United States, through long habit and long years of forbearance, has, in deference and respect to the states, refrained from the exercise of these powers, that they are now doubted.

But when, in the pursuance of a new demand for action, that body, as it did in the cases just enumerated, finds it necessary to make additional laws for the free, the pure, and the safe exercise of this right of voting, they stand upon the same ground, and are to be upheld for the same reasons.

It is said that the parties assaulted in these cases are not officers of the United States, and their protection in exercising the right to vote by Congress does not stand on the same ground.

But the distinction is not well taken. The power in either case arises out of the circumstance that the function in which the party is engaged or the right which he is about to exercise is dependent on the laws of the United States.

In both cases it is the duty of that government to see that he may exercise this right freely, and to protect him from violence while so doing, or on account of so doing. This duty does not arise solely from the interest of the party concerned, but from the necessity of the government itself that its service shall be free from the adverse influence of force and fraud practiced on its agents, and that the votes by which its members of Congress and its President are elected shall be the *free* votes of the electors, and the officers thus chosen the free and uncorrupted choice of those who have the right to take part in that choice.

This proposition answers, also, another objection to the constitutionality of the laws under consideration, namely, that the right to vote for a member of Congress is not dependent upon the Constitution or laws of the United States, but is governed by the law of each state respectively.

If this were conceded, the importance to the general government of having the actual election—the voting for those members—free from force and fraud is not diminished by the circumstance that the qualification of the voter is determined by the law of the state where he votes. It equally affects the government; it is as indispensable to the proper discharge of the great function of legislating for that government, that those who are to control this legislation shall not owe their election to bribery or violence, whether the class of persons who shall vote is determined by the law of the state, or by the laws of the United States, or by their united result.

But it is not correct to say that the right to vote for a member of Congress does not depend on the Constitution of the United States.

The office, if it be properly called an office, is created by that Constitution, and by that alone. It also declares how it shall be filled, namely, by election. Its language is: "The House of Representatives shall be composed of members chosen every second year by the people of the several States; and the electors in each State shall have the same qualifications requisite for electors of the most numerous branch of the State legislature." Article 1, section 2.

The states, in prescribing the qualifications of voters for the most numerous branch of their own legislatures, do not do this with reference to the election for members of Congress. Nor can they prescribe the qualification for voters for those *eo nomine*. They define who are to vote for the popular branch of their own legislature, and the Constitution of the United States says the same persons shall vote for members of Congress in that state. It adopts the qualification thus furnished as the qualification of its own electors for members of Congress.

It is not true, therefore, that electors for members of Congress owe their right to vote to the state law, in any sense which makes the exercise of the right to depend exclusively on the law of the state.

Counsel for petitioners, seizing upon the expression found in the opinion of the court of the case of *Minor* v. *Happersett*, 21 Wallace 162, that "the Constitution of the United States does not confer the right of suffrage upon any one," without reference to the connection in which it is used, insists that the voters in this case do not owe their right to vote in any sense to that instrument.

But the court was combating the argument that this right was conferred on all citizens, and therefore upon women as well as men.

In opposition to that idea, it was said the Constitution adopts as the qualification for voters of members of Congress that which prevails in the state where the voting is to be done; therefore, said the opinion, the right is not definitely conferred on any person or class of persons by the Constitution alone, because you have to look to the law of the state for the description of the class. But the court did not intend to say that when the class or the person is thus ascertained, his right to vote for a member of Congress was not fundamentally based upon the Constitution, which created the office of member of Congress, and declared it should be elective, and pointed to the means of ascertaining who should be electors. . . .

It is as essential to the successful working of this government that the great organisms of its executive and legislative branches should be the free choice of the people, as that the original form of it should be so. In absolute governments, where the monarch is the source of all power, it is still held to be important that the exercise of that power shall be free from the influence of extraneous violence and internal corruption.

In a republican government, like ours, where political power is reposed in representatives of the entire body of the people, chosen at short intervals by popular elections, the temptations to control these elections by violence and by corruption is a constant source of danger.

Such has been the history of all republics, and, though ours has been comparatively free from both these evils in the past, no lover of his country can shut his eyes to the fear of future danger from both sources.

If the recurrence of such acts as these prisoners stand convicted of are too common in one quarter of the country, and give omen of danger from lawless violence, the free use of money in elections, arising from the vast growth of recent wealth in other quarters, presents equal cause for anxiety.

If the government of the United States has within its constitutional domain no authority to provide against these evils,—if the very sources of power may be poisoned by corruption or controlled by violence and outrage, without legal restraint,—then, indeed, is the country in danger, and its best powers, its highest purposes, the hopes which it inspires, and the love which enshrines it, are at the mercy of the combinations of those who respect no right but brute force on the one hand, and unprincipled corruptionists on the other.

The rule is discharged, and the writ of habeas corpus is denied.

294. MUNN v. ILLINOIS
94 U. S. 113
1877

Error to the supreme court of Illinois. This was the most important of the so-called "Granger cases," and involved the validity of an act of the legislature of Illinois providing for the fixing of maximum charges for the storage of grain in warehouses in Chicago. The law was attacked as in violation of the Fourteenth Amendment. The doctrine which the court laid down in this case is one of the most important principles in American constitutional interpretation, and has never been successfully challenged since that day. Yet note in this connection the remarks of Mr. Justice Brandeis in his dissenting opinion in the Oklahoma Ice Case, Doc. No. 472. For the historical background of the case see, S. J. Buck, *The Granger Movement;* A. E. Paine, *The Granger Movement in Illinois;* Warren, *Supreme Court,* Vol. II, ch. xxxiii.

WAITE, C. J. The question to be determined in this case is whether the general assembly of Illinois can, under the limitations upon the legislative powers of the States imposed by the Constitution of the United States, fix by law the maximum of charges for the storage of grain in warehouses at Chicago and other places in the State having not less than one hundred thousand inhabitants, "in which grain is stored in bulk, and in which the grain of different owners is mixed together, or in which grain is stored in such a manner that the identity of different lots or parcels cannot be accurately preserved."

It is claimed that such a law is repugnant—

1. To that part of sect. 8, art. I, of the Constitution of the United States which confers upon Congress the power "to regulate commerce with foreign nations and among the several States;"

2. To that part of sect. 9 of the same article, which provides that "no preference shall be given by any regulation of commerce or revenue to the ports of one State over those of another;" and

3. To that part of amendment 14 which ordains that no State shall "deprive any person of life, liberty, or property, without due process of law, nor deny to any person within its jurisdiction the equal protection of the laws."

We will consider the last of these objections first. . . .

The Constitution contains no definition of the word "deprive," as used in the Fourteenth Amendment. To determine its signification, therefore, it is necessary to ascertain the effect which usage has given it, when employed in the same or a like connection.

While this provision of the amendment is new in the Constitution of the United States, as a limitation upon the powers of the States, it is old as a principle of civilized government. It is found in Magna Charta, and, in substance if not in form, in nearly or quite all the constitutions that have been from time to time adopted by the several States of the Union. By the Fifth Amendment, it was introduced into the Constitution of the United States as a limitation upon the powers of the national government, and by the Fourteenth, as a guarantee against any encroachment upon an acknowledged right of citizenship by the legislatures of the States. . . .

When one becomes a member of society, he necessarily parts with some rights or privileges which, as an individual not affected by his relations to others, he might retain. "A body politic," as aptly defined in the preamble of the constitution of Massachusetts, "is a social compact by which the whole people covenants with each citizen, and each citizen with the whole people, that all shall be governed by certain laws for the common good." This does not confer power upon the whole people to control rights which are purely and exclusively private; but it does authorize the establishment of laws requiring each citizen to so conduct himself, and so use his own property, as not unnecessarily to injure another. This is the very essence of government, and has found expression in the maxim *sic utere tuo ut alienum non lædas*. From this source come the police powers, which, as was said by Mr. Chief Justice Taney in the License Cases, 5 How. 583, "are nothing more or less than the powers of government inherent in every sovereignty, . . . that is to say, . . . the power to govern men and things." Under these powers the government regulates the conduct of its citizens one towards another, and the manner in which each shall use his own property, when such regulation becomes necessary for the public good. In their exercise it has been customary in England from time immemorial, and in this country from its first colonization, to regulate ferries, common carriers, hackmen, bakers, millers, wharfingers, innkeepers, &c., and in so doing to fix a maximum of charge to be made for services rendered, accommodations furnished, and articles sold. To this day, statutes are to be found in many of the States upon some or all these subjects; and we think it has never yet been successfully contended that such legislation came within any of the constitutional prohibitions against interference with private property. With the Fifth Amendment in force Congress, in 1820, conferred power upon the city of Washington "to regulate . . . the rates of wharfage at private wharves, . . . the sweeping of chimneys, and to fix the rates of fees therefor, . . . and the weight and quality of bread," 3 Stat. 587, § 7; and, in 1848, "to make all necessary regulations respecting hackney carriages and the rates of fare of the same, and the rates of hauling by cartmen, wagoners, carmen, and draymen, and the rates of commission of auctioneers," 9 Id. 224, sect. 2.

From this it is apparent that, down to the time of the adoption of the Fourteenth Amendment, it was not supposed that statutes regulating the use, or even the price of the use, of private property necessarily deprived an owner of his property without due process of law. Under some circumstances they may, but not under all. The amendment does not change the law in this particular: it simply prevents the States from doing that which will operate as such a deprivation.

This brings us to inquire as to the principles upon which this power of regulation rests, in order that we may determine what is within and what without its operative effect. Looking, then, to the common law, from whence came the right which the Constitution protects, we find that when private property is "affected with a public interest, it ceases to be *juris privati* only." This was said by Lord Chief Justice Hale more than two hundred years ago, in his treatise *De Portibus Maris*, 1 Harg. Law Tracts, 78, and has been accepted without objection as an essential element in the law of property ever since. Property does become clothed with a public interest when used in a manner to make it of public consequence, and affect the community at large. When, therefore, one devotes his property to a use in which the public has an interest, he, in effect, grants to the public an interest in that use, and must submit to be controlled by the public for the common good, to the extent of the interest he has thus created. He may withdraw his grant by discontinuing the use; but, so long as he maintains the use, he must submit to the control. . . .

From the same source comes the power to regulate the charges of common carriers, which was done in England as long ago as the third year of the reign of William and Mary, and continued until within a comparatively recent period. And in the first statute we find the following suggestive preamble, to wit: "And whereas divers waggoners and other carriers, by combination amongst themselves, have raised the prices of carriage of goods in many places to excessive rates, to the great injury of the trade: Be it, therefore, enacted," etc. 3 W. & M. chap. 12, § 24; 3 Stat. at Large (Great Britain) 481.

Common carriers exercise a sort of public office, and have duties to perform in which the public is interested. . . . Their business is, therefore, "affected with a public interest," within the meaning of the doctrine which Lord Hale has so forcibly stated.

But we need not go further. Enough has already been said to show that, when private property is devoted to a public use, it is subject to public regulation. It remains only to ascertain whether the warehouses of these plaintiffs in error, and the business which is carried on there, come within the operation of this principle.

For this purpose we accept as true the statements of fact contained in the elaborate brief of one of the plaintiffs in error. . . .

In this connection it must also be borne in mind that, although in 1874 there were in Chicago fourteen warehouses adapted to this particular business, and owned by about thirty persons, nine business firms controlled them, and that the prices charged and received for storage were such "as have been from year to year agreed upon and established by the different elevators or warehouses in the city of Chicago, and which rates have been annually published in one or more newspapers printed in said city, in the month of January in each year, as the established rates for the year then next ensuing such publication." Thus it is apparent that all the elevating facilities through which these vast productions "of seven or eight great States of the West" must pass on the way "to four or five of the States on the sea-shore" may be a "virtual" monopoly.

Under such circumstances it is difficult to see why, if the common carrier, or the miller, or the ferryman, or the innkeeper, or the wharfinger, or the baker, or the cartman, or the hackney-coachman, pursues a public employment and exercises "a sort of public office," these plaintiffs in error do not. They stand, to use again the language of their counsel, in the very "gateway of commerce," and take toll from all who pass. Their business most certainly "tends to a common charge, and is become a thing of public interest and use." . . . Certainly, if any business can be clothed "with a public interest and cease to be *juris privati* only," this has been. It may not be made so by the operation of the constitution of Illinois or this statute, but it is by the facts. . . .

. . . For our purposes we must assume that if a state of facts could exist that would justify such legislation, it actually did exist when the statute now under consideration was passed. For us the question is one of power, not of expediency. If no state of circumstances could justify such a statute, then we may declare this one void, because in excess of the legislative power of the State. But if it could we must presume it did. Of the propriety of legislative interference within the scope of legislative power, the legislature is the exclusive judge.

Neither is it a matter of any moment that no precedent can be found for a statute precisely like this. It is conceded that the business is one of recent origin, that its growth has been rapid, and that it is already of great importance. And it must also be conceded that it is a business in which the whole public has a direct and positive interest. It presents, therefore, a case for the application of a long-known and well-established principle in social science, and this statute simply extends the law so as to meet this new development of commercial progress. There is no attempt to compel these owners to grant the public an interest in their property, but to decline their obligations, if they use it in this particular manner.

It matters not in this case that these plaintiffs in error had built their warehouses and established their business before the regulations complained of were adopted. What they did was from the beginning subject to the power of the body politic to require them to conform to such regulations as might be established by the proper authorities for the common good. They entered upon their business and provided themselves with the means to carry it on subject to this condition. If they did not wish to submit themselves to such interference, they should not have clothed the public with an interest in their concerns. The same principle applies to them that does to the proprietor of a hackney-carriage, and as to him it has never been supposed that he was exempt from regulating statutes or ordinances because he had purchased his horses and carriage and established his business before the statute or the ordinance was adopted.

It is insisted, however, that the owner of

property is entitled to a reasonable compensation for its use, even though it be clothed with a public interest, and that what is reasonable is a judicial and not a legislative question.

As has already been shown, the practice has been otherwise. In countries where the common law prevails, it has been customary from time immemorial for the legislature to declare what shall be a reasonable compensation under such circumstances, or perhaps more properly speaking, to fix a maximum beyond which any charge made would be unreasonable. Undoubtedly in mere private contracts, relating to matters in which the public has no interest, what is reasonable must be ascertained judicially. But this is because the legislature has no control over such a contract, So, too, in matters which do not affect the public interest, and as to which legislative control may be exercised . . . the courts must determine what is reasonable. The controlling fact is the power to regulate at all. If that exists, the right to establish the maximum charge, as one of the means of regulation, is implied. . . .

We know that this is a power which may be abused; but that is no argument against its existence. For protection against abuses by legislatures the people must resort to the polls, not to the courts. . . .

We come now to consider the effect upon this statute of the power of Congress to regulate commerce.

. . . The warehouses of these plaintiffs in error are situated and their business carried on exclusively within the limits of the State of Illinois. They are used as instruments by those engaged in State as well as those engaged in inter-state commerce. . . . Incidentally they may become connected with inter-State commerce, but not necessarily so. Their regulation is a thing of domestic concern and, certainly, until Congress acts in reference to their inter-State relations, the State may exercise all the powers of government over them, even though in so doing it may indirectly operate upon commerce outside its immediate jurisdiction. . . .

Judgement affirmed.

FIELD, J. delivered a dissenting opinion.

295. COMMONWEALTH v. HAMILTON MANUFACTURING COMPANY
120 Mass. Reports, 383
1876

Massachusetts was the pioneer state in labor legislation designed to protect women and children from undue exploitation. This case involved the constitutionality of a statute limiting the hours of labor of minors and women in manufacturing establishments to sixty a week. Compare this decision to that of *People v. Williams*, Doc. No. 365. See, R. Fuller, *Child Labor and the Constitution;* G. G. Groat, *Attitude of American Courts in Labor Cases;* M. C. Cahill, *Shorter Hours: A History of the Movement Since the Civil War.*

LORD, J. The defendant contends that the St. of 1874, c. 221, under which the complaint in this case is made, is unconstitutional and void. The provision, which it is alleged is without authority under the Constitution, is, that "no minor under the age of eighteen years, and no woman over that age, shall be employed in laboring by any person, firm or corporation in any manufacturing establishment in this Commonwealth more than ten hours in any one day," except in cer-

tain cases, and that "in no case shall the hours of labor exceed sixty per week."

The learned counsel for the defendant in his argument did not refer to any particular clause of the Constitution to which this provision is repugnant. His general proposition was, that the defendant's act of incorporation, St. 1824, c. 44, is a contract with the Commonwealth, and that this act impairs that contract. The contract, it is claimed, is an implied one; that is, an act of incorporation to manufacture cotton and woolen goods by necessary implication confers upon the corporation the legal capacity to contract for all the labor needful for this work. If this is conceded to the fullest extent, it is only a contract with the corporation that it may contract for all lawful labor. There is no contract implied that such labor as was then forbidden by law might be employed by the defendant; or that the General Court would not perform its constitutional duty of making such wholesome laws thereafter as the public welfare should demand. The law, therefore, violates no contract with the defendant; and the only other question is, whether it is in violation of any right reserved under the Constitution to the individual citizen. Upon this question, there seems to be no room for debate. It does not forbid any person, firm or corporation from employing as many persons or as much labor as such person, firm or corporation may desire; nor does it forbid any person to work as many hours a day or a week as he chooses. It merely provides that in an employment, which the Legislature has evidently deemed to some extent dangerous to health, no person shall be engaged in labor more than ten hours a day or sixty hours a week. There can be no doubt that such legislation may be maintained either as a health or police regulation, if it were necessary to resort to either of those sources for power. This principle has been so frequently recognized in this Common-wealth that reference to the decisions is unnecessary.

It is also said that the law violates the right of Mary Shirley to labor in accordance with her own judgment as to the number of hours she shall work. The obvious and conclusive reply to this is, that the law does not limit her right to labor as many hours per day or per week as she may desire; it does not in terms forbid her laboring in any particular business or occupation as many hours per day or per week, as she may desire; it merely prohibits her being employed continuously in the same service more than a certain number of hours per day or week, which is so clearly within the power of the Legislature, that it becomes unnecessary to inquire whether it is a matter of grievance of which this defendant has the right to complain.

Judgment affirmed.

296. PRESIDENT GRANT'S APOLOGY

Extract from Eighth Annual Message to Congress
December 5, 1876

(Richardson, ed. *Messages and Papers*, Vol. VII, p. 399–400)

EXECUTIVE MANSION, *December 5, 1876.*
To the Senate and House of Representatives:

In submitting my eighth and last annual message to Congress it seems proper that I should refer to and in some degree recapitulate the events and official acts of the past eight years.

It was my fortune, or misfortune, to be called to the office of Chief Executive without any previous political training. From the age of 17 I had never even witnessed the excitement attending a Presidential campaign but twice antecedent to my own candidacy, and at but one of them was I eligible as a voter.

Under such circumstances it is but reasonable to suppose that errors of judgment must have occurred. Even had they not, differences of opinion between the Executive, bound by an oath to the strict performance of his duties, and writers and debaters must have arisen. It is not necessarily evidence of blunder on the part of the Executive because there are these differences of views. Mistakes have been made, as all can see and I admit, but it seems to me oftener in the selections made of the assistants appointed to aid in carrying out the various duties of administering the Government—in nearly every case selected without a personal acquaintance with the appointee, but upon recommendations of the representatives chosen directly by the people. It is impossible, where so many trusts are to be allotted, that the right parties should be chosen in every instance. History shows that no Administration from the time of Washington to the present has been free from these mistakes. But I leave comparisons to history, claiming only that I have acted in every instance from a conscientious desire to do what was right, constitutional, within the law, and for the very best interests of the whole people. Failures have been errors of judgment, not of intent. . . .

297. THE RESTORATION OF WHITE RULE IN SOUTH CAROLINA
Letter of Governor Chamberlain to William Lloyd Garrison
June 11, 1877

(W. Allen, *Governor Chamberlain's Administration in
South Carolina,* appendix III, p. 504)

In the famous 'Red Shirt' campaign of 1876, Wade Hampton was apparently successful over the carpet-bag Governor, Chamberlain. With the withdrawal of Federal support, the Chamberlain government came to a prompt end. On Chamberlain's administration see the volume by Walter Allen, above, and Chamberlain's article "Reconstruction in South Carolina," *Atlantic Monthly,* April, 1901. See also, H. T. Thompson, *Ousting the Carpetbagger from South Carolina;* E. Wells, *Hampton and Reconstruction;* C. G. Bowers, *The Tragic Era,* chs. xxiv–xxv; F. B. Simkins and R. H. Woody, *South Carolina During Reconstruction,* chs. xviii–xix.

New York, June 11, 1877

Dear Mr. Garrison. . . . Your prophecy is fulfilled, and I am not only overthrown, but as a consequence I am now a citizen of New York. It seems to me a remarkable experience indeed, though I hope I do not egotistically exaggerate it, for I am sure it will soon be forgotten by most men in the press and hurry of new events. Why I write this line now and send it to Boston when I know you are in Europe, is because I feel like putting on record my main reflections on my experiences of the last three years. . . .

First, then, my defeat was inevitable under the circumstances of time and place which surrounded me. I mean here exactly that the uneducated negro was too weak, no matter what his numbers, to cope with the whites.

We had lost too, the sympathy of the North, in some large measure, though we never deserved it so certainly as in 1876 in South Carolina.

The Presidential contest also endangered us and doubtless defeated us. The hope of electing Tilden incited our opponents, and the greed of office led the defeated Republicans under Hayes to sell us out. There was just as distinct a bargain to do this at Washington as ever existed which was not signed and sealed on paper. And the South is not to be blamed for it, if anybody is; but rather those leaders, like Evarts, who could never see their Constitutional obligations towards the South until the offices were slipping away from their party.

So the end came, but not as you expected. . . .

Daniel H. Chamberlain.

298. PREAMBLE OF CONSTITUTION OF THE KNIGHTS OF LABOR
January 1, 1878

(T. V. Powderly, *Thirty Years of Labor,* p. 243 ff.)

The Noble Order of the Knights of Labor developed out of a society of garment cutters organized in Philadelphia in 1869. The first General Assembly met in 1878 and drew up a constitution. Under Uriah Stephens and, later, Terence Powderly, the organization grew in power and strength until by 1886 it numbered some three-quarters of a million members. The Knights of Labor advocated the principle of industrial democracy, and its membership included men and women, white and negro, skilled and unskilled laborers. Membership declined rapidly after 1886. The best general discussion of the Knights is in N. J. Ware, *The Labor Movement in the United States, 1860–1895.*

The recent alarming development and

aggression of aggregated wealth, which, unless checked, will invariably lead to the pauperization and hopeless degradation of the toiling masses, render it imperative, if we desire to enjoy the blessings of life, that a check should be placed upon its power and upon unjust accumulation, and a system adopted which will secure to the laborer the fruits of his toil; and as this much-desired object can only be accomplished by the thorough unification of labor, and the united efforts of those who obey the divine injunction that "In the sweat of thy brow shalt thou eat bread," we have formed the
* * * * * with a view of securing the organ-

ization and direction, by co-operative effort, of the power of the industrial classes; and we submit to the world the object sought to be accomplished by our organization, calling upon all who believe in securing "the greatest good to the greatest number" to aid and assist us:—

I. To bring within the folds of organization every department of productive industry, making knowledge a standpoint for action, and industrial and moral worth, not wealth, the true standard of individual and national greatness.

II. To secure to the toilers a proper share of the wealth that they create; more of the leisure that rightfully belongs to them; more societary advantages; more of the benefits, privileges, and emoluments of the world; in a word, all those rights and privileges necessary to make them capable of enjoying, appreciating, defending, and perpetuating the blessings of good government.

III. To arrive at the true condition of the producing masses in their educational, moral, and financial condition, by demanding from the various governments the establishment of bureaus of Labor Statistics.

IV. The establishment of co-operative institutions, productive and distributive.

V. The reserving of the public lands—the heritage of the people—for the actual settler; —not another acre for railroads or speculators.

VI. The abrogation of all laws that do not bear equally upon capital and labor, the removal of unjust technicalities, delays, and discriminations in the administration of justice, and the adopting of measures providing for the health and safety of those engaged in mining, manufacturing, or building pursuits.

VII. The enactment of laws to compel chartered corporations to pay their employes weekly, in full, for labor performed during the preceding week, in the lawful money of the country.

VIII. The enactment of laws giving mechanics and laborers a first lien on their work for their full wages.

IX. The abolishment of the contract system on national, State, and municipal work.

X. The substitution of arbitration for strikes, whenever and wherever employers and employes are willing to meet on equitable grounds.

XI. The prohibition of the employment of children in workshops, mines, and factories before attaining their fourteenth year.

XII. To abolish the system of letting out by contract the labor of convicts in our prisons and reformatory institutions.

XIII. To secure for both sexes equal pay for equal work.

XIV. The reduction of the hours of labor to eight per day, so that the laborers may have more time for social enjoyment and intellectual improvement, and be enabled to reap the advantages conferred by the labor-saving machinery which their brains have created.

XV. To prevail upon governments to establish a purely national circulating medium, based upon the faith and resources of the nation, and issued directly to the people, without the intervention of any system of banking corporations, which money shall be a legal tender in payment of all debts, public or private.

299. THE BLAND ALLISON ACT
February 28, 1878

(*U. S. Statutes at Large,* Vol. XX, p. 25 ff.)

The demonetization of silver in 1873 inaugurated a quarter century of agitation for the free and unlimited coinage of silver. The Bland-Allison act represented a compromise between the silver west and the gold-standard East, unsatisfactory alike to both groups. The act was vetoed by President Hayes, but passed over his veto. For Hayes's veto message see Doc. No. 300. On the Bland-Allison Act see, D. R. Dewey, *Financial History of the United States,* ch. xvii; J. L. Laughlin, *History of Bimetallism,* p. 209 ff.; W. V. Byars, *An American Commoner, R. P. Bland,* ch. xii; A. B. Hepburn, *History of Currency,* ch. xv.

An act to authorize the coinage of the standard silver dollar, and to restore its legal-tender character.

Be it enacted . . . , That there shall be coined, at the several mints of the United States, silver dollars of the weight of four hundred and twelve and a half grains Troy of standard silver, as provided in the act of January 18, 1837, . . . which coins together with all silver dollars heretofore coined by the United States, of like weight and fineness, shall be a legal tender, at their nominal value, for all debts and dues public and private, except where otherwise expressly stipulated in the contract. And the Secretary of the Treasury is authorized and directed to purchase, from time to time, silver bullion, at the market price thereof, not less than two million dollars worth per month, and cause the same to be coined monthly, as fast as so purchased, into such dollars. . . . And any gain or seigniorage arising from this coinage shall be accounted for and paid into the Treasury, as provided under existing laws relative to the subsidiary coinage: *Provided,* That the amount of money at any one time invested in such silver bullion, exclusive of such resulting coin shall not exceed five million dollars. *And provided further,* That nothing in this act shall be construed to authorize the payment in silver of certificates of deposit issued under the provisions of section 254 of the Revised Statutes.

Sec. 2. That immediately after the passage of this act, the President shall invite the governments of the countries composing the Latin Union, so-called, and of such other European nations as he may deem advisable, to join the United States in a conference to adopt a common ratio between gold and silver, for the purpose of establishing, internationally, the use of bi-metallic money, and securing fixity of relative value between those metals; such conference to be held at such place, in Europe or in the United States, at such time within six months, as may be mutually agreed upon by the executives of the governments joining in the same, whenever the governments so invited, or any three of them, shall have signified their willingness to unite in the same.

The President shall, by and with the advice and consent of the Senate, appoint three commissioners, who shall attend such conference on behalf of the United States, and shall report the doings thereof to the President, who shall transmit the same to Congress. . . .

Sec. 3. That any holder of the coin authorized by this act may deposit the same with the Treasurer or any assistant treasurer of the United States, in sums not less than ten dollars, and receive therefor certificates of not less than ten dollars each, corresponding with the denominations of the United States notes. The coin deposited for or representing the certificates shall be retained in the Treasury for the payment of the same on demand. Said certificates shall be receivable for customs, taxes, and all public dues, and, when so received, may be reissued.

300. PRESIDENT HAYES'S VETO OF BLAND–ALLISON ACT
Feb. 28, 1878.

(Richardson, ed. *Messages and Papers,* Vol. VII, p. 486 ff.)

EXECUTIVE MANSION, *February 28, 1878.*
To the House of Representatives:

After a very careful consideration of the House bill No. 1093, entitled "An act to authorize the coinage of the standard silver dollar and to restore its legal-tender character," I feel compelled to return it to the House of Representatives, in which it originated, with my objections to its passage.

Holding the opinion, which I expressed in my annual message, that "neither the interests of the Government nor of the people of the United States would be promoted by disparaging silver as one of the two precious metals which furnish the coinage of the world, and that legislation which looks to maintaining the volume of intrinsic money to as full a measure of both metals as their relative commercial values will permit would be neither unjust nor inexpedient," it has been my earnest desire to concur with Congress in the adoption of such measures to increase the silver coinage of the country as would not impair the obligation of contracts, either public or private, nor injuriously affect the public credit. It is only upon the conviction that this bill does not meet these essential requirements that I feel it my duty to withhold from it my approval. . . .

The bill provides for the coinage of silver dollars of the weight of 412½ grains each, of standard silver, to be a legal tender at their nominal value for all debts and dues, public and private, except where otherwise expressly stipulated in the contract. It is well known that the market value of that number of grains of standard silver during the past year has been from 90 to 92 cents as compared with the standard gold dollar. Thus the silver dollar authorized by this bill is worth 8 to 10 per cent less than it purports to be worth, and is made a legal tender for debts contracted when the law did not recognize such coins as lawful money.

The right to pay duties in silver or in certificates for silver deposits will, when they are issued in sufficient amount to circulate, put an end to the receipt of revenue in gold, and thus compel the payment of silver for both the principal and interest of the public debt. $1,143,493,400 of the bonded debt now outstanding was issued prior to February, 1873, when the silver dollar was unknown in circulation in this country, and was only a convenient form of silver bullion for exportation; $583,440,350 of the funded debt has been issued since February, 1873, when gold alone was the coin for which the bonds were sold, and gold alone was the coin in which both parties to the contract understood that the bonds would be paid. These bonds entered into the markets of the world. They were paid for in gold when silver had greatly depreciated, and when no one would have bought them if it had been understood that they would be paid in silver. The sum of $225,000,000 of these bonds has been sold during my Administration for gold coin, and the United States received the benefit of these sales by a reduction of the rate of interest to 4 per cent. During the progress of these sales a doubt was suggested as to the coin in which payment of these bonds would be made. The public announcement was thereupon authorized that it was "not to be anticipated that any future legislation of Congress or any action of any department of the Government would sanction or tolerate the redemption of the principal of these bonds or the payment of the interest thereon in coin of less value than the coin authorized by law at the time of the issue of the bonds, being the coin exacted by the Government in exchange for the same." In view of these facts it will be justly regarded as a grave breach of the public faith to undertake to pay these bonds, principal or interest, in silver coin worth in the market less than the coin received for them.

It is said that the silver dollar made a legal tender by this bill will under its operation be equivalent in value to the gold dollar. Many supporters of the bill believe this, and would not justify an attempt to pay debts, either public or private, in coin of inferior value to the money of the world. The capital defect of the bill is that it contains no provision protecting from its operation preëxisting debts in case the coinage which it creates shall continue to be of less value than that which was the sole legal tender when they were contracted. If it is now proposed, for the purpose of taking advantage of the depreciation of silver in the payment of debts, to coin and make a legal tender a silver dollar of less commercial value than any dollar, whether of gold or paper, which is now lawful money in this country, such measure, it will hardly be questioned, will, in the judgment of mankind, be an act of bad faith. As to all debts heretofore contracted, the silver dollar should be made a legal tender only at its market value. The standard of value should not be changed without the consent of both parties to the contract. National promises should be kept with unflinching fidelity. There is no power to compel a nation to pay its just debts. Its credit depends on its honor. The nation owes what it has led or allowed its creditors to expect. I can not approve a bill which in my judgment authorizes the violation of sacred obligations. The obligation of the public faith transcends all questions of profit or public advantage. Its unquestionable maintenance is the dictate as well of the highest expediency as of the most necessary duty, and should ever be carefully guarded by the Executive, by Congress, and by the people.

It is my firm conviction that if the country is to be benefited by a silver coinage it can be done only by the issue of silver dollars of full value, which will defraud no man. A currency worth less than it purports to be worth will in the end defraud not only creditors, but all who are engaged in legitimate business, and none more surely than those who are dependent on their daily labor for their daily bread.

R. B. HAYES.

301. ENCYCLICAL LETTER, QUOD APOSTOLICI MUNERIS
December 28, 1878

(The Great Encyclical Letters of Pope Leo XIII (Benziger Brothers), p. 22 ff.)

This Encyclical Letter is recited as an illustration of the attitude of the Catholic Church towards socialism. See, W. E. Garrison, *The March of Faith;* W. E. Garrison, *Catholicism and the American Mind.*

. . . You understand as a matter of course, Venerable Brothers, that We are alluding to that sect of men who, under the motley and all but barbarous terms and titles of Socialists, Communists, and Nihilists, are spread abroad throughout the world and, bound intimately together in baneful alliance, no longer look for strong support in secret meetings held in darksome places, but standing forth openly and boldly in the light of day, strive to carry out the purpose long resolved upon, of uprooting the foundations of civilized society at large.

These are they in very truth who, as the sacred text bears witness, *defile the flesh, and despise dominion, and blaspheme majesty.* (Jude 8) They leave nothing scathless or uninjured of that which human and divine laws alike have wisely ordained to ensure the preservation and honor of life. From the heads of States to whom, as the Apostle admonishes, all owe submission, and on whom the rights of authority are bestowed by God Himself, these sectaries withhold obedience and preach up the perfect equality of all men in regard to rights alike and duties. . . . In short, spurred on by greedy hankering after things present, which is the *root of all evils, which some coveting have erred from the faith* (1 Tim. vi. 10) they attack the right of property, sanctioned by the law of nature, and with signal depravity, while pretending to feel solicitous about the needs, and anxious to satisfy the requirements of all, they strain every effort to seize upon and hold in common all that has been individually acquired by title of lawful inheritance, through intellectual or manual labor, or economy in living. These monstrous views they proclaim in public meetings, uphold in booklets, and spread broadcast everywhere through the daily press. Hence the hallowed dignity and authority of rulers has incurred such odium on the part of rebellious subjects

that evil-minded traitors, spurning all control, have many a time within a recent period boldly raised impious hands against even the very heads of States. . . .

For although the Socialists, turning to evil use the Gospel itself so as to deceive more readily the unwary, have been wont to twist it to their meaning, still so striking is the disagreement between their criminal teachings and the pure doctrine of Christ, that no greater can exist: *For what participation hath justice with injustice, or what fellowship hath light with darkness.* (2. Cor. vi. 14) They in good sooth cease not from asserting—as we have already mentioned—that all men are by nature equal, and hence they contend that neither honor nor respect is owed to public authority, nor any obedience to the laws, saving perhaps to those which have been sanctioned according to their good pleasure. Contrariwise, from the Gospel records, equality among men consists in this, that one and all, possessing the same nature, are called to the sublime dignity of being sons of God; and, moreover, that one and the same end being set before all, each and every one has to be judged according to the same laws and to have punishments or rewards meted out according to individual deserts. There is, however, an inequality of right and authority, which emanates from the Author of nature Himself, *of whom all paternity in heaven and earth is named.* (Eph. iii. 15) As regards rulers and subjects, all without exception, according to Catholic teaching and precept, are mutually bound by duties and rights, in such manner that, on the one hand, moderation is enjoined on the appetite for power, and, on the other, obedience is shown to be easy, stable, and wholly honorable. . . .

But to the end that the rulers of the people shall employ the power bestowed for the advancement, and not detriment, of those under rule, the Church of Christ very fittingly warns the rulers themselves that the Sovereign Judge will call them to a strict and speedy account, and evoking the words of divine wisdom, she addresses them one and all in God's name. *Give ear, you that rule the people, and that please yourselves in multitudes of nations; for power is given you by the Lord, and strength by the Most High, who will examine your works, and search out your thoughts; . . . for a most severe judgement shall be for them that bear rule. . . . For God will not accept any man's person, neither will He stand in awe of any one's greatness; for He hath made the little and the great, and He hath equally care of all. But a greater punishment is ready for the more mighty.* (Wisd. vi. 3 seqq.) Should it, however, happen, at any time, that in the public exercise of authority rulers act rashly and arbitrarily, the teaching of the Catholic Church does not allow subjects to rise against them, without further warranty, lest peace and order become more and more disturbed, and society run the risk of greater detriment. And when things have come to such a pass as to hold out no further hope, she teaches that a remedy is to be sought in the virtue of Christian patience and in urgent prayer to God. But should it please legislators and rulers to enjoin or sanction anything repugnant to the divine and natural law, the dignity and duty of the name of Christian and the Apostolic injunction proclaim that *one ought to obey God rather than man.* (Acts. v. 29). . . .

As regards the maintenance of public and private tranquillity Catholic wisdom, sustained by both divine and natural law, prudently provides through what it holds and teaches touching the right of ownership and the apportioning of personal property which has been accumulated for the wants and requirements of life. For the Socialists wrongly assume the right of property to be of mere human invention, repugnant to the natural equality between men, and, preaching up the community of goods, declare that no one should endure poverty meekly, and that all may with impunity seize upon the possessions and usurp the rights of the wealthy. More wisely and profitably the Church recognizes the existence of inequality amongst men, who are by nature unlike in mental endowment and strength of body, and even in amount

of fortune; and she enjoins that the right of property and of its disposal, derived from nature, should in the case of every individual remain intact and inviolate. She knows full well indeed that robbery and rapine have been so forbidden by God, the Author and Protector of every right, that it is unlawful even to covet the goods of others, and that thieves and robbers no less than adulterers and idolaters are excluded from the kingdom of heaven. Nor does she, on this account, loving mother as she is, omit solicitude for the poor or fail to provide for their needs; nay, taking them to her arms with maternal affection, and knowing that they in a manner represent the person of Christ Himself, who accounts as done unto Him any benefit conferred upon the lowliest among the poor, she holds them in great account, brings them aid to the utmost of her power, takes thought to have erected in every land in their behoof homes and refuges where they can be received, nurtured, and tended; and takes these charitable foundations under her protecting care. Moreover, she lays the rich under strict command to give of their superfluity to the poor, impressing them with fear of the divine judgement which will exact the penalty of eternal punishment unless they succor the wants of the needy. In fine, she cheers and comforts exceedingly the hearts of the poor, either by setting before them the example of Christ, who, *being rich became poor for our sakes,* (2 Cor. viii. 9) or by reminding them of the words by which Jesus pronounced the poor to be *blessed,* and enjoined them to hope for the reward of eternal bliss. Who then does not perceive that herein lies the best means of appeasing the undying conflict between the rich and the poor? For, as the evidence of things and facts clearly demonstrates, if such conclusion be disallowed or made light of, it must come about either that the vast majority of mankind will fall back into that most abject condition of bondage which through a long lapse of time obtained among pagan nations, or else that human society will be agitated by constant outbreaks and ravaged by plunder and rapine. . . .

302. POWELL'S REPORT ON THE ARID REGION OF THE WEST
1878

Major Powell was director of the U.S. Geological Survey. His report on the arid regions of the west, with recommendations for changes in the land system, though it had no immediate legislative results, was of epoch-making significance. He pointed out that the land system which had obtained from the beginning of our history and for the region east of the 100th meridian, was unsuitable to the arid lands of the west, where access to water was the basic consideration. See also, J. W. Powell, "Institutions for the Arid Lands," *Century Magazine*, May, 1890. For an appreciation of the work of Major Powell, and an elaboration of the thesis which he presented, see W. P. Webb, *The Great Plains*, esp. p. 353 ff.

. . . If the whole of the Arid Region was yet unsettled, it might be wise for the Government to undertake the parceling of the lands and employ skilled engineers to do the work, whose duties could be performed in advance of settlement. . . . Many of the lands surveyed along the minor streams have been entered, and the titles to these lands are in the hands of actual settlers. Many pasturage farms, or ranches, as they are called locally, have been established throughout the country. These remarks are true of every state and territory in the Arid Region. In the main these ranches or pasturage farms are on Government land, and the settlers are squatters, and some are not expecting to make permanent homes. . . . It is now too late for the Government to parcel the pasturage lands in advance of the wants of settlers in the most available way, so as to closely group residences and give water privileges to the several farms. Many of the farmers are actually on the ground, and are clamoring for some means by which they can obtain titles to pasturage farms of an extent adequate to their wants, and the tens of thousands of individual interests would make the problem a difficult one for the officers of the Government to solve. A system less arbitrary than that of the rectangular surveys now in vogue, and requiring unbiased judgement, overlooking the interests of single individuals and considering only the interests of the greatest number, would meet with local opposition. . . .

Under these circumstances it is believed that it is best to permit the people to divide their lands for themselves—not in a way by which each man may take what he pleases for himself, but by providing methods by which these settlers may organize and mutually protect each other from the rapacity of individuals. The lands, as lands, are of but slight value, as they cannot be used for ordinary agricultural purposes, i. e., the cultivation of crops; but their value consists in the scant grasses which they spontaneously produce, and these values can be made available only by the use of the waters necessary for the subsistence of stock, and that necessary for the small amount of irrigable land which should be attached to the several pasturage farms. Thus, practically, all values inhere in the water, and an equitable division of the waters can be made only by a wise system of parcelling the lands; and the people in organized bodies can well be trusted with this right, while individuals could not thus be trusted. These considerations have led to the plan suggested in the bill submitted for the organization of pasturage districts.

In like manner, in the bill designed for the purpose of suggesting a plan for the organization of irrigation districts, the same principle is involved, *viz,* that of permitting the settlers themselves to subdivide the lands into such tracts as they may desire.

The lands along the streams are not valuable for agricultural purposes in continuous bodies or squares, but only in irrigable tracts governed by the levels of the meandering canals which carry the water for irrigation, and it would be greatly to the advantage of every such district if the lands could be divided into parcels, governed solely by the conditions under which the water could be distributed over them; and such parcelling cannot be done prior to the occupancy of the lands, but can only be made *pari passu* with the adoption of a system of canals; and the people settling on these lands should be allowed the privilege of dividing the lands into such tracts as may be most available for such purposes, and they should not be hampered with the present arbitrary system of dividing tracts into rectangular tracts. . . .

The title to no tract of land should be conveyed from the Government to the individual until the proper survey of the same is made and the plat prepared for record. With this precaution, which the Government already invariably takes in disposing of its lands, no fear of uncertainty of identification need be entertained. . . .

. . . The general subject of water rights is one of great importance. In many places in the Arid Region irrigation companies are organized who obtain vested rights in the waters they control, and consequently the rights to such waters do not inhere in any particular tracts of land.

When the area to which it is possible to take the water of any given stream is much greater than the stream is competent to serve, if the land titles and water rights are severed, the owner of any tract of land is at the mercy of the owner of the water right. In general the lands greatly exceed the capacities of the streams. Thus the lands have no value without water. If the water rights fall into the hands of irrigating companies and the lands into the hands of individual farmers, the farmers then will be dependent upon the stock companies, and eventually the monopoly of water rights will be an intolerable burden to the people.

The magnitude of the interests involved must not be overlooked. All the present and future agriculture of more than four-tenths of the area of the United States is dependent upon irrigation, and practically all values for agricultural industries inhere, not in the lands, but in the water. Monopoly of land need not be feared. The question for legislators to solve is to devise some practical means by which water rights may be distributed among individual farmers and water monopolies prevented. . . .

The pioneer is fully engaged in the present with its hopes of immediate remuneration for labor. The present development of the country fully occupies him. For this reason every effort put forth to increase the area of the agricultural land by irrigation is welcomed.

Every man who turns his attention to this department of industry is considered a public benefactor. But if in the eagerness for present development a land and water system shall grow up in which the practical control of agriculture shall fall into the hands of water companies, evils will result therefrom that generations may not be able to correct, and the very men who are now lauded as benefactors to the country will, in the ungovernable reaction which is sure to come, be denounced as oppressors of the people.

The right to use water should inhere in the land to be irrigated, and water rights should go with land titles.

Those unacquainted with the industrial institutions of the far west, involving the use of lands and waters, may without careful thought suppose that the long recognized principles of the common law are sufficient to prevent the severance of land and water rights; but other practices are obtaining which have, or eventually will have, all the force of common law because the necessities of the country require the change, and these practices are obtaining the color of right from state and territorial legislation, and to some extent by national legislation. In all that country the natural channels of the streams cannot be made to govern water rights without great injury to its agricultural and mining industries. For the great purposes of irrigation and hydraulic mining the water has no value in its natural channel. In general the water cannot be used for irrigation on the lands immediately contiguous to the streams—i. e., the flood plains or bottom valleys. . . . The waters must be taken to a greater or less extent on the bench lands to be used in irrigation. All the waters of all the arid lands will eventually be taken from their natural channels, and they can be utilized only to the extent to which they are thus removed, and water rights must of necessity be severed from the natural channels. There is another important factor to be considered. The water when used in irrigation is absorbed by the soil and reëvaporated to the heavens. It cannot be taken from its natural channel, used, and returned. Again, the water cannot in general be properly utilized in irrigation by requiring it to be taken from its natural channel within the limits ordinarily included in a single ownership. In order to conduct the water on the higher bench lands where it is to be used in irrigation, it is necessary to go up the stream until a level is reached from which the waters will flow to the lands to be redeemed. The exceptions to this are so small that the statement scarcely needs qualification. Thus, to use the water it must be diverted from its natural course often miles or scores of miles from where it is to be used.

The ancient principles of common law applying to the use of natural streams, so wise and equitable in a humid region, would, if applied to the Arid Region, practically prohibit the growth of its most important industries. Thus it is that a custom is springing up in the Arid Region which may or may not have color of authority in statutory or common law; on this I do not wish to express an opinion; but certain it is that water rights are practically being severed from the natural channels of the streams; and this must be done. In the change, it is to be feared that water rights will in many cases be separated from all land rights as the system is now forming. If this fear is not groundless, to the extent that such a separation is secured, water will become a property independent of the land, and this property will be gradually absorbed by a few. Monopolies of water will be secured, and the whole agriculture of the country will be tributary thereto—a condition of affairs which an American citizen having in view the interests of the largest number of the people cannot contemplate with favor.

Practically, in that country the right to water is acquired by priority of utilization, and this is as it should be from the necessities of the country. But two important qualifications are needed. The *user right* should attach to the *land* where used, not to the individual or company constructing the canals by which it is used; the priority of usage should secure the right. But this needs some slight modification. A farmer settling on a small tract, to be redeemed by irrigation, should be given a reasonable length of time in which to secure his water right by utilization, that he may secure it by his own labor, either directly by constructing the waterways himself, or indirectly by coöperating with his neighbours in constructing systems of waterways. Without this provision there is little inducement for poor men to commence farming operations, and men of ready capital only will engage in such enterprises. . . .

If there be any doubt of the ultimate legality of the practices of the people in the arid country relating to water and land rights, all such doubts should be speedily quieted through the enactment of appropriate laws by the national legislature. Perhaps an amplification by the courts of what has been designated as the *natural right* to the use of water may be made to cover the practices now obtaining; but it hardly seems wise to imperil interests so great by intrusting them to the possibility of some future court made law.

303. THE PROBLEM OF "RIDERS"
President Hayes's veto of the Army Appropriation Act for 1880
April 29, 1879
(Richardson, ed. *Messages and Papers*, Vol. VII, p. 523 ff.)

The Democratic House of Representatives attached to the Army Appropriation Act for the year ending June 30, 1880 a "rider" practically repealing the acts of 1865 and 1874 which authorized the use of Federal troops in elections. The problem of the "rider" was squarely met in Hayes's veto message.

To the House of Representatives:

I have maturely considered the important questions presented by the bill entitled "An act making appropriations for the support of

the Army for the fiscal year ending June 30, 1880, and for other purposes," and I now return it to the House of Representatives, in which it originated, with my objections to its approval.

The bill provides in the usual form for the appropriations required for the support of the Army during the next fiscal year. If it contained no other provisions, it would receive my prompt approval. It includes, however, further legislation, which, attached, as it is, to appropriations which are requisite for the efficient performance of some of the most necessary duties of the Government, involves questions of the gravest character. The sixth section of the bill is amendatory of the statute now in force in regard to the authority of persons in the civil, military, and naval service of the United States "at the place where any general or special election is held in any State." . . .

The effect of the adoption of this amendment may be considered—

First. Upon the right of the United States Government to use military force to keep the peace at the elections for Members of Congress; and

Second. Upon the right of the Government, by civil authority, to protect these elections from violence and fraud. . . .

This section is, however, not presented to me as a separate and independent measure, but is, as has been stated, attached to the bill making the usual annual appropriations for the support of the Army. It makes a vital change in the election laws of the country, which is in no way connected with the use of the Army. It prohibits, under heavy penalties, any person engaged in the civil service of the United States from having any force at the place of any election, prepared to preserve order, to make arrests, to keep the peace, or in any manner to enforce the laws. This is altogether foreign to the purpose of an Army appropriation bill. The practice of tacking to appropriation bills measures not pertinent to such bills did not prevail until more than forty years after the adoption of the Constitution. It has become a common practice. All parties when in power have adopted it. Many abuses and great waste of public money have in this way crept into appropriation bills. The public opinion of the country is against it. The States which have recently adopted constitutions have generally provided a remedy for the evil by enacting that no law shall contain more than one subject, which shall be plainly expressed in its title. The constitutions of more than half of the States contain substantially this provision. The public welfare will be promoted in many ways by a return to the early practice of the Government and to the true principle of legislation, which requires that every measure shall

stand or fall according to its own merits. If it were understood that to attach to an appropriation bill a measure irrelevant to the general object of the bill would imperil and probably prevent its final passage and approval, a valuable reform in the parliamentary practice of Congress would be accomplished. The best justification that has been offered for attaching irrelevant riders to appropriation bills is that it is done for convenience' sake, to facilitate the passage of measures which are deemed expedient by all the branches of Government which participate in legislation. It can not be claimed that there is any such reason for attaching this amendment of the election laws to the Army appropriation bill. The history of the measure contradicts this assumption. . . .

. . . Upon the assembling of this Congress, in pursuance of a call for an extra session, which was made necessary by the failure of the Forty-fifth Congress to make the needful appropriations for the support of the Government, the question was presented whether the attempt made in the last Congress to ingraft by construction a new principle upon the Constitution should be persisted in or not. This Congress has ample opportunity and time to pass the appropriation bills, and also to enact any political measures which may be determined upon in separate bills by the usual and orderly methods of proceeding. But the majority of both Houses have deemed it wise to adhere to the principles asserted and maintained in the last Congress by the majority of the House of Representatives. That principle is that the House of Representatives has the sole right to originate bills for raising revenue, and therefore has the right to withhold appropriations upon which the existence of the Government may depend unless the Senate and the President shall give their assent to any legislation which the House may see fit to attach to appropriation bills. To establish this principle is to make a radical, dangerous, and unconstitutional change in the character of our institutions. The various departments of the Government and the Army and the Navy are established by the Constitution or by laws passed in pursuance thereof. Their duties are clearly defined and their support is carefully provided for by law. The money required for this purpose has been collected from the people and is now in the Treasury, ready to be paid out as soon as the appropriation bills are passed. Whether appropriations are made or not, the collection of the taxes will go on. The public money will accumulate in the Treasury. It was not the intention of the framers of the Constitution that any single branch of the Government should have the power to dictate conditions upon which this treasure should be applied to the purpose for which it was collected. Any such intention, if it had been entertained, would have been plainly expressed in the Constitution. . . .

The new doctrine, if maintained, will result in a consolidation of unchecked and despotic power in the House of Representatives. A bare majority of the House will become the Government. The Executive will no longer be what the framers of the Constitution intended—an equal and independent branch of the Government. It is clearly the constitutional duty of the President to exercise his discretion and judgment upon all bills presented to him without constraint or duress from any other branch of the Government. To say that a majority of either or both of the Houses of Congress may insist upon the approval of a bill under the penalty of stopping all of the operations of the Government for want of the necessary supplies is to deny to the Executive that share of the legislative power which is plainly conferred by the second section of the seventh article of the Constitution. It strikes from the

Constitution the qualified negative of the President. It is said that this should be done because it is the peculiar function of the House of Representatives to represent the will of the people. But no single branch or department of the Government has exclusive authority to speak for the American people. The most authentic and solemn expression of their will is contained in the Constitution of the United States. By that Constitution they have ordained and established a Government whose powers are distributed among coördinate branches, which, as far as possible consistently with a harmonious coöperation, are absolutely independent of each other. The people of this country are unwilling to see the supremacy of the Constitution replaced by the omnipotence of any one department of the Government.

The enactment of this bill into a law will establish a precedent which will tend to destroy the equal independence of the several branches of the Government. Its principle places not merely the Senate and the Executive, but the judiciary also, under the coercive dictation of the House. The House alone will be the judge of what constitutes a grievance, and also of the means and measures of redress. . . .

Believing that this bill is a dangerous violation of the spirit and meaning of the Constitution, I am compelled to return it to the House in which it originated without my approval. . . .

RUTHERFORD B. HAYES.

304. THE INDIAN PROBLEM

Extract from President Arthur's First Annual Message
December 6, 1881

(Richardson, ed. *Messages and Papers,* Vol. VIII, p. 54 ff.)

The recommendations of President Arthur foreshadowed the provisions of the Dawes Act of 1887, Doc. No. 315. In support of Arthur's characterization of our Indian policy, see H. H. Jackson, *A Century of Dishonor,* and the references listed in Doc. No. 315.

. . . Prominent among the matters which challenge the attention of Congress at its present session is the management of our Indian affairs. While this question has been a cause of trouble and embarrassment from the infancy of the Government, it is but

recently that any effort has been made for its solution at once serious, determined, consistent, and promising success.

It has been easier to resort to convenient makeshifts for tiding over temporary difficulties than to grapple with the great permanent problem, and accordingly the easier course has almost invariably been pursued.

It was natural, at a time when the national territory seemed almost illimitable and contained many millions of acres far outside the bounds of civilized settlements, that a policy should have been initiated which more than aught else has been the fruitful source of our Indian complications.

I refer, of course, to the policy of dealing with the various Indian tribes as separate nationalities, of relegating them by treaty stipulations to the occupancy of immense reservations in the West, and of encouraging them to live a savage life, undisturbed by any earnest and well-directed efforts to bring them under the influences of civilization.

The unsatisfactory results which have sprung from this policy are becoming apparent to all.

As the white settlements have crowded the borders of the reservations, the Indians, sometimes contentedly and sometimes against their will, have been transferred to other hunting grounds, from which they have again been dislodged whenever their new-found homes have been desired by the adventurous settlers.

These removals and the frontier collisions by which they have often been preceded have led to frequent and disastrous conflicts between the races.

It is profitless to discuss here which of them has been chiefly responsible for the disturbances whose recital occupies so large a space upon the pages of our history.

We have to deal with the appalling fact that though thousands of lives have been sacrificed and hundreds of millions of dollars expended in the attempt to solve the Indian problem, it has until within the past few years seemed scarcely nearer a solution than it was half a century ago. But the Government has of late been cautiously but steadily feeling its way to the adoption of a policy which has already produced gratifying results, and which, in my judgment, is likely, if Congress and the Executive accord in its support, to relieve us ere long from the difficulties which have hitherto beset us.

For the success of the efforts now making to introduce among the Indians the customs and pursuits of civilized life and gradually to absorb them into the mass of our citizens, sharing their rights and holden to their responsibilities, there is imperative need for legislative action.

My suggestions in that regard will be chiefly such as have been already called to the attention of Congress and have received to some extent its consideration.

First. I recommend the passage of an act making the laws of the various States and Territories applicable to the Indian reservations within their borders and extending the laws of the State of Arkansas to the portion of the Indian Territory not occupied by the Five Civilized Tribes.

The Indian should receive the protection of the law. He should be allowed to maintain in court his rights of person and property. He has repeatedly begged for this privilege. Its exercise would be very valuable to him in his progress toward civilization.

Second. Of even greater importance is a measure which has been frequently recommended by my predecessors in office, and in furtherance of which several bills have been from time to time introduced in both Houses of Congress. The enactment of a general law permitting the allotment in severalty, to such Indians, at least, as desire it, of a reasonable quantity of land secured to them by patent, and for their own protection made inalienable for twenty or twenty-five years, is demanded for their present welfare and their permanent advancement.

In return for such considerate action on the part of the Government, there is reason to believe that the Indians in large numbers would be persuaded to sever their tribal relations and to engage at once in agricultural pursuits. Many of them realize the fact that their hunting days are over and that it is now for their best interests to conform their manner of life to the new order of things. By no greater inducement than the assurance of permanent title to the soil can they be led to engage in the occupation of tilling it.

The well-attested reports of their increasing interest in husbandry justify the hope and belief that the enactment of such a statute as I recommend would be at once attended with gratifying results. A resort to the allotment system would have a direct and powerful influence in dissolving the tribal bond, which is so prominent a feature of savage life, and which tends so strongly to perpetuate it.

Third. I advise a liberal appropriation for the support of Indian schools, because of my confident belief that such a course is consistent with the wisest economy. . . .

305. PAN-AMERICANISM
Secretary Blaine's Invitation to Pan-American Congress
November 29, 1881

(Papers Relating to the Foreign Relations of the United States, 1881, p. 13 ff.)

James G. Blaine became Secretary of State for the first time, May 7, 1881; he at once addressed himself to the problem of our relations with the countries of Latin-America. The assassination of Garfield brought Arthur to the Presidency, and Blaine was succeeded in the State Department by Frelinghuysen. Frelinghuysen reversed Blaine's Latin-American policy, and withdrew the invitations to a Pan-American Conference. In 1888 Congress authorized a Pan-American Conference which met in Washington October 1889, and established the Pan-American Union. See, A. F. Tyler, *Foreign Policy of James G. Blaine;* D. S. Muzzey, *James G. Blaine;* S. F. Bemis, ed. *American Secretaries of State,* Vol. VII, p. 275 ff.; J. F. Rippy, *Historical Evolution of Hispanic America,* ch. xxiii.

MR. BLAINE TO MR. OSBORN.
Department of State
Washington, November 29, 1881.

Sir: The attitude of the United States with respect to the question of general peace on the American continent is well known through its persistent efforts for years to avert the evils of warfare, or, these efforts failing, to bring positive conflicts to an end through pacific counsels or the advocacy of impartial arbitration. This attitude has been consistently maintained, and always with such fairness as to leave no room for imputing to our government any motive except the humane and disinterested one of saving the kindred states of the American continent from the burdens of war. The position of the United States as the leading power of the New World might well give its government a claim to authoritative utterance for the purpose of quieting discord among its neighbors, with all of whom the most friendly relations exist. Nevertheless, the good offices of this government are not and have not at any time been tendered with a show of dictation or compulsion, but only as exhibiting the solicitous good-will of a common friend.

For some years past a growing disposition has been manifested by certain states of Central and South America to refer disputes affecting grave questions of international relationship and boundaries to arbitration rather than to the sword. It has been on several such occasions a source of profound satisfaction to the Government of the United States to see that this country is in a large measure looked to by all the American powers as their friend and mediator. The just and impartial counsel of the President in such cases has never been withheld, and his efforts have been rewarded by the prevention of sanguinary strife or angry contentions between peoples whom we regard as brethren.

The existence of this growing tendency convinces the President that the time is ripe for a proposal that shall enlist the good-will and active coöperation of all the states of the western hemisphere, both north and south, in the interest of humanity and for the common weal of nations. He conceives that none of the governments of America can be less alive than our own to the dangers and horrors of a state of war, and especially of war between kinsmen. He is sure that none of the chiefs of governments on the continent can be less sensitive than he is to the sacred duty of making every endeavor to do away with the chances of fratricidal strife. And he looks with hopeful confidence to such active assistance from them as will serve to show the broadness of our common humanity and the strength of the ties which bind us all together as a great and harmonious system of American commonwealths.

Impressed by these views, the President extends to all the independent countries of North and South America an earnest invitation to participate in a general congress to be held in the city of Washington on the 24th day of November, 1882, for the purpose of considering and discussing the methods of preventing war between the nations of America. He desires that the attention of the congress shall be strictly confined to this one great object; that its sole aim shall be to seek a way of permanently averting the horrors of cruel and bloody combat between countries, oftenest of one blood and speech, or the even worse calamity of internal commotion and civil strife; that it shall regard the burdensome and far-reaching consequences of such struggles, the legacies of exhausted finances, of oppressive debt, of onerous taxation, of ruined cities, of paralyzed industries, of devastated fields, of ruthless conscription, of the slaughter of men, of the grief of the widow and the orphan, of embittered resentment that long survive those who provoked them and heavily afflict the innocent generations that come after.

The President is especially desirous to have it understood that, in putting forth this invitation, the United States does not assume the position of counseling or attempting through the voice of the congress, to counsel any determinate solution of existing questions which may now divide any of the countries of America. Such questions can not properly come before the congress. Its mission is higher. It is to provide for the interest of all in the future, not to settle the individual differences of the present. For this reason especially the President has indicated a day for the assembling of the congress so far in the future as to leave good ground for hope that by the time named the present situation on the South Pacific coast will be happily terminated, and that those engaged in the contest may take peaceable part in the discussion and solution of the general question affecting in an equal degree the well-being of all.

It seems also desirable to disclaim in advance any purpose on the part of the United States to prejudge the issues to be presented to the congress. It is far from the intent of this government to appear before the congress as in any sense the protector of its neighbors or the predestined and necessary arbitrator of their disputes. The United States will enter into the deliberations of the congress on the same footing as the other powers represented, and with the loyal determination to approach any proposed solution, not merely in its own interest, or with a view to asserting its power, but as a single member among many coördinate and coequal states. So far as the influence of this government may be potential, it will be exerted in the direction of conciliating whatever conflicting interests of blood, or government, or historical tradition may necessarily come together in response to a call embracing such vast and diverse elements.

I am, &c.,

JAMES G. BLAINE.

306. TREATY REGULATING IMMIGRATION FROM CHINA
November 17, 1880

(Malloy, ed. *Treaties, Conventions, etc.* Vol. I, p. 237 ff.)

By the Burlingame Treaty of 1868 Chinese were given the right to immigrate to the United States; shortly after the ratification of this Treaty anti-Chinese sentiment on the Pacific coast became so strong that there was a demand for its abrogation. A bill abrogating the provision insuring reciprocal immigration privileges passed Congress in 1879 but was vetoed by President Hayes. In order to deal with the situation the President appointed a committee to negotiate a new Treaty: the Treaty of November 17, 1880 was the result. In 1882 a bill to prohibit the immigration of Chinese laborers for a period of ten years received the signature of President Arthur; the restriction was subsequently extended until it became permanent. On Oriental Immigration, see M. R. Coolidge, *Chinese Immigration;* R. L. Garis, *Immigration Restriction.*

. . . Whereas the Government of the United States, because of the constantly increasing immigration of Chinese laborers to the territory of the United States, and the embarrassments consequent upon such immigration, now desires to negotiate a modification of the existing Treaties which shall not be in direct contravention of their spirit: . . .

ART. I. Whenever in the opinion of the Government of the United States, the coming of Chinese laborers to the United States, or their residence therein, affects or threatens to affect the interests of that country, or to endanger the good order of the said country or of any locality within the territory thereof, the Government of China agrees that the Government of the United States may regulate, limit, or suspend such coming or residence, but may not absolutely prohibit it. The limitation or suspension shall be reasonable and shall apply only to Chinese who may go to the United States as laborers, other classes not being included in the limitations. Legislation taken in regard to Chinese laborers will be of such a character only as is necessary to enforce the regulation, limitation or suspension of immigration, and immigrants shall not be subject to personal maltreatment or abuse.

ART. II. Chinese subjects, whether proceeding to the United States as teachers, students, merchants, or from curiosity, together with their body and household servants, and Chinese laborers who are now in the United States, shall be allowed to go and come of their own free will and accord, and shall be accorded all the rights, privi-

leges, immunities and exemptions which are accorded to the citizens and subjects of the most favored nation.

ART. III. If Chinese laborers, or Chinese of any other class, now either permanently or temporarily residing in the territory of the United States, meet with ill treatment at the hands of any other persons, the Government of the United States will exert all its power to devise measures for their protection and to secure to them the same rights, privileges, immunities and exemptions as may be enjoyed by the citizens or subjects of the most favored nation, and to which they are entitled by treaty. . . .

307. CHINESE EXCLUSION ACT
May 6, 1882
(*U. S. Statutes at Large*, Vol. XXII, p. 58 ff.)

For references, see Doc. No. 306.

An act to execute certain treaty stipulations relating to Chinese.

WHEREAS, in the opinion of the Government of the United States the coming of Chinese laborers to this country endangers the good order of certain localities within the territory thereof: Therefore,

Be it enacted, That from and after the expiration of ninety days next after the passage of this act, and until the expiration of ten years next after the passage of this act, the coming of Chinese laborers to the United States be, . . . suspended; and during such suspension it shall not be lawful for any Chinese laborer to come, or, having so come after the expiration of said ninety days, to remain within the United States.

SEC. 2. That the master of any vessel who shall knowingly bring within the United States on such vessel, and land or permit to be landed, any Chinese laborer, from any foreign port or place, shall be deemed guilty of a misdemeanor, and on conviction thereof shall be punished by a fine of not more than five hundred dollars for each and every such Chinese laborer so brought, and may be also imprisoned for a term not exceeding one year.

SEC. 3. That the two foregoing sections shall not apply to Chinese laborers who were in the United States on the seventeenth day

of November, eighteen hundred and eighty, or who shall have come into the same before the expiration of ninety days next after the passage of this act, . . .

SEC. 6. That in order to the faithful execution of articles one and two of the treaty in this act before mentioned, every Chinese person other than a laborer who may be entitled by said treaty and this act to come within the United States, and who shall be about to come to the United States, shall be identified as so entitled by the Chinese Government in each case, such identity to be evidenced by a certificate issued under the authority of said government, which certificate shall be in the English language or (if not in the English language) accompanied by a translation into English, stating such right to come, and which certificate shall state the name, title, or official rank, if any, the age, height, and all physical peculiarities, former and present occupation or profession, and place of residence in China of the person to whom the certificate is issued and that such person is entitled conformably to the treaty in this act mentioned to come within the United States. . . .

SEC. 12. That no Chinese person shall be permitted to enter the United States by land without producing to the proper officer of customs the certificate in this act required of Chinese persons seeking to land from a vessel. And any Chinese person found unlawfully within the United States shall be caused to be removed therefrom to the country from whence he came, by direction of the President of the United States, and at the cost of the United States, after being brought before some justice, judge, or commissioner of a court of the United States and found to be one not lawfully entitled to be or remain in the United States.

SEC. 13. That this act shall not apply to diplomatic and other officers of the Chinese Government traveling upon the business of that government, whose credentials shall be taken as equivalent to the certificate in this act mentioned, and shall exempt them and their body and household servants from the provisions of this act as to other Chinese persons.

SEC. 14. That hereafter no State court or court of the United States shall admit Chinese to citizenship; and all laws in conflict with this act are hereby repealed.

SEC. 15. That the words "Chinese laborers," whenever used in this act, shall be construed to mean both skilled and unskilled laborers and Chinese employed in mining.

308. PENDLETON ACT
January 16, 1883

(U. S. Statutes at Large, Vol. XXII, p. 403 ff.)

Agitation for civil service reform dates back to the Grant administration. From 1871 to 1872 Congress appropriated money for a civil service commission, but thereafter no action was taken until 1881. A New York Civil Service Reform Association was founded in 1877, and a National Civil Service Reform League in 1881, under the leadership of G. W. Curtis of New York. The assassination of Garfield by a disappointed office-seeker dramatized the desirability of reform, and President Arthur in his message of December 6 asked for legislation on the subject. The Pendleton Act established the merit system in our national administration. Dorman B. Eaton, long active in the reform movement, drafted the Pendleton Act, and was appointed by Arthur to head the new Civil Service Commission. See, C. R. Fish, *The Civil Service and the Patronage;* L. Mayer, *Federal Service;* D. II. Smith, *The United States Civil Service Commission;* F. M. Stewart, *The National Civil Service Reform League;* J. Bryce, *The American Commonwealth,* 1893 ed. Vol. II, ch. lxv.; and bibliographies accompanying sketches of Carl Schurz, G. W. Curtis, D. B. Eaton, T. A. Jenckes, in the *Dictionary of American Biography.*

An act to regulate and improve the civil service of the United States.

Be it enacted . . . , That the President is authorized to appoint, by and with the advice and consent of the Senate, three persons, not more than two of whom shall be adherents of the same party, as Civil Service Commissioners, and said three commissioners shall constitute the United States Civil Service Commission. Said commissioners shall hold no other official place under the United States.

Sec. 2. That it shall be the duty of said commissioners:

FIRST. To aid the President, as he may request, in preparing suitable rules for carrying this act into effect, and when said rules shall have been promulgated it shall be the duty of all officers of the United States in the departments and offices to which any such rules may relate to aid, in all proper ways, in carrying said rules, and any modifications thereof, into effect.

SECOND. And, among other things, said rules shall provide and declare, as nearly as the conditions of good administration will warrant, as follows:

First, for open, competitive examinations for testing the fitness of applicants for the public service now classified or to be classified hereunder. Such examinations shall be practical in their character, and so far as may be shall relate to those matters which will fairly test the relative capacity and fitness of the persons examined to discharge the duties of the service into which they seek to be appointed.

Second, that all the offices, places, and employments so arranged or to be arranged in classes shall be filled by selections according to grade from among those graded highest as the results of such competitive examinations.

Third, appointments to the public service aforesaid in the departments at Washington shall be apportioned among the several States and Territories and the District of Columbia upon the basis of population as ascertained at the last preceding census. . . .

Fourth, that there shall be a period of probation before any absolute appointment or employment aforesaid.

Fifth, that no person in the public service is for that reason under any obligations to contribute to any political fund, or to render any political service, and that he will not be removed or otherwise prejudiced for refusing to do so.

Sixth, that no person in said service has any right to use his official authority or influence to coerce the political action of any person or body.

Seventh, there shall be non-competitive examinations in all proper cases before the commission, when competent persons do not compete, after notice has been given of the existence of the vacancy, under such rules as may be prescribed by the commissioners as to the manner of giving notice. . . .

THIRD. Said commission shall, subject to the rules that may be made by the President, make regulations for, and have control of, such examinations, . . .

SEC. 3. . . . The commission shall, at Washington, and in one or more places in each State and Territory where examinations are to take place, designate and select a suitable number of persons, not less than three, in the official service of the United States, residing in said State or Territory, after consulting the head of the department or office in which such persons serve, to be members of boards of examiners. . . . Such boards of examiners shall be so located as to make it reasonably convenient and inexpensive for applicants to attend before them; and where there are persons to be examined in any State or Territory, examinations shall be held therein at least twice in each year. . . .

SEC. 6. That within sixty days after the passage of this act it shall be the duty of the Secretary of the Treasury, in as near conformity as may be to the classification of certain clerks now existing under . . . [Section 163] . . . of the Revised Statutes, to arrange in classes the several clerks and persons employed by the collector, naval officer, surveyor, and appraisers, or either of them, or being in the public service, at their respective offices in each customs district where the whole number of said clerks and persons shall be all together as many as fifty. And thereafter, from time to time, on the direction of the President, said Secretary shall make the like classification or arrangement of clerks and persons so employed, in connection with any said office or offices, in any other customs district. And, upon like request, and for the purposes of this act, said Secretary shall arrange in one or more of said classes, or of existing classes, any other clerks, agents, or persons employed under his department in any said district not now classified; and every such arrangement and classification upon being made shall be reported to the President.

Second. Within said sixty days it shall be the duty of the Postmaster-General, in general conformity to said . . . [Section 163] . . . , to separately arrange in classes the several clerks and persons employed, or in the public service, at each post-office, or under any postmaster of the United States, where the whole number of said clerks and persons shall together amount to as many as fifty. And thereafter, from time to time, on the direction of the President, it shall be the duty of the Postmaster-General to arrange in like classes the clerks and persons so employed in the postal service in connection with any other post-office; and every such arrangement and classification upon being made shall be reported to the President.

Third. That from time to time said Secretary, the Postmaster-General, and each of the heads of departments mentioned in . . . [Section 158] . . . of the Revised Statutes, and each head of an office, shall, on the direction of the President, and for facilitating the execution of this act, respectively revise any then existing classification or arrangement of those in their respective departments and offices, and shall, for the purposes of the examination herein provided for, include in one or more of such classes, so far as practicable, subordinate places, clerks, and officers in the public service pertaining to their respective departments not before classified for examination.

SEC. 7. That after the expiration of six months from the passage of this act no officer or clerk shall be appointed, and no person shall be employed to enter or be promoted in either of the said classes now existing, or that may be arranged hereunder pursuant to said rules, until he has passed an examination, or is shown to be specially exempted from such examination in conformity herewith. But nothing herein contained shall be construed to take from those honorably discharged from the military or naval service any preference conferred by . . . [Section 1754] . . . of the Revised Statutes, nor to take from the President any authority not inconsistent with this act conferred by . . . [Section 1753] . . . of said statutes; nor shall any officer not in the executive branch of the government, or any person merely employed as a laborer or workman, be required to be classified hereunder; nor, unless by direction of the Senate, shall any person who has been nominated for confirmation by the Senate be required to be classified or to pass an examination.

SEC. 8. That no person habitually using intoxicating beverages to excess shall be appointed to, or retained in, any office, appointment, or employment to which the provisions of this act are applicable.

SEC. 9. That whenever there are already two or more members of a family in the public service in the grades covered by this act, no other member of such family shall be eligible to appointment to any of said grades.

SEC. 10. That no recommendation of any person who shall apply for office or place under the provisions of this act which may be given by any Senator or member of the House of Representatives, except as to the character or residence of the applicant, shall be received or considered by any person concerned in making any examination or appointment under this act.

SEC. 11. That no Senator, or Representative, or Territorial Delegate of the Congress, or Senator, Representative, or Delegate elect, or any officer or employee of either of said houses, and no executive, judicial, military, or naval officer of the United States, and no clerk or employee of any department, branch or bureau of the executive, judicial, or military or naval service of the United States, shall, directly or indirectly, solicit or receive, or be in any manner concerned in soliciting or receiving, any assessment, subscription, or contribution for any political purpose whatever, from any officer, clerk, or employee of the United States, or any department, branch, or bureau thereof, or from any person receiving any salary or compensation from moneys derived from the Treasury of the United States. . . .

309. JULLIARD v. GREENMAN
110 U. S. 421
1884

Error to the U.S. Circuit Court for the Southern District of New York. This notable case involved the constitutionality of the Act of May 31, 1878, providing that legal tender notes issued during the Civil War should not be cancelled, but reissued and kept in circulation. The question was whether Congress could, except as an emergency war measure, make anything but gold and silver legal tender in the payment of private debts. Mr. Warren calls the decision of the court in this case "the most sweeping opinion as to the extent of Congressional power which had ever heretofore been rendered". Immediately after the Court had rendered its decision numerous measures were introduced into Congress limiting the power of Congress as to the issue of legal tender notes. See, Warren, *Supreme Court,* 1928 ed. Vol. II, p. 652 ff. and references, p. 657 n. On the dissenting opinion

see C. B. Swisher, *Stephen J. Field, Craftsman of the Law.*

GRAY, J., . . . The act of May 31st, 1878, ch. 146, under which the notes in question were reissued, is entitled "An act to forbid the further retirement of United States legal tender notes," and enacts as follows:

"From and after the passage of this act it shall not be lawful for the Secretary of the Treasury or other officer under him to cancel or retire any more of the United States legal tender notes. And when any of said notes may be redeemed or be received into the Treasury under any law from any source whatever and shall belong to the

United States, they shall not be retired, cancelled or destroyed, but they shall be reissued and paid out again and kept in circulation: Provided, That nothing herein shall prohibit the cancellation and destruction of mutilated notes and the issue of other notes of like denomination in their stead, as now provided by law. All acts and parts of acts in conflict herewith are hereby repealed." 20 Stat. 87.

The manifest intention of this act is that the notes which it directs, after having been redeemed, to be reissued and kept in circulation, shall retain their original quality of being a legal tender. The single question, therefore, to be considered, . . . is whether notes of the United States, issued in time of war, under acts of Congress declaring them to be a legal tender in payment of private debts, and afterwards in time of peace redeemed and paid in gold coin at the treasury, and then reissued under the act of 1878, can, under the Constitution of the United States, be a legal tender in payment of such debts. . . .

The breadth and comprehensiveness of the words of the Constitution are nowhere more strikingly exhibited than in regard to the powers, over the subjects of revenue, finance, and currency, of which there is no other express grant than may be found in these few brief clauses:

"The Congress shall have power—

"To lay and collect taxes, duties, imposts, and excises, to pay the debts and provide for the common defense and general welfare of the United States; but all duties, imposts, and excises shall be uniform throughout the United States."

"To borrow money on the credit of the United States."

"To regulate commerce with foreign nations, and among the several States, and with the Indian tribes."

"To coin money, regulate the value thereof, and of foreign coin, and fix the standard of weights and measures."

The section which contains the grant of these and other principal legislative powers concludes by declaring that the Congress shall have power—

"To make all laws which shall be necessary and proper for carrying into execution the foregoing powers, and all other powers vested by this Constitution in the government of the United States, or any department or officer thereof.". . .

The power "to borrow money on the credit of the United States" is the power to raise money for the public use on a pledge of the public credit, and may be exercised to meet either present or anticipated expenses and liabilities of the government. It includes the power to issue, in return for the money borrowed, the obligations of the United States in any appropriate form, of stock, bonds, bills or notes; and in whatever form they are issued, being instruments of the national government, they are exempt from taxation by the governments of the several States. Congress has authority to issue these obligations in a form adapted to circulation from hand to hand in the ordinary transactions of commerce and business. In order to promote and facilitate such circulation, to adapt them to use as currency, and to make them more current in the market, it may provide for their redemption in coin or bonds, and may make them receivable in payment of debts to the government. So much is settled beyond doubt, and was asserted or distinctly admitted by the judges who dissented from the decision in the *Legal Tender Cases,* as well as by those who concurred in that decision. . . .

The constitutional authority of Congress to provide a currency for the whole country is now firmly established. . . .

By the Constitution of the United States, the several States are prohibited from coining money, emitting bills of credit, or making anything but gold and silver coin a tender in payment of debts. But no intention can be inferred from this to deny to Congress either of these powers. . . . The States are forbidden, but Congress is expressly authorized, to coin money. The States are prohibited from emitting bills of credit; but Congress, which is neither expressly authorized nor expressly forbidden to do so, has, as we have already seen, been held to have the power of emitting bills of credit, and of making every provision for their circulation as currency, short of giving them the quality of legal tender for private debts, even by those who have denied its authority to give them this quality.

It appears to us to follow, as a logical and necessary consequence, that Congress has the power to issue the obligations of the United States in such form, and to impress upon them such qualities as currency for the purchase of merchandise and the payment of debts, as accord with the usage of sovereign governments. The power, as incident to the power of borrowing money and issuing bills or notes of the government for money borrowed, of impressing upon those bills or notes the quality of being a legal tender for the payment of private debts, was a power universally understood to belong to sovereignty, in Europe and America, at the time of the framing and adoption of the Constitution of the United States. . . .

. . . The power of issuing bills of credit, and making them, at the discretion of the legislature, a tender in payment of private debts, had long been exercised in this country by the several colonies and States; and during the Revolutionary War the States, upon the recommendation of the Congress of the Confederation, had made the bills issued by Congress a legal tender. The exercise of this power not being prohibited to Congress by the Constitution, it is included in the power expressly granted to borrow money on the credit of the United States.

This position is fortified by the fact that Congress is vested with the exclusive exercise of the analogous power of coining money and regulating the value of domestic and foreign coin, and also with the paramount power of regulating foreign and interstate commerce. Under the power to borrow money on the credit of the United States, and to issue circulating notes for the money borrowed, its power to define the quality and force of those notes as currency is as broad as the like power over a metallic currency under the power to coin money and to regulate the value thereof. Under the two powers, taken together, Congress is authorized to establish a national currency, either in coin or in paper, and to make that currency lawful money for all purposes, as regards the national government or private individuals.

The power of making the notes of the United States a legal tender in payment of private debts, being included in the power to borrow money and to provide a national currency, is not defeated or restricted by the fact that its exercise may affect the value of private contracts. If, upon a just and fair interpretation of the whole Constitution, a particular power or authority appears to be vested in Congress, it is no constitutional objection to its existence, or to its exercise, that the property or the contracts of individuals may be incidentally affected. . . .

So, under the power to coin money and to regulate its value, Congress may (as it did with regard to gold by the Act of June 28th, 1834, c. 95, and with regard to silver by the Act of February 28th, 1878, c. 20), issue coins of the same denominations as those already current by law, but of less intrinsic value than those, by reason of containing a less weight of the precious metals, and thereby enable debtors to discharge their debts by the payment of coins of the less real value. A contract to pay a certain sum in money, without any stipulation as to the kind of money in which it shall be paid, may always be satisfied by payment of that sum in any currency which is lawful money at the place and time at which payment is to be made. . . .

Congress, as the legislature of a sovereign nation, being expressly empowered by the Constitution, "to lay and collect taxes, to pay the debts and provide for the common defense and general welfare of the United States," and "to borrow money on the credit of the United States," and "to coin money and regulate the value thereof and of foreign coin;" and being clearly authorized, as incidental to the exercise of those great powers, to emit bills of credit, to charter national banks, and to provide a national currency for the whole people, in the form of coin, treasury notes, and national bank bills; and the power to make the notes of the government a legal tender in payment of private debts being one of the powers belonging to sovereignty in other civilized nations, and not expressly withheld from Congress by the Constitution; we are irresistibly impelled to the conclusion that the impressing upon the treasury notes of the United States the quality of being a legal tender in payment of private debts is an appropriate means, conducive and plainly adapted to the execution of the undoubted powers of Congress, consistent with the letter and spirit of the Constitution, and therefore, within the meaning of that instrument, "necessary and proper for carrying into execution the powers vested by this Constitution in the government of the United States."

Such being our conclusion in matter of law, the question whether at any particular time, in war or in peace, the exigency is such by reason of unusual and pressing demands on the resources of the government, or of the inadequacy of the supply of gold and silver coin to furnish the currency needed for the uses of the government and of the people, that it is, as matter of fact, wise and expedient to resort to this means, is a political question, to be determined by Congress when the question of exigency arises, and not a judicial question, to be afterwards passed upon by the courts. . . .

It follows that the act of May 31, 1878, ch. 146, is constitutional and valid, and that the circuit court rightly held that the tender in treasury notes, reissued and kept in circulation under that act, was a tender of lawful money in payment of the defendant's debt to the plaintiff.

Judgment affirmed.

FIELD, J., delivered a dissenting opinion.

310. IN RE JACOBS
98 New York, 98
1885

Appeal from an order of the General Term of the Supreme Court. The case involved an interpretation of the New York Tenement House Law of 1882. "This decision," wrote Theodore Roosevelt, (*Autobiography,* p. 81), "completely blocked tenement-house reform legislation in New York for a score of years, and hampers it to this day. It was one of the most serious setbacks which the cause of industrial and social progress and reform ever received." For background, see R. W. De Forest and L. Veiller, *The Tenement House Problem,* 2 vols.; Jacob Riis, *The Battle With the Slum.*

EARL, J. . . . These facts showed a violation of the provision of the act which took effect immediately upon its passage and the material portions of which are as follows: "Section 1. The manufacture of cigars or preparation of tobacco in any form on any floor, or in any part of any floor, in any tenement-house is hereby prohibited, if such floor or any part of such floor is by any person occupied as a home or residence for the purpose of living, sleeping, cooking or doing any household work therein. . . . Section 6. This act shall apply only to cities having over five hundred thousand inhabitants.". . .

Generally it is for the legislature to determine what laws and regulations are needed to protect the public health and secure the public comfort and safety, and while its measures are calculated, intended, convenient and appropriate to accomplish these ends, the exercise of its discretion is not subject to review by the courts. But they must have some relation to these ends. Under the mere guise of police regulations, personal rights and private property cannot arbitrarily be invaded, and the determination of the legislature is not final or conclusive. If it passes an act ostensibly for the public health, and thereby destroys or takes away the property of a citizen, or interferes with his personal liberty, then it is for the courts to scrutinize the act and see whether it really relates to and is convenient and appropriate to promote the public health. It matters not that the legislature may in the title to the act, or in its body, declare that it is intended for the improvement of the public health. Such a declaration does not conclude the courts, and they must yet determine the fact declared and enforce the supreme law. . . . The legislature may condemn or authorize the condemnation of private property for public use, and it may, in the exercise of its discretion, determine when and upon what property the power of eminent domain may be exercised; but its exercise is not beyond the reach of judicial inquiry. Whether or not a use is a public one, which will justify the exercise of the power, is a judicial question. . . .

We will now once more recur to the law

under consideration. It does not deal with tenement-houses as such; it does not regulate the number of persons who may live in any one of them, or be crowded into one room, nor does it deal with the mode of their construction for the purpose of securing the health and safety of their occupants or of the public generally. It deals mainly with the preparation of tobacco and the manufacture of cigars, and its purpose obviously was to regulate them. We must take judicial notice of the nature and qualities of tobacco. It has been in general use among civilized men for more than two centuries. It is used in some form by a majority of the men in this State; by the good and bad, learned and unlearned, the rich and the poor. Its manufacture into cigars is permitted without any hindrance, except for revenue purposes, in all civilized lands. It has never been said, so far as we can learn, and it was not affirmed even on the argument before us, that its preparation and manufacture into cigars were dangerous to the public health. We are not aware, and are not able to learn, that tobacco is even injurious to the health of those who deal in it, or are engaged in its production or manufacture. We certainly know enough about it to be sure that its manipulation in one room can produce no harm to the health of the occupants of other rooms in the same house. It was proved in this case that the odor of the tobacco did not extend to any of the other rooms of the tenement-house. . . . To justify this law it would not be sufficient that the use of tobacco may be injurious to some persons, or that its manipulation may be injurious to those who are engaged in its preparation and manufacture; but it would have to be injurious to the public health. This law was not intended to protect the health of those engaged in cigar-making, as they are allowed to manufacture cigars everywhere except in the forbidden tenement-houses. It cannot be perceived how the cigar maker is to be improved in his health or his morals by forcing him from his home and its hallowed associations and beneficent influences, to ply his trade elsewhere. It was not intended to protect the health of that portion of the public not residing in the forbidden tenement-houses, as cigars are allowed to be manufactured in private houses, in large factories and shops

in the too crowded cities, and in all other parts of the State. What possible relation can cigarmaking in any building have on the health of the general public? Nor was it intended to improve or protect the health of the occupants of tenement-houses. If there are but three families in the tenement-house, however numerous and gregarious their members may be, manufacture is not forbidden; and it matters not how large the number of the occupants may be if they are not divided into more than three families living and cooking independently. If a store is kept for the sale of cigars on the first floor of one of these houses, and thus more tobacco is kept there than otherwise would be, and the baneful influence of tobacco, if any, is thus increased, that floor, however numerous its occupants, or the occupants of the house, is exempt from the operation of the act. What possible relation to the health of the occupants of a large tenement-house could cigarmaking in one of its remote rooms have? If the legislature had in mind the protection of the occupants of the tenement-houses, why was the act confined in its operation to the two cities only? It is plain that this is not a health law, and that it has no relation whatever to the public health. . . . Such legislation may invade one class of rights to-day and another to-morrow, and if it can be sanctioned under the Constitution, while far removed in time we will not be far away in practical statesmanship from those ages when governmental prefects supervised the building of houses, the rearing of cattle, the sowing of seed and the reaping of grain, and governmental ordinances regulated the movements and labor of artisans, the rate of wages, the price of food, the diet and clothing of the people, and a large range of other affairs long since in all civilized lands regarded as outside of governmental functions. Such governmental interferences disturb the normal adjustments of the social fabric, and usually derange the delicate and complicated machinery of industry and cause a score of ills while attempting the removal of one.

When a health law is challenged in the courts as unconstitutional on the ground that it arbitrarily interferes with personal liberty and private property without due process of law, the courts must be able to see that it has at least in fact some relation to the public health, that the public health is the end actually aimed at, and that it is appropriate and adapted to that end. This we have not been able to see in this law, and we must, therefore, pronounce it unconstitutional and void. . . .

311. CLEVELAND'S RECOMMENDATION OF THE REPEAL OF THE BLAND–ALLISON ACT

Extract from the First Annual Message to Congress
December 8, 1885

(Richardson, ed. *Messages and Papers,* Vol. VIII, p. 342 ff.)

Cleveland's plea for the repeal of the Silver Coinage Act of 1878 was not at this time successful, but he did succeed in defeating projects for free coinage of silver. On his re-election in 1893, Cleveland moved immediately for the repeal of the Sherman Silver Coinage Act, and carried his policy through to success. See Docs. No. 327, 328. On the first phase of Cleveland's silver policy, see A. Nevins, *Grover Cleveland,* ch. xvi.

. . . Nothing more important than the present condition of our currency and coinage can claim your attention.

Since February, 1878, the Government has, under the compulsory provisions of law, purchased silver bullion and coined the same at the rate of more than $2,000,000 every month. By this process up to the present date 215,759,431 silver dollars have been coined. . . .

The necessity for such an addition to the silver currency of the nation as is compelled by the silver-coinage act is negatived by the fact that up to the present time only about 50,000,000 of the silver dollars so coined have actually found their way into circulation, leaving more than 165,000,000 in the possession of the Government, the custody of which has entailed a considerable expense for the construction of vaults for its deposit. Against this latter amount there are outstanding silver certificates amounting to about $93,000,000.

Every month two millions of gold in the public Treasury are paid out for two millions or more of silver dollars, to be added to the idle mass already accumulated.

If continued long enough, this operation will result in the substitution of silver for all the gold the Government owns applicable to its general purposes. . . . The proportion of silver and its certificates received by the Government will probably increase as time goes on, for the reason that the nearer the period approaches when it will be obliged to offer silver in payment of its obligations the greater inducement there will be to hoard gold against depreciation in the value of silver or for the purpose of speculating.

This hoarding of gold has already begun.

When the time comes that gold has been withdrawn from circulation, then will be apparent the difference between the real value of the silver dollar and a dollar in gold, and the two coins will part company. Gold, still the standard of value and necessary in our dealings with other countries, will be at a premium over silver; banks which have substituted gold for the deposits of their customers may pay them with silver bought with such gold, thus making a handsome profit; rich speculators will sell their hoarded gold to their neighbors who need it to liquidate their foreign debts, at a ruinous premium over silver, and the laboring men and women of the land, most defenseless of all, will find that the dollar received for the wage of their toil has sadly shrunk in its purchasing power. It may be said that the latter result will be but temporary, and that ultimately the price of labor will be adjusted to the change; but even if this takes place the wage-worker can not possibly gain, but must inevitably lose, since the price he is compelled to pay for his living will not only be measured in a coin heavily depreciated and fluctuating and uncertain in its value, but this uncertainty in the value of the purchasing medium will be made the pretext for an advance in prices beyond that justified by actual depreciation. . . .

Those who do not fear any disastrous consequences arising from the continued compulsory coinage of silver as now directed by law, and who suppose that the addition to the currency of the country intended as its result will be a public benefit, are reminded that history demonstrates that the point is easily reached in the attempt to float at the same time two sorts of money of different excellence when the better will cease to be in general circulation. The hoarding of gold which has already taken place indicates that we shall not escape the usual experience in such cases. So if this silver coinage be continued we may reasonably expect that gold and its equivalent will abandon the field of circulation to silver alone. This of course must produce a severe contraction of our circulating medium, instead of adding to it.

It will not be disputed that any attempt on the part of the Government to cause the circulation of silver dollars worth 80 cents side by side with gold dollars worth 100 cents, even within the limit that legislation does not run counter to the laws of trade, to be successful must be seconded by the confidence of the people that both coins will retain the same purchasing power and be interchangeable at will. A special effort has been made by the Secretary of the Treasury to increase the amount of our silver coin in circulation; but the fact that a large share of the limited amount thus put out has soon returned to the public Treasury in payment of duties leads to the belief that the people do not now desire to keep it in hand, and this, with the evident disposition to hoard gold, gives rise to the suspicion that there already exists a lack of confidence among the people touching our financial processes. There is certainly not enough silver now in circulation to cause uneasiness, and the whole amount coined and now on hand might after a time be absorbed by the people without apprehension; but it is the ceaseless stream that threatens to overflow the land which causes fear and uncertainty. . . .

The so-called debtor class, for whose benefit the continued compulsory coinage of silver is insisted upon, are not dishonest because they are in debt, and they should not be suspected of a desire to jeopardize the financial safety of the country in order that they may cancel their present debts by paying the same in depreciated dollars. Nor should it be forgotten that it is not the rich nor the money lender alone that must submit to such a readjustment, enforced by the Government and their debtors. The pittance of the widow and the orphan and the incomes of helpless beneficiaries of all kinds would be disastrously reduced. The depositors in savings banks and in other institutions which hold in trust the savings of the poor, when their little accumulations are scaled down to meet the new order of things, would in their distress painfully realize the delusion of the promise made to them that plentiful money would improve their condition.

We have now on hand all the silver dollars necessary to supply the present needs of the people and to satisfy those who from sentiment wish to see them in circulation, and if their coinage is suspended they can be readily obtained by all who desire them. If the need of more is at any time apparent, their coinage may be renewed.

That disaster has not already overtaken us furnishes no proof that danger does not wait upon a continuation of the present silver coinage. We have been saved by the most careful management and unusual expedients, by a combination of fortunate conditions, and by a confident expectation that the course of the Government in regard to silver coinage would be speedily changed by the action of Congress.

Prosperity hesitates upon our threshold because of the dangers and uncertainties surrounding this question. Capital timidly shrinks from trade, and investors are unwilling to take the chance of the questionable shape in which their money will be returned to them, while enterprise halts at a risk against which care and sagacious management do not protect.

As a necessary consequence, labor lacks employment and suffering and distress are visited upon a portion of our fellow-citizens especially entitled to the careful consideration of those charged with the duties of legislation. No interest appeals to us so strongly for a safe and stable currency as the vast army of the unemployed.

I recommend the suspension of the compulsory coinage of silver dollars, directed by the law passed in February, 1878. . . .

312. PRESIDENT CLEVELAND ON PENSION LEGISLATION
Extract from Veto Message
June 21, 1886
(Richardson, ed. *Messages and Papers,* Vol. VIII, p. 437–8)

The practice of granting pensions by special legislation grew during the decade of the eighties to a positive menace. Cleveland did his best to stanch this flow of special legislation, but succeeded only in inspiring charges that he was unfriendly to the veterans of the Civil War. The Harrison administration reversed the Cleveland policy; Corporal Tanner, who was placed in charge of the pension bureau, is said to have remarked, "God help the surplus". The pension act of 1890 increased the annual pension appropriations, within two years, by $68,000,000. See, W. H. Glasson, *Federal Military Pensions;* A. Nevins, *Grover Cleveland,* ch. xix; J. W. Oliver, *History of Civil War Pensions.*

Executive Mansion,
June 21, 1886.

To the Senate:

. . . I am so thoroughly tired of disapproving gifts of public money to individuals who in my view have no right or claim to the same, notwithstanding apparent Congressional sanction, that I interpose with a feeling of relief a veto in a case where I find it unnecessary to determine the merits of the application. In speaking of the promiscuous and ill-advised grants of pensions which have lately been presented to me for approval, I have spoken of their "apparent Congressional sanction" in recognition of the fact that a large proportion of these bills have never been submitted to a majority of either branch of Congress, but are the result of nominal sessions held for the express purpose of their consideration and attended by a small minority of the members of the respective Houses of the legislative branch of Government. . . .

I have not been insensible to the suggestions which should influence every citizen, either in private station or official place, to exhibit not only a just but a generous appreciation of the services of our country's defenders. In reviewing the pension legislation presented to me many bills have been approved upon the theory that every doubt should be resolved in favor of the proposed beneficiary. I have not, however, been able to entirely divest myself of the idea that the public money appropriated for pensions is the soldiers' fund, which should be devoted to the indemnification of those who in the defense of the Union and in the nation's service have worthily suffered, and who in the day of their dependence resulting from such suffering are entitled to the benefactions of their Government. This reflection lends to the bestowal of pensions a kind of sacredness which invites the adoption of such principles and regulations as will exclude perversion as well as insure a liberal and generous application of grateful and benevolent designs. Heedlessness and a disregard of the principle which underlies the granting of pensions is unfair to the wounded, crippled soldier who is honored in the just recognition of his Government. Such a man should never find himself side by side on the pension roll with those who have been tempted to attribute the natural ills to which humanity is heir to service in the Army. Every relaxation of principle in the granting of pensions invites applications without merit and encourages those who for gain urge honest men to become dishonest. This is the demoralizing lesson taught the people that as against the public Treasury the most questionable expedients are allowable.

During the present session of Congress 493 special pension bills have been submitted to me, and I am advised that 111 more have received the favorable action of both Houses of Congress and will be presented within a day or two, making over 600 of these bills which have been passed up to this time during the present session, nearly three times the number passed at any entire session since the year 1861. With the Pension Bureau, fully equipped and regulated by the most liberal rules, in active operation, supplemented in its work by constant special legislation, it certainly is not unreasonable to suppose that in all the years that have elapsed since the close of the war a majority of the meritorious claims for pensions have been presented and determined.

I have now more than 130 of these bills before me awaiting Executive action. It will be impossible to bestow upon them the examination they deserve, and many will probably become operative which should be rejected.

In the meantime I venture to suggest the significance of the startling increase in this kind of legislation and the consequences involved in its continuance.

GROVER CLEVELAND.

313. THE SINGLE-TAX

Platform of Henry George in the Mayoralty Contest, New York 1886

(L. F. Post and F. C. Leubuscher, *An Account of the George-Hewitt Campaign of 1886*)

Henry George published his *Progress and Poverty* in 1879. Within the next six years the single-tax movement gained headway both in the United States and in the British Isles. In 1886 George was tendered the nomination for mayor by various labor and liberal groups in New York City. A fierce campaign, punctuated by unmeasured denunciation from George's opponents, resulted in the election of Abram S. Hewitt, the Tammany candidate. Hewitt was credited with 90,552 votes, George with 68,110, and Theodore Roosevelt, the Republican candidate, with 60,435: it was charged at the time that Tammany Hall counted out George, but these charges have not been substantiated. On the campaign, and Henry George, see Post and Leubuscher, above; the forthcoming biography of Abram Hewitt by A. Nevins; H. George, Jr., *The Life of Henry George*, Vol. II, ch. vii; G. R. Geiger, *The Philosophy of Henry George;* L. F. Post, *The Prophet of San Francisco;* A. N. Young, *The Single Tax Movement in the United States;* R. A. Sawyer, *Henry George and the Single Tax;* J. Chamberlain, *Farewell to Reform.*

The delegates of the trade and labor organizations of New York in conference assembled, make this declaration.

1. Holding that the corruptions of government and the impoverishment of labor result from neglect of the self-evident truths proclaimed by the founders of this Republic that all men are created equal and endowed with inalienable rights, we aim at the abolition of the system which compels men to pay their fellow-creatures for the use of God's gifts to all, and permits monopolies to deprive labor of natural opportunities for employment, . . .

2. Holding, moreover, that the advantages arising from social growth and improvement belong to society at large, we aim at the abolition of the system which makes such beneficent inventions as the railroad and telegraph a means for the oppression of the people, and the aggrandizement of an aristocracy of wealth and power. We declare the true purpose of government to be the maintenance of that sacred right of property which gives to everyone opportunity to employ his labor and security that he shall enjoy its fruits; to prevent the strong from oppressing the weak, and the unscrupulous from robbing the honest; and to do for the equal benefit of all such things as can be better done by organized society than by individuals; and we aim at the abolition of all laws which give to any class of citizens advantages, either judicial, financial, industrial, or political, that are not equally shared by all others. . . .

4. We declare the crowding of so many of our people into narrow tenements at enormous rents, while half the area of the city is yet unbuilt upon to be a scandalous evil, and that to remedy this state of things all taxes on buildings and improvements should be abolished, so that no fine shall be put upon the employment of labor in increasing living accommodations, and that taxes should be levied on land irrespective of improvements, so that those who are now holding land vacant shall be compelled either to build on it themselves, or give up the land to those who will.

5. We declare, furthermore, that the enormous value which the presence of a million and a half people gives to the land of this

city belongs properly to the whole community; that it should not go to the enrichment of individuals and corporations, but should be taken in taxation and applied to the improvement and beautifying of the city, to the promotion of the health, comfort, education, and recreation of its people, and to the providing of means of transit commensurate with the needs of a great metropolis. We also declare that existing means of traffic should not be left in the hands of corporations which, while gaining enormous profits from the growth of population, oppress their employés and provoke strikes that interrupt travel and imperil the public peace, but should by lawful process be assumed by the city and operated for public benefit.

314. WABASH, ST. LOUIS AND PACIFIC RAILROAD COMPANY v. ILLINOIS
118 U. S. 557
1886

Error to the Supreme Court of Illinois. This case involved the legality of an Illinois law prohibiting the "long-and-short-haul" evil. The Wabash Railroad had charged certain shippers fifteen cents a hundred pounds for carrying goods from Peoria, Illinois, to New York City, and twenty-five cents a hundred pounds for carrying goods of the same class for other shippers from Gilman, Illinois, to New York City, although Peoria was 86 miles farther from New York City than was Gilman. The Supreme Court of the State of Illinois upheld the constitutionality of the State law. This case seriously modified the earlier decision of the Court in *Munn* v. *Illinois,* and helped to bring about the passage of the Interstate Commerce Act.

MILLER, J. . . . The matter thus presented, as to the controlling influence of the Constitution of the United States over this legislation of the state of Illinois, raises the question which confers jurisdiction on this court. Although the precise point presented by this case may not have been heretofore decided by this court, the general subject of the power of the State legislatures to regulate taxes, fares, and tolls for passengers and transportation of freight over railroads within their limits has been very much considered recently . . . and the question how far such regulations, made by the States . . . are valid or void, as they may affect the transportation of goods through more than one State, in one voyage, is not entirely new here.

The supreme court of Illinois, in the case now before us, conceding that each of these contracts was in itself a unit, and that the pay received by the Illinois railroad company was the compensation for the entire transportation from the point of departure in the State of Illinois to the city of New York, holds that, while the statute of Illinois is inoperative upon that part of the contract which has reference to the transportation outside of the State, it is binding and effectual as to so much of the transportation as was within the limits of the State of Illinois; and undertaking for itself to apportion the rates charged over the whole route, decides that the contract and the receipt of the money for so much of it as was performed within the State of Illinois violate the statute of the State on that subject.

If the Illinois statute could be construed to apply exclusively to contracts for a carriage which begins and ends within the State, disconnected from a continuous transportation through or into other States, there does not seem to be any difficulty in holding it to be valid. . . .

The supreme court of Illinois does not place its judgment in the present case on the ground that the transportation and the charge are exclusively state commerce, but, conceding that it may be a case of commerce among the States, or interstate commerce, which Congress would have the right to regulate if it had attempted to do so, argues that this statute of Illinois belongs to that class of commercial regulations which may be established by the laws of a State until Congress shall have exercised its power on that subject. In support of its view of the subject the supreme court of Illinois cites the cases of Munn v. Illinois; Chicago, Burlington & Quincy Railroad v. Iowa; and Peik v. Chicago & Northwestern Railway,

. . . It cannot be denied that the general language of the court in these cases, upon the power of Congress to regulate commerce, may be susceptible of the meaning which the Illinois court places upon it. . . . Whatever may be the instrumentalities by which the transportation from one point to the other is effected, it is but one voyage, as much so as that of the steamboat on the Mississippi River.

It is not the railroads themselves that are regulated by this act of the Illinois legislature so much as the charge for transportation, and . . . if each one of the States through whose territories these goods are transported can fix its own rules for prices, for modes of transit, for times and modes of delivery, and all the other incidents of transportation to which the word "regulation" can be applied, it is readily seen that the embarrassments upon interstate transportation, as an element of interstate commerce, might be too oppressive to be submitted to. "It was," in the language of the court cited above, "to meet just such a case that the commerce [commercial] clause of the Constitution was adopted."

It cannot be too strongly insisted upon that the right of continuous transportation, from one end of the country to the other, is essential, in modern times, to that freedom of commerce from the restraints which the States might choose to impose upon it, that the commerce clause was intended to secure. This clause, giving to Congress the power to regulate commerce among the States, and with foreign nations, as this court has said before, was among the most important of the subjects which prompted the formation of the Constitution. And it would be a very feeble and almost useless provision, but poorly adapted to secure the entire freedom of commerce among the States which was deemed essential to a more perfect union by the framers of the Constitution, if, at every stage of the transportation of goods and chattels through the country, the State within whose limits a part of this transportation must be done could impose regulations concerning the price, compensation, or taxation, or any other restrictive regulation interfering with and seriously embarrassing this commerce. . . .

We must therefore hold that it is not, and never has been, the deliberate opinion of a majority of this court that a statute of a State which attempts to regulate the fares and charges by railroad companies within its limits, for a transportation which constitutes a part of commerce among the States, is a valid law.

Let us see precisely what is the degree of interference with transportation of property or persons from one State to another which this statute proposes. A citizen of New York has goods which he desires to have transported by the railroad companies from that city to the interior of the State of Illinois. A continuous line of rail over which a car loaded with these goods can be carried, and is carried habitually, connects the place of shipment with the place of delivery. He undertakes to make a contract with a person engaged in the carrying business at the end of this route from whence the goods are to start, and he is told by the carrier: "I am free to make a fair and reasonable contract for this carriage to the line of the State of Illinois, but when the car which carries these goods is to cross the line of that State, pursuing at the same time this continuous track, I am met by a law of Illinois which forbids me to make a free contract concerning this transportation within that State, and subjects me to certain rules by which I am to be governed as to the charges which the same railroad company in Illinois may make, or has made, with reference to other persons and other places of delivery." So that while that carrier might be willing to carry these goods from the city of New York to the city of Peoria at the rate of fifteen cents per hundred pounds, he is not permitted to do so, because the Illinois railroad company has already charged at the rate of twenty-five cents per hundred pounds for carriage to Gilman, in Illinois, which is eighty-six miles shorter than the distance to Peoria.

So, also, in the present case, the owner of corn, the principal product of the country, desiring to transport it from Peoria, in Illinois, to New York, finds a railroad company willing to do this at the rate of fifteen cents per hundred pounds for a car-load, but is compelled to pay at the rate of twenty-five cents per hundred pounds, because the railroad company has received from a person residing at Gilman twenty-five cents per hundred pounds for the transportation of a car-load of the same class of freight over the same line of road from Gilman to New York. This is the result of the statute of Illinois, in its endeavor to prevent unjust discrimination, as construed by the supreme court of that State. The effect of it is that whatever may be the rate of transportation per mile charged by the railroad company from Gilman to Sheldon, a distance of twenty-three miles, in which the loading and the unloading of the freight is the largest expense incurred by the railroad company, the same rate per mile must be charged from Peoria to the city of New York.

The obvious injustice of such a rule as this, which railroad companies are by heavy penalties compelled to conform to, in regard to commerce among the States, when applied to transportation which includes Illinois in a long line of carriage through several States, shows the value of the constitutional provision which confides the power of regulating interstate commerce to the Congress of the United States, whose enlarged view of the interests of all the States, and of the railroads concerned, better fits it to establish just and equitable rules.

Of the justice or propriety of the principle which lies at the foundation of the Illinois statute it is not the province of this court to speak. As restricted to a transportation which begins and ends within the limits of the State, it may be very just and equitable, and it certainly is the province of the state legislature to determine that question. But when it is attempted to apply to transportation through an entire series of States a principle of this kind, and each one of the States shall attempt to establish its own rates of transportation, its own methods to prevent discrimination in rates, or to permit it, the deleterious influence upon the freedom of commerce among the States, and upon the transit of goods through those States, cannot be overestimated. That this species of regulation is one which must be, if established at all, of a general and national character, and cannot be safely and wisely remitted to local rules and local regulations, we think is clear from what has already been said. And if it be a regulation of commerce, as we think we have demonstrated it is, and as the Illinois court concedes it to be, it must be of that national character; and the regulation can only appropriately exist by general rules and principles, which demand that it should be done by the Congress of the United States under the commerce clause of the Constitution.

Judgment reversed.

BRADLEY, J., delivered a dissenting opinion, in which WAITE, C. J., and GRAY, J., concurred.

315. THE DAWES ACT
February 8, 1887
(*U. S. Statutes at Large,* Vol. XXIV, p. 388 ff.)

This act marked the end of a quarter of a century of agitation for reform in our treatment of the Indian problem. It was, said one philanthropist, "the end of a century of dishonor." See, for background, F. E. Leupp, *The Indian and His Problem;* G. W. Manypenny, *Our Indian Wards;* and for the subsequent history of the act, L. F. Schmeckebier, *The Office of Indian Affairs;* L. Meriam, et al., *The Problem of Indian Administration.*

An act to provide for the allotment of lands in severalty to Indians on the various reservations, and to extend the protection of the laws of the United States and the

Territories over the Indians, and for other purposes.

Be it enacted, That in all cases where any tribe or band of Indians has been, or shall hereafter be, located upon any reservation created for their use, either by treaty stipulation or by virtue of an act of Congress or executive order setting apart the same for their use, the President of the United States be, and he hereby is, authorized, whenever in his opinion any reservation or any part thereof of such Indians is advantageous for agriculture and grazing purposes to cause said reservation, or any part thereof, to be surveyed, or resurveyed if necessary, and to allot the lands in said reservation in severalty to any Indian located thereon in quantities as follows:

To each head of a family, one-quarter of a section;

To each single person over eighteen years of age, one-eighth of a section;

To each orphan child under eighteen years of age, one-eighth of a section; and,

To each other single person under eighteen years now living, or who may be born prior to the date of the order of the President directing an allotment of the lands embraced in any reservation, one-sixteenth of a section: . . .

SEC. 5. That upon the approval of the allotments provided for in this act by the Secretary of the Interior, he shall . . . declare that the United States does and will hold the land thus allotted, for the period of twenty-five years, in trust for the sole use and benefit of the Indian to whom such allotment shall have been made, . . . and that at the expiration of said period the United States will convey the same by patent to said Indian, or his heirs as aforesaid, in fee, discharged of such trust and free of all charge or incumbrance whatsoever: . . .

SEC. 6. That upon the completion of said allotments and the patenting of the lands to said allottees, each and every member of the respective bands or tribes of Indians to whom allotments have been made shall have the benefit of and be subject to the laws, both civil and criminal, of the State or Territory in which they may reside; . . . And every Indian born within the territorial limits of the United States to whom allotments shall have been made under the provisions of this act, or under any law or treaty, and every Indian born within the territorial limits of the United States who has voluntarily taken up, within said limits, his residence separate and apart from any tribe of Indians therein, and has adopted the habits of civilized life, is hereby declared to be a citizen of the United States, and is entitled to all the rights, privileges, and immunities of such citizens, whether said Indian has been or not, by birth or otherwise, a member of any tribe of Indians within the territorial limits of the United States without in any manner impairing or otherwise affecting the right of any such Indian to tribal or other property. . . .

316. THE HATCH ACT
March 2, 1887

(U. S. Statutes at Large, Vol. XXIV, p. 400 ff.)

This important act established Agricultural Experiment Stations. See, M. Conover, *The Office of Experiment Stations;* B. H. Hibbard, *History of Public Land Policies,* ch. xvi.

An act to establish agricultural experiment stations in connection with the colleges established in the several States under the provisions of an act approved July second, eighteen hundred and sixty-two, and of the acts supplementary thereto.

Be it enacted, That in order to aid in acquiring and diffusing among the people of the United States useful and practical information on subjects connected with agriculture, and to promote scientific investigation and experiment respecting the principles and applications of agricultural science, there shall be established, under direction of the college or colleges or agricultural department of colleges in each State or Territory established, or which may hereafter be established, in accordance with the provisions of an act approved July second, eighteen hundred and sixty-two, entitled "An act donating public lands to the several States and Territories which may provide colleges for the benefit of agriculture and the mechanic arts," or any of the supplements of said act, a department to be known and designated as an "agricultural experiment station:" Provided, That in any State or Territory in which two such colleges have been or may be so established the appropriation hereinafter made to such State or Territory shall be equally divided between such colleges, unless the legislature of such State or Territory shall otherwise direct.

SEC. 2. That it shall be the object and duty of said experiment stations to conduct original researches or verify experiments on the physiology of plants and animals; the diseases to which they are severally subject, with the remedies for the same; the chemical composition of useful plants at their different stages of growth; the comparative advantages of rotative cropping as pursued under a varying series of crops; the capacity of new plants or trees for acclimation; the analysis of soils and water; the chemical composition of manures, natural or artificial, with experiments designed to test their comparative effects on crops of different kinds; the adaptation and value of grasses and forage plants; the composition and digestibility of the different kinds of food for domestic animals; the scientific and economic questions involved in the production of butter and cheese; and such other researches or experiments bearing directly on the agricultural industry of the United States as may in each case be deemed advisable, having due regard to the varying conditions and needs of the respective States or Territories. . . .

SEC. 5. That for the purpose of paying the necessary expenses of conducting investigations and experiments and printing and distributing the results as hereinbefore prescribed, the sum of fifteen thousand dollars per annum is hereby appropriated to each State, to be specially provided for by Congress in the appropriations from year to year, and to each Territory entitled under the provisions of section eight of this act, out of any money in the Treasury proceeding from the sales of public lands, to be paid in equal quarterly payments, on the first day of January, April, July, and October in each year, to the treasurer or other officer duly appointed by the governing boards of said colleges to receive the same, the first payment to be made on the first day of October, eighteen hundred and eighty-seven. . . .

317. CLEVELAND'S TARIFF MESSAGE OF 1887
December 6, 1887

(Richardson, ed. *Messages and Papers*, Vol. VIII, p. 579 ff.)

President Cleveland focussed the attention of the nation upon the problem of tariff reform by devoting his third annual message to Congress exclusively to this subject. For background, see A. Nevins, *Grover Cleveland*, chs. xvii, xxi; R. McElroy, *Grover Cleveland*, Vol. I, ch. xi; and histories of the tariff by Stanwood, Tarbell, and Taussig.

WASHINGTON, *December 6, 1887.*
To the Congress of the United States:

You are confronted at the threshold of your legislative duties with a condition of the national finances which imperatively demands immediate and careful consideration.

The amount of money annually exacted, through the operation of present laws, from the industries and necessities of the people largely exceeds the sum necessary to meet the expenses of the Government.

When we consider that the theory of our institutions guarantees to every citizen the full enjoyment of all the fruits of his industry and enterprise, with only such deduction as may be his share toward the careful and economical maintenance of the Government which protects him, it is plain that the exaction of more than this is indefensible extortion and a culpable betrayal of American fairness and justice. This wrong inflicted upon those who bear the burden of national taxation, like other wrongs, multiplies a brood of evil consequences. The public Treasury, which should only exist as a conduit conveying the people's tribute to its legitimate objects of expenditure, becomes a hoarding place for money needlessly withdrawn from trade and the people's use, thus crippling our national energies, suspending our country's development, preventing investment in productive enterprise, threatening financial disturbance, and inviting schemes of public plunder. . . .

In the present state of legislation the only pretense of any existing executive power to restore at this time any part of our surplus revenues to the people by its expenditure consists in the supposition that the Secretary of the Treasury may enter the market and purchase the bonds of the Government not yet due, at a rate of premium to be agreed upon. . . .

In considering the question of purchasing

bonds as a means of restoring to circulation the surplus money accumulating in the Treasury, it should be borne in mind that premiums must of course be paid upon such purchase, that there may be a large part of these bonds held as investments which can not be purchased at any price, and that combinations among holders who are willing to sell may unreasonably enhance the cost of such bonds to the Government. . . .

I have deemed it my duty to thus bring to the knowledge of my countrymen, as well as to the attention of their representatives charged with the responsibility of legislative relief, the gravity of our financial situation. . . .

Our scheme of taxation, by means of which this needless surplus is taken from the people and put into the public Treasury, consists of a tariff or duty levied upon importations from abroad and internal-revenue taxes levied upon the consumption of tobacco and spirituous and malt liquors. . . .

. . . Our present tariff laws, the vicious, inequitable, and illogical source of unnecessary taxation, ought to be at once revised and amended. These laws, as their primary and plain effect, raise the price to consumers of all articles imported and subject to duty by precisely the sum paid for such duties. Thus the amount of the duty measures the tax paid by those who purchase for use these imported articles. Many of these things, however, are raised or manufactured in our own country, and the duties now levied upon foreign goods and products are called protection to these home manufactures, because they render it possible for those of our people who are manufacturers to make these taxed articles and sell them for a price equal to that demanded for the imported goods that have paid customs duty. So it happens that while comparatively a few use the imported articles, millions of our people, who never used and never saw any of the foreign products, purchase and use things of the same kind made in this country, and pay therefor nearly or quite the same enhanced price which the duty adds to the imported articles. Those who buy imports pay the duty charged thereon into the public Treasury, but the great majority of our citizens, who buy domestic articles of the same class, pay a sum at least approximately equal to this

duty to the home manufacturer. This reference to the operation of our tariff laws is not made by way of instruction, but in order that we may be constantly reminded of the manner in which they impose a burden upon those who consume domestic products as well as those who consume imported articles, and thus create a tax upon all our people.

It is not proposed to entirely relieve the country of this taxation. It must be extensively continued as the source of the Government's income; and in a readjustment of our tariff the interests of American labor engaged in manufacture should be carefully considered, as well as the preservation of our manufacturers. It may be called protection or by any other name, but relief from the hardships and dangers of our present tariff laws should be devised with especial precaution against imperiling the existence of our manufacturing interests. But this existence should not mean a condition which, without regard to the public welfare or a national exigency, must always insure the realization of immense profits instead of moderately profitable returns. As the volume and diversity of our national activities increase, new recruits are added to those who desire a continuation of the advantages which they conceive the present system of tariff taxation directly affords them. So stubbornly have all efforts to reform the present condition been resisted by those of our fellow-citizens thus engaged that they can hardly complain of the suspicion, entertained to a certain extent, that there exists an organized combination all along the line to maintain their advantage. . . .

It is also said that the increase in the price of domestic manufactures resulting from the present tariff is necessary in order that higher wages may be paid to our workingmen employed in manufactories than are paid for what is called the pauper labor of Europe. . . .

By the last census it is made to appear that of the 17,392,099 of our population engaged in all kinds of industries 7,670,493 are employed in agriculture, 4,074,238 in professional and personal service (2,934,876 of whom are domestic servants and laborers), while 1,810,256 are employed in trade and transportation and 2,623,089 employed in such manufacturing industries as are claimed to be benefited by a high tariff.

Their compensation, as it may be affected by the operation of tariff laws, should at all times be scrupuously kept in view; and yet with slight reflection they will not overlook the fact that they are consumers with the rest; that they too have their own wants and those of their families to supply from their earnings, and that the price of the necessaries of life, as well as the amount of their wages, will regulate the measure of their welfare and comfort. . . .

Nor can the worker in manufactures fail to understand that while a high tariff is claimed to be necessary to allow the payment of remunerative wages, it certainly results in a very large increase in the price of nearly all sorts of manufactures, which, in almost countless forms, he needs for the use of himself and his family. . . .

In speaking of the increased cost to the consumer of our home manufactures resulting from a duty laid upon imported articles of the same description, the fact is not overlooked that competition among our domestic producers sometimes has the effect of keeping the price of their products below the highest limit allowed by such duty. But it is notorious that this competition is too often strangled by combinations quite prevalent at this time, and frequently called trusts, which have for their object the regulation of the supply and price of commodities made and sold by members of the combination. The people can hardly hope for any consideration in the operation of these selfish schemes.

If, however, in the absence of such combination, a healthy and free competition reduces the price of any particular dutiable article of home production below the limit which it might otherwise reach under our tariff laws, and if with such reduced price its manufacture continues to thrive, it is entirely evident that one thing has been discovered which should be carefully scrutinized in an effort to reduce taxation.

The necessity of combination to maintain the price of any commodity to the tariff point furnishes proof that someone is willing to accept lower prices for such commodity and that such prices are remunerative; and lower prices produced by competition prove the same thing. Thus where either of these

conditions exists a case would seem to be presented for an easy reduction of taxation.

The considerations which have been presented touching our tariff laws are intended only to enforce an earnest recommendation that the surplus revenues of the Government be prevented by the reduction of our customs duties, and at the same time to emphasize a suggestion that in accomplishing this purpose we may discharge a double duty to our people by granting to them a measure of relief from tariff taxation in quarters where it is most needed and from sources where it can be most fairly and justly accorded. . . .

The difficulty attending a wise and fair revision of our tariff laws is not underestimated. It will require on the part of the Congress great labor and care, and especially a broad and national contemplation of the subject and a patriotic disregard of such local and selfish claims as are unreasonable and reckless of the welfare of the entire country.

Under our present laws more than 4,000 articles are subject to duty. Many of these do not in any way compete with our own manufactures, and many are hardly worth attention as subjects of revenue. A considerable reduction can be made in the aggregate by adding them to the free list. The taxation of luxuries presents no features of hardship; but the necessaries of life used and consumed by all the people, the duty upon which adds to the cost of living in every home, should be greatly cheapened.

The radical reduction of the duties imposed upon raw material used in manufacturies, or its free importation, is of course an important factor in any effort to reduce the price of these necessaries. It would not only relieve them from the increased cost caused by the tariff on such material, but the manufactured product being thus cheapened that part of the tariff now laid upon such product, as a compensation to our manufacturers for the present price of raw material, could be accordingly modified. Such reduction or free importation would serve besides to largely reduce the revenue. It is not apparent how such a change can have any injurious effect upon our manufacturers. On the contrary, it would appear to give them a better chance in foreign markets with the manufacturers of other countries, who cheapen their wares by free material.

Thus our people might have the opportunity of extending their sales beyond the limits of home consumption, saving them from the depression, interruption in business, and loss caused by a glutted domestic market and affording their employees more certain and steady labor, with its resulting quiet and contentment. . . .

Our progress toward a wise conclusion will not be improved by dwelling upon the theories of protection and free trade. This savors too much of bandying epithets. It is a *condition* which confronts us, not a theory.

Relief from this condition may involve a slight reduction of the advantages which we award our home productions, but the entire withdrawal of such advantages should not be contemplated. The question of free trade is absolutely irrelevant, and the persistent claim made in certain quarters that all the efforts to relieve the people from unjust and unnecessary taxation are schemes of so-called free traders is mischievous and far removed from any consideration for the public good. . . .

318. THE INTERSTATE COMMERCE ACT
February 4, 1887
(*U. S. Statutes at Large,* Vol. XXIV, p. 379 ff.)

The exclusive character of Federal regulation of interstate commerce had been established as early as 1824 in *Gibbons* v. *Ogden,* Doc. No. 129, yet it was not until over half a century later that Congress passed any law looking to national regulation of commerce. State regulation of railroads, such as the Granger laws, had proved unsatisfactory, and the Wabash Case, Doc. No. 314, indicated the urgent necessity of national regulation. On the Act, see, D. R. Dewey, *National Problems,* ch. vi; B. H. Meyer, *Railway Legislation in the United States;* W. Z. Ripley, *Railroads: Rates and Regulation;* the Cullom Report, which largely influenced the character of the Act, is in the *Report of the Senate Select Committee on Interstate Commerce,* 49 Cong. 1 Sess. Sen. Report No. 46. See also, C. A. Miller, *Legislative History of the Interstate Commerce Act;* I. L. Sharfman, *The Interstate Commerce Commission,* 4 vols.

An act to regulate commerce.

Be it enacted . . . , That the provisions of this act shall apply to any common carrier or carriers engaged in the transportation of passengers or property wholly by railroad, or partly by railroad and partly by water when both are used, under a common control, management, or arrangement, for a continuous carriage or shipment, from one State or Territory of the United States, or the District of Columbia, to any other State or Territory of the United States, or the District of Columbia, or from any place in the United States to an adjacent foreign country, or from any place in the United States through a foreign country to any other place

in the United States, and also to the transportation in like manner of property shipped from any place in the United States to a foreign country and carried from such place to a port of transshipment, or shipped from a foreign country to any place in the United States and carried to such place from a port of entry either in the United States or an adjacent foreign country: *Provided, however,* That the provisions of this act shall not apply to the transportation of passengers or property, or to the receiving, delivering, storage, or handling of property, wholly within one State, and not shipped to or from a foreign country from or to any State or Territory as aforesaid.

The term "railroad" as used in this act shall include all bridges and ferries used or operated in connection with any railroad, and also all the road in use by any corporation operating a railroad, whether owned or operated under a contract, agreement, or lease; and the term "transportation" shall include all instrumentalities of shipment or carriage.

All charges made for any service rendered or to be rendered in the transportation of passengers or property as aforesaid, or in connection therewith, or for the receiving, delivering, storage, or handling of such property, shall be reasonable and just; and every unjust and unreasonable charge for such service is prohibited and declared to be unlawful.

SEC. 2. That if any common carrier subject to the provisions of this act shall, directly or indirectly, by any special rate, rebate, drawback, or other device, charge, demand, collect, or receive from any person or persons a greater or less compensation for any service rendered, or to be rendered, in the transportation of passengers or property, subject to the provisions of this act, than it charges, demands, collects, or receives from any other person or persons for doing for him or them a like and contemporaneous service in the transportation of a like kind of traffic under substantially similar circumstances and conditions, such common carrier shall be deemed guilty of unjust discrimination, which is hereby prohibited and declared to be unlawful.

SEC. 3. That it shall be unlawful for any common carrier subject to the provisions of this act to make or give any undue or unreasonable preference or advantage to any particular person, company, firm, corporation, or locality, or any particular description of traffic, in any respect whatsoever, or to subject any particular person, company, firm, corporation, or locality, or any particular description of traffic, to any undue or unreasonable prejudice or disadvantage in any respect whatsoever.

Every common carrier subject to the provisions of this act shall, according to their respective powers, afford all reasonable, proper, and equal facilities for the interchange of traffic between their respective lines, and for the receiving, forwarding, and delivering of passengers and property to and from their several lines and those connecting therewith, and shall not discriminate in their rates and charges between such connecting lines; but this shall not be construed as requiring any such common carrier to give the use of its tracks or terminal facilities to another carrier engaged in like business.

SEC. 4. That it shall be unlawful for any common carrier subject to the provisions of this act to charge or receive any greater compensation in the aggregate for the transportation of passengers or of like kind of property, under substantially similar circumstances and conditions, for a shorter than for a longer distance over the same line, in the same direction, the shorter being included within the longer distance; but this shall not be construed as authorizing any common carrier within the terms of this act to charge and receive as great compensation for a shorter as for a longer distance: *Provided, however,* That upon application to the Commission appointed under the provisions of this act, such common carrier may, in special cases, after investigation by the Commission, be authorized to charge less for longer than for shorter distances for the transportation of passengers or property; and the Commission may from time to time prescribe the extent to which such designated common carrier may be relieved from the operation of this section of this act.

SEC. 5. That it shall be unlawful for any common carrier subject to the provisions of this act to enter into any contract, agreement, or combination with any other common carrier or carriers for the pooling of freights of different and competing railroads, or to divide between them the aggregrate or net proceeds of the earnings of such railroads, or any portion thereof; and in any case of an agreement for the pooling of freights as aforesaid, each day of its continuance shall be deemed a separate offense.

SEC. 6. That every common carrier subject to the provisions of this act shall print and keep for public inspection schedules showing the rates and fares and charges for the transportation of passengers and property which any such common carrier has established and which are in force at the time upon its railroad, as defined by the first section of this act. . . . Copies for the use of the public shall be kept in every depot or station upon any such railroad, in such places and in such form that they can be conveniently inspected. . . .

No advance shall be made in the rates, fares, and charges which have been established and published as aforesaid by any common carrier in compliance with the requirements of this section, except after ten days' public notice, which shall plainly state the changes proposed to be made in the schedule then in force, and the time when the increased rates, fares, or charges will go into effect. . . .

And when any such common carrier shall have established and published its rates, fares, and charges in compliance with the provisions of this section, it shall be unlawful for such common carrier to charge, demand, collect, or receive from any person or persons a greater or less compensation for the transportation of passengers or property, or for any services in connection therewith, than is specified in such published schedule of rates, fares, and charges as may at the time be in force.

Every common carrier subject to the provisions of this act shall file with the Commission hereinafter provided for copies of its schedules of rates, fares, and charges which have been established and published in compliance with the requirements of this section, and shall promptly notify said Commission of all changes made in the same. Every such common carrier shall also file with said Commission copies of all contracts, agreements, or arrangements with other common carriers in relation to any traffic affected by the provisions of this act to which it may be a party. . . .

SEC. 9. That any person or persons claiming to be damaged by any common carrier subject to the provisions of this act may either make complaint to the Commission as hereinafter provided for, or may bring suit in his or their own behalf for the recovery of the damages for which such common carrier may be liable under the provisions of this act, in any district or circuit court of the United States of competent jurisdiction . . .

SEC. 10. That any common carrier subject to the provisions of this act, or, whenever such common carrier is a corporation, any director or officer thereof, or any receiver, trustee, lessee, agent, or person acting for or employed by such corporation, who, alone or with any other corporation, company, person, or party, . . . shall be guilty of any infraction of this act, or shall aid or abet therein, shall be deemed guilty of a misdemeanor, and shall, upon conviction thereof in any district court of the United States within the jurisdiction of which such offense was committed, be subject to a fine of not to exceed five thousand dollars for each offense.

SEC. 11. That a Commission is hereby created and established to be known as the Inter-State Commerce Commission, which shall be composed of five Commissioners, who shall be appointed by the President, by and with the advice and consent of the Senate. The Commissioners first appointed under this act shall continue in office for the term of two, three, four, five, and six years, respectively, from January 1, 1887, the term of each to be designated by the President; but their successors shall be appointed for terms of six years. . . . Any Commissioner may be removed by the President for inefficiency, neglect of duty, or malfeasance in office. Not more than three of the Commissioners shall be appointed from the same political party. No person in the employ of or holding any official relation to any common carrier subject to the provisions of this act, or owning stock or bonds thereof, or who is in any manner pecuniarily interested therein, shall enter upon the duties of or hold such office. Said Commissioners shall not engage in any other business, vocation, or employment. No vacancy in the Commission shall impair the right of the remaining Commissioners to exercise all the powers of the Commission.

SEC. 12. That the Commission hereby created shall have authority to inquire into the management of the business of all common carriers subject to the provisions of this act, and shall keep itself informed as to the manner and method in which the same is conducted, and shall have the right to obtain from such common carriers full and complete information necessary to enable the Commission to perform the duties and carry out the objects for which it was created; and for the purposes of this act the Commission shall have power to require the attendance and testimony of witnesses and the production of all books, papers, tariffs, contracts, agreements, and documents relating to any matter under investigation, and to that end may invoke the aid of any court of the United States in requiring the attendance and testimony of witnesses and the production of books, papers, and documents under the provisions of this section. . . .

SEC. 13. That any person, firm, corporation, or association, or any mercantile, agricultural, or manufacturing society, or any body politic or municipal organization complaining of anything done or omitted to be done by any common carrier subject to the provisions of this act in contravention of the provisions thereof, may apply to said Commission by petition, which shall briefly state the facts; whereupon a statement of the charges thus made shall be forwarded by the Commission to such common carrier, who shall be called upon to satisfy the complaint or to answer the same in writing within a reasonable time, to be specified by the Commission. . . . If there shall appear to be any reasonable ground for investigating said complaint, it shall be the duty of the Commission to investigate the matters complained of in such manner and by such means as it shall deem proper.

Said Commission shall in like manner investigate any complaint forwarded by the railroad commissioner or railroad commission of any State or Territory, at the request of such commissioner or commission, and may institute any inquiry on its own motion in the same manner and to the same effect as though complaint had been made. . . .

SEC. 16. That whenever any common carrier, . . . shall violate or refuse or neglect to obey any lawful order or requirement of the Commission in this act named, it shall be the duty of the Commission, and lawful for any company or person interested in such order or requirement, to apply, in a summary way, by petition, to the circuit court of the United States sitting in equity in the judicial district in which the common carrier complained of has its principal office, or in which the violation or disobedience of such order or requirement shall happen, alleging such violation or disobedience, as the case may be; and the said court shall have power to hear and determine the matter, on such short notice to the common carrier complained of as the court shall deem reasonable. . . .

SEC. 20. That the Commission is hereby authorized to require annual reports from all common carriers subject to the provisions of this act, fix the time and prescribe the manner in which such reports shall be made, and to require from such carriers specific answers to all questions upon which the Commission may need information. Such reports shall also contain such information in relation to rates or regulations concerning fares or freights, or agreements, arrangements, or contracts with other common carriers, as the Commission may require; and the said Commission may, within its discretion, for the purpose of enabling it the better to carry out the purposes of this act, prescribe (if in the opinion of the Commission it is practicable to prescribe such uniformity and methods of keeping accounts) a period of time within which all common carriers subject to the provisions of this act shall have, as near as may be, a uniform system of accounts, and the manner in which such accounts shall be kept. . . .

319. THE JUDICIAL REVIEW OF RAILROAD RATES

Beginning with the Granger laws of the late sixties and early seventies, many mid-western and southern States established railway commissions with the power of fixing railway charges; that the State had the power thus to regulate charges was established in the Granger Cases of 1876. See Doc. No. 294. Obviously the charges fixed by the state, or its instruments, had to be reasonable, and not confiscatory. But who was to decide whether a rate was reasonable, and what was to be the basis upon which these charges were to be predicated? These and related questions have plagued the Courts for the last half-century, and no satisfactory solution has yet been discovered. The opinions below illustrate the process whereby the Court came to insist (1) that due process requires provision for judicial review, and (2) that the rates must be high enough to yield a fair return on a fair valuation of the property. The ingenuity of the Courts, however, has not yet been sufficient to devise a means whereby a fair valuation of railroad property might be determined and a rate fixed that is fair both to the roads and to the public. For a general treatment of the problem of rate regulation, see, W. Z. Ripley, *Railroads: Rates and Regulation;* A. T. Hadley, *Railroad Transportation, its History and its Law;* F. A. Cleveland and F. W. Powell, *Railway Promotion and Capitalization in the United States.*

1. CHICAGO, MILWAUKEE AND ST. PAUL
RAILROAD CO. V. MINNESOTA
134 U.S., 418
1889

Error to the Supreme Court of Minnesota. BLATCHFORD, J. . . . This being the construction of the statute by which we are bound in considering the present case, we are of the opinion, that, so construed, it conflicts with the Constitution of the United

States in the particulars complained of by the railroad company. It deprives the company of its right to a judicial investigation, by due process of law, under the forms and with the machinery provided by the wisdom of successive ages for the investigation judicially of the truth of a matter in controversy, and substitutes therefor, as an absolute finality, the action of a railroad commission which, in view of the powers conceded to it by the State court, cannot be regarded as clothed with judicial functions or possessing the machinery of a court of justice. . . .

Under the second section of the statute in question, it is provided that all charges made by a common carrier for the transportation of passengers or property shall be equal and reasonable. Under this provision, the carrier has a right to make equal and reasonable charges for such transportation. In the present case, the return alleged that the rate of charge fixed by the commission was not equal or reasonable, and the Supreme Court held that the statute deprived the company of the right to show that judicially. The question of the reasonableness of a rate of charge for transportation by a railroad company, involving as it does the element of reasonableness both as regards the company and as regards the public, is eminently a question for judicial investigation, requiring due process of law for its determination. If the company is deprived of the power of charging reasonable rates for the use of its property, and such deprivation takes place in the absence of an investigation by judicial machinery, it is deprived of the lawful use of its property, and thus, in substance and effect, of the property itself, without due process of law and in violation of the Constitution of the United States; and in so far as it is thus deprived, while other persons are permitted to receive reasonable profits upon their invested capital, the company is deprived of the equal protection of the laws. . . .

BRADLEY, J., dissenting: I cannot agree to the decision of the court in this case. It practically overrules *Munn* v. *Illinois,* and the several railroad cases that were decided at the same time. The governing principle of those cases was that the regulation and settlement of the fares of railroads and other accommodations is a legislative prerogative

and not a judicial one. This is a principle which I regard as of great importance. . . .

It is always a delicate thing for the courts to make an issue with the legislative department of the government, and they should never do so if it is possible to avoid it. By the decision now made we declare, in effect, that the judiciary, and not the legislature, is the final arbiter in the regulation of fares and freights of railroads and the charges of other public accommodations. It is an assumption of authority on the part of the judiciary which, it seems to me, . . . it has no right to make. . . . It is complained that the decisions of the board are final and without appeal. So are the decisions of the courts in matters within their jurisdiction. There must be a final tribunal somewhere for deciding every question in the world. Injustice may take place in all tribunals. All human institutions are imperfect—courts as well as commissions and legislatures. Whatever tribunal has jurisdiction, its decisions are final and conclusive unless an appeal is given therefrom The important question always is, what is the lawful tribunal for the particular case? In my judgement, in the present case, the proper tribunal was the legislature, or board of commissioners which it created for that purpose. . . .

2. SMYTH v. AMES
169 U.S. 466
1897

Appeal from the Circuit Court of the United States for the district of Nebraska. The legislature of Nebraska by act of April 12, 1893 established a schedule of rates for railroad transportation radically reducing the rates then in effect. Bondholders of the Union Pacific and other railroads affected sought an injunction restraining the railroads from putting the new schedules into effect. The Circuit Court granted the injunction.

HARLAN, J. . . . The power to enact the statute whose validity is now assailed, . . . regulating railroads, classifying freights, fixing reasonable maximum rates, etc., in Nebraska, was referred by counsel to the general legislative power of the state as well as to the 4th section of article 11 of the State Constitution, which provides: "Railways heretofore constructed, or that may hereafter be constructed in this state, are hereby declared public highways. . . . And the legislature may from time to time pass laws establishing reasonable maximum rates of charges for the transportation of passengers and freight on the different railroads in this state." . . .

We are now to inquire whether the Nebraska statute is repugnant to the Constitution of the United States.

By the 14th Amendment it is provided that no state shall deprive any person of property without due process of law nor deny to any person within its jurisdiction the equal protection of the laws. That corporations are persons within the meaning of this Amendment is now settled. What amounts to deprivation of property without due process of law or what is a denial of the equal protection of the laws is often difficult to determine, especially where the question relates to the property of a quasi-public corporation and the extent to which it may be subjected to public control. But this court, speaking by Chief Justice Waite, has said that, while a state has power to fix the charges for railroad companies for the transportation of persons and property within its own jurisdiction, unless restrained by valid contract, or unless what is done amounts to a regulation of foreign or interstate commerce, such power is not without limit; and that "under pretense of regulating fares, and freights, the state cannot require a railroad corporation to carry persons or property without reward; neither can it do that which in law amounts to a taking of private property for public use without just compensation, or without due process of law." . . .

The plaintiffs contended that a railroad company is entitled to exact such charges for transportation as will enable it, at all times, not only to pay operating expenses, but also to meet the interest regularly accruing upon all its outstanding obligations, and justify a dividend upon all its stock; and that to prohibit it from maintaining rates or charges for transportation adequate to *all* those ends will deprive it of its property without due process of law, and deny to it the equal protection of the laws. This contention should not be passed without examination.

In our opinion the broad proposition advanced by counsel involves some misconception of the relations between the public and a railroad corporation. It is unsound in that it practically excludes from consideration the fair value of the property used, omits altogether any consideration of the right of the public to be exempt from unreasonable exactions, and makes the interests of the corporation maintaining a public highway the sole test in determining whether the rates established by or for it are such as may be rightfully prescribed as between it and the public. . . .

What was said in *Covington & L. Turnpike* v. *Sandford* is pertinent to the question under consideration. It was there observed: ". . . It is alleged here that the rates prescribed are unreasonable and unjust to the company and its stockholders. But that involves an inquiry as to what is reasonable and just for the public. . . . The public cannot properly be subjected to unreasonable rates in order simply that stockholders may earn dividends. The legislature has the authority, in every case where its power has not been restrained by contract, to proceed upon the ground that the public may not rightfully be required to submit to unreasonable exactions for the use of a public highway established and maintained under legislative authority. If a corporation cannot maintain such a highway and earn dividends for stockholders it is a misfortune for it and them which the Constitution does not require to be remedied by imposing unjust burdens upon the public."

We hold, however, that the basis of all calculations as to the reasonableness of rates to be charged by a corporation maintaining a highway under legislative sanction must be the fair value of the property being used by it for the convenience of the public. And, in order to ascertain that value, the original cost of construction, the amount expended in permanent improvements, the amount and market value of its bonds and stocks, the present as compared with the original cost of construction, the probable earning capacity of the property, under particular rates prescribed by statute, and the sum required to meet operating expenses, are all matters for consideration, and are to be given such weight as may be just and right in each case.

We do not say that there may not be other matters to be regarded in estimating the value of the property. What the company is entitled to ask is a fair return upon the value of that which it employs for the public convenience. On the other hand, what the public is entitled to demand is that no more be exacted from it for the use of a public highway than the services rendered by it are reasonably worth.

Decree of the Circuit Court affirmed.

3. REGAN V. FARMERS' LOAN AND TRUST COMPANY
154 U.S. 362
1894

Appeal from the United States circuit court for the Western District of Texas.

BREWER, J. . . . Passing from the question of jurisdiction to the act itself, there can be no doubt of the general power of a State to regulate the fares and freights which may be charged and received by railroads or other carriers, and that this regulation may be carried on by means of a commission. Such a commission is merely an administrative board created by the State for carrying into effect the will of the State, as expressed by its legislation. No valid objection, therefore, can be made on account of the general features of this act; those by which the State has created the railroad commission and entrusted it with the duty of prescribing rates of fares and freights as well as other regulations for the management of the railroads of the State. . . .

It appears from the bill that, in pursuance of the powers given to it by this act, the state commission has made a body of rates for fares and freights. This body of rates, as a whole, is challenged by the plaintiff as unreasonable, unjust, and working a destruction of its rights of property. The defendant denies the power of the court to entertain an inquiry into that matter, insisting that the fixing of rates for carriage by a public carrier is a matter wholly within the power of the legislative department of the government and beyond examination by the courts.

It is doubtless true, as a general proposition, that the formation of a tariff of charges for the transportation by a common carrier of persons or property is a legislative or ad-

ministrative rather than a judicial function. Yet it has always been recognized that, if a carrier attempted to charge a shipper an unreasonable sum, the courts had jurisdiction to inquire into that matter and to award to the shipper any amount exacted from him in excess of a reasonable rate; and also in a reverse case to render judgment in favor of the carrier for the amount found to be a reasonable charge. The province of the courts is not changed, nor the limit of judicial inquiry altered, because the legislature instead of the carrier prescribes the rates. The courts are not authorized to revise or change the body of rates imposed by a legislature or a commission; they do not determine whether one rate is preferable to another, or what under all circumstances would be fair and reasonable as between the carriers and the shippers; they do not engage in any mere administrative work; but still there can be no doubt of their power and duty to inquire whether a body of rates prescribed by a legislature or a commission is unjust and unreasonable, and such as to work a practical destruction to rights of property, and, if found to be so, to restrain its operation. In *Chicago, Burlington & Quincy Railroad* v. *Iowa,* and in *Peik* v. *Chicago & Northwestern Railway,* the question of legislative control over railroads was presented, and it was held that the fixing of rates was not a matter within the absolute discretion of the carriers, but was subject to legislative control. . . .

These cases all support the proposition that while it is not the province of the courts to enter upon the merely administrative duty of framing a tariff of rates for carriage, it is within the scope of judicial power and a part of judicial duty to restrain anything which, in the form of a regulation of rates, operates to deny to the owners of property invested in the business of transportation that equal protection which is the constitutional right of all owners of other property. There is nothing new or strange in this. It has always been a part of the judicial function to determine whether the act of one party (whether that party be a single individual, an organized body, or the public as a whole) operates to divest the other party of any rights of person or property. . . . It was, therefore, within the competency of the circuit court of the United States for the Western District of Texas, at the instance of the plaintiff, a citizen of another State, to enter upon an inquiry as to the reasonableness and justice of the rates prescribed by the railroad commission. . . .

320. THE SHERMAN ANTI-TRUST ACT
July 2, 1890
(*U. S. Statutes at Large,* Vol. XXVI, p. 209)

The growth of trusts and corporations, and some of the more notorious malpractices of big business, led to a growing demand for the regulation of trusts by the Federal Government. Both parties demanded such regulation in their platforms of 1888. December 4, 1889, Senator Sherman introduced a bill providing for the regulation of trusts. The final bill, which bears Sherman's name, was written chiefly by Senators Hoar and Edmunds. The first federal act ever passed which attempted to regulate trusts, it was couched in general and often ambiguous language. The bill contains no definition of a trust, or of a monopoly, and no indication of the meaning of the term "restraint". Nor was it clear at the time of the passage of the act whether its terms were meant to embrace combinations of labor as well as of capital. These, and similar questions, were deliberately left to the Courts. The literature on the Sherman Act is extensive. For the legislative background, see *Bills and Debates in Congress relating to Trusts,* 57th Congress, 2nd Sess., Sen. Doc. No. 147; A. H. Walker, *History of the Sherman Law;* J. D. Clark, *The Federal Trust Policy.* The most complete single volume on the trust problem is H. R. Seager and C. A. Gulick, *Trust and Corporation Problems.* The *Anti-Trust Decisions* have been collected in some twelve volumes. On the application of the Sherman Act to labor, see Docs. No. 326, 335. On the "rule of reason" see Doc. No. 375.

An ACT To protect trade and commerce against unlawful restraints and monopolies. . . .

Be it enacted

SEC. 1. Every contract, combination in the form of trust or otherwise, or conspiracy, in restraint of trade or commerce among the several States, or with foreign nations, is hereby declared to be illegal. Every person who shall make any such contract or engage in any such combination or conspiracy, shall be deemed guilty of a misdemeanor, and, on conviction thereof, shall be punished by fine not exceeding five thousand dollars, or by imprisonment not exceeding one year, or by both said punishments, in the discretion of the court.

SEC. 2. Every person who shall monopolize, or attempt to monopolize, or combine or conspire with any other person or persons, to monopolize any part of the trade or commerce among the several States, or with foreign nations, shall be deemed guilty of a misdemeanor, and, on conviction thereof, shall be punished by fine not exceeding five thousand dollars, or by imprisonment not exceeding one year, or by both said punishments, in the discretion of the court.

SEC. 3. Every contract, combination in form of trust or otherwise, or conspiracy, in restraint of trade or commerce in any Territory of the United States or of the District of Columbia, or in restraint of trade or commerce between any such Territory and another, or between any such Territory or Territories and any State or States or the District of Columbia, or with foreign nations, or between the District of Columbia and any State or States or foreign nations, is hereby declared illegal. Every person who shall make any such contract or engage in any such combination or conspiracy, shall be deemed guilty of a misdemeanor, and, on conviction thereof, shall be punished by fine not exceeding five thousand dollars, or by imprisonment not exceeding one year, or by both said punishments, in the discretion of the court.

SEC. 4. The several circuit courts of the United States are hereby invested with jurisdiction to prevent and restrain violations of this act; and it shall be the duty of the several district attorneys of the United States, in their respective districts, under the direction of the Attorney-General, to institute proceedings in equity to prevent and restrain such violations. Such proceedings may be by way of petition setting forth the case and praying that such violation shall be enjoined or otherwise prohibited. When the parties complained of shall have been duly notified of such petition the courts shall proceed, as soon as may be, to the hearing and determination of the case; and pending such petition and before final decrees, the court may at any time make such temporary restraining order or prohibition as shall be deemed just in the premises.

SEC. 5. Whenever it shall appear to the court before which any proceeding under Section four of this act may be pending, that the ends of justice require that other parties should be brought before the court, the court may cause them to be summoned, whether they reside in the district in which the court is held or not; and subpœnas to that end may be served in any district by the marshal thereof.

SEC. 6. Any property owned under any contract or by any combination, or pursuant to any conspiracy (and being the subject thereof) mentioned in section one of this act, and being in the course of transportation from one State to another, or to a foreign country, shall be forfeited to the United States, and may be seized and condemned by like proceedings as those provided by law for the forfeiture, seizure, and condemnation of property imported into the United States contrary to law.

SEC. 7. Any person who shall be injured in his business or property by any other person or corporation by reason of anything forbidden or declared to be unlawful by this act, may sue therefor in any circuit court of the United States in the district in which the defendant resides or is found, without respect to the amount in controversy, and shall recover threefold the damages by him sustained, and the costs of suit, including a reasonable attorney's fee.

SEC. 8. That the word "person," or "persons," wherever used in this act shall be deemed to include corporations and associations existing under or authorized by the laws of either the United States, the laws of any of the Territories, the laws of any State, or the laws of any foreign country.

321. THE SHERMAN SILVER PURCHASE ACT
July 14, 1890
(U. S. Statutes at Large, Vol. XXVI, p. 289 ff.)

Both the free silver and the gold elements were dissatisfied with the Bland-Allison Act of 1878. The Sherman Act of 1890 represented another compromise, but one on the whole more favorable to the silver elements, because it provided for the purchase of practically the entire domestic output of silver. The concessions made to silver were in return for western support to the McKinley tariff of 1890. See, D. R. Dewey, *Financial History of the United States,* ch. xix; A. B. Hepburn, *History of Currency,* ch. xvi; A. D. Noyes, *Forty Years of American Finance;* J. Sherman, *Recollections,* Vol. II; F. Wellborn, "Influence of the Silver Republicans, 1889–1891," *Miss. Valley Hist. Rev.,* Vol. XIV.

An act directing the purchase of silver bullion and the issue of Treasury notes thereon, and for other purposes.

Be it enacted . . . , That the Secretary of the Treasury is hereby directed to purchase, from time to time, silver bullion to the aggregate amount of four million five hundred thousand ounces, or so much thereof as may be offered in each month, at the market price thereof, not exceeding one dollar for three hundred and seventy-one and twenty-five hundredths grains of pure silver, and to issue in payment for such purchases of silver bullion Treasury notes of the United States to be prepared by the Secretary of the Treasury, in such form and of such denominations, not less than one dollar nor more than one thousand dollars, as he may prescribe. . . .

SEC. 2. That the Treasury notes issued in accordance with the provisions of this act shall be redeemable on demand, in coin, at the Treasury of the United States, or at the office of any assistant treasurer of the United States, and when so redeemed may be reissued; but no greater or less amount of such notes shall be outstanding at any time than the cost of the silver bullion and the standard silver dollars coined therefrom, then held in the Treasury purchased by such notes; and such Treasury notes shall be a legal tender in payment of all debts, public and private, except where otherwise expressly stipulated in the contract, and shall be receivable for customs, taxes, and all public dues, and when so received may be reissued; and such notes, when held by any national banking association, may be counted as a part of its lawful reserve. That upon demand of the holder of any of the Treasury notes herein provided for the Secretary of the Treasury shall, under such regulations as he may prescribe, redeem such notes in gold or silver coin, at his discretion, it being the established policy of the United States to maintain the two metals on a parity with each other upon the present legal ratio, or such ratio as may be provided by law.

SEC. 3. That the Secretary of the Treasury shall each month coin two million ounces of the silver bullion purchased under the provisions of this act into standard dollars until July 1, 1891, and after that time he shall coin of the silver bullion purchased under the provisions of this act as much as may be necessary to provide for the redemption of the Treasury notes herein provided for, and any gain or seigniorage arising from such coinage shall be accounted for and paid into the Treasury. . . .

322. CLEVELAND'S SILVER LETTER
February 10, 1891
Letter to E. Ellery Anderson of the Reform Club
(*Letters of Grover Cleveland,* ed. by Allan Nevins, p. 245–6)

This letter was one of the dramatic incidents of the silver struggle. In January, 1891, a free silver bill had passed the Senate, largely through Democratic support, and it was widely believed that Cleveland was drifting toward support of the silver cause. This letter to the Reform Club dramatically announced his unalterable opposition to free silver and aligned him with the conservative eastern wing of the Democratic Party. For background, see A. Nevins, *Grover Cleveland,* p. 465 ff.

New York, February 10, 1891

I have this afternoon received your note inviting me to attend tomorrow evening the meeting called for the purpose of voicing the opposition of the business men of our city to the 'free coinage of silver in the United States.'

I shall not be able to attend and address the meeting as you request, but I am glad that the business interests of New York are at last to be heard from on this subject.

It surely cannot be necessary for me to make a formal expression of my agreement with those who believe that the greatest peril would be initiated by the adoption of the scheme embraced in the measure now pending in Congress for the unlimited coinage of silver at our mints. If we have developed an unexpected capacity for the assimilation of a largely increased volume of this currency, and even if we have demonstrated the usefulness of such an increase, these conditions fall far short of insuring us against disaster, if in the present situation we enter upon the dangerous and reckless experiment of free, unlimited and independent silver coinage.

323. TILLMANISM IN SOUTH CAROLINA
The Shell Manifesto
January 23, 1890
(*The Charleston News and Courier,* January 23, 1890)

The century-old sectionalism in South Carolina was partially allayed by the unifying experiences of the Civil War and Reconstruction, but it came to the front again in the late eighties with the agrarian distress of that period. The Populist movement as such made little headway in South Carolina, but the revolt against the Bourbon control of the Democratic party was the political equivalent of the populist revolt

elsewhere. The leader of the agrarian and up-country revolt against the Charleston "aristocracy" was Benjamin F. Tillman of Edgefield County. In 1886 and again in 1888 Tillman lost the nomination for governorship, but by 1890 the revolt was too strong to be controlled. The campaign of 1890 was inaugurated by the famous Shell Manifesto, written by Tillman, but published over the name of G. W. Shell. the

President of the Farmers' Association. Tillman and his entire ticket were swept into office in the elections of that year. See, F. P. Simkins, *The Tillman Movement in South Carolina;* J. D. Hicks, *The Populist Revolt;* W. W. Ball, *The State that Forgot.*

THE COMING CAMPAIGN
A CONTEST PROPOSED WITHIN THE DEMOCRATIC PARTY

An Address to the Democrats of South Carolina, Issued by Order of "the Executive Committee of the Farmers' Association of South Carolina."

Mr. W. G. Shell of Laurens, president of the Farmers' Association of South Carolina, requests the News and Courier to publish the following address:

To the Democracy of South Carolina: For four years the Democratic party in the State has been deeply agitated, and efforts have been made at the primaries and conventions to secure retrenchments and reform, and a recognition of the needs and rights of the masses. The first Farmers' Convention met in April 1886. Another in November of the same year perfected a permanent organization under the name of the "Farmers Association of South Carolina." This Association, representing the reform element in the party, has held two annual sessions since, and at each of these four conventions, largely attended by representative farmers from nearly all of the counties, the demands of the people for greater economy in the Government, greater efficiency in its officials, and a fuller recognition of the necessity for cheaper and more practical education have been pressed upon the attention of our Legislature.

In each of the two last Democratic State Conventions the "Farmers' Movement" has had a large following and we only failed of controlling the Convention of 1888 by a small vote—less than twenty-five—and that, too, in the face of the active opposition of nearly every trained politician in the State. We claim that we have always had a majority of the people on our side, and have only failed by reason of the superior political tactics of our opponents and our lack of organization. . . .

The executive committee of the Farmers' Association did not deem it worth while to hold any convention last November, but we have watched closely every move of the enemies of economy—the enemies of true Jeffersonian Democracy—and we think the time has come to show the people what it is they need and how to accomplish their desires. We will draw up the indictment against these who have been and are still governing our State, because it is at once the cause and justification of the course we intend to pursue.

South Carolina has never had a real Republican Government. Since the days of the "Lords Proprietors" it has been an aristocracy under the forms of Democracy, and whenever a champion of the people has attempted to show them their rights and advocated those rights an aristocratic oligarchy has bought him with an office, or failing in that turned loose the floodgates of misrepresentation and slander in order to destroy his influence.

The peculiar situation now existing in the State, requiring the united efforts of every true white man to preserve white supremacy and our very civilization even has intensified and tended to make permanent the conditions which existed before the war. Fear of a division among us and consequent return of a negro rule has kept the people quiet, and they have submitted to many grievances imposed by the ruling faction because they dreaded to risk such a division.

The "Farmers' Movement" has been hampered and retarded in its work by this condition of the public mind, but we have shown our fealty to race by submitting to the edicts of the party and we intend, as heretofore, to make our fight inside the party lines, feeling assured that truth and justice must finally prevail. The results of the agitation thus far are altogether encouraging. Inch by inch and step by step true Democracy—the rule of the people—has won its way. We have carried all the outposts. Only two strongholds remain to be taken, and with the issues fairly made up and plainly put to the people we have no fear of the result. The House of Representatives has been carried twice, and at last held after a desperate struggle.

The advocates of reform and economy are no longer sneered at as "Three for a quarter statesmen." They pass measures of economy which four years ago would have excited only derision, and with the Farmers' Movement to strengthen their backbone have withstood the cajolery, threats and impotent rage of the old "ring bosses." The Senate is now the main reliance of the enemies of retrenchment and reform, who oppose giving the people their rights. The Senate is the stronghold of "existing institutions" and the main dependence of those who are antagonistic to all progress. As we captured the House we can capture the Senate; but we must control the Democratic State Convention before we can hope to make economy popular in Columbia, or be assured of no more pocket votes.

The General Assembly is largely influenced by the idea and policy of the State officers, and we must elect those before we can say the Farmers' Movement has accomplished its mission. It is true that we have wrenched from the aristocratic coterie who were educated at and sought to monopolize everything for the South Carolina College, the right to control the land script and Hatch fund and a part of the privilege tax on fertilizers for one year, and we have $40,000 with which to commence building a separate agricultural college, where the sons of poor farmers can get a practical education at small expense.

But we dare not relax our efforts or rely upon the loud professions of our opponents as to their willingness now to build and equip this agricultural school. . . .

All the cry about "existing institutions" which must remain inviolate shows that the ring—the South Carolina University, Citadel, Agricultural Bureau, Columbia Club, Greenville building ring—intend in the future, as in the past, to get all they can, and keep all they get. These pets of the aristocracy and its nurseries are only hoping that the people will again sink into their accustomed apathy. . . .

Is it not plain that these people intend to yield obedience to the law only when they are made to do it? The Farmers' Association demands that the land script and Hatch funds and the fertilizer tax shall be consolidated and used for the building and maintenance of a first class industrial school, with experiment stations attached, for farmers and mechanics. We hold that the experimental work, the educational work and the inspection and analysis of fertilizers can all be more efficiently and economically carried on under one board, mostly at one place, and much of it by the same corps of men who teach.

We have never and do not now want any increase of taxes to accomplish these ends. . . .

The bill prepared by the committee of the Farmers' Association for the reorganization of the board of agriculture would have secured our farmers against swindling fertilizer dealers, but it was amended to death by the lawyers in the Senate, who are attorneys for the phosphate miners and fertilizer companies, and the men who were elected on the board over the nominees of the Farmers' Convention were chosen not because they are more loyal to the agricultural interests, or better fitted for the position, but because they are friends of the University and belong or are subservient to our aristocracy —"so called"—and the phosphate miners are too well satisfied with the system of collecting the State royalty to permit a change if they can help it.

How wonderfully perfect or defective this system is, is shown by the fact that during ten years under the same officials not a single indictment has been brought against any one for attempting to swindle the State out of its dues. No wonder Charleston is in love with the agricultural bureau and cannot bear to see the "existing institutions" disturbed.

The recent proposal to sell the State's interest in the phosphate beds is fortunate, because thereby the attention of taxpayers is attracted to this most important matter. The Farmers' Association proposed in 1886 to increase the royalty as a means of lowering taxes, and we believe this can be safely done to the extent of $100,000.

A legislative committee was appointed to "investigate" and report on the subject. This was only done to give time—waiting ten months until the market had been manipulated, etc. This committee proceeded to show how well it had been chosen "not to do it." There was no honest effort made to get at the real facts as to the profits of the business and its ability to stand an increase of royalty, and after it had been "wined and dined" and brought into a suitable frame of mind that committee came to Columbia and actually proposed to give the six largest companies a monopoly for a less annual rental than the State was then receiving. Only one Senator, to whom all honor is due, dissented from this outrageous proposal. What was the result?

Of course the General Assembly did not act favorably upon it, but all thought of an increase of royalty was also abandoned, and this was what the corporation attorneys who were there in the interest of their clients and not of their constituents had been working for. "The goose that lays the golden egg" was not killed—"existing institutions" were not disturbed. Phosphate rock, which had been manipulated down to $3.40 per ton, advanced in two months after the Legislature adjourned to $6.00 and has since ruled between $5.50 and $7.50 per ton. The golden eggs are still being laid, but not in the State's nest—whether some of them have not gone into pockets which they ought not is an open question.

Now we want to warn the people that the charter of the Coosaw Company—obtained by bribery, it is said, of a Radical Legislature—expires in 1891. This Company which has grown fabulously rich, claims to have a perpetual contract, with exclusive right to mine in Coosaw River and pay only one dollar a ton for the privilege. The next Legislature must act on this question and the next Attorney General may have to test these claims in court. The whole question of phosphate management, or mismanagement, must be settled. Can the taxpayers afford to allow any but true men to go to the Senate or elect a corporation lawyer as Attorney General? Shall the politicians choose him, or shall we, casting about among the many honorable, patriotic lawyers of the State, make the selection ourselves?

The Legislature which has just adjourned has other sins to answer for, or rather the Senate must be held responsible. The people demanded that the railroad commissioners should have something to do besides draw their salaries and spend them. We want protection against the greed of the gigantic corporations owned by the North, which regard South Carolina as a lemon to be squeezed and care nothing for the welfare of our towns, our State or our people. . . .

The railroad commissioners now in office have been "tamed," so to speak, by the railroads, and men who have not been so long

under wing might have done something in the interest of the people; but that same Senate which has again and again thwarted the people, which refused to reduce salaries, which fought the Clemson College and yielded at last to necessity only, which is the stronghold of aristocracy with its non-progressive, impracticable ideas, which, in a word, is dominated by Charleston's rich politicians—that Senate resolved to maintain this "existing institution" too, status quo.

Of all the taxes we pay, the pensions to Confederate Veterans are submitted to most willingly, and we regret that we cannot increase the pittance they receive. But the continuance of men in office as political pensioners, after their ability or willingness to serve the people is gone—when the interests and even rights of the people are thereby sacrificed, this pandering to sentiment, this favoritism is a crime, nothing more and nothing less. Rotation in office is a cardinal Democratic principle, and the neglect to practice it is the cause of many of the ills we suffer.

We cannot elaborate the other counts in this indictment. We can only point briefly to the mismanagement of the Penitentiary, which is a burden on the taxpayers, even while engaged in no public works which might benefit the State. To the wrong committed against the people of many counties (strongholds of Democracy) by the failure to reapportion representation according to the population, whereby Charleston has five votes in the House and ten votes in the State Convention, which choose our State officers, to which it is not entitled.

To the zeal and extravagance of this aristocratic oligarchy, whose sins we are pointing out, in promising higher education for every class except farmers, while it neglects the free schools which are the only chance for an education to thousands of poor children, whose fathers bore the brunt in the struggle for our redemption in 1876. To the continued recurrence of horrible lynchings—which we can but attribute to bad laws and their inefficient administration. To the impotence of justice to punish criminals who have money. To the failure to call a constitutional convention that we may have an organic law framed by South Carolinians for South Carolinians and suited to our wants, thereby lessening the burdens of taxation and giving us better government.

Fellow Democrats, do not all these things cry out for a change? Is it not opportune, when there is no national election, for the common people who redeemed the State from Radical rule to take charge of it? Can we afford to leave it longer in the hands of those who, wedded to ante-bellum ideas, but possessing little of ante-bellum patriotism and honor, are running it in the interest of a few families and for the benefit of a selfish ring of politicians? As real Democrats and white men, those who here renew our pledge to make the fight inside the Democratic party and abide the result, we call upon every true Carolinian, of all classes and callings, to help us purify and reform the Democratic party and give us a government of the people, by the people and for the people.

If we control the State Democratic Convention, a Legislature in sympathy will naturally follow; failing to do this, we risk losing all we have gained, and have no hope of any change for the better. . . .

We therefore issue this call for a Convention of those Democrats who sympathize with our views and purposes, as herein set forth, . . .

By order of the executive committee of the Farmers' Association of South Carolina.

G. W. Shell,
President and Ex Officio Chairman.

324. THE OCALA DEMANDS
December, 1890

(Proceedings of the Supreme Council of the National Farmers' Alliance and Industrial Union, 1890, p. 32–3)

The Southern Alliance, the Farmers' Mutual Benefit Association, and the Colored Farmers' Alliance, all met at Ocala, Florida, in 1890. The demands drawn up presaged the entry of the Alliance into the political field, and revealed the beginnings of the disintegration of the Alliance. See, J. D. Hicks, *The Populist Revolt,* ch. viii.

1. a. We demand the abolition of national banks.

b. We demand that the government shall establish sub-treasuries or depositories in the several states, which shall loan money direct to the people at a low rate of interest, not to exceed two per cent per annum, on nonperishable farm products, and also upon real estate, with proper limitations upon the quantity of land and amount of money.

c. We demand that the amount of the circulating medium be speedily increased to not less than $50 per capita.

2. We demand that Congress shall pass such laws as will effectually prevent the dealing in futures of all agricultural and mechanical productions; providing a stringent system of procedure in trials that will secure the prompt conviction, and imposing such penalties as shall secure the most perfect compliance with the law.

3. We condemn the silver bill recently passed by Congress, and demand in lieu thereof the free and unlimited coinage of silver.

4. We demand the passage of laws prohibiting alien ownership of land, and that Congress take prompt action to devise some plan to obtain all lands now owned by aliens and foreign syndicates; and that all lands now held by railroads and other corporations in excess of such as is actually used and needed by them be reclaimed by the government and held for actual settlers only.

5. Believing in the doctrine of equal rights to all and special privileges to none, we demand—

a. That our national legislation shall be so framed in the future as not to build up one industry at the expense of another.

b. We further demand a removal of the existing heavy tariff tax from the necessities of life, that the poor of our land must have.

c. We further demand a just and equitable system of graduated tax on incomes.

d. We believe that the money of the country should be kept as much as possible in the hands of the people, and hence we demand that all national and state revenues shall be limited to the necessary expenses of the government economically and honestly administered.

6. We demand the most rigid, honest, and just state and national government control and supervision of the means of public communication and transportation, and if this control and supervision does not remove the abuse now existing, we demand the government ownership of such means of communication and transportation.

7. We demand that the Congress of the United States submit an amendment to the Constitution providing for the election of United States Senators by direct vote of the people of each state.

325. POPULIST PARTY PLATFORM
July 4, 1892

(E. McPherson, *A Handbook of Politics for 1892,* p. 269 ff.)

The Preamble, which appeared first in the St. Louis platform of March 1892, was written by Ignatius Donnelly of Minnesota. The most thorough history of the Populist movement is J. D. Hicks, *The Populist Revolt,* which contains an elaborate bibliography.

Assembled upon the 116th anniversary of the Declaration of Independence, the People's Party of America, in their first national convention, invoking upon their action the blessing of Almighty God, put forth in the name and on behalf of the people of this country, the following preamble and declaration of principles:

PREAMBLE

The conditions which surround us best justify our co-operation; we meet in the midst of a nation brought to the verge of moral, political, and material ruin. Corruption dominates the ballot-box, the Legislatures, the Congress, and touches even the ermine of the bench. The people are demoralized; most of the States have been compelled to isolate the voters at the polling places to prevent universal intimidation and bribery. The newspapers are largely subsidized or muzzled, public opinion silenced, business prostrated, homes covered with mortgages, labor impoverished, and the land concentrating in the hands of capitalists. The urban workmen are denied the right to organize for self-protection, imported pauperized labor beats down their wages, a hireling standing army, unrecognized by our laws, is established to shoot them down, and they are rapidly degenerating into European conditions. The fruits of the toil of millions are boldly stolen to build up colossal fortunes for a few, unprecedented in the history of mankind; and the possessors of these, in turn, despise the Republic and endanger liberty. From the same prolific womb of governmental injustice we breed the two great classes—tramps and millionaires.

The national power to create money is appropriated to enrich bond-holders; a vast public debt payable in legal-tender currency has been funded into gold-bearing bonds, thereby adding millions to the burdens of the people.

Silver, which has been accepted as coin since the dawn of history, has been demonetized to add to the purchasing power of gold by decreasing the value of all forms of property as well as human labor, and the supply of currency is purposely abridged to fatten usurers, bankrupt enterprise, and enslave industry. A vast conspiracy against mankind has been organized on two continents, and it is rapidly taking possession of the world. If not met and overthrown at once it forebodes terrible social convulsions, the destruction of civilization, or the establishment of an absolute despotism.

We have witnessed for more than a quarter of a century the struggles of the two great political parties for power and plunder, while grievous wrongs have been inflicted upon the suffering people. We charge that the controlling influences dominating both these parties have permitted the existing dreadful conditions to develop without serious effort to prevent or restrain them. Neither do they now promise us any substantial reform. They have agreed together to ignore, in the coming campaign, every issue but one. They propose to drown the outcries of a plundered people with the uproar of a sham battle over the tariff, so that capitalists, corporations, national banks, rings, trusts, watered stock, the demonetization of silver and the oppressions of the usurers may all be lost sight of. They propose to sacrifice our homes, lives, and children on the altar of mammon; to destroy the multitude in order to secure corruption funds from the millionaires.

Assembled on the anniversary of the birthday of the nation, and filled with the spirit of the grand general and chief who established our independence, we seek to restore the government of the Republic to the hands of the "plain people," with which class it originated. We assert our purposes to be identical with the purposes of the National Constitution; to form a more perfect union and establish justice, insure domestic tranquillity, provide for the common defence, promote the general welfare, and secure the blessings of liberty for ourselves and our posterity.

We declare that this Republic can only endure as a free government while built upon the love of the people for each other and for the nation; that it cannot be pinned together by bayonets; that the Civil War is over, and that every passion and resentment which grew out of it must die with it, and that we must be in fact, as we are in name, one united brotherhood of free men.

Our country finds itself confronted by conditions for which there is no precedent in the history of the world; our annual agricultural productions amount to billions of dollars in value, which must, within a few weeks or months, be exchanged for billions of dollars' worth of commodities consumed in their production; the existing currency supply is wholly inadequate to make this exchange; the results are falling prices, the formation of combines and rings, the impoverishment of the producing class. We pledge ourselves that if given power we will labor to correct these evils by wise and reasonable legislation, in accordance with the terms of our platform.

We believe that the power of government —in other words, of the people—should be expanded (as in the case of the postal service) as rapidly and as far as the good sense of an intelligent people and the teachings of experience shall justify, to the end that op-

pression, injustice, and poverty shall eventually cease in the land.

While our sympathies as a party of reform are naturally upon the side of every proposition which will tend to make men intelligent, virtuous, and temperate, we nevertheless regard these questions, important as they are, as secondary to the great issues now pressing for solution, and upon which not only our individual prosperity but the very existence of free institutions depend; and we ask all men to first help us to determine whether we are to have a republic to administer before we differ as to the conditions upon which it is to be administered, believing that the forces of reform this day organized will never cease to move forward until every wrong is righted and equal rights and equal privileges securely established for all the men and women of this country.

PLATFORM

We declare, therefore—

First.—That the union of the labor forces of the United States this day consummated shall be permanent and perpetual; may its spirit enter into all hearts for the salvation of the Republic and the uplifting of mankind.

Second.—Wealth belongs to him who creates it, and every dollar taken from industry without an equivalent is robbery. "If any will not work, neither shall he eat." The interests of rural and civil labor are the same; their enemies are identical.

Third.—We believe that the time has come when the railroad corporations will either own the people or the people must own the railroads; and should the government enter upon the work of owning and managing all railroads, we should favor an amendment to the constitution by which all persons engaged in the government service shall be placed under a civil-service regulation of the most rigid character, so as to prevent the increase of the power of the national administration by the use of such additional government employes.

FINANCE.—We demand a national currency, safe, sound, and flexible issued by the general government only, a full legal tender for all debts, public and private, and that without the use of banking corporations; a just, equitable, and efficient means of distribution direct to the people, at a tax not to exceed 2 per cent, per annum, to be provided as set forth in the sub-treasury plan of the Farmers' Alliance, or a better system; also by payments in discharge of its obligations for public improvements.

1. We demand free and unlimited coinage of silver and gold at the present legal ratio of 16 to 1.
2. We demand that the amount of circulating medium be speedily increased to not less than $50 per capita.
3. We demand a graduated income tax.
4. We believe that the money of the country should be kept as much as possible in the hands of the people, and hence we demand that all State and national revenues shall be limited to the necessary expenses of the government, economically and honestly administered.
5. We demand that postal savings banks be established by the government for the safe deposit of the earnings of the people and to facilitate exchange.

TRANSPORTATION.—Transportation being a means of exchange and a public necessity, the government should own and operate the railroads in the interest of the people. The telegraph and telephone, like the post-office system, being a necessity for the transmission of news, should be owned and operated by the government in the interest of the people.

LAND.—The land, including all the natural sources of wealth, is the heritage of the people, and should not be monopolized for speculative purposes, and alien ownership of land should be prohibited. All land now held by railroads and other corporations in excess of their actual needs, and all lands now owned by aliens should be reclaimed by the government and held for actual settlers only.

EXPRESSION OF SENTIMENTS

Your Committee on Platform and Resolutions beg leave unanimously to report the following:

Whereas, Other questions have been presented for our consideration, we hereby submit the following, not as a part of the Platform of the People's Party, but as resolutions expressive of the sentiment of this Convention.

1. RESOLVED, That we demand a free ballot and a fair count in all elections. and pledge ourselves to secure it to every legal voter without Federal intervention, through the adoption by the States of the unperverted Australian or secret ballot system.
2. RESOLVED, That the revenue derived from a graduated income tax should be applied to the reduction of the burden of taxation now levied upon the domestic industries of this country.
3. RESOLVED, That we pledge our support to fair and liberal pensions to ex-Union soldiers and sailors.
4. RESOLVED, That we condemn the fallacy of protecting American labor under the present system, which opens our ports to the pauper and criminal classes of the world and crowds out our wage-earners; and we denounce the present ineffective laws against contract labor, and demand the further restriction of undesirable emigration.
5. RESOLVED, That we cordially sympathize with the efforts of organized workingmen to shorten the hours of labor, and demand a rigid enforcement of the existing eight-hour law on Government work, and ask that a penalty clause be added to the said law.
6. RESOLVED, That we regard the maintenance of a large standing army of mercenaries, known as the Pinkerton system, as a menace to our liberties, and we demand its abolition; and we condemn the recent invasion of the Territory of Wyoming by the hired assassins of plutocracy, assisted by Federal officers.
7. RESOLVED, That we commend to the favorable consideration of the people and the reform press the legislative system known as the initiative and referendum.
8. RESOLVED, That we favor a constitutional provision limiting the office of President and Vice-President to one term, and providing for the election of Senators of the United States by a direct vote of the people.
9. RESOLVED, That we oppose any subsidy or national aid to any private corporation for any purpose.

10. RESOLVED, That this convention sympathizes with the Knights of Labor and their righteous contest with the tyrannical combine of clothing manufacturers of Rochester, and declare it to be a duty of all who hate tyranny and oppression to refuse to purchase the goods made by the said manufacturers, or to patronize any merchants who sell such goods.

326. UNITED STATES v. WORKINGMEN'S AMALGAMATED COUNCIL OF NEW ORLEANS ET AL.
54 Fed. 994
1893

Did the prohibitions of the Sherman Anti-Trust Act apply to combinations of labor? The wording of the act was ambiguous—perhaps purposely so—and the question was left for the courts to decide. Compare the opinion below with *Waterhouse* v. *Comer*, 55 Fed. 150, and *United States* v. *Patterson*, 55 Fed. 605. For a careful discussion of the relation of the Sherman Law to labor, see A. T. Mason, *Organized Labor and the Law;* E. Berman, *Labor and the Sherman Act.*

BILLINGS, District Judge.

This cause is submitted upon an application for an injunction on the bill of complaint, answer, and numerous affidavits and exhibits. The bill of complaint in this case is filed by the United States under the act of Congress entitled "An act to protect trade and commerce against unlawful restraint and monopolies," (26 St. at Large, p. 209.) The substance of the bill avers that a disagreement between the warehousemen and their employes and the principal draymen and their subordinates had been adopted by all the organizations named in the bill, until, by this vast combination of men and of organizations, it was threatened that, unless there was an acquiescence in the demands of the subordinate workmen and draymen, all the men in all the defendant organizations would leave work, and would allow no work in any department of business; that violence was threatened and used in support of this demand; and that this demand included the interstate and foreign commerce which flows through the city of New Orleans. The bill further states that the proceedings on the part of the defendants had taken such a vast and ramified proportion that, in consequence of the threats of the defendants, the whole business of the city of New Orleans was paralyzed, and the transit of goods and merchandise which was being conveyed through it from state to state, and to and from foreign countries, was totally interrupted. . . .

. . . The theory of the defense is that this case does not fall within the purview of the statute; that the statute prohibited monopolies and combinations which, using words in a general sense, were of capitalists, and not of laborers. I think the congressional debates show that the statute had its origins in the evils of massed capital; but, when the congress came to formulating the prohibition which is the yardstick for measuring to complainant's right to injunction, . . . the subject had so broadened in the minds of the legislators that the source of the evil was not regarded as material, and the evil in its entirety is dealt with. They made the interdiction include combinations of labor, as well as of capital; in fact, all combinations in restraint of commerce, without reference to the character of the persons who entered into them. It is true this statute has not been much expounded by judges, but, as it seems to me, its meaning, as far as relates to the sort of combinations to which it is to apply, is manifest, and that it includes combinations which are composed of laborers acting in the interest of laborers. . . .

The defendants urge (6) that the combination to secure or compel the employment of none but union men is not in the restraint of commerce. To determine whether the proposition urged as a defense can apply to this case, the case must first be stated as it is made out by the established facts. The case is this: The combination setting out to secure and compel the employment of none but union men in a given business, as a means to effect this compulsion, finally enforced a discontinuance of labor in all kinds of business, including the business of transportation of goods and merchandise which were in transit through the city of New Orleans, from state to state, and to and from foreign countries. When the case is thus stated,— and it must be so stated to embody the facts here proven,—I do not think there can be any question but that the combination of the defendants was in restraint of commerce.

I have thus endeavored to state and deal with the various grounds of defense urged before me. I shall now, as briefly as possible, state the case as it is established in the voluminous record.

. . . The question simply is, do these facts establish a case within the statute? It seems to me this question is tantamount to the question, could there be a case under the statute? It is conceded that the labor organizations were at the outset lawful. But when lawful forces are put into unlawful channels,—i.e. when lawful associations adopt and further unlawful purposes and do unlawful

acts,—the associations themselves become unlawful. The evil, as well as the unlawfulness, of the act of the defendants, consists in this: that, until certain demands of theirs were complied with, they endeavored to prevent, and did prevent, everybody from moving the commerce of the country. . . .

It is the successful effort of the combination of the defendants to intimidate and overawe others who were at work in conducting or carrying on the commerce of the country, in which the court finds their error and their violation of the statute. One of the intended results of their combined action was the forced stagnation of all the commerce which flowed through New Orleans. This intent and combined action are none the less unlawful because they included in their scope the paralysis of all other business within the city as well. . . .

327. CLEVELAND'S MESSAGE ON THE REPEAL OF THE SHERMAN SILVER PURCHASE ACT
August 8, 1893

(Richardson, ed. *Messages and Papers*, Vol. IX, p. 401 ff.)

On June 30, 1893, Cleveland issued a call for a special session of Congress to meet August 7. The struggle for the repeal of the Silver Purchase Act of 1890 was the most violent political battle of Cleveland's career. See, A. Nevins, *Grover Cleveland*, ch. xxix; R. McElroy, *Grover Cleveland*, Vol. II, ch. i; W. J. Bryan, *The First Battle*, ch. ii, iii; A. B. Hepburn, *History of Currency in the United States*, ch. xx.

EXECUTIVE MANSION, *August 8, 1893.*
To the Congress of the United States:

The existence of an alarming and extraordinary business situation, involving the welfare and prosperity of all our people, has constrained me to call together in extra session the people's representatives in Congress, to the end that through a wise and patriotic exercise of the legislative duty, with which they solely are charged, present evils may be mitigated and dangers threatening the future may be averted.

Our unfortunate financial plight is not the result of untoward events nor of conditions related to our natural resources, nor is it traceable to any of the afflictions which frequently check national growth and pros-

perity. With plenteous crops, with abundant promise of remunerative production and manufacture, with unusual invitation to safe investment, and with satisfactory assurance to business enterprise, suddenly financial distrust and fear have sprung up on every side. . . . Values supposed to be fixed are fast becoming conjectural, and loss and failure have invaded every branch of business.

I believe these things are principally chargeable to Congressional legislation touching the purchase and coinage of silver by the General Government.

This legislation is embodied in a statute passed on the 14th day of July, 1890, which was the culmination of much agitation on the subject involved, and which may be considered a truce, after a long struggle, between the advocates of free silver coinage and those intending to be more conservative. . . .

This law provides that in payment for the 4,500,000 ounces of silver bullion which the Secretary of the Treasury is commanded to purchase monthly there shall be issued Treasury notes redeemable on demand in gold or silver coin, at the discretion of the Secretary of the Treasury, and that said notes may be reissued. It is, however, declared in the act to be "the established policy of the United States to maintain the two metals on a parity with each other upon the present legal ratio or such ratio as may be provided by law." This declaration so controls the action of the Secretary of the Treasury as to prevent his exercising the discretion nominally vested in him if by such action the parity between gold and silver may be disturbed. Manifestly a refusal by the Secretary to pay these Treasury notes in gold if demanded would necessarily result in their discredit and depreciation as obligations payable only in silver, and would destroy the parity between the two metals by establishing a discrimination in favor of gold. . . .

The policy necessarily adopted of paying these notes in gold has not spared the gold reserve of $100,000,000 long ago set aside by the Government for the redemption of other notes, for this fund has already been subjected to the payment of new obligations amounting to about $150,000,000 on account of silver purchases, and has as a consequence for the first time since its creation been encroached upon.

We have thus made the depletion of our gold easy and have tempted other and more appreciative nations to add it to their stock. . . .

Unless Government bonds are to be constantly issued and sold to replenish our exhausted gold, only to be again exhausted, it is apparent that the operation of the silver-purchase law now in force leads in the direction of the entire substitution of silver for the gold in the Government Treasury, and that this must be followed by the payment of all Government obligations in depreciated silver.

At this stage gold and silver must part company and the Government must fail in its established policy to maintain the two metals on a parity with each other. Given over to the exclusive use of a currency greatly depreciated according to the standard of the commercial world, we could no longer claim a place among nations of the first class, nor could our Government claim a performance of its obligation, so far as such an obligation has been imposed upon it, to provide for the use of the people the best and safest money.

If, as many of its friends claim, silver ought to occupy a larger place in our currency and the currency of the world through general international coöperation and agreement, it is obvious that the United States will not be in a position to gain a hearing in favor of such an arrangement so long as we are willing to continue our attempt to accomplish the result single-handed. . . .

The people of the United States are entitled to a sound and stable currency and to money recognized as such on every exchange and in every market of the world. Their Government has no right to injure them by financial experiments opposed to the policy and practice of other civilized states, nor is it justified in permitting an exaggerated and unreasonable reliance on our national strength and ability to jeopardize the soundness of the people's money.

This matter rises above the plane of party politics. It vitally concerns every business and calling and enters every household in the land. There is one important aspect of the subject which especially should never be overlooked. At times like the present, when the evils of unsound finance threaten us, the speculator may anticipate a harvest gathered from the misfortune of others, the capitalist may protect himself by hoarding or may even find profit in the fluctuations of values; but the wage earner—the first to be injured by a depreciated currency and the last to receive the benefit of its correction—is practically defenseless. He relies for work upon the ventures of confident and contented capital. This failing him, his condition is without alleviation, for he can neither prey on the misfortunes of others nor hoard his labor. . . .

It is of the utmost importance that such relief as Congress can afford in the existing situation be afforded at once. The maxim "He gives twice who gives quickly" is directly applicable. It may be true that the embarrassments from which the business of the country is suffering arise as much from evils apprehended as from those actually existing. We may hope, too, that calm counsels will prevail, and that neither the capitalists nor the wage earners will give way to unreasoning panic and sacrifice their property or their interests under the influence of exaggerated fears. Nevertheless, every day's delay in removing one of the plain and principal causes of the present state of things enlarges the mischief already done and increases the responsibility of the Government for its existence. Whatever else the people have a right to expect from Congress, they may certainly demand that legislation condemned by the ordeal of three years' disastrous experience shall be removed from the statute books as soon as their representatives can legitimately deal with it.

It was my purpose to summon Congress in special session early in the coming September, that we might enter promptly upon the work of tariff reform, which the true interests of the country clearly demand, which so large a majority of the people, as shown by their suffrages, desire and expect, and to the accomplishment of which every effort of the present Administration is pledged. But while tariff reform has lost nothing of its immediate and permanent importance and must in the near future engage the attention of Congress, it has seemed to me that the financial condition of the country should at once and before all other subjects be considered by your honorable body.

I earnestly recommend the prompt repeal of the provisions of the act passed July 14, 1890, authorizing the purchase of silver bullion, and that other legislative action may put beyond all doubt or mistake the intention and the ability of the Government to fulfill its pecuniary obligations in money universally recognized by all civilized countries.

GROVER CLEVELAND.

328. REPEAL OF THE SHERMAN SILVER PURCHASE ACT
November 1, 1893

(U. S. Statutes at Large, Vol. XXVIII, p. 4)

The panic of 1893 emphasized to Cleveland the imperative necessity of the repeal of the Sherman Silver Act of 1890. On June 30, Cleveland called a special session of Congress to meet August 7 to repeal the Sherman Act. After one of the most violent debates in our legislative history, the administration was finally successful in securing repeal, but only at the cost of a split in the Democratic party which led finally to the triumph of the silver element of that party in 1896. On repeal, see Cleveland's message, Doc. No. 327, and A. Nevins, *Grover Cleveland,* ch. xxix; J. A. Barnes, *John G. Carlisle,* ch. xii; R. McElroy, *Grover Cleveland,* Vol. II, ch. i; W. J. Bryan, *The First Battle,* chs. i–iii.

An Act to repeal a part of [the Silver Purchase Act of July 14, 1890].

Be it enacted . . . , That so much of the [Silver Purchase Act of July 14, 1890], as directs the Secretary of the Treasury to purchase from time to time silver bullion to the aggregate amount of four million five hundred thousand ounces, or so much thereof as may be offered in each month at the market price thereof, not exceeding one dollar for three hundred and seventy-one and twenty-five one-hundredths grains of pure silver, and to issue in payment for such purchases Treasury notes of the United States, be, and the same is hereby, repealed. And it is hereby declared to be the policy of the United States to continue the use of both gold and silver as standard money, and to coin both gold and silver into money of equal intrinsic and exchangeable value, such equality to be secured through international agreement, or by such safeguards of legislation as will insure the maintenance of the parity in value of the coins of the two metals, and the equal power of every dollar at all times in the markets and in the payment of debts. And it is hereby further declared that the efforts of the Government should be steadily directed to the establishment of such a safe system of bimetallism as will maintain at all times the equal power of every dollar coined or issued by the United States, in the markets and in the payment of debts.

329. THE FUR-SEALING CONTROVERSY

Convention Between the United States and Great Britain for the Settlement of the
Controversy and the Award of the Tribunal
1892, 1893

(Malloy, ed. *Treaties, Conventions, etc.* Vol. I, p. 746 ff.)

The most valuable herds of seals in the world were found off the shores of Alaska and in the waters of Bering Sea, particularly on the Pribilof Islands. Russia had claimed jurisdiction over the whole of the Bering Sea, and the United States, after the purchase of Alaska, claimed that this sea was a *mare clausum.* By acts of 1869 and 1870 Congress forbade the killing of seals upon the shores of Alaska or the waters thereof except during the months from June to October. Subsequently the exclusive right of killing seals was leased to the Alaska Commercial Company under careful restrictions. The invasion of the Bering Sea by Canadian sealers led to the seizure and condemnation of three Canadian vessels. Despite the protests of Great Britain the seizures continued during the late eighties. A *modus vivendi* was arrived at by the United States and Great Britain in 1891, and the following year a convention was concluded submitting the questions of sealing and of jurisdiction to a tribunal. This Convention of February 29, 1892, presented a series of five major questions which the Tribunal was called upon to adjudicate. The Tribunal met in Paris in 1893 and decided all points of law adversely to the United States. At the same time it drew up a series of regulations designed to protect the fur seals. These regulations were only moderately effective, and on their expiration in 1898 they were not renewed. In 1906 President Roosevelt suggested the extermination of the seal herd by the United States on humanitarian grounds. Finally in 1911 Great Britain, Russia, Japan and the United States concluded a convention which afforded adequate protection to the seals. On the controversy see J. B. Moore, *International Arbitrations,* Vol. I; J. W. Foster, *Diplomatic Memoirs,* Vol. II; A. F. Tyler, *The Foreign Policy of James G. Blaine;* J. M. Callahan, *American Relations in the Pacific;* S. B. Stanton, *The Behring Sea Controversy;* S. F. Bemis, ed. *American Secretaries of State,* Vol. VIII, p. 128 ff.; J. Stanley-Brown, "The Bering Sea Controversy from an Economic Standpoint," *Yale Review,* Vol. II; T. A. Walker, *International Law,* p. 175 ff.

A CONVENTION FOR THE SETTLEMENT OF THE DISPUTED RIGHT OF THE UNITED STATES TO PROTECT THE SEALS IN BEHRING SEA.

Concluded, February 29, 1892.

The United States of America and Her Majesty the Queen of the United Kingdom of Great Britain and Ireland, being desirous to provide for an amicable settlement of the questions which have arisen between their respective governments concerning the jurisdictional rights of the United States in the waters of Behring's Sea, and concerning also the preservation of the fur-seal in, or habitually resorting to, the said Sea, and the rights of the citizens and subjects of either country as regards the taking of fur-seal in, or habitually resorting to, the said waters, have resolved to submit to arbitration the questions involved. . . .

ART. I—The questions which have arisen between the Government of the United States and the Government of Her Britannic Majesty concerning the jurisdictional rights of the United States in the waters of Behring's Sea, and concerning also the preservation of the fur-seal in, or habitually resorting to, the said Sea, and the rights of the citizens and subjects of either country as regards the taking of fur-seal in, or habitually resorting to, the said waters, shall be submitted to a tribunal of Arbitration, to be composed of seven Arbitrators, who shall be appointed in the following manner, that is to say: Two shall be named by the President of the United States; two shall be named by Her Britannic Majesty; His Excellency the President of the French Republic shall be jointly requested by the High Contracting Parties to name one; His Majesty the King of Italy shall be so requested to name one; and His Majesty the King of Sweden and Norway shall be so requested to name one. The seven arbitrators to be so named shall be jurists of distinguished reputation in their respective countries. . . .

ART. II.—The arbitrators shall meet

at Paris within twenty days after the delivery of the counter-case mentioned in Article IV and shall proceed impartially and carefully to examine and decide the questions that have been or shall be laid before them as herein provided on the part of the Governments of the United States and Her Britannic Majesty respectively. All questions considered by the tribunal including the final decision, shall be determined by a majority of all the Arbitrators.

Each of the High Contracting Parties shall also name one person to attend the tribunal as its Agent to represent it generally in all matters connected with the arbitration. . . .

ART. VI.—In deciding the matters submitted to the Arbitrators, it is agreed that the following five points shall be submitted to them, in order that their award shall embrace a distinct decision upon each of said five points, to wit:

1. What exclusive jurisdiction in the sea now known as the Behring's Sea, and what exclusive rights in the seal fisheries therein, did Russia assert and exercise prior and up to the time of the cession of Alaska to the United States?

2. How far were these claims of jurisdiction as to the seal fisheries recognized and conceded by Great Britain?

3. Was the body of water now known as the Behring's Sea included in the phrase "Pacific Ocean," as used in the Treaty of 1825 between Great Britain and Russia; and what rights, if any, in the Behring's Sea were held and exclusively exercised by Russia after said Treaty?

4. Did not all the rights of Russia as to jurisdiction, and as to the seal fisheries in Behring's Sea east of the water boundary, in the Treaty between the United States and Russia of the 30th March, 1867, pass unimpaired to the United States under that treaty?

5. Has the United States any right, and if so, what right of protection or property in the fur-seals frequenting the islands of the United States in Behring Sea when such seals are found outside the ordinary three-mile limit?

ART. VII.—If the determination of the foregoing questions as to the exclusive jurisdiction of the United States shall leave the subject in such position that the concurrence of Great Britain is necessary to the establishment of Regulations for the proper protection and preservation of the fur-seal in, or habitually resorting to, the Behring Sea, the Arbitrators shall then determine what concurrent Regulations outside the jurisdictional limits of the respective Governments are necessary, and over what waters such Regulations should extend, and to aid them in that determination the report of a Joint Commission to be appointed by the respective Governments shall be laid before them, with such other evidence as either Government may submit.

The High Contracting Parties furthermore agree to cooperate in securing the adhesion of other Powers to such Regulations.

ART. VIII.—The High Contracting Parties having found themselves unable to agree upon a reference which shall include the question of the liability of each for the injuries alleged to have been sustained by the other, or by its citizens, in connection with the claims presented and urged by it; and, being solicitous that this subordinate question should not interrupt or longer delay the submission and determination of the main questions, do agree that either may submit to the Arbitrators any question of fact involved in said claims and ask for a finding thereon, the question of the liability of either Government upon the facts found to be the subject of further negotiation. . . .

James G. Blaine.
Julian Pauncefote.

2. ARTICLES OF THE AWARD OF THE TRIBUNAL OF ARBITRATION, AUGUST 15, 1893

"ART. I. The Governments of the United States and Great Britain shall forbid their citizens and subjects, respectively, to kill, capture, or pursue at any time and in any manner whatever the animals commonly called fur seals within a zone of 60 miles around the Pribilof Islands, inclusive of the territorial waters.

"The miles mentioned in the preceding paragraph are geographical miles, of 60 to a degree of latitude.

"ART. 2. The two Governments shall forbid their citizens and subjects, respectively, to kill, capture, or pursue in any manner whatever during the season extending each year from the 1st of May to the 31st of July, both inclusive, the fur seals on the high sea in the part of the Pacific Ocean, inclusive of the Bering Sea, which is situated to the north of the thirty-fifth degree of north latitude and eastward of the one hundred and eightieth degree of longitude from Greenwich till it strikes the water boundary described in Article I of the treaty of 1867 between the United States and Russia, and following that line up to Bering Strait. . . .

"ART. 4. Each sailing vessel authorized to fish for fur seals must be provided with a special license issued for that purpose by its Government, and shall be required to carry a distinguishing flag to be prescribed by its Government.

"ART. 6. The use of nets, firearms, and explosives shall be forbidden in the fur-seal fishing. This restriction shall not apply to shotguns when such fishing takes place outside of Bering Sea during the season when it may be lawfully carried on.

"ART. 9. The concurrent regulations hereby determined with a view to the protection and preservation of the fur seals shall remain in force until they have been in whole or in part abolished or modified by common agreement between the Governments of the United States and of Great Britain. . . .

330. THE ANNEXATION OF HAWAII

Message of President Harrison Transmitting Treaty of Annexation
February 13, 1893

(Richardson, ed. *Messages and Papers,* Vol. IX, p. 348 ff.)

See Docs. No. 331, 348. For the complicated story of the Hawaiian Revolution and the attempted annexation of the Island, see E. J. Carpenter, *America in Hawaii;* H. E. Chambers, *Constitutional History of Hawaii;* J. W. Foster, *American Diplomacy in the Orient,* p. 365 ff.; D. R. Dewey, *National Problems,* ch. xix; A. Nevins, *Grover Cleveland,* ch. xxx. The official documents are in *Foreign Relations of the United States,* 1894, Appendix II.

EXECUTIVE MANSION,
Washington, February 15, 1893.
To the Senate:

I transmit herewith, with a view to its ratification, a treaty of annexation concluded on the 14th day of February, 1893, between John W. Foster, Secretary of State, . . . and Lorin A. Thurston, W. R. Castle, W. C. Wilder, C. L. Carter, and Joseph Marsden, the commissioners on the part of the Government of the Hawaiian Islands. . . .

I do not deem it necessary to discuss at any length the conditions which have resulted in this decisive action. It has been the policy of the Administration not only to respect but to encourage the continuance of an independent government in the Hawaiian Islands so long as it afforded suitable guaranties for the protection of life and property and maintained a stability and strength that gave adequate security against the domination of any other power. The moral support of this Government has continually manifested itself in the most friendly diplomatic relations and in many acts of courtesy to the Hawaiian rulers.

The overthrow of the monarchy was not in any way promoted by this Government, but had its origin in what seems to have been a reactionary and revolutionary policy on the part of Queen Liliuokalani, which put in serious peril not only the large and preponderating interests of the United States in the islands, but all foreign interests, and, indeed, the decent administration of civil affairs and the peace of the islands. It is quite evident that the monarchy had become effete and the Queen's Government so weak and inadequate as to be the prey of designing and unscrupulous persons. The restoration of Queen Liliuokalani to her throne is undesirable, if not impossible, and unless actively supported by the United States would be accompanied by serious disaster and the disorganization of all business interests. The influence and interest of the United States in the islands must be increased and not diminished.

Only two courses are now open—one the establishment of a protectorate by the United States, and the other annexation full and complete. I think the latter course, which has been adopted in the treaty, will be highly promotive of the best interests of the Hawaiian people, and is the only one that will adequately secure the interests of the United States. These interests are not wholly selfish. It is essential that none of the other great powers shall secure these islands. Such a possession would not consist with our safety and with the peace of the world. This view of the situation is so apparent and conclusive that no protest has been heard from any government against proceedings looking to annexation. Every foreign representative at Honolulu promptly acknowledged the Provisional Government, and I think there is a general concurrence in the opinion that the deposed Queen ought not to be restored.

Prompt action upon this treaty is very desirable. . . .

331. CLEVELAND'S WITHDRAWAL OF TREATY FOR ANNEXATION OF HAWAII
December 18, 1893

(Richardson, ed. *Messages and Papers,* Vol. IX, p. 461 ff.)

Cleveland came to office while the treaty for annexation of Hawaii was still pending in the Senate. He at once appointed a special agent, James H. Blount, to investigate into the circumstances of the Hawaiian revolution. Acting on Blount's report he reversed the policy of the Harrison Administration. For the ultimate annexation of Hawaii see Doc. No. 348.

Executive Mansion
Washington, December 18, 1893.
To the Senate and House of Representatives:
. . . I suppose that right and justice should determine the path to be followed in treating this subject. If national honesty is to be disregarded and a desire for territorial extension or dissatisfaction with a form of government not our own ought to regulate our conduct, I have entirely misapprehended the mission and character of our Government and the behavior which the conscience of our people demands of their public servants.

When the present Administration entered upon its duties, the Senate had under consideration a treaty providing for the annexation of the Hawaiian Islands to the territory of the United States. Surely under our Constitution and laws the enlargement of our limits is a manifestation of the highest attribute of sovereignty, and if entered upon as an Executive act all things relating to the transaction should be clear and free from suspicion. Additional importance attached to this particular treaty of annexation because it contemplated a departure from unbroken American tradition in providing for the addition to our territory of islands of the sea more than 2,000 miles removed from our nearest coast.

These considerations might not of themselves call for interference with the completion of a treaty entered upon by a previous Administration, but it appeared from the documents accompanying the treaty when submitted to the Senate that the ownership of Hawaii was tendered to us by a Provisional Government set up to succeed the constitutional ruler of the islands, who had been dethroned, and it did not appear that such Provisional Government had the sanction of either popular revolution or suffrage. Two other remarkable features of the transaction naturally attracted attention. One was the extraordinary haste, not to say precipitancy, characterizing all the transactions connected with the treaty. . . . Thus between the initiation of the scheme for a Provisional Government in Hawaii, on the 14th day of January, and the submission to the Senate of the treaty of annexation concluded with such Government the entire interval was thirty-two days, fifteen of which were spent by the Hawaiian commissioners in their journey to Washington. . . .

But a protest also accompanied said treaty, signed by the Queen and her ministers at the time she made way for the Provisional Government, which explicitly stated that she yielded to the superior force of the United States, whose minister had caused United States troops to be landed at Honolulu and declared that he would support such Provisional Government.

The truth or falsity of this protest was surely of the first importance. If true, nothing but the concealment of its truth could induce our Government to negotiate with the semblance of a government thus created, nor could a treaty resulting from the acts stated in the protest have been knowingly deemed worthy of consideration by the Senate. Yet the truth or falsity of the protest had not been investigated.

I conceived it to be my duty, therefore, to withdraw the treaty from the Senate for examination, and meanwhile to cause an accurate, full, and impartial investigation to be made of the facts attending the subversion of the constitutional Government of Hawaii and the installment in its place of the Provisional Government. . . .

The report, with its accompanying proofs and such other evidence as is now before the Congress or is herewith submitted, justifies, in my opinion, the statement that when the President was led to submit the treaty to the Senate with the declaration that "the overthrow of the monarchy was not in any way promoted by this Government," and when the Senate was induced to receive and discuss it on that basis, both President and Senate were misled. . . .

I believe that a candid and thorough examination of the facts will force the conviction that the Provisional Government owes its existence to an armed invasion by the United States. Fair-minded people, with the evidence before them, will hardly claim that the Hawaiian Government was overthrown by the people of the islands or that the Provisional Government had ever existed with their consent. I do not understand that any member of this Government claims that the people would uphold it by their suffrages if they were allowed to vote on the question.

While naturally sympathizing with every effort to establish a republican form of government, it has been the settled policy of the United States to concede to people of foreign countries the same freedom and independence in the management of their domestic affairs that we have always claimed for ourselves, and it has been our practice to recognize revolutionary governments as soon as it became apparent that they were supported by the people. . . .

As I apprehend the situation, we are brought face to face with the following conditions:

The lawful Government of Hawaii was overthrown without the drawing of a sword or the firing of a shot by a process every step of which, it may safely be asserted, is directly traceable to and dependent for its success upon the agency of the United States acting through its diplomatic and naval representatives.

But for the notorious predilections of the United States minister for annexation the committee of safety, which should be called the committee of annexation, would never have existed.

But for the landing of the United States forces upon false pretexts respecting the danger to life and property the committee would never have exposed themselves to the pains and penalties of treason by undertaking the subversion of the Queen's Government.

But for the presence of the United States forces in the immediate vicinity and in position to afford all needed protection and support the committee would not have proclaimed the Provisional Government from the steps of the Government building.

And finally, but for the lawless occupation of Honolulu under false pretexts by the United States forces, and but for Minister Stevens's recognition of the Provisional Government when the United States forces were its sole support and constituted its only military strength, the Queen and her Government would never have yielded to the Provisional Government, even for a time and for the sole purpose of submitting her case to the enlightened justice of the United States.

Believing, therefore, that the United States could not, under the circumstances disclosed, annex the islands without justly incurring the imputation of acquiring them by unjustifiable methods, I shall not again submit the treaty of annexation to the Senate for its consideration, and in the instructions of Minister Willis, a copy of which accompanies this message, I have directed him to so inform the Provisional Government. . . .

332. COXEY'S PROGRAM
1894

"General" Jacob S. Coxey of Massillon, Ohio, proposed to end the depression of 1893 by a public works program to be undertaken by federal and local authorities. This program would have the added advantage of increasing the amount of money in circulation through issues of legal tender. In order to bring these proposals before Congress, Coxey led an industrial army from Ohio to Washington. See, H. Vincent, *The Story of the Commonwealth;* D. L. McMurray, *Coxey's Army.*

1. NON-INTEREST BEARING BOND BILL
(D. L. McMurray, *Coxey's Army*, p. 302–303)

A Bill to provide for public improvements and employment of the citizens of the United States.

Be it enacted . . . That whenever any State, Territory, County, township, municipality, or incorporated town or village deem it necessary to make any public improvements, they shall deposit with the Secretary of the Treasury of the United States a non-interest bearing twenty-five year bond, not to exceed one-half of the assessed valuation of the property in said State, Territory, County, township, municipality or incorporated town or village, and said bond to be retired at the rate of four per centum per annum.

SEC. 2. That whenever the foregoing section of this Act has been complied with it shall be mandatory upon the Secretary of the Treasury of the United States to have . . . printed Treasury notes in the denomination of one, two, five, and ten dollars each, which shall be full legal tender for all debts, public and private to the face value of said bond, and deliver to said State . . . ninety nine per centum of said notes, and retain one per centum for expense of engraving and printing same.

SEC. 3. That after the passage of this Act it shall be compulsory upon every incorpo-

rated town or village, municipality, township, County, State or Territory, to give employment to any idle man applying for work, and that the rate be not less than one dollar and fifty cents per day for common labor and three dollars and fifty cents per day for teams and labor, and that eight hours per day shall constitute a day's labor under this act.

2. COXEY'S GOOD ROADS BILL
(H. Vincent, *The Story of the Commonwealth,* p. 51–52)

SEC. 1. Be it enacted . . . That the Secretary of the Treasury of the United States is hereby authorized and instructed to have engraved and printed . . . five hundred millions of dollars of treasury notes, as legal tender for all debts, public and private, said notes to be in denominations of one, two, five and ten dollars, and to be placed in a fund to be known as the "general county road fund system of the United States," and to be expended solely for the said purpose.

SEC. 2. . . . That it shall be the duty of the Secretary of War to take charge of the construction of the General County Road System in the United States, and said construction to commence as soon as . . . said fund is available . . . when it shall be the duty of the Secretary of War to inaugurate the work and expend the sum of twenty millions of dollars per month, pro rata with the number of miles of roads in each state and territory in the United States.

SEC. 3. . . . That all labor other than that of the Secretary of War . . . shall be paid by the day, and that the rate be not less than one dollar and fifty cents per day for common labor, and three dollars and fifty cents per day for teams and labor, and that eight hours shall constitute a day's labor under the provisions of this bill.

333. POLLOCK v. FARMERS' LOAN AND TRUST COMPANY
158 U. S. 601
1894

Appeal from U. S. circuit court for the Southern District of New York. Rehearing. The Wilson tariff bill of 1894 had included provision for

an income tax. The constitutionality of such a tax was challenged on the ground that it was a direct tax and therefore contrary to the Constitutional requirement that all direct taxes be apportioned among the States according to population. The issues before the Court were involved, but on the general question of the legality of a tax on the income from personal property, the court was divided four to four. The opinion below is the opinion of the court on a rehearing of the case. On the constitutionality of the tax on incomes, the Court stood five to four. Justice Jackson, who had not taken part in the first hearing, dissented from the majority opinion in the final case, while one of the other judges changed his position and voted with the majority. It was long believed that it was Justice Shiras who reversed his opinion, but lately Mr. Sidney Ratner has adduced evidence to the effect that it was Mr. Justice Brewer who reversed himself. The decision of the Court in this case aroused widespread and bitter dissatisfaction; it led, eventually, to the Sixteenth Amendment. For background, see, Warren, *The Supreme Court* (1928 ed.) Vol. II, p. 699 ff.; L. B. Boudin, *Government by Judiciary*, Vol. II, ch. xxvii; A. Nevins, *Grover Cleveland,* appendix.

FULLER, C. J. Whenever this court is required to pass upon the validity of an act of Congress, as tested by the fundamental law enacted by the people, the duty imposed demands in its discharge the utmost deliberation and care, and invokes the deepest sense of responsibility. . . .

We have, therefore, with an anxious desire to omit nothing which might in any degree tend to elucidate the questions submitted, and aided by further able arguments embodying the fruits of elaborate research, carefully re-examined these cases, with the result that, while our former conclusions remain unchanged, their scope must be enlarged by the acceptance of their logical consequences. . . .

Our previous decision was confined to the consideration of the validity of the tax on the income from real estate, and on the income from municipal bonds. . . .

We are now permitted to broaden the field of inquiry, and to determine to which of the two great classes a tax upon a person's entire income, whether derived from rents or products, or otherwise, of real estate, or from bonds, stocks, or other forms of personal property, belongs; and we are unable to conclude that the enforced subtraction from the yield of all the owner's real or personal property, in the manner prescribed, is so different from a tax on the property itself, that it is not a direct, but an indirect, tax in the meaning of the Constitution. . . .

We do not care to retravel ground already traversed, but some observations may be added. . . .

The reasons for the clauses of the Constitution in respect of direct taxation are not far to seek. . . .

The founders anticipated that the expenditures of the States, their counties, cities, and towns, would chiefly be met by direct taxation on accumulated property, while they expected that those of the Federal government would be for the most part met by indirect taxes. And in order that the power of direct taxation by the general government should not be exercised except on necessity, and, when the necessity arose, should be so exercised as to leave the States at liberty to discharge their respective obligations, and should not be so exercised unfairly and discriminatingly, as to particular States or otherwise, by a mere majority vote, possibly of those whose constituents were intentionally not subjected to any part of the burden, the qualified grant was made. . . .

Those who made it knew that the power to tax involved the power to destroy, and that, in the language of Chief Justice Marshall, in *McCulloch* v. *Maryland,* "the only security against the abuse of this power is found in the structure of the government itself." . . . And they retained this security by providing that direct taxation and representation in the lower house of Congress should be adjusted on the same measure.

Moreover, whatever the reasons for the constitutional provisions, there they are, and they appear to us to speak in plain language.

It is said that a tax on the whole income of property is not a direct tax in the meaning of the Constitution, but a duty, and, as a duty, leviable without apportionment, whether direct or indirect. We do not think so. Direct taxation was not restricted in one breath, and the restriction blown to the winds in another. . . .

The Constitution prohibits any direct tax, unless in proportion to numbers as ascertained by the census, and, in the light of the circumstances to which we have referred, is it not an evasion of that prohibition to hold that a general unapportioned tax, imposed upon all property owners as a body for or in respect of their property, is not direct, in the meaning of the Constitution, because confined to the income therefrom?

Whatever the speculative views of political economists or revenue reformers may be, can it be properly held that the Constitution, taken in its plain and obvious sense, and with due regard to the circumstances attending the formation of the government, authorizes a general unapportioned tax on the products of the farm and the rents of real estate, although imposed merely because of ownership, and with no possible means of escape from payment, as belonging to a totally different class from that which includes the property from whence the income proceeds?

There can be but one answer, unless the constitutional restriction is to be treated as utterly illusory and futile, and the object of its framers defeated. We find it impossible to hold that a fundamental requisition deemed so important as to be enforced by two provisions, one affirmative and one negative, can be refined away by forced distinctions between that which gives value to property and the property itself.

Nor can we perceive any ground why the same reasoning does not apply to capital in personalty held for the purpose of income, or ordinarily yielding income, and to the income therefrom. . . .

Personal property of some kind is of general distribution, and so are incomes, though the taxable range thereof might be narrowed through large exemptions. . . .

Nor are we impressed with the contention that, because in the four instances in which the power of direct taxation has been exercised, Congress did not see fit, for reasons of expediency, to levy a tax on personalty, this amounts to such a practical construction of the Constitution that the power did not exist, that we must regard ourselves bound by it. We should regret to be compelled to hold the powers of the general government thus restricted, and certainly we cannot accede to the idea that the Constitution has become weakened by a particular course of inaction under it.

The stress of the argument is thrown, however, on the assertion that an income tax is not a property tax at all; . . . that rents received, crops harvested, interest collected, have lost all connection with their origin, and, though once not taxable, have become transmuted, in their new form, into taxable subject-matter; in other words, that income is taxable, irrespective of the source whence it is derived. . . .

We have unanimously held in this case that, so far as this law operates on the receipts from municipal bonds, it cannot be sustained, because it is a tax on the power of the States and on their instrumentalities to borrow money, and consequently repugnant to the Constitution. But, if, as contended, the interest, when received, has become merely money in the recipient's pocket, and taxable, as such, without reference to the source from which it came, the question is immaterial whether it could have been originally taxed at all or not. This was admitted by the Attorney General, with characteristic candor; and it follows that if the revenue derived from municipal bonds cannot be taxed, because the source cannot be, the same rule applies to revenue from any other source not subject to the tax, and the lack of power to levy any but an apportioned tax on real and personal property equally exists as to the revenue therefrom.

Admitting that this act taxes the income of property, irrespective of its source, still we cannot doubt that such a tax is necessarily a direct tax in the meaning of the Constitution. . . .

The power to tax real and personal property and the income from both, there being an apportionment, is conceded; that such a tax is a direct tax in the meaning of the Constitution has not been, and, in our judgment, cannot be successfully denied; and yet we are thus invited to hesitate in the enforcement of the mandate of the Constitution, which prohibits Congress from laying a direct tax on the revenue from property of the citizen without regard to state lines, and in such manner that the States cannot intervene by payment in regulation of their own resources, lest a government of delegated powers should be found to be, not less powerful, but less absolute, than the imagination of the advocate had supposed.

We are not here concerned with the question whether an income tax be or be not desirable, nor whether such a tax would enable the government to diminish taxes on consumption and duties on imports, and to enter upon what may be believed to be a reform of its fiscal and commercial system. Questions of that character belong to the controversies of political parties, and cannot be settled by judicial decision. In these cases our province is to determine whether this income tax on the revenue from property does or does not belong to the class of direct taxes. If it does, it is, being unapportioned, in violation of the Constitution, and we must so declare. . . .

We have considered the act only in respect of the tax on income derived from real estate, and from invested personal property, and have not commented on so much of it as bears on gains or profits from business, privileges, or employments, in view of the instances in which taxation on business, privileges, or employments has assumed the guise of an excise tax and been sustained as such.

. . . Being of opinion that so much of the section of this law as lays a tax on income from real and personal property is invalid, we are brought to the question of the effect of that conclusion upon these sections as a whole.

It is elementary that the same statute may be in part constitutional and in part unconstitutional, and, if the parts are wholly independent of each other, that which is constitutional may stand while that which is unconstitutional will be rejected. And in the case before us there is no question as to the validity of this act, except sections twenty-seven to thirty-seven, inclusive, which relate to the subject which has been under discussion; and, as to them, we think the rule laid down by Chief Justice Shaw in *Warren* v. *Charlestown*, 2 Gray, 84, is applicable, that if the different parts "are so mutually connected with and dependent on each other, as conditions, considerations, or compensations for each other, as to warrant a belief that the legislature intended them as a whole, and that if all could not be carried into effect the legislature would not pass the residue independently, and some parts are unconstitutional, all the provisions which are thus dependent, conditional, or connected must fall with them." . . .

According to the census, the true valuation of real and personal property in the United States in 1890 was $65,037,091,197, of which real estate with improvements thereon made up $39,544,544,333. Of course, from the latter must be deducted, in applying these sections, all unproductive property and all property whose net yield does not exceed four thousand dollars; but, even with such deductions, it is evident that the income from realty formed a vital part of the scheme for taxation embodied therein. If that be stricken out, and also the income from all invested personal property, bonds, stocks, investments of all kinds, it is obvious that by far the largest part of the anticipated revenue would be eliminated, and this would leave the burden of the tax to be borne by professions, trades, employments, or vocations; and in that way what was intended as a tax on capital would remain in substance a tax on occupations and labor. We cannot believe that such was the intention of Congress. We do not mean to say that an act laying by apportionment a direct tax on all real estate and personal property, or the income thereof, might not also lay excise taxes on business, privileges, employments, and vocations. But this is not such an act; and the scheme must be considered as a whole. Being invalid as to the greater part, and falling, as the tax would, if any part were held valid, in a direction which could not have been contemplated except in connection with the taxation considered as an entirety, we are constrained to conclude that sections twenty-seven to thirty-seven, inclusive, of the act, which became a law, without the signature of the President, on August 28, 1894, are wholly inoperative and void.

Our conclusions may, therefore, be summed up as follows:

First. We adhere to the opinion already announced, that, taxes on real estate being indisputably direct taxes, taxes on the rents or income of real estate are equally direct taxes.

Second. We are of opinion that taxes on personal property, or on the income of personal property, are likewise direct taxes.

Third. The tax imposed by sections twenty-seven to thirty-seven, inclusive, of the act of 1894, so far as it falls on the income of real estate and of personal property, being a direct tax within the meaning of the Constitution, and, therefore, unconstitutional and void because not apportioned according to representation, all those sections, constituting one entire scheme of taxation, are necessarily invalid.

Decrees reversed and relief prayed for granted.

Justices HARLAN, BROWN, JACKSON, and WHITE delivered dissenting opinions.

334. THE ALTGELD–CLEVELAND CONTROVERSY
1894

(W. R. Browne, *Altgeld of Illinois,* p. 154 ff.)

This notable controversy arose out of Cleveland's action in sending federal troops to Chicago during the Pullman Strike. Governor Altgeld had not requested these troops, and there is no convincing evidence that the local and state authorities were not fully competent to handle the situation without outside aid. Cleveland's action broke the strike and earned him contemporary applause, but in perspective it appears unwarranted either by circumstances or by law. See *In re Debs,* Doc. No. 336. On Altgeld, see the biography by Browne; for the controversy, see A. Nevins, *Grover Cleveland,* ch. xxxiii; G. Cleveland, "The Government and the Chicago Strike," in *Presidential Problems.*

1.   Executive Office, State of Illinois
                    July 5, 1894.
Hon. Grover Cleveland, President of the
    United States,
    Washington, D. C.

Sir:—I am advised that you have ordered Federal troops to go into service in the State of Illinois. Surely the facts have not been correctly presented to you in this case, or you would not have taken this step, for it is entirely unnecessary, and, as it seems to me, unjustifiable. Waiving all questions of courtesy, I will say that the State of Illinois is not only able to take care of itself, but it stands ready to furnish the Federal government any assistance it may need elsewhere. Our military force is ample, and consists of as good soldiers as can be found in the country. They have been ordered promptly whenever and wherever they were needed. We have stationed in Chicago alone three Regiments of Infantry, one Battery and one troop of Cavalry, and no better soldiers can be found. They have been ready every moment to go on duty, and have been and are now eager to go into service, but they have not been ordered out because nobody in Cook county, whether official or private citizen, asked to have their assistance, or even intimated in any way that their assistance was desired or necessary.

So far as I have been advised, the local officials have been able to handle the situation. But if any assistance were needed, the State stood ready to furnish a hundred men for every one man required, and stood ready to do so at a moment's notice. Notwithstanding these facts the Federal Government has been applied to by men who had political and selfish motives for wanting to ignore the State Government. We have just gone through a coal strike, more extensive here than in any other State. We have now had ten days of the railroad strike, and we have promptly furnished military aid wherever the local officials needed it.

In two instances the United States marshal for the Southern District of Illinois applied for assistance to enable him to enforce the processes of the United States court, and troops were promptly furnished him, and he was assisted in every way he desired. The law has been thoroughly executed, and every man guilty of violating it during the strike has been brought to justice. If the marshal of the Northern District of Illinois or the authorities of Cook county needed military assistance they had but to ask for it in order to get it from the State.

At present some of our railroads are paralyzed, not by reason of obstruction, but because they cannot get men to operate their trains. For some reason they are anxious to keep this fact from the public, and for this purpose they are making an outcry about obstructions in order to divert attention. Now, I will cite to you two examples which illustrate the situation: . . .

It is true that in several instances a road made efforts to work a few green men and a crowd standing around insulted them and tried to drive them away, and in a few other cases they cut off Pullman sleepers from trains. But all these troubles were local in character and could easily be handled by the State authorities. Illinois has more railroad men than any other State in the Union, but as a rule they are orderly and well-behaved. This is shown by the fact that so very little actual violence has been committed. Only a very small percentage of these men have been guilty of infractions of the law. The newspaper accounts have in many cases been pure fabrications, and in others wild exaggerations.

I have gone thus into details to show that it is not soldiers that the railroads need so much as it is men to operate trains, and that the conditions do not exist here which bring the cause within the Federal statute, a statute that was passed in 1881 (1861) and was in reality a war measure. The statute authorized the use of Federal troops in a State whenever it shall be impracticable to enforce the laws of the United States within such States by the ordinary Judicial proceedings. Such a condition does not exist in Illinois. There have been a few local disturbances, but nothing that seriously interfered with the administration of justice, or that could not be easily controlled by the local or State authorities, for the Federal troops can do nothing that the State troops cannot do.

I repeat that you have been imposed upon in this matter; but even if by a forced construction it were held that the conditions here came within the letter of the statute, then I submit that local self-government is a fundamental principle of our Constitution. Each community shall govern itself so long as it can and is ready and able to enforce the law, and it is in harmony with this fundamental principle that the statute authorizing the President to send troops into States must be construed; especially is this so in matters relating to the exercise of the police power and the preservation of law and order.

To absolutely ignore a local government in matters of this kind, when the local government is ready to furnish assistance needed, and is amply able to enforce the law, not only insults the people of this State by imputing to them an inability to govern themselves, or an unwillingness to enforce the law, but is in violation of a basic principle of our institutions. The question of Federal supremacy is in no way involved. No one disputes it for a moment; but, under our Constitution, Federal supremacy and local self-government must go hand in hand, and to ignore the latter is to do violence to the Constitution.

As Governor of the State of Illinois, I protest against this, and ask the immediate withdrawal of the Federal troops from active duty in this State. Should the situation at any time get so serious that we cannot control it with the State forces, we will promptly ask for Federal assistance; but until such time, I protest, with all due deference, against this uncalled for reflection upon our people, and again ask the immediate withdrawal of these troops. I have the honor to be, yours respectfully,

JOHN P. ALTGELD, Governor of Illinois.

2.   Executive Mansion, Washington, D. C., July 5, 1894.

Hon. John P. Altgeld, Governor of Illinois, Springfield, Ill.

Sir:—Federal troops were sent to Chicago in strict accordance with the Constitution and laws of the United States, upon the demand of the postoffice department that obstruction of the mails should be removed, and upon the representations of the judicial officers of the United States that the process of the Federal courts could not be executed through the ordinary means, and upon competent proof that conspiracies existed against commerce between the States. To meet these conditions, which are clearly within the province of Federal authority, the presence of Federal troops in the city of Chicago was deemed not only proper, but necessary, and there has been no intention of thereby interfering with the plain duty of the local authorities to preserve the peace of the city.

GROVER CLEVELAND.

3.   Executive Office, State of Illinois, July 6, 1894.

Hon. Grover Cleveland, President of the United States,

Sir:—Your answer to my protest involves some startling conclusions and ignores and evades the question at issue—that is, that the principle of local self-government is just as fundamental in our institutions as is that of Federal supremacy.

First—You calmly assume that the executive has the legal right to order Federal troops into any community of the United States, in the first instance, whenever there is the slightest disturbance, and that he can do this without any regard to the question as to whether that community is able and ready to enforce the law itself. Inasmuch as the executive is the sole judge of the question as to whether any disturbance exists in any part of the country, this assumption means that the executive can send Federal troops into any community in the United States at his pleasure, and keep them there as long as he chooses. If this is the law, then the principle of self-government either never did exist in this country or else has been destroyed, for no community can be said to possess local self-government if the executive can, at his pleasure, send military forces to patrol its streets under pretense of enforcing some law. The kind of local self-government that could exist under these circumstances can be found in any of the monarchies of Europe, and it is not in harmony with the spirit of our institutions.

Second—It is also a fundamental principle in our government that except in times of war the military shall be subordinate to the civil authority. In harmony with this provision, the State troops are ordered out to act under and with the civil authorities. The troops you have ordered to Chicago are not under the civil authorities, and are in no way responsible to them for their conduct. They are not even acting under the United States Marshal or any Federal officer of the State, but are acting directly under military orders issued from military headquarters at Washington; and in so far as these troops act at all, it is military government.

Third—The statute authorizing Federal troops to be sent into States in certain cases contemplates that the State troops shall be taken first. This provision has been ignored and it is assumed that the executive is not bound by it. Federal interference with industrial disturbances in the various States is certainly a new departure, and it opens up so large a field that it will require a very little stretch of authority to absorb to itself all the details of local government.

Fourth—You say that troops were ordered into Illinois upon the demand of the post-office department, and upon representations of the judicial officers of the United States that process of the courts could not be served, and upon proof that conspiracies existed. We will not discuss the facts, but look for a moment at the principle involved in your statement. All of these officers are appointed by the executive. Most of them can be removed by him at will. They are not only obliged to do his bidding, but they are in fact a part of the executive. If several of them can apply for troops, one alone can; so that under the law, as you assume it to be, an executive, through any one of his appointees, can apply to himself to have the military sent into any city or number of cities, and base his application on such representations as he sees fit to make. In fact, it will be immaterial whether he makes any showing or not, for the executive is the sole judge, and nobody else has any right to interfere or even inquire about it. Then the executive can pass on his own application, his will being the sole guide—he can hold the application to be sufficient, and order troops to as many places as he wishes and put them in command of anyone he chooses, and have them act, not under the civil officers, either Federal or State, but directly under military orders from Washington, and there is not in the Constitution or laws, whether written or unwritten, any limitation or restraint upon his power. His judgment—that is, his will—is the sole guide; and it being purely a matter of discretion, his decision can never be examined or questioned.

This assumption as to the power of the executive is certainly new, and I respectfully submit that it is not the law of the land. The jurists have told us that this is a government of law, and not a government by the caprice of an individual, and, further, instead of being autocratic, it is a government of limited power. Yet the autocrat of Russia could certainly not possess, or claim to possess, greater power than is possessed by the executive of the United States, if your assumption is correct.

Fifth—The executive has the command not only of the regular forces of all the United States, but of the military forces of all the States, and can order them to any place he sees fit; and as there are always more or less local disturbances over the country, it will be an easy matter under your construction of the law for an ambitious executive to order out the military forces of all of the States, and establish at once a military government. The only chance of failure in such a movement could come from rebellion, and with such a vast military power at command this could readily be crushed, for, as a rule, soldiers will obey orders.

As for the situation in Illinois, that is of no consequence now compared with the far-reaching principle involved. True, according to my advices, Federal troops have now been on duty for over two days, and although the men were brave and the officers valiant and able, yet their very presence proved to be an irritant because it aroused the indignation of a large class of people who, while upholding law and order, had been taught to believe in local self-government, and therefore resented what they regarded as unwarranted interference.

Inasmuch as the Federal troops can do nothing but what the State troops can do there, and believing that the State is amply able to take care of the situation and enforce the law, and believing that the ordering out of the Federal troops was unwarranted, I again ask their withdrawal.

JOHN P. ALTGELD.

4. Executive Mansion, Washington, D. C.
   July 6, 1894.

While I am still persuaded that I have neither transcended my authority nor duty in the emergency that confronts us, it seems to me that in this hour of danger and public distress, discussion may well give way to active efforts on the part of all in authority to restore obedience to law and to protect life and property.

GROVER CLEVELAND.

Hon. John P. Altgeld,
Governor of Illinois.

335. U.S. v. DEBS ET AL.
64 Fed. 724
1894

Proceedings for contempt against Eugene V. Debs and others for violation of injunctions issued in the Pullman strike of 1894. The extract from the decision of the Circuit Court for the Northern District of Illinois bears on the application of the Sherman Anti-Trust Act to the case. The Congressional investigation of the strike can be found in *United States Strike Commission Report*, Sen. Exec. Doc. 7, 53d. Cong. 3d. Sess. See also A. Nevins, *Grover Cleveland*, ch. xxxiii; W. R. Browne, *Altgeld of Illinois*, chs. xii–xvi; and Doc. No. 334. On the use of the injunction in labor disputes see, F. Frankfurter and L. Greene, *The Labor Injunction;* E. E. Witte, *The Government in Labor Disputes;* P. F. Brissenden, "The Labor Injunction," *Pol. Sci. Qt.* Vol. XLVIII.

WOODS, Circuit Judge. . . . The question now to be considered [is] whether or not the injunction was authorized by the act of July 2, 1890. It was under that act that the order was asked and was granted; but it has been seriously questioned in this proceeding, as well as by an eminent judge and by lawyers elsewhere, whether the statute is by its terms applicable, or consistently with constitutional guaranties can be applied, to cases like this.

. . . The position of the defendants in respect to this statute, as stated in one of the briefs, is that it "is directed at capital", "at dangers very generally supposed to result from vast aggregations of capital", that "the evil aimed at is one of a contractual character, and not of force and violence.". . . It is said we may gather from the debates in congress, as from any other source, "the history of the evil which the legislation was intended to remedy." Doubtless this is often true; and in this instance it is perhaps apparent that the original measure, as proposed in the senate, "was directed wholly against trusts, and not at organizations of labor in any form". But it also appears that before the bill left the senate its title had been changed, and material additions made to the text; and it is worthy of note that a proviso to the effect that the act should not be construed to apply "to any arrangements, agreements or combinations made between laborers with a view of lessening hours of labor or of increasing their wages, nor to any arrangements, agreements or combinations among persons engaged in agriculture made with the view of enhancing the price of agricultural . . . products" was not adopted. Such an amendment, doubtless, was not necessary in order to exclude agreements and arrangements of the kind mentioned; but the offering of the proposition shows that the possible application of the statute to cases not in the nature of trusts or monopolies, and in which workmen or farmers should be concerned, was not overlooked. But it is more significant that, upon the introduction of the bill into the house, the chairman of the judiciary committee, . . . made the following statement: "Now just what contracts, what combinations in the form of trusts, or what conspiracies will be in restraint of trade or commerce, mentioned in the bill, will not be known until the courts have construed and interpreted this provision."

It is therefore the privilege and duty of the court, uncontrolled by considerations drawn from other sources, to find the meaning of the statute in the terms of its provisions, interpreted by the settled rules of construction. That the original design to suppress trusts and monopolies created by contract or combination in the form of trust, which of course would be of a "contractual character" was adhered to, is clear; but it is equally clear that a further and more comprehensive purpose came to be entertained, and was embodied in the final form of the enactment. Combinations are condemned, not only when they take the form of trusts, but in whatever form found, if they be in restraint of trade. That is the effect of the words "or otherwise". . . . Any proposed restraint of trade, though it be in itself innocent, if it is to be accomplished by conspiracy, is unlawful. . . .

I have not failed, I think, to appreciate the just force of the argument to the contrary, of my opinion,—it has sometimes entangled me in doubt,—but my conclusion is clear, that under the act of 1890, the court had jurisdiction of the case presented in the application, and that the injunction granted was not without authority of law, nor for any reason invalid. . . .

336. IN RE DEBS
158 U.S. 564
1895

Petition for a writ of *habeas corpus*. The facts of the case are stated in *U.S.* v. *Debs*, Doc. No. 335. It is important to notice that the decision of the Supreme Court was based not upon the Sherman Anti-Trust Act, but upon much broader grounds.

BREWER, J. The case presented by the bill is this: The United States, finding that the interstate transportation of persons and property, as well as the carriage of the mails, is forcibly obstructed, and that a combination and conspiracy exists to subject the control of such transportation to the will of the conspirators, applied to one of their courts, sitting as a court of equity, for an injunction to restrain such obstruction and prevent carrying into effect such conspiracy. Two questions of importance are presented: First. Are the relations of the general government to interstate commerce and the transportation of the mails such as to authorize a direct interference to prevent a forcible obstruction thereof? Second. If authority exists, as authority in governmental affairs implies both power and duty, has a court of equity jurisdiction to issue an injunction in aid of the performance of such duty?

First. What are the relations of the general government to interstate commerce and the transportation of the mails? They are those of direct supervision, control, and management. While under the dual system which prevails with us the powers of government are distributed between the state and the nation, and while the latter is properly styled a government of enumerated powers, yet within the limits of such enumeration it has all the attributes of sovereignty, and, in the exercise of those enumerated powers, acts directly upon the citizen, and not through the intermediate agency of the state. . . .

"We hold it to be an incontrovertible principle, that the government of the United States may, by means of physical force, exercised through its official agents, execute on every foot of American soil the powers and functions that belong to it. This necessarily involves the power to command obedience to its laws, and hence the power to keep the peace to that extent. . . ." Mr. Justice Bradley in *Ex parte Siebold,* 100 U. S. 371, 395. . . .

Among the powers expressly given to the national government are the control of interstate commerce and the creation and management of the postoffice system for the nation. . . .

Obviously these powers given to the national government over interstate commerce and in respect to the transportation of the mails were not dormant and unused. Congress had taken hold of these two matters, and by various and specific acts had assumed and exercised the powers given to it, and was in the full discharge of its duty to regulate interstate commerce and carry the mails. The validity of such exercise and the exclusiveness of its control had been again and again presented to this court for consideration. It is curious to note the fact that in a large proportion of the cases in respect to interstate commerce brought to this court the question presented was of the validity of state legislation in its bearings upon interstate commerce, and the uniform course of decision has been to declare that it is not within the competency of a state to legislate in such a manner as to obstruct interstate commerce. If a state with its recognized powers of sovereignty is impotent to obstruct interstate commerce, can it be that any mere voluntary association of individuals within the limits of that state has a power which the state itself does not possess?

As, under the Constitution, power over interstate commerce and the transportation of the mails is vested in the national government, and Congress by virtue of such grant has assumed actual and direct control, it follows that the national government may prevent any unlawful and forcible interference therewith. But how shall this be accomplished? Doubtless, it is within the competency of Congress to prescribe by legislation that any interference with these matters shall be offenses against the United States, and prosecuted and punished by indictment in the proper courts. But is that the only remedy? Have the vast interests of the nation in interstate commerce, and in the transporta-

tion of the mails, no other protection than lies in the possible punishment of those who interfere with it? To ask the question is to answer it. By article 3, section 2, clause 3, of the federal Constitution it is provided: "The trial of all crimes except in cases of impeachment shall be by jury; and such trial shall be held in the State where the said crime shall have been committed." If all the inhabitants of a state, or even a great body of them, should combine to obstruct interstate commerce or the transportation of the mails, prosecutions for such offenses had in such a community would be doomed in advance to failure. And if the certainty of such failure was known, and the national government had no other way to enforce the freedom of interstate commerce and the transportation of the mails than by prosecution and punishment for interference therewith, the whole interests of the nation in these respects would be at the absolute mercy of a portion of the inhabitants of that single state.

But there is no such impotency in the national government. The entire strength of the nation may be used to enforce in any part of the land the full and free exercise of all national powers and the security of all rights entrusted by the Constitution to its care. The strong arm of the national government may be put forth to brush away all obstructions to the freedom of interstate commerce or the transportation of the mails. If the emergency arises, the army of the nation, and all its militia, are at the service of the nation to compel obedience to its laws.

But passing to the second question, is there no other alternative than the use of force on the part of the executive authorities whenever obstructions arise to the freedom of interstate commerce or the transportation of the mails? Is the army the only instrument by which rights of the public can be enforced and the peace of the nation preserved? Grant that any public nuisance may be forcibly abated either at the instance of the authorities, or by any individual suffering private damage therefrom, the existence of this right of forcible abatement is not inconsistent with nor does it destroy the right of appeal in an orderly way to the court for a judicial determination, and an exercise of their powers by writ of injunction and otherwise to accomplish the same result. . . .

It is obvious from these decisions that while it is not the province of the government to interfere in any mere matter of private controversy between individuals, or to use its great powers to enforce the rights of one against another, yet, whenever the wrongs complained of are such as affect the public at large, and are in respect of matters which by the Constitution are entrusted to the care of the nation, and concerning which the nation owes the duty to all the citizens of securing to them their common rights, then the mere fact that the government has no pecuniary interest in the controversy is not sufficient to exclude it from the courts, or prevent it from taking measures therein to fully discharge those constitutional duties.

The national government, given by the Constitution power to regulate interstate commerce, has by express statute assumed jurisdiction over such commerce when carried upon railroads. It is charged, therefore, with the duty of keeping those highways of interstate commerce free from obstruction, for it has always been recognized as one of the powers and duties of a government to remove obstructions from the highway under its control. . . .

We have given to this case the most careful and anxious attention, for we realize that it touches closely questions of supreme importance to the people of this country. Summing up our conclusions, we hold that the government of the United States is one having jurisdiction over every foot of soil within its territory, and acting directly upon each citizen; that while it is a government of enumerated powers, it has within the limits of those powers all the attributes of sovereignty, that to it is committed power over interstate commerce and the transmission of the mail; that the powers thus conferred upon the national government are not dormant, but have been assumed and put into practical exercise by the legislation of Congress; that in the exercise of those powers it is competent for the nation to remove all obstructions upon highways, natural or artificial, to the passage of interstate commerce or the carrying of the mail; that while it may be competent for the government (through the executive branch and in the use of the entire executive power of the nation)

to forcibly remove all such obstructions, it is equally within its competency to appeal to the civil courts for an inquiry and determination as to the existence and character of any alleged obstructions, and if such are found to exist, or threaten to occur, to invoke the powers of these courts to remove or restrain such obstruction; that the jurisdiction of courts to interfere in such matters by injunction is one recognized from ancient times and by indubitable authority; that such jurisdiction is not ousted by the fact that the obstructions are accompanied by or consist of acts in themselves violations of the criminal law; that the proceeding by injunction is of a civil character, and may be enforced by proceedings in contempt; that such proceedings are not in execution of the criminal laws of the land; that the penalty for a violation of injunction is no substitute for and no defense to a prosecution for any criminal offenses committed in the course of such violation; that the complaint filed in this case clearly showed an existing obstruction of artificial highways for the passage of interstate commerce and the transmission of the mail—an obstruction not only temporarily existing, but threatening to continue; that under such complaint the circuit court had power to issue its process of injunction; that it having been issued and served on these defendants, the circuit court had authority to inquire whether its orders had been disobeyed, and when it found that they had been, then to proceed under section 725, Revised Statutes, which grants power "to punish by fine or imprisonment, . . . disobedience, . . . by any party . . . or other person, to any lawful writ, process, order, rule, decree or command," and enter the order of punishment complained of; and, finally, that, the circuit court, having full jurisdiction in the premises, its finding of the fact of disobedience is not open to review on habeas corpus in this or any other court. . . .

We enter into no examination of the act of July 2, 1890, upon which the Circuit Court relied mainly to sustain its jurisdiction. It must not be understood from this that we dissent from the conclusions of that court in reference to the scope of the act, but simply that we prefer to rest our judgement on the broader ground which has been discussed in this opinion, believing it of importance that the principles underlying it should be fully stated and affirmed.

The petition for a writ of *habeas corpus* is denied.

337. CLEVELAND'S APPEAL FOR A GOLD GUARANTEE ON BONDS
Message to Congress February 8, 1895
(Richardson, ed. *Messages and Papers,* Vol. VIII, p. 567 ff.)

As early as January 1895 it became apparent that the government would have to replenish its gold reserve through a third bond sale. The President and Secretary Carlisle accordingly made an arrangement with a syndicate headed by J. P. Morgan for the sale of $65,000,000 of bonds. These bonds were to yield four per cent. but if Congress would substitute the words "gold bonds" for "coin bonds" the interest rate would be reduced to three per. cent., thus saving the government some $16,000,000 in interest. Cleveland's appeal to Congress to authorize the necessary change was defeated by the silver forces, led by Bland and Bryan. The terms of the third bond deal were considered excessively hard, and both the Government and the syndicate were bitterly criticised for the transaction. See, A. Nevins, *Grover Cleveland,* p. 661 ff.; W. J. Bryan, *The First Battle,* p. 135 ff.; J. A. Barnes, *John G. Carlisle,* ch. xv; L. Corey, *The House of Morgan,* ch. xviii; the bond sale investigation is in 54th Cong. 2d Sess. *Senate Exec. Doc. No. 187.*

EXECUTIVE MANSION, *February 8, 1895.*
To the Congress of the United States:

Since my recent communciation to the Congress calling attention to our financial condition and suggesting legislation which I deemed essential to our national welfare and credit the anxiety and apprehension then existing in business circles has continued.

As a precaution, therefore, against the failure of timely legislative aid through Congressional action, cautious preparations have been pending to employ to the best possible advantage, in default of better means, such Executive authority as may without additional legislation be exercised for the purpose of reënforcing and maintaining in our Treasury an adequate and safe gold reserve.

In the judgment of those especially charged with this responsibility the business situation is so critical and the legislative situation is so unpromising, with the omission thus far on the part of Congress to beneficially enlarge the powers of the Secretary of the Treasury in the premises, as to enjoin immediate Executive action with the facilities now at hand.

Therefore, in pursuance of section 3700 of the Revised Statutes, the details of an arrangement have this day been concluded with parties abundantly able to fulfill their undertaking whereby bonds of the United States authorized under the act of July 14, 1875, payable in coin thirty years after their date, with interest at the rate of 4 per cent per annum, to the amount of a little less than $62,400,000, are to be issued for the purchase of gold coin, amounting to a sum slightly in excess of $65,000,000, to be delivered to the Treasury of the United States, which sum added to the gold now held in our reserve will so restore such reserve as to make it amount to something more than $100,000,000. Such a premium is to be allowed to the Government upon the bonds as to fix the rate of interest upon the amount of gold realized at 3¾ per cent per annum. At least one-half of the gold to be obtained is to be supplied from abroad, which is a very important and favorable feature of the transaction.

The privilege is especially reserved to the Government to substitute at par within ten days from this date, in lieu of the 4 per cent coin bonds, other bonds in terms payable in gold and bearing only 3 per cent interest if the issue of the same should in the meantime be authorized by the Congress.

The arrangement thus completed, which after careful inquiry appears in present circumstances and considering all the objects desired to be the best attainable, develops such a difference in the estimation of investors between bonds made payable in coin and those specifically made payable in gold in favor of the latter as is represented by three-fourths of a cent in annual interest. In the agreement just concluded the annual saving in interest to the Government if 3 per cent gold bonds should be substituted for 4 per cent coin bonds under the privilege reserved would be $539,159, amounting in thirty years, or at the maturity of the coin bonds, to $16,174,770.

Of course there never should be a doubt in any quarter as to the redemption in gold of the bonds of the Government which are made payable in coin. Therefore the discrimination, in the judgment of investors, between our bond obligations payable in coin and those specifically made payable in gold is very significant. It is hardly necessary to suggest that, whatever may be our views on the subject, the sentiments or preferences of those with whom we must negotiate in disposing of our bonds for gold are not subject to our dictation.

I have only to add that in my opinion the transaction herein detailed for the information of the Congress promises better results than the efforts previously made in the direction of effectively adding to our gold reserve through the sale of bonds, and I believe it will tend, as far as such action can in present circumstances, to meet the determination expressed in the law repealing the silver-purchasing clause of the act of July 14, 1890, and that, in the language of such repealing act, the arrangement made will aid our efforts to "insure the maintenance of the parity in value of the coins of the two metals and the equal power of every dollar at all times in the markets and in the payment of debts."

GROVER CLEVELAND.

338. APPEAL OF THE SILVER DEMOCRATS
March 5, 1895

(W. J. Bryan, *The First Battle*, p. 156-7)

Ever since the beginning of the second Cleveland administration, the split in the Democratic party between the silver and the gold Democrats had been steadily widening. In the closing days of the Fifty-third Congress, Bryan and Bland, the two outstanding leaders of the silver forces in the House, drew up an appeal to the Democratic party, which was signed by about one fifth of the Democratic members of the lower House and by Evan Howell, editor of the Atlanta Constitution. "This address," wrote Bryan, "was the beginning of the successful effort on the part of the silver Democrats to take control of the Democratic organization". This effort culminated in the control of the 1896 convention by the silver forces. See, W. J. Bryan, *The First Battle*, ch. vi.

An Important Document

To the Democrats of the United States:

We, the undersigned Democrats, present for your consideration the following statement:

We believe that the establishment of gold as the only monetary standard and the elimination of silver as a full legal tender money, will increase the purchasing power of each dollar, add to the burden of all debts, decrease the market value of all other forms of property, continue and intensify business depression, and, finally, reduce the majority of the people to financial bondage.

We believe that no party can hope for enduring success in the United States so long as it advocates a single gold standard, and that the advocacy of such a financial policy would be especially fatal to a party which, like the Democratic party, derives its voting strength from those who may without reproach be called the common people; and we point to the overwhelming defeat of the party in 1894, to the opposition aroused by the veto of the seigniorage bill and to the still more unanimous protest against the issue of gold bonds, as proof that the Democratic party cannot be brought to the support of the gold standard policy.

We believe that the money question will be the paramount issue in 1896, and will so remain until it is settled by the intelligence and patriotism of the American voters.

We believe that a large majority of the Democrats of the United States favor bimetallism, and realize that it can only be secured by the restoration of the free and unlimited coinage of gold and silver at the present ratio, and we assert that the majority have, and should exercise, the right to control the policy of the party and retain the party name.

We believe that it is the duty of the majority, and within their power, to take charge of the party organization and make the Democratic party an effective instrument in the accomplishment of needed reforms. It is necessary that Democrats should surrender their convictions on other questions in order to take an active part in the settlement of the question which at this time surpasses all others in importance.

We believe that the rank and file of the Democratic party should at once assert themselves in the Democratic party and place the party on record in favor of the immediate restoration of the free and unlimited coinage of gold and silver at the present legal ratio of 16 to 1, as such coinage existed prior to 1873, without waiting for the aid or consent of any other nation, such gold and silver coin to be a full legal tender for all debts public and private.

We urge all Democrats who favor the financial policy above set forth to associate themselves together and impress their views upon the party organization; we urge all newspapers in harmony with the above financial policy to place it at the head of the editorial column and assist in the immediate restoration of bimetallism.

339. UNITED STATES v. E. C. KNIGHT COMPANY
156 U. S. 1
1895

Appeal from the United States Circuit Court of Appeals. Bill by the United States against the E. C. Knight Company, and other corporations, charging violation of the Sherman Anti-Trust Act. The E. C. Knight Company, the American Sugar Refining Company, had purchased the stock of four competing sugar refining companies located in Philadelphia, Pennsylvania, and thus secured a practical monopoly on the manufacture of refined sugar in the United States. It was charged that these purchases constituted a combination in restraint of trade. The Circuit Court of Appeals dismissed the bill.

The decision in this case constituted a serious set-back to the enforcement of the Sherman Anti-Trust Act. For a discussion of the case see A. H. Walker, *History of the Sherman Law*, p. 90 ff.

FULLER, C. J. . . . In the view which we take of the case, we need not discuss whether because the tentacles which drew the outlying refineries into the dominant corporation were separately put out, therefore there was no combination to monopolize; or, because according to political economists, aggregations of capital may reduce prices, therefore the objection to concentratioh of power is relieved; or, because others were theoretically left free to go into the business of refining sugar, and the original stockholders of the Philadelphia refineries after becoming stockholders of the American Company might go into competition with themselves, or, parting with that stock, might set up again for themselves, therefore no objectionable restraint was imposed.

The fundamental question is, whether conceding that the existence of a monopoly in manufacture is established by the evidence, that monopoly can be directly suppressed under the act of Congress in the mode attempted by this bill.

It cannot be denied that the power of a State to protect the lives, health, and property of its citizens, and to preserve good order and the public morals, "the power to govern men and things within the limits of its dominion," is a power originally and always belonging to the States, not surrendered by them to the general government, nor directly restrained by the Constitution of the United States, and essentially exclusive. The relief of the citizens of each State from the burden of monopoly and the evils resulting from the restraint of trade among such citizens was left with the States to deal with. . . . On the other hand, the power of Congress to regulate commerce among the several States is also exclusive. . .

The argument is that the power to control the manufacture of refined sugar is a monopoly over a necessary of life, to the enjoyment of which by a large part of the population of the United States interstate commerce is indispensable, and that, therefore, the general government in the exercise of the power to regulate commerce may suppress such monopoly directly and set aside the instruments which have created it. But this argument cannot be confined to necessaries of life merely, and must include all articles of general consumption. Doubtless the power to control the manufacture of a given thing involves in a certain sense the control of its disposition, but this is a secondary and not the primary sense; and although the exercise of that power may result in bringing the operation of commerce into play, it does not control it, and affects it only incidentally and indirectly. Commerce succeeds to manufacture, and is not a part of it. The power to regulate commerce is the power to prescribe the rule by which commerce shall be governed, and is a power independent of the power to suppress monopoly. But it may operate in repression of monopoly whenever it comes within the rules by which commerce is governed or whenever the transaction is itself a monopoly of commerce.

It is vital that the independence of the commercial power and of the police power, and the delimitation between them, however sometimes perplexing, should always be recognized and observed, for while the one furnishes the strongest bond of union, the other is essential to the autonomy of the States as required by our dual form of government; and acknowledged evils, however grave and urgent they may appear to be, had better be borne, than the risk be run, in the effort to suppress them, of more serious consequences by resort to expedients of even doubtful constitutionality.

It will be perceived how far-reaching the proposition is that the power of dealing with a monopoly directly may be exercised by the general government whenever interstate or international commerce may be ultimately affected. The regulation of commerce applies to the subjects of commerce, and not to matters of internal police. Contracts to buy, sell, or exchange goods to be transported among the several States, the transportation and its instrumentalities, and articles bought, sold, or exchanged for the purposes of such transit among the States, or put in the way of transit, may be regulated, but this is because they form part of interstate trade or commerce. The fact that an article is manufactured for export to another State does not of itself make it an article of interstate commerce, and the intent of the manufacturer does not determine the time when the article or product passes from the control of the State and belongs to commerce. . . .

And Mr. Justice Lamar remarked: "A situation more paralyzing to the state governments, and more provocative of conflicts between the general government and the States, and less likely to have been what the framers of the Constitution intended, it would be difficult to imagine."

Contracts, combinations, or conspiracies to control domestic enterprise in manufacture, agriculture, mining production in all its forms, or to raise or lower prices or wages, might unquestionably tend to restrain external as well as domestic trade, but the restraint would be an indirect result, however inevitable and whatever its extent, and such result would not necessarily determine the object of the contract, combination, or conspiracy.

Again, all the authorities agree that in order to vitiate a contract or combination it is not essential that its result should be a complete monopoly; it is sufficient if it really tends to that end and to deprive the public of the advantages which flow from free competition. Slight reflection will show that if the national power extends to all contracts and combinations in manufacture, agriculture, mining, and other productive industries, whose ultimate result may affect external commerce, comparatively little of business operations and affairs would be left for state control.

It was in the light of well-settled principles that the act of July 2, 1890 was framed. Congress did not attempt thereby to assert the power to deal with monopoly directly as such; or to limit and restrict the rights of corporations created by the States or the citizens of the States in the acquisition, control, or disposition of property; or to regulate or prescribe the price or prices at which such property or the products thereof should be sold; or to make criminal the acts of persons in the acquisition and control of property which the States of their residence or creation sanctioned or permitted. Aside from the provisions applicable where Congress might exercise municipal power, what the law struck at was combinations, contracts, and conspiracies to monopolize trade and commerce among the several States or with foreign nations; but the contracts and acts of the defendants related exclusively to the acquisition of the Philadelphia refineries and the business of sugar refining in Pennsylvania, and bore no direct relation to commerce between the States or with foreign nations. The object was manifestly private gain in the manufacture of the commodity, but not through the control of interstate or foreign commerce. It is true that the bill alleged that the products of these refineries were sold and distributed among the several States, and that all the companies were engaged in trade or commerce with the several States and with foreign nations; but this was no more than to say that trade and commerce served manufacture to fulfil its function. . . . There was nothing in the proofs to indicate any intention to put a restraint upon trade or commerce, and the fact, as we have seen, that trade or commerce might be indirectly affected was not enough to entitle complainants to a decree. . . .

Decree of the Circuit Court of Appeals dismissing the bill affirmed. HARLAN, J. delivered a dissenting opinion.

340. CLEVELAND'S MESSAGE ON THE VENEZUELA BOUNDARY CONTROVERSY
December 17, 1895

(Richardson, ed. *Messages and Papers,* Vol. IX, p. 655 ff.)

The dispute between Great Britain and Venezuela over the boundary of British Guiana was of long standing. The efforts of Venezuela to submit it to arbitration proving vain, Venezuela broke off diplomatic relations with Great Britain in 1887. Cleveland considered that the Monroe Doctrine was involved in the dispute, and in 1895 he determined to force the issue to a conclusion. July 20, Secretary Olney sent a despatch for transmission to Lord Salisbury calling attention to the interest of the United States in the boundary dispute and insisting that the Monroe Doctrine required American intervention on behalf of arbitration. In the course of his letter, Mr. Olney said, "To-day the United States is practically sovereign on this continent, and its fiat is law upon the subjects to which it confines its interposition. Why? . . . It is because in addition to all other grounds, its infinite resources combined with its isolated position render it master of the situation and practically invulnerable against any or all other powers." And Mr. Olney concluded with a definite request for arbitration. Lord Salisbury replied, November 26, in two notes: one denying the applicability of the Monroe Doctrine to the dispute, the other maintaining the correctness of the British position in the boundary controversy. December 17, President Cleveland laid this correspondence before Congress and asked for authority to appoint an independent commission to pass on the merits of the dispute. To many it seemed that war was inevitable, but public opinion in both countries forced an accommodation. Furthermore Great Britain was faced, in 1896, with a serious outbreak of the Boers in South Africa, and on January 3 Kaiser William of Germany sent his famous telegram of sympathy to the Boer leader, Paul Kruger. Under the circumstances Lord Salisbury acquiesced in the American demand. A treaty was negotiated with Venezuela which provided for the appointment of an impartial tribunal to pass on the boundary controversy. The tribunal met in Paris in 1899 and handed down a decision which favored the British contentions. See, G. Cleveland, *The Venezuela Boundary Controversy;* A. Nevins, *Grover Cleveland,* ch. xxxiv; R. McElroy, *Grover Cleveland,* Vol. II, ch. vi; H. James, *Richard Olney;* S. F. Bemis ed., *American Secretaries of State,* Vol. VIII, p. 291 ff.; A. B. Hart, *The Monroe Doctrine;* T. B. Edgington, *The Monroe Doctrine,* ch. xvi; D. Y. Thomas, *One Hundred Years of the Monroe Doctrine.*

Executive Mansion, December 17, 1895.
To the Congress:

In my annual message addressed to the Congress on the 3d instant I called attention to the pending boundary controversy between Great Britain and the Republic of Venezuela and recited the substance of a representation made by this Government to Her Britannic Majesty's Government suggesting reasons why such dispute should be submitted to arbitration for settlement and inquiring whether it would be so submitted.

The answer of the British Government, which was then awaited, has since been received, and, together with the despatch to which it is a reply, is hereto appended.

Such reply is embodied in two communications addressed by the British prime minister to Sir Julian Pauncefote, the British ambassador at this capital. It will be seen that one of these communications is devoted exclusively to observations upon the Monroe doctrine, and claims that in the present instance a new and strange extension and development of this doctrine is insisted on by the United States; that the reasons justifying an appeal to the doctrine enunciated by President Monroe are generally inapplicable "to the state of things in which we live at the present day," and especially inapplicable to a controversy involving the boundary line between Great Britain and Venezuela.

Without attempting extended argument in reply to these positions, it may not be amiss to suggest that the doctrine upon which we stand is strong and sound, because its enforcement is important to our peace and safety as a nation and is essential to the integrity of our free institutions and the tranquil maintenance of our distinctive form of government. It was intended to apply to every stage of our national life and can not become obsolete while our Republic endures. If the balance of power is justly a cause for jealous anxiety among the Governments of the Old World and a subject for our absolute noninterference, none the less is an observance of the Monroe doctrine of vital concern to our people and their Government.

Assuming, therefore, that we may properly insist upon this doctrine without regard to "the state of things in which we live" or any changed conditions here or elsewhere, it is not apparent why its application may not be invoked in the present controversy.

If a European power by an extension of its boundaries takes possession of the territory of one of our neighboring Republics against its will and in derogation of its rights, it is difficult to see why to that extent such European power does not thereby attempt to extend its system of government to that portion of this continent which is thus taken. This is the precise action which President Monroe declared to be "dangerous to our peace and safety," and it can make no difference whether the European system is extended by an advance of frontier or otherwise.

It is also suggested in the British reply that we should not seek to apply the Monroe doctrine to the pending dispute because it does not embody any principle of international law which "is founded on the general consent of nations," and that "no statesman, however eminent, and no nation, however powerful, are competent to insert into the code of international law a novel principle which was never recognized before and which has not since been accepted by the government of any other country."

Practically the principle for which we contend has peculiar, if not exclusive, relation to the United States. It may not have been admitted in so many words to the code of international law, but since in international councils every nation is entitled to the rights belonging to it, if the enforcement of the Monroe doctrine is something we may justly claim it has its place in the code of international law as certainly and as securely as if it were specifically mentioned; and when the United States is a suitor before the high tribunal that administers international law the question to be determined is whether or not we present claims which the justice of that code of law can find to be right and valid.

The Monroe doctrine finds its recognition in those principles of international law which are based upon the theory that every nation shall have its rights protected and its just claims enforced.

Of course this Government is entirely confident that under the sanction of this doctrine we have clear rights and undoubted claims. Nor is this ignored in the British reply. The prime minister, while not admitting that the Monroe doctrine is applicable to present conditions, states:

In declaring that the United States would resist any such enterprise if it was contemplated, President Monroe adopted a policy which received the entire sympathy of the English Government of that date.

He further declares:

Though the language of President Monroe is directed to the attainment of objects which most Englishmen would agree to be salutary, it is impossible to admit that they have been inscribed by any adequate authority in the code of international law.

Again he says:

They [Her Majesty's Government] fully concur with the view which President Monroe apparently entertained, that any disturbance of the existing territorial distribution in that hemisphere by any fresh acquisitions on the part of any European State would be a highly inexpedient change.

In the belief that the doctrine for which

we contend was clear and definite, that it was founded upon substantial considerations and involved our safety and welfare, that it was fully applicable to our present conditions and to the state of the world's progress, and that it was directly related to the pending controversy, and without any conviction as to the final merits of the dispute, but anxious to learn in a satisfactory and conclusive manner whether Great Britain sought under a claim of boundary to extend her possessions on this continent without right, or whether she merely sought possession of territory fairly included within her lines of ownership, this Government proposed to the Government of Great Britain a resort to arbitration as the proper means of settling the question, to the end that a vexatious boundary dispute between the two contestants might be determined and our exact standing and relation in respect to the controversy might be made clear.

It will be seen from the correspondence herewith submitted that this proposition has been declined by the British Government upon grounds which in the circumstances seem to me to be far from satisfactory. It is deeply disappointing that such an appeal, actuated by the most friendly feelings toward both nations directly concerned, addressed to the sense of justice and to the magnanimity of one of the great powers of the world, and touching its relations to one comparatively weak and small, should have produced no better results.

The course to be pursued by this Government in view of the present condition does not appear to admit of serious doubt. Having labored faithfully for many years to induce Great Britain to submit this dispute to impartial arbitration, and having been now finally apprised of her refusal to do so, nothing remains but to accept the situation, to recognize its plain requirements, and deal with it accordingly. Great Britain's present proposition has never thus far been regarded as admissible by Venezuela, though any adjustment of the boundary which that country may deem for her advantage and may enter

into of her own free will can not of course be objected to by the United States.

Assuming, however, that the attitude of Venezuela will remain unchanged, the dispute has reached such a stage as to make it now incumbent upon the United States to take measures to determine with sufficient certainty for its justification what is the true divisional line between the Republic of Venezuela and British Guiana. The inquiry to that end should of course be conducted carefully and judicially, and due weight should be given to all available evidence, records, and facts in support of the claims of both parties.

In order that such an examination should be prosecuted in a thorough and satisfactory manner, I suggest that the Congress make an adequate appropriation for the expenses of a commission, to be appointed by the Executive, who shall make the necessary investigation and report upon the matter with the least possible delay. When such report is made and accepted it will, in my opinion, be the duty of the United States to resist by every means in its power, as a wilful aggression upon its rights and interests, the appropriation by Great Britain of any lands or the exercise of governmental jurisdiction over any territory which after investigation we have determined of right belongs to Venezuela.

In making these recommendations I am fully alive to the responsibility incurred and keenly realize all the consequences that may follow.

I am, nevertheless, firm in my conviction that while it is a grievous thing to contemplate the two great English-speaking peoples of the world as being otherwise than friendly competitors in the onward march of civilization and strenuous and worthy rivals in all the arts of peace, there is no calamity which a great nation can invite which equals that which follows a supine submission to wrong and injustice and the consequent loss of national self-respect and honor, beneath which are shielded and defended a people's safety and greatness.

GROVER CLEVELAND.

341. THE REPUBLICAN PLATFORM OF 1896
St. Louis, Missouri
June 16, 1896

(K. Porter, ed. *National Party Platforms*, p. 201 ff.)

The Republican National Convention met in St. Louis, Missouri, June 16, 1896, adopted a platform calling for the gold standard and high tariffs, and nominated William McKinley of Ohio and G. A. Hobart of New Jersey for President and Vice-President. McKinley was elected with an electoral college vote of 271 and a popular vote of over seven million. See Mark Sullivan, *Our Times*, Vol. I; H. T. Peck, *Twenty Years of the Republic*; O. S. Olcott, *William McKinley*, 2 Vols.; H. Croly, *Mark Hanna*; T. Beer, *Mark Hanna*; for the campaign, see W. J. Bryan, *The First Battle*.

. . . For the first time since the civil war the American people have witnessed the calamitous consequence of full and unrestricted Democratic control of the government. It has been a record of unparalleled incapacity, dishonor, and disaster. In administrative management it has ruthlessly sacrificed indispensable revenue, entailed an unceasing deficit, eked out ordinary current expenses with borrowed money, piled up the public debt by $262,000,000, in time of peace, forced an adverse balance of trade, kept a perpetual menace hanging over the redemption fund, pawned American credit to alien syndicates and reversed all the measures and results of successful Republican rule. In the broad effect of its policy it has precipitated panic, blighted industry and trade with prolonged depression, closed factories, reduced work and wages, halted enterprise and crippled American production, while stimulating foreign production for the American market. Every consideration of public safety and individual interest demands that the government shall be wrested from the hands of those who have shown themselves incapable of conducting it without disaster at home and dishonor abroad and shall be restored to the party which for thirty years administered it with unequaled success and prosperity. And in this connection, we heartily endorse the wisdom, patriotism and success of the administration of Benjamin Harrison.

We renew and emphasize our allegiance to the policy of protection as the bulwark of American industrial independence and the foundation of American development and prosperity. This true American policy taxes foreign products and encourages home industry. It puts the burden of revenue on foreign goods; it secures the American market for the American producer. It upholds the American standard of wages for the American workingman; it puts the factory by the side of the farm, and makes the American farmer less dependent on foreign demand and price; it diffuses general thrift, and founds the strength of each. In its reasonable application it is just, fair and impartial, equally opposed to foreign control and domestic monopoly, to sectional discrimination and individual favoritism.

We denounce the present tariff as sectional, injurious to the public credit and destructive to business enterprise. We demand such an equitable tariff on foreign imports which come into competition with the American products as will not only furnish adequate revenue for the necessary expense of the Government, but will protect American labor from degradation and the wage level of other lands. We are not pledged to any particular schedules. The question of rates is a practical question, to be governed by the condition of time and of production. The ruling and uncompromising principle is the protection and development of American labor and industries. The country demands a right settlement, and then it wants a rest.

We believe the repeal of the reciprocity arrangements negotiated by the last Republican Administration was a national calamity, and demand their renewal and extension on such terms as will equalize our trade with other nations, remove the restrictions which now obstruct the sale of American products in the ports of other countries, and secure enlarged markets for the products of our farms, forests, and factories.

Protection and Reciprocity are twin measures of American policy and go hand in hand. Democratic rule has recklessly struck down both, and both must be re-established. Protection for what we produce; reciprocal agreement of mutual interests, which gain open markets for us in return for our open markets for others. Protection builds up domestic industry and trade and secures our own market for ourselves; reciprocity builds up foreign trade and finds an outlet for our surplus. . . .

The Republican party is unreservedly for sound money. It caused the enactment of a law providing for the resumption of specie payments in 1879. Since then every dollar has been as good as gold. We are unalterably opposed to every measure calculated to debase our currency or impair the credit of our country. We are therefore opposed to the free coinage of silver, except by international agreement with the leading commercial nations of the earth, which agreement we pledge ourselves to promote, and until such agreement can be obtained the existing gold standard must be maintained. All of our silver and paper currency must be maintained at parity with gold, and we favor all measures designated to maintain inviolable the obligations of the United States, of all our money, whether coin or paper, at the present standard, the standard of most enlightened nations of the world. . . .

We denounce the practice in the pension bureau so recklessly and unjustly carried on by the present Administration of reducing pensions and arbitrarily dropping names from the rolls, as deserving the severest condemnation of the American people.

Our foreign policy should be at all times firm, vigorous and dignified, and all our interests in the western hemisphere should be carefully watched and guarded.

The Hawaiian Islands should be controlled by the United States, and no foreign power should be permitted to interfere with them. The Nicaragua Canal should be built, owned and operated by the United States. And, by the purchase of the Danish Islands we should secure a much needed Naval station in the West Indies. . . .

342. BRYAN'S CROSS OF GOLD SPEECH
July 8, 1896
(W. J. Bryan, *The First Battle,* p. 199 ff.)

Bryan, a delegate from Nebraska to the Democratic National Convention at Chicago, made the concluding speech in the debate on the adoption of the platform. This speech, the most notable of his career and one of the most notable in the history of American oratory, dramatized Bryan before the Convention and did much to bring about a nomination already highly probable. See, Bryan, *The First Battle, passim; The Memoirs of William Jennings Bryan,* ch. vi; P. Hibben, *The Peerless Leader, William Jennings Bryan,* chs. xv, xvi; M. Sullivan, *Our Times: the Turn of the Century.*

I would be presumptuous, indeed, to present myself against the distinguished gentlemen to whom you have listened if this were a mere measuring of abilities; but this is not a contest between persons. The humblest citizen in all the land, when clad in the armor of a righteous cause, is stronger than all the hosts of error. I come to speak to you in defense of a cause as holy as the cause of liberty—the cause of humanity.

When this debate is concluded, a motion will be made to lay upon the table the resolution offered in commendation of the Administration, and also, the resolution offered in condemnation of the Administration. We object to bringing this question down to the level of persons. The individual is but an atom; he is born, he acts, he dies; but principles are eternal; and this has been a contest over a principle.

Never before in the history of this country has there been witnessed such a contest as that through which we have just passed. Never before in the history of American politics has a great issue been fought out as this issue has been, by the voters of a great party. On the fourth of March 1893, a few Democrats, most of them members of Congress, issued an address to the Democrats of the nation, asserting that the money question was the paramount issue of the hour; declaring that a majority of the Democratic party had the right to control the action of the party on this paramount issue; and concluding with the request that the believers in the free coinage of silver in the Democratic party should organize, take charge of, and control the policy of the Democratic party. Three months later, at Memphis, an organization was perfected, and the silver Democrats went forth openly and courageously proclaiming their belief, and declaring that, if successful, they would crystallize into a platform the declaration which they had made. Then began the struggle. With a zeal approaching the zeal which inspired the Crusaders who followed Peter the Hermit, our silver Democrats went forth from victory unto victory until they are now assembled, not to discuss, not to debate, but to enter up the judgement already rendered by the plain people of this country. In this contest brother has been arrayed against brother, father against son. The warmest ties of love, acquaintance, and association have been disregarded; old leaders have been cast aside when they have refused to give expression to the sentiments of those whom they would lead, and new leaders have sprung up to give direction to this cause of truth. Thus has the contest been waged, and we have assembled here under as binding and solemn instructions as were ever imposed upon representatives of the people.

We do not come as individuals. As individuals we might have been glad to compliment the gentleman from New York [Senator Hill], but we know that the people for whom we speak would never be willing to put him in a position where he could thwart the will of the Democratic party. I saw it was not a question of persons; it was a question of principle, and it is not with gladness, my friends, that we find ourselves brought into conflict with those who are now arrayed on the other side. . . .

When you [turning to the gold delegates] come before us and tell us that we are about to disturb your business interests, we reply that you have disturbed our business interests by your course.

We say to you that you have made the definition of a business man too limited in its application. The man who is employed for wages is as much a business man as his employer; the attorney in a country town is as much a business man as the corporation counsel in a great metropolis; the merchant at the cross-roads store is as much a business man as the merchant of New York; the farmer who goes forth in the morning and toils all day, who begins in the spring and toils all summer, and who by the application of brain and muscle to the natural resources of the country creates wealth, is as much a business man as the man who goes upon the Board of Trade and bets upon the price of grain; the miners who go down a thousand feet into the earth, or climb two thousand feet upon the cliffs, and bring forth from their hiding places the precious metals to be poured into the channels of trade are as much business men as the few financial magnates who, in a back room, corner the money of the world. We come to speak of this broader class of business men.

Ah, my friends, we say not one word against those who live upon the Atlantic Coast, but the hardy pioneers who have braved all the dangers of the wilderness, who have made the desert to bloom as the rose —the pioneers away out there [pointing to the West] who rear their children near to Nature's heart, where they can mingle their voices with the voices of the birds—out there where they have erected schoolhouses for the education of their young, churches where they praise their Creator, and cemeteries where rest the ashes of their dead—these people, we say, are as deserving of the consideration of our party as any people in this country. It is for these that we speak. We do not come as aggressors. Our war is not a war of conquest; we are fighting in the defense of our homes, our families, and posterity. We have petitioned, and our petitions have been scorned; we have entreated, and our entreaties have been disregarded; we have begged, and they have mocked when our calamity came. We beg no longer; we entreat no more; we petition no more. We defy them!

The gentleman from Wisconsin [Vilas] has said that he fears a Robespierre. My friends, in this land of the free you need not fear that a tyrant will spring up from among the people. What we need is an Andrew Jackson to stand, as Jackson stood, against the encroachments of organized wealth.

They tell us that this platform was made to catch votes. We reply to them that changing conditions make new issues; that the principles upon which Democracy rests are as everlasting as the hills, but they must be applied to new conditions as they arise. Conditions have arisen, and we are here to meet those conditions. They tell us that the income tax ought not to be brought in here; that it is a new idea. They criticize us for our criticism of the Supreme Court of the United States. My friends, we have not criticized; we have simply called attention to what you already know. If you want criticisms read the dissenting opinions of the court. There you will find criticisms. They say that we passed an unconstitutional law; we deny it. The income tax was not unconstitutional when it was passed; it was not unconstitutional when it went before the Supreme Court for the first time; it did not become unconstitutional until one of the judges changed his mind, and we cannot be expected to know when a judge will change his mind. The income tax is just. It simply intends to put the burden of government justly upon the backs of the people. I am in favor of an income tax. When I find a man who is not willing to bear his share of the burdens of the government which protects him, I find a man who is unworthy to enjoy the blessings of a government like ours.

They say that we are opposing national bank currency; it is true. If you will read what Thomas Benton said, you will find he said that, in searching history, he could find but one parallel to Andrew Jackson; that was Cicero, he destroyed the conspiracy of Cataline and saved Rome. Benton said that Cicero only did for Rome what Jackson did for us when he destroyed the bank conspiracy and saved America. We say in our platform we believe that the right to coin and issue money is a function of government. We believe it. We believe that it is a part of sovereignty, and can no more with safety be delegated to private individuals than we could afford to delegate to private individuals the power to make penal statutes or levy taxes. Mr. Jefferson, who was once regarded as good Democratic authority, seems to have differed in opinion from the gentleman who has addressed us on the part of the minority. Those who are opposed to this proposition tell us that the issue of paper money is a function of the banks, and that the government ought to go out of the banking business. I stand with Jefferson rather than with them, and tell them, as he did, that the issue

of money is a function of government, and that the banks ought to go out of the governing business.

They complain about the plank which declares against life tenure in office. They have tried to strain it to mean that which it does not mean. What we oppose by that plank is the life tenure which is being built up in Washington, and which excludes from participation in official benefits the humbler members of society. . . .

And now, my friends, let me come to the paramount issue. If they ask us why it is that we say more on the money question than we say upon the tariff question, I reply that, if protection has slain its thousands, the gold standard has slain its tens of thousands. If they ask us why we do not embody in our platforms all the things that we believe in, we reply that when we have restored the money of the Constitution, all other necessary reform will be possible; but that until this is done, there is no other reform that can be accomplished.

Why is it that within three months such a change has come over the country? Three months ago when it was confidently asserted that those who believed in the gold standard would frame our platform and nominate our candidates, even the advocates of the gold standard did not think that we could elect a President. And they had good reason for their doubt, because there is scarcely a State here today asking for the gold standard which is not in the absolute control of the Republican Party. But note the change. Mr. McKinley was nominated at St. Louis upon a platform which declared for the maintenance of the gold standard until it can be changed into bimetallism by international agreement. Mr. McKinley was the most popular man among the Republicans, and three months ago everybody in the Republican Party prophesied his election. How is it today? Why, the man who was once pleased to think that he looked like Napoleon—that man shudders today when he remembers that he was nominated on the anniversary of the battle of Waterloo.

Not only that, but as he listens, he can hear with ever-increasing distinctness the sound of the waves as they beat upon the lonely shores of St. Helena.

Why this change? Ah, my friends, is not

the reason for the change evident to any one who will look at the matter? No private character, however pure, no personal popularity, however great, can protect from the avenging wrath of an indignant people a man who will declare that he is in favor of fastening the gold standard upon this country, or who is willing to surrender the right of self-government and place the legislative control of our affairs in the hands of foreign potentates and powers.

We go forth confident that we shall win. Why? Because upon the paramount issue of this campaign there is not a spot of ground upon which the enemy will dare to challenge battle. If they tell us that the gold standard is a good thing, we shall point to their platform and tell them that their platform pledges the party to get rid of the gold standard and substitute bimetallism. If the gold standard is a good thing why try to get rid of it? I call your attention to the fact that some of the very people who are in this Convention today and who tell us that we ought to declare in favor of international bimetallism—thereby declaring that the gold standard is wrong and that the principle of bimetallism is better—these very people four months ago were open and avowed advocates of the gold standard, and were then telling us that we could not legislate two metals together, even with the aid of all the world. If the gold standard is a good thing, we ought to declare in favor of its retention and not in favor of abandoning it; and if the gold standard is a bad thing why should we wait until other nations are willing to help us to let go? Here is the line of battle, and we care not upon which issue they force the fight; we are prepared to meet them on either issue or on both. If they tell us that the gold standard is the standard of civilization, we reply to them that this, the most enlightened of all the nations of the earth, has never declared for a gold standard and that both the great parties this year are declaring against it. If the gold standard is the standard of civilization, why, my friends, should we not have it? If they come to meet us on that issue we can present the history of our nation. More than that; we can tell them that they will search the pages of history in vain to find a single instance where the common people of any

land have ever declared themselves in favor of the gold standard. They can find where the holders of fixed investments have declared for a gold standard, but not where the masses have. Mr. Carlisle said in 1878 that this was a struggle between the "idle holders of idle capital" and "the struggling masses, who produce the wealth and pay the taxes of the country," and, my friends, the question we are to decide is: Upon which side will the Democratic party fight; upon the side of "the idle holders of idle capital" or upon the side of "the struggling masses"? That is the question which the party must answer first, and then it must be answered by each individual hereafter. The sympathies of the Democratic party, as shown by the platform, are on the side of the struggling masses who have ever been the foundation of the Democratic party. There are two ideas of government. There are those who believe that if you will only legislate to make the well-to-do prosperous, their prosperity will leak through on those below. The Democratic idea, however, has been that if you make the masses prosperous, their prosperity will find its way up through every class which rests upon them.

You come to us and tell us that the great cities are in favor of the gold standard; we reply that the great cities rest upon our broad and fertile prairies. Burn down your cities and leave our farms, and your cities will spring up again as if by magic; but destroy our farms and the grass will grow in the streets of every city in the country.

My friends, we declare that this nation is able to legislate for its own people on every question, without waiting for the aid or consent of any other nation on earth; and upon that issue we expect to carry every state in the Union. I shall not slander the inhabitants of the fair state of Massachusetts nor the inhabitants of the state of New York by saying that, when they are confronted with the proposition, they will declare that this nation is not able to attend to its own business. It is the issue of 1776 over again. Our ancestors, when but three million in number, had the courage to declare their political independence of every other nation; shall we, their descendants, when we have grown to seventy millions, declare that we are less independent than our forefathers?

No, my friends, that will never be the verdict of our people. Therefore, we care not upon what lines the battle is fought. If they say bimetallism is good, but that we cannot have it until other nations help us, we reply, that instead of having a gold standard because England has, we will restore bimetallism, and then let England have bimetallism because the United States has it. If they dare to come out in the open field and defend the gold standard as a good thing, we will fight them to the uttermost. Having behind us the producing masses of this nation and the world, supported by the commercial interests, the laboring interests and the toilers everywhere, we will answer their demand for a gold standard by saying to them: You shall not press down upon the brow of labor this crown of thorns, you shall not crucify mankind upon a cross of gold.

343. PLESSY v. FERGUSON

163 U. S. 537
1896

This case wrote the "separate but equal" doctrine into American constitutional law. It was, in effect, reversed in Brown v. Topeka, Doc. no. 617. See Vann Woodward, *The Strange Career of Jim Crow;* Gilbert Stephenson, *Race Distinctions in American Law;* Rayford Logan, *Negro in American Life and Thought 1877–1901;* and refs. to Doc. 617.

BROWN, J. This case turns upon the constitutionality of an act of the general assembly of the state of Louisiana, passed in 1890, providing for separate railway carriages for the white and colored races. . . .

The constitutionality of this act is attacked upon the ground that it conflicts both with the 13th Amendment of the Constitution, abolishing slavery, and the 14th Amendment, which prohibits certain restrictive legislation on the part of the states.

1. That it does not conflict with the 13th Amendment, which abolished slavery and involuntary servitude, except as a punishment for crime, is too clear for argument. . . .

A statute which implies merely a legal distinction between the white and colored races—a distinction which is founded in the color of the two races, and which must always exist so long as white men are distinguished from the other race by color—has no tendency to destroy the legal equality of the two races, or re-establish a state of involuntary servitude. Indeed, we do not understand that the 13th Amendment is strenuously relied upon by the plaintiff in error in this connection. . . .

The object of the amendment was undoubtedly to enforce the absolute equality of the two races before the law, but in the nature of things it could not have been intended to abolish distinctions based upon color, or to enforce social, as distinguished from political, equality, or a commingling of the two races upon terms unsatisfactory to either. Laws permitting, and even requiring their separation in places where they are liable to be brought into contact do not necessarily imply the inferiority of either race to the other, and have been generally, if not universally, recognized as within the competency of the state legislatures in the exercise of their police power. The most common instance of this is connected with the establishment of separate schools for white and colored children, which have been held to be a valid exercise of the legislative power even by courts of states where the political rights of the colored race have been longest and most earnestly enforced. . . .

It is claimed by the plaintiff in error that, in any mixed community, the reputation of belonging to the dominant race, in this instance the white race is *property*, in the same sense that a right of action, or of inheritance, is property. Conceding this to be so, for the purposes of this case, we are unable to see how this statute deprives him of, or in any way affects his right to, such property. If he be a white man and assigned to a colored coach, he may have his action for damages against the company for being deprived of his so-called property. Upon the other hand, if he be a colored man and be so assigned, he has been deprived of no property, since he is not lawfully entitled to the reputation of being a white man. . . .

So far, then, as a conflict with the 14th

Amendment is concerned, the case reduces itself to the question whether the statute of Louisiana is a reasonable regulation, and with respect to this there must necessarily be a large discretion on the part of the legislature. In determining the question of reasonableness it is at liberty to act with reference to the established usages, customs, and traditions of the people, and with a view to the promotion of their comfort, and the preservation of the public peace and good order. Gauged by this standard, we cannot say that a law which authorizes or even requires the separation of the two races in public conveyances is unreasonable or more obnoxious to the 14th Amendment than the acts of Congress requiring separate schools for colored children in the District of Columbia, the constitutionality of which does not seem to have been questioned, or the corresponding acts of state legislatures.

We consider the underlying fallacy of the plaintiff's argument to consist in the assumption that the enforced separation of the two races stamps the colored race with a badge of inferiority. If this be so, it is not by reason of anything found in the act, but solely because the colored race chooses to put that construction upon it. The argument necessarily assumes that if, as has been more than once the case, and is not unlikely to be so again, the colored race should become the dominant power in the state legislature, and should enact a law in precisely similar terms, it would thereby relegate the white race to an inferior position. We imagine that the white race, at least, would not acquiesce in this assumption. The argument also assumes that social prejudice may be overcome by legislation, and that equal rights cannot be secured to the Negro except by an enforced commingling of the two races. We cannot accept this proposition. If the two races are to meet on terms of social equality, it must be the result of natural affinities, a mutual appreciation of each other's merits and a voluntary consent of individuals. . . . Legislation is powerless to eradicate racial instincts or to abolish distinctions based upon physical differences, and the attempt to do so can only result in accentuating the difficulties of the present situation. If the civil and political right of both races be equal, one cannot be inferior (552) to the other civilly or politically. If one race be inferior to the other socially, the Constitution of the United States cannot put them upon the same plane.

Justice HARLAN, dissenting. . . . In respect of civil rights, common to all citizens, the Constitution of the United States does not, I think, permit any public authority to know the race of those entitled to be protected in the enjoyment of such rights. Every true man has pride of race, and under appropriate circumstances, when the rights of others, his equals before the law, are not to be affected, it is his privilege to express such pride and to take such action based upon it as to him seems proper. But I deny that any legislative body or judicial tribunal may have regard to the race of citizens when the civil rights of those citizens are involved. Indeed such legislation as that here in question is inconsistent, not only with that equality of rights which pertains to citizenship, national and state, but with the personal liberty enjoyed by every one within the United States. . . .

In my opinion, the judgment this day rendered will, in time, prove to be quite as pernicious as the decision made by this tribunal in the Dred Scott Case. It was adjudged in that case that the descendants of Africans who were imported into this country and sold as slaves were not included nor intended to be included under the word "citizens" in the Constitution, and could not claim any of the rights and privileges which that instrument provided for and secured to citizens of the United States; that at the time of the adoption of the Constitution they were "considered as a subordinate and inferior class of beings, who had been subjugated by the dominant race, and, whether emancipated or not, yet remained subject to their authority, and had no rights or privileges but such as those who held the power and the government might choose to grant them." The recent amendments of the Constitution, it was supposed, had eradicated these principles from our institutions. But it seems that we have yet, in some of the states, a dominant race, a superior class of citizens, which assumes to regulate the enjoyment of civil rights, common to all citizens, upon the basis of race. The present decision, it may well be apprehended, will not only stimulate aggressions, more or less brutal and irritating, upon the admitted rights of colored citizens, but will encourage the belief that it is possible, by means of state enactments, to defeat the beneficent purposes which the people of the United States had in view when they adopted the recent amendments of the Constitution, by one of which the blacks of this country were made citizens of the United States and of the states in which they respectively reside and whose privileges and immunities, as citizens, the states are forbidden to abridge. Sixty millions of whites are in no danger from the presence here of eight millions of blacks. The destinies of the two races in this country are indissolubly linked together, and the interests of both require that the common government of all shall not permit the seeds of race hate to be planted under the sanction of law. What can more certainly arouse race hate, what more certainly create and perpetuate a feeling of distrust between these races, than state enactments which in fact proceed on the ground that colored citizens are so inferior and degraded that they cannot be allowed to sit in public coaches occupied by white citizens? That, as all will admit, is the real meaning of such legislation as was enacted in Louisiana. . . .

If evils will result from the commingling of the two races upon public highways established for the benefit of all, they will be infinitely less than those that will surely come from state legislation regulating the enjoyment of civil rights upon the basis of race. We boast of the freedom enjoyed by our people above all other peoples. But it is difficult to reconcile that boast with a state of the law which, practically, puts the brand of servitude and degradation upon a large class of our fellow citizens, our equals before the law. The thin disguise of "equal" accommodations for passengers in railroad coaches will not mislead anyone, or atone for the wrong this day done. . . .

I am of opinion that the statute of Louisiana is inconsistent with the personal liberty of citizens, white and black, in that state, and hostile to both the spirit and letter of the Constitution of the United States. If laws of like character should be enacted in the several states of the Union, the effect would be in the highest degree mischievous. Slavery as an institution tolerated by law would, it is true, have disappeared from our country, but there would remain a power in the states, by sinister legislation, to interfere with the full enjoyment of the blessings of freedom; to regulate civil rights, common to all citizens, upon the basis of race; and to place in a condition of legal inferiority a large body of American citizens, now constituting a part of the political community, called the people of the United States, for whom and by whom, through representatives, our government is administered. Such a system is inconsistent with the guarantee given by the Constitution to each state of a republican form of government, and may be stricken down by Congressional action, or by the courts in the discharge of their solemn duty to maintain the supreme law of the land, anything in the Constitution or laws of any state to the contrary notwithstanding.

For the reasons stated, I am constrained to withhold my assent from the opinion and judgment of the majority.

344. HOLDEN v. HARDY
169 U. S. 366
1898

Error to the Supreme Court of the State of Utah. Compare this decision to *Lochner* v. *New York*, Doc. No. 364.

BROWN, J. This case involves the constitutionality of an act of the legislature of Utah of March 30, 1896, chap. 72, entitled "An Act Regulating the Hours of Employment in Underground Mines and in Smelters and Ore Reduction Works." . . .

The validity of the statute in question is, . . . challenged upon the ground of an alleged violation of the 14th amendment to the Constitution of the United States, in that it abridges the privileges or immunities of citizens of the United States; deprives both the employer and the laborer of his property without due process of law, and denies to them the equal protection of the laws. . . .

In passing upon the validity of state legislation under that Amendment, this court has not failed to recognize the fact that the law is to a certain extent a progressive science; that in some of the states methods of procedure which, at the time the Constitution was adopted, were deemed essential to the protection and safety of the people, or to the liberty of the citizen, have been found to be no longer necessary; that restrictions which had formerly been laid upon the conduct of individuals, or of classes of individuals, had proved detrimental to their interests; while, upon the other hand, certain other classes of persons, particularly those engaged in dangerous or unhealthful employments, have been found to be in need of additional protection. . . .

This right of contract, however, is itself subject to certain limitations which the state may lawfully impose in the exercise of its police powers. While this power is inherent in all governments, it has doubtless been greatly expanded in its application during the past century, owing to an enormous increase in the number of occupations which are dangerous, or so far detrimental to the health of employees as to demand special precaution for their well-being and protection, or the safety of adjacent property. While this court has held that the police power cannot be put forward as an excuse for oppressive and unjust legislation, it may be lawfully resorted to for the purpose of preserving the public health, safety, or morals, or the abatement of public nuisances, and a large discretion "is necessarily vested in the legislature to determine, not only what the interests of the public require, but what measures are necessary for the protection of such interests." . . .

But if it be within the power of a legislature to adopt such means for the protection of the lives of its citizens, it is difficult to see why precautions may not also be adopted for the protection of their health and morals. It is as much for the interest of the state that the public health should be preserved as that life should be made secure.

Upon the principles above stated, we think the act in question may be sustained as a valid exercise of the police power of the state. The enactment does not profess to limit the hours of all workmen, but merely those who are employed in underground mines, or in the smelting, reduction, or refining of ores or metals. These employments when too long pursued the legislature has judged to be detrimental to the health of the employees, and, so long as there are reasonable grounds for believing that this is so, its decision upon this subject cannot be reviewed by the Federal courts.

While the general experience of mankind may justify us in believing that men may engage in ordinary employments more than eight hours per day without injury to their health, it does not follow that labor for the same length of time is innocuous when carried on beneath the surface of the earth, when the operative is deprived of fresh air and sunlight, and is frequently subjected to foul atmosphere and a very high temperature, or to influence of noxious gases, generated by the processes of refining or smelting. . . . That both parties are of full age and competent to contract does not necessarily deprive the state of the power to interfere where the parties do not stand upon an equality, or where the public health demands that one party to the contract shall be protected against himself. "The state still retains an interest in his welfare, however reckless he may be. The whole is no greater than the sum of all the parts, and when the individual health, safety, and welfare are sacrificed or neglected, the state must suffer."

We have no disposition to criticise the many authorities which hold that state statutes restricting the hours of labor are unconstitutional. Indeed, we are not called upon to express an opinion upon this subject. It is sufficient to say of them that they have no application to cases where the legislature had adjudged that a limitation is necessary for the preservation of the health of employees, and there are reasonable grounds for believing that such determination is supported by the facts. The question in each case is whether the legislature has adopted the statute in exercise of a reasonable discretion, or whether its action be a mere excuse for an unjust discrimination, or the oppression, or spoliation of a particular class. . . .

345. THE DE LÔME LETTER
December 1897

(Foreign Relations of the United States, 1898, p. 1007)

This private letter from the Spanish Minister in the United States to a friend was stolen from the Havana post-office by an insurgent spy and held by the Cuban junta in the United States until it could be most effectively used. It was given to the press February 9, 1898. De Lôme at once cabled his resignation. De Lôme had been an exceptionally able diplomat, and his humiliation constitutes one of the unpleasant episodes in the annals of American diplomacy. See, W. Millis, *The Martial Spirit*, p. 96 ff.; M. A. Wilkerson, *Public Opinion and the Spanish American War*, p. 91 ff.

LEGATION OF SPAIN, Washington.
His Excellency Don JOSÉ CANALEJAS.

MY DEAR FRIEND:

You have no reason to ask my excuses for not having written to me. I ought also to have written to you, but I have put off doing so because overwhelmed with work and nous sommes quittes.

The situation here remains the same. Everything depends on the political and military outcome in Cuba. . . .

The message has been a disillusionment to the insurgents, who expected something different; but I regard it as bad (for us).

Besides the ingrained and inevitable bluntness (groseria) with which is repeated all that the press and public opinion in Spain have said about Weyler, it once more shows what McKinley is, weak and a bidder for the admiration of the crowd, besides being a would-be politician (politicastro) who tries to leave a door open behind himself while keep-ing on good terms with the jingoes of his party.

Nevertheless, whether the practical results of it [the message] are to be injurious and adverse depends only upon ourselves.

I am entirely of your opinions; without a military end of the matter nothing will be accomplished in Cuba, and without a military and political settlement there will always be the danger of encouragement being given to the insurgents by a part of the public opinion if not by the Government. . . .

I do not think sufficient attention has been paid to the part England is playing.

Nearly all the newspaper rabble that swarms in your hotels are Englishmen, and while writing for the Journal they are also correspondents of the most influential journals and reviews of London. It has been so ever since this thing began. As I look at it England's only object is that the Americans should amuse themselves with us and leave her alone; and if there should be a war, that would the better stave off the conflict which she dreads but which will never come about.

It would be very advantageous to take up, even if only for effect, the question of commercial relations, and to have a man of some prominence sent hither in order that I may make use of him here to carry on a propaganda among the Senators and others in opposition to the junta and to try to win over the refugees. . . .

Ever your attached friend and servant,

ENRIQUE DEPUY DE LÔME.

ARTICLES SUBSEQUENT TO ARTICLE XXII

Article XXIII
March 29, 1961

Sec. 1. The District constituting the seat of Government of the United States shall appoint in such manner as the Congress may direct:

A number of electors of President and Vice-President equal to the whole number of Senators and Representatives in Congress to which the District would be entitled if it were a State, but in no event more than the least populous state; they shall be in addition to those appointed by the states, but they shall be considered, for the purposes of the election of President and Vice-President, to be electors appointed by a state; and they shall meet in the District and perform such duties as provided by the twelfth article of amendment.

Sec. 2. The Congress shall have power to enforce this article by appropriate legislation.

Article XXIV
January 24, 1964

Sec. 1. The right of citizens of the United States to vote in any primary or other election for President or Vice-President, for electors for President or Vice-President, or for Senator or Representative in Congress, shall not be denied or abridged by the United States or any state by reason of failure to pay any poll tax or other tax.

Sec. 2. The Congress shall have power to enforce this article by appropriate legislation.

Article XXV
February 23, 1967

Sec. 1. In case of the removal of the President from office or his death or resignation, the Vice-President shall become President.

Sec. 2. Whenever there is a vacancy in the office of the Vice-President, the President shall nominate a Vice-President who shall take the office upon confirmation by a majority vote of both houses of Congress.

Sec. 3. Whenever the President transmits to the President pro tempore of the Senate and the Speaker of the House of Representatives his written declaration that he is unable to discharge the powers and duties of his office, and until he transmits to them a written declaration to the contrary, such powers and duties shall be discharged by the Vice-President as Acting President.

Sec. 4. Whenever the Vice-President and a majority of either the principal officers of the executive departments, or of such other body as Congress may by law provide, transmit to the President pro tempore of the Senate and the Speaker of the House of Representatives their written declaration that the President is unable to discharge the powers and duties of his office, the Vice-President shall immediately assume the powers and duties of the office as Acting President.

Thereafter, when the President transmits to the President pro tempore of the Senate and the Speaker of the House of Representatives his written declaration that no inability exists, he shall resume the powers and duties of his office unless the Vice-President and a majority of either the principal officers of the executive department, or of such other body as Congress may by law provide, transmit within four days to the President pro tempore of the Senate and the Speaker of the House of Representatives their written declaration that the President is unable to discharge the powers and duties of his office. Thereupon Congress shall decide the issue, assembling within 48 hours for that purpose if not in session. If the Congress, within 21 days after receipt of the latter written declaration, or, if Congress is not in session, within 21 days after Congress is required to assemble, determines by two-thirds vote of both houses that the President is unable to discharge the powers and duties of his office, the Vice-President shall continue to discharge the same as Acting President; otherwise, the President shall resume the powers and duties of his office.

ARTICLE XXVI
July 7, 1971

SEC. 1. The right of citizens of the United States, who are eighteen years of age or older, to vote shall not be denied or abridged by the United States or by any State on account of age.

SEC. 2. The Congress shall have power to enforce this article by appropriate legislation.

ARTICLE XXVII
Passed by Congress March 22, 1972; Not yet ratified

SEC. 1. Equality of rights under the law shall not be denied or abridged by the United States or by any State on account of sex.

SEC. 2. The Congress shall have the power to enforce, by appropriate legislation, the provisions of this article.

SEC. 3. This amendment shall take effect two years after the date of ratification.

INDEX